CHRISTIANITY

The *Cambridge History of Christianity* offers a comprehensive chronological account of the development of Christianity in all its aspects – theological, intellectual, social, political, regional, global – from its beginnings to the present day. Each volume makes a substantial contribution in its own right to the scholarship of its period and the complete *History* constitutes a major work of academic reference. Far from being merely a history of Western European Christianity and its offshoots, the *History* aims to provide a global perspective. Eastern and Coptic Christianity are given full consideration from the early period onwards, and later, African, Far Eastern, New World, South Asian and other non-European developments in Christianity receive proper coverage. The volumes cover popular piety and non-formal expressions of Christian faith and treat the sociology of Christian formation, worship and devotion in a broad cultural context. The question of relations between Christianity and other major faiths is also kept in sight throughout. The *History* will provide an invaluable resource for scholars and students alike.

THE CAMBRIDGE
HISTORY OF
CHRISTIANITY

⋆

VOLUME 6
Reform and Expansion 1500–1660

⋆

Edited by
R. PO-CHIA HSIA

CAMBRIDGE
UNIVERSITY PRESS

4/09 mh

CAMBRIDGE UNIVERSITY PRESS

Cambridge, New York, Melbourne, Madrid, Cape Town, Singapore, São Paulo

Cambridge University Press
The Edinburgh Building, Cambridge CB2 8RU, UK

Published in the United States of America by Cambridge University Press, New York

www.cambridge.org
Information on this title: www.cambridge.org/9780521811620

First published 2007

Printed in the United Kingdom at the University Press, Cambridge

A catalogue record for this publication is available from the British Library

ISBN 978-0-521-81162-0 hardback

Contents

Contents

Contents

Contents

Illustrations

Contributors

WOLFGANG BEHRINGER is Professor of Modern History at the University of Saarbrücken, Germany.

PHILIP BENEDICT is Professor of Church History at the University of Geneva, Switzerland.

ROBERT BIRELEY, SJ is Professor of History at Loyola University Chicago, USA.

ANN BLAIR is Professor of History at Harvard University, USA.

PETER BLICKLE is Emeritus Professor of Modern History at the University of Bern, Switzerland.

MIRIAM BODIAM is Associate Professor of Jewish History at Touro College, USA.

THOMAS A. BRADY is Sather Professor of History Emeritus at the University of California at Berkeley, USA.

OLIVER CHRISTIN is Professor of Modern History at the University of Lyon II, France.

SIMON DITCHFIELD is Senior Lecturer in History at the University of York, UK.

MIKHAIL DMITRIEV is Professor of History at Moscow State University, Russia.

JOHN PATRICK DONNELLY, SJ is Professor of History at Marquette University, USA.

ALEXANDER J. FISHER is Assistant Professor of Music at the University of British Columbia, Canada.

MARK GREENGRASS is Professor of History at the University of Sheffield, UK.

BRAD GREGORY is Associate Professor of History at Notre Dame University, USA.

SCOTT HENDRIX is Nichols Professor of Reformation History at the Princeton Theological Seminary, USA.

R. PO-CHIA HSIA is Edwin Erle Sparks Professor of History at Pennsylvania State University, USA.

SUSAN KARANT-NUNN is Professor of History and Director of the Division for Late Medieval and Reformation Studies at the University of Arizona, USA.

ROBERT KINGDON is Emeritus Professor of History at the University of Wisconsin at Madison, USA.

HARTMUT LEHMANN is Emeritus Director of the Max-Planck Institute of History in Göttingen, Germany.

UTE LOTZ-HEUMANN teaches in the Department of History of the Humboldt University Berlin, Germany.

R. EMMET MCLAUGHLIN is Professor of History at Villanova University, USA.

KENNETH MILLS is Professor of History at the University of Toronto, Canada.

WILLIAM MONTER is Emeritus Professor of History at Northwestern University, USA.

NICOLETTE MOUT is Professor of Modern History and Central European Studies at Leiden University, The Netherlands.

LUISE SCHORN-SCHÜTTE is Professor of Modern History at the University of Frankfurt, Germany.

NICOLAS STANDAERT is Professor of Sinology at the Catholic University of Leuven, Belgium.

ISTVÁN G. TÓTH is the late Associate Professor of History at the Central European University, Hungary.

LEE PALMER WANDEL is Professor of History at the University of Wisconsin at Madison, USA.

MERRY WIESNER-HANKS is Professor of History at the University of Wisconsin at Milwaukee, USA.

GABRIELLA ZARRI is Professor of History at the University of Florence, Italy.

INES G. ŽUPANOV is a researcher at the Centre National de la Recherche Scientifique, France.

Editor's preface

In designing the shape of this volume, which covers the crucial period of the Protestant Reformation and the Catholic response, I have attempted to achieve three goals. The first objective is to provide an authoritative and balanced exposition of the events and issues that represent the classic commonplaces of the history of the Reformation and confessional conflicts. A second aim is to present scholarship that focuses on themes that transcend the Protestant–Catholic divide, themes of social and cultural history that have animated a generation of recent historical scholarship. The third goal situates the history of Christianity in the larger world context; to this end I have solicited contributions that illuminate the relationship between Christian Europe and the non-Christian world, between Christian missions and Judaism, Native American religions, Islam, Hinduism, and Buddhism.

The thirty essays grouped in six sections correspond to these three objectives. Twelve contributions in Parts I and II cover the *loci communes* of Reformation research: the leading Protestant reformers, the interplay between politics and evangelical movement, and the Anabaptist and radical reforms. Part III is devoted to the Catholic response that included both an impulse for renewal that predated the Protestant challenge as well as specific Counter-Reformation developments. Moving from the core of confessional conflicts, the six essays of Part IV analyse first the problems of toleration, church discipline, martyrdom, Inquisition, religious colloquies and then moves beyond the frontiers of Latin Christendom to study the impact of confessional confrontations on the Eastern Orthodox churches. Topics central to the social and cultural history of religion in recent decades of scholarship comprise Part V, which attends to the relationship between religious change and the history of art, liturgy, music, science, and demonology, offering as well sociological and gender approaches to the study of the clergies and women. A final Part broadens the vision to the non-Christian world. In addition to examining the new relationship between the Christian churches and Judaism within Europe, the five contributions of

Part VI describe the frontiers of religious contact between Christian and Muslim Europe, between 'spiritual conquest' and native American religions, and between Christian missionaries and the major religions of India and China.

As a world religion, Christianity and its history are well represented in international scholarship. The thirty contributors of this volume consist of scholars of American, Belgian, British, Canadian, Chinese, Croatian, Dutch, French, German, Hungarian, Italian, and Russian backgrounds working in a dozen countries. Bringing to bear their different training and approaches, the essays illustrate the great diversity of sources and problems that pertain to this field of study.

Chronology

	• Diet of Västernås approves reforms of Swedish Church
1529	• Marburg Colloquy attempts unsuccessfully to unify Swiss and German Reformations
	• Evangelical princes issue official 'Protestation' against imperial anti-Lutheran policies at Diet of Speyer
	• Evangelical revolution in Lübeck expels city council and elects Jürgen Wullenwever as *burgomaster*
	• Imperial army defeats Turkish army at Vienna
	• Anabaptist prophet Johannes Hubmaier burned for heresy in Vienna
1530	• Diet of Augsburg attempts to reconcile Lutheran princes and cities to Emperor Charles V; Lutheran delegates issue Augsburg Confession defining Protestant faith
1531	• Civil war between Protestant and Catholic cantons in Switzerland
	• Formation of the Schmalkaldic League provides for a defensive alliance among Lutheran imperial cities and princes in event of imperial attack
	• Publication of Luther's *Warning to the German People*
1530	• Emperor-elect Charles V crowned; last officially crowned Holy Roman Emperor
1531	• Death of Ulrich Zwingli at battle of Kappel; Swiss civil war ends in Catholic victory
	• 50,000 die in Lisbon earthquake
1533	• Papal approval of Barnabite Order (Clerks Regular of Saint Paul)
1534	• Act of Supremacy institutes Henry VIII as official head of the Church of England
	• Anabaptist Kingdom of Münster established, city besieged by erstwhile prince-bishop Franz von Waldeck
	• Death of Pope Clement VII
1535	• Münster falls to Lutheran-Catholic army
	• Execution of Thomas More
1536	• Beginning of John Calvin's ministry in Geneva
	• Papal approval of Constitution of Capuchin Order
	• Attempt to unify German and Swiss reform traditions at Wittenberg Concord
	• Death of Desiderius Erasmus of Rotterdam
	• Execution of William Tyndale
1537	• Danish Church Ordinance establishes Lutheranism as official confession of Danish Church
1538	• Catholic princes form Catholic League of Nuremburg in response to Protestant Schmalkaldic League
1539	• Charles V agrees to fifteen-month truce with princes of the Schmalkaldic League by accepting Frankfurt Interim
1540	• Papal recognition of the Society of Jesus
	• Papal recognition of Order of the Somascans (Clerks Regular of Somascha)
	• First *auto-da-fé* accompanying sentencing of heretics held in Portugal

1540–1   • Religious Colloquies at Worms and Regensburg fail to reconcile
            confessional difference between Protestant and Catholic theologians in
            Empire
          • Failure to effect religious reconciliation among estates of Empire at Diet
            of Regensburg; Charles V forced to admit Protestants to Imperial
            Chamber Court
1541   • Town council of Geneva accepts Calvin's Ecclesiastical Ordinances,
            instituting the Consistory for enforcing moral discipline in the city
1542   • Inquisition reconstituted by Paul III
1544   • Papal recognition of the Ursuline Order
1545   • General Church Council opens in Trent
1546   • Death of Luther
1546–7   • Schmalkaldic War
1547   • Charles V defeats Lutheran princes at Battle of Mühlberg
          • General Church Council transferred to Bologna
1547–8   • Charles V imposes Interim on Protestant Estates at Imperial Diet at
            Augsburg
1548   • First period of Church Council concludes
1549   • Death of Pope Paul III
1551   • Death of Strasbourg reformer Martin Bucer
1551   • Founding of Jesuit *Collegium Romanum* in Rome
1551–2   • Church Council reconvenes at Trent for second period
1552   • Death of Francis Xavier in Macao
          • Collegium Germanicum founded in Rome by papal bull
1555   • Religious Peace of Augsburg officially recognizes Lutheranism as an
            official confession in the Holy Roman Empire
          • Death of Pope Julius III
1556   • Death of Ignatius Loyola
1558   • Death of Emperor Charles V; Ferdinand I elected Holy Roman Emperor
          • Death of Mary I of England ends attempts to restore Catholicism in
            England
1559   • First Jesuit mission in Japan
1560   • Protestant Confession of Faith establishes Presbyterianism as official
            confession of Scotland
1560   • Death of Gustav I of Sweden
          • Death of German reformer Philip Melanchthon, author of Confession of
            Augsburg
1562–3   • Third and final period of General Church Council at Trent
1564   • Tridentine decrees proclaimed in Spanish lands under rule of Philip II
1564   • Death of Emperor Ferdinand I; Maximilian II becomes Holy Roman
            Emperor
1565   • Archbishop Carlo Borromeo begins reforms in Milan
          • Permanent Spanish settlement instituted in the Philippines
          • Death of Pope Pius IV
1570   • Inquisition established in Mexico and Peru

1571   • Congregation of the Index created to oversee production of books
1571   • Protestant Church Ordinance officially establishes Lutheran state church of Sweden
1572   • Massacre of French Calvinists on day of the feast of St Bartholomew
       • Death of Pope Pius V
       • Papal approval of community of Hospitallers
       • Founding of first English presbytery, indicating growing influence of Presbyterians in England
1575   • Papal recognition of the Congregation of the Oratory, founded by Filippo Neri
1576   • Death of Emperor Maximilian II; accession of Emperor Rudolf II
1577   • Beginning of a wave of executions of Catholic missionaries in Elizabethan England
1578   • Oblates of Saint Ambrose founded by Carlo Borromeo
1579   • Formation of Protestant United Provinces
1580   • Jesuits establish mission in China
       • Lutheran negotiations concerning doctrine culminate in Book of Concord, providing a standardized account of Lutheran doctrine
1581   • First anti-Catholic legislation enacted in the United Provinces
1584   • Japanese Catholic emissary to Europe
1585   • Death of Pope Gregory XIII
1588   • Restructuring of papal government creates congregations of cardinals for secular and spiritual affairs
       • Papal approval of Clerks Regular Minor (Caracciolini), founded by Francesco Caracciolo
1590   • Death of Pope Sixtus V
1591   • Papal approval of Camillians (Order of Clerks Regular, Servants of the Sick)
1562–98   • French Wars of Religion
       • Papal recognition of Order of Discalced Carmelites
1595   • Death of Filippo Neri
       • Papal approval of Order of Clerks Regular of the Mother of God (Matritani)
       • Papal approval of French Doctrinaires
1598   • Edict of Nantes establishes toleration for French Protestants
1605   • Death of Pope Clement VIII
1610   • Carlo Borromeo canonized
1611   • Founding of community of French Oratorians
1612   • Death of Emperor Rudolf II; Matthias becomes Holy Roman Emperor
1614   • Japanese government begins efforts to suppress Christianity
1615   • Clerical estate of France officially recognizes Tridentine decrees
1617   • Papal recognition of Poor Clerks Regular of the Pious Schools
1619   • Capuchins (Order of Friars Minor Cap) become a fully independent order
       • Death of Emperor Matthias, accession of Ferdinand II
1621   • Death of Pope Paul V

1622	• Ignatius Loyola, Francis Xavier, Teresa of Avila, and Filippo Neri canonized as new saints of Catholic renewal
1624–9	• Repression of Protestants in Habsburg-conquered Bohemia
1626	• Consecration of the new Basilica of St Peter in Rome
1628	• Charles I of England issues Royal Declaration, requiring church ordinances to be submitted to crown approval
1632	• Papal recognition of French congregation of Vincentians (Congregation of the Mission)
1637	• Death of Emperor Ferdinand II; election of Ferdinand III
1640	• Charles I calls Long Parliament
1641	• Anti-English and anti-Protestant uprising in Ireland suppressed by Oliver Cromwell
1642	• Beginning of Civil War in England
1643	• Publication of first volumes of the *Acta sanctorum*, a Jesuit-led effort to standardize and record lives of Catholic saints
1644	• Death of Pope Urban VIII
1648	• Peace of Westphalia ends Thirty Years' War; updates Peace of Augsburg's provisions for confessional coexistence in the Empire
1649	• Execution of Charles I of England
1653	• Papal condemnation of Cornelius Jansen's *Augustinus*
	• Oliver Cromwell installed as Lord Protector of England
1655	• Death of Pope Innocent X
1657	• Death of Emperor Ferdinand III
1658	• Leopold I becomes Holy Roman Emperor
	• Death of Oliver Cromwell, succeeded as Lord Protector by son Richard
1660	• Charles II enters London; end of English Protectorate
1664	• Papal approval of French Congregation of Jesus and Mary
1685	• Revocation of the Edict of Nantes

PART I

★

LUTHER AND THE HOLY ROMAN EMPIRE

Martin Luther, reformer

SCOTT HENDRIX

Luther and reform

The catalyst of the Protestant Reformation was the German Augustinian monk and university professor, Martin Luther (1483–1546). In the late medieval church, calls for renewal were loud and persistent and some reforms were enacted in monastic orders, in church life, and in popular movements associated with the names of John Wyclif (1384–1443) and John Hus (1369–1415). Compared with those strident voices, Martin Luther's invitation to an academic debate on the power of indulgences in 1517 was a subdued summons. True, Luther had already been preaching against the indulgence practice and clerical negligence, but to call the young professor of biblical studies a church reformer prior to his circulation of the *Ninety-five Theses* would be an exaggeration. In the famous theses of 1517, the last thing on Luther's mind was reform of the entire church.

Yet Luther has gone down in history as the first Protestant *reformer* because of the conflict with the Roman curia that was ignited by those theses. It was a quarrel that Luther did not seek but also one that he did not shun once it had begun. During the three years prior to his excommunication (1521), Luther forged the identity and self-awareness of a reformer and gained the collegial and political support that would make him a leader of the evangelical movement in Germany. Even then, however, Luther was not a reformer in the sense of implementing a preconceived plan to reshape the church. Once Luther and his followers were excommunicated, a process of restructuring Christianity in Europe did ensue, but neither Luther nor his colleagues were able to envision the outcome of that process. Luther's reforming agenda had another goal altogether.

Once Luther became engaged in reform, he worked for the renewal of both theology and piety. The reform of theology was pursued at the University of Wittenberg, founded by the Saxon elector Frederick the Wise (1463–1525) and only ten years old when Martin Luther joined the theological faculty in 1512. Nevertheless, the university had attracted capable scholars who represented the various schools of late medieval thought and the humanist critique of scholastic theology. Luther, called to the chair of biblical theology, sympathized with those colleagues who wanted to replace the study of Aristotle and the scholastics with concentration on the Bible and the church fathers.[1] At the same time, he launched a critique of scholastic theology in lectures and in academic debates. Less than two months prior to the *Ninety-five Theses*, in another set of theses prepared for debate in September 1517, Luther delivered a harsh critique of the Nominalist theology in which he himself had been trained.[2]

Luther envisioned the reform of piety as a process of Christianization that he advocated in sermons, the *Ninety-five Theses*, and in German pamphlets that began to appear with regularity in 1519. Late medieval practices, like the offering of indulgence letters that would guarantee the remission of sins without contrition, were called by him not just improper but unchristian. 'Those who teach that contrition is not necessary on the part of those who intend to buy souls out of purgatory or to buy confessional privileges preach unchristian doctrine.'[3] Defending the practice of giving both elements to the laity in the sacrament of communion, Luther demanded that people first become 'real Christians' through faith and love before they approached the altar: 'Heavens, if this idea were really put across, it would mean that where thousands come to the sacrament now, scarcely hundreds would come . . . and so we would at last become a group of real Christians, whereas at present we are almost completely pagan and only Christian in name.'[4] The renewal of theology went hand-in-hand with the reform of practice and piety, and both kinds of reform were shaped by Luther's perception that late medieval religion should become more Christian than it had been. That perception had its roots in the intense religiosity of Luther's upbringing.

The roots of reform

Childhood and family

Biographers now emphasize that Luther's childhood was unexceptional for the time in which he lived.[5] He was the subject of strict discipline from both

---

1 Martin Luther to John Lang, 18 May 1517, WABr 1:99.8–13.
2 *Disputatio contra scholasticam theologiam* (1517), WA 1:221–8.
3 *Disputatio pro declaratione virtutis indulgentiarum* (1517), StA 1:180.1–2; LW 31:28.
4 *Von beider Gestalt des Sakraments zu nehmen* (1522), WA 10,2:39.1–13; LW 36:264.
5 Brecht, *Martin Luther*, vol. 1, pp. 6–9.

parents, but he was also the beneficiary of their desire to see him properly educated and religiously trained. We have few details about the relationship between Luther and his parents, but at the time of their deaths (Hans in 1530 and Margarete in 1531) Luther was deeply moved and expressed his appreciation for both of them. When he learned that his father had died, Luther confessed that seldom had he ever despised death as he did at that moment and acknowledged that through his father God had given to him all that he was and had.[6]

A quite different picture was painted by Erik Erikson in *Young man Luther*. According to Erikson, an unusually harsh upbringing alienated Luther from his father and provoked a crisis of identity which led to Luther's rebellion against the papacy and saddled him with pathological tendencies.[7] Historians have rejected Erikson's interpretation because the evidence on which it was based is unreliable, but Luther's relationship with his father did make a positive contribution to his development. The opposition of Hans Luther to Martin's decision to become a monk caused a rift between father and son, but that rift was healed by the year 1521 in a way that gave Luther entitlement to his new vocation as a reformer.[8] In the letter which dedicated the *Judgement on Monastic Vows* (1521) to his father, Luther described his separation from the cloister and the papacy not as rebellion but as liberation. Luther granted that his father had been right to oppose his monastic vocation, but he declared that Christ had now done what his father could not do – release him from scholastic theology, the cloister, and finally from the papacy. Once liberated, however, Luther felt obligated to lead a movement which, in his opinion, Christ had given into his hands. To his father Luther wrote: 'I hope that [Christ] has snatched one son from you in order that through me he might begin to help many other children of his; and I am convinced that you will not only willingly allow this, as you ought, but also rejoice at it with great joy!'[9]

Seeds of Luther's reforming vocation were also planted by his early schooling, especially during the years that he spent in Eisenach (1497–1501) around his mother's relatives.[10] Luther lived in the home of Heinz Schalbe, a prominent citizen of the town and patron of the Franciscan monastery. He attended the school of St George's parish and developed a friendship with Johannes Braun, the vicar at the foundation of St Mary, who reached out to students and with whom Luther later exchanged letters. Those contacts put Luther in touch

---

6 Martin Luther to Philip Melanchthon, 5 June 1530, WABr 5:351.20–7.
7 Erikson, *Young man Luther*, pp. 95–7, 146–50.
8 Hendrix, 'Luther's contribution to the disunity of the Reformation', pp. 51–8.
9 Martin Luther to Hans Luther, 21 November 1521, WA 8:576.18–20; LW 48:336.
10 Siggins, *Luther and his mother*, pp. 45–70; Brecht, *Martin Luther*, vol. 1, pp. 17–21.

with the late medieval piety that permeated the town and included the popular veneration of St Anne. They also anticipated the academic and religious direction of Luther's life.

The cloister

After earning the degrees of Bachelor and Master of Arts at the University of Erfurt, Luther began the study of law in the summer of 1505. A few weeks later, however, he abruptly changed his mind, sold his books, and decided to become a monk. His decision may have been prompted by a severe thunderstorm that frightened Luther on the return to Erfurt from his parents' home in Mansfeld. He cried to St Anne for help and vowed to become a monk if she protected him. True to his word, Luther spent a last evening with his friends and on 17 July 1505, at the age of twenty-one, he entered the monastery of the Augustinian Hermits in Erfurt.

Luther would remain a monk for almost twenty years, the middle third of his life. He removed the cowl for the last time in 1524, less than a year before he married and more than three years after he had been excommunicated and declared an outlaw in the Holy Roman Empire. Although historians have recognized that Luther's vow was not unusual for a young man who had been imbued with late medieval religion, the full impact of Luther's monastic experience has only gradually been appreciated. Biographers have traditionally emphasized the scruples of conscience that afflicted Luther in the monastery. He later recalled that he had been the best monk a person could be, but while he was in the cloister he doubted that he was contrite enough to appease God's wrath and to gain forgiveness. Some relief was obtained from his monastic superior and mentor, Johannes von Staupitz (1468–1524), the vicar-general of the German Augustinians whom Luther succeeded at the University of Wittenberg in 1512. Staupitz eventually gave up the office of vicar-general and decided not to support the Protestant movement, but he left an indelible personal and pastoral mark on Luther.[11]

Luther the reformer finally rejected monasticism, but his time as a monk left its mark. The intense spirituality that was nurtured in the Augustinian Order and its zeal for reform probably influenced Luther more than a specific tradition of Augustinian theology.[12] He adapted the tools of monastic spirituality for the study of scripture and recommended them in place of his own writings. *Oratio, meditatio, tentatio* – praying and meditating on the text with regularity would enable people to make the Bible a comforting resource in times of testing

---

11 Steinmetz, *Luther and Staupitz*, pp. 30–4.   12 Saak, *High way to heaven*, pp. 618–73.

and controversy.[13] Alongside his affirmation of secular life, Luther retained from the monastic ideal an element of detachment from the world that was urged on all believers. In the lectures on Genesis from the last decade of his life, Luther presented the pilgrim Abraham as a true monk and model for Christians who needed to remember that their lasting home was not on earth.[14] Historians now include Luther in their assessment of the Reformation as a 'new monasticism'[15] insofar as it sought to inspire all clergy and laity to lead an intentionally religious life in the world.

The schools

With tongue in cheek, Luther claimed in 1521 that God had taught him the sanctity of the monasteries and the wisdom of the schools so that his detractors could not later claim that he was condemning something about which he knew nothing.[16] Luther rejected much of scholastic theology, to be sure, but he was also well trained by his Nominalist teachers and steeped in the works of Augustine (354–430) whom he consulted as he prepared his early lectures. Apart from what he explicitly rejected, however, scholars have not been able to determine exactly how the theology that undergirded Luther's reforms was shaped by Nominalism, Augustine, medieval Augustinian theologians, or even by medieval mysticism. The search for the roots of Luther's theology has failed to produce a consensus.

In fact, the reformer's theology drew on all these traditions. Nominalism, whose soteriology Luther rejected, may be the source of his emphasis on the authority of scripture, and the covenantal structure of Nominalist thought may underlie Luther's correlation of promise and faith. A distinct medieval Augustinian school has yet to be discovered; most scholars have not been convinced by Oberman's detection of a *via Gregorii* (theology in the tradition of the Augustinian Gregory of Rimini [1300–58]) at the University of Wittenberg.[17] Nevertheless, anti-Pelagian themes like the primacy of grace gave Luther's thought an Augustinian cast that he was quite willing to acknowledge, but not without qualification. During his lectures on Romans (1515–16) Luther read Paul through the eyes of Augustine, whom he praised in 1518 as the apostle's 'most trustworthy interpreter'.[18] That same year Luther published

---

13 *Vorrede zum 1. Band der Wittenberger Ausgabe der deutschen Schriften* (1539), WA 50:659.3–660.16; LW 34:283–8.
14 *In primum librum Mose enarrationes* (1535–45), WA 42:548.21–32; LW 2:398.
15 Moeller, 'Die frühe Reformation in Deutschland als neues Mönchtum', p. 155.
16 Martin Luther to Hans Luther, 21 November 1521, WA 8:574.26–8.
17 Steinmetz, *Luther and Staupitz*, pp. 16–30, Saak, *High way to heaven*, pp. 691–8.
18 *Disputatio Heidelbergae habita* (1518), StA 1:213.26–30; LW 31:39.

for the second time a classic of German mysticism, the *Theologia Deutsch*, with a preface in which he asserted: 'No book except the Bible and St Augustine has come to my attention from which I have learned more about God, Christ, humanity, and all things'.[19] Luther's famous statement, 'the cross alone is our theology',[20] was made as he criticized the scholastic definition of hope and rejected the negative theology of medieval mysticism. At the same time, Luther embraced the experiential wisdom of the mystics and valued the sermons of John Tauler (1300–61) that he annotated around 1516. Even Aristotle, whom Luther blamed for the faults of scholasticism, was still able to make positive contributions to Luther's thought and under the guidance of Melanchthon continued to be studied at Wittenberg.[21]

No one is likely to discover a single irrefutable key to the formation of Luther's theology. It grew out of the academic responsibility that required Luther to bring all the resources of his education and experience to bear on the interpretation of scripture. His theology also profited from interaction and debate with his colleagues. Neither Luther's reform nor his theology originated in isolation and, if that had still been possible prior to 1517, from that point on Luther became part of a religious and political reforming movement.

The politics of reform

Wittenberg

Luther lived in the small university town of Wittenberg from 1512 until his death in 1546, all of that time in the same complex of buildings that formed the cloister of the Augustinian Hermits. When Luther and Katharina von Bora (1499–1552) married in 1525, Elector John of Saxony awarded them the cloister as their home. Wittenberg became the cradle of the Reformation only because Luther and his colleagues taught at the university and because the town was a residence of the Saxon electors. Wittenberg was also used as a political and ecclesiastical testing ground for the earliest reforms. During Luther's exile at the Wartburg Castle (1521–2), the first demonstrations of popular support took place and the first concrete changes were made by Luther's colleagues Andrew Karlstadt (1486–1540), Gabriel Zwilling (1487–1558), and Philip Melanchthon (1497–1560). Although Luther disapproved of the rapid changes and tumult that ensued, Karlstadt proposed a church order that was opposed by Elector

---

19 *Vorrede zu der vollständigen Ausgabe der deutschen Theologie* (1518), WA 1:378.21–3; LW 31:75.
20 *Operationes in psalmos* (1519–21), WA 5:176.29–33.
21 Dieter, *Der junge Luther und Aristoteles*, pp. 257–377; Frank, *Die theologische Philosophie Philipp Melanchthons*, pp. 16–23.

Frederick but eventually adopted by the town council. Luther returned to take over leadership of the Wittenberg movement and Karlstadt was ousted, but the Reformation was under way. Without advocating the reforms Elector Frederick allowed them to proceed, and he continued to protect Luther and the reputation of his university.

Electoral Saxony and the Holy Roman Empire

Reformation scholarship has long emphasized the significance of Saxon and imperial politics for the German Reformation. As an elector of the emperor, Frederick was able to exercise leverage with the papacy and the imperial court. That influence allowed Frederick to gain a hearing for Luther at the imperial diet in Worms (1521) and to shield Luther from the papal excommunication and the imperial ban that were pronounced in 1521. For the rest of his life Luther was confined to Electoral Saxony, except for the occasional safe excursion to Mansfeld, his native county, or to the Marburg Colloquy (1529) in Hesse, where Landgrave Philip ardently supported the Reformation. As a consequence, Luther participated in the work of reform mainly through his writings and correspondence and through representatives like Melanchthon, who attended the religious colloquies of the 1540s, and John Bugenhagen (1485–1558), who helped to organize the Reformation in north Germany and Denmark. At home Luther preached and lectured on a regular basis, published tract after tract, and together with his colleagues advised the Saxon court on the tactics of reform. Supported over his career by three Saxon electors, Frederick, his brother John (1468–1532), and John's son John Frederick I (1503–54), Luther's writings also served their strategies to protect and advance Protestantism.[22]

Luther thought of himself as a German reformer, even though he was ambivalent about the epithet of German prophet. After Emperor Charles V refused to accept the Confession of the evangelical territories at Augsburg in 1530, Luther issued a *Warning to His Dear German People* (1531) not to obey an imperial command to take up arms against the Protestants. The reformer had earlier sanctioned obedience to the emperor and supported a defensive war against the Turks, but after 1530 Luther reversed himself and argued that preservation of the gospel overrode civil duty to a ruler who would threaten it. He claimed: 'I am not seeking my own benefit in this, but the salvation of you Germans'.[23] By the time Emperor Charles V did attack the German Protestants and captured Wittenberg (1547), Luther was dead.

---

22 Edwards, *Luther's last battles*, pp. 38–67.
23 *Warnung an seine lieben Deutschen* (1531), WA 30,3:291.7–9, 20–9; LW 47:29.

The church

Luther the reformer never intended to start a new church, but that statement is misleading if it implies that his agenda was simply to reform the medieval church. As he pursued the goal of Christianization, Luther did not think in terms of medieval and modern, or Catholic and Protestant, churches, but in terms of Germany before and after the rule of the papacy: 'All I seek to do', he wrote, 'is to arouse and set to thinking those who have the ability and inclination to help the German nation to be free and Christian again after the wretched, heathenish, and unchristian rule of the pope'.[24] Luther's agenda was more radical than church reform. In order to Christianize Germany, he believed the church had to be liberated from 'the papacy at Rome'. As a result, Luther expanded the notion of church so that it would be equivalent to the Christian estate, or Christendom, which consisted of all believers, clergy and laity. That Christendom was not tied to Rome but included all those who lived in faith, hope, and love wherever they were found throughout the world.[25] The church was not therefore invisible, only indiscernible until each assembly of believers gathered for worship. These visible assemblies could organize themselves, but they did not form a permanent institution, because genuine Christendom could never be defined by its allegiance to a specific hierarchy like the Roman curia.

In alignment with that ecclesiology, evangelical or Protestant churches were established in the cities and territories that adopted the Reformation, and Luther played a significant role in their construction. For Saxony and other areas he recommended pastors for parishes that were making the sudden transition to evangelical status and provided those parishes with biblical arguments for their authority to judge the teaching of their leaders and to call and dismiss preachers accordingly.[26] With Roman bishops no longer exercising supervision and parishes in disarray after the Revolution of 1525, Luther petitioned Elector John of Saxony, 'out of Christian love . . . and by God's will for the benefit of the gospel and the welfare of the wretched Christians in his territory', to form a commission of visitors who would inspect the parishes and supervise their rehabilitation.[27] For the visitation Melanchthon composed guidelines for teaching, organization, and pastoral practice, and

---

24 *An den christlichen Adel deutscher Nation* (1520), StA 2:125.18–21; LW 44:161.
25 *Von dem Papsttum zu Rom*, WA 6:293.1–5; LW 39:65.
26 *Dass eine christliche Versammlung oder Gemeine Recht und Macht habe, alle Lehre zu urteilen und Lehrer zu berufen, ein- und abzusetzen, Grund und Ursach aus der Schrift* (1523), WA 11:408–16; LW 39:301–14.
27 *Unterricht der Visitatoren an die Pfarrherrn in Kurfürstentum Sachsen* (1528), StA 3:409.3–21; LW 40:271.

Luther produced catechisms, orders of worship, and hymns that were widely used outside Saxony even though he urged pastors and officials to write their own catechisms and church orders for local use.

Luther's support of the princes against the rebellious peasants and his appeal to Elector John to supervise the reordering of parish life have led to the accusation that Luther sold out the popular reformation for a reformation from above. Although he agreed with some demands of the commoners and blamed rulers for their unjust treatment, Luther did oppose the use of violence in the name of Christian justice. He was convinced that the gospel would not lead to revolt but to a Christendom in which the increase of faith and love would alleviate injustice. Nor did Luther mean to support only local religious communities when in 1523 he defended the right of parishes to resist the appointments of clergy made by Roman bishops and other patrons traditionally invested with such authority. In his eyes, evangelical teaching had to be defended at every level against authorities who did not respect it. After 1525, when many parishes were in no position to find and evaluate pastors on their own, Luther wished that evangelical bishops were available for the job, but failing that he argued that rulers like Elector John who did support the gospel could act in the stead of bishops to provide the necessary parochial supervision. The result of both decisions was the formation of territorial and confessional churches that Luther had not foreseen but also did not condemn, because they seemed to be the only stable structures through which evangelical teaching and practice could renew Christendom.

The trajectory of reform (1512–1546)

The Reformation discovery (1515–1518)

In 1545, Luther looked back at the beginning of the Reformation and described a theological insight that was crucial to his development as a reformer. That insight, often called his Reformation discovery, has been debated for decades, but no consensus on its exact nature or date has been reached.[28] As Luther framed it, the dilemma was how to understand the declaration of Romans 1:17 that the righteousness of God, taught to him as a demand of the law, was revealed in the gospel. After meditating day and night, claimed Luther, he studied its context and realized that divine righteousness could only be good news if it was a gift received through faith. 'I felt that I was altogether

---

28 Lohse (ed.), *Der Durchbruch der reformatorischen Erkenntnis bei Luther*; Bayer, *Promissio*; Härle, 'Luther's reformatorische Entdeckung'.

born again', he recalled, 'and had entered paradise through open gates'.[29] His discovery became a resource for reform because it revealed why his monastic life was unsatisfying: no matter how conscientious he was, he could never be deemed righteous if that righteousness was presented as a demand to be met. If righteousness was a gift, however, then it could release believers from anxiety about their salvation; and if he could be liberated from an existence that he found oppressive, then others could find relief and freedom as well.

Luther's earliest writings do not contain an unambiguous statement that corresponds to the flashback from 1545. Some scholars, therefore, have argued that Luther's discovery did not occur until 1518 or 1519 when clearer correlations can be found. In that case, the new insight would have provided theological support for reform only after his attacks on scholastic theology and indulgences had begun. Prior to 1517, claim other historians, passages from his lectures on Romans (1515–16) and other works supply sufficient evidence to conclude that a new theological basis for reform was in place before the conflict with Rome began. In fact, the evidence best supports a growing interaction of theology and reforming practice during the conflict with Rome. Luther may well have applied the discovery to his own struggle without yet realizing its full implications for the sacrament of penance and indulgences. In the *Ninety-five Theses*, Luther attacked the excessive claims being made for a papal indulgence, but it was the encounter with Cardinal Thomas Cajetan (1469–1534) that caused him to rethink the relationship of faith to repentance and the function of the sacraments.

In conflict with Rome (1517–1521)

After the *Ninety-five Theses* arrived in Rome, the curia opened an enquiry into the Luther affair that ended with his formal excommunication in January 1521. The trial was conducted in absentia since Luther was never allowed by the Saxon court to appear in Rome as summoned. It was filled with political intrigue and drama, nonetheless, although not the kind contained in portrayals of Luther as a Protestant hero. Only gradually did Luther realize that the claims made for indulgences and sacramental theology were not open to debate and that the curia had decided to treat his theses as an attack on papal authority. The pope's court theologian, Sylvester Prierias (1456–1523), an expert on penance and canon law, signalled that strategy in his response to the theses: *Dialogue Concerning the Power of the Pope against the Presumptuous Positions of Martin*

---

29 *Praefatio zu Martin Luther, Opera Omnia I* (1545), StA 5:637.2–3; LW 34:337.

Luther (June 1518).[30] Luther learned the same lesson from the papal legate and Thomist scholar who had examined Luther's writings and met with him at Augsburg in October 1518. Cajetan pointed out that Luther's denial of a treasury of merit as the source of indulgences contradicted a papal decree and that Luther's theology of penance departed from traditional views. In the *Explanations of the Ninety-five Theses* (1518), Luther had asserted that people receiving the sacrament of penance should trust with certainty in the words of absolution. Cajetan argued that contrite believers approaching the sacrament remained uncertain of obtaining grace because they could not be sure their contrition was sufficient. To hold Luther's view, said Cajetan, was to teach new and erroneous doctrine and to 'build a new church'.[31]

To this point, Luther had presented his challenge to indulgences as an attempt to uphold papal credibility, but the encounter with Cajetan struck a layer of theological and personal conviction that befit the experience which Luther recalled in 1545. Reporting to Karlstadt on the disagreement over faith and the sacrament, Luther declared he would rather be exiled or burned as a heretic than recant the opinion that had made him a Christian.[32] Luther began to take his vulnerability more seriously after Pope Leo X delivered the definitive defence of indulgences that Luther had requested and after John Eck (1486–1543), at the Leipzig Debate in 1519, elicited from him a declaration that the Council of Constance (1414–18) had erred in declaring John Hus a heretic. Throughout 1520 Luther became more defiant and assertive. He openly identified with Hus and attacked both the Roman hierarchy and the sacramental system of the church. In the *Address to the Christian Nobility*, Luther donned the mantle of a public reformer and called for a politically backed renewal of Christendom apart from the papacy. In response, Pope Leo threatened Luther with excommunication in June 1520, and executed that threat in January of the following year. At the imperial diet in Worms (April 1521), Luther carefully but deliberately refused to recant the views contained in his writings. After receiving twenty-four hours to consider his reply and apologizing for the harshness of his polemical tracts, Luther appealed not only to scripture and his own conscience, but also to 'the consciences of the faithful' that he described as 'miserably ensnared, vexed, and flayed' by the 'tyranny' of the papal church.[33] On their behalf he refused to recant, and the ban of the Empire was lowered over him, his writings, and all his supporters, a ban which Elector Frederick and his advisors then defied.

30 E var 1:341–77.   31 Hendrix, *Luther and the papacy*, p. 62 and p. 173, n. 74.
32 Martin Luther to Andrew Karlstadt, 14 October 1518, WABr 1:217.60–3.
33 *Verhandlungen mit D. M. Luther auf dem Reichstage zu Worms* (1521), WA 7:833.10–13, 17–19.

The conflict with Rome can be oversimplified because its outcome is well known and it wove together many strands – personal, political, religious, and theological – that are difficult to unravel. Nevertheless, the roots of the Reformation and of its significance for the history of Christianity lie buried in the fabric of that conflict and not simply in the head of Luther or in alleged deformities of the late medieval church. A different vision of Christianity, gradually articulated and accepted in some form by commoners and civil authorities, collided with a late medieval Roman Church that for centuries had invested its resources and authority in the Christianization of Europe and could hardly be expected to yield to a single professor, however firmly supported he was by colleagues and his influential prince.

The evangelical leader (1522–1530)

After Luther was surreptitiously taken to the Wartburg Castle, he assumed from a distance the responsibility for reform. Not that he wanted to accomplish it all by himself. Already in July 1521, Luther used a biblical precedent to urge his colleagues to take the message to other towns: 'You lecture, Amsdorf lectures; Jonas will lecture; do you want the kingdom of God to be proclaimed only in your town? Do not others also need the gospel? Will your Antioch not release a Silas or a Paul or a Barnabas for some other work of the Spirit?'[34] For Luther, the early Reformation was to be a missionary enterprise with himself in the lead. The assumption of a new vocation described privately to his father in 1521 also came from the Wartburg; and in the Invocavit sermons delivered after his unauthorized return to Wittenberg in March 1522, he asserted his right to change the direction of reform that had been set by his loyal colleague and supporter Karlstadt. From that point, Luther's jealous way of defending his leadership and responding to dissenters alienated potential allies. Criticizing the radical reformer Thomas Müntzer (1468–1525) in 1524, Luther said he had risked his own life for the evangelical movement and deserved to decide what doctrine was true or untrue. The followers of Müntzer, however, 'enjoy and use the fruits of our victory, such as marrying and discarding the papal laws, though they have done no battle for it and risked no bloodshed to attain it'.[35] In 1526, he accused the Swiss reformers of being fanatics inspired by the devil because they were 'blaspheming the holy and venerable sacrament.'[36] This

---

34 Martin Luther to Philip Melanchthon, 13 July 1521, WABr 2:359.112–15; LW 48:262.
35 *Ein Brief an die Fürsten zu Sachsen von dem aufrührerischen Geist* (1524), WA 15:216.21–8; 215.25–8; LW 40:54–5.
36 *Dass diese Worte Christi (Das ist mein Leib etc.) noch fest stehen wider die Schwarmgeister* (1527), WA 23:71.29–35; LW 37:18.

pattern of denouncing his opponents, which continued to the end of his life, derived from a volatile mixture of missionary zeal with the certainty of a divine call.

This mixture also fuelled Luther's vigorous pursuit of reform during the 1520s. As the evangelical movement accelerated and diversified, he and his colleagues had to adjust their vision of reform to rapid changes. According to Luther's theology of history, they also had to seize the reforming moment that had been given to Germany. 'God's word and grace are like a passing shower of rain', he wrote in 1524, 'which does not return where it once has been'.[37] If Germany ignored this opportunity, then it would fall into a more dreadful darkness than it had endured heretofore. This plea was calculated to convince city councils to establish Christian schools for young people who in the past, Luther alleged, had been corrupted by the universities and monasteries. In general, however, he viewed the emergence of reform and the unmasking of the antichrist in Rome as signs of the last days and the impending judgement of God. The devil had been provoked to a final attack on the gospel and was instigating the stubborn resistance of the papists and the opposition in Protestant ranks as well. The eschatological urgency concentrated Luther's energy and influenced his decisions about reform.

Those decisions were a combination of optimistic expectations and pragmatic politics. First, the Wittenbergers had to decide what changes should be made locally in worship and practice. How quickly should private masses be abolished, both elements given to the laity, and a new public liturgy adopted in the parishes? How should marriage be defined and regulated now that clerical celibacy was no longer required and episcopal courts were no longer available to settle disputes? To what extent should Christians obey civil authority now that princes and city councils were defying the emperor and supporting the Reformation? Should monastic vows be forbidden and what provision should be made for monks and nuns who did not leave their cloisters? If the reform was based upon biblical teaching, how should laity handle business affairs when the end was so near at hand? To answer questions about business conduct, Luther appealed to the Sermon on the Mount and asserted that true Christians should not charge interest. On the issue of civil conduct, however, Luther was more pragmatic and tempered the teaching of the Sermon with the thirteenth chapter of Romans that enjoined obedience to civil authorities. The Revolution of 1525 forced Luther's pragmatism to the forefront of reform,

---

37 *An die Ratherren aller Städte deutschen Landes, dass sie christliche Schulen aufrichten und halten sollen* (1524), WA 15:32.1–14; LW 45:352–3.

but he never gave up hope that the Reformation would produce believers that would closely correspond to the ideal described by him in *The Freedom of A Christian* (1520).

In 1523 Luther admonished communities, out of Christian love and not merely out of civic duty, to redirect the wealth of clerical chapters and monasteries to poor relief, evangelical preaching, and education.[38] Evangelical reforms in Germany endured less because of Luther, however, than because of city councils and princes who enacted them. Protestant church orders like the *Visitation Articles* for Saxony were drawn up for other towns and territories. Luther had indirect influence on these constitutions through colleagues who did in fact leave Wittenberg and supervise the installation of reform elsewhere. He also contributed to the formation of an evangelical identity through his catechisms, hymns, translation of the New Testament, and other writings that were widely circulated. By the end of the 1520s, Luther was still a leading reformer, but the evangelical movement belonged less exclusively to him than ever.

The Lutheran reformer (1531–1546)

After the 500th anniversary of Luther's birth (1983) scholarship turned its attention to the last fifteen years of Luther's life. Sometimes called the older or later Luther, this period includes his writings and political activity after the diet of Augsburg (1530) and the rise of Lutheran confessional awareness. Luther had reservations about the evangelical movement bearing his name. Reproaching overzealous followers in 1522, Luther urged them to 'abolish all party names and call ourselves Christians after him whose teaching we hold'. Luther was not preaching ecumenism, however. 'The papists', he continued, 'deserve to have a party name, because they are not content with the teaching and name of Christ but want to be papist as well'.[39] After 1530, Luther openly identified himself with the name and took stances that sharply distinguished Lutheran teaching from the convictions of Catholics and other Protestants.[40]

Luther's participation in the process of confession building started before 1530. His unyielding stance at the Marburg Colloquy (1529) helped to make the rift over the Lord's Supper into a permanent division between Reformed and Lutheran churches. Although Luther agreed to the Wittenberg Concord

---

38 *Ordnung eines gemeinen Kastens. Ratschlag wie die geistlichen Güter zu handeln sind* (1523), WA 12:11–14; LW 45:169–76.
39 *Eine treue Vermahnung M. Luthers zu allen Christen, sich zu hüten, vor Aufruhr und Empörung* (1522), WA 8:685.4–16; LW 45:70–1.
40 Kittelson, 'Luther on being "Lutheran"', p. 103.

negotiated in 1536 by the Strasbourg reformer Martin Bucer (1491–1551), he resumed his attack on the Swiss after the Concord failed to produce Protestant unity. Luther was united, however, with the Swiss in opposition to Anabaptists and other dissenters from magisterially sanctioned reform. In 1528 he wrote a revealing rejection of believers' baptism in which he claimed for his followers 'much that was Christian and good' under the papacy. Nevertheless, the papacy remained the antichrist: 'When we oppose and reject the pope it is because he does not keep to these treasures of Christendom which he has inherited from the apostles'.[41]

Luther carved out a distinct place for Lutherans on the spectrum between Protestant dissenters and the Roman Church and sharply defined that space in two ways. First, despite the continuity he alleged with medieval Christianity, Luther delineated those teachings and practices that could not be negotiated with the Roman theologians. Among those non-negotiable positions were the sacrifice of the mass, the invocation of saints, monasteries and clerical chapters, and the claim of the papacy to rule by divine right.[42] Second, he reasserted the main positions that distinguished Lutherans from other Protestants: the presence of Christ in the Lord's Supper, the legitimacy of magisterial reform and of infant baptism, and the remission of sin in both sacraments and in absolution. Luther's refusal to compromise these points during the 1530s and 1540s did not, however, prevent confessional strife among Lutherans after his death.

After 1530, the Wittenberg faculty was frequently consulted on political and ecclesiastical policy, and Luther's reforming work was integrated into the collegium of professors who issued advice both to the Saxon court and to enquirers outside Saxony. Luther continued, therefore, to participate in the organization of a different kind of Christianity, but he could not be certain that a new evangelical Christendom or Lutheran church would survive. The expanding movement of the 1530s became vulnerable in the 1540s after the leadership of Philip of Hesse was undermined by his bigamy. Luther's advice to keep the matter a secret backfired, and Catholic fortunes rose as the Council of Trent convened (1545) and Emperor Charles V turned his full attention to Germany. Luther had good reason, therefore, to be worried about the outcome of the Reformation. On the one hand, he asserted that the Reformation was God's work alone and that its future was in divine hands. On the other hand, Luther wrote against Judaism, Islam, and the Roman Church as if they were

---

41 *Von der Wiedertaufe an zwei Pfarrherrn* (1528), WA 26:147.13–18, 148.5–10; LW 40:231–2.
42 *Die Schmalkaldischen Artikel* (1536 / 1538), StA 5:354.11–388.7.

serious threats to the survival of Christendom. He repeatedly denounced Turks, Jews, and papists as enemies of the gospel and agents of the devil's last-ditch stand. The advances of the Ottoman Turks into central Europe did raise legitimate anxiety, but the concern of Luther and other reformers about the Jewish presence in Europe was irrational. It resulted in part from their disappointment that Jews had not appreciated the evangelical message and converted to Christianity in large numbers, and in part from the anti-Jewish climate of late medieval Europe that had already led to persecution and expulsions.

In the 1530s, Luther began to think of himself as belonging to the older generation, and ownership of reform and the need to protect it reasserted themselves. Lecturing on Genesis in 1536, Luther recalled life under the papacy and how difficult it was to free himself and others from it.[43] In a sermon on the Gospel of John around 1539 Luther warned: 'You young people who are not aware of the devil's powerful attacks against this article [that Christ alone is Lord] . . . must hold to it firmly. We old teachers have not yet disposed of the sects; they all rage against it, and even though they are vanquished for a while, they do not give up but rise again and grow.'[44] Luther may have viewed the Reformation as a divine operation, but he spoke as if its survival depended on the vigilance of the next generation.

Theology and impact of reform

Martin Luther did not have a theology in the form of a coherent system that a professor would publish or deliver to students. The Reformation, however, made Luther a more comprehensive theologian than he would have become if his output had been limited to biblical lectures. For the most part, his theology was shaped by the course of reform and the opposition it provoked, and Luther realized it very well. In the preface to his German writings published in 1539, Luther boasted that the assaults of his Roman opponents had made a fairly good theologian of him.[45] Owing to its controversial setting and the issues in dispute, Luther's theology concentrated on the way in which the work of Christ was mediated to believers through the word of God, the church, and the sacraments. As soon as Luther began to question his Nominalist heritage and to reconsider the sacraments, his theology was launched in a direction

---

43 *In primum librum Mose enarrationes* (1535–45), WA 42:440.33–40; LW 2:251.
44 *Auslegung des 3. und 4. Kapitels Johannes in Predigten* (1538–40), WA 47: 64.4–9; LW 22:337.
45 *Vorrede zum 1. Band der Wittenberger Ausgabe der deutschen Schriften* (1539), WA 50:657.10–14; LW 34:287.

that served the agenda of reform. If the goal was to teach believers how they could be liberated from fear of divine punishment, an evangelical theology had to explain first how forgiveness could be freely obtained through faith and still inspire those same believers to obey the commandments and serve others. Then it had to redefine the sacraments so that they served to strengthen that faith and comfort the recipients. Preaching, prayer, and absolution had to be reconceived in the same way, and the church became the community in which believers were fortified through all those means. From this pragmatic centre Luther took on the issues of sin, free will, election, the Trinity, and Christology as they were raised by opponents or in the biblical books on which he lectured. Because of the way his theology developed, it is difficult to isolate one doctrine as its centre;[46] but the hub to which everything else was linked was the conviction that Christ alone was the basis of salvation and the criterion by which all doctrine and piety was to be judged. On that theological basis, Luther became a reformer of religious practice and eventually a reformer of the church.

Martin Luther has influenced later generations through his theology, but his immediate impact was made through the concrete changes that led to new forms of Christianity. He helped to diversify the evangelical movement and to turn that diversification into an array of churches by shaping a Lutheran confession, but Luther had a great deal of help, both from colleagues and from opponents who had their own agendas for the reform of Christendom.

46 Junghans, 'Die Mitte der Theologie Luthers', pp. 190–4; Lohse, *Martin Luther's theology*, pp. 35–41.

2

Emergence and consolidation of Protestantism in the Holy Roman Empire to 1600

THOMAS A. BRADY

German Protestantism began when Martin Luther's call to reform the church, with and then against the papacy, met rejection and resistance by the Emperor Charles V, the bishops, and other rulers. The resulting evangelical movement supplied ideas and motives to allied movements in other kingdoms, some partly successful (France, Poland, and Hungary) and some generally so (England, Scotland, Denmark, and Sweden). German Protestantism was locally a success but nationally a failure, as the very condition that encouraged its survival – permanently dispersed governance – set limits to its power to spread across the Holy Roman Empire. It formed, instead, two communities of religious belief and practices, or confessions, the Lutheran and the Reformed or 'Calvinist'. Their legal coexistence with the old church was framed in 1555 by the Religious Peace of Augsburg and revised in 1648 by the Peace of Westphalia. This outcome was essentially complete by 1600.

The emergence of German Protestantism, 1526–1552

The origins of the transformation of the evangelical movement into Protestantism lie in the middle years of the 1520s: the beginning of organized Catholic resistance in 1524, the German Peasants' War between 1524 and 1526, and the imperial diet of Speyer in 1526. At Speyer the imperial diet (parliament) formulated the kernel of what would become the basis for a political treatment of the religious schism in the provision that each ruler should act 'in such a way as he will be responsible to God and the emperor'.[1] For German Protestantism, the coexistence, achieved in 1555, became the condition of its consolidation by 1600.

Struggle preceded consolidation. At the diet of Speyer in 1529, a small group of evangelical princes and cities protested – whence 'Protestants' – the

---

1 Schmauss (ed.), *Neue und vollständigere Sammlung*, vol. 2, p. 274.

majority's decision to enforce the edict of 1521 against Luther and his follow-ers. 'If we sleep and let the lamps burn out', wrote Landgrave Philip (1509–67), Hesse's twenty-year-old prince, to Jacob Sturm (1489–1553), a magistrate of Strasbourg, 'the Bridegroom will not let us in'.[2] At the diet of Augsburg in 1530, their party submitted a statement of faith, the Augsburg Confession, that would become normative for the Lutheran confession, the evangelical movement's principal heir.

After the Emperor Charles V failed to heal the schism at Augsburg in 1530, the evangelical rulers formed a defensive alliance to defend their faith. Called the 'Smalkaldic League' after the small Thuringian town where they met, it was led by the Elector of Saxony and the Landgrave of Hesse. Its pur-pose, they declared, was 'to give praise and due honour to Almighty God, to foster and spread his holy Word and the gospel, while remaining obedient members of the Holy Empire'.[3] The Smalkaldic League flourished from 1531 to 1547, and despite its military defeat at the emperor's hands, it protected the passage from an amorphous evangelical movement to a politically alert Protestantism.

German Protestantism to the death of Martin Luther

The Smalkaldic League's life coincided with the final fifteen years of Martin Luther's life. During these years, Protestant princes and magistrates:

- suppressed Catholic worship, expelled pastors, dissolved the convents, and redirected ecclesiastical properties to other purposes – public or dynastic;
- established evangelical (Lutheran) doctrine as the sole norm of preaching and practice;
- introduced reformed orders of worship and forbade all others;
- began to form an official regime for their churches;
- replaced ecclesiastical with territorial and civic institutions – marriage courts, poor relief, schools;
- encouraged the recruitment, training, ordination, and installation of a mar-ried evangelical clergy; and
- crippled the Imperial Chamber Court, the only significant judicial instance from which the Catholics could seek redress and restoration.

2 Brady, *Protestant politics*, pp. 71–2.
3 Fabian, *Die Entstehung des Schmalkaldischen Bundes*, pp. 358, line 17; p. 359, line 6.

The fruit of these measures was the Protestant state-church. As most of the changes in religious practice, personnel, and belief were illegal, the rulers required divine authority for them, which the evangelical clergy happily supplied, as they placed themselves almost without reservation under princely and magisterial authority. In return, the rulers repressed all rivals – Catholics, Anabaptists, Zwinglians. The outcome of this bargain was the Protestant state-church, the typical institutional form of German Protestantism. Although Luther had once favoured a gathered church of believers, his experience with radicalism at Wittenberg in 1522 opened his eyes, and in *On Secular Authority* (1523) he formulated his authoritative doctrine of the Christian's duty to obey a Christian ruler. True, he continued to believe, as he wrote privately in 1535, that 'whoever has been called is ordained and should preach to those who have called him, that is the ordination of our Lord God',[4] but the Peasants' War and the growth of the Anabaptist 'false brethren', who wished to serve the Protestants as they had served the Catholics, settled the issue beyond recall. 'If I had never taught or done anything else than I had enhanced and illuminated secular rule and authority', Luther wrote in 1533 (he had said the same thing in 1526), 'this alone should deserve thanks . . . Since the time of the apostles no doctor or writer, no theologian or lawyer has confirmed, instructed, and comforted secular authority more glorious and clearly than I was able to do through special divine grace'.[5] Though he had few illusions about princes – 'usually the greatest fools or the worst knaves on earth' and 'God's jailers and hangmen' – he taught that 'they alone have authority and power', and the office of priests and bishops 'consists in nothing else than in dealing with God's Word'.[6]

The central question of the early years was not whether reform could be undertaken without or against the rulers, but whether anything could be accomplished with them. How daunting the task was first dawned on Luther during the Saxon visitation of 1528 (the first under Protestant auspices). 'Dear God, help us!' he exclaimed a year later in the preface to his *Shorter Catechism*. 'What misery I have seen!' he wrote, 'the common man, especially in the villages, knows absolutely nothing about Christian doctrine, and unfortunately, many pastors are practically unfit and incompetent to teach . . . They live just

---

4 Karant-Nunn, *Luther's pastors*, vol. 69, part 8, p. 56.
5 Luther, 'Verantwortung der aufgelegten Aufruhr von Herzog Georg (1533)', in *D. Martin Luthers Werke*, vol. 38, p. 102, lines 30–3, and p. 103, lines 4–9. There is a nearly identical passage in 'Ob Kriegsleute' (1526), in *Luthers Werke*, vol. 19, p. 625, lines 15–17.
6 Rupp and Drewery, *Martin Luther*, p. 111.

like animals and unreasoning sows'.[7] His response was to advance the concept of the ruler as 'emergency bishop' (*Notbischof*), a conferral which proved permanent. No German Protestant prince or magistrate tolerated on the part of the clergy a separate authority, even to excommunicate notorious sinners. The clergy who resisted, as John Calvin (1509–59) did at Geneva, did so without success. The dissenters knew what was happening. 'You press us [Anabaptists] to abandon our faith and accept yours', the Tyrolean soap-maker Leupold Scharnschlager told Strasbourg's magistrates in 1534, but if you think it right 'to obey the emperor in such things . . . you would be obliged to reinstate all the idolatry and papal convents, also the mass and other things'.[8] This was true, and although Jacob Sturm admitted that 'laws make hypocrites',[9] he did not tolerate 'all sorts of heretical sects, unnecessary argument, and contentious opinions about the faith'.[10]

During the 1530s, Luther and his lieutenants and allies set about the task of reformation under the Smalkaldic League's protection. Most wide-ranging among them were the indefatigable Pomeranian Johannes Bugenhagen (1485–1558), chief travelling agent of Lutheran church order in the northern lands, and his southern counterparts, the Swabian Johannes Brenz (1499–1570) and Martin Bucer of Strasbourg. From Wittenberg flowed a mighty tide of materials – catechisms, sermons, and biblical commentaries – and polemics against Rome, the Zwinglians, and the Anabaptists. For years Luther steadily translated the Old Testament into German, and in 1545 'Luther's Bible', German Protestantism's rock of ages, was printed.

The Lutheran churchmen worked together, apparently without serious friction, though theological controversies were already brewing. Philip Melanchthon (1497–1560), Luther's favourite, thought that salvation must require an act of human will, a personal acceptance of God's saving grace, and argued 'that faith must be supported by means of good works, for without them it would die'.[11] This and other theological undercurrents, such as antinomianism – the law does not bind the justified – simmered until after Luther's death.

In the late 1540s, the near coincidence of the irreplaceable Luther's death (18 February 1546) with the Protestants' military defeat (April 1547) fractured the Lutheran clergy. The diet sat in 1547–8 at Augsburg, where Charles V imposed on the sullen Protestant Estates a provisional church order, called

---

7 Cameron, *European reformation*, pp. 398–97.
8 Brady, *Protestant politics*, p. 112.　　9 *Ibid.*, p. 111.　　10 *Ibid.*
11 Lau and Bizer, *A history of the Reformation in Germany*, p. 92.

the 'Interim', and extracted from them a pledge to attend the general council then sitting at Trent. Duke (now Elector) Maurice of Saxony (r. 1547–53), a Protestant but the emperor's ally and the war's chief beneficiary, was entrusted with enforcing the Interim in Saxony. In the northern city of Magdeburg, a resisting Lutheran clergy had assembled under the leadership of a fierce Croat, Matthias Flacius (1520–75), called 'Illyricus' (the Illyrian). The struggle against the Interim made him leader of an orthodox party which aimed to turn Lutheranism into a fighting faith. The party was vindicated in 1552, when Elector Maurice turned his coat to ally with the King of France and lead a group of Lutheran princes against the now helpless emperor. The insurrection was ended by an agreement (Treaty of Passau) between Elector Maurice and King Ferdinand, Charles's younger brother and heir-designate to a political *modus vivendi* in lieu of an end to the religious schism. This pact cleared the way for the second generation of German Protestantism. The 'Judas of Meissen', as some Protestants called Maurice for his actions in 1547, enabled German Protestantism to snatch victory from the jaws of their defeat.

An era of respite, 1555–1600

The Religious Peace of Augsburg demonstrated the failure of Emperor Charles's policy with respect to the Protestants, and he knew it. In his farewell address in 1556, Charles declared that he had sought 'to watch over Germany, my dear fatherland, and my other realms', but because Luther and other German heretics, plus other enemies, had embroiled him in 'perilous wars out of hatred and envy, I have not attained these goals to the degree that I have always desired'.[12] The deal with the heretics was already done. Meeting in 1555 at Augsburg, the diet endorsed the twenty-four paragraphs that came to be called 'the Religious Peace of Augsburg'. With some modification made in 1648, this agreement regulated confessional coexistence in the German lands until 1803.

The Peace declared the Protestants – adherents of the Augsburg Confession of 1530 – to be a licit religious community on the basis of the principle of 1526: the Imperial Estates – princes, nobles, and urban magistrates – possessed the *ius reformandi* (right of reformation). Each ruler might declare which religion could be practised in his (or their) lands, though dissenting subjects enjoyed the right to emigrate rather than conform. The Peace made certain other provisos, including exceptions that would play a significant role in its breakdown on the

---

12 Schilling, *Aufbruch und Krise*, pp. 253–4.

eve of the Thirty Years' War. The essential provision, the ruler's right to require the religious conformity of his subjects, was summarized in 1586 by Joachim Stephan (1544–1623), a Greifswald law professor: 'whose the regime, his the religion' (cuius regio, eius religio).

The two decades of relative religious peace that succeeded three decades of strife witnessed many acts of accommodation between the confessions. In 1584 in the bi-confessional town of Ravensburg, a spring storm set the church tower on fire, and Catholics and Lutherans formed a common fund for repairs to the house of worship they shared. Yet the peace remained uneasy, because the European reformations were surging forward. Well before the century's end there appeared a new menace to German Lutheranism in the form of a second Protestant confession, Calvinism, and not long after the astonishing recovery of the Catholic Church in the Empire began.

Meanwhile, the Protestant faith continued to advance under Ferdinand I (r. 1556–64) and Maximilian II (r. 1564–76), his son and successor. By the end of the latter's reign, the faith was officially established in three electorates, thirty-four other principalities, seventy-six counties and baronies, fifty-five or so self-governing cities, two archbishoprics, and eleven bishoprics. It threatened the Catholic position in a further thirteen principalities and three bishoprics; and its influence was growing in a further two principalities, two archbishoprics, and eleven bishoprics.[13] Most calamitous for the Catholic Church were conditions in Austria's five eastern duchies, where huge numbers of nobles and burghers had converted to Lutheranism, and it is not entirely exaggerated to say that 'by the middle of the sixteenth century the ethos of the Austrian Habsburg lands was Protestant'.[14] When Thomas Chrön (1560–1630), a convert from Protestantism, became Catholic bishop of Ljubljana / Laibach in 1599, he chose as his motto: 'The task is frightening; look [rather] to the reward'.[15] The end of the old faith in the Empire seemed near. In 1574 Lazarus von Schwendi (1522–84), an imperial general and a Protestant, advised Emperor Maximilian that 'the common man no longer has any regard for the old ways and ceremonies of the Roman clergy, except to the degree that his ruler binds him to them', so that 'the old people, who still had piety and zeal, are daily dying off, [and] the youth cannot be reined in'.[16]

Blame for this continuing decline of Catholicism is sometimes ascribed to Emperor Maximilian, who doubtless did incline to Protestant views. Yet

13 Jedin, Latourette, and Martin (eds.), Atlas zur Kirchengeschichte, p. 73.
14 Evans, The making of the Habsburg monarchy, p. 3.
15 May, Die deutschen Bischöfe, pp. 11–13.
16 Lazarus von Schwendi, Denkschrift über die politische Lage des Deutschen Reiches, pp. 18–19.

Catholicism had receded just as fast under his father, who did not. Protestantism's continued advance can be laid more to the momentum it carried out of earlier days, together with the political understanding Elector August of Saxony (1526–86), political chief of the Protestant Estates, maintained with the emperors. In and around August's lands, the fate of Lutheranism was decided, as post-Luther Lutheranism plunged into the strife and agonies that transformed it from a movement into a confession.

The creation of Lutheranism

An appreciation of German Protestantism's achievements during the three decades after Luther's death is easily obscured by the commonly expressed opinion that the first wave of the evangelical movement had produced whole populations solidly dedicated to the new faith. Luther and his fellows had no such illusion. His visitation commission reported to the Saxon elector in 1535 that 'peasants, burghers, and nobles naturally hate pastors, [and] many noblemen, and in the cities the burghers, abuse the holy Gospel without measure ... In many places the servants of the Word are held in such contempt, that unless this attitude is improved, few men will be willing to enter'.[17] This was not only a Saxon problem. Half a century after the wild 1520s, a Jesuit named Jacob Rabus surveyed – not, of course, with an impartial eye – the religious situation in his native city:

> In poor Strasbourg you now have five or six sects among the common people. One fellow is an out-and-out Lutheran, the second a half-Lutheran, the third a Zwinglian, the fourth a Calvinist, the fifth a Schwenckfelder, the sixth an Anabaptist, and the seventh lot is purely epicurean.[18]

The task of forming such peoples into a disciplined, practising, and believing community proved to be the work not of one or even several generations, but of many.

Lutheranism after Luther seemed hardly able to shoulder this burden, for its clergy had plunged into strife over doctrine, the defining mark of Lutheranism as a confession. In 1577 the peace-making authors of the Formula of Concord looked back on this terrible situation. 'It is common knowledge, obvious and no secret', they wrote, 'what kind of very dangerous situations and troublesome disturbances arose in our beloved fatherland, the German nation, soon after the

---

17 Karant-Nunn, *Luther's pastors*, p. 54.
18 Brady, 'In search of the godly city', in Hsia (ed.), *The German people and the Reformation*, p. 29.

Christian death of that highly enlightened and pious man, Dr Martin Luther'.[19] 'The enemy of the human race', they declared, 'endeavoured to scatter his seeds of false doctrine and disunity, to execute harmful and aggravating divisions in churches and schools, and thereby to adulterate the pure teaching of God's Word, to break the bond of Christian love and unity, and in this way to prevent and impede noticeably the course of the holy gospel'.[20]

They were right to blame 'the enemy of the human race', for just at this time the devil and his demons were enjoying unprecedented attention among Protestants in the German lands. Where earlier popular texts, notably Sebastian Brant's *Ship of Fools* and Erasmus's *Praise of Folly*, had attributed the world's ills to foolishness, Lutheran writers ascribed them to demons. There were beer devils, hair devils, oven devils, trouser devils, and shoe devils – enough devils to be responsible for anything and everything that could go on. In 1569 the Frankfurt publisher Sigmund Feyerabend (1528–90) and the Saxon clergyman Andreas Musculus (1514–81) teamed up to produce a *Theatre of Devils* (*Theatrum diabolorum*), the ultimate catalogue of this wicked tribe.

The demons' hegemony drew strength from the profound apocalypticism that permeated early Lutheran thought. Luther himself had set this tone, declaring that we live out our lives 'between God and the devil . . . in the shadow of the chaos of the Last Days and the imminence of eternity'.[21] Who but the devil himself could have sown the seeds of so many divisions? The plethora of doctrinal controversies is simply staggering:

- Antinomian (1520s–1570s) – whether Christians are bound by the natural and Mosaic law (Luther's 'third use of the law') or free to follow the direct impulses of the Holy Spirit (Johann Agricola [*c.* 1492–1566]);
- Adiaphorist (1548–55) – whether matters of faith, Christian doctrine, and church practice can be divided into essentials and non-essentials (Greek, *adiaphora*) ('Philippists', after Philip Melanchthon), or 'nothing is an adiaphoron in the case of confession and offence' (Matthias Flacius Illyricus [1520–75]);
- Majorist (1551–62) – whether 'good works are necessary for salvation' (Georg Major [1502–74]);
- Synergist (1550s) – whether the human will is a force in conversion (Melanchthon), or one cannot distinguish between nature as created and nature as human sin (Flacius);

---

19 Kolb and Wengert (eds.), *The Book of Concord: the confessions of the Evangelical Lutheran Church* (Minneapolis: Fortress Press, 2000), p. 5.
20 Kolb and Wengert (eds.), *Book of Concord*, pp. 5–6.
21 Oberman, *Luther: man between God and the Devil*, p. 12.

- Crypto-Calvinist – whether the human as well as the divine nature of Christ is present (as 'Philippists' alleged); and
- Osiandrist (1550s) – whether an indwelling of Christ's divine nature in the believer produces moral renewal (Andreas Osiander [*c.* 1496–1552]).

Although one is tempted, reading this list, to conclude that Luther had settled nothing, the real problem was that his successors piously believed that he had settled everything. 'The authority of the living teacher', one historian has written, 'was transformed into the written authority of the corpus of his works'.[22] Luther's authority had no rival or even parallel in Protestant history from his own day to ours. 'Our revered father and our most believed preceptor', his beloved disciple Philip Melanchthon called him, 'the horseman and chariot of Israel'.[23]

In truth, unity did not spring unbidden from Luther's heritage – nor from the Bible he had striven to restore – it had to be forged. The most important split arose from the fight over the Leipzig Interim and the Magdeburg resistance. The parties were called 'gnesio-Lutheran' (i.e., Orthodox) and 'Philippist' (after Philip Melanchthon). Their cockpit was the two Saxonys, where from their respective strongholds in the universities of Jena and Wittenberg they sought to drown their opponents in mighty rivers of print. Elector August sponsored the Philippists, who supported his policy of collaborating with the emperor to enforce the Religious Peace, while his cousins in the diminished lands called 'Ducal Saxony' (the electorate having been transferred in 1547 to August's line) harboured the Orthodox. They, the sons of the dispossessed Elector John Frederick, who had led the Protestant cause to defeat in 1547, nursed their grievances against August, the emperor, and their own fate. The eldest son, John Frederick II (1529–95), even plotted the overthrow of all their foes, until August, armed with an imperial decree of outlawry against his cousin, invaded his lands, sent John Frederick into permanent exile in distant Austria, and recouped his losses from his lands.

This melancholy story bears importantly on the history of the Lutheran doctrinal disputes, for August's victory freed him to deal with the religious split. His influence in the German Protestant world rested on his prestige as an imperial elector, as head of the Protestant Estates in the imperial diet, and as the emperor's collaborator. The elector stood at the heart of German Protestantism both politically and geographically, in the middle of the

---

22 Kolb, *Martin Luther as prophet*, p. 33.   23 *Ibid.*, p. 36.

Protestant belt of lands that stretched from Württemberg and the free cities in the south-west to Brandenburg, Mecklenburg, Pomerania, and Prussia in the north-east. Moreover, Luther's fame had transformed Wittenberg from a provincial institution into the most popular university in the German-speaking world, making August's Saxony the centre of a Lutheran culture that reached into Sweden and Prince Hamlet's Denmark.

At August's court, the Philippists, some sympathetic to Calvinism – though the name 'crypto-Calvinists' is an exaggeration – held sway until 1574, when August, a cunning and devious prince, turned on them and purged them with impressive cruelty. Orthodox theologians and laymen rejoiced.

The way to reunion now lay open. It was taken by a group of able, younger Lutheran theologians bent on ending the disunity and strife: Jacob Andreae (1529–90), a blacksmith's son from Waiblingen in Württemberg and professor of theology at Tübingen; Martin Chemnitz (1522–86), son of a Brandenburg weaver, a reformer of the duchy of Brunswick-Wolfenbüttel, and a fierce hammer of the Catholics; and Nikolaus Selnecker (1532–92), a Franconian, former (semi-Philippist) court-preacher at Dresden and superintendent-general of the church in Brunswick-Wolfenbüttel. This group shaped the Lutheran peace of 1577–80. They depended on the dukes of Württemberg and Brunswick-Wolfenbüttel, whose emergence as Lutheran powers gave Protestantism a political shape that straddled the differences between south and north. Once August had dumped the Philippists in 1574, the negotiations for unity came thick and fast: Torgau in 1576, Tangermünde in 1578, Smalkalden in 1578, and Jüterborg in 1579, plus three meetings at Bergen Abbey near Magdeburg, where the Formula of Concord was signed in 1577. Three years later, in 1580, *The Book of Concord* was produced, thirty years after the Augsburg Confession had been signed.

Nothing could have been more appropriate to the ethos of Lutheranism than a unity achieved through formulations of doctrine. The Book of Concord contains the three brief ecumenical creeds – Apostles', Nicene, and Athanasian – and the huge Formula of Concord of 1577, plus texts composed, or at least approved, by Luther, hundreds of pages of them. It presented a canonical interpretation of the Augsburg Confession, aiming

> not to manufacture anything new through this work of concord, nor to depart in either substance or expression to the smallest degree from the divine truth, acknowledged and professed at one time by our blessed predecessors and us, as based on the prophetic and apostolic scripture and comprehended in the three

Creeds, in the Augsburg Confession presented in 1530 to Emperor Charles of kindest memory, in the Apology that followed it, and in the Smalkald Articles and the Large and Small Catechisms of that highly enlightened man, Dr. Luther.[24]

Signatories pledged 'to live in genuine peace and unity with our colleagues, the electors, princes, and estates in the Holy Roman Empire'.[25] This stroke of genius – doctrinal orthodoxy wedded to political accommodation – gained the adherence of three electors, twenty other princes, twenty-eight counts and barons, thirty-five urban regimes, and 8,000 Protestant pastors. When these rulers pledged themselves not to break the restored fellowship, the Lutheran confession was born.

Lutheranism regained unity through precisely what had divided it: Martin Luther's restoration of the *vera doctrina*, true Christian doctrine. The power of his reputation was untouched by thirty years of strife. Erasmus Alber (1500–53), a priest's son from the Wetterau, Luther's student, and then pastor at Neubrandenburg, composed a song about 'the dear, pious, Luther, tender / the Germans' true prophet, / who correctly taught us God's Word'.[26] A generation later, Cyriakus Spangenberg (1528–1604) of Eisleben, Luther's home town, wrote that he

> diligently read the Holy Scripture and, alongside, its only true interpreter, Luther. But [though] indeed God did not send Luther to us Germans in vain, [He] has let many learned theologians sink and fall to such a low estimate of the writings of this precious man, the true German prophet, Dr. Luther, that they read him very little and follow them not at all.[27]

Luther's charisma and his apocalyptic vision did not die with him, but survived to inspire a Lutheranism beset by enemies within and without. From every side came fresh evidence of the devil's progress towards the end of days. 'Lord, preserve us in Your Word', runs a hymn published by Cyriakus Spangenberg, 'And send death to Pope and Turk, / Who hate Jesus Christ, Your only Son / And aim to throw Him off His throne'.[28] This, he noted, was a good song for children to sing.

Of all the terrible emanations of the Roman antichrist, perhaps the worst was the new (Gregorian) calendar that Pope Gregory XIII (r. 1572–85) introduced in 1582. The Württemberg court-preacher Lucas Osiander (1534–1604) attacked it as a tyrannical violation of 'Christian liberty' and opined that the pope

---

24 Kolb and Wengert (eds.), *Book of Concord*, p. 15.   25 *Ibid.*
26 Kolb, *Martin Luther as prophet*, p. 37.   27 *Ibid.*, p. 47.
28 Zeeden, *Konfessionsbildung*, pp. 333–6.

would do better to reform 'the errors, abuses, and terrible conditions in the papist church'.[29] In vain the Lutheran astronomer Johann Kepler (1571–1630) defended Gregory's calendar, writing that 'many proposals were made, but I don't know whether a better way could be found than the one introduced by the pope'.[30]

The restoration of Lutheran community vitally aided the task of reconstruction. At its centre lay clerical recruitment and training, a subject which, as it is dealt with elsewhere in this volume, can be treated here in a few words. Luther and his lieutenants were well aware that the noble and burgher elites scorned to send their sons into an unbeneficed evangelical clergy. 'The rich do not want to become pastors and preachers', Melanchthon observed, so 'it is necessary . . . to offer scholarships to the poor so that they can study theology'.[31] 'Poor' is, of course, a relative term. The first Protestant pastors, mostly burghers, had been recruited from former Catholic priests and monks, but soon the recruitment, training, and installation of a new clergy began. They, too, were mostly townsmen. Between 1537 and 1550, 84 per cent of the 1,117 ordinands at Wittenberg, the biggest supplier, listed their former occupations as teachers, secretaries, students, or church officials, plus 10 per cent who were burghers of unspecified occupation. Their training was an emergency measure, dictated by ceaseless calls for pastors from other territories and cities. Most of those sent out were probably less well educated than their fifteenth-century counterparts had been, though in time this, too, improved.

The supply of clergy was vital to the creation of German Protestantism's most distinctive creation, the 'pastors' church' (*Pastorenkirche*) served by a self-reproducing clerical caste bound together by intermarriage and common school experiences. The process has been studied for the years from 1585 to 1630 in the duchy of Brunswick-Wolfenbüttel, where an astonishing 77.5 per cent of the rural and 72.8 per cent of the urban clergy were either sons or sons-in-law of pastors.[32] Much the same process, though different in detail, occurred in the landgraviate of Hesse-Cassel. Over time, the creation of a biologically, socially, and culturally self-reproducing clerical caste contributed much to the extraordinary cultural flowering of German Protestant culture in the eighteenth century.

Three processes lay behind the consolidation of German Protestantism in its Lutheran form. First, the church was reformed as state-church under

---

29 Traitler, *Konfession und Politik*, pp. 141–4. He was the son of the theologian Andreas Osiander (1498–1552), a (losing) participant in a post-Luther doctrinal controversy.

30 Roeck (ed.), *Gegenreformation*, pp. 101–3.   31 Karant-Nunn, *Luther's pastors*, p. 13.

32 The figures are from Schorn-Schütte, *Evangelische Geistlichkeit*, pp. 479–88.

supervision of the prince, noble, or urban magistracy, who recruited and paid the ministers and oversaw church governance and the visitation and discipline of local churches. Second, dependent on the first, the overcoming of thirty years of doctrinal strife began with the Formula of Concord of 1577 and the *Book of Concord* of 1580. Third, the formation of a new, self-reproducing caste within the middling classes gave a social stability and continuing cultural integrity to the territorial and urban churches, while encouraging at the same time a trans-political consciousness of Lutheranism as a single religious community, a confession. By 1580, therefore, smooth sailing lay ahead for German Protestantism. Not quite, for although to this point we have looked at it as an emerging confession, since the 1560s German Protestantism was, in fact, two confessions. The second Protestant confession – Reformed or Calvinist – shared the determination of their co-confessionalists in other countries – France, England, the Netherlands, and Scotland – to form godly churches at home and to fight Rome abroad. In the Empire, ironically, the Calvinist advance took place almost entirely at Lutheran expense.

Calvinism: the bid for a second Reformation

The Calvinism that appeared in the Empire with the conversion in 1561 of Elector Palatine Frederick III (r. 1559–76), called 'the Pious', was hardly an alien faith. If newly inspired by Geneva, it also bore the heritage of Zwingli's Zurich. Heidelberg, the elector's capital, became the German Reformed confession's centre whither streamed since the late 1550s Calvinist refugees from France, the Netherlands, and German Protestant states, such as Strasbourg, that opted for Orthodox Lutheranism. Autonomous Reformed communities formed at Aachen, Metz, Trier, on the Lower Rhine, on the North Sea coast at Emden and Bremen, and in Silesia. Intended for all of them, in 1563 appeared the Heidelberg Catechism, composed by Caspar Olevianus (1536–87) of Trier and Zacharias Ursinus (1534–84) of Breslau, the founding fathers of the German Reformed confession. It came to hold the place that the Augsburg Confession held in Lutheranism. The Reformed confession nonetheless distinguished itself from the Lutheran through its political activism, especially its ties to international Protestantism. Under the Palatine regent John Casimir (1543–92), who several times campaigned with the French Protestants, Heidelberg and its university became the hub of a faith deeply engaged with the fate of international Calvinism.

In some respects, the German Reformed confession represented Zwingli's revenge on Luther's legacy. The Reformed always contended that they did not represent a new faith but a common one, and that they were merely reforming true practice as Luther had restored true doctrine. Wilhelm Zepper (1550–1607), professor of theology at Herborn and Inspector in the (Reformed) church of Nassau-Dillenburg, wrote in 1596 that the church's two pillars were its 'spiritual structure', and its 'teaching on faith' and 'teaching on life'. Luther and his colleagues had been totally engaged in reforming 'doctrine as the principal matter against the violent intrigues, rage, and insane behaviour of the pope and his crew', but now had come the time 'to take in hand a proper reformation in the other chief matter, the Christian way of life'.[33]

The Lutherans, understandably, did not see things in this light. They, after all, not the Catholics, were the chief targets of Reformed reformation, and in some states the conversion of a ruler meant the crack of doom for Lutheran belief and practice. The Reformed were known to bake hard objects in the eucharistic bread, proof that it was but mere bread. Some lands were converted more than once, the champion being the Palatinate, where a subject who had begun life as a Catholic could reckon having subsequently been twice a Lutheran and twice a Calvinist.

Relations between the two Protestant confessions resembled an inner-Protestant version of the antipathy between German Protestantism and Catholicism. Electress Anna of Saxony (1532–85), the Danish royal princess who married August I, warned her daughter, Elizabeth, not to attend Reformed services with her husband, the Elector Palatine, and when Elizabeth's baby was born dead, Anna wrote to her that the child was better off dead than a Calvinist. As the Reformed faith penetrated land after Lutheran land, the hatred deepened. While August and the other Lutheran princes hesitated to abandon the Elector Palatine to the Catholics' mercies, they knew Heidelberg was persecuting its Lutheran subjects in the Upper Palatinate, where in 1592 two Calvinist officials were lynched. Worse, among the 'Calvinists' at the electoral court were several known antitrinitarians (one was executed, another died a Muslim at Istanbul).

Soon the Protestant courts were hosting clusters of Protestant religious refugees from Protestant lands – clergymen, lawyers, and nobles. Otto von Grünrade, a Saxon noble who headed the elector's Ecclesiastical Council at Heidelberg, declared in 1586 that 'praise God, my earthly fatherland is not so dear to me, that I would not prefer to live in the Reformed Church, my truer fatherland'.[34] Shortly he would be welcome at home, for that year August died,

33 Münch, 'Volkskultur und Calvinismus', pp. 296–7.
34 Rabe, *Deutsche Geschichte 1500–1600*, p. 562.

and the Reformed faith flourished at the court of his son, Elector Christian I (1560–91). At the head of the Reformed enterprise in Saxony stood his old tutor and now chancellor, Nicolaus Krell (1550–1601), who in 1587–8 oversaw a Reformed reformation of the court, the church, and the universities. Nobles and clergy resisted this invasion of Saxony, the Lutheran Reformation's heartland, and at Christian's death Kress was arrested and, after ten years in prison, beheaded by a sword bearing the legend, 'Calvinists, beware!'

The Reformed episode in Saxony illustrates the close connection between that confession and the international Protestant crusade against Rome, the chief (as it was thought) common enemy. In 1589 Christian abandoned his father's policy of accommodation for active collaboration with the Calvinist/Reformed front that now stretched from Saxony through the Palatinate to France and the Netherlands, and in 1591 he sponsored the Union of Torgau, the first pan-Protestant league in the Empire. The nearly simultaneous deaths of John Casimir, the Palatine regent, and of Christian of Saxony, which was followed by a powerful Lutheran retrenchment, dashed this promising beginning to oblivion.

Similar efforts to guide other Lutheran principalities, notably Baden-Durlach and Schleswig-Holstein, into the Reformed fold met with similar fates, though the Nassau lands and neighbouring Hesse-Kassel were taken over to that camp. The greatest failure after Saxony, however, occurred in Brandenburg, where in 1613 the young Elector John Sigismund (1572–1619) declared his conversion to the Reformed faith but proved unable to break the confessional resistance of his Lutheran clergy and nobles. Thus the advance of the Reformed faith in the Empire was halted before the outbreak of the Thirty Years' War in 1618.

The German Reformed confession's outstanding mark was its highly authoritarian character. It had no truck with communal liberties or with the types of mixed clerical-lay governance favoured in Calvinist kingdoms abroad. The model for this came from the Palatinate, the church of which, highly centralized under the elector's Ecclesiastical Council. supplied a model to other German Reformation churches.[35] This condition ended a bitter struggle at Heidelberg between the clergy, who mostly favoured the Genevan style of co-governance, and the lay councillors, who favoured the magisterial monopoly practised at Zurich. The theorist of centralized lay governance was a son of Swiss peasants, the physician Thomas Erastus (1524–83) from Baden in the Aargau. The power to excommunicate, as always, formed the most neuralgic

---

35 Jedin, *Atlas zur Kirchengeschichte*, p. 75.

point. The clerical advocates of the 'excommunicatory fever', Erastus wrote, held that 'some certain presbyters should sit in the name of the whole Church and should judge who were worthy or unworthy to come unto the Lord's Supper'. Since the Word, but not the sacraments, was necessary to salvation, why, he asked, 'do we go about to exclude nobody from the word, while from the sacraments, especially the Lord's Supper, we would exclude some, and that contrary to, or without, the express command of God'?[36] 'Wherever the magistrate is godly', Erastus asserted, 'there is no need of any other authority under any other pretension or title to rule or punish the people – as if the Christian magistrate differed nothing from the heathen'.[37] He and his party held the day, and western-style Calvinist churches based on classes and presbyteries were hardly to be found in German Reformed territories. The German Reformed state represented an intensified form of the German Lutheran state and in this light a genuine 'Second Reformation'.

Around 1600 the Reformed confession reached the peak of its fortunes in Europe and in the German lands. The two were closely linked. Twenty years later, the Silesian pastor Abraham Scultetus (1566–1625), formerly court-preacher at Heidelberg, described the mood of the 1590s:

> I cannot fail to recall the optimistic mood which I and many others felt when we considered the condition of the Reformed churches in 1591. In France there ruled the valiant King Henry IV, in England the mighty Queen Elizabeth, in Scotland the learned King James, in the Palatinate the bold hero John Casimir, in Saxony the courageous and powerful Elector Christian I, in Hesse the clever and prudent Landgrave William, who were all inclined to the Reformed religion . . . We imagined that *aureum seculum*, a golden age, had dawned.[38]

Then, however, fortune dashed their hopes, 'for within twelve months the Elector of Saxony, the count palatine, and the landgrave all died, King Henry deserted the true faith, and all our golden hopes went up in smoke'.[39] 'The trust that one places in the most courageous, the richest, or the most skilled princes', Scultetus mused, 'is fruitless and foolish, because the honour of preserving churches is due not to this world, but to heaven; not to men, but to the Lord God'.[40]

Historians debate whether the German Reformed confession grew organically out of German Lutheranism or represented an alien intrusion into the Lutheran world. Was it a child of Luther's Reformation or the vanguard of a 'second Reformation' bearing new beliefs and practices? Suggestive is that the

---

36 Erastus, *Theses*, thesis xxxviii.   37 *Ibid.*, thesis lxxiv.
38 Cohn, 'Territorial princes', p. 135.   39 *Ibid.*   40 *Ibid.*

Reformed faith almost always represented itself as a kind of improved Lutheran Reformation. Chancellor Krell of Saxony presented himself as neither Orthodox Lutheran nor Calvinist – thus, a Philippist – though his writings and policies reveal him to have been 'a late sixteenth-century German Reformed [believer]'.[41] Krell's writings, however, prudently avoided reference to Calvinist texts. John Sigismund of Brandenburg observed a similar prudence, when he confessed his conversion to the Reformed Faith. Yet the Lutheran princes, at least, could be practical about confession. In 1566 at the diet of Augsburg, Duke Christoph of Württemberg (1515–68) complained of the 'heretical catechism' (of Heidelberg), and Elector Palatine Frederick III responded with the Reformed case for continuity with Luther's Reformation. Christoph then sheepishly admitted that if Frederick were condemned, 'the persecutions in France, Spain, the Netherlands and other similar places would grow at once by heaps, and by that condemnation we should be guilty of shedding their blood'.[42] Such pragmatism encouraged belief in the essential oneness of the two confessions and hence of German Protestantism. Not among the theologians, however, who insisted that Lutheran and Reformed were two incompatible faiths, one true and the other heretical. No one doubted how the Saxon court-preacher Matthias Höe von Höenegg (1580–1645) would answer his own question, 'whether and why one should have more to do with and trust more the papists than the Calvinists'.[43] Better Rome than Geneva.

41 Klein, *Der Kampf um die zweite Reformation*, p. 29.
42 Hollweg, *Der Augsburger Reichstag*, p. 387.
43 Neveux, *Vie spirituelle et vie sociale entre Rhin et Baltique*, p. 11.

3

The radical Reformation

R. EMMET McLAUGHLIN

Neither Catholic nor Protestant, Anabaptism and Spiritualism constituted another, more radical, Reformation in the sixteenth century.[1] Although they agreed with Catholics and Protestants in important ways, they also departed from both on essentials. Following Luther and the Protestants, they rejected the Catholic hierarchy as mediator of divine grace, authoritative source of doctrine, and gatekeeper to the Lord's sheepfold. They also agreed with Protestantism by according faith and scripture unprecedented weight. However, they rejected a purely imputed forensic righteousness[2] and refused to separate justification and sanctification as sharply as Protestantism did. In effect, they returned to the Catholic 'faith formed by love'. Distinctive teachings on the Bible, the sacraments, and the religious role of the state made them anathema to Protestants and Catholics alike. They hint at the rich variety of Christian expression with roots in the later Middle Ages that lay concealed alongside, and beneath, Tridentine Roman Catholicism and classical Protestantism.

In reappropriating Catholic elements, the radicals drew upon their general religious formation, since all first-generation reformers were, after all, Catholics. However, the radicals also made use of certain identifiable sources. Mysticism, Erasmus, and monasticism were the most important. Late medieval mysticism, particularly the anonymous *Theologia Germanica* published by Luther (1516; 1518) and the works of Johannes Tauler (*c.* 1300–61) contributed an emphasis on inwardness, suffering, and a disinterest in externals.[3] It also urged a *Gelassenheit* (resignation) that could be applied not only to mental prepossessions, but to material possessions as well. Erasmian

---

1 Williams, *Spiritual and Anabaptist writers*, pp. 19–35; Williams, *Radical Reformation*, pp. xxviii–xxxvi. I limit myself, for the most part, to central Europe, especially the Germanic-speaking lands. As a result, I do not discuss Williams's third category, Unitarianism.
2 That is, a purely 'legal' declaration of God's forgiveness not tied to any actual improvement or righteousness in the sinner. Christ's righteousness is merely imputed to the sinner.
3 Ozment, *Mysticism and dissent*; Goertz, *Innerer und äusserer Ordnung*; Packull, *Mysticism and the Anabaptist movement*.

humanism reinforced inwardness and de-emphasis on externals. Erasmus of Rotterdam (1446–1536) inspired the radicals through his Neoplatonism, defence of free will, appeal to the authority of scripture, recommendation of the Bible to the laity, emphasis upon Christ as model and teacher, preference for simplicity, and concern that principle and practice coincide. All surface repeatedly among the radicals.[4] His exegesis of the Great Commission (Matthew 28:18–20) in large measure defined Anabaptism. Finally, monasticism and ascetic thought were particularly significant for Anabaptism.[5] During the Middle Ages 'conversion' to monasticism had been equated with a second baptism. The attempt to follow in Christ's footsteps exactly, the community of goods, the use of discipline, the stringent pacifism, and the stark contrast between the monastery and the 'world' all reappear among the Anabaptists. Mysticism, Erasmian humanism, and monasticism had each implicitly challenged the hierarchical sacramental church by offering alternative visions of heartfelt religion. Unrestrained by tradition, loyalty or affection for the Catholic Church, the radicals pursued some implications of those visions to their most dangerous conclusions.

The radicals were among the earliest partisans of reform and developed their distinctive teachings during the heady 1520s before Lutheran and Reformed orthodoxies took shape. Luther's theological challenge to the Catholic Church only moved from the lecture halls to the parishes after 1520. Between 1521 and 1525 Karlstadt, Müntzer, and the Grebel circle were among the first to turn reforming rhetoric into church practice. The Peasants' War, the eucharistic controversy, and the first rebaptisms in 1525 began a second phase that extended to around 1530 and saw the full flowering of radical thought. The 1530s and 1540s were a period of trial and consolidation, but by the 1550s the heroic period had ended. Thereafter, the radicals remained discordant voices in a Europe increasingly dominated by state churches.

Karlstadt and Müntzer

The first challenges to the new Protestant orthodoxy came from Andreas Bodenstein von Karlstadt (1480–1541) and Thomas Müntzer (before 1491–1525). A colleague of Luther at Wittenberg, Karlstadt, during Luther's absence at the Wartburg, increased the pace of reform by putting Luther's teachings into practice. He also moved beyond Luther theologically. During the

---

4 Friesen, *Erasmus, the Anabaptists, and the Great Commission*.
5 Snyder, *Michael Sattler*; Davis, *Anabaptism and asceticism*.

Wittenberg Movement (December 1521–February 1522) Karlstadt celebrated the first evangelical mass, moved the city council to reorganize Wittenberg as a 'Christian City', and had images removed from churches. He was critical, however, of the dreams and visions claimed by three prophets from Zwickau who appeared in the city at that time.[6] As did Luther, Karlstadt agreed that the spirit was needed to embrace true faith, but the content of that faith was to be found in scriptures. Despite elements of Spiritualism in Karlstadt, biblicism more accurately defines him.

Suddenly returning to Wittenberg, Luther argued that reform must 'tarry for the weak' who were not yet convinced. Karlstadt's response could have been written by any of the radicals:

> When one says, 'You should be indulgent for the sake of brotherly love', it means nothing at all because it is not yet decided whether their brotherly love is not an anti-Christian cloak which is by all means as wicked and destructive as any invention of the pope . . . But I say that Christ has abolished and cut off all brotherly love if it stands against his command or turns one from God even a little. For love fulfils God's commands, and it is impossible to love Christ and act contrary to his command or not do what Christ commands. That follows from this saying: If you love me, then keep my command (John 14[:21]). 'He who is not with me is against me' (Matt. 12 [:30]). He who does not hate father and mother, wife and children cannot be my disciple, etc.   [Luke 14:26][7]

Karlstadt was silenced at Luther's urging. Moving to Orlamunde (1523) Karlstadt gave concrete form to the priesthood of all believers by instituting democratic congregationalism. Laymen elected the pastor, had the right to question the preacher, and were allowed to preach themselves. Karlstadt abandoned all academic and clerical titles and had himself called 'Brother Andrew'. He even sought for a time to support himself by farming. In Orlamunde, all images were removed, infant baptism suspended, and the real presence of Christ in the eucharist denied. Karlstadt's opposition to images and his devaluation of the sacraments rested on strict warrant of scripture and the priority of faith over rituals, not the spirit/matter dualism of the Spiritualists. Karlstadt also sought to make Orlamunde a truly Christian city by putting in place a new system of poor relief and demanding strict adherence to biblical injunctions, including many in the Old Testament. Underlying Karlstadt's innovations was the insistence that principle be translated into practice, that faith produce

---

6 Wappler, 'Zwickauer Propheten'; Karant-Nunn, *Zwickau in transition*.
7 'Whether One should Proceed Slowly and Avoid Offending the Weak in Matters that Concern God's Will' (1524) in Sider, *Karlstadt's battle*, p. 54.

visible personal improvement, that the new theology establish a new church, and that Christianity remould a corrupt society.

Exiled from Saxony in September 1524, Karlstadt went to Switzerland and the Upper Rhine. There he published treatises that ignited the eucharistic controversy between Luther and Zwingli and helped inspire the early Anabaptist movement in Zurich. Sent fleeing by the Peasants' War, he found humiliating refuge with Luther in Wittenberg (July 1525). He escaped in 1529 to Denmark and East Frisia, where he influenced the founder of Dutch Anabaptism, Melchior Hoffman. He was given a post by Zwingli in Zurich (1530–4), before becoming a professor at the University in Basel. He died in 1541.

Karlstadt was immensely influential. Second only to Luther in his use of the press, he produced some ninety works in over two hundred editions. Known throughout Germany, he was read by all the early radicals. His impact upon Anabaptism was particularly crucial. His rejection of infant baptism, his purely memorialist eucharist, his radical laicization of the church, his biblicism, his insistence upon a faith rich in works, his emphasis upon communalism and charity, and his criticisms of oath-taking were crucial for Anabaptism. However, he advocated no separation from the established church. He was also no pacifist, though he rejected the use of force in religion. In this he differed from Thomas Müntzer.

Müntzer appeared in Wittenberg during the winter semester of 1517/18 and became a fervent supporter of the reform movement. When he was substitute pastor in Zwickau (1520–1), his searing criticisms of the church and his involvement with restive elements of the population led to his dismissal. His eventual call to Allstedt (1523–4) gave Müntzer the opportunity to carry out a true reform of the church. His relationship with Luther had soured. Luther feared that Müntzer's inclination to violence would plunge the entire reform movement into disarray and disrepute. For his part, Müntzer accused the Wittenberg reformers of teaching a false faith in a sweet Jesus that avoided both the inner suffering that produced true faith and the external storms that a commitment to Christ provokes in a fallen world. Like Karlstadt, Müntzer missed in Lutheranism both serious personal improvement and visible social amelioration. Also like Karlstadt, he instituted immediate practical reforms rather than tarry for the weak. The first published Protestant mass or worship service (1524) came from his pen. Müntzer also agreed with Karlstadt that there was no real presence in the eucharist. And yet, there were profound differences from Karlstadt as well. In Müntzer, Spiritualism displaced biblicism. Müntzer criticized infant baptism, but did not abolish it. He did not share Karlstadt's concern that baptism be performed precisely as the Bible mandated.

Rather, Müntzer's Spiritualism rendered both the eucharist and baptism marginal.

Müntzer's turn to the Spirit had three causes. First, the lack of visible improvement among Luther's followers caused him to view Luther's insistence upon the written and preached Word with suspicion. The dead letter of the external Word did not engender belief and transform the sinner, only the Spirit did. Müntzer's initial move towards Spiritualism, therefore, was his equation of spirit with profound inner conversion and outward improvement. Second, given Luther's prestige as *the* interpreter of scripture, Müntzer could not challenge Luther in the biblical arena. Müntzer instead appealed to the Spirit who revealed God's will not only in the text of the Bible, but directly as well. Finally, the Spirit raised up Müntzer as an armed prophet to lead the Lord's elect against the ungodly.

Müntzer had shown violent tendencies throughout his career. While Müntzer's theology required suffering from believers, it was not to be idle suffering. In Allstedt, Müntzer organized a league or covenant (*Bund*) of 500 citizens to protect the gospel against the real threat of Catholic attack. In his infamous 'Sermon to the Princes' (13 July 1524), he sought to persuade the rulers of Saxony to lead the war against the godless. At Luther's urging, the princes silenced Müntzer instead. He fled Allstedt before worse could befall him. The break with Luther was final and Müntzer launched a series of written attacks on his erstwhile leader. Müntzer also wrote off the ruling classes and appealed instead to the 'common man' whose grinding exploitation prevented concentration upon the things of God.

Müntzer finally settled in the city of Mühlhausen (15 August 1524) where he formed an 'Eternal League of God' to protect and advance the gospel. When the tide of the Peasants' War (1524–5) reached Thuringia, Müntzer predicted a climactic victory over the powers of darkness and the establishment of an egalitarian communistic Kingdom of God. But the princes crushed the Thuringian peasant army at Frankenhausen (15 May 1525). Müntzer was captured, tortured and executed. He became a byword for violence, heresy, and fanaticism. Nonetheless, Luther and the ruling classes were haunted by the ghost of religiously inspired social upheaval.

Despite his subsequent historical notoriety, Müntzer exercised less influence than Karlstadt. The other Spiritualists owed little or nothing to him. His communistic impulses were common currency in the period and cannot be associated specifically with Müntzer. His violence, his disinterest in baptism, his use of oaths to bind together his various leagues and covenants, and his theocratic goals distinguish him from most forms of Anabaptism. Radicals appreciated his boldness in refuting the discredited Luther, though after Frankenhausen few would openly acknowledge him. Many, especially among the Anabaptists, did accept the emphasis on suffering he had learned from mysticism. Interestingly, Karlstadt had also turned to the mystics after his disappointments in Wittenberg. Both learned a deeper, more painful, but transformative faith from mysticism than they claimed to find in Luther. Although Luther had published the *Theologia Germanica*, his mature theology was defined by his rejection of mysticism and its claims of an unfallen 'ground' of the soul that made possible human improvement. In Karlstadt and Müntzer that ground was faith itself, a gift of grace to the completely fallen human, but an enabling faculty nonetheless. As a result, they agreed with the Catholics that James 2:14–17 provided a necessary corrective to Luther's 'one-sided' interpretation of Romans 3:28.

Spiritualism

Although Müntzer is usually categorized as a Spiritualist, he is anomalous.[8] Unlike other Spiritualists – including the two most important discussed here, Caspar Schwenckfeld and Sebastian Franck – Müntzer's devaluation of scripture and the sacraments was not based upon spirit/matter dualism. His conception of Spirit resembled that found in the Bible: an external force, sometimes violent, described with material imagery, producing strong emotions that result in outwardly directed action. Müntzer's dualism was based on that of flesh (fear of humans) and spirit (fear of God), or that of letter (literal understanding) and spirit (inspired interpretation, transformative faith). As a result, Müntzer could criticize infant baptism but retain it, reject the real presence but celebrate the eucharist. The other Spiritualists, however, operated with a platonic dualism in which spirit is the immaterial mind. Found in the depths of the human soul and described in abstract terms, spirit is the passive object of desire that moves the observer by attraction, and produces peace, harmony and stasis. As a result of their understanding of Spirit, Schwenckfeld and Franck were programmatic Spiritualists for whom denying the material was the basis of true religion.

Of the lower nobility, Caspar Schwenckfeld (1489–1561) was serving in the ducal courts of his native Silesia when in 1519 Luther's message provoked a 'divine visitation' (*Heimsuchung*), or conversion. By 1521 Schwenckfeld was leader of the Silesian reform movement, and by 1522 he had won over the

---

8 McLaughlin, 'Reformation Spiritualism', and McLaughlin, 'Spiritualismus'.

most powerful of the Silesian dukes. The Catholic bishop of Breslau withdrew into his own principality in 1524, allowing secular rulers to seize control of the church. By that time, however, Schwenckfeld too was increasingly disturbed by the lack of visible moral improvement among Luther's followers. Karlstadt's and Zwingli's objections to the real presence occasioned a second *Heimsuchung*. Schwenckfeld became convinced that Luther's teaching on the eucharist had blocked the awaited progress. In Schwenckfeld's experience, many Lutherans believed that since Christ was corporally present simple reception of the eucharist brought salvation. However, Schwenckfeld reasoned, Judas had shared in the bread and wine at the Last Supper and he had certainly not been saved. A vision revealed a new interpretation of Luther's proof-texts (Matt. 26:26; Luke 22:19) to Valentine Crautwald (1465–1545), a learned Silesian humanist. Armed with his own argument from Judas and Crautwald's exegesis, Schwenckfeld travelled to Wittenberg in early 1525 to present their findings to Luther and the others. Luther rejected the Silesians' position and condemned them along with Karlstadt and Ulrich Zwingli (1484–1531). In 1526 Schwenckfeld, Crautwald and the clergy of Liegnitz suspended (*Stillstand*) the Lord's Supper. Under the influence of Crautwald's Augustinianism, Schwenckfeld became increasingly spiritualistic. In yet a third *Heimsuchung* (1527), Schwenckfeld broke completely with Luther and embraced a thoroughgoing Spiritualism. Forced into exile in 1529, he spent the rest of his life in the cities and on noble estates of southern Germany, where he clashed with Zwinglians, Lutherans, Calvinists, and Anabaptists. He died in the city of Ulm (1561) leaving behind circles of followers in southern Germany and a more substantial popular movement in Silesia.

Schwenckfeld's core teaching on the Celestial Flesh of Christ argued that even in his humanity Christ had not been a creature, but rather the Son of God. He owed nothing to his mother save nurture. Sinners, by their participation in Christ's flesh, became New Men that led visibly Christian lives marked by love, patience, and forgiveness. Rebirth was the inner baptism and participation in the Glorified Christ constituted the inner supper. Since outer ceremonies were merely memorial signs of the inner sacraments, they were inessential and in abeyance until Christ's second coming would reinstitute a visible church. In the interim, Christians edified and consoled each other in small groups that Schwenckfeld denied were churches.

In Strasbourg, where many of the radicals sought a haven, he had encountered Sebastian Franck (1499–1542), the most 'modern' of the radicals. Of obscure origins in the south German city of Donauwörth, Franck witnessed Luther's Heidelberg Disputation (1518). Initially ordained as a Catholic priest, he became a Lutheran minister (1524), but he resigned (1529) when disenchanted by the immorality of Luther's followers. He settled in Strasbourg (1530–2) but was expelled when he disparaged imperial rule in print. He lived next in Ulm (1533–9) as a printer and even earned citizenship, before being expelled once again, this time for his theological views. He spent his last three years in Basel.

Franck exercised a stark scepticism that drew upon late scholasticism, mysticism, humanism, and his own unhappy experience. The proliferation of sects, both in history and in the Reformation, seemed to him a cautionary tale against any certain knowledge in religious matters. The Bible did not escape his censure. Apparent contradictions and innumerable competing interpretations convinced Franck that God used scripture only to drive despairing believers to consult the inner word in their own hearts. Franck also condemned all theology as hubris. Equivalent to Schwenckfeld's inner Christ, the inner word was less a message than a faculty of spiritual judgement. Franck's critique of the outer word extended to the entire church and all of the sacraments. Convinced that the church had fallen almost immediately after the death of the Apostles, Franck thought it wrongheaded to reinstitute it:

> I ask what is the need or why should God wish to restore the outworn sacraments and take them back from Antichrist, yea, contrary to his own nature (which is Spirit and inward) yield to weak material elements . . . And does he wish now, just as though he was weary of spiritual things and had quite forgotten his nature, to take refuge again in the poor sick elements of the world and re-establish the besmirched . . . sacraments of both Testaments? . . . nothing has been taken from the child except its doll with which it has played long enough. One must leave the nest and thereupon strive for greater and more serious things, namely faith, penitence, denial of self . . . God permitted, indeed, gave the outward signs to the church in its infancy, just like a doll to a child . . . But when the child is at length strong enough and able to throw the staff away, the father does not thereupon become angry, but rather the same is pleasing to the father.[9]

Mature Christians did not need externals and should not allow such a diversion from the inner word.

Franck was best known to contemporaries for his *Chronicle, Book of Time, and Historical Bible* (1531), a compilation of histories, in which he consistently found the heretics to have been the only good Christians. His inclusion of Erasmus in that group and his mocking portrayal of the imperial eagle as a bird of carrion

---

9 'Letter to John Campanus' (1531) in Williams, *Spiritual and Anabaptist writers*, pp. 154–5.

forced his departure from Strasbourg. Franck also collected contradictory claims from accepted authorities, including the Bible, to prove the unreliability of the outer word. As a publisher, Franck translated and reprinted ancient and contemporary texts with which he agreed, thereby making them available to wider audiences. Access to the printing press, and the volume of their publications, made both Franck and Schwenckfeld influential among radicals well into the seventeenth century.

Though the two Spiritualists shared many concerns and principles, they were different in ways that foreshadowed later developments. Franck's inner word as the sole arbiter of truth would evolve into the Enlightenment's sceptical reason. His critique of the church as a stage of development best left behind also resulted in an intense individualism. Franck had many readers but no followers, no faith companions. On the other hand, Schwenckfeld's rebirth and Inner Christ pointed towards Pietism. He was less categorical about the church, encouraging small gatherings of his followers to provide fellowship, and anticipating the reinstitution of the church at the second coming. As early as Franck and Schwenckfeld, therefore, the Spiritualist Spirit showed signs of breaking down into its component parts: mind and heart.

Nonetheless, they agreed in their fundamental differences with Müntzer. Luther, Martin Bucer (1499–1551) and other clerics had attempted to tar all Spiritualists with the Müntzerian brush. But Franck and Schwenckfeld posed no threat to the political or social order since their Spiritualism obviated a social gospel. And, in fact, they both found many disciples among the elites. They did threaten, however, the *raison d'être* of the clergy and established churches, and it was at clerical insistence that both were driven from Ulm. Lay rulers generally found them congenial, or at least not problematic, until the development of state churches and confessionalization.

Müntzer, Schwenckfeld, and Franck all came to their Spiritualism out of Luther's reform movement. There were other early Reformation Spiritualists that were the products of incipient Anabaptism: for example, Hans Denck (c. 1500–27), Hans Bünderlin (1499–after 1544), Christian Entfelder (d. after 1546), Obbe Phillips (c. 1500–68), and David Joris (c. 1501–56). Since their abandonment of Anabaptism played an essential role in its development, they will be discussed under that rubric.

In the second half of the sixteenth century, the Lutheran minister Valentin Weigel (1533–88) was the most prominent German Spiritualist. A graduate of Wittenberg and pastor of Saxon Zschopau for over twenty years, Weigel was a reader of Franck, Schwenckfeld, perhaps Müntzer, and many others (e.g. Paracelsus [1493–1541]). He escaped detection during his lifetime, but posthumous publication of his extensive writings revealed a corrosive critique of the religious coercion, academic theology, and the absence of living faith in the Saxon state church.

Weigel notwithstanding, Spiritualism found its true home in the Netherlands. Mysticism, humanism, Dutch sacramentarianism, and Anabaptism generated a practical and not necessarily consciously formulated Spiritualism. As a result, once religious coercion was removed most Netherlanders remained unaffiliated with any of the competing confessions. Whatever other reasons for refusing church membership they may have had, the absence of the unchurched made manifest their belief that the church was dispensable. The persistent and impassioned advocate of religious freedom, Dirck Volckhertsz Coornhert (1522–90), defended Franck and Schwenckfeld though he did not feel it necessary to leave the church of his birth: Catholicism. Fed by the works of Franck and Schwenckfeld, groups such as the Davidjorists, the Family of Love, and later the Collegiants maintained the speculative tradition well into the seventeenth century.

John Locke's epoch-making *First Letter on Toleration* (1689) drew extensively upon the Spiritualist tradition he had come to know from the Collegiants during his exile in Holland.[10] His religious scepticism, his placement of scripture under reason's tutelage, his dismissal of externals, his demotion of churches to mere voluntary societies, his intense religious individualism, his denial of Original Sin and his emphasis upon morality to the exclusion of doctrine reproduce Franck's Spiritualism with surprising exactitude. These traits also foreshadow much of modern Christianity.

Anabaptism

Spiritualism had addressed the lack of visible moral reform by appealing to the living Spirit over the dead letter of scripture. Although there were strong Spiritualist currents in early Anabaptism, a stringent biblicism would separate the movement from Spiritualism by the second half of the sixteenth century. As Conrad Grebel made clear to Müntzer when he rejected singing during worship services: 'Whatever we are not taught by clear passages or examples must be regarded as forbidden, just as if it were written: "This do not; sing not"'.[11] Anabaptist biblicism was distinguished by its painstaking literalness, its focus on practice as opposed to theology, and its refusal to compromise

---

10 Fix, *Prophecy and reason*; Fix, 'Radical Reformation and second Reformation'.
11 Grebel, 'Letter to Thomas Müntzer', in Williams, *Spiritual and Anabaptist writers*, p. 75.

the clear Word even in the face of terrible persecution. A life of Christian discipleship following exactly in the footsteps of the Master also embraced his fate. Christians were to live in congregations that separated from the sinful 'World'. Those congregations practised 'community of goods', accepted members only through adult baptism, and exercised the ban. The origins and implications of Anabaptism challenged not only the lack of individual moral improvement, false doctrines, and antichristian ecclesiastical institutions, but the un-Christian social structures of sixteenth-century Europe.

Anabaptism had three distinct though related geographical foci: (1) Switzerland and southern Germany, (2) the Netherlands and northern Germany, and (3) Austria and Moravia.[12]

(1) The origin of Swiss Anabaptism, also known as the Swiss Brethren, has traditionally been attributed to a group of radical Zwinglians in Zurich led by Conrad Grebel (c. 1498–1526), Felix Mantz (d. 1527), and George Blaurock (c. 1492–1529). They were dismayed by Zwingli's prudent pace and deference to the Zurich city council, in other words, his tarrying for the weak. Zwingli refused, for example, to immediately abolish the Catholic mass although he agreed with the radicals that it was an abomination – not merely an abuse or error. They also came to question the acceptability of infant baptism. Christ had clearly commanded his followers to preach and then to baptize. Nowhere in the scriptures was there an example of infant baptism. Rather, in the Gospels and the Acts of the Apostles only adults were baptized, and only after confession of faith. Although Zwingli initially shared their doubts, the political and ecclesial implications of adult baptism persuaded him to retain infant baptism. Since in Zurich, as in all of Europe, membership in the church and civil society were coterminous, believers' baptism would effectively split not only the church, but the political community. Rebuffed in Zurich, the radicals took their message to the countryside. Rural Anabaptism intensified the social implications by directly rejecting an important economic institution, the tithe, and the authority of the Zurich city council over its subject peasantry. The council used rigorous measures to suppress the movement, but with only limited success. Alerted to the danger the Anabaptists posed, the council and Zwingli moved against the urban radicals, forcing them to flee. Some (e.g. Felix Mantz) would later return and suffer martyrdom.

The genie was out of the bottle, however. The movement spread north to the city of Waldshut which became officially Anabaptist under the leadership of Balthasar Hubmaier (1480/85–1528). When the city's Habsburg overlords

---

12 Depperman *et al.*, 'From monogenesis to polygenesis'.

suppressed that experiment, it only spread the bacillus abroad. Hubmaier fled to Moravia, which quickly became the promised land of the Anabaptist movement. Another refugee may have been Michael Sattler (c. 1490–1527), an apostate Benedictine monk, who became a leader of the Strasbourg Anabaptists before meeting his death during a mission trip to Württemberg. The Schleitheim Confession (1527), which he most likely wrote, and the story of his martyrdom shaped Anabaptist identity in the south. A former prior of the monastery of St Peter's in the Black Forest, Sattler grafted monastic elements into the developing Swiss Anabaptist vision: discipleship as literal imitation of Christ life's (including martyrdom) rather than merely obedience to Christ's commands, uncompromising separation from the fallen world, refusal of oaths, and pacifism.[13]

A second stream of southern Anabaptism, initiated by Hans Denck (c. 1500–27), drew upon the mystical tradition. A student of humanism, Denck's religious development was initially moulded (1523) by Johannes Oecolampadius (1482–1531) and Erasmus in Basel. In Nuremberg (1524–5) he encountered the teachings of Karlstadt, Müntzer and some early form of Anabaptism. Most important, however, was the impact of Tauler and the *Theologia Germanica*. Unlike Karlstadt and Müntzer, he accepted not only resignation of self, but also a pronounced dualism. In direct contradiction to Luther's teaching, Denck posited a divine seed or divine image that rendered outward media, be they the Bible or the sacraments, dispensable. Humans possessed the freedom to allow God to work in them to produce a pure life. Believers' baptism attested to the inward work of God. Towards the end of his brief career, however, he became disillusioned with the divisiveness among the Anabaptists and viewed the persecution they suffered as a sign of divine disfavour. He also came to view all externals, including baptism, as mere conventions. His Spiritualism allowed him to return to Basel to live within a Reformed community without sharing its beliefs. Denck died of the plague within a few months of his arrival. Despite the brevity of his career, Denck's writings and disciples were very influential. He shaped Entfelder, Bünderlin, Franck and, indirectly, northern spiritualizing Anabaptists like Obbe Philips.

Denck also influenced Hans Hut (c. 1490–1527) though the latter owed much also to Karlstadt and, mostly profoundly, Müntzer. Hut had in fact arranged publication of one Müntzer work, had been a member of the Eternal Covenant in Mühlhausen, and had even survived Frankenhausen. In defeat he turned to Anabaptism and was baptized by Denck in 1526. He still harboured Müntzer's

---

13 Snyder, *Michael Sattler*.

hatred for the godless oppressors, but his helplessness in the wake of defeat left him hopefully predicting the imminent (1528) chastisement of the world at Christ's second coming. Rebaptism was the seal of the elect who patiently and passively awaited their deliverance. Anabaptism in these years recruited heavily among the disillusioned who wished to abandon the larger godless society and put the gospel into practice in small Christian communities. But Denck and other leading Anabaptists rejected Hut's apocalypticism at the Augsburg Martyrs Synod (1527), so-called for the fate of many who participated. Hut himself died in an Augsburg prison in December 1528 while awaiting execution for his part in the Peasants' War.

The years 1527–31 saw the end of the heady initial phase of Anabaptist development. The entire first generation of leaders had died (Grebel [1526], Mantz [1527], Blaurock [1529], Hubmaier [1528], Sattler [1527], Hut [1528]), or defected (Denck, Bünderlin, Entfelder), leaving the movement in disarray. The arrival in Strasbourg of Pilgram Marpeck (c. 1495–1556) brought stabilization and a new beginning. A native of the Tirol, Marpeck was a successful businessman. He served as Burgermeister, councilmember and magistrate in his native city (Rattenberg), before surrendering his position and possessions to embrace Anabaptism (1527). Eventually coming to Strasbourg in 1528, he bought citizenship and entered a guild of the economically vulnerable and restive segments of the populace. His usefulness as an engineer to Strasbourg, and, later, Augsburg, shielded him from the persecution that was the usual fate of his fellow believers.

Marpeck took advantage of that relative security to travel and write extensively to the scattered Anabaptist congregations in Switzerland and south Germany. Marpeck fought on a number of fronts to conserve the Anabaptist movement. But his opposition to the spiritualizing Anabaptists Bünderlin and Entfelder and the Spiritualist Schwenckfeld saved the movement from evaporation. Of the two Anabaptists, Johannes Bünderlin (c. 1498–1533) was a university trained humanist and always maintained a preference for Tauler and Erasmus. Active in Moravia (1527), he was a leading figure in the vibrant Strasbourg Anabaptist community when Marpeck arrived. His clash with Marpeck probably completed his transition to Spiritualism. Christian Entfelder (d. 1547) had arrived with Hubmaier (1526) in Moravia, where he became pastor to an Anabaptist congregation. He was associated with Bünderlin in Strasbourg and influenced by Tauler and the *Theologia Germanica* in his gradual move from Anabaptism to Spiritualism. Bünderlin and Entfelder were also acquainted with Schwenckfeld and both ended up in Prussia where the Schwenckfelders were politically well placed. Marpeck's challenge to the spiritualizing Anabaptists crystallized in a controversy with Schwenckfeld that clearly established the boundaries between Anabaptism and Spiritualism.[14]

Although Marpeck saw the outpouring of the Holy Spirit at the crucifixion as the soteriological core of Christianity, he argued that the Spirit was conveyed through the body of believers. In a real sense he sacramentalized the church, understood as the pure church whose gathered members had been sealed by believers' baptism. His emphasis on scripture alone led not to Spiritualist individualism, but to a church that interpreted the Bible and taught it to its members.[15]

In the social sphere, Marpeck advocated a critical, but not hostile, relationship to state and society. He accepted oaths, paid taxes, and served the government as long as it did not contravene the Word of God. He met the social evils of his day with a commitment to social reform and charity, not revolution or withdrawal. Though always careful to preserve their own purity, the Anabaptists were to be the Christian leaven in the larger society. His moderation applied within the community as well. He opposed a too rigorous application of discipline and the ban. In most of these positions, Marpeck differed significantly from Anabaptism in the Low Countries and Moravia. As a result, despite general good will between them, the northern and southern branches of Anabaptism would be estranged.

(2) Just at the time the torch passed from the first generation of southern Anabaptist leaders to Marpeck, Anabaptism in the lower Rhine and Low Countries began its meteoric rise. The source was Melchior Hoffman (1495?–1543). Born in the southern city of Swäbisch Hall and trained as a furrier, Hoffmann, with Marpeck, represents a change in the education and background of Anabaptist leadership. Hubmaier, Denck, and Grebel, for example, were all university educated and influenced by humanism to a greater or lesser degree. Many were also former priests or monks. Later leaders were more often laymen. Even when clerics, they often lacked advanced education. Hoffman's educational background is unknown, but clearly he had not attended university or studied with the humanists.

Hoffman's began his reforming career as a Lutheran in the eastern Baltic in Livonia, although Karlstadt had probably already begun to exercise considerable influence on him.[16] Driven from Livonia, because of iconoclasm and general intemperateness, Hoffman found refuge in Sweden for a time before fleeing to Denmark. Although initially supported by the Danish king,

---

14 Bergsten, 'Pilgram Marpeck'.   15 Boyd, *Pilgram Marpeck*.
16 Pater, *Karlstadt*, pp. 173–249.

his rejection of the real presence in the eucharist brought strong Lutheran opposition. Escaping from Denmark he worked with Karlstadt in East Frisia, a province that would harbour many radicals. For some reason, Hoffman travelled to Strasbourg in 1530. By this time, under Karlstadt's influence, Hoffman had rejected infant baptism, but he had not accepted adult rebaptism. In Strasbourg, Hoffman found himself in the forge of radical religion where Anabaptism flourished in all its many forms. Rebaptized, he returned north to find extremely fertile fields for his Anabaptist seed.

The Low Countries possessed a vibrant religious culture in the later Middle Ages particularly noted for mysticism and the Modern Devotion, a movement advocating simplicity and inner devotion that affected clergy and laity alike. Further enriched by Erasmian humanism in the early sixteenth century, the resulting religious culture diminished the role of externals in religion, although it did not put the sacraments in question. Although his movement, much to Luther's chagrin, enabled many in the Netherlands to take that final step, Luther condemned them as sacramentarians. Historians have found the term useful. They rejected the real presence, but only viewed infant baptism askance, not having progressed to rebaptism, before Hoffman brought Anabaptism from the south. Because the new Anabaptist groups possessed a firmer profile than the amorphous sacramentarianism, Catholic persecution was ferocious.

Hoffman's theology, however, had two aspects that would make northern Anabaptism distinctive. The first was a Celestial Flesh Christology that Hoffman acquired in Strasbourg, possibly from Schwenckfeld. The second was Hoffman's pronounced Apocalypticism. The rebaptized would constitute the 144,000 elect awaiting Christ's Second Coming scheduled for 1533 at the New Jerusalem, Strasbourg. In that year Hoffman travelled to Strasbourg, where he was promptly arrested and held in strict and miserable confinement until his death. Although Hoffman corresponded with his followers, the movement in the Netherlands was effectively leaderless. A new native Dutch leadership (the baker Jan Mathijs [d. 1534] and the tailor John of Leiden [1509–36]) filled the vacuum and declared Münster in Westfalia the New Jerusalem. Anabaptists flooded into Münster, took control of the Lutheran city and expelled all who refused to be baptized. A Catholic–Protestant coalition, led by the Bishop of Münster, invested the city, but was unable to take it. Within the city, the pressure of events transformed the Anabaptist movement. Although Hoffman's eschatological vision foresaw a passive role for the 144,000 elect – they were simply to await Christ's coming – the Münsterite Anabaptists adopted an active role to prepare the way for Christ by appealing to the Old

Testament. After Mathijs' death, John of Leiden made himself king, the David to Christ's Solomon, and claimed world rulership. The Old Testament also provided warrant for polygamy to control and provide for the growing numbers of unattached women. True to their New Testament roots, however, the Münsterite Anabaptists instituted a war communism that pooled all moveable wealth for common sustenance and defence. Despite dwindling numbers of able-bodied men, the city held out until 25 June 1535. Even then the city only fell through treachery. With uncommon savagery, the victors slaughtered the men and expelled the women and children. The leaders were tortured, executed and their remains hung in cages from a church steeple.

Münster branded all Anabaptists as threats to society and human decency. In the Netherlands, Anabaptism was left in ruins. Some still nourished Münsterite visions of an earthly New Jerusalem or sought revenge by brigandry and murder (the Batenburgers). Others recanted their association altogether. David Joris (c. 1501–56) and Obbe Philips (c. 1500–68), two very prominent non-Münsterite leaders, eventually retreated into Spiritualism. Both had begun as sacramentarians, were among the earliest Anabaptist leaders, but eventually evolved to Spiritualism in the manner of Denck, Entfelder, and Bünderlin in the south. Many Dutch Anabaptists, however, were chastened by the disaster but gathered around the heirs of Hoffman's non-violent vision, Menno Simons (c. 1496–1561) and Obbe's brother Dirk Philips (1504–68).

Simons had been a Catholic pastor in Pingjum and Witmarsum in Friesland as the sacramentarian and Anabaptist movements developed. Convinced by the sacramentarians (1526), he nonetheless remained in the church, but as an evangelical. Moved to search the scriptures by the steadfast martyrdom of several Anabaptists, he could find no support for infant baptism. Still, he neither left the church nor accepted rebaptism. The terrible events in Münster provoked him to condemn the leaders and the teaching that made it possible. But it was only after the fall of Münster that he was rebaptized (1536) and ordained elder (1537) by Obbe Philips. He quickly became the most influential Anabaptist leader. Despite the best efforts of the authorities to seize him, he remained free and active until his natural death.

Simons faced two internal threats. The first was the Münsterites who still had not abandoned their dreams of an earthly kingdom established by the sword. Simons wooed them, but used the ban to exclude those who refused to embrace a peaceable vision. The second problem was the Spiritualist current in Anabaptism that had cost the movement some influential leaders and many followers. Like Marpeck, Simons clearly demarcated the difference between Spiritualism and a biblicistic and communal life of witness and discipleship. The ban was crucial. But the rigorous application of discipline including shunning of banned members, sometimes even by their own families, split the movement (1556). Those who rejected the ban, or at least its more stringent use, formed a separate branch – the Waterlanders or Doopgezinde (baptist-oriented). Their tolerance produced a rich variety of groups, and their openness facilitated their influence upon English separatist Puritanism. General and particular baptists of the seventeenth century seem to stem ultimately from Dutch Anabaptism.

(3) Moravia was the final locus of Anabaptism. Fleeing after Anabaptist Waldshut fell to the Austrians, Balthasar Hubmaier arrived in Nikolsburg in 1526. Pitiless persecution drove thousands to find refuge there in the course of the sixteenth century. Hubmaier himself met a martyr's death in Vienna in 1528. Under the protection of Leonhard von Lichtenstein, who eventually accepted rebaptism, Hubmaier was able to recreate the established or magisterial Anabaptism that had existed in Waldshut. Rejecting complete pacificism, Hubmaier accepted a role for the secular authority, in this case Lichtenstein, in the Christian community and the possibility of defensive war.[17] A brief visit by Hans Hut, however, split the community on the question of the use of the sword (i.e., coercion both in war and in the administration of justice) and the relationship to the state and the larger society. Later Hutterites labelled the two parties 'Schwertler', or those who bore the sword, and 'Stäbler', or those who would only bear a staff. It is not clear whether von Lichtenstein expelled the dissident Stäbler, or they withdrew voluntarily. In any event, they found a new refuge in Austerlitz and there began a remarkable experiment in communism. They became known as the Hutterites after an early leader, Jakob Hutter (1500?–36).

As had monasticism, the Hutterites sought to recreate the community of goods practised by the first church in Jerusalem (Acts 2:44–5; 4:34–5) in order to realize true love of neighbour and oneness of heart. In this they continued early Swiss and south German Anabaptism's desire to erect a truly Christian society. Outside of Moravia, Anabaptists in both the south and the north (with the exception of Münster for a time) eventually understood 'community of goods' to be a rejection of exploitation and a remarkable charitable sharing of wealth to those in need. Private property, however, remained. In Moravia, by contrast, literal community of goods was still a live option. The result was a complex, centrally administered society in which all means of production and stores of goods belonged to the community. Protected by Moravian nobles, the Hutterite community thrived throughout the sixteenth and early

17 Stayer, *Anabaptists and the sword.*

seventeenth centuries. Under Peter Walpot (1521–78) the brethren may have numbered 30,000. The Moravian Hutterites constituted the most successful attempt to achieve that reform of individual, church and society at the heart of the Anabaptist project. But as Anabaptists had recognized, the world – including the Christian world – simply would not allow such a radically literal appropriation of the New Testament. The coming of the Thirty Years' War (1618–48) spelled the community's death knell. The Hutterites' ability to lead the fully communal life had depended on the tolerance or protection of secular lords. Under renewed persecution, they were driven at first into Slovakia. A remnant fled further to Romanian Transylvania, and finally to the Ukraine.

Conclusion

At root, the radicals' disagreement with the mainline reformers was a disagreement about what was wrong with medieval Catholicism, that is, what needed reforming. For Luther, the fundamental problem was works righteousness and the oppressed conscience. The Catholic demand that sinners should earn their own salvation exceeded the ability of fallen humanity. Because of the Fall, humans endured a bondage of the will that prevented any good work untainted by sin. The greater the effort to earn salvation was, the greater the sin. Christians, such as Luther, who realized this were plunged into despair. His discovery of 'sola fide' (faith alone) justification in the Apostle Paul unburdened consciences by denying that humans could contribute to their own salvation. Instead, they should cast themselves upon Christ who had already earned salvation for all who placed their faith in him. The result was a condemnation of any thought that a believer's efforts could improve his or her chances, since that denied the sole sufficiency of Christ's achievement and opened the doors to despair. While the doctrinal issue for Luther was the heresy of Catholic theology, the pressing practical pastoral issue was the oppressed conscience.

All the same, there is no evidence that overburdened consciences were a common problem in late medieval Catholicism. True, the church had strategies for dealing with 'scrupulosity', but in general this was a fringe phenomenon usually associated with monks like Luther. Medieval critics of the church, both heretics and Catholic reformers, had seen the problem quite differently.[18] Consciences were not burdened enough. Catholicism was not too demanding; rather it was not demanding enough. Though theologians had argued about the roles of human freedom and God's grace, even the

18 Oakley, *Western Church in the later Middle Ages*; Lambert, *Medieval heresy*.

most Augustinian (like Augustine himself) saw individual repentance and reform, not faith, as the key. Personal and institutional reform, therefore, entailed renewed commitment to the pursuit of holiness. Not surprisingly, other Protestant leaders put Luther's reform of doctrine in service to the universally desired reform of the church. For all of its power, therefore, *sola fide* justification was the answer to a problem that few knew they had. In fact, the doctrine could be, and was, viewed as exacerbating the sinful lives and corrupt institutions that were the targets of earlier reformers.

> . . . every man wants to be saved by superficial faith, without fruits of faith . . . without love and hope, without right Christian practices, and wants to persist in all the old manner of personal vices . . .[19]

The radicals addressed the problem by making faith itself the principal of good works. Protestant churches, for their part, undercut *sola fide* by emphasizing church discipline, the necessity of visible fruits of faith, and the 'Third Use of the Law'.[20] Thus, justification by faith alone proved no more 'practical' than the radicals' demand for exemplary Christians.

In one of the ironies with which history abounds, the magisterial Protestant churches that officially taught *sola fide* actually moulded individual behaviour for centuries to come, most famously in the Protestant ethic. Their alliance with the state made that possible. The rejection of that alliance by most Anabaptists deprived them – another irony – of the very means to achieve their highest goal, the visible moral reformation of society. Nonetheless, their discipline reproached the other churches, especially the reformed, into greater rigour. The Spiritualists, for their part, were seeds within the churches of later Pietism and Enlightenment Deism, both of which fed the common modern equation of religion with morality. Like many radicals, therefore, the Anabaptists and Spiritualists influenced developments indirectly, though no less powerfully, despite their apparent failure.

19 Grebel, 'Letter to Thomas Müntzer', in Williams, *Spiritual and Anabaptist writers*, p. 74.
20 The divine law served to guide saved Christians although it had no power to condemn. The first two uses were civil law and to convict consciences.

4

Lutheranism in the seventeenth century

HARTMUT LEHMANN

Luther's legacy contested

When Martin Luther died unexpectedly in 1546, Philip Melanchthon was his obvious heir. But as we know from bitter disputes among Lutherans that erupted almost immediately after Luther's death and which lasted for several decades, Melanchthon's authority was never accepted by all of Luther's disciples. Indeed, it seems only a minority considered him to be Luther's true successor. How can this be explained? First, in all of his writings Luther produced no systematic summary of his theology. He addressed specific problems, discussing at great length controversial issues which were brought to his attention, and spelled out in his answers many specific positions which served to characterize his theological approach. But he never wrote a large treatise explaining dogmatic matters in a comprehensive way, a piece which could be compared to Calvin's *Institutio*. Perhaps one could say that his translation of the New Testament and later also the Old Testament, together with the longer and the shorter versions of the Catechism, represented the sum of his theological insight. But just as Luther had always insisted on his own understanding of the biblical texts, after 1546 others, including some of his students, friends and followers, were tempted to do so also. Luther's German Bible and the two Catechisms were a solid base on which all of his disciples stood, but this base did not provide them with a common theological approach.

Philip Melanchthon certainly believed that he understood Luther's true intentions better than anyone else. Melanchthon had deputized for Luther at the Augsburg negotiations in 1530. Here the text which Lutherans would accept as the very foundation of their faith for centuries to come was formulated: the Augsburg Confession. Melanchthon had also been close to Luther since 1518. Because of his excellent knowledge of Greek he had played a major part in translating the Bible. Furthermore, Melanchthon had written the first survey of Luther's life after Luther passed away. But these accomplishments did not convince all of Luther's disciples. As is well known, and this is the other side of the story, Melanchthon's own approach to theology had been deeply influenced by a variety of humanism that incorporated key ideas from classical learning. Melanchthon, it seems, was more interested in matters of education and in building the kinds of institutions that provided opportunities for learning than in doctrinal matters. He was not a person close to simple believers nor did he possess the kind of charisma that would have enabled him to convince all of those who doubted his leadership.

For the congregations of Lutherans in central Europe the 1560s and 1570s were decades characterized by theological strife, unending controversies, and even division. While no new leader appeared on the scene who would have been able to reunite Luther's obstinate spiritual children, the sovereigns ruling in the territories which had decided to subscribe to Luther's exposition of the Christian faith in the Treaty of Augsburg in 1555 increasingly took control of the Lutheran churches. When on the occasion of the fiftieth anniversary of the Augsburg Confession the church leaders of some Protestant territories signed a compromise formula in 1580, the *Formula Concordiae*, this was more the result of political pressure than a sign of theological insight or restored theological harmony. In this context, two matters have to be distinguished. First the *Formula Concordiae*, second the Book of Concord. Since the 1560s and 1570s, leading Lutheran theologians had attempted to interpret the *Confessio Augustana* in a way that bridged the obvious differences of theological opinions concerning, for example, Original Sin, the role of good works, justification by faith alone, and Christology. Compromises were formulated by some and rejected by others. It is only in 1580 that a majority of Lutheran theologians was ready to agree and sign the *Formula Concordiae* that, in turn, was published as a part of the Book of Concord that contained all the symbolical books of Lutherans, including the most important creeds of the ancient church as well as those defined by Luther and Melanchthon. Not surprisingly, however, the Book of Concord never formed a theological platform for all followers of Luther. Within the religious life of Lutheran communities, Luther's Small Catechism and to a certain extent also his Large Catechism were much more important than the Book of Concord, even though leading Lutheran theologians such as Jakob Andreae had signed this document.

The spectacular success of the reform movement first led by Calvin, and after Calvin's death inspired by the writings of the great theologian from Geneva, proved to be a further challenge for Lutheran communities and Lutheran theologians. Calvin's disciples time and again claimed that Luther's reformation had not achieved what Luther had promised and that a Second Reformation, namely the true reformation, was necessary. This was to be a reformation of doctrine as well as of religious practice and of the moral conduct of the believers. Furthermore, Calvin's followers were able to gain influence all over Europe, not only in some cities close to Calvin's Geneva, but most notably in France, Scotland, the Netherlands, in some territories within the Holy Roman Empire and even in faraway Hungary. As regards the political situation within the Holy Roman Empire, nothing demonstrated the power of Calvin's ideas more clearly than the decision of the Elector of the Palatinate to join Calvin's movement. As a result, within the Empire, Heidelberg became the most influential centre of reformed theology. In sum, by the 1580s, many observers had the impression that Calvin's churches and the congregations and universities which followed his theology were a success, while Luther's movement stagnated.

But the situation was even more complicated because both the followers of Calvin as well as the followers of Luther had to witness the revitalization and reorganization of the Roman church following the negotiations at the Council of Trent. Even though the programme that had been accepted at Trent was implemented only step by step, what had been resolved at Trent was comprehensive, ambitious, and proved to be most effective. Many of the peculiarities and doctrinal points within Catholicism that had aroused Luther's opposition, such as the various steps involved in attaining sainthood, and the various customary ways of venerating saints, were abolished. Catholic liturgy was reformulated, and even the institutions of the Vatican were reorganized. Above all, with the Jesuits a new religious order appeared on the political scene of Europe after 1560 which was able and ready to reclaim much of the territory which the Catholic Church had lost in the 1520s and 1530s. On the one hand the Jesuits were the pope's obedient soldiers; on the other hand they excelled in virtues such as erudition and asceticism that were quite foreign to Renaissance Rome. Like Melanchthon, the Jesuits were strongly interested in matters of education. They founded schools and established universities that soon excelled as centres of rejuvenated Catholic life. Within the Holy Roman Empire, the duchy of Bavaria became the point of entry for the Jesuits into German politics and German cultural life, and quite soon became a stronghold of Jesuit activities. By the last decade of the sixteenth century, therefore, the Catholic revival was vibrant and impressive in Germany also. While the Habsburg rulers failed to lead this movement, appropriately labelled the Counter-Reformation, the Bavarian dynasty of the Wittelsbacher, together with the Jesuits, was prepared to limit any further expansion of Protestant influence in central Europe. The Wittelsbacher rejoiced when they were able to stop Protestant reform efforts in the archdiocese of Cologne and managed, in turn, to establish a member of their dynasty as archbishop in this key city on the Rhine.

In the same time period, within the Protestant territories of the Empire, foremost in states like Saxony and Wuerttemberg, the role of the Protestant churches was significantly strengthened as it was being reformulated. Both the sovereigns and the church leaders were committed to convince, even to force, all congregation members – meaning, they believed, all inhabitants of their respective states – to adopt fully the Protestant doctrine in either the Lutheran or the Calvinist form. Historians have designated this policy 'confessionalization'. Within the Lutheran territories of the Holy Roman Empire in particular, but also in states like Denmark or Sweden, which were governed by sovereigns who adhered to the Lutheran faith, this policy of confessionalization rested on three principles.

(1) The Lutheran church was supposed to be an integral part of the state and the sovereign was considered to be the true head of the church. Consequently, the leaders of the church were not only obliged to spread and consolidate the Lutheran faith but were also expected to support the political aims of their princes.

(2) The major Lutheran states passed detailed church ordinances (*Kirchenordnungen*) in which all aspects of Lutheran church life were explained in detail and regulated with much attention to all aspects of ordinary life. No aspect of religious practice, it seems, was left to local decision-making or to personal initiative. Regular inspections, so-called visitations, were part of what the ordinances demanded. In this manner, the consistories wanted to ensure that all paragraphs of the ordinances were carried through as intended and that local pastors observed their duties properly.

(3) To guarantee both allegiance to the state and the execution of the ordinances, a body of loyal and well-trained pastors was crucial. Therefore, much of the emphasis of Lutheran church policy was placed on finding young men willing to become pastors, on training, educating and examining them before, finally, entrusting to them the post of a pastor in a congregation.

Much energy was spent on establishing bodies that would be able to guarantee church discipline. In the different territories of the Holy Roman Empire that observed the Lutheran faith, different solutions were found. Some princes entrusted this task to consistories and to superintendents who had to supervise deans who in turn were expected to control the pastors. In other territories a church council (*Kirchenrat*) was established that was entrusted not only with disciplinary matters but also with matters of church property and finance. In the early years of the Reformation, to be sure, local congregations had formed the vital centres of the new faith; by 1580, however, and certainly by 1648, the structure of evangelical churches resembled more and more the political set-up of absolutist states, that is to say: what we can observe is a distinct hierarchy in which the theologians and lawyers at the top controlled all church matters, including matters of faith, obedience, and finance.

Confessionalization, therefore, meant not only demanding confessional loyalty but also bureaucratization. It consisted of the professionalization as well as the disciplining of the clergy. In short, the policy of confessionalization was well suited to support early absolutist rule. One could even argue that without confessionalization any attempt to dispossess the estates in Protestant territories of their political influence and to establish the absolute power of the princes according to the theory of the divine rule of all sovereigns (*Gottesgnadentum*) would not have been successful. As recent research has shown, there were, however, clear limits to the policy of confessionalization. While the norms which were spelled out in the various paragraphs of the ordinances were strict, religious life in Lutheran congregations did not follow these rules. Not only did many Lutheran pastors have their own ideas about doctrine and proper church procedures, but also many ordinary church members did not observe the ordinances or the requirements of the consistories, proclaimed in a never-ending series of edicts. More often than not, the visitations proved that pastors were unaware of key elements of the Lutheran faith and that people who were officially Lutheran did not live according to Lutheran church ordinances, not so much because they refused to do so but because they did not know any better. To build homogeneous and spiritually strong Lutheran congregations, was, therefore, an uphill struggle, as was the professionalization of the Lutheran clergy. Before the outbreak of the Thirty Years' War, moreover, some people with a strong interest in religion took the liberty of moving from one confession to another, and some did so more than once. For a certain period of time, it seems, before the strict rules of absolutist church regimes were enforced, there existed for some people a kind of market in religions, offering not only the confessions represented by Wittenberg and Geneva, but also the views of Spiritualists, antitrinitarians, and Anabaptists. It is not surprising, therefore, that even after the turn of the century Lutheran church officials were especially strict in eliminating the influence of all of those movements that had developed in the course of the radical Reformation.

Continuing crises

Even before the process of confessionalization had achieved some conclusive results, Lutheran believers were confronted by an additional challenge that they found extremely hard to handle. This new challenge was especially severe because it came from a direction which was totally unexpected and contained dimensions which threatened the very lives of people as well as the foundations of their belief. The core of the matter was that from the 1570s, climatic conditions in large parts of Europe had begun to deteriorate. The average temperature fell by some degrees. As a result, winters were harder than before and lasted longer; spring came later and the season for planting had to be postponed; very often, summers were unusually cold and wet; early frost came before grain and other fruits were ripe and could be harvested, and soon after came snow and ice. As we know from recent research by Christian Pfister and others, during this phase of inclement weather conditions, labelled the 'Little Ice Age', not all years were the same. In some years, normal harvests could be produced. But all in all, from the early 1570s, food became scarce in many European countries, and as it became scarce, it also became expensive. For the poor, especially, hunger became a constant companion. Hardship also affected the middle classes of society. Almost everybody had to struggle for survival.

In Lutheran congregations and beyond, but particularly in Lutheran congregations which felt threatened by the advances of Calvinism as much as by the Catholic Counter-Reformation, many people asked why God permitted such a sudden turn of events. Was this the hand of an angry God, they wondered, who punished them because they lived a more sinful life than their ancestors and because they no longer adhered strictly to His commandments? Lutheran pastors were ill-equipped to give plausible answers.

In retrospect, as the crisis became increasingly severe, we can observe and should distinguish several different reactions within the Lutheran congregations and churches of central Europe. Some of these reactions were mutually exclusive, others occurred simultaneously. In almost all cases, members of the educated middle classes with a strong religious affinity were the ones who tried to come to terms with the new situation.

First, beginning in the 1580s, we can find in the circles of pious and educated Lutherans an ever-increasing production of hymns, prayers, and edifying tracts.

Key elements of these literary texts are captured in an abbreviated but much used German phrase, 'Not, Angst und Pein'. The term 'Not' stood for the hardship of the times; 'Not' expressed hunger as well as the various illnesses that afflicted bodies weakened by insufficient food; 'Not' also alluded to the harshness of the authorities who did not care enough for the common people in great need. By contrast, the term 'Angst' exemplified the fear of a sudden death without the spiritual consolation of a promise of salvation. The most vivid and frequently used expression for 'Angst' was the example of Christ dying on the cross and asking His father whether he had forgotten him. It is interesting to note in this context that in the decades before and after 1600 Lutheran churches began to observe Good Friday more than in the preceding period. Just as passion plays became more and more popular, Good Friday was soon considered to be the most important Protestant holiday. This day was supposed to exemplify how fear could be overcome, and that there was a way for sincere Christians, as if in a rite of passage, to move from the fear of being doomed to salvation. Finally, the term 'Pein', in English pain, was supposed to point to purgatory. 'Pein' suffered here and now meant that God allowed the devil to inflict on people the kind of pain that they would suffer once they had been sent to hell on the day of the Last Judgement.

Second, in all hymns and prayers, but especially in the edifying tracts, Lutheran believers were told how they should live if they wanted to be sure to gain ultimate salvation. These works contain a large body of advice concerning Christian virtues and Christian values. While most of these exhortations were relatively short, some were presented in the form of very long and elaborate studies. No work was longer, or cited and reprinted more often, than Johann Arndt's (1555–1621) four and later six *Books of True Christianity*. On the one hand, Arndt used material that he had found in the writings of medieval mystics, for example Bernard de Clairvaux. On the other hand, many of his arguments were inspired by late sixteenth-century Spiritualism, for example the books of Valentin Weigel (1533–88), who in turn had been influenced by late medieval mystics like Johannes Tauler. According to Arndt, indoctrination in dogmatic matters counted for little; by contrast, those striving to become true Christians should concentrate on prayer and on what he called the growth of inner spiritual life. Arndt was translated into Latin, English, French, Dutch, Swedish, Danish, Czech and even into Russian and Icelandic. Between 1605 and 1740, Arndt's *Book of True Christianity* was printed in no fewer than 128 editions. As a consequence, for many devout seventeenth-century Lutherans, Johann Arndt became the true father of their church, just as Lutheran faith seemed to find its purest and most beautiful expression in the hymns written by Paul Gerhardt (1607–76) a generation later.

For many Lutherans, the concentration on edification in light of the subsistence crisis people were facing had two consequences. First, especially well-educated Lutherans began to differentiate between piety and confession. While they were striving to become more pious, and while sanctification became the main aim of their religious endeavours, they began to ignore the very meaning of dogmatic and confessional factors as explained to them, for example, by a theologian like Johann Gerhard (1582–1637). In addition, those Lutherans who were seeking spiritual advice in Arndt's works no longer really needed a pastor. They believed that they were able to satisfy their religious wishes, needs and aspirations by reading the right kinds of edifying tracts and books. As a result, they tended to become somewhat independent of the congregation to which they officially belonged. Perhaps one could speak of the beginning of the individualization of their lives as Christians.

Third, a special aspect of edification that one can find in many of these tracts is the exhortation to fulfil one's duties in private as well as in professional life. God expected that one work hard in whatever profession one was in; He did not demand quietism but activism, that is, unceasing work, for the community of all good Christians and in particular for one's own congregation and family. That exemplary Christians had supposedly been working harder than other people was a topos found frequently in the funeral sermons of the time which since the late sixteenth century had become a literary genre of peculiar and strong influence. Through this kind of hagiography what was believed to be proper Protestant faith received a special interpretation. In sum, as part of the edifying literature, and clearly in a direct relationship to the crisis of the time, ethical values and in particular what Max Weber called innerworldly asceticism, meaning a new emphasis on work ethic and an ethical conduct of life, became part not only of Calvinism, as Weber has stressed, but also of the lives of many devout Lutherans. To be Lutheran was not to be idle, but to use the time God had given to each one of His children who knew only too well that death could come unexpectedly. The premiums which they needed to collect in order to gain eternal salvation had to be collected while they had a chance to do so, and that meant every day.

Fourth, not only some Calvinists, but also many Lutherans were most worried that the hardship they experienced possessed an unmistakable eschatological meaning which they should not miss. They believed that salvation history had progressed since Luther had revealed the true text of the Bible to all of those who wanted to know God's word, and they were convinced that the end of time was rapidly approaching. While some argued that Christ would return soon to execute the Last Judgement, others maintained that the returning Christ would together with His faithful children erect a glorious regime lasting a thousand years before Judgement Day. For the members of both of these groups, those who believed in the immediate execution of the apocalypse and those who were convinced of chiliasm, the political, economic, social, cultural, and moral changes of their time had a special eschatological significance. These changes were 'signs of the times', and it was the duty of good Christians to observe and decipher these signs and to draw the right kind of conclusion. Some Protestant circles even believed that God's beautiful creation had lost much of its inner strength as the apocalypse was approaching. To them, the various climatic effects of the 'Little Ice Age' were proof that Christ was returning soon. In a similar manner others interpreted the Catholic revival and the political oppression exerted by early absolutist regimes as proof that the end of times was near because as eager readers of the Bible they knew that God allowed the devil to rage so that he could test the belief of God's children before the glorious return of His son. For many Protestants, the military success of the Turkish armies in the Balkans in the last decades of the sixteenth century was a further irrefutable indication that God allowed the antichrist to punish His disobedient children even before His son would execute the Last Judgement. Yet others began to interpret the various numbers they found in the books of the Bible in order to find out exactly when Christ would be returning. Even high-ranking church members like Philip Nicolai (1556–1608) participated in these kinds of speculations. Some Lutherans came to the conclusion that Judgement Day would be soon, as early as 1630, while others pointed to the year 1666 and yet to even later dates, for example 1692. No doubt, for all Lutherans who were taken in by eschatological speculations in one way or another, their fear ('Angst') was transformed into hope ('Hoffnung'). They were convinced that the returning Christ would bring an end to the misery they were experiencing: that he would elevate them from the valley of tears (the *Jammertal*) to the glory of His realm (His *Freudensaal*).

For a long time church historians writing in the tradition of Lutheran orthodoxy failed to perceive, or perhaps consciously ignored, the degree to which eschatological speculations had modified Lutheran belief even before 1618. This is no longer so today, although some church historians still have difficulties in acknowledging the far-reaching effects of climatic change and like to think that Lutherans were safe and secure in the era of Lutheran orthodoxy up until the beginning of the Thirty Years' War. As we now know, this was certainly not so.

Fifth, as the subsistence crisis affected their lives more and more, many Lutherans, like many Catholics and Calvinists, adopted yet another explanation, and this explanation was certainly much less strenuous than adopting a strict work ethic in accordance with Protestant asceticism, and certainly simpler than eschatological calculations. These circles were sure that witches as the devil's agents had caused all the misery which they were experiencing. Witches were able to kill cattle and cause the miscarriage of children, they believed, just as they were capable of destroying a harvest with a hailstorm. To them, the answer was straightforward and simple: if one were able to detect all of the persons who had entered into a contract with the devil, and were able to catch them, make them confess and then deliver them to the fire or the stake, one would bring an instant end to hardship. Hunting witches, therefore, looked like an obligation for all good and devout Christians, Protestants and Catholics alike, and these actions seemed to be in complete agreement with God's demands. When plague hit European societies in the fourteenth century, the persecution of Jews became a widespread phenomenon within just a few years. In a similar manner, from the 1570s and 1580s, European Christians, including Lutherans of all walks of life, began to suspect their closest neighbours of witchcraft, and they were ready to denounce them and deliver them to torture and even to death. Before 1618, there were only a few Lutherans who opposed this view.

The Thirty Years' War

At the beginning of the sequence of battles called the Thirty Years' War, Lutherans in central Europe were not affected, or perhaps one should say that they believed that they had nothing to do with the decisions that had precipitated these events. When in 1618 the estates of the kingdom of Bohemia chose the Elector of the Palatinate, a Calvinist, as their new king and seriously provoked the Habsburgs in Vienna, key Lutheran states such as Saxony or Wuerttemberg were not directly involved. But this quickly changed. Once the Habsburg emperor Ferdinand had defeated the Bohemian estates in the battle of the White Mountain in 1620, he began to carry through the Counter-Reformation in Bohemia with military force and with unprecedented vigour. As a result, the delicate confessional balance between Catholic and Lutheran territories in the Holy Roman Empire, constructed as part of the Peace Treaty of Augsburg in 1555, and which came to include also the Calvinists, though not as yet officially, was severely threatened. As the Habsburgs brought Bohemia back into the Catholic camp, Lutherans as well as Calvinists within the Empire feared that this would be just the beginning of Catholic use of military force and that the Catholic Reconquista would continue, just as Emperor Ferdinand and his military advisors after 1620 developed plans to move beyond Bohemia.

The first Lutheran power which decided to oppose any extension of Habsburg power into northern Germany was the crown of Denmark. With Denmark's defeat, northern Germany was left wide open to Habsburg influence. In the following years, considerable parts of southern, central and northern Germany were occupied by imperial troops. By the end of the 1620s, the non-Catholic territories of the Empire were in a desperate situation. As the emperor dreamed of bringing back all non-Catholics into the fold of the Catholic Church and even made plans to establish absolute imperial rule in the Holy Roman Empire, some Lutheran rulers, for example the Duke of Wuerttemberg, went into exile, while others, most notably the Duke of Saxony, attempted to accommodate themselves to the new situation. Most probably, Lutheranism in central Europe would have been extinguished within a decade or two, had King Gustav Adolphus of Sweden not decided to intervene, and had not the French also taken up arms against the emperor in the mid-1630s. In 1632, at the battle of Luetzen, the Swedish king suffered a hero's death. Soon he was being venerated by German Lutherans as a martyr and a saint of the Lutheran cause. It is equally important that even after their king's death, the Swedish army remained in central Europe, while the French troops decidedly limited the range of activities of the emperor's army.

After unheard-of misery, after many battles, and after the senseless slaughter of thousands of civilians, the peace treaties of Muenster and Osnabrueck were signed in 1648, allowing for the political balance of power in the Empire to be redefined. This also involved a new confessional balance which now officially included Calvinist territories in addition to Catholics and Lutherans. In 1648, therefore, Lutheran princes could start to reorganize the administration and also the church life in their territories. Lutheran subjects rejoiced, prayed, and thanked God for peace at last.

In the decades between 1618 and 1648 the death toll had been shockingly high. In some parts of central Europe, and especially in some of the Lutheran territories, the population had been decimated. Whole villages were wiped out, many cities had been destroyed. In some areas the number of people had declined by 40 or even 50 per cent. Extreme violence and brutal killings had become everyday events, and those who were not victims of the large armies or of marauding bands of soldiers moving from place to place in hope of finding some kind of booty often became victims of disease such as the plague. What had triumphed in central Europe during the Thirty Years' War was the fatal combination of hunger, war, and plague. For men, women and children alike, the experience of mass death and of imminent and sudden death had become familiar. No one, it seemed, had been excluded from this most catastrophic turn of events. Not since the fourteenth century, and not again until the first half of the twentieth century, had uncurtailed violence, uncontained diseases, and the sheer lust for killing changed the lives of so many people so drastically as during the Thirty Years' War. Especially for German Lutherans, this conflict, which over the course of several decades involved almost all the great powers of Europe, was the ultimate imaginable catastrophe.

It is not surprising, therefore, that in the three decades between 1618 and 1648 the culture, the church life, and even the world-view of Lutherans changed significantly and Lutheran orthodoxy was thoroughly transformed as a result of the war. In dealing with sorrow, pain and death, for example, poets with an affiliation to the Lutheran church found new forms of expressing themselves. *Memento Mori* became the appropriate slogan for many of them, as was reprimanding the *vanitas* of their contemporaries as the principal cause of all the misery. Andreas Gryphius (1616–64), Simon Dach (1605–59) and many others attempted to find artistic and symbolic ways of dealing with the horrors of their time. Their poems are a lasting tribute to those Lutherans who had lost their lives in the course of this bitter and, as it must have seemed to many of those who were not in power, senseless conflict.

Among the Lutheran clergy in the course of the war some concluded that the answers they had given prior to 1618 in order to explain the misery of that time were no longer sufficient. In a similar manner to the Jesuit Friedrich von Spee, the Lutheran Johann Matthaeus Meyfart (1590–1642), for example, severely criticized witch-hunting. Hunting witches was a foolish injustice, he explained, which God would punish on the Day of the Last Judgement when God himself would sort out the sinners. Rather than hunting witches, Meyfart wrote, people should observe the signs of the times and prepare themselves for Christ's return. Not surprisingly, among common folk millenarianism became very popular. Itinerant self-appointed prophets wandered from village to village. When they proclaimed that the end of time had come, they received much attention. No one dared to contradict them. The horrors of the war, it seems, were as close to the apocalypse as anyone could imagine.

Among some well-educated circles, in cities like Nuremberg or Augsburg, finally, the pre-Christian teaching of stoicism served as a suitable guideline for psychological survival. The wheel of fortune (*Fortuna*) turned, the followers of neo-stoicism contended, and just as times had become extremely bad they would surely change and become better again. In some circles the teachings of hermeticism, or hermetics, also offered relief. The Lutheran pastor Johann Rist (1607–67), for example, combined his interest in nature with speculations derived from hermeticism, and both of these approaches taught him on the basis of eschatological belief that as salvation history had progressed God allowed, even offered, insight into the laws of creation which had hitherto been undisclosed. On this basis Rist conducted what he considered scientific experiments that in retrospect should be classified as significant first steps towards modern natural science, even though Rist never attained the insights of his more famous contemporaries in other countries, foremost in Great Britain. Compared to the other ways of coping with the catastrophe of the Thirty Years' War, therefore, Rist's endeavours should not be overestimated. As a pastor in a rural parish who had to care for his flock, Rist was just as helpless as were most of his colleagues. More valid, and perhaps also more typical of the reaction to the hardship of the times than Rist's modest scientific experiments, were the hymns that he wrote in which he admonished true Lutherans to prepare for the coming of Christ's kingdom.

How much of Lutheran orthodoxy survived throughout the catastrophe of the Thirty Years' War is hard to assess. Lutheran pastors had been affected by despair, misery, hunger, and the experience of sudden, premature and violent death as much as anyone else. No visitations were held, and the church ordinances contained no advice for survival, nor did the learned compendia of Lutheran dogmatic teaching offer spiritual help. The famous city of Magdeburg, a proud symbol of Protestant culture, had been destroyed by imperial troops during the war, as had many other Protestant cities. Because many church archives were also burned it is difficult, even today, to reconstruct the history of Lutheranism in some places prior to the Thirty Years' War. In retrospect, perhaps, the one theological notion which deserves special attention is the belief that the number of God's true and faithful children is small and that persecution serves as proof that they are the elected. This notion is not restricted to the Thirty Years' War. It is, however, certainly the one theological tenet that helped to preserve Lutheran faith during the time of the war and for some time thereafter. Theophil Grossgebauer (1627–61) from Rostock, among others, came to this conclusion. A generation later, in a somewhat different context, this idea of the small group of God's true children was taken up by the Pietists.

Old problems and new beginnings

For a long time historians have postulated that 1648 marked the end of war and the beginning of a long period of peace. This view can no longer be upheld. After 1660 a new series of wars began which raged through the north-east of the Empire and shortly thereafter wars erupted which afflicted the south-west. In both of these regions we find many Lutherans, and in both areas whatever had been rebuilt shortly after 1648 was destroyed in these new wars. Hunger, plague, and killing returned. These wars lasted, with short intervals, into the early eighteenth century. The process of rebuilding and of finding a way back to some kind of normalcy was very slow, therefore, and was characterized by many setbacks. No wonder that in all Lutheran communities feelings of insecurity persisted. In many Lutheran circles even after 1648 the interest in apocalyptical matters remained strong. What the future seemed to hold, many people believed, was more hardship rather than peace and prosperity. Typically, Lutheran pastors produced masses of edifying tracts, while Lutheran communities consumed this kind of literature in the hope of finding spiritual guidance. A strong interest in funeral sermons also continued.

The continuity of the combination of hardship, despair and interest in strategies to save one's soul during this time cannot be disputed, but within Lutheran territories, just as within territories ruled by Catholic or Calvinist princes, the decades after 1648 should also be seen as the beginning of a new period. Now that the question of how much power would be exercised by whom within the Holy Roman Empire had been settled by the Peace Treaty of Westphalia, and now that a new confessional balance between Lutheran, Calvinist and Catholic principalities within the Empire had been achieved, all territorial princes possessed a firm basis for stabilizing their rule. Wherever this was possible, princes abolished the participation of the estates in governmental and administrative affairs. As soon as some financial means were available, because taxes began to flow again, the princes, including those in Lutheran territories, expanded the operations of the court. They demonstrated their new power by exhibiting a new measure of luxury. Even princes in Lutheran territories were tempted to follow the example of Louis XIV and to imitate the court life of Versailles. For them, the Baroque artistic style that had originated in the Italian Catholic Counter-Reformation seemed to be the appropriate expression of their rule.

For the Lutheran churches, the rise of most princes to absolute power was a mixed blessing. On the one hand the sovereigns supported the consistories in bringing back 'law and order' to their churches and congregations. They strengthened the role of the superintendents, and thus of hierarchy within the church government; as a result, the social and cultural distance between those at the top who claimed responsibility for church affairs and the pastors, especially pastors labouring in rural villages, grew. The training of pastors was supervised more closely, and, as a rule, the general education of the clergy was much improved. Visitations were carried out again regularly and nonconformists and dissenters who were detected in the course of these visitations were rebuked and, if they did not promise to conform to Lutheran rules, were expelled. In some cases they also very deliberately used the *jus emigrandi* that the Peace Treaty of Westphalia had stipulated and emigrated in search of a place where they would not suffer persecution. It was then, only in the decades after 1648, that the rule of territorial princes over the churches (the 'Landesherrliche Kirchenregiment') was fully implemented. Only then could one begin to speak of homogeneous Lutheran states within the Holy Roman Empire.

On the other hand most absolute princes – with the exception of a figure like Ernst der Fromme from Sachsen-Gotha, for example – had no interest in the sincere devotion of pious Christians. These Lutheran princes of the post-1648 era liked, and supported, this-worldly pleasures, not inner-worldly asceticism. What they expected from their subjects was obedience and hard work, not knowledge of the Bible or the teachings of Luther. In line with the theory of mercantilism, they believed that people should produce goods which could be sold and which would bring revenue and taxes, as advocated by economic advisors, and that young men should also be willing to be trained as soldiers in the new standing armies which the princes were building. Of course, Lutheran princes also hired court-preachers. These court-preachers were expected to take part in court life. Lutheran princes, as a rule, did not like to hear sermons in which they were admonished to live a sincere life as Christians. As we know, some court-preachers did deliver such sermons, and as we also know, some of them were soon replaced by pastors who had a wider view of the ethical standards as they should be applied to the life of princes. It is not wrong, therefore, that historians have concluded that absolute obedience leading to authoritarianism was an integral part of Lutheranism, while Calvinism tended to produce the kind of spirit which led to democratic forms of government, even though in most cases only indirectly. However, further research will have to look more closely into the cases in which Lutheran pastors, and Lutheran court-preachers, openly and decidedly opposed the new worldly life-style of princes, in which they supported people who were unjustly punished by some agencies within the absolute government of the princes, or in which Lutheran theologians or pastors resisted, as a matter of principle, the temptation to take part in the new secular way of life within Lutheran principalities. Perhaps such research will find out that the close connection between Lutheranism and authoritarianism is more a matter of nineteenth-century Lutheran ideology than a matter of seventeenth-century Lutheran political practice and has to be seen as a notion which was projected back from the later period into the earlier.

The lasting legacy of seventeenth-century Lutheranism may therefore not be, if all aspects are considered, blind obedience towards worldly power and a tendency towards authoritarian forms of government. Unlike seventeenth-century dissenters in England, seventeenth-century German Lutherans did not discover and practise freedom of religion as a basic human right, and as a right that could be transferred from the religious world into that of politics and power. By contrast, the lasting legacy of seventeenth-century German Lutherans can be found, and cherished, in the edifying tracts that they wrote, in their hymns, their prayers, and their poems. Driven by the wish to counsel spiritually those of their contemporaries who were worried that they would die a sudden death without having been saved and who were struggling to find ways to save their souls, Lutheran pastors produced moving cultural and literary monuments. This is the spirit in which Johann Arndt wrote his *Books of True Christianity*. Deeply disturbed by the misery of their times, and in search of what God might wish to tell the people through the tribulations to which they were exposed, Andreas Gryphius and a number of his friends composed some of the best poems of seventeenth-century German literature. Trusting that God's goodness was not failing, and that they were still God's chosen people as they lived in the tradition of Luther to whom God had entrusted the task of reforming His church, Paul Gerhardt wrote his most beautiful hymns. In the course of the seventeenth century, these hymns became the centre of the services and in this way the centre of spiritual life of many congregations in Lutheran territories.

What we can observe, therefore, and what we should underline, in conclusion, is a close, even productive, relationship between the enormous misery of the seventeenth century and the way some Lutherans found in artistic, symbolic and literary forms a means of dealing with their unique experience. It is not surprising, perhaps, that some of these seventeenth-century Lutheran hymns and poems have been especially appreciated in the first half of the twentieth century, that is, in another time of extreme hardship in which many people were in need of consolation. And for some twentieth-century writers, for example Jochen Klepper (1903–42), the hymns written by Paul Gerhardt served as an inspiration as he wrote his own hymns in which he attempted to guide pious Christians as they were confronted with the horrors of twentieth-century totalitarianism. It was not until the twentieth century that the full extent of the catastrophe of the seventeenth century was understood by historians. It took the experience of another catastrophe before the dimension of despair and misery and the experience of mass-death of the seventeenth century could be grasped. This is not to say that we will ever be able to understand what people in the seventeenth century, and in particular Lutherans, had to come to terms with. God, it must have seemed to them, had deserted His chosen flock. As they rallied to prove to God that they were His chosen people after all, and as they trusted that the progress of salvation would lead them through the misery of their own world to eternal bliss, they needed a degree of courage and a measure of determination which is hard to imagine in retrospect. Only few lived to see peace return. In this sense, one would not wish to need their cultural legacy for spiritual consolation once again, even though such consolation may be much in need in times of secularization and the ever-renewed misuse of political power.

PART II

★

THE SECOND
REFORMATION

5

Communal Reformation: Zwingli, Luther, and the south of the Holy Roman Empire

PETER BLICKLE

In the German historical tradition, the Reformation has for centuries been interpreted as a 'national' event. Leopold von Ranke, the co-founder of critical historical science in the first part of the nineteenth century and one of its most profound proponents, greatly influenced conventional wisdom on this subject up until the 1960s.[1] According to this, Martin Luther's theology was the purest form of Christianity and was promoted throughout the world by the efforts of the German nation.[2] 'Nation' and 'the people' (*das Volk*) were frequently used synonymously despite the fact that neither the question as to how the people were incorporated into the reformers' theology nor how the people were thought to have supported it have been adequately examined. This, however, has changed over the last thirty years. The Reformation was one of the most prominent subjects of social history in Germany, as well as in England and the United States. Under close scrutiny it became obvious that both urban inhabitants and rural peasants were the most ardent supporters of the Reformation and that neither the nobility nor the majority of the clergy were in favour of it. Contemporary sources attribute the support of the Reformation to the 'common man' (*der gemeine Mann*),[3] a category that included those sections of society involved in manual labour and not in any way wielding 'power', in particular peasants and burghers, or, as European social theory has labelled them, the estate of the 'laboratores'. The prime social and political context for both the rural and the urban common man was the community.

The Reformation led to unrest in the cities and countryside which ultimately culminated in the most serious popular uprising before the French Revolution.

---

1 Walther Peter Fuchs, 'Das Zeitalter der Reformation', pp. 43–52, 77–81.
2 von Ranke, *Deutsche Geschichte*, vol. 1, p. 165.
3 Blickle, *Revolution*, pp. 122–5; Blickle, *Communal Reformation*; *passim*; Lutz, *Der gemeine Mann*.

It was not until the reformatory movement reached its climax in 1525 that the imperial princes became involved in order to restore law and order and to secure their own power.

The following analysis deals with this first phase of the Reformation. The primary concern will be the process and success of the Reformation in the Holy Roman Empire as evinced by its acceptance in the cities and countryside. It will become obvious that the 'community' as an organizing frame for everyday life played a crucial role in the endorsement of the Reformation. The reformatory process itself went through a period of radicalization which directly led to the Peasants' War of 1525. The term 'Peasants' War' (*Bauernkrieg*) itself has, in modern historical science, ceased to be the preferred term for an event that today is recognized to have crucially incorporated the burghers of princely cities. Thus, the expression's social emphasis on peasants and its terminological limitation to war ignores the fact that the conflict was aimed at changing the very core of political and social life. Indeed, due to the research of the last thirty years, the Peasants' War is nowadays seen as being in every way equal with other European uprisings in revolutionary history[4] and as being a crucial and integral part of the Reformation.[5] To conclude, the way in which the 'peasants' Reformation' and the 'burghers' Reformation' have merged at an interpretational level in modern historical science will be shown by the use of the term 'communal Reformation'. Contemporary historians unanimously agree that it is necessary to be aware of the concept of princely, or territorial, reformation due to the fact that 1525 marks a caesura.[6]

The Reformation as a social event in urban and rural communities

In the early 1520s, Martin Luther's and Huldrich Zwingli's theology rapidly spread by way of sermons, theatre plays, and especially its dissemination by pamphlets, the new medium of the day.[7] Mass was replaced by the 'pure gospel' (*das reine Evangelium*) in form of sermons, and justification purely for the sake of the Creed usurped the sacraments and the 'good works' (*die guten Werke*). The new message was that no priests were necessary to achieve eternal salvation

---

4 Wende (ed.), *Grosse Revolutionen der Weltgeschichte*; Bookchin, *The third revolution*, pp. 38–60.
5 Oberman, 'Gospel of social unrest'.
6 Reinhard, *Reichsreform und Reformation*, pp. 313–20.
7 Scribner, *Simple folk*; Köhler, 'Meinungsprofil'; Edwards, *Printing*; Burkhardt, *Reformationsjahrhundert*.

and that the Word of God was intelligible without any kind of dogma.[8] Neither Luther nor Zwingli disagreed in principle in their interpretation of the 'iustitia dei' and the principle of justification by faith derived therefrom: to believe is a God-given blessing and mankind can only hope to approach true belief by admitting to his own innate sinfulness, his 'natura corrupta'. However, Luther and Zwingli did disagree upon the nature of the relationship between, on the one hand, 'law' (*Gesetz*) and 'gospel' (*Evangelium*), Old and New Testament, and, on the other hand, the nature of the Holy Communion. It will be necessary to return to these conflicting notions in a later systematical section because they are crucial to the explanation of 'communal Reformation'.

In the cities the burghers increasingly became more interested in this new form of Christianity from 1521 onward.[9] The preachers' offices present in every larger town were generally staffed by young, academically educated priests who often sympathized with Luther and Zwingli and hence urged their rectories to adopt changes. It is proven that in Kaufbeuren, a medium-sized southern German town half way between Munich and Lake Constance, the burghers demanded the proclamation of the 'pure gospel' after 1524 and thus the abolishment of mass and the Catholic rites of the town. At Christmas 1524, protests were directed against the town priest and the pressure exerted upon him was great enough to induce the town council to call a religious disputation on 30 January 1525 at which the Catholic priesthood was expected to defend itself against the ideas of one Lutzenberger, a reformed priest, and this despite explicit prohibition by the nearby Bishop of Augsburg. Both the town councillors and a committee of burghers chosen specifically for this debate were summoned. The religious disputation resulted in the council permitting the preaching of the gospel and promising to install a new church ordinance because, according to the community's judgement, the established ceremonies had been proven to be the work not of God but rather of Man.[10]

The towns adopted the reformatory impetus to a surprisingly large degree, and in southern Germany and Switzerland it was even adopted by the majority of the imperial cities. It is possible to construct an ideal archetype of the reformatory process in the towns by supplementing the example of Kaufbeuren with information gathered from a plethora of other examples.

Based on numerous case studies, it is today a widely accepted assumption in historical science that urban reformation took place through 'bottom-up'

8 Schwarz, *Luther*; Locher, *Zwinglische Reformation*, pp. 197–225.
9 Moeller, *Reichsstadt*; Ozment, *Reformation in the cities*; Schmidt, *Reichsstädte*.
10 Thomas Fuchs, *Konfession*, pp. 278–91.

processes.[11] This is based on the theoretical concept of different social groups adopting ideas in different ways. Thomas A. Brady's examination of the case of Strasbourg represents an innovative example of research into this concept by showing that the burghers and councillors had a very different attitude to the Reformation, seeing it as 'a story of attack and threat from below'. According to Brady, the assault on mass and its imagery endangered the chapels and altars donated by the politically and economically powerful. Likewise, the withholding of tithes and payments of interest was a heavy economic blow to the patricians just as the closure of monasteries and religious foundations threatened their sons' and daughters' supply structures. It was purely to secure their own political survival that the upper classes of Strasbourg in the end decided to join the reformers' ranks.[12]

The supporters of the Reformation in urban areas agreed upon the fact that the 'gospel' was the quintessence of Christianity.[13] Thus, the 'pure gospel', already the reduced form of 'the gospel without human augmentation' (*Evangelium ohne menschlichen Zusatz*) and meaning the abnegation of the dogmas and canon law of the church, was further abbreviated to just 'the gospel'. By doing so, the urban reformation adopted the guidelines of the scripture, thereby inducing urban communities to require preachers so as to be able to guarantee sermons and, as attested by the many religious disputations, to make decisions regarding the correct form of teaching. Despite the fulfilment of these demands, political decisions regarding the church were once again being made by the council, and the church ordinances were all reminiscent of magisterial mandates.

The commonly held view that urban reformation was a process 'from below' was corroborated by the analysis of the way in which it evolved and proceeded. Despite initially developing in small, heterogeneous circles frequently influenced by the poorer lower classes, the movement rapidly came to symbolize the tensions between the communities and the councils. In conflictual situations, communities would nominate a committee which in its debates with the councils would invariably insist on pressing ahead with the Reformation;[14] depending on the constitutional realities of the individual cities, these committees consisted of guild members, parishioners, or citizens of urban districts. Following the famous example of Zurich in 1523 (Zwingli's disputation),[15] it was also frequently these committees that arbitrated on the confessional unity

---

11 Schmidt, *Reichsstädte*; Blickle, *Communal Reformation*, pp. 63–97.
12 Brady, *Strasbourg*, pp. 234–5, 291–3.   13 Schmidt, *Reichsstädte*, pp. 72–4.
14 Blickle, *Reformation*, pp. 101–30; Rammstedt, 'Stadtunruhen 1525'.
15 Moeller, 'Zwinglis Disputationen'.

of the city by acting as communal representatives and forming a kind of court of law together with the council and judging the merits of the correct form of teaching.[16]

Thus, it also becomes possible to explain the endorsement of certain parts of reformatory ethics. It had always been the urban Reformation's aim to achieve equality between both secular priests and priests in religious orders, and burghers in respect to rights and duties. In effect, this obliged priests to pay taxes and participate financially in the town guard; furthermore, having equal rights entailed the abolishment of the special status priests had had at the ecclesiastical courts and subjected them to the authority of the city courts.

The urban Reformation did commence in 1521 based upon Luther's justificatory teachings but very soon mutated to propagating demands stemming from Zwingli and the upper German reformers for the changing of the world order. It is the 'common man' who was at the core of this demand for change and who thereby became what Heinrich Richard Schmidt has called 'the patron' of the Reformation.[17] The councillors, responsible for law and order in the cities, solely enacted the majority of the community's decision by 'introducing' the Reformation by church ordinance.

In the countryside, historical science was for long remiss in analysing the reformatory process given that the Reformation was regarded as the domain of priests and humanists and therefore a purely intellectual event. This attitude has since been thoroughly revised.

The case of the community of Wendelstein in Franconia serves as a prime example to show what is meant by 'peasants' Reformation'. Wendelstein was a village with a typical southern German form of self-government. At community meetings it elected the two mayors of the village and eight jurors, managed the community's financial affairs, regulated the use of forests and common land, and organized village security.[18]

The priest, who had been in office since 1510, was so slovenly when attending to his duties that the patronage lord forced him to resign. His deputy introduced new taxes designed to benefit the clergy when performing rites that demanded the wearing of the stole, for example, for marriages and funerals. The community did not accept the legality of these taxes and took the case all the way to the ecclesiastical court of the Bishop of Eichstaett which resulted in years of tension. Finally, in October 1524, Kaspar Krantz was ordained as the new priest. On the occasion of his ordination the community representative

16 Fuchs, *Konfession*; Schmidt, *Reichsstädte*; Schilling, *Stadt*, pp. 96–7.
17 Schmidt, *Reichsstädte*, p. 332.
18 Endres, 'Die Reformation im fränkischen Wendelstein'.

made a speech designed to instruct Krantz on his rights and duties: 'And so we will recognize you not as a lord but only as a servant of the community . . . and hereby command you to preach the gospel and the Word of God sincerely and scrupulously in a pure, clear, and veracious manner [i.e., without any interpretation by the Roman Church]'.[19] Furthermore, the benefices were to serve as appropriate income and the community would therefore no longer be contributing any kind of sacrificial donations or endowments for the soul's salvation (*Seelgerätsstiftungen*). Should Krantz, however, require anything else from the villagers then he would have to take them to the local court and not to the bishop's ecclesiastical court.

Other villages must have witnessed similar events.[20] It is possible to speak of a 'peasants' Reformation' from 1523 onward. It started in the territory of the imperial city of Zurich and within the following two years had rapidly spread to Salzburg in the east, to Alsace in the west, southwards to Trentino, and northwards all the way to Thuringia and Saxony. The demands the peasants directed at the church were more or less unanimous. Their understanding of the Reformation was manifest in their desire for (1) the preaching of the 'pure gospel'; (2) the priest's appointment by the community; (3) the community to decide on which form of teaching should be pursued; (4) the priest's residentiary; (5) an affordable and sustainable church, and (6) the abolishment or the restraint of the ecclesiastical court (the bishopric).[21]

Originally, peasants and their urban counterparts used the term 'pure gospel' synonymously. The peasants repeatedly emphasized that they did not believe they would be able to achieve salvation without hearing the gospel being preached. Yet, in addition, they also recognized its practical effect on everyday life: as the gospel demands the promotion of the 'common good' (*gemeiner Nutzen*) and 'brotherly love' (*brüderliche Liebe*) it must also have an equalizing tendency and thereby aim at Christianizing society. Hence, it was paradigmatic for the structuring of the political and legal order and increasingly came to resemble the 'lex'. This interpretation of the gospel in regard to the rhetorical device of 'divine law' (*göttliches Recht*) was to become a crucial element in the Peasants' War. In time, the priest's appointment by the community became just as important a demand as the 'pure gospel' because this alone, or so the argument went, guaranteed the correct form of preaching as dictated by the community. The priest's residentiary was mandatory to

---

19 Franz (ed.), *Quellen Bauernkrieg*, pp. 315–16.
20 Conrad, *Reformation in der bäuerlichen Gesellschaft*, pp. 49–85; Bierbrauer, 'Die Reformation in den Schaffhauser Gemeinden'; Bierbrauer, *Unterdrückte Reformation*.
21 Blickle, *Communal Reformation*, pp. 11–40.

ensure salvation through sermons. If the priest was adequately financed by endowments and tithes there was no need for surcharges on baptisms, weddings, funerals, or any other spiritual or ritualistic services. If canon law was solely the work of man and not based upon the gospel it seemed straightforward to transfer the authority of the ecclesiastical courts to local and village courts.

Generally speaking, the Reformation in both urban and rural society conspicuously attempted to communalize the church.

The Peasants' War as the revolution of the 'common man'

The Peasants' War commenced after the unrest stretching from Basle to Lake Constance in the summer of 1524 and the revolts in Upper Swabia in January 1525. Tens of thousands of peasants formed three large bands. When the lords induced the writing of letters of complaint so as to begin negotiations, the peasants, who had had enough of the meddlesome courts, demanded to be judged according to 'the divine right which dictates the appropriate course of action to each estate.'[22] In effect, this meant employing the gospel to judge the secular order and thereby making judges of the theologians. The most famous peasant letter of complaint and very symptomatic of the times was the 'Twelve Articles of the Upper Swabian peasants' (die Zwölf Artikel der oberschwäbischen Bauern),[23] passed by a kind of peasants' parliament in Memmingen in March 1525. It demanded a reduction in taxes, the priest's appointment by the community, freedom (abolishment of villeinage), liberalization of hunting and fishing regulations, and the enhancement of communal rights. To settle the question whether the demands corresponded to the spirit of the gospel, Luther, Zwingli, and the majority of the other well-known reformers were called upon as 'judges'. Simultaneously, the Upper Swabians formulated a 'Federal Ordinance' (Bundesordnung) for the 'Christian Union', the name they gave their organization.[24] Twelve councillors and three captains were designated to represent a government for all the communities in the region between Lake Constance and Ulm. It would have been a small step indeed to the proclamation of a republic along the lines of a Free State (Freistaat). Wolfgang Hardtwig has detected the incipience of civil society in this chain of events and in similar

22 Franz (ed.), Quellen Bauernkrieg, pp. 146–7; Scott and Scribner (eds.), Peasants' War, p. 124.
23 Franz (ed.), Quellen Bauernkrieg, pp. 174–9; Scott and Scribner (eds.), Peasants' War, pp. 252–7.
24 Seebass, Artikelbrief, pp. 77–88; Scott and Scribner (eds.), Peasants' War, pp. 130–2.

processes in other periods of German history, and sees in them a crucial challenge to the system of the *ancien régime*'s political authority in Europe as a whole.[25]

Another important fact to bear in mind is that contemporary sources were already aware of the republican spirit of the Peasants' War and quickly developed political theories connected to the revolutionaries' ideals of 'freedom', 'divine right', and the 'pure gospel'. In particular, this does not refer to the well-known ideas of Tirolean peasant leader Michael Gaismair[26] or Utopians such as Hans Hergot,[27] but rather to concepts developed by, for example, Christoph Schappeler. Schappeler probably committed them to paper in March or April 1525 and published them anonymously in Nuremberg in May. The title read 'To the Assembly of Common Peasants' (*An die Versammlung gemeiner Bauernschaft*)[28] and it definitely matched Luther's and Zwingli's thoughts on political theory in regard to its intellectual integrity and argumentative consistency.

Schappeler had won Memmingen as the first Upper Swabian imperial city for the Reformation at Christmas 1524. He was the preacher at St Martin's Church and both an ardent supporter and a personal friend of Zwingli, whose theology he defended in his theses of religious disputations presented to the council and guilds at Epiphany 1525. Schappeler was born in St Gallen and was thus Swiss. His close affiliation with the peasants who were meeting in Memmingen in March 1525 to discuss and approve the Twelve Articles is indisputable.

Schappeler's politico-theoretical vision was of a kind of republic based on the immediacy of the burghers and peasants to the emperor. His argument hinges on the conviction that the peasants were being tyrannized and that this called for resistance. The new political order designed by him ideally emulated the structures of the Roman republic and the Confederation of Switzerland. Schappeler's notions of politics were further reinforced by Huldrich Zwingli's theological Zurich school of thought which held that the gospel showed both the way to salvation and the way to the amelioration of the political and social order.[29] Schappeler radicalized this notion and insisted on the indivisibility of gospel and law, Old and New Testament. Just as if he had been addressing Martin Luther and his friends, he let his arguments in favour of the radical renewal of the world through the spirit of Christianity culminate in the passage:

---

25 Hardtwig, *Genossenschaft*, pp. 102–58.   26 Politi, *Statuti*.
27 Seibt, *Utopica*, pp. 90–104.   28 [Schappeler,] *An die versamlung gemeyner Pawerschaft*.
29 Hamm, *Zwinglis Freiheit*, pp. 108–10.

And even if they [probably the theologians around Luther] for all times speak of two commandments, the 'divina' which concerns itself with the soul's salvation, and the 'politica' which is for the common good. O God, these commandments should not be separated because the commandments of politica are also divina and promote the common good. This specifically means to retain brotherly love, which is the greatest victory for the spirit's bliss.[30]

Politica and divina thus serve the common good and only those who promote them are legitimately in power.

Furthermore, Schappeler included villeinage and freedom as central elements of his argumentation and assessed them in light of God's commandments. God demands that he who wields political power should employ His commandments meticulously.[31] Tyranny develops only when the powerful fail to do this. One may depose tyrants similarly to the way the Swiss drove out the brutal nobility. Tyranny always leads to villeinage and enslavement. Rome's prestige waxed during the republican era but when this successful 'common regiment' declined, subjects were degraded to villeins (*Eigenleut*). The Israelites were no different insofar as 'God gladly lived' amongst them as long as they had a 'common regiment', but as soon as it declined they 'in their misery and clamouring introduced villeinage and the like' (*Elend und Jammer mit Leibeigenschaft und anderem*).[32] Tyrants are always those who make villeins of men and if they are not driven forth they will make life everlasting hell by causing villeins to become 'servi' and, as slaves so Schappeler feared, eventually be 'sold as cattle, as horses and oxen'.[33] Tyrants must 'own everything, body and property'.[34]

According to Schappeler, these conditions could only be improved by the gospel. In his essay, divine law is called 'divine jurisprudence' (*göttliche Juristerei*),[35] and the evangelists and apostles are 'divine jurists' just as alluded to in the Old and New Testament. The notion of a republic consisting of free peasants and burghers loyal to an imperial sovereign was an attempt to base this on the Bible. Indeed, it is there that the legitimation for freedom in terms of divine law originates. By quoting the first Epistle to the Corinthians (1 Cor. 7), Schappeler states that he who is a villein and has the opportunity to liberate himself should not hesitate to do so.

Christoph Schappeler attempted to justify the Peasants' War as a throwing off of tyranny. His essay conspicuously contains partly the drafts and partly the

---

30 [Schappeler,] *An die versamlung gemeyner Pawerschaft*, p. 181, lines 12–19.
31 *Ibid.*, p. 162, lines 24–9.   32 *Ibid.*, p. 188, lines 41–4.   33 *Ibid.*, p. 186, lines 27–33.
34 *Ibid.*, p. 168, lines 11–12.   35 *Ibid.*, p. 177, line 34.

final versions of the material published by the peasants: the Twelve Articles and the Federal Ordinance. Schappeler adopted their demand for freedom and increased communal autonomy and supported it by referring to the Roman republic just as the Swiss did in the early sixteenth century. He also adopted Zwingli's call for the gospel to be employed to improve the world. The 'Two Kingdoms' were merged into a single Christian commonwealth in which there was to be only freedom and in which the free were to have political rights, thus enabling every peasant and every cobbler to wield power. However, as the text admonished, 'often hold communal meetings amongst yourselves' (*haltet oft Gemeinden untereinander*) as this alone could guarantee a lasting and just order. Finally, Schappeler tied freedom to divine law in precisely the way the peasants had hoped: evangelists as jurists.

With the publication of the Twelve Articles (another twenty-seven editions were to follow), the revolt spread rapidly.[36] The Twelve Articles were the organizing programme and the Federal Ordinance was the organizing framework. The winning over of the archbishopric of Mainz to the Twelve Articles in May 1525 was seen as particularly spectacular and was followed shortly by numerous cases of urban unrest originating in Mainz and Frankfurt, reaching northward to Cologne,[37] and leading to the fall of bishoprics and monasteries all the way to Saxony with barely any resistance offered. The inhabitants of Bamberg claimed to not want 'a single castle or monastery to remain standing' and proceeded to burn down 200 castles in just three days. The unrest spread from Upper Swabia to the Alps, and Tyrol, Salzburg, and Grisons became key areas in the revolts.

The prelates and nobility were paralysed by the peasants' successes. Monks fled from their monasteries and nobles abandoned their castles because they no longer felt safe within those walls. It was the princes of Bavaria, Lorraine, Hessen, and Saxony who decisively put an end to the nightmare. On 15 May the charismatic Thomas Münzler was reading the sermon in the peasants' camp in Thuringia when the princes' united army fired their first cannonballs at them. The peasants, who had staunchly believed in an imminent act of God on their behalf, panicked. With 5,000 of the 6,000 peasants killed, the battle was in reality a massacre. The battle of Frankenhausen was fought simultaneously with a battle at Zabern in Alsace and one at Böblingen in Württemberg and sealed the peasants' fate. Contemporary sources state that 100,000 people died in the Peasants' War.

36 Franz, *Bauernkrieg*; Scott and Scribner (eds.), *Peasants' War*, pp. 1–64.
37 Rammstedt, 'Stadtunruhen 1525'.

What were the reasons and what were the effects of the Peasants' War? There had already been increasing waves of peasant unrest in the late Middle Ages. The level of tension was undoubtedly great in commoners' circles, partly as a reason of increasing economic and social pressure, but certainly also due to rising political expectations.

In addition to this, the lords increasingly standardized their use of statutes, thereby exerting considerable political pressure on their subjects. Specifically, this fundamentally interfered with the traditional system in which criminal cases and legal disputes were resolved by courts depending on regional and local laws, significance of the case, and the judge's own ethics. Judges had never been university-educated jurists but instead laymen, peasants, and burghers from the villages and towns. Now, however, trials were being relocated away from local courts and their verdicts made void.[38]

The desire for freedom as the ultimate aim of the Peasants' War lay not only in the intensification of villeinage but also in a growing awareness of man's dignity which developed alongside the desire for more political rights in the decades leading up to 1525. In noble and ecclesiastical estates villages were constituted as communities with extensive rights to regulate agriculture, the use of forests and common land, and the establishment of infrastructure (smithies, public baths, taverns). Loosely organized neighbourhoods were converted into coherently structured corporations (statutes, self-administration). Due to these newly created corporational constitutions it had now become possible to attend parliament as a member of a distinct and separate political estate (Tyrol, Salzburg, Baden, Chur, the Habsburg regions in the west of the Empire) or to constitute political representation (*Landschaft*) in the body politic. This was connected with the right to levy taxes and present complaints (*gravamina*) to the princes by ratifying laws. Thus, the intention was to develop rights through laws and not through unilateral decree by the lords. Divine law could be regarded as a universal legal principle and therefore had to be applicable everywhere and at all times. This supported the expectation and hope that society and political authority could with the aid of the Bible be influenced to become more binding or even sacrosanct by way of the dignity of divine will.

Inasmuch as 'the gospel' had also influenced the reformatory movement in the cities, solidarity was able to supersede political estates. This happened without friction in all those territories in which cities and villages were united by the same dependence on a particular political authority and in which economic

---

38 Blickle, *Bauernkrieg*, pp. 70–86.

problems such as the monocultural specialization on vineyards created common interests (Alsace, Württemberg, Frankonia, Thuringia, Tyrol). There was also solidarity to be found between the suburbs and the poorer classes of the imperial cities (Heilbronn, Rothenburg ob der Tauber, Weissenburg in Alsace) in cases where they were closely connected by agriculture (guild of gardeners, guild of vine-dressers) and finally also with the miners (Tyrol, Salzburg).

All revolutions, even failed ones, have consequences. The princes and lords were exceedingly displeased and therefore a solution had to be found. Contracts represented by far the best way of resolving this problem. King Ferdinand himself opted for this and enacted an ordinance for Tyrol based on peasants' and burghers' complaints at the Innsbruck parliament. In other cases contracts were drawn up, especially in smaller territories such as in southern Germany. Spectacular events such as the transformation of the ecclesiastical estate of Chur, which was immediately adjacent to the Empire, into the republic of Grisons, an event that would probably never have occurred without the Peasants' War, were very exceptional. Generally speaking, the peasants' farmsteads were accorded legal rights regarding inheritance law, now theoretically enabling families to retain their farmsteads over generations, and subjects were given a clear, personal status which, albeit with regional variations, allowed the freedom of marriage and freedom of movement, both of which had been heavily curtailed under villeinage.[39] Winfried Schulze's thesis on the 'juridification of social conflicts' (Verrechtlichung sozialer Konflikte)[40] deals with this process and is based upon the observation that from the late sixteenth to the eighteenth centuries peasants increasingly decided to go to court to protect and promote their own interests.

Communal Reformation

The proposal to describe the Reformation as 'communal Reformation' in the Upper German area prior to the mid-1520s and its 'integration into the state' (Verstaatlichung) by the princes is rooted in the fact that both peasants and burghers made the same demands of the church and of religion in general: that the pure gospel be preached as a condition for salvation and that the priests, chosen by the commune, were to arbitrate on the correct form of teaching in cases of schism. This logically led to the equality of priests and

39 Blickle, Bauernkrieg, pp. 108–18; Reinhard, Reichsreform und Reformation, pp. 307–8.
40 Schulze, 'Die veränderte Bedeutung'.

the other members of the community in respect to rights and duties and the strengthening of the legal status of the villages and cities due to the abolishment of ecclesiastical courts.

The support of the Reformation by millions of people in southern Germany, Switzerland, and Austria is probably best explained by the fact that both city and village communities had greatly advanced the degree of self-administration during the fourteenth and fifteenth centuries. The community had become the primary form of political organization for peasants and burghers. This was most visibly expressed by the fact that the community employed statutory laws in its own affairs (use of forests, common land, village communal installations such as bakeries, public baths, taverns) by calling upon its own institutions (like the Vierer modelled on city councils).[41] Legitimation for this style of action was seen in the 'common good'.[42] Historical science has recently started to use the term 'communalism' to circumscribe this revitalization of communal Christianity theoretically and ideologically infused by the Reformation.[43] The 'revolution of the common man' is directly aligned with 'communal Reformation' due to the striking similarities between the regional identities of the two movements.

The term 'communal Reformation', however, refers not only to the way in which Luther's and Zwingli's teachings were received but also to the actual theology developed by Luther and Zwingli themselves.[44] Both of them made communal Christianity the crux of their theology by discounting the entire hierarchical structure of the church and thereby transforming 'priests' into believers. Bishops, archbishops, and the pope himself vanished in this ecclesiology just as did canon law with its hierarchical organization of courts from the parish court to the bishop's court and even the Rota. Luther had developed this theological stance in 1523, the main assertion of which was that the community had the right to arbitrate on the correct form of teaching and to appoint its own priests. The community, and thus the church, was 'where the pure gospel was preached' (wo das reine Evangelium gepredigt wird).[45] Zwingli had gone a step further and attached a communal denotation to the Holy

---

41 Blickle, *Kommunalismus*.
42 Cf. Simon, 'Gemeinwohltopik in der mittelalterlichen und frühneuzeitlichen Politiktheorie'.
43 For the reception of the 'communalism'-concept, see Brady, 'Sacral community'; Edwards, 'Die Gemeindereformation als Bindeglied', pp. 95–103; Hardtwig, *Genossenschaft*, pp. 149–58; Reinhard, *Reichsreform und Reformation*, pp. 90, 168–70; Dilcher, 'Kommune'; Ehrenpreis and Lotz-Heumann, *Reformation*.
44 Peter Blickle, in Dixon (ed.), *German Reformation*, pp. 133–67.
45 Luther, *Werke*, vol. 11, pp. 401–16, 408 (for the quotation).

Communion. Thus, it signifies rather a commemorative communal celebration than the transubstantiation itself. Holy Communion was a sacrament in which all the believers present at the ritual publicly communed with one another. According to Zwingli, this was analogous to the political unification of people in the form of a 'coniuratio'. The oath sworn by the founders of the Swiss Confederation was originally recognized as the equivalent of a church sacrament. The burghers of Zurich constituted such a confederation and annually reiterated their burghers' oath in Zurich's cathedral.[46] Thus, it is more than reasonable to regard the reformers' theology as, among other things, a theoretical discussion of the preceding communalization of the late Middle Ages.[47]

Berndt Hamm's expression 'normative centring' (normative Zentrierung) approximates this meaning although he only explicitly uses it for cities. Normative centring 'generally describes the theological, social, and political impetus of the Reformation and confessionalization as regards the orientation of religion and society as a fundamentally accommodating and organizing centre with normalizing, legitimizing, and regulatory powers'. The reformatory school of thought and communal values converge in the following paradigms: most significantly, 'the importance of community-oriented ethics' arising from the theological criterion of brotherly love. This suffices to explain the 'distance to Luther's dialectics pertaining to the conflict between God's law and the gospel' or, expressed in a more positive manner, an attitude 'that interconnects both the gospel and law and the law and spirit'. Hence, the political order was intended to be changed or even improved by the law of Christ.[48]

Hans Jürgen Goertz uses the term 'anti-clericalism' to characterize the Reformation. In his opinion, cities and villages were both crucial to the reformatory movement but no more influential than 'anti-clerical, humanistic, reformatory, radically reformatory, imperial knightly, rural, and urban movements'. These 'movements' all incorporated two major elements: on the one hand, the support of the gospel with its 'relentless normativity for spiritual and secular life' (unerbittlichen Normativität für das geistliche und weltliche Leben) and, on the other hand, its 'anti-clericalism'. Due to the priesthood of all believers, this required the abolishment of the priestly estate, thereby presupposing

---

46 Zwingli, Werke, vol. 1, pp. 537–8; vol. 2, p. 120; vol. 3, pp. 64, 535; vol. 4, pp. 427, 860; Schmidt, 'Häretisierung'.
47 Seebass, 'Reformation', pp. 400–1; Gatz, 'Gemeinde'; Reinhard, Reichsreform und Reformation, pp. 292–3.
48 Hamm, Bürgertum, pp. 73, 133–4 (for the quotation).

anti-clericalism, and at the same time dictated that anti-clericalism should lead to the disappearance of priests in general.[49]

'Communal Reformation' is an expression that must also be seen as the product of the great controversies dealing with the appropriate interpretation of the Reformation and European history in general during the Cold War. This is related to debates on the scientific theory of how best to conceptualize the driving forces behind historical processes, which led to the rise of structuralism over historicism and the novel focus on history as the history of society. Research on the history of the Reformation must be seen in connection with these processes. Marxist research in particular succeeded in connecting the two formerly isolated phenomena of Reformation and Peasants' War and coined the term 'Early Bourgeois Revolution', thereby empirically supporting Karl Marx's historical materialism and interpreting the reformers' theology as a superstructural phenomenon of economic and social change: the crisis of feudalism set in motion by nascent capitalism.[50] The continuity constructed from the Early Bourgeois Revolution in the sixteenth century to late twentieth-century socialism was politically especially contested as it was seen in the West as an attempt to usurp its history. This helps to explain the fascination the history of the reformatory era has exerted upon modern researchers despite the rapid and unprecedented decline of the Christian churches in Europe. Historical materialism as a methodological tool has not proved sufficient to plausibly analyse and firmly connect the empirical material. However, the subject at hand was a challenge to attempt to causally connect the numerous phenomena of an era so as not to let them remain elements of an incomprehensible history of isolated events.

49 Goertz, *Pfaffenhaß*; Goertz, *Antiklerikalismus*.
50 Smirin, *Münzer*; Steinmetz, 'Charakter der Reformation'; Vogler, *Gewalt* translated by Steven Parham.

6

The Calvinist Reformation in Geneva

ROBERT M. KINGDON

The Reformation in Geneva began as a political revolution, quickly followed by a religious revolution, both directed against the power of a prince-bishop. For centuries Geneva had been ruled by a prince-bishop as the headquarters of a large diocese extending over much of what is now south-western France. He had ruled this diocese in close collaboration with the duchy of Savoy. Many bishops had come from the ducal family. A concrete symbol of the Savoyard role in the city was the office of *vidomne*, an agent of Savoy sent into the city to regulate the administration of justice. Much of the strictly internal government of the city had been granted by earlier bishops to the local inhabitants, organized into a hierarchy of councils and represented before the bishop by agents called syndics.

There had been an important shift in the economy of Geneva late in the fifteenth century, away from trade in good part with Italy to trade increasingly with Germany and the Germanic areas making up the Swiss Confederation. This helped lead to a political alliance between the local government of Geneva and the Swiss governments of Fribourg and Bern. That alliance made possible the revolution against the prince-bishop and Savoy, although it was the militarily powerful republic of Bern alone that supported Geneva in the final climactic stages of revolution. Change was accomplished in a number of steps. One of the first was the creation of a new council, called the Council of Two Hundred, in imitation of a similar council in Bern, to increase local participation in government. Another was the abolition of the office of *vidomne* and its replacement with the new office of lieutenant, selected from among local citizens rather than being brought in from outside. Finally the bishop himself was driven out of the city, along with an entourage of several hundred people, including canons in the cathedral chapter, priests in all the city's parish churches, and members of several religious communities both male and female. All that was left of the ecclesiastical establishment was a handful of chantry priests, who were allowed to keep collecting their benefice income providing that they no longer said the masses that were the reason for that income,[1] and a single nun who took the city up on its offer to provide a dowry for any nuns who would agree to leave their community and marry. Troops dispatched by Bern conquered much of the area around Geneva, protecting it from retaliation by the bishop and Savoy for these changes. Geneva managed to keep control of a relatively small group of villages in its immediate neighbourhood that could provide some of the supplies of food and drink needed to sustain life within the city. Most of the rest of the diocese remained under the control of the bishop. A few parts of it were taken over by Bern.

The departure of the bishop and his agents left a tremendous void in Geneva's civic life. It had lost most of the wealthiest and best-educated people in town. It had lost all of those who supplied it with religious services. It had lost almost all of its educators and administrators of charity. This void was soon filled by religious refugees – primarily from France, secondarily from Italy, eventually from other countries as well. Refugees began flowing into the city as it adopted Protestantism, along with its other changes. The flow increased sharply in the following decades, until it reached a peak about 1560. From a pre-Reformation population of about 10,000, the city's population dropped to about 8,000, then climbed again to about 20,000. That proved to be unsustainable, and the population then dropped to about 15,000, and stayed at that level. Of these refugees, the most prominent was John Calvin.

During the early stages of Geneva's revolt against its bishop, Protestantism had spread into Switzerland and had been adopted by Bern. Bern in turn had tried to spread the new faith further by sending Protestant agents into neighbouring areas including Geneva. The most important of these agents was a preacher named William Farel, whose inflammatory sermons against what French Protestants labelled the 'idolatry of the mass' won considerable support within Geneva. That led to civic decisions to abolish the mass and to live, in the words of the Reformation ordinance of 21 May 1536, 'according to the Gospel and the Word of God'.[2] A few months later, John Calvin happened to be passing through Geneva, and Farel persuaded him to stay. Calvin had recently published a manual entitled the *Institutes of the Christian Religion*, designed to elaborate for the literate public, particularly in France, the basic meaning of the catechisms being adopted by Protestant regimes all over northern Europe. Farel thought he would be an ideal person to explain to Genevans what the

---

1 For more on these priests, see Cahier-Bucelli, 'Dans l'ombre de la Réforme', pp. 367–90.
2 *Sources du droit*, vol. 2, pp. 312–13.

change they had voted for really meant. The government agreed to appoint Calvin as a public lecturer with this charge.

Two years later, in 1538, Farel, Calvin, and others were thrown out of Geneva by a faction then controlling the government that did not like many of the changes in liturgy and discipline they were trying to introduce. Farel moved to Neuchâtel, another state in alliance with Bern, to supervise its Reformation. Calvin moved to Strasbourg and became pastor of its church of French refugees. That brought him into close contact with Martin Bucer, one of the leaders of the urban Reformation in German-speaking lands. It also gave him a chance to become personally acquainted with how a Protestant church could be organized.

Three years later, in 1541, after another shift in Genevan local politics, Calvin alone was invited back to Geneva to superintend its Reformation. That began a period of reformation that was to have consequences well beyond Geneva, to create a model that was followed by an entire branch of Protestant churches that called themselves Reformed, in distinction from the churches that called themselves evangelical and looked to Luther for inspiration.

Unlike the leaders of Protestant churches in most of Germany, Calvin had never been ordained as a priest and was not even trained in theology. He had been born in the town of Noyon in northern France, not far from Paris. His father was a notary whose most important client was the bishop of Noyon. John had received his earliest education in a small private school created primarily for the benefit of the nephews of the bishop and the children of other local dignitaries. As a boy, Calvin was named to benefices connected to a couple of local churches. Vicars ran these churches on his behalf and part of the income was used to support his advanced education. This was a common method of supplying financial support to university students in the period. For that advanced education, Calvin was sent to Paris, and studied in a couple of colleges there, absorbing the usual introduction to what was then called the humanities and what we would call the classics. When it came time for professional education, however, Calvin's father decided to take him out of the obvious successor studies in theology and instead have him study law. He continued studies in law at the universities of Orleans and Bourges, finally earning the degree of *licence* from Orleans in the early 1530s. In the final stages of his study, Calvin returned to Paris and took advantage of the courses taught by the newly established royal lecturers in advanced humanities, notably in Greek and Hebrew. These studies could well have been by-products of his legal studies, since many of the most important texts in the body of Roman law that constituted the essential part of the legal curriculum in those days had been originally drafted in Greek at the command of Roman emperors then resident in Constantinople.

At some point in these years that scholars still have trouble identifying, Calvin became a Protestant. He associated with other Protestants in and around Paris. With the general crackdown on Protestants in 1534, following the Protestant posting of placards attacking the mass that infuriated the king and the leaders of the Roman Catholic Church, Calvin decided to take refuge abroad. He resigned his benefices in Noyon and moved to Basel. There he plunged into intensive study, perhaps for the first time in his life, of theology and the Bible. He read voraciously in the writings of church fathers like Augustine. He read a good deal of Luther. And he used his developed knowledge of Greek to study scripture more closely than ever before. He did not register in the university and this programme of study was not formal. Calvin was really an autodidact in theology.[3] The end result of this period of study was his book, the *Institutes of the Christian Religion*, and the consequent call to teach in Geneva.

When Calvin returned to Geneva, the city wanted him to resume teaching and also begin preaching in the city's churches. He became a member of a body called the Company of Pastors, and quickly became its unofficial leader. He convened its weekly meetings and represented it at meetings of the governing councils. His position eventually developed into what was called Moderator of the Company of Pastors. The city also, however, wanted Calvin to use for their benefit his skills as a lawyer. One of the first things he did on returning to Geneva in 1541 was to write a set of ecclesiastical ordinances that provided a kind of constitution for the city's Reformed Church.[4] He was then asked to join a committee of local legal experts to write several sets of laws defining the offices of the secular government, creating a kind of constitution for it as well. That work was largely completed with the Edict of the Lieutenant adopted in 1542, and the Ordinances of Offices and Officers in 1543.[5] Calvin also drafted, in 1545, an Ordinance on Marriage,[6] but it was not adopted immediately by the city government. Even though it had not been adopted, however, research reveals that its provisions were in fact followed by the local courts.

All of these laws reveal a commitment to collective government, by select groups of people. The Genevans had become thoroughly disillusioned with government by any one person, by monarchic government, with its tendencies

---

3 Ganoczy, *Le jeune Calvin*, ch. 2.   4 *Registres de la Compagnie des Pasteurs*, vol. 1, pp. 1–13.
5 *Sources du droit*, vol. 2, pp. 394–408, 409–34. See Roget, *Histoire du peuple*, vol. 2/1, pp. 62–8, on Calvin's role in drafting these laws.
6 *Calvini Opera*, vol. 10, cols. 33–44.

to tyranny. Even though most Europeans at that time thought monarchic government was easily the best and most natural kind of government, Geneva wanted no part of it. It instead followed a model similar to that of many other city-states of the period. At the base of its secular government was a General Council of all the male inhabitants of the city over the age of twenty. It met at least once a year to elect other officers in the government. At its peak were four syndics elected for terms of only one year to be the chief executives of the government. In between was a series of councils made up only of members of two more privileged castes within the community, all of whom were expected to hold substantial pieces of property, including their own houses, and to practise honourable professions. They were called citizens, if they were born in the city, bourgeois if not. One could gain the status of bourgeois by petition, usually but not always accompanied by payment of a sum of money that could be quite substantial, depending on the resources of the applicant. The payment could be waived for people expected to serve the community in some important way, for example as ministers or jurisconsults.

The intermediate councils running the city government included the Council of Two Hundred, the Council of Sixty, and the Small Council. The Small Council, including the four syndics, had twenty-five members, all of them citizens, and met at least three times a week. It was the real executive of this government. The other two councils, made up of bourgeois and citizens both, met at the call of the Small Council to consider certain kinds of problems. The Two Hundred could be called to hear appeals from judicial decisions made by the Small Council. It was also often asked to ratify certain kinds of laws. The Sixty generally considered problems of relations with foreign powers. The General Council in these annual elections also ratified slates of nominees by the Small Council for members of a number of committees that reported to the Small Council. These committees handled problems like keeping the city's accounts, maintaining a system for watching the walls and supplying defence when necessary, supervising the city's grain supplies. Two of these committees were regarded as semi-religious in character. One was a board of Procurators for the General Hospital which supervised the administration of charity in the city. The other was the Consistory, which was supposed to handle all problems involving marriage, and, in general, to see to it that everyone in town lived in a truly Christian manner.

Membership on the councils tended to be relatively stable, and to change only slightly in the annual elections. The two most important councils elected each other, with the Two Hundred electing the Small Council and the Small Council electing the Two Hundred. When people were not reelected to a council and replaced, it often indicated a significant political shift. Membership on the committees tended to be less stable, but people often served on them for several consecutive years. The syndics were always replaced every year, but were often elected again after a lapse of several years.

Just as Geneva was committed to collective rule in its government, so was it committed to collective rule in its church. The city did not want any trace of episcopal government to survive. Although Calvin clearly became the dominant figure in this church, he never held any formal position of authority. The church was run by a collective, the Company of Pastors, including all the pastors called to service in the city parishes and in the villages dependent on Geneva. It met once a week, to plan services, to engage in mutual correction, and for other purposes. Although Calvin presided over its meetings and negotiated for it with the city government, he never acted on his own authority. He always spoke for the Company as a whole. Outsiders uninformed about this arrangement sometimes called him the 'bishop of Geneva'. This was a title he emphatically rejected.

Calvin's Ecclesiastical Ordinances had created four orders of ministry, each organized into a collective body: pastors, doctors, elders, and deacons. The first order, of pastors, called to proclaim the Word of God from the pulpit and administer the sacraments, was organized, as we have seen, into a Company. The second order, of doctors, was called to discover the Word of God in all its detail by study and to teach it to those preparing for the ministry. In the beginning Calvin was virtually the only doctor. In 1559, however, an academy was created to offer fuller training in theology, and its faculty became the corps of doctors. It was headed by a rector, Theodore Beza, who was called from Lausanne for this purpose. Beza, like Calvin, also served as a pastor. Most of the other members of the faculty were doctors alone. They normally met with the pastors in their weekly meetings, and the Company thus became a Company of Pastors and Doctors.

Beza was much like Calvin in his background, except that he came from an even higher social stratum. He was of a minor noble family located in Vézelay, Burgundy, and had been trained in the humanities and in law. He, too, had earned a *licence* in law from the University of Orleans. He was also a brilliant student of Greek, and spent much of his life in improving translations of the Greek New Testament. And he was also an accomplished poet, the author of sometimes risqué Latin poems in his pre-Protestant youth, and of translations into poetic French of the Old Testament psalms after his conversion. He had also held minor ecclesiastical benefices in France, and had married secretly before even resigning from them. One of the first things he did on arriving in

Geneva in 1548 was to make public his marriage. He then was appointed to a teaching position in the academy in nearby Lausanne which he held from 1549 to 1558, and then returned to Geneva when its new academy was created to provide it with leadership. After Calvin's death, in 1564, Beza was elected Moderator of the Company of Pastors, and was reelected annually until 1580, when he insisted on retiring for reasons of health. He lived on, however, continuing to preach and to teach until he finally died at the unusually ripe old age for that period of eighty-six, in 1605. He was really Calvin's successor as leader both of the Genevan Church and the international Reformed movement.

The other two orders of ministry created by Calvin's Ecclesiastical Ordinances, the elders and deacons, were also agents of the state, members of committees reporting to the Small Council which we have already mentioned. The term deacon was applied by Calvin to the Procurators of the General Hospital. This was a body created before Calvin's arrival in Geneva to supervise the administration of charity. The General Hospital was an all-purpose charitable institution. It housed several dozen orphans and abandoned children, with a staff to provide for their needs and education, until these children were ready to be placed in city homes as apprentices or servants. It also housed severely handicapped people of several varieties whose families could not care for them. It also provided rations of bread once a week to heads of households in significant need scattered throughout the city. The board of Hospital Procurators met once a week to establish a list of people deserving a bread ration and for other purposes. The General Hospital provided charity only to native residents of the city. The growing groups of refugees had to create separate institutions of charity to meet the needs of their members. The largest was a *Bourse française* which provided charity, mostly in the form of cash grants, to the needy among the community of French refugees.[7] The administrators of these bodies, drawn from among the wealthier members of these communities, were also called deacons.

The term elder was applied by Calvin to the Commissioners to the Consistory. There were twelve of them, elected to represent the governing councils of the city. Two came from the Small Council and ten from the Council of Two Hundred, with four of the latter usually also from the Council of Sixty. One of the syndics presided over the Consistory. It also possessed a secretary and a summoner. All of the pastors, led by Calvin, were also supposed to attend meetings of the Consistory. It met once a week, for sessions which before long took hours. It was remarkably intrusive, summoning between 6 and

---

7 See Olson, *Calvin and social welfare*, on this institution.

7 per cent of the entire adult population every year. It was no respecter of class status. Nobles and patricians were called before it as well as servants and day-labourers. It was supposed to see to it that Genevans not only accepted true Christian belief but also behaved in a truly Christian manner. In its early years, it spent a good deal of time trying to root out surviving Catholic practices. It would summon elderly women, for example, for praying in Latin during church services instead of listening to the sermon. It would scold people for using rosaries and votive candles. It would question people who stopped eating meat during Lent. It would discipline people who had dared to attend a mass elsewhere or have a baby baptized by a Catholic priest.[8]

The Consistory would also try to iron out marital problems. In later years that took up an increasing percentage of its time. It would handle the not infrequent breach of promise cases that had probably been the most important task of the bishop's court before the Reformation. It would handle petitions for dissolution of marriage, with authority to go beyond the annulments and permanent separations that Catholic law permitted, to recommend divorce of the modern sort with permission to remarry. And it would handle many cases of sexual deviance, most commonly of pre-marital fornication, also of adultery.

Even more of the Consistory's time, however, was spent in resolving disputes, within families, among neighbours, among business partners. In this capacity it acted as a kind of compulsory counselling service. A petition for divorce, for example, would usually be handled at first by an attempt to arrange a reconciliation. A claim by an elderly woman, that her children were ignoring her and not supporting her properly, would be handled by an attempted reconciliation. A quarrel between two brothers over a business deal gone sour would be handled in the same way. These problems would often be resolved at Consistory sessions. If the quarrel had become too public, the Consistory would arrange a public ceremony of reconciliation that would accompany a church service.[9]

The Consistory had only limited powers of enforcement. The typical case would involve a person summoned, informed of the reason for the summons, asked questions about it, and then scolded in an 'admonition' or 'remonstrance' by one of the ministers in attendance. A high percentage of these scoldings were administered by Calvin himself, although not quite all, as one of his biographers claimed.[10] If the case seemed particularly serious or the sinner

---

8 For examples, see *Registres du Consistoire*, vol. i.
9 For examples, see *Registres du Consistoire*, vol. i.
10 Nicolas Colladon in *Calvini Opera*, vol. 21, col. 66.

insufficiently repentant, the Consistory could proceed to excommunication. This was a step that was much more serious than we might imagine. Many still believed that it placed one's eternal soul in jeopardy by depriving one of a sacrament generally perceived to be essential to salvation (if not technically in Calvinist theology). It also shamed one before one's neighbours and business associates, inhibiting normal social relations. It could also lead, under Genevan law, to perpetual banishment of someone who remained excommunicate and was never readmitted to communion.

If the Consistory felt that the sin being explored deserved further investigation and punishment, it would refer a case to the Small Council. The docket of the Small Council on Mondays often included a number of cases referred by the Consistory on Thursdays. Occasionally the Council would dismiss these charges as frivolous. If the charges seemed minor, the Council might hear the parties immediately and decide on an appropriate resolution. If the charges seemed major, the Council would refer them to the lieutenant for full investigation and a formal trial. Of these penalties, the most controversial was excommunication. In most Protestant communities, excommunication was not widely practised by church authorities. Its frequent use by Catholic church authorities was regarded as a major abuse that should be suppressed. Catholic courts, for example, had sometimes used excommunication to force the payment of debts, or for other purposes that had nothing to do with religious behaviour. A faction of Genevans devoted to Protestantism and initially strong supporters of Calvin formed in protest to the practice of consistorial excommunication. They called themselves the 'children of Geneva'. Calvin called them 'Libertines'. Their leader was Ami Perrin, sometime captain of the republic's armed forces. These protestors thought that at least there should be provision for a right of appeal to the councils responsible for all of Geneva's government from a sentence of excommunication. They thought that it should be possible for the governing councils to modify or even lift such a sentence. This was a possibility Calvin and the other pastors flatly refused to allow. As those responsible for administering communion, they simply refused to consider tendering the communion elements to sinners who had not been formally pardoned by the Consistory. They said they would resign their ministry and leave Geneva if they did not get their way on this issue. Argument over consistorial excommunication continued for years. It finally reached a climax in a riot in 1555. Calvin's opponents were decisively routed in that riot, most of them chased out of the city, some put to death, others removed from public office. From then on there was no effective challenge to Calvin's leadership within Geneva.

Calvin's victory in this controversy was due in good part to the growing role of refugees in Geneva's government. Increasing numbers of them had flooded into Geneva in the crucial years in the 1550s when consistorial excommunication was being discussed. Many of them were people of wealth and talent. A significant number of them bought membership in the bourgeoisie, and with that a chance to participate actively in government. They came from all ranks of society. Perhaps the most prominent refugee was Galeazzo Caracciolo, called the Marquis, of a prominent family of Neapolitan aristocrats. One of his great-uncles was a particularly intolerant pope, Paul IV. Caracciolo summoned his wife to follow him, and when she refused the summons, he sued for divorce on grounds of desertion. After considerable argument he won his suit, and remarried a wealthy French widow.[11] He was given a special seat of honour in the worship services held in the cathedral church of St Pierre. He also became an elder in the Consistory.

Among the refugees to Geneva were almost all the city's pastors. We know for sure of only one pastor who was recruited from the pre-Reformation Catholic religious community and he was soon sent off to a village church. A high percentage of these pastors, furthermore, were noblemen, including Beza. This made the Genevan corps of pastors unusual when compared to groups of Protestant pastors in other communities. Most of these noble pastors, to be sure, did not stay in Geneva indefinitely. Many of them returned to France and assumed positions of leadership in French Reformed churches. It seems to have been a significant reason for the unhappiness of the 'children of Geneva' that they were being pushed around by foreign pastors, insensitive to local customs and traditions.

Among the refugees to Geneva, in addition, were almost all of the city's printers and publishers. Where before the Reformation Geneva housed only an occasional jobbing printer, with the Reformation the city developed a major printing industry, second only to Paris and Lyon among centres for the publication of books in French. The star among these printers was Robert Estienne, who had been printer to the king of France, and the owner of a remarkable set of fonts permitting him to publish in Hebrew and Greek as well as Latin and French. All of that material Estienne had successfully smuggled out of Paris along with most of his family, leaving behind one branch of the family who kept working for the crown and remained in touch with its Protestant relatives.[12] Estienne and his son Henri, who surpassed his father as a scholar of the classics, became the lead printers for Geneva's most important prestige

11 See Kingdon, *Adultery and divorce*, ch. 6.   12 See Armstrong, *Robert Estienne*.

publications, including Beza's editions of an annotated New Testament. Other prominent printers included Jean Crespin, from Artois in what is now northern France, who became most famous for his martyrologies,[13] and Antoine Vincent, from nearby Lyon, who organized international syndicates that published Reformed psalters for Calvinist worship in tens of thousands of copies. One could also add Laurent de Normandie, a publisher rather than a printer, who hired a good many printers who operated on a smaller scale, and then arranged for sale of their books through a network of 'colporteurs' or travelling book salesmen.

Also among the refugees were a number of lawyers and notaries with some training in the law. The most prominent of them was Germain Colladon. He had studied law at about the same time as Calvin and Beza at the same universities, Orleans and Bourges. He had gone even further than they had, however, becoming a doctor of both laws (civil and canon) at the University of Bourges and then teaching law there for almost a dozen years, from 1531 to 1542. He had then gone into private practice as a lawyer and jurisconsult. When he arrived in Geneva in 1550, he immediately re-established his practice there, and did a lot of legal work for their government, including negotiations with foreign powers. He took over much of the legal and political work that Calvin had done in the beginning. There are literally hundreds of memoranda in the Geneva State Archives recording his opinions. He was often called upon by judicial authorities when a case seemed difficult on whether it was permissible to administer torture. And once a judgement had been reached he was often called upon again to render an opinion on the appropriate penalty, particularly if the death penalty seemed indicated. He tended to be quite severe in his opinions, often recommending both torture and the death penalty. But he always gave detailed reasons for his opinions, often citing relevant passages in the Roman *Corpus Iuris Civilis*, the body of Roman law, sometimes citing the Catholic *Corpus Iuris Canonici*, the body of canon law, occasionally even citing the customary law of his native province, Berry. Colladon's career reached a climax in 1568, when he presided over the drafting of both a set of Civil Edicts, codifying laws, and a new Edict on Offices, replacing the one Calvin had helped draft back in 1543.[14] These laws remained in effect until 1792, when the city's government collapsed on the invasion of French armies during the French Revolution.

13 See Gilmont, *Jean Crespin*.
14 For the texts of these laws, see *Sources du droit*, vol. 3, pp. 176–232, 233–59. For more on Colladon, see Kaden, *Germain Colladon*.

Among the people accompanying Colladon on his arrival from Bourges in Geneva was a talented notary named Jean Ragueau. He was soon notarizing for deposit contracts for many of Geneva's most prominent residents. He was only one of a number in similar occupations.

Another family of prominent refugees were the wife and children of Guillaume Budé, a royal professor and maître de requêtes at the court of the king of France. Jean Budé, his son, soon became the most prominent deacon running the *Bourse française* on behalf of his fellow refugees, actually accumulating so much money in it that he could use some of it for other purposes, like smuggling Protestant books into France.

This pool of prominent refugees not only helped Calvin win control of Geneva. It also helped spread his religious ideas to other countries. The greatest effort launched from Geneva was to convert France to Protestantism. Dozens of refugees were trained to become missionaries who could take the Reformed faith back to their native country. They would follow Calvin's lectures on the Bible as a beginning. Every year he would pick a book of the Bible for intensive study, and then deliver a series of talks on its content, pericope by pericope, both as sermons in French for the general population and as commentaries in Latin for those with scholarly inclinations. It was in this form that Calvin's theological research was most fully developed and displayed. When the academy was organized, many of these prospective missionaries signed up as students, taking the full range of available courses, now including additional lectures on biblical theology by Beza, and instruction in Greek and Hebrew by others. Many of these people then gained some experience in the pastorate, often in village churches in the countryside around Geneva, or in the neighbouring Pays de Vaud around Lausanne, now under Bernese control, or in the nearby but independent entity of Neuchâtel. Others served as teachers or tutors in wealthy Genevan families.

When these people were ready for their missions back to France they would appear before the Company of Pastors, present evidence of their training and abilities, and receive a letter certifying their qualifications for serving in the Reformed ministry. Some of them would even receive fake credentials from the government, identifying them as travelling merchants. They then would be smuggled back into France, into communities in which Reformed worship was often still technically illegal, often accompanied by couriers from underground churches seeking their services. This 'mission to France' reached a climax in the early 1560s. In those years the royal government relaxed its pressure on Protestants, and actually invited a delegation of prominent Reformed pastors led by Beza to a colloquy sponsored by the crown and held in 1560 in the village of Poissy near Paris, on the religious issues then threatening to tear the kingdom apart. That was followed by a royal edict in 1561 permitting Protestant worship in certain towns and other places under strict limitations. This edict of partial toleration so enraged conservative Catholics that it provoked the first of a series of religious civil wars. They tore France apart for the rest of the century.[15] Never again did Geneva have as good an opportunity to spread its faith in neighbouring France.

Similar attempts to spread the Calvinist faith to yet other countries were generated in these years. There was an English community of refugees in Geneva between 1555 and 1560, led organizationally by William Whittingham, and ministered to spiritually by John Knox. It helped spark the chain of events that led to a thoroughly Calvinist Reformation in Scotland, led by Knox himself, and a partially Calvinist Reformation in England, led by others. It was within this community that the translation into English known as the Geneva Bible, presenting a full text with marginal glosses explaining passages in a sense that was usually Calvinist, was prepared and first printed. That Bible came to be the most widely used Bible in English-speaking areas throughout the rest of the century, and even beyond, although gradually replaced in the seventeenth century by the Authorized King James version of the Bible. And even the King James Bible reveals some traces of Genevan influence. One of the most important early manuscript copies of the New Testament upon which it was based had been given to Cambridge University by Theodore Beza, who had himself received it as war loot from a French monastery, lifted by a Protestant armed force during the first war of religion. It is now known as the *Codex Bezae* and still remains in the university library of Cambridge.[16]

In succeeding years, others relayed Calvinist ideas and practices to their home countries. From the Netherlands came the Marnix van St Aldegonde brothers, for example, both of whom were students in the Geneva academy briefly. They both took an active part in the ensuing Dutch revolt against the Spanish crown. One of them, Jean, became a military commander and died at a fairly early stage in that revolt. The other, Philippe, joined the staff of William of Orange, the eventual leader of the Dutch revolt, and in that position became a very important publicist and propagandist for the Reformed cause.[17] From Germany came Kaspar Olevianus, who became Protestant while studying law

---

15 On this 'mission to France', see Kingdon, *Coming of the wars*.
16 See Beza, *Correspondance*, vol. 22, pp. 245–57, for Beza's letter to Cambridge University accompanying this gift.
17 *Livre du recteur*, vol. 4, pp. 440–1.

in Orleans and Bourges, who visited Geneva, although before creation of the academy, and who remained in touch with its ecclesiastical leaders by letter. On his return to his native Germany, he first tried to reform the ecclesiastical principality of Trier, his home town. When that did not work, he moved on to Heidelberg where he became one of the principal religious advisers to the government of the Palatinate. He persuaded that government to follow Calvinism both in thought and in practice, even to adopt a system of discipline featuring consistorial excommunication, over the vehement objection of a local group of Zwinglians led by Thomas Erastus.

There were even a number of east Europeans who came to Geneva to absorb its ideas and to learn from its example. Early in 1582, for example, the Czech nobleman Karel de Zerotin arrived from Bohemia for a couple of years of study as part of a tour of western universities. He then returned to central Europe, became a governor of Moravia, and oversaw the creation of a number of Reformed churches in that area. He remained active in Reformed politics until the first stage of the Thirty Years' War led to a triumph of Habsburg Catholicism in Bohemia and a catastrophic collapse of the Reformed movement there.[18]

There is some irony in the fact that in the areas where Geneva tried the hardest to win people to the Calvinist vision of Reformed Protestantism, notably in France, it ultimately failed. In areas where its efforts were less massive, it ultimately succeeded. Thus the Netherlands, Scotland, and German states like the Palatinate became Calvinist and have preserved that faith in one form or another down to the present. And even more surprising, English colonies, like those in New England, and American missions, like those in Korea, have taken Calvinism even further.

In Geneva itself, Calvinism survived and flourished, although with a massive scare in the late sixteenth and early seventeenth centuries, when Savoy made a serious attempt to reconquer the city. That attempt ultimately failed, in the abortive Escalade attack of 1602. Beza, Calvin's successor, was still alive to see that happen. He would die three years later, confident in the belief that Calvinism would survive in its native city.

---

18 *Livre du recteur*, vol. 6, p. 288.

7

The theology and liturgy of
Reformed Christianity

MARK GREENGRASS

The historians of early modern science have taught us the postmodern lesson that there is a 'social history' of truth. The claims to scientific knowledge
based on experiment and observation that were advanced by the protagonists of the 'new science' in the later seventeenth century were reliant on
suppositions about whose observation was to count, what experiment was to
be relied on, and what constituted a scientific truth.[1] Although the Protestant
theologians and divines of the age of the Reformation would have rejected any
such notion – God's truth being revealed, eternal, and immutable – the fact is
that the Reformed Protestant theological and liturgical tradition was framed
in a context in which the reformers themselves redefined what constituted
religious truth and how it was validated.

'By faith alone' (*sola fide*) was Luther's redefinition. 'Scripture alone' (*sola
scriptura*) was the Protestant reformers' sensational means of validating it. The
latter was the route by which Protestants proclaimed that the church could
return to its roots – the gospel of Christ and the church of His earliest followers. The doctrine was corrosive of the accretion of normative traditions
in the councils of the church, the proclamations of Rome and the works of
scholastic theologians. Luther's central critique of the Roman Church was that
it was weighed down with human traditions that popes, cardinals and ecclesiastical authorities claimed as 'holy', confusing the divine with the human,
and arrogating to themselves an authority to proclaim truth that belonged
to God alone. Only the word of God constituted the true 'tradition' of the
church. The Bible was the record of his verbal promise to mankind from the
beginning of the world, renewed in the Old Testament and fulfilled in Christ.
From Christ, the promise was passed on to the church through the preaching
of the gospel and the sacraments that embodied Christ's fulfilment of that
promise. Nothing is more 'literally' true than this promise since God Himself

---

1 Shapin, *Social history of truth*.

is to be trusted in faith. From this reductionist and startling truth-claim, so much else descended – and, in particular, a monumental, Protestant division of theological opinion as to how 'literally' it was to be taken.

The origins of this division of opinion lie in the remarkable community of Bible scholarship in the upper Rhineland. Its centres were in Basel, Zurich and Strasbourg. Basel was the great university city where Erasmus completed work on his Greek New Testament (*Novum instrumentum*) in 1515 (published by Johann Froben in February 1516), the year Wolfgang Capito (G: Wolfgang Köpfel [1478?–1541]) became cathedral preacher, professor and Erasmus's assistant. Also in 1515, Johannes Oecolampadius (G: Johannes Huszgen [1482–1531]) arrived in Basel at the invitation of Erasmus's printer, Johann Froben. Oecolampadius helped Erasmus finish the notes and commentary to the New Testament. At around the same time, Huldrych Zwingli (1484–1531) visited Basel to meet that 'most learned of all scholars' (Erasmus), purchasing the New Testament and settling down to learn Greek to master it. Four years later, Zwingli would mount the pulpit at the Grossmünster of Zurich, capital of the large, easterly Swiss canton. Eight years on, Capito took up his post as provost of the collegiate church of St Thomas in Strasbourg, being joined there by Martin Bucer (G: Martin Butzer [1491–1551]), Caspar Hedio (G: Caspar Seiler [1494/5–1552]) – another Basel graduate – and Matthias Zell (1477–1548). Between them, these were the movers and shakers of the Reformation in the upper Rhineland. They delineated a distinctive theological approach to the truth-claims of the Protestant Reformation advanced by the Saxon Martin Luther. Their theology is at the origins of what, for historical convenience rather than strict accuracy, is called the 'Reformed tradition'.

Theology in the sixteenth century was, first and foremost, an activity of reading, writing, and reflection. Since the divine touched every branch of human knowledge, it was the queen of sciences. Theologians wrote in a diffused number of genres. But *sola scriptura* placed the emphasis on biblical truth; and what that truth was, how it was accessed and by whom, and to what effect, were the central questions of the Protestant Reformation. The answers were influenced by the literary and intellectual culture of the period, and especially by literary humanism, textual scholarship and philology. Erasmus's New Testament was a triumph of that literary culture. It presented the Christian scripture in Greek, boldly proclaiming on the title-page that this was the original and true text, carefully construed against others. It also provided a new Latin translation in parallel with the Greek to supersede the official version of St Jerome. Then, in the part of the work which cost Erasmus dearest and of which he was most proud, came the 'Annotations'. The latter were not glosses in the accepted scholarly mode. Instead they formed a discursive commentary on the Vulgate New Testament. Its prefaces, the *Paraclesis* ('Summons'), *Methodus* and *Apologia* were manifestoes to a newly recovered truth. In this newly edited text, said Erasmus, 'the truth itself *(ipsa veritas)* is revealed to us. Christ is the author. He is truly present for us in what He writes. His presence is the guarantee of truth. The New Testament presents a living 'image of the holy mind and the speaking, healing, rising Christ himself'.[2] Read with a 'pious and open mind' and a 'pure and simple faith', Christ makes His presence felt within us. Erasmus's metaphors were seductive and his resulting theology alluring.[3] But the work contained the ammunition with which to mount an attack upon its own integrity.

Luther's critique of Erasmus's exegetical methods and theology does not concern us directly here. But he raised the central issues of the relationship between 'grammar' and 'grace' (as one recent expositor has put it) to which Reformed theologians would return over the next century and a half: Original Sin, free will, predestination.[4] Luther sensed all sorts of dangers; the historicizing of holy scriptures, the relativizing of truth, and the constraint of God's sovereign power. As was his way, he defined his own position as the defence of truth against those in error. For the theologians of the upper Rhineland, however, the potential of Erasmus's method and the capacity of the unleashed word of God, rightly understood, to change people's lives remained undiminished. They shared Erasmus's approach to biblical hermeneutics and exegesis. Whereas Luther and the Wittenberg school constructed their biblical commentaries in terms of linked theological themes, or 'commonplaces' *(loci communes)*, in Basel, Strasbourg and Zurich, the commentaries of Martin Bucer, Capito, Oecolampadius and Zwingli divided the text into pericopes, or sections, each section being then the subject of comment in various ways.[5] Sometimes it was paraphrased. Philological issues were discussed in annotations on the Erasmian model and larger theological issues were treated as separate asides. The commentaries were learned, well informed by the latest rabbinic and patristic scholarship, and sympathetic to the figurative language of the Bible. This was biblical scholarship with a sense of an uncovering of God's truth, and one with practical consequences. Zwingli's commentary on Isaiah, published in 1529 (under the pseudonym 'Christianus Theodidactus'),

---

2 Erasmus, *Les préfaces*, p. 88; translated in Olin, *Christian humanism*, p. 106.
3 Boyle, *Erasmus on language*; Bentley, *Humanism and holy writ*; Rabil, *Erasmus and the New Testament*.
4 McSorley; Cummings, *Literary culture*, esp. ch. 4.
5 Bedouelle and Roussel (eds.), *Les temps des Réformes*, esp. table, pp. 228–32.

was entitled *The First Hatching of the Planing Smooth of Isaiah* (*Complanationis Isiae prophetae fœtura prima*) and the words 'Fœtura' and 'Complanatio' in the title were intended, as Zwingli noted in his prefatory letter of dedication to the newly formed confederate cities of the Christian Civic League (*Christliche Burgrecht*) of the upper Rhine, as plays on words: 'genesis' / 'new growth'; 'getting the meaning straight' / 'making straight' the way of the Lord.[6] In his early writing on *The Clarity and Certainty of the Word of God* (1522), Zwingli borrowed from Erasmus the metaphors of light and truth. He describes his own experience of being led by the spirit of God to that enlightenment.[7] We must, he says, be '*theodidacti*, that is, taught of God, not of men: that is what truth itself said [John 6:45] and it cannot lie'.[8] We must have faith in the spirit of God, leading us to that truth.[9] These were the mainspring behind the *Prophezei*, the weekly biblical lectures begun at the Grossmünster in Zurich in June 1525, in which the scriptures were expounded in Latin, Greek and Hebrew by 'prophets' (the word itself was chosen from the cue in 1 Corinthians 14:3). The practice resulted in the publication of the Zurich Bible. It would become embedded quite widely within the Reformed tradition in the sixteenth century – in Bucer's Strasbourg, Lambert's Hesse, Calvin's Geneva, in East Friesland and brought thence to London by John à Lasco.[10] Prophesying reflected the centrality the Reformed tradition accorded a learned, regular, preaching office.[11]

Sixteenth-century theologians raised issues that were also central to public policy and debate. New ways of understanding the Bible had profound consequences, especially if worship was to be derived solely from the words of scripture. These effects began to become evident from 1523, the year of Zwingli's two public disputations in Zurich, and then, in due course, in the upper Rhineland cities.[12] Fasting, feast days, pilgrimages, signs and images were all, declared Zwingli, false to the spirit of God, revealed in His word, a theft of Christian freedom.[13] Images, the cult of saints, music too, had the power to seduce us and obscure God's truth. They must be abandoned or replaced. Liturgical books in Zurich, Basel and Bern were destroyed or sold on to grocers and pharmacists. In Zurich, a censorial board, headed by Zwingli, determined

---

6 *Fœtura*, in Zwingli, *Sämtliche Werke*, vol. 14, pp. 5 etc. Cf. Hobbs, 'Zwingli'.
7 Christ, 'Das Schriftverständnis', pp. 111–25.
8 Zwingli, *Sämtliche Werke*, vol. 1, p. 377; translated Potter, *Zwingli*, p. 30.
9 Stephens, *Theology of Huldrych Zwingli*, ch. 2.
10 Denis, 'La prophétie', pp. 289–316; Locher, 'In spirit and in truth', pp. 27–30.
11 Snavely. 12 Moeller, 'Zwingli's Disputationen'.
13 Gäbler, *Huldrych Zwingli*, ch. 6; Potter, *Zwingli*, ch. 9; Sunderland, 'Zwingli's Reformation'.

what to keep.[14] Zwingli's friend, the Hebrew scholar Leo Jud (1482–1542), had pointed out in a sermon of September 1523 that there were contrasting ways of numbering the Ten Commandments. In the Judaic tradition and in Eastern Christianity, the Commandment: 'you shall not make yourself a graven image, or any likeness of anything', was a separate second Commandment, whereas Augustine had successfully championed the numbering of the Commandments to make this simply a subordinate part of the first. Zwingli and, in due course, the Reformed tradition more generally, followed that pattern, whilst Luther and the Lutherans maintained the old Augustinian ordering and, with it, the view that images were neither here nor there. There is no better example of the extent to which biblical scholarship, and the literary culture which sustained it, had a dramatic impact on the world around. As a result of the second disputation in October 1523, triptych altar paintings were closed for good by the church authorities and silver, gold and other ornaments banned from wedding services.[15] When people took the law into their own hands and pulled down local images and shrines, the city authorities intervened on 15 June 1524 and all Zurich's churches were officially 'cleansed' of religious images and stained glass, leaving the walls, as Zwingli exclaimed, 'positively luminous . . . beautifully white'.[16] Meanwhile, in printed devotional literature, woodcuts and engravings depicted ordinary, pious people in place of the saints as images of the divine.[17] In 1527, Johannes Copp issued a new church 'Kalendar' in which saints' days were abolished in place of Old Testament figures and distinguished reformers – a calendar that would find its way around Reformed Europe in the sixteenth century, reaching England, for example, in the 1563 edition of John Foxe's *Book of Martyrs*.[18] Meanwhile Zwingli banned instrumental and choral music from the liturgy in Zurich in 1525 on the scriptural grounds of Matthew 6:6 and Ephesians 5:19.[19] He regarded church choirs as ostentatious and distracting. The practical implementation of these changes varied across Reformed Europe – Basel, for example, never banished hymnody as happened in Zurich until 1598.[20] But the visual impact of the removal of religious imagery in Reformed churches is still evident upon church architecture as one moves across Europe. Scriptural injunctions against idolatry became

---

14 Germann, 'Zwischen Konfiskation', pp. 63–77.
15 Egli, *Actensammlung*, p. 186.
16 Eire, *War against the idols*, pp. 79–81; Garside, *Zwingli and the arts*, p. 156.
17 Wandel, 'Reform of the images', pp. 105–24.
18 Sunderland, 'Zwingli's Reformation'; Foxe, *Acts and Monuments*.
19 Jenny, *Luther, Zwingli, Calvin*, p. 175 ff.; Garside, *Zwingli and the arts*, pp. 43–6; Aeschbacher, 'Zwingli und die Musik'.
20 Marcus, 'Hymnody and hymnals'.

developed into theological objections to a wide range of religious representation. The first use of the familiar 'deus absconditus' to represent God first
appeared in Reformed circles in Strasbourg in around 1529. Dutch paintings of
Reformed church interiors by Pieter Jamnsz Saenredam present an ordered,
clean, cold space, cleansed of images save for those that recalled civic virtue
and republican pride.[21] It is difficult to ignore the iconophobic tendencies in the
Reformed tradition, or its chromophobic and phonophobic allergies either.
'Literal' truth was best expressed plainly, in black and white.

At the second disputation of October 1523, there was an allied question for
debate: the mass. The implication was clear – was the mass also to be regarded
as an idolatrous image? Zwingli's initial approach to the question reflected the
imprint of Erasmus.[22] If the New Testament could be historicized in such a
way that Christ's words, although spoken at a particular moment, could be as
'real' (Erasmus dared to say: 'even more real') and present as when he had said
them, why was not the same also true of the central sacrament of the church?
One of Zwingli's favourite biblical proof-texts was John 6:63 ('The Spirit gives
life, but the flesh is of no use') and his theological insights were grounded on
a distinction between the overwhelming power of the spirit on the one hand,
and the deadening impact of the flesh on the other. He readily followed Luther
in agreeing that the mass was not a sacrifice and that transubstantiation was
absurd. Why not, therefore, abandon any notion of Christ's physical presence
in the bread and wine of the eucharist? If we wanted to retain the notion of
the mass as a sacrament, Zwingli reasoned (and, since it was nowhere in the
Bible, the word was perhaps redundant), we must regard it as a 'pledge' or
'oath' from God – 'the word by which the mind is nourished . . . hence the
bread of the soul is the word of God, for man does not live by bread alone but
by every word that comes from the mouth of God', a 'sure sign and seal' of
the forgiveness of our sins by Christ.[23] Two years later came Zwingli's major
theological statements on the eucharist. They coincided with the year in
which the 'form or manner of the Last Supper' to replace the mass was decided
in Zurich. 'The appointed ministers carry round the unleavened bread, and
each believer takes with his own hand a morsel or mouthful from it, or has it
given to him by the minister. And . . . other ministers likewise follow behind
them with the wine' went the rubric. The evangelical communion service was
born, and it was 'biblical' bread and ordinary wine in plain wooden cups that

21 Janson, 'Public places, private lives'.
22 The bibliography on this central question is enormous; see Pipkin, 'Positive religious
   values', and Stephens, Theology of Huldrych Zwingli, pp. 218–59 for overviews.
23 Zwingli, Sämtliche Werke, vol. 2, pp. 583–4; translated Potter, Zwingli, p. 33.

was given out from the altar (yet to be repositioned) in the Grossmünster at Eastertide in Zurich, April 1525. By 1525, Zwingli's eucharistic understanding had become more complex. To the 'pledge' (*Pflicht*) of the forgiveness of our sins contained in God's act of instituting the sacrament became conjoined our remembrance of the sacrifice once made for us, and our testimony to one another when we receive it. So the eucharist was not simply about what God does for us; but also about what we do for God, and for one another. By 1525, Zwingli's philological training had sent him to the origins for the Latin word 'sacramentum'. He discovered in Varro that it had been adopted early in the Latin church for a pledge deposited by a litigant before an altar and recovered when the suit was successful and that it had originated in the word used by the Roman army for a soldier's oath. This resonated, as Diarmaid MacCulloch has pointed out, in the heartland of Europe's mercenary armies. Receiving the eucharist was the equivalent of a contingent of troops reverently giving the salute before the flag.[24] By doing so, we strengthened our inward faith and inscribed in our hearts the reality of what the Bible had told us of Christ's once-for-all sacrifice for all humanity on the Cross.

What was true of the eucharist must also be true for the other biblical sacrament, baptism. Here, Zwingli had initially found it difficult to develop a coherent, biblically based argument, consonant with his developing theology, to counter the emerging Anabaptist arguments in favour of adult (re)-baptism. In 1525, however, he could argue that infant baptism was a covenant-sign or pledge 'by which a man proves to the church that he either aims to be, or is, a soldier of Christ, and which informs the whole church rather than yourself of your faith'.[25] This was set out in the scriptures, initially in the rite of circumcision, given by God to Abraham and his descendants, not in order to confirm Abraham's faith but as a pledge that Abraham would lead his children to God. Since Zwingli was not convinced by original guilt, baptism was not a washing away of sin. It was simply the entering into a new life and community. In practical terms, baptism was thus to take place during Sunday worship. As with the eucharist, there was a reductionist simplicity at work. The baptismal font and gold or silver accoutrements were replaced by an earthenware, zinc, copper or glass bowl and plain ewer – liturgical ware that would eventually become widespread in the Reformed tradition in France, the Netherlands, and Scotland. And the salt, oil, candles and exorcism of the Roman rite were banished for good.

24 MacCulloch, *Reformation*, pp. 147–8.
25 Stevens, *Theology of Huldrych Zwingli*, p. 198.

By 1525, Zwingli had sight of an open letter, written by a humanist from Delft, Cornelisz Hoen, who had taken up the argument of a fifteenth-century Frisian, Wessel Gansfort, and developed it. In the version published in Zurich, Hoen's argument was brief and to the point. When Christ said: 'This is my body', He did so metaphorically, as He had so often before to the disciples. 'Is' means 'symbolizes'. Transubstantiation – or whatever the 'word-bemused scholastics' cared to choose for the bread and the wine turning into something else – was as irrelevant as not eating sausages in Lent. This was the background to that most notorious non-meeting of minds that brought Zwingli, Oecolampadius, Luther and Melanchthon together under the princely eye of Philipp of Hesse in late September 1529 in the castle above Marburg. In their acrimonious exchanges on the eucharist (in German, at Luther's insistence, perhaps so that he could mock Zwingli's *Zweizerdeutsche* dialect), Oecolampadius (whose eucharistic theology was subtly different from that of Zwingli) asked Luther: 'Where, doctor, does it say in the Bible that we should close our eyes to its meaning?' Luther replied: 'If we debated for a century it would make no difference. Show me the text and I will be satisfied. We must not gloss the words of our beloved Lord'.[26] The essence of their division was there; and in the following century, when the Reformed confessions were consolidated, all the theological debates in the world would not, as Luther predicted, make it go away.

*

The next generation saw the unfolding of this upper Rhineland theology, partly responding to the pressures of events and partly evolving under the impact of dominant personalities. The events, referred to elsewhere in this volume, included the death of Zwingli at the battle of Kappel (1531) and the subsequent struggle, successfully conducted by his statesmanlike successor as Zurich's *antistes* (or church leader), Heinrich Bullinger (1504–75), to stabilize and defend the pattern of Zwinglian reform and reinforce it intellectually and politically by winning support for it on a wider stage. On that stage, the dominant religious events were a gathering political and institutional Catholic reaction to the Protestant message, especially in its 'radical' (i.e., Anabaptist) and 'sacramentarian' (i.e., Zwinglian) forms. The result was the creation of a 'refugee reformation' in the political and linguistic interstices of western central Europe, from Emden and Wesel southwards down the Rhineland to the upper Rhine and the Swiss cantons. In most of these cities, the 'strangers' were a minority and on the margins. In Geneva, however, the 'strangers' transformed the city, providing Jean Calvin (1509–64) with a unique platform.

26 Köhler, *Das Marburcher Religionsgespräch*, no. 13, p. 65.

Bullinger *and* Calvin: the basis for the Reformed tradition (and hence the historical necessity for the term) was bicephalous. The amalgam of Bullinger's and Calvin's views was the most remarkable development of the period up to Calvin's death (1564), and one which provided a solid and defensible theological heritage at a time when Lutheran theological arteries were also hardening.

Bullinger's most distinctive theological insights developed that aspect of Zwingli's theology that had emphasized the notion of a Covenant (G: *Bund*; Fr: *Alliance*: L: *Foedum*), a bond between God and humanity. Although there were parallel explorations of Covenant theology in Philippist Lutheran theology, its imprint was much more enduring in the Reformed tradition. Bullinger's most single-minded exploration of the subject came in his *De testamento seu fœdere Dei unico et æterno* (1534) although the subject frequently occurred in his other writings, including his published collection of fifty sermons, organized by groups of ten, the *Hausbook* (in German) or *Decades* (in Latin and English) (1549–51), which had a widespread impact on Reformed preaching in Europe, just as his later hundred sermons (1557) launched apocalyptic writing in the Reformed tradition.[27] The Covenant also played its part in Bullinger's major confessional formulations, especially the second Helvetic confession.[28] The difficulty was that the Old Testament presented different notions of God's Covenant. Sometimes they were binding agreements between God and his chosen people, with consequences when they were broken – Adam in Eden (Genesis 2:15–17) or Moses on Mount Sinai (Exodus 34:27). At other times, they appeared as unconditional legacies, 'bequeathed' by God to mankind, as when Noah was told that God would never flood the world again (Genesis 9:8–17). Bullinger attempted to reconcile these elements into one Covenant determining the course of human history, conditional and invariant. God would keep his promises if humans kept His laws: to have faith in Him, and love their neighbours. So the responsibilities were mutual, although much was laid on the shoulders of the preachers and magistrates – successors to the Old Testament prophets and kings – to keep the faith and discipline the Christian community. Covenant theology would find its adherents in the later sixteenth and seventeenth centuries. It appealed to those who laid claim to having the 'seal' of being God's chosen people. It offered an important role to the laity and, in the later sixteenth century, the Reformed tradition bred numerous, distinguished theologians among the laity – Philippe Du Plessis Mornay (1549–1623), Philip Marnix van Saint Aldergonde (1540–98) and Thomas Erastus

27 McCoy and Baker; Hollweg, *Bullingers Hausbuch*; Büsser, 'H. Bullingers 100 predigten'.
28 Koch, *Der Theologie*.

(G: Thomas Lüber (1524–83)), for example. It had political resonances when it came to justifying revolt, in defined circumstances, against a legitimate ruler. And Covenant theology sat conveniently in polities like the Swiss cantons and later the Dutch republic, whose federal state-like structures were based on complex patterns of shared mutual responsibilities. Only gradually towards the end of the sixteenth century did the Reformed scholastic theologians at Heidelberg (especially Girolamo Zanchi (1516–90)) and English academic theologians (Dudley Fenner (1558–87), Thomas Cartwright (1535–1603) and Robert Rollock) begin to formulate the notion of a 'Covenant of Works', what was expected by way of human action under the Covenant, a complement to the 'Covenant of Grace'.[29]

For all Bullinger's influence as a Biblical commentator, the Reformed tradition only produced one pre-eminent theological systemizer: Jean Calvin. It is difficult to do justice to Calvin's theological impact in brief compass, not least because his theology cannot be dissassociated from his persuasive brilliance as a writer of Latin and (even more so) French, or from the effect of the refugee reformation in Geneva upon a generation of exiles from western Europe. Calvin's overwhelming ambition was to create a single, overarching theological framework that would unite God's truth and human wisdom. To that objective, he brought a formidable humanist talent for grammar, logic and rhetoric by which he sought not to 'demonstrate' God's truth (that had been the objective of the medieval scholastics and they had failed) but to 'educate' the world to 'hear' God's Word. The latter, for Calvin, was not a dead, aloof and institutionalized truth, but a personal, dynamic, life-changing one.[30] Calvin's theological system was supported by three fundamental, mutually reinforcing pediments: refined texts of the Bible, an interlocking exegetical framework in his commentaries on the books of the Bible, and the theological *summa* of the *Institutes of the Christian Religion (Christianae Religionis Institutio)* – 'institutio' in the sense of 'instruction' (as in Quintilian's rhetorical textbook) but also in the sense of 'institution' or 'establishment'.

All three components witnessed to Calvin's command of humanist technologies of learning, exposition, and logic. The brilliant French-exiled printer Robert Estienne devised the system of numbered verses (we now take it for granted) in addition to the normal chapter-numbering. It appeared for the first time in his Genevan Greek New Testament. In time, Geneva Bibles would be complemented by marginal glosses and footnotes, exploitations of humanist

---

29 McGiffert, 'Grace and works' and 'From Moses to Adam'. Cf. Letham, 'The *Fœdus operum*', and Weir, *The origins of the federal theology*.
30 Millet, *Calvin et le dynamisme*.

literary technology. Calvin added his biblical commentaries, based on and (in turn) contributing to his massive activity as a preacher. He preached three times a week on weekdays at 5pm and three times on Sundays, with additional lectures to the Friday congregation, or company, of pastors, until 1549 – Calvin's sense of regimented time tells us much about the man himself. Thereafter the regime was altered to one every weekday in each alternate week and twice on Sundays and the texts taken down by two successive short-hand scribes. There must have been over 2,000 of them in the years from 1549 to Calvin's death (1564) but the volumes were sold off by the Genevan magistrates in 1805 and almost two centuries later, they are still being recovered.[31] Calvin commented and/or preached on all the books of the Bible with the exception of Revelation. The commentaries, published from 1551 onwards, provided the exegetical foundation for his theology. His methodology was announced in the commentaries on Romans, published first in March 1540 by the Strasbourg printer, Wendelin Rihel. He aimed at 'lucid brevity' (perspicua brevitas) and began with an introduction that laid out the 'theme' of the epistle that used the inner 'method' of the text to elucidate the 'exact sense of the words' and 'unfold the mind of the writer'.[32] Behind the words lay the 'genuine sense' that was in accord with the writer's mind; alongside ephemeral 'signs' lay the real, embedded 'signified'.[33]

The Institutes served as the theological keystone. The first edition (published in 1536) was written fast and in Latin in the first year of his exile from France, in Erasmus's heartland of Basel. Successively transformed and expanded until the final 1559 edition, he explained its complementary relationship to his commentaries and the Bible thus:[34]

> it has been my purpose in this labour to prepare and instruct candidates in sacred theology for the reading of the divine Word in order that they may be able both to have easy access to it and to advance without stumbling. For I believe that I have so embraced the sum of religion in all its parts, and have arranged it in such an order, that if anyone rightly grasps it, it will not be difficult for him to determine what he ought especially to seek in scripture and to what end he ought to relate its contents. If, after this road has, as it were, been paved, I shall publish any commentaries on scripture, I shall always condense them, because I shall have no need to undertake long doctrinal discussions and digress into commonplaces . . .

31 Gilmont, 'Les sermons de Calvin'.
32 Calvin, New Testament Commentaries, vol. 8, p. 1.
33 Girardin, Rhétorique et théologique.   34 Calvin, Institutes, pp. 3–5.

Calvin's ambition is recorded in the famous opening sentence of the *Institutes of the Christian Religion*, already present in 1536: 'Tota fere sapientiae nostrae summa, quae vera demum ac solida sapientia censeri debeat, duobus partibus constat, Dei cognitione et nostri' ('Almost the whole sum of our wisdom, that is to say, true and sound wisdom, consists of two parts: the knowledge of God and of ourselves'). In 1536, Calvin organized the remainder of the text into six sections, derived from Luther's Short Catechism. By 1559, this material had become subsumed and reorganized into four books. The more it grew, the more difficulty Calvin experienced in holding on to the rhetorical impact of the crucial sharp contrast of the first two books of the *Institutes*. This lay between the God who is revealed to us in the Bible: eternal, the creator of the universe and of men, perfect in wisdom and goodness, omnipotent, a spirit transcendent everywhere, a sovereign ruler and righteous and merciful judge on the one hand, and human beings as miserable, shameful specimens on the other.[35] Calvin's language about the human condition is rhetorically charged. We are imprisoned by a 'yoke', a 'maze', an 'abyss' (a 'deep, dry well', as described in the psalms) of sin.[36] We run around 'like rats, pell-mell in straw' (and 'paille' has a double meaning in sixteenth-century French: 'straw' and 'sin'). It is an inherited 'corruption' and 'depravity', the 'original' sin of Adam.[37] By our own wisdom, we can do nothing: 'Scripture teaches that man was estranged from God through sin and is an heir to wrath, subject to the curse of eternal death, excluded from all hope of salvation, beyond every blessing of God, the slave of Satan, captive under the yoke of sin, destined finally for a fearful destruction and already involved in it'.[38] Sin is a generalized corruption, manifested in particular 'works' and 'fruits'. Calvin typically obliges with revealing lists of the latter: 'adultery, fornication, theft, hatred, murder, revellings [*comessationes*] . . .'.[39] Sin was the result of miscibility ('adulteration') and the logic behind Calvin's theology was to create firewalls that separated the holy from the profane, the sacred from the sinful, the saved from the damned. So to think that we have any part in our own salvation is itself an adulteration. Only an act of special, free grace from God can save us: 'Free will is not sufficient to enable man to do good works, unless he is assisted by grace . . . We need the promise of grace which can testify to us that the Father is merciful; since we can approach him in no other way and upon grace alone can the heart of man have repose'.[40] Calvin took the central theological Augustinian perspective that Luther had restated and sought to integrate it into the methodology and

---

35 Dowey, *Knowledge of God*, esp. ch. 3.   36 *Institutes*, II.xvi.9.   37 *Institutes*, II.i.8.
38 *Institutes*, II.xvi.2.   39 *Institutes*, II.i.8.   40 *Institutes*, II.ii.6–7.

perspectives of the Rhineland biblicists. Where Erasmus had dodged, Calvin did not flinch, hoping thereby (as he saw it) to recall the Catholic France from which he was now estranged to its real Christian roots. Throughout Calvin's theology, an 'antithetical structure' is woven into its logical fabric at every turn so that he can apply what one scholar has termed a 'calculus fidei', a logic of scripturally based distinctions until the boundaries have been defined.[41]

Predestination was the uncomfortable logical consequence of Calvin's Augustinian 'double wisdom of God' (*duplex cognitio domini*) – God the creator and redeemer, one that Luther had acknowledged and Zwingli and Bullinger had begun to explore too.[42] It could not be ducked: 'No one dares simply deny predestination, by which God adopts some to hope of life, and sentences others to eternal death'.[43] God's providence – the force behind the Hebrew exile, the prophets of the Old Testament, and Calvin's understanding of his own refuge – belonged to the central nervous system of his theology. And it cut both ways, a 'double predestination' (*duplex predestinatio*): 'For all are not created in equal condition; rather eternal life is foreordained for some, eternal damnation for others'.[44] Calvin called on his humanist techniques of understanding and exposition to limit the speculative theological horizon that this afforded. This was a 'baffling question' to humans, quite simply because human knowledge could not adequately comprehend it. Try to unravel the secrets of divine providence and theologians would become astrologers – whom Calvin denounced – and fall back into the 'abyss' of adulterated knowledge.[45] 'First, then, when they enquire into predestination, let them remember that they are penetrating into the recesses of divine wisdom, where he who rushes forward securely and confidently, instead of satisfying his curiosity, will enter into an inextricable labyrinth'.[46] The 'they' in question is a bruise-mark in the 1559 edition, left by Calvin's run-in with the French refugee theologian and former Carmelite, Jérôme Bolsec, who had delivered a lecture to the Company of Pastors in 1551 declaring that Calvin's 'double predestination' made God into a tyrant and the author of sin. The Company subsequently abstracted thirteen propositions from the text and Bolsec was imprisoned by the Genevan magistracy on charges of offensive language, blasphemy, and heresy.[47] Within months he was declared *persona non grata* and banished from Geneva, which did not stop him, or indeed others (in private, Bullinger too), from expressing their fundamental unease with Calvin's predestinarian logic. From the

41 Battles, 'Calculus Fidei', in Neuser (ed.), *Calvinus Ecclesiae Doctor*, pp. 85–110.
42 Dowey, *Knowledge of God*, ch. 2.   43 *Institutes*, III.xxi.5.   44 *Ibid.*
45 Calvin, *Advertissement contre l'astrologie judiciare* (1549).   46 *Institutes*, III.xxi.1.
47 CR, vol. 36, cols. 147–9; partially translated in Potter and Greengrass, *John Calvin*, p. 98.

1539 edition of the *Institutes* onwards, Calvin drew on Bucer's insights on the subject.[48] All Christian communities have a 'variable geometry' to them; a 'leaven' and, moving outwards in an expanding circle of faith-community, an 'outer penumbra' of those who have been scarcely drawn to the faith or not at all.[49] That was why the Protestant Reform had succeeded in some places, and was embattled in others – the reality of suffering for one's faith being never far away from the theology of the mature Calvin. It was that incontestable reality that Calvin drew on to underscore his discussion of predestination in book 3 of the *Institutes*: 'In reality, the covenant of life (*foedus vitae*) is not preached equally to all, and among those to whom it is preached, it does not always meet with the same reception. This diversity displays the unsearchable depths of the divine judgment . . .' Learned ignorance (*docta ignorantia*) was a defensible Renaissance approach to knowledge, whether it was a matter of divining the deepest *arcana* of nature or the workings of God's inscrutable providence. It was a full-stop explanation as to why some – those in the congregations 'under the cross' in France, the Netherlands, Marian England and Scotland – suffered for the faith whilst others did not.

The greatest challenge to Calvin's systemizing instincts came with the eucharist. The issue defined the agreement he reached with Bullinger in 1549 and consolidated the confessional fault-lines emerging across Protestant Europe. Calvin approached it circumspectly – his earliest developed statement was a treatise of 1541 in French rather than Latin directed to a lay rather than a theological audience.[50] Only gradually did his views filter into the broader corpus of his writings. He was initially suspicious of Zwinglian notions, aware of the central criticism they had already attracted: that they made the eucharist into a 'naked' or 'empty' sign. Zwingli and Oecolampadius, he said in an aside in 1541 'sont plus efforcez de ruiner le mal, que d'edifier le bien'.[51] At the same time, he could not bring himself to accept Lutheran eucharistic theology because it mixed things up: the secular and the sacred; the corporeal and the spiritual. That way lay idolatry. Gratefully falling back on Augustine's definition of a sacrament as a 'visible sign of a sacred thing', Calvin then deployed his humanist artistry to refine the distinction between the 'sign' and the 'signified'.[52] Once more the issue was the relation between thought and language,

---

48 Spijker, 'Prädestination bei Bucer und Calvin', in Neuser (ed.), *Calvinus Theologus*, pp. 85–111; Kroon, *Martin Bucer und Johannes Calvin*, ch. 1.

49 Spijker, 'Bucer's influence on Calvin', in Wright (ed.), *Martin Bucer*, pp. 32–45; cf. Hammann, *Entre le secte et la cité*; Höpfl, *Christian polity*.

50 Elwood, *The body broken*, ch. 3.   51 Higman, *Three French treatises*, p. 129.

52 Fitzer, 'The Augustinian origins', pp. 69–86.

between *sensus* and *littera, res* and *verba*. (No surprise that the founder of postmodern linguistic theory, Ferdinand de Saussure, was Genevan.) The sign is not the reality, but it stands in a corresponding relationship with reality as an 'analogy' between the visible, material sign and the invisible, spiritual reality of the sacrament, an analogy so close as to be a 'metonymy'. A relationship of analogy is necessary to prevent the adulteration of the sacred and the secular, the confusion of the sign with the signified. But the reality of the signified is so strong that it 'vivifies' us. That is why the sacrament involves the ingestion of the sacrament, rather than simply the viewing of it. God is really 'ingrafted' in us by the 'mystery' (and Calvin retained that sense of the 'sacrament') of the eucharist.

It took several years of theological correspondence, a personal visit, and a good deal of tact on both sides before Calvin and Bullinger were able to put their names to a joint statement on the sacraments of the eucharist and baptism in 1549. Known later as the 'Zurich Accord' (*Consensus Tigurinus*), its twenty-six articles defined the eucharistic theology of the 'Reformed tradition'. There was give and take, and room to read aspects of it both ways. But, with Lutheran opposition to its basic formulations hardening, the agreement formed the basis of the statements on the subject of the confession of faith of the churches over the next generation – in Poland (1557), France (1559), Scotland (1560) and the Rhine Palatinate (1563). A Reformed consensus had been achieved.

In one important liturgical respect, however, Calvin's contribution to the emerging Reformed tradition was overwhelming: that of the vernacular, metrical psalter. Paraphrasing the psalms into vernacular verse for private devotion had been part of the inherited Christian tradition. The Protestant Reformation transformed them into a constituent element of public worship. The first collections of Lutheran chorales (1524) included, for example, a number of psalm paraphrases among its devotional hymns. The Rhineland biblicist reformers insisted, however, that only God's word in the Bible was suitable for the purposes of public worship and attempted to confine the texts to paraphrases of the psalms and a limited range of other biblical texts. They adopted the verse forms of popular song to assist the process of learning them, but also in the hope that people would be persuaded to abandon the sensual, silly songs they knew and sing psalms instead. Calvin, unlike Zwingli or his successor in Zurich, put his weight behind the tradition that was emerging in Strasbourg. In 1539, he published his first compendium there, which included thirteen of the brilliant rhymed translations of the French poet Clément Marot as well as a further six psalms and three canticles in his own verse paraphrases, several of the melodies being borrowed from earlier Strasbourg songbooks.[53] Once back in Geneva, Calvin published his second psalter (*La forme des prières et chantz ecclesiastiques* (1542)) which contained more of Marot's and Calvin's settings, an important preface by Calvin on the sacraments and on psalm singing, and keystone liturgical prayers to be read at worship.[54] The complete edition of the Geneva metrical psalter was finally published in Geneva in 1562. It included 125 different melodies for 152 texts (150 psalms and two canticles).[55] Antoine Vincent, the printer in charge of its publication, master-minded the publication and distribution of the work on a large scale from presses in Geneva, Paris (twenty-four printers published editions of it there alone), Lyon, Caen, St Lo and elsewhere – over forty-four editions are accounted for in the three years 1562–4 alone.[56] It was quickly translated into other languages too. The German translation by Ambrosius Lobwasser, completed in 1565 and published in Leipzig in 1573, was popular with Lutheran as well as Calvinist congregations. The Dutch translation by Petrus Dathenus, published in 1566, was accepted by the synod of Wesel in 1568 and remained the official songbook of the Dutch Calvinist church for over two centuries. The Genevan psalter exercised its influence, too, on the important metrical psalm tradition of the Reformed in Scotland and England. It was the biggest single success that linked liturgy and printing in the history of the Protestant Reformation.

*

From Calvin's death (1564) to the outbreak of the Thirty Years' War (1618), Reformed theology was affected by the remarkable expansion of its confessional base. By 1600, there were established Reformed churches in Scotland, England, Béarn and a clutch of German statelets. In addition, there were legally tolerated congregations of Reformed churches in France, Poland-Lithuania, Hungary, Bohemia and the Rhineland. How these churches related to one another and managed their affairs was, as another chapter in this volume makes clear, very variable. The major Reformed confessions emerged rapidly (French (1559); Belgic/Dutch (1561); 39 Articles (1563); Heidelberg Catechism (1563)) and reflected common theological approaches, albeit with local variations. But the existence of enemies from without, coping with the problems of expansion, and the impact of the disciplinary framework within the majority of the Reformed churches were as important as the confessions in sustaining theological unity. They were, as Joseph Hall put it in 1645, 'Sisters of the Reformation' and 'harmonizing' their confessions proved more a well-meant

53 Douen, *Clément Marot*; Bovet, *Histoire du Psautier*; Terry, *Calvin's first psalter*.
54 Pidoux (1959).   55 Pidoux (1962).   56 Droz, 'Antoine Vincent'.

illusion than a realizable goal.[57] Reformed liturgies and patterns of worship certainly differed quite widely, even in the eucharist. The English who conformed to the liturgical tenets established by the Elizabethan episcopacy knelt at an altar rail and were served 'holy communion' from a minister wearing a surplice who reminded them as he did so of how they should regard the sacrament. But there were plenty who did not choose to conform. These – Elizabethan puritans, in due course 'separatists', and later Caroline Presbyterians – sat to receive communion 'about' a table. The Scots sat 'at' a table as the elders passed round the bread and wine, and they were followed by Caroline Presbyterians in England too – the question was discussed at length at the Westminster Assembly in the 1640s. Confessing members of the Dutch church at the 'heilig avondmaal' did the same, twelve by twelve about a table in the chancel in a practice that seems to go back to the pattern established by Zwingli at Zurich. Meanwhile, members of French congregations who were able to receive the 'cène' lined up and gave their tokens (*méreaux*) to wardens or elders before receiving the bread and wine in silence from their minister, the latter dressed in a simple gown, perhaps not wearing the collar 'tabs' that would become standard dress for a Huguenot pastor later on. In German lands there were disputes over the 'breaking' of the bread, the use of wafers, and baptismal liturgies between Reformed and Lutheran confessions that reached the streets.[58]

One inescapable result of this expansion was the need to provide a well-trained ministry. In French-speaking lands, this was perforce mainly outside the traditional universities, in newly formed academies, copying the Lausanne (1537) and Genevan (1559) models. By 1620, the academies at Montauban, Nîmes, Die, Saumur and Sedan were acknowledged and supported by the French synods. In the Netherlands, new academies were founded to commemorate signal events in the Dutch Revolt (Leiden in 1575; Ghent in 1580, though it later moved to Franeker) and, in the seventeenth century, the academies of Utrecht (1636), Harderwijk (1647), and Groningen (1647) played a major part in training Reformed ministers for the Netherlands and northern Europe more generally. In Germany, Calvinist places of learning enjoyed a place in the sun before the Thirty Years' War, the model academy at Herborn eventually becoming a university alongside Calvinist Heidelberg, Marburg, Frankfurt a/d Oder and (briefly) Königsberg too. To these we should add the universities of

---

57 Milton, *Catholic and Reformed*, ch. 8, esp. p. 377.
58 Nischan, *Prince, people and confession*, pp. 137–45; also 'Exorcism controversy'; and '"Fractio panis"'.

Scotland, England, the newly formed Trinity College, Dublin, and, in North America, the college at Harvard.

A theology of the schools was different from that of the study. It was influenced by the demands of a student curriculum: textbooks, methodical study, examinations. Calvin had published more than Bullinger and he was translated and reprinted more in the second half of the sixteenth century.[59] His biblical commentaries were the subject of controversy. That on Romans was praised by Théodore de Bèze, accused of 'judaizing' influences by the Lutheran Aegidius Hunnius in 1593, defended by David Pareus, and then attacked anew for inaccuracy and worse by the exiled English Catholic at Louvain, Thomas Stapleton, in 1594.[60] The *Institutes* were abridged and tabulated for an audience which found them ambiguous and difficult.[61] Calvin's writings were the subject of chair appointments and lecture courses in their own right. Caspar Olevian (1537–86), who was appointed to just such a post at Herborn, explained to Théodore de Bèze (1519–1605) that he lectured on a book of it each term. What may have been something like the lectures was published in 1586 – Calvin in his own words, shorn of anti-Catholic polemic. Three years later, his colleague at Herborn, Johannes Piscator (1546–1625), published his *Aphorisms*, drawn from Calvin's works – summaries of his lectures in a form that invited student dissertations.[62] The term 'aphorism' was consciously adopted in preference to 'thesis' since the latter implied an Aristotelian method of study – a proposition that had to be 'demonstrated' rather than a topic to be 'discussed'. Many, perhaps the majority of, Reformed academies tended to a Ramist approach to study in the later sixteenth century. Pierre de la Ramée (L: Ramus [1515–72]) had formulated a radical reform of the undergraduate curriculum to simplify the teaching of logic and amplify the study of rhetoric. Ramist influences were therefore present in the theological teaching of many of those who had been through the schools in those years and came to dominate Reformed theology in the early years of the seventeenth century. But teaching fashions come and go. Faced with Lutheran and Catholic opponents who deployed the forces of systematic theology, reinforced by the tools of scholastic logic, Reformed theologians found themselves obliged to respond, especially in German lands.[63] Chairs in rhetoric gave way to chairs in philosophy. Professorial reputations were made around formal expositions of Reformed doctrine. And

59 See the tables in Benedict, *Christ's churches*, pp. 60 and 92.
60 Girardin, *Rhétorique et théologique*, pp. 52–7.
61 Fatio, 'Présence de Calvin', in Neuser, *Calvinus ecclesiae doctor*, pp. 171–207.
62 Piscator, *Aphorismi*.
63 For difficulties in using the term 'scholasticism', see Muller, 'Calvin and the Calvinists'.

academic enquiry tended to expose in time the inner weaknesses of belief systems.

Jacob Hermanszoon (L: Jacobus Arminius [1559–1609]) was just such a doctor of theology at Leiden. His credentials were impeccable – a childhood marked by family bereavement at the siege of Leiden in 1575, student days at its new Calvinist university, an obligatory 'peregrinatio academica' to Geneva, and a stint as pastor in an Amsterdam city church. Predestination was the issue which, in Arminius's reluctant hands, turned Reformed theology into a force for division rather than unity. At Geneva, Arminius heard Théodore de Bèze probe the theological soft tissue of a subject that Calvin had said was best left alone. Even before Adam and Eve had sinned, God had a divine plan ('supralapsarianism' or 'antelapsarianism'). And, when Christ died for all, he died for the elect only. These views were already causing disquiet among the Reformed who wore their predestination more lightly. Dirck Volckertszoon Coornhert (1522–90), a self-taught notary from Haarlem with a populist streak, denied that the doctrine had any scriptural basis at a synod in Leiden in 1578. A synod in the little Protestant enclave of Montbéliard in 1586 brought Beza face to face with critics over the same issue, among others. In England, Samuel Harsnett preached a Paul's Cross sermon at London in 1585 that questioned double predestination and was duly told to hold his tongue. The debate gradually widened and deepened, especially in manuscript treatises and private discussion. Arminius's initial engagement with the issue was as a minister called in by the consistory at Delft to refute a treatise by two of its ministers against Beza's antelapsarianism. His fullest direct consideration of the issue was in the form of a response to William Perkins's treatise *On the Order and Mode of Predestination* (1598), completed by 1600 but only published after Arminius's death in 1612. Arminius was nothing if not refined in his soteriological distinctions. God appointed Christ as redeemer. He then promised to receive those who believe in Him. He further provided the means necessary for their faith. And He finally chose to save those whom He knew would accept and persevere in this faith – a divine 'foreknowledge' rather than a 'predestination'. These distinctions allowed Adam and Eve to invent sin before God granted salvation to those who willed its acceptance, whilst retaining His grace alone as the source for all salvation.

Arminius's views were too subtle by half, especially when (as became the case after his death in 1609) they became the object of theological, political and ecclesiological conflict that reached its climax at the famous national synod of the Dutch Reformed church at Dordrecht (Dordt or, in English, 'Dort'), opening on 13 November 1618. Attended by fifty-eight ministers and elders from Dutch churches, eighteen civil delegates from the States General of the Netherlands to represent the civil interest, five theologians from Dutch universities as well as twenty-six Reformed theologians from foreign countries, it was the nearest that the Reformed theological tradition would ever come to a rally. The thirteen Arminian Remonstrants, led by Simon Episcopius (D: Simon Egbertszoon (1583–1634)), arrived on 6 December, summoned not as delegates but to witness the condemnation of their views which, despite 154 formal sessions over six months, was the foregone conclusion of the synod. The synod was an acrimonious affair in which the periodic pleas for toleration and ecumenism have to be read in the context of the complex divisions among delegates and the awareness that the 'jarring of churchmen' did nothing for the edification of the churches. Yet delegates found the Reformed tradition far from united. Even the inclusion of the Apocrypha in a new translation of the Dutch Bible generated heated arguments. Foreign visitors thought the liturgical customs of the Dutch churches a bit strange. Edward Davenant, for example, noted the custom of leaving a wisp of straw under a stone at one side of the door of a recently deceased person: 'Bells are never ronge for them, nor any sermon made, but 2 or 3 invite the persons neighbours & frends, at a certaine hower to come and accompany him to his buriall: neither is there any woman admitted among them'.[64] In return, Dutch delegates referred to the English and Scottish sabbatarianism as the 'figmentum Anglicanum'. A Swiss delegate was bemused to discover that, at the house where he stayed, the mother and daughter were Calvinists, but the grandmother was a Mennonite and the uncle a Jesuit.[65]

Eventually a committee of nine drew up the famous five 'canons' (or 'chapters'), with their attendant articles, remembered from the seventeenth century by the appropriately Dutch acrostic 'TULIP'. Often presented as the high-water mark of Calvinist predestinarianism, the decrees were, in reality, mild in their doctrinal formulations.[66] They did not link creation and election in a narrowly supralapsarian framework to safeguard the 'eternal decrees'. They sought to express 'received doctrine' in formulae that would be understood and approved. Nor was it the case that moderate Remonstrant theologians were faced by intolerant scholastic Calvinists. If anything, it was Arminians who brought scholastic distinctions to the synod.[67] But Dort was not a 'universal synod', simply a national assembly of the Dutch church with significant foreign participation. Its decrees had no binding authority over other Reformed

---

64 Cited in A. Milton (ed.), *The British Delegation and the Synod of Dort (1618–1619)*, p. 106.
65 Cited in Pollmann, 'Public enemies', p. 184.   66 Patterson, *King James VI*, pp. 276–9.
67 Sinnema, 'Reformed scholasticism'.

theologians. They did not curtail Reformed theological arguments, especially around the issue of universal grace, in the Netherlands, in England (where the synod's decisions became a matter of Arminian dispute) and in France (where Moïse Amyrault and his adherents advanced the arguments of 'hypothetical universalism'). Calvin's and Bullinger's works remained on the shelves of the theologians of the Reformed tradition in the seventeenth century. But what, to take just one comparison, the independent-minded English puritan Richard Baxter (1615–91) made of them was very different from his confessionally engaged contemporary, Abraham de La Cloche (d. 1656), pastor at Metz.[68] The divergences would only grow greater in the generation of sceptical biblical scholarship and rationalist theology that emerged in the later seventeenth century.

68 Kadane, 'Les bibliothèques'.

8

The second wave of Protestant expansion

PHILIP BENEDICT

Although the Reformation was a pan-European event from the start, its initial epicentre was the Germanic cultural world: the Holy Roman Empire and those Baltic and Nordic regions tied closely to it by language, trade, and patterns of university attendance. Here, as the magnificent anarchy of the early Reformation gave way to confessionalization, the centrality of Luther's writings and persona in early evangelical propaganda, as well as the political process by which Protestant territorial churches came to be established and defended, ensured that the great majority of the new Protestant churches would be Lutheran.

Elsewhere in Europe, the Reformation's spread and institutionalization took longer. In Hungary, it appears to have been during the 1530s and 1540s that the process of change by parish and seigneurial initiatives got underway that by the century's end had brought the majority of the population into the Protestant camp. Henry VIII divorced the Church of England from obedience to Rome in 1534, but only during the mid-century reign of his son and successor Edward VI (r. 1547–53) did the church's doctrines and liturgy assume a clearly Protestant cast. Between 1550 and 1566, networks of Protestant churches formed and proliferated in defiance of governmental repression in Poland, Scotland, France, and the Netherlands. Religious wars soon followed in the last three lands. The party of Reformation triumphed quickly in Scotland. It took it until the 1590s to achieve a less complete victory in the northern provinces of the Netherlands that gained their independence from Spain. Despite three dozen years of civil war, the cause never attained more than the status of a tolerated minority in France. It quickly attained the same status in Poland without civil war.

Strikingly, this second wave of Protestantism's expansion and institutionalization eventuated above all in the multiplication of Reformed churches – churches that their enemies called 'Calvinist'. To be sure, exceptions existed.

Lutheran churches predominated among the Protestants of the German-speaking regions of Poland and Transylvania. Small numbers of Lutheran congregations also emerged among the Polish speakers of the Polish-Lithuanian Commonwealth, in Magyar and Slovakian-speaking portions of Hungary, and in the Netherlands, where Anabaptism also made its presence felt. Antitrinitarian churches took root in Poland and Transylvania. But the new state church of Scotland, the legally privileged state-supported church of the United Provinces, all of the Protestant churches in France, and the majority of Protestant churches in Poland and Hungary ultimately adopted Reformed confessions of faith. Even within the Holy Roman Empire, a number of German rulers of lands that had previously established Lutheran state churches altered these to align them more closely with the Reformed tradition. When this second wave of Protestant expansion had run its course, England, Scotland, the Dutch Republic, Béarn, and more than a dozen German territories had joined Switzerland's Protestant cantons as places where Reformed worship was established by law. Hundreds of tolerated Reformed congregations existed in France, Poland, and Hungary. From Pau to Poznán, perhaps ten million people worshipped in these churches.

These new Reformed churches spread and became established in a variety of ways. In some countries, a 'revolutionary reformation' swept the Reformed churches into power. In others, the movement spread through a largely spontaneous process of diffusion but never involved armed efforts to protect and extend it. In still others, princes imposed its characteristic doctrines and practices on their subjects by fiat. Since their manner of establishment varied so, any explanation of why the Reformed tradition dominated the second wave of Protestant expansion must be correspondingly complex. In some cases, it would appear to have been the cause's ability to spur large numbers of converts to form independent churches and to organize to advance and defend them that were critical to its success. In others, its spokesmen's ability to convince princes and their chief theological advisers that they offered the most compelling exegesis of scripture and that their doctrines reinforced rather than undermined established systems of political authority evidently held the key. Compounding the difficulty of the problem is the fact that contemporaries rarely set forth their reasons for adopting one set of doctrines rather than another. All the historian can do is explore with care the process whereby the faith spread and compare contrasting outcomes to isolate determining factors.

Eastern Europe: ecclesiastical transformation by parish and seigneurial initiative

It is not surprising that the two large kingdoms on Latin Christendom's eastern marches, Hungary and Poland-Lithuania, were the first areas other than Germany, Scandinavia, and Switzerland where Protestant worship established itself with a degree of permanence. Both polities contained important pockets of German speakers whose towns and mining settlements offered entry points for Protestant ideas. Many students from both countries attended German universities. The power of the nobility and relative weakness of the crowns also offered noble converts or privileged communities unusual latitude to found new congregations or experiment with new forms of worship. Indeed, religious change here would be above all a matter of spontaneous manor house and parish reformations that only slowly assumed clear confessional definition and standardized liturgical practices. When they did so, the majority of non-German speaking Protestant congregations adopted Reformed practices, although important groups of Antitrinitarians, Lutherans, and, in Poland, Czech Brethren also took shape. The reasons for the special appeal of Reformed practices are unusually hard to pinpoint here since little evidence has been found that sheds light on key moments of choice between competing alternatives. It is nonetheless clear that confessional choices mirrored linguistic differences to a considerable degree, and that particularly important support for the Reformed cause came from the nobility.

Protestantism took root especially quickly and became especially strong in Hungary, with the stunning Ottoman triumph at Mohács in 1526 providing the essential backdrop. Seven of Hungary's sixteen bishops perished alongside King Louis II at that fateful encounter, tearing holes in the ecclesiastical hierarchy. A disputed succession followed that led to twenty years of intermittent war and ultimately split the kingdom into three parts: the central Hungarian plain under direct Ottoman rule; a band of territory under Habsburg control around the country's northern and western borders; and an independent Transylvania under Ottoman protection. The decades of conflict hardly facilitated the efficient repression of heresy. The subsequent decades of relative peace found the country's new rulers uninterested in doing so. The Ottomans had no stake in religious disputes among Christians. The Zápolyai princes of Transylvania had been excommunicated during the succession struggle and were hostile to Rome. The first Habsburgs to rule their portion of Hungary were religious moderates who depended on imperial taxation and could not alienate the Protestant princes of the Empire.

The exact pace and character of Protestantism's spread amid this vacuum of religious authority are hard to trace, but it appears that the movement first found adherents in German-speaking towns in the 1520s and among certain magnates in the 1530s before expanding more widely from the 1540s onward. One leading preacher, Mihály Sztárai, told a correspondent in 1551 that he had been able to circulate without impediment through Ottoman Hungary for the previous seven years, during which time he founded 120 congregations.[1] Evangelists in Habsburg Hungary faced imprisonment on occasion but still circulated widely thanks to noble patronage and protection. The local printing industry was slow to reorganize itself after the Ottoman invasions, but a short-lived press in Sárvár produced the first Hungarian New Testament between 1539 and 1541, and more permanent presses in a number of cities after 1550 produced upwards of 140 Protestant polemical, doctrinal, and catechetical texts in Hungarian over the next two decades.[2]

While Luther and Melanchthon were major influences on early Hungarian Protestantism, the writings of Zwingli, Oecolampadius, and Bullinger also circulated. The first attempt to organize a Protestant church order on a regional scale in the mid-1540s in the privileged Saxon towns of Transylvania received Luther's direct approbation. Melanchthon had so many contacts and former pupils in the country that he spoke of taking refuge there during the Interim crisis. But when new laws against heresy issued in the wake of Mühlberg outlawed sacramentarian but not Lutheran opinions in Habsburg Hungary, the resulting efforts of Lutheran clerics to denounce their sacramentarian rivals touched off debates within the clerical districts of the northern and eastern portions of the country that ended in the 1560s with majorities in three districts voting to embrace Genevan confessions of faith or the Heidelberg Catechism. No sooner had these decisions given the church districts of the north-east a clearly Reformed cast than the arrival of the antitrinitarian doctor Giorgio Biandrata at the Transylvanian court split that region's church over the doctrine of the Trinity. The schism proved permanent. Between 1557 and 1571 Reformed, Lutheran, and antitrinitarian views all were accorded formal rights of worship here. The Reformed became dominant in Ottoman Hungary and much of the Habsburg-controlled portion of the kingdom, although Lutheranism had determined supporters in these areas as well, especially in the

---

1 Quoted in Fata, *Ungarn*, p. 121.
2 Gedeon Borsa, 'Le livre et les débuts de la Réforme en Hongrie', in Gilmont, *Réforme et le livre*, pp. 389–90.

German-speaking towns and Slovak regions. The confessional orientation of the Protestant churches in the north-western portions of the kingdom remained imprecise until the 1590s, when disputes over the Lutheran Formula of Concord precipitated a clear division between Reformed and Lutheran church networks in these areas.

Estimates of the country's religious composition at the end of the sixteenth century testify to the remarkable penetration of Protestant ideas and to the preponderance of the Reformed among those won to the cause. Reformed Protestants made up roughly 40 to 45 per cent of the total population. Lutherans formed another quarter of the population, while the remaining third of the population was divided between antitrinitarianism, Orthodoxy, and Roman Catholicism, a small minority in every region except Croatia. The new ideas took particularly deep root among the high aristocracy: all but three of the roughly thirty-six magnates who sat in the upper house of the Hungarian diet were Protestant.[3]

Protestantism would never make as deep inroads into Poland, but here too an important fraction of the elite converted for at least a generation, and it looked for a moment as if the king might embrace the faith. As in Hungary, evangelical ideas first spread among the German-speaking population. Polish Prussia was swept by the same initial agitation for the cause in the early 1520s as the other German-speaking regions around the Baltic. By mid-century, perhaps half of the region's communities had altered their worship along Lutheran lines. It took a decade for the cause to cross the linguistic divide and another decade before the first evangelical propaganda began to appear in Polish from a press in Königsberg in 1544. The first known contacts between Polish adepts and Zurich date from 1546 and with Geneva from 1549.

Multiple influences shaped early Protestantism in the Polish-speaking areas. Melanchthon was again widely read and respected. One of the first attempts to organize a regional church order took as its model his draft order for Hermann von Wied's aborted Cologne Reformation, written jointly with Bucer. But again Reformed influences ultimately dominated, with, as in Hungary, several of the most influential local figures moving from Lutheran to Reformed or even antitrinitarian positions over time, without it being possible to identify for certain the considerations that prompted their change of outlook. The new orientation became evident when an assembly of churches in the heartland of Poland near Krakow wrote to Geneva and Lausanne in 1555 to ask Beza and Calvin to come and take charge of the church-building process there.

3 Benedict, *Christ's churches purely reformed*, pp. 279–80 and 602, n. 38.

They refused the mission but commended the native aristocrat John Laski/a Lasco (1499–1560), who had broken with Rome while studying in Louvain and subsequently moulded Emden and the London 'strangers' church' into model Reformed churches. He returned to Poland and dedicated the last years of his life to advancing the cause.

The 1550s proved to be the critical decade for Protestantism's fate in Poland. Powerful noblemen began to shelter preachers on their vast domains. Evangelicals assumed a prominent place at court, urged the king to take in hand the reform of the church, and presented him with Protestant confessions of faith. Protestants were chosen to preside over the Chamber of Deputies at every session of the Sejm from 1552 to 1565. The assembly suspended ecclesiastical jurisdiction over laymen, proclaimed the sovereignty of the crown over ecclesiastical affairs, and urged the king to call a national council to consider alterations in the liturgy. But while individual noblemen and some townsmen profited from the suspension of ecclesiastical jurisdiction to establish Protestant churches, Sigismund II ultimately rejected on grounds of conscience the call to reform the church. Protestantism's brief moment of high hopes and rapid expansion ended soon thereafter as debates over the Trinity split the Reformed and a vigorous Counter-Reformation got underway. The trinitarian disputes were touched off by Biandrata's arrival from Switzerland in 1558 and the adoption of antitrinitarian ideas by one of the region's most prominent early Reformed spokesmen, Francis Stancaro. By 1565 a breakaway 'Minor' church had formed that attracted the majority of native Polish ministers, while the Nicene Major church attracted the majority of noble converts. While the quarrels between them discredited the larger cause, Cardinal Stanislas Hosius's return from the last sessions at Trent accompanied by a number of Jesuits initiated a campaign to renew Catholic loyalty to Catholicism. It proved so successful that Polish Protestantism was thrown on the defensive by the second half of the 1560s.

With the antitrinitarian enemy looming on the left, the Major Reformed churches of the region were able to broker a rapprochement with the Lutherans and the small groups of Czech Brethren (one of the offshoots of the Hussite movement) that had moved to Poland around 1550. The Sendomir Consensus of 1570 established inter-communication among the three faiths and decreed that their ministers were to refrain from polemics against one another – a rare instance of intra-Protestant ecumenicism that would be widely cited by advocates of this cause in subsequent generations. The nobility of Poland also gained confirmation of its right to shelter Protestant churches on its lands with the Warsaw Confederation of 1573; the Protestant churches of Polish Prussia and Lithuania had already purchased confirmation of their rights of worship from the perennially cash-starved crown between 1557 and 1562.

During Protestantism's brief moment of expansion throughout the Commonwealth, the cause never penetrated much below the nobility and urban elite except in Polish Prussia. At the height of its strength, thirty-six of the sixty-nine members of the upper house of the Polish diet were Protestants of different kinds: twenty-eight Reformed, seven Lutheran, and one member of the Czech Brethren. Among the second estate as a whole in Poland and Lithuania, perhaps one-sixth of the class embraced the cause. But in the churches that these noblemen established on their lands, few peasants turned up regularly for services, rarely more than one in ten. In Krakow, 15 per cent of the population, mainly from the capital's wealthier families, adhered to the cause. In all, at least 700 Polish-language Protestant churches were established during the sixteenth century: 500 of them Reformed, 100 antitrinitarian, forty Lutheran, and forty of the Czech Brethren. A large but uncertain number of German-language Lutheran churches also took shape in Polish Prussia and Great Poland.[4] The lack of social depth of these churches meant that they would be vulnerable to Counter-Reforming efforts to win back the aristocracy to Catholicism and would dwindle to a small fraction of their initial numbers over the next century.

Scotland, the Netherlands, and France: revolutionary Reformations

A similar phenomenon of spontaneous diffusion led to the creation of Reformed churches in Scotland, France, and the Netherlands, but the stronger state structures of western Europe meant that these churches, once established, faced a greater threat of persecution and even eradication. They consequently adopted more forceful measures of self-defence and agitated more aggressively to become the new state church. Their efforts were quickly crowned with success in Scotland, took a generation to bear fruit in the Netherlands and then only in half of the region, and never resulted in more than the acquisition of rights of worship as a tolerated minority in France. In every instance they were accompanied by violence and bloodshed.

Echoes of the initial agitation in Germany over the Luther affair were slow to reach Scotland, but from the first moment when proselytization for the

---

4 Merczyng, *Zbory I senatorowie protestanccy*; Tazbir, 'Géographie du protestantisme polonais'; Jobert, *De Luther à Mohila*, pp. 142–4; Schramm, *Polnische Adel und die Reformation*, pp. 107–8; Schramm, 'Reformation und Gegenreformation in Krakau', p. 30.

Reformation became intense, it was accompanied by aggressive noble support and the recourse to arms. Scotland's first crown edict against Lutheran heresy was not promulgated until 1525, an exceptionally late date by comparison with the rest of Europe and therefore a probable sign of the limited initial reception of early evangelicalism. Several iconoclastic incidents and executions for heresy in the 1530s testify to stirrings of dissent in that decade. But it was only with the regency government that followed on the accession of the infant Mary in 1542 that Protestant propaganda and preaching circulated widely. The first regent, the earl of Arran, legalized vernacular Bible reading, chose evangelical chaplains whom he allowed to preach publicly, and initially pursued a policy of alliance with Henry VIII's England. But Henry VIII's brutal effort to ensure Mary's marriage to his son Edward by sending troops across the border alienated Scottish opinion, forced Arran to reconcile with the Catholic hierarchy, and strengthened the party of alliance with France. In the war that followed, a number of Scottish noblemen not only took the English side but allowed Protestant ministers to preach in their wake. One group stormed Saint Andrews castle in 1546, killed the archbishop, and took control of the town for over a year, during which time worship was transformed in a Protestant manner. The arrival of French troops put an end to this first moment of aggressive Protestant proselytization, ensured Mary's marriage to the future Francis II of France, and strengthened the place of the queen's mother Mary of Lorraine in the regency government. The emerging leaders of Scottish Protestantism spent the better part of the next decade at the galley oar or in exile.

New twists in the political situation allowed them to return in the latter half of the 1550s when Mary of Lorraine loosened the repression of heresy as part of a broader campaign to gain the support of the political nation for a power-sharing arrangement between her daughter and Francis II. At the encouragement of ministers who now dared to return to the country, 'the Lords and Barons professing Christ Jesus' banded together in December 1557 to protect them and 'to maintain, set forward and establish the most blessed word of God and his Congregation'.[5] Churches were formed in a number of localities. John Knox issued open letters in July 1558 urging the queen regent to embrace the Reformation and telling the common people that they shared in the responsibility to punish idolatry, could maintain and defend preachers of God's word if their superiors would not do so, and need not pay tithes to false teachers. The Beggars' Summonds of 1 January 1559 nailed to the

---

5 Knox, *History of the Reformation in Scotland*, vol. 1, pp. 136–7.

doors of the religious houses denounced the monastic life as fraudulent and called on the religious orders to surrender their property by Whitsun or face forcible expropriation. Mary of Lorraine was confident that she could deal with the gathering storm once the affair of the crown matrimonial was resolved, but within a month of the settlement of this affair late in 1558, the death of Mary Tudor restored a Protestant regime to England that soon showed itself willing to send aid to the Lords of the Congregation. In the confrontation that followed, stormy weather and internal turmoil in France prevented the French crown from sending as many troops as Mary of Lorraine had hoped to receive from that quarter. The queen regent died in June 1560. Her Guise relatives who were acting as the chief advisers of the teenaged Francis II and Mary Stuart were preoccupied with France's own Protestant problem and could only accept an agreement that placed the government of Scotland in the hands of a regency council dominated by parliament. The religious question was referred to an upcoming gathering of that assembly that the Lords of the Congregation made sure to control. In 1560 it voted to abolish the mass and accept a new confession of faith. An unpredictable concatenation of events thus produced the surprisingly sudden triumph of a cause initially supported only by important sections of the nobility and a fraction of towns and townsmen.

The leading preachers of the Scottish Reformation and key drafters of the new confession of faith had spent time in exile in England, Emden, and Geneva, this last 'the most perfect school of Christ since the time of the apostles', in Knox's famous phrase. The new church consequently followed these models. The eucharistic theology of its confession of faith was close to Calvin's. The new liturgy was similar to Geneva's. Nearly a generation of experimentation and conflict would be required to work out the parameters of what always proved to be an unstable system of church government, but from the beginning it included a system of consistorial discipline involving elders similar to that found in both Geneva and Emden. Superintendents like those employed in Emden to oversee the reorganization and functioning of parish worship were part of the first church order. Bishops also survived the ecclesiastical revolution as in England and eventually displaced the superintendents with the blessing of the secular authorities, while elements of the presbyterial-synodal church structure that came to be normative among the Reformed churches in France and the Netherlands were added to the mix as well. Those who manned all of these various institutions displayed a combination of force and flexibility that enabled this new church order to gain first the participation and ultimately the assent of the near entirety of the population, even though only an activist minority had ensured its initial triumph.

The early history of the Reformation in the Netherlands was very different from Scotland, for this region's close trade ties with Germany and location within the Empire meant that it experienced the first wave of evangelical enthusiasm with full force. An extraordinary variety of heterodox ideas – Lutheran, sacramentarian, Spiritualist and Anabaptist – circulated quickly through this highly urbanized region. Only repression of an unparalleled severity that began with the execution of Europe's first Protestant martyrs in 1523 and claimed over 1,300 victims by 1566 kept these ideas from eventuating in established Protestant churches during the Emperor Charles V's lifetime. The wide circulation of heterodox ideas and growing revulsion at the repression did, however, weaken attachment to the Roman church and create an audience of potential adherents for the Reformed churches once these began to organize in secrecy within the region. This they did from some point around 1555 on, with aid from Geneva and the important refugee churches and exile communities in Emden, the Rhineland, and England.

The continuing force of government repression kept these churches rare and small for the first decade after 1555, but when aristocratic protest against the government's religious policy led to a temporary suspension of the laws against heresy in 1566, the volatility of the religious situation was rapidly revealed. Open-air preaching quickly began and soon drew vast crowds. Iconoclasm swept across the region. The suddenly proliferating Protestant churches offered to purchase permanent rights of worship. When this offer was rejected, Reformed synods endorsed armed defence of the changes they had made. The stunning expansion of this Wonderyear ultimately proved ephemeral, for once the regent Margaret of Parma regained her nerve and assembled her forces, she was able to reassert the laws against heresy, overcome the resistance of the most disobedient cities, put an end to open Protestant worship, and drive the majority of preachers back into exile. The arrival in the region of the Duke of Alva with a large contingent of troops intensified the heresy hunt, but Alva's aggressive disregard of the region's political privileges also alienated public opinion, so that when a small group of seafaring Reformed exiles who had taken to piracy against Spanish shipping landed on the Dutch coast in 1572, they were able to seize control of the greater part of Holland and Zeeland with the aid or acquiescence of the local population. Holland had not previously been a centre of Reformed strength, but a rapid transformation of the religious order nonetheless followed. Church revenues were seized for the benefit of the rebel cause. The mass was outlawed and Reformed worship instituted. Revolt spread through the entire region when the unpaid Spanish troops mutinied in 1576 and sacked Antwerp, forcing the seventeen provinces to assemble the

States-General on their own initiative and decree new measures for the region. The new religious settlement created another opportunity for Reformed churches to come out into the open, which they did with particular vigour and aggressiveness in Flanders and Brabant, only to be dispersed once again after the Spanish army reconquered the region in the 1580s. The seven northern provinces, however, successfully defended the independence proclaimed throughout the rebellious regions in 1581. The Reformed church became the legally privileged church throughout these newly independent United Provinces.

The religious settlement defining the rights and duties of this church was unique within Europe. While it was the sole legally recognized church and received the income from tithes and ecclesiastical property, liberty of conscience had been one of the Dutch revolt's great rallying cries, and the Reformed cause had been relatively weak prior to 1572 in the provinces that ultimately won their independence. At the same time, during the lean years of exile and underground struggle, the Reformed church had established a clear structure and confession of faith for itself that defined consistorial discipline as one of the essential attributes of the church. Following the rebels' triumph in the north, few of the region's inhabitants were eager to place themselves under this discipline, nor were the ruling authorities inclined to compel people to join the church. The Reformed were not prepared to renounce their discipline. The compromise solution that was gradually negotiated and that varied slightly from place to place opened Sunday worship and baptism to all, but allowed only those who accepted the discipline of the church to partake of the Lord's Supper and be considered full church members. Some regions instituted civil marriage as an alternative to church marriage. The upshot was a quite remarkable pattern of religious practice. Local studies recurringly reveal that in the first decades after Dutch independence, full members of the Reformed church rarely exceeded a quarter of the adult population. Another important fraction of the population turned up in the public church on Sundays to listen to Reformed sermons but abstained from communion. Once the threat of Spanish reconquest receded, the authorities turned a blind eye to Catholic worship so long as it did not take place in too visible a setting. A large Catholic minority took shape under the care of missionary priests overseen by a papal vicar. Smaller Mennonite, Lutheran, and, later, Remonstrant churches also formed. Some people lived outside the formal structures of any church whatsoever.

In none of the countries where Reformed churches took shape in defiance of governmental prohibitions during the 1550s did as many congregations form as quickly as in France. Here, however, the unpredictable course of political events proved less favourable to the cause. The early French Reformation stood somewhere between the Scottish and Netherlandish extremes. More evangelical propaganda circulated than in Scotland, and a higher percentage of French than Scots paid with their lives for embracing heterodox ideas, but neither the volume of evangelical buzz nor the intensity of crown repression was as great as in the Low Countries. As Calvin's birthplace, France was also a particular focus of the Genevan reformer's attention. He addressed many of his letters and treatises of pastoral advice to a French audience, encouraged those who had seen the light of the gospel to form their own churches, oversaw the dispatching of over 200 ministers from Geneva to take charge of organizing these churches, and even helped raise men and money for political efforts to advance the cause that he considered legitimate.[6] The ministers dispatched from Geneva proved to be just a fraction of the pastors needed to staff the new French churches, for when the sudden death of Henry II in 1559 led to a series of child kings and contests over who should offer them counsel, the confused situation offered the churches an ideal situation to grow. In that same year, delegates from the initial underground churches met secretly in Paris, drew up a common confession of faith, and confederated together through an interlocking system of regional and national synods. Over the next three years these collaborated with the chief ministers in Geneva to act as midwives for as many as a thousand additional congregations. These churches proved to be particularly successful in the cities and among the nobility. Overall, they gained the adherence of perhaps 10 per cent of the population. So unstoppable did their growth appear that the unsteady government around the queen mother Catherine de Medici felt it had no choice but to grant them legal rights of worship in January 1562.

But the religious settlement of this Edict of January did not hold, for the Reformed were poised unsteadily between hope for their complete triumph and fear that the Catholics were conspiring to eliminate them, while determined Catholic preachers were able to tap into the powerful national myths associating the preservation of the 'most Christian kingdom' with its purity from heresy to rally an important fraction of the population to the defence of the church. Incidents of violence had already begun to multiply between Huguenots and papists in the localities as early as 1560. When new massacres of Protestants followed the Edict of January, the Huguenots replied by seizing control of roughly a third of the kingdom's major cities in what they claimed

---

6 Kingdon, *Geneva and the coming*; and especially Dufour, 'Affaire de Maligny'.

was a defensive measure to protect their lives and rights of worship, but that resulted in the mass being driven from these cities and the king's agents being denied entry. It was the first act of a cycle of bloody civil wars and unsteady peace settlements that lasted for thirty-six years until exhaustion and Henry IV's rare combination of military genius and personal charm ended the cycle in 1598. The wars and accompanying massacres reduced the strength of the Reformed churches in most of the kingdom but reinforced their situation in certain portions of the south and centre-west. The Edict of Nantes that ended the conflicts gave these churches special military privileges and guaranteed the civil rights of their members. At the same time, it restricted Reformed worship to specified localities and effectively ended the faith's ability to proselytize and expand. Roughly 700 churches with just under a million members operated under the terms of this edict in the early seventeenth century.[7]

If the reasons why the majority of Hungary and Poland's Protestant churches took on a Reformed cast largely escape detection, some of the reasons why Reformed churches took the lead in the revolutionary Reformations of Scotland, the Netherlands, and France emerge clearly from the close scrutiny of the events in these countries. The geography of influence was one important factor. The first French-speaking territories in Europe where Protestantism became established were the francophone borderlands of Switzerland from Neuchâtel to Geneva, where the Reformation occurred under Bernese auspices and was consequently Reformed in character. These subsequently became the great centres for the production of evangelical propaganda in French. Emden, a little outpost of Reformed influence in the Empire, likewise became the greatest centre of Dutch-language evangelical printing. Direction and shelter for the underground churches in the Netherlands also came from the refugee churches across the channel in England, likewise Reformed. The theologians of the Scottish Reformation were shaped in Geneva, Emden, and England.

In situations of persecution, Reformed doctrines also had a greater capacity than Lutheran to inspire believers to establish churches of their own. The leading Reformed theologians of the second generation, Bullinger, Calvin, and a Lasco, urged those who had seen the light of the gospel to renounce Roman worship far more insistently than did their Lutheran counterparts. Calvin's doctrine of the four-fold ministry, in suggesting that the Bible set forth the proper institutions of a Christian church, also tendered believers a pattern for organizing churches of their own. From 1554 or 1555 onwards, Calvin's letters

---

7 Benedict, *Huguenot population*, p. 76; Garrisson-Estèbe, *Protestants du Midi*, p. 83.

regularly began to encourage groups of the faithful in contact with him to do just this. Once established, these churches became magnets for all those disaffected with the established ecclesiastical order. Furthermore, the consistories and synods established by these churches proved to be effective agencies for organizing the further spread and defence of these churches; in both France and the Netherlands, they raised money and troops and corresponded with one another to coordinate political action. Last of all, in the Netherlands, the lone case among the three just examined where organized Lutheran churches took shape alongside Reformed ones, the Lutherans adopted a stance of non-resistance when faced with government repression in 1566, while the Reformed proved willing to have recourse to arms to defend their churches. A greater proclivity to legitimize resistance was thus a final reason why the Reformed assumed a leadership role in these cases.

England and the second Reformations of the Empire: Reformed churches by princely fiat

The revolutionary manner in which the Reformation unfolded in Scotland, France and the Netherlands caused Calvinism's Lutheran and Catholic rivals to brand it as seditious. As the Lutheran Johannes Brenz informed Duke Christopher of Württemberg in 1568, it was predictably accompanied by 'iconoclastic rampages, the alteration of ordinary and useful ceremonies, and the deposition of ordained magistrates'.[8] But in fact the leading Reformed theologians walked a fine line. They counselled believers to set up churches of their own even where these were not permitted by law, since they believed that the Bible set forth clear rules about the forms of worship that were pleasing and displeasing to God that it was incumbent upon Christians to obey. At the same time, they insisted that converts obey the duly constituted authorities in all things that did not contravene divine law. Calvin and Bullinger (although not Knox) warned their followers sternly against taking the law into their own hands and purifying churches of their idols without magisterial approval. Furthermore, they directed many of their treatises and letters to encouraging rulers to embrace their point of view.

In some instances, their appeals met with success. At the same time that Reformed Protestantism spread across most of continental Europe and Scotland through a spontaneous process that depended on the cause's capacity to galvanize discontent with the established church into a coherent, effective

---

8 Quoted in Hollweg, *Augsburger Reichstag von 1566*, p. 122.

alternative, it won establishment in England and a number of German principalities thanks to its ability to convince rulers and their chief theological advisers that it offered a more persuasive exegesis of the biblical text than that of any of its rivals, and that it was not seditious as they claimed. These latter cases were all reformations from above, not below. In the parlance of German historiography, they were also all 'second reformations,' i.e., further transformations of the church orders of territories that had already broken with Rome and implemented an initial set of changes.

England's sixteenth-century Reformation was consistently driven from the top down and evolved according to a distinctive pattern. Henry VIII's desire to divorce Catherine of Aragon led him to proclaim himself supreme head of the church in 1534, but clearly Protestant forms were not imposed on the church until more than a decade later during the short reign of Edward VI, whose untimely death interrupted the restructuring of the church in midstream and yielded a curiously truncated reformation. While established church doctrine was thoroughly altered, the shape of the liturgy was modified far less completely, and the system of church government was scarcely transformed at all, except that the supremacy of Rome was cast off. Despite repeated efforts by purists to inspire further reformation under Elizabeth I, the virgin queen steadfastly preserved this settlement, at first out of fear that further change could provoke opposition, then in the name of tradition and expediency, and finally with certain theologians justifying its worship forms positively as ideally fitted to God's majesty.

Although Henry VIII's rejection of papal church leadership did not lead to a reformation of church doctrine, his need to find cooperative churchmen did create a new latitude for evangelical preaching and publication and even yielded for a time measures cutting back saints' days and ordering an English Bible to be placed in every church. It also created a strong likelihood that the church would move in a Protestant direction after his death, since of his three children only Mary was a child of his first wife. The others, Edward and Elizabeth, could not accept the Catholic position that their father's divorce was illegitimate, for that would make them bastards and destroy their claims to the throne. It was hardly foreordained, however, that the changes to come under Edward would be aligned theologically with the Reformed tradition, since Luther was at least as powerful an influence on early English evangelical propaganda as any Reformed or Lollard figure. Two interrelated developments chiefly determined the confessional coloration of the Edwardian changes. The first was the evolution of Thomas Cranmer's eucharistic theology from a position close to Luther's to one closer to Calvin's between 1546 and 1548.

Since Cranmer was Archbishop of Canterbury and the key drafter of the new prayer books and articles of faith imposed on the church, his views on this critical question passed into these documents. The second was the coincidence of Edward's reign with the Interim crisis in Germany, which spurred a number of continental theologians of a prestige unmatched in England to seek refuge there. The English offered asylum to Protestant leaders of many theological orientations, including Melanchthon and Brenz, but only those of a Reformed inclination, with their stronger sense that no compromise could be brooked with papist forms of worship, accepted. Bucer, a Lasco, and Peter Martyr Vermigli all crossed the channel to assume key teaching or leadership positions. Their views influenced Cranmer's change of heart on the eucharistic question. Their instruction formed the next generation of church leaders. The key documents of the Edwardian Reformation consequently assumed a Reformed stamp, even if they retained special vestments and more feast days than in the continental Reformed churches. So, the new liturgy of the Book of Common Prayer removed from baptism the formula of exorcism retained by Germany's Lutheran state churches and celebrated the Lord's Supper by breaking regular bread at a table set in the body of the church, rather than by distributing special communion wafers at an altar as the Lutherans did. The Forty-Two Articles of the church taught Christ's spiritual instead of physical presence in the eucharistic elements. The brief Catholic interlude under Mary further oriented English Protestantism towards the Reformed tradition, since Reformed communities on the continent proved far more hospitable to the Marian exiles than Lutheran ones, and these exiles returned to take charge of the Elizabethan church with grateful memories of their time spent in places such as Zurich and Geneva.

If Reformed ideas had circulated in Germany since the earliest days of the Reformation and even managed to survive the pressure to conform to the emerging Lutheran orthodoxy in a few corners of the Empire such as Bremen and East Friesland, the Palatinate was the first major German principality whose initially Lutheran church order was changed in a Reformed direction following the 1555 Peace of Augsburg. Located astride the trade routes of the Rhineland, this territory drew many of its administrators from the free cities of south-western Germany where Reformed ideas had been strongest in the initial decades of the Reformation. Several theologians of Reformed inclinations taught at its prestigious university in Heidelberg. When the debates sparked by the second sacramentarian controversy set them to quarrelling with their orthodox Lutheran colleagues, the pious, independent-minded Elector Frederick III felt that he had to resolve the issue himself. He undertook a careful study of the Bible and of different treatises on the eucharist that led him to side with the Reformed and see the Lutherans as given to excessive theological nit-picking and invective. Between 1563 and 1571, he instituted a new church order with simplified eucharistic and baptismal services, sponsored the drafting of the Heidelberg Catechism that espoused a spiritual understanding of Christ's presence in the eucharist and a strict interpretation of the Second Commandment as prohibiting all images in church, and, after intense local debate, accepted a system of parish-based church discipline that gave elders the power to suspend people from communion.

Over the next three decades, second reformations also took place in Nassau-Dillenberg, Anhalt, Hesse-Kassel, and a number of smaller territories between Heidelberg and the Dutch border. In some of these cases, the changes merely involved liturgical transformations and the introduction of the Heidelberg Catechism. In others consistorial discipline and a presbyterial-synodal form of church government was introduced as well. Imposed from above, the changes met increasing resistance with each passing decade from populations primed by the advance of Lutheran confessionalization to reject them – so much so that when the elector of Brandenburg personally embraced Reformed ideas in the first decade of the seventeenth century, he thought it wiser not to risk imposing a new church order on his entire territory, but merely sponsored Reformed preaching and worship in the vicinity of the court. The prime period for these second reformations came between 1580 and 1600, as the campaign to impose the Formula of Concord throughout the Protestant regions of the Empire alienated rulers formed in the Melanchthonian tradition and spurred them to consider alternatives, and as growing Spanish and papal intervention in imperial affairs in defence of Catholic interests made Protestant rulers increasingly receptive to the call to pan-Protestant solidarity that the Reformed articulated with particular insistence. While they all ultimately hung on individual rulers' decisions of conscience, they were particularly likely to occur in territories where Melanchthonian or Swiss and south German currents of thought were influential in the entourage of the king and high administration, or where the local rulers fought alongside the Reformed in France or the Netherlands. Thus, as in the case of the revolutionary reformations, the geography of influence was important in accounting for these instances where princely fiat enshrined Reformed instead of Lutheran doctrines and practices within territorial state churches. The Reformed cause also benefited from the aggressive insistence of the orthodox Lutheran theologians of this generation on the rightness of their interpretations of certain contested fine points of doctrine, which made them look to those less interested in the details of theology like narrow-minded zealots who refused the hand of reconciliation that the Reformed extended to them to facilitate political cooperation against Rome.

The label of 'Calvinist' became attached to all of the Reformed churches that proliferated across Europe in the second wave of Protestant expansion, but the story of their establishment has shown us that Calvin was not the only theologian guiding and inspiring the process, nor Geneva the only cradle of Reformed expansion. Already in the early 1530s in south German cities such as Augsburg or Ulm where Reformed ideas coming from Zurich competed on a relatively equal footing with Lutheran ideas coming from Wittenberg, the former's denial of the real presence and more uncompromising rejection of the presence of images in churches won more supporters, suggesting that these fundamental ideas of the Reformed tradition had a capacity to convince lay audiences that predated Calvin's emergence as a reformer. In the next generation, Bullinger was nearly as prolific an author as Calvin and maintained an even more extensive correspondence than his Genevan colleague. His writings, like Calvin's, encouraged those who had seen the light of the gospel to shun the worship of Rome; at the same time they defended the Zurich Reformation's distinctive merger of church and civic community against the autonomous system of ecclesiastical discipline advocated by Calvin and illustrated in Geneva. Their influence was felt particularly strongly in Hungary, England, and the Netherlands. Further north, the refugee centres of Emden and London acted as alternative Genevas for the Low Countries and Scotland. A Lasco was another prominent Reformed champion whose writings encouraged believers to leave the Roman church and whose work as a church organizer was important for Poland, England, and the Netherlands. While these and still other figures must be accorded their proper importance, it remains the case that Calvin gave to the Reformed cause a set of theological writings of unmatched clarity, vigour, and utility that defined and defended an original middle ground in the eucharistic debate that had divided Lutherans from the early Swiss Reformed. His success in transforming his adopted home into a model Christian community made it the most important single base for further Reformed expansion abroad. His zeal for encouraging and sustaining the formation of 'churches under the cross' abroad was exceptional. The Reformed churches came to be called Calvinist for good reason.

PART III

★

CATHOLIC RENEWAL

9

Redefining Catholicism:
Trent and beyond

ROBERT BIRELEY, SJ

About four o'clock on the afternoon of 4 December 1563, the 235 voting members of the Council of Trent processed from the Palazzo Thun across to the cathedral where the Bishop of Catania celebrated the Mass of the Holy Spirit. There followed a vote approving overwhelmingly the five reform decrees that had been formulated in the previous weeks. Next, the full text of the doctrinal decrees that the council had approved over the last eighteen years was read out, followed by the initial paragraphs of the reform decrees. The bishop then put two questions to the assembled fathers: were they agreed that the council be declared at an end and that confirmation of all its decrees be sought from Pope Pius IV in Rome? To the first the fathers reiterated the affirmative response given the previous day. Their similar response to the second question, with one dissenting vote, implied a clear recognition of papal authority and signified a notable victory for the papacy. To the unrestrained joy of the assembly, the council's president, Cardinal Giovanni Morone, then declared the council ended.[1] So the movement for reform and renewal within the Catholic Church reached a major milestone.

Historians have employed different terms over the years to designate sixteenth- and seventeenth-century Catholicism. 'Counter-Reformation' considered the developments within the Catholic Church to have been basically a reaction to the Protestant Reformation, and it evoked images of the Inquisition and the Index of Prohibited Books as well as the political and military measures of the religious wars. Many Catholics long countered this one-sided view with a similarly partisan position. They preferred 'Catholic Reform' and argued that the church had begun the necessary process of reform long before 1517. The Protestant Reformation accordingly bore the responsibility for the division within the Christian body. A compromise solution found widespread acceptance in the ecumenically minded post-World War II decades: the movements

---

1 Jedin, *Geschichte des Konzils von Trient*, vol. 4:2, pp. 187–9.

for reform within the church prior to 1517 were likened to streams that only merged into a river after the shock of Luther's attack, eventually to reach the papacy and provoke the convocation in 1545 of the Council of Trent. Both Catholic Reform and Counter-Reformation then described the Catholic Church until the end of the seventeenth century.[2] Yet there still existed no single term to characterize the Catholicism of the period, and though both Catholic Reform and Counter-Reformation designated important aspects of the Catholic Church in the early modern period, they defined it largely in relation to the Reformation and overlooked many developments in sixteenth-century Catholicism that had little to do with Protestantism, such as the rise of new religious orders and missionary endeavours across the seas. Furthermore, reform implied that the church was steadily deteriorating on the eve of the Reformation, a view that much recent research has challenged. So the admittedly prosaic yet more inclusive term 'Early Modern Catholicism' seems to be gathering acceptance.[3] Perhaps the most fruitful approach sees in both the Catholic and Protestant movements competing efforts to update the Christian church to the changing world of the early sixteenth century: significant growth of the modern state; demographic and economic expansion; the coming of the first European colonial empires; the Renaissance including the invention of printing and the Scientific Revolution; and, of course, for the Catholic Church the challenge of Protestantism. Once again in the sixteenth century as so often in the past, Christianity faced the need to adapt to a changing culture and society. So it should not surprise us to find early modern attitudes and values reflected in the Catholicism of the period.[4]

Well before the Council of Trent and with little attention to events in the north, new religious orders and congregations sprang up from below under the leadership of charismatic individuals, to initiate innovative forms of religious life and ministry; foremost among them were the Capuchins, the Jesuits, and the Ursulines. The Italian Observant Franciscan Matteo da Bascio gathered about him a small group with a view to reviving the primitive Franciscan spirit; they received initial papal approbation in 1524 and the approval of their Constitutions in 1536. Soon known as the Capuchins because of the pointed cowl (*capuche*) that they wore, they numbered nearly 30,000 in their 'golden age' in the seventeenth century. The new Society of Jesus or Jesuits grew initially out of the spiritual experience of the Spanish nobleman Ignatius Loyola. He and ten companions arrived in Rome in late 1537, where they preached and

2 Jedin, *Katholische Reform oder Gegenreformation?* pp. 26–38.
3 O'Malley, *Trent and all that*, esp. pp. 140–3.   4 Bireley, *Refashioning of Catholicism*.

ministered to the poor in the dreadfully cold winter that followed, and in 1540 they received formal approval as a new religious order from Pope Paul III. By the death of Ignatius in 1556 they counted roughly 1,000 members spread over much of Europe and reaching into Asia and the Americas, and their foundation of thirty-three colleges by that time illustrated a turn to education, an innovative form of ministry characteristic of the period. At about the age of forty, the pious, unmarried laywoman Angela Merici moved to Brescia in 1516 from her home in the Veneto; soon in association with the local Oratory of Divine Love she began to assist in the women's section of the new hospital for incurables. Her activities gradually expanded to include care for orphans and instruction of young girls in Christian doctrine, and soon her goal became a community of virgins and widows who would serve in the world as had their forebears in the early church. Their group of about thirty-five first formally organized in 1535, and their initial rule received papal approbation in 1544 five years after Angela's death. In the following years they expanded into other Italian cities and then, above all, into France where they turned increasingly to education and, under pressure, took on features of an enclosed order.

After prolonged negotiations among Emperor Charles V, King Francis I of France, and Paul III, the council initially summoned by the pope in 1536 finally convened in Trent, a town on the Italian side of the Alps but still within the Empire, on Laetare Sunday, 15 December 1545. It was to meet in three distinct periods: from December 1545 to March 1547; from May 1551 to April 1552; and then after a ten-year interruption, January 1562 to December 1563. Only four archbishops, twenty-one bishops, and five generals of religious orders attended the opening session as voting members under the guidance of three papal legates. At the start the council confronted the issue whether to give priority to doctrinal clarification and definition or to reform legislation. Emperor Charles wanted the council to deal first with disciplinary matters, in the hope that once a clear will to reform was made manifest, the Protestants would come to the council, thus opening the way to doctrinal understanding. But the pope insisted that the council first clarify Catholic doctrine, in order to overcome the widespread uncertainty among the faithful, and he likewise feared dubious theological compromises in an effort to conciliate the Protestants. Eventually the parties agreed to take up matters of doctrine and matters of reform alternately. Subsequently, Trent was criticized for obstructing a reconciliation with the Protestants, but this is to overlook the institutionalization of the Protestant churches by that time as well as the failure of the religious colloquies held at Worms and Regensburg in 1540 and 1541.

The council's historical significance consisted in two achievements, as its great historian Hubert Jedin asserted.[5] First, it clarified Catholic teaching on most doctrines contested by the Protestants, and secondly, it put forth a series of reforms that aimed not only at the elimination of abuses but at a renewed pastoral programme that placed the bishop and the parish priest at the centre of the church's mission. To the Protestant notion of 'scripture alone' it countered with the claim that divine revelation was transmitted in two forms, unwritten traditions dating from the apostles as well as scripture, and it insisted on the right of the church authoritatively to interpret scripture. The decree's initial formulation indicated that revelation was contained partly in the written books and partly in the unwritten traditions, implying that these were two separate vehicles of revelation. But a few fathers objected that scripture included in some way all revelation and so came closer to Luther's position. The words were then changed to render the relationship between the two channels more vague.[6] In fact, most of the bishops probably did understand the traditions to be a supplement to the scriptures and most subsequent Catholic theology clearly did. Many bishops, led by the Spanish cardinal Pedro Pacheco, Bishop of Jaen, wanted to prohibit vernacular translations of the Bible as the mother of heresies, as had already been decreed in Spain, France, and England by ecclesiastical or secular authorities. But opposition to this led by the prince-bishop of Trent, Cristoforo Madruzzo, prevented passage of the measure. Later, as we shall see, the Inquisition returned to the issue.

The most important dogmatic decree, on justification, responded to Luther's position of 'faith alone' and was to influence significantly Catholic spirituality. The council fathers and their theologians worked on this issue from late June 1546 until the formal, unanimous acceptance of the decree on 13 January 1547. Carefully crafted and preceded by at least four drafts and drawing heavily on scripture, it is often considered a theological masterpiece. The decree was composed of not only thirty-three canons or anathemas condemning various positions but sixteen chapters setting forth a positive doctrine that explained the canons and was intended to serve as a basis for preaching. Three main features characterized the final decree. While stressing the utter inability of the sinner to secure justification on his own and its complete gratuity as a gift

---

5 *History of the Church*, vol. 5, p. 496.
6 Session 4, 8 April 1547, *Decrees of the Ecumenical Councils*, ed. Giuseppe Alberigo and Norman P. Tanner (Washington, 1990), vol. 2, pp. 663–5. 'The council clearly perceives that this truth and rule [that is, the gospel] are contained in written books and in unwritten traditions which were received by the apostles from the mouth of Christ himself, or else have come down to us, handed on as it were from the apostles themselves at the inspiration of the Holy Spirit.'

of God and attributing all initiative to God, it affirmed the need for cooperation on the part of the individual and so an active role for free will in the process. Secondly, it declared that justification involved not only the remission of sin but an inner transformation and renewal that followed from the individual's union with Christ and the infusion of the Holy Spirit, as opposed to a mere application of the merits of Christ or the benefit of divine favour. Finally, the council asserted that the justified individual must continue to perform good works which, precisely because of his union with Christ, merited an increase of grace and eternal reward, this merit itself being a gift.[7]

Two issues stirred considerable debate among the fathers. The council eventually rejected but did not condemn the novel notion of the so-called two-fold justification; a formula intended as a compromise with the Lutherans, it had been proposed by Cardinal Gasparo Contarini and accepted by Philip Melanchthon at the Colloquy of Regensburg in 1541 only to be rejected by Rome and by Luther, and was presented to the council by the Augustinian superior general Girolamo Seripando. Secondly, the fathers condemned Luther's position that justifying faith included complete certitude of one's own personal salvation; they struggled to find the formulation that 'no one can know by that assurance of faith which excludes all falsehood, that he has obtained the grace of God' or that he is among those predestined to eternal life (apart from a special revelation).[8]

The council also reaffirmed Catholic positions on the real presence of Christ in the eucharist and the sacrificial character of the mass. Other decrees laid out the nature of a sacrament and enumerated seven including penance with auricular confession, holy orders, and matrimony. For the validity of a marriage free consent of both parties was declared to be necessary, in the face of what the fathers felt to be undue social pressures. For a long time severe pastoral problems had emerged from the so-called clandestine marriages, that is, marriages that were concluded on the basis of the consent of the two parties alone, which indeed did constitute the essence of the sacrament of marriage, without any proper public recognition. According to a Portuguese theologian in Trent, of the 100 confessors in the diocese of Lisbon, ninety-four had had to deal with issues following from clandestine marriages. Only after long debate and despite the opposition of a significant minority did the fathers issue the decree 'Tametsi' that required for the validity of a marriage the presence of the parish priest or his delegate and two or three other witnesses. Much of the opposition argued that such a measure exceeded the authority of the church.

7 Session 6, 13 January 1547, ibid., 2, pp. 671–81.   8 Ibid., p. 674.

Bishops and parish priests were to be not only ecclesiastical officials but effective pastors and preachers who lived among their flocks. The bishops of an ecclesiastical province were expected to meet in a provincial council triennially under the chairmanship of the archbishop. The council strengthened the position of the bishop within his diocese, and so attempted to respond to the frequent excuse of bishops for non-residence, that they were not masters in their own house. The bishop now controlled who was to be ordained in his diocese, and he was granted greater oversight in pastoral matters such as preaching and the hearing of confessions. Diocesan synods were to take place annually, and bishops were to carry out regular visitations of their dioceses. Parish priests for their part were also to reside in their parishes and preach regularly. The decree on Holy Orders included a provision that a seminary for the formation of priests be established in every diocese. Other decrees passed in the last days of the council aimed to end abuses regarding religious images, the veneration of saints and relics, purgatory, and indulgences while reaffirming their role for Catholic piety.

Yet the council also avoided taking a position on important issues. Many of the fathers foresaw a decree on the reform of princes, but Catholic rulers showed little enthusiasm for this, and so the fathers, aware of their need of princely support for church reform, desisted. So the council made no statement on the relationship between church and temporal government, and it did not try to challenge the privileges of many princes regarding ecclesiastical appointments. Nor did the fathers succeed in legislating the thorough reform of the Roman curia that late medieval reformers had intended with their call for 'reform in head and members'. Neither the new religious orders and congregations nor the expanding missionary activity of the church in Asia and the Americas received serious attention from the council.

Above all the council did not address the role of the papacy and its relationship to the bishops as a body. One certainly would have expected it to do so given the Protestant attacks on the papacy. Papalists at the council endeavoured, successfully for the most part, to keep the issue off the agenda because they feared a resurgence of conciliarism. Twice the issue did emerge in connection with the discussion of residence for bishops. The Spanish bishops in particular argued that only a declaration that divine law itself required the presence of a bishop in his diocese would truly prevent the pope from conceding dispensations and would speak with adequate force to episcopal consciences. Cardinals and other curial officials opposed such a declaration because many of them lived as absentee bishops, and they saw in it a limitation on papal power. Later a proposed decree failed to state that the office of bishop itself existed by divine right, leaving open an interpretation that the papacy served as the source of episcopal authority. Stress over the tension that arose concerning this issue seems to have contributed to the death of two papal legates in March 1563. Pius IV then dispatched Cardinal Morone to Trent as the new president of the council, and he succeeded in working out a compromise. The council declared in the decree on orders that the church's hierarchy existed 'by divine appointment', and in an accompanying decree, that bishops were required to reside in their dioceses by 'divine command', without commenting further on the nature of the obligation. It applied this explicitly to the officials of the curia but allowed that under certain circumstances Christian charity and the greater good of the church permitted episcopal absence.[9]

The council did result in a substantial increase in papal authority. The fathers sought papal confirmation for their decrees, which Pius IV granted with his bull *Benedictus Deus*, backdated to 26 January but only published on 30 June 1564 after Roman officials secured recognition for the pope of the right to interpret the council's decrees and the establishment of a new Roman Congregation for the Interpretation of the Council. Vigorous popes after the council, Pius V (1565–72), Gregory XIII (1572–85), and Sixtus V (1585–90), bolstered the papal position, and the papacy found allies in the international religious orders, especially the newly founded Capuchins and Jesuits. As the council came to an end, it entrusted tasks to the pope that enhanced his prestige. At the council's behest Pius IV published an Index of Prohibited Books in March 1564, and later that year there appeared the Tridentine Profession of Faith which summarized Trent's doctrinal decrees and included a promise of obedience to the pope. Subscription to it was henceforth required from all bishops, religious superiors, pastors, professors, and degree candidates before they took up their office or received their degrees. In 1568 under Pius V there appeared a new version of the breviary prayed daily by most clerics and two years later a new Roman Missal.

Eventually there followed in the wake of Trent a gradual upswing in the quality of bishops across the church. Many provincial and diocesan synods were conducted after the council, to translate its decrees into regional and local programmes, yet their number differed vastly across Europe and definitely waned by 1600 apart from in France. Episcopal visitations showed more staying power, and they have left behind a rich source of documentation about early modern church life. Yet bishops saw their authority decline *vis-à-vis* secular power as well as the pope. Frequently popes sided with princes against bishops

---

9 Session 23, 15 July 1563, *ibid.*, pp. 744–5.

because of the need for princely support against the Protestants and in the cause of reform. Charles Borromeo, the saintly, austere Archbishop of Milan from 1565 to 1584, has long been considered the embodiment of the model Tridentine bishop, but recent research has come to see him as an advocate of an episcopalist interpretation of Trent that failed to prevail. Though faithful to Rome, Borromeo chafed under Roman supervision, especially under Gregory XIII. The pope's hesitation to support him enthusiastically in his conflicts with the Spanish secular authority annoyed the archbishop. Gregory also concluded a concordat with Duke William V of Bavaria in 1583, which did not please the local bishops. He conceded to the duke rights to tax clergy, make many ecclesiastical appointments, and supervise extensive church property. Despite the prohibition of Trent, Gregory permitted pluralism in Germany, especially in the case of the Habsburgs and Wittelsbachs, staunch allies of the church, because they supplied episcopal candidates who could strengthen politically a shaky German Catholicism. Under Sixtus V new regulations were issued for the regular *ad limina* visits to Rome of the bishops across the world, but these only gradually came into practice after 1600. Sixtus also restructured the Roman curia, that had outgrown its medieval administrative capacity. The pope established six congregations or ministries for the governance of the Papal States and nine for the universal church, each with a cardinal at its head. He greatly increased the number of cardinals to seventy; these were becoming almost exclusively Italian, and they gradually became ecclesiastical bureaucrats rather than councillors who met regularly with the pope. This reorganization reduced the quasi-constitutional role of the College of Cardinals as an international representative body. Consistories decreased from two or three a week to twice a month after 1600, with decision-making authority concentrated more in the pope himself.

Nepotism and patronage persisted at the papal court. But this did not rule out improvement of the situation. Piety became fashionable. Pluralism among papal officials decreased, but rules for residence were often relaxed, for example, for nuncios. Other means of financing them simply did not exist. With the trend towards a monarchical papacy, which dated from the mid-fifteenth century, came the trappings of a seventeenth-century court. The pope did, in fact, also govern a principality. Outright gifts, pensions, and non-ecclesiastical offices funnelled funds to members of the papal family and their clients. The family of Paul V Borghese (1605–21) rose from Roman patricians to one of the great land-holding families in Italy. A new Roman aristocracy arose dependent upon papal favour. Others sought at the papal court more modest social and political advancement. The Counter-Reformation popes, like their Renaissance predecessors, worked to assert Rome's rightful status as the centre of Christendom, and they directed an unrivalled programme of urban renewal and artistic patronage that encouraged the dramatic, monumental Baroque style. The new basilica of St Peter's – begun under Julius II in 1506, consecrated by Urban VIII in 1626, and the colonnades of its square completed under Alexander VII in 1666 – exemplified the best of their efforts. Both Michelangelo and Bernini left their mark on it.

At the top of the list of the papal congregations as reorganized by Sixtus V stood the Inquisition. It had been created in 1542 by Paul III as a reorganization of the medieval Inquisition, to counter the Protestant threat, and it was joined in 1571 by the Congregation of the Index whose function was to oversee the publication and censorship of books. Originally the Inquisition was foreseen as a network of courts that would proceed against heretics throughout Christendom. But Spain and Portugal already had functioning Inquisitions, and France and most other Catholic states were not about to allow it to operate in their territories. In practice, its ability to implement its decisions was limited to areas of Italy; still, these decisions as well as those of the Index were meant by Rome to be normative for the whole church, as are the decisions of its successor, the Congregation for the Doctrine of the Faith, up to the present day.

Inquisition courts functioned most actively in Italy from about 1580 to 1620. By 1580 heresy had receded as a threat there, and the courts looked more to 'illicit magic' and other deviations more moral than theological. According to recent research and counter to long-standing myths, the Roman Inquisition generally followed careful legal procedures and showed more respect for suspects' rights than other contemporary courts. Scholars have recognized that, frequently, sentences were not to be taken literally; for example, 'perpetual imprisonment' could mean three years of incarceration. The most reliable figures indicate that the Inquisition executed roughly 100 victims between 1542 and 1761, the most famous being Giordano Bruno who was burned at the stake on the Campo dei Fiori in 1600.[10] Perhaps the most harmful effects of the Inquisition lay in fear and in an intimidation of intellectual life, but these are difficult to measure reliably. In 1596, after long hesitation, the Index of Pope Clement VIII prohibited translations of the Bible into Italian, because of the frequent association of the vernacular scriptures with heresy, and so it

---

10 Tedeschi, *The prosecution of heresy*, pp. 104, 125 (this chapter was co-authored by E. William Monter), p. 147.

followed the Spanish and Portuguese Inquisition. But this prohibition did not apply to the lands north of the Alps.[11]

Catholic Reform, like the Protestant Reformation, aimed to evangelize ordinary people. Religious belief escapes measurement, but it probably relates generally to religious knowledge and practice. Growth took place in some areas by 1600 and in others only after the turn of the eighteenth century. Just as the Protestant Reformation first took root in cities and towns, so did the Catholic Reform, in cities like Munich, Lyon, and Barcelona, often fostered by the foundation of a Jesuit college. Gradually, the movement reached into the hinterland and then further on into the countryside. Regionally, north Italy, the Spanish Netherlands and the Rhineland, Alsace, Lorraine and surrounding territories, Bavaria, and parts of the Iberian peninsula first experienced its effects. Much of France did so in the first half of the seventeenth century and most of the Habsburg Austrian and Bohemian lands only in its second half.

Both Catholics and Protestants realized the need to win over the youth, and both saw in the school a principal means of evangelization. Few historical movements have taken education as seriously as did the Reformation and the Catholic Reform, and both shared the enthusiasm of the Renaissance for it. Members of the new religious orders and congregations often served as schoolmasters and schoolmistresses. This characterized both the Jesuits and Ursulines, and it marked a new development in the history of religious life. The Jesuits established their first college at Messina in Sicily in 1548; by 1600 there were 236 in existence, and estimates of the number of their students in France in 1630 reach 40,000. The social composition of the student bodies varied. In Italy the proportion of students from the nobility seems to have been high, but this was not the case elsewhere. In the 1620s at Châlons-sur-Marne in France, a centre of the wool trade, the office-holding, merchant, and artisan families all sent sons to the college in significant numbers. The colleges owed their success to several factors. They were free, endowed usually by princes, ecclesiastics, or municipalities, and they offered a means to social advancement. Benefactors favoured them as a source of government officials as well as diocesan and religious priests. Many families and students were sold on the programme of studies that combined Christian, humanist, and, at the higher levels, scholastic elements for the formation of young men in learning and piety. Other religious groups followed the Jesuits into the foundation of colleges: the Barnabites, who were founded initially in Milan in 1533 for pastoral and catechetical purposes; the Piarists, whom the Spaniard Joseph Calasanz established in Rome in 1602,

---

11 Fragnito, *La Bibbia al rogo*, pp. 217–24.

originally to provide free elementary education for poor boys; and the French branch of the Oratorians, an affiliate of the society founded in Rome by St Philip Neri in 1575, which under papal pressure had come to conduct thirty-one colleges by 1631.

With regard to women, the Ursulines of Angela Merici turned to education when in 1567 Charles Borromeo called them to Milan to assist in his programme of religious instruction. The papal territory of Avignon served as their spring-board into France in 1598, and they spread out from there into the Spanish Netherlands. Two actions of the Paris community in 1612 proved decisive. It accepted monastic enclosure, partly under pressure from the French hierar-chy and from French society which frowned on single women living outside the home or cloister, partly from their own desire to follow the example of the Discalced Carmelites of Teresa of Avila who were then being established in France. On the other hand, the Paris Ursulines secured papal approval to take a special vow committing themselves to the work of education. So there evolved a new form of women's religious life that combined contemplation with classroom teaching. The Ursuline schools became a major factor in the effort to Christianize the population of Catholic Europe. By 1700 they pos-sessed over 300 houses in France; so the Ursulines served as a vanguard of the feminization of the church in France in the seventeenth century.[12] Many other congregations followed, including the Daughters of Charity of Louise de Marillac and Vincent de Paul who traced their origins back to 1629 and devoted themselves to care for the poor rather than to education.

Between 1551 and 1650 forty-five new Catholic and twenty-six Protestant uni-versities were founded or restored.[13] Prominent among them was the Jesuits' Roman College first established by Ignatius Loyola himself in 1551 for Jesuit seminarians and re-established on a firm financial basis by Pope Gregory XIII in the 1580s and hence called the Gregorian University today. Soon associated with it was the German College, founded in 1552, which served as the model for the Greek College (1577), the English College (1578), and the other national colleges which were intended to prepare clergy for largely non-Catholic areas. So Rome became a centre for clerical education.

The fathers at Trent realized the formation and education of the diocesan clergy were key for reform; hence their decree that each diocese establish its own seminary. This decree eventually had far-reaching effects, but its imple-mentation took decades, even centuries. The quality of diocesan clergy did

12 Rapley, *The dévotes*, esp. pp. 5, 20–2, 60, 165, 193.
13 Willem Frijhoff, 'Patterns', in Ridder-Symoens, *A history of the university*, p. 71.

improve in some regions by the early seventeenth century. Whilst this was probably due in part to other factors, such as the Jesuit colleges, the seminaries deserve much of the credit for the substantial improvement of parish priests by the early eighteenth century. Tridentine seminaries came to enjoy their greatest success in France, though here too improvement was initially slow: by 1620, sixteen seminaries existed, most of them residences with as few as ten students who attended the local Jesuit college, but forty new ones were founded between 1642 and 1660. Seminary education in France was greatly aided by a new phenomenon, the societies of common life, that is, associations of priests who lived in community and practised evangelical poverty, chastity, and obedience but without taking formal vows: the French Oratory founded by Pierre de Bérulle in 1611; the Congregation of the Mission or Lazarists founded by Vincent de Paul in 1625; the Sulpicians dating from 1642, and the Eudists from 1643. They came to run many of the seminaries in France. Their spirituality focused on the priesthood. According to Bérulle, 'there are two types of persons, those who receive and those who communicate the spirit, the light, and the grace of Jesus. The first are all the faithful, the second are the priests.'[14] The common *esprit* increasingly evident in the French diocesan clergy grew in part out of this exalted view of the priesthood. Yet this conception of the priest's role, along with his education, the soutane now faithfully worn, and his more reserved deportment set him off more from his parishioners.

The early modern church employed many methods, some new, some old, to evangelize the faithful. The mendicant orders had long sent out preachers among them. What was now new in the popular missions undertaken first by Capuchins and Jesuits and then, especially in France, by Lazarists, Eudists, and Oratorians, was a clear strategy and method. Home missionaries preached first in towns and later to the populace in the countryside, which Jesuits in both Italy and Spain called their 'Indies' because of the religious ignorance and the uncouthness of the population. Still more crucial was the regular preaching in urban and rural parishes. Trent had insisted that the principal task of bishop and pastor alike consisted in preaching. The decades after Trent saw the publication of a number of works on preaching which suggested a variety of rhetorical styles. In addition, sermon collections were published to help pastors fulfil their obligation to preach on Sundays and feast days, for example the 600-page volume in Catalan of Andreu Capella, Bishop of Urgell, published in 1593.[15] Yet much time would elapse before pastors, especially in

---

14 Bérulle, cited in Taveneaux, *Catholicisme*, vol. 1, p. 60.
15 Kamen, *Phoenix and the flame*, p. 360.

rural areas, would be adequately prepared and willing to preach regularly. The burden of preaching remained with the religious orders, especially for the popular Advent and Lent series of sermons in the cities and towns.

Overlapping with the school and the sermon as a means of Christianization was regular religious instruction, or catechism. One can characterize the sixteenth century as the age of the catechism. In 1536, the Italian priest Castellino da Castello had launched in Milan his initiative of popular catechetical instruction for the young that resulted in the Confraternity of Christian Doctrine. By the death of Cardinal Borromeo in 1584, the archdiocese of Milan counted about 40,000 boys and girls in 740 schools, nearly one per parish, instructed by nearly 3,000 teachers.[16] Trent imposed upon pastors the duty of teaching catechism to children regularly, at least on Sundays and feast days. A number of catechisms came on the market intended to assist pastors and other religious educators, perhaps the most prominent being those of the German Jesuit Peter Canisius, who between 1555 and 1566 published separate catechisms for university students, adolescents, and children that, altogether, went through more than 200 editions before his death in 1597. But catechism instruction often encountered opposition from pastors as well as parents, who argued against keeping children indoors on Sunday afternoons. Some pastors taught catechism after the homily at mass. The effort at systematic instruction in preparation for first confession and first communion, which was introduced at this time, seems to have met with more success. Yet by mid-century many French pastors taught catechism regularly.

The mass, especially the Sunday and feast-day mass in the parish, remained the centre of Catholic worship, above all in rural areas. In towns and cities, the churches of the religious orders competed successfully with the parish churches, offering the faithful a choice in liturgical style and spirituality and sometimes engendering rivalry with the parish clergy. For the devout, confession and communion each month or at least four times a year became the standard by the early seventeenth century. Some historians have seen in the careful examination of conscience before confession a step in the direction of systematic, orderly thinking. The popular handbook for confessors composed by the Jesuit Juan Polanco at the direction of Ignatius Loyola, and published in 1564 at the urging of Roman authorities, considered a principal fruit of the sacrament to be the consolation of the penitent.[17] More frequent confession brought the faithful into regular contact with the clergy and augmented the

---

16 Paul F. Grendler, 'Borromeo and the schools of Christian doctrine', in Headley and Tomaro (eds.), *San Carlo Borromeo*, p. 165.
17 *Breve directorium ad confessarii ac confitentis munus recte obeundum*, pp. 3, 4, 16.

clergy's role. New and revived devotions came to the fore, many associated with confraternities. They often involved practices or doctrines that distinguished Catholics from Protestants and so promoted confessional identity, such as adoration of Christ present in the eucharist, veneration of the Virgin Mary, and prayer for the souls in purgatory. With more or less success, authorities attempted to banish profane or superstitious elements from processions, pilgrimages, and other observances. Catholics generally tolerated local customs and folk ways more readily than Protestants. Religious authorities and local leaders often reached tacit understanding.

Confraternities came to play an even more vital role in Catholic life in the course of the sixteenth century, just as church authorities attempted to submit them to greater control. Christopher Black has estimated that by 1600 in the large urban areas of Italy, every third or fourth male belonged to a confraternity at some point in his life, as did a lesser number of women and adolescents.[18] There existed a vast variety of these confraternities. Their expansion in number and membership, and their new emphasis on works of charity, represented to a degree a response to the growing number of poor and unfortunate, especially in the cities. Many confraternities were associated with religious orders and offered an alternative to the parish, especially in cities and towns. Bishops often fostered the foundation of at least one confraternity in each parish, even isolated ones, as a way of securing support for the pastor. Undoubtedly, friction arose between pastors and lay leaders of confraternities, but it is not clear how regularly this happened.

Both the Catholic Reform and the Reformation asserted the validity of the worldly, or lay, vocation. This affirmation, along with the attempt to demonstrate how to live a Christian life in the world, constituted a further effort to accommodate Christianity to early modern times. It reaffirmed the position of Renaissance humanism as well as of the renewed Thomism that spread out from Paris to Spain and Rome and produced outstanding theologians like the Dominican Domingo de Soto and the Jesuit Francisco Suarez. Both humanism and Thomism proposed an optimistic vision of human nature and a widespread harmony between nature and its completion in grace. A persistent strain of Augustinian pessimism, with an emphasis on man's sinfulness, ran counter to this and came to the fore particularly in French Jansenism, but it did not prevail. Ignatius Loyola had studied in Paris from 1528 to 1534, and not surprisingly the Jesuit Constitutions later recommended Aquinas's *Compendium of Theology* for the study of theology. His *Spiritual Exercises* fostered

18 Black, *Italian confraternities*, p. 270.

a world-affirming spirituality. God's creation remained fundamentally good even after original sin and humankind's later abuse of God's gifts. It also implied that the Christian could follow Christ in any career or state of life.

More important still than Ignatius in this regard was the gentle but firm Bishop of Geneva, Francis de Sales. Francis carried on spiritual direction through a vast correspondence, especially with women whose aspirations for a more profound Christian life impressed him. Among those was Louise de Chastel, twenty-year-old wife of the ambassador of the Duke of Savoy to the republic of Bern in whom Francis recognized a call from God to a life of 'devotion', as he put it. In 1607, he drew up a set of instructions to guide her in the ways of the spirit that were published in 1609 as the *Introduction to a Devout Life* addressed to a fictional 'Philothea', that is, to souls loving or in love with God, men or women, who 'live in town, within families, or at court, and by their state of life are obliged to live an ordinary life as to outward appearances'.[19] His descriptive, psychological method reminds one of Montaigne's *Essays*, which Francis knew well. At least forty editions of the *Introduction* appeared by Francis's death in 1622; it was read by Protestants as well as Catholics, often in expurgated versions, and it remains a Christian classic today.

Many others wrote in the same vein as Francis, if not with the same lucidity of style, illustrating how one could, and indeed ought to, live as a Christian in the world. From 1612 to 1615, four volumes came from the pen of the Spanish Jesuit Luis de la Puente entitled *Perfection in All the States of Christian Life*. The French Jesuit Nicholas Caussin published *The Holy Court* at Paris in late 1624, and editions and translations followed in all the major European languages until the century's end. Even courtiers and ladies-in-waiting, he contended, could live as good Christians, and he introduced a wealth of examples to prove his point. To this genre belonged the Antimachiavellian tradition that aimed to refute the declaration of Machiavelli in *The Prince* that a ruler or man of politics who consistently adhered to Christian moral principles could not achieve political success measured in terms of the acquisition and maintenance of power. Two authors founded this tradition, both publishing in 1589: the Flemish humanist Justus Lipsius with his *Six Books of Politics or Teaching on the State* and the Italian priest Giovanni Botero in his *Reason of State*. They attempted to meet Machiavelli on his own grounds of political practice and to show that his programme would only bring a state to ruin, whereas one based intelligently on Christian moral principles could, and indeed would, lead to a stable and powerful state. The popularity of these two books – they were the two most

---

19 De Sales, *Introduction to the devout life*, p. 33.

widely read political works of the first half of the seventeenth century – shows the extent to which the relationship between religion, morality, and politics engaged contemporaries as they became aware of the growth of the state.

The prolonged, painful dispute in France between the Jesuits and the Jansenists revolved around the relationship between the Christian and the world: more specifically, the value of human activity *vis-à-vis* divine action in the process of salvation and the need of the church to accommodate its moral teaching to a changing world. The Louvain theologian Cornelius Jansen's *Augustinus*, published in 1640, two years after his death, was imbued with a profound theological pessimism about the effects of original sin and seemed to deny the role of free will in human salvation. To Jesuit theologians this appeared to revert to the position of the Protestant Reformers. In addition, the priest and associate of Jansen, Jean Duvergier de Hauranne, Abbé de Cyran, and Antoine Arnauld, son of a prominent *parlementaire* family, questioned contemporary and especially Jesuit moral theology. Trent's insistence that confessors be better instructed had led to the composition of treatises on moral theology that aimed to prepare priests for the cases of conscience that they might expect to encounter, that is, to instruct them in casuistry. Occasionally these tomes, in their desire for thoroughness, laid out instances of unusual complexity that might seem inane. Yet these casuists performed a crucial function: the application of traditional principles to a changing society regarding, for example, the charging of interest on loans, or the freedom of a girl to choose her marriage partner. In his scintillating but one-sided *Provincial Letters*, published serially and anonymously in 1656/7, the mathematician and scientist Blaise Pascal held up to ridicule the Jesuit position on grace and a lax moral theology that he attributed to them. Jesuit authors responded, but they could not match Pascal's polemical skills. The Jansenist controversy long remained alive in France, but after the 1650s it became more a matter of politics than of theology. Pascal for his part seems to have feared that his *Provincial Letters* may have harmed not only the Jesuits but the cause of Christianity itself and so undertook to compose his own apology for the faith which, as his *Thoughts*, remained unfinished at his death in 1662.

Princes played a significant role in advancing the cause of Catholicism, and their militance also helped inflame the religious wars of the period. The church needed the support of the state, and the state for its part exercised increasing control over the church. Prominent as Counter-Reformation rulers were King Philip II of Spain (1556–98), Duke and then Elector Maximilian of Bavaria (1598–1651), and Emperor Ferdinand II (1619–37). All three aimed sincerely at the triumph of Catholicism, which they tended to equate with their own political advantage. Shortly after his assumption of rule in late 1596 as archduke in Inner Austria, Ferdinand embarked on a rigorous, often harsh recatholicization of the territory, despite warnings from councillors that such a campaign was politically unwise. Encouraged by Jesuits, Ferdinand felt himself called by God to restore Catholicism in his lands and was then confirmed in this sense of mission by his unanticipated success in Inner Austria. Soon after the dust settled following the Bohemian rebellion of 1618 and he was elected emperor in 1619, he initiated Counter-Reformation measures in the Austrian and Bohemian lands that would lead to the effective restoration of Catholicism, but not until the end of the century. Catholicism came to constitute one of the three pillars of the multi-ethnic Habsburg monarchy, along with the dynasty and the aristocracy.

Drawn increasingly into the conflict in Germany that became the Thirty Years' War, his forces and those of his ally Maximilian controlled much of north and central Germany by late 1627. Urged on by his Jesuit confessor, William Lamormaini, and supported by the Catholic electors, he promulgated in 1629 the fateful Edict of Restitution. It reclaimed for the Catholic Church the extensive church lands that had been seized, illegally according to the Catholics, by Protestants since the Peace of Augsburg in 1555. This extremist measure revealed the religious nature of the war for Ferdinand and Maximilian, alienated Protestant states hitherto loyal to Ferdinand, especially Saxony and Brandenburg, and helped provoke the Swedish invasion of 1630. Gustav Adolf's decisive victory over the Catholic forces at Breitenfeld in September 1631 reversed the whole course of the war. After the military balance had been re-established by the battle of Nördlingen in 1634, Ferdinand retreated from his militant programme, compromised on the Edict of Restitution, and concluded with Saxony in 1635 the Peace of Prague, to which most German states subsequently adhered. This agreement prepared the way for the Peace of Westphalia of 1648 which finally put an end to the religious wars on the Continent. After their disruption in many areas of Europe by the long war, the processes of reform and confessionalization would continue at least until early into the eighteenth century.

10

New religious orders for men

JOHN PATRICK DONNELLY, SJ

Introduction

Historians stress what is new in history, so the new religious orders of the Catholic Reformation attract more attention than reform movements in the older traditional orders of monks and friars. Since these older orders were much larger than most new orders, their efforts to reform probably contributed even more to reforming Catholicism. Some older orders, however, virtually disappeared. The crusading orders in Baltic lands, Spain and Portugal largely lost their reason for existence, and civic rulers took over most of their assets. Many bishops and cardinals felt that religious orders should be phased out altogether or amalgamated into four or so different types. Many bishops hated the exemptions from episcopal control and the privileges the papacy had conferred on the orders. Despite such attitudes, the period saw the creation of new male and female orders and congregations that reshaped Catholicism in the next 500 years.

The creation of new religious orders is usually a sign of Catholic vitality. The thirteenth century saw five new major orders of friars. The aftermath of the French Revolution and Napoleon saw dozens of new orders, especially of women. The fifteenth century was almost barren, while this chapter traces the rise of eighteen men's orders during the Catholic Reformation. None of these new orders were started by popes and few by bishops. Their founders were sometimes priests, sometimes laymen, who saw social and religious needs and gathered followers to answer those needs. Except possibly for the Spanish Discalced Carmelites, all the new orders stressed active ministry more than prayer, although none saw work and prayer as either/or alternatives. Many new orders added a fourth vow to the traditional ones of poverty, chastity and obedience, for instance to teach or care for orphans or the sick. Some took solemn vows, some took simple vows which were easier to dispense. Some congregations took no vows but did live in communities so that their lifestyle was similar to that of religious orders. Some new orders wore distinctive habits, as had earlier religious orders, but others adopted the cassock of parish priests. Often the new orders required a longer and more rigorous training than did the medieval orders. Most had both priests and lay brothers. Some, notably the Jesuits, were highly centralized; in others each community enjoyed considerable autonomy. Seven of them made teaching their main or only ministry. Most of the new orders tended to work with the poor and needy. Most encouraged frequent confession and weekly communion for both their own members and pious lay people. Most were confined to a single country during their formative decades, but almost all gradually spread to other countries. Many spread to Asia, Africa or the Americas, but all were slow to recruit new members from outside Europe. All were short on funds, but that had some advantages, notably that they rarely had to worry about interference from *in commendam* superiors who were not members of the order but controlled their finances.

Members in most of the new male religious orders fall into two groups: lay brothers who did low-skill jobs, largely around the community (e.g., cooks, porters, secretaries), and the priests and men in training for the priesthood. That division largely reflected social and class divisions in the larger society. Lay brothers usually came from the peasantry or urban working classes and seldom knew Latin, which was a prerequisite for priestly training. Some lay brothers were widowers who entered later in life; thus Giovanni Tristano, a respected architect, entered the Jesuits at forty. Most candidates entered religious orders between fifteen and twenty-two. The Theatines were probably the most aristocratic orders. Many of their candidates were already priests, as were those of the Roman Oratory. Most candidates of the teaching orders, the Jesuits and the French Oratorians, came from their students. Most were sons of merchants, administrators, lawyers and doctors. Younger sons of the nobility often entered the religious life. Thus the good manners of the Jesuits and the fact that three of their first five Generals were noblemen made the Jesuits an acceptable career for the nobility, especially after Duke Francis Borgia became a Jesuit. But many noble and wealthy families feared losing their sons and threatened to withdraw them from Jesuit schools, so Loyola barred accepting students from a Jesuit school without their parents' permission. In Spain only the Jesuits would accept candidates of Jewish ancestry; many such men entered, but in 1593 the Jesuits too, under pressure from Philip II, barred their doors. The Capuchins, who often worked among the peasantry and urban poor, and the Piarists, who taught their children, attracted many gifted young men from the lower classes.

The new Italian religious orders

The rule of St Francis of Assisi (*c.* 1181–1226) set such a high standard of poverty that its application resulted in numerous schisms among later Franciscans. Leo X in 1517 tried to consolidate various Franciscan factions in two juridically separate orders, the Conventuals and the stricter Observants but renewed calls for even stricter observance continued and resulted in four additional schisms during the sixteenth century. The most important of these led gradually to the full independence of the Capuchins (OFM Cap) as an order in 1619.

Unlike most of the other orders studied here, they have no canonized founder – rather they have always looked back to St Francis himself for inspiration. The first Capuchin vicars-general were flawed leaders. In 1525 Matteo da Bascio (*d.* 1552) left the Observants looking for a more austere life; he grew a beard and wore a habit with a pointed hood (cappuchino, whence Capuchins), practices which he traced back to St Francis and which the Capuchins later embraced. Matteo did not want to start a new order and later returned to the Observants. Ludovico da Fossombrone (*c.* 1498–*c.* 1560), a former soldier, took his place, drew up constitutions in 1529 and secured from Clement VII a bull that authorized the new lifestyle and conferred considerable privileges. But Ludovico alienated so many friars that he was forced to resign and was later expelled. Meanwhile many zealous Observants joined the Capuchins, who began expanding from their original base in the Marches of east-central Italy. This alarmed the Observants, who secured a new bull ordering former Observants to return, but the new pope, Paul III, did not enforce the bull, partly because two influential noble women, Vittoria Colonna and Caterina Cibo, supported the Capuchins. The new vicar-general, Bernardino d'Asti (1484–1554), although not charismatic, governed well, revised the constitutions and secured solemn papal approbation in 1536. Troubles returned with the fifth vicar-general, Italy's most charismatic preacher, Bernardino Ochino (1487–1564). His preaching took on a Protestant tone, and when he was asked to report to Rome and the Inquisition in 1542, he fled to Calvin's Geneva. The whole Capuchin order fell under suspicion, and calls for its dissolution arose. The order was exonerated after an investigation but was restricted to Italy until 1574.

Most of the early Capuchins lived on the outskirts of small towns and begged their food. They did street preaching and encouraged frequent confession and communion, but they rarely heard confessions lest they seem to intrude on the work of parish priests. They won universal favour for their heroic, even reckless, devotion to helping those stricken by plague. Of all the new orders the Capuchins grew the fastest, especially after 1574. Their membership grew to 8,803 by 1600 and 27,336 by 1700. They did not go into teaching and did not produce many scholars, but they did produce popular religious writers, and they cultivated a common touch which made them extremely effective preachers in missions to rural parishes. Their greatest preacher was St Lorenzo da Brindisi (1559–1619), who served as vicar-general (1602–5) and healed divisions within the order. He was also a learned theologian, gifted in seven languages; he doubled as a diplomat and military chaplain. Most of his later years were spent in central and eastern Europe, and his work carried him from Poland to Portugal, where he died.

During the sixteenth century the spiritual and material needs of the Italian people, ravaged by plague and war, inspired several leaders, most of them canonized saints, to found many small active religious orders or congregations. Meeting the Protestant challenge was seldom a major concern. Most of these orders are called Clerks Regular because they were clergy who followed the rule (*regula*) of a religious order. Because of their small size most of these orders attempted unions with other orders, but almost all these attempts proved abortive. Their history is traced here chronologically.

The first community of the Theatines or Clerks Regular (CRT, OT or OTheat) was started at Rome when four men took the traditional vows of poverty, chastity and obedience at St Peter's on 14 September 1524. Their leaders were Gaetano Thiene (1480–1547) and Giampietro Carafa (1479–1559, later Paul IV). Carafa came from a wealthy Neapolitan noble family and was an accomplished humanist and the Bishop of Chieti (Theate in Latin, whence the name Theatines). Carafa resigned his bishopric and served as the first superior. Later Paul III named him a cardinal and put him in charge of the newly founded Roman Inquisition, whose repressive measures he backed with all his heart. Later as Pope Paul IV (1555–9) he strove to uproot heresy and clerical abuse throughout Italy. He even suspected several leading cardinals of heresy. Gaetano (known as Saint Cajetan) was a more gentle soul. Before his vows he had travelled through northern Italy where he established confraternities to help poor people and victims of syphilis. He also encouraged people to frequent confession and communion, a cause that his followers embraced.

The first Theatines obtained papal authorization in 1524. Later Theatines took the three traditional vows after a year of novitiate; some were already priests, some were still in training, and some were lay brothers. Two things distinguished them from earlier religious orders: first, they recited the traditional priestly office in common, but without singing it; second, their vow of poverty forbade them to hold benefices or to beg. Rather they tried to live from alms which people offered spontaneously, and so they were chronically short of funds. Their main priestly work was aimed at the poor and the sick. Carafa drew up a letter of regulations which largely governed the order; after gradual modifications to his regulations official Constitutions were drawn up and published in 1604.

The Theatines fled to Venice from Rome in 1527 when Spanish soldiers sacked the city. Six years later they established a second community in Naples. They returned to Rome in 1557, and by 1570 they had also opened houses in Milan, Cremona and Piacenza. During the seventeenth century they had fifty communities in the Italian cities and had spread to Spain, Portugal, France, Germany, and Poland. During the last seven decades of that century they did some missionary work in Russia and India. By 1700 there were 1,400 Theatines, but then their number slowly declined. Many reforming bishops came from their ranks.

The mother church of the Clerks Regular of Saint Paul (CRSP) in Milan was dedicated to St Barnabas, so they quickly became known as the Barnabites. Saint Antonio Zaccaria (1502–39) with eight disciples started living as a community in 1530. Although trained in law and medicine, Zaccaria became involved in charitable work in his native Cremona; after ordination to the priesthood in 1528 he shifted his work to Milan. Initially the Barnabites took no vows, but in 1533 they successfully requested papal permission to take the three traditional vows and live as a religious community. Their rule, first drafted in 1542, received its final form in 1579. Their spiritual mentor was the Dominican friar Carione de Crema, but he became suspected of heresy, and the public self-flagellations practised by Zaccaria and his disciples alienated many people. They were expelled from Venetian territory in 1551. Although Paul III vindicated them after an examination in 1535, suspicion and hostility slowed their growth.

Not until 1557 were they able to set up a new community in Pavia. By 1567 they had eighty-one members scattered in six small communities in the Po Valley and one in Rome, but St Charles Borromeo, the Cardinal-Archbishop of Milan, supported them strongly and put them in charge of a minor seminary. Thereafter their numbers began to climb – 322 men by 1608 and 726 by 1700. Communities were established in France (1610) and Austria (1626). In Italy they concentrated on preaching, stressing moral reform, and on encouraging frequent confession and communion and devotion to the eucharist. They held mental prayer sessions in common both mornings and evenings and made daily use of the discipline. In France they also staffed some schools. Because of their small numbers the Barnabites sought mergers with the Jesuits, the Somascans, the Oratorians and the French Fathers of Christian Doctrine, but nothing came of these proposals. In 1623 they did absorb a still smaller congregation, the Fathers of Our Lady of the Assumption.

The Clerks Regular of Somascha (CRS, also known as the Somascans or the Order of Saint Jerome Aemilian) traced their roots to a group of clerks and laymen at Venice who began living as a community in 1528. Their leader was St Girolamo Emiliani (1481–1537), who remained a layman and died at Somascha, a town near Bergamo, whence the name of the order. He was a former soldier whose religious conversion led him to devote his life to helping the many orphans created by war and plague. He brought together a small group of clergy and laymen to care for the orphans. Although orphans remained the main focus of the nascent order, the Somascans gradually began working in parishes, training seminarians, and teaching catechism. A female branch was soon formed. Paul III approved the Somascans in 1540. In 1568 Pius V gave a fuller approval to the Somascans and to their work in seminaries, colleges and parishes as well as with orphans, and they began taking solemn vows. The Somascans, urged by Giampietro Carafa, entered into a union with the Theatines, but that only lasted from 1547 to 1555. Discussions about uniting with the Capuchins or the Jesuits came to nothing. The seminary at Venice and colleges at Como and Rome were among their more important communities. By 1600 the Somascans had 438 members, but their numbers barely increased during the seventeenth century. In 1616 the Somascans entered a union with the Congregation of Christian Doctrine of France (Doctrinaires), but the two groups separated in 1647.

No saint of the Catholic Reformation was so attractive as Filippino Neri (1515–95), the founder of the Oratorians (Filipini or Congregation of the Oratory, CO). Born and raised in Florence, in 1533 he tried a business career at Naples for a few months and hated it. He went to Rome where he spent eighteen years as an urban hermit wandering the streets, now smiling and mirthful, now deep in prayer. He was ordained there in 1551. He gathered young men, encouraged them to frequent confession and communion, and discussed the gospels with them. As his audience grew, he secured a room, called the Oratory, at the church of San Giovanni dei Fiorentini, where they could meet for discussion and prayer. In 1567 he and a group of priests and laymen began living together as a community, but without taking vows or having an official superior. The members contributed to the community expenses from their income or patrimonies. Community living, which is more central to the religious life than vows of poverty, chastity and obedience, largely implies those vows. Neri saw his followers as models for diocesan priests. They heard confessions, preached and sponsored participation in religious music, from which sprang the musical genre of the oratorio. Gregory XIII recognized them as a congregation of priests in 1575. Neri himself wrote no rule, but later rules based on his practices were redacted several times. The Oratorian constitutions, which Paul V approved in 1612, owed much to Francesco Maria Tarugi.

After 1575 the Oratorians began setting up communities in various Italian cities, most notably at Naples in 1586. There conditions were far different than at Rome. Most of the Roman Oratorians were well-educated and mature priests when they entered. At Naples they were young laymen, often from lower-class backgrounds. They needed a novitiate for spiritual formation as well as training in theology. For Neri the superior was to serve as a role model, a first among equals rather than a person in command. At Naples the superior gave orders. Although the Naples Oratorians did not take religious vows, they were closer to the practice of religious orders, and most of the sixty-one Oratorian communities set up in Italy between 1591 and 1700 followed the Naples model. By the end of the seventeenth century there were some 150 Oratorian communities around the world, strongest in Italy, Spain and Portugal, but also in Latin America, Poland, Belgium, and even India. Each community was autonomous. The French Oratorians, who were even closer to traditional religious orders, will be discussed later.

In 1573 St Giovanni Leonardi (1541–1609) founded at Lucca the Clerks Regular of the Mother of God (also known as the Matritani or Leonardini, CRMD). In 1603 the order's first general congregation elected Leonardi superior general for life and approved the rules he had gathered and organized over the previous thirty years. The papacy approved the congregation in 1595 and raised it to the status of an order in 1621. The Matritani worked in parishes but lived as communities. They dedicated all their churches to Mary and celebrated her many feast days with great pomp. By the time of Leonardi's death they had communities in only two cities, Lucca and Rome (established in 1601), and their work remained restricted to Italy for the next two centuries. Protestants were stronger in Lucca than any other Italian city, so the Matritani tried to oppose Protestantism by preaching on the decrees of the Council of Trent and teaching catechism. A short-lived union with the Piarists between 1614 and 1617 fell apart because the Matritani stressed parish work and the Piarists were dedicated to teaching.

In 1578 St Carlo Borromeo founded at Milan a small local order named the Oblates of Saint Ambrose after Milan's early bishop. Nine years previously Borromeo had tried to persuade St Philip Neri to send Oratorians to work in his archdiocese, but Neri sent only four men and then abruptly withdrew them when the imperious Borromeo insisted on controlling them. After consulting Neri about Oratorian practices Borromeo introduced some key differences in the rules he drew up for his Oblates. They were to recite the daily office in community and were directly under obedience to the bishop. Gregory XIII approved their rule. The Oblates spread to France and England in the nineteenth century.

The only new order begun in southern Italy was the Clerks Regular Minor (Chierici regolari minori, Caracciolini, CRM) founded at Naples by St Francesco Caracciolo together with Giovanni Agostino Adorno. Sixtus V approved them in 1588. Their communities included both priests and brothers under superiors elected for three-year terms. They tried to stress humility, ministry to prisoners, especially those condemned to death, and the perpetual adoration of the eucharist, at which members of a community took turns. Their second community was set up at Rome in 1595, and in the early seventeenth century they spread to Madrid, Valladolid, Alcalá, and Salamanca. In addition to the three usual vows, the Caracciolini added a fourth, not to seek church dignities.

St Camillus de Lellis (1550–1614) was another former soldier. After gambling away his possessions in 1575 he worked for the Capuchins and then joined them briefly as a lay brother, but he was dismissed because he had a war wound that refused to heal. Next he served in a hospital at Rome. There St Philip Neri was his confessor and encouraged him to devote his life to the sick. He studied for the priesthood at the Jesuit Roman College. In 1584 he gathered some followers and started a small congregation of priests and brothers without vows. In 1591 the pope raised them to the status of an order; they took the usual three vows plus a vow to serve the sick, including plague victims. They were known officially as the Order of Clerks Regular, Servants of the Sick, but more popularly as the Camillians (OSCam). In 1594 their communities started living right within the hospitals where they worked. Their main community was established at Naples in 1588, and the order grew fairly rapidly. When Camillus died there were 330 professed members in fifteen Italian cities. Gradually they began to minister to sick people in their own homes. They were not on the cutting edge of medical science, but they did insist on cleanliness, no minor matter in the hospitals of the time. Camillians wore a habit with a distinctive red cross, later taken over by the modern Red Cross.

The Piarists or Scolopi (Poor Clerks Regular of the Pious Schools) were founded at Rome in 1597 by a Spaniard, St José de Calasanz (1557–1648, known in Italy as Calasanzio). José studied both law and theology and was ordained in Spain before he came to Rome seeking a post in the papal curia; there he worked

with confraternities which helped the poor and taught catechism. Although the
Jesuit colleges scattered through Italy did not charge tuition, they did demand
that prospective students could read and write. Seldom could working-class
parents pay for elementary schooling, so their children usually could not
attend Jesuit schools. Here was an obvious need, and Calasanz together with
some companions started a school at Rome that taught poor students the
four Rs – religion, reading, writing and arithmetic – plus enough Latin for
students to get into the Jesuit colleges. They financed the school by begging
and donations from wealthy churchmen. By 1610 they had 700 students, more
than most Italian Jesuit colleges. The twenty members of the teaching staff
included priests and pious laymen living together as a community. In 1617 Paul
V authorized them to set up as a separate religious order whose members took
a fourth vow to teach. During the next seventeen years they started thirteen
schools in Italian cities. In 1631 they opened a school in Moravia. Fifteen years
later there were thirty-seven communities with 500 Piarists.

Their classes usually met for five hours a day, with a break for lunch, and continued all year round except during the hottest part of summer. The growing
demand for teachers, however, induced Calasanz to lower admission standards and require less training among his men. Most of the Piarists were lay
brothers and taught elementary courses in Italian; the priests taught advanced
students in Latin. This created divisions and tensions in the communities. The
Jesuits, Barnabites and Somascans, who were also involved in teaching, often
resented the Piarists. Noble patrons were their main source of financing, but
some noblemen felt that educating the working class would lead to unrest.
When critics questioned the orthodoxy of the order a commission of cardinals
investigated it in 1642 and relieved the aging and autocratic Calasanz of office.
Worse was to follow. The Piarists were forbidden to accept novices, and those
with vows were permitted to seek entry into other orders. Two hundred left,
three hundred stayed. But the Piarists also had supporters, and these prevailed.
The papacy recognized them as a religious congregation in 1656 and as a religious order with solemn vows in 1669. Again they could take in novices, and
their numbers reached 950 by 1676. Catholics who opposed the Jesuits invited
the Piarists to Habsburg lands in Germany in the 1630s. During the eighteenth
century they spread to Spain and the Polish-Lithuanian Commonwealth.

The Jesuits

The Society of Jesus (the Jesuits, SJ) was the most important religious order
founded during the sixteenth century; it quickly outnumbered the other new

orders except the Capuchins. At the death of their founder Ignatius of Loyola (1491–1556) there were a thousand Jesuits, by 1600 there were some 8,500, and by 1700 they counted 20,000. Their impact was greater than that of the Capuchins, who largely worked among the peasantry. The Jesuits tended to work in cities and among the middle and upper classes. Their range of ministries was more diversified than that of other orders.

Loyola was a Basque courtier and not a soldier, but he did serve several weeks as a gentleman volunteer. In 1521 he was wounded fighting for Charles V against the French at Pamplona and underwent a religious conversion while convalescing at his family's castle. After a pilgrimage to Jerusalem and learning Latin at Barcelona, he briefly attended the universities of Alcalá and Salamanca before transferring to the University of Paris (1528–38) where he gathered six companions. In 1534 the seven took a vow to work for souls in Jerusalem. They and three new recruits from Paris gathered at Venice in 1537, but war between Venice and the Turks prevented their sailing. These first ten companions included five Spaniards, two Frenchmen, two Savoyards and a Portuguese. Of the Spaniards, all but Francis Xavier remained in Italy most of their remaining years. The other orders discussed previously were confined to Italy during their opening decades; the Jesuits were international from the start and quickly spread through Catholic Europe and beyond. Since they could not go to Jerusalem, they put themselves at the service of Paul III, who gave them permission to be ordained and sent them to preach in the cities of north Italy. Rather than work as so many freelance priests, the companions decided to form a religious order, the Society of Jesus, which Paul III approved in 1540. They elected Loyola their superior general (later called simply the general) and commissioned him to draft constitutions.

The constitutions, which were approved by the first Jesuit General Congregation in 1558, contained many innovations. The general was to serve for life and appoint all other important superiors so that authority was far more centralized and less democratic than in other orders. How to live the vow of poverty has always caused tensions in religious orders and repeatedly split the Franciscans. Loyola's stress on centralized authority and obedience rather than on poverty helped keep the Jesuits united. Yet Loyola frequently urged flexibility in applying the rules. Jesuits were divided into four groups: lay brothers who engaged mainly in physical work within the communities, scholastics in training for the priesthood, coadjutor priests, and the professed fathers. Only the professed fathers, men noted for zeal and learning, were allowed to take solemn vows. In other religious orders, all members took solemn vows. Jesuits with only simple vows could be easily dismissed if they wanted to leave or if they failed to live up to high standards. Voting rights were restricted to the professed fathers, only 3 per cent of all Jesuits at Loyola's death. That percentage grew sharply during the coming decades as more Jesuits completed their studies. Professed fathers took a fourth vow, to go on missions when the pope sent them. This was not a vow of unrestricted obedience to the pope, but it did encourage Jesuit loyalty to the papacy.

Jesuits kept their family names. They did not wear a distinctive habit. They read the divine office privately to save time for their ministries and did not sing or recite it in common, as did other religious orders. They had no obligatory physical penances. They had no parallel order of nuns. Their novitiate and later training were considerably longer than in most religious orders. Their Constitutions were far longer and more detailed than the previous rules for monks and friars. These innovations and the seeming arrogance of the Jesuits in calling themselves the Society of Jesus often fostered resentment among other religious.

Several new orders restricted their ministry: to serving the sick, helping orphans, or teaching. The Jesuits embraced an unprecedented range of ministries. Jesuit churches were usually attached to their colleges and were rarely official parishes, but the Jesuits did engage in preaching, encouraging frequent confession and communion, teaching catechism, and giving the *Spiritual Exercises*.

Jesuits esteemed missionary work beginning with St Francis Xavier, and by Loyola's death they were working in Brazil, Ethiopia, India, Indonesia, Malaysia, and Japan. Later the Jesuits spread their work to Spanish America, opening pioneer colleges in Lima (1568) and Mexico City (1573). To evangelize native Americans and protect them from Spanish and Portuguese raiders, they established reductions, semi-independent colonies where Indians attended schools, learned catechism, reading, and new agricultural techniques, and developed music which blended native and western traditions. Matteo Ricci (1552–1610), a gifted linguist, entered China in 1583; in 1601 he set up a Jesuit house at Beijing, where he won favour with the emperor. The Jesuits continued to enjoy imperial favour for nearly two centuries, and this provided a shield for Christian missionaries working elsewhere in China. The court Jesuits proved key middlemen in teaching the Chinese about the West and vice versa. Ricci and his Jesuit successors adopted the clothing of court mandarins and argued that most of Chinese culture, for instance ancestor worship, needed only slight modification to become compatible with Christian faith and practice. Other missionaries objected, and a papal declaration of 1710 agreed with their objections.

The Jesuits encouraged all their missionaries to send reports to Rome; these were often published to foster financial support and attract young men to the order, but they also spread knowledge of other cultures to the West. Their records remain important historical sources today.

The Jesuits also worked in 'the other Indies', rural Europe, where the peasants had only a rudimentary grasp of the Christian faith. Thus in 1590 the Jesuit General Claudio Aquaviva ordered every Jesuit Province to assign six to twelve Jesuits to evangelizing rural areas. They were sent out in pairs to villages where they preached, taught catechism and heard confessions. In this work the Jesuits were second only to the Capuchins. Jesuits also worked in city hospitals and prisons. Although again second to the Capuchins, Jesuits often served as military chaplains. It was dangerous work: thus ten Jesuit chaplains died at the siege of Ostend in 1600. Jesuits often served as royal confessors or court-preachers at Paris, Vienna, Lisbon, and Munich, but not at Madrid. Royal confessors had considerable influence in moral and religious questions. The Jesuits tried to avoid serving as inquisitors, not because they objected to the Inquisition, but because their participation would increase tensions with the Dominicans, who supplied most inquisitors.

The first communities that Loyola envisioned for the Jesuits were called Professed Houses where the professed fathers would live; attached would be a church where the Jesuits would preach, give the *Spiritual Exercises* and administer the sacraments. Professed Houses, largely because they were forbidden to have fixed income and depended on alms, enjoyed little success.

Loyola and his first companions did not originally plan to become educators, but Jesuit schools gradually became the main Jesuit ministry. Jesuit colleges could have fixed incomes and were initially residences for Jesuits in training who took courses at nearby universities, for instance at Coimbra and Padua. The real pioneer Jesuit college for lay students, not young Jesuits, was opened at Messina in 1548. Encouraged by the Spanish viceroy, the city government provided funding. Loyola sent a team of gifted Jesuits to get the college off to a good start. Soon other Sicilian towns were asking for colleges, then requests from Italian and Spanish cities came flooding in. Loyola usually declined requests that did not provide funding for at least fourteen Jesuits. Claudio Aquaviva, General of the Society from 1581 to 1615 when Jesuit influenced peaked, claimed he refused 150 requests for colleges between 1581 and 1590. By 1615 the Jesuits had 372 colleges, at first mainly in Italy, Portugal and Spain, then gradually spreading to France, Germany and Poland. The colleges became the main recruiting ground for young Jesuits, but many had to be turned away because funds to train and feed them were short during the first century. The Jesuit colleges remained the largest and most coherent educational system in the world till the Bourbon monarchs pressured the papacy into suppressing the Jesuits in 1773. The new Jesuit colleges, which charged no tuition, threatened the jobs of lay teachers everywhere. Universities also felt threatened by the Jesuit colleges, which gradually expanded their curriculum upward so that it overlapped with university courses. At Paris, Louvain, Padua, Lima and elsewhere opposition from the universities forced the Jesuit colleges to scale back or close.

Loyola was much struck by the superiority of the organized, step-by-step curriculum at the University of Paris compared to the more haphazard and ineffective training he got at Alcalá and Salamanca; his Jesuit Constitutions laid down rules for Jesuit education which drew on his Paris experience. The new Jesuit colleges, most of which trained students from roughly ten to eighteen years old, largely followed the new humanistic studies. Usually students needed some skill at Latin before admission. The curriculum stressed Latin authors and skill at writing and speaking Latin; Greek literature was less emphasized. Catechism was usually taught only once a week, but Catholic students were expected to attend mass daily and go to confession monthly. These last requirements did not apply to Protestant students, who were not uncommon in eastern Europe and Germany, where the Jesuits had colleges at Cologne, Munich and Vienna even before Loyola's death. Students took part in frequent classroom disputations, and Jesuit schools drummed up support by inviting parents and town elites to public orations by both students and faculty. Later Jesuit colleges were famous for elaborate dramas which stressed religious themes. As the number of colleges grew, so did the need to systematize their curricula. Initially distinguished Jesuit scholars drew up model curricula which the generals encouraged colleges to follow. In 1586, 1591 and 1599 committees drew up a plan of studies (*Ratio Studiorum*). The 1599 *Ratio Studiorum* remained in effect till the Jesuits were suppressed in 1773 and was revised when the Jesuits were restored in 1814. In 1599 the Ratio was on the cutting edge of training for the upper classes, but it became increasingly outmoded as the decades passed. It did allow for some flexible application, with special rules for different countries. During the eighteenth century the Jesuits introduced more mathematics, science and history into their colleges.

During the fourteenth and fifteenth centuries the *via moderna* based on the writings of Scotus and Ockham dominated the study of philosophy and theology. Several factors led to a revival of the *via antiqua*, especially of Thomism, in the sixteenth century. Lutheranism pushed out Nominalism at many German universities where it had been strong. Several eminent Dominicans led a revival of Thomism, especially Cardinal Cajetan (Tommaso de Vio, 1469–1536) in Italy and Francisco de Vitoria (c. 1483–1546) in Spain. The *Summa theologiae* of Aquinas quickly replaced the *Sententiae* of Peter Lombard as the standard text in theology. The Capuchins chose St Bonaventure as their official theologian. The Discalced Carmelites and the Jesuits chose Aquinas. Loyola's choice of Aquinas was critical, given the spread of Jesuit schools. Although only the small advanced classes in those colleges taught philosophy and theology, many leading philosophers and theologians in Catholic Europe came from those schools.

The most influential early Jesuit theologians were St Peter Canisius (1521–97) and St Robert Bellarmine (1542–1621); both wrote polemical works against Protestants, catechisms republished in hundreds of editions, and popular devotional books. Francisco Suarez (1544–1606) was a major theologian but even more important for his philosophical and legal treatises.

Spiritual writings have always been more popular than theological works. Ironically Loyola's *Spiritual Exercises* (Latin edition at Rome in 1548) is the most influential and popular book ever written by a Jesuit; it has gone through some 5,000 editions in virtually all modern languages. Ironically, because Loyola was a precise but not a gifted writer; the book was not meant to be read, and Loyola ordered that it should not be given to anybody who had not already made the *Spiritual Exercises*. Those who have not made the *Exercises* will find it a maze of rules and meditations – it is somewhat like reading a cookbook: one must first bake the cake and eat it, and only then judge the recipe. The *Spiritual Exercises* is a manual to help directors guide people through thirty days of meditation and prayer (the *Exercises*) designed to reform their lives. In this the *Exercises* have proved amazingly successful, although those willing to dedicate thirty days were already well on the way to reform. Almost from the start, Jesuits have used shorter versions of the *Exercises*, three days to a week, for people who had less time available. Jesuit novices usually made the full *Spiritual Exercises* shortly after joining the order; later Jesuits made an annual eight-day retreat based on the *Exercises* so that the *Exercises* became the foundation of their spiritual lives. Among the many other Jesuit spiritual writers were Alfonso Rodriguez (1538–1616) and Luis de la Puente (1554–1624). The multi-volume works of them both were translated into many languages and were printed in more than 300 editions.

Most religious orders had ties to lay confraternities. Thus Loyola set up three Roman confraternities for the wealthy to help ex-prostitutes, young women in danger of becoming prostitutes, and impoverished noblemen. At Seville the Jesuits set up a confraternity to teach black slaves catechism. The most important Jesuit-sponsored confraternities were the Marian sodalities. These were usually linked to Jesuit colleges where the students elected their lay prefect but the Jesuit superior appointed the Father Director. All these sodalities worldwide were linked to that at the Collegio Romano, and the Jesuit General theoretically had the final voice on membership. Different groups – nobles, lawyers, people working in various trades and crafts – had their own sodalities for greater solidarity. Thus the Jesuit college at Naples in 1595 had seven different sodalities, one with 600 members. It was not unusual for half the students at a Jesuit college to belong to the college sodalities, and the alumni continued to belong. The sodalities were a major force in spreading Jesuit spirituality.

New orders in Spain

Spain played the commanding military role in the Counter-Reformation but supplied only two new male religious orders, the Brothers Hospitallers and Discalced Carmelites. Neither fit the Counter-Reformation image of soldiers of God.

José Cuidad (1495–1550, known as St John of God), who founded the Hospitallers, was a Portuguese ex-soldier who ran a religious bookstore in Granada and took poor people into his home. In 1537 he and some friends formed a community. Its members worked in hospitals and were not ordained, but they did take the three traditional vows of poverty, chastity and obedience plus a fourth vow to help sick people. Constitutions were drawn up after his death, and the order received papal approval in 1572. The new order, which soon spread to the Spanish colonies in the Americas, had 626 members by 1600 and 2,046 by 1700.

Most of the new religious orders were started by men for men; later they added a branch for women. The reverse was true for the male Discalced Carmelites. Teresa Sánchez de Ahumada y Cepeda (1515–82, known as St Teresa of Avila) was the sixteenth century's greatest mystic and arguably its greatest woman writer. She entered the Carmelite convent at Avila in 1536 and over the next twenty years her deepening religious experiences convinced her that the Carmelite order badly needed reform in both its female and male branches. By 1567 St Teresa had succeeded in establishing two reformed convents for

Carmelite nuns. She felt her nuns needed Carmelite confessors who shared their ideals, so she discussed a parallel reform among male Carmelites with Giovanni-Battista Rossi, general of the Carmelites, who was then visiting and trying to reform the male Carmelites in Spain. He supported her project, and a tiny convent of male Discalced Carmelites opened at Avila in 1568. It had only three members, among them St John of the Cross (1542–91), the great poet and premier theologian of mysticism. The name Discalced Carmelites comes from the sandals its members wore instead of the shoes worn by the unreformed Calced Carmelites. Sandals became a symbol, but the new branch of Carmelites insisted on many other austere features of the original rule approved by Innocent IV in 1247. They faced the same opposition from the Calced friars that the Capuchins had faced from the Observant Franciscans, partly because the new branch was drawing off many excellent friars, partly because its austerity seemed a reproach to the older branch. The tensions increased when Jerome Gracián was appointed visitor to reform the order in Spain and proceeded to establish more Discalced convents. The Calced fought back and even kidnapped and imprisoned John of the Cross at Toledo for eight months till he escaped. Philip II granted the Discalced the right to establish a separate province in 1581. They held their first general chapter in 1588; Clement VIII recognized them as an independent order five years later. Gradually they spread, but differences arose so that there were soon two almost independent orders, one in Italy and later in France, Germany, Belgium and Poland where the friars emphasized pastoral ministries, the other in Spain, Portugal and their colonies where the friars stressed prayers and the mystical tradition enshrined in the writings of St Teresa and St John of the Cross. The Discalced friars grew from 1,000 in 1600 to 5,000 by 1700, but the Calced Carmelites remained far more numerous in early modern Europe.

France

Eight religious wars between Catholics and Huguenots ravaged France from 1562 to 1598 and slowed efforts to reform French Catholicism. A remarkable religious revival during the next fifty years gave rise to several new religious orders in France, most of which drew inspiration from Philip Neri and the Oratorians. The spiritual writer (and later cardinal) Pierre de Bérulle (1575–1629) founded the first French Oratorian community at Paris in 1611; by 1651 there were 431 French Oratorians. The French communities were less independent and more homogeneous than those in Italy. They had a superior general elected for life and held triennial General Chapters, but like the Italian Oratorians they were technically societies of common life, not religious orders, since they did not take the three traditional vows. Unlike the Italians, their main work was teaching and not pastoral ministries. They had twenty-two colleges by 1700 and were training priests in nineteen of the seminaries mandated by Trent, which the French bishops were slowly establishing. The French Oratorians gradually became rivals of the Jesuits, partly because many of them were inclined to Gallicanism or Jansenism, partly because their rival colleges offered a more modern curriculum and featured a galaxy of fine scholars.

In 1592 César de Bus (1544–1607) and Jean Baptiste Romillon (1543–1622) founded the Doctrinaires (Pères de la doctrine chrétienne) at Avignon to teach poor people. Five years later they received papal approval. But their communities split when de Bus urged that they take a vow of obedience, something Romillon opposed. As a result Romillon and eleven communities which supported him joined the French Oratorians in 1619. De Bus's supporters joined the Somascans until 1647, when they broke away. They began taking simple vows of poverty, chastity and obedience in 1659 and devoted themselves mainly to teaching.

The most successful of the new French congregations was the Vincentians (Congregation of the Mission, Lazarists, VSC). In 1626 their founder, St Vincent de Paul (c. 1581–1660), established their first community in Paris at the priory of St Lazarus. They received papal approval in 1632 and counted 500 members and twenty-three communities by 1660. After 1636 they slowly spread to Italy, Ireland, and Poland. A general assembly in 1668 mandated that they take simple vows, but they continued wearing the traditional soutane of French priests. Their superior general was elected for life. Their main work, as their title suggests, was giving revivalist missions in the countryside, but they also staffed fifteen seminaries, directed retreats and continued their founder's ministry to galley slaves of the French Mediterranean fleet.

St Jean Eudes (1601–80) was an Oratorian working in Normandy and Brittany, but he founded the new Congregation of Jesus and Mary (CJM, Eudists) in 1643 at Caen after his superiors opposed his plan to establish a seminary at Caen. Members did not take public vows. By 1670 the Eudists were teaching at six seminaries in Normandy and Brittany and preaching parish missions throughout France. Similar to the Eudists were the Sulpicians (Society of Priests of St Sulpice) which the spiritual writer Jean Jacques Olier (1608–57) founded at Paris in 1642. They were diocesan priests but lived in community; by 1657 they were operating five seminaries in France. Their constitutions were approved in 1664.

Despite the loss of many countries to Protestantism the Catholic Church was in better shape in 1650 than in 1500. For the first time it could claim to be a worldwide church. Most of its clergy were better educated and more zealous. The laity knew their faith and practised it better than during the Middle Ages. In this the reform of old religious orders and the work of new ones played a crucial role.

Female sanctity, 1500–1660

GABRIELLA ZARRI

Introduction

During the Renaissance and early modern period, female religious life emerged with extreme vivacity. Scholars agree that both the socio-economic and juridical condition of women's lives deteriorated during the Renaissance. They also agree that religion, on the other hand, provided a means for different forms of female affirmation to offset and even-out the misogynist cultural currents that were present and driven by churches.[1] Socially, sanctity was valued and was pursued both by licit means, that is, means relevant to the very nature of religious faith, and by illicit.

Between 1500 and 1660, women expressed their religiousness according to traditional models that were valued differently as the political, social, and cultural situations proposed and imposed new conditions of life upon them. At the same time, religious conflicts and the plurality of religions generated new models of sanctity but at times reproduced the old ones. Considering the universality of the aforementioned problems, I intend to trace the evolutionary lines of female sanctity, starting with the most representative experiences of religious life during the period indicated, and to proceed in chronological order. I will not consider the approved model of sanctity exclusively, but will bear in mind the proscribed as well, while also referring to counter-models.

In outlining the evolution of female sanctity, I will avail myself of traditional representations of Christianity while demonstrating the active role of women in interpreting such representations or in generating new ones. The models can be found in some principal chronological periods: the first decades of the sixteenth century; the period of the Protestant Reformation and the Council of Trent; and the period of the Counter-Reformation and Catholic renewal.

---

1 Kelly, *Did women have a Renaissance?* pp. 19–50; Herlihy, 'Did women have a Renaissance?' pp. 15–16; Ottavia, *Introduzione*.

Models of female sanctity in the first decades of the sixteenth century: mystical and prophetic sanctity

Between the fifteenth and sixteenth centuries, contingent historical elements favoured the continuation of the mystical model of female sanctity that was asserted in the late Middle Ages, and in particular extolled the aspect of political prophecy exemplified by Bridget of Sweden and Catherine of Siena.[2] Indeed, the fall of Constantinople in 1453 and the start of the Italian Wars in 1494, which gave way to the broader conflicts between France and the Empire, were events that awakened fear at a popular level and that put the Italian seignories in danger and caused conflict among them. The fall of the Medici in Florence and the declaration of the liberal government supported by the Ferrarese Dominican Girolamo Savonarola, who presented himself as a prophet sent by God to reform the city, facilitated and justified the resumption of political prophecy.[3] It is in this context that the visions of the Blessed enlightened by God and endowed with mystical gifts were particularly venerated, to the point of giving rise to attempts on the part of princes to hoard charismatics who demonstrated prophetic gifts or who were marked on their bodies by some sign of God's blessing, such as stigmata. Thefts of sacred relics during the medieval period happened later in regard to living saints. The most famous case is that of the abduction of the stigmatized tertiary Lucia Brocadelli da Narni by Ercole I d'Este, Duke of Ferrara.[4] Kept in a tertiary convent in Viterbo, the nun was considered a precious treasure by the rulers of the city, and not even the repeated briefs of Pope Alexander VI, who ordered she be handed over to Ercole I d'Este, could induce the people of Viterbo to give up their saint. Ercole I therefore put a plan into action that was also proof of his astuteness as a skilled combatant. Without attacking the city, he sent his archers under the walls to retrieve the stigmatized woman, smuggling her out in a basket. After reaching Ferrara with the procession that accompanied Lucrezia Borgia, future bride of Alfonso I d'Este, Lucia was for many years a valued counsellor of the prince, and the blood that flowed from her wounds was an ever-fertile source of new relics.

A contemporary of Lucia was the Dominican tertiary Colomba Guadagnoli who, being already known for her rigidly austere life, decided to travel from her native city of Rieti to Perugia, where she was received as a saint by the

---

2 Vauchez, *La sainteté en Occident*; idem, *Sainthood in the later Middle Ages*.
3 Weinstein, *Savonarola and Florence*; Polizzotto, *The elect nation*.
4 Geary, *Furta sacra*; Zarri, *Lucia da Narni*, pp. 99–116; Matter, *Prophetic patronage*, pp. 105–19.

populace and by the Baglioni. The Baglioni were the lords of that land and they begged her to stay in their city as protector and patroness. There were also cases in Mantua: Osanna Andreasi, a Dominican tertiary who suffered each Friday the pains of the Passion, lived among the Gonzaga family, while nearby, in a convent of the duchy, the Blessed Stefana Quinzani led a religious life. Each of these mystical and penitent women was also subject to revelations and visions and each exerted herself to promote a reform of customs and the church in direct relationship with the princes of central Italy and the Po Valley. This movement, which represents an explicit example of the political use of prophecy, has generally been associated with the Italian female living saints, but it appears as a paradigmatic model applicable also in other countries and other historical periods. Particularly marked in the small Italian seignories from the beginning of the sixteenth century to around 1530,[5] the movement had offspring all over Europe. In New Castile, the Blessed of Piedrahita, known by the name of Maria de Santo Domingo and protected by the dukes of Alba, was familiar with and imitated Lucia da Narni;[6] in the territories of the Empire, a false saint, Anna Laminit, found a position as counsellor at the court of Maximilian I and was protected by the Welsers, the imperial bankers;[7] in France, the example of Joan of Arc was certainly not extinguished with her burning at the stake, even though the living saint of the French court at the start of the sixteenth century was male: the venerated founder of the Minims, St Francis of Paola.[8]

Although exceptional penitents and mystics, the living saints drew their principal power from their prophetic and thaumaturgic ability. According to the hagiographic construction of their biographies, which combined a position of struggle à la Savanarola with judicial astrology, as prophetesses they were able to foresee events with greater certainty than were the astrologers who had great influence at the courts of the princes. Their thaumaturgic power also represented an inestimable treasure for the princes who, through having a saint in their court, assumed the sanctity that the kings of France and England possessed directly.[9]

The cult of the living saints also had, as I have said, a popular element based on the preceding anorexic model of female sanctity[10] that was related to the

5 Zarri, *Pietà e profezia*, pp. 201–37, now in Zarri, *Le sante vive, Cultura e religiosità*, pp. 51–85; Zarri, *Le sante vive: Per una tipologia*, pp. 372–445, now *ibid.*, pp. 87–163; English translation: Zarri, *Living saints*, pp. 219–303.
6 Bilinkoff, 'Charisma and controversy', pp. 55–66; Sastre, 'Proceso de la beata', pp. 350–401; Sastre, 'Proceso de la beata (II)', pp. 337–86.
7 Dinzelbacher, *Heilige oder Hexen?*   8 Pietro, *San Francesco*.
9 Bloch, *Les rois thaumaturges; idem, The royal touch.*
10 Bell, *Holy anorexia*; Walzer, *Holy feast and holy fast.*

example of Catherine of Siena, who had been recently elevated to the honours of the altars (1461); it was fuelled also through preaching and hagiographic scripture. Immediately after the deaths of the charismatics mentioned above, their confessors composed the legend of their lives and miracles. Not all of the legends made it to the printing press, but in some cases different versions of them, which included contradictory points of view and sensibilities, were produced and printed. In the case of Osanna Andreasi, for example, the Dominican Francesco Silvestri composed and had printed in a short amount of time both a Latin legend (1505) and a vernacular one (1507). At about the same time, Don Girolamo Scolari, of the Congregation of Monte Oliveto, published his vernacular legend, which was much richer in Savonarolian accents than that of the Ferrarese Savonarola's fellow brother (1507). This hagiographic and editorial commitment was directed at the immediate promotion of the cult of the holy counsellor of the Gonzaga family. The goal was reached when the beatification of Osanna was obtained in 1515 by papal brief.[11]

Different, but just as significant, is the story of the life of Colomba da Rieti. Written in two versions – Latin and vernacular – by the tertiary's confessor, Brother Girolamo Bontempi, the legend of Colomba is interwoven with references to the model of Catherine and contains apologetic elements in defence of Savanarola. Neither of Bontempi's versions was printed. Some years later, however, in 1521, the educated Bolognese Inquisitor Leandro Alberti, an important spokesman of the Observant Lombard Congregation of the Order of Preachers, published an abbreviated version of the life of Colomba, carefully expunging any reference to the burdensome figure of the Florentine prophet but authorizing thereby the cult of female living saints.[12]

The prophetic model of sanctity was represented in Italy during this period first and foremost by the tertiaries who had begun to live in communities, according to the example of Colomba da Rieti, and who were therefore more easily controllable by the ecclesiastical institutions. In Spain an analogous process of convent organization was started in New Castile,[13] but the majority of the *beatas*, as the women belonging to the Third Orders were called, lived in their own homes. It is perhaps for this reason that their behaviour was carefully observed and their visions and revelations subjected to the scrutiny of the Inquisition: such was the case, for example, with Tecla di Tarragona, who about 1469 was forced to marry a man named Guillem Servent. Servent did not appreciate the extraordinary religious experiences of his wife, but

---

11 Zarri, *Le sante vive*, pp. 65–71.   12 *Ibid.*, pp. 92–5.
13 Muñoz, *Beatas santas neocastellanas*, p. 93.

rather opposed them by reprimanding and striking her. She fled from home, perhaps in 1492, and went to Valencia, where she acquired fame as a prophet and was called to the court of the Duke of Gandia to pray for the birth of an heir. The content of her prophecies is known through the acts of the inquisitional trial to which she was subjected in 1495–6. An accredited prophet in the city, she dared to preach against the sins of laymen and ecclesiastics and described the particulars of one of her visions in a letter that she wanted to send to the pope himself. The images and content of the vision were similar to those transmitted by popular hagiographic literature such as the *Legenda aurea*, by illustrated texts such as *Lo specchio di Umana Salvazione* (*The Mirror of Human Salvation*) and by apocalyptic sermons; the contemporaneous visions of some Italian mystics were also similar. Perhaps it was because of her condition as a single woman, separated from her husband, that the tribunal of the Spanish Inquisition convinced itself that the visions of Tecla Servent were 'tot ficcio' y simulacio' y falsi' (all fictitious and simulated and false), and they condemned her to abjuration and the obligation of never revealing again to anyone what was communicated to her by God.[14] A few years later, numerous other *beatas* were investigated in Spain. However, by that time the indictment had changed: they were no longer suspected of false sanctity but were accused of *alumbradismo*, the mystical current initiated at the start of the sixteenth century by the Blessed Isabel de la Cruz and condemned by the church because it saw in the movement the pretension of obtaining personal perfection through direct contact with God.[15]

The mothers of the soul

In their capacity as counsellors of princes, the living saints in Italy and the *beatas* in Spain carried out a significant role in the first decades of the sixteenth century in the religious context of the *Cura animarum*. Even without ever arriving at, to our knowledge, the practice of priesthood, women acquired sacerdotal prerogatives within the medieval and modern church by virtue of their extraordinary gifts. Through prophetic announcement they were allowed to hold a public role in preaching; through *consilium* they were recognized as having the authorization to exercise the function of spiritual direction, normally carried out by the confessors.[16]

14 Surtz, *Writing and sodomy*, pp. 197–213.   15 Hamilton, *Heresy and mysticism*.
16 Ranft, *A woman's way*.

In the fifteenth and sixteenth centuries, both within the convents, where the institutional version prevailed, and without, where the charismatic aspect was rather more present, a particular form of female teaching, which we could define as spiritual maternity, was present and active as a recognized element of sanctity. It is well known, in fact, that a nun from the convent of Santa Croce in Brescia was considered mother by Gaetano da Thiene, one of the founders of the Order of the Clerics Regular Theatines; so too, Paola Antonia Negri, first teacher of the Angelics, a female branch of the first Regular Clerics of Saint Paul (known as the Barnabites), who kept, until her imprisonment in a convent, the title of Divina Madre Maestra (Divine Mother Teacher), which she had been called due to unconditional faith in her charisma as spiritual guide.[17] Not even the Jesuits were exempt from the influence of charismatics, whom they considered examples, until the authority of the Roman Church regarded such an inversion of roles as suspect and reduced the most influential mothers to silence.

Among these mothers of the soul was the controversial figure of the Bolognese Elena Duglioli. Known from 1506 as a married virgin and remembered later as the commissioner of a painting by Raphael depicting the ecstasy of St Cecilia, the devout woman was said to have the gift of *lactatio Virginis* and to have materially nursed her disciples, to the great admiration of some and decided suspicion of others.[18]

The role of other women who lived in Italy at the start of the sixteenth century, such as Margherita da Ravenna and Gentile da Russi, was more decentralized than that of the figures noted above, but not less important for the full inclusion of requests which were widely felt as reforms of the church from below. As in Milan and Rome, where Companies of Clerics Regular were formed that later gave birth to religious orders, so too in Ravenna a Company of Clerics Regular was formed by the son of Gentile da Russi, the devout woman who was the epitome of a natural mother and mother of the soul.[19]

And yet the mothers of the soul cannot be considered during this period as merely the expression of an exceptional divine grace or a recognized prophetic charisma. In the late Middle Ages spiritual maternity was recognized as a particular element of sanctity that did not acknowledge differences of gender. As Caroline Bynum has observed, not only the Virgin but also Christ nursed the disciple Bernard;[20] the act of *lactatio* came to assume a symbolic

---

17 Baernstein, *A convent tale*; Bonora, *I conflitti della Controriforma*.
18 Zarri, *L'altra Cecilia*, pp. 83–118, now in Zarri, *Le sante vive*, pp. 165–96.
19 Zarri, *Le sante vive*, pp. 98–9. 20 Bynum Walker, *Jesus as mother*.

significance that meant to underline birth to new life, and therefore nurturing in the path embarked upon: whether this was the religious profession or a simple conversion. The tradition of the Mothers of the Church, as Kari Børresen calls the medieval female theologians who made a notable theoretical contribution to the idea of the maternity of God,[21] did not stop with the mystics of the fifteenth century, but flowed quietly into the cloisters of the Observant convents where abbesses and learned religious women, accustomed to reading the Bible and texts of mystic spirituality, passed on their teachings to their sisters and to a large group of disciples whom they reached by letter. Of these women we must at least mention the Poor Clare Camilla Battista da Varano, who wrote an instructional treatise on spiritual life for her confessor,[22] and also the Dominican Caterina de' Ricci, whose correspondence demonstrates a network of relationships between nuns, laymen, and important prelates.[23]

Nor is there a lack of attempts to understand those phenomena such as the *lactatio* of Elena Duglioli, which seemed strange even to their contemporaries. Lyndal Roper applies an interpretive hypothesis of utopian belief to the radical sect of the Dreamers, which was born in the bosom of the Protestant Reformation.[24] In applying Roper's hypothesis to the case cited, Gianna Pomata includes the experience of Elena – who nursed her spiritual sons – within a religious context that refers to the Christian root of the redeemed body and its destination for resurrection, and that works towards the reconstitution of a broken unity, to the detriment of the worth of the body.[25]

Divine Love between the West and the East

The mystical model of sanctity was not always identified exclusively with contemplative life. In the Italian cultural context at the start of the sixteenth century, active life and contemplative life were joined in the religious experience of Caterina Fieschi Adorno, a noble Genovese widow who founded the first hospital for the Incurables to give aid to people stricken with syphilis, the plague of the new century. She worked in the bosom of a spiritual confraternity of Divine Love, which was characterized by the participation of women and men, laypersons and priests, whose goal was to give aid to the sick, to orphans, and to the *poveri vergognosi* (disgraced poor), through a method of

21 Børresen and Vogt (eds.), *Women's studies.*
22 Bucuré, 'Camilla Battista Varano da Camerino', pp. 263–338.
23 Scattigno, '*Carissimo figliolo in Cristo*'.   24 Roper, *Oedipus and the devil.*
25 Pomata, *A Christian utopia of the Renaissance*, pp. 323–53.

secrecy. From Genoa the company spread to Rome, Brescia, and other cities. It opened and ran hospitals everywhere and administered great sums of money for aid. The secret character of the Company and the involvement of business-men and government has led some historians to emphasize the managerial aspect rather than the spiritual aspect of the brotherhood, but there is no doubt that many of the followers made radical religious choices, as is brought to light by the prosopographical analysis of the members of the Roman Com-pany, which has come to us through the unofficial list of a brother.[26] Some of the members of the Roman Divine Love were, in fact, among the founders and first practitioners of the Clerics Regular Theatine, while others adhered to spiritual groups subsequently accused of heresy. What emerges from the Roman documents is also the proliferation of institutions that seemed to want to give aid to all people at risk of death in those decades that were torn apart by disease, famine, and by wars that produced a disproportionate increase in mendicants and false mendicants. They, too, caused a rift in some aspects of civil and social solidarity.

Instituting hospitals for the poor in the countries of the Empire accompanied increasing prohibition of begging. This idea joined humanists such as Vives and More and reformers such as Luther and Calvin, but in Italy charity continued to be seen as an expression of divine love. Caterina Fieschi Adorno can therefore be considered an extreme case. Her charitable style was a cross between mystical sanctity, which would be suspected of *alumbradismo* after the break of Christian unity with the spread of the Protestant Reformation, and an active life, where the ideas of perfection in almsgiving and helping one's neighbour were based on the traditional teaching of the church. In the period between the founding of the Genovese Hospital of the Incurables and the publication of the life and mystical writings of Caterina Fieschi (1551), the definitive division of European Christianity had come to a head and the options of individual believers were at that point finished. In Protestant countries the doctrine of *sola fide* and the refusal of vows and almsgiving signalled a reversal in the way charity or divine love was conceived. Almsgiving remained a way of exercising charity that characterized the Catholic Church and Mediterranean Europe, while northern countries were moving slowly towards the concept of welfare as a responsibility of the state.

The active life and charity towards one's neighbours model of sanctity also characterizes the Orthodox Church, which was rather more stingy than the Catholic Church in conceding official recognition of sanctity. It is important

---

26 Solfaroli Camillocci, *I devoti della carità*.   27 Fedotov, *I santi dell'antica Russia*.

to note that two of the fourteen saints recognized by the churches of ancient Russia, before the dramatic events of the twentieth century enriched the hagiology, lived in the sixteenth century. Both were named Juliana; both belonged to the category of the just – that is, laypersons who belonged neither to the category of martyrs nor to that of nuns – but both had very different lives and were venerated for different reasons. The young princess Juliana Olshanskaya died at the age of sixteen in about 1540. She enjoyed the reputation of sanctity that accompanies those who die young. However, a true cult developed at the start of the seventeenth century when, during an excavation, her tomb was opened and her body was found uncorrupted. That a thief who took some jewels that had covered her body died soon after was interpreted as divine punishment and served to reinforce faith in the sanctity of the woman. Shortly thereafter Juliana Olshanskaya was incorporated in the martyrology of the Russian Church.

The story of Juliana Lazarevskaya, the daughter of a functionary of the tsar Ivan the Terrible, is quite different. She was orphaned at six and taken in and raised by her maternal grandmother. She married and had thirteen children. Her life story was written by one of her children and, although keeping in mind traditional hagiographic commonplaces, revealed new information. She was a devout woman, and she conducted a life of asceticism and penitence during the years of her childhood and marriage. She administered the household in periods when her husband was in service to the tsar. She was generous with alms, but did not eat into the familial patrimony. During a famine that had greatly increased the number of poor, Juliana, who practised habitual fasting, pretended to give up the habit in order to be able to donate a little more food to the needy. After her husband's death she led a semi-monastic life at home. During the famine of 1601–2, which hit Russia during the reign of Boris Godunov, she used up all the reserves in her possession, retired to her property in the country, released all her servants, fell ill, and died a few years later in 1604.[28]

The religious experience of Juliana Lazarevskaya, although different from the life and concept of Divine Love of Caterina Fieschi Adorno, was distinguished by the conviction that charity towards one's neighbour was pleasing to God and the way to salvation. Prior to the new ideas of the reformers of continental Europe, the oldest Christian churches of Europe reconfirmed their attachment to tradition.

28 Rudi, *La santità*, pp. 211–28.

The primitive church: the evangelical model

Among the spiritual persons who were inspired by Christian humanism and who made allusion to Erasmus and Thomas More, and among those who entrusted themselves rather to the hopes for a renewal of the church as expressed by Girolamo Savonarola, there were many who were sensitive to the creation of spiritual companies that had the primitive church as reference, and that considered women as active participants in the apostolic mission. One of these groups acquired particular importance. A group was formed in Brescia around a woman who had dedicated her life to prayer and to the instruction of poor young female workers who, while wanting to consecrate themselves to a religious life, were unable or unwilling to enter a convent. The institute that was founded in 1535 by Angela Merici took the name of the Company of Saint Ursula. It was inspired by the apostolic church and was modelled on the group of women who surrounded St Jerome. The letters that the father of the church addressed to them show that those women, widows and virgins, materially aided Jerome in his preaching, and were at the same time participants in his mission. The founding of the Company of Saint Ursula represented, therefore, a new model of female sanctity: that of a life consecrated to God but lived in the world without institutional ties to a religious order. Such a model strongly felt the effects of the decidedly utopian cultural air of the period that gave birth to it. In fact, the Company earned approval by the Roman Church only after having accepted a form of institutionalization that subjected it to the guidance of a diocesan bishop and which imposed a distinguishing mark upon the habit that allowed those belonging to the company to be identified. In spite of this, the movement put forth the most innovative petitions of the female religious world of the sixteenth century, which called for the recognition of sanctity and individual perfection also for the lay condition, together with active participation in the mission of the propagation of the faith.[29]

Quite similar were the premises that induced Ludovica Torelli, Countess of Guastalla, to form in the same years a female religious company, that of the Angelics, which stood with the Barnabite Clerics Regular in the mission to reform convents and found institutions for the protection and education of women. Even if in this case, unlike in that of the Ursuline Company, we have no documentary proof referring to Jerome and to the primitive church,

---

29 Zarri, *Ursula and Catherina*; Prodi, Zarri, Mezzadri, and Castenetto, *Angela Merici*.

it is sufficient to consider that the two recognized leaders of the movement of the Angelics, Torelli and the Divine Mother Paola Antonia Negri, were laywomen.

I have mentioned two female religious movements that remained in the circle of the institutional Roman Church and that were destined, particularly in the first case, to have a notable importance in the period of the Catholic renewal. The fact remains that these movements had their origin in, and developed from, a root – that of the return to the primitive church – that led other groups or individuals to break loose from Roman orthodoxy.

Many of the women who in Italy, England, or France adhered in the same years or the next decade to the Protestant Reformation were moved by similar intellectual motives and morals to those expressed here. I am not speaking of spiritual women such as Vittoria Colonna or Caterina Cybo, who lived in the convent but refused monastic vows and sought to attain individual salvation within a church of the chosen, but who in fact did not reject Roman Christianity; I am speaking of women such as the Ferrarese humanist Olimpia Morata, who left their homelands for religious motives,[30] or of others such as the Englishwoman Mary Askell, who confronted martyrdom with the Bible in hand,[31] and others still, such as the women of Lyon, who adhered to Calvinism in order to be authorized to read the Bible together with their husbands.[32] All these women were in some way won over by a model of apostolic life that deprived the monks of the prerogative of individual perfection and also recognized institutionally an active participation of women in the mission of the church.

Between contestation and restoration:
the martyr model

The fights for the affirmation and spread of the Protestant Reformation, with its resultant wars, religious intolerance, inquisitional trials, and summary sentences, did not delay in bringing back to the forefront a high model of adherence to Christianity: that of the martyr. The ambition of a return to the true religion and to the primitive church was made concrete in the middle of the sixteenth century with the proposal of new sanctity for those martyred for faith. Even those religions that had rejected the cult of the saints, such as the Lutheran religion, began to keep alive the memory of their dead.

30 Bainton, *Women of the Reformation.*   31 Beilin (ed.), *The examinations of Anne Askew.*
32 Zemon Davies, *Society and culture in early modern France.*

The compilation of the martyrologies of the most diffuse reformation religions occurred almost simultaneously in the middle of the sixteenth century. A quick look at these compilations of Reformation martyrs demonstrates that at the beginning those affected were, above all, priests and monks who had abandoned the Roman Church; with regard to gender, one can note that the martyrs of the first generation of reformers were almost exclusively male; in the second generation, however, women who faced their martyrdom were many, and in some cases exceeded the number of men.

Among the female English martyrs, one must at least mention Anne Askew (1521–46), daughter of a gentleman of Lincolnshire and wife of a Catholic, who probably converted to Protestantism due to the influence of her brothers. She moved to London to be nearer to her companions in faith, was arrested in 1545 for heresy, and subjected to two interrogations before being condemned to the stake. Her execution occurred in 1546, under the reign of Henry VIII. While in prison she wrote the account of her interrogations, which was published in 1547 by the Protestant editor John Bale. He used the text for propaganda purposes, portraying Anne as a saint who crushed the head of the papal beast. On the title-page of the book, in fact, there was a xylography of the young woman with a halo, holding a Bible in her right hand and the palm of martyrdom in her left, while at her feet lay an impotent dragon whose head was covered with the papal tiara. To the left of the figure a verse from Psalm 116 reminded the reader that the truth of the Lord lasts forever, and to the right an inscription commented that Anne Askew stayed firm in the truth of God until the end.[33]

Naturally there were martyrs among Catholics as well. In England especially, first the establishment of Anglicanism, then the reaction to the sentences handed down by Mary Tudor, led to a strict repression that hit above all the Catholic clergy. Besides Margaret Pole, the mother of Cardinal Reginald, who was executed in 1541 after years of detention, there were only three Englishwomen who suffered martyrdom for their faith. Among these the most notable was Margaret Clitherow, who was stoned to death.[34]

Quantitatively, women were struck less than men by torture and martyrdom. However, the model of martyrdom was still present not only in the liturgical celebration, but also in hagiographic literature. In Italy the most widespread hagiographic text in the vernacular in the sixteenth century was a booklet entitled *Il leggendario delle santissime Vergini* (*The Legend of the Most Holy*

---

33 Beilin (ed.), *The examinations of Anne Askew*, p. 1.
34 Gregory, *Salvation at stake*, p. 280.

Virgins), a collection of stories taken from the *Legenda aurea*. It was printed numerous times until late into the eighteenth century.

The Catholic renewal: founding female saints

The Council of Trent not only set the foundations for redefining Catholic identity in opposition to Protestantism but it also made decisive changes to the traditional institutions, in particular those regarding the condition of women: the reforming of marriage and the cloistering of convents.

Monastic cloistering was a drastic and unexpected provision. To the fathers at the Council, however, it seemed the only way to restore discipline in the convents. In Italy it was mostly the bishops who were charged with supervising the cloistering and they did it with more or less severity in agreement with political and city power. In the countries where the general curia of the religious orders were seated, there were no significant changes. It was rather in the nations directly upset by the wars of religion that religious orders demonstrated new vitality and creativity.[35] At times the nuns themselves took the initiative for reform, as happened in the case of the Order of Our Lady of Mount Carmel. The work of the Spaniard Teresa de Cepeda de Avila was an emblematic case.

Teresa de Jesus, who had Jewish ancestry, was educated and had accentuated mystical inclinations. She was endowed with a practical spirit and proposed to reform, in a rigorous sense, the organization of the Carmelites. She did not limit herself to the professed nuns, but extended the reform inside the order. With the assistance and the approval of confessors and confidants of exceptional culture and spirituality, such as brother John of the Cross and the Dominican Louis de Granata, and with the support of Philip II himself, Teresa and some of her sisters began to visit the convents, reforming them above all from the point of view of poverty. The Order of the Discalced Carmelites was quickly born, and in the favourable climate of the Counter-Reformation it enjoyed support and protection that gave birth to new foundations. Philip II looked favourably on the expansion of convents in France, in the Low Countries, and in Italy, and considered them political outposts of a more profound cultural penetration. The personality of Teresa asserted itself everywhere with its deep mysticism, but her writings were submitted to the scrutiny of the Inquisition some time before they were printed.[36]

---

35 Hsia, *Catholic renewal*.
36 Weber, *Teresa of Avila*; Slade, *St Teresa of Avila*; Ahlgren, *Francisca de los Apostoles*, pp. 119–33.

The new French foundations corresponded to social rather than political needs. The Bishop of Geneva, Francis de Sales, already had a reputation as an educated preacher and author of texts on spirituality. When he proposed to the noble widow Jeanne Françoise Fremyot de Chantal that she found a convent at Annecy, in Savoy, he had a well-defined plan in mind. He wanted to create an institution that would respond to the religious exigencies of a spiritual elite, made up for the most part of widows and gentlewomen not entirely free of familial problems. The convent was to have less rigid rules than the traditional ones, because it was to welcome women of delicate constitution or precarious health. It was not to be cloistered, so that it could, for short periods of time, host gentlewomen who wanted to carry out spiritual exercises, and so that it could allow religious women the possibility of looking after the essential affairs of their families. Jeanne de Chantal agreed and began to write the constitution of the new convent with Francis de Sales. On the problem of cloistering, however, it was not possible to compromise. Either one renounced the religious profession, creating a college for laywomen, or cloistering had to be applied. The inventors of the new foundation yielded to the Roman provisions but obtained a partial compromise. Non-practising women entered for short periods of time, and there was less rigidity in the abstinences and in the rules of communal life. Thus the Order of the Salesians was born, which in the first half of the seventeenth century spread rapidly in Savoy, Piedmont, and southern France, and even penetrated various Italian states.[37]

The religious order founded in France by Louise de Marillac (1591–1660) and St Vincent de Paul, called the Daughters of Charity, had different goals, which were dictated rather by the desire to transform charity into an efficient social system. Louise was also a widow of the high French nobility, and she alternated her duties as mother with exercises of devotion, but was attentive to the needs of the very poor. After visiting some of the works begun in Champaign and in French villages by Vincent de Paul, she agreed formally to establish the Daughters of Charity, a female company with simple vows, like the Ursuline companions of Angela Merici; its members wore grey and were dedicated to helping the poor of the villages, providing in particular for the care and raising of abandoned children.[38]

The existence of the combative Englishwoman Mary Ward is conceivable only in the heated climate of the Counter-Reformation, aimed as it was at reaffirming its religious identity in the desire for a spiritual recovery. Catholic

---

37 Devos, *Vie religieuse feminine et société*; Mellinghoff-Bourgerie, *François de Sales*.
38 Rapley, *The dévotes*; Ryan and Rybolt (eds.), *Vincent de Paul*.

and marginalized, if not also persecuted, Mary Ward considered herself a missionary with respect to the official Anglicanism and insistent Puritanism of early seventeenth-century England. She wanted to found a female company along the lines of the Order of Jesuits, to open colleges for the instruction of young noblewomen in England, in the Low Countries, and in the German territories: in short, in all those countries where Roman Christianity had to reaffirm itself on the basis of Catholic renewal. In this sense she did a lot: she opened colleges in York, in Munich and in the Low Countries, until the Roman curia granted her permission to create a centralized religious congregation analogous to those of the male religious orders. This experience was brief, however. As Mother Superior of the Congregation she was obliged to visit the colleges, and the female practitioners were obligated to participate in the general chapters of the Congregation, all of which were in opposition to the laws of the cloister. The Congregation was dissolved in 1631 and an order of female Jesuits was not realized.[39]

Forbidden models of sanctity and counter-models

In 1558 the Congregation of Rites was instituted and was charged with preparing the reform of the process of canonization. Even in the field of sanctity, however, the Holy Office operated directly, contributing, with its repressive action, to the establishment of a change in direction in the very concept of officially recognized sanctity.

Women, above all, were the object of special attention on the part of the Roman Holy Office and it was mysticism still alive among the faithful that was put under scrutiny. Many female mystics were investigated for simulated sanctity: a very subtle accusation that addressed conscience and faith, and as such was able to be prosecuted by the Inquisition, unlike the preceding false sanctity, which could be classed as fraud.[40] The accusation of simulated sanctity was one of the ways of undermining mysticism and bringing it down from the high position it held in the goal of *fama sanctitatis*. Such accusation was also the pretext for investigating the habits of the clergy and the relationships between female mystics and their confessors.[41] Through this battle against simulated sanctity, which made mysticism the proscribed model, a new prescribed model

---

39 Grisar, *Maria Wards Institut*; Konrad, *Zwischen Kloster und Welt*.
40 Zarri (ed.), *Finzione e santità*; Prosperi, *Tribunali della coscienza*; Schutte, *Aspiring saints*.
41 Romeo, *Esorcisti, confessori e sessualità femminile*; Prosperi, *Tribunali della coscienza*.

for ascertaining *fama sanctitatis* was affirmed: that is behaviour where Christian virtues are possessed to a heroic degree.

The accusations of simulated sanctity were directed at first towards female mystics who enjoyed a reputation of sanctity both among the nobility and also among the religious orders. This was, for example, the case with Orsola Benincasa, who was subsequently cleared of the charges. Others did not escape, such as female prophets and visionaries who in Italy or Spain followed the paths of sanctity that were indicated by Catherine of Siena and were still regarded as female living saints during the first part of the sixteenth century. Philip II himself heeded the counsel of a mystic who was later accused of simulation.[42] The line between approved and simulated mysticism became ever more evanescent and difficult to define according to doctrine. Where there are records, one can deduce from the inquisitional trials conducted between the end of the sixteenth and the start of the seventeenth centuries that the accusation of simulated sanctity was directed above all against tertiaries or *beatas* who practised in non-cloistered female institutions, or against laywomen who followed the path to perfection under the guidance of a spiritual father. This was the case in Toledo, where in 1575–6 there was a trial against the tertiary Francisca de los Apostoles, who sought to found a *beaterio* and a hospice for female converts, and who declared that the task had been entrusted to her by God, who spoke to her in a vision.[43] The same happened some years later in Venice, where Cecilia Ferrazzi, a woman of humble origins who had built a conservatory for poor girls, was called by the Inquisition to respond to the charge of simulated sanctity.[44] The sociological analysis of the women charged with simulated sanctity leads us to conclude that the *inquisitio* also had the goal of disciplining the behaviour and habits of semi-religious women not protected by the cloister. However, we must not underestimate the fact that the accusation of simulation could also correspond to a real occurrence, as the episode of Ana Domengo da Barcellona seems to prove: she was a Dominican prophetess who claimed to want to be the St Teresa of the Order of Preachers.[45] Since at the end of the sixteenth century the reputation of sanctity was still socially significant, there was no shortage of cases of fraud that even at the highest levels went undetected. For example, the levitation of a mystic achieved through the use of a wooden device deceived even the General of the Dominicans.

As we have mentioned, the inquisitional fight against the mystical model aimed to advance the development and acceptance, on the part of the faithful,

---

42 Kagan, *Lucrecia's dreams*.   43 Ahlgren, *Francisca de los Apostoles*, pp. 119–33.
44 Schutte (ed. and trans.), *Autobiography of an aspiring saint*.
45 Rhodes, 'Y yo dije', pp. 134–54.

of a model of sanctity based on behaviour rather than on a direct relationship with God, or on signs of the body, or on miracles. In accordance with the humanistic tendency, which had already emerged in the fifteenth century, of considering as illustrious the men and women who had distinguished themselves by possessing virtue to a heroic degree, and with the intent of responding to Protestant critiques, the heads of the Church of Rome, in particular the Congregation of Rites, had decided to canonize saints to give more prominence to their lives, to their virtues, and to their fulfilment of professional and familial duties. The idea of sanctity was thus profoundly transformed compared with the medieval concept. It aimed at becoming a verification of an individual journey towards perfection taken by a believer under the guidance of a spiritual father and of the same believer's adjustment to the precepts of the church.

Besides contributing to the proscription of the mystical model of sanctity, the inquisitional tribunals sought also to reduce, if not to eliminate, the countermodel of such sanctity: that is, the heretical image of the witch that had been born and asserted in the Christian West in close connection with the spread of female mysticism. The phenomena of mysticism and witchcraft were strictly correlated, and they represented contrasting models of two powers in competition: the power of God and that of the devil. The first was aimed at miraculous works, the second at evil works. Not only at the level of the powers, but also at that of models, the saint and the witch incarnated two precise representations of woman: the one who follows the paths of God, and she who rejects them.[46] At the end of the sixteenth century, when the Roman Church undertook its work of reconverting the model of sanctity, belief in witches was still alive and functioning, as in the rest of Christian Europe. However, by then the Renaissance idea that the sect of witches had to be eradicated with fire was more contentious. In the Catholic Church the conviction became stronger that one ought first to proceed with the art of exorcism. The treatises by Girolamo Menghi, to give only one example, were printed at various times throughout Europe between about 1580 and the first half of the seventeenth century.[47] In addition, the idea that both a woman's visionary activity as well as her possession by the devil could be the effect of a female illness – a sickness of her uterus – became popular at the beginning of the seventeenth century, partly because of the progress in medicine and in the scientific knowledge of the human body. The directives given in 1621 by

---

46 Craveri, *Sante e streghe*; Zarri, *Le sante vive*; Dinzelbacher, *Heilige oder Hexen?*
47 Maggi, *Satan's rhetoric*.

an authoritative member of the Congregation of the Holy Office, Cardinal Scaglia, counselled Inquisitors to proceed with caution in judging cases that concerned the imaginings of female mystics,[48] simulators, possessed women, and witches. Their protestations began to be considered illnesses.

Hysteria would very soon become a scientific mode for discriminating against women, but in the short term this new attitude of the Roman Inquisition saved lives. The fact that a large number of these female living saints, simulators of sanctity, possessed women, and witches were also anorexic or hysterical was an idea that began to be discussed in the seventeenth century. There is no doubt that for those who had created the myth of the witch, and for those who were living it or who perceived it in those years, these women were above all the wives of the devil, dangerous and needing to be wiped out because they were able to generate other witches.

What can we say of the possessed women? Possession by the devil is one of the typical cases classified by psychoanalysts as collective hysteria; in fact, Freudian theory has been authoritatively applied by De Certeau to explain the events of the possessions at Loudon, although other studies have brought to light the political components of the case.[49] But how can we call the possessed women of Carpi hysterics? The situation happened shortly after that of Loudon and was certainly put in motion by the skill of the Princess of Este, Abbess at Santa Clara, in order not to submit to provisions that would have put the convent under the jurisdiction of the archpriest of the local Pieve.[50]

Perhaps one could cautiously put forth the hypothesis that, as it was possible in the monasteries to resort to simulations of sanctity to cover occurrences of homosexuality,[51] so too simulated possession by the devil could attract attention and force the superiors to concede benefits or to withdraw orders: a result which would not otherwise have been achieved. In this last case, hysteria would not be an attribute of the nuns, but of the exorcists and of those who gave credence to the event.

The post-Tridentine canonizations: the monastic model

As we have said, both the Congregation of the Holy Office and the Congregation of Rites were active in defining the prescribed model of sanctity. According to the investigation of Christian Renoux,[52] thirty-two canonizations took place

---

48 Tedeschi, *The prosecution of heresy.*   49 Certeau, *Le possession de Loudun.*
50 Lavenia, *I diavoli di Carpi e il Sant'Uffizio*, pp. 77–139; Ori, *La principessa.*
51 Brown, *Immodest acts.*   52 Renoux, *Canonizzazione e santità femminile*, pp. 731–51.

in the seventeenth century, the highest number achieved in a century. But there was also another novelty: the geographic range broadened. In the seventeenth century, in fact, the sanctity of the New World was presented to the Catholic world by the canonization in 1679 of Rosa da Lima, who died in 1606. From the point of view of gender, there was a clear preponderance of men, even if the number of women canonized in the seventeenth century was the highest in absolute terms. There were, in fact, six female saints. Two of these had been queens: Elizabeth of Portugal, proclaimed a saint in 1625, and Margaret of Scotland, who lived in the eleventh century. She received an equipollent canonization, which ratified a local cult of long duration. The other saints were nuns: Francesca Romana, who lived during the fifteenth century and was made a saint in 1604; Teresa d'Avila, who died in 1582 and was canonized in 1622; Maria Maddalena de' Pazzi, who died in 1607 and was canonized in 1669 after having been beatified; and, finally, the aforementioned Rosa da Lima. In addition to the canonizations, one may count the beatifications and the *casus excepti* – that is, the ratifications of the cults of those women who were venerable, who had died more than 100 years before the decrees of Pope Urban VIII and who had always enjoyed a local cult. Among the beatifications the female presence is very low (one in ten) but it is very high (one woman to every four men) in the *casus excepti*. To understand this inequality it is necessary to remember that beatification was a process introduced by the Congregation of Rites in the seventeenth century. Therefore, beatification was possible for those whose process had opened shortly after their death. If the beatified women were few, the most plausible explanation is the one indicated by Renoux: the church was more cautious (or, it would be better to say, it had become more cautious) in recognizing female sanctity. The assumption is confirmed by the high number of *casus excepti* that hark back to the sanctity of the Middle Ages and Renaissance, before 1540; that is, to the period in which, as we have seen, female mystical sanctity still enjoyed the full approval of the church.[53]

However, if we consider analytically the female saints promoted to the honours of the altar, I would not be inclined to share Renoux's classification. He places these canonizations under the category of mystical sanctity; I would rather favour a monastic model. It is quite true that all the women named above were mystics, although at diverse levels of intensity and culture, but it is also true that they became saints above all because they were nuns, and among the justifications for their sanctity, the *status* of nun or of founder prevailed over that of mystic. It is interesting in this regard to compare, as Giulia Barone has

---

53 *Ibid.*, p. 739.

done, the fifteenth-century process of canonization of Francesca de' Ponziani with the seventeenth-century papal bull on canonization: before founding the Congregation of the Oblates of the Tor de' Specchi, Francesca was a wife and mother. This was recalled during the testimony of the fifteenth-century trial, but was completely silenced in the seventeenth-century justifications of her sanctity, which took into consideration only her monastic status.[54]

What can we say of the other saints? If the most important image of Teresa d'Avila is Bernini's statue that depicts her in ecstasy, it is also true that she was canonized in 1622 together with Ignatius of Loyola, Francis Xavier, Isidore the Farmer, and Filippo Neri, that is, with two fellow Spaniards and two founders of orders. No one could deny that Ignatius was also a mystic. The autobiography he dictated to his secretary in the last months of his life proves that he remained faithful to himself until death; yet mysticism was not the founding element of his sanctity. With these simultaneous canonizations, the Roman Church wanted on the one hand to indicate the contribution given by Spain to the cause of the Counter-Reformation, and on the other to encourage the imitation of those who had contributed to the reform of the religious orders and to the renewal of the church. Perhaps the mystical model had a greater weight in the canonization of Maddalena de' Pazzi but, even in this case, one must not forget that she was a cloistered nun, living in the post-Tridentine period, and that her visions, which had a theological rather than a prophetic content, were rarely made public.[55]

In the case of Rosa da Lima the problem is certainly greater, because the difficulty of the relationship between the representation of her sanctity by her first biographers and the perception of sanctity in areas as totally different as the Old and New Worlds is complex. As a Creole who imitated Catherine of Siena by living in a hermitage built in a garden, Rosa da Lima submitted herself to fasting and penitence, refused both marriage and the convent, and is a welcome exception that we would not have expected to encounter in the seventeenth century. Investigated and released without being subject to punishments nor to injunctions to change her life, Rosa's destiny was quite different from that of the group of female companions who surrounded her. These last were investigated and forced to take vows in a cloistered convent.[56]

To conclude, I would like to recall attention to the evolution that the mystical model of female sanctity, certainly the most diffuse since the eleventh century,

54 Barone, *La canonizzazione di Francesca Romana (1608)*, pp. 264–79.
55 Pozzi (ed.), *Maria Maddalena de' Pazzi*; Maggi (intro. and trans.), *Maria Maddalena de' Pazzi*.
56 Cantù, *Rosa da Lima*.

suffered between the Middle Ages and the early modern period. Catherine of Siena's model of prophetic sanctity was reduced in the modern period, although not extinguished completely, and it became the prerogative of cloistered nuns[57] and no longer of lay tertiaries. The mysticism of these last was discouraged and often condemned under the accusation of simulated sanctity. There was also a form of apolitical mysticism, tied to mental or quiet prayer, which was developed in the seventeenth century in relation to the diffusion of spiritual direction and personal prayer. This mysticism flowed into the quietist condemnation of 1678. The condemnation appears to have been dictated more by the desire to cut off a behavioural practice than a doctrinal deviance. As records of the trials against the quietists prove, what appeared dangerous to the cardinals of the Holy Congregation was the relationship that was established between women and confessors who practised the prayer of quietism. The seventeenth-century mysticism of the cloisters is less problematic. It could testify to, depending on the interpretations, deviations or mental illnesses but the majority of the time it was controlled and did not involve or compromise ecclesiastical dignity.

57 Matter, 'Prophetic patronage as repression', pp. 105–19.

12

Tridentine worship and the cult of saints

SIMON DITCHFIELD

1. Introduction – reforming liturgy after Trent

Central to the Tridentine reaffirmation of the divinely-ordained nature of the Holy Roman Church was the assertion of papal *magisterium*. While conflicts with the secular authorities over rights of ecclesiastical patronage in general, and episcopal appointment in particular, have long received the attention of scholars, considerably less notice has been taken of an area in which the papacy took a highly visible lead in the immediate aftermath of Trent. This concerned the reform of liturgy, which the Council of Trent in its final (25th) session had left entirely to papal discretion. In the space of less than fifty years, from the publication of the revised Roman Breviary (1568) to the issue of the revised Roman Ritual (1614), the Roman Church undertook the unprecedented step of providing texts which were to possess *universal* validity and authority. In what follows, discussion will be focused on the reform of the breviary, not only because the issues raised most directly concern the cult of saints, but also because the processes involved tell us much about the reception and interpretation of Tridentine reforms in general.

Members of the reforming commission sought not to innovate but 'to strip the office back to its antique [simplicity]' (*ridur l'officio all'antico*). In Pius V's words, the aim was to reclaim 'the original standard of the Fathers' (*pristina patrum norma*) so as to permit the more frequent saying of the daily ferial (i.e. non-feast day) office.[1] The latter was centred on readings from the psalms (all 150 of which were meant to be covered each week), together with other key passages from scripture (many of which were accompanied by short homilies, not infrequently of patristic authorship). All these scriptural readings (with their commentaries) were suppressed on feast days, when

---

[1] The fullest published account still remains Bäumer, *Histoire du Bréviaire*, vol. 2, pp. 160–291, but see also Batiffol, *History of the Roman Breviary*, pp. 177–235. Cf. Ditchfield, 'Giving Tridentine worship back its history', *passim*.

the space freed up was given over to hagiographical readings from the life of the saint or saints in question whose memory was being celebrated. Over the centuries, the ever-increasing number of additions to the saints' calendar (circa 200 between 1100 and 1500) had resulted in the fact that by the sixteenth century, the daily (ferial) office had become effectively marginalized by the festal office to commemorate the saints.[2] Users of the breviary thereby neglected much of the psalter and significant parts of the Bible with their related homilies in favour of hagiographical readings. The implications such an unbalanced use of the breviary had for the instruction of the religious and devout in Roman Catholic doctrine and devotion are obvious but need restating, since the didactic function of liturgy, prayer and the cult of saints has been overshadowed by historians' preoccupation with determining the effectiveness of the Council of Trent's requirement that every diocese establish a seminary for the training of secular priests.

Much space was cleared for the recitation of the ferial office by restating the connection between the importance of a saint's feast and the number of hagiographical readings s/he merited. In the case of an ordinary, simple feast (*simplex*), this was restricted to one (out of three, including one scriptural and another homiletic), while for a double or semi-double feast (*duplex, semi-duplex*) the ceiling was fixed at three readings (out of nine, including three homiletic and three scriptural). Importantly, simple feasts were no longer permitted to use their own specially written offices in place of the ferial one. This ranking of feasts had been made necessary to decide who had priority on the not infrequent occasions when several saints enjoyed the same feast day. This was a particular problem when a feast fell on a Sunday during Advent or Holy Week or during the week's celebration (known as an *octave*) enjoyed by major feasts relating to the life of Christ: Epiphany, Circumcision, Pentecost, Ascension, Corpus Christi, or the patronal day of a church or diocese, when the observance of lesser feasts was transferred to the next available day. The overall result was to leave some 157 days a year for the recital of the ferial office, which were particularly concentrated during Lent.

It must be emphasized that this concern to prune back the calendar of saints was not new. It had come up for discussion, for example, during the Council of Constance (1414–18) and underlay Cardinal Quiñones' far more radical *Breviarium sanctae crucis* (1535/36), which, designed for private devotion rather than for spoken recitation by religious communities in the choir of their churches,

---

2 For this and related relevant figures see Klauser, *A short history of the Western liturgy*, pp. 125–6. Cfr. Focke & Heinrichs, 'Das Kalendarium des Missale Pianum vom Jahre 1570 und seine Tendenzen'.

enjoyed over one hundred editions before its placing on the Indexes of 1557 and 1559. However, a reading of the papal bull *Quod a nobis*, which prefaced the new Tridentine Breviary of 1568, reveals at once a different order of ambition. For by explicitly forbidding the continued recitation of all existing local variants of the breviary which could not prove at least 200 years of uninterrupted use, it set out to provide a calendar of universal application. Nevertheless, several breviaries which were specific to particular religious orders did satisfy the 200-year rule, and so continued to be legitimately used. For example, no fewer than eighty-five editions of the Benedictine breviary and twenty-six editions of the Dominican counterpart were printed between 1568 and 1660.[3] Also preserved were certain liturgies of undisputed ancient lineage such as the Ambrosian rite of Milan.[4] Turning to diocesan breviaries, France, in particular, persisted in respecting local traditions on a scale unmatched elsewhere in Europe, with some thirty-nine dioceses printing their own breviaries over the same period, (in a total of ninety-eight editions).[5] Moreover, the revised Roman Breviary itself went through two further editions in little over sixty years (1602 and 1632), each of which had to accommodate new and restored saints' cults in its calendar, so that by the close of the period covered by this volume the number of those saints' feasts which took precedence over the ferial office had increased from 104 listed in 1568 to 145 by 1686.

Taken together, these factors point to the inappropriateness of adopting a crude top-down model of liturgical reform. Furthermore, we are not dealing with a straightforward case of aspirations for uniformity by the centre frustrated by practical obstacles at the periphery. Rather, from the earliest years after Trent, there exists evidence not only that bishops petitioned Rome for licence to continue the recital of offices in honour of their local patrons, but also that figures of the highest rank and intellectual significance in the Roman hierarchy directly concerned themselves with the necessary textual revisions and responded creatively and flexibly to the challenge of reconciling the devotions of particular dioceses with universal precept. For example, letters

---

3 Though in both cases, revised texts were published (the Dominican breviary in 1596 and the Benedictine one, known as the *Breviarium monasticum*, in 1612), in a conscious effort to impose uniform practice within their respective orders. In the case of the Benedictine text, this was the outcome of a papal commission (1608–11) set up by Paul V. (See Bäumer, 2, pp. 277–8.) The only other orders to have ten or more editions of their breviary published (1568–1660) were the Premonstratensians (twelve) and Franciscans (ten). The numbers of breviary editions are based on Bohatta, *Bibliographie der Breviere*, pp. 84–5, 92–8, 139, 149–50 with the update by Amiet, *Missels et Bréviaires imprimés*, pp. 145, 150–4, 198, 206.

4 Twelve editions of the *Breviarium Ambrosianum* were printed during the period 1568–1660. See Bohatta, pp. 160–2 and Amiet, p. 217.

5 Bohatta, pp. 156–274 and Amiet, pp. 213–306.

addressed to Cardinal Guglielmo Sirleto (*inter alia* a prominent member of the commission responsible for the revision of the Roman Breviary in 1568) reveal that some twenty-two dioceses in Italy alone sought the cardinal's assistance on this matter (1570–84).[6] After the foundation in 1588 of the body specifically to deal with this issue (and the related area of canonization procedure) – the Congregation of Rites and Ceremonies – one finds high profile figures such as Roberto Bellarmino and Cesare Baronio devoting themselves to such minutiae with a scrupulous attention to detail.[7]

However, to understand how necessarily extensive the dialogue was between the local dioceses and Rome one needs to appreciate the composite structure of the office book which constituted the ultimate point of reference for discussion: the Roman Breviary. As its very name suggests, this office book was in fact several books in one and its overall structure reflected this. First the reader encountered the calendar of saints (together with tables to calculate the dates of moveable feasts, such as Easter); next came the psalter; then came the proper offices of the season (*Proprium de tempore*), containing the prayers, responses, scriptural and homiletic readings for the recital of the daily, ferial offices. This was followed by the special offices (including hagiographical readings) which had been written in honour of particular saints to be recited on their feast day (*Proprium sanctorum*) and, after that, by a sequence of generic offices for different categories of saint, such as confessors or martyrs, which were to be recited for those who did not have their own office (*Commune sanctorum*). The final main section of the Roman Breviary consisted of additional services, such as the office for the dead and the so-called little office of the Blessed Virgin Mary.

Coordination between these separate parts was facilitated by a prefatory list of general instructions or rubrics (the *Rubricae generales*), which guided the user back and forth in the text so that s/he could assemble the correct combination of readings, prayers and psalms for each day. But in addition to these main sections there was frequently to be found a *second* proper of saints, but this time restricted to the offices of those who enjoyed either special or exclusive devotion in a particular region or diocese. The existence of these local propers (*propria*) – and Rome's acknowledgement of the issues raised by their continued relevance – is strongly implied in the very first column of

---

6 Ditchfield, *Liturgy, sanctity and history*, pp. 60–6. Cf. Schmid, 'Weitere Beiträge zur Geschichte des römischen Breviers und Missale', pp. 624–7.

7 E.g. Bellarmino's report on the texts of offices to be included in the revised *Officia propria sanctorum ecclesiae placentinae* found in ACCS, *Positiones decretorum et rescriptorum 1798*. Cf. Ditchfield, *Liturgy, sanctity and history*, pp. 111–12.

the General Rubric to the revised Roman Breviary. Here it was written that, provided sanction has been given by Rome, 'even if [the aforesaid] feasts be not found in the Roman calendar' they could be celebrated.[8] The subordinate and vulnerable position of these local saints' offices; sometimes bound at the end of the main text of the breviary, and sometimes printed separately, has meant that they have come to the attention of bibliographers only relatively recently. The most comprehensive, though certainly incomplete, catalogue lists some 197 *propria* shared between 100 dioceses and regions of Western Europe for the period 1568–1660.[9]

2. The Counter-Reformation and the cult of saints

At first glance, the link between the Counter-Reformation and the cult of saints appears too self-evident to require much comment. After the initial dismay and disorientation caused by the Lutheran and Calvinist Reformations, which by 1555 had left more than half of Central Europe in Protestant hands, the Catholics, armed with the clarity and focus provided by the doctrinal decrees resulting from the Council of Trent (1545–63), went on the counter-attack so that by the end of the century they had not only halted the advance of heresy, but regained lost ground.[10] As a symbolic counterpart to this recovery of confidence, papal canonization was resumed in 1588 after a hiatus of sixty-five years.[11] The following seventy-seven years (down to 1665) were to see no fewer than fourteen canonizations.[12] In addition, there were twenty-seven beatifications,

8 'etiamsi praedicta festa in hoc calendario non sint descripta'. Although this phrase is absent from the 1568 Plantin, Antwerp edition of the Roman Breviary, it is already present in the Plantin edition of 1585 and is reprinted thereafter.
9 This figure includes the *propria* of three countries, Spain (in fifteen editions), Poland (three) and Portugal (one). Amiet, pp. 310–437. Illustrative of the difficulty of tracing all editions of such an elusive liturgical genre is the fact that for the N. Italian diocese of Piacenza, Amiet lists neither the 1619 nor the 1624 editions (p. 399). Evidence also exists for editions of 1598, 1608 and 1610. See Ditchfield, *Liturgy, sanctity and history*, p. 136.
10 Geoffrey Parker sees the War of Cologne (1583–8) as the turning point in the struggle between Protestantism and Catholicism in Germany. See his *The Thirty Years War*, p. 20. Cf. D. MacCulloch, *Reformation*, pp. 449–57.
11 Burke, 'How to be a Counter-Reformation saint', p. 49.
12 In the case of Andrea Corsini, the actual bull of canonization was only proclaimed in 1724. There were seven Spaniards: the Franciscan Diego of Alcalá (c.1400–63) in 1588, the Dominican Raymund Peñaforte (c.1175–1275) in 1601, the Jesuit founder saints Francis Xavier (1506–1552) and Ignatius Loyola (1491–1556), the layman Isidore Agricola (c.1080–c.1130), the Spanish Discalced Carmelite Teresa of Avila (1515–82) all in 1622, the Spanish Augustinian Thomas of Villanova (1486–1555) in 1658; four Italians: Francesca Ponziani (1384–1436) in 1608, Carlo Borromeo (1538–84) in 1610, the founder of the Oratorians Filippo Neri (1515–95) in 1622, the Carmelite Andrea Corsini (1302–73) in 1629 and one each from Poland: Jacek Odrovaz (d.1257) in 1594; Portugal: the Franciscan tertiary Queen

(fifty-one if one includes the twenty-four martyred companions of the Jesuit Paolo Miki and Franciscan Pietro Battista Blásquez, who were all put to death in Nagasaki, Japan).[13] Finally, there were two confirmations of universal and eight of non-universal cult as well as two proclamations of 'equivalent (*equipollent*) beatification'.[14] This revival in saint-making was accompanied by an unprecedented attempt at the regulation of cults. As has been seen, this was first undertaken in the immediate aftermath of the Council of Trent by Cardinal Guglielmo Sirleto. It was then placed under the jurisdiction of the new Congregation of Rites; but their authority in the area was contested by the Congregation of the Holy Office (better known as the Inquisition, founded 1542).

Just as the traditional top-down view of Tridentine liturgical reform needs to take account of 'reciprocity within inequality' (to borrow William Taylor's crisp formulation), so consideration of the cult of saints simply in terms of a 'revival accompanied by an increase in central control of the sacred, or the

Elisabeth (1271–1336) in 1626 and France: Francis of Sales (1567–1622) in 1665. All except Diego of Alcalá are listed in the *Index ac status causarum*, pp. 547–9. Nine of the above had been beatified before being canonized. Ignatius Loyola was the first to undergo this treatment (in 1609). Carlo Borromeo was the last saint to be canonized without previously being beatified.

13 Until 1662, with the first formal beatification ceremony conducted by the Pope in St Peter's, this status was conferred simply by means of a bull. They were (in chronological order): the Spanish Augustinian, John (González) of Sahagún (c.1430–1479) in 1601; the French reformer of Poor Clare monasteries, Colette Boilet (1381–1447) in 1604; the Jesuits Stanislaus Kostka (1550–68) and Aloysius Gonzaga (1568–91) in 1605; the Spanish Franciscan, Salvatore (Grionesos) of Horta (1520–67) in 1606; the Spanish Dominican, Louis Bertrán (1526–81) in 1608; Ignatius of Loyola and the Italian Dominican tertiary Margaret of Città di Castello (1287–1320) in 1609; the Italian Capuchin Serafino of Montegranaro (1540–1604) in 1610; Teresa of Avila (1614); Philip Neri (1615); the Spaniards Thomas of Villanova (1486–1555) and Paschal Baylon (1540–92) in 1618; Isidore the Farmer and Francis Xavier (1619); the Spanish Franciscan Peter (Sanabria) of Alcántara (1499–1562) in 1622; the Italian Franciscan Giacomo delle Marche (c.1394–1476), the Italian Theatine Andrea Avellino (1521–1608), the Spanish Jesuit Francisco de Borja (1510–72), the Italian Capuchin Felix (Porri) of Cantalice (1515–87) all in 1625; the Italian Carmelite Maria Maddalena de Pazzi (1556–1607) in 1626; the Franciscan Pedro Baptista Blásquez and his twenty-two companions together with the Jesuit Paolo Miki and his two companions (all of whom were martyred in 1597) in 1627; the Italian founder of the Theatines, Gaetano (Cajetan) of Thiene (1480–1547) in 1629; the Spanish founder of the Brothers Hospitallers, John of God (1495–1550) in 1630; the Savoyard Bishop of Geneva, Francis of Sales (1567–1622) in 1662; the Spanish Augustinian canon, Peter of Arbués (1440–1485) in 1664. This list is based on that given in Levillain, *Dictionnaire historique*, p. 192, which has been cross-referenced with the *Index ac status causarum* and *Bibliotheca sanctorum*.

14 The *equipollent* beatifications were of the hermit Romuald of Ravenna (c.950–1027?) and the founder of the Mercedarians, Peter of Nolasco (d.1249). For the former see ACCS, *Decreta servorum dei*, vol. 1, pp. 146–7, dated 8 February 1594. For Nolasco this had been prefaced by official recognition of his local cult in 1628. The relevant *Decretum casus excepti* was dated 30 September 1628. See *Index ac status causarum*, p. 457.

right to define the sacred' needs to be nuanced.[15] To begin with, we need to move beyond the identification of the history of the cult of saints with the history of canonization and appreciate that during the period never had so many saints (from *all periods* of Christian history) been integrated into Roman Catholic worship and devotion. Moreover, the inclusion of those whose non-universal cults were approved by Rome in the list of those who received papal recognition 1588–1665 points to the issue which Trent placed centre stage: how to reconcile particular, local practice with universal, Roman precepts.

3. Making saints – politics and procedure

It is important not only to remember that the reform of canonization procedure postdates Trent, but to understand that its complexity, combined with the fact that jurisdiction over it was a shared (and not uncontested) responsibility between the Congregation of Rites and the Holy Office, makes it difficult to date the introduction of changes to a single innovation or year. The traditional date given for the advent of a new age in the history of canonization is 1588, which saw both the first papal canonization since 1523, that of the Spanish Franciscan missionary Diego of Alcalá and, later that year, the founding of the Congregation of Rites. But as this order of events suggests, the revival of canonization predated the creation of the agency which was involved in overseeing changes in procedure. Moreover, the first four canonizations processed by the Congregation – those of Jacek (Hyacinth) Odrovaz, Raymund Peñaforte, Francesca Ponziani and Carlo Borromeo – were dealt with according to long established procedure that was essentially unchanged since the Middle Ages.[16] Moreover, it is important to remember that this hiatus in canonizations was not accompanied by corresponding inactivity on the part of papal recognition of non-universal cults. Between 1524 and 1588, no fewer than fourteen holy men and women were so honoured.[17]

---

15 Burke, 'How to be a Counter-Reformation saint', p. 50. Cf. Taylor, *Magistrates of the sacred*, p. 6, where the author acknowledges the influence on his thinking here of the historian E. P. Thompson and the anthropologist James Scott.
16 Papa, 'La sacra congregazione dei Riti', pp. 29–33. Cf. Finucane, 'Saint making at the end of the sixteenth century' *passim*.
17 I follow here the data compiled by Christian Renoux, *Sainteté et mystique féminines à l'âge baroque*, annexe no. 2, pp. 771–2 with dates cross-referenced with the *Bibliotheca sanctorum*. They were: the Venetian nobles Lorenzo Giustiniani (1381–1456) in 1524 and Giacomo Salomoni (1231–1314) in 1526; Jacek Odrovaz, Peter of Luxembourg (1369–87) and Louis Aleman (d.1450) all in 1527; aristocratic Poor Clare Catherine of Bologna (1413–63) in 1530; the Dominican noble Agnes of Montepulciano (1274–1317) in 1532; the noble hermit from Noto Guglielmo Cuffitelli (1309–1404) in 1538; Raymund Peñaforte in 1542; the Portuguese

Papal reservation in matters of canonization had been unambiguously asserted as far back as the papal letter to King Canute of Sweden, *Audivimus* (ca.1170) and enshrined in canon law as long ago as 1234 (Gregory IX, *Decretales*, III, 45, 1). Moreover, the two-tier model of trials to collect testimony was also centuries old. This consisted of the *processus ordinarius* (sometimes referred to as the *processus inquisitionis et informationis*), which was instigated at the initiative of the bishop (*ordinarius*) of the diocese where the candidate had died or lived in order to establish the candidate's saintly reputation (*fama sanctitatis*), on whose positive outcome, in combination with an effective lobbying campaign consisting of postulatory letters from supporting individuals or institutions addressed to the pope, depended the next stage: the *processus apostolicus*. This was sometimes referred to as the *processus remissorialis et compulsorialis* after the name given to the special letters of instruction required from Rome before such a trial could take place. These were frequently drawn up by senior members (*auditori*) of the highest court of the Roman Curia – the Rota. Although this trial often made use as far as possible of the same witnesses as the *processus ordinarius*, it subjected them to a more rigorous series of questions (*interrogatorii*) ascertaining their trustworthiness and knowledge of the candidate in both the processes ordinarius and apostolicus being investigated. Questions about the life, virtues and miracles of the candidate followed a set pattern predetermined by a series of propositions (*articuli*), which could run to several hundred in number, about the holy man or woman under study. A selected number of these propositions were put to each witness, who was thereby asked to corroborate the propositions s/he could comment upon. These sets of questions were both generated by legal officers of the Sacred Congregation of Rites. The *interrogatorii* were invariably drawn up by the most senior canonist in the Congregation, who from 1631 was the *promotore della fede*, (promoter of the faith, perhaps better known by the sobriquet of the devil's advocate), while the *articuli* or *positiones* were the product of the postulator or procurator appointed by the order or institution which was sponsoring the case in question. Trials could be conducted simultaneously in more than one geographical location. The latter were determined by where the candidate had lived and died. The resultant documentation was then examined by two or three members of the college of cardinals before the latter's report was submitted to the pope. By the sixteenth century the auditors of the Rota

noble hermit Gonsalvo of Amarante (c.1187–c.1259) in 1560; Princess Marguerite of Savoy (1382?–1464) and the Dominican tertiary Colomba of Rieti (1467–1501) both in 1566; the noble founder of the Premonstratensians Norbert of Magdeburg/Xanten (1085?–1134) in 1582; the child 'martyr' Simon 'Simonino' of Trent (d.1475) in 1588.

were also crucially involved in summarizing the material in a report (*relatio*). However, the sheer volume of cases post-1634, combined with the increased professionalization of the relevant legal officers in the Congregation of Rites, in particular the promoter of the faith, increasingly marginalized the auditors' role. At a meeting of the Congregation of 24 August 1632, for example, there arose a dispute between the auditors of the Rota and the promoter of the faith over the latter's assertion of his right to draw up the headings (*positiones*) under which cases were summarized for consideration by the Cardinal-members in the summary report (*relatio*).[18] The significance of this dispute can be seen from the fact that how the *relatio* was structured largely determined the order of business in subsequent meetings of the congregation. In broad terms, it tended to have a tripartite structure. After a brief outline of the candidate's life together with a history of the cult, there followed a listing of his/her virtues, first theological (faith, hope and charity), then cardinal (justice, prudence, fortitude and temperance), before concluding with a detailed account of the evidence for miracles (those *post mortem* receiving the lion's share of attention).

What *was* new post-Trent was a resolve on the part of the papacy to differentiate more clearly than ever before between the local nature of the ordinary trial and the universal authority of the apostolic trial and furthermore to ensure, through tighter regulation, that the former in no way constituted official recognition of sanctity (of whatever degree) nor prejudged the outcome of the second stage. Papal preoccupation with this problem can be dated with some precision, to Clement VIII's creation of a special 'Congregazione de Beati' in 1602.[19] This committee was made up initially of nine theologians and seventeen cardinals; including, interestingly, only one from the Congregation of Rites besides no fewer than eight from the Holy Office and a further two from the Congregation of the Index. This temporary committee was brought into being precisely to deal with the problem of how to cope with pressure on the part of various interest groups – from religious orders to royal houses – to canonize those recently deceased who enjoyed degrees of saintly reputation that led to their effectively enjoying public cult without papal dispensation. Clement revealingly termed them the 'new blesseds' (*beati moderni*), so as to differentiate such potential candidates for canonization clearly from those for whom evidence of a long-established local or regional cult (*ab immemorabili tempore*) could be found. The particular case which appears to have precipitated the pope's action, by making him uncomfortably aware of the power

18 Gotor, *Chiesa e santità*, p. 81.
19 Gotor, 'La fabbrica dei santi', 696–708 and Gotor, *I beati del papa*, pp. 127–253. Cf. Papa, *Le cause di canonizzazione*, pp. 57, 61–3.

of pressure groups to support embarrassing and controversial candidates, was that of the Ferrarese Dominican preacher Girolamo Savonarola (1452–98), whose candidacy (and orthodoxy) was vigorously, if unsuccessfully, championed not only by his own order but also by the Oratorians, led by Filippo Neri.[20]

However, the problem of how to control such cults was wider and it can be argued that it is not until the mid-1620s that the papacy got a grip on the problem.[21] Until then, the situation was fluid and papal policy far from consistent. For example, in 1600 official permission was granted for the publishing of two engravings depicting Francis Xavier and Ignatius Loyola with haloes, surrounded by depictions of their miracles. In addition, both men were clearly labelled 'beatus' before official grant of this title had been given.[22] Rather than permission being revoked, the pope willed that the images already printed should continue to be publicly sold, but that no more be printed. In the case of two young Jesuits who had died in the odour of sanctity, Stanislaus Kostka and Aloysius Gonzaga (in 1568 and 1591 respectively), in 1605 Pope Paul V granted them both the title of 'beatus', even though trials had only recently been under way for the latter (1603–4) and were not to start before 1621 for the former. It is in such an atmosphere of flux that one should situate the manuscript treatise written by the Oratorian hagiographer and *consultor* to the *Congregazione de Beati*, Antonio Gallonio, in 1596 which was explicitly entitled: *How one should present those who are not yet canonized.*[23]

The pragmatic and, above all, moderate tenor of Gallonio's treatise may be seen by the fact that he argued for the legitimacy of private cults, even to the extent of using images and candles, but that publicly the deceased's tomb should only be decorated with lamps. Although the term 'saint' could be used and their deeds could be celebrated in print immediately after death, public acknowledgement of the cult should otherwise be limited to a mass to commemorate the day of the candidate's decease. Gallonio also asserted the Pope's complete authority in the matter of canonization, including his capacity to add the names of holy men and women to the catalogue of saints

---

20 See now S. Dall'Aglio, *Savonarola e il savonarolismo*, pp. 185–8.
21 Beginning with the decree of 13 March 1625 issued by the Holy Office, for the details of which see below.
22 Bury, *The print in Italy*, pp. 130–1 (fig. 11 Ignatius) and Leuschner, *Antonio Tempesta*, p. 229 (fig. 7.15 Xavier).
23 *De his quae prestari possunt non canonizatis*, BVR, ms *H. 14*, ff. 272r–307r. Another copy may be found at BVR, ms. *G. 91*.

immediately after their death should they so wish.[24] Gallonio went on to trace an unbroken succession of no fewer than sixty-eight papal canonizations from Pope Stephen III's recognition of the cult of the hermit Trudpert in the mid-eighth century down to Clement VIII's canonization of Jacek Odrovaz in 1594.[25] Although, interestingly, Gallonio did concede a degree of overlap in his admission that episcopal recognition of cults continued up until 1159 and the accession of Alexander III when papal monopoly in this area of competence was asserted.[26]

The limits of the debate that occurred in the *Congregazione dei Beati* were marked at one extreme by the hardliner Francisco Peña, an auditor of the Rota who was involved in all the trials which resulted in canonization at this period. His other roles as *consultor* of the Index and editor of Nicolaus Eymerich's fourteenth-century inquisitorial manual remind us of the symbiotic relationship between investigation of sanctity and investigation into heresy; between canonization and censorship. Peña believed that local commissaries of the Holy Office should decide whether or not the unofficial cult of someone who had died with a 'reputation for sanctity' (*fama sanctitatis*) should be suppressed for its 'whiff of heresy' (*sapore di eresia*).[27] At the other end of the wide spectrum of opinion were those who believed that such decisions lay within the authority of the local bishop, which was essentially the traditional position which the Council of Trent had left undisturbed. This was essentially the view of Cardinal Roberto Bellarmino, who concurred with the line of argument put forward by his adviser Gallonio in a memo dated 5 December 1602.[28] They argued that those figures who had not yet been formally canonized could enjoy devotion, so long as the latter was conducted in private. At the same time, in order to exercise closer control over intermediate, non-universal cults, Peña and others pressed for an extension of papal reservation to embrace beatification as well as canonization. Although there are several examples of early sixteenth-century popes authorizing non-universal cults, such as Clement VII in the case of Jacek Odrovaz, whose veneration was permitted only within the dominions of the King of Poland, there was not yet any consistent use of and differentiation between the terms *beatus* and *sanctus*. On 19 June 1601 Clement VIII granted

---

24 'possunt [papae] statim ab eorum obitu sanctorum cathalogo ascribi'. BVR, ms. *H. 14*, f. 289r.
25 Gallonio, *De his quae prestari*. ff. 297r–307r.   26 Gallonio, *De his quae prestari*. f. 294r.
27 Gotor, 'La fabbrica dei santi', 699.
28 BVR, ms. *H. 14*, ff. 378r–85r with a response on ff. 386r–87r and Gallonio's own replies to these objections ff. 388r–89r. Cf. R. Bellarmino, *De controversiis*, pt. IV lib. 1, cap. VIII.

an *indultum* in favour of a strictly localized cult in honour of Juan de Sahagún, initially restricted to the diocese of Salamanca, but whether this should be considered a 'beatification' as such is a moot point.[29] Doubts on this point would appear to be backed up by the fact that in the same year Angelo Rocca, in the first treatise on canonization published post Trent, *De canonizatione sanctorum commentarius*, used the term 'semi-canonization' (*semicanonizatio*) when discussing this very case in an effort to reflect its intermediate status. The first treatise expressly to discuss 'beatification' is Felice Contelori's *Tractatus et praxis de canonizatione sanctorum* (1634), although by this date he was describing a term which had been in public use since at least 1608 when Paul V declared that the Dominican missionary Louis Bertrán 'could be called blessed'.[30] It is well known that the first beatification ceremony to take place in St Peter's was that of François de Sales in 1662; what is less well known is the fact that papal permission for ceremonies to mark the beatification of several founders of religious orders had been granted to specified churches in Rome since 1609 when the Jesuits celebrated their founder's beatification that year in the Gesù, (although as if to make as clear as possible the intermediate nature of this honour, Paul V prohibited the participation at mass of the cardinals present at the ceremony: 'so that the liturgy did not take on the appearance of a [formal cardinals'] chapel', [an honour] which is due only to canonized saints').[31]

Teresa of Avila's trial saw two innovations of considerable future import. Firstly, her apostolic trial was clearly divided into two stages: *in genere* (1604–6), where the emphasis was on demonstrating her saintly reputation and *in specie* (1609–10), which was focused on her virtues and miracles. (Although subsequently, where a candidate's holy reputation was beyond doubt, as was the case with St Francis of Sales, the *in genere* trial was omitted.) Secondly, in a postulatory letter from the University of Salamanca to Clement VIII of 2 February 1602 in support of Teresa's cause, we have what appears to be the first occasion where the term 'heroic' was applied to the degree of a candidate's exercise of virtues.[32] By 1614–16 the term found its way into the reports of the

---

29 Papa, *Le cause di canonizzazione nel primo periodo della congregazione dei riti (1588–1634)*, p. 190. Cf. *Bibliotheca sanctorum* VI, col. 899 which is then reported by Gotor, *Chiesa e santità*, p. 47.

30 'beatus noncupari possit'. Veraja, *La beatificazione*, pp. 101, 103. Cf. F. Contelori, *Tractatus*, pp. 14–21.

31 '. . . ma Nostro Signore giovedì sera fece intendere a tutti, che andassero a far oratione ma non assistessero alla messa, acciò non paresse una Cappella, che conviene solo alli santi'. *Avviso* dated 1 August 1609 in BAV, *Urbin. Lat. 1077*, ff. 244v–245r. Cf. Papa, *Le cause di canonizzazione*, p. 195 n.285.

32 'Nullis enim praeceptis aut institutis facilius et certius homines ad vitae rectitudinem excitantur quam heroicarum virtutum ad imitandum propositis exemplis.' *Acta SS,*

auditors of the Rota, until in 1624 the following formula was used for the first time (with reference to Francesco Borgia): 'sanctity and heroicity of virtues to be approved' (*constare de sanctitate et heroicis virtutibus*).[33] The essence of this quality is to be understood in terms of the repeated and apparently effortless carrying out of virtuous acts.[34] Much has been made of this innovation, to the extent of regarding its advent as evidence for the modernization of sanctity: from a magical conception of the exercise of miracle-working powers to a more purely ethical one. This could be more easily distinguished by contemporaries from pretence of sanctity (*finta ò affettata santità*), which in the seventeenth century was receiving unprecedented attention from local tribunals of the Holy Office.[35] However, for all its significance, the fact remains that from the point of view of the overwhelming majority of consumers of sanctity throughout not only the period covered by this chapter, the efficacy of a saint was measured above all by his or her capacity to deliver miraculous cures. Moreover, for the first century or so after Trent, at the height of confessional polemic over the cult of saints, the miracle played an important role as an authenticating sign of Roman Catholicism as the one and only *vera ecclesia*.[36] Finally, once a candidate had been beatified, s/he only qualified for canonization by virtue of further *miraculous* activity.

For the *real* watershed in the history of canonization procedure we must look to the legislation that rendered the work of the *Congregazione de Beati* superfluous.[37] The most important item here was the decree of 13 March 1625 issued not by the Congregation of Rites but by the Holy Office. This measure not only prohibited the placing of lights or votive offerings before (painted or sculpted) images of holy men and women whose holiness had not been officially recognized by the pope, but also banned the printing and possession of accounts of any miracles or visions such unofficial candidates for sanctity claimed to have experienced.[38]

This decree led to the formalization of what was effectively a preparatory trial for all future candidates for canonization at which it was necessary to prove that they enjoyed no public cult. In view of the simultaneous requirement to

Octobris VII, section LVI, p. 350. Cf. Papa, *Le cause di canonizzazione*, p. 168 and R. De Maio, 'L'ideale eroico nei processi di canonizzazione della Controriforma' in R. De Maio, *Riforme e miti nella chiesa del '500*, pp. 253–72.

33 ACCS, *Decreta servorum Dei*, vol. I, p. 234 (dated 24 August 1624). Cf. Papa, *Le cause di canonizzazione*, p. 169.

34 Benedict XIV, *De servorum dei*, bk. III, ch. XXII, n. 8.

35 Prosperi, *I tribunali della coscienza*, p. 461–2. Cf. Schutte, *Aspiring saints*, passim.

36 Ditchfield, *Liturgy, sanctity and history*, pp. 117–34.

37 Papa, *Le cause di canonizzazione*, pp. 319ff.

38 BAV, *Urbin. Lat. 1095*, fol. 219r. Cf. Castellino, *Elucidarium theologicum*, pp. 120–3.

demonstrate a candidate's *fama sanctitatis*, this decree, *super non cultu*, meant that campaigners had to strike a particularly difficult and fine balance. The effect of this decree was to remove from episcopal control all but the initial stage of canonization: the *processus ordinarius*. Either side of this decree had been published two new restrictions by the Congregation of Rites itself that represented further attempts to control the cults of the *beati moderni*. On 28 September 1624 *Per decem annos* introduced the requirement that there be a pause of ten years between the closure of the ordinary trial and the opening of the apostolic trial; while on 20 November 1627 a decree prohibited discussion of a candidate's virtues or martyrdom until the candidate had been dead half a century (the so-called 50-year rule). However, the right of local bishops to instigate and oversee the collection of eyewitness testimony immediately after the death of the candidate was respected. The sole exception to these restrictions was made for those candidates who could prove continuity of cult for at least one hundred years (*ab immemorabili*). By a decree of 20 November 1628, however, it was deemed insufficient simply to demonstrate 'immemorial' veneration in general terms. Rather such devotion had to have been expressed liturgically in the uninterrupted practice of recitation of the candidate's office and the saying of mass in his/her honour. Moreover, the approval of such 'equivalent canonizations' (*canonizzazione equipollente*), though permissive in nature, had to be explicitly decreed by the Congregation of Rites. Only in this way could papal reservation be asserted over non-universal as well as universal cults.

The following years were to see further modifications to the operation of the Congregation of Rites. The most important of these was that on 27 January 1631 it was decreed that there were to be only three meetings a year (in January, May and September) at which the Congregation would meet to discuss candidates for beatification and canonization in the presence of the pope. (Although less important business relating to prospective candidates could be discussed without the pontiff's presence.) Furthermore, at about the same time, the individual cardinals who by now were required as sponsors for each candidate (*cardinale ponente*) were only permitted to put forward at each meeting a single miracle for consideration. The year 1631, as has been already noted, also saw the formal institution of the office of the *promotore della fede*, whose raising of problematic questions (*dubia*) relating to the evidence presented in favour of a candidate's cause (which were written down in the form of formal replies (*animadversiones*) to the arguments put forward) now took on a more consistent format. Such was the number and import of these decrees that Urban VIII had them collected together and republished on 5 July 1634 as a papal brief, *Coelestis Ierusalem cives* and then, with a few further relevant decrees, again as *Decreta servanda in canonizatione et beatificatione sanctorum* on 12 March 1642. These decrees of 1642 constituted the overall framework for procedure in beatification and canonization until the publication of *Divinus perfectionis magister* in 1983.

Such legislation evidently had the desired effect, for already during the 1630s the considerable activity of the Congregation of Rites, relating to no fewer than eighty-eight cases, failed to result in a single papal canonization, beatification or even recognition of existing cult *ab immemorabili* in the same period. One of the unsuccessful cases before the Congregation at this time was that of Gregory X (pope, 1272–6), whose case had been reopened in 1622. The grounds on which his cause was halted in 1645 – the doubtful historical status of the medieval parchment attached to his tomb on which were listed his miracles – reveals the overwhelming importance of legal-historical criteria in post-1634 canonization procedure.[39] Equally, the grounds on which his regional cult finally received papal recognition in 1713 – proof of continuity of cult *ab immemorabili* (from before 1534, i.e. a century before *Coelestis Ierusalem cives*) whereby Gregory's case was exempted from Urban VIII's regulations – demonstrates the great significance placed by the papacy on the need, wherever possible, to find official place even for those local and regional cults which did not satisfy the legal criteria for inclusion in the universal calendar of saints; even if this was achieved by officially sanctioned circumvention of the relevant legislation, as was reflected in the very title given to such acts where a universal cult was being recognized: 'equivalent canonization' (*canonizzazione equipollente*). As has already been seen, between 1588 and 1666 just two candidates fitted into this category: Romuald of Ravenna in 1594 and the founder of the Mercedarians, Peter Nolasco (in 1664).

Any numerical analysis of the pattern of papal canonization during this period has to be combined not only with an awareness of those whose cult was confirmed, but also of the more numerous group of those whose cases never got further than a diocesan *processus ordinarius*. The literally *hundreds* of men and women who merely enjoyed local *fama sanctitatis* throughout the Roman Catholic world during the period (not an unreasonable supposition given that the Kingdom of Naples alone had fifty-seven such cases 1540–1660) should therefore be set beside the mere fourteen who were papally canonized (1588–1665).[40] Given the difficulties placed in the way of canonization, it is unsurprising to discover that of these fourteen, Isidore Agricola was the only

---

39 Ditchfield, *Liturgy, sanctity and history*, p. 255.   40 Sallmann, *Naples et ses saints*, p. 132.

layperson (Elisabeth of Portugal was a Franciscan tertiary). Among the dozen religious, there were no fewer than five founders of religious orders. This constituted the most important road to canonization. The next most important route was that of the good shepherd (Carlo Borromeo, Andrea Corsini, Francis de Sales and Thomas of Villanova). The gender imbalance was very marked; with just three women (Francesca Romana, Teresa of Avila and Elisabeth of Portugal) to eleven men. A final point to note is the fact that with twelve out of the fourteen canonized from Italy and the Iberian peninsula, this period sees a dramatic reassertion of the Mediterranean heartland of Roman Catholicism over Europe north of the Alps, with the hegemonic Roman Catholic superpower of the period – Spain – taking the lead, with no fewer than seven successful candidates. The canonization of Diego of Alcalá, for example, may be justifiably seen as a conscious gesture by Sixtus V to reward Philip II for undertaking the Armada against the heretic Queen Elisabeth.[41] Similarly, as Ron Finucane has shown in his important reconstruction of the canonization of Jacek Odrovaz, it was the desire by both Sixtus V and Clement VIII to create a united front against the Turk, in which a strong Catholic Poland was seen to play an important geo-strategic role, which proved decisive. Finucane is undoubtedly right to argue that in the confessionally divided early modern world, papal canonization became ever more a political act, in which dynastic power and geography spoke louder than favoured models of sanctity or even tighter judicial procedure. Turning to the control of non-universal cults, however, such a top-down explanatory model needs to be combined with an understanding of how cults were produced and consumed at a local or regional level.

4. Counting saints – censuses of the sacred

What legitimate place was there in the Tridentine Church for those who enjoyed only local or regional devotion? To set the issue in particularly stark terms, the saints' calendar for January from the Roman Breviary of 1568 lists twenty-five individually named saints plus feasts for the Circumcision of Jesus, Holy Innocents and Epiphany; while the first two volumes dedicated to the same month in that most comprehensive census of the sacred ever undertaken, the collection of saints' *vitae* with detailed critical commentary begun under the auspices of the Jesuit Jean Bolland in 1643, the *Acta Sanctorum*, provided lives of no fewer than 1,170 saints. Moreover, the rediscovery (in 1578) and

---

41 Villalon, 'San Diego de Alcalá', 713–15.

subsequent exploration of the Roman catacombs brought 'on stream' what appeared to contemporaries to be an inexhaustible supply of early Christian martyrs' relics, a high proportion of whom had never been listed in official martyrologies (and whose acts never made it even into the *Acta SS*). This phenomenon, in turn, inspired bishops not just within the Mediterranean historical heartland of Roman Catholicism, during the century and a half after the close of the Council of Trent, to become amateur archaeologists and demonstrate, frequently in a spirit of fierce competition, that their local churches also possessed these priceless *vestigia* from the most heroic period of ecclesiastical history.

The problem of reconciling local devotions to the universal calendar of saints was essentially resolved through the creation of mechanisms whereby universal cults were carefully distinguished from local and regional ones: the *sanctus/a* from *beatus/a*. In the Middle Ages the assertion of the papal monopoly over universal cults had not been accompanied by any corresponding attempt by Rome to regularize and oversee systematically the particular devotions of diocese and region. The response post-Trent, by contrast, was founded not only on making a clear distinction between the universal and particular cults, but also on ensuring that even the latter followed universal guidelines. The fruit of this new approach was to refurbish the already existing term *beatus/a* to signify a clearly defined intermediary status. The latter not only existed as a half-way house to canonization and sainthood, but also, crucially, came to have an autonomous existence to indicate cults that in a local or regional context enjoyed all the honour owed to fully-fledged saints *and also* all the obligations to obey universal canonical regulations. It is in this way that one can talk of a simultaneous development: of the particularization of the universal – in the sense that the offices of local saints had to obey a universal, standardized rubric – on the one hand, and of the universalization of particular practices, on the other. The latter was symbolized with particular clarity by the Sacred Congregation of Rites' *Decretum pro patronis in posterum eligendis* of 23 March 1630, which demanded that the patron saints of particular confraternities, villages, towns, or nations only be elected from amongst candidates who had been canonized by the pope or whose names were already to be found in the Roman Martyrology, official evidence that they enjoyed a universal cult.

Such a carefully differentiated hierarchy of sanctity stands at the very heart of the Tridentine reform of the cult of saints, whereby local practice was to be brought into line with universal norms. However, *outside* the liturgical context, dioceses and religious orders throughout the Roman Catholic world were able to give full expression to their local patriotism. This was achieved by means of affixing an author's disclaimer (*protesto dell'autore* to give the Italian version of the phrase) at the front of books containing accounts of the *vitae* of men and women with saintly reputation from towns, regions, nations or religious orders the length and breadth of the Roman Catholic world. This disclaimer explicitly stated that the terms *beatus* and *sanctus* to be found in the text which followed were not to be understood in the official, canonical sense. In this way, just as the equipollent canonization permitted confirmation of the cult of numerous holy men and women who had not met the rigorous legalistic criteria newly refined by Urban VIII, so the *protesto dell'autore* adroitly sidestepped the Holy Office decree of 1625 that had disqualified from further consideration for canonization all those cults which by exhibiting evidence of public cult had anticipated apostolic decision in this matter.

In this way Rome kept a space for the process whereby universal virtues were particularized in local saints with whom their compatriots could more easily identify. As the leading hagiographer of the Kingdom of Naples, Paolo Regio, put it in the preface to his *Vita de'sette santi protettori di Napoli* (1572): 'these saints [of ours] intercede more than ever in heaven next to the Protector of the World in the name of their compatriots'. Almost a century later, the picture was unchanged when one of the numerous antiquarians who saved for posterity their local devotional particularities, the Umbrian Ludovico Jacobilli, author of a massive, three-volume survey of his province's holy men and women (1647–61), referred to his work as a 'mine of sanctity' rich with examples from every station in life for his compatriots to imitate. What is more, their imitability was greater since 'they were composed of the same stuff (*medesima massa*) as us'.[42]

5. Enjoying the saints – producing and consuming devotions in a world religion

The almost ceaseless processing of relics, images and sacred bodies intensified during the early modern period. The work of Peter Brown has enabled us to see such activity as characteristic of the cult of saints ever since St Ambrose's realization that by such acts 'more power could pass through stronger and better insulated wires towards the bishop as leader of the community'.[43] In a confessionally-divided world, devotion to saints was a highly visible badge of Catholic identity (along with the ever more elaborately gilded and shaped

---

42 Jacobilli, *Vite de'santi e beati dell'Umbria*, vol. 3, p. 540.
43 Brown, *The cult of the saints*, p. 37.

monstrances used to carry the Eucharistic Host in procession). It is thus perhaps more appropriate to consider 1580 rather than 1588 as marking the post-Reformation revival of the cult of saints. For in that year the Wittelsbach rulers of Bavaria engineered what is surely the most symbol-laden 'holy rescue' (*furta sacra*) of relics since the Venetian sack of Byzantium in 1204, when they removed the body of Benno of Meissen (significantly, one of the last two saints to have beeen canonized, in 1523) from Protestant Saxony to adorn their capital, Munich.

The early modern counterpart to Brown's wizard of sacred circuitry, the fourth-century bishop of Milan, was, appropriately enough, the Cardinal Archbishop of the same city, Carlo Borromeo, who linked the cult of saints directly to issues of ecclesiastical governance and devotional 'best practice'. The processing of his saintly early Christian predecessors, Simpliciano and Benigno, together with their martyr contemporaries Sisinio, Martirio and Alessandro, in May 1582 served not only to remind the prelates attending the Sixth Provincial Council of the antiquity and historical continuity of their metropolitan's office and his authority over them (a point underlined by the presence of portraits of all previous prelates of Milan adorning the archiepiscopal palace). It also provided occasion for the populace at large, from nobles to the *popolo minuto*, to engage in spiritual preparation for a very public act of devotion that brought the city and its hinterland together in a procession that carefully reinforced social hierarchy and ecclesiastical precedent. It was an act, furthermore, which was accompanied by the singing of psalms and prayers whose texts had been specially composed and printed for the occasion. All that is missing from the extract is reference to the sermon which we know was later given by San Carlo himself in the basilica of San Simpliciano.[44]

In this respect, the Milanese example points also to the importance of realizing to what extent devotion to the cult of saints was a multi-media experience; a *Gesamtkunstwerk*, in which art, architecture, sculpture, word, music and print were deployed to move heart and soul through eye and ear. S. Carlo Borromeo's processing of relics is not only a classic example of the genre, it also became an influential model for imitation that was disseminated not only via Bascapè's Latin *vita* (and Giussani's Italian one), but also in the highly influential collection of episcopal legislation that was the *Acta Ecclesiae Mediolanensis* (1582), which continued to be read and consulted in both the Old and New Worlds right down into the eighteenth century. However, if it is true to say that similar, if frequently less splendid, processions regularly punctuated the ritual

---

44 Bascapè, *Vita e opere di Carlo Arcivescovo di Milano*, pp. 559, 561.

year of dioceses the length and breadth of the Roman Catholic world, it is also important to realize that their celebration of civic concord and distinctive diocesan traditions did not occur in a vacuum, but in relation to rival, often conflicting, interpretations.

On 15 January 1648, the hagiographer and ecclesiastical historian Pietro Maria Campi (1569–1649) interrupted the long-delayed printing of his life's work, *Dell'historia ecclesiastica di Piacenza*, to incorporate a detailed account of the arrival in the N. Italian city, between 1643 and 1647, of some twenty bodies of early Christian martyrs, together with the relics of a further eighty-eight.[45] Their provenance was the catacombs under and around the churches of S. Saturn[in]o, S. Lucifero and SS. Mauro and Lello, just outside the city walls of Cagliari in Sardinia. These had begun to be excavated in 1614 under the personal initiative of Archbishop Francisco de Esquivel, in direct response to the discovery earlier the same year, by his opposite number in Sassari, Archbishop Gavino Manca de Cedrelles, of the bodies of SS. Gavino, Proto and Gianuario, who had been martyred under Diocletian, beneath the basilica of S. Gavino in Porto Tórres, near Sassari itself. At issue here was the perennial dispute over which archbishopric enjoyed historical primacy over the island: Cagliari or Sassari? In this context, the discovery of relics from the most heroic period of Christian history was presented as tangible evidence in support of their respective claims. De Esquivel's campaign (and that of his successor, Ambrogio Machin, who succeeded him in 1624) was orchestrated with assurance and aplomb: from the moment on the feast day of S. Saturn[in]o (6 November 1614) when, in the presence of a notary and many leading citizens of Cagliari, he uncovered the inscription 'SINNU' or 'SINUM' (taken as the abbreviated form for 'SANCTI INNUMERABILES') that led to the excavation of no fewer than 338 bodies, to the carefully supervised distribution of umpteen relics not only to Piacenza but also to several other cities in the Western Mediterranean, including Alassio in Liguria (which received the earliest shipment of 86 martyrs in 1624), Catalonia and Naples.[46] This was complemented by a sustained publicity campaign, which was marked by the successive appearance of De Esquivel's personal account of the happy rediscovery (in 1617), the Capuchin Stefano Esquirro's more detailed 'archaeological' treatment (in 1624) and finally of Dionigio Bonfant's exhaustive 'historical' account (in 1635), all of which were published in the (Spanish) vernacular. D'Esquivel and Machin thereby hoped to enlist the support of the Spanish king (who then ruled the island) in their

45 Campi, *Dell'historia*, vol. 1, pp. 181–3; vol. 3, pp. 208–14.
46 Mureddu et al., *'Sancti innumerabiles'*, passim. Cf. Ditchfield, 'Martyrs on the move'.

campaign. The latter's successful conclusion was marked by a series of decisions by the highest court in the Roman Curia, the Rota, between 1637 and 1640, which unambiguously rebuffed Sassari's pretensions to the title.

The next case study, by contrast, examines the ways in which the cult of a single saint – S. Geneviève, Patron of Paris – could simultaneously bear several meanings. In his revealing study of her cult from the later Middle Ages to the French Revolution, Moshe Sluhovsky has shown how readily it responded to the pressures of a rapidly expanding city.[47] Although traditionally associated with protection from flooding, from 1552 S. Geneviève came to be increasingly invoked as the city's patron saint of subsistence; supplier of grain to the city. The saint's image as a nurturing patron was associated with a new gendered appeal of the saint to women as nurturers and supervisors of the family bread supply at precisely a time when women's roles were being redefined and increasingly circumscribed. However, if we are to appreciate on just how many levels the cult of S. Geneviève could work simultaneously at times of unrest and conflict, we need to consider the processing of her relics that took place on 11 June 1652. It was a time of dramatic political conflict known as the *Fronde*, which had been aggravated that year by a severe drought. The procession was invoked by a coalition of merchants, *parlementaires* and the saint's confraternity in the teeth of fierce opposition from the Archbishop of Paris, who, wishing to assert his authority not only over the nearby Abbey of Sainte-Geneviève and that of his own rebellious canons, argued, *inter alia*, that such a procession should not take place during the octave of the feast of Corpus Christi when it necessarily distracted attention from devotion to the Eucharist. Once under way, the ceremony was then hijacked for political purposes by the leading *Frondeur*, Le Grand Condé, who in a successful effort to curry the favour of the *menu peuple* pushed his way through the crowds to kiss the sacred reliquary of S. Geneviève numerous times, before rushing to the West Door of Notre-Dame, where he reviewed the approaching procession – thereby simultaneously honouring the protectress of Paris and being honoured by the participants as *de facto* ruler of the city. The various uses made of the saint by these groups is illustrative of the frequent inability of any single authority, however powerful, fully to control and appropriate the cult. Here, effectively, no one was in charge.

As well as playing an important role in the assertion of municipal and regional identity, both vis-à-vis internal parties and in relation to external challenges, devotion to saints could also constitute an important 'weapon of

---

47 For what follows see Sluhovsky, *Patroness of Paris*, pp. 126–36.

the weak' in the armoury of those for whom conventional expressions of power and authority were denied. In the year 1662 a community of Franciscan nuns in Munich succeeded – via the assistance of a Capuchin friar – in securing from that rich mine of sanctity that was the Roman Catacombs the complete body of a certain S. Dorotea. According to the persuasive analysis of Ulrike Strasser, the nuns sought to use this new, very fashionable addition to their sacred treasury in order to secure for themselves a public presence in the city which had been denied them ever since their enforced claustration some forty years before, in 1621.[48] In spite of the best efforts of Modestus Reichart, Provincial of the Reformed Franciscan Order that enjoyed spiritual responsibility for their convent, the nuns succeeded in preventing him from examining the body of the saint in private. This would have necessitated breaking the authenticating seals to the casket containing the saints' bones, thereby preventing the bishop from officially recognizing their genuine status. Interestingly, the nuns invoked their cloistered status in order to prevent Reichart's gaining access. In this way, the sisters were able to open the casket on their own terms with the necessary witnesses, before lavishing due care and attention on preparing the saint for public display. The outcome was that although it was the Franciscan friars who carried the saint in procession through the streets of Munich, the nuns could claim sole responsibility for S. Dorotea's rich adornment and benefit from her presence in their church, whose efficacy as a 'prayer factory' for the souls of purgatory was thereby strengthened and reasserted.

The emphasis here has been on movement; not just in the physical sense, but also in semantic terms. Saints were signs or, better, signifiers, whose precise meanings were informed by context so that a single saint, as we have seen in the case of S. Geneviève, could mean different things to different people, even in the same time and place. In itself, this is an obvious point, but one whose important implications for our understanding of 'local' religion have all too often been left unexplored. For the capacities of saints to be simultaneously bearers of more than one meaning or embodiments of more than a single identity should remind us that devotion to saints and sacred space in general could never be exclusively 'local'.

Elsewhere, in the New World, it has been remarked that by the mid-seventeenth century at the latest, religion for the Nahua people of modern-day Mexico was in practice about saints: 'no other aspect of Christian belief and ritual had a remotely comparable impact on the broad range of [Nahua] activity (especially if we consider that Jesus Christ and often the cross were treated

---

48 Strasser, 'Bones of contention'.

as so many more saints)'.[49] Once the Nahua had learned the significance of the cult of saints, almost everything they wrote without supervision and thus for their own eyes and purposes – including wills, municipal decrees, property sales, leases or annals – reflected belief in the active agency of saints or invoked their intercession and aid. The latter were regarded as the parents of their people and as the true owners of a community's land. In fact, so closely bound up were the celestial protectors with the settlements they were patrons of that the general term for a named subentity of the basic indigenous unit of colonial government – the *altepetl* – which was known as the *calpolli*, was simply referred to as *santopan*, literally 'where a saint is'.

A particularly eloquent example of how the cult of saints could be appropriated and made to work for non-Westerners who had been recently converted comes from Japan, whose Christian community experienced the fiercest religious persecution seen anywhere in the world during this period. Conducted by the Tokugawa Bafuku regime and reaching its greatest intensity 1614–45, it resulted in the martyrdom of some 2,000 Christians (including seventy-one Europeans). Survival of Christian belief was only achieved at the price of the complete elimination of public cult. The latter was replaced with the domestic veneration by the *Kakure Kirishitan* ('Crypto-' or 'Hidden Christians'), who were forced to live outwardly as Buddhists, of *nandogami* (lit. 'closet-gods'), which included pictorial depictions of saints and martyrs called *gozensama*. These most commonly took the form of painted hanging scrolls (*kakemono*), which could be rolled up for safekeeping and concealment, where the image was framed by textiles such as figured silk or brocade.[50] That of the Madonna of the Snows, whose prototype was ultimately the Borghese Madonna in S. Maria Maggiore, is a particularly fine early example of this genre, painted, so argues convincingly Gauvin Bailey, by an indigenous, Japanese artist who had been trained at the Jesuit-run Niccolò academy. It shows how despite clear adherence to a European model, the artist had transformed 'every element of his image into equivalent Japanese style and technique', as can be seen most strikingly in the Madonna's high, arched eyebrows and narrow eyes.[51] Such a refined appropriation of Western religious art is eloquent testimony to the fact that the cult of saints did not merely function as a vector of religious propaganda for missionary endeavour but could also take root in the hearts and minds of non-Western Christians.

49 Lockhart, *The Nahuas after conquest*, p. 235.
50 Turnbull, 'The veneration of the martyrs of Ikitsuki'.
51 Bailey, *Art on the Jesuit missions*, pp. 75–6 (and fig. 35).

These examples of appropriation of saints' cults by their consumers in the New World should not be taken to imply that this process was unknown in the Old. The work of David Gentilcore, in particular, has eloquently described the ways in which saints both *in vita* and *post mortem* in the early modern Terra d'Otranto were fully integrated into the 'system of the sacred', whereby their healing power could be drawn on. In doing so, he has drawn attention to the existence of a shared community of belief in the potential to access supernatural powers between so-called 'élite' and 'popular' cultures, which are personified for him by the bishop and the witch, who coexist in a continuum rather than inhabiting distinct zones of belief.[52] Meanwhile, Jean Michel Sallmann's emphasis on the perceptions of sanctity adopted by consumers in the Kingdom of Naples has firmly placed the role of the saint as shamanic healer and miracle worker centre stage.[53]

6. Conclusion: religion as a verb not a noun

It has been a central contention of this chapter that a fuller understanding of the reform of liturgy and, specifically, its impact on the cult of saints can help us to see that the reforms adumbrated by the Council of Trent cannot be understood in terms of centre/periphery (or, for that matter, élite/popular) and that, to return to William Taylor's phrase quoted earlier, one should be alive to the dynamic of reciprocity within inequality. If such a perspective is adopted, one stands a better chance of shedding a still lingering obsession with asking what Roman Catholicism *was* during this period (i.e. what noun or label should we attach to it) and, instead, ask ourselves what it *did* (i.e. what cultural work did it undertake and what are the active verbs that can be used to describe the interactions involved).[54] If we did so, it might be easier for us to understand the protean forms local Roman Catholicisms took in the emergence of this planet's first world religion.

52 Gentilcore, *From bishop to witch*, passim.   53 Sallmann, *Naples et ses saints*.
54 Ditchfield, 'Of dancing cardinals and mestizo madonnas'.

PART IV

⋆

RESOLVING CONFESSIONAL CONFLICTS

13

Peace without concord: religious toleration in theory and practice

NICOLETTE MOUT

In the seventeenth century René Descartes (1596–1650) defended the philosopher's right to distinguish between the spheres of faith and reason, claiming practically unlimited intellectual freedom for reason. Where faith owed nothing to reason, being illuminated by divine revelation, reason owed nothing to faith: therefore, philosophy ought to be radically separated from revealed theology. This conviction had direct consequences for the practice of religious toleration, for it meant that the emphasis was shifting from the struggle for or against freedom of religion to a struggle for or against freedom of thought. Descartes claimed the right to think unconstrainedly about fundamental religious concepts and, moreover, to formulate these with equal liberty.[1] In his clash with the Dutch theologian Gisbertus Voetius (1598–1676), who opposed this notion with much fervour, Descartes interpreted the problem of free philosophical discussion not in ideal, but in moral and legal terms. Such liberty should not so much be considered a necessary philosophical condition for discovering hidden truths, but first and foremost a political right guaranteed by the government. Whoever blackened the reputation of an individual infringed this liberty, as Voetius had done when he attacked Descartes – or so the latter argued. Under a political system which guaranteed, at least in theory, equal liberties to every inhabitant of the Republic of the United Provinces, the theologian Voetius was not in a position powerful enough to oppress the philosopher Descartes. For, according to the latter, no theologian was privileged to overrule the magistrates, who were bound to protect philosophers like Descartes against aggression and calumny and, by so doing, were upholding law and order.[2]

Such emphasis on the importance of reason combined with arguments in favour of a species of toleration which resulted in freedom of thought was

---

1 Verbeek, *De vrijheid van de filosofie*.
2 Verbeek, 'Descartes et les exigences de la liberté'; Verbeek, 'Le contexte néerlandais'.

naturally not well received by everyone. The English theologian William Chillingworth (1602–44), who argued for religious toleration because no human being is infallible and therefore sincere disagreement of opinion should be acceptable, was accused of having 'runne mad with reason'.[3] Nonetheless, reason would become a very powerful concept in the debate concerning toleration during the early Enlightenment.[4] Advocating a 'reasonable' approach to religion, Benedictus de Spinoza (1632–77) zealously defended freedom of thought and speech. He was willing to accept, however, certain political limitations to religious toleration in case of a threat to public peace. Although, according to Spinoza, the individual thus could be obliged to curb his actions in deference to his legitimate rulers, he unquestionably had the right to liberty of thought and expression, both in speech and in writing.[5]

Reason, however, played a very different role in the debate about religious toleration in the previous century. Michel de Montaigne (1533–92) criticized those who overstepped the boundaries of reason during the French Wars of Religion and were responsible for decisions which were sometimes 'unjust, violent and also rash'.[6] But he did not propose to solve the problem of religious diversity through the propagation of toleration – far from it. He considered those who defended the ancient Roman Catholic faith and the existing form of government as having chosen the best and most sensible side in the civil wars that ravaged France.[7]

In Montaigne's days this view was shared by many. Traditionally, heresy was considered a danger to both the secular and the spiritual or ecclesiastical order. This did not prevent the odd ruler from tolerating dissidents, but such exceptional policy usually led to major problems. Suppression of heretics by the Roman Catholic Church was the rule, and its chosen instrument, the Inquisition, became better and better organized from the mid-thirteenth century onwards.[8] And there was yet another problem to deal with: the presence of non-Christians. Before the Reformation, relatively undisturbed coexistence of different religions had occurred in certain parts of Europe. In the case of

---

3 Quoted by Ayers, 'Theories of knowledge and belief'; Orr, *Reason and authority*.
4 Grell and Porter (eds.), *Toleration in Enlightenment Europe*.
5 Laursen, 'Spinoza on toleration'; Israel, 'Spinoza, Locke'; Israel, *Locke, Spinoza*.
6 '. . . il s'en voit plusieurs que la passion pousse hors les bornes de la raison, et leur faict par fois prendre des conseils injustes, violents et encore téméraires'. Montaigne, *Essais*.
7 'En ce debat par lequel la France est à présent agitée de guerres civiles, le meilleur et le plus sain party est sans doubte celuy qui maintient et la religion et la police ancienne du pays.' Montaigne, *Essais*.
8 Lambert, *Medieval heresy*; Hamilton, *Medieval inquisition*.

Spain, for instance, Jews, Muslims and Christians lived more or less peacefully together until a wave of persecutions and conflicts started in the late fourteenth century. Elsewhere the presence of Jewish communities in the midst of a predominantly Christian society was at best permitted, seldom welcomed.[9] Muslims became widely feared and even detested after the Ottoman Turks extended their conquests and military successes into east-central Europe and the Mediterranean.[10] With the emergence of the Reformation, however, the debate on toleration tended to focus on a regrettably disunited Christendom and, consequently, on the problem of internal religious pluriformity. Henceforward, the question of Christian coexistence with Jews and Muslims was usually considered a separate issue. In comparison, the lack of concord among Christians – which contrasted sharply with the ancient ideal of religious peace and unity – seemed to be far more troubling.[11]

The problem of how this ideal of peace and unity was to be preserved or newly attained occupied adherents of every shade of Christian faith from the Reformation onwards. Should it be done through punishment of heretics and schismatics, following the ecclesiastical tradition which was securely founded on teachings of St Augustine and included in the *Decreta Gratiani*? Or should one fall back on equally venerable and ancient opinions defending leniency towards religious dissidents on the strength of several biblical passages, of which the parable of the tares among the wheat (Matthew 13:24–30, 36–43) remained the most popular?[12] The issue became as perplexing in theory as in practice once sizeable dissenting groups sprang into existence during the early stages of the Reformation. Nor was it confined to religion alone; the nascent modern state was seeking political stability for itself by trying to suppress or resolve religious tensions, as it was generally convinced of the necessity to allow only one faith in one state. Moreover, as the state was lending the ecclesiastical powers a hand in punishing dissidents, it became necessary to rethink the reasons for persecution or toleration on a political level.

Behind this lurked an even more fundamental problem: where exactly was the line to be drawn between heresy and orthodoxy? What was the role of individual conscience? Should the definition of heresy be left to the theologians? In 1519, Desiderius Erasmus (1469?–1536) gave a pertinent answer to this last question in a letter about Martin Luther (1483–1546):

9 Kriegel, *Les Juifs*; Hsia and Lehmann (eds.), *In and out of the ghetto*; Katz, *Exclusiveness and tolerance*.
10 Coles, *The Ottoman impact*.   11 Sutherland, 'Persecution and toleration'.
12 Lecler, *Histoire de la tolérance*, pp. 82–8; Bainton, 'The parable of the tares'.

In the old days a heretic was one who dissented from the Gospels or the articles of the faith or things which carried equal authority with them. Nowadays if anyone disagrees with Thomas he is called a heretic – indeed, if he disagrees with some newfangled reasoning thought up yesterday by some sophister in the schools. Anything they [i.e., the theologians] do not like, anything they do not understand is heresy. To know Greek is heresy; to speak like an educated man is heresy. Anything they do not do themselves is heresy. It is, I admit, a serious thing to violate the faith; but not everything should be forced into a question of faith.[13]

The best solution was, according to Erasmus, to distinguish the few fundamental Christian doctrines from the many man-made teachings not vital for attaining salvation. Only in this way was it possible to preserve the concord of the faithful. In 1523, when Luther's defiant attitude to ecclesiastical and secular authorities was the talk of the town, Erasmus wrote in a famous letter: 'The sum and substance of our religion is peace and concord. This can hardly remain the case unless we define as few matters as possible and leave each individual's judgement free on many questions.'[14]

This was the voice of Christian humanism, which had been steadfastly gaining in influence since Jacques Lefèvre d'Etaples (c. 1460–1536) and Erasmus advocated a combination of classical, biblical, and patristic scholarship as the foundation for an aspiring programme of moral and religious reform. The aim was ecclesiastical renewal, leading the church back to the spiritual power and theological purity that had been its hallmarks in its early days. On the eve of the Reformation, Erasmus and his disciples were decidedly optimistic about the future: peace, justice, and religious reform were about to conquer the world with humanist learning in a leading role. Hateful religious disputes and persecution of heretics had no place in this golden dream. Preachers should deal patiently and gently with persons harbouring erroneous convictions, because people are weak, needing guidance to greater perfection.[15] Hence Erasmus's commentary on the parable of the tares: 'The servants who wished to gather up the tares before it was time are those who think that pseudo-apostles and heretics should be destroyed by the sword and put to death; whereas the Master did not wish them destroyed, but rather tolerated so that perchance they might repent and from tares become wheat'.[16] An exception was made

---

13 *Collected works of Erasmus*, vol. 7, p. 115, lines 257–65: Erasmus to Albert of Brandenburg, 19 October 1519.
14 *Collected works of Erasmus*, vol. 9, p. 252, lines 232–4: dedicatory letter by Erasmus to Jean Carondelet, 5 January 1523.
15 Augustijn, *Erasmus en de Reformatie*, pp. 13–21; Bateman, 'From soul to soul'.
16 Ferguson, 'The attitude of Erasmus toward toleration', p. 179.

for irremediable and seditious heretics posing a threat to civil law and order, as punishing blasphemers and rebels is necessary to protect the peace.[17]

The very real problem of how to put a theory of toleration, however limited, into practice in a strife-torn world can be demonstrated by Luther's changing attitude. In his early writings Luther defended religious ('Christian') liberty to the degree of strongly arguing against any interference by secular authorities in matters of faith. Besides, in his treatise *On secular authority* (*Von Weltlicher Obrigkeit*, 1523) he wrote: 'The use of force can never prevent heresy. Preventing it requires a different sort of skill; this is not a battle that can be fought with the sword. This is where God's Word must fight. And if it does not win, then secular power can certainly not succeed either, even if it were to fill the world with blood.'[18] However, the Peasants' War in Germany and the appearance of radical reformers like Thomas Müntzer (*d.* 1525) championing not only religious and moral, but also social and political reforms, forced Luther to reformulate his position. Apparently, there was in reality a certain osmosis between the otherwise strictly distinct spiritual and temporal kingdoms. Secular authority, Luther now argued, was obliged to punish public blasphemy and sedition because these posed a threat to society. Princes were to protect the true faith and the newly reformed evangelical churches enjoying Christian liberty. They were also obliged to suppress false doctrines, but at the same time Luther warned the princes not to 'try to change and be masters of the Word of God'.[19] In 1536 Luther conceded that liberty of conscience for dissidents was an option, as long as they refrained from any public profession of their faith as this would amount to the crime of blasphemy.[20]

Toleration of dissent was rejected altogether by Jean Calvin (1509–64). He favoured punishment of heretics and false prophets, the much-debated execution of the Spanish antitrinitarian Michael Servetus in Geneva (1553) being a case in point. He abhorred the idea that an individual would make up his own mind in matters of faith. According to him, Christian worship was tied to the life of the community and had direct bearing on the social and political order. The defence of pure doctrine and the godly condition of the church and, consequently, the prevention of heresy was one of the ends of secular government.[21] 'I approve', Calvin wrote in his *Institution*, 'a political order that makes it its business to prevent true religion, which is contained in the

---

17 Hoffmann, 'Erasmus and religious toleration'; Margolin, 'La tolérance et ses limites'.
18 Höpfl, *Luther and Calvin*, p. 30.   19 Rupp, 'Luther and government', p. 146.
20 Cargill Thompson, *Political thought of Luther*, pp. 155–62; Lienhard, 'De la tolérance'; Estes, 'Luther's first appeal'.
21 Bouwsma, *John Calvin*, pp. 101, 216–17; Bainton, *Travail of liberty*, pp. 54–72.

law of God, from being besmirched and violated with impunity by public and manifest sacrilege'.[22] So at first sight a juxtaposition of Calvin and the concept of toleration is not an obvious one. Nevertheless, it must be noted that in one all-important regard Calvin's stance did not differ from Erasmus's or Luther's positions: all three viewed heresy as profoundly disruptive to society and none accepted religious pluriformity as a normal condition. The propagation of certain limited forms of toleration by Erasmus and Luther, and Calvin's outright rejection of them, had the same conceptual background: the sense that Christendom was severely endangered by the loss of religious concord. Erasmus, Luther, but also Calvin fought for the re-establishment of that concord, albeit with different theological, social, and political ideals in mind.

Luther's early warnings to the secular powers that they should not intervene in the religious life of their subjects may have been incited by the wish to prevent persecution of evangelical believers. Not surprisingly, this point of view was shared by those, like the early Anabaptist Hans Denck (c. 1500–27) or the theologian sui generis Sebastian Franck (1499–1542), who regarded an indwelling force of the soul as the only true religious authority. Faith, they believed, revealed itself through spiritual, not temporal means, persecution was pointless and so was, to a degree, persuasion. According to Franck no man was able to judge whether his fellow-man is a heretic or not, as no one can be sure of knowing the truth in its divine entirety. He extended his religious tolerance to non-Christians, who had a right to their own views and should be met in a spirit of brotherhood, not censure. It might even be useful, he argued, to read their books, as 'no book is so evil that a Christian – who is incorruptible – may not learn from it'.[23]

Sebastianus Castellio (Sébastien Castellion, 1515–63) took up some of these ideas. He was also attracted to Erasmus's aforementioned reductionist theology based on the concept of the concord of the faithful. His thoughts about toleration were first formulated in reaction to the burning of Servetus: he published a volume of historical texts, ranging from early Christianity to his own time, in which killing for religious reasons was condemned. The book ignited lengthy and bitter polemics with Calvin and Theodore Beza. Castellio pleaded in favour of toleration of heretics because he believed that gentle persuasion together with an appeal to human reason would eventually lead them back to the fold. According to him, secular power had no right to label people as heretics.[24] Castellio also condemned their execution: 'To kill a human being

22 Höpfl, *Luther and Calvin*, pp. 50–1.
23 Furcha, 'Turks and heathen are our kin', p. 90; Barbers, *Toleranz bei Sebastian Franck*.
24 Guggisberg, *Sebastian Castellio*, pp. 80–150; Castellion, *De haereticis*.

is not to defend a doctrine, but to kill a human being. When those Genevans killed Servetus they did not defend a doctrine, but killed the man.'[25] Killing heretics he interpreted as an act against God's will, as only God was qualified to judge the hearts of men. In Castellio's opinion many would be damned on the Last Day because they had killed innocent people, but no man would be damned because he had killed nobody.[26] Eventually, these views were echoed by many contemporaries, especially by Italian evangelical refugees. One of them, Mino Celsi (1514–75), offered a similar condemnation of capital punishment of dissidents in his writings. Contrary to Castellio, however, he allowed the secular powers to interfere in religious matters as long as justice was tempered by mercy.[27]

Celsi had been an administrator and politician in his native Siena before he became a religious refugee eking out a meagre existence in exile. From the 1560s onwards, politicians came to the fore in the debate on toleration. By that time, religious pluriformity had become a permanent feature of Christendom. So, politicians of all persuasions, having to deal with an seemingly irreversible situation, often chose a way out whereby the ideal of doctrinal concord was given up in favour of restoration of political order: the religious settlement. The most famous one was the Peace of Augsburg (1555), which granted religious liberty to the Roman Catholic and Lutheran princes of the Empire, but not to the individual believer. Nevertheless it functioned, as did an earlier settlement (the second Peace of Kappel, 1531) between Catholics and Protestants in the Swiss Confederation.[28] Settlements could also be concluded at a local level. These existed for instance in France, especially in the south, during the Wars of Religion. Undoubtedly they not only testify to a politically inspired desire for prudent coexistence in times of trouble, but also to a truly Christian aspiration to peace within a community of fellow-Christians, however different their religious leanings might be. In 1568, the council of a small town near Avignon affirmed before a notary that it was resolved 'to make a good and holy confederation between all the people, to swear peace and friendship to each other, and to help each other in full brotherhood, nothing being more wished by the common body of the said council than to live together as brothers in concord and friendship'.[29]

25 Castellio, *Contra libellum Calvini*, fol. E1.
26 Guggisberg, *Sebastian Castellio*, pp. 130–1.
27 Celsi, *In haereticis coërcendis*; Fimpel, *Mino Celsis Traktat*.
28 Brady, 'Settlements: the Holy Roman Empire', pp. 349, 352–5; Berner, Gäbler, and Guggisberg, 'Schweiz', pp. 297–302.
29 Bossy, *Peace in the Post-Reformation*, p. 35.

The degree to which politicians abhorred religious strife is well expressed by Thomas More (1477/78–1535) in his *Utopia* (1516):

> Even before he took over the island, King Utopus had heard that the natives were continually squabbling over religious matters . . . As soon as he had gained the victory, therefore, he decreed that every man might cultivate the religion of his choice, and proselytize for it, too, provided he did so quietly, modestly, rationally and without bitterness towards others. If persuasions failed, no man might resort to abuse or violence, under penalty of exile or slavery. Utopus laid down these rules not simply for the sake of peace, which he saw was being destroyed by constant quarrels and implacable hatreds, but also for the sake of religion itself.[30]

This remarkable degree of religious toleration in Utopia (where the Christian faith had not been revealed) seldom applied in the real world. Later on, More himself, as Lord Chancellor of England, strictly enforced the laws against heresy, stating that as a judge he was 'relentless towards thieves, murderers, and heretics'.[31]

Statesmen began to search for political solutions which were not based on King Utopus's idealistic views, but on a generally rather reluctant acceptance of toleration as a lesser evil than permanent political and social disorder caused by religious issues. This can be clearly observed in France shortly before and during the Wars of Religion. Toleration was not regarded in a positive light nor viewed as a safe path leading to the reunion of churches.[32] Formal discussions between the warring parties in the form of theological colloquies about contested issues, however, did not bring tangible results: the most important one, the Colloquy of Poissy (1561), failed because neither party was disposed to reconciliation.[33] Repression of Protestantism by a French monarchy committed to defending the Roman Catholic Church did not work either. Royal policy towards Protestants then took a startlingly new form, which has been formulated in the words: 'un roi, une loi, deux fois'. In 1562 Catherine de Medici issued the Edict of Saint-Germain granting the Protestants freedom of worship as long as religious unity was not yet reattained in order to 'keep our subjects in peace and concord'. The edict, however, was rejected by a majority of the nation's body politic. Civil war broke out soon, and lasted for decades. Not only French Catholics were extremely reluctant to accept the notion that people of different religions could coexist in peace; many Protestants also

---

30 More, *Utopia*.   31 Kenny, *Thomas More*, p. 61.
32 Huseman, 'The expression of the idea'.
33 Nugent, *Ecumenism*; Wanegffelen, *Ni Rome, ni Genève*, pp. 99–208.

professed hostility to it, believing that it was the duty of the secular authorities to suppress heretics and support the true faith.[34] Royal toleration policy in the early 1560s was theoretically underpinned by the chancellor, Michel de L'Hôpital (1505–73), and others. The preservation of the unity of the kingdom and its law was presented as more important than religious unity and uniformity. The lynchpin was the monarch himself: he was celebrated as the impartial ruler to which all subjects, regardless of their religion, owed allegiance. In return, the monarch protected all his subjects and worked for their reconciliation.[35]

Discussions about tolerating two faiths in France and its practical consequences continued for over a century. Those defending toleration of Protestant worship rarely acknowledged the fundamental right to religious freedom. Pragmatic arguments bearing on the problem of how to end the Wars of Religion dominated the exchange of views. In due course, broader arguments in favour of the principle of religious liberty for all were put forward by some. In his treatise *Six livres de la République* (1576) the jurist Jean Bodin (1529/30–96) propagated the preservation of religious uniformity in a state even if the religion in question was not the 'true' one, while leaving open for the individual the possibility to exercise his faith in private. The general attitude of political, theological and legal thinkers remained, however, averse to a generalized defence of toleration based on those liberties.[36]

In practice, therefore, the vicissitudes of the Wars of Religion and the local balance of power determined the presence or absence of toleration until King Henry IV (1589–1610) managed to introduce a reasonably balanced policy allowing for coexistence of the two faiths in his kingdom. His Edict of Nantes (1598) was a royal settlement forced on the warring parties, not a decree aiming at systematic toleration. Henry's objective was religious concord; as long as this was not effectuated, he was willing to protect the rights of Protestants in a Catholic state in order to achieve the desired public peace. Henry's successors repeatedly restricted the rights of Protestants within the framework of the Edict of Nantes. When King Louis XIV took personal charge of the government in 1661 this meant the onset of a policy of increasing, relentless pressure on the Protestants, whittling away their rights and encouraging or even coercing their conversion to the Catholic faith. The end of pragmatic toleration of

---

34 Benedict, '*Un roi, une loi, deux fois*', pp. 68–71; Stegmann, *Edits*, pp. 8–14, quotation on p. 10.
35 Christin, 'From repression to pacification'; Wanegffelen, *Ni Rome, ni Genève*, pp. 214–20.
36 Benedict, '*Un roi, une loi, deux fois*', pp. 70–4; Roellenbleck, 'Jean Bodin et la liberté de conscience'.

the two faiths in France came with the revocation of the Edict of Nantes in 1685. At last, the monarchy had gained enough strength and the Protestants had become so weak that the necessary, but nevertheless regrettable, evil of toleration could be done away with.[37]

The Dutch intellectual debate about toleration and its practical outcomes were undoubtedly mainly shaped by the experience of the revolt (since *c*. 1566) against their overlord Philip II, King of Spain. Emperor Charles V had refused, as lord of the Netherlands, to extend the Peace of Augsburg (1555) to that part of his realm, and his son and successor Philip II was confident he could stamp out heresy there without having to rely on religious settlements with his subjects. Lower magistrates, however, usually took a more lenient view and did not want to punish heretics too severely as long as they were not seditious. In defence of such an attitude it was pointed out that toleration could have a stimulating effect on the economy. Just before the outbreak of the Dutch Revolt the leader of the opposition against the central government, Prince William of Orange (1533–84), designed a programme for religious peace. It would have involved toleration in the form of a strictly circumscribed religious pluriformity, but it failed: the revolt broke out before either government or opposition had been able to put their ideas into practice, or before a compromise between these two parties had been worked out.[38]

By 1572 the Dutch rebels were holding a sizeable part of the northern Netherlands, where they had to come up with a solution to the problem of religious diversity. At first, the leaders of the revolt proposed a form of toleration which included freedom of conscience for everybody and freedom of worship together with protection of their clergy for Catholics. But this was not acceptable to those staunch Calvinists who wanted to ban Catholic worship altogether. Catholics were, moreover, suspect as potential allies of the enemy, the King of Spain. However, seven years later, the Union of Utrecht (1579) – the military alliance of the Dutch rebel provinces – did guarantee freedom of conscience stating that 'nobody shall be persecuted or examined for religious reasons'. The estates of the provinces were free to arrange public religious life as long as this was respected. Freedom of worship was not granted: in some places not only Catholics, but all dissidents were suppressed. The issue of state control over religious life was hotly debated. The lay theologian Dirck Volckertszoon Coornhert (1522–90) pleaded for religious freedom together with freedom of discussion and a free press. Justus Lipsius (1547–1606) defended

37 Garrisson, *L'Edit de Nantes et sa révocation*; Garrisson, *L'Edit de Nantes*; Benedict, 'Un roi, une loi, deux fois', pp. 82–3; Wanegffelen, *L'Edit de Nantes*, pp. 19–58.
38 Mout, 'Limits and debates', pp. 37–9; Guggisberg, 'Wandel der Argumente', pp. 469–70.

in true humanist fashion the virtues of religious uniformity and considered toleration a sure sign of an imperfect state.[39]

The Dutch Republic developed into a religiously pluralist society in which a limited amount of religious freedom seemed to be perfectly compatible with a well-ordered state. Protected by the secular powers, Mennonites, Lutherans, Jews, and others acquired the status of tolerated religious communities. Catholics remained officially banned, but were in practice allowed to worship in private and have their own pastoral care, sometimes even their own schools and poor relief. As long as they accepted the limits set by the local magistracy and paid handsome sums of protection money, Catholics had not much to fear. For many strict Calvinists, however, their ideal had been a strong church exercising a profound influence on public and private life, and this was not given up lightly. During the seventeenth century, strict Calvinists reopened from time to time the public debate about religious pluriformity and concomitant toleration in Dutch society. Such discussions, though, were often but academic skirmishes between theologians, lawyers and historians. The controversial issue – toleration and the place of non-Calvinists in society – had been attended to in a pragmatic way, although a detailed and comprehensive religious settlement laid down by law was missing. Religious pluralism and toleration were often associated with economic prosperity and social and political stability. In daily life, however, both the breadth and the limits of Dutch toleration were manifest: where Mennonites, Jews and even Catholics could thrive, self-made prophets and enthusiasts together with followers of out-of-the-way beliefs, antitrinitarianism for instance, were sometimes severely repressed.[40]

In the Holy Roman Empire the Peace of Augsburg (1555) did not solve the religious problems. Territorial rulers represented in the estates were given the *ius reformandi* – the right to determine the religion of their subjects. No ruler was obliged to tolerate adherents of a religion different from his own, but in practice he was free to come to an understanding with his subjects about a pragmatic form of toleration, and sometimes he did. Calvinism was not recognized as an established religion, and other dissidents – Anabaptists, Zwinglians, etc. – were also excluded. The granting of equal rights to Catholics and Lutherans meant, however, that the canonic laws concerning heresy could no longer be applied to Lutherans. Imperial free towns harbouring both Catholics and Lutherans were guaranteed freedom of worship for both parties. Other towns

39 Mout, 'Limits and debates', pp. 40–1; Pettegree, 'The politics of toleration', pp. 184–7; Güldner, *Das Toleranz-Problem*.
40 Po-Chia Hsia and Van Nierop (eds.), *Calvinism and religious toleration*.

and knights could stay Lutheran if they wished, but freedom of worship was not granted to individual subjects of the Empire. If they disagreed in religion with their ruler, they had the right to emigrate: 'Modest as this beneficium emigrandi appears today, this freedom of religion in the guise of freedom of domicile is the first universal human right guaranteed by the Empire in written constitutional form to every German'.[41]

In sum, from the point of view of toleration, the Peace of Augsburg was flawed and incomplete. Nevertheless it functioned quite well until the late 1570s, after which period a process of swift confessional polarization set in. Both Lutherans and Catholics were keen on extending their territories and rights at each other's expense, while Calvinist princes sometimes tried to buttress their insecure position by seeking support from foreign powers. In the last decades of the sixteenth century three confessional power blocs were developing, each of them trying to gain advantage over the others. The Thirty Years' War (1618–48), being in part a war of religion, made it clear that a better and more comprehensive settlement than the Peace of Augsburg was needed.[42] The Peace of Westphalia (1648) which ended the war was, like the Peace of Augsburg, fundamentally a religious settlement. It gave the Empire a highly durable legal and constitutional foundation for a form of toleration, however limited. There were three established churches with equal constitutional rights: Catholic, Lutheran, and Calvinist. Territorial rulers kept the *ius reformandi*, but were not allowed to interfere with members of non-dominant churches, insofar as these churches had been established in their lands before 1624. The dominant church was allowed to present itself as the public church with all kinds of rights attached to it, the non-dominant received strictly circumscribed rights of so-called 'private worship'. Adherents of other faiths were free to worship in their homes ('domestic devotion'), had the right not to be forced into conversion, and should be allowed to emigrate without loss of property. Under these provisions, religious persecution declined markedly, although it was often difficult to maintain a clear distinction between the three types of freedom of worship: public, private, and domestic. At the highest political level, in the imperial diet and other imperial institutions, decisions about religious matters could only be taken by agreement, not by majority vote. In certain places, for instance in Augsburg and Osnabrück, where Catholic and

---

41 Heckel, *Deutschland im konfessionellen Zeitalter*, p. 48; cf. also Simon, *Der Augsburger Religionsfriede*.
42 Schilling, 'Confessionalization in the empire', pp. 210–32; Schormann, *Der dreissigjährige Krieg*; Schmidt, *Der dreissigjährige Krieg*; Dickmann, 'Das Problem der Gleichberechtigung'.

Lutheran presence was more or less in balance, the two confessions existed side by side with equal rights. Such parity between Catholics and Protestants did not, however, automatically lead to a more tolerant view of each other and certainly not to toleration of other faiths.[43]

Through all these provisions, the rights of the non-Catholic minority were sufficiently protected, but toleration *per se* was not granted nor intended. Like the Peace of Augsburg, the Peace of Westphalia was only designed to ban religious conflicts in the Empire, not to reunite the different Christian churches in a spirit of toleration. Nevertheless, toleration became an issue because of the different interpretations of the provisions of the Peace in the various religious camps. For the Catholic estates, freedom of domestic worship did not mean a total freedom for all to organize family devotions as they saw fit, as it did to the Protestant estates. Moreover, some Protestant princes were inclined, on pragmatic as much as on legal grounds, to interpret the *ius reformandi* in such a way that also religious groups outside the dominant public church could be given certain privileges. This was the case, for instance, in parts of the dukedom of Brandenburg-Prussia.[44]

In one specific part of the Holy Roman Empire, the Kingdom of Bohemia, the debate about religious pluralism and the possibility or impossibility of toleration preceded the sixteenth-century Reformation. In the previous century, the Hussite movement had resulted in the Czech Reformation. After the dust of the Hussite wars had settled down, a Catholic minority and a Hussite Utraquist majority coexisted in legally recognized churches of equal status – each with its own ecclesiastical organization – since the Compactata of Jihlava (Iglau) (1436). This politically, not theologically, inspired settlement was the work of the Catholic Bohemian king, Emperor Sigismund of Luxemburg, and moderate Hussite politicians. However, it did not bring lasting peace: the Catholics tried to win back the lost field and the Utraquists tenaciously defended their hard-won positions. In 1485 the Bohemian nobility concluded the Peace of Kutná Hora (Kuttenberg) at their diet. The underlying principles were freedom of conscience for everybody, rejection of religious persecution, and freedom for every community to stick to its faith, regardless of its lord's religion. There was only one drawback to this remarkable step in the direction of fully acknowledged religious toleration within a given state: other groups than Catholics and Utraquists, particularly the new radical Hussite church called the Unity of Brethren, were excluded. The principle of freedom

---

43 Schmidt, 'Der Westfälische Friede als Grundgesetz', p. 452; Schindling, 'Andersgläubige Nachbarn'; Whaley, 'A tolerant society?' pp. 180–2.

44 Jahns, 'Die Reichsjustiz als Spiegel'; Schindling, 'Andersgläubige Nachbarn', pp. 468–9.

of conscience became an empty slogan as far as the Brethren were concerned, because especially in the first decades of the sixteenth century they were heavily persecuted.[45]

The coming of the Reformation to Bohemia added yet other groups to the spectrum: Lutherans, Anabaptists, antitrinitarians, Calvinists. A number of Protestant churches reached a theological compromise in 1575: the Bohemian Confession, which can be considered a manifestation of inter-Protestant tolerance excluding, however, Catholics and sectarians. True religious toleration was reached only in 1609, when Emperor Rudolf II (1576–1612) issued the Letter of Majesty under heavy political pressure of the largely non-Catholic Bohemian estates. Religious dualism changed into pluralism, but not for long. The Bohemian Revolt (1618–20) – the first stage of the Thirty Years' War – was soon crushed by Emperor Ferdinand II (1619–37). His victory also meant the abrupt end of religious toleration and the beginning of a policy of violent and, in the end, successful recatholicization of the Bohemian kingdom.[46]

Early manifestations of religious pluralism, concomitant theological considerations and toleration settlements are also found in the Polish-Lithuanian state and in Hungary, including Transylvania. Further to the east, in Orthodox Russia, indigenous theories about religious toleration did not come up, but from the beginning of the seventeenth century foreign merchants and diplomats were usually granted, for economic reasons, freedom of worship within their own precincts.[47] In Poland-Lithuania, the Catholic monarchy reigned in an expanding state over religiously very diverse groups. Freedom of religion was granted to the nobles in order to strengthen their affiliation to the crown. In the Confederation of Warsaw (1573) the nobles swore to 'keep the peace among ourselves, and neither shed blood on account of differences of faith, or kinds of church, nor punish one another . . .'[48] A moot point was the relation between noble lord and subject: did the lord have the *ius reformandi* or not? Other groups, especially the inhabitants of predominantly Protestant royal towns like Danzig, were granted certain religious freedoms by the crown. Local and regional privileges given to Protestants or Jews led to pragmatic toleration of these groups, while others, for instance Orthodox peasants or Muslim Tatars in the eastern part of the kingdom, were simply left alone although there was no legal basis for toleration. To stem the rising tide of anti-Protestantism in a still predominantly Catholic kingdom, Calvinists, Lutherans and Bohemian Brethren concluded the *Consensus Sendomiriensis* (1570). This agreement was

---

45 Šmahel, *Husitské Čechy*; Pánek, 'The question of tolerance', pp. 231–6.
46 Pánek, 'The question of tolerance', pp. 238–48; Válka, 'Tolerance, či koexistence?'
47 Nolte, *Religiöse Toleranz in Russland.*   48 Davies, *God's playground*, p. 160.

not only a fruit of political pragmatism, but also of a sincere desire to foster Christian unity, although it was directed against the Catholics and excluded the numerous Polish antitrinitarians. However, legal toleration of non-Catholics was slowly but steadily eroded under the reign of Sigismund III (1587–1632), who even repudiated the oath of toleration sworn at his accession. By 1660 Poland-Lithuania was closely bound to a more and more intransigent Catholic Church.[49]

The degree of tolerance exercised by the rulers of Hungary and Transylvania was primarily determined by political considerations. A main factor was the permanent Ottoman threat which made rulers dependent on their subjects for an effective defence. There existed, however, a medieval tradition of toleration towards Greek Orthodox believers. After the coming of the Reformation, rights of church patronage did not automatically lead to the imposition of a particular religion on the faithful by the patron – the local lord or the town magistracy. Those in power responded very often positively to petitions for freedom of worship by Protestants in order to preserve the public peace, because they were convinced that a tolerant attitude would work better than the exercise of a *ius reformandi* or a confrontational policy. Churches of different denominations were allowed to coexist; the village church was sometimes shared by adherents of different faiths.[50] Legal toleration went furthest in Transylvania, which was, with one exception, ruled by Catholic princes until the succession of the Calvinist István Bocskai in 1604. In 1564, the diet recognized the Lutheran and Calvinist churches. The diet of Torda (1568) granted four churches complete freedom of worship: Roman Catholic, Lutheran, Calvinist, and antitrinitarian. The Greek Orthodox church was left out, but not impeded in its *de facto* freedom of worship. Ministers were free to preach the gospel and congregations were allowed to decide whom they wanted to hear. Faith was described as a gift of God to the individual believer and forced conversion was prohibited. Disagreements over religious issues did arise from time to time, but also under the Calvinist princes ruling Transylvania until 1690 the principle of legal toleration was upheld.[51]

England is rather unique in the history of toleration as it acquired a Protestant state religion, but at the same time harboured many dissidents of different faiths. Thomas Cranmer (1489–1556), Archbishop of Canterbury, thought that concord ought to be furthered by dialogue, persuasion or even coercion, but

49 Müller, 'Protestant confessionalisation', pp. 263–70; Tazbir, *A state without stakes*; Jordt-Jørgensen, *Ökumenische Bestrebungen*; Wyrwa, 'La liberté de conscience en Pologne'.
50 Péter, 'Tolerance and intolerance', pp. 250–5.
51 Binder, *Grundlagen und Formen der Toleranz*.

preferably not by persecution.[52] Since the Elizabethan Settlement (1559) had defined Anglicanism, toleration in England had been discussed in the guise of considerations about Anglican doctrinal latitude, so that concord among the faithful could be attained through accommodation.[53] However, penalizations for religious reasons and persecutions did occur during Elizabeth's reign, as dissidents could be seen as troublesome, not so much because of their false doctrines, but because they might endanger public order in a state requiring religious conformity by law. Against defenders of the government's policy Catholics never ceased to demand toleration of their worship, perhaps even hoping that this would eventually lead to a return of England to Rome. Catholics were not regarded as heretics, but could nevertheless be persecuted under the guise of treason, as William Allen pointed out in his *True, sincere and modest defence of English Catholics* (1584).[54] On the other hand, foreign Protestant refugees were allowed to have their own churches. However, the moving force for the crown here was economic gain, not religious toleration.[55]

In the first half of the sixteenth century, England had had its share of writings in which persecution was rejected and spiritual weapons for spreading the gospel propagated.[56] Later, Jacobus Acontius (*c.* 1520–67), an Italian Protestant refugee, supported individual freedom of choice in religion and the narrowing of fundamental doctrines to an absolute minimum in his influential book *Satanae stratagemata* (1565), dedicated to Elizabeth I. In his view, full toleration might at first create chaos, but would eventually help the crystallizing of truth, which would, in due course, be commonly accepted.[57] Meanwhile, Catholics and Puritans requested the right of freedom of worship for themselves, but generally not for others, while acknowledging that faith cannot be compelled.[58]

Religious toleration became an important public issue during the seventeenth-century English Revolution when government repression through censorship broke down and sects started to flourish. The government's religious policy during the Protectorate wrestled with arguments about liberty of conscience and its consequences for social and political life, because even the staunchest Puritan admitted that conscience should not be forced. Cromwell's aim was the re-establishment of Christian concord, not of

52 MacCulloch, 'Archbishop Cranmer'.
53 Jordan, *The development of religious toleration*, pp. 82–238.
54 Elton, 'Persecution and toleration', pp. 180–2.
55 Pettegree, *Foreign Protestant communities*.
56 Jordan, *The development of religious toleration*, pp. 57–81.
57 Briggs, 'An apostle'; Jordan, *The development of religious toleration*, pp. 303–65.
58 Jordan, *The development of religious toleration*, pp. 239–99, 372–420.

toleration.[59] However, advocates of full toleration were about: the London merchant Henry Robinson (1605–64) defended in his treatise *Liberty of conscience* (1643) the right to free judgement, assuming that religious truth was not ascertainable. He stated that toleration would bring much-needed public peace and economic prosperity to England. Roger Williams (c. 1603–83), theologian and founder of Rhode Island, advocated rigorous separation of church and state, as the latter should never be allowed to tyrannize over the former in his book *The bloudy tenent of persecution* (1644) and its sequel *The bloudy tenent yet more bloudy* (1653). Consciences should never be forced, freedom of worship should be granted as a natural right to 'all men in all nations and countries'.[60] With the Restoration (1660), Charles II had expressed his preference for a religious settlement including toleration of dissidents, hoping this would make him the ruler of a united nation. However, dissenters in Restoration England were living in what has been called 'a persecuting society', until the royal Declaration of Indulgence (1672) granted toleration to Catholics and Protestant dissenters, foreshadowing the Toleration Act of 1689 – which still left out antitrinitarians.[61]

The history of religious toleration in theory and practice is usually told on the basis of official government policies, scholarly theories of toleration, and the printed works of zealous pamphleteers. It is much harder, however, to sketch the level of tolerance or intolerance in daily life. Assuming that the 'cohabitation of the faithful with the unfaithful'[62] would have led to occasional or even permanent tension, it is not easy to assess its general outlines and consequences, if any. Did religious differences contribute to dislike, hatred, or inimical actions springing from those feelings, on a local level? Or were those differences generally ignored because people wanted, first of all, to live in peace and quiet, perhaps having a rather pragmatic tolerant attitude to those who were adherents of a different religion from their own? Examples of all kinds of reactions, stemming from a multitude of different situations, locations and periods, can be extracted from the sources.[63] However, a general picture of toleration or the lack of it in daily life, valid for European history from the beginning of the Reformation until 1650, still remains to be drawn.

59 Worden, 'Toleration and the Cromwellian Protectorate'.
60 Williams, *The bloudy tenent*, p. 341; cf. also Carlin, 'Toleration for Catholics'.
61 Tyacke, 'The "rise of Puritanism"'; Fletcher, 'The enforcement'; quotation in Goldie, 'The theory of religious intolerance', p. 331.
62 Collinson, 'The cohabitation', p. 51.   63 Collinson, *The birthpangs*, pp. 148–55.

14

Imposing church and social discipline

UTE LOTZ-HEUMANN

Social and church discipline are historiographical concepts which have been developed to describe a general trend exhibited by all states and confessional churches during the early modern period of establishing control mechanisms over their subjects or flock. Originally, the concept of social discipline (or disciplining) was developed by Gerhard Oestreich as an alternative to the etatistic term 'absolutism'. Oestreich described 'social disciplining' (*Sozial-disziplinierung*) as a process in which, based on neo-stoic philosophy, the early modern state strove to control the behaviour of its subjects in all areas of life, thus turning them into 'obedient, pious, and diligent subjects'.[1] The concept of 'social discipline' was also taken up by historians working on the religious history of early modern Europe. 'Church discipline', the very diverse measures used by the confessional churches of early modern Europe to discipline their flock, was consequently regarded as part of the larger process of 'social disciplining'.[2]

Church and social discipline are very complex phenomena and their complexity has to be taken into account in at least four aspects: first, the development of church and social discipline between the late Middle Ages and the period of the Reformation and Counter-Reformation; second, the confessional variations of church discipline, i.e., the attitudes to and expectations of church discipline were decisively influenced by the Protestant reformers' theological attitudes and by the Catholic reform movement and the decisions of the Council of Trent; third, as a consequence of different religio-political

---

1 Hsia, *Social discipline*, p. 2.
2 On social disciplining, see Schulze, 'Gerhard Oestreichs Begriff "Sozialdisziplinierung in der frühen Neuzeit"'; on the relationship between social and church discipline, see Gorski, *The disciplinary revolution*, pp. 1–38; Hsia, *Social discipline*; Schilling (ed.), *Kirchenzucht und Sozialdisziplinierung*, especially the introduction by Schilling, 'Die Kirchenzucht im frühneuzeitlichen Europa'; Schilling (ed.), *Institutionen, Instrumente und Akteure sozialer Kontrolle und Disziplinierung*, especially the introduction by Schilling, 'Profil und Perspektiven'.

structures in different parts of Europe, there came into existence a wide variety of institutions and procedures of church discipline.

The biblical origin and the medieval history of church discipline

The idea of church discipline is derived from the New Testament, especially Matthew 18:15–18, where it says:

> Moreover, if thy brother shall trespass against thee, go and tell him his fault between thee and him alone: if he shall hear thee, thou hast gained thy brother. But if he will not hear thee, then take with thee one or two more, that in the mouth of two or three witnesses every word may be established. And if he shall neglect to hear them, tell it unto the church: but if he neglect to hear the church, let him be unto thee as an heathen man and a publican. Verily I say unto you, Whatsoever ye shall bind on earth shall be bound in heaven: and whatsoever ye shall loose on earth shall be loosed in heaven.[3]

By the late Middle Ages, the church had developed a more complicated system of church discipline than this simple biblical model implies. Church discipline was executed by a hierarchy of church courts, beginning with the archidiaconal courts at the lowest level, the consistories of the bishops, the archbishops' tribunals and, at the top of the hierarchy, the papal curia. The most important measures of church discipline were the minor and the major excommunication (*excommunicatio minor* and *excommunicatio maior*). A minor excommunication resulted in the exclusion from the sacraments of the church, whereas a major excommunication meant the exclusion from the benefits of being a member of the Christian community, but not a complete exclusion from the church. The ecclesiastical courts were responsible for judging the laity as well as the secular clergy. They 'adjudged the validity of marriages, punished fornicators and adulterers, and dealt with the condition of church buildings, the proper administration of the sacraments, ministerial conduct, and lay attendance at church services'.[4] The system of church courts was variously criticized during the later Middle Ages for its alleged abuses, but recent research has also shown that it performed many necessary and worthwhile tasks for the community, for example the resolution of conflicts.[5]

---

3 See Leith, '1. Begriff, 2. Theologischer Überblick', in 'Kirchenzucht', p. 175; Wandel, 'Church discipline', p. 328; Friedeburg, 'Kirchenzucht', col. 1368.
4 Greaves, 'Church courts', p. 435.
5 See Greaves, 'Church courts', p. 435; Wandel, 'Church discipline', p. 328; Link, 'V. Reformation und Neuzeit', in: 'Bann', pp. 182–4.

Church and social discipline after the Reformation:
an overview

Although social and church discipline was thus not an invention of the early modern period, the Reformation and Counter-Reformation led to an intensification of the disciplining measures of church and state. As a consequence of the Lutheran Reformation in Germany and the spread of Protestant ideas all over Europe, the medieval universal church was broken up. This led to the formation of early modern confessions which were clearly defined in terms of theology and doctrine, the three major confessions being Lutheranism, Calvinism and Catholicism. Anglicanism can be added to this list, although it may be doubted that it was a confessional church in the strict sense of the word. This process has been called 'confession building' or 'confessionalization' in historiography. To different degrees, the new confessional churches allied with the states and thus became state churches. In any case, the existence of different confessional churches as well as numerous sects led to a new situation of rivalry. Each church had not only to formulate its doctrine unequivocally, but it also had to make sure that its confessional norms were propagated and enforced among its flock and it often did this with the help of the state.

At this point, social disciplining in a broader sense was implemented to ensure the unity – and ideally homogeneity – of the confessional church on the one hand and its demarcation from rival churches on the other. Measures like confessional oaths and subscription enabled the churches to remove dissidents and to ensure the religious orthodoxy of personnel in important positions, in particular theologians, priests, teachers and secular officials. Propaganda and censorship were also essential in order to use the printing press for one's own purposes while preventing rivals from access to the printing press. While scholars engaged in controversial theology, catechizing and sermons were used to influence the people. Education was one of the major measures of social disciplining during the confessional age. By founding new educational institutions – parish schools, grammar schools and universities – all confessional churches hoped to keep their flocks from attending their rivals' institutions and to 'indoctrinate' future generations. In view of the importance of rites for the coherence of a confessional church, participation in such rites, especially baptisms and marriages, was closely monitored through the keeping of registers. The expulsion of religious minorities also served the end of ensuring the unity of the confessional church. And last but not least, the regular visitations of parishes and a variety of other measures of church discipline were used to control the morals and behaviour of the individual which were thought to reflect on the confessional group as a whole.[6]

The increased confessional rivalry from the sixteenth century onwards and the confessional churches' parallel attempts to effectively control their flocks thus led not only to the implementation of social and church discipline in all confessional churches, but also resulted in heightened awareness of the necessity of church discipline. There was, therefore, an intensification of church discipline after the Reformation. In spite of the fact that, as we shall see in more detail later, the different churches used very different institutions and measures to inculcate and control the laity's beliefs and behaviour, these were all a mixture of old, i.e., medieval, instruments and new.

Historical and historiographical problems

All religious communities in the early modern period – including those which were separated from or even persecuted by the state – strove to maintain a system of discipline among their flocks. In state, territorial, or city-state churches, however, the government (the monarch, prince, or city council) always became closely involved in the administration of the church and thus also in the implementation of church discipline. This was not only the case in Protestant state churches, but also in Catholic territories because the universal Catholic Church needed the state as an ally to realize its Tridentine reform programme. This leads to two problems, which were not only historical problems of institutionalization and execution of church discipline, but which have also triggered historiographical discussions.

First, in many historical as well as historiographical discussions a clear theoretical distinction 'between state sanctions and church discipline'[7] is made. Accordingly, the state is seen as responsible for the persecution of secular 'crimes', whereas the church is responsible for the disciplining of 'sin'. Again in theory, the state's secular institutions are therefore seen as strictly separated

---

6 On the connections between social disciplining and confessionalization, see Reinhard, 'Zwang zur Konfessionalisierung?'; Reinhard, 'Reformation, Counter-Reformation, and the early modern state'; Reinhard, 'Was ist katholische Konfessionalisierung?'; Schilling, 'Confessionalization in the Empire'; Schilling, 'Confessional Europe'; Schilling, 'Die Konfessionalisierung von Kirche, Staat und Gesellschaft'; on confessionalization and its historiography, see Lotz-Heumann, 'The concept of "confessionalization"'.

7 Hsia, *Social discipline*, p. 123.

from the churches' ecclesiastical institutions, including those administering church discipline. However, this was not at all the case in practice, where church discipline was, in fact, less tidy. On the one hand, there were some basic preconditions governing the relationship between church and state in the area of church discipline. It was easier for the church discipline of minority churches and secret churches to operate free of state influence. In contrast, territorial churches frequently came under strong state influence, not least in matters of church discipline. This is why, as we shall see below, Calvinist church discipline appeared in very different – and basically incompatible – shapes and sizes all over Europe. On the other hand, the relationship between a particular church and a particular state also evolved over time with a consequent effect on church discipline. This was particularly the case in the early Reformation when reformers' ideas had to be transformed into workable procedures and institutions. But it was also the case when political circumstances changed so that a new *modus vivendi* had to be found between state and church.[8]

Second, the concept of social disciplining which has informed much research into church discipline implies measures taken by the state and ecclesiastical authorities from 'above' and imposed upon the people 'below'. It implies a 'top-to-bottom' process, in which the people were at the receiving end of demands and actions from church and state. This model has been severely challenged in recent years. Consequently, historians have come to realize that the common people were not passive 'victims' or obedient recipients of disciplining measures. Rather, they often found ways to work with, negotiate, or avoid them. It is now clear that disciplining measures in the early modern period were far from successful. On the contrary, some scholars think that they were successful only if there was also a need for self-regulation among the people, so that the institutions of church discipline were used by them to cater to that need. It is now clear that the small social entities of the early modern period, especially the congregation and the neighbourhood, have to be taken into account when the workings and effects of social and church discipline are investigated.[9]

---

8 For the historiographical debate about the relationship between secular criminal justice and church discipline, see Schilling, '"History of crime" or "history of sin"?'; Ingram, 'History of sin or history of crime?'; Schnabel-Schüle, 'Kirchenzucht als Verbrechensprävention'; Benedict, *Christ's churches purely reformed*, pp. 482–4.

9 See Schmidt, *Dorf und Religion*, with an English summary, pp. 377–400; Schmidt, 'Sozialdisziplinierung?'; Schmidt, 'Pazifizierung des Dorfes'; Roodenburg, *Oonder censuur*; Roodenburg, 'Reformierte Kirchenzucht und Ehrenhandel'; Münch, 'Kirchenzucht und Nachbarschaft'.

The theory and practice of church discipline in early modern Europe

In order to understand the different theoretical concepts of church discipline and the wide variety of forms of church discipline which resulted from these concepts, it is useful to look at the attitudes of the Protestant and Catholic reformers on the subject before turning towards the different confessional institutions and measures which were established in practice.[10] The following sections will first look at Catholic church discipline, but will then concentrate on Protestant Europe, as the most important institution of church discipline in Catholicism, the Inquisition, is covered in a separate chapter of this volume.[11] In the discussion of Protestant Europe this chapter concentrates on those measures and institutions whose principal purpose was the administration of church discipline, i.e., the control of the religious orthodoxy and morals of clergy and laity. Other measures, for example poor relief, which also served the social disciplining purposes of church and state, will not be taken into account.[12]

Catholic church discipline

Post-Tridentine Catholic church discipline was quite a different phenomenon from the Protestant ideas and their realizations which will be discussed below. Catholic church discipline as it developed in the context of the Catholic reform movement of the sixteenth century was a varied phenomenon which is still under-researched. However, it should not be assumed that it was either less active or less effective than any of the Protestant systems. The most striking aspect of church discipline in post-Tridentine Catholicism is the fact that it

---

10 A bibliography of literature on church discipline in Europe up to 1994 is provided in Schilling and Scherneck, 'Auswahlbibliographie'; for short overviews of church discipline in early modern Europe or early modern Germany, see Hsia, Social discipline, esp. pp. 122–42; Schilling, 'Confessional Europe', esp. pp. 651–2; Schilling, 'Die Kirchenzucht im frühneuzeitlichen Europa'; Schmidt, 'Gemeinde und Sittenzucht', esp. pp. 187–95; Venard, Geschichte des Christentums, pp. 1003–11; Gorski, The disciplinary revolution, pp. 114–55. The following encyclopaedia articles are also instructive: Goertz, '3. Reformationszeit', in: 'Kirchenzucht'; Friedeburg, 'Kirchenzucht'; Wandel, 'Church discipline'; Greaves, 'Church courts'; Link, 'V. Reformation und Neuzeit', in: 'Bann'; Schmidt, 'Visitation'.

11 See Chapter 16, below.

12 There is a rich historiography which reflects the fact that church and state were involved in poor relief to varying degrees of intensity and cooperation. See, for example, Grell and Cunningham (eds.), Health care and poor relief; Prak, 'The carrot and the stick'; Davis, 'Poor relief'; Fehler, Poor relief and Protestantism; Grell, 'The religious duty of care'; Jütte, 'Disziplinierungsmechanismen'; Lindberg, Beyond charity; Parker, The reformation of community; Pullan, 'Catholics and the poor'.

did not so much invent new institutions and procedures of church discipline as intensify medieval ones. Catholic church discipline can be differentiated into two broad approaches, one focusing on the individual's interior, the other operating in the *forum externum*.

On the one hand, there was the confession by the individual believer, focusing on the *disciplina interna*. Confession as an obligation which every Catholic had to perform at least once a year at Easter had already been established by the Fourth Lateran Council in 1215. However, the Catholic Reformation of the sixteenth century stressed the necessity of confession, especially if sins had been committed, and sought to lay more emphasis on the individual as confessant and on the personal relationship between the confessant and the confessor. As a consequence, handbooks for confessors became very important in order to establish a new practice of confession: confessors were advised as to which questions to ask their confessants and how to lead confessants to repentance. The most influential of these handbooks were the Instructions for Confessors by the famous Milan archbishop Carlo Borromeo, published in 1583. In contrast to these normative sources, we know very little about the actual practice of confession in early modern Catholic Europe because – in contrast to the Calvinist consistorial minutes – confessing was a secret affair between two persons without record-keeping.[13]

On the other hand, there were many different forms of external discipline in the Catholic Church, ranging from the Inquisition in Spain and Italy (see Chapter 16, below) to different kinds of visitations, a hierarchy of ecclesiastical courts and – as a new 'invention' of the Catholic Reformation – the so-called 'Marian sodalities' of the Jesuits. Visitations, which had fallen into disuse or proved to be ineffective in the late medieval church, were reanimated by the Council of Trent. On the one hand, the authority of the bishop was strengthened because he was entitled to include exempt persons and institutions in his visitations. On the other hand, the bishop was obliged to conduct regular visitations in his diocese. Once again, the Archbishop of Milan, Carlo Borromeo, set an example for Catholic reform in the rest of Europe by meticulously employing visitations in his diocese. In the Catholic territories of the Holy Roman Empire, for example in Bavaria and the Habsburg territories, visitations subsequently became one of the most important instruments of church discipline, targeting the clergy as well as the laity. Regarding the church courts, the medieval system of diocesan courts was in fact left in place, but the

---

13 See Delumeau, *L'aveau et le pardon*; Delumeau, *Sin and fear*; Bossy, 'The social history of confession'; Bossy, *Christianity in the West*; Tentler, 'The summa for confessors'.

Council of Trent suppressed the archidiaconal tribunals, thus resting this aspect of church discipline firmly in the hands of the bishops. The pope remained the final instance of appeal in the Catholic Church. In addition, the religious orders, notably the new-founded Jesuits, participated in the disciplining efforts. The Jesuit order's own internal organization and practices of piety were very strict and attuned to an almost military discipline. Jesuits were active as teachers and confessors, and they founded the 'Marian sodalities', a new type of religious fraternity geared to inculcating the principles of reformed Catholicism.[14]

Lutheran church discipline

Luther was at first deeply suspicious of church discipline. As the abuse of ecclesiastical justice by the medieval Catholic Church was a major gravamen of the Protestant Reformation, he placed his trust in the gospel as a sufficient force to reform the people. Soon, however, he realized that this was an unrealistic position; he himself was repeatedly in conflict with the Wittenberg congregation about morals and adequate behaviour. Without taking a fundamental decision on church discipline, Luther held the view that only the exclusion from communion, the so-called lesser excommunication, should be imposed, while he regarded the greater excommunication as a secular punishment. According to Luther, the pastor of the parish was to be responsible for the disciplining of his flock through catechizing and preaching. In this context, the pastor was also meant to have the power of enforcing a lesser excommunication. However, similar to the fate of Luther's general idea about the separation of the ecclesiastical and the secular sphere (Zwei-Reiche-Lehre), which often proved to be untenable in practice, Lutheran church discipline became more and more influenced by the state. Church discipline came under the control of the so-called consistories (Konsistorien), ecclesiastical governing bodies which were established by princely ordinances.

It is very difficult to generalize about the different forms of church discipline developed in Lutheran territories in the Holy Roman Empire and there is still a need for more research, but a basic model can be identified, on which church discipline was based in major Lutheran territories like electoral Saxony or

14 See Becker, *Konfessionalisierung in Kurköln*; Freitag, *Pfarrer, Kirche und ländliche Gesellschaft*; Heiß, 'Konfessionsbildung'; Holzem, *Religion und Lebensformen*; Holzem, 'Katholische Konfession und Kirchenzucht'; Lang, 'Reform im Wandel'; Châtellier, *The Europe of the devout*; Black, *Italian confraternities*; Donnelly and Maher (eds.), *Confraternities and Catholic reform*; Zeeden and Molitor (eds.), *Die Visitation im Dienste der kirchlichen Reform*; Zeeden and Lang (eds.), *Kirche und Visitation*; Headley and Tomato (eds.), *San Carlo Borromeo*; Bossy, *Christianity in the West*.

Württemberg. For the development of this model of church discipline, Justus Jonas's work of 1538 entitled *Bedencken der Consistorien halber* (*Thoughts about Consistories*) was decisive. In contrast to Luther he argued that church discipline should be referred to consistories and that excommunicated persons should also face secular punishments. Pastors should have only the power to initiate proceedings with the consistories and to announce rulings in their parishes. They were not to have the power to pronounce a parishioner excommunicate. Accordingly, a central consistory under the direct supervision of the prince (as in Saxony) or regional consistorial courts (as in Württemberg) were established. Central consistories widened their sphere of responsibility and added visitations, censorship and the day-to-day control and administration of the church to church discipline. Sometimes, pastors resented the loss of power resulting from this and exceeded their authority, which led to conflicts with the central institutions.[15]

In some cases, Lutheran territories developed different institutions of church discipline. For example, in Hohenlohe, a small territory in south-western Germany, and in the city of Magdeburg the parish clergy had the right to impose lesser excommunications. In other Lutheran territories of the sixteenth century, notably those which later converted to Calvinism, the system of church discipline was closer to Calvinism, focusing on the congregation. For example, in Hesse, Pfalz-Zweibrücken and Nassau-Dillenburg there existed committees of laymen of the parish (so-called presbyters or elders; see below for an explanation of the Calvinist presbyterial system) who were responsible for church discipline. Even in Württemberg, a territory which remained Lutheran, communal church convents, i.e., church courts on the level of the parishes, were established in the middle of the seventeenth century.[16]

However, although consistories and even presbyters in some cases existed as institutions of church discipline in Lutheranism, they were far from being the major instruments of church and social disciplining. Rather, besides preaching, catechesis and private confession,[17] visitations played a very important role in the control of the clergy and the laity. Therefore, the following section will

---

15 See Brecht, *Kirchenordnung und Kirchenzucht*; Brecht, 'Lutherische Kirchenzucht'; Brecht, 'Protestantische Kirchenzucht'; Schnabel-Schüle, 'Der große Unterschied'; Götze, *Wie Luther Kirchenzucht übte*; Franz, *Die Kirchenleitung in Hohenlohe*; Gorski, *The disciplinary revolution*, p. 119; for an example of an urban Lutheran Reformation analysed from a gender perspective, see Roper, *The holy household*.

16 See Tolley, *Pastors and parishioners in Württemberg*; Schnabel-Schüle, 'Calvinistische Kirchenzucht in Württemberg?'; Gorski, *The disciplinary revolution*, p. 120; Schmidt, 'Gemeinde und Sittenzucht', pp. 190–2.

17 See Schilling, 'Die Kirchenzucht im frühneuzeitlichen Europa', p. 34.

provide an introduction to the practice of visitations in the Lutheran territorial churches in the Holy Roman Empire.

The general Lutheran practice of visitations grew out of the first major Saxon visitation in 1528–9. For this visitation, Melanchthon wrote the *Instruction of the Visitors to the Pastors in the Electorate of Saxony*, and in his preface to this work Luther stressed that by taking up visitations the Reformation church was returning to the ancient apostolic custom of 'visiting'. As visitations could only be carried out successfully with the help of the state, Luther once again laid aside his doubts and reservations about such state involvement in the church. In the future, visitations of the church thus 'served the state as effective tools for enlarging, solidifying, and perpetuating its dominion'.[18] Visitations could be of different scopes, from local visitations to general visitations of the entire territory. The aim of a visitation was two-fold: first, it was to provide information on the general situation of the church regarding church fabric, personnel and finances; second, it was to control and promote the religious orthodoxy and morality of the clergy and the laity.

Visitations were comprehensive bureaucratic processes resulting in the production of a lot of written material which is important source material for Reformation historians. Visitations began with a formal announcement, the visitation order, in which the names of the visitors – a mixture of clerical and lay personnel – were also given. The visitors then received an instruction on how they were supposed to carry out the visitation. Visitors were provided with a list of questions (*interrogatoria, Fragstück*) which they had to put to each person. When the visitors came to the towns and villages, the inhabitants assembled in the parish church where they first heard an opening address by the visitors and were then interrogated. Besides the pastor, sextons, schoolmasters, mayors, town councillors or village elders, a representative sample of the common people was questioned: men and women of different ages and social standing, children and youths.

The questions that were put to clerical and secular officeholders and to the people were manifold: up to seventy or eighty questions were on the printed questionnaires of the visitors. The pastor was questioned about his parishioners as well as other pastors, the parishioners were questioned about their pastor as well as about other parishioners: everybody was to inform on everybody else. The visitors gathered information about the fulfilment of pastoral duties by the clergy as well as their personal life. They looked into the religious knowledge of the parishioners and their moral behaviour. They recorded conflicts in the

18 Strauss, *Luther's house of learning*, p. 258.

parish, and checked on the school and its schoolmaster. Record-keeping was very thorough: visitors were accompanied by a scribe who wrote the answers to the questions in booklets (so-called *Kladden*). These were later transcribed into protocols of the visitation which were headed by a synopsis listing the problems which prevailed in many or all of the parishes. As these protocols were still large documents, they were often summarized in so-called 'relations' (*Relationen*) in order to provide the secular and ecclesiastical authorities with quick and easy information on the results of the visitation.[19]

Calvinist church discipline: Geneva, France, Scotland, and the German territories

For Calvin, church discipline had a very different meaning than for Luther. From the point of view of his theology, church discipline was indispensable in a truly reformed church because only through church discipline could the purity of the congregation at the Lord's Supper be ensured. This idea thus provided a strong impetus to establish institutions of church discipline on the level of the congregations. In his Genevan *Ordonnances ecclésiastiques* of 1541, Calvin therefore created two institutions on which church discipline in all Calvinist churches came to be based: the so-called presbyters or elders, respectable members of the congregation, were elected by the congregation and formed the so-called consistory which was responsible for administering church discipline in the congregation. (The Calvinist consistory should not be confused with the Lutheran consistory; the same term is employed to mean two very different things!) The second major influence on Calvin's conception of church discipline was his sphere of activity, i.e., the independent city-state of Geneva. As the Reformed church established there by Calvin was not a church of voluntary membership, but a city-state church, Calvin accepted that the church needed the support of the secular arm in order to enforce discipline. Therefore, the Genevan consistory consisted of the Genevan ministers and some ministers from the surrounding villages as well as twelve laymen who were members of the city council, but had to be confirmed as presbyters by the congregations.[20]

---

19 See Strauss, *Luther's house of learning*, pp. 249–67; Strauss, 'Success and failure'; Strauss, 'Visitations'; Kittelson, 'Successes and failures'; Kittelson, 'Visitations and popular religious culture'; Dixon, *The Reformation and rural society*, esp. pp. 60–5; Müller, 'Die Konfessionalisierung in der Grafschaft Oldenburg'; for a territory that was transferred from Lutheranism to Calvinism, see Konersmann, 'Kirchenvisitation als landesherrliches Kontrollmittel'.

20 See Kingdon, 'The control of morals in Calvin's Geneva'; Kingdon, 'Calvinist discipline'; Kingdon, 'The Genevan consistory'; Kingdon, *Adultery and divorce*; Monter, 'The

In accordance with Geneva's role as a mother church to international Calvinism, Calvin's system of church discipline was spread, modified and in some cases changed beyond recognition in communities and states of Reformed faith all over Europe, to the Netherlands, France, Scotland and parts of Germany, as well as in the New World. The Calvinist presbyterian system of church discipline was, compared to Lutheranism and Catholicism, the most coherent in early modern Europe. Calvinist consistories produced a string of minutes, in which they meticulously recorded their sessions and thus the perceived 'sins' of their flock as well as the disciplining measures imposed on those called before the consistory. Because of this richness of sources, Calvinist church discipline has been at the centre of historiographical interest for several decades.[21]

Calvinist consistories were concerned with two major areas of church discipline: first, church discipline in a narrow sense of the word, i.e., religious conformity and piety. Consistories strove to eliminate remnants of Catholic beliefs and practices as well as magic and witchcraft. While on the one hand warning their church members to avoid 'idolatry' and discouraging them from recourse to magic like cursing and casting spells, consistories also made sure that their flock learned and adhered to Calvinist doctrines and devotions. For example, regular attendance at catechesis was a major concern of the consistories and they valiantly fought against Sabbath breach. In areas of Europe where members of different confessional churches lived closely together, for example in the Netherlands, consistories warned their flock against too much contact with members of other churches.

The second major area of church discipline was concerned with all offences concerning the social community. Here, consistories concentrated their activities in three sub-areas: sexual conduct, marriage, and neighbourhood relations. Sexual discipline was the main sector of activity in this context. Consistories were mostly concerned with adultery and 'harlotry' i.e., extramarital relationships resulting in unmarried women becoming pregnant. Consistories also censured anticipation, i.e., sexual relationships of engaged couples before

---

consistory of Geneva'; Naphy, *Calvin*; Cameron, 'Godly nurture', pp. 264–8; Neuser, 'Dogma und Bekenntnis in der Reformation', pp. 265–8.

21 See Schilling, 'Reformierte Kirchenzucht'; Schilling, 'Sündenzucht'; Schilling, 'Calvinism'; Schilling, 'Die frühneuzeitliche Formierung'; Schilling, 'Reform and supervision of family life'; Schmidt, *Dorf und Religion*; Konersmann, 'Presbyteriale Bußzucht'; Pfister, 'Reformierte Sittenzucht'; Münch, *Zucht und Ordnung*. The church discipline of Calvinist stranger churches has also received some attention. See, for example, Houston, 'The consistory of the Scots church, Rotterdam'; Littleton, 'Ecclesiastical discipline'; Pettegree, *Foreign Protestant communities*, pp. 182–215.

marriage, often resulting in childbirth too soon after the wedding. Severe cases of sexual misconduct like prostitution, homosexuality, incest and rape also occur in the consistories' minutes, but to a much lesser degree. Another major area of consistory activity was the matrimonial order. Although a Calvinist marriage could theoretically be divorced if there were serious grounds, for example adultery, madness, impotence and permanent abandonment, consistories generally tried desperately and repeatedly to reconcile spouses to one another. Their activities in this area were inspired by the general conception of the well-ordered, hierarchical household, in which the father was the head of the household and thus held the responsibility for order and peace within his realm. Therefore, more men than women were summoned before the consistories in such cases, and, in addition, consistories then often sided with the women. Men were censured in particular for drinking, which implied wastefulness, and for domestic violence. The third major sector of activity, neighbourhood relations, had a similar leitmotif to the consistories' concern with marriage: friendliness and Christian love. Reconciliation between the parties was the major aim of the consistories because social unity was, as we have seen above, regarded as an essential precondition for communion. As a consequence, all forms of quarrelling, violent behaviour, maledictory magic, defamation, etc. came under the scrutiny of the consistories. As in marriage cases, the consistories often brokered resolutions between the parties concerned and thus performed an important social function. However, as can be seen from the many cases that came before the consistories repeatedly, compromises were often fragile. Although historians are still arguing about the real impact and long-term behavioural changes brought about by Calvinist ecclesiastical discipline, it cannot be denied that Calvinist consistories became deeply involved in the lives of church members, and it is hardly imaginable that their regulating impetus did not have at least some influence on the societies around them.[22]

As already mentioned above, the Calvinist system of church discipline spread from Geneva throughout Europe. In France, where the Huguenots, the French Calvinists, organized their church either under conditions of persecution or with a grudging toleration by the state, the Presbyterian system was taken over from Geneva. However, in contrast to the Genevan city-state church, the Huguenots needed further institutions in order to build a church that spanned

---

22 On the areas of activity of Calvinist consistories, see in more detail Benedict, *Christ's churches purely reformed*, pp. 460–82, 484–9; Kingdon, *Adultery and divorce*; Schilling, 'Calvinism'; Schilling, 'Reform and supervision of family life'; Schilling, 'Sündenzucht'; Schmidt, *Dorf und Religion*.

the whole of France. Therefore, a hierarchy of so-called synods – provincial and national – was established above the consistories by the Huguenot church order of 1559. The synods acted as appeal courts for the consistories. The Huguenot consistories were composed of the minister of the congregation and elected lay elders, and the synods also had lay as well as clerical members.[23] The system of synods was then taken over by other Calvinist churches, notably in the Netherlands[24] and in Scotland.

In Scotland, where the Calvinist Reformation first established itself in the form of 'privy kirks' in the households of lairds (gentry) or urban elites, and where the Presbyterian system of church government was under constant pressure by the Episcopalian system supported by the crown, the Presbyterians nevertheless managed to establish and sustain a system of church discipline centring on the kirk session. The kirk session staffed by the minister and the elders was the equivalent of the consistory in other Calvinist churches, i.e., the body responsible for administering church discipline in the congregation. In addition to the local kirk sessions, there were also the so-called presbyteries. These were regional assemblies of the ministers which also acted as disciplinary courts and decided on serious or difficult cases referred to them by the kirk sessions. Above these were the synods, which also acted as appeal courts, the national synod in Scotland being called the general assembly.

In theory, church discipline in the Scottish Presbyterian church was construed as completely independent of the secular authorities. For example, excommunications were pronounced by the kirk sessions without involvement of the state. However, in practice, especially in the towns, there was an overlap between church and civil authorities because the urban elite often staffed the town council as well as the consistory.

The church discipline administered by the kirk sessions in Scotland was in some cases even more strict than that in Geneva. For example, while in Geneva fornicators only incurred a lesser excommunication, in Scotland, where the kirk sessions concentrated much of their effort on fornication and adultery, punishment of sexual sins was much harsher. The offenders had to endure public penitence by sitting on a Stool of Repentance in the church on several Sundays dressed in sackcloth. In addition to extra-marital sex, kirk sessions

---

23 See Neuser, 'Dogma und Bekenntnis in der Reformation', pp. 266–7. On church discipline among the Huguenots, see Mentzer, 'Disciplina nervus ecclesiae'; Mentzer, 'Ecclesiastical discipline'; Mentzer, 'Marking the taboo'; Chareyre, '"The great difficulties one must bear to follow Jesus Christ"'; Vogler and Estèbe, 'La genèse d'une société protestante'; Benedict, *Christ's churches purely reformed*, pp. 470–2.

24 See, for example, Parker, 'Two generations of discipline'; Kooi, 'Pharisees and hypocrites'; see also note 21 above.

concentrated their disciplining measures on marriage and family problems like domestic disputes, on Sabbath breach, on disputes between neighbours and violent behaviour, on magic and witchcraft. One of their regular tasks was closely connected with the above-mentioned Calvinist concern about the purity of the congregation at the Lord's Supper. Before the communion, the kirk session visited all families in the parish and questioned all members who wanted to participate in the Lord's Supper in order to determine whether they were free of sin. Only then would the kirk session issue a token of admission for communion.[25]

In spite of the striking differences between the Calvinist and the Lutheran model of church discipline, it has been argued for the territorial states in the Empire that the differences between Lutheran and Calvinist church discipline were limited in practice because the church government of Calvinist princes was as state-centred as that of Lutheran princes, and Calvinist church discipline could therefore never be truly communal. When we look at the system of church discipline in one of the major Calvinist territories of the Empire, the Palatinate, we find that a compromise was in fact established by the church discipline order of 1570: while consistories were created on the parish level, the presbyters were not elected by the parishioners, but chosen by the authorities. The consistory had only the right to impose a lesser excommunication, while the greater excommunication was in the hands of the prince. This meant that church discipline in the Palatinate was in fact strongly controlled by the state. On the other hand, as we have seen above, there were also forms of presbyterial church discipline established in some Lutheran territories. In fact, only in areas of Germany where Calvinism did not become the official confession of a territory but developed as a church independent of the state – in the territories of Jülich-Cleve-Berg on the Lower Rhine, in the city of Emden in East Friesland and in the sixteenth-century Calvinist refugee communities in cities like Frankfurt, Strasbourg, and Cologne – were the presbyters elected by the members of the congregation.[26]

25 See Cameron, 'Godly nurture', pp. 271–6; Greaves, 'Church courts', pp. 437–8; Graham, 'Social discipline in Scotland'; Graham, *The uses of reform*; Parker, 'The "kirk by law established"'; Kirk, '"The polities of the best reformed kirks"', pp. 29–31; Lenman, 'The limits of godly discipline'; Benedict, *Christ's churches purely reformed*, pp. 469–70. For a detailed account of the everyday workings of Calvinist church discipline in Scotland, see Todd, *Culture of Protestantism*, esp. pp. 84–126, 127–82, 265–314.

26 See Konersmann, *Kirchenregiment und Kirchenzucht*; Schaab, 'Obrigkeitlicher Calvinismus'; Münch, *Zucht und Ordnung*; Schnabel-Schüle, 'Der große Unterschied'; Goertz, '3. Reformationszeit', in: 'Kirchenzucht', pp. 181–2; Greaves, 'Church courts', p. 437; see also note 21 above.

Other varieties of church discipline: Zwinglianism, the Anabaptists, and Anglicanism

In contrast to this wide reception of the Calvinist model, Zwingli's ideas about church discipline were first realized in Zurich and afterwards became a model mainly for the German-speaking areas of Switzerland, for example Bern. Zwingli proceeded from the same aim as Calvin: ensuring the purity of the congregation at communion. However, in contrast to Calvin, Zwingli left the execution of church discipline to the secular authorities. Although the Zurich marriage court, which was staffed by members of the city council and ministers, quickly expanded its purview to include lay morality and behaviour in general, it could only pronounce recommendations, while the execution of church discipline lay with the city council.[27]

In terms of church discipline, the Anabaptists held very similar views to the Calvinists: Anabaptists saw church discipline as an essential instrument to ensure the purity of the congregation at the Lord's Supper. It was essential to them that their church, being composed of voluntary members, be kept free of sin. As the Anabaptists kept aloof from the state, their church discipline was completely centred on the individual congregation and free of secular influence or intervention. In practice, there were very different degrees of institutionalization of church discipline in the Anabaptist communities. For example, in the central and upper German congregations there were no institutions of church discipline at all, whereas the Hutterites as well as the Anabaptists of lower Germany, the Netherlands and Switzerland instituted church discipline formally.[28]

The Anglican churches, the Protestant state churches of England and Ireland, can be described as Janus-faced. While their theology and doctrine were Calvinist, these churches retained many institutions, for example a hierarchical church structure, and outward traditions like vestments, from the medieval Catholic Church. Another medieval institution which was thus retained were the church courts: as a consequence, church discipline in the established churches in England and Ireland was administered by the ecclesiastical courts which were under the control of the bishops and archbishops. In the parishes, the role of the churchwardens, laymen elected by the parish, was important because in addition to the clergy they could bring a case before the ecclesiastical courts. In sixteenth- and seventeenth-century England the

---

27 See Gordon, *Clerical discipline*; Gordon, 'Die Entwicklung der Kirchenzucht'; Köhler, *Zürcher Ehegericht*. On Bucer, see Burnett, 'Church discipline'.
28 See Davis, 'No discipline, no church'; Goertz, 'Kleruskritik, Kirchenzucht'; Goertz, '3. Reformationszeit', in 'Kirchenzucht', pp. 179–80.

church courts came under severe criticism by the so-called Puritans, members of the Church of England who wanted the state church to become more clearly Calvinist. Puritans aimed for a Calvinist system of church discipline with consistories on the parish level, and some Puritans also aimed for a synodal system. These aims and wishes were never fulfilled in the national church in England, although Puritans from England did institute a Calvinist church discipline in the New World. The bad press which the ecclesiastical courts received from the Puritans in early modern England convinced historians for several centuries that the courts did not function properly. In recent decades, however, detailed investigations into the workings of the church courts have shown that – like their medieval predecessors – they did perform a useful function for the community by, for example, settling disputes.[29]

Conclusion

All in all, we have seen that not only did the Protestant and Catholic reform movements have very different ideas about church discipline, but there resulted an even wider variety of institutions and practices from these ideas. As the history of early modern church discipline is not only an on-going growth area of historiographical research, but has inspired numerous controversies, it remains difficult to make any definitive statements about the effectiveness of the institutions and measures of church discipline described above. It seems no longer likely that church discipline contributed to a successful process of social disciplining, as was held by an older historiography. However, it is also not yet clear how far church discipline was dependent upon the cooperation of the common people. This question will undoubtedly inspire further research and debates in the future.

29 See Houlbrooke, *Church courts*; Ingram, *Church courts, sex and marriage*; Marchant, *The Puritans and the church courts*; Marchant, *The church under the law*; Sharpe, *Defamation*; Friedeburg, 'Reformation of manners'; Friedeburg, 'Anglikanische Sittenzucht'; O'Day, 'Geschichte der bischöflichen Kirchenvisitation'; Lotz-Heumann, 'Social control'. For a comparison between England and North America, see Friedeburg, *Sündenzucht*.

15

Persecutions and martyrdom

BRAD S. GREGORY

Christian martyrdom was dramatically reborn in the sixteenth century, as devout men and women proved willing to die for their respective, divergent views of God's truth. Depending upon national and local contingencies, Anabaptists, magisterial Protestants, and Roman Catholics were subjected to judicial trials for their violation of laws that prescribed correct religious belief and practice. Those who refused to recant were often executed. From the 1520s into the seventeenth century, this basic confrontation between capital judicial procedure and committed religious belief resulted in some 5,000 deaths for religion in Europe, the majority of which occurred in the Low Countries, France, and England.[1] The extensive memorialization of these deaths by martyrologists and the communities of faith to which they belonged played an important role in the shaping of distinct, separate Christian traditions in early modern Europe and beyond.

Viewed broadly, the thrust of executions for religion during the era shifted from Anabaptists in the 1520s and 1530s to Reformed Protestants in the 1540s and 1550s, to Roman Catholics after 1580 in England, Asia, and the Americas. Nearly 500 known or 'probable' executions of Anabaptists had occurred in central Europe, including Switzerland and Bohemia, within a decade of the first deaths in 1525.[2] In the Low Countries, the followers of David Joris and Menno Simons would experience more of the same in the years just after the fall of the Anabaptist kingdom of Münster in 1535. The number of Protestant martyrs grew with the proliferation of Calvinism in the 1540s and 1550s. In France, the Parlement of Paris issued only twenty-three death sentences for heresy from 1536 through 1543, for example, but 112 from 1544 through 1549.[3]

---

1 The approximate figure of 5,000 executions for religion is compiled from data in Monter, 'Heresy executions', pp. 48–65; Nuttall, 'English martyrs', pp. 191–7; and Moreau, *L'Eglise de Belgique*, vol. 5, pp. 172–206.
2 Clasen, 'Executions of Anabaptists', pp. 118–19.
3 Monter, *Judging the French reformation*, pp. 253–62.

Between 1555 and 1558, some 300 executions were carried out in England under Mary Tudor. After Charles V reorganized the Inquisition in the Low Countries in 1546 and promulgated the so-called 'bloody placard' in 1550, inquisitors such as Pieter Titelmans went to work and the number of trials and executions for heresy increased in tandem with the spread of Calvinism in both the French- and Dutch-speaking Netherlands. If one takes not merely a European but a global perspective that includes Roman Catholic missionaries and converts abroad, there were more Catholic than Anabaptist or Protestant martyrs in the sixteenth and seventeenth centuries. In Japan alone, over 2,100 Catholics were executed in the early seventeenth century, most of them between 1614 and 1639.[4] In Europe, however, at the hands of other Christians, fewer Catholics than Anabaptists or Protestants were put to death: only in Britain beginning in 1535, primarily during the reigns of Henry VIII and Elizabeth I, were Roman Catholics judicially tried and executed for religious treason. Other Catholics were also celebrated as martyrs, mostly members of the clergy who perished during the violence of the Dutch revolt or the French wars of religion, of whom the best known are probably the nineteen Gorcum martyrs, killed in 1572.

Persecution or prosecution?

'Persecutions and martyrdom' might be considered as a straightforward description of this phenomenon. Such a characterization, however, is not analytically neutral, but rather reflects what has become the predominant, modern moral judgement in the West concerning the judicial treatment of religious and political nonconformists in general. Based upon a widespread acceptance of religious toleration and pluralism, 'persecution' has come to mean oppression for one's convictions regardless of their content, while 'martyrdom' refers to death endured for those convictions, again irrespective of content. Yet in the sixteenth century this was not so. Content mattered. Certainly those Christians who were suffering at the hands of others – Huguenots in France, for example, or Dutch Mennonites in the Low Countries, or Elizabethan Catholics in England – regarded themselves as persecuted, and their deaths as martyrdoms. Yet the application of these very terms was as sharply contested as the doctrines about which early modern Christians disputed so vigorously. If a chapter covering the same subject matter were to consider the perspective of sixteenth-century ecclesiastical and secular authorities, rather

---

4 Hsia, *World of Catholic renewal*, pp. 184–5.

than only a generalized perspective on those who regarded themselves as the victims of persecution, it might be entitled 'Prosecutions and executions of religious criminals'. Such a title would serve to remind us that the ecclesiastical and political authorities who were responsible for upholding orthodoxy (however defined) and for maintaining order (whatever its particularities) regarded neither themselves as persecutors nor the deaths that they procured as martyrdoms. On the contrary, they believed that they were protecting their subjects against the dangerous purveyors of deadly ideas by discharging a divinely entrusted duty. Religious heterodoxy was a crime, and it was treated as such. This was true not only of Catholic authorities, who inherited a centuries-old tradition of protecting the church against its internal and external enemies, but also of Lutheran, Zwinglian, and Calvinist authorities who took legal action against Anabaptists and other Christian dissidents.

The contingent nature of moral and legal categories such as 'persecution' and 'prosecution', 'execution' and 'martyrdom', is among the insights to be gained when we consider the dramatic resurgence of Christian martyrdom in the Reformation era from the perspective of authorities as well as martyrs, and as a cross-confessional whole that includes Anabaptists, Protestants, and Catholics. Analysed in this manner, the study of early modern Christian martyrdom offers powerful correctives both to traditional confessional history, with its concentration on a single tradition to the exclusion of others, as well as to much social history of the Reformation, with its tendency to marginalize doctrine, theology, and devotion in favour of an emphasis on the social and political motivations that are purportedly the explanatory mainsprings of human behaviour. The comparative, cross-confessional study of martyrdom reveals similarities as well as differences among Catholic, Protestant, and Anabaptist martyrs that remain hidden if the martyrs of different traditions are studied apart from one another. And the demographic diversity of Christian martyrs across confessional divides disrupts any obvious social scientific explanation for their actions: some were well-educated clergy, others simple artisans; some were men, others women; some were married, others single; some were teenagers, others middle-aged, still others septuagenarians. Martyrs were as socially diverse as the devout sixteenth-century Christians of which they comprise a small subset. Numerically, to be sure, they were exceptional in dying for their beliefs – but the content of their beliefs, deeply held, made them similar to their much more numerous, committed co-religionists.

On the eve of the Reformation, it would not have occurred either to ecclesiastical or secular authorities to question their duty to protect the faith by correcting those who had strayed from the church's teachings and practices.

They might as well have considered decriminalizing murder, theft, or rape (even though such crimes touched only other people or their property, not God or the faith). In theory, at least, theirs was a cooperative enterprise in late medieval Europe. Duly delegated churchmen, usually episcopally appointed inquisitors or papally appointed Dominicans, were charged with investigating whether or not a given person suspected of heresy – that is, of wilful error in Christian doctrine – was in fact guilty. Suspicion almost always derived from some conspicuous, concrete action that reflected heretical beliefs – the dishonouring of a religious image, a refusal to attend mass, or speech against a priest or prelate, for example – since purely private, unexpressed ideas, however heretical, would have been undetectable. Mere ignorance, superstition, or confusion was not heresy and was distinguished from it. If a heresy suspect was tried and found guilty, he or she was instructed accordingly, ordered to abjure, usually given some sort of penance and punishment, and received back into the church. Only in the case of those who refused to recant, or who relapsed after having previously been reconciled, were secular authorities to become involved: because in canon law the clergy were forbidden to shed blood, obstinate heretics were 'relaxed' to the secular arm for capital punishment, most commonly by burning, but sometimes by beheading or hanging. This judicial severity 'was neither singular nor extreme' in late medieval or early modern Europe when set alongside the use of the death penalty for other felonies, including theft, arson, counterfeiting, murder, and treason.[5] Lest punishment for crimes against religion be arbitrarily abstracted from its historical context, these harsh judicial realities must be kept in mind. They were crucial to the ways in which theologians, rulers, and magistrates made sense of the prosecution for heresy, which seemed to demand capital punishment for the sake of legal consistency: if traitors, for example, were put to death for betraying their human masters, how much more should heretics be executed for committing treason against God by betraying His church, the body of Christ?

The most important bodies in the execution of Protestants, Anabaptists, and Roman Catholics for religious crimes were the inquisitorial institutions within France, the Low Countries, and England, overseen by individual rulers and supported by laws and local political authorities. In all three countries, the unmistakable trend was towards a decreasing ecclesiastical and an increasing state influence in the prosecution of heresy or what might be called (in the case of Roman Catholics in Henrician or Elizabethan England, for example) religious treason. Inquisitorial institutions, whatever their specific form,

5 Mentzer, *Heresy proceedings*, pp. 122 (quotation), 127.

were as far from omnipotent as 'absolutist' regimes were distant from concretely absolutist rule in early modern Europe. Despite the fearsome capital
punishment that could be and sometimes was imposed upon heretics or religious traitors, the limitations of early modern technology, communication,
and travel placed enormous constraints on the exercise of judicial measures
against them by ecclesiastical or civil officials. Even if kings such as Henry II
of France or Philip II of Spain had wanted to root out every heretic from their
lands, they lacked any realistic means of doing so. The profusion of anti-heresy
legislation in France and the Low Countries from the 1520s through the 1560s
provides eloquent, indirect testimony to the ineffectiveness of prosecutorial
measures. The territories were too large, the means of communication too
slow, the prospects for evasion too numerous, the local authorities too often
uncooperative.

Modern historical scholarship has sought to correct mistaken stereotypes
about the character of judicial enquiry for religious heterodoxy, which popular
opinion still widely assumes to have been nothing but brutal and bloodthirsty.
The small number of people who were even suspected (let alone convicted)
of heresy overturns any notion that even the most active inquisitorial officials
were antagonizing large swaths of the population in a 'persecuting society'.[6]
More people were executed for religion in the Low Countries under Charles V
and Philip II than anywhere else in Europe, yet the most extensive study
of the Inquisition there in the sixteenth and seventeenth centuries reveals
that well under 1 per cent of the population was investigated for suspicion
of heresy.[7] Among those who were tried as suspected heretics, only small
minorities were executed, which dispels any idea that inquisitors were ruth-
less exterminators who sought merely to slaughter 'the other'. One of the
most zealous sixteenth-century inquisitors, Pieter Titelmans, spent twenty
years criss-crossing Flanders and heard over 1,100 and perhaps as many as
1,600 heresy cases, yet only 127 (8–11 per cent) resulted in executions.[8] Indeed,
Titelmans and members of the Council of Flanders broke what by then was
imperial law in order to save penitent Anabaptists in the 1550s, and Titelmans
himself interceded with secular authorities in order to block the execution
of others.[9] Overwhelmingly, ecclesiastical and civil authorities sought not to
kill but to correct those whom they regarded as religiously wayward, and so

---

6 The quoted phrase refers to the title of Moore, *Persecuting society*, a work that has been
   important for debates concerning these issues in medieval Europe.
7 Goosens, *Inquisitions dans Les Pays-Bas*, vol. 2, pp. 190–1.
8 van de Wiele, 'Inquisitierechtbank', pp. 59–61.
9 Decavele, *Dageraad van de reformatie*, vol. 1, pp. 26, 26 n. 77, 439, 440–2, 449.

to save them from themselves, as it were, in reclaiming them for orthodoxy. Notwithstanding his blatantly heretical views, for example, the religiously eccentric wool carder of Cardenete, Bartolomé Sánchez, met dozens of times between 1553 and 1558 in Cuenca, Spain, with remarkably patient inquisitorial judges, who were keenly sensitized to questions about his mental stability and who reasoned and pleaded with him to change his views and be reconciled to the church.[10]

Despite the repeated enactment of anti-heresy and religious treason legislation, such laws were dead letters unless they were put into practice. The actual course of prosecutions for religious heterodoxy was highly contingent on particular circumstances, the most important of which was probably the attitude of local magistrates charged with implementing the laws. Some magistrates enforced anti-heresy laws rigorously, others leniently, and still others not at all. In this respect, laws pertaining to religious heterodoxy were no different from other sorts of legislation. In no European country was there a constant, systematic prosecution of heresy suspects throughout the Reformation era. Rather, prosecution tended to be localized and to come in spurts – immediately after the suppression of the Anabaptist kingdom of Münster or the Iconoclastic Fury in certain Dutch cities, for example, or just after the Affair of the Placards in Paris, or in Essex and London during the brief reign of Mary Tudor. Not every region had a dedicated inquisitor such as Pieter Titelmans. In many instances, factors such as social standing and personal relationships with local civil officials influenced whether or not prosecution would proceed, and if so, what punishment would be imposed. The widespread judicial tendency to treat women as less than fully responsible for their actions was partly responsible for considerably fewer executions of women than men. In England, this pattern reached its extreme when coupled with the anti-treason legislation directed especially against the Catholic clergy (who were of course exclusively male): there were only four women among the 314 Catholics executed for religion between 1535 and 1680 among those whom the Roman Catholic Church officially recognizes as saints, blessed, or venerable.[11] Other women would like to have joined them, but were denied: when the priest Roger Dicconson and layman Ralph Milner were sentenced to death in 1591, for example, 'eight or nine young damsels' were condemned but not sentenced, whereupon they 'with open outcries and exclamations urged the Judges most constantly that, as they were all culpable of the same crime, viz. of hearing mass, relieving a priest, confessing their sins and serving their Saviour after the rite of the

---

10 Nalle, *Mad for God*.   11 Nuttall, 'English martyrs', p. 191.

Catholic Church, so they might drink all of the same cup, with such fervour and vehemence that they made the whole assembly astonished'.[12] Had the judges decided to execute only these women on this single occasion, they would have tripled at a stroke the number of female Catholics executed for religious treason in early modern England. Yet the women's desire to join the men went unrequited, demonstrating that even openly confessed guilt and subsequent conviction were not always punished according to the law.

The late medieval roots of the renaissance of Christian martyrdom

The renaissance of Christian martyrdom in the sixteenth century depended not only on magistrates who were willing to enforce laws against religious crimes, but also on men and women who, when judicially pressured, were willing to die rather than to relinquish their beliefs. Even when all prosecutorial contingencies are considered, the fact remained that to refuse to abjure one's convictions was to invite death. Without question, the men and women in such circumstances understood themselves to be unjustly persecuted rather than rightly prosecuted, and they anticipated death as martyrdom, not as an execution for criminal behaviour. In this self-understanding and anticipation of martyrdom, Christians from all three of the main martyrological traditions that took shape or persisted in the Reformation era – Anabaptists, Protestants, and Roman Catholics – were heirs to a late medieval Christianity saturated with sensibilities related to martyrdom. The story of martyrdom in the Reformation era therefore begins in the late Middle Ages. Despite the dearth of contemporary Catholic martyrs in late medieval Europe (a lack attributable to the successful institutionalization of Christianity over centuries), fifteenth- and early sixteenth-century Christians were keenly attuned to a host of ideas, attitudes, and practices related to martyrdom. Each of the three main traditions is better understood in the light of this common religious inheritance, far from all of which was rejected by Protestants and Anabaptists when they turned to scripture as the authoritative foundation for Christianity.

At the heart of Christianity – in contrast to Judaism, Islam, or Buddhism – there stands a martyr-saviour, Jesus Christ, whose physical suffering and painful death are integral to the religion's narrative and logic of salvation. Human beings can be saved because Christ, himself both man and God the Son,

---

12 John Cecil to Robert Persons, 1 November 1591, in Pollen (ed.), *Unpublished documents*, p. 200.

accepted a violent, humiliating death in a stunning act of obedience to God the Father that righted the primordial disobedience of Adam. The early sixteenth century was the apex of a long, late medieval crescendo in which the passion and death of Christ by crucifixion was depicted, honoured, and employed as an aid to devotion. In late medieval Christianity the central image of the religion and the primary focus of every church and chapel was the crucifix, the depiction of the dead Christ on the cross, which also dangled in miniature from the end of that new form of beaded prayer-chain, the rosary.[13] The stages of Christ's passion that culminated in crucifixion, whether based on scripture or derived from pious custom, were re-enacted in urban passion plays and processions, especially during Holy Week. They were formalized and affixed to the naves of churches in the fourteen stations of the cross, which functioned as visual aids to prayerful meditation detached from dependence on human actors or community processions. The tenor of late medieval devotion to Christ's passion was concrete and corporeal, highlighting the mystery of the Incarnation. A late fifteenth-century Flemish devotional pamphlet published in 1518, for example, comprised a weekly cycle of prayers and indulgences, set forth 'so that cold hearts might be kindled in the warm blood of Christ, because he so willingly suffered his bitter passion for us'.[14]

Passion and patience have the same Latin root, and they were linked in the 'imitation of Christ' – one of the chief religious practices among devout Christians in late medieval Europe, and not coincidentally the title of one of the best-selling books in the early decades of printing, with more than 120 editions in the half-century between 1470 and 1520 besides more than 800 surviving manuscripts.[15] Thomas à Kempis wrote in the *Imitation* that 'There is no thing more profitable for thy self and acceptable to God than to be patient and glad to suffer for the love of him. . . . For by adversity thou art made conformable to Christ and all his saints.'[16] Suffering was not only the means to salvation, but through Christ's death it was made holy, an experiential training ground through which Christians exercised the virtue of patience that they acquired by following in the footsteps of their Lord. 'For thy holy life that thou lead is a way to us to follow. And by holy patience we walk to thee that art our crown. For if thou haddest not gone afore us and had shewed us the ways of patience and virtue, who should have followed thee?'[17]

---

13 See Winston-Allen, *Stories of the rose*.   14 *Devote meditacie*, p. 326.
15 Lovatt, '*Imitation of Christ*', p. 118; De Backer, '*De imitatione Christi*', pp. 1–9, 34–5, 107–11, 127–9, 149, 155–6, 174; Pollard (ed.), *Short-title catalogue*, vol. 2, p. 303.
16 [Thomas à Kempis], *Imytacyon*, sig. [F6r–v].
17 [Thomas à Kempis], *Imytacyon*, sig. [J5].

Martyrdom had of course been instrumental in the spread of Christianity under hostile Roman emperors in ancient times, but had waned in Europe with the forging of medieval Christendom, which eventually rendered martyrdom a phenomenon of extra-European mission fields. Already in late antiquity, church fathers such as Cyprian, Augustine, Jerome, and Gregory the Great had distinguished between 'spiritual' or 'white' martyrdom and actual martyrdom, which helped to lay theological foundations for Christian asceticism as a form of sublimated martyrdom absent active persecution.[18] Integrated into medieval monastic life, it was this sublimated martyrdom as ascetic desire and practice that transcended monastic walls and was increasingly adopted by devout late medieval laity as well as religious in movements such as the *devotio moderna* – the most famous member of which was Thomas à Kempis. The movement's founder, Geert Grote, was deeply imbued with the desire to imitate Christ through persistent meditation on his suffering, as the means to acquire patience: 'the passion of our Lord Jesus Christ is ever to be before our minds. Reflect upon it as often as possible, for in this way no adversity can strike that will not be borne with an even-tempered soul.' Grote cautioned that 'remembrance of the passion avails little, if it is not accompanied by an overpowering desire to imitate Christ'.[19]

Among Christ's closest imitators were the early Christian martyrs, paragons of patience on whom late medieval Christians called so assiduously for help with everything from finding lost belongings to protecting themselves from the plague. The omnipresence of martyr-saints as intercessors meant that even though Christianization had largely rendered martyrdom dormant in the late medieval present, Christians across the social spectrum called on holy friends who in the distant past had died violent deaths in imitation of Christ. Two-thirds of the saints in the era's most important hagiographical collection, the thirteenth-century *Golden Legend*, are martyrs,[20] and many of them, including Barbara and Blaise, Stephen and Sebastian, Peter and Paul and Margaret, were among the most popular late medieval saints. Plentiful depictions of martyr-saints from the fifteenth and early sixteenth centuries, too, whether in woodcuts, paintings, or sculptures, strongly imply that their mimetic deaths remained a lively part of the religious awareness of late medieval Christians.[21]

---

18 Gougaud, *Dévotions*, pp. 200–19; and Rush, 'Spiritual martyrdom', pp. 569–89.
19 In Van Engen (ed.), *Devotio moderna*, pp. 87–8.
20 Reames, *Legenda aurea*, pp. 98, 256 n. 44.
21 For some examples of martyr-saints in woodcuts, see Field, *Fifteenth-century woodcuts*; and Geisberg, *German single-leaf woodcut*.

Although their opportunities for dying similar deaths within the church were practically nonexistent, by the 1520s late medieval Christians in Europe had for a century prepared for their deaths through the *Ars moriendi*, another important strand in Christian religious practice prior to the Reformation. One of the most popular works (and *the* most popular woodblock book) of the fifteenth century, the *Ars* sought to enable Christians to face death with composure, mindful of Satan's snares while resisting his seductions, remaining faithful to God while focusing on the life to come. Considering the inescapability of death, it is difficult to imagine a more practical genre with such universal applicability. Fundamentally, the 'art of dying' applied the virtue of patience to the deathbed, or, indeed, to whatever situation a Christian might confront in facing death. Trials for heresy and stone prison cells would be no exception.

Around 1520 late medieval Christians lived in a religious culture in which reminders of Christ's passion and death, exhortations to imitative patience and virtuous suffering, depictions of and prayers to martyr-saints, and an emphasis on 'dying well' were pervasive and intertwined with one another. These aspects of Christian belief and practice coalesced in the widespread revival of Christian martyrdom, the catalyst for which was the application and expansion of medieval anti-heresy laws to evangelicals and Anabaptists in the 1520s, followed in the mid-1530s by Henry VIII's startling definition of religious loyalty to the pope as treason. To be sure, late medieval Waldensians, Lollards, and Hussites had already regarded the smaller numbers of their respective executed fellow believers as martyrs in the late fourteenth and fifteenth centuries, but the scope of Christian martyrdom in the sixteenth century was to be much wider and its long-term consequences vastly greater. For the first time since antiquity, the spread of anti-Roman forms of western Christianity would be neither contained nor controlled by the Roman church in alliance with political rulers.

Early evangelicals and Anabaptists rejected Roman ecclesiastical authority on the basis of their respective understandings of scripture, but they made nothing like a clean break from the sensibilities related to martyrdom that so deeply marked late medieval religious culture. Given their insistence that Christian belief and practice be based on the Bible alone, such a break might have been easier had the late medieval sensibilities in question themselves not been so thoroughly biblical. Christ's passion and death are central to all four gospel narratives as the necessary prerequisite for His resurrection and the means of redemption for sinners, all of which remained no less important to Protestants or Anabaptists than they had been and continued to be for Catholics. The example of martyrs being persecuted and dying for their fidelity to Christ, too, is rooted in scripture – consider the Christian protomartyr Stephen (Acts 7) or the apostolic martyr James (Acts 12:2) – a precedent not about to be ignored by those who claimed that scripture alone provided the authoritative warrant for Christian faith and life. And the Bible is filled with passages about the blessedness of those who endure persecution for righteousness and the reward for those who follow Christ no matter the cost. The 'imitation of Christ' is a pervasive biblical notion, whatever its particular theological or devotional valence. 'Blessed are those who are persecuted for righteousness' sake', Jesus says in his Sermon on the Mount, 'for theirs is the kingdom of heaven' (Matt. 5:10). Indeed, when sixteenth-century Anabaptists or Protestants turned to scripture, they found their Lord telling them explicitly to *expect* persecution for his sake: 'Remember the word that I said to you, "Servants are not greater than their master." If they persecuted me, they will persecute you' (John 15:20). Small wonder, then, that when early members of the Swiss Brethren found themselves before Zwinglian authorities in Zurich, for example, or when early English Protestants faced trial for heresy during the reign of Henry VIII, they understood their predicament as the realization of biblical predictions made by Christ himself. The Reformation's turn to the word of God as a critical tool against the authority of the late medieval church led not to a repudiation, but rather to an intensification, of the same sensibilities pertinent to martyrdom that had been so prevalent among late medieval Christians.

At the same time that the various groups of Protestants and Anabaptists adopted such attitudes, they also rejected a great deal in the late medieval church, including any authoritative role for its tradition alongside that of scripture. The Bible, however, despite claims about its self-sufficient, self-interpreting character by many Protestant and Anabaptist leaders, proved empirically to be nothing of the sort from the very outset of the Reformation. From the early 1520s, Christians who had rejected the authority of the Roman Church disagreed among themselves literally about what Christianity was, because they disagreed about what the Bible meant. In practice, scripture was not a clear, self-evident foundation on which to reconstruct a single, purified Christianity, but rather an intractable hermeneutic can of worms and the source of endless disputes among Protestants and Anabaptists, just as it was between them and Catholics. It would be a serious interpretative misstep to downplay these differences, for which Christian authorities proved willing to kill and Christian martyrs willing to die. Doctrinal differences were carried over into martyrdom, in which deaths were wedded to specific teachings that divided Christians from one another, despite their shared attitudes about suffering and the hope of eternal reward. Martyrdom dramatically concretized religious controversy. It gave doctrinal dispute an irreducibly human face. In so doing, it helped simultaneously to create and sustain divergent Christian traditions, because co-believers were not disposed to minimize the convictions for which their respective martyrs had given their lives. On the contrary, the martyrs were celebrated in a wide variety of genres, visual and musical as well as verbal.

Anabaptists

In Europe there were more Anabaptist than either Protestant or Catholic martyrs, in large part because they were the most politically vulnerable. With the exception of the fragile protection afforded the Hutterites by members of the Moravian nobility and the *de facto* toleration of Mennonites in the northern Netherlands beginning in the last quarter of the century, Anabaptists were executed at the hands of Catholic, Zwinglian, and Lutheran authorities, whether in Switzerland, the Low Countries, or Germanic territories within the Holy Roman Empire. After a few early, tentative experiments with civic Anabaptism, the principled rejection of the alliance between churches and states seemed calculated to alarm political authorities, especially in the aftermath of the German Peasants' War (1524–5) and the Anabaptist kingdom of Münster (1534–5). The Anabaptist repudiation of infant baptism as unbiblical, too, seemed to signal a repudiation of Christian society as such – and indeed, according to Anabaptists, the whole point was that society was anything but Christian. Baptism presupposed self-awareness and knowledge of what faith *was*, just as had been true of Jesus' first followers, a knowledge that infants could not possibly possess. In the wake of the Peasants' War, authorities' violent rejection of any substantive social or political changes inspired by the gospel seemed to leave separatism as the only viable alternative for Christians unwilling to compromise with state power. Exhortations to perseverance in the midst of persecution are pervasive in the writings of early Anabaptist leaders, including Conrad Grebel, Jörg Blaurock, Michael Sattler, Balthasar Hubmaier, Hans Hut, Hans Schlaffer, Leonhard Schiemer, and Jakob Huter. In a certain sense, Anabaptists collapsed the distinction between ordinary and extraordinary Christians implicit in the medieval divide between the mass of the baptized and the saints.

With a few exceptions such as Balthasar Hubmaier, early German-speaking Anabaptists had less formal education and less access to print technology than did their Protestant and Catholic contemporaries, who made such extensive use of print in memorializing their respective martyrs. As a result, a dramatic contrast exists between the many Anabaptists executed between 1525 and 1535, and the small number of printed accounts of their deaths. In fact, only two early Anabaptist martyrs, Michael Sattler and Jörgen Wagner, both of whom were killed in 1527, seem to have been publicized in print by means of the pamphlets that were such a characteristic means of propaganda and communication in the early German Reformation.[22] In the absence of print, early Swiss, south German, and Austrian Anabaptists relied on oral communication, letters, handwritten accounts, and songs in order to spread the news and preserve the memory of their martyrs. Wilhelm Reublin, for example, wrote and sent copies of a letter about the execution of several Swiss Anabaptists in the summer of 1527 to Anabaptist communities in Zollikon, Basel, Grüningen, and Appenzell.[23] When the former priest Julius Lober was apprehended in the duchy of Ansbach on his way to Moravia in the spring of 1531, he had with him a list of more than 400 Anabaptists put to death in fifty-two different territories and towns.[24] Such lists and accounts, as well as oral reports from surviving family members and fellow believers, must have contributed in later years to the formation of the manuscript Hutterite chronicles, in which the stories of the martyrs from the 1520s and 1530s are so prevalent. The Philipite Anabaptists (followers of Philip Plener) wrote at least fifty-three songs about persecution and suffering for Christ in the years after their imprisonment in Passau in 1535, even though the songs were not published until 1564, in the first-known printed hymnal of the Swiss Brethren.[25] It seems that for nearly three decades, the songs were kept alive either through memorization or manuscript copies of the lyrics coupled with *contrafacta* denoting the tunes to which they were to be sung, or a combination of the two.

Anabaptist martyr hymnology occupies a special place within the revival of Christian martyrdom in the sixteenth century. Although there were Catholic and Protestant martyr songs, in neither tradition did they assume anywhere near the importance that they held for the Swiss Brethren, Hutterites, and Mennonites. Numbering in the hundreds, the two principal kinds of Anabaptist martyr songs were those which recounted in narrative form the interrogations, responses, condemnation, and steadfastness of the martyrs themselves, and those which urged fellow Anabaptists to remain stalwart despite oppression, reminding them of the promises of Christ to his faithful followers. The first type preserved the stories of those already slain; the second type urged those facing persecution to stand fast. Individual Anabaptist songs circulated as printed

---

22 See *Eyn new warhafftig geschicht*; [Graveneck], *Ayn newes wunderbarlichs geschicht*; and [Sattler], *Brüderlich vereynigung*.
23 Muralt and Schmid (eds.), *Quellen*, p. 250.   24 Schornbaum (ed.), *Quellen*, pp. 278–9.
25 *Etliche schöne christliche Geseng*; Packull, *Hutterite beginnings*, pp. 89–98.

broadsheets as early as the late 1520s. The Swiss Brethren reprinted fifty-one of the fifty-three songs from the 1564 hymnal as the second half of the *Ausbund*, apparently first published around 1570 (although the oldest extant edition dates from 1583). The first half of the collection consists of eighty songs, forty-two of which – in succession – are either about, written by, or attributed to martyrs.[26] By this time the Swiss Brethren were borrowing and translating songs from Dutch Mennonites about their martyrs, who by 1563 had not only a martyr hymnology but also a published martyrology of their own.

Het offer des heeren was the most successful Anabaptist martyrology of the sixteenth century, with eleven editions from 1562–3 through 1599. Devoted almost exclusively to Dutch Anabaptists, the collection has two parts: the first half consists mostly of prison letters written by martyrs, the second half of songs written about them.[27] Only a handful of published accounts of Dutch Anabaptist martyrs had appeared prior to the first printing of *Het offer des heeren*, but by 1559 the Mennonites had already appropriated the hymn collection known as the *Veelderhande liedekens*, which already included over 200 songs and continued to grow.[28] After the United Provinces declared their independence from Philip II of Spain, the persecution of Mennonites declined, and numerous martyrological pamphlets were published in the northern Netherlands. In combination with *Het offer des heeren*, these became the core of several seventeenth-century martyrologies that would culminate in Thieleman Jans van Braght's *Martyrs' mirror*, by far the best-known Anabaptist martyrological source because of its later translations into modern German and English.

The *Martyrs' mirror* scarcely resembled *Het offer des heeren* in size, historical scope, hymnology, or the roll-call of its Anabaptist martyrs. Its first edition (1660) was a massive folio volume that dwarfed its tiny, palm-sized predecessor of the sixteenth century and cost considerably more, a material transformation that paralleled the sharply altered place of Mennonites in golden-age urban Dutch society. The two-volume second edition of 1685 included over 100 intricate engravings by Jan van Luyken. Unlike *Het offer des heeren*, which skipped straight from the stoning of Stephen in the Acts of the Apostles to the martyrdom of Michael Sattler in 1527, the *Martyrs' mirror* offered an Anabaptist version of Christian history from New Testament times to the present. In an alternating, century-by-century exposition, this history coupled the doctrine of believers' baptism with those who had been persecuted for (ostensibly) upholding it. The hymns had disappeared, reflecting the seventeenth-century

---

26 *Aussbund*, pp. 9–246.   27 Cramer (ed.), *Het offer des heeren*.
28 Hofman, 'Gereformeerden en doopsgezinden', pp. 63–5.

preference of Dutch Mennonites for singing the psalms rather than martyr hymns in their now-secure surroundings. Most significantly, the *Martyrs' mirror* was a much broader, more inclusive collection than *Het offer des heeren*. Van Braght followed the Waterlander Hans de Ries, who had been the principal editor of martyrological collections published in 1615 and 1631–2, in internationalizing the heavily Dutch emphasis of *Het offer des heeren* to embrace martyrs from all the major non-violent Anabaptist traditions of the sixteenth century. As a result, the schisms among the Dutch Mennonites in the late sixteenth and seventeenth centuries, as well as the doctrinal and other differences that set Anabaptist groups against one another in general, were rendered all but invisible in the single most important source about Anabaptist martyrs bequeathed to modern Mennonites.[29]

Protestants

Many fewer early evangelicals than Anabaptists were put to death, but much more about them appeared in print. At least a dozen men executed between 1523 and 1529 were memorialized in *Flugschriften*, sometimes in several publications, and often in multiple editions of each title.[30] In the towns and territories of the Holy Roman Empire or Switzerland in which local political authorities adopted one or another form of the Reformation, early Protestant leaders enjoyed the protection and access to print that was almost wholly lacking among Anabaptists. The very first martyr pamphlet of the Reformation, which recounted the burning of the former Augustinian monks Hendrik Vos and Johann van den Esschen in Brussels on 1 July 1523, saw no fewer than sixteen editions by at least eight different printers working in seven different cities.[31] Luther himself wrote a pamphlet about them, and subsequently published pamphlets about Hendrik van Zutphen, who was killed in 1524, as well as about Georg Winkler and Leonhard Keyser, respectively, both of whom were executed in 1527.[32] He and other early martyrological writers were keen to announce to the world that the recovery of the gospel – understood fundamentally as the embrace of the doctrine of justification by faith alone – was

---

29 For more on this point and the transformation of the Dutch Mennonite martyrological tradition in the seventeenth century, see Gregory, *Salvation at stake*, pp. 240–8, and Gregory (ed.), *Forgotten writings*, pp. xxxiv–xl.

30 Gregory (ed.), *Forgotten writings*, pp. 143–4.

31 *Der actus und handlung*, pp. 15–19; for the editions, see Hebenstreit-Wilfert, 'Märtyrerflugschriften', pp. 432–6.

32 Martin Luther, *Ein Brief* (on Vos and Van den Esschen); *Von Bruder Henrico* (on Hendrik van Zutphen); *Tröstung an die Christen* (on Georg Winkler); and *Von Er Lenhard Keiser*.

capable of producing witnesses to its truth despite the cost. News of the early evangelical martyrs also spread via oral communication, written correspondence, and songs, as we have seen was true among Anabaptists. Because many early evangelical leaders had been learned members of religious orders with international connections, such news more easily crossed national and linguistic boundaries than was the case for Anabaptism (which never established anything close to its Dutch or Germanic following in either England or France).

As among Anabaptists, early evangelical martyrological sources made the connection between the martyrs' deaths and the doctrines for which they died. Johannes Heuglin, for example, who was interrogated in the diocese of Constance and executed in May 1527, held that good works added nothing to right belief, that masses were not to be said for the dead, and that priests could marry (as he had done).[33] Other important themes in Protestant martyrological sources were present from the 1520s, and reveal not only a reliance on scripture, but also continuities with late medieval sensibilities relevant to martyrdom. Parallels were drawn between present persecutions and those endured by early Christians, the apostles, and Christ himself, the rediscovery of the gospel provoking hatred no less than had its first proclamation. Direct use of scripture bolstered exhortations to steadfastness, as in so many Anabaptist songs, much in the same way that late medieval Christians had been urged to exercise the virtue of patience more generally. William Tyndale advised oppressed fellow believers in his commentary on Matthew 5:8, blending *ars moriendi* with *imitatio Christi*: 'comfort thyself with the hope of the blessing of the inheritance of heaven, there to be glorified with Christ, if thou here suffer with him. For if we be like Christ here in his passions, and bear his image in soul and body, and fight manfully, that Satan blot it not out, and suffer with Christ with bearing record to righteousness, then shall we be like him in glory.'[34] Resistance to the gospel's rediscovery and the execution of some of its most heroic proponents were perceived as harbingers of the impending apocalypse.

The same attitudes persisted as the number of executions climbed in the 1540s and 1550s. In these same decades, a host of Reformed Protestant writers, most famously John Calvin and Pierre Viret, but also Richard Tracy, George Joye, Wolfgang Musculus, John Hooper, Heinrich Bullinger, Peter Martyr Vermigli, and others, published anti-nicodemite treatises condemning capitulation to Catholic authorities and prompting persecuted Protestants to persevere.[35] This context of increased numbers of executions for heresy, the

---

33 *Warhaffte hystorien*, sigs. [A4v], B1.   34 [Tyndale], *Exposicion uppon Mathew*, fol. 22v.

35 On these treatises and the importance of Protestant anti-Nicodemism for martyrdom, see Gregory, *Salvation at stake*, pp. 154–62.

product of more militant Catholic opposition to the spread of Calvinism in particular, as well as to the defeat of German Lutherans in the Schmalkaldic War, was the backdrop for the publication of the major Protestant martyrologies of the mid-sixteenth century, all of which were first published between 1552 and 1559.

Perhaps the best-known martyrological source of the Reformation era is John Foxe's *Acts and Monuments*, better known by its nickname title, the 'Book of Martyrs'. The work first appeared in 1563, having been preceded by two shorter works in Latin devoted to martyrs (1554, 1559) which the Oxford-trained Foxe wrote and saw through publication during his voluntary exile on the Continent. There would be three further editions of his English-language martyrology before his death in 1587, then five more through the final seventeenth-century edition of 1684. Foxe had his French analogue in Jean Crespin, a lawyer who had fled his native Arras and relocated in Geneva, where by 1550 he had changed careers and become a printer. His own *Histoire des martyrs* was the most famous work to issue from his press. First published in 1554, the work appeared under various titles and grew by instalments into the early 1560s, then Crespin finally published it as a gigantic folio volume akin to Foxe's in 1564. Six additional French folio editions were published from 1565 through 1619, three Latin editions from 1556 through 1560, and thirteen editions of two different German translations between 1590 and 1682, as Calvinism grew in central Europe after the Peace of Augsburg.[36] In the Low Countries, the principal mid-century Protestant martyrologist was the Calvinist pastor in Antwerp, Adriaen Cornelis van Haemstede, forced to flee shortly before his Dutch-language martyrology was published in Emden in early 1559.[37] Exceeding the pace of publication of either Foxe or Crespin, his *Geschiedenis ende den doodt der vromer martelaren* would run through fifteen editions by 1616, twenty-three by 1671.[38] Less durable in its influence but part of the same cluster of major Protestant martyrologies, the *Historien der heyligen, außerwölten Gottes Zeügen, Bekennern und Martyrern* by the Lutheran pastor Ludwig Rabus appeared in eight parts between 1552 and 1558, then in one folio edition in 1571–2.[39]

Despite their bulk, historical sweep, and considerable influence, the major Protestant martyrologies did not differ fundamentally in their major themes from the publications of the 1520s. They synthesized a vast amount of material

36 Gilmont, *Jean Crespin*, pp. 166–82; *Bibliotheca belgica*, vol. 1, pp. 966–82.
37 Jelsma, *Adriaan van Haemstede*, pp. 28–81; Pettegree, *Emden*, pp. 63–4, 93–4, 275.
38 *Bibliotheca belgica*, vol. 1, pp. 374–94; Vander Haeghen et al. (eds.), *Bibliographie*, vol. 2, pp. 271–364.
39 Kolb, *For all the saints*, pp. 46–7, 50.

into a powerful, Augustinian version of history centred on the proclamation and persecution of the gospel, which was cresting in the apocalyptic raging of the pope and his minions in the sixteenth century. In the cosmic conflict between Christ and antichrist, good and evil, martyrs provided the dramatic, human heart of the story of the persecuted church through time. Despite this shared historical framework, however, the national and confessional contexts for each of the major Protestant martyrologies in the later sixteenth and seventeenth centuries entailed widely different legacies. Foxe's became an important ideological prop of a triumphalist Elizabethan establishment, Crespin's took its place as a pillar in the identity of an embattled Huguenot minority during the French wars of religion, and van Haemstede was appropriated by Dutch Calvinists concerned to uphold the witness of their own martyrs over against those of Mennonites and Catholics in the Low Countries. Much as Hans de Ries and Thieleman Jans van Bragh would do among Dutch Mennonites in the seventeenth century, Protestant martyrologists identified a body of witnesses to 'the gospel' that downplayed, ignored, or edited away the doctrinal differences that had plagued magisterial Protestants from the 1520s. When rival Protestant confessions were perceived as a threat greater than Catholicism, as in certain territories within the Holy Roman Empire in the late sixteenth century, Lutherans accused executed Calvinists of being 'the devil's martyrs'.[40]

Roman Catholics

Ironically, although less had changed doctrinally and devotionally for Reformation-era Catholics than for their Anabaptist or Protestant contemporaries – indeed, Catholic martyrs under Henry VIII such as John Fisher and Thomas More *were* late medieval Christians who died for the unity of the late medieval church – Catholic martyrdom in Europe had been dormant for so long that its re-emergence seems initially to have stunned would-be memorializers into a sort of paralysis. Obscure evangelicals such as Casper Tauber were celebrated in multiple pamphlets whereas Fisher and More, despite international reputations, inspired little recognition in the years immediately after their deaths, especially in England. Early Protestants and Anabaptists, however, saw their respective martyrs as apocalyptic confirmation of their daring embrace of Christian truth without compromise. By contrast, the meaning of the return of Catholic martyrdom in Europe was unclear at first, at the hands

---

40 Rab, in [Crespin and Goulart], *Märtyrbuch*, sig.[]:(7).

of a king who had now defined as treason fidelity to the pope whose authority he had previously defended in print against its evangelical detractors.

During the Marian restoration of Catholicism, members of the clergy such as Nicholas Harpsfield and Reginald Pole waxed eloquent about the heroic witness of More and the other Henrician Catholic martyrs.[41] The Carthusian Maurice Chauncy had done likewise in his *Historia aliquot nostri saeculi martyrum*, the first published account of the Henrician martyrs, which appeared in Mainz in 1550. Mary's death and Elizabeth's assumption of the throne brought renewed persecution, however, particularly in the second half of her reign, after the failed northern rebellion of 1569 and the papal bull *Regnans in excelsis*, in which Pius V excommunicated Elizabeth and threatened the same for all English Catholics who obeyed her. Post-Tridentine Catholic Europe was a different world from the 1530s, a contrast evident not only in the clarity of interpretation regarding the Henrician martyrs, but also in the resolve of the seminary priests being trained as missionaries to England at Douai-Rheims and in Rome, where Pope Gregory XIII founded the English College in 1576. Sloughing off the uncertainty of Henry's reign, the 1580s and 1590s in England represented the peak of Catholic martyrological awareness in early modern Europe. Dozens of treatises about martyrdom and stories about the martyrs poured openly from presses on the Continent and secretly from others in England, not only in Latin and English, but also in French, Italian, Spanish, German, and Dutch.[42] They included works such as William Allen's *Brief History of the Glorious Martyrdom of Twelve Reverend Priests* (1582), which was incorporated along with many other sources by the Jesuit John Gibbons in the *Concertatio ecclesiae catholicae in Anglia* (1583, 1588). Other treatises urged English Catholics to remain steadfast and even yearn for martyrdom, such as Thomas Hide's *Consolatory Epistle to the Afflicted Catholics* (1579, 1580) and Robert Southwell's *Epistle of Comfort* (1587/8). Members of religious orders, including the Franciscans and Jesuits, contributed to publications whose latinity facilitated international communication. There were no direct Catholic counterparts to Foxe or Crespin – that is, sweeping ecclesiastical histories in which martyrdom was made the centre of the story of Christian truth besieged yet triumphant – although Richard Verstegan's popular *Theatrum crudelitatum haereticorum nostri temporis* (1587) combined graphic martyr engravings with texts about sixteenth-century Catholic martyrs from England, France, and the Low Countries.

---

41 Harpsfield, *Life and death*; and Pole, 'Cardinal Pole's speech', pp. 490–7.
42 See Allison and Rogers (eds.), *Contemporary printed literature*.

The longstanding Catholic emphasis on visual representation as an aid to devotion and catechesis found a vibrant outlet in depictions of martyrs both ancient and recent. In Rome several series of martyr paintings were commissioned in the 1580s, two of which were in turn copied as sets of engravings.[43] Those in the chapel of St Thomas of Canterbury in the English College were expressly intended to inspire in seminarians a willingness to die for the faith. Flanders enjoyed a vogue for graphic martyrdom paintings as well, especially after Alexander Farnese reclaimed the southern Netherlands for Spain and Catholicism in 1585.[44] Post-Tridentine martyrological celebration was not limited to paintings and engravings, however: Jesuits wrote dozens of plays about martyrs, songs were written and sung in their honour, and their relics were venerated and eagerly sought among lay Catholics as well as the clergy.[45] The desire for relics was inflamed after 1578 by the rediscovery of the Roman catacombs, where pilgrims could see for themselves the material remains of early Christian martyrs and the inscriptions carved in their honour. A great deal of evidence makes clear that Catholics did not wait for official recognition from Rome in the form of canonization before acknowledging their slain fellow believers as saints, to whom they prayed as intercessors and whom they credited with healing miracles. For example, immediately after his fellow priest Thomas Ford had been hanged, drawn, and quartered in front of him at Tyburn in London on 28 May 1582, John Shert knelt down and prayed, 'O Tom, O happy Tom, O blessed soul, happy art thou, thy blessed soul pray for me'. As the head of the seminary at Douai-Rheims, William Allen, noted, 'His martyrdom and innocencie proved him to be a saint'.[46] Unlike the more arduous and ambiguous path of the exercise of conspicuous virtue, which could make one a candidate for sainthood, heroic death by martyrdom conferred it instantly. Provided, of course, that one died for the right reasons.

True vs. false martyrs

'Not the punishment, but the cause, makes a martyr' – Augustine as the heir to Cyprian had articulated this principle in the course of his dealings with the Donatists in the fifth century, and it would dominate the controversy about

---

43 For the paintings, see Herz, 'Imitators of Christ', pp. 53–70; for the engravings, see Circignani, *Ecclesiae militantis triumphi* and *Ecclesiae Anglicanae trophaea*.
44 Freedburg, 'Representation', pp. 128–38.
45 For the plays, see McCabe, *Introduction to Jesuit theater*, pp. 37–46, 171; Valentin, *Théatre des jésuites*, vol. 1, pp. 373–9, 421–7; ibid., vol. 2, pp. 558–9, 602–11.
46 [Allen], *Briefe historie*, sig. [A6].

true and false martyrs in the Reformation era. When the very issue in question was the content of Christian truth, death for one's religious beliefs *per se*, however impressive, was ordinarily a necessary but never a sufficient condition for recognition as a martyr. Otherwise, the impressive displays of stalwart behaviour in the face of death by Jews, Muslims, or even pagans would have made them true martyrs as well – a patent absurdity, according to Christian controversialists, who often mentioned these groups alongside heretical martyrs. Among Christians, if one was executed for true beliefs, then one was a martyr, a heroic witness and close imitator of Christ; if one was killed for false beliefs, one was a justly executed heretic or religious traitor, misled by Satan, who 'disguises himself as an angel of light' (2 Cor. 11:14). Because men and women were executed for their religious convictions, fellow believers linked their deaths to the doctrines for which they had given their lives no less than had the authorities responsible for their deaths. Yet because Anabaptists, Protestants, and Catholics believed incompatible teachings to be God's own revelation, their respective martyrological communities inevitably developed in mutual exclusivity. So long as martyrology turned on doctrinal incompatibilities that were judged important, it necessarily excluded as it included. And so we are brought back to the difference between persecution and prosecution, the steadfast death of martyrs or the just execution of religious criminals. There developed correlatively within early modern Christianity a vigorous literature about true and false martyrs, one that eventually provoked anti-martyrological works nearly as massive as the martyrologies that they sought to refute: Robert Parsons's anti-Foxean *Treatise of Three Conversions of England* (1603–4), for example, or Jacques Sévert's *L'Anti-Martyrologe* (1622), an attack on Crespin. Yet because the dispute hinged on doctrines that divided the various groups from one another to begin with, it could not but add another, martyrological strand to the era's massive production of doctrinal controversy. This particular strand was stained with the blood of several thousand deaths that had helped to forge divergent traditions.

In martyrdom the religious, political, and social history of the Reformation came together in dramatic fashion and with far-reaching consequences. Shared convictions about the nature of reality in a Christian world-view – including notions of divine revelation and divine judgement, of the Bible as God's word and of providence as His guiding hand in human history – inspired devout men and women to die rather than to renounce their faith. Yet discrepant, fiercely held convictions about what God had revealed and how specific events were to be interpreted under the rubric of providence guaranteed that these men and women would die for different versions of what it was to be a Christian. The result was supremely ironic: the formation of early modern Christian pluralism as the successor to medieval Latin Christendom, an outcome diametrically opposed to the wishes of virtually every committed Christian in the sixteenth century. 'The way, the truth, and the life' was not recentred at the heart of a purified Christian society, but obscured within a fragmented Europe bloodied by persecution and religious wars. Western Christians dragged one another into doctrinal diversity despite themselves.

16

The Mediterranean Inquisitions of early modern Europe

WILLIAM MONTER

There are good reasons to separate the Inquisitors of Heretical Pravity, who had been operating under papal commissions in several parts of Europe since the thirteenth century, from their modern successors. Of course, one must recognize that several fundamental continuities connected medieval inquisitors and modern holy offices. Their purposes were identical: all Inquisitors always sought primarily to uncover and punish heretics. Because both used legal procedures taken from canon law, their *modus operandi* was essentially identical: no new general handbooks for inquisitors were needed to replace the fourteenth-century models by Bernard Gui or Nicolas Eymeric, which were reprinted centuries later with relatively minor changes for use by their successors. But holy office organization became radically different after 1500 and their activities expanded in new directions, as they began investigating such offences as owning heretical books, homosexuality, or even (for a short time and in a few parts of Spain) horse smuggling.

The early sixteenth century also marks a watershed in inquisitorial history because jurisdiction over heresy, always the principal business of Inquisitions, had passed into the hands of secular courts almost everywhere north of the Alps and Pyrenees around the time of Luther's Reformation. For anyone accused of heresy, this was an ominous development. In an extreme but significant instance, two successive southern French Inquisitors were themselves indicted as Protestant heretics by the Parlement of Toulouse and the second man was actually burned in 1538.[1] Overall, more than 3,000 Protestants, mostly Anabaptists, were burned for heresy throughout western Europe in the sixteenth century. However, fewer than 10 per cent of them perished at the hands of Inquisitorial courts in Mediterranean Europe.

Unlike their medieval predecessors, modern Inquisitions were permanent governmental institutions with specialized bureaucracies. The first and best

---

1 Monter, *Judging the French Reformation*, pp. 78–9.

known is the Spanish Inquisition, chartered under Ferdinand and Isabella in 1478 and already staffed and operating in Seville two years later. More than half a century later, its smaller Iberian cousin, the Portuguese Inquisition, obtained a founding charter in 1536 and held its first public *auto da fé* in Lisbon four years later. The youngest of the three, the Roman Inquisition, created in 1542, was a governmental institution only in the papal states, and its early activities remain largely unknown because a Roman mob burned its central records in 1559. All three Inquisitions operated for an extremely long time, lasting into the nineteenth century. The Portuguese finally abolished their holy office in 1821; the Spanish Inquisition was abolished on three separate occasions between 1808 and 1837; and the Roman Inquisition still languishes in vestigial form as the *Dicastero*. During their long existence, all three extended their jurisdictions over many other matters besides their original targets – 'Judaizing' by baptized Christians for both Iberian tribunals and 'Lutheranism' for the Roman system, founded decades after the Protestant Reformation had begun.

Inquisitions and witchcraft

An excellent way to illustrate both the success of Inquisitors in broadening the scope of their efforts and the differences between their medieval and modern forms is through examining the complicated relationship between Inquisitions and witchcraft. Historians seldom study both medieval and early modern history, and in this instance, the gulf between them has led to an interesting paradox: while medievalists stress the significance of Inquisitors both in defining the crime and punishing it by burning witches, early modernists note that Inquisitions rarely handled witchcraft cases after 1530 and when they did, punished the crime with remarkable leniency compared with secular courts. Both groups are correct.

Fourteenth-century Inquisitors did not investigate what we now call witchcraft. Our clearest evidence is that neither author of Inquisitors' manuals, Bernard Gui or Nicolas Eymeric, mentions anything other than necromancy when discussing illicit magical practices.[2] Inquisitors played a significant but not dominant role when the doctrine of the witches' sabbath took shape in the western Alps in the 1430s; only one of the five central texts was composed by a practising Inquisitor, whose name we do not know. We know that Ulric de Torrenté, an Inquisitor based in Lausanne, was arresting Waldensian heretics in the 1420s and arresting witches a decade later in the same region. Although

2 Bailey, *Battling demons*, p. 36.

only a handful of practising fifteenth-century Inquisitors discussed witchcraft theoretically, they include the best-known author, Jacob Kramer, a German Dominican who composed the infamous *Malleus Maleficarum* (1486). Some of his information came from an Italian colleague working in the southern Alps; the last practising Inquisitors to write about witchcraft were Dominicans from northern Italy, like Bernardo Rategno (*De Strigiis*, 1510) or the official papal spokesman against Luther, Silvestro Mazzolini alias Prierias (*De Strigimagarum*, c. 1525).

When Kramer published his *Malleus*, the newly founded Spanish Inquisition began operating in witch-infested Pyrenean districts. By 1494, the guidelines for Aragon's holy office mentioned witchcraft, and its preserved witch-trials begin in 1498. Such cases spread slowly across northern Spain while Inquisitors like Rategno or Mazzolini were active in northern Italy. In the mid-1520s, a major crisis in Spanish Navarre provoked the Supreme Council into appointing a blue-ribbon panel to offer guidelines for inquisitorial intervention in witch-hunting, and it ignored the *Malleus Maleficarum*. Ever since Henry Charles Lea, historians have praised the Spanish Inquisition for its caution and restraint in pursuing witches. It consistently tried to re-educate rather than punish them. Despite occasional failures, as in Catalonia in 1549 or a momentary lapse into severity in Navarre in 1609–10, the Spanish Inquisition generally maintained its relative leniency towards accused witches. In the early seventeenth century, the Inquisitor Salazar y Frias made the first attempt in Europe to disprove the reality of witchcraft empirically.[3]

After 1530, the history of inquisitorial involvement in witch-hunting diverged north and south of the Alps. In Mediterranean Europe, all three major state Inquisitions claimed jurisdiction over it as a form of heresy and apostasy to the devil. Jurists agreed with the *Malleus* that witchcraft was a 'mixed' crime and could be tried by either Inquisitors or secular judges. However, because Inquisitors were basically unconcerned with their harmful magic or *maleficia*, both the Portuguese and Roman Inquisitions also treated accused witches leniently. Even during its campaigns against all forms of illicit magic after 1580, there is no clear evidence that the Roman Inquisition ever ordered anyone to be executed for witchcraft.[4] The Portuguese Inquisition tried nearly 300 people for practising malevolent witchcraft between 1540 and 1774. Death sentences were rare but not unknown; Portugal's holy office executed only four people for witchcraft, although twenty-seven more, mostly women, died in prison.[5]

3 Henningsen, *The witches' advocate*.   4 Romeo, *Inquisitori*.
5 Paiva, *Bruxaria e superstição*, p. 219.

Meanwhile, north of the Alps and Pyrenees, papal Inquisitors were marginalized almost everywhere after the Lutheran Reformation. Even when they survived, they had their hands full coping with more dangerous kinds of heretics than witches. One veteran Inquisitor, an expert in torturing Alpine witches, moved to southern France in 1530 and began torturing heretics instead.[6]

New Inquisitions in Spain, Portugal, and Italy

A recent comparative analysis by a Portuguese scholar[7] integrates many significant advances made in inquisitorial scholarship during the past generation and offers institutional portraits of the three major holy offices of early modern Europe. Using it to inform our discussions about their similarities and differences, we will examine some fundamental and closely related questions about their operations: how did they actually function? how severe were they? and how well did they succeed in their self-imposed task of eliminating what they perceived as the most dangerous forms of religious dissent?

*

All three permanent systems employed a relatively small staff of full-time officials supplemented by large numbers of volunteers. Two or three Inquisitors usually staffed tribunals in the Spanish or Portuguese Inquisitions, although the Roman version often required only one. It seems clear that both in their organization and their primary purpose, the Spanish and Portuguese Inquisitions resembled each other far more closely than either of them resembled the Roman Inquisition. Both Iberian institutions were essentially state-run bureaucracies – in fact, royal councils – operating under papal charter, but normally completely independent of Roman influence. Nearly all Spanish and Portuguese Inquisitors were trained in canon law; but after Torquemada's time they were almost never monks, and several had little formal training in theology. We should see these Iberian Inquisitors as career public servants, bureaucrats hoping for promotion to the governing boards of their national holy offices or else serving their respective royal governments in different capacities. On the other hand, Italian Inquisitors were always Dominican or Franciscan monks who could not possibly expect to be promoted to their organization's governing board or congregation, composed entirely of cardinals. Nevertheless, Inquisitors from all three major systems shared one frequent

---

6 Monter, *Judging the French Reformation*, pp. 76–7.
7 Bethencourt, *L'Inquisition à l'époque moderne*.

career path: successful service in a significant location gave an Inquisitor about one chance in five of eventually becoming a bishop.[8]

The volunteers, among whom the familiars (yet another medieval legacy) form the best-known group, were selected only after elaborate probationary enquiries and served in exchange for various legal privileges, including tax exemptions and the right to bear weapons. Their numbers varied widely at different times and in different places. In Spain, they apparently reached their peak under Philip II, simultaneously with an increase in holy office business generally; their numbers declined sharply after 1640, paralleling a general decline in inquisitorial activity. But in Portugal their numbers mushroomed throughout the eighteenth century, although holy office business stagnated or even declined sharply after mid-century. Information about familiars is scarce in Italy, although a few samples from Bologna or Modena suggest a far more strongly aristocratic composition than anywhere in Iberia.

Compared with its older Iberian cousins, the Roman Inquisition had far more branches (forty-three, including Malta and Avignon, against only twenty for Spain and its colonies and only four for Portugal), yet at the same time it seems institutionally underdeveloped. For example, unlike its Iberian predecessors, the Roman Inquisition never developed an autonomous system of emblems.[9] Italian Inquisitors, unlike those of Spain or Portugal, never visited their districts (which, however, were generally far smaller). Compared to Iberian Inquisitors, they were installed with minimal pomp, had smaller budgets and supervised smaller staffs. The occasional public punishments inflicted by the Roman Inquisition seem vastly less dramatic than Spanish or Portuguese *autos da fé*. Significantly, the closest Italian approximation to an Iberian-style *auto da fé* took place long before the Roman Inquisition was founded, with a Spanish-born pope punishing immigrant Spanish *conversos* at Rome in 1498.[10]

Research trends

During the past generation, scholarship on the three major Inquisitions has moved in different directions. Much of the best work by Spanish Inquisition scholars investigates individual tribunals (for example, Garcia Cárcel 1976, 1980; Contreras 1982; Dedieu 1989; Haliczer 1990), studying their organization, administration, and relations with the *Suprema*, the Inquisition's governing council, in addition to their repressive activities. Portuguese scholars have

8 *Ibid.*, pp. 119, 130–1, 139–41.   9 *Ibid.*, p. 94.   10 *Ibid.*, p. 308.

investigated individual offences, for example Judaizing, witchcraft, or sodomy, across their national system. Meanwhile, Italian experts, without a usable central archive, have preferred the in-depth case study. It has sometimes been manipulated with extraordinary brio, above all in the brief but dense examination of the mental universe of a Friulian miller, condemned to death by the Roman Inquisition in 1599;[11] this study provides our best example of 'victim-based' inquisitorial history and simultaneously created the prototype for the current fashion of microhistory. The once-obscure Menocchio, today a cultural hero both locally and abroad, has received a critical edition of his two inquisitorial trials.[12] Meanwhile, a 'Spanish Menocchio', who was ultimately judged insane rather than burned, has been unearthed and discussed.[13] In both these and other explorations, early modern scholars interested in the finer nuances of discourse and dialogue have found few materials as valuable and reliable as inquisitorial records, above all those from late Renaissance Italy.

Almost anyone, including even Spanish grandees, could be arrested by an Inquisition. A very different type of case study therefore investigates internationally prominent defendants whose abundant paper trails require much of a scholar's lifetime to examine. Two good examples are Cardinal Morone, later rehabilitated to become a key figure at the Council of Trent, and the unlucky Archbishop of Toledo, Bartolomé Carranza, who was imprisoned for seventeen years, first in Spain and then at Rome, although never convicted of any serious offence; their combined trial records fill thirteen printed volumes.[14] Of course, the trial of Galileo (which was sufficiently important to be returned to Rome after Napoleon's fall) remains an apparently inexhaustible 'case study' of European significance. Revisionist scholarship[15] uses fresh holy office archives to refurbish the old argument that Galileo was a self-made victim who was treated so severely because he was actually guilty of extremely serious theological errors.

Self-presentation and external descriptions

The general European population was never opposed in principle to the establishment of an Inquisition in the Middle Ages and rarely so in the early modern

---

11 Ginzburg, *The cheese and the worms*.   12 Del Col, *Domenico Scandella*.
13 Nalle, *Mad for God*.
14 For the former, see Firpo and Marcatto (eds.), *Il processo inquisitoriale*; for the latter, see Tellechea Idigoras (ed.), *Fray Bartolomé Carranza*.
15 Redondi, *Galileo heretic*.

centuries, which helps explain why they were so difficult to abolish even after 1800. The great Iberian holy offices maintained an enviable degree of prestige and popular favour through a mixture of absolute secrecy in their everyday operations and skilful propaganda at their well-advertised and dramatically staged *autos*, which were occasionally attended by reigning monarchs since the time of Ferdinand and Isabella; for example, Philip II witnessed five of them between 1559 and 1591, while João V of Portugal saw seven at Lisbon between 1716 and 1748. The Roman Inquisition shared their passion for secrecy, but minimized the shaming rituals associated with such public punishments, which were beneath papal dignity to attend.

Preceded in Spain by elaborate processions with the famous green cross of the holy office and opened in Portugal by sermons which were often printed afterwards, Iberian *autos* consisted primarily of lengthy public readings of the crimes committed by the defendants. Most but not all major public *autos* included death sentences. But it is rarely realized that about half of those condemned to be burned were not physically present. Instead, they were represented by effigies with individual portraits wearing the customary *sanbenitos*, which were saved and hung in churches while the effigies themselves were thrown onto the same bonfire as the living victims, thus providing a 'fairly sophisticated notion of images and their concrete efficacity'.[16] We should also realize that many smaller *autos* were held inside a church rather than outdoors in a public plaza. Because most of our printed and pictorial representations of Spanish *autos de fé* derive from very late examples, we should remember that such ceremonies became increasingly elaborate in proportion as they became less frequent.

Published discourse on the Inquisition came mostly from enemies. Although Jews and Muslims generally lacked access to printing presses, its Protestant victims began attacking it as early as the 1560s, using its methods as prime illustrations for their 'Black Legend' of Spanish cruelty; a remarkable work by a well-informed Spanish refugee, published in several languages after 1567, offered an incisive and extremely critical analysis of its procedures. At the same time, however, Protestants knew too little about most individual Inquisition victims to include their sufferings in their various martyrologies. Ironically, the first former prisoner to publish a best-selling version of his troubles with an Iberian Inquisition was a French Catholic. Arrested in 1674 by the Portuguese in India and sentenced at an *auto* at Goa in 1676, Charles Dellon returned to France and published his account in 1687; by 1750, it had gone through

---

16 Bethencourt, *L'Inquisition à l'époque moderne*, p. 281.

thirty editions in four languages, although it has yet to be printed in full in Portuguese.[17]

How severe were they?

The order of seniority among the major modern Inquisitions – Spain, Portugal, Rome – corresponds to our relative level of information about their primary common activity, the detection and punishment of heretics. The central archives of both Iberian institutions have been remarkably well preserved, and we possess considerable information about their colonial branches as well. However, not only were the early archives of Rome's holy office destroyed by a mob after the death of an unpopular pope in 1559, but many of its key documents, especially its original trials, were later stolen by Napoleon and never returned.[18] Only a handful of its forty-three branches (Friuli, Siena, Venice, Naples, Malta) are known to possess significant numbers of trials. Experts on the Roman Inquisition, unlike their colleagues working on Spain or Portugal, remain understandably reluctant to venture comprehensive overviews of its operations, despite a controversial and isolated pioneering attempt[19] to compare the patterns of its trials and punishments with those of its older Iberian counterparts.

It is now very old news that the Spanish Inquisition did not burn vast numbers of prisoners at its *autos de fé* – at least not after 1540, when reliable evidence about its overall activities becomes abundant (we will discuss its earliest years later in relation to Sephardic Judaism). The first results of the path-breaking *relaciones de causas* project, begun by a Danish anthropologist in 1972, were published more than twenty-five years ago.[20] These annual reports of cases resolved, submitted by each tribunal in the Spanish system in order to get a substantial *ayuda de costa* or salary bonus, summarize more than 40,000 trials, with relatively few lacunae, which it judged between 1540 and 1700. The results (not yet available electronically) show a sharp rise in the Spanish Inquisition's activities after the Council of Trent, followed by an equally sharp decrease after the expulsion of Spain's Moriscos in the early seventeenth century.

To the best of our knowledge, about a thousand people were burned at Spanish *autos de fé* between 1540 and 1750, accompanied by an equal number of effigies representing convicted heretics who had either died or fled. We

---

17 Amiel (ed.), *Relation de l'Inquisition de Goa par Charles Dellon*.
18 Tedeschi, *The prosecution of heresy*.   19 Monter-Tedeschi, 1986.
20 Henningsen, 'El "banco de datos" del Santo Oficio', pp. 547–70.

should realize that a thousand victims spread over nearly two centuries works out to only five public executions per year for the entire system: a relatively small number for a land of over six million people, not counting its possessions in Italy and America. During this period the Inquisition's victims were far outnumbered by the thousands of Spaniards executed by royal courts for different capital crimes; Spain's largest city, Seville, averaged fifteen public executions annually, with Madrid close behind. Moreover, the Inquisition's capital punishments were unequally distributed. Nearly half of them occurred outside the kingdom of Castile, which held almost five-sixths of Spain's population in this era. Instead, they clustered in the Inquisition's north-eastern and Mediterranean branches belonging to the crown of Aragon. During their peak activity between 1570 and 1625, five main tribunals of this region (Barcelona, Saragossa, Valencia, Navarre, and Sicily) held 150 *autos de fé* at which almost 400 people died, almost double the number executed at *autos* in Castile's nine major tribunals.[21] It also seems noteworthy that almost 40 per cent of those burned by the Aragonese tribunals of the holy office were not 'heretics' in the usual sense of the term, but had been convicted of such crimes as bestiality, witchcraft, or armed resistance to the Inquisition (for example, by murdering informers).

Although Portugal was far smaller than Spain and its holy office contained only four tribunals, including one in India, the Portuguese Inquisition held as many trials as its older Spanish cousin between 1540 and 1760, and even burned more people at its *autos da fé*. Portugal's trial records seem nearly complete and can be supplemented after 1680 by a remarkably rich list of printed pamphlets describing its *autos*. They confirm that every Portuguese tribunal handled far more accusations, arrests and convictions each year than any of their Spanish counterparts. Portugal's lone overseas tribunal in Goa, which was established simultaneously with the first Spanish-American tribunals in Mexico and Peru, held over 13,000 trials, or five times as many as the three Spanish-American tribunals combined; at least twice as many people were executed by order of European-trained Inquisitors in India as in the Americas. (One key to this discrepancy is that, while Portugal subjected all baptized Christians in Asia to the jurisdiction of its holy office, Philip II of Spain excluded pure-blooded native American converts from inquisitorial jurisdiction, although subjecting half-breed *mestizos* to it.) They also confirm that, unlike Spain, Portugal experienced no decline in inquisitorial activity after 1640, but continued its patterns of *autos*

21 Monter, *Frontiers of heresy*, pp. 48, 326–7.

and executions at the same high levels until the 1760s. There are good reasons why Voltaire's satire in *Candide* was directed more at the Portuguese than the Spanish Inquisition and why English usage prefers the Portuguese phrase *auto-da-fé* over the Spanish form.

Once again the situation of the Roman Inquisition is different, because the scarcity of its trial records makes it far more difficult to determine how many of its prisoners were condemned to death. In the important case of Venice, all executions were carried out in absolute secrecy, despite occasional objections from papal nuncios.[22] Nevertheless, it seems possible – particularly at Rome itself, where the largest numbers of heretics died – to overcome these difficulties through using parallel sources, especially records from the special confraternities who accompanied prisoners to the place of execution. Overall, one can estimate slightly over a hundred heresy executions carried out through the Roman system before 1620, mainly against Protestants.[23]

Did they accomplish their main purposes?

This question elicits a wide range of answers, not only because their main purposes were originally quite different, but also because they changed considerably over time, especially as the Protestant threat receded throughout Mediterranean Europe after the Council of Trent. We must remember that these institutions held jurisdiction only over baptized Christians (non-Christians cannot commit heresy), and realize that every major Inquisition followed a different trajectory. Both Spain and Portugal created their holy offices in order to attack the problem of 'Judaizing' among baptized Christians of Jewish ancestry, whereas the Roman Inquisition was created in order to deal with the menace of Protestantism in the Italian peninsula. Of course, Spain and Portugal also encountered Protestantism as a major problem by the mid-sixteenth century. Moreover, we must not forget the enormous Muslim presence throughout Fernand Braudel's 'Mediterranean world' in the early modern period. Although only Spain created a monumental religious problem for itself by forcibly baptizing its remaining Muslim population in 1526, all three Inquisitions encountered Islam as a major source of heresy. Therefore the best way to approach this problem is by asking first how well each holy office resolved its original problem, and then finding out what each did subsequently on related matters.

22 Martin, *Venice's hidden enemies*.   23 Monter, 'The Roman Inquisition'.

Judaism

The Spanish Inquisition has been a veritable mine-field for Jewish historians, whose evaluations depend on largely preconceived notions of whether or not to consider Spain's remarkably large and influential *converso* population as genuine Jews when Ferdinand and Isabella's new Inquisition began persecuting them. On the one hand, not only were these Spanish *conversos* frequently third-generation Christians, several of whom held important posts in the Spanish church, but Sephardic rabbis outside Spain overwhelmingly considered them apostates and told practising Jews to shun them.[24] On the other hand, the so-called 'Catholic kings' were sufficiently persuaded of the extent of Judaic practices among many *conversos* that they lobbied a reluctant papacy to create a holy office in order to punish them for enjoying the privileges of Christians while behaving like Jews. If we say that the truth lies in between, we are still bedevilled by insoluble historical problems, the most important one being that the Inquisition itself provides virtually our only source of information about Spanish *conversos*. We have no reliable estimates of how many *conversos* (or even how many practising Jews) lived in Spain in 1480 or 1492. But we know that Torquemada's holy office punished thousands of *conversos* ruthlessly, mainly during the time that Ferdinand and Isabella were campaigning in Grenada to destroy the last non-Christian state in western Europe.

After Granada fell in 1492, practising Jews were expelled from Spain, yet the Inquisition continued to discover and punish *conversos* for Judaizing. Around 1500, several messianic outbreaks and the discovery of a clandestine synagogue in Valencia, run by an uncle of Juan Luis Vives, Spain's most famous Renaissance humanist, gave the holy office a patina of continuing legitimacy. Its early reign of terror was therefore prolonged until around 1530. Even the most conservative estimates suggest that the Spanish Inquisition burned 1,500 adults at the stake during its first half-century, along with an approximately equal number of effigies (Torquemada's earliest regulations insisted that 'trials of the living must never take precedence over trials of the dead'). Several thousand more *conversos* endured lesser punishments. We know that many fled Spain to avoid persecution. But we will never know how many thousands of *conversos* stayed and, like the ancestors of St Teresa or the Jesuit general Diego Laynez, assimilated quietly into mainstream Spanish Christian society. After a persecution at Murcia in the late 1550s, driven by local political factionalism,[25]

---

24 Netanyahu, *Origins of the Spanish Inquisition.*   25 Contreras, *Sotos contra Riquelmes.*

most 'Judaizers' punished by the Spanish Inquisition came from Portugal, while other heretics, Protestants or Muslims, replaced them as its primary targets. Perhaps, after two generations of terrorist tactics, Spain's holy office had basically accomplished its original purpose of eradicating external vestiges of Judaism among its *converso* population without exterminating them.

Because Portugal's 'New Christians' were often descended from Jews who had fled Spain in 1492 only to be forcibly baptized shortly afterwards in the so-called 'Great Conversion' of 1497, its Inquisition faced a crypto-Jewish minority with far less desire for assimilation into Christian society than the Spanish *conversos*. Not surprisingly, Portugal's holy office compiled a much bloodier record than the Spanish Inquisition between 1540 and 1760, without eliminating crypto-Judaic practices among Portuguese 'Marranos'. It has been proposed that, in order to justify its continued existence, Portugal's holy office deliberately provoked such behaviour through constant public reiterations of 'Judaic' practices at its *autos da fé*, simultaneously fanning anti-Semitism among the general population and instructing its principal clients, who had been unable to practice Judaism in public since 1497, about their religious heritage.[26] Not until the 'Enlightened' ministry of the Marquis de Pombal was the problem solved by destroying all registers of 'New Christian' family names in 1768 and then removing all legal distinctions between them and 'Old Christians' five years later.

The Roman Inquisition burned copies of the Talmud and encouraged the formation of ghettoes to intimidate practising Jews, but it confronted no serious indigenous *converso* problem and 'Judaizers' therefore never became a major concern. A handful of immigrant Iberian crypto-Jews living in Spanish-controlled regions of Italy were executed at Rome (for example, five in 1572). Meanwhile, in cosmopolitan Venice, the Inquisition investigated several Iberian *conversos* who practised Judaism openly in Italy, but never executed any of them.[27]

Protestantism

Although the Roman Inquisition was the first to make 'Lutheranism' its principal target, by the late 1550s all three holy offices had become deeply involved in repressing Protestantism. Here it seems safe to say that, although they employed somewhat different tactics, all three succeeded fully, with general

26 Saraiva, *Inquisição e critãos novos*.
27 Pullan, *The Jews of Europe*; Ioly Zorattini, *Processi del S. Uffizio*.

public support; they can claim credit (or blame) for erasing this movement throughout Mediterranean Europe by 1580. Given the weakness of indigenous Protestantism, their task was not extremely difficult and did not require extensive bloodshed. By way of comparison, the tribunal of Flanders in the Low Countries, under a particularly vigorous Inquisitor, executed almost as many native Protestants in the 1550s as all three major Mediterranean Inquisitions combined in the following decade – yet Protestantism triumphed (at least temporarily) in Flemish cities shortly after the holy office had stopped functioning there.

The Italian experience must be addressed first, because the problem was most serious here. Experts agree that Protestantism was suffocated rather than burned out in Italy. Most prominent Italian Protestants had already fled abroad by 1560, where they played a major role in shaping Protestant radicalism in eastern Europe. The most stubborn obstacle Italian Inquisitors faced was the practice of Nicodemism, or concealing one's private heretical opinions. An influential recent explanation[28] argues that the Roman Inquisition's most effective tactic for overcoming it was its practice of co-opting confessors, ordering them to refuse absolution to penitent heretics unless they repeated their confessions to the holy office.

Spain's encounter with 'Lutheranism' provides a clear illustration of the holy office's effective use of force to destroy a dissident religious movement. Until the accidental discovery of Protestant sympathizers in Spain's economic capital (Seville) and political capital (Valladolid) in the late 1550s, the Inquisition had believed that Spaniards were immune from this disease. Once aware of the problem, they acted quickly. Using a special privilege issued by the notoriously anti-Spanish Pope Paul IV, allowing them to execute even penitent first offenders if they saw fit, the Spanish Inquisition proceeded to burn out both groups through a few spectacular *autos de fé* in 1559 and 1560. About seventy Spaniards, half of them women, died. As H. C. Lea noted a century ago[29] barely half a dozen of them would have been executed under ordinary rules of inquisitorial procedure, but exemplary severity was used precisely because most defendants came from prominent families. In this instance, brutal but brief repression succeeded in eliminating Protestantism in Spain, although a hundred foreigners were subsequently burned at various Spanish *autos* until the early seventeenth century. In Sicily, which belonged to the Spanish rather than Roman Inquisition, French Calvinists were still executed in 1628 and 1640.

---

28 Prosperi, *Tribunali della coscienza*.
29 Lea, *A history of the Spanish Inquisition*, vol. 3, pp. 337–47.

Although Portugal had no significant native Protestant movement, by 1570 its holy office had prosecuted well over a hundred 'Lutherans', three-quarters of them foreigners, and burned five: an English merchant, a French cleric, a Flemish workman, a Venetian, and the French ambassador's pastry-cook.[30] Overseas, its tribunal at Goa in India continued to execute an occasional Dutch or English Protestant in the early 1600s.

Islam

However, after succeeding in eliminating Protestantism, all three major Inquisitions failed miserably in their encounters with Islam. Unlike Protestantism, this was a religion which converted large numbers of Mediterranean Christians, but whose members could rarely be made into Tridentine Catholics. Samples from 1582 and 1603 show that Protestants were almost twice as likely as Muslims to abjure their apostasy at the Vatican. Inquisitors learned that the number of Muslim converts to Catholicism was tiny compared with the number of Christian converts to Islam. Every seaport between Venice and Lisbon possessing an inquisitorial tribunal encountered numerous 'renegades', baptized Christians who had more or less willingly converted to Islam before being examined by the holy office, usually after being captured at sea; between 1560 and 1620, nearly 500 of them were questioned at Palermo and another 200 at Naples. A sample of 1,550 ex-Christian renegades processed by various holy offices between 1550 and 1700 included almost 200 Frenchmen and fifty Englishmen; because fewer than 20 per cent of them were eastern Europeans, the authors suggest that this number represents less than 1 per cent of their total numbers.[31]

Obviously, confrontations with Islam were most acute in Spain, which had created hundreds of thousands of 'New Christians' of Muslim ancestry through forced baptisms between 1500 and 1526 but subsequently failed to assimilate them culturally. As late as 1570, the Inquisitors found Moriscos in Valencia who could not remember their Christian names, and professional circumcisers were still working there in the 1580s.[32] The most serious attempt to make them behave like proper Christians came shortly after the Council of Trent, but it led to a major rising in Granada which required two years to extinguish, with the survivors being forcibly dispersed throughout small communities in Castile. Overall, the Spanish Inquisition put about 8,000 Moriscos on trial between

---

30 Bethencourt, 'Les hérétiques et l'Inquisition portugaise', pp. 103–17, 115–16.
31 Bennassar, *Les Chrétiens d'Allah*, p. 147.　　32 Vincent, *Minorias y marginados*.

1540 and 1615, sending several hundred men to the galleys and burning about 200 'Mohammedans' at public *autos*. However, its severity had little effect apart from hardening Morisco fear and loathing of an institution which they sometimes called *la cosa*, 'the thing'.

Morisco resistance to the Spanish Inquisition was both direct and passive. On one hand, they were the only group in Spain bold enough to murder several informers and even a few inquisitorial familiars. On the other hand, as the Inquisition's standardized religious tests imposed on all prisoners after 1570 demonstrate, Moriscos stubbornly resisted becoming confessionalized Catholics. At Cuenca, among a variety of offenders, 71 per cent of the Old Christians charged with doctrinal errors could recite all their essential prayers correctly; accused Judaizers did even better (78 per cent), but Moriscos scored only 54 per cent.[33] In the end, the Inquisition enthusiastically promoted the expulsion of Spain's Moriscos in 1609. Their descendants returned to Europe only a few decades ago.

Inquisitorial censorship

Controlling the flow and content of printed information was an important concern of every holy office. In this instance, we know much more about how censorship worked under the Roman system than in the Iberian peninsula. The nearly complete archives of the Vatican's Congregation of the Index, created in 1572, abolished in 1917, and officially open to scholars since 1998, reside in the old palazzo of the Roman holy office, alongside those from the Congregation of the Inquisition: although they were sometimes uneasy neighbours, one supposedly directed censorship policy while the other implemented it. Roman censors had spies at every Frankfurt book fair and thus possessed fresher and more accurate information than their Iberian counterparts. Papal censorship, a cornerstone of Tridentine Catholicism, exercised an influence far beyond the Italian peninsula. Early lists of prohibited books approved by the Vatican (made by the Roman Inquisition in 1559, by Tridentine bishops in 1564, and finally by the Congregation of the Index in 1597) resonated throughout Catholic Christendom. Scholarship about censorship should become a 'growth sector' within inquisition studies; as an investigation of Cardinal Bellarmine's complicated thirty-year involvement with Roman censorship shows, it has already begun.[34]

33 Nalle, *God in La Mancha*, p. 129.   34 Godman, *The saint as censor*.

How effective was Roman censorship? The first important investigation of inquisitorial enforcement examined the heart of Italian publishing, Venice, where over a third of Italy's books were produced, and provided an optimistic assessment of its weaknesses.[35] However, early Venetian searches resulted in lengthy trials of twenty-eight booksellers, one of whom had more than a thousand books confiscated, and prosecutions for possessing prohibited books were more frequent here than elsewhere. Subsequent investigations of such major aspects as Italian censorship of Erasmus[36] or the confiscation and destruction of vernacular bibles[37] have concluded that it was relatively thorough and effective. Overtly obscene works, previously an Italian specialty, were driven underground. Expurgations of 'provisionally' forbidden works were rarely made; the official Index finally issued in 1607 covered only fifty-three of several hundred titles.[38] In a few areas of Italian culture, for example judicial astrology or duelling, post-Tridentine censorship could never be enforced. But long before Galileo encountered it, the Index had completed its primary task by erasing all traces of Reformation literature in Italy, and had inflicted serious damage on some other aspects of Italian culture.

In Portugal and Spain, censorship and its enforcement remained entirely in the hands of the holy office.[39] Both systems developed almost identical methods for controlling printed matter (Portugal usually slightly sooner than Spain): each produced its own lists of prohibited books, which they updated frequently, and after a large number of Protestant books were accidentally discovered at Seville in 1557, both tried to maintain comprehensive inspections of both booksellers and incoming foreign ships. The Portuguese system of visiting ships was so regular that economic historians have used it to measure port traffic.[40] Despite claims that in Spain 'neither the Index nor the censorship system produced an adequate machinery of control',[41] considerable evidence of its indirect and direct impact on science and culture exists, for instance in its stock of 3,021 books confiscated by 1634, including many not on the Index.[42] Portugal's holy office confiscated far fewer books, but a 1606 sample from Lisbon shows targets which were often Italian or Spanish: Castiglione, Ariosto, Cervantes, Lope de Vega, plus books on magic and even Erasmus.[43]

---

35 Grendler, *The Roman Inquisition*.   36 Seidel Menchi, *Erasmo in Italia*.
37 Fragnito, *La Bibbia al rogo*.   38 Fragnito (ed.), *Church, censorship and culture*, p. 6.
39 Bethencourt, *L'Inquisition à l'époque moderne*, pp. 215–28.   40 *Ibid.*, p. 221.
41 Kamen, *The Spanish Inquisition*, p. 131.   42 Pardo Tomás, *Ciencia y censura*.
43 Bethencourt, *L'Inquisition à l'époque moderne*, p. 218.

Other spheres of jurisdiction

Although inquisitions always considered combating formal heresy to be their primary occupation, indeed their reason for existence, they did much more than struggle against major threats from followers of Moses, Luther, or Mohammed. Each of the major systems also investigated a wide range of problems only indirectly related to religious deviance. It is difficult to reduce these additional pursuits to a clear system. In the early 1970s, following the language of the holy office itself as far as possible, scholars trying to map the overall activities of the Spanish Inquisition from 1540 to 1700 created six large subdivisions: 'heretical propositions and blasphemy', 'bigamy', 'solicitation in the confessional', 'opposition to the Holy Office', 'superstitions and witchcraft', and 'miscellaneous'. These offences can also be found in both Roman and Portuguese inquisitorial sources, although usually in smaller numbers than Spain ('sodomites', who formed the largest group within Spain's 'miscellaneous' category, can also be found in Portuguese, but not Roman, trials).

Aligning these Iberian categories with Italian inquisitorial evidence has required some rearrangement. Although there is much overlap, one finds, for example, that Italian sources contain many more charges of owning prohibited books and include problems rarely encountered in Iberia, such as investigations of 'materialism' or 'atheism' (usually a belief that the soul died with the body) or of bogus living saints.[44] Even the verbal content of trials for 'heretical blasphemy' seems somewhat stronger in Italy than in Iberia. Perhaps the best way to approach the issue of inquisitorial business apart from major heresy is to divide it into a few major subgroups. First, we will examine the attempt to enforce Tridentine theological norms, to 'confessionalize' Mediterranean Catholics, through prosecuting such minor erroneous propositions as the widespread Spanish belief that fornication between consenting adults was not sinful, or the Italian belief that homosexuality was a venial rather than a mortal sin. Second, we will look at their increasing preoccupation – visible in all three systems, but earliest and strongest in Italy – to uproot all kinds of popular magical practices. And finally, we will inspect the Iberian campaigns against homosexuality (in Italy, 'sodomy' was tried exclusively in secular courts).

In Castile, the Spanish Inquisition played a significant role in refining confessional discipline, complementing catechistical training from the secular clergy by punishing speech crimes against Tridentine doctrines. Such offences, for which ordinary people were punished comparatively lightly, accounted

---

44 Schutte (ed. and trans.), *Autobiography of an aspiring saint.*

for almost 40 per cent of Castile's inquisitorial business between 1560 and 1614. However, we can safely say that Philip II's Spain had been successfully confessionalized; at Cuenca, hundreds of ordinary inquisitorial prisoners, usually accused of doctrinal irregularities and often illiterate, demonstrated an impressive mastery of their basic prayers, usually in Spanish.[45] Matters were apparently similar in post-Tridentine north-central Italy. During its most active phase (1580–1640), Siena's holy office, one of the few Roman tribunals with complete records, investigated 1,725 such cases; as in Spain, the bulk of them concerned either 'heretical propositions', eating meat on fast days, irreverence towards the clergy, or blasphemy (44 per cent), while the largest single cluster (34 per cent) investigated illicit magical practices.[46]

As Siena's figures illustrate, illicit magic became the primary target of the Roman Inquisition after the Protestant threat had disappeared, and disciplining this type of offender became an important aspect of the Catholic Reformation. However, relatively few investigations led to formal trials and few punishments were severe. Consider the now well-known Friulian *benandanti*, a group of magical healers 'diabolized' by Inquisitors:[47] eighty-five of them were investigated, but only fifteen trials proceeded to sentencing. Between 1615 and 1700, Spanish inquisitorial tribunals judged over 2,500 cases of 'superstitions' (the overwhelming majority of them unrelated to maleficent witchcraft), roughly one-sixth of their total business at this time, or about half as large a share as in Italy. Before 1774, Portugal's holy office tried over 900 people (only about 4 per cent of its recorded cases) for performing various kinds of illicit magic. Its punishments seem relatively more severe than in Italy or Spain; but it seems worth noting both that a large share of these defendants (almost 30 per cent) were charged with maleficent witchcraft, and that in over 30 per cent of them we have no evidence that their sentences, usually banishments, were ever carried out.[48]

'Sodomy' was punished severely wherever it fell under Holy Office jurisdiction. Both the Spanish and Portuguese Inquisitions tried 'sodomy', but its definition was narrower in Portugal. Although judged by inquisitorial courts in only three tribunals of the crown of Aragon, 'sodomy' accounted for 170 deaths between 1570 and 1625 (almost half of their capital punishments) and for about 300 condemnations to the galleys. Defendants were often immigrants, slaves, or Moriscos, people whose fate aroused little public sympathy.[49]

45 Nalle, *God in La Mancha*, pp. 118–33.
46 Di Simplicio, *Inquisizione Stregoneria Medicina*.
47 Ginzburg, *The night battles*; Nardon, *Benandanti e inquisitori*.
48 Paiva, *Bruxaria e superstição*, pp. 208–9.
49 Carrasco, *Inquisición y represión*; Monter, *Frontiers of heresy*.

Portugal's Inquisition recorded about 4,500 denunciations for homosexual 'sodomy'. Over 450 men were tried for this offence; thirty of them were punished with death, making it Portugal's second-ranking inquisitorial capital crime, although far behind Judaism.

*

The major early modern Inquisitions continue to resist easy generalizations. We can see several aspects of all three systems far more clearly than a generation ago, but paradoxes abound everywhere. Concerning the crucial issue of its treatment of Sephardic 'New Christians' in Spain and Portugal, scholars wrestle inconclusively with apparently insoluble problems of cultural assimilation. Sometimes, as in their approach to witchcraft or Protestantism, old assessments of their behaviour and its probable effects seem more accurate than ever. The Spanish holy office's approach to its Morisco minority was an outright failure, while its assistance with post-Tridentine 'confessionalization' among other Spaniards emerges as a significant and successful concern. Although their officials must often be understood as career bureaucrats, the holy offices sometimes look like precocious experts in public relations. On the other hand, civil rights experts lament their well-organized enthusiasm for censorship, feminists have little patience with them, and gay activists rank them among Europe's most determined and bloodthirsty prosecutors. Boring and irrelevant they are not.

17

Religious colloquies and toleration

OLIVIER CHRISTIN

It is paradoxically from a double absence that the history of toleration and coexistence between confessions during the Reformation can be written. Not only were its partisans and artisans few in number, so much so that traditional historiography always seems to enumerate the same names – Erasmus, Schwenckfeld, Franck, Celsi, Castellion, Coornhert, or Hoen – and their texts just as rare and confidential,[1] but the very vocabulary in which they evoked questions that seem to us to concern directly liberty of conscience and worship, protection of clerics, religious buildings and burials, and confident dialogue between members of different faiths, is a far cry from our own. 'Toleration', for example, is very seldom found, in French or in German, except with a negative connotation such as Luther and most of the French authors gave it in 1542:[2] to tolerate is to endure, suffer, and accept in bad faith something that cannot be fixed or abolished in the immediate future. Significantly, the expression 'tolerate', or 'toleration', cannot be found in the texts that concretely organized the great experiments of peaceful coexistence in the Empire or in France: these terms are absent from the texts of the Peace of Augsburg (1555), from most of the Landesordnungen, as well as from the Edict of Nantes (1598). When they evoked the possibility of establishing a form of coexistence between rival confessions that vied for control in Europe from the beginning of the 1520s, contemporaries willingly spoke of *concordia*, of *mansuetudo*, *caritas* or, in a different register and often with different intentions, of *pax* and *amicitia*.[3]

---

1 It is therefore necessary to recall that the famous *Colloquium Heptaplomeres* by Jean Bodin, often given as a model of thinking on toleration, remained in manuscript.
2 Quoted Schulze, 'Concordia, Discordia, Tolerantia', pp. 43–79. For France, see Huseman, 'The expression of the idea of toleration', pp. 294–310.
3 Guggisberg, 'Wandel der Argumente für religiöse Toleranz'; Schreiner, 'Tolerantz'; and Wanegffelen, *L'Edit de Nantes*.

This double absence does not, however, forbid us from describing the theoretical justifications and the concrete measures that were taken by some sixteenth-century Christians in an effort to master a situation which had remained unprecedented until that point – the long-term confessional break-up of a large part of Europe, increasing the occasions of confrontations and face-offs – who, in doing so, invented new tools. But this absence inspires caution and, at the very least, the dismissal of a teleological history in which toleration and freedom of conscience progressed step-by-step in the course of the sixteenth century, and is interpreted in the modern sense given by the Enlightenment. It suggests, on the contrary, a certain perspective on ideas that were expressed in texts written in precise circumstances and with definite ends in mind, to ask questions about the actors, individuals, collective or institutional, who called up such projects as meetings between churches, legal recognitions or peaceful debates between theologians from both sides, and to identify the movement of people and works; for instance the presence of the famous 'moyenneur' François Bauduin at the colloquy of Worms in 1557 and Poissy in 1561 where rival confessions seemed to be on the verge of an agreement.

How to communicate with the heretic?

It is therefore necessary to remember that it was only gradually, through controversy and following the evolution of the religious and political situation (at least until the opening of the Council of Trent in 1545), that the places, arguments and examples around which supporters and adversaries of coexistence or peaceful reunion of the churches fought each other finally emerged. As early as the 1520s the first arguments and biblical points of difficulty were already emerging as the first elements of controversy were being voiced.

Luther was compelled to fight on two fronts, against the attacks of Carlstadt and the Schwärmer (enthusiasts) but also against the persecution that was orchestrated by the Church of Rome and the princes who supported her, and he was thus led to lay the foundations of a systematic critique of the use of force in matters of faith. In the *Letter to the German Nobility* (1520), he rejected the use of force against religious dissidents, because 'if to overcome heretics by fire is an art, executioners would be more learned than doctors'. At Wittenberg, in the second sermon on *Invocavit* of 1522, he condemned in similar terms the violence that was exerted this time by the followers of Carlstadt in the hope of toppling the Catholic mass more speedily: for him, 'one must preach, write and proclaim that the mass celebrated in this manner is a sin; but one must not tear anyone away from it by force'.[4] Luther returned several times to these questions, distinguishing for example between largesse granted to the weak and the rigour necessary against the obstinate,[5] adding essential indications on the role of temporal authority: 'the latter must stay still, mind its own business, but leave everyone to believe this or that' (1523).[6]

After 1525, however, in reaction to the Peasants' War but also as a result of the institutionalization of the first Lutheran churches, the reformer went back on what he had initially written extolling Christian freedom and the free gift of salvation. At the beginning of that crucial year, the pamphlet *Vom Greuel der Stilmesse* fustigated mass anew and concluded that 'authority has the duty to defend and punish such public blasphemy'. And in 1526, Luther asked the Elector of Saxony to forbid mass on his estates in order to avoid the disorder which would not fail to emerge from the plurality of religion. Despite this U-turn, the first interventions of Luther nonetheless allowed some arguments and biblical passages that would be at the heart of later debates to emerge: the nature of faith and the possibility of violating consciences, running the risk of leading the flock to adhere through fear to a doctrine that they did not understand or adopted superficially; the role of secular authorities and the question of public scandals, distinct from individual freedom of conscience and private worship; the true interpretation of the parable of the wheat and the chaff, which became one of the predominant fighting grounds of toleration. Erasmus, notably, gave it a central role, refusing to interpret it as a justification for persecution: the chaff of the false prophets and the heretics should be tolerated, that is, suffered, in anticipation of their ultimate conversion: 'if they fail to amend themselves, let their judge take the care of chastising them one day'. In 1524, B. Hubmaier came to an even more radical conclusion of the parable of Matthew in asserting that in wanting to build their church in blood, 'the Inquisitors are the greatest heretics'. Gradually, different topical positions took shape, well formed, but that cannot be assimilated to schools of thought or parties, even if, in certain specific circumstances, as in the Empire in 1539–41 or in France in 1560–62, these new positions drew together groups of theologians, lawyers, peers of the realm and courtiers whose interests and projects temporarily converged. Recent historiography has offered to distinguish between different ways of thinking on the necessary resolution of the religious rift:[7] on the one hand, projects of religious concord that veered towards the union or the peaceful

---

4 *WA* 10,3, pp. 15–18. 5 Hartweg, 'Luther et l'autorité temporelle', p. 541.
6 Luther, *On temporal authority* (1523). 7 Notably Turchetti, *Concordia o tolleranza*.

reunion of the churches at the cost of reforming abuses and making more or less important concessions like discipline and ecclesiology on the sacraments and doctrine; on the other, toleration *per se*, namely the acceptance of the very principle of religious pluralism and the diversity of worship, and civil concord that only contemplated the establishment of a legal framework for the coexistence of confessions without making any pronouncements on issues of dogma. This distinction is nothing more than a tool for the classification of concrete situations, debates, opinions in a situation that remained extremely fluid and complex, but allows nonetheless for the identification of diverse solutions that were elaborated by contemporaries to conceive and surmount the confessional rift. A call to a 'union of hearts' and largesse towards those who, not causing scandals or professing inadmissible beliefs, were in the wrong can be found in the writings of Erasmus: in order to recover Christian concord, Erasmus enjoined a return to the text of the gospel and the staving off of theological speculations as much as possible, in order to determine what was essential, what should unite all Christians, and indifferent things, adiaphora, that cannot suffice to draw a line between heresy and orthodoxy. For Sebastian Franck, Mino Celsi, or Schwenckfeld, however, the rejection of the use of force and defiance towards rival churches led them to question the very notion of heresy, because it is not for men to determine who errs and who is in the right, and consequently dissidence in general should be accepted without attempting to reach a doctrinal compromise. Even more starkly, the Peaces of religion that emerged in a large number of territories, explicitly renounced, even if provisionally and with ill will, the doctrinal stakes and thought about the nature of faith in order to instigate specific political and judicial solutions.[8] The text of a decision of the *Reichskammergericht* (the Imperial Chamber of Justice that dealt with territorial, and, after 1555, with religious peace) states: 'Religion-Fried non est res spiritualis, sed politica et secularis.' For the contemporaries themselves, these different ways of thinking were indeed distinct and partly irreconcilable. One only needs to follow the successive battles waged by Johann Gropper, central artisan of the religious colloquies of 1540–1 and their prospects of concord, and acerbic critic of the peace of 1555, to be convinced. But one can also go back to the very texts of the Peaces of religion instigated in the Empire, in France, or in the Low Countries. According to article 25 of the Peace of Augsburg, the emperor and the imperial states pledged to instigate 'a state of peace . . . in order to preserve this venerable nation from the complete shipwreck that threatens it, in order to come all the quicker to a friendly and

8 With an exception in Siebenbürgen.

305

definitive Christian reunion of religion'. *Friedstand* is, whenever possible, only a step towards *Vergleichung*. Similarly, the famous preamble to the Edict of Nantes of 1598 specifies that the peace has no other ambition than to ensure that 'God . . . can be worshipped and prayed to by all [the] subjects' of the King of France, even if it displeased God to 'allow that it be still in one and the same form of religion'.

It would be perilous, however, to invent imaginary parties of concord, of peace or toleration or to establish too tight a chronology that would place the disenchanted and cautious of period political peace that followed generous hopes of a humanist concord. The same individuals indeed brought forward projects that today seem contradictory, pursuing parallel strategies in the hope that at least one of them would succeed, as can be observed at the French court from the time of Michel de L'Hôpital's appointment to the chancellorship. Under the influence of Erasmian humanism,[9] L'Hôpital inspired or at least supported some of the most significant projects of concord of the mid-sixteenth century, in backing the 'moyenneurs'[10] of the Colloquy of Poissy and Saint Germain-en-Laye in 1561 (Claude d'Espence, François Bauduin, Jean de Monluc). At the same time he also led a policy of reform of the judiciary and restoration of the king's authority that led the king to make him the secular arm of pacification devoid of a dogmatic agenda. In March and May 1560, and again in January and July 1561, royal edicts established a clear distinction between sedition and heresy and guaranteed amnesty to the Protestants as long as they did not indulge in scandalous behaviour, which opened the way to a temporary judicial solution. And in January 1562, and in March 1563, two very different settlements were agreed upon that led the kingdom to a long-term period of institutionalized confessional coexistence.[11] As L'Hôpital himself said in his famous speech 'it is possible to live at peace with those who have a different opinion'.[12]

In order to uncover the historical stakes of the efforts that were deployed in the hope of overcoming the devastating effects of the rift between religions, it is not enough to describe the arguments that were gradually voiced by unlikely inventors of toleration before toleration took a hold. It is not only necessary

---

9 Crouzet, *La sagesse et le malheur*.
10 The word is Calvin's, who denounced by it those who sought a middle way between Reform and Catholicism and end up, in his eyes, by confessing but 'half of Jesus Christ': Wanegffelen, *Ni Rome ni Genève*, p. 131.
11 Benedict, 'Un roi, une loi, deux fois'; Christin, *La paix de religion*, p. 327.
12 Descimon (ed.), *Michel de l'Hopital*.

to understand how the new forms of debate and negotiations took shape, in what circumstances, by whom and why, it is also necessary to determine who the authors of these confrontations were, who created the habits and practices of peaceful clashes, through controversy or law, for example. New forms of discussion, destined to play a decisive role in the history of attempts at religious pacification, took shape against the grain of the mutual interdicts and cautions, that nipped in the bud any contradictory exchanges that would have given the respective parties a chance to express their opinions:[13] the religious colloquies or public conferences or disputes, to repeat some of the expressions used by contemporaries. Even before the break from Rome, Martin Luther was directly attacked by opponents in a series of public jousts: in the spring of 1518 in the Augustinians' chapter house, in the autumn of the same year against Cardinal Cajetan, and in the summer of 1519 in Leipzig opposite the Vice-Chancellor of Ingolstadt, Johannes Eck, and lastly at the diet of Worms in 1521. The public disputes between doctors of different confessions, the confrontation and contradictory discussion were from the outset a fixture of the spread of new ideas and the attempts by the followers of Rome to stem their flow.[14] None of these formal meetings was intended to bring together different points of view and find a meeting ground. On the contrary, many of them, partly inspired by the academic tradition of disputation, intended to unmask the adversary and to unveil his lies. This was notably the case for the French disputes during the first war of religion[15] and after the Edict of Nantes: their organization, hotly contested and modelled on academic controversy, and the virulence of the words exchanged between adversaries, made it an arena for confessional fighting and enterprises of conversion, rather than a tool for peace. The hundreds of disputes that took place throughout the kingdom after the Edict of Nantes of 1598 pursued in their own way the wars of the second half of the sixteenth century and the bolstering efforts of confessional churches.[16] In Switzerland, many public clashes between theologians of different confessions seemed to fulfil the needs of both polemic and the strengthening of confessional identities. Some of the most famous of these clashes even marked the official

---

13 An idea of the tenacity of the interdicts opposed to all forms of discussion with heretics is provided in an anonymous French work, *Discours de l'Erinophile* (1594), pp. 238–9: 'It is in good cause that I complain about several light Catholics who, in order to bolster I do not know what common freedom between men, say that there is no danger in mixing with them, to listen to them, or question or hear their opinion'.

14 Fuchs, *Konfession und Gespräch*.

15 Foa, 'Le métier de la dispute'; Dufour, 'Das Religionsgespräch von Poissy'.

16 Christin, 'La formation étatique de l'espace savant'.

beginning of the Reformation in the territories where they took place. The secular authorities who had called them chose their side according to the outcome of the debate and made sure that there was indeed a winner, as in Zurich in 1523 or in Lausanne in 1536.[17] The disputations were the official tool of the triumph of the Reformation.

But other public meetings obviously followed different principles, closer to those that Erasmus had hoped would rule over the exchanges regarding matters of faith. Refusing the dangerous allure of rhetoric and dialectic, preferring, in his own terms, to be a pious theologian with Jerome than an invincible one with Duns Scotus, Erasmus indeed considered religious debate to be a courteous, friendly, relaxed and sincere exchange of views.[18] Moreover, in a letter to the Elector Prince of Saxony in 1526, he underscored that he had given his book on free will 'a very careful title, calling it a discussion or confrontation . . . or a well-meaning treatment'. It is easy to understand then that certain humanist princes and some theologians inspired by the thinking of Erasmus had seen in the organization of genuine religious colloquies an ideal way of peacefully and sincerely resolving the religious conflict: they believed that during these carefully planned meetings an ideal of concord and its specific requirements of largesse and compassion could emerge. And at the beginning of the 1540s, the political and religious context of the Holy Roman Empire proved suddenly favourable to the organization of such colloquies: the pope had indeed just pushed back once more the opening of the council, and its first session (1545) had not yet put an end to all hopes of a reunion of churches through discussion and negotiation. Three important meetings followed one another, in Haguenau, Worms, and Regensburg in the space of a few months in 1540–1. Protestants (Melanchthon, Bucer, Pistorius, Pflug, and Creutziger) and Catholics (Gropper, and the cardinals Contarini and Campeggi) seemed then close to an agreement, notably around a text of compromise that had been drafted by Bucer and Gropper at the request of Granvelle, the *Book of Ratisbonne*. The latter offered formulations, for example on the question of justification by faith, that were susceptible to convincing both sides. But the union failed, for reasons that have as much to do with persistent disagreements about doctrine, about the sacraments and ecclesiology, as about political stakes. Luther and Melanchthon on one side, Fabri and Eck on the other, finally rejected the *Book of Ratisbonne*, called it a 'falsity' and even the work of the devil.

---

17 Augustijn, 'Die Religionsgespräche'.
18 Quoted by Margolin, 'L'apogée de la rhétorique humaniste', p. 215.

At peace

It is not, however, in the debates between humanists and spiritualist theologians nor in the religious colloquies that concrete forms of confessional coexistence and the modern vocabulary of pluralism originated. They originated from the experience at once banal and unprecedented, singular and diversified, of the Peaces of Religion, as they were known notably in France, the Empire, the Swiss confederacy, the Low Countries, Poland, and Transylvania. What the contemporaries themselves designated by the expression Peace of Religion (*Religionsfried, Paces Religionis*, etc.) emerged as early as the Peace of Cappel as a solution, unsatisfactory but effective, to the troubles raised by religious division. This first agreement of 1531[19] (that established the sovereignty of all cantons in religious matters, with the exception of particular situations such as that of the confessionally mixed Glaris and Appenzell, and forbade resorting to violence, even in the common bailiwicks that were the most concerned with the concrete effects of religious coexistence, insults and verbal violence) was soon followed by other agreements that loosely took inspiration from it. In the negotiations that led to the Peace of Augsburg, in 1555, the Swiss precedent was thus explicitly cited.

In fact, at Augsburg, the principles at work in the imperial recess that dealt with religious problems in the context of territorial peace and put doctrinal questions proper aside were very similar to what had been instigated at Cappel: religious autonomy (*Freistellung*) of the imperial states (*Stände*), to which the right to reform their territory and consequently to impose the confession of the prince on the subjects (*ius reformandi*) was conceded; interdiction of violence, including verbal violence, and all forms of intervention in the religious affairs of another state; concessions to the subjects of a right to emigrate (*ius emigrandi*) to another territory in cases where they refused to follow the religion of the prince; transformation of the composition and the operating mode of the imperial tribunal of the Reichskammergericht so that it could apply parity to the instruction of religious cases opposing the states of the Empire; and, lastly, implementation of the terms of article 27, of zones of mixed confession where, theoretically, the two confessions included in the recess – excluding Anabaptists and Calvinists – would be able to celebrate their cult freely. It was therefore, as in Switzerland, an *a priori* territorial solution to the religious conflict that was instigated in the Empire, partly due to the institutional structure of the Reich and the balance of power that prevented any given side from totally imposing its

---

19 Walder (ed.), *Religionsvergleiche des 16. Jahrhunderts*.

conditions: the attempt at rolling back Protestantism and Catholic reconquest that the Interim of 1548 had embodied had, after all, failed. In the course of the 1570s, Lutheran lawyers summarized this internal arrangement specific to the Peace of Augsburg in a derogatory formula that survived the test of time: 'cujus regio, ejus religio'.

Later, however, things were more complex. On the one hand, the question of *ius reformandi* of certain states of the Empire and certain magistrates remained ambiguous and were the object, after 1555, of bitter negotiations and judicial battles: as recipient of the Freistellung, did the immediate knighthood benefit from the *ius reformandi* as well? Could the urban magistrates also claim it and impose, by the same token, on the occasion of a change of regime in city councils, a religious revolution for their inhabitants? Could the Catholic prelates who converted to Lutheranism also convert their territories with them, at the risk, in the case of the elector princes of Trier, Mainz, or Cologne, of tipping the balance of the imperial college of electors? This latter eventuality was *de facto* excluded by a disposition of the peace that instituted an ecclesiastical reservation (*Geistliche Vorbehalt*), but the Protestants did not accept it and sought to have it abolished, or subverted it. But in the case of cities, the interpretation of the Peace was more difficult and the situations of instability were multiplied, for example when cities such as Mühlhausen, Haguenau, or Colmar sought late in the day to benefit from the dispositions of article 27, even of a genuine *ius reformandi* over their inhabitants. Lastly, contrary to what is sometimes suggested in the historiography, the Peace did not bring a definitive end to the projects of reconciliation and doctrinal compromise, since in 1557 a new colloquy was organized in the context of the diet of Regensburg, which reflected the dissatisfaction that the Friedstand had failed to alleviate.

If the issue of religious peace is similar in the Kingdom of France – the rapid progress of Protestantism, failure of the colloquy of Poissy/Saint-Germain, troubles and menace of a civil war as early as 1560–1 – the solutions that were tried by Catherine de Médici, Michel de L'Hôpital and some other councillors from 1562 onwards were by force of circumstances different from the territorial model. What was at stake in France was the negotiating between the restoration of the authority of the Catholic king and theoretical defender of the church, and the diversity of religion of his subjects. In jettisoning the precept 'One king, one law, one faith' in 1562 to launch onto a novel path of coexistence extending to almost the whole kingdom, France began (as was shown by Philip Benedict) a new era in the history of Peaces, serving as a model in turn to subsequent pacifications such as in the Low Countries in

1576 and 1578. The Edict of January 1562 implicitly guaranteed freedom of conscience to the king's Protestant subjects, and, moreover, authorized the celebration of the Calvinist cult in the whole kingdom, 'in daylight, outside the cities', thus going beyond the concessions, albeit considerable, granted by the preceding Peaces, in Switzerland or in the Empire, that were limited geographically or socially. As the chancellor L'Hôpital declared concisely in his speech of January 1562: from now on, according to the new arrangement of the *Res Publica* and religion established by law, 'even the excommunicate does not cease to be a citizen'. The aims of the state were no longer exactly the same as those of the church and it was this conviction that lay at the basis of the arguments of those who began to be called 'Politiques' and who would play a central role in the Henrician Pacification and the Edict of Nantes.

It is true that the wars of religion would throw into question the dispositions made in 1562: the edicts of pacification that followed (1563, 1568, 1570, 1573, 1576, 1577, 1580, and lastly 1598) would be more constraining, reflecting the awakening of French Catholicism in the 1560s[20] but also the establishment of a political and military tussle or struggle that did not favour the Reformed: if freedom of conscience continued to be declared, if the insults and threats were condemned, if the Protestants eventually obtained military (*place de sûreté*) and judicial (mixed tribunals) concessions that were not stipulated in the edict of January 1562 or even the Peace of Amboise (1563), freedom of worship was limited to a number of specific cases. As early as 1563 the edicts distinguished three possibilities: the cult of domains, conceded to lords who become at once the beneficiaries and the guarantors of the peace in an obvious ploy to demobilize the Protestant armies; the worship of possession, namely those that were already in existence when the peace was proclaimed (in this instance on 7 March 1563 for the Peace of Amboise); and lastly the right to worship that was granted by the king and his council in one or more localities by bailiwick, though not without some restrictions (Paris, cathedral towns, etc.).

Despite these restrictions, which make the Edict of January 1562 the most liberal of all the edicts ever granted to the French Reformed, the edicts of pacification of the kingdom evidently rested on a very different mode of operation for the settlement of religious conflict than the one in force in the Empire and in the Swiss Confederacy: in addition to the territorialization of confessions and to the establishment of a complex system of weights and counterweights, of barriers (such as the ecclesiastical reservation), of sharing and arbitration,

20 Harding, 'The mobilization of confraternities'.

France upheld a supra-confessional co-citizenship under the protection of the monarch and the *Res Publica*, placed outside and above confessional differences. The Common Good was identified with peace, with the continuity of the state, to the safeguard of the motherland against the plotting of foreign princes, and religious affairs were relegated to the rank of a laudable but private sphere. Many contemporaries grasped from the outset what it was that separated these ways of envisaging a solution to the wars of religion and inter-confessional violence: if both followed 'peace through law'[21] they were founded, it seems, on two different judicial practices and ideas. The imperial councillor Lazarus von Schwendi, totally familiar with the French situation and the writings of Michel de L'Hôpital, could therefore offer to the emperor in the 1570s some modifications, inspired by the French model, of the Peace of Augsburg granting to all the subjects of the Empire a general Freistellung: this radical measure would have put an end to the territorialization of the Empire and, moreover, would have strengthened the emperor by placing him in the position of referee. Schwendi's utopian project would not have had much weight if it did not reflect at once the pursuance of different solutions for peaceful coexistence in the Empire after 1555 and also the will to make policies of pacification a tool for strengthening central power, which created the success of Henry IV.

These ideas can also be found in the Habsburgs' policies on their hereditary lands, before the Catholic backlash at the end of the century, or in the gradual recognition, from 1543 onwards, of four great confessions (Lutheran, Catholic, Calvinist, and antitrinitarian) in the principality of Transylvania that was caught in a vice between the Habsburgs and the Ottomans. Transylvania was a principality whose independence was fragile, being under the authority of Catholic princes, except John Sigismond, who successively embraced different Protestant confessions, knowing full well that they had no chance of being obeyed by their Protestant subjects unless they acted as patrons and protectors.[22] The absence of organized persecution, and also some of the princes' concrete decisions, clearly demonstrate the progressive recognition of the great Confessions that had spread in the principality: in 1557, for example, during the diet that bolstered the freedom of the Lutheran Church, the Regent Isabel Jagellon stressed that 'by virtue of our position and royal offices, we are forced to protect all the churches'.[23] On several occasions, Etienne Bathory himself acted as Protector of the different Confessions: in 1571, for example,

21 Scheurmann (ed.), *Frieden durch Recht.*
22 Binder, *Grundlagen und Formen der Toleranz.*
23 Quoted by Peter, 'Tolerance and intolerance', p. 256.

he accepted the election of a first antitrinitarian superintendent; in 1579, he insisted that the diet should not oppose the arrival of the Jesuits.[24]

In several instances it is obvious that the religious division was imposed on the prince, but he could attempt to make himself its impartial referee and to find, in the same movement, a new legitimacy. Between territorialization, strengthening of the autonomy of states, sovereign cantons, great nobles and the ideals of a *Res Publica* that would peacefully rally at its heart different churches as in Bodin, the larger part of Europe would, in the second half of the sixteenth century, make the experience more or less long term, and effective, as the Peace of religion based on law: Switzerland, the Empire, France, Transylvania, but also Lower Austria (oral declaration of the diet in favour of the Confession of Augsburg in 1568; decreed in 1571), Poland (compromise of Sandomir 1570, confederation of Warsaw in 1573), the Low Countries (Pacification of Ghent 1576, Religionsfried in 1578). Like the situation in Transylvania, where the confessional allegiances partly followed the complex ethnic mosaic of the principality, the Polish situation reveals this diversity of concrete forms of coexistence. It is at once distinct from the model of impartiality of central government incarnated by the French experiments and the territorial solutions which are characteristic of the Holy Roman Empire and Switzerland. According to the terms of the religious clause of the confederacy of Warsaw, concluded in anticipation of the election of Henri of Valois to the crown, he could forbid in advance any attempts at Catholic repressive measures. The Polish nobility (half of which had converted to Protestantism, including a large proportion of the most important) benefited from such religious freedom, that proved to be its most lasting and important attribute.[25] But the outline of this individual freedom – specific to this republic of nobles that made up Poland – remained ambiguous. The text of the confederacy does not indicate which confessions are included in the agreement; it remains elusive on the question of a possible *ius reformandi* conceded to the lords over their subjects; it could have been applied to the royal cities, but the king and the clergy refused them the benefices.[26] Despite these uncertainties and while the Counter-Reformation began to upset the balance of power at the expense of Protestantism, the agreements made at the beginning of the 1570s temporarily protected a situation of complex confessional pluralism in Poland where Catholics rubbed shoulders with Lutherans in the big cities and the Duchy of Prussia, Calvinists in Little Poland and Lithuania, protected by great magnates such as Nicolas Radziwill,

24 Barta *et al.* (eds.), *Kurze Geschichte Siebenbürgens*, p. 292.
25 Tazbir, *Geschichte der polnische Toleranz*, pp. 52–67.
26 Müller, 'Protestant confessionalisation'.

Bohemian Brethren, mainly in Greater Poland, Greek Orthodox defended by the Prince Konstanty Ostrogski, and Jews. Regardless of the legal dispositions and the definitions of religion and faith that they embraced, these Peaces all shared in common the task of permanently changing the confessional map of Europe: far from the schematic representations given by textbooks and atlases, the latter was characterized by the multiplicity of the situations of coexistence and local confrontations. While travelling through Augsburg in the 1580s, Montaigne was surprised by the banality of relations between confessions in the city and even within families: 'weddings between Catholics and Lutherans are common . . . there are thousands of such weddings: our host was Catholic and his wife Lutheran'. With polemical intentions and avowed exaggeration, Carlo Carafa also noted the complexity of the religious situation in the small town of Austerlitz, 'so full of heretics of different stripes and so many sects, that it is said that in the same house, the father is of one faith and the son of another, the wife has her opinion on questions of faith and her husband another'. Fifty years later, coexistence of confessions in several communities of Dauphine or the Drôme still attracted the attention of astonished and scandalized chroniclers, pastoral visitors, and royal officers: at Besse, for example, the pastoral visitor was indignant at the fact that the priest, 'plays bowls with them [the Protestants], often eats in their company, [is] very friendly with the minister'.[27]

Coexist, cohabit, and collaborate

If it is impossible to render through cartography the new complexity of the religious situation in sixteenth-century Europe, because of documentary uncertainties, sudden changes of the status of minorities, ambiguous cases of official prohibition that went hand-in-hand with unofficial toleration, judicial cover-ups and fictions, it remains true that these numerous cases of local coexistence generally raise identical problems. Observance or the abolition of Catholic feast days and holidays, competition for burial sites and buildings reserved for worship, the taking-up of urban space by processions, funerals or images at street corners, on squares or at the city gates, membership of militias or city councils, were among the many occasions for frictions, and even violence between confessions. Could the Protestants, for example, have tolerated the unfolding of Catholic processions in cities with their singing, their banners, their images, and reliquaries? Should they themselves have accepted the need

27 Dompnier, Le venin de l'hérésie, p. 140.

to decorate the front of their houses along the processional path, or let the Catholics do it for them, even if they disapproved of this practice? Should they have closed their shops and workshops on the Roman Church's feast days, and participated, by default, in the devotions of their adversaries? But was not to refuse to do so the cause of public scandals, breaking the peace, and unlawful competition at the expense of the Catholic artisans and merchants? Did refusal not risk new quarrels? Can Catholics in turn have imposed their specific calendar on the Protestants and claimed the religious use of the theoretically common urban space? Legislation obliging shops to close on feast days was imposed on all the inhabitants regardless of their confession by the Catholic authorities, but in the space of a few months in 1562–3 in Lyon, the rule gave way to compulsory opening decreed by the new Protestant magistrate who took power at the outset of the first war of religion.

The concrete stakes of confessional coexistence only marginally cross the grand doctrinal and ecclesiological questions that were debated in the religious colloquies and in the treatises on toleration. And in order to bring seeming simple practical answers to these problems, the actors and partisans of peace had to find new arrangements, offer new compromises and to that effect mobilize theoretical resources that were far from those expressed by partisans of concord or tolerance. The very texts of the Peaces of religion, like those of the concrete measures that accompany them locally, reflect a different use of categories and principles of justification. The preambles of the French edicts of pacification, for example, invoke 'peace and union', 'public rest', or the 'conservation of the kingdom', and mostly 'friendship' between the king's subjects,[28] and the same vocabulary is found in the recess of 1555 (article 14: 'we ordain that each has regarding the other the spirit of true friendship and Christian love') or in the letter of majesty conceded in 1609 by Rudolph II to the Estates of Bohemia ('every person has to entertain good friendship').

But the most blatant proof that the concrete forms of coexistence in sixteenth-century Europe were much more organized, for the contemporaries themselves, around the idea of *amicitia* rather than tolerance or concord, and mostly on the basis of practical resources and concrete procedures known to the urban elite, local lawyers, merchants, and artisans, is provided by the existence of many local agreements between members of different confessions to solve any conflicts between them, or to prevent violence from erupting. These pacts of genuine friendship, which can be traced in communal deliberations and judicial archives, celebrated the civic ideals of friendship, of good

28 Carbonnier-Burkardt, 'Les préambules des édits de pacification'.

neighbourhood and fraternity as antidotes to the wars of religion and the use of force. The Catholics and Protestants of the village of Zizers in the Grisons, for example, pledged in 1612 to 'live honourably as neighbours and fellow citizens';[29] those of Montélimar in the Rhone valley promised in 1567 to be 'in peace, friendship and perpetual fraternity as true citizens of one city should behave, keeping and defending each other'.[30] Surprisingly frequently such agreements can be found in many French localities during the 1560s and 1570s – a complete count has yet to be done.[31] From the 1560s it was no longer possible to envisage the collective as a community of salvation, united by the same faith and the same rituals, so the civic values and the urban ideals were revived and served as a new basis for the organization of life in common: proof can be found in different iconographic programmes such as the Cologne City Hall or in an engraving by the ES master glorifying the *Res Publica* and equitable peace at Nuremberg, or else in the resurgence of procedures of friendly arbitration that took root in the tradition of the 'peacers' or 'appeasers' at the end of the Middle Ages, namely those notables of good will that mediated between clans and factions. For example, in Lyon in 1561, the municipal magistrate organized on several occasions, in the face of Calvinist proselytizing, assemblies of notables in order to find a *modus vivendi* in the city. On these occasions, the council invited both sides to be moderate and condemned verbal violence.

The importance of these pacts of friendship and what they tell us about the mobilization of extremely varied resources by the artisans of religious coexistence pose questions which have been neglected by the historiography until now – for example the non-St Bartholomew's Day Massacre, namely the absence of massacres or exceptional violence against Protestants in many cities of the kingdom that were nonetheless confessionally mixed in 1572 – and, more generally on the practices of Peace and not only the ideas that surround it.

It is not easy to describe these practices, however, given how much they depended on the local balance of power, institutions, civic traditions and the social make-up of the city or the village and the degree of autonomy it enjoyed from central government. But this does not prevent us noticing a number of recurrent tracks that can be found couched in almost the same terms

29 Head, 'Religious coexistence and confessional conflict'.
30 Christin, 'Peace must come from us'.
31 These treatises are well documented for Nyons, Montélimar, Annonay, Orange, Vienne, Saint-Laurent-des-Arbres, Saint-Affrique, Caen, Le Vigan, Tulette, Luçon, not counting more ambiguous cases such as Lyon.

in the zones of confessional mix and contact. The concrete apportioning of places of worship and burial was very often the main concern of the religious communities involved and, by the same token, one of the most frequent occasions for friction and conflict. Because as soon as the inhabitants of one area – and not only travellers or mobilized soldiers who raised problems of their own – and different confessions coexisted for any length of time, it was necessary to find solutions for the celebration of worship and for the burial of the dead. Otherwise there was a danger of forcing the minority underground, sometimes at the cost of openly contradicting the official Peace treaties, that forbade the use of constraint and intervention in the affairs of the confessions, at the risk of creating fresh excuses for violence to erupt. This work of peace, which involved the local authorities, the clergy and the faithful of rival churches, and sometimes the agents of central government (royal officers, imperial commissioners, or delegates from sovereign cantons), was always fragile. It was relentlessly questioned by radical groups, instigating wars, or the transformation of the religious context, notably the Counter-Reformation, and led to very varied outcomes. At one end, there was the official rule against minorities celebrating their cult or burying their dead, with only one potential concession being made to those who wanted to go to mass or communicate outside the cities (like the Parisian Protestants who had to travel to Charenton at the beginning of the seventeenth century). There was also the organization of the places of worship theoretically clandestine, but often known to all, like the Schuilkerk of the Catholics of Leiden or Amsterdam.[32] At the other end, there was the simple sharing of the buildings, both established or new: by virtue of the Edict of Amboise of 1563, Lyon Protestants were authorized to build two temples within the city, one of which was the famous Paradis of which two precise illustrations remain; similarly in the Vateline, the Grisons leagues decreed, in 1557, that 'where there are two churches, one must be given to the pastor, the other to the priest'.[33] The urban landscape at Augsburg was characterized after 1555 by the misleading proximity of Catholic and Lutheran places of worship.[34] Between the two was the whole range of partial solutions and unequal accommodations: witness the exercise of *simultaneum*, namely the organization of both cults in the same building at the cost of sometimes important architectural modifications, to

---

32 Kaplan, 'Fictions of privacy'.
33 Head, 'Religious coexistence and confessional conflict'; the same author gives examples of *simultaneum* for Thurgau in a forthcoming article 'Fragmented dominion, fragmented churches: the institutionalization of the Landfrieden in the Thurgau, 1531–1660'.
34 Warmbrunn, *Zwei Konfessionen in einer Stadt*.

the development of seignorial chapels and suburban temples. There was also the Protestant occupation of buildings that were theoretically still Catholic, or the celebration of mass within the walls of a totally isolated monastery in the middle of a Lutheran city, as in Strasbourg.

The conflicts, the negotiations, and the accommodations regarding places of worship, however, only generated part of the conflict between confessions about the symbolic use of space. It is therefore necessary to remember the importance of tensions that surrounded the question of burial and funeral marches or processions. These tensions arose because rival confessions tried to keep for themselves these particular forms of public expressions of faith that translated into the appropriation of territory, the rogation of sacralizing space, the visible delimitation of the community of believers.[35] In many Protestant-controlled areas the processions, and particularly that of Corpus Christi, which associated religious definition of the community with the eucharistic miracle, were forbidden:[36] in Augsburg, for example, from 1555 to 1606, or again in La Rochelle after the Edict of Nantes. In 1599, the magistrate of La Rochelle agreed to concede the question of the mass and to authorize it anew, but he obstinately refused to let the Catholics of the city restart their processions. Similarly, it is possible to note in many Catholic territories and cities the increase in disruption of Protestant funerals: in 1563, for example, the Protestants of Mâcon petitioned the governor Gaspard de Saulx-Tavannes for a place 'where they can bring and bury the dead in all safety, peace, and modesty', in keeping with the Edict of Amboise. Tavannes conceded and gave them the place called Saint-Etienne, outside the walls, on condition that they did not meet in a group of more than eight people at a time, that they abstained from singing and from sermons, and that they made do with burials 'at daybreak'. In France, the story of the pacifications is often mixed with that of the invention, in law but also in the practice of local actors, of compromise on these at once banal and controversial, simple, and inextricable questions: to authorize the Catholics to organize their processions without forcing the Protestants to join them, even passively; to let the Protestants bury their dead without upsetting Catholic customs and their concern for being buried in consecrated and possibly *ad sanctos* ground, in the church, close to the relics. But it is precisely their nature of compromise, of provisional agreements that were always at the mercy of a sudden change in the balance of power, that rendered confessional coexistence in the sixteenth century so fragile in the face of the deepening of the confessional disagreements

---

35 Koslofsky, *The reformation of the dead*; and Luria, 'Separated by death?'
36 Duffy, *The stripping of the altars*, particularly pp. 43–4.

and the advent of the Counter-Reformation. Not only its partisans' critics grew in importance, notably regarding the question of whether Christian subjects or their prince were really bound by agreements concluded with heretics,[37] that directly jeopardized the contractual dimension of many pacifications, but the institutional mechanisms that guaranteed that they ran smoothly became rusty. So, for example, in the Empire, at the end of the century, the Reichskammergericht was no longer in a position to impose an outside ruling on confessional parties that were strengthened and fought each other within it.[38] The boundless energy of some religious orders that emerged from the Catholic Reformation (Jesuits, Capuchins, and Theatines), the outpouring of controversy, the resort to violence by princes or monarchs who could not renounce the idea that religious unity within their borders was the mark of power, also greatly contributed to this process of erosion of the Peaces: in the mixed canton of Appenzell, for example, the arrival of the Capuchins in 1586 and the Catholic magistrates' concern for bringing about an alliance with Spain precipitated the schism in 1588 between Inner Rhodes (Catholics) and Outer Rhodes (Protestants).[39] In Styria as well, the policy of Catholic reform engaged in by the archdukes brutally questioned the balance that had been reached between confessions: the settling of the Jesuits in Graz in 1573 and building of their college and university in the following decade, and the expulsion of the Protestant pastors from the city. From a tool of peace-making, the *ius reformandi* had become a weapon of aggression.

It is easy to understand why it is necessary to couple the history of ideas or Begriffsgeschichte, always tempted by *a posteriori* conclusions, with a true social history and anthropology of the work of peace, of the daily confrontation and negotiation between Christians and local magistrates and not only between theologians and pious humanists. It is not only that thereby one is given the means to understand the institutional means and the moral, psychological, and political dispositions that prevented the confessional rift from becoming all-out war, abolishing all contact with neighbours, the running of the state, or commerce, but that the true measure of the exchanges between confessions in the sixteenth century can be taken. In France, for example, dozens of cities and towns experienced parity from 1563 onwards and instigated mixed consulates, shared between Catholics and Calvinists: Caen, Gap, Montélimar and even Lyon. And new institutions were explicitly created with

37 For a discussion of the maxim 'Nullam haereticis esse fidem servandam', see Lecler.
38 Heckel, 'Die Reformationsprozesse im Spannungfeld des Reichskirchensystems'.
39 *Appenzeller Geschichte*, vol. 1, *Das ungeteilte Land*, pp. 479 ff., and Fischer (ed.), *Appenzeller Land*, pp. 24 ff.

the intention that religious adversaries would work together at their centre, like the academy of poetry and music that Jean-Antoine de Bäif created in 1570 and wanted to participate in a 'festive creation of peace'.[40]

One should perhaps celebrate the absence of the word 'toleration' in the writings of the sixteenth century. Against a retrospective rewriting of history for the sixteenth and seventeenth centuries of concepts and representations that only saw the light with Hoen, Bayle, or Locke, and particularly the Enlightenment, this absence is an invitation to ponder the importance and singularity of the practices of coexistence and to bring out the true mechanisms for moving out of the wars of religion: the recognition of dissidence in law and the daily work of living together.

40 Jouanna (ed.), *Histoire et dictionnaire*, pp. 140 and 188–9.

18

Western Christianity and Eastern Orthodoxy

MIKHAIL V. DMITRIEV

Throughout the Middle Ages, the relationships between Western and Eastern Christianity were characterized by two tendencies. On the one hand, there was estrangement, while on the other hand, there were the links between Rome and the Eastern churches, as well as between Catholics and Orthodox people in all European countries, that were never interrupted and sometimes even intensified. Both tendencies were reflected in the history of the Florentine Union (1438–9), which was the last attempt in the Middle Ages to overcome the estrangement. However, the rejection of the Florentine Union in Orthodox societies showed that the development of confessional self-consciousness both in the West and in the East had increased the distance between the two churches and their cultures. Were these growing tendencies towards estrangement replaced by others between 1500 and 1660? There are numerous studies of the subject: the main points of contact between Western and Eastern Christianity in the sixteenth and early seventeenth centuries are more or less clearly described, although there remains much that has not been studied or is open to dispute. This chapter provides a brief overview of how the relations between Rome and the Orthodox East developed in this period, how the dialogue between Catholicism and Orthodoxy in Eastern Europe and in the Balkans continued, traces the relationship between Protestants and the Orthodox, and studies the interaction between Eastern and Western Christianity in the 'epoch of confessions'.

Papacy, Polish Catholicism and Orthodoxy in the east of Europe

The Florentine Union did not lead to a rapprochement between Catholicism and Orthodoxy. The links between the Orthodox churches and Rome weakened noticeably during the century following 1438–9, but began to be restored in the mid-sixteenth century after France had obtained the right to establish a Protectorate over the Catholics of the Ottoman Empire (in 1535). Later, in 1583, the Jesuits arrived in Constantinople, followed by other orders and congregations.

Greek 'colonies' under the rule of Italian states played a very important role in the interaction between Catholicism and Orthodoxy. In the fifteenth century, Greeks of Cyprus, Chios, the Ionic Islands, and Crete became subjects of the Venetian state, and the centre of Greek studies moved to the University of Padua. In 1463, the first chair of Greek 'philology' was established for Demetrius Chalcocondylis in Padua. Twenty Greek professors taught there between 1572 and 1600.[1] After 1499, many Greek writings were published in Venice and these considerably influenced the development of Western scientific thought.

Venetian laws guaranteed religious freedom for the Greeks,[2] and Rome was unable to interfere in their activities. Though conversions to Catholicism did occur, in general the relations between the Orthodox and Catholics in the Greek Islands under Venetian rule remained quiet. There were advocates of church union among the Italian Greeks. However, during the periods of anti-Lutheran campaigns the Inquisition tried a number of Greeks as schismatics.[3] In 1564, a papal bull prohibited academics from taking a degree without first professing their Catholic faith. As a result, a well-known advocate of union, M. Margunius,[4] chose to decline his doctoral degree.[5] On the other hand, some leaders of the Greek community argued for abstention from any kind of critique of Catholicism, preferring instead to prepare for a new 'Crusade' against the Ottoman Empire.[6]

In the mid-sixteenth century, the papal curia established contacts with Patriarch Dionysius II of Constantinople, and, later, with Patriarch Metrophanes. A number of patriarchs and prelates seemed to favour the idea of rapprochement with Rome. At the same time, relations with Christians of the Middle East were re-established. In 1553, Pope Julius III recognized Patriarch John Sulaqa of Chaldea, but the latter was obliged to accept the Catholic Creed, which was based on the decrees of the Florentine Council, although the concessions concerning *filioque*, purgatory, and the pope's supremacy in the East that had been made to accommodate Greeks were not included in its text. The curia followed the same lead in contacts with Jacobite Patriarch Ignatius.[7] A few sporadic contacts with the Georgian Church and Ethiopian Christians also took place.

---

1 Sherrard, *The Greek East and the Latin West*, p. 175.
2 Fedalto, *Ricerche storiche sulla posizione giuridica.*   3 *Ibid.*, pp. 86–93.
4 Fedalto, *Massimo Margunio.*   5 Fedalto, *Ricerche storiche sulla posizione giuridica*, p. 89.
6 Runciman, *The great church in captivity*, p. 229.
7 Vries, *Rom und die Patriarchate des Ostens*, pp. 306–7.

The Roman policy towards all these 'schismatics' was shaped by certain imperatives predetermined by Tridentine decrees and by Catholic Reform in general.[8] Pope Pius IV annulled the right of Greeks under Roman jurisdiction to keep non-Latin rites. One of the important aspects of this policy was missionary expansion to the Orthodox East. A 'Greek congregation' was founded in 1573 in Rome[9] and four years later the 'Greek College' was established to educate missionaries. The Roman Catechism was translated into Greek, and 12,000 copies were sent to the Levant in 1576.[10] In 1577, a treatise on the Union of Florence, which was falsely attributed to Gennadius Scholarius, was published in Greek, together with Florentine decrees and a special epistle to the Orthodox.[11]

Initially, all efforts at church union were aimed at Patriarch Jeremiah of Constantinople. The known contacts of the patriarch with Protestants were followed by almost simultaneous attempts of the Roman curia to strengthen its influence in Constantinople. In 1575, a group of Dominicans, Franciscans, and Jesuits was sent to Constantinople. Contact with Jeremiah was established, and the patriarch approved the foundation of the Greek college in Rome and sent two of his nephews there.

In the late 1570s and early 1580s it was thought that a union with the Russian Orthodox Church was possible. The Jesuit Antonio Possevino explored the possibility during his mission to Poland and Russia at the end of the Livonian War.[12] Possevino concluded that a 'universal union' was impossible, and proposed to establish connections with the Orthodox world in other ways and to attempt union with the Kievan Metropolitan see. Projects of church union with the Moscow Patriarchate reappeared during the years of dynastic crisis in Moscow and Polish intervention (1604–13), but they proved to be unrealistic. During the first half of the seventeenth century the attitude of Russian clergymen to Rome and Catholicism was, in general, openly hostile.[13] However, relations between Catholics and Greeks and other

---

8 Heyberger, *Les chrétiens*; Heyberger, 'Réforme catholique', pp. 292–8; Peri, 'Chiesa latina', pp. 271–469; Peri, 'La lettura del Concilio di Firenze', pp. 593–611; Peri, 'Berestei͏̈ska uniia u rims'komu bachenni'. In B. Gudziak (ed.), *Istorichnii kontekst, ukladennia berestei͏̈skoi unii i pershe pounïine pokolinnia* (Lviv, n.d.), pp. 7–25.

9 Peri, 'La congregazione dei Greci', pp. 129–256.

10 Chodynicki, *Kościół prawosławny a Rzeczpospolita Polska*, p. 204.

11 Peri, *Ricerche sull'editio princeps*, pp. 78–101 ('La stampa degli atti greci di Firenze ed il programma pontificio; l'*editio princeps* del 1577 come strumento per l'unione').

12 On Possevino, see Pierling, *Antonio Possevino*; Pierling, *La Russie et le Saint-Siège*, vol. 2, pp. 48–237; Polcin, *Une tentative d'Union au XVIe siècle*.

13 T. A. Oparina, *Ivan Nasedka i polemicheskoe bogoslovie Kievskoi͏̈ mitropolii* (Novosibirsk: Nauka, 1988).

Orthodox communities in the Mediterranean, Middle East, and the Balkans developed differently.

Under Pope Gregory XIII (1572–85) the Greeks who were united with Rome received a special Creed where *filioque*, purgatory, and transubstantiation were included, and the autonomy of patriarchs within a united church was not stated. Sixtus V went further to subject Orthodox Christians to Roman supremacy. In a letter to Gabriel, the Coptic Patriarch, he wrote: 'You have to understand that the Roman Church judges all, but cannot be judged by anybody; she has a power of both swords and delegates her right to judge to others'. By accepting the union the patriarch would gain in dignity, 'for through the subjecting itself to the Roman Church it would not be diminished but, on the contrary, would be increased'.[14]

In 1622, the Congregatio Propagandae Fidei was founded in Rome. Its aim was not only to disseminate Catholic doctrine but also to establish and develop connections with those Eastern churches which recognized Roman supremacy. Interaction between Catholics and the Orthodox was most intense in the Balkans and in the Danube region. The relationship between these confessions in Dalmatia was particularly tense as the major part of the province, which housed an influential Greek Orthodox community, was governed from Venice. An Orthodox archbishopric was founded there in the second half of the sixteenth century. In 1577 in Constantinople, Gabriel Severus was ordained as Archbishop of Philadelphia and was sent to Lidia. He kept the title, but moved to Venice where he became the leader of a local Greek community. To make things more complicated, a part of the Orthodox population in continental regions of Dalmatia were under the jurisdiction of Serbian or Bosnian bishops. This situation led to continuous tension between the Orthodox and Catholics, which intensified when Franciscans began their missionary campaign and made converts among the Orthodox population of Dalmatia.[15] On the other hand, in Ottoman territories some Catholics converted to the Orthodox faith.[16]

In 1611, a bishop of the Serbian enclave in Croatia declared his subjection to the see of Rome; he went to Rome, signed a formula of the Catholic Creed and was ordained as a bishop for the second time. This initiative, however, did not gain support from the clergy and the laity of his diocese.[17] In Transcarpathia

---

14 Cited as in Przekop, *Rzym-Konstantynopol*, p. 83.
15 Milash, *Pravoslavna Dalmatsiia*, pp. 244–8.
16 Draganovic, 'Massenübertritte von Katholiken zur "Orthodoxie"', pp. 181–232.
17 Vries, *Rom und der Patriarchate des Ostens*, pp. 108–9.

(at that time part of a province of the Hungarian Kingdom), a movement for church union began in the diocese of Mukachevo. The movement could be seen as a form of resistance against forced conversions of the Orthodox undertaken jointly by Count George Druget, an early seventeenth-century Catholic convert from Calvinism, Athanasius Krupetsky, a Uniat bishop of Peremyshl', and Jesuit missionaries in Mukachevo. Their attempt resulted in bitter tension, and the union did not take place. During the 1630s and 1640s Vasily Tarasovich, Bishop of Mukachevo, favoured the idea of union. It led to conflict with the Calvinist prince of Transylvania, G. Rakoczi, who was a lay patron of Mukachevo. Tarasovich relied on support from Vienna and declared his acceptance of the union. As a result of this action he could not return to Mukachevo. His successor, Parpheny Petrovich, led a pro-union campaign and secretly recognized Roman jurisdiction. In 1651, he became Bishop of Mukachevo and preached the union in his diocese, but initially it was recognized only in Slovakia. The relationship between Catholics and the Orthodox in the Balkans[18] was not limited to attempts at church union. Franciscan and Jesuit missionaries worked in all the Balkan regions and influenced the development of vernacular languages.

In 1601, a Catholic bishopric of Sofia was established; in 1642, it became an archbishopric. In the first half of the seventeenth century, four archbishops of Ochrid (Parphiry Paleologos, Athanasios, Avrahamy, and Melethy) were told to support the union with Rome secretly.[19]

In Chiprovtsy, a school for Catholic missionaries was founded where students were taught philosophy, logic, theology, and the 'Illiric' language. In the 1660s to 1680s, the school had between 100 and 120 students, and some of them continued their education in Italy.[20]

A Catholic diocese had existed in Bosnia since the twelfth century, and in the mid-fifteenth century up to 20 per cent of its population was Catholic. In the sixteenth and seventeenth centuries, Franciscan missionaries succeeded in converting a substantial number of Bosnians to Catholicism.[21]

Between 1500 and 1650, Serbian Orthodoxy demonstrated signs of renewal followed by the intensification of contacts not only with Russia but also with Catholics, particularly under Patriarch Iovan Quantul (1592–1614). The

---

18 Bogovic, *Katolicka crkva*; Radonih, *Shtamparije i shkole*; Radonih, *Rimska kuriya*; Simrak, *De relationibus*; Simrak, *Crkevna uniija*; Milev, *Katolishkata propaganda*; Stanimirov, *Politicheskata deïnost*.

19 Snegarov, *Istoriia na Okhridskata*, pp. 95–105.

20 N. Genchev, *Blgarskata kultura XV–XIX v.* (Sofia, 1988), pp. 131–3.

21 Milash, *Pravoslavna Dalmatsiia*, p. 233.

contacts with the West continued under the patriarchs Paysios (1614–1647), Gabriel Raic (1648–1655), and Maxim (1655–1674), who supported contacts with Catholic missionaries.[22]

The most important event in the relationship between Rome and the Orthodox East in the late sixteenth to early seventeenth centuries was the Union of Kiev Metropolitanate and the Roman curia, signed in 1595 in Rome and proclaimed in 1596 at the Council of Orthodox and Catholic clergy at Brest. The union resulted from the religious policy of the Polish state or Roman curia in eastern Europe on the one hand, and, on the other, from internal conflicts in the Orthodox Church in Ukraine and Belarus. In the sixteenth century the Polish rulers did not force Kievans to recognize the Union of Florence. In 1500–70, the policy of the state towards the Orthodox was characterized by unprecedented toleration.[23] In 1573, the Polish parliament (sejm) recognized the freedom of religious belief in Poland. It must be noted, however, that the policy of the Polish state towards the Orthodox did not always coincide with that of the Catholic Church. In the late fifteenth to the early sixteenth centuries the attempts of the Orthodox to establish a close connection with Rome faced opposition from the Polish Catholic hierarchy, who saw only one way of uniting the two churches: conversion. A treatise written by a Cracovian theologian, Jan Sakran,[24] known for its hostility towards Orthodoxy, demonstrated the hostility in Polish Catholics' attitudes towards the Orthodox people. This hostility showed itself in later Polish Catholic writings and documents where Orthodox churches were called 'synagogues', and the Orthodox were denied the name of Christians. Until 1560, the Polish Catholic hierarchy insisted on rebaptizing Orthodox converts.[25]

A well-known treatise by Peter Skarga, SJ, On the Unity of God's Church under One Shepherd (1577),[26] reflected the attitude of the Catholic clergy in general. Skarga understood union as an unconditional subjugation of the Orthodox Church to Rome. The idea of union (i.e., a union as an 'agreement') was not considered by the Catholic missionaries in Orthodox territories. They aimed at

---

22 Slijepchevih, Istorija srpske, pp. 320–95.
23 V. Bednov, Pravoslavnaia cerkov' v Polshe i Litve po Volumina Legum (Ekaterinoslav, 1908); Chodynicki, Kościół prawosławny a Rzeczpospolita Polska; Lapinski, Zygmunt Stary; Vodoff, 'La tolérance religieuse'.
24 Published in Lasicki, De Russorum, Moscovitarum et Tartarorum religione, pp. 184–98. See also Krajcar, 'A report on the Ruthenians'.
25 Sawicki, 'Die "Rebaptizatio Ruthenorum"', pp. 142–6; Przekop, 'Die "Rebaptizatio Ruthenorum"'.
26 P. Skarga, O iednosci kościóła Bozego pod iednym pasterzem. Russkaia istoricheskaia biblioteka, 7 (St Petersburg, 1882) (= Pamiatniki polemicheskoï literatury v Zapadnoï Rusi, 2), cols. 223–526.

the establishment of Roman jurisdiction over new regions and the conversion of 'schismatics'. The final goal was not merely Ukraine and Belarus, but Russia and beyond.

In 1569, the Jesuits founded a college in Vilnius; in 1574, another was established in Jaroslav. Stephan Bathory backed the projects of disseminating Catholicism in Russia and converting the Orthodox to the 'true faith'.[27] Although tolerant towards the Orthodox Church in Poland through necessity, he was not 'indifferent' to the Orthodox 'schism'. During his reign, missionaries were active within the Orthodox community, and Possevino's projects to preach Catholicism to Russian prisoners of war[28] were supported by the court. The same tendencies continued during the first years of Sigismund III's reign (1587–1632).

During that period, missions to the Orthodox were quite successful. Catholic schools were founded at which Orthodox youth was educated,[29] Catholic doctrine was disseminated through printed propaganda and possibly also through preaching.[30] Members of the most powerful noble and upper-class families became objects of conversion.[31] Finally, there was an attempt to introduce the Gregorian calendar among the Orthodox population.[32] It provoked resistance and revolts in L'vov, Lutsk, Vilno, and other places with mixed populations. As a result, the Polish government made concessions, and the Orthodox were permitted to use their old calendar.[33]

The 1580s saw a sharp conflict within the Orthodox Church in the Ukraine and Belarus. It was a conflict between Orthodox bishops, the Patriarch of Constantinople, and the Orthodox laity united into confraternities.[34] This

---

27 Chodynicki, *Kościół prawosławny a Rzeczpospolita Polska*, pp. 223–5.

28 *Ibid.*, pp. 225–6.

29 On Jesuit and other Catholic schools, see K. Kharlampovich, *Zapadnorusskie pravoslavnye shkoly XVI i nachala XVIIv., otnoshenie ikh k inoslavnym, religioznoe obuchenie v nikh i zaslugi ikh v dele zashchity pravoslavnoi very i tserkvi* (Kazan, 1898), pp. 1–140; A. A. Savich, *Narisi z istorii kul'turnikh rukhiv na Ukraini ta Bilorusi u XVI–XVII v.* (Kiev, 1929).

30 A particularly aggressive pamphlet was compiled by B. Herbest (*Wiary kościoła Rzymskiego wywody y greckiego niewolstwa historya dla iednosci. Russkaia istoricheskaia biblioteka*, 7 (St Petersburg, 1882) (= *Pamiatniki polemicheskoi literatury v Zapadnoi Rusi*, 2), cols. 581–600).

31 On efforts to convert the Orthodox nobility to Catholicism, see Krajcar, 'Konstantin Basil Ostrozski'; Krajcar, 'The last princes of Sluck'.

32 N. F. Sumtsov, 'Istoricheskii ocherk popytok katolikov vvesti v iuzhnuiu i zapadnuiu Rossiiu grigorianskii kalendar'', *Kievskaia starina* 5 (1888): 235–72; Plokhy, *Papstvo*, pp. 33–40; Chodynicki, *Kościół*, pp. 188–92, 245–8.

33 Plokhy, *Papstvo*, p. 34; Chodynicki, *Kościół*, pp. 189–91.

34 On the conflict between Orthodox bishops and confraternities, see A. S. Krylovskii, *Lvovskoe stavropigialnoe bratstvo (opyt tserkovno-istoricheskogo issledovaniia)* (Kiev, 1904), pp. 136–57; I. D. Isaievich, *Bratstva ta ikh rol' v rozvitku ukrainskoi kulturi XVI–XVIII st.* (Kiev,

conflict led a number of bishops to send a declaration to Rome in June 1590 on their readiness to accept Roman jurisdiction. In 1595, a delegation of Orthodox bishops left for Rome, and in December 1595 the union was proclaimed in Rome and then, in October 1596, the decision was confirmed by a synod of Ruthenian clergy in Brest. The paradox of the Brest Union is that it resulted from the sincere aspirations of both the Catholic and Orthodox churches to overcome the schism and to combine efforts in reforming Christian culture and deepening Christianization. However, after the promulgation of the Church Union, a religious war broke out in the Ukraine and Belarus. In 1623 Jozafat Kuncewicz, the Uniate archbishop of Polock, was murdered in Vitebsk by an Orthodox mob. Leaders of the Orthodox community were executed and the city lost its liberties as a punishment.[35] The confrontation culminated in the Twenty Years' War (1648–67) between Poland and the Cossacks, who were backed by large sections of the population in both the Ukraine and Belarus.[36] Many Uniate clergy and followers were massacred by the Cossacks; reprisals by the Catholics and Uniates followed.

This violence ran contrary to the generally peaceful relationship between Catholics and Orthodox Christians in the sixteenth century. In seeking to explain the religious wars in eastern Europe, some historians have blamed the Orthodox clergy; others have looked for national motives behind religious strife and clashes; still others focus on the mistakes and miscalculations of the Polish government and the Roman see. In this context, the following questions are significant: how was the Union concluded in 1595/6 understood by the Roman and the Orthodox clergy? How significant were differences in comprehending church reunification?

From documents preceding the union, and stemming from Orthodox and Catholic circles between 1590 and 1595, we can reconstruct their views. First, the union was understood as a shift of supreme authority over the Kievan Metropolitanate from Constantinople to Rome – with no other changes in doctrine, institutions, and liturgical practices of the Orthodox Church.

1966); Isaievich, 'Between Eastern tradition and influences from the West'; Gudziak, *Crisis and reform*, pp. 148–67, 196–207; Dmitriev, *Mezhdu Rimom i Tsargradom*, pp. 92–132; Dmitriev, 'Les confréries de Ruthénie', pp. 208–20; S. S. Lukashova, *Miriane i cerkov': religioznye bratstva Kievskoï mitropolii v kontse XVI veka* (Moscow: Institut slavianovedeniia, 2006).

35 Zhukovich, *Seĭmovaia bor'ba ... (s 1609 g.)*, part 4, pp. 69–104; E. A. Vernikovskaia, 'Vitebskoe vosstanie 12 noiabria 1623 g.'. In *Slavianskiĭ almanakh 2001* (Moscow: Indrik, 2002), pp. 108–32.

36 For a recent overview, see Plokhy, *The Cossacks and religion*. See also Praszko, *De Ecclesia Ruthena*; T. Iakovleva, *Getmanshchina v drugiĭ polovini 50-kh rokiv XVII stolittia. Prichiny i pochatok Ruiny* (Kiev: Osnovi, 1998); Platania, 'Politica e religione'.

Basically, the union amounted to the replacement of patriarchs by popes and the relationship between Kiev and Rome would have been identical to that between Kiev and Constantinople. Second, the preservation of all doctrinal traditions, customs, rituals, and institutions was of primary importance for those who initiated and supported the union. Third, the union was not seen as an unconditional submission of the Kievan church to the popes. Conditions of union had to be negotiated and approved by the Orthodox Church, preferably by a special synod (*sobor*). In exchange for submission to Rome, the Orthodox clergy claimed assistance from the Polish state in strengthening the positions of the Orthodox Church in Ukraine–Belarus and sought guarantees of the rights and privileges of the Ruthenian clergy. The desires and claims of the Orthodox clergy found their most coherent and complete expression in thirty-two articles signed by all bishops and sent to Rome in 1595.[37] First, the Ruthenian bishops wanted the preservation of all ancient Orthodox traditions in rituals, in doctrine, and in church organization. Second, a number of measures aimed to strengthen the position of the Orthodox clergy; the Ruthenian clergy after the union were to be given the same rights and privileges as the Catholic clergy. Third, the authority of the Ruthenian clergy within the Orthodox Church was to be strengthened by royal decrees. The bishops wanted their authority asserted against local lay patrons, brotherhoods, and the laity in general. The union was viewed as a means of carrying out internal reforms in the Orthodox Church. Fourth, there were provisions to stop the Latinization of Orthodox society: in particular the Uniates were forbidden to convert to Catholicism (art. 15), and excommunications in the Orthodox Church were valid in Catholic areas as well (art. 30). Finally, the metropolitan was to be chosen from among four candidates suggested by the *sobor*, the synod (art. 10), and confirmed by the pope; the papal blessing, in turn, required confirmation by two Orthodox bishops (art. 11). However, if the new metropolitan was already ordained as bishop prior to his election, there was no need for papal approval.

Rome appointed a commission to study the articles. Its reaction to the 32 articles was cool. As the Dominican Saragosa, who was one of the committee members, put it: to be received in the Holy Church is a deed indispensable for salvation; therefore entering the church must be disinterested and unconditional.[38] The Ruthenian bishops were welcomed in Rome, but neither Pope

---

37 *Artykuly na które.*
38 'Nel primo, è necessario che si conformino omninemente con la determinatione della Chiesa Latina, e quanto alla sostanza, et quanto alla forma delle parole, non concernendo questo punto riti o ceremonie, nelle quali sarebbe tolerabile qualche alteratione, ma l'essenza della fede' (*Documenta Unionis Berestensis*, no. 37, p. 194).

Clement VIII nor Vatican officials had talked to Potij and Terleckij about conditions for a union. On 23 December 1595 the Ruthenians signed an act of obedience to Rome recognizing not only the supreme authority of pontiffs but also all things Tridentine. In 1596, the metropolitan was given the right to consecrate bishops, on condition of subsequent papal approval. Papal documents reveal that the union was comprehended by the Catholic side as an act of repentance, conversion, and unconditional recognition of papal authority by schismatics. Especially telling are the formulas used in the sixteen letters sent by Pope Clement VIII to Poland, which used the words 'conversion' and 'heresy'.

After the Ruthenian delegation departed for Rome, the Polish king proclaimed his support for the union. Meanwhile, an Orthodox anti-union movement appeared. When the union was declared in Brest in October 1596 two councils – the Orthodox and the pro-union – confronted one another and issued excommunications.

The events of 1595–6 signified the beginning of religious conflict in Ukraine and Belarus. Advocates and opponents of the union faced each other at the *sejm* sessions and the Sejmiks, at law courts, in towns and cities, in parishes and monasteries. The Greek hierarchy (including the Patriarch of Constantinople) played an increasingly important role in the conflict between the Orthodox and the Uniats. In 1620, the Patriarch of Jerusalem, Theophan, arrived in the Ukraine and secretly ordained new Orthodox bishops and the metropolitan. In 1634–5, King Vladislav IV and the Sejm had to recognize this new hierarchy, though Rome refused to accept it. Thus every Ukrainian and Belarusan diocese had two bishops: the Orthodox and the Greek Catholic (Uniat) ones.

With mounting religious and social tension in the Ukraine and Belarus, many local nobles supported the Orthodox Church and 'Greek religion'. In the 1620s, the anti-union movement gained the support of the Cossacks. The crisis climaxed in 1648, during the Cossack uprising led by Bohdan Khmelnytsky. Foreign visitors to the Ukraine thought that 'Cossacks fought the Poles for their faith'. The rebels identified their enemies unambiguously with the alien non-Orthodox (i.e., Catholics or Jews), and they themselves with the Orthodox. The Uniat clergy took a pro-Polish position. Uniats were seen as 'Poles', that is, Catholics, and were persecuted by rebellious Cossacks and their allies.

The rebels demanded the dissolution of the union and the restoration of all rights and possessions of the Orthodox Church. The union was saved mostly by the uncompromising position of Vatican diplomats.

It is important to note that during the first half of the seventeenth century some Orthodox clergymen advocated the rapprochement with Rome and with Polish Catholics, despite all the bitter division provoked by the union.[39] But these groups of clergy did not accept the conditions of union defined by the Vatican in 1596. The first-known project of the joint council of the Orthodox and the Uniats was proposed to the Sejm of 1623.[40] A commission of the Sejm invited two leaders of the Orthodox movement, Iov Boretskij and Melethius Smotritskij, to its meetings. But both flatly refused the proposition of peace. The king then sent the monk Jan Dubovich to Kiev. The Orthodox were ready to submit to the pope but wanted to remain under the immediate jurisdiction of the Patriarch of Constantinople. As for the papal primate, the Orthodox bishops were said to be ready to accept it *jure ecclesiastico* but not *jure divino*. The Catholic side rejected this project, but the search for compromise continued.

In 1626, King Sigismund III sanctioned the holding of a synod of the Uniat Church in Kobrin and invited the Orthodox clergy, though he failed to secure Rome's support. The pope and the congregation thought that a joint synod would be more harmful for the union because there could not be anything in common between Uniats and the Orthodox, just as there could be no communication between light and darkness. The Orthodox also rejected the idea of a joint council.

Nonetheless, new steps towards the rapprochement were made by both sides at the Warsaw Sejm of 1629, though the Roman curia continued to reject the initiative of the Orthodox and the Uniats. The nuncio had to forbid the Uniats to participate in the council. It was also forbidden to discuss any points of doctrine with the Orthodox.[41] Metropolitan Rutskij declared his submission to the nuncio, but the council was summoned. The Orthodox, however, did not come to L'vov; they held their council in Kiev. Thus another attempt at reconciliation failed.

After the Polish state recognized the Orthodox hierarchy in 1634–5, the latter took the initiative and suggested the creation of a Kiev Patriarchate under Roman jurisdiction.[42] In February 1636, the Roman curia formed a secret commission of three cardinals to deal with this proposal. On 11 April

39 Zhukovich, *Seïmovaia bor'ba ... (do 1609 g.)*; Zhukovich, *Seïmovaia bor'ba ... (s 1609 g.)*; M. S. Grushevskiï, *Istoriia Ukraini Rusi*, vol. 7: *Kozacki chasi do roku 1625* (Kiev Lviv, 1909; new edn Kiev, 1995), vol. 8: *Roki 1626–1650* (Kiev, 1995); Chodynicki, *Kościół*, pp. 449–512; Dziegielewski, *O tolerancje dla zdominowanych*; Plokhy, *The Cossacks and religion*.
40 Zhukovich, *Seïmovaia bor'ba ... (s 1609 g.)*, part 4, pp. 54–5. See also J. Pietrzak, *W przygaszonym blasku viktorii chocimskiej. Sejm z r. 1623* (Wrocław, 1987).
41 Shmurlo, *Rimskaia kuriia*, pp. 63–8. See also I. Khoma, 'Ideia spilnogo sinodu 1629 r.'. In I. Khoma, *Kiïvska mitropoliia v beresteiskim periodi* (Rome, 1979), pp. 77–108.
42 Shmurlo, *Rimskaia kuriia*, pp. 96–106; Plokhy, *Papstvo*, pp. 139–48.

1636, a papal nuncio in Poland was sent an instruction: he was to learn about the position of Uniats and to estimate how real were the plans of a new union. In response both Kievan metropolitan Peter Mohyla and Rutskij declared their readiness to summon a joint council of the Orthodox and Uniats. They won the support of King Wladyslaw IV, who promised the Uniat metropolitan and bishops positions in the senate.[43] Once again, the new initiative led to nothing. In the end, the curia rejected the idea of a new patriarchate and forbade Uniats to participate in a council.[44]

The king tried again to get papal permission to summon a joint council of Uniats and the Orthodox, most likely under the influence of the Cossacks' rebellions of 1637–8. This question was discussed at four meetings of the commission of the *Congregatio propagandae fidei* in June and July 1638. Finally it was decided to reject the king's demand. From his side, the nuncio Filonardi followed the congregation's decision and forbade Uniats to participate in an Orthodox council. It seems that after this the Orthodox never returned to the idea of a general council.[45] In 1644 (or in early 1645), a special envoy of Wladislaw IV, Valerian Magni, went to Rome with two projects for a new union – that of Peter Mohyla and the Orthodox magnate Adam Kisel'.[46] The Orthodox were ready to compromise on many points, but papal primacy remained a stumbling-block. This time, no one proposed the creation of a new patriarchate, yet a new union was to be proclaimed at the general council of the Orthodox and Uniats. The conditions of this proposed 'new union' were to guarantee more autonomy for the Orthodox Church than was given by the Union of Brest.[47] The *Congregatio propagandae fidei* held a meeting to discuss the proposal on 16 March 1645. The final decision was postponed for several reasons. As earlier, the union was understood as direct submission of the Orthodox Church to Rome, with conditions which were in accord with the ecclesiological principles of post-Tridentine Catholicism.

The death of Peter Mohyla changed the situation dramatically. The Orthodox Council, which gathered in April 1647 in Vilnius, proposed to start negotiations for a union on the principles that had been formulated by Peter Mohyla

43 Dziegielewski, *O tolerancje dla zdominowanych*, p. 178.
44 Shmurlo, *Rimskaia kuriia*, pp. 104–6; Plokhy, *Papstvo*, pp. 143–7.
45 Shmurlo, *Rimskaia kuriia*, pp. 254–5, note 228; Dziegielewski, *O tolerancje dla zdominowanych*, pp. 186–7.
46 Shmurlo, *Rimskaia kuriia*, pp. 108–24; Welykyi, 'Un progetto anonimo'; Zhukovskii, *Petro Mogila*, pp. 143–68; Jobert, *De Luther à Mohila*, pp. 395–400.
47 Shmurlo, *Rimskaia kuriia*, pp. 98, 101–4; Golubev, *Kievskii mitropolit*, vol. 2, pp. 138–49; Zhukovskii, *Petro Mogila*, pp. 125–43.

in his memorial. Orthodox envoys to the Sejm of May 1647 agreed that the problems of the Orthodox Church were to be dealt with by the king himself. In the second half of 1647, the king promoted intensive negotiations on a new union and the summoning of a general synod of the Orthodox and Uniats in Warsaw in July 1648. The nuncio knew about the negotiation. The major contradiction remained unsolved: the *Congregatio propagandae fidei* and the Orthodox understood the union in different ways, although the Orthodox made many concessions to accommodate Catholics.

It is important to realize that conflicts of Orthodoxy and the union in Ukraine and Belarus did not prevent the Orthodox clergy from using the pastoral experience and doctrines of the Catholic Church. Catholic influence over the religious thought of Ukraine and Belarus became particularly strong in mid-seventeenth to early eighteenth centuries, especially if one considers the activities of the Metropolitan Peter Mohyla and the Kiev Academy founded by him.[48] Later, the Ukrainian and Belarusan clergy introduced these new ideas into Russia.[49]

Reformation and the Orthodox communities of eastern and south-eastern Europe

It is known that in his fight against 'papism', Luther appealed to the experience of the Orthodox Church and the Hussites. Melanchthon and other Protestant leaders showed an interest in Orthodoxy. The most interesting and characteristic episode consists of the contacts of Jeremiah, Patriarch of Constantinople, with German Protestants.[50] A few Orthodox Greeks came to Germany and even converted to Protestantism; from their side, Protestants tried to disseminate their ideas among the Orthodox population. In the 1560s, Jean Basilikos

48 On Peter Moghila and his Academy, see Golubev, *Kievskii mitropolit*; A. Jablonowski, *Akademia Kijowsko-Mohilanska. Zarys historyczny na tle rozwoju ogólnego cywilizacji zachodniej na Rusi* (Kraków, 1899–1900); M. Korzo, 'Prawoslawne wyznanie wiary Piotra Mohyly. Kilka uwag w sprawie wplywów zachodnich na teologie kijowska XVII w.', *Odrodzenie i Reformacja w Polsce* 46 (2002): 141–9; P. Lewin, 'A select bibliography of publications on the Kiev Mohyla Academy by Polish scholars, 1966–1983', *Harvard Ukrainian Studies* 8 (June 1984), no. 1/2: 223–8; Moghila, *La confession orthodoxe*.

49 Kharlampovich, K., *Malorossiiskoe vliiane na velikorusskuiu cerkovnuiu zhizn'* (Kazan, 1914), vol. 1; Okenfuss, *The rise and fall of Latin humanism in early-modern Russia. Pagan authors, Ukrainians, and the resiliency of Muscovy* (Leiden: Brill, 1995).

50 Wendebourg, *Reformation und Orthodoxie*; G. Florovsky, 'An early ecumenical correspondence (Patriarch Jeremiah II and the Lutheran divines)'. In *World Lutheranism of today. A tribute to Anders Nygren* (Oxford, 1950), pp. 98–111; Runciman, *The great church in captivity*, pp. 248–56.

Heraclides tried to propagate Lutheranism in Moldavia aggressively, relying on the help of German Protestants.[51] Hans von Ungnad established a printing press in Urach, Germany, in order to publish books destined for the Ortho-dox population of the Balkans. Other German Protestants also tried to convert Orthodox south-eastern Europe.[52] All these attempts failed. Hungarian Calvin-ists who propagated their faith in Transylvania were more successful.[53] Later, antitrinitarians and Judaizers obtained limited success in Orthodox regions of eastern Europe.[54]

The most famous Protestant success was the secret conversion of the Patri-arch Cyril Lukaris to Calvinism. Lukaris began his church career in Lithuania and in western Ukraine, then moved to Alexandria. He established contacts with Dutch Calvinists and, in about 1613, became a crypto-Calvinist. In 1620, Lukaris became a Patriarch of Constantinople and attempted to reform the Orthodox Church. In the late 1620s to early 1630s he published his Calvinist 'Confession of Faith' in Switzerland. At that time and also later, Lukaris remained at the centre of religious and political conflicts; several times he was deposed from the patriarchal see, and he was executed in 1638 on the sultan's order. His religious views have been repeatedly refuted by Orthodox councils.

Information on the Reformation first appeared in Russian texts in the 1550s.[55] In 1552, the Danish King Christian responded to the request from the Russian government to help with their printing process in Moscow by sending a Protes-tant missionary, Hans Missinheim. Later, a number of Protestants served Ivan the Terrible. During the 1550s and 1560s, a Protestant district was formed in Moscow, and later in other Russian cities too. The Russian Protestant com-munity had difficult times but in general did not face persecution[56] and num-bered about 30,000 by the 1670s. In Moscow, Protestants lived mostly in the 'German quarter', and played an important role at the court of the Tsar Alexy

---

51 Benz, *Wittenberg und Byzanz*, pp. 34–58.
52 *Ibid.*, pp. 141–246.
53 Suttner, *Beiträge*.
54 J. Juczczyk, 'O badaniach nad judaizantyzmem', *Kwartalnik historyczny* 1 (1969): 141–51; M. Mieses, 'Judaizanci we wschodniej Europie', *Miesięcznik żydowski* 4 (1934): issues 1–5; Z. Pietrzyk, 'Judaizers in Poland in the second half of the sixteenth century'. In A. Polonsky (ed.), *The Jews in medieval Poland, 1000–1795* (Oxford, 1993), pp. 24–35; L. Szczuczki, 'Polish and Transylvanian Unitarianism in the second half of the sixteenth century'. In *Antitrinitarianism in the second half of the sixteenth century* (Budapest/Leiden, 1982), pp. 231–41.
55 N. A. Kazakova, *Zapadnaia Evropa v russkoï pis'mennosti XV–XVI vv.* (Leningrad: Nauka, 1980), pp. 213, 238–9.
56 H.-H. Nolte, *Religiöse Toleranz in Russland, 1600–1725* (Göttingen, 1969).

Mikhailovich in the third quarter of the seventeenth century.[57] It is quite likely that Russian dissident groups of the mid-sixteenth century were influenced by Protestants. Matvej Bashkin's heresy is a case in point.[58] Bashkin was descended from minor gentry and occupied a prominent position at Ivan IV's court. His 'heretical' views became known in church circles in 1553 when a group of dissidents had formed around his leadership. Bashkin asked his confessor to interpret some questions which arose from reading the gospel, and to explain how to fulfil the Commandments in everyday life. In his opinion, the clergy had to be a model for laymen and encourage all believers to learn the Command-ments. According to Bashkin, all the Commandments of Christ consist of the precept of loving one's neighbour, which was not compatible with the insti-tute of serfdom in Russia, for Christ had called all people 'brothers'. Following New Testament norms, Bashkin emancipated his serfs. He told his confessor Simeon that priests should visit their parishioners more often and exhort them to treat their subjects properly, sparing them suffering whenever possible.

Bashkin was arrested and repented, and gave the names of his partisans. He said that he adopted the 'evil doctrine' 'from Lithuania'. In the charter setting forth the motives of Bashkin's condemnation,[59] he and his followers were accused of insulting Christ and denying his equality to God-the-Father. They allegedly considered the eucharist to be plain bread and wine, denied the authority of the Holy Apostolic Church, and maintained that the true church was the very gathering of believers. They viewed icons of Christ, God's Mother, and the saints as idols. They denied any importance to penance, claiming that all sins were forgiven as soon as sinning ceased, rendering any confession to the clergy unnecessary. They qualified church traditions and the lives of saints as fables and criticized seven ecumenical councils for pride.

'Feodosij Kosoi's Heresy'[60] appeared at the same time and, possibly, under Protestant influence as well. Feodosij himself was most probably of common

57 On Protestants and Protestantism in Russia, see D. V. Tsvetaev, *Protestantvo i protestanty v Rossii do epokhi preobrazovaniï* (Moscow, 1890); E. Amburger, *Geschichte des Protestantismus in Russland* (Stuttgart, 1961).

58 M. V. Dmitriev, *Dissidents russes. II. Matvej Baskin. Le starec Artemij* (Baden-Baden: V. Koerner-Verlag, 1999) (= A. Séguenny (ed.), *Bibliotheca dissidentium. Répertoire des non-conformistes religieux des seizième et dix-septième siècles*, 20), pp. 15–60.

59 *Akty, sobrannye i izdannye arkeograficheskoï ekspedicieï*, 1 (239) (St Petersburg, 1836), pp. 249–56.

60 On Kosoj, see A. I. Klibanov, *Reformacionnye dvizheniia v Rossii v 14–pervoï polovine 16 vv.* (Moscow, 1960); A. A. Zimin, *I. S. Peresvetov i ego sovremenniki. Ocherki po istorii russkoï obshchestvenno-politicheskoï mysli serediny XVI veka* (Moscow, 1958); R. M. Mainka, *Zinovij von Oten'. Ein russischer Polemiker und Theologe der Mitte des 16. Jahrhunderts* (Rome, 1961) (= *Orientalia Christiana Analecta*, 160); M. V. Dmitriev, *Pravoslavie i reformaciia. Reformacionnye dvizheniia v vostochnoslavianskikh zemliakh Rechi Pospolitoï vo vtoroï polovine XVI v.* (Moscow, 1990); Dmitriev, *Dissidents russes. I. Feodosij Kosoj* (Baden-Baden: V. Koerner-Verlag, 1998)

birth. Towards the end of the 1540s he, along with a group of followers, fled from Moscow to the north of Russia. Taking monastic vows, Feodosij and his partisans began to propagate their 'new teaching'.

About 1554–5 he was arrested, conveyed to Moscow, and placed in one of Moscow's monasteries. He and a number of dissidents managed to flee to Belarus. They preached their ideas as they travelled, and this propaganda, as Russian polemicists stated, had great success with the Belarusan population. In 1557, Russian dissidents crossed the Russian–Lithuanian border and began to preach in Vitebsk. According to a contemporary Protestant chronicle, the dissidents threw out icons from houses and churches and called for the worship of God through the sole mediation of Christ. In spring 1557, seven Russian dissidents met the Calvinist reformer Joannes a Lasco (Jan Laski) in Vilnius. They agreed on the main religious issues, in particular on the eucharist. The Russian dissidents told Lasco that seventy 'noblemen' had been imprisoned in the Russian state for their religious beliefs, and they knew more than 500 'brethren' in Russia who supported the true religion. Russian dissidents were taken under the protection of Mikolaj Radziwill Czarny, Chancellor of the Great Duchy of Lithuania. It is also known from a letter from John Burcher to H. Bullinger of 16 February 1558, that the émigrés' leader (called by Burcher 'a second Luther or, better, Zwingli') published his creed 'in all respects' in line with the Protestant one. Burcher emphasized that the author of this creed did not know any of the languages in which the Reformation teaching was propagated in Europe, and had elaborated his own religious programme with no influence from any Protestant doctrine.

The subsequent fate of Russian dissidents was closely connected with the Reformation movement in Ruthenian lands. They became preachers in Protestant communities and spread Reformation ideas among the Orthodox population. In the second half of the 1550s, Russian dissidents were active in Vitebsk and Vilnius. Foma (Thomas), the closest associate of F. Kosoi, preached in Polock, and was drowned in an ice-hole on the orders of Ivan IV after the town had been captured by Russian troops in 1563.[61] In 1567, the documents of the Kraków Protestant community recorded that Isaja from Moscow, 'one of those seven priests, who, when the Gospel light began to gleam, fled from Moscow . . . to Poland from the cruelty of other priests and the Muscovite

(= A. Séguenny (ed.), *Bibliotheca dissidentium. Répertoire des non-conformistes religieux des seizième et dix-septième siècles*, 19); L. Ronchi de Michelis, *Eresia e riforma nel Cinquecento. La dissidenza religiosa in Russia* (Turin: Claudiana, 2000).
61 For details, see Dmitriev, *Pravoslavie i reformacii*, pp. 91–2.

prince himself',[62] came to Lublin, after serving as preacher (*minister*) on the estate of a Polish nobleman. Feodosij himself and his associate Ignatij settled in Volynia on the estate of Kadian Czaplic in the early 1570s. In 1625, the Uniat Archbishop of Polock Antony Sielawa wrote that 'those Muscovite monks' were largely responsible for the 'heretical corruption' of Lithuania. 'They poisoned many in Russia, and many of those who knew them, drank and ate with them and listened to their sermons are still alive'.[63]

All this was possible because Protestantism became an important factor in the religious life of the Orthodox lands of the Polish–Lithuanian Commonwealth. The Reformation drew the attention of the Orthodox people to questions which were considered earlier as irrelevant or marginal. An important role was given to the spread of Protestant printings among the Orthodox population. One of the most important episodes was the attempt of Szymon Budny[64] to publish Protestant books in Russian ('rus'ka mowa'). 'Njagovsky sermons', published by A. L. Petrov,[65] and the recently discovered collection of sermons from Yavorky's materials[66] reflected the Protestant influences on the Ruthenian Orthodoxy. J. Janow ascertained a very strong influence of Mikolaj Rej's 'Postylla' on the Ukrainian–Byelorussian handwritten homiliaries.[67] In this respect, an enquiry into documents of local chancelleries (*ksiegi grodzkie i ziemskie*), begun by O. Levitski, which provided a great deal of new information on antitrinitarian communities in the Ukraine in the first half of the seventeenth century,[68] would be especially promising.

---

62 M. Sypałło (ed.), *Akta synodów różnowierczych* (Warsaw, 1972), p. 216.

63 A. Sielawa, *Antelenchus, to jest odpis na skrypt uszczypliwy zakonnikow Cerkvie odstepney S. Ducha, Elenchus nazwany, napisany przez Oyca Anastazego Sielawe, przelozonego monastyra Wilenskiego S. Troyce zakonu S. Basilego* (Wilno, 1622). Arkhiv Iugo-Zapadnoï Rossii, Part I, vol. 8, pt 1. *Pamiatniki literaturnoï polemiki pravoslavnykh iuzhnorussov s protestantami i latino-uniatami v Yugo-Zapadnoï Rusi za XVI i XVII stol* (Kiev, 1914), p. 717.

64 Z. Pietrzyk, *Budny S.* In A. Séguenny (ed.), *Bibliotheca dissidentium. Répertoire des non-conformistes religieux des seizième et dix-septième siècles*, 13 (Baden-Baden, 1991), pp. 95–136; S. Kot, *Szymon Budny. Der grösste Häretiker litauens im XVI Jh.* Wiener Archiv für Geschichte des Slaventums und Osteuropas, vol. 2 (Graz, 1956).

65 A. L. Petrov, 'Pouchenie na Evangelie po Niagovskomu spisku'. In A. L. Petrov (ed.), *Pamiatniki tserkovno-religioznoï zhizni ugrorussov XVI–XVII vv.* (Petrograd, 1921) (= *Sbornik Otdelenia russkogo iazyka i slovesnosti Akademii nauk.*, vol. 97(2)), pp. 1–226.

66 M. V. Dmitriev, 'K istorii reformatsionnoï propovedi v vostochnoslavianskikh zemliakh Rechi Pospolitoï vo vtoroï polovine XVI v.', *Sovetskoe Slavianovedenie* 2 (1989): 15–26.

67 J. Janów, 'Problem klasyfikacji ewangeliarzy "uczytelnych" (kaznodziejskich)', *Sprawozdania Polskiej Akademji Umiejetnosci* 8 (1947): 296–306; Janów, 'Ze studiów nad ewangeliarzamy "uczytelnymi" XVI–XVII w.', *Slavia* 19 (1950) nos. 3–4: 317–35; Dmitriev, *Mezhdu Rimom i Tsargradom*, pp. 57–72.

68 O. Levitskii, *Sotsinianstvo v Polshe i Iugo-Zapadnoï Rusi v XVI i XVII vv.* (Kiev, 1882) (= *Kievskaia starina* 4–6 (1882)).

One can hardly doubt that the new traces of Protestant influences will be found in the activities and ideology of Orthodox brotherhoods (*bratstva*) of the Polish–Lithuanian Commonwealth[69] between 1580 and 1640. Orthodox confraternities of a new type appeared in the Ukraine and Belarus in the second half of 1580s as a result of a reform sanctioned first by Patriarch Joachim of Antioch and, later, by Jeremiah of Constantinople. The reform could be understood through the foundation charter of the L'vov confraternity.[70] In its first part, the rules for entering into the confraternity were defined, as well as the main aims of its activity. In the second part Joachim gave 'to this confraternity the right to denounce all things contradictory to the law of Christ and to excommunicate all who would offend against it'. The confraternity had an unprecedented authority to punish offenders. Bishops and priests were to refuse their pastoral blessing to those who were excommunicated by the confraternity through its 'own priest'. The confraternity had the right to 'denounce in preaching or writing' those who would live 'not in accordance with the law', persons 'either lay or clerical', be it a priest, a deacon, or a junior deacon. Those who resisted were to be brought before a bishop. Priests were placed under strict control. They were to be brought before a bishop for entering a tavern, for usury, fornication (priest–adulterers were mentioned), bigamy, visits to sorcerers; the accusations should be confirmed by two 'Christian witnesses'. All other confraternities were to be subjected to that of L'vov. A bishop had no jurisdiction over offending confraternity members. Moreover, the confraternity had the right to resist an unworthy bishop: 'If a bishop rejects the law and the truth, if he does not build up the Church according to the rules of the Holy Apostles and our Fathers, if he corrupts the faithful into sin, and assists those who violate the law, such a bishop should be resisted by all as an enemy of the truth.' On the other hand, a bishop had no right to resist the confraternity. Any Christian who opposed the confraternity would lose the blessing of the confraternity and of all patriarchs.

A similar charter was presented by a confraternity of Vilno to the Metropolitan Onisiphor Devochka in 1588. It was confirmed by the Patriarch Jeremiah during his visit to Vilno in 1588. Confraternities arose in numerous cities and towns: in Krasny Stav and Rogatin (1589), Brest, Grodk, and Gologory (1591), Komarna, Bel'sk, and Ljublin (1594), Galich (about 1594), etc. New confraternities appeared after 1596: in Staraja Sol' (1600), Mohilev, and other places. In

---

69 See Dmitriev, *Les confréries de Ruthénie.*

70 W. Milkowicz (ed.), *Monumenta confraternitatis stauropigianae Leopoliensis*, 1 (L'vov, 1895), pp. 113–19; *Pamiatniki, izdannye vremennoï Komissieï dlia razbora drevnikh aktov*, 3(1) (Kiev, 1852), pp. 3–11.

the early seventeenth century, confraternities existed in Drogobych, Sambor, Sanok, Kamenets, Strumilova, and Zamost'e. Their charters reproduced the pattern shaped by those of Vilno and L'vov. In fact, it meant that the relationship between clergy and laity changed radically and the latter usurped power in the church. But this usurpation was not thought of as a break with tradition by the Orthodox Church. Members of confraternities were not, and did not see themselves as, 'Protestants within the Orthodox Church'. Their claims were specifically based on Eastern Christian ecclesiology inherited from Byzantium. The absence of an 'Orthodox kingdom' in Poland led to the reinterpretation of the *symphonia* of secular and spiritual powers in such radical forms.

A number of documents produced by the confraternities reveal the motives, which look similar to those of European Protestants. It shows itself first in the laity's claim to govern the church and even its clergy. There is no doubt that, externally, such a claim questions the basis of traditional church order and is surprisingly similar to the famous Protestant doctrine of a 'priesthood of all believers'. In a document from the Lutsk confraternity,[71] the definition of the laity's responsibility for their church was expressed in a general statement of equal participation of laity and clergy in salvation: 'As members of two bodies of the Church of Christ laity and clergy alone cannot be sufficient for human salvation, and in order to gain it they enter in mutual charity and equal efforts, as there is neither Jew nor Greek, bond nor free, clerical nor lay, noble nor common, wise nor illiterate: but all are united in Jesus Christ'. K. Sakovich, a preacher of the Orthodox confraternity in Lublin, said that the Orthodox Church was governed 'in an unnatural way' (*contra naturam*) because 'it was not the clergy that directed the people but, on the contrary, the people who directed the clergy'.[72] On the other hand, after the 1590s the Orthodox community in Poland established lasting connections with Polish Protestants and were their natural allies in the struggle against the union.

How was Protestantism seen by Russian and Ruthenian authors in the sixteenth and seventeenth centuries? Russian chronicles of the sixteenth century reduced Lutheranism solely to iconoclasm and profanation of churches.[73] In the epistle of Patriarch Ioasaf, included in chronicles, characteristics of 'Luther's heresy' are as follows: the denial of sacraments of eucharist and

---

71 'Postanovlenie ob obsheezhitel'stve v bratstve Lutskom'. In *Pamiatniki, opublikovannye Kievskoï arkeograficheskoï kommisieï*, vol. 1 (Kiev, 1945), pp. 55–82.

72 Golubev, *Kievskii mitropolit*, vol. 1, p. 122.

73 Kazakova, *Zapadnaia Evropa* (note 55), pp. 213–14.

consecration; rejection of fasting and icons; refusal to venerate saints and relics.[74]

The most representative sources for the study of Orthodox views of Protestantism are the voluminous polemics against Protestant doctrines. Polemic was waged since the moment of encounter with Protestantism in the middle of the sixteenth century and lasted over many decades. In the seventeenth century, written and oral debates with Protestants were common. One of the best-known events was the 1570 dispute between Ivan the Terrible and Jan Rokita, representative of Czech Brethren.[75]

A typical example of the Orthodox perception of Protestantism is contained in *starets* Artemij's epistles.[76] He was a learned Russian monk, adviser to Ivan IV, and abbot of the famous Trinity monastery. In the mid-1550s Artemij was accused of deviating from Orthodoxy and fled to Ukrainian–Belarusan lands. He became involved in polemics with Protestants and compiled a number of polemical epistles. Especially revealing in this respect are his epistles to one of the leaders of the Calvinists in Poland–Lithuania, Szymon Budny, who in 1562 published his 'Cathechism' in the Ruthenian language.[77]

Answering Budny's question of which traits of the Calvinist church appealed to the Orthodox, Artemij responded with a sharp criticism of Protestantism. 'We', wrote Artemij on behalf of Orthodox believers, 'do not dare call your communities a church because we believe in the Holy Apostolic Church. And in your apostate godless communities there is no consent, except eating meat and denying fasts. Your entire teaching consists in defaming Christ's Church and true Christians.' Artemij denies 'Lutherans' the right to be called Christians.[78] In another epistle to Budny, Artemij declared that the new doctrines revealed the hand of the Antichrist.[79] 'People with corrupt minds are seduced by their teaching. They destroy the Christian faith, betray the traditions passed on by the apostles and introduce their own false ideas instead of divine rules.'[80] In

---

74 *Polnoe sobranie russkikh letopisej*, 13: *Vtoraja polovina* (St Petersburg, 1904), pp. 334–9.

75 V. A. Tumins, *Tsar Ivan IV's reply to Jan Rokyta*. Slavic Printings and Reprintings, 84 (Paris/The Hague: Mouton, 1971).

76 P. A. Giltebrant (**Hildebrand(t)?**) (ed.), [Artemii], *Poslaniia starca Artemiia*. Russkaia istoricheskaia biblioteka, 4 (St Petersburg, 1878) (= *Pamiatniki polemicheskoï literatury v Zapadnoï Rusi*, 1), cols. 1201–1448. On Artemii, see Dmitriev, *Dissidents russes. II* (note 58); G. Schulz, *Die theologiegeschichtliche Stellung des Starzen Artemij innerhalb der Bewegung der Besitzlosen in Russland der ersten Hälfte des 16. Jahrhunderts*. Oikonomia: Quellen und Studien zur Orthodoxen Theologie, 15 (Erlangen, 1980).

77 S. Bydnyï, *Katikhizis, to est nauka starodavnaya khristianskaya ot svetogo pisma dla prostykh liudeï jazyka ruskogo v pytaniakh i otkazekh sobrana* (Nesvizh, 1562).

78 [Artemii], *Poslaniia* (note 76), cols. 1426–7.   79 *Ibid.*, col. 1289.

80 *Ibid.*, cols. 1290–1.

other epistles, Artemij calls 'Lutherans' pneumomachs, who debased divine service as 'sorcery and dancing' and Christ's flesh as plain bread; they substitute the true faith by misleading reason, their thought is guided by their flesh, they do not understand Christ's gospel and preach the Decalogue instead of the gospels.[81]

'The epistle to Lutheran teachers' shows how Protestantism was perceived by Artemij. It is very characteristic that Protestant doctrines were represented in such an inadequate manner. They did not consider the essence of Protestantism (justification by faith, *sola scriptura*, denial of papal authority, the role of laymen in the church, the rejection of most sacraments, specific conception of the eucharist); instead, issues of peculiarly Orthodox doctrine, raised in polemics with dissidents within the local East Slavic milieu, were placed at the forefront by Artemij. Artemij sets forth the teaching of his opponents in the following way. They claim to preach the evangelical doctrine and call children of the gospel those who follow them. However, the central place in their teaching is taken by the Decalogue. Besides, they demand the giving up of the veneration of icons, which are nothing but pagan idols, created by men. The Holy Cross must not be revered either, for that is a gibbet; the sign of the cross should not be made, the liturgical services should be abolished as well as singing and fasting; internal repentance for sins suffices and no expiatory punishments are needed; all ancient prayers should be dismissed as useless; monasticism makes no sense and in the New Testament nothing is said about it.[82] It is clear these had peripheral significance in Protestantism, whereas for East Slavic Orthodoxy all these issues were central to confrontation between dissidents and church authorities in Russia, Ukraine and Belarus. Almost all Orthodox authors understood Protestantism one-sidedly, noticing what was important for Orthodoxy and ignoring debatable points that were central to the confrontation between Protestants and Catholics. Orthodox polemicists after Artemij saw in Protestantism iconoclasm, above all, denial of sacraments and rituals, an assault on monasticism. Iconoclasm was introduced in the first place because in the Orthodox tradition the issue of icons was understood as a Christological problem. The theme of justification by faith did not attract attention because this theme was irrelevant for the Orthodox tradition.[83] It should be underlined that the misunderstanding was mutual: Protestants were not aware of many fundamental peculiarities of the Byzantine–Orthodox

81 *Ibid.*, cols. 1276–8. 82 *Ibid.*, cols. 1211, 1250–1.
83 See J. Meyendorff, 'La signification de la Réforme dans l'histoire du christianisme'. In J. Meyendorff, *Orthodoxie et catholicité* (Paris: Seuil, 1965), pp. 109–29.

tradition. An illustration of that mutual misunderstanding is the correspondence between Jeremiah, Patriarch of Constantinople, and Tübingen theologians in the 1570s.

On the whole, the materials of the east European polemical writings confirm J. Meyendorff's conclusion that Orthodoxy and Protestantism were centred on different problems and the languages they used were profoundly different.[84]

---

84 *Ibid.*, p. 120.

PART V

RELIGION, SOCIETY, AND CULTURE

19

The Reformation and the visual arts

LEE PALMER WANDEL

The theology of Incarnation and the visual arts

Any consideration of the visual arts in the Reformation must begin with the Incarnation.[1] Throughout their history, Christians have struggled with what it means that, in the words of the Gospel of John, 'the Word was made flesh' (1:14, KJV). The Incarnation overthrew the opposition many different schools of classical thought, from the presocratics through the Stoics, had posited: of flesh to spirit, matter to mind. For no Christian could 'flesh', or matter, be completely severable from 'the Word' or God – the two were bound together in Christ, and to state otherwise was heresy.

The Incarnation also overthrew the Jewish prohibition of images. As both Rome and Constantinople declared during the iconoclastic controversies of the eighth and ninth centuries, if God could take on the flesh, then material representations of Christ in some essential way belonged on a continuum in which matter could serve to make divinity present to the eyes of the faithful. With the rise of the cult of the saints in the high Middle Ages, that continuum came to encompass images of saints, which revealed God's hand in the lives of Christians after the life of Christ. Thomas Aquinas, explicating the consequences of those pronouncements, explicitly located visual representations on an unbroken line that began with Jesus, then Mary, and then the saints, and ended with man-made visual representations, first of Christ, then Mary, and finally, the saints.

The proliferation of images in churches[2] coincided with the increasingly important function accorded images in a number of medieval theories of memory and cognition. For several theorists, images were central to the

---

1 The text of the Nicene Creed sets forth the doctrine of the Incarnation. For the text, see Tanner, *Decrees of the ecumenical councils*, vol. 1, p. 5.
2 For close studies of the interplay of incarnational theology and medieval art, see Kessler and Wolf, *The holy face*, for the West, Pelikan, *Imago Dei*, for the East. More generally, see Hans Belting, *Bild und Kult*.

organization and retention of received knowledge.[3] For them, human beings both remembered their learning and made sense of it through images in their minds, which themselves could be drawn from visual experience. Such a position provided powerful support for images, from illuminated prayer books for the laity through carved altar retables in churches in the use of contemplation and devotion.

For Christians, whether one was Protestant or Catholic, Reformed or Lutheran, Roman or Orthodox, 'representation' was never a simple problem of perspective and proportion. The visual arts were viewed within the context of how one understood Christ – and God – to be present in the physical world. Sixteenth-century Christians were divided on the question, not if God revealed himself through matter, but if and how human hands could have any part at all in that revelation. In the sixteenth century, Christians asked the agonized and agonizing question: could any human-made 'representation' reveal anything of God's, or Christ's, nature or truth? Their answers, revealed in their catechisms and in their preaching, divided them. To be 'Catholic' was to align oneself with a tradition reaching back to the eighth- and ninth-century iconoclastic controversies, which repeatedly endorsed the centrality of representation to Christian culture. To be 'Lutheran' was to hold images to be indifferent to worship. To be 'Reformed' was, foremost, to reorganize the Ten Commandments, such that the prohibition against human-made images was a commandment unto itself.

In the sixteenth century, the formal Catholic position echoed the conceptualization of images and their relationship to divinity worked out in the iconoclastic controversies and most fully articulated by Thomas Aquinas.[4] That position, as it was decreed at Trent, had two central components. First, it affirmed the closely defined place of images in devotion:

> And they must also teach that the images of Christ, of the virgin mother of God and the other saints should be set up and kept, particularly in churches, and that due honour and reverence is owed to them, not because some divinity or power is believed to lie in them as reason for the cult, or because anything is to be expected from them, or because confidence should be placed in images as was done by pagans of old; but because the honour showed to them is referred to the original which they represent: thus, through the images which we kiss and before which we uncover our heads and go down on our knees, we give adoration to Christ and veneration to the saints, whose likeness they

3 Carruthers, *The book of memory.*
4 For a summary of older literature and an influential formulation of the question, see Prodi, 'Ricerche sulla teorica delle arti figurative'.

bear. And this has been approved by the decrees of the councils, especially the second council of Nicaea, against the iconoclasts.

Second, it affirmed the cognitive function of images in the complex of education in Christianity:

> Bishops should teach with care that the faithful are instructed and strengthened by commemorating and frequently recalling the articles of our faith through the expression in pictures or other likenesses of the stories of the mysteries of our redemption; and that great benefits flow from all sacred images, not only because people are reminded of the gifts and blessings conferred on us by Christ, but because the miracles of God through the saints and their salutary example is put before the eyes of the faithful, who can thank God for them, shape their own lives and conduct in imitation of the saints, and be aroused to adore and love God and to practise devotion. If anyone teaches or holds what is contrary to these decrees: let him be anathema.[5]

For the Church of Rome, images had a long-standing and carefully delineated place within the economy of worship, serving not only the illiterate – the great majority of Christians in the early modern world – but all Christians through their capacity to 'put before the eyes of the faithful' manner, bearing, acts of faith, expressions of devotion; to 'remind', to call to mind again, the 'gifts' of the Incarnation.

Martin Luther himself held all images to be adiaphora, unimportant.[6] His radical emphasis on faith did not accord images, *qua* matter, the same potency as did either Catholic or even Reformed positions – images, for Luther, by their very materiality, were not capable of seducing or illumining the soul. Others, who largely agreed with the major tenets of his theology, strongly disagreed with his position on images. While Luther was in hiding at the Wartburg, for instance, Andreas Bodenstein von Karlstadt preached iconoclasm in Wittenberg and published 'On the Removal of the Images', in which he listed all the biblical injunctions against any representations of God.

Karlstadt's position echoed that of the most radical evangelicals – those who took the commandment against images absolutely. Most of those groups met clandestinely – and therefore had no sites where images might have been placed. Some of the most outspoken iconoclasts number among their

---

5 Tanner, *Decrees of the ecumenical councils*, vol. 2, p. 776, Latin text, p. 775.
6 'Bilder / glocken / Messegewand / kirchenschmueck / allter liecht und der gleichen / halt ich frey / Wer da wil / der mags lassen / Wie wol bilder aus der schrifft und von guten Historien ich fast nuetzlich / doch frey und wilkoerig halte / Denn ichs mit den bildestuermen nicht halte.' Martin Luther, *Vom Abendmahl Christi*, p. 514.

members, however, which suggests that many of those who broke with Luther and Huldrych Zwingli found images anathema to worship.[7]

John Calvin was not hostile toward the visual arts *per se*:

> And yet I am not gripped by the superstition of thinking absolutely no images permissible. But because sculpture and painting are gifts of God, I seek a pure and legitimate use of each, lest those things the Lord has conferred upon us for his glory and our good be not only polluted by perverse misuse but also turned to our destruction.[8]

For Calvin, the problem was not images themselves, but what those images represented and who created them.[9] Insofar as all images were made with human hands, they reflected human conceptions of God and Christ; insofar as human beings directed devotion towards those images, they were worshipping their own conceptions of God and Christ. The danger lay not in the images themselves, but in human presumption that the images revealed God transparently. For Calvin, God 'represented' himself in light, in the ordering of nature – materially, but not artificially.

Iconoclasm

Perhaps most striking, the theologians' positions were largely formulated in reaction to violence against images.[10] None of the theologians, other than Karlstadt and, possibly, Martin Bucer in Strasbourg, condoned that violence. Unlike Luther, Calvin, or Zwingli, lay Christians, ordinary men and women, held the question of images to be absolutely urgent – souls were at stake – even as they voiced a wide range of different understandings of images and their place in worship. In community after community, Christians polarized, some calling the acts of verbal or physical violence against the images in their churches 'blasphemy', an assault against God, others calling those same images 'idols', and calling for their destruction 'for the honour of God'. These debates were framed not in terms of proportion or craftsmanship or aesthetics, not in any aesthetic terms at all, but in terms of worship: how does one best honour God? At no other time had images been so central to so many Christians in the determination of true worship.

---

7 Klaus Hottinger of Zurich, for example; see Wandel, *Voracious idols and violent hands*, pp. 72–80.
8 Calvin, *Institutes*, p. 112.
9 On Calvin's position on images more generally, see Wencelius, *L'esthêtique de Calvin*.
10 Wandel, *Voracious idols and violent hands*.

In parishes throughout Europe – from Poland on the east to south-western France, from Switzerland to Scotland and Sweden – individual Christians 'took down the idols'.[11] For many, in doing so, they were putting their own lives at risk: blasphemy was, in many communities, a capital crime. For many, iconoclasm, violence whether verbal or physical, was an act of faith, an act, moreover, which put them at risk of becoming martyrs. 'Iconoclasm' encompassed a range of acts. The earliest iconoclasts might attack a single altar retable in the middle of the night. Some simply carried the objects out of the churches. Those objects might be returned to the families of the original donors or, more often, simply 'disappear'. More often, iconoclasts smashed images in their places, breaking representations into the material of which they had been made, stone or wood. Indeed, in communities which legalized iconoclasm, the wood was frequently given to the poor to heat their homes, the stone reused as cobblestones, and the cloth given to the poor for clothing. And in spectacular cases, such as Basel in 1529 and throughout the provinces of the Low Countries during the Wonderyear in 1566, crowds contemporaries numbered in the hundreds broke into churches, smashed all the objects associated with worship – representational art, liturgical implements, stained glass windows, altars, and missals.

For many Christians, iconoclasm was inseparable from 'Reformation'. Removing the false idols was essential to the institution of true worship. Those 'idols' participated in a number of affronts against God, as delineated by different iconoclasts. Crucifixes and altars participated in a particular conceptualization of the mass as a sacrifice, a sacrifice that Luther, Zwingli, Calvin, and dozens of other evangelicals preached had been made once for all time at the crucifixion. Images of the saints as well as their relics participated in the cult of saints, which distracted the devout from concentrating exclusively and intensively on the life of Christ alone as the model of sanctity and the revelation of divine mercy. Images of Mary also drew the attention of the faithful away from the central salvific meaning of Jesus's life, as well as diminishing Christ's divinity and majesty. All the different kinds of images – from representational art through the golden chalices, the jewelled missals, and the oil lamps – embodied wealth that ought to have been spent in 'love of one's neighbour', for the care of the poor. For those who tore them down and destroyed them, images were 'powerful' certainly: capable of drawing the faithful away from God and towards human conceptions of worship, of the meaning of Christ's life, and of God.

---

11 For literature on iconoclasm in different nations, see Wandel, *Voracious idols and violent hands*, p. 13, note 31. For the most recent study, see *Macht und Ohnmacht der Bilder*.

In the years between the Edict of Nantes and its Revocation in France, 1598–1685, *de facto* after 1572 and legally after 1648, in the United Provinces, where specific Reformed churches or congregations had the legal authority and the local power to so institute, they removed 'idols' from their churches. Which specific images constituted 'idols' was not consistent from congregation to congregation, but the generally accepted definition of 'idols' was anything – not simply representational art, but also liturgical objects, altars, vestments – that led to false worship, that led the faithful, in other words, from close attention to the Word of God as it was preached and lived. The political situation within the Empire was even more volatile, and any number of churches witnessed 'cleansing', then 'recatholicization', in which the interiors of Catholic churches were consciously and explicitly reclaimed with sculpture, panel paintings, altar retables, as well as putti and prophets and apostles carved right into the architecture.

The production of images

Christians were divided on the content of religious images and the sites, but Catholic, Lutheran, and Reformed Christians all continued to commission religious art. Protestant and Catholic art alike continued to be produced in workshops, each with a master, journeymen, and apprentices. Artists used the same substances – ink, chalk, oil, marble, stone, wood, copper, iron – for Protestant and Catholic commissions alike. While new media, such as oil, and new techniques, such as etching, emerged in this period, those media and techniques do not seem to belong to one church or another: Rembrandt van Rijn used the technique of chiaroscuro he had seen in the work of Caravaggio to render evangelical biblical scenes. Most artists, moreover, worked in multiple media.

Modes of production played a role in the history of the visual arts in the Reformation – not reflecting confessional divides so much as the changing character of 'Reformation' over the course of the period. We can trace a shift, from the early years, when print served the immediacy of polemics, to the years of the establishment of churches, when patrons commissioned more durable and stable forms of art.

The earliest Reformation images were printed. In the 1520s and 1530s, Protestants took up woodcuts foremost. Woodcuts were perhaps the cheapest image of all to produce – in part because of the materials involved, in part because of the lesser value of the skilled labour – and therefore affordable for a greater number of people. They were certainly the quickest to produce, far more easily appropriated for the polemics of the early years, when Christians were defining theological positions, liturgy, and ethics in opposition to one another.

Printed images were produced in a way that set them and how they functioned apart from painted and sculpted images.[12] Printed images were produced on a less-durable material, paper. The subject of early sixteenth-century prints was itself more transient: their polemics were very much of the moment. There is evidence that printed images were hung – in taverns as well as homes and churches. But prints seem to have functioned in ways that the majority of sculpted and painted images could not: while private devotional diptychs and triptychs might travel with their wealthy patrons, printed images travelled on the road, in a pocket or knapsack, from hand to hand, into the workplace, and into the homes of artisans and peasants. They carried visualizations to places where no other images might be found.

In the 1520s, many communities north of the Alps ceased the production of painted and sculpted images. When painted and sculpted images were again produced, largely using traditional methods and materials, their commissions, their placement, their content, and the ways in which they were understood to function in devotion all reflected a divided Christendom.

Patronage and sites for images

Patronage was very much an expression of confession. For Catholics, images were an important means of proselytizing and conversion. Catholics invested capital, cultural and financial, in images. Rome and Antwerp were major centres of artistic production. Catholic families, both great and humble, paid to replace images, altarpieces, choir screens, stained glass windows in churches that were 'recatholicized'. The great papal families – the Farnese, the Borghese – were also great patrons of the arts, endowing monumental sculptural programmes for more public spaces in churches, altarpieces from major artists for their 'private' chapels, into which all the faithful could look, as well as more intimate forms of devotional art. Politically powerful Catholic families, such as the Medici and the Habsburgs, also demonstrated their faith through the endowment of chapel altarpieces and more public sculpted or painted images, as well as the construction of chapels and the renovation or restoration of churches. Catholics, lay and clerical, commissioned richly illuminated devotional books and private devotional images. Those commissions were themselves acts of devotion, efforts to promulgate the faith, at first among the

12 Griffiths, *Prints and printmaking.*

Flemish, Bavarians, and Polish, but soon among the Inca, Aztec, Chinese, and other indigenous peoples of the Americas and Asia.

Lutherans, like Catholics, continued to commission images for their churches, but those images were more narrowly didactic. We know less of individual patrons: images were not evidence of their devotion, so the record of commissions is less public, and their patronage is less studied than that of the great Catholic families. With the institution of Lutheran churches, Lutherans commissioned painting for the interiors of their churches, and after the Peace of Augsburg, funerary sculpture, architectural sculpture, and friezes of biblical narratives.[13] Within Luther's lifetime, Lucas Cranach the Elder produced a number of altarpieces for Lutheran churches in Saxony, each one of which seems to have been paid for by local Lutheran families. So, too, Cranach, Holbein, and others were commissioned to produce illustrations – woodcuts and engravings – for Luther's translation of the Bible.[14]

The Reformed tradition does not present a uniform pattern of patronage. French Huguenot bourgeois eschewed, apparently, all public religious art. Dutch Reformed merchants, on the other hand, were the market for Rembrandt's paintings and prints of biblical figures and narratives – though those images were neither commissioned, nor placed in public places of worship. Those merchants did commission both funerary sculpture for some of their churches and painted wooden panels depicting the Ten Commandments.

Christians from all three of the major traditions patronized the arts. Patronage differentiated confessionally over whether art belonged within the public space of worship. Catholics commissioned religious art for both public and domestic spaces, both technically 'civic' and ecclesiastical domains, ranging from monumental to intimate in scale. Lutherans, too, commissioned art for their churches, as well as illustrated bibles. Both Catholics and Lutherans commissioned images that were placed where laity and clergy alike worshipped, where anyone, therefore, who wished to see them might have access to them, to gaze at them, to kneel before them, to pray. Only Catholics, however, saw images as very much central to the project of missionizing in Europe, the Americas, and Asia. Catholics and Lutherans commissioned images for different purposes.

Of the major traditions, the Reformed Church sought most to circumscribe where and how religious images were to be seen. Huguenots barred paintings, statues, and stained glass from the buildings in which they worshipped.[15]

13 Smith, *German sculpture of the later Renaissance*.
14 Schmidt, *Die Illustration der Lutherbibel*, pp. 93–161.
15 Mentzer, 'The Reformed churches of France' *Seeing Beyond the Word*, p. 228.

Dutch Reformed congregations, insofar as their political situation allowed them to act, 'cleansed' their churches of medieval paintings, relics, and altars; reoriented the space itself around the pulpit; and some hung on the walls boards painted with the Ten Commandments.[16] Reformed churches were largely distinguished by those white-washed walls that Zwingli had found so 'beautiful' – their visuality lies outside the scope of this essay. Most Reformed art was commissioned for private homes, for a different viewership and with a different function.

Confession and the content and function of images

Annibale Carracci, Peter Paul Rubens, and Bernini were 'Catholic' artists, Cranach, 'Lutheran', and Rembrandt, 'Reformed'. All sought to articulate in matter – in mass and texture and line and colour – religious visions. They did not differ in the materials they used or in the process of production. The major traditions divided on what might be represented and, inseparable from that prescription of content, how an image might function in devotion.

The printed image and 'Reformation'

Even as they were removing 'idols' from their churches, Protestants promulgated 'Reformation' through printed images.[17] Printed images differed from the images in the churches in important ways. They were two-dimensional, and therefore never 'life-like'. They were linear, closer in appearance to the printed page than to the sensuous image. They were usually printed on paper, a substance that deteriorated rapidly, its transience also undercutting the potential for an image to become an idol. Finally, the subject of Protestant printed images was largely polemical, as distinct from devotional, the images of Christ, for example, set within biblical narratives and next to scripture itself, or in explicit contrast to the conduct of clergy and pope.

Protestants used printed images in two contexts that were linked in the larger project of promulgating the evangelical message: printed bibles and visual polemics. Protestant bibles, which were put on the Roman Index, sought to reach populations of mixed literacy; many, therefore, carried hundreds of images, sometimes beautifully hand-coloured. And two of the most successful artists of the sixteenth century, Holbein and Cranach, designed images for Zwingli's and Luther's translations of the Bible, respectively. The woodcuts

---

16 Section on the Netherlands, Finney, *Seeing beyond the word*, pp. 343–425.
17 Scribner, *For the sake of simple folk*.

from these bibles were taken up, copied, used in other contexts, carrying the evangelical message in ways that their designers may never have intended.

Protestants printed images in unprecedented numbers, not only to carry visually the Holy Scripture to the world, but also to challenge Rome's claim to primacy, to dispute a range of practices of the medieval church, to delineate clerical abuses, and to articulate in minute visual detail the contrast between the 'True Church' and the Church of Rome. It may be that printed images were the most effective tool of a group who began as both a demographic and a political minority, but Catholics, whether German, Roman, Flemish, or French, never took up printed images with the same intensity or sheer proliferation for the purposes of polemics.

While printed images were simpler, lacking colour or plasticity, they shared with painting, sculpture, and performances complex visual languages of symbols, signs, clothes, objects, gestures, faces, and articulated physical relations.[18] Printed images drew upon a plethora of symbols, both traditional and new to the sixteenth century, from the ubiquitous cross with its complex theological meaning, as well as its immediate connotation of Christianity, or the dove, to the *fleur de lis* of France or the two-headed eagle of the Empire, to Luther's rose, for some a symbol of faith and true Christianity. Thousands of familiar objects served as signs: the thresher or the pike, for example, signalled kinds of labour; the sceptre, relations of secular power; the altar, or the chalice or the host, which could signal either the mystery of the mass or blasphemy and idolatry, depending on the viewer. Analogous to these signs were what we might call visual metaphors: the monk's belly, signalling a life lived too well; the nun's sidelong glance, signaling a promiscuity that contradicted the oath the habit signalled; the uplifted face, signalling luminous faith; the hands pressed together in prayer. Clothes might signal rank, such as fur or the royal ermine; or office, the key of the magistrate or the cardinal's hat; or labour, the artisan's tunic or the peasant's clogs; or character, the fool's cap. Some pieces of clothing could stand for the person or the office: the pope's tiara served frequently to signal one or the other. One of the most effective and famous Catholic polemical images, 'The Seven-headed Luther', published as the title-page of a 1529 pamphlet by Johannes Cochleus, used the turban of the Turk, the hood of the Eastern Orthodox patriarch, flies or 'Schwärmerei', and the head of Barrabbas to link Luther to the most feared enemies of Christendom. Two of the most popular polemical single-sheet images, the monk calf and the papal ass, linked two famous monstrous births, the one through the cowl to

18 Andersson, 'Popular imagery'.

the religious, and the other, through the physical setting of the Tiber, to the pope.

The polemic of Reformation prints most often operated through oppositions, which were articulated in the visual terms of gesture, facial expression, and relations between figures. The woodcut, 'The Godly Mill', for instance, articulated contrast through the language of placement: those who were 'evangelical', Erasmus and Luther, were close to the gospels, and the cardinals, monks, and curia, signalled by their habits, were remote. Lucas Cranach the Elder's *Passional Christi und Antichristi*, a series of thirteen paired woodcuts published in Wittenberg in 1521, contrasted Christ's gesture, demeanour, and relation to his followers, to those of the pope (Fig. 1). It was all the more effective for recalling the thousands of images of Christ's humility and poverty, so familiar to Christians from their own churches, and articulating explicitly in line and placement how papal gesture, conduct, demeanour, dress, and court contrasted. Some Dutch engravings contrasted the two major forms of papal idolatry – the mass and the use of images in worship – to Reformed iconoclasm, which removed altars as well as images. Many polemical prints heightened the contrast through the exaggeration of gesture or the addition of physical attributes, such as a belly, that connoted inner character.

Gesture, facial expression, and relations between figures were also the corporeal language of devotion. Even as they contrasted evangelical demeanour and bearing to the superstitious attending mass, Protestant printed images depicted the proper demeanour of the faithful, as in those that showed the pious listening to evangelical preachers. In some broadsheets, the audience stands, in some the women are seated on the floor, but in all their persons are oriented towards the pulpit, their faces turned upward towards the preacher's face and mouth. Hands are folded in the laps of the seated, neither holding rosary beads nor knitting. On the evangelical side of these prints, no one prays the rosary, speaks to a neighbour, knits, carves, and/or performs any other forms of manual production.

Images 'spoke' in a language rich in allusion to other images. A particular position of the head or hand, rendered in line or shadow, pointed to other images in other media; the outlined forms of shepherds or lambs 'represented' figures the viewer had seen in colour and mass elsewhere. Painted and sculpted images might refer to an arrangement of figures, a background, a particular rendering of Christ's agency in printed biblical illustrations, caricatures, or broadsheets; wooden retables reproduced the gestures, figural arrangements, and facial expressions of biblical illustrations. All images, whether printed, painted, or sculpted, moreover, in capturing a gesture, an angle of the head,

Figure 1. Lucas Cranach the Elder, *Passional Christi und Antichristi* (1521)

Antichristi.

Antichristus.

Der Babst maßt sich an itzlichen Tyrannen vnd heydnischen fursten / so yre fueß den leuten zu kußen dar gericht/nach zu volgen/damit es waer werde das geschrieben ist.Wilcher dießer Bestien Bilde nicht anbettet/sall getödt werden Apocalip.13.
Ditz kußens darff sich der Bapst yn seyne decretalen vnnorschemßt rümen.c.cū olī depri.cle.Si summus pon.de sent.excō.

Figure 1. (cont.)

a particular expression of the hand, reached beyond themselves to human actors – some, in representing the carefully dictated movements of the liturgy, reached out to its lived performance; some, in representing the grasping hand of the monk, reached out to living religious. The play of visual allusion did not stop with images. The visual tropes of character that printed images attached to their representations – the belly to the monk, the glance to the nun, the hauteur to the pope – could attach to the persons of living human beings. That was their efficacy and their power.

Lutheran art

Lutherans commissioned paintings and sculpture for their churches, but those representations were no longer to be understood on a continuum of revelation: even if medieval representations of saints might survive within the churches, those images provided models of behaviour, not foci for the cult of saints. In both function within worship and in content, Lutheran images differed from Catholic.[19] Lutheran images were, in Luther's own words, 'for the sake of simple folk', a part of a larger didactic enterprise. As such, they served along with catechisms to teach the fundamentals of Lutheran doctrine: the Ten Commandments, God as merciful Father, Christ's central salvific role, the Lord's Prayer, the nature and proper celebration of the sacraments. In the sixteenth and seventeenth centuries, the Ten Commandments, in particular, but also the Lord's Prayer, were painted on boards that hung along the nave.

The first and most prolific of the early Lutheran painters, Cranach the Elder, also rendered in oil visualizations of fundamental tenets of Lutheran doctrine.[20] In both printed image and in oil, he gave visual articulation to Luther's conceptions of law and grace, rendering their opposition allegorically. In a series of major altarpieces, he rendered the Lutheran formulations of the sacraments of baptism and communion. In the 'Reformation Altar', completed in 1547 for the church of Mary in Wittenberg, Cranach represented the three sacraments in three panels, left to right: baptism, communion, confession (Fig. 2). The representation of baptism made visible the infancy of the recipient, a simple font, and the presence of the community. The representation of confession made visible its public and open character, with Luther's own

---

19 Martin Scharfe differentiated specific kinds of Protestant images – biblical history, divinity, saints and ideal Christian behaviour, sacred acts and history, and the ideal Christian life and death – each of which existed in a distinctive relationship to its viewer, and was intended to invoke different responses. Scharfe, *Evangelische Andachtsbilder*. See also Christensen, *Art and the Reformation*.

20 Thulin, *Cranach Altäre der Reformation*; Hoffmann, *Luther und die Folgen für die Kunst*.

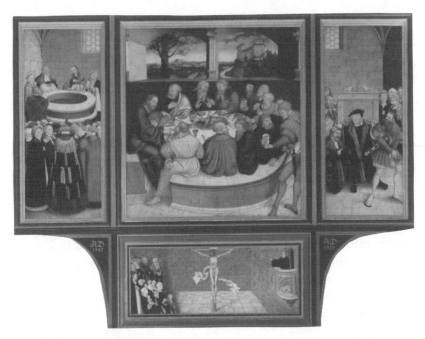

Figure 2. Lucas Cranach the Elder, Reformation Altar, Wittenberg (1547)

'confessor', Johannes Bugenhagen, holding the keys of absolution, which come from heaven. In the middle panel, the largest of the three, Cranach represented the Lutheran communion. While the other two could be set in a church – the stone walls in the background suggest such a setting – the Supper is in an open room. Luther turns to hand a knight the cup, even as Christ places the bread soaked in bitter wine in Judas's mouth, Judas signalled by his pouch of money, clutched in his hand. In the very centre of the table is the paschal lamb, and bread is distributed all around. Cranach placed Luther at the circular table of the Last Supper itself, among Christ's apostles, using oils to render the persons of Luther, Christ, and the disciples realistically fleshly and present – all simultaneously present in the same moment, with the same fleshiness. Cranach was able to render in paint Luther's difficult – for his closest followers, as well as for artists – theology of consubstantiation. Transubstantiation, as many Catholic artists knew, could be rendered visible in a number of ways: through the image of the crucified Christ, through the traditional image of the Mass of St Gregory; or alluded to, through images of Incarnation.

Reformed art

There is considerable debate as to what constitutes a 'Reformed' religious image, given that no images were commissioned for churches – the easiest way to define the religious identity of an image.[21] Here, Rembrandt may serve as representative: the son of one member and the husband of another, Rembrandt seems always to have had a Bible in his house and to have been a churchgoer, but he was himself not a member of the Dutch Reformed congregation in Amsterdam.[22] In an extraordinarily productive career, Rembrandt rendered in print and paint dozens of biblical scenes and figures (Figs. 3 and 4).[23] All, whether painted or printed, are historical, that is, unlike medieval predecessors, dress and setting were of biblical times, as the seventeenth century understood it. All are explicitly situated within time, historical – by their very temporality and contingency resisting iconic use. Rembrandt's biblicism, however, was not 'typical' in some ways: his rendering of biblical scenes reflected both a deeply personal interpretation of those narratives and his own engagement with the philosemitism of a broader community of biblical scholars.[24]

Catholic art

The twenty-fifth session of the Council of Trent stipulated what the precise nature of each viewer's relationship to images was to be. It was formulated in conscious response to the Protestant critique, with its particular understanding of the human mind and its vulnerabilities both to human creations and to matter of all kinds. That position did not capture all the ways that images were integral to Catholic devotion. It did not capture the significance of commissioning art. It did not capture the particular understanding of the relationship between God's agency and revelation on the one hand and the physical world on the other that Catholic art, scrutinized for its theological orthodoxy and approved, 'represented' in oil and marble, colour and mass.

Even as Trent echoed ancient arguments for the didactic purposes of religious images, artists in service of the church brought new techniques of light and shadow, a new monumental scale to the representation of Catholic saints and martyrdom. Artists explored in chalk, oil, marble, wood, and stone a complex interplay of spirit and flesh.[25] They rendered in the heavy substance of oil

---

21 See, for example, Egbert Haverkamp-Begemann's comment, in Finney, *Seeing beyond the word*, pp. 423–5.
22 Arius Theodorus van Deursen, quoted in Zell, *Reframing Rembrandt*, p. 6.
23 Visser t' Hooft, *Rembrandt and the gospel*; Halewood, *Six subjects of Reformation art*.
24 See Zell's compelling interpretation in *Reframing Rembrandt*.
25 Smith, *Sensuous worship*.

Figure 3. Rembrandt Harmensz van Rijn, Saint Anna (1639),
Kunsthistorisches Museum, Vienna

or marble dimensions of the mystery of Incarnation – the import of gravity, the
consequences of materiality for luminosity, 'apotheosis', a particular subject
of Reformation Catholic art, and flight.

Scholars have long debated the relationship between the Catholic Reformation and the Baroque style. Lutherans certainly adopted the Baroque style

Figure 4. Rembrandt Harmensz van Rijn, Saint Paul (1633?),
Kunsthistorisches Museum, Vienna

for their own churches in the seventeenth and eighteenth centuries. But the
great artists of the Counter-Reformation were also integral to the articulation of the Baroque style: Carracci, Bernini, Rubens, Tintoretto, Caravaggio.
The Baroque style of art, like its counterpart in theatre, is more expressive
of a nuanced range of emotions and spiritual states than were its medieval

and Renaissance predecessors.[26] In both painting and sculpture, artists of the Catholic Baroque articulated in gesture and in posture just how the presence of the Holy Spirit was made visible in the human body – the presence of the Holy Spirit was manifested corporeally, not only in the face, but through the arms, the hands, the torso, the legs, even the feet (Fig. 5). Sanctity was made known precisely through the solid materiality of the human body, that same 'flesh' that could be represented in the substances of oil or marble.

Bernini's work in the Cornaro Chapel, of the Church of Santa Maria della Vittoria, Rome exemplifies the particular interplay of embodiment, representation, and epideic, in the Baroque (Fig. 6).[27] The centrepiece of the chapel is the sculpture, 'The Ecstasy of St Teresa', but the sculpture is integrated, first within its own stage, set above the altar in the chapel, and then within a complex theatre of piety. That 'ecstasy' takes place before other human beings. The sculpture itself gives expression in marble to many of the qualities of Teresa's piety. It renders in visible matter – gold, marble, dimension, weight – one of her frequent visions:

> It pleased the Lord that I should see this angel in the following way. He was not tall, but short, and very beautiful, his face so aflame that he appeared to be one of the highest types of angel who seem to be all afire. They must be those who are called cherubim . . . In his hands I saw a long golden spear and at the end of the iron tip I seemed to see a point of fire. With this he seemed to pierce my heart several times, so that it penetrated to my entrails. When he drew it out, I thought he was drawing them out with it and he left me completely afire with a great love for God. The pain was so sharp that it made me utter several moans; and so excessive was the sweetness caused me by this intense pain that one can never wish to lose it, nor will one's soul be content with anything less than God.[28]

The two figures of angel and saint hang before golden rays, which serve also to carry light from a hidden source – giving visible form to a particular notion of divine emanation. The marble of the saint's robes and the angel's renders motion – precisely the opposite of the mass and solidity of the substance marble – even as the saint's body, beneath those folds, is the site for transport: had she sat still and alone in her cell, such transport would never have been visible to another human being. In his particular rendering of her body, Bernini

---

26 Norman, *The theatrical Baroque.*
27 Lavin, *Bernini and the unity of the visual arts*, Part II.
28 *The life of Teresa of Jesus*, pp. 274–5.

Figure 5. Michelangelo Merisi da Caravaggio, 'Madonna of the Rosary' (1606/7), Kunsthistorisches Museum, Vienna

Figure 6. Gian Lorenzo Bernini, 'The Ecstasy of Saint Teresa', Cornaro Chapel, Rome

alludes to the connection mystics had made between ecstasy and death.[29] The placement of her transverberation over the altar links in marble and gold sacramental liturgy and saints and their cults.

What distinguishes this particular sculpture, however, is its setting: this is no free-standing grouping of two, but an event represented within a larger context. To the left and right of the sculpture are prie-dieus, which look very much like theatre boxes (Fig. 7). In each are four male figures in curial dress. Not all look at the saint; indeed one reads. Her 'visibility', in other words is not something physical, but a more complex seeing. The import of those corporeal manifestations of the presence of the Holy Spirit is not transparent – nor is embodiment to be transparently read.

Catholic art also represented core precepts of Catholic doctrine, such as pur- gatory,[30] transubstantiation, and the unique honour due the Virgin Mother.[31] These images articulated in the visual terms of colour, line, mass, and texture

29 'In other words, Teresa was a martyr, not in the physical sense of dying *for* her faith, but in the spiritual sense of dying *of* her faith', Lavin, *Bernini and the unity of the visual arts*, p. 114.
30 Göttler, *Die Kunst des Fegefeuers nach der Reformation*.
31 For surveys of Counter-Reformation iconography, see Mâle, *L'art religieux*; and Knipping, *The iconography of the Counter-Reformation*.

Figure 7. Gian Lorenzo Bernini, 'The Ecstasy of Saint Teresa', Cornaro Chapel, Rome

specific implications of orthodox doctrines at the centre of Catholic identity. In so doing, they gave visual definition to complex theological doctrines and were, therefore, themselves subject to close scrutiny for their orthodoxy.[32] Indeed, in the wake of Trent, contemporary humanists and theologians scrutinized a number of paintings for theological orthodoxy.[33] Those humanists and theologians were aware that theological doctrine not only could be rendered in oil and marble, but that those substances, like the printed word, could give expression to false or wrong doctrine.

These representations were, like Bernini's Cornaro Chapel, not transparent or literal, but engaged fully with the artistic implications of Incarnation. Many artists and patrons chose as an affirmation of the Catholic doctrine of transubstantiation one moment in the crucifixion. These paintings, normally hung over the high altar, would then participate in the performance of the mass, their represented motion a counterpart to the performed celebration, with the elevation, of the mass. Rubens, for example, painted the Raising of the Cross[34] for the parish church of St Walburga in Antwerp.[35] The church no longer exists, but a painting by Anthoon Gheringh depicts the altarpiece, a triptych, over the high altar, which was itself on a raised apse – a series of elevations, of sacred apse, of altar, of altarpiece, and then of the body of Christ. As in all Rubens's paintings, the colour of flesh dominates, Christ's flesh lighter, more luminous, also forming in this image a diagonal line from the lower, sinister side to the upper right. The backs of the six labourers, as well as the arms and legs of the two soldiers, manifest in muscle the physicality of raising the cross. Here is no simple chemical transformation, but an event worked out through human bodies, realized in human agency, of central sacred meaning.

Jesuit art

Of all the orders of the sixteenth century, the Jesuits embraced most fully the 'power' of images.[36] Jesuit devotional woodcuts and engravings articulated carefully and in detail in line the particular facial expressions of devotion, transport, illumination.[37] In rendering again in that same careful line the specific gestures of Christ and the distinctive relationships that he, and other biblical figures, had to others, these images provided the faithful with eloquent representations of embodied faith: how it looked, how it moved, how it existed

---

32 Dempsey, 'Mythic inventions'.
33 Ibid.; and Hall, Renovation and Counter-Reformation.
34 On the theme of the Raising of the Cross, see Lawrence, 'Before The raising of the cross'.
35 Belkin, Rubens, pp. 103–13.   36 Wittkower, Baroque art: the Jesuit contribution.
37 Melion, 'The art of vision'.

in relationship to others. Those simple linear images were integrally a part of Jesuit 'discipline', showing the faithful, in line, how that faith, when so enacted, so brought into conformity with the demeanour and bearing and manner and conduct, would come to be embodied in a deeper sense, 'disciplined' in the Jesuit sense of a lived and conscious enactment of faith.

Jesuits explicitly took up images as a part of their programme of conversion of the peoples of Asia and the Americas and of reconversion of the peoples of Europe.[38] They drew upon images to translate central Christian theological ideas to non-European cultures.[39] They built new churches in Asia and the Americas, in the process connecting European visual traditions to local, at once preserving and transforming both.[40] In the recatholicization of Bavaria, they commissioned new images for churches that had been 'cleansed', and built new churches, which were also visually rich (Fig. 8).[41] In each milieu, the Jesuits both carried with them and commissioned from local artisans images that might bring to Europeans and to cultures whose languages the Jesuits had not yet mastered central theological concepts of Catholicism. When Pierre Biard arrived in 1610 with the first Jesuits at Acadia in Canada, for instance, 'I took the occasion to give them images and to place a cross before their cabin, singing a Salve Regina'.[42] The 'neophytes' among the Algonquins in the mid-seventeenth century turned their eyes to an image of the Virgin in times of suffering.[43] So, too, the Jesuits foremost among the missionizing orders took up gold, its particular physical properties, to convey in material language qualities of God – no material captured quite so dramatically the 'glory of God'.

In a number of devotional works, Jesuits suggested how they understood images to function in the processes of conversion and of deepening piety. Jerome Nadal commissioned a series of extraordinary images whose function was not to illustrate the text, but to focus the mind of the reader, to reach the soul through the eyes, not to 'aid meditation', but to bring the entire body into the act of meditation – eyes to heart.[44] Jesuit art rested on the conviction that images might shape the perception of the world itself, through exercises;

---

38 Gagnon, *La conversion par l'image*.
39 Spence, *The memory palace*. On the complex interaction of native cultures and European missionizing Christianity, see Bailey's excellent study, *Art on the Jesuit missions in Asia and Latin America, 1542–1773*.
40 For specific examples of the complex interplay of European Christian and indigenous cultures, see Bailey, *Art on the Jesuit missions*; and Vargas Ugarte, *Los Jesuitas del Peru y el arte*.
41 Baumstark, *Rom in Bayern*; Smith, *Sensuous worship*.
42 Gagnon, *La conversion par l'image*, p. 15.   43 *Ibid.*, p. 55.
44 Melion, 'Artifice, memory, and Reformatio' and 'The art of vision'.

Figure 8. Peter Paul Rubens, 'The Miracles of Saint Ignatius of Loyola' (1615/16), Kunsthistorisches Museum, Vienna

train human cognition itself to attach immediately and, after time, without conscious decision, pious associations to visual stimuli, and thereby discipline a lived state of contemplative *and visual* devotion. Images, moreover, could teach that discipline to the illiterate and to non-Europeans.

Conclusion

Both the Catholic and Reformed churches construed the question of images within the context of the Incarnation and the representation of God in the world. The Reformed Church, in keeping with its conception of human nature and of sin, circumscribed the use of images – which were human-made creations, reflecting human values and perceptions – in worship. The Catholic Church, in keeping with its understanding of the operation of grace, took up images as important in a massive project of proselytization and conversion – images could touch the spirit, could render in matter the multiplex meaning of the Incarnation for humanity. Luther, with his radical emphasis on faith, gave images the least weight: in the tradition that looked to him as its founder, images remained, but they existed apart from the great drama of Incarnation.

20

Ritual in early modern Christianity

SUSAN C. KARANT-NUNN

All the observances of the temple have to be learned by the person, for the visible ceremonies or practices announce the invisible.[1]

Throughout the history of Christianity, leaders of the faith have found in ecclesiastical ritual an indispensable means of inculcating correct doctrine upon the unlettered and theologically uninitiated masses. As the religion of small communities and face-to-face acquaintance gave way in the western Roman Empire to territorial conversion, increasingly bishops sought to unite those in their care within a framework of observances that reinforced pastoral teachings. Indeed, through long ages of clerical under-instruction for their duties, mastery of the rites of the church constituted the core of professional preparation for the priesthood. For nearly two millennia, Christian authorities have assigned paramount importance to the proper understanding and execution of central observances, such as baptism and the eucharist.

As attractive and useful as the invocation of a ritual's antiquity is, however, scholars in many disciplines have noticed the marked changes introduced as a result of theological controversy, as well as of changed historical circumstances. The recitation of creeds, those summaries of belief, followed the bishops' taking of positions that formally set them apart from their challengers.[2] Peter Cramer has traced the evolution of baptism in the West during nearly a thousand years.[3] Medievalists are aware that the Fourth Lateran Council of 1215 elevated marriage to sacramental status, requiring the consent of both bride and groom.[4] This same council played a significant part in compelling all

---

1 'Eine katechismusartige Schrift unter dem Namen von Johann Landsperger', reprinted in Seebaß, *Müntzers Erbe*, p. 508.
2 For a simple presentation of the background, see Gonzalez, *The story of Christianity*, vol. 1, pp. 165–6; on the origins of the 'Apostles' Creed', pp. 63–4, 265. Also Pelikan, *The Christian tradition*, vol. 1: *The emergence of the Catholic tradition*, pp. 201–2.
3 Cramer, *Baptism and change*.
4 Pelikan, *Christian tradition*, vol. 3: *The growth of medieval theology*, pp. 211–12.

Catholics to confess to their priests and receive Holy Communion a minimum of once a year.[5] Most consequential for the later Reformation era, it fixed into Catholic theology the precept of transubstantiation. Just as hard, then, as leaders of the churches have attempted to preserve what they regarded as the authentic practice of the early church, they have sought to explicate and elaborate the past in ways that, in the aggregate, have transformed ritual assumptions. Liturgy has ever been, in the end, in a state of slow dynamism, responding to and reflecting the concerns especially of those who governed it. Many of those concerns were about the convictions and the life-style of the laity. Religious celebrations, whether taking place in the sanctuary or out upon planted fields during Rogation Days, sought to impress upon ordinary people the embedded quality of all aspects of life within the comprehensive design of the Creator.[6]

To a substantial degree, they succeeded. At the end of the Middle Ages, the majority of Europeans everywhere, whether pious in their behaviour or not, marked off their lives by the saints' feast days of the ecclesiastical calendar and duly confessed during Holy Week and received the Host. Their universe was a mixture of folkish and Christian principles, of whose combinations churchmen themselves had often been the deliberate agents. The Catholic faith, as it spread, had not shunned creative syncretism in the service of conversion.

On the eve of the Reformation, charismatic preachers had already begun to stress to their hearers the greater importance of basic principles, such as the imitation of Christ as found in the gospel, over the myriad available penitential acts, such as purchasing indulgences or undertaking pilgrimages. The great fourteenth- and fifteenth-century preachers, from Jan Milic and Jan Hus to John of Capistrano, Girolamo Savonarola, and Johann Geiler von Kaisersberg all believed that they founded their messages upon the truth of scripture, which they aggressively taught to their hearers. They were pre-Reformation evangelists. They, too, along with intellectuals like Erasmus who mainly abstained from homiletics in favour of scholarship, sought a return to biblically based faith. Although they were critics of prevailing practices, they did not attempt themselves to cleanse, or to urge the people to cleanse, what they may have thought was an Augean stable of scripturally unauthorized liturgical accretions. As 'forerunners', they concentrated upon the transmission of Holy Writ, particularly the life of Christ, to their hearers, and upon inspiring the faithful to bring their hearts and lives into closer conformity with it.

5 Philip Hughes, *Church in crisis*, p. 243.
6 A collection of forty-three essays on medieval religious and social rituals of all kinds is Altenburg, Jarnut, and Steinhoff (eds.), *Feste und Feiern im Mittelalter*.

The reformation of the sacraments

The early reformers were not so moderate. Martin Luther, Johannes Bugen-hagen, Ulrich Zwingli, Johannes Brenz, Berchthold Haller, Joachim Vadian, Johannes Oecolampadius, Guillaume Farel, and John Calvin were just as rad-ical in the transformations they sponsored as any Anabaptist leader.[7] The root of revolution as well as of the lasting subdivision among all these devout men was their very adherence to that fundamental Reformation principle, *sola scriptura*. From 1518 forward, the self-appointed leaders of the movement to return to the alleged practices of the early church came to differing con-clusions on what scripture said. The full spectrum of ritual variety within Protestantism reflected these differences. Only Catholicism, with its reiter-ated emphasis upon the equality of tradition to the literal Word of God, was exempt from this endeavour to conform, even at the peak of its own reforming efforts.

Martin Luther and Ulrich Zwingli, in their respective regions, emerged as the predominant voices – and this is an apt metaphor inasmuch as both loved to sing – in the early Reformation chorus. The path to transformation was much more complicated for Luther because Ernestine Saxony was a far-flung territory; Zwingli's agenda could be effected much more easily in the Swiss city that presided only over its immediate hinterland.[8] In Wittenberg, a colleague of Luther, Andreas Bodenstein von Karlstadt, made the first decisive gesture towards the revision of the eucharist when, on Christmas Day 1521, he admin-istered both bread and wine to the gathered communicants, in violation of the Catholic distribution only of the Host. Simultaneously he urged the removal of icons from the churches, and many Wittenbergers, with the approval of the city council, joined in the undertaking. Luther was sufficiently alarmed to return from his hiding place at the Wartburg by Eisenach in March 1522, and to insist on the revocation of these precipitous innovations. In his opinion, change should come gradually, as people became used to the idea of receiving the chalice too. He was categorically opposed to iconoclasm and advocated the removal (and not the destruction) only of those images that were not bib-lically attested. Crucifixes, manger scenes, and apostles could stay; Sts Ursula, George, and Christopher, along with myriad others, must ultimately go.

7 I take issue here with the old label of the Anabaptists as 'radical reformers', employed, of course, by Williams in his *The Radical Reformation* (Philadelphia: Westminster Press, 1962). Its 3rd edn appeared as *Sixteenth Century Essays & Studies* 15 (Kirksville, MO: Sixteenth Century Journal Publishers, 1992).
8 For the perspective of a leading historian of theology, see Junghans's essay, 'Luthers Gottesdienstreform – Konzept oder Verlegenheit?'

Luther's will prevailed, with the necessary consent of his princes, Elector Frederick the Wise (d. 1525), and Frederick's brother and successor, John the Constant (d. 1532). The observant churchgoer in Wittenberg might have noticed the alterations that crept into the administration of the sacraments during the 1520s, whereas indifferent participants in ecclesiastical celebrations might not.[9] By 1526, the Reformer had translated the mass into German (following the pattern already provided by Thomas Müntzer as well as several other men) and written his own baptismal rite (*Taufbüchlein*) in the vernacular, including several departures from Catholic precedent. That all the laity could comprehend the wording was significant – although there was already a tendency in late medieval liturgy to make the proceedings intelligible to the uneducated. But even given this advance, few ordinary people understood the distinction between the Catholic *transubstantiation* and Luther's doctrine of *consubstantiation*. Even if the priest no longer pronounced his 'hocus pocus' (*hoc est corpus meum*) and transformed the bread and the wine into the actual body and blood of Christ, Luther taught that when communicants came to the altar (soon to be moved to the front of the dais so that the presiding clergyman could face the congregation), they continued to ingest the true flesh and blood of their Saviour. The supernatural magnitude and power-to-move of this experience very likely remained the same as before: the Divine, with its unspeakable power, physically entered the mundane realm. The elevation of the eucharistic elements persisted until 1542; and although the officiating cleric did not wear elaborate vestments any longer, he still donned what appears to us as a simple choir robe. Every altar displayed its retable and candles, even if monstrances, pyxes, reliquaries, and thuribles now disappeared. Furthermore, auricular confession continued as a prerequisite of participating in communion.

In Lutheran sanctuaries, organ music and song gained new ground during the sixteenth century. The first hymnal appeared in 1524, and Luther himself contributed to the following editions German translations of key parts of the Latin mass: 'Jesaja dem Propheten das geschah', 'Christe, du Lamm Gottes', and 'Herr Gott Vater im Himmel, erbarm dich über uns', to be sung by the congregation.[10] From 1528, pastors were required to preach weekly from the new Lutheran catechisms, and this was clearly an innovation.

---

9 For consideration of the elements of continuity and discontinuity within Luther's liturgy of the mass, see Wendebourg, 'Luthers Reform der Messe – Bruch oder Kontinuität?' pp. 289–306.

10 Oettinger, *Music as propaganda*, pp. 44–7; Veit, *Das Kirchenlied in der Reformation*.

The adoption of Luther's baptismal rite represented relatively little discomfiture to parents and godparents. The father's select representatives carried the newborn to church, as before, as soon after birth as could be arranged, and they met the pastor there.[11] Although they could now enter the church without an initial lustral rite of greeting, the small party still gathered at the old christening font, whether inside the west entrance or in a chapel closer to the altar. The godparents still demanded baptism on the child's behalf and renounced Satan and all his minions. They provided their little charge's name. Luther retained but reduced the incidence of exorcism, regarding unbaptized infants still as 'children of wrath'. He introduced to the ceremony baptism as a counterpart in the individual's life to the collective flood in the time of Noah. He preferred infants to be disrobed and either dipped in the font or manually aspersed. Philip Melanchthon is shown performing the latter in the altar-painting in the city church in Wittenberg.[12] He retained the use of a white baptismal dress or bonnet, with which the baby was garbed at the end. The sacrament as a whole, along with the preservation of 'emergency baptism' by the midwife within the birthing chamber, reveal quite clearly that Luther continued to regard baptism as essential to salvation *despite* the doctrine of justification by faith. Apart from what he selected for the services over which he presided in the Wittenberg city church, where he was not the pastor Luther left room for other officiants to make their own choices; he thought that apart from core transactions, the liturgy should be flexible.

The Reformer of Zurich, by contrast, in the alterations he wrought, left no doubt, even among his illiterate charges, that Catholic ritual was now at an end. Auricular confession was abolished. The city fathers consented to the suspension of the mass in 1525. What supplanted its rendition of the eucharist was a Lord's Supper of stark simplicity. Zwingli's conviction that Jesus's instruction to his disciples that 'this *is* my body' meant 'this *signifies* my body', and that, therefore, the supper was strictly a commemorative event, showed itself in the breaking up and distribution of plain table bread.[13] Kneeling and making the sign of the cross were no longer permitted. Song too was banned – although not every Swiss Reformed city was willing to follow Zurich to this extreme.[14]

---

11 Karant-Nunn, *The reformation of ritual*, pp. 43–71; Karant-Nunn, 'Suffer the little children to come unto me'.
12 This painting can be seen in many places, among them Junghans, *Wittenberg als Lutherstadt*, p. 132, plate 68.
13 For a subtle discussion of the ways in which images and gestures communicated with lay worshippers in Zurich, see Wandel, 'Envisioning God'.
14 Garside, *Zwingli and the arts*; Ehrstein, *Theater, culture, and community*, pp. 247–88.

Violent iconoclasm led the way to the total removal of religious images and any artefacts thought to be sacrally charged. Here God was indeed spiritual and transcendent, unavailable to the five senses. Zwingli preferred to have ministers preside in regular apparel rather than clerical vestments. Calvin would share in his predecessor's sense of liturgical and decorative propriety, although he would have liked to celebrate the eucharist each week. The magistrates would not permit this but adhered to Zwingli's provision of four annual suppers, one per quarter. Calvin did, however, adopt the Strasbourgers' singing of metrical psalms.

A principle that underlay Zwingli's and later Calvin's rubrics was the representation of the godly community. Even though in the theology of both men (in contrast with the Anabaptists), the visible and invisible churches could not be clearly distinguished on earth, sacraments united the members of the congregation in time and space, and also in a perdurable sense, as part of the eternal church of God. This is especially visible in the enactment of baptism. Whereas well into the longer early modern period, Lutheran christenings could occur in isolation from the gathered parishioners, Zwingli, and then Calvin, abolished emergency baptism and insisted that the sacrament could only take place during a regular service. Zwingli pointedly noted that with baptism the child is engrafted into the body of Christ.[15] The prayers of all the faithful should surround the infant, and the entire congregation should commit itself to assisting in the production of a faithful and upright adult.

Further, from an early date infants' natural fathers were required to take part – although most likely their mothers remained 'confined' at home. All 'superstitious' remnants of Catholicism were now eliminated – exorcism and the application of breath, spittle, salt, oil, candles, specially consecrated water, and the sign of the cross. Fonts were often removed in favour of simple basins. At the nexus between ritual and social practice, Calvin's prohibition of the use of certain saints' names in baptism caused tension and even riots in Geneva.[16] Preserved was, along with key Bible readings, a core Christian ceremony in which the officiant applied water while declaring, 'N., I baptize you in the name of the Father, and of the Son, and of the Holy Spirit'.[17] Not all newborns would attain a simultaneous inner washing with the water

---

15 *Hundreich Zwinglis sämtliche Werke* (hereafter ZW), ed. Emil Egli, vol. 4, pp. 243–4.
16 Naphy, 'Baptism, church riots and social unrest'. On the persistence of Catholic elements in Geneva, see Spierling, 'Daring insolence toward God?'
17 ZW, vol. 4, pp. 680–2; available in modern German translation in Mira Baumgartner (comp.), *Die Täufer und Zwingli*, pp. 133–6.

of grace. That all hoped they might receive it was reflected in prayers and admonitions.[18]

Hughes Oliphant Old has studied the development of Reformed baptismal rituals during the remainder of the sixteenth century and found them to be anything but inflexible. Alterations reflected in part a response to the Anabaptists' voluntarism and their conviction that God would ultimately save few people. Above all, the prompt initiation of infants, whether strictly necessary for salvation or not, had to be maintained in the face of the Anabaptist advocacy of adult believers' baptism. Also spurred on by the Anabaptist challenge was the revival of ritual confirmation after young people had demonstrated their mastery of the pertinent new catechism and professed to accept its terms. Confirmation marked the individual's acceptance of the oaths made by godparents on his behalf at christening.

The Anabaptist ceremony of baptism departed the most radically from established practice. Without standard rubrics, it must have occurred somewhat differently on each administration. Hans Hut enquired of each candidate whether he or she would desist from sin. On receiving a positive reply, he then dipped one finger in a bowl of water and with it made three signs of the cross on the baptisand's forehead. In some manner, he invoked the Trinity, but possibly not using the familiar sentence, 'I baptize thee in the name of . . . '[19] A contemporary ink-drawing from Anabaptist Münster shows a man applying a fair volume of water from a plain wooden keg to a woman's head as others kneel nearby. Christ walks among the group.[20] Little research has been done on any category of Anabaptist ceremony. Most of its leaders regarded marriage as so completely secular that its sealing should not take place in a religious setting. Indeed, there may have been little ceremony beyond public mutual consent.

The sermon

A means by which clergymen disseminated their inmost convictions was the sermon. Preaching was no novelty in the Reformation era, and yet prior to the evangelical movement the sermon was a regular event chiefly in major urban centres. Wherever it occurred, the sermon was a ritual artefact. As long

18 Old's *The shaping of the Reformed baptismal rite* takes up Switzerland and the German south-west and is rich in detail. See at least Chapter 10, 'The washing and the word', 249–82.
19 Seebaß, *Müntzers Erbe*, pp. 243–4.
20 Reproduced in von Greyerz, *Religion und Kultur*, p. 255.

as the signal role of the priest was to serve as the channel through which the body and blood of Christ entered the telluric sphere, the homily paled in comparison to this transubstantiation. The Reformation transformed formal worship by replacing this supernatural act with the explication of the Word. Both in time consumed and attention demanded, the sermon became the central component of Sunday and many weekday services.[21] Christians were asked not just to submit to the programmes presented by their pastors; they were to understand salient doctrines and consciously reaffirm their adherence to them each time they attended church. Spreading, large, prominently placed pulpits symbolize the centrality of preaching throughout the Protestant world, from Scandinavia to Switzerland, from Massachusetts to eastern Europe. The Lutheran world developed two homiletical subgenres from the mid-sixteenth century that quickly became virtually obligatory: funeral and wedding sermons. Catechetical sermons were novel but far fewer in published form. Printed burial and nuptial homilies have survived in the hundreds of thousands, for pious, literate men and women were expected to purchase them for their and their families' ongoing edification between services. In this way, as well as by means of the proliferating prayerbooks, the word of scripture and of the pastor extended beyond formal worship and into many households. Calvinist communities put equal stress upon the preached word, but their leaders perceived a danger in wedding and funeral sermons and did not adopt them. Curiously, too, Reformed sermons found their way into print far less often than Lutheran ones – possibly because of the fear in France that such books could provide incriminating evidence of nonconformity.

There was never such a thing as a 'pure' Lutheran or a 'pure' Reformed liturgy of divine worship. Despite the influential rubrics of the great Reformers, cities and territories considered their own preferences and often combined elements of more than one model in the ordinances they adopted. There was much disagreement over which liturgical usages were 'adiaphora' or 'indifferent matters' that could be carried out or not, as a presiding clergyman or a community wished. The Augsburg Interim, imposed in 1547 by the victorious Catholic Emperor Charles V, was a bitter pill in that it imposed upon Protestant churches within the Holy Roman Empire practices that they by no means considered matters of choice but rejected out of hand. Among these were the re-establishment of the mass, the recognition and practice of all seven sacraments, and obedience to the pope and bishops. Philip Melanchthon was

---

21 Taylor (ed.), *Preachers and people* contains valuable essays on both specific denominations and regions.

willing to compromise, which made him objectionable in the eyes of such fellow Lutherans as Matthias Flacius Illyricus.[22] Tensions over what constituted *adiaphora* remained.

The Catholic Church

Today historians discuss whether the label Counter-Reformation has any validity.[23] In the flowering of Catholic preaching from the middle of the sixteenth century, however, I still choose to see a certain urgent acknowledgment that Protestant pedagogical tools must be adopted and adapted in order to prevent the further spread of 'heresy'. The Society of Jesus and the Capuchins honed their homiletic skills, developing formal methods of training for those who would go out as missionaries to the common people of Europe. As a result of the Catholic Church's new emphasis on preaching, despite the remaining centrality of the traditional mass, the elaborate and costly pulpit became a Catholic symbol too.

The post-Tridentine Catholic Church strove not so much to revise Catholic ceremony as to make it uniform. The so-called Tridentine Missal was its first effort to ensure liturgical purity. In 1588 Sixtus V founded the Congregation of Sacred Rites, which was to oversee the introduction and maintenance of approved practice. Finally, the *Rituale Romanum* of 1614 laid down a pattern for the mass that contained the long-familiar core and that remained fundamentally intact until the second Vatican Council. Eliminated in the improved rubrics were the most fanciful of the local and regional tropes that had crept in over many centuries, as well as nearly all votive masses.[24] The Church also cast a disapproving eye at retables and statues whose contents hinted at unorthodoxy. Carlo Borromeo (1538–84), Archbishop of Milan, who after his death came to be regarded as a model bishop and was canonized in 1610, set out regulations governing everything from the running of the bishop's own household to the interior decoration of churches.[25] His influence was considerable. Nonetheless, the political obstacles and the popular defence of custom meant that much remained as it had before. Foremost among the aspirations of the missionizing orders, whether in southern Germany, France,

---

22 Manschreck, *Melanchthon*, pp. 287–92; Scheible, *Melanchthon: Eine Biographie*, pp. 196–201, 218–26.

23 O'Malley, *Trent and all that*.

24 The indispensable work on the history of the mass is Jungmann, *The mass of the Roman rite*.

25 Deroo, *Saint Charles Borromée*.

or the New World, were the orderly inculcation of fundamental credal precepts upon the people and their firm identification of themselves as Catholic Christians. These orders and the parish clergy as well often exploited familiar rituals in the service of these greater ends. Holy Week observances with their long and elaborate programmes of sermons, Corpus Christi processions, and supervised pilgrimages were regular occurrences.[26]

The Baroque style afforded reforming Catholics a ready aesthetic for appealing to the masses. Deliberately elaborate and arousing, the newly adorned churches drew the people by their senses into a fresh appreciation of the link between the priesthood and the Divinity.[27]

Common elements in Catholicism and Protestantism

Throughout Europe, whether in Catholic or Protestant territories, leaders of both church and state, in wary alliance with each other, participated in defining acceptable belief and practice. Initially, they had to ensure that the pastorate was firmly in command of approved doctrine so that its members could, in turn, instruct the laity. The process of improving the clergy took virtually the whole of the sixteenth century. Bishops, superintendents, consistories, synods, and inquisitions all played their parts. They supported requirements for advanced education for young men becoming priests or pastors, the production of catechisms and pastoral handbooks to define belief and the symbolism of the liturgy for clerics and laypeople alike, pre-ordination testing of clergymen, parish inspections at regular intervals, and the revival of confirmation (which had fallen into desuetude during the Middle Ages) before admission to communion. The mechanisms of punishment for infractions ranged widely. In Calvinist Geneva and Scotland, exclusion from the eucharist was so regular an event that it acquired ritual implications. The laity had to show coin-like tokens as evidence of pastoral approval, in order to be admitted to communion. Banning also took place in Lutheran churches. Before readmission, the accused were displayed during services and compelled to express heartfelt remorse for their transgressions.

An aspect of the general reform impulse that is expressed in liturgical revisions was the effort, across emerging denominations, to curtail, control, and

---

26 Soergel, *Wondrous in his saints*; Christian, Jr, *Local religion in sixteenth-century Spain*; Châtellier, *The Europe of the devout*.
27 Smith, *Sensuous worship*. Note the confessional boxes, figs. 56 and 184, respectively on pp. 85 and 185.

even eliminate the universal extensions of ecclesiastical ritual into the social sphere. Authorities widely agreed that what was sacred must be exclusively so – although Catholics were consistently more tolerant of festivities than Protestants. Lutheran and Calvinist divines, along with the magistrates and princes who agreed with them, strove to moderate post-wedding, -baptismal, and -confinement celebrations. Lutheran churches left modest observances in place, but Calvin, by means of the Genevan consistory, was able to cleanse outward expression more completely by means of close oversight and enforcement.[28] Lutherans still danced at their wedding dinners, but Genevans did not, or at least not with impunity. Other Reformed communities, however, left 'modest dancing' in place. Lutheran wives still held and attended post-churching ales, but Calvin eliminated the purification of women after childbirth together with the accompanying get-togethers of neighbouring housewives.

The programmes of prelates and princes to install the creeds of their choices, including the liturgies that embodied them – which Wolfgang Reinhard and Heinz Schilling have identified as part of confessionalization – were most effective in city-states and small, compact territories where the enforcing eye could be keen and the arm of the law consistent.[29] The freedom to move between emergent belief systems and ritual practice is most noticeable in two settings: along geographic boundaries and in lands where, in the end, no denomination came to be established. Nominally Protestant peasants living within easy reach of a Catholic land crossed over to avail themselves of alternative rituals. Some pregnant women sought out papist midwives because these were able to invoke the patron saints of childbirth, Anna and Margaret, and to apply such folk aids as the Virgin's belt to mothers in labour. Other parents desired the exorcism used by priests in administering baptism. Catholics came in the other direction, to hear sermons or to visit saints' shrines that through happenstance were now located on Protestant properties. Protestant authorities evidently everywhere ordered the immediate disposal of baptismal water so that it could not be collected and used for 'superstitious' purposes.

In the post-Reformation period, the appropriation of the ceremonial practices of other denominations slowly becomes evident. This phenomenon requires further study. Lutheran churches widely adopted, for example, the

---

28 Lambert and Watt (eds.), *Registers of the Consistory of Geneva*, vol. I.
29 Reinhard, 'Gegenreformation als Modernisierung?'; Reinhard, 'Konfession und Konfessionalisierung in Deutschland'; Schilling, 'Confessional Europe'; Schilling, *Konfessionskonflikt und Staatsbildung*; Schilling, 'The Reformation and the rise of the early modern state'. See also Lotz-Heumann, 'The concept of "confessionalization" '.

Reformed insistence on burying unbaptized infants along with their relatives and 'other Christians' on the grounds that the parents' faith was effective for their child. Some Calvinist congregations mitigated their prohibition on instrumental music and reintroduced organs from the end of the sixteenth century. Overall contrasts remained, to be sure, but ecclesiastical ceremony continued its visible evolution.

Religious choices

In the Netherlands, because no single religious group was able to ally itself with the governing echelons and become the one permissible creed, citizens had the tacit liberty – in an age that did not advocate such liberty – to select among several available churches, including Anabaptist. In the great cities of the northern Low Countries, especially in Amsterdam, liturgical contrasts were in evidence. Catholic congregations carried on their multiple masses in as highly ornamented surroundings as the wealth of the people allowed. The Virgin Mary and other saints retained their iconic prominence, and women other than the Virgin were well represented in the holy precincts. The churches taken over by the Calvinist-minded were completely reconfigured, their altar-steads boarded up, walls whitewashed, pulpits placed high along one side of the sanctuary, with a plain communion table at their base. Huguenots in some circumstances were able to build new churches, and these were architecturally innovative, embodying Reformed theology.[30] Pews proliferated in all denominations from the mid-sixteenth century. In Calvinist churches, these were gathered around and faced the pulpit. In such a mixed and densely populated setting, Christians may have gained a casual familiarity with a range of liturgical styles and the teachings that they were intended to bespeak. Not even those congregations that desired to bar non-members from their sacred premises could always succeed. In time, godparents and courting couples crossed confessional lines and had to be allowed. Church discipline could be imposed only with the consent of the targeted members.[31]

Patterns of influence can be traced between Zurich and Geneva and between Geneva and the Huguenot churches of France, the Reformed congregations of the Low Countries, Presbyterian parishes of Scotland, and Puritan pastors

---

30 Raymond A. Mentzer, Jr, provides an especially fine overview in 'The Reformed churches of France and the visual arts'.
31 See, for example, Houston, 'The Consistory of the Scots Church, Rotterdam', and Catterall, 'The rituals of Reformed discipline', *Archive for Reformation History* 94 (2003), 194–222.

and their followers in England. Ecclesiastical rites could still be bones of avid, sometimes murderous, contention in an age in which theologians and princes led their followers towards the passionate certainty that only one monolithic Truth existed. The ideals put forward could be unbending even when practice was pragmatic.

The English Church

Nowhere was ritual more hotly contested than in England. Henry VIII's theological vacillations produced only a few permanent changes. Among those that must be included are the destruction for their wealth of liturgical artefacts, monasteries, and shrines across the country; and the expansion of the use of English in worship services. Despite the king's early opposition to the translation of the Bible, he ultimately authorized what came to be called the Great Bible (1539). Scriptural texts were henceforward to be read from this rather than the Vulgate. During Henry's lifetime, tensions existed chiefly between Roman Catholics and those who conceded to the king.

During young Edward's reign, however, the two successive Calvinist lords protector acted to impose Geneva's radical changes on both existing conservative categories. The Duke of Somerset immediately declared, among much else,

> that they shall take away, utterly extinct and destroy all shrines, coverings of shrines, all tables and candlesticks, trundles or rolls of ware, pictures, paintings and all other monuments of feigned miracles, pilgrimages, idolatry and superstition, so that there remain no memory of the same in walls, glasses, windows or elsewhere within their churches or houses.[32]

Thomas Cranmer intended his second prayerbook (1552) to be a moderate doctrine. In its introduction, the archbishop declared,

> The mindes of menne are so diuerse, that some thynke it a greate matter of conscience to departe from a pece of the least of their Ceremonies . . . and again on the other side, some be so new fangled, that thei would innouate all thyng, and so do despise the old, that nothyng can like them, but that is new: it was thought expedient, not so much to haue respect how to please and satisfie either of these parties, as how to please God, and profyte them both.[33]

32 From 'The Edwardian injunctions, 1547', in Bray (ed.), *Documents of the English Reformation*, p. 255.
33 *The first and second Prayer Books of Edward VI*, p. 324.

In this rubric, Cranmer omits the more traditional words of distribution, 'The body of our Lorde Jesus Christe whiche was geuen for thee . . . The bloud of our Lorde Jesus Christ which was shed for thee . . .' that had appeared in his first prayerbook.[34] He now recommends exclusively, 'Take and eate this, in remembraunce that Christ dyed for thee, and feede on him in thy hearte by faythe, with thankesgeuing . . . Drinke this in remembraunce that Christ's bloude was shed for thee, and be thankefull.'[35] He favours, like his governing patrons, spiritual nourishment. Even though the predominant influence upon Anglican theology was Calvinist, Queen Elizabeth I preferred a more Catholic ceremony. The modifications of the Edwardian Prayer Book that she sponsored combined the language of eucharistic institution so that either Christ's bodily presence or commemoration could be understood.

The Puritans arose within the Church of England during the second half of the sixteenth century. After the return of the so-called Marian exiles, their spokesmen expressed the great fault that they found in the Book of Common Prayer, at the meeting of Convocation in 1563, among other venues. They were narrowly defeated. Richard Hooker later summarized the Puritan position, which was that the Prayer Book had

> too great affinity with the Form of the Church of Rome; it differeth too much from that which Churches elsewhere reformed allow and observe; our attire disgraceth it; it is not orderly read, nor gestured as beseemeth; it requireth nothing to be done which a child may not lawfully do; it hath a number of short cuts or shreddings, which may be better called wishes than Prayers; it intermingleth prayings and readings in such manner, as if suppliants should use in proposing their suits unto mortal Princes, all the world would judge them mad; it is too long, and by that mean abridgeth Preaching; it appointeth the people to say after the Minister; it spendeth time in singing and in reading the psalms by course, from side to side; it useth the Lord's Prayer too oft . . . These and such like are the imperfections whereby our form of Common Prayer is thought to swerve from the Word of God.[36]

Hooker himself favoured the Prayer Book and regarded ceremonial as an inducement to holiness.[37] Curates who were inclined towards a greater degree of reformation than the Prayer Book and the Anglican establishment (with notable exceptions like Archbishop Edmund Grindal) encouraged took it upon themselves to bring the usage of their congregations in line with the Bible as they interpreted it. The sermon occupied a longer, more central

---

34 Ibid., p. 225.   35 Ibid., p. 389.
36 Hooker, Of the laws of ecclesiastical polity, Book 5, Chap. 27, Sec. 1.
37 Cited by Lockyer, Tudor and Stuart Britain, p. 202.

position than it did elsewhere – where it was not neglected. These clerics dispensed with vestments, strictly employed communion tables, favoured the singing of metrical psalms alone, frowned on the use of wedding rings, and urged their parishioners not to indulge in Christmas festivities. Where it proved possible, Puritans reorganized church interiors to conform to their teachings.[38] Elizabeth I despised both the Catholic and Puritan ends of what in reality was a religious spectrum. Her fear of their destabilizing power was realized during the reigns of her successors: the differences between the defenders of the Anglican style of worship and the Puritan styles, including in the seventeenth century Presbyterians and Independents, would be a factor in the English Civil War. The former were able to appreciate historical accretions along with scripture, whereas the latter strove to hold services that accorded with their biblical literalism. Throughout Albion, local ritual preferences waxed and waned. From the death of Henry VIII, what we refer to as 'high church' and 'low church' Anglican liturgical styles could be found. A lack of mobility as well as the parish system no doubt prevented many parishioners from selecting the type of service that they preferred.

Conclusions

Each Reformer sought to rectify the theological errors that he attributed to the late medieval Catholic Church. As we know, from an early date it was evident that the principle of *sola scriptura* – not to mention the conviction held by some that direct communication by the Holy Spirit surpassed the contents of Holy Writ – guaranteed a widespread diversity of belief. Accompanying that diversity were infinite variations in its symbolic representations. Differences among religious ceremonies and artefacts spread across Europe, until their variety far surpassed those available within late medieval Catholicism. These developments, conceived and led by theologians and secular governors, often did not reflect the preferences of the ordinary laity. Nevertheless, as Catherine Bell has assured us, the intentions of the organizers of the Reformation did not necessarily coincide with the interpretations of ordinary participants in ritual.[39] How the laity perceived and appropriated the liturgy for its own purposes deserves further attention.

38 See Stell, 'Puritan and nonconformist meetinghouses in England'.
39 Bell, *Ritual theory, ritual practice*, esp. 'The power of ritualization', pp. 197–223.

21

Music and religious change

ALEXANDER J. FISHER

Introduction

Between the beginning of the Lutheran Reformation and the end of the Thirty Years' War sacred music in early modern Europe underwent several waves of transformation, responding partly to the dramatic religious upheavals of the period and partly to changes in aesthetic taste and compositional technique. The most fundamental aspect of these changes – significant both to religious context and musical structure – was a new relationship of music to the word, whether scriptural or otherwise. Late medieval composers, writing music for the mass liturgy and motets for a variety of sacred functions, had focused their energies on exploiting the possibilities of intricate, and to the listener obscure, musical structures, abstract patterns of sound based on tunes whose provenance (secular or sacred) or inherent significance was of relatively little importance. Likewise, for the medieval laity the Latin words sung by church choirs had represented the sacred authority of scripture and liturgy, but their unavailability in the vernacular had hindered their capacity for inspiration and edification.

Throughout the early modern era the clear presentation and musical interpretation of words became a defining feature of church music, both Roman and Reformed. The Lutheran Reformation elevated the significance of the word in sacred music, but in fact the concern with the meaning and comprehension of words was widely shared among humanists and church leaders across the confessional divides of the early modern era. Erasmus of Rotterdam, Philip Melanchthon, and Pietro Bembo, for example, sought through the study of ancient texts the revival of some aspects of classical civilization; in music the interest in theories of rhetorical oratory (inspired by works of Quintilian and Cicero) affected entire genres, ranging from sacred music to the secular Italian madrigal and, eventually, opera. For church reformers of the sixteenth century the popular access to and understanding of sacred words was of greater importance. The Lutheran and Calvinist Reformations granted lay access to scripture and other religious texts in the vernacular; the texts of Lutheran chorales, for example, became as essential as their musical settings and indeed enjoyed quasi-scriptural status. While the Catholic Church retained the Latin language, church leaders and composers focused on the appropriateness of texts and musical models (the Council of Trent resolved that all 'lascivious or impure' associations were to be avoided in church music), and many insisted on the clear declamation of words, achieved through careful attention to textual accentuation and by ensuring that the clarity of the words would not be disturbed by the intricacy of musical counterpoint.

In all three of the major confessional churches – Lutheran, Calvinist, and Catholic – sacred music reflected and helped to define the emerging doctrinal and cultural differences between them. From an early stage Lutheran and Calvinist music was defined by the combination of vernacular texts with relatively simple and memorable tunes, providing a vehicle for the rapid spread of new religious thinking. These repertories aided in religious edification and provided a means of collective devotional expression. In the contested areas of central Europe along the divide between the Reformed and Catholic faiths, such music took on the undeniable quality of propaganda. The Catholic Church, too, eventually embraced vernacular song as a counterweight to Lutheran chorales and Calvinist psalms, but on the whole its music strengthened the links between the Latin language, the authority of Rome, and the venerable spiritual and liturgical traditions of the medieval church. If Reformation church music sought to grant the laity a more meaningful and participatory role as a 'priesthood of believers', Catholic church music more fully embraced a representational mode in which the aural splendour of choirs and instruments impressed upon the listener the drama of the sacraments and the glory and authority of the universal church. In these ways sacred music, both popular and sophisticated, reflected and contributed to the process of European confessionalization.

Music and the Reformation

Music in early modern Lutheranism

The distinctive musical traditions, both popular and learned, of the early modern Lutheran church reflect its founder's conviction that music was second in importance only to theology.[1] Music facilitated the meaningful participation

---

1 Luther, Tischreden, nos. 968, 7034, 3815. A comprehensive overview of Lutheran music may be found in Blume (ed.), Protestant church music.

of the laity in the divine service while serving as one of the most effective tools of propaganda. In turn the heritage of the chorale informed the more elaborate traditions of Lutheran polyphony that flourished through the eighteenth century in the hands of composers like Heinrich Schütz, Dietrich Buxtehude, and Johann Sebastian Bach.

The promotion of the vernacular chorale (variously called *Kirchenlied, geistliches Lied, geistlicher Gesang,* and by other names in its early years) by Luther and his colleagues was a step of fundamental importance for the subsequent history of church music. Seeking to breach the artificial barriers between the clergy and laity that characterized the contemporary church – symbolized by the inaccessibility of the Latin liturgy as well as the physical separation of the celebrant from the congregation – Luther and his associates composed and assembled some two dozen songs for congregational singing in the winter of 1523/4. Luther is generally acknowledged to have authored the texts, although debate continues on whether he, or his colleague Johann Walter (1496–1570), composed the melodies as well[2] (Luther's well-documented musical interests and abilities suggest that he was capable of this step; *Ein feste Burg ist unser Gott* is the best-known chorale generally attributed to him). Few of Luther's melodies were entirely original: German translations of Latin chant, medieval German spiritual songs (*Leisen*) and popular Latin sacred songs for major feasts (*cantiones*) served as musical resources and ensured that contemporary congregations would quickly recognize and learn the new music; the skilful adaptation of the traditional melodies to the demands of the German language is also a hallmark of Luther's work. The texts address all aspects of Christian life, and range from *de tempore* settings to texts on themes of faith, dogma, penance, comfort, suffering, death, and eternal life.[3] In searching for a model for this repertory Luther may have drawn inspiration from the vernacular songbooks of the Bohemian Brethren, three editions of which were published by 1519 (Luther was a friend of Michael Weisse, a member of the Brethren who would contribute twelve songs to the 'Bapst' hymnbook [1545], the earliest large-scale publication of Lutheran chorales).

Luther's radical move to involve the laity in the divine service by encouraging communal singing in the vernacular should not obscure the continuing role of more elaborate polyphony in the Lutheran Church, a role that is consistent with the reformer's reluctance to dispense with the received Latin liturgy. Called the 'Nightingale of Wittenberg' by the *Meistersinger* Hans Sachs, Luther

---

2 On Walter's contribution see Blankenburg, *Johann Walter: Leben und Werk.*
3 For a systematic examination of thematic imagery in the early Lutheran chorales, see Veit, *Das Kirchenlied in der Reformation Martin Luthers.*

had a fine tenor voice, played the lute and flute, and had a decent understanding of music theory; his favourite composers included Jacob Obrecht, Heinrich Isaac, and Josquin des Prez. Traditional plainchant and polyphony continued to find a place in the mostly Latin liturgy outlined in Luther's *Formula missae* (1523), intended to serve as a model for urban congregations. For the main service, or *Hauptgottesdienst*, Luther retained the chief items of the Catholic mass, eliminating only the offertory (which unacceptably symbolized the 'sacrifice' of the mass) and the canon; traditional Latin-texted music would have been sung by the choir in the expected places while the congregation would sing German hymns at specified points in the service (the Gradual hymn, or *Graduallied*, emerged as the primary chorale in the Lutheran service). Luther offered a simplified version of this formula for rural congregations in his *Deutsche Messe* (1526), which established authorized German alternatives to the standard items of the mass ordinary, including the replacement of the Gloria with *Allein Gott in der Höh' sei Ehr*, the Credo with *Wir glauben all an einem Gott*, and the Agnus Dei with *Christe, du Lamm Gottes*. The heritage of the chorale exerted a major influence on Lutheran polyphonic traditions in the sixteenth century and beyond, resulting in various genres of sacred music in the vernacular that took the chorale melody as a basis for compositional elaboration: characteristic are Johann Walter's polyphonic hymns for four or five voices, in which the original tune appears in long notes in one or more of the parts. Nevertheless, both the *Hauptgottesdienst* and the *Vespergottesdienst* (vespers, the other chief service in the Lutheran tradition) continued to allow significant scope for Latin polyphony as well; the Magnificat, for example, enjoyed numerous settings by Lutheran composers throughout the early modern era.

On the whole, the numerous hymnbooks published for the Lutheran church in the sixteenth century illustrate the dual purposes of providing music not only for the lay congregation, but also for trained choirs, composed largely of schoolboys, that were expected to lead the congregational singing. Thus a work like the entirely monophonic *Etlich Cristlich Lieder* (Nuremburg, 1523/4, also called the *Achtliederbuch*), containing eight chorale texts and four simple melodies for use by the laity, was balanced by efforts like Johann Walter's *Geystliches Gesangk Buchleyn* (the so-called *Chorgesangbuch*, Wittenberg, 1524), containing four- to five-voice settings of chorale melodies. Pupils in urban Latin schools would have learned these compositions partly for their own edification (Luther hoped that this music would 'wean them away from love ballads and carnal songs') and partly for the purpose of leading church congregations. While the Wittenberg printer Joseph Klug focused on the publication of chorale collections for popular use (his comprehensive and well-organized

Geistliche Lieder of 1529 went through eight subsequent editions), Georg Rhau concentrated on the polyphonic repertory, issuing several new editions of Walter's *Chorgesangbuch*, a large anthology of vernacular sacred polyphony in 1544 (the *Newe deudsche geistliche Gesenge*), as well as Latin-texted music for the mass ordinary, proper, and vespers. In most of these latter publications the distinct enunciation in one or more of the voices of the pre-existing tune – be it a Lutheran chorale or plainchant – underlines the functional basis of the music. Especially in the case of music based on vernacular chorales, the close connections between the simple monophony for the congregation and the more elaborate polyphony for the choir commonly resulted in the alternation of the two bodies of singers in successive stanzas of the chorale. The organ would aid the congregation not only by direct accompaniment, but also by introducing the chorale with a *chorale prelude* that signalled to the laity the precise chorale to be sung as well as its pitch and tempo. Eventually the chorale prelude would develop into one of the most elaborate forms of Lutheran church music, culminating in the some 170 preludes by the Leipzig cantor Johann Sebastian Bach in the eighteenth century.

The publication of the so-called Bapst hymnbook in Leipzig in 1545, containing a comprehensive collection of some 120 chorales and establishing the core Lutheran repertory for the next two centuries, signalled a new phase of consolidation and rationalization in Lutheran music, spurred partly by confessionalization in the face of new challenges from the Catholic Counter-Reformation and the Calvinist faith. Large-scale hymnbooks like Nikolaus Selnecker's *Christliche Psalmen, Lieder und Kirchengesang* (Leipzig, 1587) abandoned the earlier practice of organizing songs by their respective authors in favour of a stricter *de tempore* format, and included hymns clearly delineating Lutheran dogma from that of other faiths. At the same time, the pressures of economic decline and eventually of confessional conflict brought about a gradual change in tone, as collective statements of faith and praise (emphasizing 'we' or *wir*) gave way to more subjective reactions (emphasizing 'I' or *ich*) to themes of sin, repentance, death, the Second Coming, eternal life, and comfort in the face of adversity. The Passion chorale *O Haupt voll Blut und Wunden* (O sacred head, bloody and wounded) by one of the leading hymn composers, Paul Gerhardt (1607–76), typifies the vivid imagery and personal feeling of these new compositions, which were intended at least as much for private devotional usage as for worship services. Johann Crüger (1598–1662) was the most prominent of the mid-seventeenth-century hymn composers; his *Erbauungslieder* (edifying songs) and *Trostlieder* (songs of comfort) from his *Newes vollkömliches Gesangbuch* (1640) demonstrate how the devastation of the

Thirty Years' War gave rise to new and more intimate contexts for Lutheran sacred music.

Performance contexts for the Lutheran chorale included not only the church, but also schools, streets, taverns, and private homes. Luther and his colleagues Philip Melanchthon and Johann Walter promoted the chorale repertory in Lutheran schools not only to train competent church choirs, but also as a means of spiritual edification. A distinct repertory of chorales (such *Dies sind die heiligen zehn Gebot* [the Ten Commandments] and *Wir glauben all an einem Gott* [the Lutheran Credo]) were frequently sung during the course of catechism instruction, which was offered regularly in both schools and churches. Increasingly during the course of the sixteenth century, choirs of Lutheran students in German cities earned extra money by singing music in the streets and in front of private residences (*Kurrendengesang*), music which likely included or was based on Lutheran chorales. Cheap printed matter furthered the dissemination of these songs among the populace. While some songbooks with musical notation were aimed towards musically literate individuals, it was much more common for songbooks merely to offer the successive stanzas of text, indicating at the outset only the name of the tune to which the words were to be sung. This process of contrafacture – by which new texts were adapted to existing melodies – ensured the rapid transmission of religious ideas by exploiting an existing, and broadly known, body of music. The popularity and relative simplicity of the tunes aided the memorization of these new texts and enabled common persons to learn the music through oral transmission.

The broad appeal of the chorale granted it a central role in the process of Lutheran confessionalization, and also made it a potent weapon in the confessional struggles that increasingly characterized central Europe in the decades leading up to the Thirty Years' War.[4] Catholic territorial rulers (such as the dukes of Bavaria) and the patrician councils of cities with Catholic populations (the biconfessional city of Augsburg is the most prominent example) sought to control strictly the creation, dissemination, and performance of the more inflammatory chorales such as *Erhalt uns Herr bei deinem Wort*, or *Lobt Gott, ihr frommen Christen*, recognizing that songs with explicitly anti-Catholic or anti-imperial content could be politically destabilizing.[5] The challenge of eradicating popular Lutheran chorales from Catholic contexts is suggested

---

4 On the political aspect of Lutheran song, see Oettinger, *Music as propaganda in the German Reformation*. Music played an important role in a broader Lutheran education programme; see Strauss, *Luther's house of learning*.

5 For the case of Augsburg, see Stetten, *Geschichte der Heil. Röm. Reichs Freyen Stadt Augspurg*, vol. 2, p. 599; see also Fisher, *Music and religious identity in Counter-Reformation Augsburg*.

by Albrecht V of Bavaria's 1569 school ordinance, which banned forbidden songs 'because in our time many seductive new songs and falsified psalm [translations], which are not permitted in the Christian, Catholic mass, have come among the common people'.[6] Fifty years later the Jesuit Adam Contzen, confessor to Maximilian I of Bavaria, continued to lament that 'the hymns of Luther have killed more souls than his writings or declamations';[7] indeed, by that time the Jesuits had developed an analogous Catholic repertory (see below). The inclusion of Lutheran chorales in mid-century Catholic song-books like the *Catholische Geistliche Lieder und Psalmen* of Johann Leisentrit (1567) illustrates the popularity and tenacity of the genre only two decades after the reformer's death.

Even if the congregational chorale expressed most fully Luther's philosophy of the 'priesthood of believers', his musical interests had ensured a place for more elaborate music for trained singers in the divine service; it is telling, for example, that Walter's polyphonic *Geystliches Gesangk Buchleyn* (1524) had been among the very first Lutheran music publications. By the end of the seventeenth century, in the major urban churches at least, the balance between simple congregational song and complex choral polyphony had shifted gradually towards the latter, with Latin art music and elaborate German chorale settings assuming an ever-greater role in the liturgy.[8] In the early seventeenth century composers like Michael Praetorius (1571–1621) and Johann Hermann Schein (1586–1630) continued to provide chorale-based compositions for the liturgy; the former's nine encyclopaedic volumes entitled *Musae Sioniae* (1605–10), for example, include some 1,200 pieces based on chorales. The gradual but perceptible shift from a collective to a subjective focus in the chorale literature, however (see above), paralleled the rise of the church composer as an individual voice, providing music as much for spiritual edification as for the liturgy. It is significant that the leading Lutheran composer of the seventeenth century, the Dresden chapel-master Heinrich Schütz (1585–1672), based hardly any of his music on chorales, preferring instead to provide musically affective settings of biblical passages. The two volumes of *Kleine geistliche Konzerte* (1636 and 1639), set for a small number of vocal soloists with instrumental accompaniment, are particularly skilful examples of how contemporary German composers exploited the fashionable idioms of Italian secular music to provide emotive

---

6 Quoted in Ursprung, *Münchens musikalische Vergangenheit*, pp. 55–6; see also Hsia, *Social discipline in the Reformation*, p. 115.
7 From Contzen's *Politicorum libri decem* (Mainz, c. 1620); see Moser, *Verkündigung durch Volksgesang*, pp. 15–16.
8 On this phenomenon, see esp. Blume, *Protestant church music*, pp. 121–3.

depictions of these concentrated texts. In Germany, however, the trend towards smaller groups of vocal soloists and away from the substantial choirs of the sixteenth century also reflected the pressures of economic crisis and eventually of warfare, which severely affected church musicians and princely chapels throughout the region.

Music in Reformed communities

While sacred music to the Lutheran orthodoxy amounted to *adiaphora* – a phenomenon unnecessary to salvation but welcome as an expression of faith – other Reformed churches restricted music severely. Ulrich Zwingli, despite his own musical talents and interests that were documented by contemporaries (he was a singer and could play lute, harp, viol, and various wind instruments), strove to eliminate music entirely from the sacred space. For Zwingli and his followers in the northern Swiss cantons the seductions of church music were an obstacle to the popular understanding of religion, and the years following his first published revision of the liturgy (*De canone missae epicheiresis*, 1523) saw the elimination of music and the silencing of organs in churches under his influence. On the other hand, Zwingli's approval of musical instruction in schools and seminaries, and indeed his own composition of several songs (including *Hilff, Herr Gott, hilff in diser Not*, a plague song), suggests that the popular view of Zwingli as entirely opposed to religious music needs modification.

John Calvin promoted a practice of much greater consequence for Western sacred music, the congregational singing of psalms, often in strict metrical versions that ensured the clear enunciation and perception of the words. Exiled from Geneva (which had embraced the Zwinglian version of the liturgy) in 1538, Calvin came into contact with French refugees in Strasbourg who cultivated psalm singing in the vernacular, and familiarized himself with the French psalm translations of Clément Marot (1497–1544). In 1541, the year that Calvin returned to Geneva, the first Genevan Psalter was published. Melodies for the psalm translations were drawn from existing Latin hymns and sequences, as well as from German hymns and secular songs; they were organized into successions of long and short notes, corresponding carefully to the accentuation of the French text. Although Calvin himself did provide translations of the canticle *Nunc dimittis* ('Lord, now lettest thou thy servant depart in peace'), the Credo, and several psalms, Marot and Théodore de Bèze (1519–1605) were responsible for most of the psalm translations; in 1562 the scholar and music theorist Loys Bourgeois (c. 1510/15–c. 1560) published all 150 psalm translations and provided 125 different melodies, some of which were likely of his own composition.

It is difficult to overestimate the popular enthusiasm shown for vernacular psalmody in various parts of Europe from the mid-sixteenth century onward. While congregations sang strictly monophonic versions of the psalms (to the melodies of Bourgeois, for example) during church services, amateur musicians in private contexts enjoyed polyphonic settings of the psalms by composers like Claude Goudimel (*c.* 1514/20–1572), who was associated with reformists in Metz and eventually died in the St Bartholomew's Day Massacre. Like Lutheran chorales, Calvinist psalms served not only as spiritual edification but also as religious propaganda in confessionally mixed areas: in 1551, for example, printers' journeymen in Lyon organized armed crowds of artisans and their families to process through the streets and sing vernacular psalms in defiance of the local Catholic authorities.[9] In France, this popular psalmody was strictly forbidden once official persecution of the Huguenots intensified in the late 1560s.

Sometime shortly after the first publication of the first Genevan Psalter in 1541, Ambrosius Lobwasser (1515–85), professor of law at the Prussian university in Königsberg, embarked on a German version which was published in Leipzig and Heidelberg in 1573 and 1574 respectively. Although Lobwasser himself was Lutheran and translated the psalms as a literary endeavour, his psalter would become standard fare for Reformed churches in Germany and in German-speaking Switzerland. The Genevan Psalter, by contrast, dominated in Reformed congregations in France, French-speaking Switzerland, and indeed even as far east as Bohemia, Moravia, and Hungary.

Like their counterparts elsewhere on the Continent, Calvinist congregations in the Netherlands sang psalms in unison, unaccompanied by instruments (organs in Dutch churches were not dismantled, but were not used in the divine service until the early seventeenth century). Simon Cock of Antwerp published a Dutch translation of the psalter in 1540 (probably by the nobleman Willem van Zuylen van Nyevelt) that would be disseminated in some thirty editions; the simple melodies to which these psalms were sung would come to be called *souterliedekens* ('psalter songs'). While Cock's inclusion of the corresponding Vulgate texts of the psalms indicates that the collection was not initially meant to be exclusive to the Reformed church, the *souterliedekens* were much more closely identified with Protestantism in the later sixteenth century and were strictly prohibited in the Spanish Netherlands. Another Antwerp printer, Tylman Susato (*c.* 1500–1561/4), issued a series of 'music booklets' (*Musyck boexken*) beginning in 1551 that included the influential three-voice

9 Davis, 'Strikes and salvation at Lyon', pp. 4–5.

settings of the *souterliedekens* by Clemens non Papa (*c.* 1510/5–1555/6). Like Goudimel, Clemens aimed his polyphonic settings towards musical amateurs in domestic contexts.

Traditions of sacred music in early modern England reflected the distinctive and complex religious history of the realm, as native late medieval traditions intermingled with developments redolent of both Calvinism and Catholicism.[10] The religious upheavals of Henry VIII's reign (1509–47) may be responsible for the lack of extant sources for sacred music in that period, but that which survives (by Robert Fayrfax, William Cornysh, John Taverner, and a few others) suggests continuity with the intricate counterpoint of late medieval traditions. Reforms instituted by the Archbishop of Canterbury, Thomas Cranmer (1489–1556), during the reign of the young Edward VI (1547–53) brought far-reaching consequences for English sacred music. The promulgation of the Act of Uniformity and the introduction of the *Book of Common Prayer* (1549) cemented liturgical changes that would shape religious music in the subsequent decades: the establishment of the communion service (formerly the mass), matins, and evensong as the principal services and contexts for sacred music in the Anglican tradition.

The relative sobriety of music in the Chapel Royal during Edward VI's reign reflected the mood of religious reform, but with the accession of Elizabeth I after the short and ill-fated Catholic restoration under Mary I (*r.* 1553–8), sacred music appeared to divide into two parallel streams, the elaborate – and to some observers, 'popish' – church polyphony of the Chapel Royal and the popular embrace of metrical psalmody in the countryside. Elizabeth's complete control over the Chapel Royal ensured its position as the pre-eminent English context for sophisticated polyphony. Composers affiliated with the Chapel (William Mundy, Orlando Gibbons, and the Catholic William Byrd are among the most prominent names) wrote polyphonic 'services', comprising entire or partial settings of texts drawn from the communion service, matins, and evensong, as well as 'anthems' (derived from the pre-Reformation 'antiphon') that would be performed paraliturgically at the conclusion of matins or evensong. Both types of music were written in versions for unaccompanied choir (short service, great service, full anthem) and for alternations of soloist(s), choir, and instruments (verse service and verse anthem), a development that would exploit the ideal of contrasting musical forces characteristic of the seventeenth century. The churches of St Paul's, Westminster Abbey, and St George's Chapel at Windsor,

---

10 On sacred music during the English Reformation, see Le Huray, *Music and the Reformation in England, 1549–1660.*

being closely associated with the royal court, followed the musical lead of the Chapel Royal to a greater or lesser extent.

Outside the Chapel Royal and its satellite churches, however, the zeal of reformers tended to limit elaborate church music, as musical expenses were reduced and organs were neglected or, in some cases, done away with entirely. In London parish churches congregations were singing metrical psalms by the 1560s, a development analogous to the metrical psalmody of Calvinist churches on the Continent; Bishop John Jewel would write in 1560 that after the service at Paul's Cross there were 'six thousand persons, old and young, of both sexes, all singing together and praising God'.[11] A key moment was the publication of all 150 psalms in English translation by John Day in 1562. The sources for Day's melodies included Bourgeois' Genevan Psalter, Lutheran tunes, and others of English origin. Day's collection would be supplanted only by the Scottish *Psalms of David in Meeter* (1650), whose dissemination benefited greatly from the mandate for Presbyterianism in the realm between 1647 and 1652. The *Whole Booke of Psalms* for four voices published by Thomas East in 1592 formed a polyphonic counterpoint to Day's collection and was likely performed in domestic contexts. In the English Puritan colonies of North America metrical psalmody, sung in unison by the congregation, represented the first significant tradition of sacred music: the *Bay Psalm Book* (1640) was the first published book of any kind in the colonies. Although the earlier editions of the book lacked melodies, indications of tunes were provided that had already appeared in Thomas Ravenscroft's *The Whole Booke of Psalmes* (London, 1621). The Scottish *Psalms of David in Meeter* would also be widely adopted in seventeenth-century New England.

The institutional musical traditions of Lutheranism and Calvinism should not obscure the important role of popular hymnody in the religious and cultural life of the early modern West. An instructive example is provided by the well-developed hymn tradition of the Anabaptists, who in their period of greatest persecution in the sixteenth century relied on simple hymns for spiritual succour and communal expression. Many of the earliest Anabaptist hymns were written by prisoners or martyrs, and indeed the most significant contemporary published collection, the so-called *Ausbund* (*Etliche schöne Christliche Geseng, wie sie in der Gefengkniss zu Passaw im Schloss von den Schweitzer Brüdern durch Gottes gnad geticht und gesungen worden*, 1564), contained hymns purportedly composed and sung by a group of Swiss Anabaptists who were imprisoned during their return journey from Moravia, another stronghold of

---

11 Robinson (ed.), *The Zurich letters*, vol. 1, p. 71.

the movement. The appearance of specific hymns in printed and manuscript collections of widely separated communities demonstrates the vital connections between Anabaptists in the Low Countries, Switzerland, south Germany, and Moravia, and suggests the important role of hymnody in facilitating communication and exchange in troubled times.

Music and early modern Catholicism

The debate between proponents of a fundamentally reactive Catholicism in the post-Reformation era (the 'Counter-Reformation') and proponents of a Catholicism whose reforms and characteristic religious expressions responded to both internal and external stimuli (Jedin's 'Catholic Reform', O'Malley's 'Early Modern Catholicism', Hsia's 'Catholic Renewal') has important consequences for music historians, who have traditionally viewed Tridentine censures as the driving force behind subsequent developments in Catholic music.[12] However, the diversity of Catholic musical repertories and practices in the early modern era suggests that a more comprehensive view requires attention not only to the restrictions mandated by the Council of Trent and their consequences for composers of polyphony, but also to ways in which the Catholic renewal channelled new energies into sacred music, both sophisticated and popular. Furthermore, much is to be gained from examining the ways in which music (not only Catholic, but also Lutheran and Calvinist) both reflected and contributed to the gradual process of European confessionalization.

If the significance of the Council of Trent's discussions on music has been overemphasized, the Council is nevertheless a suitable starting point for a discussion of Catholic sacred music. The delegates shared with contemporary humanists a general concern with the intelligibility of the text in polyphonic compositions, something which was easily obscured by the complex interweaving of voices in traditional counterpoint (the humanists' emerging views on the relative importance of music and text would later become a key stimulus for the development of Baroque opera). Furthermore, many prelates disapproved of the use of secular tunes as models for church polyphony, a common practice since the mid-fifteenth century. Despite detailed preliminary discussions, however, the Council resolved only that all things 'lascivious or impure' should be eliminated from church music, and that responsibility for reforms would fall upon local dioceses. Although some reformers connected with Trent – chief among them Carlo Borromeo and Vitellius Vitellozo, members

---

12 See Jedin, 'Catholic Reformation or Counter-Reformation?'; O'Malley, 'Was Ignatius Loyola a church reformer?'; and Hsia, *The world of Catholic renewal*.

of a commission of cardinals (1564–5) charged with the implementation of the decrees – gave more detailed prescriptions for composers, the overall vagueness of the Tridentine directives left ample room for a striking diversity of musical practices in subsequent decades.[13] The legend of Giovanni Pierluigi da Palestrina's 'saving of church music' through a performance of his *Pope Marcellus Mass* before the Council has long been discredited by scholars,[14] but in fact there was little to save: by no means did the Council intend to ban polyphony from the church, and if Palestrina did shy away from secular models and enhance the clarity of text declamation in his music, there were many other Catholic composers who ignored these desiderata or modified them for their own purposes.

Palestrina, who worked in Rome and its environs, Tomás Luis de Victoria, a Spaniard who worked for both Italian and Spanish patrons, Orlando di Lasso in Munich, and William Byrd in England were four outstanding figures whose careers and works reflected the varied political and cultural profiles of Catholicism in sixteenth-century Europe. Of the four Palestrina (1525/6–1594) has been most closely linked with the aims of Tridentine Catholicism, a consequence not only of the above-mentioned 'legend' but also of his music itself, in which secular influences are rare and the careful balance and control of harmony and melody lend it a sobriety consistent with the atmosphere of reform. As the most prominent composer in the hub of the Catholic world (he worked in some of Rome's most prestigious institutions, including the Capella Giulia, S Maria Maggiore, and St John Lateran) Palestrina would exert enormous influence during his lifetime, and indeed after his death would come to embody a stereotype of a 'sanctioned' Roman musical style that was imitated in some circles (particularly within the Sistine Chapel) during the next three centuries. His leading position among late sixteenth-century Roman composers led to a papal commission (along with Annibale Zoilo) to reform the body of Gregorian chant along the lines of humanist principles of textual accentuation, but in the end the radical nature of the revisions would lead to the project's failure (a revised Gradual published in 1614/15 was never endorsed by the pope).

Palestrina's seeming embarrassment at having once composed secular madrigals (his apology to Gregory XIII appeared in a 1584 book of motets) was not shared by Tomás Luis de Victoria (1548–1611), who published exclusively sacred music. Beginning his career as a choirboy in Avila, Victoria established

---

13 On the general and open-ended nature of the Council's resolution on music, see Monson, 'The Council of Trent revisited'.

14 The legend was widely popularized by Baini in his *Memorie storico-critiche della vita e delle opere di Giovanni Pierluigi da Palestrina* (1828).

his musical reputation in Rome at S Maria di Monserrato (1569–74), the Jesuit Collegium Germanicum (1571–6), and S Girolamo della Carità (1578–85) before returning to Spain in the service of the dowager empress Maria. Liturgical concerns determined the nature of Victoria's output, which stresses hymn and Magnificat settings for vespers, masses, and motets organized by liturgical function; his collection of music for Holy Week, the *Officium Hebdomadae Sanctae* (1585), is characteristic of his output in its rich textures, expressive use of harmony, and, befitting the atmosphere of Catholic reform, complete lack of secular influence. The sombre mysticism seen by some critics in his works has been linked to the spiritual intensity of contemporary paintings by Velazquez and El Greco, although in truth the bulk of his output tends towards the joyous. 'His disposition being naturally sunny', wrote João IV of Portugal in 1649, 'he never stays downcast for long'.[15]

Orlando di Lasso (1532–94), a Netherlander who was brought to the Bavarian court by Duke Albrecht V in 1556, presents a contrasting image to Palestrina and Victoria in that he never neglected the fashionable secular repertories of his time: German drinking songs, French songs, and Italian madrigals all found a home beside his prodigious sacred output. Nevertheless, the accelerating pace of Catholic confessionalization in Bavaria in the late sixteenth century, promoted greatly not only by the Jesuits but also by the court itself, exerted its influence on the composer, who responded with numerous polyphonic settings of the Magnificat, Marian litanies, and his swansong, the *Lagrime di San Pietro* (Tears of St Peter, 1594), a cycle of Italian-texted sacred madrigals that express the saint's remorse at his own denial of Christ through vivid, wrenching harmonies and characteristic turns of phrase.[16] This work illustrates a fundamental difference from the music of Palestrina, especially, in that the clear presentation of words is augmented by their interpretation through melody, harmony, and texture. The increasing Marian fervour of the Bavarian court – symbolized by the official promotion of the Altötting pilgrimage and ultimately by Maximilian I's designation of Mary as the patroness of Bavaria – found greater resonance with Lasso's musical successors in Munich, whose embrace of Catholic textual imagery could not be more explicit.

William Byrd (1543–1623) was alone among the major Catholic composers in practising his art in a confessionally hostile atmosphere. As a Gentleman of the Chapel Royal (from around 1572) he was expected to write music for Anglican

---

15 See Stevenson, 'Victoria, Tomás Luis de', p. 535. The leading musical figures in the Spanish Counter-Reformation are discussed at length in Stevenson, *Spanish cathedral music in the golden age.*
16 On Lasso's Magnificats, see Crook, *Orlando di Lasso's imitation Magnificats.*

services, and some of the period's finest service music and anthems (including verse anthems for choir and soloists with the accompaniment of instruments) came from his pen. The increasing persecution of Catholics in the 1580s – and notably, the execution of Edmund Campion and two Jesuits in 1588 – may have strengthened his commitment to Catholicism, and in the subsequent decades he and his family were charged with recusancy several times. However, the personal favour of the queen protected Byrd from any serious consequences during his tenure with the Chapel Royal, and after 1593 he retired to Stondon Massey in Essex, where he could attend secret services in the home of Catholic leader Sir John Petre. Much of his music for Catholic services (including three settings of the mass ordinary and the mass proper settings of his *Gradualia* [1605]) and Latin motets would likely have been performed in these contexts; many of his motets expressing themes of sin, repentance, and deliverance may refer to the increasingly difficult position of Catholics as the century drew to a close.[17] The text of Byrd's first published composition (1575), the motet *Emendemus in melius*, begs for remission from sin and deliverance from the cares of this world; the composer responded with one of his most intense efforts, declaiming the words clearly and employing harmonic tension to heighten the piece's fervent intensity.[18]

Despite a tendency in some circles to canonize the unaccompanied liturgical polyphony of Palestrina as a model for church music, the turn of the seventeenth century brought fundamental changes that reflected the consolidation of state power, the intensification of Counter-Reformation spirituality, and the influence of secular styles. Sacred music was increasingly drawn into visual / aural spectacles that represented the glory and authority of temporal rulers and the ecclesiastical hierarchy. In Venice, where the liturgy venerated not only God but also the temporal authority of the republic, composers like Giovanni Gabrieli (c. 1555–1612) achieved massive sonic effects through the employment of multiple choirs of voices and instruments dispersed among the balconies of San Marco.[19] Forming a musical counterpoint to the spaciousness and emotional impact of contemporary Catholic art, this polychoral style was adopted mainly in Italian and German centres (regardless of confessional orientation) whose resources could support large numbers of singers and instrumentalists. In Rome church composers of the later seventeenth century extended the idiom to embrace ever-larger numbers of choirs in dialogue, resulting in an overwhelming musical display sometimes referred to as the

17 On the political implications of Byrd's motets, see Monson, 'Byrd, the Catholics, and the motet'.
18 Kerman, 'On William Byrd's *Emendemus in melius*'.   19 Arnold, *Giovanni Gabrieli*.

'colossal Baroque'. Apart from the mass, the increasing musical importance of vespers demanded works of this kind, and the early seventeenth century saw an expansion of large-scale psalm and Magnificat settings for this office (Claudio Monteverdi's *Vespro della beata Vergine* of 1610, containing a variety of traditional and modern music for vespers, is a key work).

The growth of charitable confraternities and religious congregations also gave impetus to the composition of music for their devotional services and activities.[20] From the 1550s Filippo Neri's Roman Congregazione dell'Oratorio had hosted lay devotional meetings that featured the singing of monophonic or polyphonic *laude*, simple devotional songs in the vernacular whose origins go back to the thirteenth century. However, the growing humanist interest in the possibilities of dramatic narrative, along with the rising demand for spiritual edification in groups such as Neri's, led to the cultivation of more elaborate musical forms involving dramatic dialogue between biblical characters, and including solo and choral singing and the inclusion of instruments. Emilio de' Cavalieri's *Rappresentatione di Anima e di Corpo* (1600) for the oratory of the Chiesa Nuova closely resembles the earliest forms of secular opera in its fully musical setting, use of dramatic recitation, and use of scenery, costumes, and acting, but most works later classified as 'oratorios' (the term 'oratorio' first emerged only around 1640 to describe unstaged sacred dramatic works) were less ambitious in scope and did not typically involve such visual aids. Giovanni Francesco Anerio's *Teatro armonico spirituale* (1619) included dramatic dialogues closely resembling the late sixteenth- and early seventeenth-century secular madrigal in style, but the full-blown oratorio, involving instrumental passages, alternations of recitative (dramatic recitation) and aria, and choral commentary did not emerge until Giacomo Carissimi (1605–74) composed works like *Jephte* (*c.* 1649) at mid-century. By this time the genre fell into distinct vernacular and Latin forms (the *oratorio volgare*, heard in Rome primarily at the Chiesa Nuova and S Girolamo della Carità, and the *oratorio latino*, heard primarily at the aristocratic Oratorio del S Crocifisso, respectively).

Occupying a middle ground between liturgical music for mass and vespers and the non-liturgical oratorio was a massive quantity of smaller-scale music that could both substitute for liturgical items in the mass and serve as 'spiritual recreation' in private contexts. In order to fill out the musical texture when all of the required singers were not present, late sixteenth-century church

---

20 A recent study on music in a Roman confraternity may be found in O'Regan, *Institutional patronage in post-Tridentine Rome.*

composers (particularly in Rome) began to provide their compositions with organ accompaniments. By the early seventeenth century these instrumental accompaniments evolved into independent and indispensable parts of the musical texture, usually supporting a small group of voices whose character was more soloistic and virtuosic than in the motet of the previous century. The sacred concerto for few voices and instrumental bass (*motetto, concerto, geistliches Konzert*; the term 'concerto' may be taken to mean the union of contrasting vocal and instrumental sonorities) flourished especially in early seventeenth-century Italy and Germany, where its relatively modest performance requirements and textual flexibility suited it for the church, the devotional gatherings of confraternities, and domestic contexts. Although their origins were different, the sacred concerto and early secular opera drew upon a common musical vocabulary: the independent instrumental bass (*basso continuo*, or 'continuous bass'), the gradual distinction between dramatic recitation (recitative) and melodies (arias), dramatic dialogue between the voices, and the vivid expression of textual imagery through melody, harmony, and other means. The increasing differentiation in styles within a single piece would eventually lead to the sacred cantata in multiple movements.

Much of this music, it must be stressed, was designed for and performed in relatively narrow circles, although the laity could hope to hear some of it passively in the context of worship services. By the late sixteenth century, however, Catholic elites in northern Europe, especially, began to perceive a need for a popular repertory of edifying and dogmatic songs that would parallel the spiritual role that the Lutheran chorale had fulfilled since the 1520s. Sixteenth-century Catholic songbooks like Michael Vehe's *New Gesangbüchlin geystlicher Lieder* (Leipzig, 1537) and Johannes Leisentrit's *Geistliche Lieder und Psalmen* (Bautzen, 1567) retained a relatively ecumenical profile, including a significant proportion of Protestant songs. However, as they expanded their educational and missionary activities the Jesuits and their sympathizers began to publish and promote a body of confessionally specific music narrating the lives of model saints, recounting miraculous phenomena such as Marian apparitions and eucharistic healing, and celebrating the lives of Catholic martyrs. The new repertory, contained in books like Nikolaus Beuttner's *Catholisch Gesang-Büch* (Graz, 1602), David Gregor Corner's *Gross Catholisch Gesangbuch* (Bamberg, 1625), and Georg Vogler's *Catechismus in auserlesenen Exempeln* (Würzburg, 1625), differs from earlier Catholic song in its explicitly confessional tone and intention not only for worship services, but especially for school catechism and household devotion. The promotion of social discipline may be seen most explicitly in these latter contexts, where the singing of designated songs throughout the day – upon waking, at mealtimes, during work, and before retiring – represented a form of musical and spiritual regulation. Jesuit songs, often deliberately simple and direct in both text and music, tended to reflect the missionary goals of that order; other orders, however (notably the Franciscans), began to publish collections of more artfully conceived vernacular songs in the seventeenth century that spoke more to the development of inner spiritual values.[21]

Despite its importance from the standpoint of European confessionalization, the relative exclusion of Catholic vernacular song from the liturgy made it impossible to base a tradition of church music upon it, as was the case in Lutheran music based on chorales. However, Catholic song would prove instrumental to the Jesuit-led Christianization of non-Western peoples in Asia and the Americas.[22] Missionaries translated Christian doctrine into local dialects, combining the words with indigenous or European melodies that facilitated memorization; notable in this regard is Bernardo de Sahagún's *Psalmodia christiana* (1583), showing hymn texts in the local Nahuatl language (South America) with native-derived melodies. Catholic missionaries in North America resorted to similar measures. It is remarkable that highly elaborate musical traditions, sometimes involving the collaboration of indigenous people and European colonizers, quickly developed in several of the Jesuit missionary locales. By the late sixteenth century polychoral music involving multiple choirs of voices and wind instruments was heard at Goa, while Manila witnessed gigantic devotional exercises and processions organized by the Jesuits, the music for which was performed by troupes of indigenous and Spanish instrumentalists and singers. Polyphony by European composers, notably Francisco Guerrero, was known to Filipino choirs.[23] Orchestras also developed in Paraguay, where the Jesuits designated certain Guaraní towns ('reductions') for the manufacture of instruments and the training of musicians (relatively little is known about this repertory, however).[24] In Mexico the traditions of Spanish Renaissance polyphony were influential through the early modern era, beginning with Hernando Franco (1532–85), who arrived in Guatemala in 1554 and eventually became *maestro di capilla* at Mexico City. As in certain places in South America, Mexican churches saw a rapid expansion of church

---

21 For a survey of thematic ideas in the songs of the Jesuits, Franciscans, and other orders, see Moser, *Verkündigung durch Volksgesang*.

22 An overview of Catholic church music outside of Europe in the early modern era may be found in Dyer, 'Roman Catholic church music', VI.

23 See Summers, 'The Jesuits in Manila'.

24 See, however, Nawrot, *Música de vísperas*. A broader survey of Jesuit art in the reductions may be found in McNaspy, *Lost cities of Paraguay*.

orchestras from the late sixteenth century.[25] Scholars are only beginning to uncover the richness of early modern sacred music in the New World, which aside from its musical significance raises important questions of cultural conflict, adaptation, and assimilation.

Conclusion: music and confession in the early modern West

There is little doubt that sacred music in its myriad forms closely reflected the changing religious cultures and politics of the early modern era. The explosion in the number of vernacular chorales in the Lutheran tradition would have been unthinkable without the decisive influence of Luther's interest in *musica practica*; the renewal of post-Tridentine spirituality clearly manifested itself in the diversity, confessional orientation, and emotional intensity of Catholic polyphony; and the rise of multilingual devotional singing and church orchestras in the Americas cannot be divorced from the context of Jesuit ministry. The integral role of music in the religious experience of early modern subjects, however, demands further research into the distinct ways in which sacred music and musical practice in turn contributed to confessional awareness and the process of confessionalization in general.

The relationship of music and confession is complex and cannot be subjected to a single explanatory narrative that will be valid for all types of repertories and audiences. Vital to its investigation, however, are approaches that place musical repertories within specific social, political, and religious contexts, as well as a sensitive consideration of the popular and amateur sacred music that has typically eluded scholarly attention. The interface of oral and print culture, for example, will continue to be fruitful in the study of vernacular traditions ranging from the Lutheran chorale to Catholic devotional song in Europe and abroad. The role of vernacular songs, litanies, and simple polyphony in the context of Catholic ritual practices like processions and pilgrimages will remain a vital area of inquiry, one that can benefit from historical as well as anthropological methodologies; the nature of music-making in these events will certainly contribute to the debate on whether such practices represented spontaneous popular religious expression, enforced confessional discipline, or a combination of both. Much remains to be written, as well, on the changing demands on composers of sacred polyphony in the period under discussion:

25 For an overview of musical activity in the Mexican colonial era, see Stevenson, *Music in Mexico*.

while the Council of Trent's discussions on music and their practical ramifications have been well documented, we know relatively less about the ways in which post-Tridentine Catholic spirituality shaped sacred repertories, and encouraged a rapprochement between deeply devotional texts and new musical and dramatic forms arising out of the secular sphere. Most important, perhaps, is an understanding of how the merging of secular and sacred authority in the early modern confessional state led to, and was buttressed by, distinctly Catholic, Lutheran, and Calvinist forms of musical expression. It is within this context that the music history can be most closely integrated with the broader process of early modern confessionalization.

22

Demonology, 1500–1660

WOLFGANG BEHRINGER

Literally, demonology is the science of demons and their actions. The word 'daimon' is Greek and simply means a supernatural being, or a lesser divinity. In classical ancient Greece 'daimones' were perceived as guardian spirits, or as either good or evil spirits who try to influence the human psyche. However, in Christian theology, demons were always considered evil, whereas angels were thought to serve as God's messengers or agents. Since the evil spirits were conceived as being masters of deception, an elaborate procedure of evaluation – the discernment of spirits (*discretio spirituum*) – was deemed necessary. This produced a science of angels – angelology – distinct from demonology. Theologically, demonology was based upon numerous references in the Bible, both in the ancient Jewish tradition and in the New Testament. A belief in spirit beings was fairly universal, as was a belief in related phenomena such as inspiration, spirit possession, and the struggle against possession by exorcism. Archaic religious systems such as shamanism were based on communication with spirits or spirit helpers. Inspiration was an important aspect of Christianity, and still is, as the feast of Pentecost indicates. To the dismay of the authorities, indigenous prophets continued to emerge from all corners of Europe, and various forms of spiritualism and prophecy remained part of European everyday life. Between 1500 and 1660 the medieval concept of demonology remained largely intact. It was shaped by St Augustine's (354–430) idea that interactions between demons and humans were based on a contract, either explicit or implicit. This assumption was inspired by Roman law which viewed contracts as being mutually binding agreements. The idea of an implicit pact was based upon a kind of semiotic theory that interprets superstitious acts as signs that could call up demons and invoke their support without using words to conjure them up. At the core of Augustinian demonology was the concept of a metaphysical triangle. On one side there are supernatural evil agents (demons) acting with the permission of (or even commissioned by) an almighty God, trying to tempt and seduce human beings to commit evil deeds. The consequences of this approach were radical and far-reaching: for Augustine and most theologians in his wake,[1] including the Dominican philosopher St Thomas Aquinas (1225–74), the mere use of an amulet signified that the user was an implicit ally of the devil, and the implicit pact was still considered a spiritual crime.[2] However, from about 1400, implausible superstitions such as the belief that witches could fly were increasingly considered as being possible if God allowed the devil to intervene. These reports of witch trials and demonological treatises were summarized in the fifteenth century by Heinrich Kramer/Institoris, a Dominican Inquisitor, doctor of theology, and author of The Witches' Hammer (Malleus Maleficarum; Speyer, 1486). He considered the demons' allies to be members of a sinister conspiracy against Christian society. Witchcraft by then had become the main focus of demonology since, according to scholastic theology, it required demonic assistance and was considered the most common expression of demonic intervention. Most demonologies between 1500 and 1660 dealt with witchcraft.

Although Reformers such as Martin Luther and John Calvin argued for predestination and denied the concept of free will, which meant it was logically impossible for a human willingly to make a deal with a demon, they still felt it necessary to state that a pact with the devil was a deadly sin and a capital crime. Mainstream Reformers (unlike Waldensians, Hussites, or most Anabaptists and spiritualists) remained traditionalists with respect to demonology, even when Calvin abandoned baptismal exorcism. After the Reformation, demonology seemed to have become a universally accepted branch of theology. Because it involved collecting and discussing ancient, medieval, and contemporary stories of extraordinary events, demonology also turned into a science of the exotic and the unusual to explain those phenomena in society and nature that could not easily be understood by the paradigms of Aristotelian physics, Galenic medicine, Thomistic theology, or common sense. While natural magic (magia naturalis) was used to explore and understand natural phenomena, as a kind of proto natural science, demonology dealt with the remaining 'unnatural' phenomena that could only be explained by either divine or demonic intervention. Although we can assume that a good number of contemporaries did not share any of the basic assumptions of demonology, as demonologists were constantly complaining, these continued to prevail in the public arena until the apparent consensus was questioned

---

1 Augustine, Civitas Dei (City of God), 10, 21f.
2 Aquinas, Summa Theologiae, III, q. 71, a. 3.

by the powerful new philosophies of René Descartes and Thomas Hobbes in the mid-seventeenth century. Cartesian physics and Hobbesian materialism left no space for demons.

From about 1500, an increasing number of people outside the church engaged in the debate about demonological issues hoping to reduce the potential danger of inquisitorial demonology on society. An obvious example is the *Witches' Hammer* (*Malleus Maleficarum*), which is a compilation of ideas drawn from medieval dogmatic theology (Augustine, Thomas Aquinas, Antoninus of Florence), on the one hand, and canon law and inquisitorial practice (Nicolaus Eymeric), on the other. In contrast with earlier demonologies such as Johann Nider's (*c.* 1380–1438) *Formicarius* (*c.* 1436), which gave descriptions of all kinds of vices and crimes cumulating in deeds inspired by demons, the *Malleus Maleficarum* was more practical. Nider, the author of *Formicarius*, was a scholastic theologian who had taught at several universities and had served as a prior of the Dominican convent of Basel. In contrast, Henry Kramer (1430–1505), the author of the *Malleus*, was an active papal Inquisitor. It was he who urged Pope Innocent VIII (*r.* 1484–1492) to issue the bull *Summis desiderantes affectibus* in 1484 in order to gain a wide public for his demonological fantasies in inquisitorial action. Kramer saw demonological theory primarily as a tool used to legitimize persecution of the supposed allies of the devil. The *Malleus* consists of three parts. The first two concentrate on theological issues of demonology. One is on the existence of demons and their power in relation to God and human beings, in particular the *permissio Dei* and demonic action as necessary requirements of harmful magic. The other gives examples of harmful magic and the ways to fight off demonic attacks. The third part deals with the 'killing of the witches', as Kramer writes, in particular the practice of witch trials. Its purpose was to enable judges to try witches effectively, without having to work out the correct legal formulae or procedures each time. Kramer's writings on the power of demons and the reliability of human senses are both stimulating as well as contradictory. Kramer concludes that for humans reality is unintelligible and the success of demonic deception illustrates that human senses are untrustworthy and therefore humans are not equipped to judge the truth of any phenomena. Nevertheless, he does accept the validity of eyewitness accounts in court, based on a mood of apocalypticism, as he himself states in the 'Apologia', the Preface to the *Witches' Hammer*.

The *Malleus* is a striking example for the claim that demonologies only make sense when seen in context. It was written following a campaign of witch persecution that took hold in Innsbruck. The local authorities – the bishop, the duke, the Tyrolean Estates, and the magistrate – all tried to defuse the situation. The bishop invalidated all accusations and threw Henry Kramer out of his diocese on the grounds that he was a lunatic. It was this crushing defeat and fundamental disagreements about demonological issues that prompted Kramer to compile his extensive work on demonology (256 pages in folio). The *Malleus Maleficarum* was welcomed by a curious audience as the first printed handbook of demonology. The upsurge of witch trials in the early 1490s in central Europe has been interpreted as a direct result of the publication of the *Witches' Hammer* and there are incidents indicating that it certainly had an impact. A chronicler reported that the region near the monastery of Eberhardsklausen on the Mosel River had been plagued by witches for some time, but as no one knew how to define a witch's behaviour it was impossible to do anything about them.

Only after reading the *Witches' Hammer* was it clear to the authorities how to proceed in dealing with witches – and this method was carried out. Here we do indeed have a kind of conversion experience, but this is a rare example, and it is not at all clear how the *Malleus* was generally received. In the light of the many sceptics that Kramer so often complains about in the *Malleus*, it seems highly unlikely that any of them were convinced by this desperate text. It is striking that opposition publications were frequent during the 1490s. Ulrich Molitor (1442–1507), a lawyer of the Bishop of Constance and courtier at Archduke Sigmund's court in Innsbruck, challenged the central assumptions of the *Witches' Hammer*. Molitor fashioned his text (*De laniis et phytonicis mulieribus*; Constance, 1489) in the style of a dialogue between a fanatic believer in witchcraft with himself as opponent and Archduke Sigmund as the wise arbiter. The protagonists always came to rational conclusions and flatly denied the possibility that witches could fly, shape-shift or influence the weather and they denied the existence of a witches' sabbath.

Their discussions would be the standard subject matter of all future demonologies. However, Molitor did not depart from the consensus of Augustinian demonology, since this was exactly the traditional attitude of the Catholic Church that had hitherto prevented witch persecutions. Canon law considered the more fantastical elements of witchcraft to be based on superstition, not on real practices. What other humanists thought about witches is not really known.

Even from within the religious orders, Franciscans like Samuel de Cassinis questioned the assumptions underpinning Kramer's inquisitorial demonology (*De lamiis, quas strigas vocant*; Milan, 1505).

However, there were also several Dominicans who defended Kramer and the Inquisitors of their order against Cassinis, as for instance Vincente Dodo

(*Apologia Dodi contra li defensori de le strie*; Pavia, 1506), and with Bernardo Rategno (*c.* 1450–1510), the chief Inquisitor of the diocese of Como, one of those responsible for the Italian persecutions raised his voice, adding many new examples to the debate (Bernard of Como, *De Strigibus*, 1508). There was a political rift between the church and states that tried to curb witch hunts wherever possible, for instance the Republic of Venice. This conflict was mirrored in the intellectual sphere; for example, philosophers sharply criticized the mass persecutions in the Italian alpine valleys in short treatises, such as that written by Gianfrancesco Ponzinibio (*De Lamiis*, 1520) from the University of Padua, who was famous for his denial of the immortality of the soul.

As a consequence of this treatise, the debate in Italy flared up again with even more Dominicans defending their cause. These included writers such as Bartolomeo de Spina (1479–1547) in his *Quaestio de strigibus* (Venice, 1523), Paulus Grillandus (*Tractatus de hereticis et sortilegiis* [1525–1673]; Lyon, 1536–1673) and, interestingly, Silvester Mazzolini da Prieri (1460–1523), a leading papal theologian and one of the first strong opponents of Luther (*De strigimagarum demonumque mirandis libri tres*; Rome, 1521), but also Prince Giovanni Francesco Pico della Mirandola (1469–1533), who referred to witch trials in his own territory (*Strix*; Bologna, 1523). The Italian witch hunts were fiercely criticized by the famous humanist lawyer Andrea Alciati (1492–1550), who labelled these, largely illegal, procedures the 'new holocaust' (*De lamiis seu strigibus*; 1515–1642, reprinted 1530), and by contemporary scientists such as Henricus Cornelius Agrippa von Nettesheim (1486–1535), who created and promoted the idea that witchcraft was an inquisitors' invention. Their arguments were on legal and compassionate grounds and not, it seems, related to doubts about demonology itself. The 'Art of Inquisition' was certainly described as a vain art by Agrippa, but he said this about all the arts and sciences, and his 'murderous inquisitor' referred to the inquisitorial theory of the *Malleus* rather than demonology in general.[3]

Demonology was not a fashionable topic in the Reformation era, presumably because the demonological consensus remained largely intact. No major work on demonology was published between 1520 and 1560, and there were no reprints of the *Malleus Maleficarum*. It was not until the early 1560s, when social hardship increased and witch hunting became more common again, that the need for explanations re-emerged. Johann Weyer (1515–88), a student of Agrippa and physician at the court of the dukes of Jülich-Kleve, came up with a completely new counter-argument to Henry Kramer's views on witch confessions.

---

3 Agrippa, *De incertitudine et vanitate scientarum*, cap. CXVI.

Like his teacher Agrippa, he called Kramer a 'bloodthirsty monk'. Weyer, the author of what was to become the most influential early modern book against witch persecutions, viewed so-called witches as melancholic females who needed leniency, love, and medical care to cure their mental illness. These 'witches' were not strong and dangerous, but weak, deceived, and tricked by demons into believing that they could indeed do harm or fly through the air. But these poor women were not evil, but sick, and they did not need punishment, but love. Killing them could not be justified under any circumstances as this would be a 'massacre of the innocents'.[4] What Weyer did was to alter fundamentally the discourse on witchcraft. Nevertheless, his massive demonology of almost 600 pages in folio format on *The Deceits of the Devils* is structured in the traditional way. The first book is on the origins, the nature, and the intentions of demons. The second book deals with those sorcerers who voluntarily conjure up demons. However, in the third and largest book Weyer writes about witches. He claims that even if these women admit to performing harmful magic, they should not be considered evil, but insane, and therefore physically and mentally incapable of bearing any legal responsibility for their supposed deeds. Weyer explains how it is impossible to class witchcraft as a crime, drawing on arguments from juridical, theological, and medical sources as well as from ancient philosophy, and supported this with evidence from experience and experiments. However, the scores of examples of demonic interference into worldly affairs that he provides in the remaining books – the fourth on the devils' activities, the fifth on possession, and the sixth on dealing severely with sorcerers, witches, and poisoners – tend to undermine his more liberal arguments. Weyer concludes that women accused of witchcraft are not guilty of a crime and therefore may not be burned to death. Finally, he states that burning witches is a heinous crime in itself. Weyer's publication signifies a paradigm shift on the side of the opponents of witchcraft persecution. His hidden agenda was to protect women against judges influenced by the *Malleus Maleficarum*, and to change the legal system by introducing medical arguments in general, and the insanity defence in particular. In order to popularize his point of view, Weyer translated his volume into the German vernacular.[5] The strong demand for this text is witnessed by the fact that there were two more unauthorized translations into German, and frequent reprints of the Latin original.

Weyer's second book on demonology triggered a similarly strong reaction (*De lamiis liber*; Basel, 1577). The European denial of witchcraft is

---

4 Weyer, *De praestigiis daemonum*, Preface.
5 Weyer, *De praestigiis daemonum. Von Zauberey, woher sie ihren Ursprung hab* [. . .]. Trans. from Latin by Johann Weyer.

firmly rooted in this pre-Cartesian opposition to atrocity, which was soon adopted by the representatives of European spiritualism, rationalism, and Enlightenment.

The sudden increase in witch panics from the 1560s onwards saw new demonologies emerging from all religious camps. This was in part a direct response to Weyer's attacks but also reflected the need to reshape the old teachings of the *Witches' Hammer* for Protestant purposes. This endeavour started within the Reformed camp. In Switzerland, the execution of witches was commonplace, though not everybody was convinced that this bloodshed was justified. Zwingli's successor Heinrich Bullinger (1504–75) felt it was time to confirm, in what was to be the first Reformed publication on the matter, the consensus on demonology as based upon the gospel, without referring openly to scholastic theology or the *Malleus* (*Von Hexen*, Zurich, 1571). A year later Calvin's successor in Geneva, Lambert Daneau (1530–96), followed Bullinger's example. According to his dialogue, *Les Sorciers* (Lyon, 1572), witches were apostates, traitors, and poisoners and deserved the severest possible prosecution. The Genevan pope's treatise was immediately translated into Latin and English (*A Dialogue of Witches*; London, 1575) and, a little later, into German. In the same year, Thomas Erastus (1524–83) published his view of witchcraft in the Calvinist Palatinate, obviously to alert his government, which denied the existence of witches and forbade any trials (*Disputatio de lamiis et strigibus*; Basel, 1572). The first Lutheran demonology was compiled in Denmark in response to the witch panics that flared up in the 1570s. *Admonishment to Avoid Magical Superstitions* (*Admonitio de superstitionibus magicis vitandis*) by Nils Hemmingsen (1513–1600) was published in Copenhagen in 1575. King James VI of Scotland (1566–1625; *r.* Scotland 1567–1625; *r.* England 1603–25) met Hemmingsen while in Copenhagen on his wedding trip. Scottish witch hunts increased in 1590 simultaneously with Danish witch hunts, partly to explain the many mishaps that occurred during the royal voyage. Inspired by Hemmingsen, King James wrote a *Daemonologie* that was divided into three books, dealing with magic, witchcraft, and the manifestation of troublesome spirits (demons). Despite the unusual structure, the content is entirely conventional, apart from the addition of the idea that the witches' pact with the devil mirrors the Calvinists' covenant with God. In the Preface, King James's deliberations were explicitly directed against the demonologies of Weyer and Scot.[6] However substantial, compared with Weyer's massive demonology these were all small booklets.

---

6 James VI, *Daemonologie, in forme of a dialoge*, Preface.

The first major post-Reformation Catholic demonology was drafted by a lawyer, the French intellectual Jean Bodin (1529–96). Bodin is usually known as the author of reasoned publications on historical method (*Methodus ad facilem historiarum cognitionem*, 1566), on economy (*Réponse aux paradoxes de M. de Malestroit*, 1566), on political theory (*Les six livres de la République*, 1576), and a proponent of religious toleration (*Heptaplomeres*, 1593). His work ranged across a rather disorderly selection of topics but his most shocking publication was to be *On the Demon-Mania of the Witches* (*De la Démonomanie des Sorciers*; Paris, 1580), in which he felt the need to refute the theories of Weyer and the related sceptics and Pyrrhonists, as he indicates in his Foreword. Bodin was able to see the resemblance between Weyer and Nicolas of Cusa (1401–64), who had doubted the reality of witchcraft in the fifteenth century, as could be expected by a philosopher who was able to conceive God mathematically as *coincidentia oppositorum*. After the Preface, in which Bodin articulates his commitment to defeat Weyer and his followers, he continues in the role of a dogmatic theologian starting with a lengthy chapter on the discernment of spirits. *On the Demon-Mania of the Witches* is divided into five books, dealing with: the nature of the demons; the crime of witchcraft; antidotes against witchcraft; the punishment for witchcraft; and, finally, a refutation of Weyer. On the whole, Bodin endorses traditional Catholic inquisitorial demonology, but is far more radical in his rather shocking attitude to what are clearly illegal forms of prosecution. He even approves of trials at Ribemont in 1576, which had been condemned by the parliament of Normandy as unlawful. Bodin's rather extreme position on witchcraft was the reason that his political career ground to a halt. The French edition of the *Démonomanie* was reprinted at least four times between 1580 and 1604 (Paris, Antwerp, Rouen), the Latin translation of 1581 was reprinted at least twice (Basel, Frankfurt), the German translation of 1586 was also reprinted twice (Strasbourg, Augsburg) and there was an Italian translation (1587). By the first decade of the seventeenth century, Bodin's *Démonomanie* was replaced by new demonologies.

Until the mid-1580s, witch trials were still rare in Europe, but the frequency of witch panics was increasing. In 1586 the Frankfurt publisher Nicolaus Basse (?–1599) commissioned Abraham Sawr (1545–93) to compile a comprehensive reader on witchcraft and demonology for the book fair. This book, the *Theatre of the Witches* (*Theatrum de Veneficis*; Frankfurt, 1586), was a selection from seventeen earlier demonologies and pamphlets on the subject. The final version was almost as large as Weyer's demonology. The title was a play on the *Theatre of the Devils* (*Theatrum Diabolorum*; Frankfurt, 1569), a summary of Protestant literature on the devil. However, whereas this earlier work mainly presented moral satires, the later concentrated on demonology. *The Theatre of the Witches* contains Johannes Trithemius's (1462–1516) famous answers to Emperor Maximilian I on witchcraft, a piece of traditional demonology (*Johannes Trithemii zu Spanheim Antwortt* [1508]), and Molitor's dialogue of 1489, but focuses on Protestant opinion leaders like Daneau, Lavater, and Bullinger, contrasting their traditional viewpoints with the position of Weyer and some of his followers, like Johann Ewich (1525–88) from Bremen (*De Sagarum Natura et Potestate*, 1584), or Herman Wilcken, called Witekind (1522–1603), a professor of mathematics at the University of Heidelberg, whose *Christlich Bedencken von Zauberey* (Heidelberg, 1585) had first been published as a booklet under the pseudonym 'Augustin Lercheimer', and succeeded with half a dozen reprints. All of these authors denied the existence of witchcraft and of witches in the inquisitorial sense, partly arguing from traditional theology, partly by introducing new arguments such as human reason and the laws of nature. However, Saur's collection leaves it to the reader to draw conclusions, supporting this endeavour by adding texts on demonology using every biblical quote he could find on the subject, as Adrian Rheynmann does in his dialogue *On Evil Angels and Unclean Spirits*,[7] Ludwig Lavater (1527–86) does in his treatise *On Ghosts* (*De Spectris*; Zurich, 1570),[8] and Leonhard Thurneysser (1531–96) in his work on exorcism.[9]

The two most radical opponents of inquisitorial as well as traditional demonology emerged at the very end of the sixteenth century and gave Weyer's approach a distinctive twist. The Calvinist minister Anton Praetorius (*c.* 1560–1614), who had courageously intervened in trials in the Calvinist county of Isenburg-Birstein in 1598 putting his position as court preacher at risk, and finally ending up in the Electoral Palatinate, surprised the public with a fundamental criticism of both belief in witches and witch trials even more radical than Weyer in that he proposed the abolition of torture in general (*Gründlicher Bericht von Zauberey und Zauberern*; Lich, 1598).

The English gentleman Reginald Scot (1538–99), seemingly a Puritan, now believed to have been a member of the Family of Love, a secret network of spiritualists, considered Bodin to be the most serious adversary, perhaps because the French scholar had launched the strongest attack against Weyer. But Scot acknowledged that the authority of the *Malleus Maleficarum* was always in the background. Protestant demonologists like Daneau, Erastus, and Hemmingsen were perhaps less vigorous authors than Bodin, but equally dangerous

---

7 In Sawr, *Theatrum de Veneficis*, pp. 97–114.   8 *Ibid.*, pp. 115–92.
9 *Ibid.*, pp. 193–202.

(*The Discoverie of Witchcraft*; London, 1584). Both Praetorius and Weyer apply the laws of nature and reason to support their argument. They both deny the physical power of demons and ridicule this basic assumption within Christian demonology, arguing that if weak old hags were able to do as much harm as was attributed to them, armies would be unnecessary. Witchcraft was reduced to a spiritual error, irrelevant to secular justice. Whereas Praetorius's booklet was of a smaller (quarto) size and aimed at a more popular audience, with at least four editions until 1629, Scot's learned demonology added up to several hundred pages and was written for an educated English audience. Scot's *Discoverie of Witchcraft* was translated into Dutch in 1609 and this edition was reprinted 1637. The English version was reprinted only during the Commonwealth, in 1651 and 1653, and the final edition of 1665 was intended to fuel the public debates on witchcraft at that time.

In Catholic countries, the prosecution of witches reached a hitherto unknown high in the late 1580s, with extensive burnings occurring from Catholic southern Germany to the Duchies of Lorraine and Luxembourg, into the Spanish Netherlands. It was from within this area that new Catholic demonologies arose, starting with the *Treatise on the Confessions of Male and Female Witches* (*Tractatus de confessionibus maleficorum et sagarum*; Treves, 1589), published by the driving ideologue of the persecution, the suffragan bishop Peter Binsfeld (1545–98). His demonology was divided into two parts, the first demonstrating the existence and efficacy of demons and witches, the second arguing that the witches' confessions were to be taken as circumstantial evidence in court, a claim denied by Weyer and Witekind. As a Catholic, Binsfeld could refer to the *Witches' Hammer*, to Spina and to Grillandi, but his aim was to reshape demonology by comparing theory and practice, as represented in the confessions of convicted minions of the devil. In pursuing this ambitious project, Binsfeld managed to leave behind some of the more monstrous ideas of his Dominican predecessor, such as lustful fantasies about sexual relations between demons and women. Furthermore, Binsfeld condemned some of the superstitious practices tolerated or even recommended in the *Malleus*, such as water ordeals or pricking tests. He also dismissed the practice of relying on diviners, witch-doctors or executioners to identify witches by characteristics such as their eyes, or special physical marks, as these marks were based upon superstition. However, Binsfeld replaced these transgressions with absurdities of his own, denying suspects the right of defence, and – like Bodin – he allowed repeated, and thus unlimited, torture and using child witnesses in court. Binsfeld drew his examples from the confessions in the trial records, that is, he worked from experience. As a consequence the treatise doubled in size within a few years.[10] As with Kramer and Bodin, the hidden agenda was to make witch hunting easier. The Catholic zealot Binsfeld did not refrain from quoting the Calvinist Daneau whose demonological approach appeared to be congenial.

During the reign of Duke Charles III of Lorraine (1543–1608, r. 1552–1608) the largest witch hunt in Francophone Europe by far took place. His *procureur général* Nicolas Rémy (c. 1528–1612) boasts of 900 witch burnings over fifteen years of office.[11] Rémy carried on burning witches for another ten years and was succeeded by his son Claude Rémy (in office 1606–31), who continued the burnings, adding a praise poem to his father's demonology. Whereas Bodin and Binsfeld tried to give the impression that they merely built on classical examples, Rémy fills his books with hundreds of examples of his own trials, taking pride in providing 'the exact and clear designation of the events, persons, places and times'.[12] Rémy was aware of the learned references, but examples of witchcraft and demonic action from the Bible, classical authors or recent demonologists like Bodin were far outnumbered by the account of his own first-hand observations. Demonology began to overlap with ethnography. Rémy was methodologically skilled enough to know the significance of using the word 'experience' as the first word of the first chapter of the first book. Rémy was well aware of the objections against demonology but he did not attribute them to particular authors but referred to atheists who claimed that his stories were 'contrary to the laws of nature'. In response, Rémy referred to the 'mighty power of demons', whose actions, by God's permission, are 'entirely inconsistent with the normal limitations of nature'.[13] Rémy was aware of the dangers of credulity, but was convinced that reason and experience were on his side. Rémy includes new shocking and graphic details concerning the sexual relationships between witches and demons, for instance, descriptions of the size, form or temperature of the devil's *membrum virile* and accounts of the women during intercourse. No wonder this demonology was instantly translated into Latin and German and saw about half a dozen reprints in the 1590s (Lyon, Frankfurt, and Cologne), as well as two very late ones in Hamburg (1693 and 1698). The witch persecutions in the Spanish Netherlands inspired another demonology, which built on the expertise of Kramer, Binsfeld, and Rémy, but was crafted more elegantly, authored by one of the most prolific scholars of the period, the Jesuit Martin Antoine Delrio (1551–1608). Born in Antwerp, the son of a high Spanish-Dutch official, Delrio studied law

---

10 Latin editions: Trier, 1589; Trier, 1591; Trier, 1596; Trier, 1605; Cologne, 1623. There are two independent translations into the vernacular: Trier, 1590, and Munich, 1591, which were both reprinted.
11 Rémy, *Daemonolatriae*, Preface.　12 *Ibid.*　13 *Ibid.*

in Paris, Douai, and Salamanca, where he received his doctoral degree in 1574. Delrio gained administrative and political experience through his appointment as *procureur général* of Brabant in 1577. Soon after, he was made vice-chancellor and Philip of Spain's chief fiscal officer for the province of Brabant in the years 1578 to 1580. At this stage, for unknown reasons, Delrio abandoned his political career, joined the Jesuit Order, and studied theology in Valladolid, Louvain, and Mainz. He was soon to be recognized as an erudite writer by one of the cleverest minds of the period, the neo-Stoicist philosopher Justus Lipsius (1547–1606), who praised Delrio as 'the wonder of our time'. Delrio served from 1591 as teacher in Liège and Louvain, and from 1600 in Graz and Salamanca. His *Six Books of Investigations into Magic* (*Disquisitionum magicarum libri sex*; Louvain, 1599/1600) were published in twenty-five Latin editions between 1600 and 1755, and almost immediately replaced the *Witches' Hammer* in importance. The six books deal with magic in general, magic involving evil spirits, harmful magic, divination, the duty of judges, and the duty of a confessor. Like the *Malleus Maleficarum*, the *Disquisitiones Magicae* combined demonology with practical guidelines. It was meant to serve as a handbook for judges, providing numerous examples from contemporary legal practice, mostly collected in the Spanish Netherlands, with updates in later editions up to the author's death, taken from his Europe-wide correspondence. The *Disquisitiones Magicae* contained the first coherent and comprehensive account of a Witches' Sabbath. Delrio's massive demonology, with more than a thousand pages, outgrew all earlier works: it was the demonology of all demonologies that was quoted approvingly by Protestants. Even the opponents of witch hunting, like Robert Filmer (1588–1653), acknowledged Delrio's authority and he referred to the *Disquisitiones Magicae* in order to demonstrate that the demonological assumptions of Puritan divines like William Perkins (1558–1602) (*A Discourse of the Damned Art of Witchcraft*; Cambridge, 1608) are exactly the same as those of the Belgian Jesuit (*An Advertisement to the Jurymen of England*; London, 1653).

After Delrio's massive compendium, there were no publications that added any new ideas or concepts. It seemed that the subject of demonology was exhausted. However, scores of new examples were added from hitherto neglected territories, which were now drawn to the European public's attention. Henry Boguet (1550–1619), grand judge of the lands of the Abbey of St Claude from 1587, and chief judge of Burgundy, wrote about persecutions in the Franche Comté in *Discours des Sorciers* (Lyon, 1602). Like Luxembourg and the area currently known as Belgium, the Franche Comté was under Spanish rule, but the population, as well as the legal system and the lawyers, were French, with the Parlement at Dole as the High Court. Boguet refers to the *Malleus*, to Bodin, Binsfeld, and Rémy as his main sources but he adds many examples from his own trials as evidence from experience. Unlike Rémy, Boguet seems more driven by apocalyptic feelings, and in an appendix to his book he claims it is 'A manner of procedure of a Judge in a case of Witchcraft'. However, by this time, the French Parlements had become sceptical about witchcraft as a crime. Nevertheless, Boguet's demonology was a bestseller in France, with three different editions (Lyon, 1602, 1603, 1610), which were all reprinted six times (Paris and Rouen, 1603; Lyon, 1605, 1607, 1608, 1611).

Monter assumes that Boguet feared that his publication might damage his aspirations to a see in the Parlement at Dole, and therefore stopped further reprints.[14] However, it was far beyond the capacity of a provincial judge to prevent printers in France, Switzerland, or the Holy Roman Empire from reprinting his booklet. It seems more likely that new and more thrilling publications rendered further reprints unattractive, very much as in Bodin's case. Rémy and Delrio had set new standards for future demonologists. For instance, Francesco Maria Guazzo (?-*c*. 1640), an Ambrosian monk from Milan, published a *Compendium Maleficarum* (Milan, 1608), which was illustrated with attractive woodcuts that are still being printed in the present day.[15] Guazzo's demonology is divided into three books: the first on demonology, the second on the various kinds of witchcraft, and the third on divine remedies for those who are bewitched. In contrast to Binsfeld, Rémy, and Boguet, Guazzo was not directly involved in any persecutions, as far as we know. However, like Delrio, he had a personal interest in the subject, as he was an internationally renowned exorcist. When he was called to Düsseldorf to exorcise the mad Duke Johann Wilhelm of Jülich, Cleves, and Berg (1562–1609), Guazzo, perhaps unsurprisingly, first diagnosed demonic possession as the cause of the poor duke's mental illness. However, after five months of unsuccessful attempts at treatment in the middle of 1604, he changed his diagnosis to bewitchment.

What makes this episode so striking is that Guazzo had been sent by Duke Charles III of Lorraine on behalf of his daughter Antoinette (1569–1610) who was Duke Johann Wilhelm's wife. Guazzo had exorcised several members of the house of Lorraine before, namely the bewitched Cardinal Charles of Lorraine (1567–1607), as well as Eric de Lorraine, the Bishop of Verdun.

In his book, Guazzo used examples from Lorraine's leading lawyer and demonologist, Rémy. It is striking to see all these Lorraine examples turn

14 Monter, *Witchcraft*, pp. 69–74.
15 Guazzo, *Compendium Maleficarum*, lib. II, chap. 13; Summers (ed.), p. 130.

up again in an Italian demonology with exactly the same names and dates, mostly from the late 1580s and early 1590s. Guazzo also included examples from Binsfeld and Delrio but only a few from Italy, which were mostly from the beginning of the sixteenth century.

Exorcisms were often the trigger for witch trials throughout the period and some of the most scandalous were actually initiated by possession cases, for instance the trial against Louis Gaufridy (1572–1611) from Marseille, who had served as a confessor in a monastery of Ursuline nuns at Aix. The Catholic Church remained sceptical with regard to exorcism and Pope Paul V (Camillo Borghese) (1552–1621, r. 1605–21) published the *Rituale Romanum* in 1614 to try to restrict its use. Nevertheless, possessions continued to be exorcised. A well-known case took place in the Ursuline nunnery of Loudon, which resulted in the execution of the priest Urbain Grandier (?–1634) and had repercussions all the way up to Cardinal Richelieu, who had become involved in the case.

Another French lawyer, Pierre de Lancre (1553–1631), member of the Parlement de Bordeaux, caused a stir with a huge volume on his inquisitions in the French Basque territories. His book on the *Inconstancy of Demons* (*Tableau de l'Inconstance des mauvais Anges et Démons*; Paris, 1612), was a preliminary attempt to reformulate the subject. He brought out a more extensive publication ten years later (Pierre de Lancre, *L'incrudelité et mescréance du sortilège*; Paris, 1622). In 1609, De Lancre was commissioned by King Henry IV of France to investigate a witch panic and he became deeply entangled in the business of witch hunting himself. This is all the more surprising since the Spanish Inquisition had enquired into a similar witch panic in the Spanish Basque territories. The Spanish Inquisitor in charge, Don Alonso de Salazar Frias (1564–1635), performed such a thorough analysis that it reads like a piece of sociological research, and the outcome was that all accusations were judged fabrications and that therefore all imprisoned suspects should be released at once.

Salazar suggested forbidding witch trials throughout the Spanish Empire and the Spanish Inquisitors took Salazar's advice. However, De Lancre, a committed and erudite humanist and theologian, concealed the outcome of this Spanish enquiry and built on the ideas of demonologists like Delrio arguing that the demons recently driven out of Japan and 'India' (the Americas) had returned to the Labourd, where there were now more witches than anywhere else in Europe. De Lancre does not merely label the Labourd as a witch-infested area in the way Binsfeld had done with Trier or Boguet did with Burgundy. He attempted to discuss the reasons and specific conditions for the presence of witches in the same way as the two men he quoted, Diego de Landa (1524–79), Bishop of Yucatan (*Historia de las Cosas de Yucatan* [1566]; Merida, 1990), and

José de Acosta (1540–1600), rector of the Jesuit College in Lima (*Historia Natural e Moral de las Indias*; Seville, 1590), who both worked as ethnographers of their respective American territories. De Lancre drew his examples mainly from his own trials and those of three other French lawyers and demonologists – Bodin, Rémy, and Boguet – adding a few stories from Delrio but completely dismissing the accounts of other theologians. As de Lancre admits, the lawyers he quoted considered witchcraft to be an extraordinary crime (*crimen exceptum*), unlike the French Parlements.

The first great wave of witch hunts was responsible for an ill-fated confessional polarization. To the Catholic theologians it seemed that the main critics of witchcraft persecutions were all Protestants (Weyer, Ewich, Witekind, etc.). The result was that the Protestants were labelled as heretics and opposition to inquisitorial demonology was outlawed. In 1592, the Catholic theologian Cornelius Loos (1546–95) was detained in Treves because he had tried to publish a radical critique of the ongoing witch hunts. There is a certain irony here, since Loos had been commissioned by Binsfeld to refute Weyer but he had come to the conclusion that Weyer was right. Loos wrote a radical pamphlet on *True and False Magic* (*De vera et falsa magia*, 1591), indicating that the kind of witchcraft described by demonologists did not actually exist: it was therefore fictitious and false, whereas turning blood into gold by confiscating the property of convicted witches was real magic. This ironic twist was lost on the Catholics, and Loos was forced to recant his heretical ideas by suffragan bishop Binsfeld. A transcript of his recantation was to be included in Delrio's authoritative demonology (1600). The discussion of demonology, and witchcraft in particular, had always been problematic, but by the 1590s Catholics had to be extremely careful of saying anything critical. To question the existence of witchcraft was considered to be heretical, and could even serve as circumstantial evidence in court. With the main channels of criticism blocked, Catholics had to look for new ways to put their arguments forward. They found it in the criticism of the judicial procedures in witch trials, which were usually cruel and often illegal. Interestingly, this meant taking and mixing arguments from various academic disciplines. Bodin the lawyer had argued theologically, Weyer the medical doctor had argued on theological grounds, and now the Catholic theologians started to argue as lawyers. They referred to Johann Georg Goedelmann (1559–1611), jurist at the University of Rostock, who had developed an efficient argument that made it very difficult to justify torture or capital punishment in cases of witchcraft. Although Goedelmann was presumably a supporter of Witkind, in his *Treatise on Magicians, Poisoners and Witches* he avoided demonological issues completely and focused on the legal issues, denying the acceptance of denunciations as circumstantial evidence in court, and calling for material proof or eye-witness accounts which, of course, could hardly ever be provided (*Tractatus de magis, veneficis et lamiis*; Nürnberg, 1584).

This approach was adapted by Adam Tanner (1572–1632), a Jesuit theologian who published his carefully constructed objections against witch trials in a theological standard work on scholastic theology. In his dogmatic chapter on angelology Tanner remains entirely traditional, although he questions the claimed number of demon-induced flights. However, in the chapter on 'Justice' (*De iustitia et iure*) in his moral theology, he emphasized the rule of law, denied the acceptance of any irregular procedures in court in the sense of Goedelmann, and deliberately expressed his compassion for the persecuted victims of witch hunts (Quaestio 5: *De processu adversus crimina excepta; ac speciatim adversus crimen veneficii*).

According to Tanner, the persecutions were clearly far more dangerous than the witchcraft itself, and he emphasized their lawlessness to the point of comparing them to Nero's persecutions of the Christians.[16] Tanner's work encouraged a number of Jesuits to join the radical opponents of witch persecutions. The most famous of these was Friedrich Spee (1591–1635), who quoted Tanner extensively in his work *Cautio Criminalis* (Rinteln, 1631) as being the only Catholic writer with enough authority to refute the dangerous suggestions of Binsfeld and Delrio. Spee's *Cautio Criminalis* is an exercise in Ciceronian rhetoric: the author states in a first paragraph 'once forever' that the teachings of Christian demonology cannot be doubted, witches therefore do exist, and it is unnecessary to pursue this issue any further. In the rest of his book, Spee systematically undermines the assumption of the existence of witchcraft, without explicitly questioning or ever returning to his introductory statement on demonology.

On two occasions in his book, having excluded the possibility that the cases of witchcraft discussed could be proven as real in an ordinary legal trial, Spee says there was one more truth too risky to articulate in these dangerous times. This vividly reminds us that publications from this period must never be taken at face value.[17] Having clearly stated that *all* the convicted were innocent, Spee's dangerous truth could only be that witchcraft did not actually exist at all. This implied that authorities were, in fact, committing mass murder. This was exactly what Weyer, whom orthodox Catholics were forbidden to quote, had claimed earlier.

16 Tanner, *Theologia scholastica*, vol. 3, cols. 981–1022. 17 Zagorin, *Ways of lying*.

The end of witch hunting was not an explicit act since the political actors preferred not to provoke strange alliances between reactionary theologians and an angry populace. How easy it was for moral entrepreneurs to incite the people's rage can be seen in the English Civil War, when the self-appointed witch-hunter general Mathew Hopkins (?–1648) single-handedly provoked a terrible witch hunt in East Anglia (*The Discoverie of Witches*; London, 1647). Written justifications by Hopkins and his assistant John Stearne show that their demonological assumptions were completely in line with continental mainstream demonology. For these witch hunters the witches' 'League and Covenant with the devil' provided details to identify characteristic criminal behaviour such as evidence of sexual intercourse with the devil or visible stigmata *diaboli*, the devil's marks. (The familiar spirits in animal shape, or imps, unique in European witchcraft, were also a token of their alignment with the devil.) In their 'confessions', the witches not only admitted to simple malevolent magic, they also gave details of their pact, and devilish assemblies, which took place 'in our owne Kingdome', as 'in all countries' where they worshipped the devil. Stearne tried to conceal the Catholic origins of his ideas by referring exclusively to biblical citations and his own trial records (*A Confirmation and Discovery of Witchcraft*; London, 1648).

Just as the witchcraft persecutions reached their climax in the second quarter of the seventeenth century, demonology started to fall out of favour. Leading intellectuals like Gabriel Naudé (1560–1653), the librarian of Cardinal Richelieu, carefully defended suspected magicians (*Apologie pour tous les grands personnages, qui ont esté sopconnez de magie*; Paris, 1625). After the mid-seventeenth century, when the frenzies of religious wars, hunger crises, and rebellions were over, the common mood changed completely. Increasing secularization affected disciplines like demonology first. Not content with merely defending those accused of witchcraft, intellectuals began to attack the supporters of witch hunts and demonology, ridiculing and taunting them publicly, for instance Cyrano de Bergerac (1619–55) in his work *Lettre contre les sorciers* (1654). Only three years after the English witch hunters had published their reports, Thomas Hobbes (1588–1679) devoted the fourth part of his *Leviathan* to questions of demonology, ridiculing the 'fabulous doctrine concerning demons' in an unprecedented manner, and portraying the Catholic Church as the 'Kingdome of Darknesse'.[18] Although Anglicans and Presbyterians shared this view, they were shocked by the notion that Hobbes did not discriminate much between the churches and that his criticisms could apply to them as well, as

---

18 Hobbes, *Leviathan*, chapters 44–7.

was acknowledged by the Cambridge Platonist Henry More (1614–87) in his *Antidote against Atheisme* (London, 1653).

Three years later, More's viewpoint was taken even further by the English physician Thomas Ady, who denied the physical power of devil and witches alike. He considered poor health care and social tensions in the villages as fuelling suspicion and fear (*A Candle in the Dark, or, a Treatise concerning the Nature of Witches*; London, 1656). The public exchange between Hobbes, More, and others served as a starting point for later debates. Suddenly it was no longer just demonology that was being debated, but a much wider issue: religion. This paralleled the debate between Joseph Glanvill (1636–80) (*Some philosophical considerations touching the Being of Witches and Witchcraft*; London, 1665; *A Blow at Modern Sadducism*; London, 1668) and John Wagstaffe (*Question of Witchcraft Debated*; London, 1669), since, 'if the Notion of a Spirit be absurd, as is pretended, that of God, and a Soul distinct from matter, and Immortal, are likewise Absurdities' (Joseph Glanvill, *Philosophical Considerations*; London, 1676).

Early modern demonology, between 1500 and 1660, could be seen as a science in the sense that it produced a coherent body of texts, discussing over and over again the same or similar examples of unexplainable phenomena and observations, by supposing supernatural interference. Stuart Clark defines demonology as 'a composite subject consisting of discussions about the workings of nature, the processes of history, the maintenance of religious purity, and the nature of political authority and order'. However, his assumption that 'demonology as a working system of belief at the height of its powers to persuade' was based upon the assumption that demonologists were basically using the same language and were engaging in the same discourse (Clark, *Thinking with demons*, Preface) seems exaggerated. If demonologies were so closely related to contemporary debates on science, history, religion, and politics, it makes little sense to analyse their contents as if they were representing a unified system of thoughts. Rather it seems that not all contemporaries agreed on the subject. Although the linguistic code appears to rest on common assumptions this does not necessarily mean that their authors applied the same meaning to certain words. It seems rather that basic categories meant different things to different authors, even those of the same generation, depending on the authors' own agenda. Demonic possession, for example, would have meant different things to a Galenic doctor, interpreting the humours of the body, or a lawyer, balancing his legal knowledge against the Dominican Inquisitors' ideas about demonic signs. Authors could discuss demons without believing in their existence or talk about witches without believing in witchcraft. Or they could confirm their belief in witchcraft as a rhetorical device, and argue against persecution, or even the existence of witches.

Demonology was a dangerous subject that could result in physical harm not only by the demons but also the ecclesiastical and secular authorities. Delrio claimed that the witches' patrons were worse than the witches themselves and they were the first that should be prosecuted. Heinrich Schultheis rightly suspected that Spee engaged in an entirely different discourse and openly threatened him with torture and execution (*Ausführliche Instruction, wie in Inquisition Sachen des grewlichen Lasters der Zauberey zu procedieren*; Cologne, 1634). To conclude, a meaningful discussion of demonological texts has to be set in the context of the interests these texts served and the particular situations they were related to.

23

Science and religion

ANN BLAIR

The period of religious transformations covered in this volume corresponds closely in time to a series of major scientific developments traditionally known as the 'Scientific Revolution', which is commonly considered to extend from the publication of Copernicus's heliocentric thesis (in *De Revolutionibus*, 1543) to that of Newton's laws of physics (in the *Principia*, 1687).[1] In the course of these 150 years, Aristotelian natural philosophy, which had been dominant since its introduction to the Latin West *c.* 1200, came under attack in many quarters and gradually lost its hold on the curriculum. Various alternative authorities and new interpretations of nature were advanced, but by 1650 the new philosophy which had become dominant was a mechanical philosophy premised on the notion that all phenomena could be explained as particles of matter in motion, according to mathematical laws open to empirical observation and experimentation. The historiography on the Scientific Revolution is vast.[2] Alongside detailed studies of the central figures and texts of the Scientific Revolution, we have a rich array of studies which highlight the role of the social, cultural, and intellectual contexts of these developments. Among these, religion has long been and continues to be acknowledged as a particularly important factor.

The historiography on science and religion across the centuries predates the professionalization of the history of science and has from the beginning singled out the early modern period for developments which were

I am grateful for helpful comments to Anthony Grafton, Mordechai Feingold and the editor of this volume.

1 I will use the term 'science' for convenience, as historians of science often do, to designate the various forms that the study of nature took in early modern Europe, which are often quite different from the practices and assumptions we associate with modern science. Since the term is anachronistic, I will also use terms that correspond better to the categories of the historical actors, such as natural philosophy, natural history, astronomy, mathematics, and medicine.

2 See Daston and Park (eds.), *Cambridge history of science*, vol. 3: *Early modern science* including an article on 'Religion' by Rivka Feldhay.

taken as paradigmatic both of conflict (the Galileo Affair) and of cooperation ('Protestantism and science'). Although recent work on the interactions
between science and religion has moved away from such starkly articulated
theses, the early modern period remains a particularly rich area of study.[3] In the
sixteenth and seventeenth centuries new developments in both religion and
science undermined the solidity of the scholastic synthesis of Aristotelianism
and medieval Christianity and triggered a wide range of new interactions.

The legacy of the Middle Ages

The scholastic synthesis of Aristotelianism and Christianity was made possible
by the reception of Aristotelian philosophy into the newly founded universities
of Europe during the thirteenth century. This reception was not unproblem-
atic. The early teaching of Aristotle in the Latin West triggered a series of
condemnations culminating in 1277 when the Bishop of Paris, Etienne Tempier, condemned as impious 217 theses which he feared were being drawn
from Aristotle.[4] The condemnations of 1277 highlighted a number of points of
tension between Aristotelian philosophy and Christian beliefs. Aristotle could
be read as supporting both the eternity of the world and the mortality of
the soul, although Thomas Aquinas skilfully averted conflict by arguing that
Aristotle concluded that these points could not be decided from reason alone;
without impugning reason or the authority of Aristotle, Aquinas argued that
these human sources had to be supplemented with the authority of revelation,
with its doctrines of Creation and of the immortality of the soul. The necessity
of natural law was another major point of tension, which continued to surface
in various forms even as Aristotelianism gave way to new philosophies in the
early modern period. The scholastic distinction between the absolute and the
ordained power of God served to acknowledge both that God had the power
to suspend the laws of nature and that in practice God chose to abide by them.
This distinction legitimated the naturalistic study of God's ordained power
without seeming to deny divine omnipotence.[5]

Thanks to these resolutions of points of conflict, developed by Thomas
Aquinas among others, by 1325 Aristotle was fully entrenched in the curriculum

3 For the most recent studies, see Helm and Winkelmann (eds.), *Religious confessions and
the sciences*; Fatio (ed.), *Les églises face aux sciences* and *Sciences et religions de Copernic à
Galilée*. On science and religion more generally see especially Brooke, *Science and religion*,
Lindberg and Numbers (eds.), *God and Nature* and Ferngren, *Science and religion*.
4 See Grant (ed.), *A source book in medieval science*, pp. 45–50. For the debates surrounding
these theses, see Thijssen, 'What really happened on 7 March 1277?'
5 On this theme see Courtenay, *Capacity and volition*.

of the arts faculty at the University of Paris and at most other universities. The institutional separation between the faculty of theology and the lower-ranked arts faculty gave philosophers a variable amount of independence from theological constraints, depending on the context. At Paris, the Sorbonne was powerful and philosophers abided by the condemnations of 1277. At the University of Padua, which had no theology faculty, but only a higher faculty of medicine, the philosophers enjoyed great independence and were noted for their radical Aristotelianism. This Paduan tradition survived into the sixteenth century, when it generated increasing ecclesiastical reaction. Pietro Pomponazzi (1462–1525), professor at Padua, concluded in his *On the immortality of the soul* (1516) that the soul could be shown on purely rational grounds to be mortal rather than immortal. After a papal condemnation in 1518 Pomponazzi published a *Defensorium* including orthodox proofs of the immortality of the soul and refrained from publishing his other highly naturalistic treatments of astrology and miracles.[6] Even later in the century Cesare Cremonini (1550–1631) left un-Christianized his interpretation of Aristotle's position on the eternity of the world and denied the intervention of God in the sublunary realm; for this he was investigated by the Inquisition, but he still retained his high-paying position at the University of Padua.[7]

The opportunities for institutional and intellectual independence afforded to philosophers by some scholastic contexts were on the wane in the sixteenth century. Throughout the sixteenth and seventeenth centuries natural philosophy was justified by religious motivations and informed by religious beliefs. Already at the Fifth Lateran Council (1512–17), the church called on philosophers to play an active role in supporting religious doctrines and mandated philosophical demonstrations of the immortality of the soul, for example.[8] The Reformers devised new curricula in which natural philosophy would serve the needs of religious doctrine. The post-Tridentine Catholic Church tightened its control on the religious orthodoxy of philosophical works through education on the one hand and the Inquisition and Index of Forbidden Books on the other. The impetus behind this renewed emphasis on the need for philosophy to be pious was not only religious in origin. The humanist movement was equally hostile to scholasticism and the perceived impieties of Aristotelianism. Petrarch (1304–74) mocked Aristotelianism as sterile and raised the classic Christian objections to Aristotle as articulated in 1277. Petrarch did not propose any philosophical alternatives to Aristotle, but he opened the way for others

---

6 See Pine, *Pietro Pomponazzi*.
7 Kraye, 'The philosophy of the Italian Renaissance', p. 42.
8 Mercer, 'The vitality and importance of early modern Aristotelianism', p. 47.

to do so, by objecting to an excessive reliance on Aristotle and Aristotelian method.[9]

The Renaissance search for a pious philosophy

The humanists are well known for their efforts in bringing to light long-lost ancient texts. Among these there were ancient commentaries on Aristotle, which offered new and often critical perspectives on the Philosopher, but also texts from quite different philosophical traditions – particularly Stoic, Epicurean, or Platonist – and doxographical works like Diogenes Laertius who reported the opinions of still other thinkers whose works were often no longer extant, such as the Pre-Socratics and the Pythagoreans. With all these alternatives available for study and imitation, Aristotle was no longer the only option; the long-standing religious objections to Aristotle could be adduced to justify turning to other authorities who might seem more readily reconciled to Christian doctrines.

Marsilio Ficino (1433–99) championed Plato in developing a philosophical system complete enough to rival Aristotle's. In addition to voluminous translations of and commentaries on Plato, Ficino offered his own synthesis of Christianity and Platonism in his *Theologia platonica* (composed around 1474, published in 1482). He contrasted this 'pious philosophy' with what he considered the impieties of scholastic Aristotelianism.[10] Ficino revived the arguments of St Augustine in claiming that Plato's teachings on the individual immortality of the soul and on the creation of the world by a divine Demiurge made his philosophy more easily reconciled with Christianity. But the fit was not perfect, given Plato's belief in the transmigration of souls and the fact that the creation described in the *Timaeus* was not a creation *ex nihilo*, but rather from pre-existing matter. Platonic philosophy remained an option which appealed to a few thinkers like Symphorien Champier in France (*c.* 1470–1539) or Jakob Boehme in Germany (1575–1624), down to the 'Cambridge Platonists' Henry More (1614–87) and Ralph Cudworth (1617–88) who saw Platonism as a weapon against materialist interpretations of the mechanical philosophy.[11] But the renewed emphasis on traditional orthodoxy in the Counter-Reformation church resulted in the condemnation of the writings of

9 See Menn, 'The intellectual setting', p. 41.
10 Hankins, 'Marsilio Ficino as a critic of scholasticism'.
11 For detailed bibliographical references on these and other figures, see my contribution on 'Natural philosophy', in Daston and Parks (eds.), *Cambridge history of science* vol. 3: *Early modern science*.

Francesco Patrizi, for whom professorships in Platonic philosophy had been founded in Ferrara (1578) and Rome (1592), and the subsequent suppression of these positions by Robert Bellarmine who concluded that Platonism was more dangerous to Christianity than Aristotelianism.[12]

Another scientific authority brought to the fore by the humanist movement was Lucretius, whose *De rerum natura* presented the Epicurean theory that the natural world is formed by the random movement and coalescence of atoms. Although Epicureanism continued to be associated with immorality and impiety in the minds of many, Lucretius found a Christianizing champion in the French Oratorian Pierre Gassendi (1592–1655). Against Lucretius, Gassendi maintained that atoms were divinely created and endowed with motion by God and introduced angels and rational souls to complement the materialistic structure of the world. Gassendi concluded that his system was more pious than Aristotle's, because, among other virtues, it could account better for the transformation involved in the eucharist.[13] Although Gassendi's particular type of atomism did not find many followers, his arguments smoothed the way for the acceptance of Descartes' mechanical philosophy, which, despite differences on various specifics, also rested on the assumption that the world can be explained as particles of matter in motion.

The Stoics appealed to Justus Lipsius, who applied them not only to political but also to natural philosophy, again with the claim that the results were more pious than Aristotelianism.[14] The Pre-Socratic philosophers, known for their naturalism, were also used as the basis for 'new philosophies' which proclaimed their superior piety. For example Bernardino Telesio (1509–88) explained the natural world as the interaction between the two principles of hot and cold and Christianized his system by introducing a universal spirit of divine origin which infused the world. Tommaso Campanella (1568–1639), a disciple of Telesio, carried the idea of the world-spirit to a pansensist extreme of envisioning the whole universe as a living animal in which God was omnipresent and immanent. Nature was thus full of correspondences and divine messages which the natural philosopher could interpret, especially through astrology. But neither of these claims to piety seemed convincing to the post-Tridentine church: Telesio's works were condemned posthumously in 1593 and Campanella spent most of thirty years in Italian jails and fled to France after his release in 1634.[15]

---

12 Firpo, 'The flowering and withering of speculative philosophy', p. 278.
13 Osler, 'Baptizing Epicurean atomism'.
14 Barker, 'Stoic contributions to early modern science'.
15 On these and other anti-Aristotelian philosophers, see Kristeller, *Eight philosophers of the Italian Renaissance*.

Amid the plethora of philosophical experimentation unleashed by the Renaissance a different strategy was to turn not to ancient philosophical authorities, but rather to religious inspiration and the Bible to ground a truly pious natural philosophy. Theophrastus Bombastus von Hohenheim, who styled himself 'Paracelsus' for surpassing the ancient medical encyclopaedist Celsus, claimed support from divine inspiration as well as empirical observation for his rejection of the traditional medical synthesis of Aristotle and Galen in favour of chemical remedies. Paracelsus was held in contempt by many throughout the early modern period and associated, at times unfairly, with dissolute habits, heresy (Arianism), and magical activities.[16] Nonetheless his writings, published from manuscripts gathered by followers after his death, elicited an enthusiastic following among non-conforming Protestant thinkers marginalized and radicalized by religious persecution, particularly in central Europe. These radical Paracelsians hailed his works as uniting both theological and philosophical truth by drawing on the lights of grace and of nature.[17] Millenarianism was often present in this utopian vision of religious and philosophical reformation, as it was in more mainstream Protestant thought.[18] Other, less radical attempts to ground a 'most Christian' natural philosophy in biblical authority can be identified among thinkers, both Catholic and Protestant, who rejected Aristotelian explanations in favour of biblical ones, attributing for example the origin of underground springs not to the condensation of watery vapours (as Aristotle explained) but to the oceans returning to their sources, as mentioned in Ecclesiastes 1:7.[19] 'Most Christian' strategies also included stressing the greatness of God as creator of such abundance and variety and, by contrast, the incompetence of reason to understand many natural phenomena. Confessing human ignorance in order better to praise God's glory remained a trait of religiously inclined natural theologies through the seventeenth century.[20]

The explosion of new and often explicitly anti-Aristotelian philosophies in the Renaissance did not affect the standing of Aristotle as the authority of choice in traditional pedagogical settings, such as schools and universities.[21]

---

16 Gunnoe, 'Paracelsus's biography among his detractors'. Paracelsus never left the Catholic Church nor faced any persecution, but expressed a spiritualist and anti-clerical conception of religion in works he left in manuscript.

17 See Gilly, '"Theophrastia Sancta"', p. 166.   18 See Hotson, Paradise postponed.

19 Blair, 'Mosaic physics'.

20 On the confession of ignorance, see Blair, The theater of nature, pp. 92–3, 144–6.

21 Aristotelianism in the schools often acquired new eclectic features, incorporating elements from outside the Aristotelian tradition; for more on this eclecticism, see Schmitt, Aristotle and the Renaissance.

The Council of Trent elevated the Thomist synthesis of Aristotelianism and Christianity to the status of orthodox doctrine, so that in most Catholic institutions to deviate from Aristotle was to risk charges of impiety. The Jesuits in particular took an explicit oath of allegiance to Aristotle.[22] In Protestant universities, despite early attempts to find alternatives, Aristotle was soon established as the backbone of the curriculum.[23] But as they packaged Aristotle for student consumption during the great educational expansion of the sixteenth century, both Catholics and Protestants placed Aristotelian natural philosophy in the context of Christian piety. One early textbook, by a Franciscan, intermingled philosophical presentations with psalms of praise to God. This format, which did not become the norm, is evidence of the uneasiness of the author at presenting Aristotle 'straight up', especially to the broad and inexperienced readership targeted by an introductory textbook.[24] Protestant textbooks, following the lead of Melanchthon, typically praised natural philosophy as an incitement to piety for revealing the benevolent providence of God.[25]

Whether they were Aristotelian or anti-Aristotelian, Renaissance natural philosophers proclaimed the piety of the study of nature. Natural philosophy offered justification for the existence, greatness and worship of God and could serve as a bulwark against impiety and atheism, which many contemporaries feared were on the rise.[26] In some instances these statements may have been rhetorical reiterations of long-standard arguments; but most often religious motivations were central to inspiring the innovations of the anti-Aristotelian philosophies of the Renaissance.[27] In any case, pious motives and natural theological justifications long outlived both Aristotelianism and the 'new philosophies' of the Renaissance grounded in other ancient authorities. As the mechanical philosophy of the seventeenth century prevailed over these rivals, it too was couched in terms of Christian piety and praise of the greatness and providence of God.[28] Christians of all confessions used natural theological arguments to justify the study of nature throughout the early modern period. Claims that one particular strand of Christianity, such as Lutheranism

22 See Ariew, 'Descartes and scholasticism', pp. 64–5.
23 On the brief attempt by Melanchthon to teach natural philosophy from Pliny instead of Aristotle, see Kusukawa, *The transformation of natural philosophy*, 175.
24 Frans Titelmans, *Compendium naturalis philosophiae* (1542). See Schmitt, 'The rise of the philosophical textbook'.
25 Philip Melanchthon, *Doctrinae physicae elementa* (1552).
26 For an introduction to the vexed question of the existence of atheists in this period, see Hunter and Wootton (eds.), *Atheism from the Reformation to the Enlightenment*.
27 See Cunningham, 'How the *Principia* got its name'.
28 See Feldhay and Heyd, 'The discourse of pious science'.

or Calvinism, was more open than others to the study of nature seem dubious; although less well known, Catholic natural theologies would also repay further study.[29]

Protestantism and science

The historiography on science and religion originated during the early decades of the reception of Darwin when religious objections to the theory of evolution were intense. The debate is best known for the conflict thesis articulated bluntly by John William Draper, *The History of the Conflict between Science and Religion* (1874) and somewhat moderated by Andrew Dickson White, *A History of the Warfare of Science with Theology in Christendom* (1896). But those same decades elicited some equally classic historiographic statements about the cooperation of science and religion, including Pierre Duhem's argument that the condemnations of 1277 opened the way for the modern rejection of Aristotle and the claim that Protestantism was particularly favourable to science, first made by the Genevan naturalist Alphonse de Candolle.[30]

The notion of a special relationship between Protestantism and science had a long career, fuelled by Max Weber's linkage of Protestantism with capitalism and articulated in most detail by Robert Merton in *Science, Technology and Society in Seventeenth-Century England* (1937–8). Over the following decades a remarkable number of scholars, most of them specialists of seventeenth-century England, debated various formulations of the Merton thesis.[31] These debates helped to sharpen some historical categories, including the range of Protestantisms in seventeenth-century England, from strict Puritans often hostile to the study of nature to the Broad-Churchmen or latitudinarians whose desire to avoid religious controversy was characteristic of the core group of natural philosophers at the Royal Society. But the lengthy discussions about

29 For example, a special impetus for natural theology has been attributed to the Lutheran doctrine of real presence in Barker, 'The role of religion in the Lutheran response to Copernicus', p. 61, or to the Calvinist sense of obligation to study God's creation in Knoeff, *Herman Boerhaave (1668–1738)*, p. 10. But Catholic natural theology also thrived in the multi-volume *Spectacle de la nature* by the Abbé Antoine Pluche, which was among the most widely owned books in mid-eighteenth century Parisian private libraries; see Mornet, 'Les enseignements des bibliothèques privées (1750–1780)', p. 460.

30 On Duhem, see Wallace, 'The philosophical setting of medieval science', pp. 105–6. Alphonse de Candolle first published his claim in *Histoire des sciences et des savants depuis deux siècles* (1873).

31 For a convenient sampling of the debate, see Cohen (ed.), *Puritanism and the rise of modern science*; for a recent re-assessment see *Science in Context* (1989).

what features essential to Protestantism might have been favourable to science (which variously attributed to Protestantism greater rationalism, valuation of manual labour, optimism, rejection of received authority, of demons and the supernatural) no longer seem viable.[32] On the one hand historians now tend to reject on principle essentialist characterizations of religious movements; in addition the much-increased geographical range of historical studies, European and otherwise, has reinforced the dangers of generalizing from a particular case like seventeenth-century England. On the other hand the creationist movement and its religious arguments against Darwinian evolution have become increasingly visible to the public since the 1980s, especially in the English-speaking world, and offer clear evidence of the potential for conflict between Protestantism and science. Finally, as I will elaborate in the next section, a number of recent studies focused on science in Catholic contexts in early modern Europe undermine the initial quantitative assumptions of Protestant superiority that drove the claims of de Candolle and Merton.[33]

Even if we set aside many of the earlier arguments about 'Protestantism and science' and their frequently confessional motivations, it is reasonable to consider under this heading the considerable body of research on specific cases of the interaction between religion and science in Protestant contexts. Protestantism took different forms in different contexts and its lack of unity and of a central religious authority is one of its defining characteristics. Protestantism involved no particular predisposition towards scientific innovation. Luther and Calvin are noted for their general lack of interest in the study of nature.[34] But pedagogical demands in both confessions led to the institutionalization of the teaching of natural philosophy. By the 1550s in Strasbourg and the 1570s in Geneva Hieronymus Zanchi and Lambert Daneau respectively taught natural philosophy and published textbooks with a stated preference for the authority of the Bible over philosophers and yet an emphasis on finding agreement between the Bible and Aristotle.[35] In building the model curriculum for use in Lutheran institutions Melanchthon gave an important place to natural philosophy which would show the providence of God in the natural

32 For a classic set of such arguments, see Hooykaas, 'Science and Reformation', and *Religion and the rise of modern science*.
33 This point was already made by Russo, 'Le rôle respectif du catholicisme et du protestantisme'.
34 Kusukawa, *The transformation of natural philosophy*, pp. 188–9, 205. For more detailed discussion, see Gamble, *Calvin and science*.
35 On Zanchi, see Harrison, *The Bible, Protestantism and the rise of natural science*, p. 138; and Donnelly, 'Calvinist Thomism'.

world.[36] Melanchthon had a particular interest in astronomy, notably as an aid to astrology; his presence at Wittenberg was no doubt instrumental in fostering interest there in Copernicus.[37] Wittenberg was the site of the first group of astronomers to master Copernicus's system and use it to draw up new astronomical tables, the Prutenic tables of 1551. The 'Wittenberg interpretation' of Copernicus, centred around Erasmus Reinhold, was a fictionalist one which used Copernicus's theory for computational purposes but denied that heliocentrism was a real physical phenomenon.[38]

One of the earliest convinced Copernicans, Johannes Kepler, was a Lutheran too, trained at Tübingen, where Melanchthon had established the curriculum.[39] Kepler's deeply religious motivations in seeking the mathematical harmonies underlying the distribution, size and distances of the planets are well known. He first explained the arrangement of the planets by a series of perfect Platonic solids in the *Mysterium cosmographicum* (1596). But Kepler's own exacting empirical standards led him to question his use of the planetary data, notably in detailed footnotes in a later edition of the *Mysterium*, and ultimately to reject this scheme in favour of another one, based on musical harmonies, in his *Harmonices mundi* (1619), which also contained in passing the mathematical relationships later known as 'Kepler's laws' of planetary motion.[40] Kepler laboured intensively with the observational data gathered by Tycho Brahe, driven by the conviction that God must have created the heavenly planets and their motions according to a beautiful mathematical plan. A devout and orthodox Lutheran, Kepler even tried to identify the logic of the Trinity in some triadic features of the heavens, without showing any concern for specific biblical passages which seemed to contradict heliocentrism.[41]

Scriptural objections certainly did play a role in the rejection of Copernicanism by other Lutherans, such as Tycho Brahe himself, who prided himself on offering a geo-heliocentric cosmology which offered the advantages of Copernicanism without its signal disadvantages of flying in the face

---

36 Kusukawa, *The transformation of natural philosophy*, p. 187. For a study of Melanchthon's manuscript 'Physicae seu naturalis philosophiae compendium' (1543), see Bellucci, *Science de la nature et Réformation*.
37 Barker, 'The role of religion', pp. 65–8.
38 Westman, 'The Melanchthon circle'. For further research on this topic, see Gingerich and Westman, *The Wittich connection*, and Gingerich, *An annotated census of Copernicus' De revolutionibus*.
39 Methuen, *Kepler's Tübingen*.
40 See Johannes Kepler, *Secret of the universe*; Field, *Kepler's geometrical cosmology*; and Stephenson, *The music of the heavens*.
41 Westfall, 'The rise of science and the decline of orthodox Christianity', in Lindberg and Numbers (eds.), *God and Nature*, pp. 222–4.

of all known physics and of the straightforward interpretation of various biblical passages.[42] Protestant opposition to Copernicanism continued to surface down to the late seventeenth century when conservative Dutch Calvinists invoked scriptural objections to reject Copernicanism and the Cartesianism with which it had become associated; these intellectual positions were often driven by the politics of power struggles within church and state and resulted in the condemnation of Cartesianism by the theology faculty of Leiden in 1659.[43] Protestant exegetical principles allowed for a broad range of interpretations of problematic passages like Joshua 10:12 and, unlike Catholic principles, did not require adherence to an interpretation because it was traditional. While some Protestants favoured literalism, on the grounds, given for example by the conservative Calvinist Gisbert Voetius, that it was invidious to imply that the Holy Ghost either could not or would not speak the truth in the Bible, many explained the passage as accommodated to the understanding of its Hebrew audience. In addition to Calvin's own use of the principle of accommodation, Galileo's arguments concerning Copernicanism were available in a Latin translation of his 'Letter to the Grand Duchess Christina' published in 1636. Other explanations advanced by Calvinists included Grotius's suggestion (following Jewish exegesis) that the passage was a poetic exaggeration or the claim that the standstill of the sun was an optical illusion.

Given that some Catholics too favoured heliocentrism before and even after and despite the condemnation of Galileo in 1633, cosmological positions cannot be correlated with particular religious affiliations. The deep religious commitments characteristic of early modern thinkers led individuals in each confession to different positions on Copernicanism depending in part on their preferences in admiring God for the beauties of mathematical order and rational simplicity or rather for a more mysteriously complex natural order supported by literal and traditional readings of the Bible.

Seventeenth-century England, which served as the principal evidence for a special relationship between Protestantism and science, continues to offer a rich field of investigation. A wide range of scientific activity, from the utilitarian pursuits of 'mathematical practitioners' to the experimentation at the Royal Society designed to elucidate aspects of the mechanical philosophy, can be attributed to a vision of the benefits of science that was most famously articulated by Francis Bacon (1561–1626). In his unfinished *Instauratio magna*, Francis Bacon envisioned a plan for moral and philosophical reform which

---

42 Blair, 'Tycho Brahe's critique of Copernicus'.
43 Vermij, *The Calvinist Copernicans*, pp. 239–31, 309–13; for the interpretations by Voetius and Grotius which follow, see pp. 249–51 and 243–6.

would restore Adam's lost dominion over nature; Bacon distinguished ethical mastery, which had been denied the human race after the Fall, from natural and technical mastery, which had never been forbidden – indeed it was a divine injunction which had never been fulfilled. Bacon outlined a method for collective scientific endeavour which would reach reliable generalizations about nature by confronting a plethora of individual facts or 'instances' gathered from observation and purposeful experimentation.[44] Though Bacon never completed any such investigation himself nor managed to secure the royal funding for his project that he had hoped, his methodological manifesto proved a powerful inspiration for generations to come, particularly but not exclusively in England. Bacon was careful to warn against an intermingling of science with theology, although his utopian vision in *New Atlantis* depicts the ranks of scientific workers on the model of an ecclesiastical hierarchy. Bacon's various followers agreed with him on the close link between moral and philosophical reform, but conceived of it in different ways.[45]

One group inspired by Bacon's vision, the Office of Address formed around the Polish-born Calvinist Samuel Hartlib, harboured radical visions for social and religious reform, often millenarian in tone, and in natural philosophy focused on Paracelsianism, astrology and the pansophy of Comenius; after flourishing during the Interregnum, they were marginalized and dispersed under the Restoration. In 1662 the members of two other informal groups (the '1645 group' in Oxford and the 'Invisible College' around Robert Boyle) requested approval from the king to form the Royal Society in 1662. The Royal Society included a large and dispersed membership but was run by a core of some twenty active London members who focused on making natural philosophy safe from political and religious controversies and the potential for royal disfavour.[46] They specialized in reporting on 'matters of fact' – accounts of observations and experiments – about which they hoped there would be no disagreement.[47] The members of the Royal Society embraced a mechanical philosophy adapted from Descartes, which interpreted all natural phenomena as the motions of inert particles of matter. True to Bacon's vision they presented their experimental mechanical philosophy as the bulwark of good Christian piety. Their demonstrations of the workings of divine providence throughout nature were offered as an antidote against atheism, which was perceived as an

---

44 For an introduction to Bacon see Peltonen (ed.), *Cambridge companion to Bacon*.
45 For a detailed account of Bacon's legacy, see Webster, *The great instauration*; also Gieryn, 'Distancing science from religion' and Kroll *et al.* (eds.), *Philosophy, Science and religon*.
46 Hunter, *The Royal Society and its fellows*.
47 Shapin, *A social history of truth*, pp. 308–9.

ever-increasing threat. Their sober research into facts was an antidote against religious enthusiasm, with its hasty 'imaginings' (e.g., about supernatural interventions) and the risk of dangerous social disturbances.[48]

The English experimentalists dwelt at length on the intricate beauty of the organic world, as examined for example under the microscope in Hooke's *Micrographia* of 1665, and the mathematical regularities of the planets, as magisterially demonstrated in Newton's *Principia* of 1687. 'Physico-theology' came to be used to describe the many works of physics or natural philosophy couched as demonstrations of divine providence, power and benevolence in nature.[49] Some formulations of natural theology emphasized the rationalization of divine actions to such an extent that revelation could seem to serve only as a confirmation of truths derived from natural religion.[50] Others, like Robert Boyle, emphasized the greatness of God by insisting on the limits of human reason.[51] The lecture series which Boyle endowed at his death in 1691 would perpetuate his project of proving Christianity against infidels and atheists without engaging in internecine doctrinal disputes – natural theology was a favourite theme of Boyle lecturers for decades to come. Recent studies of the oeuvre of Isaac Newton, from his famous mathematical works to his abundant theological and alchemical manuscripts, have emphasized his deeply religious motivations.[52] In establishing the laws of physics Newton was striving to uncover the workings of God throughout nature and history; these included not only regular laws but also occasional direct interventions, required for example to insure the continuity of the planetary motions, and miraculous moments in history. But Newton kept his religious views private and for good reason, since they were antitrinitarian – an unorthodoxy that could not have been officially tolerated at the time.[53]

Seventeenth-century England proved fertile ground for the development of experimental mechanical philosophy and natural theology. Restoration England was tolerant of a range of Protestant beliefs, from high church

---

48 See Joseph Glanvill, *Philosophia pia or a discourse of the religious temper and tendencies of the experimental philosophy of the Royal Society* (1671), as discussed in Westfall, *Science and religion in seventeenth-century England*, p. 130.

49 Major examples include John Ray, *The wisdom of God manifested in the works of Creation* (1691) and William Derham, *Physico-theology* (1713).

50 For example in the case of John Locke who moved close to a rational religion in *The reasonableness of Christianity* (1695). For a short survey of this movement, see Lagrée, *La religion naturelle*.

51 See Wojcik, *Robert Boyle and the limits of reason*; Sargent, *The diffident naturalist*.

52 See, for example, Dobbs, 'Newton as final cause and first mover'.

53 See Westfall, 'The rise of science', pp. 228–34. More generally, Cohen and Westfall (eds.), *Newton*.

Anglicanism to Puritanism, though not including Catholics, dissenters or Arians. A Puritan like Samuel Hartlib, a conservative Anglican like Robert Boyle, an Arian who concealed his views (like Isaac Newton) and one who tended towards natural religion (like John Locke) could each bring their religious commitments to their philosophical work and feel that they were participating in one broadly Baconian project of reforming society through the study of nature. Natural theology proved such a successful framework precisely because it too encompassed a wide range of motivations, from the rationalistic to the more purely religious. Seventeenth-century England offers a fine example of the harmonious cooperation between science and religion, and yet it also put in place structures of thought that would later prove problematic for the relationship. Natural theology proposed scientific grounds on which to rest religious faith, based on assumptions about an act of creation which proved divine power, wisdom and providence. When this assumption was challenged by Darwin's notion of evolution by natural selection, science and religion suddenly seemed irreconcilable enemies to many in the late nineteenth century and since. For over 200 years English natural theology had been so successful in its broad appeal that it masked tensions generated by complex changes in the status of theology and of the natural sciences, which had become increasingly independent and professionalized, and between various strands within Protestantism; when these tensions burst into the open under the impact of Darwin, the metaphor of a warfare between science and religion became predominant.

Catholic science

Although Draper and White, both Protestants, were delighted to point to Catholicism as the first source of the conflict between science and religion, there was no indication of such a conflict prior to the Galileo Affair. In many ways the Catholic Church and its medieval antecedent offered a favourable context for the development of natural philosophy – though not, as Duhem had argued, through the condemnations of 1277. Those early condemnations had been meant to thwart the entry of Aristotle into the university curriculum and might well have done so, had they not been undercut by the success of the skilful Christianization of Aristotle offered by Thomas Aquinas. Instead the church fostered the development of science by adopting many features of Aristotelian methodology and in posing questions about nature in the teaching of theology itself, spurring debate and discussion on, among other questions, the intension and remission of forms or the qualities of motion.[54] Furthermore the church offered opportunities for education and life-long careers to secular and regular clergy which often gave them the freedom to pursue scientific interests. Finally, the institutional separation between the theology and the arts and medical faculties left philosophy and medicine often free from explicit theological regulations. As noted above, the church showed an interest at the Lateran Council in harnessing philosophy to serve the needs of theology, by demonstrating the immortality of the soul. But aside from the condemnation of Pomponazzi and the condemnation and arrest of Pico della Mirandola (1488), which were resolved by the publication of apologies, the church had intervened little in philosophy before the Counter-Reformation.

In response to the threat of Protestantism the church issued the first Index of Forbidden Books in 1559; early indexes included all works by heretics, including works of science, but later versions were moderated, so that, for example, the natural histories by Protestants like Gesner and Fuchs could be read after emendation.[55] Scientific works were often published, distributed and read across the Protestant–Catholic divide in both directions. More damaging were the decrees of the Council of Trent concerning biblical interpretation, which were designed to ensure that the Catholic Church would remain united against Protestantism: the Catholic laity was not allowed to interpret the Bible; Catholic interpretation must respect the traditional interpretations of the church fathers and doctors. These principles were the result of theological conflicts with Protestantism and were not directed at nor motivated by issues in natural philosophy, but they came to have a large impact on astronomy and natural philosophy through the condemnation of Galileo.

The historiography on the Galileo Affair is vast and ranges from interpretations which lay the blame solely on the Counter-Reformation church to those which hold Galileo and his acerbic personality responsible. The historiography has examined the complex politics of church factions (Jesuits and Dominicans) and philosophical ones (Galileo's disputes with Scheiner, Grassi and the Aristotelian 'pigeonists' around Ludovico delle Colombe), and the role of individual personalities, including Urban VIII (who felt his trust in Galileo had been betrayed), Robert Bellarmine (who had a special interest in natural philosophy), and Galileo, with his ambitions for a career at the

---

54 See Grant, 'Science and theology in the Middle Ages', in Lindberg and Numbers (eds.), *God and Nature*, pp. 49–75.
55 See Fragnito (ed.), *Church, censorship and culture in early modern Italy*.

Medici court.[56] The Galileo Affair involved a tangled web of causes, many of them contingent. But it also resulted from a deep intellectual conflict over the control of biblical interpretation and the kind of scientific evidence that the Counter-Reformation church required to justify relinquishing a traditional interpretation of the Bible. These tensions were bound to play themselves out at some point on the issue of the motion of the earth, and the timing of Galileo's *Dialogue concerning the two chief world systems* (1632) precipitated a conflictual outcome. Copernicanism did not yet have the support of a large number of astronomers nor of a physics that explained it (like Newton's) – Galileo's *Dialogue* helped to foster both – and the Counter-Reformation church was inclined to enforce rigidly the interpretative principles laid out at Trent.[57]

Even before Trent, Nicolaus Copernicus had been fearful of the reception of his heliocentric theory by the Catholic Church in which he served as a cathedral canon (in Frombork, Poland). Copernicus delayed publication of his work until the year of his death and offered it to Pope Paul II as a contribution to the church's project of calendar reform; he also included a letter of support from Bishop Schönberg. Unbeknownst to Copernicus the Lutheran Andreas Osiander, probably at the behest of the printer, tried to facilitate the reception of the work by explaining in an additional preface, against Copernicus's own realist claim, that the heliocentric hypothesis was not a description of reality but only an elegant computational device. As it happened, and perhaps thanks to these preventive measures, the publication of *De revolutionibus* elicited no ecclesiastical reaction from either Catholics or Protestants. It was a difficult, technical work which few were able or inclined to read. Two early Catholic responses attest to the breadth of possible responses: a pre-Tridentine manuscript by the Dominican Tolosani was critical, while in 1584 the Spanish Augustinian Diego de Zuñiga published a favourable assessment of heliocentrism and an interpretation of some of the problematic biblical passages. But Zuñiga's interpretations were condemned in 1616.[58]

Galileo prudently never published his own arguments for biblical interpretations to allow for or even support the motion of the earth. But Bellarmine was

---

56 For a brief account of the Affair, see William Shea, 'Galileo and the Church', in Lindberg and Numbers (eds.), *God and nature*, pp. 114–35.

57 There is no evidence to support the claim that Galileo was condemned for atomist views rather than heliocentrism, as advanced in Redondi, *Galileo heretic*. See, among other refutations, Ferrone and Firpo, 'From Inquisitors to microhistorians'. Redondi nonetheless offers a vivid portrait of many of the people and places involved in the Galileo Affair.

58 For more detailed treatment of the material I survey here, along with related primary texts, see Blackwell, *Galileo, Bellarmine and the Bible*.

aware of the arguments of Galileo's 'Letter to the Grand Duchess Christina' which circulated in manuscript in 1615. Galileo adduced the authority of Augustine to argue that passages which seemed to indicate that the earth was stationary were accommodated to the understanding of the Hebrews and should be reinterpreted in light of evidence for the motion of the earth.[59] Bellarmine on the contrary maintained that though the church fathers had not addressed the question of the motion of the earth, their traditional interpretations were binding until and unless demonstrative proof was made of the motion of the earth – a proof that Bellarmine was convinced would be impossible. The condemnation of heliocentrism in 1616 as 'foolish and absurd in philosophy and formally heretical since it explicitly contradicts in many places the sense of Holy Scripture', made no mention of Galileo.[60] It was precipitated by the imprudent publication of new biblical interpretations in support of Copernicanism by the Carmelite priest Paolo Antonio Foscarini. Some fifteen years later, after friendly conversations with Urban VIII and armed with a written certificate that cleared him of any suspicion of wrongdoing, Galileo was confident that he had demonstrative proof of Copernicanism and was authorized to publish a discussion of Copernicanism as a hypothesis. In the *Dialogue* Galileo did indeed devote the final page to a confession of ignorance on the question of cosmology, but only after writing hundreds of pages mocking Aristotelian objections to the motion of the earth and attempting to prove heliocentrism from the motion of the tides. In 1633 Galileo was charged with disobeying both the decree of 1616 and an unsigned injunction which summoned him in particular to cease teaching Copernicanism, which was found in the files of the Inquisition, unbeknownst to Galileo. Galileo was found guilty of 'strong suspicion of heresy' and condemned to house arrest. He died in 1642, after composing in his last years a treatise on the physics of motion.

The condemnation of Galileo had a lasting impact on what cosmology Catholics could teach and defend. Catholics were forbidden to support heliocentrism publicly until 1833 when Copernicus was finally taken off the Index.[61] For early modern Catholics the solution of choice to the cosmological question was to adopt the observationally equivalent Tychonic geoheliocentric system, in which all the planets except the earth revolved around the sun, which in turn

---

59 'Accommodation' refers to the message of the Bible being accommodated to its audience, not to philosophy being reconciled with religion, although the principle of accommodation was often useful in achieving that end.

60 See Finocchiaro (ed.), *The Galileo affair*, p. 146.

61 On the attempt to remove Copernicus from the Index in 1757, see Mayaud, *La condamnation des livres coperniciens*.

revolved around a stationary earth. Better yet, as Newton sealed the acceptance of heliocentrism in 1687, Catholics most often opted to engage in other kinds of scientific work. The Jesuits were noted for producing fine astronomers in the seventeenth century, who devoted their efforts to observations and avoided cosmology altogether.[62] The Jesuits had long been particularly active in mathematical sciences, following the efforts of Christopher Clavius to elevate the status of mixed mathematical disciplines, and they continued to be at the forefront of teaching and research in many mathematical disciplines.[63] The buildings of many a Catholic church were used as instruments of astronomical measurement.[64] Despite his public humiliation, Galileo himself fostered a school of followers in Italy who worked on the physics of motion, not cosmology.[65] Francesco Redi (1626–98) and Marcello Malpighi (1628–94) also carried on the tradition of anatomical and medical research which played an essential role in William Harvey's work on the circulation of the blood (*De motu cordis*, 1628).[66]

Outside Italy the church fostered the careers of innovative natural philosophers like the Minim Marin Mersenne and the Oratorian Gassendi. Blaise Pascal did his work in physics (e.g. on barometric pressure) before his conversion to a more austere religious outlook and Jansenism (to which the church was consistently hostile). René Descartes, who was condemned by both Protestants and Catholic institutions for the potentially irreligious consequences of mechanical philosophy, thought of himself as a devout Catholic; indeed his motivation to develop a new philosophy is attributed to a conversation with the Counter-Reformation cardinal Bérulle.[67] Descartes sent copies of his work to the Jesuits at La Flèche where he was educated, evidently in the hope that they would adopt his ideas in the curriculum. Descartes was careful to remain a Catholic in good standing; he explicitly alluded to the condemnation of Galileo in explaining why he did not publish his cosmological system, *Le monde*. But the spread of Cartesianism played a major role in diffusing Copernicanism; after initial resistance and condemnation, even the University of Paris adopted Cartesianism for its curriculum in the 1690s. There is no identifiably Catholic character to the variety of scientific pursuits and results achieved by early

---

62 See Feingold (ed.), *The new science and Jesuit science*.
63 On Clavius, see Lattis, *Between Copernicus and Galileo*; for recent work on the Jesuit polymath Athanasius Kircher, see Findlen (ed.), *Athanasius Kircher*.
64 Heilbron, *The sun in the Church*.   65 Segre, *In the wake of Galileo*.
66 See Bertoloni Meli, 'Francesco Redi e Marcello Malpighi'.
67 On the condemnation of Descartes, see Jolley, 'The reception of Descartes' philosophy'. Baillet, *Vie de Monsieur Descartes*, vol. I, ch. 14, pp. 160–5.

modern Catholics – they did not even agree on rejecting Copernicanism as the church had decreed.

Coda

In keeping with the dominant orientation of the historiography on science and religion, this brief survey has focused mostly on the impact of religion on science, as studied especially by historians of science. It would take another kind of expertise to disentangle the role of science from among the many forces shaping changes in religion in the early modern period, but the new confidence in scientific explanation was no doubt an important factor driving the rationalization of religion and the development of natural religion in the late seventeenth century.

24

The new clergies

LUISE SCHORN-SCHÜTTE

As the title of this volume suggests, the long-prevailing division of the history of the European Reformation into 'Reformation' and 'Counter-Reformation' has been overtaken by more recent research. The older model has been replaced by that of a single reform movement, one which resulted in the formation of confessional churches on the one hand and a deferred Catholic reform movement on the other; thus, it makes more sense to talk about a 'Catholic reform' or 'renewal'. At times parallel and at times interdependent, these developments are vividly illustrated by the history of confessional office-holders – both the Protestant clergy and the Catholic 'reform clergy'. Strong arguments suggest that from the mid-seventeenth century on, there remained few significant differences, in terms of educational and/or socio-economic backgrounds, between Protestant pastors and the Catholic pastoral clergy. This effectively contradicts Max Weber's thesis that Protestants enjoyed an educational advantage over Catholics.[1]

Medieval traditions

Visitation reports from a number of European regions, dating back to the mid-sixteenth century and offering an insight into the educational levels of the clergy on the eve of the Reformation, record an urgent need for improvement. Much was left to be desired regarding the theological training of both the lower clergy and those theologians who, although ordained to higher orders, served merely as holders of benefices and failed to carry out their spiritual duties. Similar deficits existed concerning their pastoral abilities and preaching skills. In addition, the personal conduct of all clergy groups remained a constant bone of contention in the eyes of the congregation as well as of secular and

---

1 Schorn-Schütte, 'Priest'.

ecclesiastical authorities. Most of these deficiencies clashed with even the medieval ideal of a priest. Yet, theological competence and preaching skills were not part of the 'job description' for pastoral clergy: 'Their main functions were sacramental and disciplinary, not doctrinal'.[2] Thus, the majority of pre-Reformation clergy did not need profound theological training; their task was to facilitate the accomplishment of good works as a path towards spiritual salvation – a task requiring primarily practical and technical skills. Only the higher clergy were expected to perform theological duties. Technical skills and theological knowledge were supposed to be taught at schools and theological seminaries and faculties; in reality, however, this was not done adequately, if at all, in the late fifteenth and early sixteenth centuries. After all, appointment to a clerical office was closely tied to the assumption of a benefice, and only in the rarest of cases did this selection depend on spiritual-pastoral abilities. Rather, in the late Middle Ages, the pursuit of personal income and patronage were the decisive factors in these decisions. All pre-Reformation efforts to redress these deficiencies were aimed at the full realization of the clerical ideal. Thus, they were not anti-clerical, but rather were marked by a singular esteem for the sanctity of priesthood.

But it was exactly this sanctity of office that was brought into question by Luther's justification doctrine. The need for technically able assistants in the quest for salvation by way of good works had become superfluous; hence, Luther's teachings on the priesthood of all believers. With this doctrine, the Wittenberg reformer was actually building on medieval traditions (among others, those of the Lollards and the followers of Wyclif). In sum, the reformist cause can be seen as the sacralization of the secular and the secularization of the sacral; a separate clerical estate was to be abolished. Social historians have found that the first two generations of the new Protestant clergy were recruited largely from the clerical estate (former monks or priests); and, moreover, that numerous pastors' wives had previously been their illicit companions, or were, as in the famous case of Katharina vs Bora, former nuns.[3] A complete replacement of the clerical personnel in all the territories where the Reformation had taken hold would have led to a failure to supply the populace with spiritual care, and was therefore out of the question.

---

2 Swanson, 'Protestant clergy', p. 40.
3 Despite the large volume of social-historical studies, an unevenness of sources has meant that the depth of coverage varies greatly from one territory to the next: for the Old Reich, see Schorn-Schütte, *Geistlichkeit*; and Wahl, *Lebensplanung*; for England, O'Day, *English clergy*; for France, Bergin, *Episcopate*; for central Europe, Bahlcke, 'Geistlichkeit'; for southern Europe, Paiva, 'Portuguese'; and for Switzerland, Fischer, *Reformatio*.

Basic outlines of a social biography of
the 'new clergy'

Few historical studies compare the European clergy across confessions and regions. In large measure, this reflects the unevenness of the sources, as not all records provide mass data of equal significance. But it also reflects a problem of interpretation, as it is still generally assumed that an unbridgeable gap existed between Protestant priests and Catholic clerics, both in their perception and execution of office and in their social backgrounds. However, more recent regional studies in social history – including confessionally mixed regions – clearly show that both the Protestant clergy and the majority of the Catholic pastoral clergy belonged to the European bourgeoisie. Therefore, the following comparative study of the new, post-Reformation clergy in Europe begins with more detailed information on these groups.

Undoubtedly, there are also other aspects of social origin (such as peasant backgrounds), particularly at the outer edges of Europe (in the south and central-east), which need to be taken into account as exceptions to the rule. And the high clergy in the Catholic Church still came from the European nobility.

Social and regional origin and integration

The common image of the peasant origin of Catholic priests has given way to a much more differentiated one, as a result of numerous studies of the pastoral clergy in the Old Reich since the late sixteenth century.[4] The term 'pastoral clergy' applies to the lower secular and regular clergy at the parochial level, which – as a result of the reform of clerical education launched by the Council of Trent (1545–63)[5] – increasingly had to take on spiritual responsibilities that went beyond the technical-practical task of pastoral care (*Seelsorge*). Despite inadequate sources, the following can be concluded about the sixteenth and early seventeenth centuries: just like Protestant pastors of the second and third generations, the majority of the Catholic pastoral clergy appear to have come from the urban or territorial bourgeoisie. The evolution of this social pattern was probably closely related to the introduction of ordination titles (proof of financial security in terms of money or landholdings in order to be ordained) at the end of the sixteenth and beginning of the seventeenth

---

4 For more literature, see Schorn-Schütte, *Geistlichkeit*.
5 The education of the clergy was one of the main topics on the agenda of the first session of the Council 1545–7. For the ideal image of the Reform priest formulated at the Council, see Jedin, 'Leitbild'.

century. Thus, entrance to clerical office was barred to the great majority of poor, independent peasants, while it remained open for the more affluent urban bourgeoisie and wealthier peasants, as well as for the territorial civil servants (court, administration, university).[6] These findings are confirmed by the Jesuit Order's tendency to recruit its members from the more affluent and/or highly educated bourgeoisie.[7] The foundation of the Jesuit Order (1540), as well as that of other reform orders (such as the Capuchin Order in 1525/8 and the Collegium Germanicum in Rome, 1552),[8] was the Catholic response to the redefinition of clerical office within the Protestant Church and to its strong pedagogical influence over the secular sphere. The debates about the specialization of the education of boarding students in the Germanicum that arose at the end of the sixteenth century confirm this conclusion about social origins in a remarkable manner. For while parts of the first generation of pupils still came from the bourgeoisie, after the 1670s a new practice prevailed: the Germanicum was now dedicated exclusively to the education of the nobility in order to reform the higher echelons of the territorial church.[9]

These observations on the social origins of the new pastoral clergy apply to France and Italy as well. According to Joseph Bergin, '[o]ne of the most significant features of the French Counter-Reformation parish clergy is how large a proportion of it was drawn from the bourgeoisie of town and country'.[10] In the mid-seventeenth century, the bourgeoisie supplied up to 85 per cent of all secular and regular clerics who were employed as parish pastors. Just as in the Old Reich, social groups below the level of the urban and territorial bourgeoisie were barred from entering clerical office.[11] The proportion of aristocrats among the parish clergy nearly equalled their proportion among the overall population. This 'bourgeois' dominance, found in France from the late sixteenth century on, can be explained at least in part by the material incentives involved. Exempted from taxes and dues, the parish clergy enjoyed a privileged status in an economically overburdened society.[12] Moreover, the French Catholic Church itself contributed to social change through persistent efforts to improve existing standards of education.

Developments in Italy were very similar to those in France. A number of recent studies have shown that members of the urban elites turned towards

---

6 Cf. Becker, *Kurköln*; Hahn, *Pfarrerideal*; Freitag, *Kirche*; and Holzem, *Religion*.
7 Cf. Hsia, *Discipline*, pp. 48–50.
8 For the history of the Germanicum, see Schmidt, *Germanicum*.
9 *Ibid.*, pp. 44–6, 78–80, and figure 3 on p. 79.   10 Bergin, 'Estate', pp. 76–7.
11 However, Bergin points out that in some French dioceses, sons of wealthy peasants could indeed enter clerical office. Bergin, 'Estate', p. 77.
12 Bergin, 'Estate', pp. 77–8.

clerical office for economic reasons. This applies to both the pastoral clergy and the clerical elite; numerous bishops of the seventeenth century were patricians from large Italian cities.[13] From the mid-seventeenth century on, this development was reinforced by the fact that the episcopal seminary-colleges that had been founded exclusively for the education of future clergy opened their doors to the affluent urban bourgeoisie, as well as to interested aristocratic laymen.[14] Although the majority of students from these social groups remained laymen, quite a few actually found their way into clerical office.

Just as before the Reformation, the aristocracy remained the social recruiting pool for the higher clergy (such as bishops and cardinals) within the old church throughout Europe. In contrast to Protestantism, the Catholic clergy remained an independent social and political estate, retaining its political function in the estate assemblies in the Catholic regions of Europe. Furthermore, until the late eighteenth century members of the higher clergy often maintained their functions as political leaders or advisers to the court and were part of the inner circle around the monarch (as in the cases of Richelieu and Mazarin).[15] Since these structures no longer existed within the Protestant Church, the Catholic clergy was far more diverse; that is, its membership was recruited from a much wider social scale. The number of aristocratic boarding students educated in the above-mentioned Germanicum rose to a good 60 per cent by the middle of the seventeenth century, and to 70 per cent by the middle of the eighteenth century.[16] This group comprised members of the hereditary nobility, as well as those who had attained their noble status by office; the latter would gain numerous leading positions in the old church during the seventeenth and eighteenth centuries.[17]

A glance at the regional backgrounds of the Catholic pastoral clergy in the Old Reich confirms the above conclusions about social origins. From the late sixteenth century on, the pastoral clergy in the countryside came only rarely from rural areas or the parish itself. In the case of the diocese of Würzburg, it has been shown that the country pastors came predominantly from neighbouring cities, often the seats of the court and territorial administrations or of

---

13 Cf. Papenheim, *Karrieren*, pp. 221–3.
14 Cf. Julia, 'Prete'; and Fantappie, 'Istituzioni'.
15 Asch, 'Lumine solis'; Millet and Moraw, 'Clerics'; Schorn-Schütte, 'Revolution'; and Reinhard, *Staatsgewalt*, p. 187.
16 Schmidt, *Germanicum*, pp. 80–9.
17 For the bishopric of Chur as an example, see Fischer, *Reformatio*; for the Old Reich in general, see Aretin, *Römisches Reich*, pp. 76–82. For similar results in France, see Bergin, *Episcopate*, p. 196 and *passim*.

the military.[18] Even for such ecclesiastical territories as the prince-bishopric of Münster or the bishoprics of Hildesheim and Chur – in which the Tridentine reforms requiring that the pastor reside in his parish had proven hard to implement – this pattern of regional origin holds true.[19] The confessionally reliable candidates needed for the stabilization of a Catholicism renewed by the Tridentine measures – figures who often were members of the new reform orders[20] – came from distant regions and were mostly of urban background. From the mid-seventeenth century on, the so-called 'local' clergy continued to be of mainly urban origin. It can therefore be asserted for Catholic Germany as well that due to the cultural gap 'between the urban-minded priest and the rural environment of the faithful . . . the gulf between pastor and parishioners' grew ever wider over the course of the seventeenth century.[21] Only seldom was there an actual family connection between the village community and the pastor's relatives. In areas where the parish office was filled by members of religious orders, their short-term residence contributed to this situation.[22] Still, this did not necessarily make the pastor an outsider.[23]

As early as the seventeenth century, the regional mobility of the Catholic parish clergy in France was apparently more pronounced than that of the pastoral clergy in the Old Reich.[24] There was a clear disparity between the various church provinces in terms of supply of clergy members, which could be described as over- or undersourcing. The south, in fact, drew upon the north for its supply of young clergy. The 'geography of clerical recruitment' can be observed as clearly in the seventeenth century as in the nineteenth.[25] Its basis was economic in nature: due to extremely permeable diocesan borders, clerics could always move to places where they could find the highest paying benefices (*Versorgungsmobilität*). This is an indication of both the clergy's regional independence and an absence of supraregional qualifications for the admission to clerical office, the latter continuing until the late eighteenth century. The conclusion that from the early seventeenth century on the rural parish clergy came largely from cities applies to France as well. Thus, here – as in other European regions – the gulf between laymen and pastoral clergy

18 Knetsch, 'Geistlichen', p. 159.
19 For more on this, see Freitag, *Kirche*, pp. 185–7, and table 8; Dürr, *Kirchenräume*, pp. 196–202; and Fischer, *Reformatio*, pp. 544–52.
20 Dürr, *Kirchenräume*, p. 200; evidence for the Grisons in Wendland, 'Konfessionalisierung'.
21 Becker, *Kurköln*, p. 82.   22 Dürr, *Kirchenräume*, pp. 198, and 201–2.
23 *Ibid.*, This revises the predominant opinion in existing research.
24 Bergin, 'Estate', pp. 72–4.   25 *Ibid.*, p. 72.

was growing. Whether this led to mistrust and rejection, however, is not at all certain.[26]

Despite the reform decrees of the Council of Trent, in the Italian regions, more than anywhere else, clerical office continued to be regarded as a private domain and could be filled according to private law. This custom was facilitated and further promoted by the great diversity of church patrons who were endowed with different local privileges. The families of prebends saw clerical benefices as a legitimate way to provide for their own.[27] Thus, the extent of regional mobility among the pastoral clergy remained rather limited.

The social integration of the Protestant clergy has been much better documented, at least for the period since the late sixteenth century.[28] As a result of comparative research on the Old Reich, the Swiss Confederation and the Polish aristocratic republic, the commonly accepted idea of self-recruitment to clerical office must be thoroughly revised in regard to the late sixteenth and the seventeenth centuries. Instead, it has been shown that the urban and territorial administrations played a rather important role both in the recruitment of pastors and their wives, and as an occupational field for their sons or sons-in-law. In some regions, the occupations of 'craftsman' and 'merchant' continued to have significant functions.[29] This illustrates that the Protestant clergy became integrated into the group of (often legally trained) non-aristocratic office-holders in the service of territorial or city authorities, a group that was becoming increasingly influential from the late sixteenth century on. A growing network of personal and familial relations connected these different groups.[30] Upward mobility within this group of civic office-holders was possible over the course of two or three generations; clerical office proved to be a 'springboard profession'. This trend was even more pronounced in the case of pastors' wives. The figures point to the early modern nature of marriage, which proved to be an important element in the social integration of the Protestant clergy. Aside from the financial advantages it offered both spouses, marriage promoted social establishment, and social ascent.[31]

Developments in the Protestant cantons of the Swiss Confederation did not differ much from those in the Old Reich. The oft-cited occupational continuity

---

26 For more on this, see Hsia, *Gegenreformation*, pp. 163–4.   27 Cf. Julia, 'Prete'.
28 *Pfarrerbücher* are a good source of relevant documents for the German-speaking areas.
29 Cf. the tables in Schorn-Schütte, *Geistlichkeit*, and Schorn-Schütte and Dixon, Introduction, tables on pp. 7–10. See also Strom, *Orthodoxy*, pp. 32–7 and table A.2; as well as Riegg, *Konfliktbereitschaft*, pp. 75–110.
30 Cf. Wahl, *Lebensplanung*; and Riegg, *Konfliktbereitschaft*.
31 Cf., among others, Schorn-Schütte, 'Matrimony'; Riegg, *Konfliktbereitschaft*, pp. 84–91; and Strom, *Orthodoxy*, pp. 32–4.

among the clergy is not to be found here either. In some of the researched areas, clergy members proved even less willing to remain in their profession over a long period of time than did artisans. What is remarkable here is the consistently high proportion of craftsmen recruited to the clergy in the Swiss cities. From the mid-eighteenth century on, the Swiss cantons witnessed a high influx of new clergy; as a result, entry into office was blocked for candidates from the lower ranks. In the Old Reich, this development began a full generation later, and did not achieve comparable results until the first decades of the nineteenth century.[32]

A glance at England confirms the observations concerning the social integration of the Protestant clergy on the Continent. In the late sixteenth and early seventeenth centuries, following a period of insecurity and instability, the new Anglican and Puritan clergy succeeded in getting socially established. Their new social status meant that now the gentry sought entrance to clerical office as well, so that the opportunities for upward mobility for yeomen's sons, which had existed since the mid-sixteenth century, began to dwindle.[33] This does not mean, however, that a new aristocratic church was established within English Protestantism. Instead, the close connection between gentry and urban bourgeoisie helped create a new middle social group in England as well, from which, as on the Continent, academically trained office-holders were recruited. The Protestant clergy was part of this group. Both in England and on the Continent, the clerical elite also belonged to this 'middle class'. Anglican bishops, for example, were 'sons of merchants, clothiers, tailors, yeomen, and small gentry. They succeeded in becoming the equals of the lower gentry and of urban middle classes but never of the nobility, which they could not enter even by marriage.'[34]

In this respect, there remained a significant difference between the Protestant and the Roman Catholic Church.

A glance at regional and academic mobility in the Old Reich confirms these conclusions concerning social mobility. To be sure, a discernible change took place between the late sixteenth and the early eighteenth centuries. For as the first two generations of the Protestant clergy experienced steady recruitment from outside, after the confessional borders were consolidated an increasing number of clerical office-holders came from within the territories themselves. This was, on the one hand, the result of the recently introduced scholarship system that required theology students to study at a university in their home

---

32 Schorn-Schütte, 'Amt', pp. 7–9; and Gugerli, *Pfrund*. For the problem of shortages and surpluses, see Titze, 'Überfüllung'.
33 Barrie-Curien, 'Clergy', pp. 453–4.   34 *Ibid.*, p. 454.

territory. On the other hand, it was a result of the patronage system which remained unchallenged in the Protestant territories and which made clerical employment conditional upon the candidate's personal client-like relationship with the aristocratic, urban or parish patrons. In the larger territories, however, foreign theologians still made up a significant segment of clergy, even in rural areas. Throughout the entire early modern era, regional mobility remained most discernible among the ecclesiastical leadership (such as superintendents, *Oberpfarrer*, deans, and theology professors).[35]

While similar developments can be observed in England,[36] in Switzerland a certain regional containment (*begrenzte Kleinräumigkeit*) was predominant from the late sixteenth century on.[37] At least two-thirds of future pastors had studied either at the University of Basel or the academic gymnasium (Scola Tigurina) in Zurich. If there were any cross-regional contacts in the area of education at all, these remained within clearly defined confessional limits.

At least among the Protestant rural clergy, such regional ties certainly contributed to a positive relationship with the parish; after all, local traditions of piety were much more accessible to those who had experienced them first hand.

Training and educational levels of clergy; access to clerical office; economic provisions

With the onset of the Reformation, existing criticism of the Church turned into demands for well-trained pastors. Therefore, even contemporaries understood the Reformation as an educational movement. Over the course of the early modern period, the ideal of the clerical office was being realized within all three Christian confessions in similar ways, however long it took to achieve this goal.[38] A look at the educational levels and the criticism of the conduct of both the Protestant and the Catholic clergy in the Old Reich at the end of the sixteenth century reveals striking similarities between the two 'camps'. This shows that the Catholic norms that evolved in response to the Tridentine reforms coincided largely with the Protestant ideal of a pastor in the last third of the sixteenth century. At the time, university-educated pastors constituted only a negligible number of parish clergy in both Catholic and Protestant regions of Europe.[39] Each side displayed a colourful mixture of theological

---

35 Schorn-Schütte, 'Priest'; Strom, *Orthodoxy*; and Kaufmann, *Universität*.
36 Barrie-Curien, 'Clergy', pp. 545–5.   37 Gugerli, *Pfrund*.
38 Cf. the stimulating research by O'Day, *Clergy*; and the important work by Vogler, *Le Clergé*.
39 On developments in Protestantism, see Schorn-Schütte, *Geistlichkeit*; in Catholicism, Holzem, *Religion*, pp. 46–7.

positions, rooted in both Catholicism and Protestantism and founded on a combination of pastoral care and parish piety. The reforms, or rather the institutionalization, of the educational system – which had started originally in the Protestant regions but in the seventeenth century began taking hold in the Catholic territories as well – were aimed at enhancing theological knowledge and the 'preservation of clerical dignity' within each confession. On both sides, educational goals were tied to an ethos of clerical office that prescribed a certain way of life. The particulars of these prescribed life styles, however, differed from one confession to the other. The formal differences between the respective educational systems were significant, but did not necessarily translate into lower educational levels for Catholics.

Since the secular authorities had for the most part failed to implement the reform decrees of the Council of Trent, the activities of the reform orders (such as the Franciscans, the Capuchins,[40] and above all the Jesuits) can hardly be over-emphasized. Where initiatives by the territorial rulers had fallen short, the Jesuits often succeeded in establishing seminaries for preachers (*Predigerseminare*) to help redress the lack of clerical and sacral schooling for the aspiring pastoral clergy. However, that goal was only partly achieved.[41] Therefore, the period until approximately 1650 must be considered a transitional phase for the Catholic clergy in the Old Reich, characterized by lingering shortcomings in the educational levels, perceptions of office, and the official and private conduct of clergy members. With the image of the 'pastor bonus' (which corresponded to the church fathers' ideal image of the bishop) the Tridentine reform movement developed a new approach under which the pastor became the 'leader of the parish, proclaimer of God's word, and dispenser of sacraments'.[42] These criteria became the basis of the Jesuits' educational concept, and correct execution of the duties of their office and moral integrity became the central focus of Jesuit 'education'.[43] This went hand in hand with the institutionalization of education, suitably referred to as 'churchification'.[44] In accordance with the provisions of the Order's *Ratio Studiorum*, all Jesuit gymnasia taught in their five grades the 'studia inferiora', along with Catholic doctrine and specific forms of piety that varied from one confession to the next. In most cases, the gymnasia were attached to philosophical-theological institutes that provided further education for aspiring priests. There students

---

40 For the activities of the Capuchins in the Swiss Confederation, see Wendland, 'Konfessionalisierung'.
41 Cf. Holzem, *Religion*; Hahn, *Pfarrerideal*; and Fischer, *Reformatio*.
42 Holzem, *Religion*, pp. 238–9; Freitag, *Kirche*; and Dürr, 'Images'.
43 Holzem, *Religion*, pp. 239–40; and Jedin, 'Leitbild'.
44 Schindling, 'Schulen'; and Freitag, *Kirche*, p. 163.

were taught the 'studia superioria' – that is, the basic knowledge of theology, the Old and the New Testaments and the church fathers.[45] Graduates could choose to attend either a nearby faculty of arts or a theological seminary. Students at the seminary often had to practise the delivery of sermons, in order to master the practical application of their knowledge. After four years, the candidates were ordained to higher orders. Following ordination, they would often sit in on the catechetic exercises the Jesuits offered in the city parishes.

A glance at the reality of pastoral training in some of the prince-bishoprics in the north of the Old Reich and Switzerland shows that the qualifications of the aspiring pastoral clergy increased slowly but steadily from the first third of the seventeenth century on.[46] Thus, in the early seventeenth century more than half of the clergy in a north German deanery had indeed attended the local Tridentine gymnasium, and there is evidence that a great majority also attended a local Jesuit college. Yet only a few of the aspiring clergymen earned academic degrees; as a rule they spent four years in study at a Jesuit college. Thus, they received a uniform specialized training, while – in contrast to contemporary Protestantism – a university degree remained the exception to the rule.[47]

Professional training and ordination did not, however, guarantee entrance into office. After all, only the patron could grant a benefice, that is, appoint a candidate to a parish that would generate a liveable income. These patronage rights, though, remained widespread among secular and ecclesiastical rulers in the Old Reich. Ultimately, since the Tridentine seminary system was not established to the same extent in all parts of the Old Reich, no common standard of clerical training emerged. Therefore it is not possible to refer to the pastoral office as a 'profession', as the term would be understood in the nineteenth and twentieth centuries. In the end, this much can be said: professional qualifications were handled very differently across the various regions of the Old Reich.[48] The early modern combination of formal qualifications with client-like and/or familial connections remained the basis for employment throughout the existence of the Old Reich.

As late as the sixteenth century, it was not uncommon for Catholic pastors to seek an income for 'their' own sons. This use of family connections faded away

---

45 For the Jesuit course of studies, see Hengst, *Jesuitenuniversitäten*, pp. 70–1. For the Catholic schools, see Dickerhof, 'Gelehrtenschulen'.
46 The following is based on Freitag, *Kirche*; Holzem, *Religion*; and Fischer, *Reformatio*.
47 Freitag, *Kirche*, p. 189.
48 Cf. the various case studies by Holzem, *Religion*; Freitag, *Kirche*; and Fischer, *Reformatio*.

with the gradual implementation of the Tridentine clerical reform. Instead of trying to arrange positions for immediate kin (a habit referred to as 'Pfarrfamiliensinn') the pastor was now taking care of nephews and grand-nephews.[49] While the ensuing change in elites took off in the first half of the seventeenth century, it was during the eighteenth century that these transformed family networks were consolidated.

The implementation of the clerical reform introduced by the Council of Trent turned out to be very problematic in France, Italy, and Spain as well. Just as in the Old Reich, these difficulties were due to the persistence of traditional institutions such as the patronage system on the one hand, and the lack of funds experienced by the proposed episcopal seminaries for preachers on the other. 'Bishops and Church authorities were both obliged to, and proved perfectly capable of, working within traditional institutions and the benefice-system to produce change'.[50] In the south-west of France and in parts of Italy and Spain, clergy members were appointed not by the bishop or the curia, but rather by local holders of patronage rights and administrators of benefices. Therefore, it was extraordinarily difficult for reform-minded bishops to ensure that the criteria for appointment of pastoral clergy were met, both in form and in content.[51] According to the decrees of the Council of Trent, the main requirement was graduation from a preacher seminary. As a rule, however, dioceses in both the Old Reich and other European regions lacked the financial resources to establish episcopal seminaries of adequate quality. Seminaries founded in the late sixteenth century in France, for example, had to be closed down during the religious wars, and even as late as the eighteenth century such institutes failed to develop educational standards that would exceed those of the academic gymnasia.[52] Moreover, strong competition between these seminaries and the educational institutions of the reform orders developed; instead of cooperating in a useful manner, they hindered each other in their work. The results in France, to begin with, were very similar to those in the Old Reich. Since the schools and seminaries led by the reform orders (Jesuits, Franciscans, Capuchins) were so dominant in the education of future pastoral clergy, their curricula remained largely free from episcopal influence. Only when the interests of church and royal authorities collided at the end of the seventeenth century did French bishops get the chance to exercise more power over the allocation of benefices, with the result that the church gained greater

---

49 Freitag, *Kirche*, table II: clerical family, on p. 198.
50 Bergin, 'Estate', p. 78.   51 Julia, 'Prete', pp. 410–12.
52 Bergin, 'Estate', pp. 82–3. For more on France, Italy, and Poland, see also Hsia, *Gegenreformation*, pp. 144–64.

influence over the qualification requirements for aspiring clergy.[53] Over the course of the seventeenth century appointment to clerical office finally became contingent upon the fulfilment of certain minimal requirements (such as minimum age at first ordination and proof of education at an academic gymnasium). Regional studies show that in those dioceses where the majority of patronage rights lay in the hands of the church, more extensive qualification requirements in the form of the so-called 'concours' (that is, proof of basic theological knowledge) were put into effect. It was not the disbanding of the clientele and benefice system – so characteristic of the early modern period – that led to increased educational levels of the clergy. Rather, it was the combination of that system with new forms of control on the part of the bishops, who relied in no small measure on the capacity of clerical candidates to provide a minimum of economic self-sufficiency. Just as in the Old Reich, the 'ordination title' proved to be an instrument with a positive long-term impact on the quality of clerical office.

Unlike in France, the training seminaries of the various orders in Italy as well as in Spain were firmly integrated into the dioceses. As a result, the bishops had much greater input into the clerical and spiritual content of the curricula. In Italy, the large increase in the number of candidates for clerical office led to an expansion of the episcopal seminary system from the mid-seventeenth century on. The financial situation of these seminaries, however, remained highly precarious. The exemplary works of the Archbishop of Milan, Carlo Borromeo (1538–84), in the late sixteenth century aimed primarily at the implementation of the Tridentine clerical reforms in his diocese.[54] In addition to founding a new community of priests, he was responsible for the establishment of new schools and the initiation of synods and provincial councils to help put the reforms into effect. After his death, many of these activities lost their significance, and only at the beginning of the seventeenth century were the Tridentine reforms brought back to life. The Milanese model was adopted in Spain as well. Here, the bishops had implemented the Tridentine reforms right from the beginning. Supported by the Spanish king, they succeeded in their efforts even against the will of reluctant patrons. Similar developments occurred in Portugal.[55]

Due to the great importance Protestantism placed on preaching the Word, the increasing of theological knowledge among aspiring pastors went to the heart of all educational plans in the Protestant parts of Europe. In the German imperial cities as well as in the territories that had become Protestant, it was hoped that qualifications could be improved through the creation of an

---

53 Hsia, *Gegenreformation*, p. 78.   54 *Ibid.*, pp. 144–51.   55 Cf. Paiva, 'Portuguese'.

integrated system of Latin schools, cloister or chapter schools, and universities (such as in Württemberg and Hesse). The Latin schools taught elementary Latin, church hymns, and Luther's catechism. In some territories, the church funded a system of scholarships to support talented but underprivileged students, who were expected to meet the additional need for junior clergy. North Germany provides a typical outline of the various steps in this process: as early as the late sixteenth century, 80 per cent of the pastors whose education can be traced through the records had studied at one of the regional universities.[56] This did not mean, however, that all aspiring pastors enjoyed a more profound theological education than had the first generation of Protestant clergy. After all, despite the stipulations of the church ordinance of 1569 proof of an academic degree, even if only from a faculty of arts, was not mandatory for appointment to a parish position. Studies of the educational levels of second- and third-generation Protestant theologians suggest a clear discrepancy between those in church leadership positions and regular clergymen.[57] Duration of studies and academic degrees are useful indicators; according to these, up until the mid-seventeenth century the great majority of the regular Protestant pastors had attended university, but had not necessarily been required to attend lectures in the theological faculty, or even to provide any certification of their studies at the faculty of arts.[58]

Despite this latitude regarding university qualifications, by the mid-seventeenth century clear requirements for appointment to a parish position had been established: the church ordinances of the late sixteenth century had had normative effects in this area. The typical clergyman began his training – assuming he had already spent about seven years in school – at the age of twenty at a faculty of arts, from which he would graduate three or four years later. During the first half of the seventeenth century, it was customary for the graduates to go on to a non-ecclesiastical post (such as private tutor), before assuming an entry-level church position such as adjunct pastor or school rector. Therefore, it can be assumed that the average age of a newly appointed pastor in the late sixteenth and the early seventeenth centuries was 33.4 years.[59] Detailed studies of the late seventeenth and early eighteenth centuries have shown that there must have been alternating periods of over- and undersupply of Protestant clergy, leading to ongoing changes in these age specifications.[60]

56 For more details, see Schorn-Schütte, *Geistlichkeit*.
57 Cf. Strom, *Orthodoxy*, pp. 77–9; and Kaufmann, *Universität*, pp. 145–51.
58 For variations in length of studies, see Schorn-Schütte, *Geistlichkeit*.
59 Schorn-Schütte, *Geistlichkeit*, pp. 199–210; and Wahl, *Lebensplanung*, pp. 88–90.
60 Titze, 'Überfüllung'.

Applicants for parish office were examined by the consistory only after having been presented by the patron. As a result, this examination was essentially reduced to a formality, a trend which in some places only changed with the Pietist reform initiatives of the late seventeenth century. After having been presented and examined, the candidate stood to be inaugurated into office at a church service.

Thus, in Protestantism as well, the typical early modern fusion of traditional factors with those aimed at change remained a key feature of clerical office. Assignment to a clerical post still generally depended on clientage or family connections, so that here, just as in Catholicism, these positions continued to be seen as sources of income (in other words, as prebends). Since in numerous territories of the Old Reich patronage rights lay in the hands of noble families, city councils, or the parish itself, no centralized employment policy emerged before the late eighteenth century.[61] Thus, access to a parish office was affected as much by the applicants' personal career strategies as by local political decisions, which remained largely unaffected by the preferences of territorial rulers. Thus, there can be no talk of a 'professionalization' of the clerical office (in the sense of modernization theory) until the end of the eighteenth century. At the same time, however, the nature of the office did gain a good measure of constancy.[62]

These mechanisms were based on the integration of the clergy into certain groups through marriage and education. After all, even though the thesis of exclusive self-recruitment has been proven untenable, the social networks clerical candidates established through their families or alma maters played a decisive role in the bestowal of office and benefice. On average, newly appointed clergymen got married within three months.[63] The prospective pastors were apparently well aware of how indispensable a wife was for the practical management of the parsonage, and how important the choice of a spouse was for the social recognition of the new office-holder. Then again, the search for a position was not always linked to a favourable marital connection; access to office was often facilitated by contacts the candidate had made at school, university, or during educational travels.[64]

In England as well, the Anglican and Puritan clergy experienced a remarkable increase in educational standards from the late sixteenth century on, a

---

61 Wahl portrays Württemberg as an exceptional case. See Wahl, *Lebensplanung*, pp. 97–132.
62 Cf. Riegg, *Konfliktbereitschaft*, pp. 119–21.
63 Wahl, *Lebensplanung*, pp. 97–132; and Schorn-Schütte, *Geistlichkeit*, pp. 295–304.
64 Schorn-Schütte, *Geistlichkeit*, pp. 162–4; and Riegg, *Konfliktbereitschaft*, pp. 75–110.

pattern reflected, for example, by the great number of academic degrees held by pastors.[65] 'The policy of educating the clergy thus bore its fruits on the eve of the Civil War in practically the whole of England.'[66] This rise in educational levels, however, did not result in higher remuneration for pastors: at the end of the sixteenth century, 40 per cent of pastoral offices failed to provide adequate support for the pastor's entire family. This situation – along with a rising number of highly qualified university graduates – heightened the competition for well-endowed prebends, a phenomenon that grew ever more intense from the first decades of the seventeenth century on. Hence, patronage and personal connections continued to play a dominant role in the allocation of clerical positions. Here, too, the meaning of clerical office as a vocation continued to coexist with its traditional function as largely a source of income – again, there can be no talk of professionalization.[67] This dynamic is confirmed by the consolidation of the English system of patronage rights after the Reformation. The gentry had profited considerably from the dissolution of the monasteries; centralization of power by way of a 'Reformation from above' did not occur. Here is another reason why the long-term process of raising clerical qualifications cannot primarily be regarded as the expression of a 'disciplinary urge' on the part of the authorities. The predominantly aristocratic patrons remained strictly concerned with their own regions, usually installing only such clergymen into pastoral office as were residents there, and/or were willing to conform to the patron's theological and political expectations. The conflict between Puritans and Anglicans was an extension of the wider conflict between gentry and crown, and patronage rights became an instrument of church politics – a development that could also be observed on the Continent.

A comparison of the clergy of all three Christian confessions in Europe with regard to their material circumstances shows that even after the Reformation clerical office remained integrated into early modern agricultural structures. The Council of Trent explicitly required that a pastor reside in his parish, which meant – as the accumulation of several benefices was expressly prohibited – that it had to be feasible for him to actually earn enough to live on. Despite all difficulties, most pastors in the seventeenth century apparently managed to make a living. Those city pastors and, to an even larger degree, rural pastors who were responsible for cultivating their own land, with or without the help of servants, shared their daily agricultural returns with their parishioners.

65 Barrie-Curien, 'Clergy', p. 452.   66 *Ibid.*, p. 452.
67 Collinson, *Religion*, pp. 98–9, 114–15, and *passim*.

But those leasing out their property remained firmly tied to the cycles of an agricultural economy as well. The pastors' income in the early modern pastoral system remained anchored in medieval structures – in the Protestant as well as in the Catholic Church. The problems inherent in this system could only partially be solved since the complexity of the parish revenue structure made it difficult for the pastor to secure a steady income on the one hand, and led to conflicts between parishioners and pastor on the other. After all, the pastor's different roles were constantly at odds with each other, as he had to fulfil his duty as spiritual role model and handle the challenges of agricultural self-sufficiency at the same time.[68] This remained a constant source of conflict within both Protestantism and Catholicism.

The local revenues of both the Catholic and Protestant clergy derived from the crops of the land that had always, by tradition, belonged to the parsonage, the tithe, and the taxes and fees charged for clerical services. In addition, the parsonage itself with its gardens and/or surrounding meadows and fields (that made up what can be referred to as a pastor's farmstead) provided an economic foundation.[69] These basic features varied considerably from region to region. Even within each individual confession differences existed, and one could find 'poor' and 'prosperous' parishes everywhere. In the big cities (just as in the imperial cities of the Old Reich), cash income played an additional role. In general, however, it can be stated that the monetarization of clerical income only began to develop during the eighteenth century, and in many places was not completed before the nineteenth. Thus, the income of both Catholic and Protestant pastors remained highly dependent upon the cycles of agricultural economy, the parishioners' ability and willingness to contribute their share, and demographic developments, since payments for clerical services rose and fell with the population. Fluctuations in income were the rule; a standardized system of remuneration based on education and experience scarcely existed before the end of the eighteenth century.[70]

'Truly poor pastors were . . . rather the exception.' This statement characterizes the material conditions within all Christian confessions from the early

68 This problem recurs through contemporary literature under the headings 'Verbauerung des Klerus' or 'Vom Sinken des geistlichen Standes'. Cf. Holzem, *Religion*, pp. 249–50; and Schorn-Schütte, 'Amt'.

69 For more details (which have been studied on a regional basis, but have not yet been combined in a comprehensive overview for the whole of Europe), see Hahn, *Pfarrerideal*, pp. 134–253; Freitag, *Kirche*, pp. 202–11; Holzem, *Religion*, pp. 249–59; Schorn-Schütte, *Geistlichkeit*, pp. 49–83; Wahl, *Lebensplanung*, pp. 39–43; Strom, *Orthodoxy*, pp. 45–63; and Riegg, *Konfliktbereitschaft*, pp. 155–7.

70 This conclusion is not shared by all researchers. For a different interpretation, see Freitag, *Kirche*, p. 206.

seventeenth century on – a period when the situation even of Protestant pastors, who had to provide for legitimate families, gradually stabilized. Within the Catholic Church, differences in income were most pronounced between the higher and the lower clergy. But even among the pastoral clergy incomes varied, as they did, for example, between chaplains or vicars on the one hand and pastors on the other.[71] In the Protestant realm, these differences were particularly discernible between urban and rural clergy.[72] Compared to the financial situation of the parishioners, clergy in rural areas were generally well provided for. The income of urban clergy in the Old Reich, for example, was often equivalent to that of councilmen or jurists employed by the city magistrate.[73] Protestant clergy in leadership positions could always negotiate increases in salary with their respective patrons. More and more, they also received payments in cash and benefited from the introduction of a widows' pension plan. Yet existing differences in income did not generally reflect the clergy member's position in the church hierarchy. Rather, they resulted from the varying endowments of individual parishes, a tradition that, in most cases, continued to exist even after the Reformation.

Pastor and parishioners

The laity's expectation that the clergy lead an exemplary life – described as 'clerical conduct' – was not new. It is generally known that such demands, hopes, and expectations stood in an old tradition of criticism of the clergy, long predating the reform movements of the sixteenth century. The criteria used to measure such model behaviour remained essentially unchanged since the Middle Ages, based as they were on the norms of the Old and New Testaments: pastoral care, intercession, and propagation of the Word, which included the clergy's admonitory and warning functions. However, since Protestantism denied the necessity and legitimacy of a clerical estate, stressing instead the value of all human activity as worship, the clergy was gradually integrated into the daily world of the faithful; thus, the clerical estate was robbed of its sacral character.[74] In contrast, the Council of Trent had actually reinforced the dogmatic foundations of priesthood: the sacral character bestowed on the office through ordination on the one hand, and the sacrificial nature of the

---

71 Hahn, *Pfarrerideal*, p. 134; Freitag, *Kirche*, pp. 215–20; and Holzem, *Religion*, pp. 259–63.
72 Schorn-Schütte, *Geistlichkeit*, pp. 227–86.
73 With regard to the purchasing power of clerical income in the sixteenth and seventeenth centuries, Hahn points out that a pastor earned as much money by reading a mass as a labourer for a whole day of work. Hahn, *Pfarrerideal*, pp. 200–1.
74 For more details, see Fagerberg, 'Reformationszeit'.

mass – which could be celebrated only by an ordained priest – on the other.[75] A notable consequence of this difference was that the two confessions had completely opposite concepts of model clergy conduct. While Protestants expected the ideal pastor to be a living example for all other family fathers and mothers, Catholics envisioned the ideal life style as one that situated the pastor above the everyday life of the parish. Celibacy was supposed to make the priest stand out from daily life, to make him a model by virtue of his removal from secular matters. In contrast, the Protestant pastor was expected to be not only the 'father of the congregation', but the best 'father of the family' as well. He was not removed from the daily world of the parishioners, but rather was part of it in a distinctive way, expected as he was to be perfect at all times.

Accordingly, the perception of self and of office on the part of the Catholic clergy 'concentrated on their sacramental powers',[76] while from the mid-sixteenth century on the Protestant clergy developed its own unique self-awareness (*Sonderbewusstsein*), drawing upon the early Christian practices of exceptional erudition and model behaviour of the 'bishops' in their everyday conduct.[77] It is therefore remarkable that with the image of the 'good shepherd', Catholicism also readopted a pastoral ideal that was characterized by the humanist-inspired return to the church fathers and their ideal of a bishop.[78] The realization of this ideal began, as mentioned above, over the course of the Catholic reform of the early seventeenth century.

The relationship between pastor and parishioners was not as deeply affected by these theological divergences as one might expect. Although the confessional differences maintained and embodied by the pastor – the fact that the Protestant pastor could have a legitimate family, while the Catholic priest was at least theoretically committed to celibacy – were ever-apparent to parishioners in the sixteenth and seventeenth centuries, relations between the pastor and his congregation did not change. The reason for this could be found in the continuing interconnectedness of economic dependence and spiritual duty that marked daily life in Protestant as in Catholic parishes and which could (but did not necessarily have to) render the pastor a supplicant to a congregation more inclined to refuse than to fulfil its obligations. 'All spiritual contact between the clergy and the congregation remained caught in an interpretative

75 Jedin, 'Leitbild', pp. 110 and 115; and Holzem, *Religion*, pp. 238–40.
76 Holzem, *Religion*, p. 239; and Dürr, 'Images'.
77 On the development of the perception of clerical office in Protestantism, see Baur, 'Amt'; for the term *Sonderbewusstsein*, see Schorn-Schütte, *Geistlichkeit*.
78 Jedin, 'Leitbild', pp. 110 and 115.

network of give and take'[79] – this applied to Protestantism and Catholicism alike. The pastor's office created distance and demanded respect, since he was seen as the representative of both ecclesiastical and secular authorities. At the same time, he was part of the parish, and as such was no less tied to the traditional subsistence economy of the early modern period than any-one else. The demand for improved execution of office, on the rise since the late sixteenth century, did not bring about any change. Conflict usually arose when the clergy's 'otherworldly' duties had to be compensated by secular ser-vices, mostly of an economic nature, on the part of the congregation. What the pastor considered a requisite for his pastoral-admonitory work could be viewed by his parishioners as a burdensome obligation, especially when they were already confronted with material shortages. In such cases, the clergy's demand for economic support could be construed by the congregation as a sign of greed, and as indifference towards the poor.

In the late sixteenth century such demands increased in those parishes that had become Protestant, as most pastors there were now married and thus had greater material needs. These conflicts arose from opposing legal claims as well as divergent conceptions of the relationship between pastor and parish. While the parishes repeatedly invoked their established traditions, the Protestant pastors emphasized their own rights, derived from territorial church ordinances. Moreover, the old dispute over the equivalence of clerical service and material contributions remained seemingly unsolvable. A good example of these structural problems is the parishioners' assumption that model behaviour had to involve a diffidence regarding material status. In contrast, the pastors themselves considered it a Christian duty on the part of the parish to meet their economic needs; in their opinion, such support showed appropriate respect for the clerical office as commanded in the Bible.[80]

The social distance between pastor and parishes, particularly in rural areas, could aggravate these conflicts even more. Thus, in the first decades of the seventeenth century, pastors' calls for full payment of the tithe were repeat-edly met with disgruntlement and at times outright refusals on the part of the parishes – this was a European reality. The parishioners justified their behaviour on the grounds that the pastor acted superior to them; in their eyes, his demands showed that he was ignorant about agricultural crops, and the difficulties involved in producing them. Similar conflicts were recorded in Catholic parishes as well. In the seventeenth century these conflicts were

79 Holzem, *Religion*, p. 266.
80 For examples, see Schorn-Schütte, *Geistlichkeit*, pp. 272–3.

regularly the topic of printed sermons, used to offer possible solutions to the problem.[81]

The credibility of clerical office and hence its ability to advance the political interests of the authorities depended largely on the credibility of the office-holders. Their spiritual and moral education therefore became a central concern of secular and ecclesiastical authorities. But not all of the structural problems arising between pastor and parish could be addressed through thorough training. In the end, the differences in the educational goals of Catholics and Protestants may have been few, but these remained significant. Catholicism did not aspire to 'establish a general state of subservience designed to level out the differences between the clergy and the laity'.[82] Rather, the 'prominence' of clerical office-holders was to be emphasized, as a way to accentuate both religious barriers and boundaries between the estates, the existence of which was justified with reference to biblical sources. This attitude was at times directed against secular authorities themselves, showing the pastor to be a less-than-reliable mediator in the process of social disciplining.

The same is true for the Protestant Church as well, except that here the clergy did not invoke the sacrality of office. The model conduct of the pastor did not involve his acting as a particularly obedient subject; rather, the clergy developed a special perception of itself and its office that could be referred to as a unique self-awareness – as a result, the Protestant pastor became more immune to the demands of both the authorities and the parish.[83] This unique self-awareness found justification in the traditions of the New Testament as well as in the continuing validity of the doctrine of the three estates. As it turned out, this clerical self-perception could become either a source of conflict between the pastor and the parish, or an integrative force – the latter when directed against claims by authorities that were regarded as inappropriate by pastor and congregation alike. Therefore, the image of the Protestant pastor as an 'agent of the state' fails to reflect the reality.

81 Moser-Rath, *Kirchenvolk*, pp. 187–8. 82 Holzem, *Religion*, p. 277.
83 For parallel developments in England, see Collinson, *Religion*.

25

Women and religious change

MERRY WIESNER-HANKS

Every religious tradition has ideas about proper gender relations and the relative value of the devotion and worship of male and female adherents; every one stipulates or suggests rules for the way men and women are to act. In many religions these messages are contradictory and ambiguous, providing ideas that support gender hierarchy as well as complementarity and equality. This was true in Christianity from New Testament times onward, and was certainly true in the early modern period. On the one hand, God was thought of as male, the account of creation was understood to ascribe or ordain a secondary status for women, women were instructed to be obedient and subservient, the highest (or all) levels of the clergy were reserved for men, and religious traditions were used by men as buttresses for male authority in all realms of life, not simply religion. On the other hand, women used the language of religious texts and the examples of pious women who preceded them to subvert or directly challenge male directives. For Christian women of all classes and all denominations, religion provided a powerful justification for independent action; women who were not Christian also found support in their own religious traditions – Judaism, Islam, and in colonial areas indigenous religions – for actions opposing or undermining Christian authorities.

The Protestant Reformation

Scholars differ sharply about the impact of Protestantism; some see it as elevating the status of most women in its praise of marriage, others see it as limiting women by denying them the opportunity for education and independence in monasteries and stressing wifely obedience, and still others see it as having little impact, with its stress on marriage a response to economic and social changes that had already occurred, and not a cause of those changes.

Whatever their opinion about the Protestant Reformation's larger impact, however, historians agree that the period in which women were the most active was the decade or so immediately following an area's decision to break with the Catholic Church or while this decision was being made. During this period, many groups and individuals tried to shape the new religious institutions. Sometimes this popular pressure took the form of religious riots, in which women and men destroyed paintings, statues, stained-glass windows or other objects which symbolized the old religion, or protected such objects from destruction at the hands of government officials; in 1536 at Exeter, for example, a group of women armed with shovels and pikes attacked workers who had been hired by the government to dismantle a monastery. Sometimes this popular pressure took the form of writing when women and men who did not have formal theological training took the notion of the 'priesthood of all believers' literally and preached or published polemical religious literature explaining their own ideas.

Women's preaching or publishing religious material stood in direct opposition to the words ascribed to St Paul (1 Timothy 2:11–15) which ordered women not to teach or preach, so that all women who published felt it necessary to justify their actions. The boldest, such as Argula von Grumbach, a German noblewoman who published eight works in 1523 and 1524, including a defence of a teacher accused of Lutheran leanings, commented that the situation was so serious that Paul's words should simply be disregarded: 'I am not unfamiliar with Paul's words that women should be silent in church but when I see that no man will or can speak, I am driven by the word of God when he said, He who confesses me on earth, him will I confess and he who denies me, him will I deny'.[1] Ursula Weyda, a middle-class German woman who attacked the Abbot of Pegau in a 1524 pamphlet, agreed: 'If all women were forbidden to speak, how could daughters prophesy as Joel predicted? Although St Paul forbade women to preach in churches and instructed them to obey their husbands, what if the churches were full of liars?'[2] Marie Dentière, a former abbess who left her convent to help the cause of the Reformation in Geneva, published a letter to Queen Margaret of Navarre in 1539 defending some of the reformers exiled from that city, in which she gives ringing support to this view:

---

1 Peter Matheson (ed. and trans.), *Argula von Grumbach: a woman's voice in the Reformation* (Edinburgh: T. & T. Clark, 1995), p. 23.
2 Translated and quoted in Paul A. Russell, *Lay theology in the Reformation: popular pamphleteers in southwest Germany 1521–1525* (Cambridge: Cambridge University Press, 1986), p. 203.

I ask, didn't Jesus die just as much for the poor illiterates and the idiots as for the shaven, tonsured, and mighty lords? Did he only say, 'Go, preach my Gospel to the wise lords and grand doctors?' Did he not say, 'To all?' Do we have two Gospels, one for men and the other for women? . . . For we ought not, any more than men, hide and bury within the earth that which God has . . . revealed to us women?[3]

Katherine Zell, the wife of one of Strasbourg's reformers and a tireless worker for the Reformation, supported Dentière in this, asking that her writings be judged, 'not according to the standards of a woman, but according to the standards of one whom God has filled with the Holy Spirit'.[4]

Zell's wish was never granted, and women's writings were always judged first on the basis of gender. Argula von Grumbach's husband was ordered to force her to stop writing, and Marie Dentière's pamphlets were confiscated by the very religious authorities she was defending. Once Protestant churches were institutionalized, polemical writings by women (and untrained men) largely stopped. Women continued to write hymns and devotional literature, but these were often published posthumously or were designed for private use.

Women's actions as well as their writings in the first years of the Reformation upset political and religious authorities. Many cities prohibited women from even getting together to discuss religious matters, and in 1543 an act of parliament in England banned all women except those of the gentry and nobility from reading the Bible; upper-class women were also prohibited from reading the Bible aloud to others. Class as well as gender hierarchies were to be maintained at all costs, though from women's diaries it is clear that this restriction was rarely obeyed.

The ability of a woman to act out her religious convictions was largely dependent on class in reality as well as theory. Though none of the reformers differentiated between noblewomen and commoners in their public advice or writings, in private they recognized that noblewomen had a great deal of power and made special attempts to win them over. Luther corresponded regularly with a number of prominent noblewomen, and Calvin was even more assiduous at trying to win noblewomen to his cause. Their efforts met with results, for in a number of cases, female rulers converted their territories to Protestantism or influenced their male relatives to do so. In Germany, Elisabeth of Brunswick-Calenburg brought in Protestant preachers and established a new

---

3 Translated and quoted in Thomas Head, 'Marie Dentière: a propagandist for the reform', in Katharina M. Wilson (ed.), *Women writers of the Renaissance and Reformation* (Athens, GA: University of Georgia Press, 1987), p. 260.
4 Elsie Anne McKee, *Katharina Schütz Zell*, 2 vols. (Leiden: Brill, 1999), vol. 2, p. 79.

church structure; in France, Margaret of Navarre and her daughter Jeanne d'Albret supported Calvinism through patronage and political influence; in Norway, Lady Inger of Austraat, a powerful and wealthy noblewoman, led the opposition to the Norwegian archbishop who remained loyal to Catholicism. The most dramatic example of the degree to which a woman's personal religious convictions could influence events occurred in England, of course, when Mary Tudor attempted to wrench the country back to Catholicism and Elizabeth created a moderately Protestant Church. In all of these cases political and dynastic concerns mixed with religious convictions, in the same way they did for male rulers and nobles.

Once the Reformation was established, most women expressed their religious convictions in a domestic, rather than public, setting. They prayed and recited the catechism with children and servants, attended sermons, read the Bible or other devotional literature if they were literate, served meals that no longer followed Catholic fast prescriptions, and provided religious instruction for their children. Women's domestic religion often took them beyond the household, however, for they gave charitable donations to the needy and often assisted in caring for the ill and indigent. As it had been before the Reformation, most women's charity was on a case-by-case basis, but there are also examples from Protestant areas of women who established and supported almshouses, schools, orphanages, funds for poor widows, and dowry funds for poor girls. In a few places, such as Amsterdam, women who assisted widows and other poor women were given the title of female deacon (*deaconessen*), but they did not participate in church governing bodies as male deacons did.

Such domestic and charitable activities were widely praised by Protestant reformers as long as husband and wife agreed in their religious opinions. If there was disagreement, however, continental Protestants generally urged the wife to obey her husband rather than what she perceived as God's will. She could pray for his conversion, but was not to leave him or actively oppose his wishes. English Puritans were less restrictive, urging their female followers to act as 'domestic missionaries' and attempt to convert their children, servants, and husbands. During the first decades after the Reformation, marriages between spouses of different faiths were much more common than they would be later in the century when the lines of religious confession hardened. Such mixed marriages occasioned less comment than one would assume given the violence of religious disagreements in general, because for the nobility and gentry, dynastic concerns continued to override those of religion, and even among middle-class urban dwellers, neither spouse appeared to feel the need necessarily to convert the other.

The women whose domestic religious activities were most closely scrutinized in the first generation of the Protestant Reformation were the wives of the reformers. During the first few years of the Reformation, they were still likened to priests' concubines in the public mind and had to create a respectable role for themselves, a task made even more difficult by the fact that many were former nuns themselves. They did this largely – and quite successfully, within a generation or so – by being models of wifely obedience and Christian charity, living demonstrations of their husbands' convictions whose households were the type of orderly 'little commonwealths' that their husbands were urging on their congregations in sermons. Whereas priests' concubines had generally been from a lower social class, by the second generation Protestant pastors had little difficulty finding wives from among the same social class as themselves, a trend that further aided the acceptance of clerical marriage. Maintaining an orderly household was just as important for Protestant pastors as teaching and preaching correct doctrine, with visitation teams and other officials investigating charges of sexual improprieties or moral laxness just as thoroughly as charges of incorrect doctrine. The women whose status was most tenuous were the wives of English bishops. Not only were many forced into exile or, worse yet, repudiated by their husbands during Mary's reign, but their marriages were not formally approved by Elizabeth, so that their children could always be declared bastards. Bishops were expected to live like wealthy noblemen and were accorded high rank at all ceremonial occasions, but their wives had no rank whatsoever. Long after continental pastors' wives had succeeded in making theirs a respectable position, bishops' wives in England still had not achieved even legal recognition despite all of their efforts at maintaining pious households.

No matter how much it was extolled in Protestant sermons and domestic conduct books, the vocation of mother and wife was not enough for some women, whose religious convictions led them to leave their husbands and continue to express their religious convictions publicly, even at the cost of their lives. One of the most famous of these was Anne Askew, an Englishwoman who was tortured and then executed for her religious beliefs in 1546. Like Argula von Grumbach and Marie Dentière, she defended her actions, using the Bible against her inquisitors effectively throughout her trial; her standard response to their questioning was one that affirmed the right of every Christian to read and interpret the Bible on her own. Askew was one of the few women martyrs to come from a gentry or middle-class background. Of the people martyred during the reign of Mary, one-fifth were women, and most of these were quite poor; wealthy people who opposed Mary fled to the Continent.

Most of the women executed for religious reasons in early modern Europe were Anabaptists, religious radicals who were hated and hunted by Catholics and Protestants alike. Most Anabaptist groups were very small, and they had widely divergent ideas, so it is difficult to make generalizations that apply to all. Some groups emphasized divine revelation and spiritual experiences, and took the visions of women prophets very seriously. Others allowed believers to leave their unbelieving spouses, but women who did so were expected to remarry quickly and thus come under control of a male believer. In 1534, Anabaptists took over the northern German town of Münster, and attempted to create their vision of a perfect community. Part of this vision was polygamy and enforced marriage for all women, for the male Anabaptist leaders took literally the statement in the Book of Revelation that the Last Judgement would come once 144,000 'saints' (true believers) were in the world. These most radical of Anabaptists looked to the Old Testament, rather than the Gospels, for their models of gender relations.

The interrogations of Anabaptists are one of the few sources available for the religious ideas of people who were illiterate; from these records, it is clear that many women could argue complicated theological concepts and had memorized large parts of the Bible by heart. As Claesken Gaeledochter, who was drowned at Leeuwarden in 1559, put it, 'Although I am a simple person before men, I am not unwise in the knowledge of the Lord'.[5] Anabaptist women actively chose the path of martyrdom, often against the pressure of family members, and the records of their trials, which often appeared in print shortly after their executions, reveal a strong sense of determination. Their actions were praised after their deaths in special hymns that were later sung by fellow believers, full of the details about their martyrdoms and testimonies to women who were 'in their faith strong, as men might be'.[6]

Along with providing new roles for women – religious polemicist, pastor's wife, domestic missionary, martyr – the Protestant Reformation also rejected many activities that had given women's lives religious meaning. Religious processions that had included both men and women, such as that of Corpus Christi, were prohibited, and sumptuary laws restricted the celebrations of baptism, weddings, and funerals, all ceremonies in which women had played a major role. Lay female confraternities, which had provided emotional and economic assistance for their members and charity for the needy, were also

---

5 Translated and quoted in Hermoine Joldersma and Louis Grijp (eds. and trans.), 'Elisabeth's manly courage': testimonials and songs by and about martyred Anabaptist women (Milwaukee: Marquette University Press, 2001), p. 42.
6 Translated and quoted ibid., p. 63.

forbidden, and no all-female groups replaced them. The reformers attempted to do away with the veneration of Mary and the saints, though women continued to pray to Mary and Saints Anne and Margaret, the patron saints of childbirth, for centuries. The Protestant martyrs replaced the saints to some degree as models worthy of emulation, but they were not to be prayed to and did not give their names to any days of the year, which stripped the calendar of celebrations honouring women.

The Protestant rejection of celibacy had the greatest impact on female religious, both cloistered nuns and women who lived in less formal religious communities. One of the first moves of an area rejecting Catholicism was to close the monasteries and convents, either confiscating the buildings and land immediately or forbidding new novices and allowing the current residents to live out their lives on a portion of the convent's old income. In England and Ireland, where all monasteries and convents were taken over by the crown, most nuns got very small pensions and were expected to return to their families, though not all did. Many Irish and English nuns fled to religious communities on the Continent, or continued to fulfil their religious vows in hiding while they waited for the chance to emigrate. In many cities of the Dutch Republic, the convents were closed, their assets liquidated, and the women given their dowries and a pension. Though some returned to their families, others, called *kloppen* or *geestelijke maagden* (holy maidens), continued to live together in small, informal domestic groups.

Even when prominent families did become Protestant, they sometimes continued to support convents because of long-standing traditions. The convent at Vadstena in Sweden, for example, had long housed female members of the Swedish royal family, and when Swedish rulers became Protestant in the 1520s they thought it inappropriate simply to close it down. Instead they attempted to convince the nuns to accept Protestantism willingly, but the nuns resisted, stuffing wool and wax in their ears when they were forced to attend Lutheran services. The convent survived until the 1590s, when royal patience gave out; the nuns were then forcibly evicted and the convent's treasures and library confiscated.

This link between convents and prominent families was most pronounced in the Holy Roman Empire, where many convents had been established by regional ruling houses or by the wives and daughters of emperors. Many of them had been reformed in the fifteenth century, and long traditions of power, independence, and prestige combined with a reinvigorated spiritual life to make reformed convents the most vocal and resolute opponents of the Protestant Reformation. The nuns' determination had social and political as well as religious roots, for they recognized that as women they could have no office in any Protestant Church; the role of a pastor's wife was an unthinkable decrease in status for a woman of noble standing.

In some territories of central Germany, the nuns' firmness combined with other religious and political factors to allow many convents to survive for centuries as Catholic establishments within Protestant territories. In the bishoprics of Magdeburg and Halberstadt, which became Protestant, half of the female convents survived, but only one-fifth of the monasteries. Some of this was certainly due to the women's zeal, but it also resulted from the fact that religious and political authorities did not regard the women's institutions as as great a threat as the men's. The marriage market for upper-class women also played a role. The cost of dowries was rising in early modern Germany, and even wealthy families could often not afford to marry off all their daughters to appropriate partners.

Some convents also survived as religious institutions by accepting Lutheran theology except for its rejection of the monastic life. Anna von Stolberg, for example, was the abbess of the free imperial abbey of Quedlinburg, and so governed a sizable territory including nine churches and two male monasteries. When she became Protestant in the 1540s she made all priests swear to Luther's Augsburg Confession and turned her Franciscan monastery into an elementary school for both boys and girls, an interesting gender reversal of the usual pattern of male authorities transforming female convents into schools or using convent property to fund (male, of course) scholars at universities. She continued to receive both imperial and papal privileges, for Catholic authorities were unwilling to cut off support from what was, at any rate, still a *convent*. She was also not uniformly criticized by Lutheran leaders, however, who emphasized that she was, at any rate, *Lutheran*. Quedlinburg was not the only abbey in this situation. At least fourteen Lutheran convents in the relatively small territory of Brunswick/Lüneburg survived into the nineteenth century, most of which are still religious establishments for unmarried women today.

It is very difficult to determine how many convents throughout the Empire were able to survive as either Catholic or Protestant institutions, because their existence was in some ways an embarrassment to secular and religious authorities attempting to enforce a policy of religious uniformity. Many of the urban convents in south Germany, such as those in Strasbourg and Nuremberg, fought disbanding as long as they could, despite being forced to listen to daily sermons, being denied confessors and Catholic ceremonies, and even having residents forcibly dragged out by their families. (The few male monasteries that actually opposed the Reformation were simply ordered shut and their residents banished from the territory, an action that could not be used against convents as their residents were usually the daughters of local families and would have nowhere outside the territory to go.) Finally urban authorities often gave up their direct attacks, and simply forbade the taking in of new novices so that the convents slowly died out. A few also followed the central German pattern of becoming Protestant; one convent in Ulm, for example, survived as a Protestant institution until the nineteenth century.

The distinction between Protestant and Catholic that is so important in understanding the religious and intellectual history of sixteenth-century Europe may have ultimately been less important to the women who lived in convents or other communal groups than the distinction between their pattern of life and that of the majority of lay women. Evidence from convents in Brunswick and Augsburg indicates that Protestant and Catholic women lived together quite peacefully for decades, protected by the walls of their convent from the religious conflicts surrounding them. Women in the Netherlands and England, denied the possibility of continuing in their convents, continued to live together, letting their formal religious affiliation remain a matter of speculation, both for contemporaries and for historians. The Protestant championing of marriage and family life, which some nuns accepted with great enthusiasm as a message of liberation from the convent, was viewed by others as a negation of the value of the life they had been living; they thus did all in their power to continue in their chosen path.

The Catholic Reformation

The response of the Catholic Church to the Protestant Reformation is often described as two interrelated movements. One, a Counter-Reformation that attempted to win territory and people back to loyalty to Rome and prevent further spread of Protestant ideas, and the other a reform of abuses and problems within the Catholic Church that had been recognized as problems by many long before the Protestant Reformation. Thus the Catholic Reformation was both a continuation of medieval reform movements and a new crusade. Women were actively involved in both movements, but their actions were generally judged more acceptable when they were part of a reform drive; even more than the medieval crusades, the fight against Protestants was to be a masculine affair.

The masculine nature of the Counter-Reformation was intimately related to one of the key aspects of church reform – an enforcement of cloistering for women. Reforms of the church beginning with the Gregorian in the eleventh

473

century had all emphasized the importance of the control of female sexuality and the inappropriateness of women religious being in contact with lay society; claustration was a key part of the restrictions on Beguines in the fourteenth century and of the fifteenth-century reform of the convents. The problem became even more acute after the Protestant Reformation, for numerous women in Europe felt God had called them to oppose Protestants directly through missionary work, or to carry out the type of active service to the world in schools and hospitals that the Franciscans, Dominicans, and the new orders like the Jesuits were making increasingly popular with men. For example, Angela Merici founded the Company of St Ursula in Brescia, Italy. The Company was a group of lay single women and widows dedicated to serving the poor, the ill, orphans, and war victims, earning their own living through teaching or weaving. Merici received papal approval in 1535, for the pope saw this as a counterpart to the large number of men's lay confraternities and societies that were springing up in Italy as part of the movement to reform the church.

Similar groups of lay women dedicated to charitable service began to spring up in other cities of Italy, Spain, and France, and in 1541, Isabel Roser decided to go one step further and ask for papal approval for an order of religious women with a similar mission. Roser had been an associate of Ignatius Loyola, the founder of the Jesuits, in Barcelona. She saw her group as a female order of Jesuits that, like the Jesuits, would not be cut off from the world but would devote itself to education, care of the sick, and assistance to the poor, and in so doing win converts back to Catholicism. This was going too far, however. Loyola was horrified at the thought of religious women in constant contact with lay people and Pope Paul III refused to grant his approval. Despite this, her group continued to grow in Rome and in the Netherlands, where they spread Loyola's teaching through the use of the Jesuit catechism.

The Council of Trent reaffirmed the necessity of the cloister for all women religious and called for an end to open monasteries and other uncloistered communities. Enforcement of this decree came slowly, however, for several reasons. First, women's communities themselves fought it or ignored it. Followers of Isabel Roser, for example, were still active into the seventeenth century, for in 1630 Pope Urban VIII published a bull to suppress them, and reported that they were building convents and choosing abbesses and rectors. The residents of some of Roser's communities and other convents that fought strict claustration were often from wealthy urban families who could pressure church officials. Second, church officials themselves recognized the value of the services performed by such communities, particularly in the area of girls' education and care of the sick. Well after Trent, Charles Borromeo, a reforming archbishop in Milan, invited in members of the Company of St Ursula, and transformed the group from one of lay women into one of religious who lived communally, though they still were not cloistered. From Milan, the Ursulines spread throughout the rest of Italy and into France, and began to focus completely on the education of girls. They became so popular that noble families began to send their daughters to Ursuline houses for an education, and girls from wealthy families became Ursulines themselves.

The very success of the Ursulines led to the enforcement of claustration, however, as well as other Tridentine decrees regulating women religious. Wealthy families were uncomfortable with the fact that because Ursulines did not take solemn vows, their daughters who had joined communities could theoretically leave at any time and make a claim on family inheritance. (Solemn vows bound one permanently to a religious establishment, and made an individual legally dead in the secular world.) Gradually the Ursuline houses in France and Italy were ordered to accept claustration, take solemn vows, and put themselves under the authority of their local bishop, thus preventing any movement or cooperation between houses. They were still allowed to teach girls, but now only within the confines of a convent. Some houses fought this as long as they could, though others accepted claustration willingly, having fully internalized church teachings that the life of a cloistered nun was the most worthy in the eyes of God.

Extraordinary circumstances occasionally led church leadership to relax its restrictions, but only to a point. The situation of English Catholics under Protestant rulers was viewed as a special case, and a few women gained approval to go on their own as missionaries there. One of these was Luisa de Carvajal y Mendoza, a Spanish noblewoman who opposed her family's wishes and neither married nor entered a convent. She was quite effective at converting non-Catholics and bolstering the faith of her co-religionists, and later commented that being a woman helped her, as the English never suspected a woman could be a missionary. Paul V, pope from 1605 to 1621, was relatively open to female initiatives and in 1616 granted Mary Ward, who had run a school for English Catholic girls in exile in the Spanish Netherlands, provisional approval for her Institute of the Blessed Virgin Mary. She wanted women in her Institute to return to England as missionaries, for 'it seems that the female sex also in its own measure, should and can . . . undertake something more than ordinary in this great common spiritual undertaking'.[7]

7 Quoted in Elizabeth Rapley, *The Dévotes: women and church in seventeenth-century France* (Montreal and Kingston: McGill-Queen's University Press, 1990), p. 29.

She openly modelled the Institute on the Jesuits and began to minister to the poor and sick in London, visiting Catholic prisoners and teaching in private homes.

The reports of Ward's successes proved too much for church leadership, and she was ordered to stop all missionary work, for 'it was never heard in the Church that women should discharge the Apostolic Office'.[8] Undaunted, Ward shifted her emphasis, and the Institute began to open houses in many cities throughout Europe in which women who took no formal vows operated free schools for both boys and girls, teaching them reading, writing, and a trade. The Institute needed constant donations, for which Ward and her associates travelled extensively and corresponded with secular and church authorities. Ward recognized that this public solicitation of funds was necessary in order for her schools to flourish, and so asked that the Institute never be under the control of a bishop, but report directly to the pope. Her popularity and independence proved too much for the church hierarchy, however, and the year after the bull was published against Roser Ward's schools and most of her houses were ordered closed, and Ward herself imprisoned by the Inquisition in Munich.

Thus the only active apostolate left open to religious women was the instruction of girls, and that only within the convent. No nuns were sent to the foreign missions for any public duties, though once colonies were established in the New World and Asia cloistered convents quickly followed. The exclusion of women from what were judged the most exciting and important parts of the Catholic Reformation – countering Protestants and winning new converts – is reflected in the relative lack of women from the sixteenth century who were made saints. Luisa de Carvajal was raised to the status of Venerable, the first rung on the ladder to sanctity, but only 18.1 per cent of those who reached the top of the ladder from the sixteenth century were women, whereas 27.7 per cent of those from the fifteenth century had been female. Most of the women who did achieve sainthood followed a very different path, one of mysticism or reforming existing orders, a path in some ways set by the most famous religious woman of the sixteenth century, Teresa of Avila.

Teresa was a Carmelite nun who took her vows at twenty, and then spent the next twenty-five years in relative obscurity in her convent at Avila. During this time of external inaction, she went through great spiritual turmoil, similar to that experienced by Loyola and Luther, but came to feel the presence of God not through founding a new denomination or new order, but by

8 *Ibid.*, p. 31.

mystical union with the divine. She went through extremes of exaltation and melancholy, suffering physical effects such as illness, trances, and paralysis. Her mystical path was not one of extreme mortification of the flesh, but of prayer, purification of the spirit, and assistance to the women of her convent. At other times or places she might have spent her life unnoticed, but this was Spain during the sixteenth century, when the Spanish crown was using its own Inquisition to stamp out any sign of humanist, Lutheran, or other deviant ideas. Other nuns and lay women who felt a sense of religious vocation had been accused of heresy and questioned, so Teresa's confessors ordered her not only to describe her mystical experiences in writing, but to reflect on them and try to explain why she thought these were happening to her. Though Teresa complained about having to do this, she also clearly developed a sense of passion about her writing, for she edited and refined her work, transforming it into a full spiritual autobiography. She manipulated stereotypes of femininity, conceding women's weakness, powerlessness, and inferiority so often that it appears ironic, and using informal language both to appeal to a wider audience and deflect charges that she was teaching theology.

Like Angela Merici and Mary Ward, Teresa also yearned for some kind of active ministry, and explicitly chafed at the restrictions on her because of her sex: 'Lord of my soul, you did not hate women when you walked in the world; rather you favoured them always with much pity and found in them as much love and more faith than in men. Is it not enough, Lord, that the world has intimidated us . . . so that we may not do anything worthwhile for you in public?'[9] In part she solved this by interpreting her prayers and those of other nuns as public actions: 'we shall be fighting for Him [God] even though we are very cloistered'.[10] When she was fifty-two, she also began to reform her Carmelite order, attempting to return it to its original standards of spirituality and poverty. To do this she travelled all around Spain, founding new convents, writing meditations, instructions for monastic administrators and hundreds of letters, provoking the wrath or annoyance of some church authorities; a papal nuncio called her a 'restless gadabout, a disobedient and obstinate woman, who invented wicked doctrines and called them devotion . . . and taught others against the commands of St Paul, who had forbidden women to teach'.[11]

---

9 Teresa of Avila, *The way of perfection*, quoted in Alison Weber, *Teresa of Avila and the rhetoric of femininity* (Princeton: Princeton University Press, 1990), p. 41.

10 Teresa of Avila, *The way of perfection*, quoted in Jodi Bilinkoff, *The Avila of St. Teresa: religious reform in a sixteenth-century city* (Ithaca: Cornell University Press, 1989), p. 136.

11 Quoted in Weber, *Teresa of Avila*, pp. 3–4.

Teresa's success in reforming the Carmelites won her more supporters than critics within the church, however, for, unlike Angela Merici and Mary Ward, she did not advocate institutionalized roles for women outside of the convent. Her frustration at men's alterations of Christ's view of women did not lead her to break with the male church hierarchy, and church censors expunged the words expressing that frustration quoted above from her works. The version of Teresa which was presented for her canonization proceedings, held very shortly after her death, was one which fitted her into the acceptable model of woman mystic and reformer, assuming a public role only when ordered to do so by her confessor or superior; only recently has it become clear that Teresa thought of herself as a Counter-Reformation fighter, viewing the new religious houses she established as answers to the Protestant takeover of Catholic churches elsewhere in Europe.

It is easy to view Teresa as a complete anomaly, but in many ways she fits into a pattern of women's religious experience that was quite common in Spain, the Spanish colonies, and Italy, that of the holy woman (*beata*) discussed elsewhere in this volume in the chapter by Gabriella Zarri. The respect accorded to Teresa and other 'holy women' did not lead to any lessening of the call for the cloistering of religious women, however. Their separation from the world lessened the ability of women's communities to solicit funds, and the post-Tridentine emphasis on the sacraments meant that most benefactors preferred to give donations to a male house whose residents could say mass. Thus many female houses grew increasingly impoverished, or more interested in the size of the dowry of a prospective entrant than the depth of her religious vocation. By the seventeenth century, convents in many parts of Europe were both shrinking and becoming increasingly aristocratic; in Venice, for example, nearly 60 per cent of all women of the upper class joined convents. The long-range effects of claustration were not an increase but a decrease in spiritual vigour.

The effects of the Catholic Reformation on religious women were thus to a great degree restrictive. What about lay women in Catholic Europe? Here the balance sheet is more mixed, in large part because of the ambivalent attitude of church leadership about marriage. Catholic authors did begin to publish manuals for husbands and wives to counteract those written by Protestants, and emphasized their continued view of the sacramental nature of marriage. On the other hand, virginity continued to be valued over marriage, and spouses who took mutual vows of chastity within a marriage or left marriage to enter cloisters were praised. Catholic authors criticized the veneration of Anne, seeing the intercession of an older woman as no longer an appropriate avenue to God; the depiction of an all-female trinity disappeared from religious pamphlets, replaced by illustrations of Mary with both of her parents.

In Italian cities, Catholic reformers began to open institutional asylums for repentant prostitutes (*convertite*), and also asylums for women who were felt to be at risk of turning to prostitution or losing their honour, such as orphans, poor unmarried women and widows, or those whose marriages had failed, called *malmaritate*. Women in these institutions were taught basic skills with which to support themselves, usually weaving, and given large doses of religious and moral instruction. The drive to cloister all women's communities affected them as well, though some were able to remain uncloistered, with the residents even allowed to keep any wages earned, because it was seen as so important to prevent the women from landing back on the streets. In Catholic theory marriage was indissoluble, but in practice the Malmaritate houses offered women who had been abandoned or victimized by their husbands a respectable place to live, an alternative that was unavailable in Protestant areas.

No Catholic author went so far as to recommend that Catholic wives leave Protestant husbands, but in practice Catholic authorities put fewer blocks in the path of a woman who did. Catholic writers were also more open in their support of women working to convert their Protestant or indifferent husbands than were continental Protestant writers, or even of daughters converting or inspiring their parents: 'Young girls will reform their families, their families will reform their provinces, their provinces will reform the world'.[12] The confessional box came to be used more widely during this period, for the Counter-Reformation church saw private confession as a way to combat heresy. Catholic women married to Protestant men could find in the priest hearing their confession a man who could give them a source of authority to overrule or disobey their husbands. The husbands recognized this, for court records in Venice indicate that men charged with heresy often beat their Catholic wives after they came home from confession.

England and Ireland provided the most dramatic example of the importance of Catholic women's domestic religious activities. In 1559 Queen Elizabeth ordered that everyone attend services in the Anglican Church or be penalized with fines or imprisonment. Many English and Irish Catholics outwardly conformed, but others did not, becoming what were termed 'recusants'. Among these was a large percentage of women, who posed a special problem for royal officials. A single woman or widow found guilty of recusancy could be fined,

---

12 Quoted in Rapley, *Dévotes*, p. 157.

but a married woman, according to common law, controlled no property, and imprisoning her would disrupt her family life and harm her husband, who might not even share her religious convictions. The crown tried a variety of tactics to solve the problem, but only the most adamant Protestant men were willing to back measures that would allow a wife to be legally responsible as an individual for her religious choices and put her husband's property at risk. Catholic husbands often outwardly conformed and attended services, leaving their wives to arrange for private masses held in the home, or even to shelter illegal Catholic missionaries. Because of this, while continental Catholicism was becoming increasingly parish-oriented after the Council of Trent, Catholicism in England and Ireland grew increasingly domestic.

Non-Christian women in Europe and the European colonies

Women as well as men were questioned, tortured, physically punished, and in some cases executed during the repressions of Jews by Christian political authorities. Women were often particularly suspect in the eyes of authorities because they were responsible for religious rituals that took place in the home, such as lighting the sabbath candles or observing dietary restrictions, or that involved their own bodies, such as taking a ritual bath after menstruation, both more difficult to control than the public rituals that were the province of men. In 1492, Ferdinand and Isabella of Spain ordered all Jews to leave Spain or convert, and during the next several centuries those who converted and their descendants (termed 'New Christians') were frequently targets of the Inquisition, leading Jews in other parts of Europe to make special efforts to help women of Jewish ancestry leave Spain and Portugal. Portuguese Jews in Amsterdam, for example, set up a special dowry fund in 1615 for poor women and girls from the Iberian peninsula who were willing to migrate to Amsterdam, readopt Judaism and marry Jewish men, though women often had to wait ten years before enough money became available for them.

Jews lived in many parts of Europe during the early modern period, but Muslims lived primarily in the Iberian peninsula and south-eastern Europe, where the Ottoman Turks were expanding their territory. At roughly the same time that they ordered Jews to leave or convert, Spanish and Portuguese authorities also outlawed the practice of Islam, and gave the Inquisition jurisdiction over those suspected of Muslim practices as well as Jewish. In places where Islam was heavily persecuted, such as Aragon, women were extremely important in its survival. Like English recusants and Jews, Spanish Muslim women (termed

'Moriscas') carried out religious rituals in their homes and taught them to their children. According to the records of the Inquisition, Moriscas observed the Muslim holy month of Ramadan, performed daily prayers, wore Muslim dress while Morisco men adopted Christian-style clothing, hid religious books and amulets written in Arabic in their clothing and furniture, taught Muslim ideas and practices to Christian women who married Muslim men, and organized funerals, weddings, and other ceremonies. Muslim midwives circumcised baby boys, and failed to report births to Christian priests, as they were required to do. Though they generally stayed away from controversy, a few Moriscas publicly argued with their Christian neighbours about points of theology; through this, or other actions, they came to the attention of the Inquisition. Like Muslim men, they were whipped, imprisoned (often in convents), subjected to rituals of public humiliation, and occasionally executed at ceremonies termed *autos de fé*. In Saragossa, the inquisitors complained that 'the Moriscas of this kingdom are worse than the men, many of whom do not dare drink wine or eat bacon [both practices forbidden to Muslims] or do other Christian things from fear of their wives'.[13]

The Inquisition paid special attention to marriages between Christians and Moriscos, which were generally allowed, and at times even promoted, as long as the Muslim spouse converted; in 1548, for example, an edict of the Spanish crown ordered converted Muslims to marry Old Christians. (Old Christians were those whose ancestors were not known to have been Jewish or Muslim.) At the same time, however, laws which favoured 'purely' Old Christian families (generally termed 'purity of the blood' laws) worked against intermarriage, and also led couples in which the husband was of Muslim background to adopt the wife's Christian surname in order to disguise his Muslim ancestry.

The first wave of European colonization occurred concurrently with the Protestant and Catholic Reformations, and the conversion of indigenous people was one of the primary justifications for conquering new territories. Christian officials tried to impose European gender patterns – monogamous marriage, male-headed households, limited (or no) divorce – but where these conflicted with existing patterns they were often modified, and what emerged was a blend of indigenous and imported practices. In some areas, such as the Andes of South America and the Philippines, women had been important leaders in indigenous religions, and they were stronger opponents of conversion than were men; this pattern was enhanced by male missionaries' focus on

---

13 Translated and quoted in William Monter, *Frontiers of heresy: the Spanish Inquisition from the Basque lands to Sicily* (Cambridge: Cambridge University Press, 1990), p. 227.

boys and young men in their initial conversion efforts. In other areas, women became fervent Christians, confessing and doing penance for their sins so intensively they harmed their health, and using priests and church courts to oppose their husbands or other male family members.

Most scholars of colonization and imperialism view the activities of Christian authorities and missionaries as leading to a sharpened gender hierarchy, for religious leaders paid little attention to women's activities and either misunderstood or opposed women's power. They were also complicit in the establishment and maintenance of racial hierarchies, regulating marriage and other types of sexual activities so as to maintain boundaries between population groups.

In the early modern period, the domestic nature of women's acceptable religious activities was reinforced. The proper sphere for the expression of women's religious ideas was a household, whether the secular household of a Catholic or Protestant husband, or the spiritual household of an enclosed Catholic convent. Times of emergency and instability offered women opportunities to play a public religious role, but these were clearly regarded as extraordinary by male religious thinkers and by many of the women who wrote or spoke publicly during these times. Both Protestant and Catholic men, even those who otherwise broke with tradition or questioned existing structures of power, concurred that gender hierarchy was ordained by God. Women occasionally ignored their subservient status when their religious convictions were at stake, but only a handful directly challenged that status in the name of religion, and even fewer left any record of that challenge. In the period of the Reformations and colonialism, the words of Paul in Ephesians (5:22) – 'Wives, be subject to your husbands' – and ascribed to Paul in 1 Timothy (2:11) – 'Let a woman learn in silence with all submissiveness' – were repeated more often and heard more clearly by both men and women than Paul's words in Galatians (3:28) – 'In Christ . . . there is neither male nor female'.

PART VI

*

CHRISTIANITY AND OTHER FAITHS

26

Christianity and Judaism

MIRIAM BODIAM

A population map of the Jews in Christian lands in the year 1500 would reveal a striking fact – namely, that in vast areas of Christendom there *were* no Jews. Practising Jews were permitted to live in only three regions of Europe: the Italian states, the Holy Roman Empire, and Poland-Lithuania. (Even in these regions, they were excluded from many towns and principalities.) Beyond these areas, Jewish life existed only clandestinely, mainly in Spain and Portugal, where members of a population of unwilling converts to Catholicism practised crypto-Judaism.

Where Jewish settlement was permitted, insecurity was a reality of every-day life. Jewish communities were organized as autonomous corporate entities, and did enjoy basic protections, but their members were burdened with numerous restrictions and special taxes. The socio-cultural environment was dominated by images and rituals that conveyed hostility to Jews and Judaism (and evoked a hostile response in Jews themselves). Periodically, the equilibrium was broken by a paroxysm of popular anti-Jewish fury, stirred by clerical incitement or false accusations of ritual crimes. Local expulsions were common. In general, only Christian dependence on the Jews' economic services ensured the Jews' continued right to settlement.

Between 1500 and 1660, patterns of Christian–Jewish interaction were pro-foundly impacted by two major transformations: humanism and the Reformation, on the one hand, and the rise of the Atlantic state-system, on the other. This chapter will focus on changing patterns of Christian–Jewish interaction in the religious sphere, while keeping in mind the political and economic context.

Poland-Lithuania

Over the entire period, the largest Jewish population in Europe was that of Poland-Lithuania. (By 1660, it numbered perhaps 300,000 persons.) By the late medieval period it had become a refuge for Jews fleeing persecutions in central

Europe. The commonwealth of Poland-Lithuania remained a relatively welcoming place for Jews until the fateful disruptions of the mid-seventeenth century. This was due in part to its religious and ethnic heterogeneity, which diffused anxiety about religious difference. Well before the Reformation, the Christian population of Poland-Lithuania was split between Catholics, Orthodox, and Armenians; the non-Christian population included rabbinite Jews, Karaite Jews, and Muslims. By the second half of the sixteenth century, it included Lutherans and Calvinists, as well as Polish Brethren (Arians) and foreign sectarian refugees. Furthermore, in 1596 the ranks of the Orthodox were split when many joined the newly established Uniate church. Catholic rulers took half-hearted measures to suppress heterodoxy within the Latin Christian camp, but by 1544 even these ceased. In 1573, the Confederation of Warsaw promulgated a general guarantee that coercion would not be used in religious matters; such a guarantee was the first of its kind in Europe.

The Catholic Church – the predominant ecclesiastical entity – was certainly not pleased by the Jewish presence. But, faced with a wide spectrum of non-Catholics (as well as a Polish ruling class that resisted discipline and was jealous of its freedom), it favoured compromise and persuasion over coercion, and did not focus obsessively on Jews. Blood libel and host-desecration charges were less prominent in ecclesiastical writing than elsewhere in Europe.[1] Church synods did attempt to restrict contact between Jews and Christians (an aim shared by the Jewish leadership). But characteristically, statutes passed by the diocese of Chelm in 1624, while including anti-Jewish restrictions, also included a clause prohibiting preachers from inciting Christians to violence against Jews.[2] The mildness of the Polish religious ethos was apparent even into the first half of the seventeenth century, when the retreat from tolerance had begun.

To be sure, a hostile pamphlet literature was produced (mainly in burgher circles), associating Jews with demonic activity. Popular violence against Jews did occur, often spurred by ritual murder or host-desecration charges.[3] Jews were routinely assaulted, and they experienced considerable psychological insecurity.[4] But their *relative* security and absence of degradation were remarkable for the time. In a period of prosperity and economic expansion, Jews were allowed, despite burgher opposition, to engage in a variety of socially acceptable occupations. They were never required to wear a distinguishing mark

1 Kalik, 'Attitudes towards the Jews', p. 183.   2 Goldberg, 'Poles and Jews', p. 254.
3 Guldon and Wijaczka, 'Accusation of ritual murder', pp. 101–21; Tazbir, 'Anti-Jewish trials'.
4 Rosman, 'Jewish perceptions', pp. 19–27.

or badge. Even though a number of cities received privileges *de non tolerandis Judaeis*, Jews were often able to settle within, or near, the city limits of these places. The relative attractiveness of Poland was famously recognized by the great rabbinic scholar Moses Isserles, who wrote, when a student refused a lucrative post in Germany to return to Poland, that eating dry bread crust in security was perhaps better than a comfortable life amidst gentile hatred.

Polish tolerance, however, did not mean cosiness. Social barriers between the estates in Poland were rigidly maintained. It would not have occurred to an educated Polish noble, conditioned to the insular ethos of his class, to take an interest in the spiritual and ritual life of the Jews. In fact, among Christians in general there was little of the intense scrutiny of Jews and Judaism that became a feature of early modern European culture elsewhere. This is striking, since Jewish culture was in a period of unparalleled flowering in early modern Poland-Lithuania. Local gentiles were hardly aware of this efflorescence.[5] As for the Jews, who in traditional Ashkenazi fashion tended to cultural introversion, the indifference, for the most part, was mutual.

Given the circumstances, it is not surprising that Jewish conversion to Christianity was rare. For the clergy of Poland-Lithuania, Jewish culture was essentially impenetrable; the most successful proselytizers tended to be Jewish converts themselves, but they, too, had little success. Marcin Czechowic, a leader of the Polish Brethren, wrote in the sixteenth century that to convert a Jew was 'more difficult than luring a wolf from dead sheep, a cat from a mousetrap'.[6]

Jews first faced large-scale popular violence in Poland-Lithuania in 1648, during the so-called Chmielnicki rebellion in the Ukraine. The anger of the Orthodox rebels – mostly Cossacks and Ruthenian peasants – was actually directed not at Jews, but at a wider exploitative social and religious structure, of which Jews were only a part – one that was dominated by Polish Catholic landowners, and included Catholic clergy and Uniates. Despite the loss of tens of thousands of Jewish lives, little attention was paid to the Jews in Cossack chronicles of the uprising.[7] Still, 1648 marks a turning point after which the general conditions of life in Poland steadily deteriorated, with inevitable adverse effects for Jews. The Chmielnicki revolt was suppressed, but it was followed by the destructive invasions of Swedes and Russians, along with epidemics, famine, and economic ruin. Moreover, since the late sixteenth century

---

5 See Tazbir, 'Images of the Jew', p. 20, for a single vague example of such recognition.
6 Goldberg, 'Die getauften Juden', p. 58.　　7 Kohut, 'Khmelnytsky Uprising', p. 144.

the influx of Jesuits had begun to put its mark on Polish society, reshaping its religious culture to conform increasingly to post-Tridentine Catholic ideals. Ominously, the Sejm, which had already placed heavy restrictions on the Arians of Raków in 1638, expelled all antitrinitarians in 1658, depriving Poland of its most outspoken advocates of religious toleration.

It was these Arians – along with other radical sectarians – who for a few decades (1570s to 1590s) engaged in some of the most interesting interactions with Jews in eastern Europe, not only in Poland but in Bohemia as well.[8] Extant polemical works indicate actual contacts between sectarians and Jews mainly in the towns of Troki, Raków, and Lublin. The Jews involved were intrigued by the appearance of Christians who rejected the Trinity and the divinity of Jesus (and, in some cases, even the New Testament). In Prague, the Jewish chronicler David Gans expressed his wonder from afar at the beliefs of 'the great scholar' Michael Servetus who was burned at the stake in Geneva because he 'denied the divinity of their Messiah and wanted to revive the faith of the [early Christian] Arians'.[9] The Karaite Jew Isaac of Troki engaged throughout his adult life in debates with Catholics, Lutherans, Calvinists, and Arians – 'with anyone who wanted to debate with me',[10] as he put it – and was familiar with the antitrinitarian works of the Lithuanian Hebraist Simon Budny and the Italian Nicholas Paruta. The antitrinitarians, for their part – most notably Simon Budny, who produced a Polish translation of the Bible – made use of Jewish exegesis to support their doctrines. It is clear, however, from surviving documentation that both sides felt a strong need to distance themselves from the other – the sectarians, in order to defend themselves against accusations that they were 'judaizers'; the Jews, in order to head off possible Jewish conversions to a 'purified' form of Christianity.

The contact between Jews and antitrinitarians in eastern Europe, however intense, was marginal and short-lived. The eastern regions of Christendom may have possessed the largest Jewish populations, but they were not the stage for the most dynamic and historically significant Christian–Jewish interactions. Only when we move westward to lands that had expelled all or most of their Jewish populations in the medieval period do we find a set of dynamics that eventually impelled Christians (and, in response, Jews) to reconsider in fundamental ways the nature of their relationship. Let us turn, then, to central and western Europe, and to the unfolding of vital developments there.

---

8 See Dán, 'Isaac Troky'; Rosenthal, 'Marcin Czechowic and Jacob of Belzyce'; Ben-Sasson, 'Jews and Christian sectarians'.
9 Gans, *Zemah David*, p. 398.   10 Troki, *Hizzuk Emunah*, p. 10.

Central and Western Europe

Demystification

One of the fundamental shifts in Christian perceptions of Jews in these lands had to do with the wider phenomenon of 'disenchantment' in the early modern period – that is, the general erosion of the place of the supernatural in popular consciousness. Late medieval Christians had produced quite a repertory of terrifying representations of Jews. Jews were not only unbelievers, but dangerous plotters, co-conspirators of the devil or the antichrist, intent on exploiting and destroying Christian society. To some extent phobic feelings about Jews were a negative counterpart to late medieval emotionalism about Christ's passion. But they were also fuelled by economic resentment and concerns about the 'pollution' of an otherwise Christianized orbit. Fantastic narratives were spun around the basic motif of a crime against Christians committed by Jews: the ritual murder of a Christian boy, the desecration of a host, an episode of well-poisoning, or the practice of malevolent forms of magic. Such accusations were most prevalent in German lands, but they surfaced wherever Jews lived, and were part of popular lore even where Jews had long been expelled.

Reformation theology did not immediately lower the volume of anti-Jewish rhetoric. In fact as the invective of the pamphlet wars escalated, Jews – the ultimate infidels – were exposed to sharpened attacks. Moreover, apocalyptic expectations, which since late antiquity had entailed a dramatic conversion of the Jews to Christianity, drew the Jews more deeply into a conflict that had little to do with Judaism *per se*. Martin Luther was persuaded in the 1520s that the Jews were poised for just such a conversion. But he was soon disillusioned, and responded by consigning the Jews to the apocalyptic counter-world of popes, bishops, Turks, and the devil.

In the long run, however, religious trends in Reformation Europe had the effect of reducing the demonic perception of the Jews, in both Protestant and Catholic lands. This did not necessarily result in a reduced level of *hostility* towards Jews and Judaism, but it did result in a reduced tendency to blame Jews for such phenomena as plagues, local misfortunes, and the death of Christian boys.

Interestingly, in Spanish lands the Inquisition became one of the agents of 'disenchantment'. It did so by teaching Spaniards that extravagant belief in the miraculous and supernatural lay outside the boundaries of correct belief. While its prosecution of 'New Christians' or 'conversos' (baptized Jews and their descendants) for 'judaizing' entailed great injustices, it is worth noting that inquisitorial lists of crypto-Jewish practices consisted of matter-of-fact catalogues of actual ritual practices, such as observing the sabbath, refraining from eating pork, and reciting 'Jewish' prayers. The Inquisition's prosecutions unquestionably reinforced anti-Jewish feeling (and racialism) in Spanish society; but they did not perpetuate grotesque fantasies.

In lands where Protestant theology put down roots, the effort to suppress magical thinking was more sweeping. The anti-Catholic propaganda that rolled off Protestant presses ridiculed an entire way of believing, and played a key role in persuading a wide public that the Church's endorsement of pilgrimages, devotion to saints, indulgences, masses for the dead, and so on, was all a huge swindle. A public that came to scorn supposedly supernatural acts performed by priests was less likely to give credence to bizarre tales of secret Jewish rituals. In particular, the Protestant demystification of the eucharist – the rejection of the doctrine that the host actually became in substance the body of Christ – rendered ludicrous the notion that Jews were in the habit of ritually stabbing it and causing it to bleed.[11]

Demystification of a certain kind was also an outgrowth of Christian Hebraism, which was given great impetus by the Reformation and by Hebrew printing in the sixteenth century. Christian interest in the Talmud and other rabbinic works was by no means motivated by brotherly impulses towards the Jews. On the contrary, Talmudic passages became grist for the mill of anti-Jewish polemics and conversionist efforts. But Christian researches into Jewish texts had the unintended effect of undermining the sort of fantasies that had flourished in the absence of concrete knowledge. Johann Buxtorf the Elder's *Synagoga Judaica* (1603), which appeared originally in German and later in other languages, provides a good example. This detailed description of Judaism by a learned Hebraist drew from classical rabbinic texts, but also incorporated material about contemporary Ashkenazi practices. Certainly Buxtorf's overall tone was hostile and sarcastic. His aim was to demonstrate that post-biblical Judaism was essentially a human innovation and a distortion of the Law of Moses. ('It is just about as appropriate for a Jew to interpret Holy Writ', he remarked, 'as for a wild pig to dig up a vineyard'.[12]) Moreover, he made no distinction between talmudically ordained precepts and naïve Jewish folk practices. But however negative his views, Buxtorf did not ascribe to the Jews demonic supernatural powers. On the contrary, he portrayed them as superstitious *believers* in magic, not as dangerous practitioners of magic.

In some places the development of Protestant culture had the indirect effect not only of demystifying, but of actually humanizing the perception of the

---

11 See Hsia, *Myth of ritual murder*, pp. 146–51.   12 Buxtorf, *Synagoga Judaica*, p. 40.

Jews. This was true particularly in the Netherlands, England, and New England. A strong contributing factor appears to have been the Protestant ethos of Bible-reading. Christian Hebraism had already drawn educated Christian readers into the world of Jewish exegesis, with its focus on the concrete narrative meaning of the text. But the Protestant doctrine of *sola scriptura*, along with concerted efforts to provide vernacular texts of the Bible, resulted in a new familiarity with Old Testament narratives. Sixteenth-century readers were certainly aware of the theological intricacies of the biblical text. But scripture was most accessible to them as a series of stories; and the compelling human dramas of the patriarchs' lives, with their moments of grandeur, their squabbles, their lapses, and their travails of old age, became enmeshed in popular consciousness. The integration of Jewish elements into Christian life – whether in the form of vernacular Bibles, Hebrew grammars, the adoption of Old Testament first names, or the display of paintings of Old Testament scenes – foreshadowed developments that will be discussed further below.

Church and state

The utility of the Jews to rulers had always been the basis for their settlement in Christian lands. (Not until the late eighteenth century were Jews granted a place in any Christian society that was independent of their utility.) However useful the Jews might be, though, rulers were compelled to consider the demands of clergy and burghers to restrict (if not to expel) them. To be sure, Jewry policy was complicated by the fact that rulers were also believers, and did not want to offend God (or the pope); while bishops were frequently rulers, and did not want to sacrifice their material interests.

The Reformation dramatically disrupted established church–state relations. Early on, this caused the Jews of Germany some consternation. In 1543 Martin Luther called for anti-Jewish measures more hostile than anything ever proposed by Rome. In his work *On the Jews and their Lies*, he proposed setting fire to the Jews' synagogues and homes, confiscating their prayer books and talmudic writings, prohibiting their rabbis from teaching, outlawing their practice of usury, and confiscating their wealth. Eventually, he believed, they should be driven from 'our land'.[13] Such a programme (which was never implemented) constituted a striking breach of both traditional Roman church policy and customary law. The Jews' intercessor at the imperial court, Josel of Rosheim, wrote in desperation to the authorities, 'Never has any scholar contended that we poor Jews should be treated with violence in this tyrannical way – that no

---

13 *WA* 53:523–9.

one need honour an obligation with us or maintain the peace of the land – just because we don't want to believe what Martin Luther believes'.[14]

The Reformation did, in fact, usher in a new wave of local expulsions in Germany. But in the long run, the upheaval set off by Luther had the unintended consequence of *weakening* ecclesiastical power and influence. The fragmentation of ecclesiastical power proved to be an irreversible and continuing process. Clerical authority was further weakened in states whose governments were becoming great fiscal-military machines. The consolidation of these states was accompanied by a changed understanding of statecraft and political values. From a mercantilist point of view, the particularistic objectives of the clergy and the guilds were a genuine hindrance to the aims of state. When clerics or local merchants protested at the presence of Jews in their towns, their protests increasingly fell on the deaf ears of bureaucrats who *valued* the competitive practices of these newcomers, and did not much care what religion they practised.

The reassessment of the Jews by rulers and bureaucrats in the context of a new political framework had major consequences for patterns of Jewish settlement. By the 1570s Jews in Slavic lands, most of whose ancestors had come from Germany, began trickling back into towns and villages of the Holy Roman Empire. As Jewish lending and mercantile activity expanded in central Europe, further spurred by the Thirty Years' War, a new Jewish type emerged, the 'court Jew', who supplied financial and mercantile services to territorial princes and in return received unprecedented privileges. The major figures in this period – Marcus Meysl and Jacob Bassevi in Prague, Reuben Elias Gomperz in Berlin, Samuel Oppenheimer in Vienna – became indispensable because of their ability to marshal large quantities of cash and army provisions at short notice. Around them Jewish communities developed, patronized and dominated by the court Jews.

The most brilliant of these communities was Jewish Prague under the Habsburg emperor Rudolf II (1579–1612). That Jews played a role at the Rudolfine court is remarkable, in view of the fact that Jewish life in Bohemia had been utterly devastated by the end of the fifteenth century. It continued to suffer setbacks in the sixteenth century as well, including short-lived expulsions from the crown cities. But under Habsburg domination the Bohemian Jews, who possessed a virtual monopoly on the marketing of agricultural surpluses, were able to benefit from centralization and commercial expansion. Consequently, while early in the century there was only a handful of Jews in Prague, by 1600

14 Joseph of Rosheim, *Historical writings*, p. 378.

there were many thousands. It was the prosperity of a fast-growing population that laid the economic foundations for the emergence of court Jews, in Prague as elsewhere in central Europe.

Conversion to Christianity was rare among Jews in this region. It tended to occur, when it did, among persons who had little to lose materially or socially. Many converts were men and women who lived at the fringes of Jewish society – vagabonds, petty thieves, and the like – who went to the baptismal font in order to receive the immediate monetary reward (*Taufgeschenk*) this act brought. (Often they travelled elsewhere to repeat the procedure.) Others, such as Johannes Pfefferkorn and Antonius Margaritha, became prominent in ecclesiastical circles as proselytizers to the Jews and vehement opponents of Judaism.

When we move south to the Italian states, we find that patterns of Christian–Jewish interaction underwent a somewhat different development. The papacy, though weakened abroad by the Reformation, had begun to reassert its power in Italy well before the Protestant upheaval. It pursued aggressive measures to expand its own territories, and became closely intertwined with princely rule in other Italian states. In the face of Habsburg and French threats, the relationship between the pope and the Italian princes was one of constant negotiation and a relatively high degree of cooperation.

The conventional account of Italian Jewry in the Reformation period has differentiated sharply between a Renaissance 'golden age' of Christian–Jewish cultural exchange and a Counter-Reformation 'age of the ghetto'. This picture has undergone considerable modification in recent years.[15] To be sure, the shift in papal policy in the 1550s had a deleterious impact on all Italian Jewish communities (concentrated, by the mid-sixteenth century, in northern and central Italy). It was not, however, papal policy alone, but a multiple set of factors, which led to the sharp decline of these communities by the late seventeenth century. In fact, in the century or so that followed the issuance of the bull *Cum nimis absurdum* (1555), Italian Jewish life demonstrated conspicuous vigour.

The mainstay of Jewish life in the papal territories, as elsewhere in Italy, had long been loan banking. By the late fifteenth century, the attack on Jewish 'usury' became a key element in the anti-Jewish fulminations of the Franciscan friars. These friars called for the elimination of Jewish 'usury' (and the Jews) by means of the establishment of *monti di pietà*, or free-loan associations. But the *monti* were able to provide credit to only a limited sector of the population,

15 See, *inter alia*, Bonfil, 'Change in cultural patterns'.

and Jewish banking, while hard hit, persisted as the only source of credit for most of Italy's poor.

In the sixteenth century a new element appeared in Italian Jewry – the Sephardim, or Jews of Iberian origin. By the 1530s, Sephardi merchants had become important in Italian trade with the Levant, and soon dominated it. They were able to parlay the demand for their services into settlement privileges from Italian rulers who were competing among themselves to gain an edge in this trade.[16]

Initially, the papacy shared with other Italian rulers a purely utilitarian interest in these merchants. In 1532, the papal state gained an important commercial asset when it assumed direct control of Ancona. In order to help Ancona compete with other Adriatic ports (particularly Ferrara and Venice), Pope Paul III allowed Sephardi Jews – among them former New Christians – to settle and trade in Ancona, and even offered them protection against inquisitorial molestation. His successor, Julius III, confirmed this protection.

But it was also Julius III who inaugurated the Tridentine offensive against the Jews when, in 1553, he approved the Roman Inquisition's call for the confiscation of copies of the Talmud. (In Rome, the confiscated volumes were burned publicly in the Campo de' Fiori.) This episode was of passing consequence. More importantly, Paul IV, shortly after he ascended to the papacy in 1555, issued the bull *Cum nimis absurdum*, breaking sharply with regnant papal policy. Jews in the papal state were to wear 'in full view' a distinguishing mark; they were to be subjected to new restrictions in their occupational activity; they were to live in designated, segregated quarters; they were not to have Christian servants; and they were to sell all their real estate to Christians. What was most startling, perhaps, was that these measures (not all of them new) were actually enforced.

As a result, ghettos were established in Rome, Bologna, and Ancona – a clear signal of the papacy's willingness to sacrifice profit for the sake of religious scruples. Yet it came as a shock to many when, shortly after the creation of the Ancona ghetto, the pope initiated proceedings against the baptized *ex-conversos* who had settled there. While some managed to escape, fifty-two of them were arrested and tried as heretics. To the horror of Sephardi exiles everywhere, twenty-four were burned at the stake in the spring months of 1556.

Following Paul IV's death, that pope's policies were moderated in response to various pressures. Pius IV reduced the severity of some of the Roman ghetto restrictions. Jewish appeals to the Council of Trent to lift the ban on the

---

16 Ravid, 'Tale of three cities'.

Talmud resulted in a revised Index of 1564, permitting circulation of expurgated copies of the Talmud with the title 'Talmud' removed. Although the ban on the Talmud was subsequently reintroduced, many Italian Jews continued to own copies. Other rabbinic works, once they were expurgated by Jewish converts who specialized in Hebrew censorship, circulated freely. The last of the sixteenth-century anti-Jewish excesses was the expulsion of the Jews in 1569 from all parts of the papal territories except Rome and Ancona. The Jews who remained in the latter communities were subjected from 1577 onwards to compulsory conversionary sermons.

One scholar has argued that the underlying intent of all Tridentine papal policy regarding Jews was conversionary.[17] Be this as it may, the foundation in 1543 of a *domus catechumenorum* in Rome to house Jewish neophytes certainly reflected such an aim. (Starting in 1554, the Jews of Rome were required to contribute for its upkeep.) However, converts were generally held in low esteem in Italy, and their numbers were apparently not high. Few of them achieved prominence, with the exception of Sixtus of Siena and Giulio Morosini, both of whom proselytized vigorously among their former coreligionists.

Perhaps the most permanent ramification of Tridentine papal policy was the establishment of ghettos almost everywhere in Italy by the mid-seventeenth century. But it is important to note that this occurred only because papal segregationist motivations dovetailed with the interests of early modern rulers, who welcomed an arrangement that would allow for greater supervision of Jewish immigration and economic activity. When interests did not mesh in this way – particularly when papal restrictionism collided with princely mercantilist interests – Italian rulers were liable to defy papal pressure. In 1570, for example, the Duke of Savoy welcomed Jews who had been driven from the Duchy of Tuscany by severe measures advocated by the pope. The duke thereby gained a mercantile asset for his port city of Nice that apparently more than compensated him for incurring the pope's wrath.

In Venice, mercantile interests eventually overcame both papal protests and a long history of local hostility to Jewish settlement. In fact it was the Venetian authorities who in 1516 had first grudgingly created a 'ghetto', permitting Jewish money-lending (and residence) within a walled area of the city known by that name. (Prior to this, Jewish money-lending had been confined to the Terraferma.) But in the wake of the Venetian–Ottoman war of 1537–40, which had diverted the Levant trade, the Senate recognized the need to fend off increasing commercial competition, and was inevitably drawn into the scramble to attract

17 Stow, *Catholic thought*, pp. 3–59.

and hold Sephardi merchants. At first, in 1541, the Senate agreed to admit only 'Levantine' (Ottoman) Jewish merchants, and then only as transients; but by 1589 it had granted full rights of residence not only to 'Levantine' Jews, but also to 'Ponentines' (*ex-conversos* from Spain), with a guarantee to the latter of protection from inquisitorial interference. The papacy immediately objected. But Fra Paulo Sarpi, adopting an increasingly persuasive logic, argued that it was in the interest of Christendom to allow *ex-converso* merchants to settle in Venice as Jews, since otherwise they would take their capital to Constantinople where they would benefit the infidel Turk.[18]

By the second half of the sixteenth century Italy was no longer an attractive destination for Jewish migration. Yet particularly in Venice, Jewish life continued to demonstrate considerable vitality, as well as a relatively high level of social and cultural interaction with Christian society. In Hebrew printing establishments (which Jews could not own), Jews, along with Jewish converts to Christianity and other Christians, collaborated routinely on the publication and censorship of Jewish works. Christians employed Jews to teach them Hebrew, music, and dancing; Italian polyphonic music even found its way experimentally into the synagogue. Jews from all over Europe studied medicine at the University of Padua in a cosmopolitan and intellectually advanced social orbit.[19] Christians, for their part, paid sightseeing visits to the ghetto, especially on Jewish holidays. The prodigious seventeenth-century Venetian rabbi Leon Modena was proud of the 'many esteemed friars, priests, and noblemen' who came to the ghetto on sabbaths to hear him preach.[20] To be sure, the ghetto walls clearly marked the boundary between Christian and Jewish space, and the gates were locked at night. But this did not inhibit a steady stream of people and ideas in and out of the ghetto.

By the second half of the sixteenth century, opportunities for interaction were opening up elsewhere. The decades between 1550 and 1600 saw a demographic shift that was to be of the greatest significance for Christian–Jewish relations. A key role was played by Iberian New Christians. The creation of this population (whose presence in Italy we have discussed) was one of the unanticipated consequences of late medieval Spanish religious repression: a population of thoroughly Hispanized families of Jewish origins, some of whose members persisted in rejecting a Catholicism they believed was forced on them and held to a belief in 'the Law of Moses', as well as a sense of belonging to the Jewish people. The activity of the Spanish and Portuguese Inquisitions, along with

18 Ravid, 'Venetian government', pp. 18–19.
19 Ruderman, *Jewish thought*, pp. 100–17.   20 Modena, *Autobiography*, p. 96.

widespread stigmatization of the 'New Christians' for generations after the last conversions in 1497, contributed to the perpetuation of a crypto-judaizing population, and to the steady emigration of its members.

In the course of the sixteenth century, the *converso* merchant elite in Iberian lands became involved in the Atlantic colonial trade, operating from Lisbon, Oporto, Seville, and Antwerp. In 1550, hoping to attract some of these merchants to his own realm, Henri II of France issued *lettres patentes* to 'the merchants and other Portuguese called New Christians'. ('Judaizing' had by this point died out among Spanish *conversos*, who thus had less incentive than the Portuguese to emigrate.) In France, New Christian émigrés settled in Bordeaux and Bayonne, abetted by royal authorities who turned a blind eye to the newcomers' barely concealed 'judaizing'. By the end of the sixteenth century, small numbers of 'Portuguese' had settled as Christians elsewhere in northern Europe as well.

It was in Amsterdam that the 'Portuguese' were able to bring about a dramatic religio-cultural self-transformation. The New Christians who settled there, after testing the waters briefly, discovered that they would be allowed to live openly as Jews, with no concern about their prior baptism and with only minor economic restrictions. After 1609, when a truce was negotiated between the Netherlands and Spain, New Christians began flocking in large numbers to the Dutch entrepôt, where they 'returned' to Judaism. A Jewish community was established that was composed almost entirely of neophytes to Judaism; it was to become the site of unparalleled testing of Christian–Jewish boundaries.

The Dutch Republic in the early seventeenth century was a new society whose public consciousness had been shaped by the recent struggle against Spain. The place Jews were eventually granted in its great commercial centre was shaped not by any pre-existing Jewry policy (there was none), but by deeply ingrained attitudes among members of the regent class who served as the city's magistrates and burgomasters. The main concern of these men was to preserve civil peace among Christians of different confessions. The Portuguese Jews were hardly relevant to this problem (and, more importantly, were not *regarded* as relevant), and their appearance on the scene did not cause particular anxiety among the ruling class.

The Reformed clergy, on the other hand, as leaders of the officially recognized 'public church', were alarmed by the presence of deniers of Christ. They exerted pressure on the magistrates, first to prohibit the practice of Judaism in Amsterdam, then to prevent the building of a synagogue. In a pattern that was to become routine, the magistrates and burgomasters responded evasively to the complaints of the Reformed clergy, allowing the Jews to proceed. It was only in 1616 that Amsterdam's burgomasters felt compelled officially to acknowledge this community by issuing a set of regulations for it. The Jews, they instructed, were 'not to speak or write anything . . . that may, in any way, tend to the disparagement of our Christian religion'; they were not to convert to Judaism persons outside their own ethnic group; and they were not to have sexual relations with Christian women. (The latter provision was rarely enforced.) The 1616 regulations, which governed the Jews of Amsterdam for almost two centuries, left the Jews free to live where they chose and to engage freely in commerce; moreover, they were not burdened with special taxes. (As elsewhere in Europe, though, most of the Amsterdam guilds excluded them.)

The extraordinary conditions enjoyed in Amsterdam by the Portuguese Jews (who were soon followed by Ashkenazi Jews from the east) resulted from a convergence of factors. Jews had never lived in the northern Netherlands in significant numbers; the region thus lacked the legacy of venomous anti-Judaism so common elsewhere. Most Netherlanders, in the wake of their protracted and bloody struggle with the Spanish, had little appetite for internal religious strife. Indeed, by 1581 Dutch political thinkers and pamphleteers had produced a considerable literature arguing against the use of coercion in matters of conscience.[21] While Jews did not figure in the ongoing debate, the terms and logic of the discourse created an atmosphere favourable to them. It was also advantageous to the Portuguese Jews that Netherlanders shared with them a fierce antipathy to Spanish 'tyranny' and the Inquisition.

In the second half of the seventeenth century, the northern Portuguese-Jewish diaspora fanned out to include England, the Caribbean, and British America. The settlements in south-west France, though still officially Catholic, in effect became part of a far-flung network of Jewish communities whose members were vitally involved in the transformation of European society.

Narrowing the divide

Throughout western Europe, and to some extent in central Europe as well, the sixteenth and seventeenth centuries saw an erosion of the barriers between Christians and Jews. As traditional frameworks of thought and practice lost their hold, possibilities opened for new modalities of exchange.

This is not the place to dwell on the profound ruptures in mental continuity among early modern Europeans – ruptures set off by the fragmentation of the Western Church, the humanist study of scripture, the print revolution, and so on. In terms of Christian–Jewish relations, the most profound innovations

21 See Van Gelderen, *Political thought*, pp. 217–28.

occurred among three sometimes overlapping groups: Christian Hebraists, radical Christian sectarians, and the descendants of Iberian *conversos*. Let us focus on those.

In the late fourteenth century, it became almost routine for Christian scholars to undertake the study of Hebrew. (Jews or Jewish converts provided the tutoring.) The motivations driving Christian Hebraists were diverse. In Protestant lands, Hebraism was closely bound up with the recovery of the Bible. Humanists had developed techniques to recover the texts of ancient works; their curriculum provided Protestants with the tools to produce better Bible translations and a more philologically grounded exegesis. Such work naturally required a scholarly knowledge of Hebrew.

But Hebrew was also cultivated by Christians for spiritual and nostalgic reasons. It was the sacred Ur-language, the tongue that had been spoken in the Garden of Eden. A sixteenth-century Italian abbot went so far as to translate the Office of the Blessed Virgin Mary into Hebrew, believing that a prayer recited in that language would be more efficacious.[22]

Belief in the supernatural properties of Hebrew was related to another branch of Christian Hebraism: Christian Kabbalah, a field of study pioneered by Pico della Mirandola. Pico set the agenda for generations of Christian Kabbalists when he identified the corpus of Jewish Kabbalah as key in the search for the *prisca theologica* – the universal core of (Christian) truth that was concealed, it was believed, in all ancient theologies and philosophies. Whether or not the hermetically inclined Habsburg emperor Rudolf II actually met with the great rabbinic scholar Judah Löw ben Bezalel of Prague to discuss 'esoteric matters',[23] there was logic to such a rumour. (The emperor's confessor, Pistorius, had himself published a compendium of kabbalistic texts in Latin.) The prospect of uncovering the secret scaffolding of a comprehensive system of revealed truth concealed in kabbalistic texts nourished one of the most powerful dreams of Reformation thinkers: to unite mankind in a truly 'catholic' sacred tradition and to bring religious turmoil to an end.

But perhaps the most commonly cited justification for studying Hebrew was to proselytize the Jews more effectively. Particularly when Portuguese-Jewish rabbinic scholars appeared on the scene with an extensive knowledge of Christianity and Latin sources, Christian scholars found themselves at a disadvantage. As the seventeenth-century Dutch scholar Gerhard Johann Vossius put it, 'We often defend a most excellent cause with play arms rather than real

---

22 Stow, 'Conversion, Christian Hebraism, and Hebrew prayer', pp. 222–3.
23 Gans, *Zemah David*, p. 145.

ones'.[24] Only a Christian disputant with extensive knowledge of the Hebrew Bible and rabbinics was properly equipped.

Such a brief survey does not do justice to the truly protean forms Christian Hebraism assumed. But Christians who studied Hebrew, whether they were hostile or friendly to Jews, marginal eccentrics or cardinals in Rome, mystics or grammarians, became intimately acquainted in a new way with Jewish texts and rabbinic approaches. The intensity of Christian–Jewish dialogue in early modern Europe would be unthinkable without these figures. Equally unthinkable would be the appearance of such intellectual giants as Guillaume Postel or Jean Bodin, who, despite their vastly different minds, shared a breathtaking detachment from traditional Christian thinking about Judaism.

Protestant biblicism at a more popular level was no less important. The new accessibility of the Bible in the vernacular, and the Protestant emphasis on the sovereign authority of the Bible, stimulated innovative thinking at all levels of society. As the Old Testament text became familiar, so did its narrative, historical, and apocalyptic contents. It became a basis for speculation not only about true doctrine, but also about such matters as the proper structure of secular government, issues of everyday morality, the history of mankind, and the nature of the coming apocalypse. In some radical sectarian circles – even among dissidents in Catholic lands[25] – a combination of radical anti-Catholicism and literalist Bible reading led to a kind of 'Judeo-tropism', an adoption by believing Christians of doctrines and practices that seemed 'Jewish' to contemporaries. This occurred even in lands where there were no Jews to imitate. In England, for example, certain nonconformist Baptists, eager to appropriate the literal sense of the Old Testament, drew the conclusion that the Roman Church's abolition of the Jewish sabbath on the seventh day had been unjustified. These 'Saturday sabbatarians' were re-evaluating the validity of Old Testament law years before professing Jews were readmitted to England.[26]

Whether they lived in the vicinity or not, Jews played a role in the various millenarian scenarios that germinated in Protestant and radical sectarian circles. Particularly in the Netherlands, England, and New England, there was a strong tendency to conflate eschatological scenarios from the vernacular Bible with unfolding contemporary events – events which included an escape from 'Babylon' and the establishment of a 'New Jerusalem'. The extravagant apocalyptic expectations that sprouted on this soil invariably involved the

---

24 Katchen, *Christian Hebraists*, p. 163.
25 See Bodian, 'In the cross-currents', pp. 85–90, 95–100.
26 Katz, *Philo-semitism*, pp. 9–42.

Jews, whose imminent conversion was an integral part of the script. Jews thus became objects of the millenarians' possessive and benevolent interest.

For their part, the Portuguese Jews who were settling in Atlantic commercial and cultural centres arrived from Iberian lands with an unprecedented knowledge of Catholic Christianity. Though most of them regarded themselves as believers in the 'Law of Moses', they were at first largely ignorant of rabbinic law as it was practised in the early modern period. Their encounter with rabbinic Judaism, on the one hand, and with Protestant Christianity, on the other, raised stubborn issues about Jewish tradition and its relationship to the Christian world. Some *ex-converso* thinkers became staunch and learned defenders of the rabbinic tradition, leaders of their communities. While many among the rank-and-file vacillated, unsure where their loyalties lay, most integrated with reasonable ease. But a few bold individuals, dissatisfied with existing orthodoxies of all sorts, developed radically critical views of traditional Judaism. They drew from sceptical currents in European society, as well as from crypto-Jewish criticisms of Catholicism they had cultivated in the Iberian peninsula – criticisms which, they found, could be applied with equally demolishing effect to rabbinic tradition.[27]

The encounter of mentally adventurous Christians and Jews in early modern Europe was highly charged and fraught with ambiguities that continue to vex scholars. The participants included both orthodox and heterodox thinkers, as well as radicals and sceptics, on both sides. Their interests intersected in numerous ways, and their controversies touched on some of the central issues in European thinking at the time.

Much of the interchange consisted of polemic and counter-polemic. This had been the characteristic mode of encounter between Christian and Jew for centuries. But both sides were now better informed than they had ever been about the other. Moreover, the particularly great need felt by Portuguese Jews to repudiate Christian teaching and to 'reclaim' wavering fellow New Christians for Judaism led them to produce a body of polemical literature that was unprecedented in volume. (Most of it circulated in manuscript.) The central aim of the Christian controversialists was, as always, to bring about Jewish conversion.[28]

In reality, the polemics tended to reinforce the boundaries on both sides. But while both Jews and Christians engaged in polemical boundary-marking, they generally also participated in the gradual demystification and 'de-pollution' of

27 Bodian, *Hebrews*, pp. 118–23; *idem*, 'In the cross-currents', pp. 102–4.
28 On polemics, see Yerushalmi, *From Spanish court*, pp. 352–5, 408–12; Kaplan, *From Christianity*, pp. 235–62.

one another, and consequently in a reduction in the level of mutual hostility. The Ashkenazi chronicler David Gans of Prague, whose interest in astronomy gained him the acquaintance of Tycho Brahe and Johannes Kepler, encouraged his fellow Jews to become conversant in gentile learning, and, to ease their fears, he minimized the role of Christian violence in Jewish history.[29] In fact, of course, Jews still faced considerable Christian hostility, so Jewish apologetes were also quick to identify, when they could, with new secular values in Christian society. Christian interest in Old Testament government, for example, led some Portuguese Jews to identify the 'government' of the Israelites (as well as contemporary governance of Jewish communities) with republican ideas.[30] Simone Luzzatto in Venice and Menasseh ben Israel, among other defenders of the Jews, consciously tailored their apologetic works to resonate with a mercantilist sensibility, emphasizing the value to the commonwealth of a Jewish population of international merchants.[31]

A more delicate issue was that of religious rapprochement. Despite their wariness of Christian conversionism, some prominent Jews were willing and even eager to collaborate with Christians in lowering the barriers. In Amsterdam, Menasseh ben Israel, who had contacts with numerous unconventional Christians, was at the centre of efforts to make rabbinic works available in translation to Christian readers. He believed (as did other contemporary Jews) that by reading such works Christians would recognize the true value and character of Jewish learning.[32] The Venetian rabbi Leon de Modena, no stranger himself to the learned Christian world, published a book in Italian that offered Christian readers a systematic account of Jewish ritual practice. His aim was to rebut disparaging works by Buxtorf and others, and to offer an authoritative alternative. At the same time, he sought to moderate Jewish hostility to Christians: in a Hebrew work for Jewish readers he adopted a conciliatory view not only towards the historical Jesus, but even towards the doctrine of the Trinity and the Christian belief that Jesus was the messiah.[33] But involvement in millenarian 'politics' was another matter. While millenarian theologians were anxious to engage Jews in dialogue about shared expectations (since Jews were to play a key role in bringing about the millennium), Jews were less eager to reciprocate (since that role entailed conversion). The redoubtable Menasseh

---

29 See Breuer, 'Modernism and traditionalism', pp. 70–4.
30 See Bodian, 'Biblical Hebrews'.
31 Ravid, 'How profitable the nation of the Jewes are'.
32 See Katchen, *Christian Hebraists*, pp. 101–290; cf. Fishman, 'Early modern Jewish discourse', pp. 184–5.
33 See Cohen, 'Leone da Modena's Riti'; Fishman, 'Early modern Jewish discourse'.

ben Israel nevertheless engaged in extensive discussion and diplomacy with millenarians throughout Europe. He may have concluded, after reading Isaac la Peyrere's remarkable *Rappel des Juifs* (1655), that Jewish messianism and Christian millenarianism could in some complex way be reconciled.[34]

Oddly enough, one of the towering figures in early modern intellectual life, Benedict Spinoza, *was* a Portuguese Jew by birth. How this affected his philosophy has long been a matter of debate. It is true that Judaism and Jewish history figured centrally in Spinoza's work. But they also figured centrally in the work of such figures as Jean Bodin, Thomas Hobbes, and James Harrington. More specifically, it is true that Spinoza was excommunicated from the Amsterdam Portuguese Jewish community for holding sceptical ideas similar to those held by a few other 'heretics' in that community – ideas that may have had specific roots in the Portuguese-Jewish experience. But the rejection of clerical authority and revealed religion was a subterranean current in European society as a whole.

The fact is that by the seventeenth century, Judaism had become inextricably entangled in European philosophical and religious discourse. Never had so many Jews and Christians penetrated so deeply into each other's religio-cultural spheres. It was a remarkable moment. But it was about to fade. In fact, Spinoza's work can be said to mark the beginning of the retreat of innovative thinking from the realm of theology. It thus also marks the concomitant decline in mutual curiosity about traditions that were, in large part, medieval.

---

34 On Menasseh and millenarians, see Popkin, 'Some aspects'; essays in Kaplan *et al.* (eds.), *Menasseh ben Israel and his world.*

27

The naturalization of
Andean Christianities

KENNETH MILLS

I enquire in this chapter into what images of Christ, the Virgin and other saints meant to the emergence and 'fruition' of local Andean Christianities in the sixteenth and seventeenth centuries.[1]

On one level, saints were the favourite creatures of churchmen and colonial officials and thus might seem to have invited the 'withering' and 'erasure' of native Andean forms before the force, 'surveillance and discipline' of Spanish Christian impositions.[2] They were approved patrons of lay groups and parish-based neighbourhoods, and they immediately authorized not only chapels and churches, but entire towns and cities. There were careful rules for saints' veneration, systems for how the copies of images and other sacred material would circulate, and regular moments set aside for the promotion and observance of their cults. Official inspectors and representatives set themselves against the saints' unsupervised proliferation, their untetherings.

And yet, however much saints were meant to play in tune with the universal ambitions of the church and the demands of a colonial system, they joined even more surely to their new people and places. What William A. Christian Jr has found so seminally both in the case of the late medieval and early modern Spanish kingdoms, and in his ethnographic investigations of the same regions, proves as persuasive abroad.[3] Many saints could not keep their distance; they invited social appropriations and personal connections, and they were remembered through increasingly localized stories of apparitions

My thanks for questions, suggestions, and provocations to William B. Taylor, Simon Ditchfield, Ronnie Po-chia Hsia, Catherine J. Julien, Izumi Shimada, Cynthia Milton, Daviken Studnicki-Gizbert, and Ines Županov in particular.

1 On the fruitions of early modern visual forms, see Elisabetta Corsi, 'Masons of faith'. My explorations in the Andean colonial religious imagination build upon remarkable foundations: see the Bibliography.

2 Abercrombie, *Pathways*, pp. 188–9, who notably also sees a 'reinscription of Andean social memory'.

3 Esp. *Apparitions, Local religion*, 'De los santos a María', *Person and God*. Also Ditchfield, 'La santità' and *Liturgy*.

and miracles, and by iconographic syntheses. Saints built particular reputations as the advocates of individuals and special causes. Bits of them, and material associated with their sacred places, could, like memories, be carried away by devotees and activated elsewhere. Saints could be quite instrumental, offering remedies for extraordinary strain, crisis, desire and despair in individuals' lives. But healings and other miracles attributed to saints' intercessions with God were interpreted metaphorically, too, and not only by theologians and preachers drumming upon the value of contrition or the hope of eternal salvation. Saints' representative images had human faces and bodies, which could be approached spontaneously through prayer. They might be attentive, dismissive and vengeful in equal measure. And they competed jealously, asking to be first, to replace one another, to be honoured, invoked, visited, nourished and prayed to, promising to secure favours and salvation from a sometimes more distant God.

The attraction of indigenous peoples in much of Andean Peru to the Christian cult of the saints was partly one of familiarity. Native Andeans had grown accustomed to the consultation of ancestral originators who asserted themselves across overlapping sacred landscapes. There was a changeable spiritual hierarchy of divine personalities in pre-Hispanic times, divine forces which, like Christian saints, moved within power and people: pre-Hispanic 'devotees' distinguished between original divinities and their 'offspring', between hugely powerful and more limited beings, and between generalist personalities and more specialized ones. Andeans were familiar, too, with visible representations of the holy, and with ways of knowing, recalling and stirring their divinities through the performance of sacred narratives, offerings and visits to special places. Because saints could sometimes seem so known, the steps towards veneration in chapels, in newly constructed shrines, and towards pilgrimages and parish-church-based religiosity in colonial times were not impossible ones. The cult of the saints invited a number of key ancestral modes and patterns to continue, even if continuity soon grew less conscious and gradually sensible. Saints came to partake of originally non-Christian understandings of territory, if not of the older sacred personalities themselves.

Yet this was a fluid kind of familiarity. The emergence and fruition of Andean Christianities is simultaneously about the capacity for novelty and innovation, about the allure and utility of the new. The attraction of some originally unfamiliar expressions of sacred power – the visual and narrative personalities of Christ, the Virgin Mary, and other saints were foreign in this way – was in part tied to these personalities' perceived ability to summon valuable powers from 'outside'.[4] The attraction of this spiritual and practical power for many native Andeans has been insufficiently studied within a larger history of Catholic Christian transformations.

I contend two things in what follows. First, that the chasm which many Spanish Christian commentators detected and attempted to open between key dimensions of the non-Christian Andean past and a Christian Andean present and future either opened differently for many native Andeans or was effectively closed by them in favour of emerging and localized options. My interest in the aptitudes of native Andean peoples for stretching beyond any single cultural and religious tradition towards new syntheses leads simultaneously towards the capacities of other actors and ideas. Thus, I endeavour to show, second, how the production and reproduction of emerging kinds of 'religious commonsense' developed through the interactions and transformations of many kinds of people in a variety of Christian 'microcosms' across the colonial Andes.[5] This multi-ethnic array included thinkers, promoters, and mobilizers on different planes, in different ways, many of them unintended. Some of the clergy feared and persecuted as 'error' the very fusions they and their fellows helped bring to life, and of which they partook. But all participated in a vibrant circulation of religious ideas, forms and practices around the images of Christ and the saints, and, together, brought about an emerging Andean interculture.

A proliferous past

There was an Andean system of meaning that appears to have encouraged native reception and understandings of Christian sacred images more than any other. I refer to beliefs surrounding, and the interrelationships between, Andean divinities known in the Quechua tongue as *huacas*. And I refer, even more, to the ways in which such beliefs and interrelationships were coming to be understood in colonial times.

In understanding *huacas* we are mostly the prisoners of post-conquest reflections upon these much older and diverse phenomena,[6] however much the work of historical archaeologists such as John Topic and others, featured below, seems to bolster and extend the surviving written record. To the best of our knowledge, pre-Hispanic *huacas* were extraordinary physical things and places often imbued with the power of ancestral personalities, cultural originators

---

4 Helms, *Craft*.   5 Peter Brown, *The rise*, esp. ch. 16, but *passim*.
6 Julien, *Reading*; Graubart, 'Indecent living'.

for surrounding peoples. They were, importantly, part of a broader range of special or sacred natural phenomena I cannot treat here.[7] The fact that most understandings of *huacas* departed from the pre-Hispanic, and became 'hybridic' – which is to say, both authentically native Andean *and* infiltrated, to one degree or another, by the understandings and vocabularies of Spanish Catholic Christianity – is integral to the colonial processes and realities to be explored here. Two originally disparate systems cease only to continue or repeat themselves, and were instead finding shared territories and conjoining to generate new understandings and religious forms.[8] This is a case of a gradually developing interculture in which even the exceptions suggest the rule. By mid-colonial times in the Andes, steadfast native opponents of the growing presence of Christian images in the hearts and minds of Indian commoners tellingly incorporated within their rejections and counter-teachings the very characterizations employed against their *huacas* by Spanish evangelizers.[9]

We do well to begin at what we can discern as the top of the hierarchy of pre-Hispanic Andean *huacas*. These pinnacles became magnets to post-conquest comment and enquiry. The encounter of Hernando Pizarro and his advance raiding party with Pachacamac, the 'oracular' divine force of pan-Andean proportions in the Lurin Valley just south of what became the Spanish capital of Lima in January of 1533, offers an early and evocative case in point.

In crossing over the final threshold at the top of the divinity's pyramid-shrine, the first Spaniards at the place faced what their Judeo-Christian tradition and experience had fully prepared them to identify as an 'idol', a male figure atop a wooden pole that struck them as both sad and hideous. It took no effort and less theology to perceive Pachacamac as Miguel de Estete did. Here was a thing beneath contempt, a vile material form crafted by human hands and pilfering the adoration human beings ought to reserve only for the Christian God. The precious offerings, reportedly piled around the figure and adorning the site, only proved how much Andean peoples had been hoodwinked by an active devil who 'appeared to those priests and spoke with them', conspiring to siphon 'tribute' from up and down the entire coast, and demanding a respect that in Inca times was rivalled only by the temple of the Sun in Lake Titicaca.[10] It mattered most particularly to establish whether the famous voice and oracular

---

7 For more, see esp. Mills, *Idolatry*, chs. 2, 3, 4; Salomon, 'Introductory essay', in Salomon and Urioste (eds.), *The Huarochirí manuscript*. Inspiring on the related *mallqui* complex: Gose, 'Converting'.
8 Sahlins, *Islands*.
9 Mills, *An evil*, pp. 106–7, and *passim*; Cummins, *Toasts*, pp. 159–60; Estenssoro Fuchs, 'Les Pouvoirs'.
10 Pizarro, 'Relación'; Estete, 'Noticia'.

utterings of Pachacamac were the handiwork of the devil speaking through him, or – as Hernando Pizarro sought to prove through brutal interrogation of an Indian minister – artifice worked by the false god's attendants. So went an early and coldly archetypal narrative of spiritual conquest of a high Andean religious form.

It was not long, however, before the figure of Pachacamac gave pause to different minds. Pedro de Cieza de León, who blended his own observations and enquiries with information about the coastal region gained from the Dominican Domingo de Santo Tomás, among others, represents an uneasy and telling transition in the 1540s and 1550s. While still content to label the oracular divinity on the coast the 'devil Pachacamac', Cieza pushed harder. He was among the first of the Spanish voices in Peru to practise what would prove a long-lived writerly tradition in the Americas, that of uncovering far more than he could resolve.[11] Cieza wrestled with the *huacas*' multifaceted natures and with the manner of best expressing the apparent relationships between an evident hierarchy of divine Andean forms. While consistently described across coastal and Andean regions as a predominant creative force 'who gives being to the earth',[12] it was abundantly clear that Pachacamac coexisted with other divine figures. Other *huacas*, too, were creative founders who rooted deeply. Sacred oral histories recounted these ancestral beings' origins, featured their contributions to local and regional civilization, in many cases told of their lithomorphosis into the regional landscape, and, importantly, explained their interrelationships with other divine beings. Explanations of the natural environment and entire histories of conflict and interaction between human groups might be encapsulated within the durably fluid form of the *huacas*' oral narratives, which themselves were remembered and enacted by ritual tellers, singers, and dancers.[13]

In Pachacamac's coastal midst, for instance, Dominican friars from the convent at Chincha in the 1540s and 1550s learned about Chinchaycama. This ancestral originator was revered by the Yungas people at a certain rock from which the divinity was said to have sprung. It emerged that Chinchaycama had been one of a number of divinities 'who responded' to the requests and entreaties of his Yunga people; this is precisely how the Dominicans put it. According to what the friars learned and managed to express about this set of relationships

<hr />

11 Cieza de León, *Crónica*, ch. lxxii, 214–15.
12 Castro and Ortega Morejón, 'Relación y declaración', p. 246; Santillán, 'Relación', 111b; MacCormack, *Religion*, pp. 351–2, 154–9.
13 Salomon and Urioste (eds.), *The Huarochirí manuscript*; Dedenbach-Salazar Sáenz, 'La comunicación'.

between people and divinity, the Yungas made choices and assigned precedence according to their own changing requirements. The people effectively moved between *huacas* 'who responded', the Dominicans explained, and 'this not always, but only when they had need of them'. How do we see the apparently selective horizontality of Yunga religiosity? It did not much impress Spanish commentators, and it has struck at least one modern historian similarly, as an approach that treated 'matters of religion somewhat casually'.[14]

In fact, this glimpse of Chinchaycama's position, and of Yunga attitudes towards an array of divine beings, suggests Andean religious understandings that were anything but casual. Divinity was tied not only to the people's sense of themselves and their meaning, but more immediately to political, economic and environmental stresses, to developing needs and to survival itself. The Dominicans were doing their best to see, within a decade of their arrival in the region, and this fact needs thinking about. Their conception of Chinchaycama and other *huacas* as critical intermediaries who might reward or punish, and from whom answers, benevolence and protection might be sought through regular ritual invocations and offerings emerges within an explanation and refutation of Yunga religious inclinations. That pre-contact Andean traditions of divine multiplicity were being distorted by early Spanish Christian descriptive inclinations should be suspected, if not assumed. But, distortion coexists with at least three other possibilities. First and most basically, that information about pre-Hispanic *huacas* slips through in spite of awkward cross-cultural terms of reference. Second, and more deeply, that a Christianizing terminological and imaginative frame linked to the cult of the saints clearly enabled Spanish understandings, descriptions, and denunciations of actual Andean forms, both in the mid-sixteenth century and for years to come. And third, that these understandings of *huacas* were increasingly informed by native Andeans themselves, people who had shared in their creation.

The idea of horizontal levels of *huacas* beneath the likes of Pachacamac, beings 'who responded' to Indians and addressed local and specific needs, fast became a preachable concept for Spanish priests and missionaries. This kind of popular broadcasting of an emerging early colonial understanding of *huacas* from the pulpit cannot be romanticized. It was brutally connected to an enduring slur about the fickleness and inconstancy of native Andean worshippers, as well as to other concentrated assertions about the *huacas*'

---

14 Castro and Ortega Morejón; Anonymous, 'Aviso de el modo'; MacCormack, *Religion*, p. 155.

impotence or the charlatanry of their ministers.[15] Yet these denunciations, like a far broader 'pastoral of fear' in this and many other contemporary evangelization settings,[16] spurred emotional and creative responses from their hearers that were notoriously uncontrollable. Preachers and confessors of sins could not curtail the resonance of their messages about *huacas* with the popular Christian conceptions of simultaneously coexisting diabolic forms and competitive saintly cults from which their descriptive concepts and metaphors had, at least in part, sprung. An instructive precedent for the increasingly active and unsanctioned convergence of ideas about *huacas*, devils and saints is further suggested if we linger just a little more on the Pacific coast.

When the Incas entered the central coastal region of what is now Peru in force, bringing integrative settlers from other zones, they built a shrine to their principal divinity the Sun, impressing upon newly subjected peoples the importance of this divinity's attributes and consecration of themselves as his children. But almost everything we know about Inca expansionism suggests that the Incas attempted to incorporate rather than erase important local cults, effectively smoothing over necessary conflict and injecting themselves into longer regional mythohistoric trajectories. Cieza and the Dominicans found, for example, that the aforementioned cult of Chinchaycama had continued for the natives of Chincha, operating alongside those of other divinities, including those favoured by the arriving Incas.[17] The fact that these commentators had little to gain by finding such religious complexity – and, in the Dominicans' case in particular, may have wished for a more concentrated 'enemy' to be curious about – suggests that the *huaca* complex was at least as interconnected and layered as they understood. Thus, quite apart from the issue of whether or not Spanish descriptors and metaphors did adequate justice to pre-Hispanic Andean understandings (which they surely did not), plastic and practical relationships between divine beings, and between *huacas* and their peoples, appear to have been something of a ruling principle.

One multiply informative bit of colonial learning on the subject was produced by the lawyer Hernando de Santillán amid a 1563 response to a royal decree enquiring about Inca taxation. Along his purposeful way, Santillán rendered an oral tradition about Topa Inca Yupanqui on the eve of Inca expansion into the very coastal valleys of the Yunga with which our examples have been

15 Mills, *Idolatry*, pp. 189–210.
16 Jean Delumeau, *La peur en Occident*; Dominique Deslandres, *Croire*; Ines G. Županov, *Disputed mission*, ch. 3; Eugenio Menegon, 'Deliver us'. For contemporary Peru, see Andrew Redden; Estenssoro Fuchs, *Del paganismo*, esp. pp. 286–91.
17 Cieza de León, *Crónica*, p. 220.

concerned.[18] While Mama Ocllo was pregnant with the child who would become Topa Inca, his voice was said to have issued from within her belly to inform her that a great 'creator of the earth' lived on the coast, in the 'Irma valley' (today the valley of Lurín, south of Lima). When Topa Inca was older, his mother told him of the experience, and he set out to find this creator. His wanderings led him to the coast and the sacred place of Pachacamac. Once in the presence of the great *huaca*, the story stresses, the Inca's gestures were those of a respectful supplicant, for he spent 'many days in prayer and fasting'.

After forty days, Pachacamac was said to have broken the silence, speaking from a stone. He confirmed that he was the 'maker of the earth' whom Topa Inca sought. Yet Pachacamac also explained that he was not alone as this kind of force. He explained that while he had made (literally 'given being') to all things 'down here', that is to say on the coast, the Sun, who 'was his brother', had performed the same creative function 'up there', in the highlands. Not surprisingly delighted to hear that such an understanding had been struck, the Inca and his travelling companions sacrificed llamas and fine clothing in honour of Pachacamac. Their tone, according to Santillán's reporting, continued as gratitude, 'thanking him [Pachacamac] for the favour he had bestowed'. The Inca even asked Pachacamac if there was anything else he particularly desired. The great coastal divinity replied that since he had a 'wife and children', the Inca should build him a house. Topa Inca promptly had a 'large and sumptuous' house for the *huaca* constructed. But the gifting in the interests of his progeny had only begun. Pachacamac also spoke of his 'four children'. They, too, would require houses, shrines. One was in the valley of Mala just to the south, another in Chincha, and there was a third in the highlands, in Andahuaylas near Cusco. A fourth child of Pachacamac was conveniently portable, and would be given to Topa Inca for his safekeeping, and so that he could 'receive responses to that for which he asked'.[19]

Santillán's story merits both caution and close attention, and not only because of Christian understandings of what 'creation' meant and entailed. Notably, privilege is granted an Inca point of view, and to the origin of relatively recent Inca constructions at a cultic centre that was over half a millennium old. Thanks to Santillán's aims and the bias of his informants, one is being treated to an explanatory narrative of political and religious incorporation in the interest of Inca overlordship. Yet scholars from a variety of disciplines have recently added valuably different perspectives which suggest that this kind of action was

18 See Julien in *Die Inka*, esp. pp. 64–5.
19 Santillán, 'Relación', p. 111; Rostworowski, *Pachacamac*; Patterson, 'Pachacamac'.

representative of how the Incas proceeded in expansion, at least attempting to adopt the services of certain *huacas* in accordance with their need for effective regional influence, oracular advice in war, and an increasingly complex imperial governance.[20] Moreover, there is a muted but simultaneous demonstration here of the corresponding benefits of Inca sponsorship for divine beings such as Pachacamac: alliance and support was the surest way to ensure that Pachacamac himself might survive and spread across the land. Later Spanish observers consistently referred to the great *huaca*'s new expressions of himself as 'children', a description in accordance with the wider cluster of intimate and familial terms applied to related groups of regional *huacas* and other divinities by interpreters and notaries who recorded Quechua-speaking Indian testimonies before inspectors of 'error' in the seventeenth- and eighteenth-century rural parishes of the archdiocese of Lima.[21] In Pachacamac's case, one such expression needed no fixed location and was to be carried about by the travelling Inca, evoking its divine centre, and ready to be consulted if the ruler should require a response.

The story invites us to contemplate further just how Andean *huacas* related to one another. Evidence of Pachacamac's proliferous quality beyond his regional landscape and original pilgrimage site had struck and clearly troubled Hernando de Santillán and prompted a bit of extended analysis for the benefit of his courtly readers back in Spain. His commentary is important enough for our purposes to merit quotation in full. 'The Devil, who speaks through them [the *huacas*], makes them believe that they [the *huacas*] have children', Santillán explained. 'And thus', he continued,

> they [native Andeans] built new houses for them, conceived of new forms of worship to the *huacas* from whom they believed themselves descended, and understood them all to be gods. Some they worshipped as men, others as women, and they assigned devotions to each one according to a kind of need: they went to some in order to make it rain, to others so that their crops would grow and mature, and to [still] others to ensure that women could become pregnant; and so it went for all other things. What happened with so much multiplication is that soon almost every thing had its *huaca*. And through the *huacas* the Devil had them [the Indians] so thoroughly deceived that herein lies the chief obstacle in that land to lodging the faith firmly among native peoples . . . to make them understand the deception and vanity of it all [reverence for these *huacas*].[22]

20 Patterson, 'Pachacamac'; Gose, 'Oracles'; Topic *et al.*, 'Catequil'.
21 On the latter see Mills, *Idolatry*, esp. chs. 2 and 3.
22 Santillán, 'Relación', pp. 111–12.

Santillán's mixing strands of firm opinion, curiosity, and evident preoccupation in the first decades after the conquest can be detected in many interpretations of Andean sacred phenomena. Indeed, the Dominicans' earlier discovery about the Yungas' shifting loyalties between *huacas* represented only the beginning of the problem from the point of view of the most attentive Catholic Christian purveyors. Individual *huacas* had the ability to enjoy multiple selves, to propagate beyond original territories, take over new specializations, and win local loyalties by making themselves differently indispensable.

Conquest and efforts at evangelization seemed not to extinguish but perhaps even to quicken these capacities for multiplication. Santillán himself noted the findings of his contemporary and fellow lawyer Polo de Ondegardo, who claimed in 1561 to know of more than 400 temples (*adoratorios*) within one and a half leagues of Cusco at which offerings to *huacas* were actively being made.[23] Closer to the ground of an emerging early colonial local religiosity than either of our enquiring and well-informed lawyers was the first set of Augustinian friars stationed in Huamachuco in the northern Andes in the 1550s. While they faced and attempted to destroy a number of provincial *huacas* in what had clearly been a bustling pre-Hispanic religious landscape, they found themselves particularly embedded within the realm of a powerful divinity named Catequil.

As with Pachacamac on the central coast, the oracular fame of Catequil had been fanned by close association with the Inca dynasty and, in his case, with the Inca Huayna Capac. Despite the fact that this Inca's son, Atahuallpa, had turned against this *huaca* after unfavourable news and attempted his destruction, Catequil's essence in a large hill and high rocky cliffs had proven impossible to extinguish. Yet because the 'children' or new expressions of Catequil had already begun to spread, the *huaca* enjoyed a great number of ways to endure. Sometimes he moved with resettling peoples and as part of the resettlements tied to Inca political policies.[24] What is more, the pattern of cultic diffusion appears only to have expanded as more and more of Catequil's children – chips off the old block, tangible 'pieces' of the divinity in the wake of the physical assault upon his physical abode by the Inca Atahuallpa – were spread by other mobilizing devotees. A perplexed Fray Juan de San Pedro, writing on behalf of the divinity's newest enemies, the Augustinians, claims to have discovered some 300 of Catequil's 'sons' arrayed through various towns and smaller settlements in the region. Most were particularly beautiful stones that seemed easy enough to confiscate and grind into dust, but there was the

23 *Ibid.*, p. 112 and n. 1.   24 Topic *et al.*, 'Catequil', p. 326.

story of the *huaca's* apparent disregard for his own physical destruction to consider. Catequil seemed to be everywhere at once; San Pedro believed that this multiplication of 'idols' only continued 'after the arrival of the Spaniards in the land'.[25]

The words of these post-Pizarran commentators acknowledged in one way or another that *huacas'* cults were various and overlapping, unlikely to cancel each other out completely even if one or another cult's rise to prominence was promoted and secured. Further, while one divine being might remain rooted in a precise physical landscape and connected to a certain association and responsibility (often as a founding ancestor), others developed multiple roles and personalities that allowed them to transcend local beginnings and associations. In the celebrated cases of Pachacamac and Catequil, there is high spiritual and political intrigue to factor in. An already considerable translocal significance and power was something that might be augmented through association with members of the Inca line. And even when such relationships went sour, as in the case of Catequil, patterns of transformation and proliferation secured survival of the form. Not only Pachacamac's renown, but his children, too, were flourishing far afield.

In these matters, as in many others, pre-Hispanic continuities recombine with post-conquest realities. Nowhere is this more evident than in the ways in which Spanish Christian expressions of concern and alarm about the *huacas* were often accompanied by attributions of diabolic authorship, as seen in Santillán's account. These diabolic attributions signal broader religious transformations, as I shall endeavour to show further below. But, for the moment, let us see the attribution in action.

More than a decade after Santillán wrote about his findings, the Jesuit José de Acosta claimed to have received a priest's report from Chuquisaca (today Sucre, Bolivia) in the south-central Andes about a *huaca* named Tangatanga. That region's Indians purportedly believed that their *huaca* represented three divine identities in one and one in three, like the Christian Holy Trinity. 'When the priest shared his astonishment at this', Acosta wrote,

> I believe I told him that the Devil always stole as much as he could from the Truth to fuel his lies and deceits, and that he did so with that infernal and obstinate pride with which he always yearns to be like God.[26]

Here is perhaps the neatest, most straightforward expression and enduring answer to the problem of *huaca* multiplicity: the devil as unseen author of

25 San Pedro, *La persecución*, pp. 179–80.   26 *Historia*, bk. 5, ch. 28, p. 268.

myriad errors and deceptions, insinuating himself within an Andean divine being, and through this false god misguiding native converts into believing there were certain convergences between Catholic Christian and native Andean religious traditions.

But it did not end here. On account of the wide diffusion of Acosta's writings, the story of 'Tangatanga' turned up in subsequent discussions of religious matters in colonial Peru. Writing in the early seventeenth century, the Mestizo humanist El Inca Garcilaso de la Vega went to considerable trouble to point out the fragility of the evidence upon which Acosta had relied. But what stands out even more is Garcilaso's contention that the understanding of an Andean divinity filtered by Acosta, in fact, represented an invention of the Indians of Chuquisaca in colonial times, something 'constructed after they had learned of the Trinity and of the unity of Our Lord God'.[27] Garcilaso enters the fray both sceptical of what Acosta actually learned without an understanding of indigenous languages, and disapproving of what may have been a blatant effort by the Indians of the Chuquisaca to impress Spaniards and gain from the supposed resemblance between the poly-selved *huaca* Tangatanga and the Trinity. We cannot know for certain that 'Tangatanga' existed, or existed in quite the way he was described. But other *huacas*, for whom evidence is more certain, clearly did. In the mid-seventeenth-century village of Acas, Cajatambo, for instance, the regional *huaca* Vicho Rinri was linked ritually by his people to their image and festival of St Peter.[28] In this sense, El Inca Garcilaso would seem to have been a few steps behind the unfolding story of Andean religious change he himself uncovered in suggesting that colonial 'inventions' and fusions were commonplace among Indian peoples. What happens if we question the assumption about the Indians' conscious cunning upon which his explanation relies?

Seeing the devil in a colonial present

This exploration of the emerging significance of beliefs and practices surrounding *huacas* in colonial times pushes beyond contemplation of a surviving fixity of ideas about them, and beyond the physical survival of their forms. Evidence bearing upon the colonial Andean religious imagination requires that we especially ponder the divine personalities who appeared and continued to hear people, and communicate with them. A number of Spanish

---

27 Garcilaso de la Vega, *Comentarios*, bk. 2, ch. 5, pp. 54–5.
28 Mills, *An evil*; also 'Limits'.

churchmen who were commissioned as inspectors of indigenous 'idolatry' in the seventeenth- and early eighteenth-century archdiocese of Lima claimed to have found precisely what an earlier Santillán or Acosta would have guessed they would find: the latest, elastic deceptions of the devil among a vulnerable because credulous new laity. Of course, in making the *huaca*–devil association as automatically as some of them did, the mid-colonial inspectors of idolatry only amplified a message that had long been central to official Christianity's attempt to convince Indians of the evil of their ways and the guile of their deceiver. Diabolic explanations for the *huaca* complex of beliefs and practices in pre-Hispanic and emerging colonial Andean religious life had, for generations, been broadcast in Quechua in schools for the sons of regional nobles, during confession, and from the pulpits in small adobe churches. Christianization had embraced demonization within it.

An evangelizer's insistence upon the perceived connection between a *huaca* and the devil in the mid-colonial Lima region was meant to frighten people. Both Francisco de Avila's and Hernando de Avendaño's mid-seventeenth-century cycles of sermons in Quechua and Spanish conjured word-pictures of the unforgettable enemies of humankind, diabolic deceivers who could assume any form. With graphic imagery and through fear, evangelizers sought to nip 'idolatry' – both surviving Andean traditions and rogue interpretations of Christian elements – in the bud. But it proved difficult to maintain, much less control, fear and such awakening connections. The unintended effects of preaching emerged, among them fruits of an explicit connection between the devil and the native Andean *huacas*, and of theatrically coercive attempts to demonstrate the powerlessness of devil-*huacas* to defend themselves and, by extension, to answer the entreaties of anyone in need. With the stakes raised by the challenges to their relevance and efficacy, the *huaca*-devils of the mid-colonial era began to respond. They began, quite literally, to 'appear' to their people.

There are chilling accounts of indigenous peoples' nightmare visions and apparent inner torment at the prospect of what Spanish and Hispanicizing authors called their 'conversions'. Some of these apparition-visions fell conveniently into step with Catholic Christian edifying genres, culminating in death-bed scenes such as the one endured famously by Cristóbal Choque Casa of Huarochirí.[29] But a good number of Indians' testimonies before seventeenth-century inspectors of 'error' in the central Andes were less tailored for

---

29 See *The Huarochirí manuscript*, chs. 20 and 21, and Salomon, 'Nightmare'. More in Redden's 'Satan's fortress' and 'The Sun God'; and in Mills, *Idolatry*, esp. ch. 7 and 'A very subtle'.

consumption. In 1650, one professed Andean Christian, Juana Ycha of Poma-cocha in the mountain province of Canta, told in detail of the frequent appari-tions of an Andean 'demon' Apo Parato; he came to her 'as a whirlwind with much noise', dressed in an Indian's cloak, demanding a customary meal, spout-ing heretical Christian teachings, and summoning the woman to leave with him for the high sierra, 'above Cajapalca [a village nearby] to a great hill, the one with the lake called Cochayoc on top'.[30] Testimonies such as Juana Ycha's featured apparitions by culturally ambiguous beings whom Andrew Redden has aptly called 'Devils of the in-between'.[31] These apparitions and their messages engaged directly with people's current beliefs, hopes and fears, prompting what some Spanish investigators were quick to identify as Indians' 'pacts' with the devil.

The rise of these frequently reported religious phenomena in the Andes speaks volumes about the unintended processes of transformation we are investigating. These 'devils' reflected the intercultural realities of many native Andean peoples. Their very existence, their names, features, purported words and actions, picked up the pieces of an assaulted, often tattered, but still adaptive vocabulary and language of the *huacas*. These are 'devils' whose labels ulti-mately ought to concern us less than their multiform apparitions and broader significance ought to open our minds to an analytical space in which the ori-gins of a given religious or cultural form have become less important than its emergence and fruition in the local and often personal terms of indigenous peoples.

In a path-breaking article published in 1992, Monica Barnes examined what we might call the afterlives of key proselytizing texts authorized and dis-tributed after 1584-5 by decree of the Third Provincial Council of Lima. She contended that such texts operated as 'distorting mirrors' which reflected, as she put it, 'warped images of Andean life back to the people themselves'.[32] For our purposes, Barnes's sense of what was being 'warped' through the multi-headed processes of evangelization and response might profitably swell to include ideas and aspects of Catholic Christianity. Indeed, a significant part of what the devil and demonic signs represented in emerging local religious realities in the colonial Andes is fruitfully explored beneath the broader rubric of self-Christianization. That is to say that the presence, mobility, and wild omnipresence of 'diabolic' *huaca* forms and features are intimately related to the trajectories of other Catholic Christian ideas and practices, all of them the

---

30 Mills, *Idolatry*, ch. 7, esp. pp. 228–42.   31 Redden, 'The Sun God'.
32 'Catechisms', p. 67.

developing by-products of evangelization, response, and fruition. The devil was an originally Spanish Christian idea which – through insistent and some-times violent teachings, steady persistence of association, and gradual pro-cesses of selective appropriation and reinvention – had been internalized and transformed by Indians, and which had lodged within a transforming *huaca* complex. That the reconfigured devils seem to have appealed especially when men and women were threatened, vulnerable, and marginalized, should not surprise.[33]

Promoting sacred images, surmounting problems

'Devils' were taken in and reconfigured by native Andeans in ways that mirrored their acceptance of the saints. Disagreement flourished among early and mid-colonial churchmen on how best to Christianize native Andeans, but the careful proliferation of the saints seemed to some clerical onlookers the best solution to the continuing riddle of sparking and maintaining an Indian Christianity. Saints' images and the regular rhythms of paraliturgical devotion that surrounded them offered a motor of change and antidotes to error with established track records in the evangelization settings of the deeper Christian past. Accordingly, a colourful and changing cast of saintly personalities were, over generations, presented to Indians didactically through images, doctri-nal instructions, and sermons. In the eyes of their promoters, they were the accessible examples of appropriate Christian behaviour and the ready advo-cates in the celestial court of the Christian God. As we have seen, older and newer terminologies merged, unevenly and imperfectly, depending on local circumstances, and of course not only in the Andes.[34]

A great variety of commentators reassured themselves and their readers that the flourishing Indian devotion to holy images had been won entirely at the expense of loyalties to local and regional *huacas* and the devil. In the first few decades of the seventeenth century, the Seville-born poet Diego Dávalos y Figueroa, for instance, joined the far better-known Augustinian voices of Alonso Ramos Gavilán and Antonio de la Calancha in trumpeting

---

33 Redden, 'The Sun God'; also Cervantes, *The devil*, esp. chs. 1, 2.
34 Esp. Dedenbach-Salazar Sáenz, 'La terminología', transcending Borges, *Métodos* (esp. pp. 521–5) and Marzal in *La transformación* (esp. pp. 57–63). Note Durston, 'El *Aptay-cachana*'. On Francisco de Avila's preaching on the example of saints in matters of sexual abstinence, *Tratado*, fols. 45–53; translation in Mills *et al.* (eds.), *Colonial Latin Amer-ica*, selection 35. Another view is presented in Cussen, 'The Search'; On New Spain, Burkhart, *The slippery*, esp. pp. 187–90, *passim*, also *Holy Wednesday*, and *Before Guadalupe*, also Duverger, *La conversion*, pp. 150–2, *passim*.

the accomplishment of a transition from ancient sacrality in meaningful environs such as Lake Titicaca and Pachacamac.[35] The keys to the transition, for all, were newly rooted, miraculous images of the Virgin Mary. Here was a divine positioning, Calancha assured his readers, simultaneously joining his Augustinian order to the miraculous origins and spiritual jurisdictions of three of the most powerful Marian images in the land. The Virgin of Guadalupe in the north coastal valley of Pacasmayo, the Virgin of Copacabana in Chucuito, and the Virgin of Pucarani (towards La Paz), had been spread out just so, 'to bless [beatificar] the different territories in which they are venerated, and so as not to tire travellers and pilgrims when they go in search of them'.[36] In the telling, each of these advocations of Mary looked out especially for native Andean devotees, appearing most powerfully and often to them and favouring the Indians with God's miracles.

Such authors saw something happening, even if the miraculous cleansings of a pre-Hispanic landscape and the neat, saintly substitutions they theorized seemed to twist conveniently away from deeper consideration of experiences and meanings for native Andean recipients of God's favours in Andean places. Certainly Calancha and Ramos Gavilán, and to a limited extent even Dávalos y Figueroa, would have been aware that native Andean devotees had once moved across these same vast territories according to earlier divine markers and divisions. Yet they muted the issue, artfully covering it in feats of exegesis and multiple Virgins' skirts. Not everyone packaged and published their findings as expertly as the Augustinians and their sympathizers were doing.

Consider the representations left by the Jesuit provincial P. Rodrigo de Cabredo in 1600 as he described in a letter to his Father General the work of *padres* from the Jesuit college at Cusco in towns and villages in the region of Huamanga (modern Ayacucho). In one such place (most probably San Francisco de Atunrucana), in 1599, the Jesuits had began to build a new church to replace one struck by lightning and burnt to the ground. In the presence of a great assembly of people, including the regional native lord, sacred images of the town's patron San Francisco and the Baby Jesus were enshrined and a sermon was offered in thanks that the local people had been freed from their blindness and the clutches of the devil. 'One of the principal fruits of this mission', insisted the summarizing Cabredo from his perch in Lima,

---

35 Dávalos y Figueroa, *Miscelánea austral*, esp. fols. 139v–142r; Ramos Gavilán, *Historia*; Calancha, *Corónica moralizada*.
36 *Corónica moralizada*, vol. 4, bk. 3, ch. 14, p. 1362.

was teaching the Indians about the veneration [*adoración*] of images, telling them [first] not to worship [*adorar*] them as Indians do their *huacas*, and [second] that Christians do not think that virtue and divinity resides in them [the images] themselves but, rather, look to what they represent. . .

He could hardly have been more true to the Tridentine decree which in 1563 had affirmed and defended the veneration of sacred images and relics among believers and against all critics. Yet there was something more particular at issue that day than church construction and the clarification of Catholic orthodoxy in a Reformation world. Instructing the Indians in the proper veneration of images of the saints 'is of the utmost importance', Cabredo noted, 'because a bad Christian with little fear of God had sowed a very pernicious and scandalous doctrine in this *pueblo*, saying many things against the honour and reverence that the images deserve'. Cabredo employs his provincial's distance from the actual evangelizing setting at this juncture. His emphasis falls on what he might just be able to control: the process of instruction that Jesuit *padres* would need to begin in order 'to remedy the poison the Devil had sown through his minister.'[37]

The Jesuit retrospective of events in Huamanga in 1599 is easy enough to discern: a singular corrupter is blamed and soon put on the run. A church is reconstructed, images are re-enshrined, preaching on the proper invocation and veneration of sacred images is intensified. A slip is averted; everything is put back up again, in more ways than one. Yet the silences are deafening. Even if a single person such as the Jesuit's wandering 'bad Christian' did exist, the reader's mind wanders away from the correspondent Cabredo's smooth constructs, and towards the still-exposed and rougher edges. What about the far more numerous Indian audience for the purported rogue's alleged teachings, the native Andean people about whom the Jesuits are so obviously concerned? Is it not the Indians' hearts and minds as fertile soil for heterodox ideas about sacred images and their veneration that is really at issue here?

Nascent Christianities which developed and embraced localization and deviation have often disappeared beneath blanket terms such as 'error' and 'idolatry', and with them can go the vital and creative hearts of colonial Andean religious culture. It is almost as if heterodoxy happened to Indians,

---

37 'Carta anua de la provincia del Perú del año de 1599', doc. 6, 73–6. 'On invocation, veneration and relics of the saints, and on sacred images', Council of Trent, Session 25 (3–4 December 1563) in Tanner (ed.), *Decrees*, vol. 2, pp. 774–6.

like an arriving foreign governor, a natural disaster, or an epidemic. Acculturation and destructuration have proven powerful twin interpretations of what happened.[38] It has long been apparent that the era of intensified indigenous labour exaction and resettlement of native Andean kin groups into nucleated towns and villages ushered in by the Viceroy of Peru Francisco de Toledo in the early 1570s wrought brutal and destructive changes in the Andes. Less apparent have been the many things that Indians and non-Indians began to construct in these times, and, even more so, in the decades to follow. Some of the creativity, of course, was the stern stuff of utter desperation, survival, and making do. But this was a historical moment of surprises, too. A time when native Andean women displaced with mine-working husbands to parishes on the slopes of the Rich Mountain of Potosí entered and controlled an entire multi-ethnic network of petty commerce and credit in the largest city of the New World.[39] This was the era when local church construction, sponsored by native Andean elites as much as by Spanish and Creole churchmen in head-towns and their remote annexes, began to flourish. And it was when sacred images and their apparitions started to become – as the historical anthropologist Thomas Abercrombie discovered to his initial surprise in Santa Bárbara de Culta, in what is today Bolivia – defining features of local Andean memory and self-understanding.[40] Even as large numbers of the resettled Andean communities failed in the wake of depopulation, late sixteenth-century epidemics, abandonment on account of excessive tribute exactions, exploitative native lords, and Spanish and Mestizo interlopers, key transformations began and persisted around naturalizing Catholic Christian forms.

Within and around the local churches, lay religious associations, the *cofradías*, became principal rallying points both for groups of indigenous people whose corporate identities had survived the transition of extended-kin-based *ayllu* networks and for those who had gathered together in the new places because of work regimes, need, and opportunity. New religious allegiances were sometimes coaxed directly out of older ones, as in the cases in which lay associations of Indians took over the herds and lands once dedicated to a kin group's ancestors and regional divinities, the *huacas* and *mallquis*. At baptism, native individuals, like their new towns, took on favoured or patronal saints' names in ways that people had formerly associated themselves with pre-Hispanic beings.

38 Wachtel, *La vision des vaincus*.   39 Mangan, *Trading roles*.
40 *Pathways*, passim.

Yet if the rise of an image-centred, confraternity Christianity was encouraged by a convergence with Andean forms of ascription and social organization such as the *ayllu*,[41] it becomes just as important to examine critically a static interpretation of the colonial *cofradía* that sees in it only or primarily an opportunity for indigenous clandestinity – in Rafael Varón's words, 'a setting for disguised pre-Hispanic beliefs'.[42] *Cofradías* and their images facilitated new kinds of belonging especially for displaced individuals and kin groups in parts of the colonial world where older kinship ties had fragmented or were threatened, or where resettlements and work regimes kept individuals and families far from their home territories for generations. A parish-based town and, within it, a *cofradía*, often became more than an imposed institution and structure. They offered new indigenous spaces in which members might also come together, practically and imaginatively, for the good of each other and of themselves. In the process, Indians themselves steadily reinforced saints' cults as authentically Andean forms.

It bears remembering that these indigenous Christian spaces were not uniformly encouraged by Spanish Christian officials. Indeed, Indian *cofradías* around sacred images had multiplied in such numbers by the late sixteenth century that many churchmen worried openly about their lack of supervision and about the kinds of devotion they fostered within. Prelates from the time of the Third Provincial Council of Lima (1582–3) reflected the rise in concern, actively discouraging new foundations of confraternities among Indians.[43] Yet, the fact that the late sixteenth-century's official discouragement of Indian lay associations was neither shared nor honoured by large numbers of churchmen, let alone by indigenous *cofrades*, needs also to be emphasized. Proponents of the images and institutions argued from local vantage points that here, around the saints' images and in the *cofradía*, was Indian Christianity – precisely the popular, flourishing results they had been charged to bring into being and nurture.

The frustration on this point registered in Potosí in 1600 by a Jeronymite alms-collector and orchestrator of Marian devotion named Diego de Ocaña was shared by a number of his contemporaries. Ocaña railed, first, against

---

41 Celestino and Meyers, *Las cofradías*; Garland Ponce, 'Las cofradías'; Varón, 'Cofradías de indios'.

42 'Cofradías de indios', p. 133. Varón's study encompassed seventeenth-century *reducción* of Huaylas. The idea of an autochthonous religion enduring beneath the cover of the external forms of the Catholic Christian cult was conceptualized influentially by Mariátegui in the 1920s, *Siete ensayos*, p. 173.

43 Vargas Ugarte, *Concilios Limenses*, vol. 1, p. 360, Tercera acción, cap. 44, De las cofradías; see also Saignes, 'The colonial condition'.

the shortage of cheap printed images of the Virgin of Guadalupe from Extremadura, *estampas* he wished to distribute to the faithful in exchange for alms. Prospective Indian devotees – whose alms, Ocaña noted with calculated venom, easily surpassed those given by Potosí's wealthier Spanish citizens – had quickly depleted his authorized supply. He complained, second, about the official opposition he met in attempting to found an Indian *cofradía* in the venerable Guadalupan Mary's name in Potosí.[44] Ocaña's solution was to paint a portrait image of Guadalupe's sculpted original, an image that would appeal especially to Potosí's native Andean majority. Ocaña enshrined the image in a chapel most likely to secure its future, orchestrated local devotions, and an alms-collection scheme with similarly bright prospects, and, finally, set to recording a surge of popular devotion in Potosí, crowned by miracles through which God showed his distinct favouritism not only for the Jeronymite promoter's populism, but more particularly for the Indian mine-workers and their families.[45]

The journey of particular saints into native Andean imaginations and local settings involved a multitude of non-Indian sparks and promoters such as Diego de Ocaña, people whose sensuous and participatory brands of Catholic Christianity defied ecclesiastical concerns about just what was best advised among indigenous American peoples. Just when (from an official standpoint) they should not have done, late sixteenth- and early seventeenth-century Jesuits also reported vibrant *cofradías* of Indians around images of Christ and the saints in their churches across the Andes. Even though we must negotiate the seemingly requisite dollops of Jesuit self-congratulation and self-defence in these reports, there is more than calculated self-puffery here. The Jesuit provincial Rodrigo de Cabredo's claim that the principal Jesuit-sponsored confraternity of Indians in Potosí consisted of 'more than 1,000 Indian men and women' in 1602 is corroborated by contemporary observers. One of these, who was not inclined to admire Jesuit approaches and achievements in Potosí or anywhere, was the Jeronymite Ocaña. Undoubtedly thinking about his own goals in the populous mining centre, he confirmed the impressiveness of the Jesuit lay association, noting the religious leadership shown by wealthy Indian women, as well as these pious women's exemplary care for their image of the Baby Jesus in the Jesuit church.[46]

---

44 Ocaña, fol. 159r–159v; Mills, 'Diego de Ocaña's hagiography'.
45 See Mills, 'Diego de Ocaña's hagiography'.
46 Archivum Romanum Societatis Iesu, Peru 12, tomo 1, Lima, 28 April 1603, 'Carta anua de la provincia del Perú del año de 1602'. A published transcription in *Monumenta Peruana* VIII (1603–4), ed. Fernández (Rome, 1986), Doc. 82: 231–3; Ocaña, fol. 181r.

What is appearing?

'Problems' involving indigenous people and sacred images only mounted in official Christian thoughts, actions, and explanations through this period. Among the challenges which the Archbishop of Lima and the official initiator of a concerted campaign to eradicate idolatry in his jurisdiction, Bartolomé Lobo Guerrero, and other Peruvian prelates identified in their synod of 1613 was the need to chase down and remove unauthorized sacred images from Indian parishes.[47] It seemed similarly clear to Lobo Guerrero's contemporary and extirpating ally, the Jesuit Pablo José de Arriaga, that in some parishes saints' images represented as much, if not more, of a problem as any surviving *huaca*. So-called extirpators of 'idolatry' were reining in saints' images and monitoring what Andean parishioners were doing in their lay religious associations. What precisely was happening inside native Andeans' hearts and minds? For the churchmen who are our principal sources and filters, the answer to this question depended on how one interpreted the indigenous Christians' experience of apparitions, visions, and related spiritual phenomena. Were they, optimistically, the stuttering but no less miraculous starts of God's unfolding plan for the Americas? Or more of the devil's dark and disfiguring work?

The early seventeenth-century Augustinian chroniclers in the southern Andes, Alonso Ramos Gavilán and Antonio de la Calancha, noted above, were particularly assiduous reporters of prodigious happenings – apparitions, miracles, and miracle-working – among native peoples.[48] Contemporary Jesuits, too, transmitted scores of such reports in regular correspondence back to Rome and, effectively in some cases, to their brethren in Jesuit colleges across the world. Because the Augustinians' approaches to this difficult and contentious bounty are better traversed by scholars and more accessible to students of their published chronicles,[49] I will draw here from the archival evidence of the Jesuits.

At the turn of the seventeenth century, Padre Pedro Vicente Pizuto, who had worked for years among the Lupaqa peoples at Juli on the shores of Lake Titicaca, was struck by the fervent devotion he found upon his early seventeenth-century transfer to Potosí. In taking over supervision of the

---

47 Lobo Guerrero, *Constituciones synodales*, fol. 77r.
48 Calancha, *Crónica moralizada* [1638], esp. vol. 1, pp. 24–38, and vol. 5, pp. 2005, 2010–2011, 2015–2107. On the 132 miracle narratives gathered by Alonso Ramos Gavilán in his *Historia*, see Salles-Reese, *From Viracocha to the Virgin*, esp. pp. 159–63, and MacCormack, 'From the sun of the Incas'.
49 Salles-Reese, *From Viracocha*; MacCormack, 'Antonio de la Calancha' and 'From the sun of the Incas'.

famously burgeoning *cofradía de indios* of San Salvador in the Jesuit church, Pizuto wrote immediately to his provincial Rodrigo de Cabredo in Lima to tell of the remarkable things he was seeing and hearing about. Among the information selected and relayed by the synthesizing Cabredo to Rome in 1603 was Pizuto's report of the experience of a native woman who abandoned her sinful life after an apparition of the Christ Child. The baby Jesus had appeared to her in a vision during a moment of danger, with a stern expression on his face and a lance in hand – a perfect copy of the sacred image before which Indian *cofrades* prayed in Potosí's Jesuit church. With the sacred image and the personal vision etched in her mind, and the woman's life miraculously spared in this way, she was said to have reformed her ways.[50]

Another Indian woman in the Cusco region in the 1640s told Jesuits of how she, a companion and their llama were walking home from their fields one day only to be gathered off a hillside by a furious wind and transported to a mountain top. There, according to the Jesuit correspondent, the devil appeared to the bewildered party as a pretender, in the beautiful form (*figura*) of the Virgin Mary, seated on a resplendent throne of lights. The fiend even managed to feign a sweet voice as he explained to the Indian woman that she had been chosen as the redeemer of her *pueblo*. She would from this day forward become the possessor of great powers, the worker of great marvels, all of which she would derive from her devotion to an image of the Virgin Mary. Just then, the woman said that the apparitional figure had given her 'a little idol or small image' with which, the Jesuit claimed, the woman still communicated constantly. The figure which the Jesuit insisted had been the Devil-as-Mary then sent the woman, her friend and the animal on their way. Word of the happening, of the gifted image, and of the Indian woman's fast-proven powers soon spread, the Jesuit stressed, and 'in the town, all the people recount what happened'.[51]

The Jesuit ambivalence which surfaces in this pair of stories about apparitions and miracles among Indians is common, and thus important to consider before one peers beneath and around the needful tellings. On the one hand, just like Padre Pizuto among the Indian women of the *cofradía* in Potosí – or Alonso Ramos Gavilán chronicling the miraculous power of his order's

---

50 Archivum Romanum Societatis Iesu, Peru 12, tomo 1. Carta anua de la provincia del Perú del año de 1602. Lima, 28 April, 1603, fol. 274r–274v.
51 Archivum Romanum Societatis Iesu, Peru 15, tomo 4, Carta anua de la provincia del Perú de los años de 1641, 1642 y 1643, fol. 182r–182v. Note Serge Gruzinski's attention to the figures of Gregorio Juan, Juan Coatl, and Antonio Pérez, colonial wonder-workers in New Spain: *Man-Gods in the Mexican highlands.*

beloved image at Copacabana, for that matter – evangelizers can be trusted to promote and edify if humanly possible. They often awaken genuine signs of God's favour and deserving Indian faithful in their evangelization settings because they must. On the other hand, they worry simultaneously and openly about all manner of Indian misinterpretation and vulnerability to diabolic deception. All that really separates a 'positive' story such as the one about the apparitional Christ Child in Potosí from the 'negative' one involving the diabolic Mary of the mountain-top near Cusco is the tip towards further details and an interpretational 'spin' in the latter case. Pizuto's story from Potosí is contained, direct and edifying, and carefully maintained as such, whether by the reporting *padre*, by an editing Cabredo, or both we cannot know. In the case of the second story such containment is wanting. As Cabredo filters and transcribes Pizuto's internal report from Cusco into his annual letter to Rome, everything seems in place for another celebration of the dramatic favour shown by the Virgin Mary through a wondrous vision to a pious Indian woman.

But the details are allowed to intrude. The story swells, worryingly both in popular Christian and in deep Andean directions. It had long been surmised in these Jesuits' learned and popular traditions that apparitions were far more likely to be diabolic and misguiding – if not feigned and evil in more human ways – than they were to be celestially sent.[52] The apparition's utterances may well have sealed the Jesuit rejection. Too much was promised to the Indian woman by her apparitional Mary – including curative and wonder-working powers of the sort that might well have been guaranteed by the devil through a *huaca*! Even Mary's seemingly surest iconographic and auditory signals of celestial beauty and glory are interpreted as the devil's traps. As twenty-first-century readers of the account, even we can feel the tipping point between an apparitional vision that might be sanctioned and championed, and one that will not. We fathom why the second story's apparitional *figura has* to be the devil. And yet the Indian woman's Andean Christian Mary hovers just as freely for us to ponder as Juana Ycha's Apo Parato (discussed above) has done. This Virgin appears to have taken advantage of the room to manoeuvre afforded by her recipient's seventeenth-century religious imagination. An uncertain but emerging Andean interculture of which she is a part is so very thinly cloaked by the Jesuit's suspicious interpretation of the evidence before him.

52 Mills, *Idolatry*, esp. pp. 212–18; MacCormack, *Religion*, esp. pp. 225–40; Elliott, 'The discovery', esp. pp. 59–60; and for broader contemporary foundations, Clark, *Thinking with demons*.

An Andean Christian interculture

The cross-cultural thinkers, promoters, and mobilizers of the colonial Andes are a diverse bunch. They include a learned Mestizo humanist who spent much of his adult life among his books and Spanish godchildren in Andalusia, a Creole extirpator of idolatry, a Franciscan preacher, a Castilian Jeronymite image-maker, a hopeful Jesuit with his eye on an urban Christian future, and a native Andean healer and ritual specialist from the Andean province of Conchucos, and many others besides. Only by considering such figures together can we begin to reach what the cult of the saints meant in the development of local Andean Christianities.

El Inca Garcilaso de la Vega may have grown short-tempered in considering the interpretative needs of colonial Indians in Chuquisaca, as noted in the above case of the supposedly triune *huaca* Tangatanga. But it did not prevent him from unleashing a brilliantly searching definition of the concept of *huaca* that ought to give us pause here. The paths it suggests into intercultural colonial understandings are far more than perhaps Garcilaso intended. At the centre of El Inca's discussion was his unabashed Inca apologetic. He insists that in spite of the confusion of an unfortunate earlier age in which Andeans had worshipped a great many 'vile objects' as if they were divinities, people in Inca times had not understood *huacas* to be gods in the sense that they would have been rivals to the notion of a single creator. Other views which generalized about the 'idolatry of the Incas', he assured his readers, were mistaken, only arising because of Spanish misunderstanding and a mounting prejudice against their increasingly homogenized subject peoples. Garcilaso was most concerned to vanquish petty rivals to the idea of a singular 'God' in the Incaic Andean context, and to renovate how anyone might think of indigenous people's spiritual capacities. What he attached to his argument and portrayal of the *huacas* is even more interesting for our purposes. He shows that the appeal of the saints as represented in holy images and miracle stories ought to have followed on naturally for native Andeans.

Garcilaso wrote of an ancient marble object in the shape of a cross, which he claims had somehow weathered the conquest and subsequent waves of worry about diabolic mimicry of Christian symbols and rituals. The pre-Hispanic marble cross hung in the sacristy of Cusco's cathedral when he left Peru as a young man in 1560, a mysteriously meaningful American relic. The kind of form that led other authors to plumb contemporary evidence and theories about feats of pre-Hispanic evangelization carried out by a wandering St Thomas or Bartholomew did not much distract our Mestizo humanist. Garcilaso saw Inca devotional restraint and more Christian pathways. He stressed that although the 'cross' had been kept by the Inca rulers in a consecrated chamber in a royal house, 'they did not worship it, but rather [had] held it in reverence'. The cross in its special place 'attracted the Indians to our holy religion through their own things', he explained, things 'which they could compare with ours'.[53]

Garcilaso was not alone in pondering the pre-contact foundations the Catholic Christian cult of saints might enjoy in Peru. Informed by indigenous testimony and his own experiences, a mid-seventeenth-century parish priest and sometime extirpator of idolatry Estanislao de Vega Bazán arrived more uncomfortably at a remarkably similar conclusion. Vega Bazán's investigations of what the surviving ancestral being Huari meant to people in the Andean province of Conchucos and Guamalíes led to the following revelation: 'Until now, it has been understood that the Indians worshipped hills', Vega Bazán asserted, but '[now] it has been discovered that they do not worship them, because offerings are made to the said Huari, and not to the hills. And they [the Indians] have idols as representations of Huari . . .'[54] While Vega Bazán believed in diabolic authorship of error, and certainly did not intend his statement about multiple 'representations' of Huari to be part of a case for the legitimacy of native Andean beliefs concerning huacas or mallquis, he has learned more than the reigning condemnations can contain. In the end, he questions a distinction between Catholic veneration of sacred images and native Andean 'idolatry' that had long been a central plank in the refutation of the native Andean religious system. And he did so at a time when official preoccupation about the meaning and roles of images (sculpted or painted) of saints, crosses, and sacred objects in Indian devotions had grown ever more acute.[55]

As someone collecting native Andean testimonies about colonial beliefs and practices, and closely involved in the scrutiny and gauging of religious change, Vega Bazán was as conditioned as his peers to see in terms of error and quandary. Yet he was simultaneously trying to understand what was in process on the mid-colonial ground of this set of rural parishes. He began partaking of common conceptions and of the unsanctioned relationships that were developing between Indian idolatry and Christian images and symbols.[56]

53 *Comentarios reales*, bk. 2, esp. ch. 3, pp. 49–50; developed over chs. 1–5, 45–55.
54 Vega Bazán, *Testimonio autentico*, fols. 3v–4r. I discuss this text in detail in Mills, '"A very subtle idolatry."'
55 'Constituciones sinodales, Lima, 1614', in Duviols (ed.), *Cultura andina y represión*, app. 1, 517. Now see Duviols *et al.*, *Procesos*.
56 On the developing communications through images, see Cummins, 'El lenguaje del arte'; Estenssoro Fuchs, *Del paganismo* and, for Mexico, esp. Taylor, 'Santiago's horse', and Gruzinski, *La Guerre*.

Vega Bazán gave concrete examples and used them to explain that native Andeans in mid-colonial times were thinking of *huacas* in terms of physical things that represented holy intercessors with God, and thus in terms of connections to larger forces and continuing sacred histories – as material things in a special place, a shrine, beings who might be visited, seen, consulted and called upon in times of general and specific need. We do well to recall that Hernando de Santillán had railed against native understandings of *huaca* cults in remarkably similar terms about a century earlier, raising the possibility that what Vega Bazán was perceiving was not necessarily *either* a colonial synthesis *or* pre-Hispanic survival, but something of *both*.

This much said, Vega Bazán had his own interpretative needs. He was principally concerned with sorting between the physical forms which Spaniards had long treated monolithically as 'idols' and the physical manifestations of the ancestral beings which native Andeans had long held in reverence. The intellectual Garcilaso had been concerned in this way, too, making appropriate distinctions, as MacCormack once put it succinctly, 'between different kinds and degrees of holiness and veneration'.[57] Although such determinations asserted Andean difference in discussing so confidently what had and had not been 'holy' in pre-Hispanic times, the evidence offers us new grounds for thinking over how 'sacrednesses' were coming together in the colonial period. In Conchucos y Guamalies we are far from Garcilaso's Córdoban study, but we are thinking of similar subjects. From the *huacas'* physical forms in the landscape, it was not much of a leap to consider the sacred narratives which gave these forms meaning. Names, narratives, sacred histories that linked to people's needs and local identities – all were things that *huacas* and saints also shared. Saints, just like the extraordinary ancestral beings of old in Peru, had stories collected, conveyed and retold and performed by special humans. I have been suggesting that we call these people not simply thinkers and actors, but also mobilizers and promoters of an Andean interculture – in the hope of giving capaciousness to who and what they were, and to what they did.

Luis Jerónimo de Oré was a Creole (a person of Spanish descent but born in the Americas) and an experienced Franciscan evangelizer who approached such matters directly. Engraved images of the Virgin Mary begin and end his missionary manual, the *Symbolo Catholico Indiano* of 1598, accompanied by words composed in Quechua to guide indigenous contemplation and songs in praise of this foremost of the saints. Mary was also a principal concern in the book itself, as Oré translated her and other selected aspects of the Roman

---

57 *Religion*, p. 337.

Catholic faith through a series of prayers and hymns expounding doctrine and mysteries for Quechua-speaking Christians. Oré is one instance of an evangelizer who made the most of a deep Andean tradition of sacred song and dance in honour and reverence of regional divine forms that, by his example, he showed to have been unthinkingly vilified rather than capitalized upon in the process of evangelization.[58] Among the many projects of his life was the preaching in Quechua he did in Potosí in 1600–1601 on behalf of the Virgin of Guadalupe from Extremadura. Oré had been recruited for the task by the peninsular Jeronymite alms-collector and orchestrator of devotions, Diego de Ocaña. Oré helped Ocaña to promote the reception of the latter's newly painted portrait copy of the Spanish Mary of Guadalupe, and to orchestrate a miraculous beginning for her cult.[59]

The so-called 'anonymous Jesuit' of the late sixteenth or early seventeenth century offers another evocative case in point.[60] In this case, we encounter again an insistence that the Quechua language and an Incan Andean religious system forged a wonderful groundwork for Catholic Christianity. The anonymous Jesuit's vision of this best-of-all-possible-worlds led directly to Christian living environments for Indians such as Santiago del Cercado, the famously enclosed resettlement on the edge of central Lima. The Cercado had seen brutal beginnings and, in the author's day, still rested contentiously in the supervisory hands of the Jesuits. Yet the anonymous Jesuit saw the place as heroic and exemplary, like others that might be hoped for, positive and even miraculous spaces in which Indian Christians could be safe and secure amid an abusive colonial world.

He held that the only mode of entry into Christianity that was actually working for native Andeans in the late sixteenth century depended upon individuals' uneven education in the faith being sustained by personal access to newly available divine forces (the saints) and, when possible, a regular experience of key sacraments. That which was working was arguably what, following Brown's formulations, we have been calling 'self-Christianization'. Certainly, in the Jesuit's opinion, native people benefited from priests fluent in the Quechua language to explain didactically with winning formulations and

---

58 Oré, *Symbolo*. On pre-Hispanic ritual dance and broader festive traditions in honour of the lively regional *huacas* Pariacaca, Chuquisuso and Chaupiñamca, as recorded in the sacred narratives of Huarochirí, see esp. Dedenbach-Salazar Sáenz, 'La comunicación con los dioses'. Also, Abercrombie, *Pathways of memory and power* examines the vilification and underestimation of native Andean song and dance in colonial times.

59 Mills, 'Diego de Ocaña's hagiography' and 'La "memoria viva"'.

60 Jesuita Anónimo, Biblioteca Nacional de España, Madrid, MS 3177; Urbano, 'Introducción'; Hyland, *The Jesuit and the Incas*.

to administer to their souls. Moreover, Indians still required good examples to excite their faith, just as his contemporary Acosta had insisted more famously. 'But when they lack someone to instruct them', the anonymous Jesuit added powerfully, 'they look for ways to pick up what is required and teach it to their children'. His further identification of Indian women and their family units as keys in the transmission and growth of Andean Christianities among an Indian laity is significant.

Like Oré, this Jesuit looked beyond the vertical and direct instrumentality of the ordained Spanish and Creole priests who could indoctrinate effectively in the Quechua (or another relevant indigenous) tongue. However much they might continue to depend on non-Indians for depth and breadth of understanding, the aftermaths of evangelizing beginnings are presented here as largely the Indians' own to resolve. What opens up as the core portions of a medium- and long-term transformation is a selective, necessarily horizontal, and less-supervised understanding of Christianization. If many Indian Christians remained vulnerable to error, in the anonymous Jesuit's view, this did not make them any less genuine additions to the fold or any less able to learn and ultimately succeed as God's own. On this matter, the Jesuit would have been well aware of purportedly miraculous events he was perhaps best advised not to discuss: that Archbishop of Lima Toribio Alfonso de Mogrovejo – then engaged in a prolonged battle with the Jesuits over spiritual jurisdictions in the Cercado – had launched ecclesiastical investigations to determine the veracity of a show of divine favour in a chapel in the neighbourhood. It was claimed that on 28 December 1591 the face of a sculpted copy of Our Lady of Copacabana had grown flushed and she and the Christ Child in her arms had shed tears and perspired, and that further miracles had been worked by God through the image.[61] The anonymous Jesuit may have shared the view of local powers in his order concerning the suspicious character of the purported original miracles, or he may not have been able to discuss the affair for political reasons. But what was clear, for him and for others, was that the moment when the pace and character of religious change would be set by God and by the Indians' own devotion, efforts and controls was already at hand in places such as the Cercado, even if further work was needed to maintain the momentum.

Near the heart of such further evangelization, in the anonymous Jesuit's opinion, should be 'historical narration and . . . personal conversations in which the saints' lives are told and matters of virtue are treated'. The emphasis upon

---

61 'Información, calificación y aprobación'.

'*conversaciones particulares*' about the saints captures this author's understanding both of the intimate and ultimately horizontal manner in which sacred images and their cults had been entering the hearts and minds of many native Andeans for some three generations, and of the way in which processes of self-Christianization would see the phenomena continue.

Lest we confine such a vision to a single Jesuit's wishful mind or to a precious few urban zones, we do well to zoom out from the streets and plazas of Lima's *Cercado*, and focus in again on developments in the rural province of Conchucos and Guamalíes. The pessimistic 'spin' that Estanislao de Vega Bazán puts on the evidence of Andean Christianities he uncovers is very different from the earlier Jesuit's realm of hope. And yet we are, by now, accustomed to reading through and around this and other kinds of spin. The two participant-tellers, in fact, come to remarkably similar conclusions. Near the end of his mid-seventeenth-century *Testimonio auténtico*, Vega Bazán introduced two native Andean religious offenders, male ritual specialists, healers and sometime ministers of the persistent *huaca* Huari. It becomes clear that these men have been the extirpator's chief informants, the fount of many of his revelations, all along. We learn from Vega Bazán that one of the men, Felipe Ramos, was regularly visited by 'the devil' for the purposes of instruction in healing and other arts. The author's renderings of Felipe Ramos's pedagogical abductions strongly resemble other contemporary descriptions of the choosing, appointment, and training of Indian 'dogmatizers' and specialist ministers often carried out through visions or dreams involving a growing complement of Andean and Christian spiritual beings, among whom, as we have seen, the devil was only one such emerging force.[62]

At night, Vega Bazán related, Felipe Ramos was in the habit of constructing altars for images of the saints and of Our Lady the Virgin. Before his makeshift constructions, he would make consultations, learning from the saints what was needed for his curing of the sick. According to Vega Bazán, Ramos would say: 'now the saints will come, and tell us what we have to do'.[63] His acts of supplication and petition before the sacred images recall what he had also revealed were his ritual invocations to the *huaca* Huari (who also had 'altars' near an ancient stone seat), sometimes identified as the devil. Viewed from the angle of our investigations in this chapter, and with Vega Bazán's own realization about emerging Indian understandings of *huacas* in mind, Ramos's raising of makeshift altars in honour of the images of Mary and other saints

---

62 Mills, *Idolatry*, esp. pp. 61–2, 221–4, 240, 226, 234; Redden, 'Satan's fortress'; Salomon, 'Nightmare victory'; Mannheim, 'A semiotic of Andean dreams'.

63 *Testimonio autentico*, fol. 4v.

comes into focus rather differently. Here, arguably, is a regional Indian holy man's expressions not only of his growing trust in Christian divine personalities, but also of his perceived need to show gratitude and beg favours before them. The fact that images of the saints and makeshift shrines were hardly alone in the fulsome sacred repertoire of Ramos and, presumably, his clients in Conchucos bothered Vega Bazán greatly – just as the answering and gifting Virgin Mary from near Cusco had so troubled the contemporary Jesuit provincial. But the state of the religiosity expressed in these mid-colonial moments captures a complex religious and cultural reality coming into being for many native Andean contemporaries. Their Christianization had been left partly, and sometimes largely, to themselves, their families and neighbours.

Back in the viceregal capital the anonymous Jesuit was, of course, serving his purpose. He kept his eye trained on what the Society of Jesus and Indians might achieve together in the urban settings he knew best such as those in Lima, Potosí, and Cusco. He remained his own brand of mobilizer, bound to filter out inconveniences in a particular way. For him, a stubborn older generation of Indians and the content of their oral traditions remained a quite singular obstacle to his vision of self-Christianizing Andean futures with saints at their centres. But for this challenge, too, he had a two-pronged and extremely Jesuitical remedy: the recruitment of Indian children and the utilization of Christian song. He recommended that children should begin 'to sing before them [the resistant elders] so that in this way they [will] forget the ancient songs'.[64]

The 'ancient songs' might stand in here for the *huacas* in general, and, in a certain sense, for the pre-Hispanic religious complex as a whole. This Jesuit's sense of his late sixteenth-century present and his glimpse into the future posit a gradual substitution of one set of meanings by another, a slow but inexorable displacement of the old by the new. Yet his acknowledgements *en route* point just as surely in other directions. He sees, first, a creative tension between deep patterns and modes of religious understanding, and, second, situations in which ritual memories are in motion through narrative expression. The acknowledgements seem far more remarkable than his hopeful prognostication. What these very different contemporary commentators, mobilizers, and promoters were turning up in the late sixteenth and seventeenth centuries merges with the evidence we have been sifting for clues from the Pizarran raids on Pachacamac in 1533 and thereafter. We are investigating what Thomas Cummins – with his eye on other, but related, visual

---

64 Jesuita Anónimo, BNM MS 3177, fols. 74, 80–1, respectively.

matters – has characterized as a 'cultural area between Catholic intention and Andean reception'.[65]

A native Andean tradition of selective horizontality, as once exercised within dynamic *huaca* hierarchies, proves elastic and enduring. In what they both had and had not reached for people, *huacas* provided paths along which some of the most supple and localizable dimensions of Catholic Christianity would flourish in the colonial Andes. Native appreciation for practical, reciprocal, horizontal relationships between people, and between people and their divinities, were easy to denigrate for early Spanish commentators upon Andean religious understandings and practices, as captured in the examples of Santillán and his informing Dominicans. Yet what they presented as the earthy practicality and inconstancy of Indians content to move between differently responsive *huacas* according to need and whims was seriously undervalued, and invites careful consideration against the breadth of what was offered – both in authorized and in highly unsanctioned ways – by the incoming religious system epitomized in the cult of the saints. As appears to have been the case with *huacas* to whom people felt connected and to whom they gave reverence, saints became repositories for a great range of hopes and fears, from the mundane request for safety while travelling away from home to the metaphysical contemplations of communal life beyond nature. William B. Taylor has written recently about the 'kinetic' character and development of devotional landscapes in colonial Mexico, and his presentation of how saints appealed to and worked for contemporaries is instructive for fathoming Andean selective horizontality. 'People were likely to be interested in more than one shrine or saint', Taylor writes, 'and felt a more intense devotion to one or another at a particular time, as the array of saints' images available in most churches suggests; and devotees may never have actually visited the shrine of a favorite image or relic'.[66] People chose and responded to and promoted divine expressions for particular reasons. In this way, a variety of officially disqualified understandings and practices around *huacas* and *mallquis* became effectively revalued in colonial times, contributing to the particular fruitions of saints' cults.

Like ambitious pre-Hispanic *huacas* who, through their ministers and often out of necessity, tied their fortunes to Inca rulers or speculated through 'children' they rooted in ever-widening locations, Christ, Mary and the other saints were long before designed to be co-opted, copied, and re-energized in new

---

65 *Toasts with the Inca*, p. 159; also elaborated in 'From lies to truth'.
66 Taylor, 'Process in place', unpublished MS.

environments. Saints from foreign and Andean places gained their own volitions and became renewed in Andean settings, as they were elsewhere across the early modern world.[67] No amount of demonization, denigration, or omission of this fact in the service of some narrowing vision of what constituted religious truth could arrest the developments of an Andean interculture, as Catholic Christian saints and their multiple 'copies' became local and personal repositories of authentically Andean beneficence and power.

67 Dean, 'The renewal', p. 174; see also her 'Familiarizando'; Taylor, *Magistrates*, ch. 11, pp. 265–300; Gruzinski, *La Guerre*.

28

Between Islam and Orthodoxy: Protestants and Catholics in south-eastern Europe

ISTVÁN GYÖRGY TÓTH

The Ottoman Empire, which in the fourteenth and fifteenth centuries had conquered one after another of the Balkan states, pushed the imperial frontier forward to the environs of Vienna. At the Battle of Mohács in 1526, the Turks defeated the Hungarian army and during the following decades the Turkish province of Hungary was established around the former royal Hungarian capital of Buda. The frontier of the Ottoman Empire – and thus of Islam – reached to the very heart of Europe. Meanwhile, in the eastern half of the medieval Kingdom of Hungary, a new state was created: the Principality of Transylvania, which existed from 1556 until 1690 as a vassal of the sultan. Nevertheless, in spite of the Ottoman conquest and following Islamization of south-eastern Europe, a large Catholic and Orthodox population lived in the Turkish provinces. In the world history of Reformation, the success of the Lutheran, Calvinist, and antitrinitarian churches in the lands of Islam, in the Ottoman Empire, represents an interesting case.

In the sixteenth century, Muslims still formed minorities in all of the European provinces of the Ottoman Empire. From Buda to Istanbul and from Sarajevo to Sofia, many Catholics were living in these territories; in Bosnia they were particularly numerous. In the Balkan territories, however, most Christians were Orthodox; since the Reformation had arisen within Rome-based Latin Christianity, Protestants were rare here. In Moldavia and Wallachia, two vassal principalities of the sultan, most people were Orthodox. However in Moldavia, Catholics and, in the sixteenth century, Protestants were also quite numerous.

The political and religious circumstances of Ottoman Hungary differed from those of all the other provinces of Ottoman Europe. While the independent kingdoms of Serbia, Bosnia, and Bulgaria had ceased to exist with the Turkish conquest, in Hungary the Turks occupied and annexed to their empire merely the middle third of the country. And even in this area the influence of the Kingdom of Hungary, a part of the Habsburg Empire, remained considerable: the counties of Habsburg Hungary levied taxes and passed judgements in an area extending several hundred kilometres into Turkish territory. In Ottoman Hungary the Catholic hierarchy of bishops remained, unlike in the Turkish Balkan territories. Thus – uniquely amongst the provinces of the Ottoman Empire – Catholic bishops living 'in exile' in Habsburg Hungary collected tithes from their congregations subjected to Turkish rule on the other side of the border. In such frontier regions, the Muslim share of the population was much smaller than it was at the heart of the Ottoman Empire or in the Balkan provinces: the 50,000–70,000 Muslims comprised just 6–8 per cent of the population of Ottoman Hungary. The settlement of Serbs – initially fleeing from the Turks and later advancing alongside them – increased the Orthodox share of the population, while the arrival, in similar waves, of Croatians added to the Catholic camp. In some parts of Ottoman Hungary – particularly the catchment areas of the Franciscan monasteries at Gyöngyös and Szeged, which continued to operate under Turkish rule – Catholic Hungarians were still numerous even in the second half of the sixteenth century, and this was also true in southern Transdanubia. Nevertheless, the great majority of Hungarians living under Turkish rule followed the Calvinist branch of the Reformation and there were many antitrinitarian villages in the area too.

The victory of Reformation

The religious composition of the population was quite different in Habsburg Hungary, Transylvania (an Ottoman vassal state), and Turkish Hungary from the Ottoman provinces in the Balkans. At the end of the sixteenth century, in the territory of medieval Hungary, Protestants formed a large majority, alongside Orthodox, Catholic, and Muslim minorities. In contemporary propaganda, the Turks were often called 'Christendom's natural enemies'. However, the Turkish conquest helped the spread of Reformation by weakening the Catholic Church as well as its main patron, royal power. Half of the Hungarian Catholic bishops were killed in the Battle of Mohács, and, during the following years, the Turks occupied most bishops' seats and many monasteries. The two simultaneously ruling kings of Hungary, Ferdinand of Habsburg (1526–64) and his Hungarian rival, John of Szapolyai (1526–40), both fervent Catholics, could not put up any effective resistance to the spread of Reformation as they were too occupied by the fight against the Ottomans and by the civil war fought between them.

These events made the progress of Reformation easier in Ottoman Hungary; however, the hopes of early reformers about the Turks helping to 'spread the gospel' quickly proved to be illusionary. Initially, Protestants often considered the Ottomans to have been sent by God to punish the papists, and nursed a variety of illusions about the Turks, hoping that under Ottoman rule Protestantism would spread freely. In 1557, the Calvinist priest Gál Huszár wrote enthusiastically to Heinrich Bullinger that in Hungary the Turks 'are so much inclined to the servants of the gospel (i.e. the Protestants) that they never disturb them. Indeed, sometimes even Turkish soldiers are present at the church services, stay up to the sermon to the Christian faithful, and leave only when the Lord's Supper begins.' In 1549, the Lutheran pastor of the town of Ozora, under Turkish occupation, wrote about his struggle against the 'papists', declaring that 'God defended us in our heavy fight with the help of the Turkish lords and governors who really favour us in the same way as the Turkish judges called Kadi also favour our religion'. However, as Protestant pastors gained more experience with the Turkish authorities, their illusions vanished.

In the 1520s and 1530s, the teaching of Martin Luther spread rapidly in Hungary, first among the German-speaking burghers of the cities, and later in all strata of society, from the great landlords to the poorest peasants. Many early reformers in Hungary came from mendicant orders, mainly from the Observant Franciscans. There were several Franciscan friars who became Protestant pastors: Mátyás Dévai Bíró (c. 1500–c. 1545), who had the greatest influence in the first generation of reformers, the priest and poet Mihály Sztárai, author of Hungarian dramas, as well as István Benczédi Székely, author of the first Hungarian world history, all belonged at one time to the Franciscan Order. Other early reformers in Hungary frequented Wittenberg University, where they became followers of Luther. Thus Imre Ozorai and Imre Farkas began to study at Wittenberg University as Catholic priests but soon became Luther's adherents. Under their influence, many Catholic parish priests in Hungary accepted the 'new faith', too; for example, the above-mentioned Gál Huszár who turned from a Catholic priest into a Protestant pastor and later founded a printing house in the service of Lutheran teachings.

From the middle of the sixteenth century, Calvinism also spread rapidly in Hungary, both under Habsburg and Ottoman rule. Many Hungarian-speaking Christians regarded the Lutheran Reformation as 'too Germanic'. The centre for Hungarian Calvinism became Debrecen in eastern Hungary, inhabited by Hungarians. This large and rich town was on the border of three countries – Habsburg Hungary, Transylvania, and Turkish Hungary – therefore here the control of state power was less strongly felt than in the middle of these states. Influenced by Péter Melius Juhász (*d.* 1572), who later became the Calvinist bishop of Debrecen, priests of this region sympathizing with Calvin's teaching joined forces with the soldiers and nobility of the nearby town of Eger. They outlined their teachings and professed their faith at a common synod of Eger-Debrecen in 1562. This was followed by the 1567 synod of Debrecen, which accepted the Second Helvetic Confession of Faith. With this, after many hesitations and doctrinal uncertainty, the young Hungarian Reformed Church joined the mainstream of European Calvinism. The new Calvinist Church gained adherents in Habsburg Hungary, in Turkish Hungary, and in Transylvania.

The Ottoman authorities did not impede the spread of Reformation in their provinces. Therefore, the first reformers had already achieved great success in the Turkish-occupied villages: the ex-Franciscan Mihály Sztárai, later Protestant pastor, claimed to be the founder of Lutheran congregations in no fewer than 120 villages in Turkish Hungary. The initial enthusiasm of the Protestant pastors for the Turks, however, soon disappeared as they realized that Turkish tolerance towards Lutherans and Calvinists was relative, and that the Turkish authorities often persecuted or harassed Protestant pastors. In 1561, the Ottomans kept the leading Calvinist pastor and church organizer, István Szegedi Kis (1505–72), in captivity for two years. In the first decades after the Turkish occupation, Turkish officials had some interest in the disputes on Protestantism and the Christian faith; at this time, even Turkish beys participated in religious disputes, often deciding themselves whether the Lutheran or Calvinist pastor was right. In 1574, after a religious dispute between Calvinist and antitrinitarian pastors at Nagyharsány, the Turks did not hesitate to hang the losing side, the antitrinitarian priest, on the pretext that he made disdainful remarks about the Qur'an.

The Ottoman Empire did not have a consistent policy towards Christian churches in its territories, therefore the actions of different vesirs and pashas often seem contradictory or confused. The fact that some pashas allowed Christians to do what others strictly prohibited often confused contemporaries. The Turks looked on with obvious satisfaction when quarrelling Protestants and Catholics appealed to their new rulers for justice. Conflicts arising between Christian priests of different denominations were often resolved by a pasha who would decide on matters of religion often unfamiliar to him. At the same time, the Turks also had an interest in provoking differences between the Catholics, Protestants, and Orthodox. Bitter rancour among the non-Muslim populations reduced the likelihood of a united Christian uprising against Turkish rule. A united stand by Christians that ignored denominational differences was a constant fear of the Turks. Events during the great wars at the end of the sixteenth and seventeenth centuries proved that this fear was not without foundation.

According to Islam, Christian teaching was stuck halfway along the true path. Thus Christians, whether Protestants or Catholics, were seen as living under the protection and leadership of Islam; however, they had to pay a substantial poll tax for this. Christians were allowed to retain their churches where they had already existed prior to Ottoman occupation, and, if necessary, could also undertake repairs. However, new churches, or churches larger than those already in existence, could not be built. Ostentatious expressions of Christian faith, processions, bell-ringing, and outdoor sermons, were also forbidden. As most Christian churches were transformed into mosques, Turkish pashas often decided that the only remaining Christian church in town should be divided by a wall to allow access to Catholics as well as Protestants, or to Calvinists and antitrinitarians, as happened in the former capital, Buda, at nearby Pest and at the Catholic bishops' one-time residence, Pécs.

As the Turkish authorities did not persecute them, the radical movements of Protestantism survived better under Ottoman than under Christian rule. The antitrinitarians were not accepted as a church in the Hungarian territory ruled by the Habsburgs, but they thrived in the Ottoman part of Hungary, especially in the southern region of Baranya around the city of Pécs, where there were several antitrinitarian communities; indeed, a large number of the inhabitants of this important town belonged to the antitrinitarian church. When, at the end of the seventeenth century, the Habsburgs liberated this region from the Turks, the antitrinitarians' peaceful existence came to an end.

Protestants and Catholics in the Ottoman provinces

Christians in northern parts of the Balkan peninsula under Turkish rule lived under very different circumstances in the various provinces.

In Istanbul, Christians lived dangerously close to the secular and religious authorities of the Turks, but at the same time enjoyed the protection of the Christian powers' ambassadors, who were living in the capital. A substantial Catholic and Protestant community resided in the sultanic capital – above all, in the Christian merchants' quarter of Galata (Pera). The Catholics in Istanbul counted on the protection of the French and Habsburg ambassadors, while Protestants were protected by the Dutch and English envoys. The assistance and mediation of the French ambassadors in local matters was even sought (in vain) by the missions to Hungary, from a distance of many hundreds of kilometres. The Catholic missions and monasteries of several religious orders provided for the Catholics living in Istanbul and its environs. All of the Catholic priests in Istanbul were members of one or another of the religious orders. There were Conventual and Observant Franciscans, Capuchins, Jesuits, and Dominicans – mostly Italians but some French, too.

Some of the Greek Mediterranean islands were under Turkish, thus Muslim, rule, whilst others belonged to Catholic Venice. Catholic missionaries were active, however, both on the Turkish-occupied islands as well as on the islands under Christian rule. Since the crusades and the Venetian conquest, a large Greek-speaking 'Latin' – that is, Catholic – population had been living on the islands, as well as many Catholic seamen, merchants, and slaves, all of whom required priests. Catholic missionaries also operated on the Venetian islands of Zante (Zakynthos), on Crete (Venetian until 1669, thereafter Turkish) and on Corfu and Cefalonia. Most of them were Conventual Franciscans, Dominicans, or Augustinians.

In Serbia, most people were Orthodox. As in earlier and later centuries, under Turkish rule too, Serbian identity and Orthodox religion were closely linked. Just like the Greek Orthodox Church of Constantinople, the Serbian Orthodox Church established far closer relations with the Turkish authorities than did Catholics. In 1557, the Patriarchate of Peć (Ipek) in Kosovo, abolished after the Turkish conquest of 1459, was restored as the centre of the Serbian Orthodox Church, as a result of the effective assistance of the Ottoman grand-vizier, Sokollu Mehmed, a man of Bosnian Serb descent who had converted to Islam. (In a similar way, after the conquest of the island in 1669, the Turks re-established the Orthodox metropolitan's office in Crete abolished by the Venetian 'Latin' rulers, much to the satisfaction of the Orthodox population.) Catholic missions in Serbia were unsuccessful, because here the Orthodox Church preserved the identity of the Serbs under Turkish rule. Serbs were loyal to the Orthodox Church and, as missionaries frequently complained to Rome, were rarely receptive to Catholic propaganda. Many Catholics lived in the southern part of Serbia, in Kosovo, however (many of them Albanian immigrants).

Catholics living in Bulgaria were few in number but played a very important role in the life of the province, owing to their geographical concentration and relative wealth. Although most people in Bulgaria, which had fallen to the Turks at the end of the fourteenth century, were Orthodox, the missions of the Franciscans arriving from Bosnia led to the establishment of several significant Catholic enclaves in the western half of the country centred on Ciprovci.

Missionaries working in the country could also count on the support of Saxon (German) and Ragusan Catholic craftsmen and merchants. The number of Catholics in Bulgaria also grew with the conversion of many Paulician heretics; members of this Near Eastern sect, named after either the Apostle Paul or a heretic leader of the same name, had been settled in Bulgaria by Byzantine emperors in the twelfth century.

The Catholic mission was more successful in Bulgaria than in Serbia. In Bulgaria there was no independent (autocephalous) Bulgarian Orthodox Church comparable with the Serbian Orthodox Church after the restoration of the Peć Patriarchate. Bulgarian Orthodox priests, who were subordinated to the Patriarch of Constantinople, were not as influential as Orthodox bishops in Serbia. The Bulgarian Catholic mission, which had begun with the arrival of Bosnian Franciscans at the end of the sixteenth century, soon consisted of Bulgarian Franciscans, many of whom had studied in Italy and thus conveyed modern ideas and knowledge to the people in their own language. For this reason, Catholic missionaries were far more popular here than in Serbia. From the mid-seventeenth century, the Bulgarian Franciscans became important missionaries in other Turkish provinces.

In Albania, which lay on the boundary between Latin and Greek Christianity, Orthodox Christians were numerous in the south while in the north there was a sizeable Catholic community. At the same time, Albanians converted to Islam in larger numbers than any of the other Balkan peoples. Indeed, many leaders of the Ottoman Empire were Islamicized Albanians, including twenty-five grand viziers and numerous pashas. Meanwhile the diocesan bishops of Albanian Catholics, who were subordinated to the archbishops of Durazzo and Antivari (Bar), lived in Venice or Ragusa rather than on Ottoman territory. Nor did the archbishops of Antivari reside at their seat, which had been under Turkish rule since 1571. Instead, they lived in Budva, an Adriatic port ruled by the Venetians. The absence of these bishops rendered the role of the Catholic missionaries in Albania a crucial one. Two Observant Franciscan provinces, that of Bosnia in the north and Rome on the other side of the Adriatic, maintained missions in Albania, and missionaries from near Ragusa were also active. Several Franciscan missionaries died as martyrs in Albania: during the war with Venice, the Turks impaled them as spies. Under Turkish rule, an increasing number of Albanian Catholics resettled in neighbouring provinces, including Kosovo, adding to the numbers of Catholics there.

Like Transylvania and the Ragusan Republic, Moldavia and Wallachia were Christian vassal states of the sultan. The princely rulers and the majority of both populations were Orthodox. In Wallachia, Catholics and Protestants numbered just a few hundred. In Moldavia, however, there was a whole series of Catholic towns and villages inhabited by Saxons (Germans) and by Hungarians who had migrated from Transylvania. In the sixteenth century, in many of these Moldavian towns and villages, priests from Transylvania spread Lutheran and Calvinist ideas. In the seventeenth century, however, a strengthened Catholic Church was able to oust supporters of the Reformation from the parishes. In this effort the Catholic Church was supported by the Moldavian princes who were fearful of Transylvanian political influence accompanying Protestantism. Thus, the remaining Latin priests were Catholic, even if many of them had wives and had little education. From the fourteenth century, many Armenians also lived in Moldavia, and they were often persecuted by the Orthodox Church. Both the Catholic and the much more powerful Orthodox Church tried to force these 'Gregorian' or monophysite Armenians into a union.

In Bulgaria, the Catholic Church was strengthened by the Catholicization of the Paulician heretics, while in Bosnia – another predominantly Orthodox province – a similar consolidation was achieved through the mass conversion to Catholicism of the Bogumil heretics. Amongst all the European territories of the Turks, it was in Bosnia that the Catholic Church and the Catholic missions were most influential. The missionaries of the Bosnian Observant Franciscan Province were the most important representatives of Western culture in the country during its rapid Islamicization after the Turkish conquest.

Friars appeared in Bosnia at the end of the thirteenth century. They were given the task of challenging the Bogumil heretic church. The pope declared the whole of the Bosnian Kingdom to be a missionary territory and appointed the Franciscans as local Inquisitors. Friars arrived in Bosnia from many different countries: English, German, Italian, and Catalan Franciscans converted the Bosnian heretics, and the famous Inquisitor St Jacob of Marche, too, worked here. During the golden age of the Order in Bosnia in the middle of the fifteenth century, Franciscan friars were living in about sixty monasteries throughout the country. Owing to the popularity of Bogumil heresy, the number of Catholic secular priests in the country was small. Therefore, in accordance with their papal privileges, the Franciscans in Bosnia worked as parish priests too.

The end of the golden age of the Bosnian Kingdom and of the Franciscan Order in Bosnia came with the country's occupation by the Ottomans, which was completed by 1463. Following the incorporation of Bosnia into the sultan's empire, local Franciscans chose to remain in the province. The Ottoman administration tolerated and even assisted Bosnian Franciscans because it needed them to keep the peace, to control the tax-paying Catholic populations, and prevent their emigration.

Transylvania: a Turkish vassal with three Protestant state churches

The religious situation in Transylvania, the sultan's Christian vassal state, developed in a particularly peculiar manner. In the sixteenth century, several branches of the Reformation were simultaneously successful in Transylvania. In this multi-ethnic country, language differences contributed to religious divisions. The Germans (Saxons) of Transylvania followed Lutheran teachings, while Hungarians inclined towards Calvinism; other, more radical, branches of the Reformation were also successful. Transylvanian Romanians were Orthodox, while many Hungarians remained Catholic – this was particularly so amongst the Hungarian-speaking Szekler frontiersmen: their province, forming a compact Catholic area in the east, was sometimes referred to as 'Transylvanian Rome'.

German-speaking Saxons in Transylvania were quickly converted to the teaching of Luther. The most important Saxon city, Brassó (Kronstadt or Brasov), was won over by Johann Honterus (1498–1549), a schoolmaster who had studied at Wittenberg. His successor, Valentinus Wagner (1510–57), was also a former student of Melanchthon at Wittenberg University. Luther's teaching was popular not only among the Saxons, but in many non-Saxon parts of Transylvania too, especially around the predominantly German-speaking Kolozsvár (Cluj). In this rich town, the reformer Kaspar Helth (c. 1500–74) preached in the spirit of Luther. Helth was himself a Saxon, but he later Hungarianized his name to Gáspár Heltai and became an important Hungarian writer, chronicler, and printer under his new name. For some time, the Hungarian Lutherans and the Saxon Lutherans had two separate bishops in Transylvania. Around 1550, however, the Calvinist Reformation arrived from eastern Hungary in Transylvania, and Hungarian Lutherans living there turned to Calvin.

The Transylvanian laws, adopted between 1548 and 1571, recognized several religions. At the outset, Catholicism was not included among them; however, this changed with the rule of the Polish king and Transylvanian prince, the Catholic Stephen Báthory (1571–76), the great patron of the Jesuits. From this time, the Transylvanian law-book recognized no fewer than four denominations – Catholic, Lutheran, Calvinist, and antitrinitarian, the latter also called 'Unitarian' – as 'accepted religions' of equal status. The Orthodox Church of Romania was not included, but it also had a broad range of rights. In multi-national Transylvania, no one denomination had the strength to declare itself the one true church that the majority should be forced to follow.

Although Catholicism was one of the four accepted religions in Transylvania, in many respects the circumstances of local Catholics were worse than those of the merely tolerated Orthodox. In Transylvania, from 1556 until the beginning of the eighteenth century – excluding one four-year period – there was no Catholic bishop, there were few parish priests, and no Catholic training of priests. The flourishing religious orders of Transylvania in the Middle Ages had ceased to exist: there was just one remaining Catholic Franciscan monastery, at Csiksomlyó in the Szekler region. In the 1660s and 1670s, Transylvania's religious and ethnic composition became even more complicated with the arrival of large numbers of Armenians from Poland and Moldavia. Their subsequent union with Rome was supported by the Armenian bishop Oxendius Verzerescul, who studied at the Rome college of the Holy Congregation for the Propagation of Faith ('Propaganda Fide'). As the seventeenth-century princes (with only two ephemeral exceptions) were all fervent Calvinists, Calvinism became a *de facto* state religion, and in Transylvania the court pastors of the princes held the Calvinist bishops' office, too.

Catholic reform in the Ottoman Empire

Following its revival at the Council of Trent, the Catholic Church took steps to provide for the spiritual needs of Catholics living in the Ottoman Empire; the ecclesiastical reform measures also applied to them. Rome attempted to help Catholics initially by dispatching apostolic, or papal, visitors, then by sending missionaries, and, finally, by appointing missionary bishops.

In 1580, Pope Gregory XIII sent two apostolic visitors to the Turkish Balkan provinces. The Catholics of Istanbul and Bulgaria were visited by Pietro Cedulini, Bishop of Nona. Assisted by the French ambassador to Istanbul, Cedulini drew up a detailed report on the Catholics in the sultanic capital. Cedulini sent one of his companions, a Greek Franciscan, to Wallachia and another, an Italian Dominican, to the Catholics of the Crimean peninsula. Meanwhile, Cedulini travelled around Bulgaria, where he found Paulician heretics and Catholic villages alongside the Orthodox majority.

The other visitor, Boniface of Ragusa, was guardian to earlier Franciscans in Jerusalem. In 1581, Boniface first visited Bosnia and its Franciscan monasteries, then travelled to Ottoman Hungary. He found here not only an 'endless number' of Protestants, but also many faithful, even though ignorant, Catholics. Boniface decided to continue his travels to Moldavia and Wallachia, but in 1582 he died in Temesvar (Timişoara), in Ottoman Hungary.

In 1584, Pope Gregory XIII appointed a further apostolic visitor, Alessandro Cumuleo (Komulović), Canon of Split, and sent him to the Ottoman Balkans. Cumuleo travelled around the southern Balkans, Serbia, Bulgaria, Wallachia, Moldovia, and Istanbul from 1584 to 1587. In 1607, commissioned by Pope Paul V, two Benedictine monks from the monastery on the island of Mljet near Ragusa, the missionaries Antonio Velislavi and Ignazio Alegretti, carried out an apostolic visitation to the southern part of Hungary under Turkish rule. Here they found many Catholics who had remained faithful to the pope in Rome but who were rather ignorant, given the lack of priests: many of them were unable even to recite the Lord's Prayer and died without baptism.

A fundamental turn in the direction of Catholic missions both worldwide and in the Ottoman Empire came when, in 1622, Pope Gregory XV founded the Holy Congregation for the Propagation of Faith, a body in charge of missions throughout the world. Prior to this, missions had been directed, according to the prevailing balance of power, either by the papal state secretary or by an influential cardinal or, later on, by the Holy Office, that is the Inquisition. From this time, one of the most influential offices of the papacy, an autonomous council of cardinals, with solid finances and qualified staff, was responsible for organizing Catholic missions in the most effective manner possible.

The next apostolic visitor to Ottoman Hungary was Pietro Massarecchi (Mazarek), an Albanian priest from Kosovo, who had been at one time the Bishop of Sofia's vicar for Serbia. Subsequently, from 1631 until his death in 1634, Massarecchi led the Catholics of Ottoman Hungary in his position as the Archbishop of Antivar (Bar) in Montenegro, and the apostolic administrator of Ottoman Hungary.

Massarecchi prepared a detailed description of all four countries listed in his instructions: Bulgaria, Serbia, Bosnia, and Hungary. However, having described in detail Bulgaria, Serbia and Bosnia, Massarecchi performed visitations only along the southern fringe of Ottoman Hungary as well as of parishes in the Belgrade area. Thus, he had only a superficial knowledge of Hungary. In subsequent years, the Holy Congregation formed its policy in the European provinces of the Ottoman Empire based on Massarecchi's apostolic visitation, and on the conclusions and proposals that he had made.

The apostolic visitation to Transylvania took place some time after the visitation to the Ottoman Balkan territories. It was only in 1635 that the first visitation to Transylvania was made by the Sicilian Conventual Franciscan missionary Francesco Leone da Modica, who had been working in Habsburg Hungary. Then, in 1638, the Bosnian Franciscan Stefano a Salina (Tuzlak), who was working as a missionary in Transylvania, drew up a detailed report about the Transylvanian Catholics. He spoke in harsh terms of the Transylvanian priests; he had found celibate priests in just 15 per cent of parishes: but Protestant teachings had 'infected' only one of the parish priests. Even though they were living with women, local Catholic priests conformed to the other rules prescribed by the Council of Trent. Another transgression was their superficial knowledge, which was hardly surprising given the absence of a Catholic seminary in Transylvania.

The reports from the apostolic visitors sent to the various Turkish provinces informed the papacy about the existence – even in the predominantly Orthodox European provinces of the Turkish sultans – of large and sometimes flourishing Catholic populations. The papacy also became aware of the need to assist these Catholics, who were in ever-greater need of the assistance of missionaries.

Rome sent missionaries to the European Turkish provinces from three different directions: some arrived from the Habsburg Empire in the north. The Habsburg Empire was a Catholic power bordering the Ottoman Empire. Still, the frequent wars fought with the Turks did not favour the work of the missionaries. Another group of missionaries came to the Balkans from the Ottoman capital of Istanbul (Constantinople), where there were flourishing Catholic communities and several important monasteries and missionary centres. The third and most successful path of approach was from the Adriatic, with missionaries from Venice, Spalato (Split), and Ragusa travelling to the Balkan hills.

The city-state of Ragusa (Dubrovnik) – autonomous but obliged to pay a tribute to the sultan – reached its golden age in the sixteenth century, because its merchants could move freely in both the Christian world and on Ottoman territory. The city-state received far-reaching privileges from the Turks and, as a consequence of the Ottoman conquests, the whole of the Balkan Peninsula, from Istanbul to Buda, opened up to its merchants. For this reason, the citizens of Ragusa were particularly suited to carrying out the tasks of missionaries and apostolic visitors in the European provinces of the Ottoman Empire. The Ragusans were ardent Catholics and were well acquainted with the Ottoman-administered Balkans: they knew how to deal with the Turkish authorities. Catholic priests of the Ragusan merchant colonies became secure points of support for Catholic missionary work from Belgrade to Sofia. Thus, initially, Rome sent mostly Ragusan priests to carry out missionary work in the Balkans and Ottoman Hungary after the Council of Trent. The colonies of the Ragusan merchants formed a network across the Balkan Peninsula; the largest and most important was in Belgrade, which had been under Turkish rule since 1521. Wealthy Catholic merchants of the Ragusan colonies and their priests became supporters of the Catholic renewal in the Balkans: merchants and priests conveyed money and correspondence intended for the missionaries and missionaries reached their posts by joining the caravans of Catholic merchants on the perilous Balkan roads.

Catholic missionaries in the Turkish territories

Catholic missionaries working in the Ottoman Empire constituted a tiny but influential elite. In the Balkans, it was only in Bosnia that there was a larger number of Catholic priests: in the mid-seventeenth century, about 300 Franciscans were living in the Bosnian Franciscan Province. There were no secular parish priests in Bosnia; the Franciscans fulfilled the needs of all Catholic parishes. In the other provinces, however, missionaries wrote in shocking terms of the lack of priests. By the second half of the seventeenth century, the situation had improved considerably, but in Ottoman Hungary in the late sixteenth century and the first half of the seventeenth century, some Catholic villages had to make do with half-yearly or annual visits from priests. In 1622, Péter Pázmány, Archbishop of Esztergom (1616–37), informed Rome that only twenty priests were covering several hundred parishes in Ottoman Hungary.

In this ecclesiastical vacuum, a few well-trained and learned missionaries, fervent and fearless, could almost perform a miracle for Catholic believers. These missionaries took the place of priests in dozens of villages, demonstrating that the church in Rome had not abandoned the territories under Turkish rule. The missionaries began a wide range of activities: baptisms, masses, sermons, visitations, theological debate with Protestants and Orthodox, missionary work, training young monks to be their successors, and founding schools. This small number of missionaries made an enormous difference in this region under Turkish rule.

Thanks to the effective organization of the Holy Congregation for the Propagation of Faith (founded in 1622), by the mid-seventeenth century a network of missions had formed across the European provinces of the Ottoman Empire. Just as the situation of Catholics differed substantially amongst the various provinces, so also the missionaries had to work under very diverse circumstances, occasionally achieving success but sometimes suffering failure.

The missions in Istanbul were very important, because many Catholics lived in or passed through the city. The missionaries in Istanbul not only provided for the Christian merchants residing in the city, for the staff of embassies of the Catholic hierarchy, or for seamen arriving at the port; they also tried to serve the needs of the large numbers of Christian slaves who had been brought to Istanbul by force. Furthermore, the missions in Istanbul became the point of departure for missionaries travelling to the Balkans – Wallachia, Moldavia, Bulgaria, and Hungary – and to the East: the Crimean Peninsula, Asia Minor, the Holy Land, and even Persia.

The success of missionaries on the Greek Islands is demonstrated by the fact that many Greeks subsequently became missionaries to the Turkish provinces. Cretan Franciscans worked as missionaries in Wallachia, Moldavia, and Transylvania, and Greek Franciscans served in missions in Ottoman Hungary. A particularly important contribution to the more remote missions was made by Catholic missionaries from Chios (Italian: Scio). This island, which had belonged to the Genoese Republic, fell to the Turks in 1566. Even under Turkish rule, however, the monasteries on the island continued to train large numbers of local inhabitants as priests, with some of these then becoming missionary bishops – not just on the island of Chios, but further afield, too: in the course of the seventeenth century, thirty-three bishops serving in the Greek Islands and two apostolic vicars of Constantinople were from Chios. The Chian Greek priests also reached other, more distant, missions: Girolamo Arsengo (d. 1610), a Conventual Franciscan, worked as a missionary in Poland, Constantinople, and Wallachia, before becoming missionary Bishop of Bacau in Moldavia. Giacinto Macripodari (d. 1672), a Chian Dominican, heard the confessions of the imperial ambassador to Istanbul and then became the Bishop of Csanád in Ottoman Hungary – as a Turkish subject, even as bishop he was able to enter the Ottoman Empire. Another native of Chios and a bishop, Josef De Camelis, worked as a missionary in Italy, having graduated from the Collegio Greco in Rome. Then, in 1689, he became apostolic vicar in Munkács (Mukacevo) in eastern Hungary (today Ukraine), where he achieved the union of the Orthodox Ukrainians with Rome.

In Bulgaria, all missionaries were Observant Franciscans: in 1623, twenty-five Franciscans were working there. The missionaries were particularly successful in western Bulgaria, centred on the monastery of Ciprovci, where between ten and fifteen Franciscans lived. The Bulgarian mission became independent of the Bosnian Franciscan Province. In 1624, an autonomous Franciscan custodia was formed, and in 1676 it became an independent Bulgarian province. The Franciscan archbishops from the Bulgarian missions, the Bulgarian Pietro

Diodato (Bogdan-Bakčić) and Pietro Parchevich, made an important contribution to Catholic missionary work in the Balkans. At the same time, their literary efforts did much to preserve Bulgarian culture under Turkish rule. Bulgarian Franciscans worked as missionaries in other areas of the Ottoman Empire – in Ottoman Hungary and in Transylvania.

The flourishing of Bulgarian Catholicism and the Franciscan mission came to an end with the Ciprovci Uprising of 1688. At the time of the Balkan campaign of the imperial Habsburg troops, Bulgarian Catholics, hoping for the expulsion of the Turks, rose up against the Ottomans. The Turks suppressed the uprising by brutal means: whole Catholic villages were destroyed, churches and monasteries were burnt, and many missionaries and Catholic laymen were either murdered or sold as slaves. The Observant Franciscans, the Archbishop of Sofia Stefano Conti, as well as many of the Catholic faithful, fled to Wallachia and from there to Transylvania. Thereafter the mission to the Bulgarians of Transylvania constituted an important task for the Holy Congregation for the Propagation of Faith.

Of all the Turkish Balkan territories, it was in Bosnia that the Catholic missions were most successful. The Franciscans in Bosnia continued their influence, even after the country fell to the Turks. Indeed, in certain respects they even benefited from the fact that the kingdom no longer had a Christian ruler. Similar to Bosnian merchants, for whom the Turkish advance meant the creation of a uniform commercial territory without frontiers stretching from Buda to Istanbul, the Bosnian Franciscans – as members of the only Catholic institution in the Balkans that was recognized by the Turks – were also able to extend their influence under Turkish rule.

At the heart of the Ottoman Balkans, in the area between Belgrade and Istanbul, the Bosnian Franciscan Order was the only Catholic institution to be tolerated by the Turks. Even though the Bosnian Franciscan province was itself in difficulties – following the loss of numerous monasteries and the conversion of large numbers of local Catholics to Islam – Bosnian Franciscans began to expand their missionary activity in the second half of the sixteenth century. They travelled to areas far from Bosnia. Indeed, by the middle of the seventeenth century, Bosnian Franciscans were operating in Transylvania, Moldavia, and Bulgaria, as well as in Buda and Pest in Hungary. In this way they upheld the Catholic faith in areas that were also subject to Turkish taxation but were situated far from the borders of the medieval kingdom of Bosnia.

The Turks kept a firm hand on the leadership of the Franciscan province. Permits had to be obtained from the pasha of Bosnia for the provincial chapters held every three years, and such permits were never issued free of charge. The

Turks also interfered in elections for the Bosnian provincial: thus, for example, in 1637, Mariano Maravich (d. 1660), who later became Bishop of Duvno, was elected as provincial only after pressure from a Turkish bey – who was in fact a relative of the Franciscan missionary Maravich.

The Catholic missionaries played an important role in Transylvania, a Christian vassal state of the Ottomans. In 1579, Stephen Báthory, Prince of Transylvania and King of Poland, sent Jesuits from Poland to Transylvania, who in turn established a mission and college at Kolozsvár (Cluj). After the death of the monarch, however, a law adopted in 1588 banned the Jesuits from Transylvania; although they subsequently resettled in the principality, their college in Cluj was destroyed by the antitrinitarians in 1603 during the Transylvanian civil war. Nonetheless, a Jesuit mission began operating in Transylvania once more from 1616. Although Gabriel Bethlen, Prince of Transylvania (1613–29), was a Calvinist, he nevertheless made several gestures towards the Catholic Church, inviting, amongst others, Jesuit missionaries to Transylvania. Wearing secular clothes for the sake of appearances, the Jesuits performed successful missionary work in the capital of the principality, Gyulafehérvár (Alba Iulia), as well as in three other places. From 1630, two Bosnian friars established a mission in Transylvania, assisted by the Catholic Transylvanian aristocracy, while Hungarian friars settled in the last remaining Transylvanian Franciscan monastery at Csiksomlyó. The Bosnian and Hungarian Franciscan missionaries revitalized the Catholic Church in Transylvania; soon, five monasteries were operating in the principality. However, the constant battle between Bosnian and Hungarian missionaries could only be ended by the armed intervention of the authorities in Rome and the Transylvanian aristocracy. In 1666, the Catholic lords and the Italian missionaries used soldiers to occupy the Bosnian Franciscan monastery at Mikháza. Due to the outbreak of the Habsburg–Turkish war in 1683, the mission of the Italian Conventual Franciscans in Moldavia became impossible, and the missionaries went across to Transylvania where they ran a missionary station and successful school amongst the Szeklers.

Catholic missionaries travelled to Ottoman Hungary both from the north – the Habsburg Empire – and from the south – the Ottoman Empire. From the 1580s, the Bosnian Franciscan Province sent missionaries to Ottoman Hungary too, and Benedictine missionaries from Ragusa also operated there. In 1612, having been commissioned by the pope, a Jesuit mission with priests from Ragusa began operating in Ottoman Hungary, Belgrade, and then Temesvár (Timişoara), and there were Jesuit missions in Pécs and the Balaton region. Jesuit missionaries travelled around almost all of Ottoman Hungary, but they increasingly found themselves in conflict with the Bosnian Franciscans and, by the mid-seventeenth century had abandoned several of their missions. The Jesuit missionaries travelled to Ottoman Hungary from two directions: from the south came Dalmatian priests belonging to the Roman Province and, from the north came Hungarian and Croatian priests belonging to the Austrian Province.

The Bosnian Franciscan Province sent ever-larger numbers of missionaries to Ottoman Hungary and to the Croatian-inhabited areas of the country in particular. Generally, missions world-wide receive financial aid from their centres, but here, the Franciscan monasteries in impoverished Bosnia expected contributions from their missionaries operating in the wealthier Turkish Hungary. In the 1650s, thirty-eight Bosnian Franciscan missionaries were working as parish priests in Croatian-inhabited villages in Ottoman Hungary. In the town of Karaşevo, close to Temesvár (Timişoara), a Bosnian Franciscan mission began operating in 1626; the monks residing at the mission visited the surrounding area and even Transylvania. In addition to the Bosnian Franciscans, Greek and Bulgarian monks worked as missionaries here too; indeed, from 1659 to 1667 the mission was run by Bulgarian Franciscans.

Bosnian Franciscan missionaries also provided for the Catholics of Buda and Pest, as the only Catholic priests of these two adjacent towns in the seventeenth century. In the second half of the sixteenth century, Ragusan priests had been present in Buda, but during the Long War (1593–1606) the Turks banned Catholic priests, whom they considered to be enemies, from living in Buda, which was their most important fortress. In 1633, the Bosnian Franciscans established a mission in Pest, on the other side of the Danube. Two Bosnian friars proceeded to take over the small Calvinist church in Pest (the only Christian church in Pest and Buda) and convert Calvinist families. In subsequent periods, until the recapture of the towns in 1686, two Bosnian Franciscans were generally at work in Pest.

The Bosnian friars were very effective in the southern parts of Ottoman Hungary amongst Catholics of Croatian descent. At the same time, in the northern part of Ottoman Hungary, the Hungarian Observant Franciscans arriving from Hungary were similarly successful: in Szeged, Gyöngyös, Kecskemét, and the surrounding area they kept Catholicism alive.

The so-called 'licenciati' both assisted and competed with the missionaries working in Ottoman Hungary. They were part of an institution peculiar to the Catholic Church of Hungary under Turkish rule. These men, called 'half-priests', were in fact married laymen. In the absence of priests in a village, and with the permission of a bishop (this is why they became known as 'licenciati'), they recited devout readings to Sunday congregations and presided at baptisms, weddings, and funerals; they sometimes even celebrated mass, in spite of the protests of missionaries. Similar half-priests worked in the Catholic villages of Transylvania and Moldavia. The number of licenciati in Ottoman Hungary significantly exceeded the number of ordained Catholic priests. When, in 1675, György Pongrácz, Bishop of Vác, drew up a record of priests working in his diocese, fifteen priests and thirty licenciati were serving local Catholics, even though in the second half of the seventeenth century, the situation of the Catholic Church in Ottoman Hungary was far more consolidated than it had been in the sixteenth or the early seventeenth centuries.

Apostolic vicars and secret bishops

Having organized the missions, Rome faced the important task of developing missionary bishoprics. The papacy did everything to ensure that bishops should also care for Catholics living under Muslim rule, because only consecrated bishops could consecrate churches and altars; more importantly, only consecrated bishops could ordain priests – and without 'real' bishops there would be no replacement priests. However, in territories under Turkish rule, the bishops' activities were subject to severe restrictions. Moreover, in many Turkish provinces and in some areas of the Turkish vassals, a dual system of episcopal hierarchy had come into existence.

The Polish kings – who considered themselves to be the vassal lords of Moldavia – appointed Catholic bishops to the Băcau diocese in Moldavia. However, they remained in their poor and dangerous seat for just a few months, behaving – according to the complaints of believers – 'more like wolves than as pastors', because they were more concerned with exploiting the treasures of the bishopric than caring for the faithful. The Habsburg emperors, as kings of Hungary, also appointed bishops to Ottoman Hungary, Transylvania, and Bosnia, the former vassal state of the medieval Kingdom of Hungary. The Holy Congregation for the Propagation of Faith called upon the bishops of the Turkish territories to resign (which they were unwilling to do) or to occupy their seats (which the Turkish authorities refused to permit them to do). These bishops were unwilling to visit the Catholic populations living under Ottoman rule. In response, the pope refused to confirm their nomination and therefore they were not consecrated and enthroned. The papacy then attempted to provide for the Catholic faithful in areas under Turkish rule by sending missionary bishops. For this reason, several of the territories, such as southern Hungary and Bosnia, had both an absent bishop and a missionary bishop.

The missionary bishops of Ottoman Hungary had their seats in Belgrade. The geographical, commercial, and administrative centre of Ottoman Hungary was Buda, and it would have made sense for the missionary bishops of the territory to have their seats there. It was Buda's very importance, however, that made this impossible – because the Turks would not have tolerated an excessive Christian population in this crucial military centre and seat of the pashas. Belgrade, on the other hand, lay at the outermost edge of Ottoman Hungary; at first sight it appears unsuitable as a seat for a bishop who has no congregations to the south but who must hold visitations over an area stretching several hundred kilometres to the north. Free of pashas, however, the city was one of the most important commercial centres in the northern Balkans, with a large and wealthy colony of Catholic merchants.

In order to avoid conflict with the Habsburg emperors, who had a right to appoint bishops, the papacy applied a variety of solutions when appointing missionary bishops. The Dalmatian Pietro Catich, missionary Bishop of Belgrade (1618–22), was given the title of Bishop of Prizren in Kosovo, while his successor, the Ragusan Franciscan missionary Alberto Rengjich (1625–30), held the title of Bishop of Smederevo in Serbia. The next missionary Bishop of Belgrade, the Italian Franciscan Giacomo Boncarpi, received the title of Bishop of Himeria in Mesopotamia (1640–7). From 1647, the pope and the emperor negotiated and agreed upon appointments to the post of Bishop of Belgrade; thereafter each bishop held the title of his real seat. At this time both the emperor and the papacy accepted that if they wanted to provide effectively for the Catholics of Ottoman Hungary, they would have to abandon the policy of bringing in missionary bishops. Instead, the bishops would have to be selected in the Turkish territories, that is, they would have to appoint Bosnian Franciscans who were well acquainted with the land, language, parishes, and the Turks. Thus the medieval bishopric of Belgrade was established once more.

Reflecting the fact that Bosnian Franciscans became increasingly important in the missions of Ottoman Hungary, the next missionary bishops – Marino Ibrishimovich (1647–50), Matteo Benlich (1651–74), and Mattia Berniakovich (1675–1707) – were all Bosnian Franciscans. These bishops performed many visitations and ordained many priests whose task was to look after the Catholics under Turkish rule. The Turkish authorities were also more tolerant of these missionary bishops who originated from the Ottoman Empire. In Temesvár in 1653, the Bosnian friar Matteo Benlich, Bishop of Belgrade, was spared the punishment of being impaled for his 'espionage' on behalf of the pope, when Bosnian merchants from Sarajevo, who were resident in the town, proved to the pasha that Benlich was a subject of the sultan rather than a 'suspicious person' from outside the Turkish Empire.

As a result of the strengthening of the Catholic Church in Habsburg Hungary, by the mid-seventeenth century the bishops living there were able to exercise greater influence on the Hungarian territories under Turkish rule, too. Bishops living in the Habsburg part of the country appointed vicars for the Turkish area. Generally, these vicars were missionaries: Franciscan or Jesuit monks who directed parish priests and churches on behalf of the bishops. The Bishop of Vác, András Tarnóczy (d. 1655), planned to travel in disguise through the villages of his diocese under Turkish rule, but in the end he only reached as far as the Ottoman–Hungarian border. In 1675, György Pongrácz, Bishop of Vác, summoned a diocesan synod for priests living under Turkish rule, which was held in the first fortress beyond the border, in the immediate vicinity of Ottoman Hungary.

The Habsburg emperors also appointed bishops to Bosnia – generally speaking, priests living in Vienna. For this reason, the Bosnian missionary bishops appointed by the pope received the titles of other dioceses nearby (Scardona, Duvno). The missionary bishops of Belgrade directed the dioceses in Ottoman Hungary as apostolic vicars (appointed directly by the pope) in place of the absent bishops, living in exile in Habsburg Hungary. The Bosnian missionary bishops did the same in the Bosnian diocese.

Just as the bishops appointed by the Habsburgs were unable to enter the Turkish territories, so too were they prohibited from entering the Turkish sultan's Calvinist vassal, the Principality of Transylvania. Thus in 1618, Gabriel Bethlen, Prince of Transylvania (1613–29), placed a canon with the title of general vicar at the head of Transylvanian Catholics, who then governed the orphaned diocese of Transylvania in lieu of a bishop – although as a non-bishop he was unable to ordain priests. In terms of ecclesiastical law, it is quite extraordinary that a secular ruler – moreover a Calvinist one! – should appoint a Catholic bishop's vicar, but this solution proved to be both wise and lasting. Nevertheless, the Transylvanian Catholics were in need of a consecrated bishop. Therefore in 1668 the pope consecrated the Franciscan missionary Kázmér Damokos (1606–78) as Bishop of Koron in Greece, simultaneously nominating him as the apostolic vicar of Transylvania. However, Damokos, Transylvania's only missionary bishop, was required to keep his title of bishop secret from the Prince of Transylvania.

The Holy Congregation for the Propagation of Faith was entitled to appoint 'in partibus infidelium' Latin bishops to the Greek territories under Turkish rule: this was how the aforementioned Transylvanian missionary bishop received the title of Bishop of Koron. Similarly, the Italian Franciscan Francesco Antonio Frascella da San Felice (d. 1653), formerly a missionary in both Istanbul and Hungary, was sent to India and Japan as apostolic vicar with the title of Archbishop of Myra.

The apostolic vicars of Moldavia were the Franciscan missionary archbishops of Marcianopolis in eastern Bulgaria, while the Franciscan missionary Archbishop of Sofia in western Bulgaria looked after the Catholics of Wallachia as apostolic vicar. The Archbishop of Sofia held his seat in the Franciscan monastery at Ciprovci, rather than in the city of Sofia (where hardly any Catholics were living and where the Turks had converted the old church into a mosque). The Catholic population in southern Serbia was steadily growing due to the constant influx of Catholic Albanians. The papacy therefore established two new missionary archbishoprics: Ohrid (in Macedonia) on the Albanian border became a missionary archdiocese in 1647, while Skopje (currently the Macedonian capital) became a missionary archdiocese in 1656; here too, the missionary archbishops were usually Franciscan friars.

The sultanic capital of Istanbul also received a missionary bishop. There had been a Catholic patriarch of Constantinople alongside the Orthodox patriarch dating from the crusade of the thirteenth century, but since the reoccupation of the city in 1261 by Byzantium he had not been permitted to reside there. Since that time, an official of the Roman curia had held the office. The patriarch's vicar was generally a missionary living in Istanbul, the Guardian of the Conventual Franciscan monastery in Constantinople and at the same time the Provincial of the local Franciscan province. However, he was not a bishop and could not consecrate churches or ordain priests; he merely had rights of supervision *vis-à-vis* clerics in Istanbul. Amongst these vicars we find Italian missionaries who had earlier been sent to Hungary: for example, Angelo Petricca da Sonnino and Andrea Ridolfi. From 1652, however – parallel to the papacy's attempts to send apostolic vicars to all missionary areas from the Portuguese colonies to Transylvania – the former vicars were replaced by apostolic patriarchal vicars. The similarity in name concealed an enormous difference: the new apostolic vicars were consecrated bishops; they could therefore ordain priests, and had the power of bishops, just like the other apostolic vicars sent to the Balkans or to Hungary.

Conclusion

Islam was the ruling ideology of the Ottoman Empire and the sultans stressed repeatedly in their letters that, by conquering Christian kingdoms and fighting against the infidel, they spread the true faith of Mohammed. However, the Catholic Church not only survived under Ottoman rule but, through the work of its missionaries, even Catholic reform arrived in Turkish lands. The tolerance, or rather indifference, of the Turks for their Christian subject came, however, at a heavy price: Christians had to pay a burdensome poll tax. To avoid this tax, more and more Albanian and Bosnian peasants converted to Islam, as their hopes of Christian reconquest were not fulfilled. This Islamization of the Balkans had lasting consequences. In the northern provinces, however, in Ottoman Hungary, Transylvania, Wallachia, and Moldavia, conversions remained exceptions: these countries kept their Christian identity.

Christianity shaped by the Chinese

NICOLAS STANDAERT

Introduction

There are different ways of writing the history of the expansion of Christianity and its evangelization of the non-Christian world. The common approach is to write it from the perspective of the European missionary, whereby the process of Christianization is primarily perceived as the result of the missionary's action. Another approach is to take the receiving community as the starting point of discussion; thereby emphasizing this community's role as an active participant in the conversion process. This chapter will adopt the latter approach.[1] By focusing on the Chinese, both Christian and non-Christian, it will show how these actors, in interaction with the respective missionaries, shaped the form of Christianity in seventeenth-century China.

The account of this historic interaction begins with the year 1583, the first time local Chinese authorities granted missionaries permanent residence in mainland China. During the preceding thirty years, i.e., since 1552, the year in which Francisco Xavier (1506–52) died on an island off the Chinese coast, some fifty missionaries had been trying in vain to settle in China.[2] The closing date of this account is 1666. In that year, Chinese authorities banished all but four missionaries to confinement in Canton. During a period of approximately five years, all churches in the provinces were closed and Christianity forbidden. Although 1666 therefore represents a closing date that fits elegantly within the time-frame set by this volume of the *Cambridge History of Christianity*, the events that took place during this time should not necessarily be considered the most significant in the process of evangelization in China. From the point of view of Chinese secular history, 1644 is a more important date. It was the year

---

1 This chapter only contains a limited bibliography. For an extensive bibliography, including primary and secondary sources, both in Chinese and Western languages, see *Handbook of Christianity in China*.
2 Sebes, 'The precursors of Ricci', p. 30.

in which the Manchus captured the capital Beijing, thus bringing to an end the Ming dynasty that had reigned for nearly 300 years (1368–1644), installing in its place the new Qing dynasty (1644–1911).

In general, Christianity was a rather marginal phenomenon in seventeenth-century China, certainly from a numerical point of view.[3] Compared to Japan, the number of converts grew slowly in China. In 1610, there were c. 2,500 Chinese Christians, in contrast with Japan where in 1579, also after thirty years of Christian presence, there were c. 130,000 baptized Japanese. While there were still only 13,000 Chinese Christians in 1627, their number grew more rapidly in the 1630s. By 1665 they were probably c. 70,000–80,000. The number of missionaries, however, was limited. During the first fifty years, the only missionaries were Jesuits who came under the Portuguese Padroado. When Matteo Ricci SJ (1552–1610), often considered the main initiator of the mission, died in Beijing in 1610, there were but sixteen Jesuits in China: eight Chinese brothers and eight European fathers.[4] Only in the 1620s did the number of Jesuits exceed twenty. With the arrival of Franciscan and Dominican friars under the Spanish Patronato in the 1630s, and a slight increase of Jesuits in the same period, the number of foreign missionaries grew to over thirty. During the next thirty years, the total number of foreign missionaries remained constant: between thirty and forty. There were no Chinese priests active in China in this period, except for the Dominican Luo Wenzao (1616–91), known in Western sources as Gregory López, who was ordained in the Philippines in 1654.

The late Ming and early Qing context

At the end of the sixteenth century, the Ming dynasty seemed at the height of its glory; it would decline only in the 1620s and fall in 1644.[5] Its achievements in culture and the arts were remarkable, urban and commercial life proliferating to new levels of prosperity, and considerable amounts of porcelain and silk of outstanding quality being produced. With a population much larger than that of Europe – c. 150 million inhabitants versus 60 million, in 1600 – China was not divided into multiple states like Europe, but was a unified country with an

---

3 Standaert, 'Number of missionaries', in *Handbook of Christianity in China*, pp. 300–5; Standaert, 'Number of Christians', in *ibid.*, pp. 380–6.
4 Lamalle, 'La propagande du P. N. Trigault', p. 53 n. 11, based on a contemporary report by N. Longobardo.
5 For a short description, see Spence, *The search for modern China*, chs. 1–3; and Spence, *The memory palace*; for an extensive description of the Ming dynasty, see *The Cambridge history of China*, vols. 7 and 8; for a contemporary description, see d'Elia, *Fonti Ricciane*, and Trigault and Ricci, *De Christiana expeditione*, book 1.

efficient bureaucratic system bonded by an immense body of statutory laws and provisions. One segment of this bureaucracy lived in Beijing, serving the emperor in an elaborate hierarchy that divided the country's business among six ministries dealing respectively with finance, personnel, rituals, justice, military affairs, and public works. The other segment of the Chinese bureaucracy consisted of those assigned to posts in the fifteen major provinces, which were further divided into prefectures and counties. Officials were selected by an examination system, which started at the county level and culminated in the three-year Metropolitan Examination in which *c*. 300 new officials were selected for the highest positions.

The demands of this civil examination system shaped the lives and thinking of the learned elite (*shi*) (often rendered into English as 'literati').[6] These were sufficiently literate to read and write passable examination essays but had not necessarily succeeded in the examinations. Many indeed were employed as local clerks and private tutors. This notwithstanding, the examination system was most significant in aiding to institutionalize a stable, but not static, system of ideas that became known as the 'Learning of the Way' (*daoxue*) (often referred to as 'Neo-Confucianism' in Western literature). The education system centred on selected classical texts with accompanying commentaries by the Neo-Confucian thinker Zhu Xi (1130–1200). Zhu Xi's systematic interpretation of all major Confucian texts dating from before 200 BC determined real moral values that formed the basis of all proper relations between humans and thus the proper means for establishing social order. In his eyes, such values could be adequately apprehended through a process of learning. Since the examinations required the memorization and recapitulation of the Confucian texts and their interpretations, all civil officials and literati were also Confucians (*ru*) in the broad sense of the word. However, despite this training, many literati showed strong personal involvement in what were clearly 'other' teachings with definable doctrines, such as Buddhism and even Christianity.

After the fall of the Ming, the new Manchu leaders vowed to uphold China's traditional beliefs and social structures. While maintaining their own Manchu traditions, they were quick to restore the national examination system and to promote Confucian learning.

This general cultural and intellectual setting is important in several regards to understanding the process of evangelization in China. The image of the

---

6 Peterson, 'Confucian learning in late Ming thought', in *The Cambridge history of China*, vol. 8, pp. 708–88, esp. pp. 708–11, 771.

Chinese mission in contemporary and modern sources is predominantly one of an elite mission. This image is evoked by several factors: the general policy of the Jesuits to propagate 'from the top down', the underlying idea being that if this elite, preferably the emperor and his court, were converted, the whole country would be won to Christianity; the actual conversion of some high officials in late Ming who are referred to in many Chinese and Western books as examples of the success of this policy; the publication of many books, including scientific texts, by both missionaries and converts, indicating a notable activity among a literary elite; and, finally, general knowledge of Christianity in late Ming and early Qing, predominantly based on published sources that inevitably draw attention to literary groups. Given these factors, the majority of this chapter will focus on this elite. It will show, on the one hand, how the Chinese cultural environment shaped Christianity in such a way that it became associated with the elite, the sciences and book learning, and also, on the other hand, how Christians belonging to this elite creatively shaped Christian thought. As the final section will indicate, however, the strongest and most durable embedment of Christianity did not in fact take place among the elite but among the popular levels of society where it took the form of communities of effective rituals.

Association with the elite of literati

A first characteristic is that the late Ming socio-cultural context allowed Christianity to become associated with the elite of literati.[7] In fact, the early Jesuit missionaries' policy underwent a change from adaptation to Buddhists to adaptation to Confucians (and the subsequent rejection of Buddhism).[8] Originally, probably inspired by their policy in Japan, Jesuits dressed like Buddhist monks. The accommodation to the Buddhist life style had not been without advantages. It enabled the Jesuits to make contact with the majority of the Chinese population relatively easily and allowed them to focus conversation specifically on religious matters. But there had also been disadvantages. From a Confucian perspective, Buddhism and Christianity had many religious elements in common, such as belief in an afterlife, the idea of heaven and hell, and the practice of celibacy, which were considered very un-Confucian. Moreover, Buddhist monks were regarded as very low on the social ladder. Precisely this similarity to the Buddhists forced the Jesuits to differentiate themselves from

---

7 Standaert, 'Jesuit corporate culture', pp. 355–6.
8 Bettray, *Die Akkomodationsmethode des P. Matteo Ricci S.J.*

them and inflate the differences. As a consequence, they turned to Confucianism. In fact, it was Confucian literati like Qu Taisu (Qu Rukui) (1549–?) who encouraged Ricci to institute this change. Consequently, Jesuits dressed like Chinese scholars, studied the Chinese classics and participated in intellectual debates in the academies of the literati.

This association with the Confucian elite not only influenced the way in which Christian faith became expressed in Chinese, but also greatly influenced the way Christianity actually spread in China.[9] A short comparison with Buddhism makes this clear. Due to the central place of the monastery, Buddhism spread in the way the roots or branches of a tree expand, by gradually moving outward, constantly developing new shoots that penetrated into new territories and filled up the empty spaces. Christianity, on the contrary, had a weak local nucleus, yet underwent rapid territorial expansion. It is true that the Jesuits' guiding strategy was a choice for the centre over the periphery and for the city over the countryside. But the establishment of Christian communities was determined by another factor that did not depend on the active decision-making of the missionaries: the *guanxi* or personal relationships with the Chinese literati (converts). Owing to their social function, the elite were potentially highly mobile, since official appointments changed every three years and were fulfilled in provinces other than the native region. Consequently, the spread of Christianity followed the path of the transfer of Chinese Christians who were first to move to a new region and who subsequently invited the foreign missionaries. As a result, Christianity spread in a relatively short period to the centres of many different regions, first Nanjing, the southern metropolis, and Beijing, the northern metropolis, followed by the Fujian and Shanxi regions. After the key economic macroregions had been reached, local sedentarism became more important, and the relationship with the mobile elite diminished. At the local level, too, as is well illustrated by the Dominicans in the Fujian province, missionaries moved to new places at the invitation of local Christians.

Members of the literati elite adopted differing attitudes towards Christianity: a very small minority converted to Christianity; others sympathized with the missionaries and their teachings and adopted an open, positive, or curious attitude; others still actively opposed their teachings; most people, however, adopted a position somewhere between these extremes or remained neutral or indifferent.

9 Zürcher, 'Bouddhisme et christianisme'; Standaert, 'The creation of Christian communities', in *Handbook of Christianity in China*, pp. 567–72.

The number of degree-holders who converted to Christianity in the seventeenth century and whose names have been identified totals around sixty.[10] The earlier period in this time-frame (1600–1620s) was the period in which most of the highest degree-holders are recorded to have converted. Well known are four converts: Xu Guangqi (1562–1633; baptized as Paul in 1603), Li Zhizao (1565–1630; baptized as Leo in 1610), Yang Tingyun (1562–1627; baptized as Michael probably in 1611), and Wang Zheng (1571–1644; baptized as Philip c. 1616).[11] They not only lived during the same period and were baptized around the same age (all in their forties), but they also developed a relationship among themselves. In public life they all pursued an average official career, with the exception of Xu Guangqi who at the end of his life became Grand Secretary, one of the highest positions in the civil administration. As co-authors with the missionaries or as authors themselves, they shaped Christianity by producing a considerable number of works in the field of what became known as 'Heavenly Studies' (*tianxue*), which comprised a wide range of theological, philosophical, ethical, and scientific topics. As a result, both their story of conversion and their thought as such have been rather well documented.

Their conversion to Christianity was not an abrupt event, but a long process during which they actively sought answers to their life questions. The socio-cultural context in which they lived was to a large extent in crisis and allowed scholars to seek alternatives. In general, they shared the following characteristics with many contemporary scholars: an interest in 'solid' or 'practical' learning (*shixue*); a renewed interest in the study of the Chinese Classics (*jingxue*); the search for an objective morality against the intuitionist tendencies of their times; a critical attitude towards the Zhu Xi Neo-Confucian school and a return to the learning of the Han dynasty (206 BC to AD 221); a search for fulfilment of the ethical-religious needs in their lives, accompanied by a rejection of Buddhism after their conversion to Christianity. This was the context of their quest to maximize meaning and purpose in life.

Distinguishing between affective, intellectual, ethical, religious, and socio-political conversions,[12] Xu Guangqi's and Li Zhizao's conversions can be considered primarily intellectual conversions. In their search for meaning they

10 Dudink, 'Table of Christian degree-holders', in *Handbook of Christianity in China*, pp. 399–403.
11 Standaert, 'Chinese Christians: well-known individuals', in *Handbook of Christianity in China*, pp. 404–20; Peterson, 'Why did they become Christians?'; Xu Guangqi: Jami, *Statecraft and intellectual renewal*; Übelhör, 'Hsü Kuang-ch'i und seine Einstellung zum Christentum'; Li Zhizao: Leung, 'Towards a hyphenated identity'; Yang Tingyun: Standaert, *Yang Tingyun*; Wang Zheng: Zürcher, 'Christian social action'.
12 Rambo, *Understanding religious conversion*, pp. 146–7; see also pp. 14–15.

were dissatisfied with the orthodox tradition, and examined alternatives, such as Han commentaries. The option presented by the 'Heavenly Studies' in all their aspects (discussion about Heaven, personal and moral cultivation, practical sciences) convinced them in a logical and rigorous way. In the case of Wang Zheng it was primarily an ethical conversion. He was very much influenced by a treatise on the 'Victories over the Seven Capital Sins' (*Qike*, 1614) of Diego de Pantoja SJ (1571–1618). Moreover, the moral dimension of Wang's commitment is well illustrated by the 'Humanitarian Society' (*renhui*) that he established in Xi'an around 1634. Though these three scholars experienced conversion as religious, it is most conspicuous in Yang Tingyun's life. The response to what was experienced as Ultimate Reality received an intellectual expression in his writings that discuss Christian doctrine in depth. Though these four converts are primarily known for their scientific, moral and theological writings, it should be emphasized that Christian faith was not merely an intellectual experience for them, since they participated fully in the ritual and devotional life of Christianity.

But it was not only literati converts who contributed towards shaping the development of Christianity. Christian expansion depended to a large extent on the actions and reactions of non-Christian literati.[13] This literati support and the missionaries' attitude to it also underwent a gradual evolution during the seventeenth century. In the initial period, the doubts concerning traditional values and openness for other traditions facilitated the Chinese scholars' contacts with people from other cultures. The period before 1616, when a persecution took place in Nanjing, constituted the peak of literati sympathy, as is indicated by the many prefaces to books written by missionaries on scientific, moral or philosophical subjects. In the 1620s and early 1630s, literati support diminished and Christianity moved on to different areas, such as the Fujian and Shanxi provinces. During the 1630s, however, when Christianity became increasingly locally embedded, there was less need to propagate it with the help of sympathizing literati. In fact, there was a double shift in the relationship of missionaries with the elite. In the capital, they diverted their activity from literati and officials to the imperial court to which, after earlier unsuccessful attempts, they finally gained access; outside the capital they turned their attention from literati and officials to the lower officials and common people. In the early decades of the Qing, the contacts between literati circles and missionaries transformed significantly. Instead of intellectual companions

---

13 Dudink, 'Sympathising *literati* and officials', in *Handbook of Christianity in China*, pp. 475–91.

of the literati, missionaries became expert advisers to the throne and literati support almost completely vanished.

Not all literati, however, sympathized with Christianity. Some were opposed to it and even took (legal) action against converts and missionaries.[14] The first major anti-Christian incident took place in Nanjing in 1616–17 and was initiated by Shen Que (1565–1624), who was Minister of Rites in Nanjing. It resulted in the arrest of the missionaries and several converts, the expulsion of four missionaries and the temporary retreat of the other missionaries from the public scene in the Hangzhou region. This incident was an attempt to bring Christianity under the control of the government and state orthodoxy, just as Buddhism and Taoism had been, and to keep the missionaries away from the two capitals, where they had begun to influence officials with their ideas. The sole example of an anti-Christian movement or campaign was initiated by Huang Zhen (fl. 1630s) in the Fujian and Zhejiang provinces in 1634. It culminated in the publication of the anti-Christian 'Collection for the Destruction of Heresies' (Poxie ji, 1640), but not in actions taken by the government, probably because it was mainly a campaign by Buddhist monks and literati against the strong anti-Buddhist attitude of missionaries and converts. Finally, the best-known incident is the Calendar Case of 1664, initiated by Yang Guangxian (1597–1669). Yang attacked both Christian doctrine and Western astronomy and geography. Johann Adam Schall von Bell SJ (1592–1666) and seven officials (among whom were five Christians) at the Astronomical Bureau were sentenced to death (April 1665). Although Schall was pardoned, the five Christian officials were executed. The Calendar Case was a combination of several factors, some of which had been smouldering before Yang's attack took place: personal rivalry among the Jesuits, tensions between pro- and anti-Christian factions at the court, Schall's dismissal of Muslim astronomy, and the Confucian roots of Yang's thinking. This incident also had consequences for Christianity outside Beijing as churches were closed and Christianity was forbidden. Except for Schall, Ferdinand Verbiest (1623–88), Lodovico Buglio (1606–82) and Gabriel de Magalhães (1610–77), all other missionaries, twenty-one Jesuits, three Dominicans and one Franciscan, were sentenced to confinement in Canton. Four Dominicans remained in Fujian. As a result, most communities were left to their own devices. Some vanished, others were contrarily consolidated. In effect, these various anti-Christian incidents contributed in their own way to the expansion of Christianity since they forced missionaries to

---

14 Dudink, 'Opponents', in *Handbook of Christianity in China*, pp. 503–33; Gernet, *Chine et christianisme*.

move to other places and converts to further embed Christianity within local communities.

Sciences

A second characteristic of Christianity in late Ming China, closely linked with the role of the elite, is that it became associated with the introduction of Western sciences.[15] Here also the Ming context played a significant role in shaping Christianity.

Indeed, if Chinese scholars became interested in the sciences brought by the Jesuits, it was because *prior* to their arrival Chinese literati had developed an interest in practical learning.[16] The search for 'solid learning' or 'concrete studies' (*shixue*), also characteristic of the four well-known converts, was a reaction against some intuitionist movements originating from the Wang Yangming school in the late sixteenth century. According to the Neo-Confucian thinker Wang Yangming (1472–1528), the principles for moral action were to be found entirely within the mind-and-heart (*xin*) and not in the outside world. In the early seventeenth century, the intellectual and political movement of the thinkers of the Donglin school re-established the importance of 'things in the world'. Officials and scholars searched for concrete ways to save the country from decline. It is this preceding quest that fostered the interaction between them and the Jesuits in the field of the sciences.

It should be pointed out that most of the early missionaries had no particularly advanced training in the sciences in the modern sense of the word and were initially not sent for the purposes of propagating them. All Jesuit missionaries had attended classes in natural philosophy (or *physica*), which included subjects such as astronomy and ballistics and was taught in the second year of philosophy. This was an integral part of the Jesuit curriculum in preparation for theology. In fact, Matteo Ricci happened to have attended courses by Christophorus Clavius SJ (1538–1612). The latter had been among those responsible for the reform of the Gregorian calendar and the inclusion of mathematics in the Jesuit *Ratio Studiorum*.[17] It was, however, due to the insistence of converts such as Xu Guangqi that Ricci engaged in the translation of Clavius's commentaries on Euclidean mathematics (especially 'Elements of Geometry' (*Jihe yuanben*), 1607). Other converts such as Li Zhizao and

---

15 Jami, 'Science and technology: general reception', in *Handbook of Christianity in China*, pp. 689–710.
16 Übelhör, 'Geistesströmungen der späten Ming-Zeit'.
17 Engelfriet, *Euclid in China*.

Yang Tingyun and missionaries such as Sabatino De Ursis SJ (1575–1620) and Manuel Dias SJ (1574–1659) joined them in translating works on astronomy, hydraulics, and geography. By 1626, Li Zhizao compiled these works, together with theological and moral writings, in the 'First Collection of Heavenly Studies' (*Tianxue chuhan, c.* twenty works). After these spontaneous initiatives, the translation of western works became a real project due to the initiative of Niccolò Longobardo SJ (1565–1655) and Nicolas Trigault SJ (1577–1628). In 1620, after Trigault's recruitment trip to Europe, new books and new missionaries with an advanced scientific training arrived in China, better equipped to meet the intellectual demands of the Chinese literati. They engaged in time consuming and long-enduring activities, such as the calendar reform, again an initiative of Xu Guangqi. That reform resulted in the publication of the voluminous collection of astronomical writings 'Calendar Compendium of the Chongzhen Reign' (*Chongzhen lishu*, 1635). This persistent demand of the Chinese (both converts and non-converts) for practical learning was one of the reasons why Jesuits did not engage in other translation projects such as a translation of the Bible, despite having received permission to do so from Rome in 1615. Aside from mathematical and astronomical writings, Chinese converts and missionaries collaborated on the publication of a wide range of other scientific subjects, including cartography, cannon-making, technology, and medicine.[18] They also translated and published books in the field of humanistic writings or Aristotelian philosophy. Moreover, the transmission of knowledge did not flow in only one direction: Jesuit writings on China informed Europe about the Chinese political and religious system, cartographic discoveries, and medical practices. With the appointment of Schall von Bell in an official position at the Bureau of Astronomy in 1644, scientific contacts took a new turn. Missionaries with specific training were sent and became technical advisers at the service of the emperor in order to guarantee the Chinese court's protection of Christianity.

The link between science and religion that characterized Christianity in seventeenth-century China is an issue widely disputed by modern scholars, mainly due to their own tendency to clearly separate science and religion. Though Jesuit missionaries of the seventeenth century distinguished – like their Renaissance contemporaries in Europe – between mathematics, natural philosophy, and theology, they did not separate them as such. They conceived of them as forming a hierarchical structure in which natural philosophy was a necessary preparation for theology. In their eyes, one needed to know

18 *Handbook of Christianity in China*, pp. 711–808.

mathematics well, so as to master astronomy well, so as to understand the whole cosmos and ultimately God. As a result, the introduction of sciences was for them more than merely a means for achieving a religious aim. Gradually, however, events such as the Nanjing incident in 1616 more or less forced them to disconnect the introduction of Western sciences from that of their religious message and a division of labour occurred among the missionaries. Some were predominantly employed as technicians in the function of court officials, while others were primarily involved in pastoral activities. Converts such as Xu Guangqi had probably also advised such disconnection. In that way they thought they would guarantee the introduction of the sciences. There were also literati, however, who explicitly rejected Christian religious teachings but remained interested in Western sciences.

Cultural imperative expressed in book learning

Other characteristics of late Ming society shaped Christianity in a way different from the European encounters in other countries at that time. In many ways, Chinese culture was relatively similar to Europe as regards the means of reproduction and circulation of knowledge,[19] and to a certain extent these means were developed even further in China. Whereas European missionaries were often the first to introduce printing and formal education in other areas, China already had a widely available printing system in place and the culture of the book was an integral part of late Ming intellectual life. The flourishing of the publishing and printing industry played an important role not only in the intellectual changes of that time[20] but also in the spread of Christianity. Indeed, by making dissenting views widely available, publishers and writers helped to create an intellectual environment conducive to the spread and reception of other streams of thought than the orthodox 'Learning of the Way'.

As a result, the 'apostolate through books' became one of the major means of spreading Christianity among the elite.[21] Moreover, in addition to the numerous writings that made Christian doctrine and Western sciences known to a large public, writings directed at an inner-church public increased as the number of Christians grew. The number of texts produced in Chinese by missionaries and Chinese Christians is quite impressive. For the seventeenth

---

19 Brook, 'The circulation of knowledge', in *The Cambridge history of China*, vol. 8, pp. 635–70.
20 Chow, 'Writing for success', pp. 145–6.
21 Dudink and Standaert, 'Apostolate through books', in *Handbook of Christianity in China*, pp. 600–31.

century, in addition to some 120 texts dealing with the West and its sciences, some 470 texts can be identified that are mainly related to religious and moral issues (most of which have been preserved). These include treatises on a very wide variety of topics: catechetical texts for neophytes, theological writings destined for both Christian and non-Christian literati audiences, apologetic writings by Chinese converts, biographies of saints and sages used as exempla to encourage and convince converts, (illustrated) biblical narratives, writings explaining the sacraments and liturgy, prayer books and spiritual writings.

This large collection of texts also gives the clearest indication of the Chinese strategy of 'cultural imperative' that obliged the foreigner to accommodate to the native culture. Noteworthy was the predominance of the Chinese language in the evangelization process. It was necessary for the foreign missionary to learn the Chinese language in order to proclaim the gospel. Contrary to the Christian expansion in Japan, where the Japanese learned Portuguese or Latin, in China no one involved in the interaction learned a foreign language, except for a small number of Chinese who were educated for the priesthood. As a result, before Christian ideas could evoke any response, they were filtered through Chinese language and thought patterns.

Yet, the cultural imperative not only required that foreign missionaries learn Chinese or dress like Chinese scholars, but more fundamentally, in interaction with Chinese converts, that they adapt Christianity to some of the foundations of Chinese thought. No marginal religion penetrating from the outside could ever expect to take root in China (at least at that social level) unless it conformed to that pattern of thought that in late imperial times was more clearly defined than ever. Confucianism represented what is *zheng*, 'orthodox', in a religious, ritual, social, and political sense; in order not to be branded *xie*, 'heterodox', and thus to be treated as a subversive sect, a marginal religion had to prove that it was on the side of *zheng*.[22] The authority, sheer mass and attractive power of Confucianism were such that any religious system from outside was caught in its field, and was bound to gravitate towards that centre. In other words, when Ricci started to apply the method of accommodation, he probably did not realize the full weight of that cultural imperative. He must only gradually, with a rare combination of intelligence, intuition, and a growing knowledge of the Chinese situation, have come to realize that adaptation to the imperative of Confucianism was the only viable way. Those opposing his policy denied the very principle that Christianity, in order to take root, had to be based on the Chinese heritage.

22 Zürcher, 'Jesuit accommodation', pp. 40–1.

As a result, Christianity in China lost some of its European monopolistic character and developed into a small but not negligible religious movement by grafting itself on to the dominant Confucian tradition. Chinese Christian texts from the seventeenth century show all the characteristics that were typical of the responses of marginal religions such as Buddhism, Judaism, or Islam to the cultural imperative: the emphasis on congruity and complete compatibility between the minority religion and Confucianism; the notion of complementarity; the foreign creed serving to enrich and fulfil the Confucian doctrine; the tendency to ground the existence of the foreign doctrine upon historical precedent, sometimes reaching back to the very beginning of Chinese civilization; the adoption of Chinese mores and rituals.[23] Several of these characteristics can be observed in the writings of missionaries, such as Ricci's well-known treatise, 'The True Meaning of the Lord of Heaven' (*Tianzhu shiyi*, 1603).[24]

It is among the Christian scholars, such as Yang Tingyun, Wang Zheng, Zhu Zongyuan (*c.* 1616–60) but also the brothers Li Jiugong and Li Jiubiao from the Fujian community and the brothers Han Yun and Han Lin (*c.* 1600–49) from the Shanxi community, that one finds the clearest expressions of this Confucian–Christian synthesis: a kind of 'Confucian monotheism' centred upon the belief in the Lord of Heaven, the one omnipotent creator and stern judge.[25] The integration of Christian monotheism into the Confucian tradition took place through a daring reinterpretation of some ancient cultic terms (*tian*, 'Heaven'; *shangdi*, 'Sovereign-on-High') that occurred in key passages of the Confucian classics. The use of those terms to denote the Christian God was controversial even within the Jesuit order, but it was fully accepted by Chinese converts. The most basic element in this Christian–Confucian synthesis was the transformation of the abstract, impersonal 'Heaven', the highest cosmic force or principle, into a personal 'Lord of Heaven' (*tianzhu*). To Chinese Christians the worship of that *tianzhu* was the very essence of their creed; in every exposition of the doctrine it forms the first and most fundamental theme. The complex of incarnation–passion–resurrection, which was duly explained by the missionaries, only played a secondary role. Another focus of interest concerned the ethical message: the excellence of Christian morals and their congruence with Confucian norms of social conduct. Sin and retribution loomed large in the Chinese Christian discourse: converts could assume that their burden of Original Sin was to be eliminated by baptism; but the steady

23 *Ibid.*, p. 36.   24 Ricci, *The true meaning of the Lord of Heaven*.
25 Zürcher, 'Key theological issues', in *Handbook of Christianity in China*, pp. 641–2, 644–5, 648.

accumulation of guilt in daily life required a rigorous programme of intro-spection and penitence, and the performance of good works as a means to accumulate 'merit' in order to redress the moral balance. There was the strong conviction that Christian morals could play a positive role in society because of their concrete applicability, their 'solidity' (*shi*). Some prominent converted scholars are known to have been active in promoting charity and social har-mony along Christian lines. In short, both metaphysically and ethically, many Chinese Christians were convinced that Christianity was a 'complement' to the original teachings of Confucianism.[26]

The cultural imperative and accommodative attitude of both the mission-aries and the Chinese Christians also led to tensions.[27] The name of God, and other important concepts such as angels and the soul, formed the core issues in what would later be called the 'Term Question'. The major ques-tion was whether these terms taken from the Chinese classics could convey the Christian concept of God. Another set of questions of what became the 'Rites Controversy' was related to the ceremonies in honour of Confucius, performed by the literati class in temples and halls dedicated to him, and the cult of ancestors, which was embedded in the social structures on all levels and manifested by such forms of piety as prostrations, incense burning, and food serving, before the corpse, grave, or commemorative tablet. The question was whether one should forbid Christians from participating in these acts, or whether one should regard them as not having any religious significance, or at least none contrary to Christian belief, and therefore to be tolerated? Or could the missionaries still take a third position: while condemning some features, permit converts to perform the rites with modifications and expect that they would eventually abandon them?

The scope of this Controversy in the period up to the 1660s was rather limited. It was restricted to the discussions among the small number of mis-sionaries in China and to reactions by the inner circle of church officials in Rome. Only at the end of the seventeenth century did it develop into intense negotiations back and forth between missionaries and legates sent to China or Europe, papal decrees and public discussions among European intellectuals. In the first fifty years of their stay in China, the Jesuits had expressed very different opinions about the rites.[28] One of the key moments had been the conference of Jiading (1628) at which Chinese converts and Jesuits reached a compromise, accepting a moderate and open attitude towards the terms to be used and the

---

26 *Ibid.*, p. 637.
27 Standaert, 'Rites Controversy', in *Handbook of Christianity in China*, pp. 680–8.
28 Rule, *K'ung-tzu or Confucius?* chs. 1–2.

participation in the rites. The beginning of the Controversy outside the circle of China Jesuits is usually associated with the initiatives taken by Juan Bautista de Morales OP (1597–1664), who was one of the first Dominicans to arrive in China in 1633. After having left China and returned to Rome in 1643, he presented 'Seventeen Questions' that basically attacked the Jesuit approach. A first decree approved by the pope (12 September 1645) prohibited the practices described by Morales. In reaction, the Jesuits dispatched Martino Martini SJ (1614–61) to Rome in 1651 to show that de Morales had not described their missionary practices accurately. A favourable decree followed on 23 March 1656 giving sanction to the practices as described in a statement by Martini. After the 'Canton Conference' held among representatives of the Jesuits, Dominicans and Franciscans during their confinement around January 1668, which aimed at arriving at a uniform missionary method, Juan de Polanco OP (?–1671) asked if the decision of 1656 had annulled the decision of 1645. The Holy Office responded on 20 November 1669 that both were still in effect and to be observed 'according to the questions, circumstances, and everything set down in them'.[29]

Communities of effective rituals

This image of Christianity as primarily an elite mission is cast in a different light if one looks at the statistics of the Christian population.[30] A rather rare and very specific statistic of 1636 gives the following figures: among 38,300 Catholics, there were fourteen high-level officials, ten doctor-degree holders (*jinshi*), eleven licentiates (*juren*), 291 bachelors (*shengyuan* or *xiucai*), more than 140 family members of the emperor, more than forty eunuchs and some court women. Including the court people, this elite represents only 1.33 per cent of the total Catholic population. Even if one presumes that the relative number of literate people who did not succeed in the examinations among the Christians was similar to those in the national population, the number of literati probably did not exceed 10 per cent of the total Catholic population. In other words, by far the largest group of Christians were illiterate commoners. Missionaries often complained about the fact that most Christians were *pauperes* (people with little property). But they also saw it as proof that it was more difficult for the rich to enter the Kingdom of God since they were too attached to the world, to their wealth, and to their concubines. Primary sources on these

29 For a translation of the Roman Documents, see *100 Roman Documents*, documents 1–4.
30 Standaert, 'Social stratification', in *Handbook of Christianity in China*, pp. 386–91.

commoners, however, are much more scarce in comparison to material on the elite.

At this level also, Christianity was shaped by Chinese religious culture. The clearest example of this is the organization of the church. Aside from monasteries, Chinese religious organization was centred around 'associations' (hui), which were one of the most important ways of lay participation in the merit-making clerical life. Some associations had a more formal structure and met at regular times, others were looser assemblies. The activities included devotional practices, works of charity, or support of the local temple. Likewise, in the seventeenth century, Chinese Christians were not organized in parishes, i.e., geographical units around a church building, but in hui (assembly or association), often according to age, sex, and social background, with lay people as leaders (huizhang).³¹ In the late Ming period, Chinese Christians patterned their communities on Confucian or Buddhist models, some of them with an explicitly charitable purpose. In the early Qing, associations were a mixture of a Chinese type of social organization and European-inspired congregations, actively promoted by Francesco Brancati SJ (1623–71). Most congregations were open to people from different classes, but there were also special ones for women, for children, for literati, and for catechists. Such groups seem to have been widespread. For instance, around 1650, Shanghai counted seventy-nine congregations of Our Lady and twenty-seven of Our Lord; around 1665, there were around 140 congregations in Shanghai while there were more than 400 Christian congregations in the whole of China.

These communities of Christians (christianitas), however, were not only located in intellectual and administrative centres, but were spread all over the country, both in cities and villages. The embedment of Christianity at this local level took place in the form of what can be described as 'communities of effective rituals': groups of Christians whose lives were organized around certain rituals (mass, feasts, confession, etc.).³² These rituals were related to faith and doctrine, and were organized by a liturgical calendar. They were 'effective' both in the sense that they built a group and that they were considered by the members of the group as bringing meaning and salvation.³³

---

31 Standaert, 'Social organisation of the church: associations for lay-people', in Handbook of Christianity in China, pp. 456–61.
32 Standaert, 'Christianity as a religion in China', pp. 8–15.
33 For descriptions of the functioning of these communities in Fujian, see Zürcher, 'The Jesuit mission in Fujian'; Menegon, 'Ancestors, virgins, and friars'; in the Jiangnan region, see Golvers, François de Rougemont; Brockey, 'The harvest of the vine'; in Shanxi, see Margiotti, Il Cattolicismo nello Shansi.

Effective rituals were patterned according to the Christian liturgical calendar, which included not only the major liturgical feasts (Christmas, Easter, Pentecost, etc.), but also, similar to Buddhist or Taoist calendars, celebrations of the saints. The introduction of a 'Sunday' and of Christian religious feasts caused people to live according to a rhythm far different from the one practised in Buddhist or Taoist communities of effective rituals. The most apparent rituals were the sacraments, especially the celebration of the eucharist and confession. But common prayer, particularly reciting the rosary and the litanies, and fasting on specific days, also constituted important ritual moments. Occasionally there were also rituals accompanied by miraculous interventions through which they proved their immediate efficacy. In most cases, the happy discovery that the rituals 'work' appeared to be a primary motive for conversion.[34] This regular intervention of the supernatural in Christian communities, by way of miraculous healing, rescue from disaster, appearance of auspicious objects, or revival from temporary death constituted the way in which the efficacy of the faith was sustained. Christianity was in this way not just an intellectual construct but a living minority religion, a complex of beliefs, rituals, prayer, magic, icons, private piety and communal celebrations, in which both the elite and commoners alike participated. In that whole sphere of religious practice, Christianity was by no means a semi-Confucian hybrid; in fact, in many respects it was much closer to devotional Buddhism than Confucianism.[35] It is also at this ritual level where itinerant missionaries most strongly competed with Buddhist monks, Taoist priests, or local shamans and where they often inflated their differences.

While these characteristics form an essential part of European religiosity, it was in many respects the Chinese religious environment and the local ethos of religious tolerance that made it possible for Christian rituals to become part of the daily religious and social experience of Chinese Christians.[36] Indeed, these Christian communities also reveal some essential characteristics of Chinese religiosity: communities that are very much lay oriented and that have lay leaders; the important role of women as transmitters of rituals and traditions within the family; a service-oriented concept of priesthood (travelling priests present only at important feasts or celebrations); a doctrine expressed in a simple manner (recitative prayers, simple and clear moral principles, a pastoral fighting all kinds of fear supplemented by relief through confession); a belief in the transformative power of rituals (patterned in accordance with a liturgical

34 On this efficacy, see Zürcher, 'The Lord of Heaven and the Demons', p. 371.
35 Zürcher, 'Confucian and Christian religiosity', p. 650.
36 Menegon, 'Ancestors, virgins, and friars'.

calendar with feasts and yearly gatherings; the intervention of miraculous events). It seems that just in the same way that Chinese popular devotions and rituals were shaping the lives of common people, Christian practices also provided awe-inspiring ceremonies that mediated the quest for salvation within the daily struggle for survival.

Communities gradually came to function on their own. An itinerant priest would visit them once or twice a year; in certain cases, the communities themselves moved to the city for one day of liturgical activity. Ordinarily the leaders of the community brought the members together once a week and presided over the prayers, which most members knew by heart. They also read the sacred texts and organized religious instruction. There were often separate meetings for women. Moreover, there were itinerant catechists who instructed the children, catechumens, and neophytes. In the absence of a priest, these leaders administered baptism. During his annual visit of a few days, the missionary exchanged conversation with the leaders and members, received news from the community, enquired about ill people and catechumens, etc. He heard confessions, celebrated the eucharist, preached, baptized, and prayed with the community. After his departure, the community continued its common practice of saying the rosary and litanies. The ordinary Christian therefore only met the missionary once or twice a year. The real centre of Christian life was not the missionary but the community itself with its leaders and catechists as the major link. Once a Christian community was established in a given place, it tended to survive as a tolerated part of the local religious panorama over long periods of time, even if it was isolated from direct pastoral care as was the case during the confinement of missionaries in Canton in 1666–71.

If the 'real measure of Christian religious culture on a broad scale must be the degree to which time, space, and ritual observances came to be defined and grasped essentially in terms of the Christian liturgical year',[37] then the existence of these Christian communities of effective rituals is a confirmation of the 'Christian' embedment in China.

Conclusion

Christianity, as shaped by the Chinese in the seventeenth century, has often been used as a case study by theologians, missiologists, and various researchers interested in cultural contact in general. Scholars are continually fascinated by such aspects as Ricci's accommodation method, the inculturation of Christian

37 Van Engen, 'The Christian Middle Ages', p. 543.

thought by the Chinese Christians, or the way in which science spread in China. However, while these aspects of the historic exchange can still serve as objects of reflection for the scholar, for many Chinese in present-day China, the shape of Christianity in the seventeenth century has yet another significance: it is the origin of their identity. Indeed, present-day Christians trace their origins by a direct line of descent to the seventeenth century, and the rituals they practise and the prayers they chant today are still those of their ancestors.

Reception of Hinduism and Buddhism

INES G. ŽUPANOV AND R. PO-CHIA HSIA

In 1585, the Third Ecclesiastical Council of Goa, the hub colonial town of Portuguese India, issued an official declaration stating that some of the native Christians, who were recent converts, kept on moving out of the Portuguese territory into the 'infidel' hinterland in order to 'return to the caste [tomar casta]' by performing 'diabolical rites of the gentiles'. The way this is done is by going on a pilgrimage to some Pagodas (the temples) and by carrying out ceremonies of expiation helped by their Brahman priest (bragmanes sacerdotes) and, finally, by drinking 'foul drinks [immundicias]'. These apostates then return to Goa and live among the Christians, which causes scandal, because performing such rituals was considered an act in 'detestation of the faith [em detestação da fé]'.[1]

What may appear as a confusion for our contemporary sense of conversion and apostasy is the fact that in the sixteenth and seventeenth centuries caste and religious beliefs of the non-Christian population in India seem to be confounded and interchangeable according to the Portuguese colonial and ecclesiastical administrations. Moreover, the name and concept of 'Hinduism' as a religion of all Hindus does not exist during this period. Even the name 'Hindu', or 'indo', is a scarce word in Portuguese texts and deserves a history of its own.[2] In spite of the lack of use of familiar terms, it is safe to claim that the Portuguese did have a sense that these people, whom they simply called the gentiles (gentios), practised some kind of separate religion, but what exactly it was and how to go about uncovering its secrets was far from clear. On the other hand, the Portuguese identified instantly other religious groups such as the Muslims (mouros) and the Jews (judios) and the St Thomas Christians (cristãos de São Thomé).[3]

---

1 Rivara, *Archivo Portuguez Oriental*, fasc. 6, p. 125.
2 Delgado, *Glossário Luso-Asiático*, vol. 1, pp. 456–7.
3 Also called Syrian, Syro-Malabar Christians or Nazareni.

If we jump chronologically and cast a glance at the ideas of the British Orientalists and administrators in the nineteenth century, Hinduism, as a concept, as cultural practice and as a full-fledged religion, had already been constructed. Therefore to write a historical account of Hinduism is not possible without a history of its coming into being as a heterological construction negotiated between various Indian and foreign colonial actors.[4] Moreover, it has been argued by scholars like Smith that even the concept of religion with which we operate today had not yet been reified in European epistemological tradition and thus meant something else than a unified religion.[5] In fact, it usually meant a religious order, while terms such as 'law' (*lei*), 'sect' (*seita*), 'confession', 'science' (*sciencia*) carried the notion of adherence to religious ideas and practices. Paganism (*gentilidade*) was the name given to the unknown, although the generic term *gentio*, or *ethicus*, used for those who practised these yet unnamed 'superstitions', was sometimes confounded with 'infiel', which is used for the Muslim.

In the period under discussion and from the Portuguese Christian perspective, the religious practices of the gentiles in India were conceived as a plural religious world, in which demonic gods in all shapes, and innumerable rites and ceremonies performed by the gentile priests, were geared to keep in darkness and in ignorance the free will of the people and thus prevent them from acquiring salvation offered by Christianity. This negative assessment of paganism remained throughout the seventeenth century, but the increasing familiarity with specific religious doctrines, cosmologies and ritual gestures opened the way to cultural interaction, to hybridity, mimesis and the sense of religious relativism. The texts and documents produced in this exchange contributed, though not always in a straightforward way, to the modern construction of Hinduism.

From the Middle Ages and possibly before, European travellers to the East took home an image of India as a land of wonderful and 'maligned monsters'.[6] When the Portuguese went to India at the very end of the fifteenth century, they had, therefore, a bag full of chimerical expectations and visual templates. On the one hand, in their wishful thinking and nourished by a widespread millenarianism that reigned at the court of Dom Manuel in Portugal, they expected to find Oriental Christians ruled, as it was believed, by the Prester John.

4 King, *Orientalism and religion*.
5 Smith, *The meaning and end of religion*. Sweetman, 'Unity and plurality', pp. 209–24.
6 Mitter, *Much maligned monsters*.

Throughout the first half of the sixteenth century, Portuguese officials in Goa, settler-merchants (*casados*) and various other foreign travellers and adventurers steadily provided bits and pieces about the ethnography of the gentile religion.[7] In his *Livro*, Duarte Barbosa provided a minute description of the caste structure and its connection with religious rites of the societies encountered on the Malabar coast.[8] Domingo Paes and Fernão Nunes gave fascinating accounts about state religious culture at the court of the kingdom of Vijayanagara, situated at the heart of the Deccan plateau.[9]

Not all was expressed in words. The most formidable early pictorial account of Indian idolatry is found in the Códice Casanatense, a collection of seventy-six coloured drawings representing ethnographic scenes from Africa to China. It has been dated by Georg Schurhammer to around the 1540s. Besides purely secular themes at least eight of them can be identified as acts of religion. One depicts a chariot procession on the Konkan coast: a terrifying portrayal of a three-storey chariot full of people pulled by half-naked men with mighty ropes. Under the wheels of the chariot lie scattered two bleeding dismembered bodies. These sacrifices became famous in all learned and casual descriptions of Hindu fanaticism. The famous Jaganath temple in Puri (Orissa) became especially notorious for this kind of practice (picture XLIII);[10] hence, the English word 'Juggernaut'.[11] An unavoidable topos in all representations of Indian paganism is the custom of sati: the burning of women on their husband's death pyre. In one Casanatense picture, there is a somewhat different custom in which a still-living woman and her dead husband are buried alive.[12]

The authorship of the Casanatense collection is still disputed, although recently scholars have agreed that it was painted by a Gujerati or a Deccani artist and the legends were written by two different Lusitanian literati in Goa.[13] Who the patrons and the audience of these paintings were may not be easily answered. Whilst it has been suggested that it was the Jesuits who commissioned these images, if one closely examines the narrative content there is absolutely no mention of any proselytizing and conversion.

Whatever the case, the Jesuits accelerated and intensified the 'uncovering' of Indian 'paganism'. With a fine eye for detail and with superior theological

---

7 Loureiro, 'O Descobrimento da Civilização Indiana nas Cartas dos Jesuítas', pp. 107–25.
8 Barbosa, *O Livro do Duarte Barbosa*.
9 Rubies, *Travel and ethnology in the Renaissance*.
10 Matos (ed.), *Imagens do Oriente no século XVI*.
11 Yule and Burnell (eds.), *Hobson-Jobson: a glossary of colloquial Anglo-Indian words*, pp. 466–8.
12 Matos, *Imagens*, p. 83. 13 Mota, 'Códice Casanatense', pp. 34–46.

and cosmological tentacles, they went straight to the bottom of Indian idola-try. From Francis Xavier to Alessandro Valignano, many important and less-important Jesuit missionaries provided fragments of descriptions combined with theological intuitions and speculations. Their early letters record a jum-bled collection of superstitions, often likened to those encountered in Europe. In spite of stereotyping, some basic cultural traits that continue uninterrupt-edly into contemporary psychological make-up of the communities observed by the Jesuits stand out clearly in these early reports. One of these is demonic possession, which in South India in particular is closely connected with heal-ing.[14] In 1547, Manuel de Moraes wrote from Kanniyakumari, at the extreme end of the Indian peninsula, that:

> The Brahmans and some gentiles do their ceremonies [cyrymonyas], and one man makes himself into a figure of a demon, saying that he would cure and facilitate the birth; [there is] loud drumming and feasts, much painted cloth; and the one who made himself into the devil [diabo] . . . appears like the real demon.[15]

Various things are collapsed in this description and the Brahmans were already identified as Indian idolatrous priests. In Moraes's view, all non-Christian reli-gious activities were nothing but witchcraft, that is, manipulation of objects in order to obtain some earthly reward. Devoid of any spirituality and tran-scendentality, such practices were considered perilous and damaging. This perspective changed with the 'linguistic turn' that occurred around the 1570s, that is, with the first concerted efforts by the Jesuit missionaries to learn Indian vernacular languages.[16]

With the mastery of local idioms missionaries acquired a new understand-ing of the nature of Indian religious practices. The arrival of learned, aris-tocratic and non-Portuguese Jesuits from 1575 onwards, such as Alessandro Valignano and others, was also important because they applied a theologico-anthropological (i.e., Thomistic) grid to non-Christian religious sensitivities.[17] Not just blind idolatry, but the natural reason was thus detected in local rit-ual actions. Finally, some of the Brahmans who had converted in Goa and elsewhere cooperated willingly with European priests and Portuguese state officials. Brahman books written in Sanskrit, considered as the language of their 'science' by the Portuguese, were coveted and procured – by force, purchase or

---

14 Nabokov, *Religion against the self.*
15 Moraes to the members in Portugal, Cap Comorim, 15 December 1547, *Archivum Romanum Societatis Iesu*, Rome, N.N. 66 I, fol. 226v.
16 Wicki (ed.), *Documenta Indica*, vol. 10, pp. 827–31.
17 Pagden, *The fall of natural man.*

theft. Although Brahmans comprised only a fraction of the population, their definition of the situation had increasingly been taken into account. The 'Brahmanization' of the Portuguese and missionary perceptions of Indian religion took root at this time.

Interest in Brahmanical life-cycle rituals, their 'sciences' and sacred books grew and reached its apogee by the end of the sixteenth and in the early decades of the seventeenth centuries. There was a small number of Jesuit writers who had access to vernacular or Sanskrit texts. The majority of missionary corps resided in Goa and in places where Portuguese secular and ecclesiastical administration held sway. It was in the experimental (accommodationist) missions, where missionaries had to use persuasion rather than force and coercion, that the first accounts of Indian religion as a pan-Indian system started to take shape.[18]

One remarkable non-Jesuit account is by Frey Agostinho de Azevedo (1603), whose text was then very faithfully plagiarized by Diogo do Couto in his *Fifth Decada* (1612).[19] Azevedo's text, written as part of a report for the royal council of Philip III, presents Indian paganism as a system, not just a muddle of various rites, ceremonies, cosmogonies and scattered texts. Thus, he says, the gentiles recognize 'one and the only opinion concerning God, creation and corruption of the creatures', which they teach in their Brahmanical schools. All of these religious precepts are contained in books written in 'their Latin', which he calls Geredão (i.e., Sanskrit). Thus he identified Vedas, Sastras, Puranas and Agamas as the most sacred texts in which all gentile rites and ceremonies were classified and enumerated. Among the major themes of these Indian books we find typically Christian scholastic and theological concerns, such as 'the first cause, the first matter, the angels, the soul, the good and the bad' and similar. But as soon as the system is thus established, it is turned upside-down, because, as the author says, those are all 'lies'. Paganism is thus constructed as a Christian antipode.

Azevedo probably did not know any of the southern Indian languages and, therefore, relied entirely on his sources. Jacome Fenicio, whose manuscript 'Livro primeiro da Seita dos Indios Orientais, e principalmente dos Malauares' (1609) was also used by various plagiarizers such as Philippus Baldaeus and Manuel de Faria y Sousa, knew Malayam and Tamil very well.[20] For Fenicio, the 'Brahmenes in India' are like philosophers and geologists who have

---

18 Županov, *Disputed mission.*
19 Rubies, 'The Jesuit discovery of Hinduism', p. 228. Couto, *Da Asia*, pp. 1–48.
20 Charpentier, *The* Livro da Seita dos Indios Orientais *of Father Jacobo Fenicio*; Baldaeus, *A true and exact description*; Sousa, *Asia Portuguesa.*

'buried for others the true doctrine that the Philosophy and natural Geology teaches, and invented for the others one sect much devoid of reason'. Fenicio's stories of deeds and misdeeds of Indian gods, goddesses, demons and other supernatural beings are all infused with metaphors and allegories of sexual desire. The episodes of divine debauchery and fornication are strung together in overlapping stories.[21]

The reading of Hindu cosmology and theology as unspiritual, profane and dirty is shared by Fenicio's contemporary Diogo Gonçalves, who was also a Jesuit missionary in the Kerala region. His treatise, *História do Malavar* (1615), deals with 'political' customs and with 'the errors of the Malabars concerning the cult and adoration of God'.[22] This is a very militant Portuguese 'nationalist' text with no empathy for Hindu cosmogony and peculiar social practices, such as polyandry and caste (pollution) rules. What is interesting about the treatise is the fact that he divides Indian customs into political and religious, the division that became an important, albeit controversial, epistemic tool for approaching paganism after the famous dispute between Roberto Nobili and Gonçalo Fernandes Trancoso.

Neither Roberto Nobili nor Gonçalo Fernandes Trancoso intended to write an account of the paganism that they observed in the Madurai Mission, at the heart of the Tamil country, at the beginning of the seventeenth century. It was through their personal, political and 'ideological' clash that they forged two different perspectives on paganism. By establishing a separate, high-caste, 'aristocratic' mission in the same town, Nobili tried to dissociate Christianity from its image of low-caste religion practised by the Portuguese, the 'impure', meat-eaters and alcohol-drinkers, and by the pearl-fishing community of Parava Christians. Nobili's accommodationist mission was to target Brahmanical and the highest castes by presenting himself as a teacher of a new spiritual religion. Thus he lived and behaved as a Brahman *sannyasi* (hermit), he started learning Sanskrit from a Brahman teacher who later became his first convert, and he employed Brahman, vegetarian cooks. His method was inspired by Alessandro Valignano in Japan and Matteo Ricci in China and, moreover, had full approval from his superior in Cochin, the Provincial of the Malabar Province, Alberto Laerzio. Another Italian Jesuit missionary, Antonio Rubino, also started an accommodationist mission at the court of the King of Vijayanagara at Vellore at around the same time as Nobili in Madurai (1606). Political turmoil on the Coromandel coast, the order by the King of Spain and Portugal to end the mission in 1611, and Laerzio's change of heart as to the economic

---

21 Charpentier, *Livro da Seita*, p. 8.
22 Wicki (ed.), *P. Diogo Gonçalves S. I. Historia do Malavar*, p. 108.

viability of keeping two accommodationist experiments at the same time ended this experiment.[23]

The dispute between Nobili and Fernandes Trancoso, which began in 1606, outlived its first protagonists. Throughout the seventeenth century, the papacy and the newly established Congregation for the Propagation of Faith (1622) wavered between condemnation and celebration of the Jesuit accommodationist missions in India and China. In the eighteenth century, this complex history came to be known as the Malabar and Chinese Rites Controversy.

The Malabar Rite Controversy began in 1610 when Fernandes Trancoso denounced Nobili's turning of himself into a 'pagan' and a Brahman:

> His manner [was] to make believe that there are some or even big differences between us in religion . . . None of them [Nobili's Christian converts] designate themselves otherwise than as disciples of the Aiyer . . . because when they know who is their Curu [Guru] they know which is their sect and what [God] they venerate. The dress of the Father is that worn by the pagan Saneazes [sannyasis] of certain sects and he also wears a string . . . Neither myself, nor my servants, nor the Portuguese, nor the Christians [Paravas] go to his church or to his house.[24]

For Fernandes Trancoso, 'paganism' was, as he recorded a few years later (1616) in his *Tratado*, a 'brahmanical machine' and contrary to natural reason.[25] While to the Portuguese, missionary conversion consisted in annihilating all vestiges of paganism – something that was practically impossible in the missions beyond Portuguese administrative control – for Nobili, conversion was the grafting of Christianity onto pre-existing cultural and social patterns. Just as Matteo Ricci in China selected Confucianism as the best analogical vehicle for introducing Christianity, Nobili chose the Brahmanical cultural model as a way through which to propagate the 'true Christian faith'.

Under the burden of the Controversy, Nobili developed an adiaphoristic appraisal of Indian 'paganism', defining it as consisting mostly of 'indifferent', external customs that did not stand in the way of Christianization. In this way, Nobili opened a path for diversity and respect for local cultures within the global project of Christianization. This was then one of the first efforts at 'provincializing' European Christianity and thus promoting the universal character of the Christian religion. However, other colonial missionary actions realised that this was also a way to introduce cultural and religious relativism. That Christianization was not Portugalization was a statement that made not

23 Rubies, 'The Jesuit discovery of Hinduism'.
24 *Archivum Romanum Societatis Iesu*, Rome, Goa 51, fols. 29r–31v.
25 Wicki (ed.), *Tratado do Pe*, p. 3.

only the Portuguese state officials, but also Portuguese Jesuit missionaries, nervous.

In his three lengthy texts, *Responsio* (1610), *Informatio* (1613) and *Narratio* (1619), Nobili developed the thesis that there was no Hindu religion and that Indian paganism was simply 'civility'. Armed with theological theories developed in Europe by both Catholic and Protestant thinkers, Nobil 'proved' that, 'these people have one civility (or civil cult) and, in truth, multiple religions [*hi populi unum habeant civilem cultum, religionem vero multiplicem*]'.[26] The term 'religio' in this passage is used in the sense of religious order or religious sect; it does not mean a single religion in the contemporary sense of the word.

In the work Fernandes Trancoso wrote in response to Nobili in 1616, 'paganism' receives a name that comes closer to the notion of Hinduism: a unified religion of the Hindus. Under the heading 'bramanismo' he describes a series of prescriptive superstitious life-cycle ceremonies and thus added the first '-ism' to an 'Indian' word in an effort to make it into a concept.[27] It was a solitary effort and without immediate followers, but it signalled the uniqueness of the religion practised by the Indian gentiles.

While Jesuit missionaries debated the nature and origin of Indian customs and religious practices, by the end of the seventeenth century Dutch and German missionaries entered the scene and often used or plagiarized Jesuit texts. One of these was Philippus Baldaeus, who published '*Afgoderye der Oost-Indische heydenen* [*Idolatry of the East-Indian Heathens*]' (Amsterdam, 1672), which is considered as having borrowed much of its content from Fenicio's text. The Dutch Calvinist missionary Abraham Roger's book *De Open-Deure tot het verborgen Heydendom* (Leiden, 1651) became something of a bestseller and was translated into many European languages; this was a product of his research in Pulicat, a Dutch enclave on the Coromandel coast where he was helped by Brahman interpreters, 'Padmanaba' and others.[28] The Moravian missionary Bartholomäus Ziegenbalg (1682–1719), active in Tranquebar in the early eighteenth century, appreciated and used Roger's book when composing his own *Genealogie der malabarischen Götter* (written in 1713 and first published in 1791) and *Ausführliche Beschreibung des malabarischen Heidentums* (published in 1926).[29]

---

26 Rajamanickam (ed.), *Roberto de Nobili on adaptation*, p. 112.
27 *Ism* is a suffix that transforms an ordinary verb or a noun into a name, a 'concept' or a doctrine. It started its career in the loan words from Greek.
28 Halbfass, *India and Europe*, p. 46.
29 *Ibid.*, p. 47; Valle, *The travels of Pietro della Valle in India*; Castro and Bouchon (eds.), *Voyage de Pyrard de Laval aux Indes orientales*; Castro and Couto (eds.), *Voyage à Mozambique & Goa*; Carletti, *Ragionamenti del mio viaggio intorno al mondo*.

Besides missionaries, European travellers and Portuguese, French, Dutch and English administrators also contributed their 'secular' descriptions of Indian religious practices. As a rule, these descriptions focus on particular sensational and visual effects of paganism and they often copy each other's stories. In the seventeenth century, customs like *sati* and other blood sacrifices boosted a newly cherished moral superiority over the 'natives'. In fact, from the late sixteenth and early seventeenth centuries, foreign travellers such as Pietro della Valle, John Huyghen van Linschoten, Francesco Carletti and Pyrard de Laval trumpeted the fact that the Portuguese settlers in Goa and elsewhere were 'going native' and turning into pagans.[30] This was attributed to mixed marriages between Portuguese *casados* and Asian women. Idolatry and paganism were thus gendered, a characteristic that continued for several centuries.

While the Portuguese and their missionaries pondered over paganism and its social ramifications (caste, *sati*, hook-swinging, temple ceremonies), famous travellers in the middle of the seventeenth century, such as Jean-Baptiste Tavernier, Jean Bernier, Abbé Carré and others, cast their glances further inland towards the kingdom of the Great Moguls.[31] Comparison between the gentiles – with their Brahmans, temples and ceremonies – and the Islam of the Moguls became more frequent and gave food for thought to those in Europe who avidly read their books and correspondence.

At the turn of the eighteenth century, Indian paganism slowly turned into a 'Brahmanical System' as Filip Ivan Vesdin, alias Paulinus a Sancto Bartholomaeo (OCD), entitled his major work on the subject.[32] With this and efforts by other European and Indian scholars and reformers to define the totality of Indian religious practices and mythologies as a unified whole, what was once called idolatry, or paganism, arrived closer to its modern destiny, its name and place as one of the world religions: Hinduism.

Jesuit perceptions of Chinese Buddhism

It is well known that the first two Jesuits to reside in China, the Italians Ruggieri and Ricci, arrived in Zhaoqing, the capital of the Governor of Guangdong and Guangxi, dressed as Buddhist monks. For that reason, and on account of their claim of origins (from the West, from Goa, i.e., India), Ruggieri and Ricci

---

30 Burnell, *The voyage of J. H. van Linschoten to the East Indies.*
31 Tavernier; *Les Six voyages de Jean-Baptiste Tavernier*; Carré, *The travels of the Abbé Carré*; Bernier, *Travels in the Mogul Empire.*
32 Paulinus a Sancto Bartholomaeo, *Systema Brahmanicum.*

were treated by everyone as foreign Buddhist monks. In the initial years, then, the Jesuits led a double existence. While viewed by most as bearers of a new Buddhist teaching from India,[33] Ruggieri and Ricci tried their best to dispel that mistaken identification and to clarify the distinct teachings and rituals of Christianity in numerous conversations with curious visitors. The first result of that encounter with Buddhism left a mark in the very first Chinese work composed by the Jesuits, the *Tienzhu shengjiao shilu* (Veritable Records of the Holy Teachings of the Lord of Heaven), a catechism that Ruggieri probably began composing while he was still in Macau and completed in Zhaoqing in early autumn 1584. Cast in the form of a dialogue between a Confucian scholar and a missionary (in the preface Ruggieri signed off as Tianxu Zheng, a monk from India), one particular question was raised about the more than 4,000 *juan* of Buddhist sutras composed by the Buddha. The missionary replied the sutras were all wrong and ridiculous, singling out the doctrines of reincarnation and vegetarianism, and criticized the widespread popularity of the *Lotus Sutra*, the recitation of which supposedly gained the paradise of Pure Land for its devotees.[34]

By the time of Ruggieri's return to Europe and Ricci's assumption of leadership in the incipient mission, the imperative to distinguish Christianity from Buddhism was paramount. But even when the Jesuits moved in 1589 to Shaozhou (today Shaoguan) in northern Guangdong, the label of *heshang* (i.e., Buddhist monks) still haunted them. Directed by the magistrates to lodge first at the Nanhua monastery south of the city, famous on account of its erstwhile seventh-century monk Weineng, honoured as the Sixth Patriarch of Chinese Buddhism and founder of the southern school of Chan, Ricci and his associates resisted, having no intention to remain secluded in the hilly monastery; their mission was to evangelize in the city. The Nanhua monks were equally eager to see the Jesuits leave for they feared a takeover. Eventually, the Jesuits were given permission to settle in the city and reside in the Guangxiao monastery before finally acquiring their own residence. It was during their apprenticeship years in Shaozhou that the idea crystallized: a change of identity was necessary to promote the Christian faith. In the winter of 1593/4, Ricci secured permission from the Visitor in Macau, Alessandro Valignano, to grow a beard

---

33 Wang Pan, magistrate of Zhaoqing, graced the Jesuit residence with an engraved platform 'qien hua si' (The Moved Wondrous Flower Monastery); the chapel had a board with the characters 'xi lai zhen tu' (Pure Land of the West). See Table 12 and n. 254 in *Storia dell'introduzione del Cristianesimo in Cina*, ed. Pasquale M. D'Elia, 3 vols. (Rome, 1942–9), vol. 1.

34 *Tianzhu shengjiao shilu* 7a–b.

and short hair; the missionaries would shed Buddhist garb for scholar's cloak, wear the scholar's four-cornered hats instead of shaven heads; silk garments and berets were added to their wardrobe for ceremonial visits to officials.[35] In this, Ricci benefited much from the advice of one of the first prominent converts, the scholar Qu Rukui (Taisu),[36] whose brothers Qu Ruqi and Qu Ruyue were fervent Buddhist laymen.[37] From the same Qu Rukui, Ricci most likely gathered some knowledge of Buddhist doctrines. In later polemics with Buddhists, Ricci would deny the need of full textual knowledge of the sutras before refuting their doctrines.

We now enter the crucial phase of the Jesuit–Buddhist encounter, from *c.* 1595 to 1610, the year of Ricci's death. The most intense and sustained contact between Christianity and Buddhism occurred during these years, which shaped subsequent Jesuit and Chinese Christian attitudes towards Buddhism. The crucial factor was the new alliance with Confucianism, Ricci's progressive mastery of the Confucian classics, his new persona as a Western scholar, his widening network of friendship with the academic and official elites, and his growing reputation. It was precisely this expanding network with the Confucian elites that enabled a more intense encounter with Buddhism.

The nexus of Buddhist–Confucian synthesis was located in the Jiangnan region, in the southern capital of Nanjing and cities such as Hangzhou. When Ricci gained access to the elites after 1597, he was likewise drawn into closer contact with Buddhist intellectuals. Many of his Confucianist admirers were lay Buddhist devotees. One of them, Yang Tingyun, became a Christian convert; and together with Xu Guangqi and Li Zhizao were lauded as the Three Pillars of Christianity in China in early Jesuit sources. Yang's intense involvement and interest in Buddhism is well documented in Nicolas Standaert's study.[38] Xu Guangqi, likewise, was once interested in Buddhism, like many of his intellectual and social peers. Both would later compose anti-Buddhist tracts. In this world where Buddhist and Daoist texts were fashionable among the Confucian literati, Ricci found himself engaged in many dialogues with potential Confucian neophytes about the differences between Christianity and Buddhism. We have an example of this interlocution in the Chinese language account of the conversion of Yang Tingyun, *Yang Qiyuan xiansheng chaoxing shiji* (The

---

35 *Storia dell'introduzione del Cristianesimo*, n. 429.
36 On Qu Rukui and Catholicism, see Shen Dingping, 'Qu Taisu de jiahi', *Zhongguoshi yanjiu*, 1 (1997), pp. 135–46.
37 HCC, p. 602; Yü, *Kuan-yin*, pp. 138, 140; Shi Sengyan, *Mingmo Fojiao yanjiu* (Taipei, 1987), pp. 262, 269, 283; Huang Yilong, 'Qu Rukui (Taisu) jiashi yu shengping kao', *Dalu zazhi*, 895 (1994), pp. 8–10.
38 Standaert, *Yang Tingyun*.

Achievements of the Surpassing Nature Yang Qiyuan), compiled after Yang's death by Ding Zhilin.[39] Yang met Ricci in Hangzhou at the home of Li Zhizao, who had already received baptism. Attracted by Christian doctrines and Ricci, Yang suggested to Ricci that indeed the Lord of Heaven should be worshipped; but since Sakyamuni Buddha was also reputed to be a saint of the West, what harm was there in worshipping him as well? Ricci, who saw the spirit of toleration and religious synthesis among the Chinese as a weakness rather than a virtue,[40] retorted that Buddha disobeyed God and was nothing but a rebellious official and a bandit (luan chen zei zi).[41]

In early 1599, Ricci met and debated with the Buddhist monk Xuelang Hongen in an episode that made him a celebrity among literati circles. In spite of his generally dismissive attitude towards Buddhism – a false doctrine, borrowed Greek philosophical concepts, and plagiarized Christian ideas of heaven and hell;[42] 'a babylon of doctrines so intricate that no one can understand or explain it well'[43] – Ricci recognized the qualities of the eminent Buddhist monk. 'He was sufficiently different from the other heshang', wrote Ricci, 'because he was a great poet and learned, and knowledgeable of all the sects and practised in his own.'[44]

The years of Ricci's ascent witnessed a hardening of attitude towards Buddhism. His most famous work, Tianzhu Shiyi, 'True Meaning of the Lord of Heaven', written over four to five years prior to his settlement in Beijing, appeared in 1603.[45] More than a catechism, Tianzhu Shiyi offered a philosophical explanation of Christianity, using Confucian terminology and perspectives. Sprinkled with citations from the Confucian classics, it was simultaneously a savage attack on Buddhist doctrines and practices. One of the eight chapters in Tianzhu Shiyi (ch. 5) is entirely devoted to refuting Buddhism with the title 'Refutation of the false teachings concerning reincarnation in the Six Directions and the taking of life, and an explanation of the true meaning of fasting.' Ricci ascribed the origins of the idea of reincarnation to Pythagoras, who created it to restrain the evil of his times. After his death, Ricci asserted, this notion spread to India, where Sakyamuni Buddha, in the midst of creating his own sect, appropriated it to add to his teachings of the Six Directions. In his refutation of Reincarnation, Ricci relied primarily on the Platonic notion of distinctions in the soul. No Buddhist sutra was cited; Buddhist beliefs were

39 On this source see ibid., p. 51.   40 Storia, n. 199.
41 Yang Qiyuan xiansheng chaoxing shiji, 1b.   42 Storia, n. 183.
43 Ibid., n. 186.   44 Ibid., n. 557.
45 A convenient bilingual edition in Chinese and English is The true meaning of the Lord of Heaven (T'ien-chu Shih-I), trans. Douglas Lancashire and Peter Hu (St Louis and Taipei, 1985).

stated summarily, and the objections verged on caricature. Nonetheless, there are two points worth remarking in Ricci's anti-Buddhist refutation: Greek philosophy, especially Plato, served as his intellectual foundation; and Confucian social ethics was invoked as a new ally in this battle against Buddhism.

The new alliance with Confucianism, as we have seen, acquired an intellectual content, as Ricci and his closest Chinese Christian associates developed a Christianized Confucianism as the intellectual template for conversion. Invoking the authority of the Song dynasty neo-Confucian master Zhu Xi, who was himself critical of Buddhism, served to double the new legitimacy claimed by the Jesuit mission. This strategy of conversion – 'to cleanse pure Confucianism of Buddhist corruption', 'to harmonize Christianity and Confucianism' – had different effects. For sympathetic literati, such as Yang, Xu, Li, and many others of their generation, it served as the intellectual justification for conversion. For sceptical literati, such as Wang Zheng, it was nothing but a disguise to undermine tradition and introduce a foreign evil. For Buddhists, it amounted to a declaration of war. The Jesuit/Christian polemic against Buddhism provoked a spirited rejoinder: three works by leading monks, the *Tianshuo* (*c.* 1615) by Zhuhong (1535-1615), the *Pixie ji* (1643) by Ouyi Zhixu (1599–1665), and the *Piantian sanshuo* by Miyun Yuanwu (1566–1642); and the influential collection *Poxie ji* (1640) by the layman Xu Changzhi.[46]

All of these works, of course, appeared after the death of Ricci. Instigated by his attack, the Christian–Buddhist polemic reached a climax in the years between 1610 and 1640. This period witnessed the publication and compilation of the major Buddhist anti-Christian treatises, as well as the most extensive Christian refutations of Buddhism, the *Tianshi mingbian*, 'Clear Discussion on Heaven and Buddhism' (1621) by Yang Tingyun and the *Pi Shishi zhuwang*, 'A Critique of the Various Errors of Buddhism' by Xu Guangqi.[47] With the Manchu conquest, a new epoch cooled polemical passions. No anti-Christian tracts seemed to have been composed by Buddhists after 1648, while only a handful of specifically anti-Buddhist treatises were published, all by Chinese converts.[48]

---

46 On this literature, see the introductory remarks in *HCC*, vol. 1: *635–1800*, pp. 511ff; Kern, *Buddhistische Kritik am Christentum im China*; Shi Shengyan, *Mingmo Zhongguo Fojiao zi yanjiu*, pp. 49–56; Cha Shijie, 'Ming mo fo jiao dui Tianzhu jiao de pi xie yun dong chu tan.'

47 For editions of Yang's work, see Standaert, *Yang Tingyun*, p. 69. HCC argues that *Pi Shishi zhuwang* was an attributed work and not actually by Xu, composed probably after 1670. There is, however, no supporting argument to this assertion. See HCC, p. 617.

48 The works in question are: 1. *Shen mi pian*, 'On awakening from confusion' (1667) by Luo Guangpin; 2. *Pi lüeshuo tiaobo*, 'Abridged refutation of several disputable points' (1589), compiled by Zhang Xingyao and Hong Ji. There is a detailed discussion in D. E.

For European missionaries, knowledge of Buddhism seemed to have stabilized at a functional level. In other words, by the mid-seventeenth century, the Jesuit Mission knew enough about Buddhism for catechism and evangelization, while avoiding confrontation in polemical debates. All energies were focused on the appropriation and translation of the Confucian canon.[49] And, like the Confucian elites they professed to emulate, the Jesuits also adopted a socially superior and condescending attitude towards their former arch-rivals. In *Tianxue luyi*, 'A Brief Synopsis of the Learning of Heaven', composed by the Portuguese Jesuit João Monteiro in 1642, the anti-Buddhist Confucian–Christian front was clearly articulated: 'The Confucian today also views Buddhism as ridiculous. If there are any well-known Confucian scholars who believe in Buddhism and Daoism, not only do they sin against the Lord of Heaven but they turn their back on the precepts of Confucius and Mencius as well.'

Throughout the seventeenth century, Jesuit missionaries continued to offer short descriptions of Buddhism in compendia on China destined for European audiences. Among these works, the most perceptive insight was offered by the Portuguese Alvaro Semedo, who gave a succinct and even-handed description of Buddhism in his *Relação da Grande Monarquia da China* (1637), a work devoid of the triumphalism and defensiveness in Ricci's memoirs. The reader is offered brief but succinct information on many subjects: the legend of Sakyamuni's birth and enlightenment; the date of Buddhism's first introduction into China; the current status of the Buddhist clergy, under the supervision of the Board of Rites; the appearance, fasting, and rituals of the Buddhist clergy; their further division into monastic, mendicant, and ascetic ways of life; a brief summary of the doctrine of the transmigration of souls and rebirth; and the ten realms of being. While Semedo pointed out some mendicant monks were no more than thieves and criminals, it was also a critique that resounded in the writings of leading Buddhist monastic reformers of the time such as Zhuhong and Zhixu. All in all Semedo viewed the Samgha in a surprisingly positive light: 'The majority of these monks do not give scandal, being very patient, docile, and respectful, coming from the fact they live a humble life or from the little estime that keeps them feeling lowly'.[50] The aim of the monastic life was to do penance in this life in the hope of betterment for the future. After describing the Buddhist logic of rebirth, Semedo observed that

Mungello, *The forgotten Christians of Hangzhou*, pp. 122–41. 3. Liu Ning, *Juesi lu* (after 1690).
4. Yu Xianghua, *Xing shi mi bian*, 'A treatise to awaken the confused world' (1714).
49 Rule, *K'ung-tzu or Confucius.*
50 Semedo, *Relação de Grande Monarquia da China*, p. 170.

the most cultivated or the most given to atheism abandoned this way, which they call exterior, to follow an interior and secret [way] . . . concentrating entirely on knowing the First Principle (which is the actual doctrine of the Buddha), believing all things are the same, all things being the same with him, without any essential distinction, working, always, through extrinsic qualities that he is subject to, like wax made into various figures that melt and turn to liquid, remaining hardly wax itself.[51]

Beyond a common Christian mode of understanding, the Jesuits in China did not necessarily share a common assessment of Buddhism, even if they came from a similar background. The example of Antonio de Gouvea is a case in point. Following his countryman Semedo, Gouvea arrived in the Jesuit Vice-Province in China through Goa and Macau. While Semedo still participated in the heady days of early Jesuit success (he arrived in 1613), Gouvea got to Hangzhou in 1636 and lived through the tumult of Manchu conquests and rebellions, which almost wrecked the foundations of the mission. The times were very different. While Semedo witnessed the Buddhist revival in full swing, by the 1630s, when Gouvea learned of China, three of the four great Buddhist monks central to the revival had long passed away.[52] In his manuscript *Asia Extrema*, written in 1644 and never published in full,[53] Gouvea too recounted the introduction of Buddhism into China and its fluctuating historical fortunes. He had little regard for its philosophy or doctrine: the first was borrowed from the Greeks, including Pythagoras's idea of the transmigration of souls, a common view shared by other Jesuits as we have seen, such as Ricci and Semedo; the latter represented only the shadow of truth and full of lies and falsehoods. 'They confuse the place of rewards and punishments, and do not place souls in heaven or on earth.'[54] Their doctrine of reincarnation, while tied to the idea of reward for the good life and chastisement for an evil one, served mainly to enrich the Buddhist clergy. Sounding like a Protestant reformer, Gouvea castigated Buddhist monks for staging all sorts of ceremonies and works of charity in order to fleece the faithful of their money, promising to liberate the souls of departed loved ones. Although they possessed a large number of

51 *Ibid.*, p. 171.
52 Zhuhong died in 1615, Zhengho died in 1603, Hanshan Teqing died in 1623, and only Zhixu was alive. For biographies of the four monks, see Chün-fang Yü, *The renewal of Buddhism in China*; Hsu, Sung-peng, *A Buddhist leader in Ming China*; Shi Shengyen, *Mingmo Zhungguo Fojiao di yenjiu*; Shi Guoxiang, *Zi bo da shi yanjiu*; Fan Jialing, *Zi bo da shi shengping ji qi sixiang yanjiu*. For brief biographical sketches, see He Qimin, *Zhongguo mingdai zhongjiao shi*, pp. 24–31.
53 There is a modern edition being prepared by Horácio P. Araújo. Only Book I of Part I has so far been published by Fundação Oriente Lisbon in 1995.
54 Gouvea, p. 293.

books, they propagated confusing and obscurantist doctrines, a criticism that echoed Ricci's critique of the profusion of Buddhist texts.[55]

The overall impression is that Gouvea understood little of Buddhist ideas and liturgies. While noting the important soteriological function of chanting Buddhist monks at Chinese funeral rituals, Gouvea betrayed his ignorance of its foundational idea when he remarked that monks in temples continued to chant the following words: 'nanwu amituofo', which, according to Gouvea, 'has no more sense than to say: the pagodas are not from the South, which is China, but from the West, which is India, therefore we will go there'.[56] The chant, 'nanwu amituofo', literally meaning 'I beseech you Amitabha Buddha', signified the devotee's desire to be reborn in the Pure Land of the West, the Land of Amitabha Buddha. The enormous popularity of Buddha recitation 'nien-fo' ranged in practice from quiet meditation, visualization, to audible chanting, and was widely popular in lay Buddhism.[57]

If Buddhist doctrines still represented a shadow of truth, the Buddhist clergy, in Gouvea's opinion, had no redeeming qualities. In stark contrast to Semedo, Gouvea wrote:

> they are all villainous, from the people, more vicious than the average, whence they are neither esteemed nor respected. They are sold or given for some cause as children to the temples, and are raised by the monks. Each one has his own disciples, and inherits the mantle of the master upon his death, with the obligation to buy disciples in order to propagate and multiply themselves, as each day large numbers who go about without any relatives or desire for betterment in life become monks, except for some literati who, in order to have quietude or work, cut their hair and live like monks, but not amongst them. And not a few of these same monks, repenting [of their decision], grow their hair and turn to their old ways. They are all normally uncultivated, vulgar, unlettered, leading an indolent life verging on vices, and debasing themselves in such a way that they debase and discredit very much the Buddhist sect that they profess.[58]

The paradoxical position of the Buddhist clergy versus the state was noted by Gouvea: the mandarins considered them inferior and did not hesitate to administer corporal punishments; but while regulated by the state, the Buddhist clergy flourished in the last decades of the Ming dynasty thanks to the patronage of palace eunuchs and members of the imperial household.[59]

55 *Ibid.*, p. 294.   56 *Ibid.*, p. 293.   57 Yü, *Renewal of Buddhism*, pp. 11, 45–6.
58 Gouvea, p. 294.   59 *Ibid.*, pp. 294–5.

For the missionaries, the Confucian–Christian synthesis, or the Jesuit way of proceeding in China, remained very much the guiding intellectual and conversion strategy throughout the seventeenth century. That they succeeded in becoming courtiers in the new Qing dynasty – as astronomers, engineers, mathematicians, painters, and musicians – surpassed perhaps the expectations of the first generation of fathers. It was from this elevated position in the midst of the Forbidden City that the Jesuits viewed the Buddhist clergy. The Portuguese Gabriel de Magalhães was an example.

Arriving in China during the last years of the Ming dynasty, Magalhães survived captivity by the brutal rebel leader Zhang Xianzhong in the 1640s and the persecution against Jesuit court astronomers instigated by the mandarin Yang Guangxin in 1664–5, the so-called Calendar Case.[60] To gather information for his book on China, which he finished in 1668 but only published later in French translation in 1688,[61] Magalhães used his contacts at the imperial court. On the Buddhist clergy, Magalhães turned to a friendly colleague at the Board of Rites, who consulted bureaucratic records before giving the Portuguese Jesuit the figures of 480 important Buddhist temples and 350,000 registered Buddhist clerics. In Beijing alone, Magalhães was told, there were 10,668 registered monks. Since for every patented monk there were six or seven unlicensed ones, Magalhães concluded there were well over one million Buddhist monks in the entire empire.[62] This, in fact, constituted the only remark on Buddhism in a long discourse on Chinese civilization and government, one page out of more than 230 in a modern edition. For Magalhães, Chinese civilization was synonymous with Confucian culture and the Confucianist state, with which the Jesuit mission was firmly identified.

In the late seventeenth century, before the so-called 'Edict of Toleration' issued by Emperor Kangxi in 1692, the apogee of the Catholic mission, the Jesuit position on Buddhism, and on Chinese religion and civilization in general, was well summarized by Louis Le Comte, missionary in China from 1687 to 1691, procurator of the China Mission in France thereafter, famous for his treatise, *Nouveaux mémoires sur l'état présent de la Chine* (Paris, 1697),[63] whose statements

---

60 See HCC, pp. 513–15.
61 The original Portuguese manuscript is lost. The book was published under the title *Nouvelle relation de la Chine* (Paris, 1688). I used a modern Portuguese edition: Gabriel de Magalhães SJ, *Nova Relação da China*, trans. Luís Gonzaga Gomes (Macau: Fundação Macau, 1997).
62 Magalhães, *Nova*, p. 96.
63 The edition cited here is from the 1697 English edition: *Memoirs and observations topographical, etc. made in a late journey through the Empire of China* (London: Benjamin Tooke, 1697).

on Chinese religion were condemned by the Sorbonne. Describing the ancient and modern religions of the Chinese, Le Comte speculated that the children of Noah in all probability founded the empire and transmitted the knowledge of the true God. Ancient Chinese religion was pure, as reflected in the teachings of Confucius, and became corrupted only by Daoism.[64] But a more pernicious danger to this corrupted religion was Buddhism. In his words:

> This poison began at court, but spread its infection thro' all the provinces, and corrupted every town; so that this great body of men already spoiled by magick and impiety, was immediately infected with idolatry, and became a monstrous spectacle for all sorts of errors. Fables, superstitions, transmigration of souls, idolatry and atheism divided them, and got so strong a mastery over them, that even at this present, there is no so great impediment to the progress of Christianity as is this ridiculous and impious doctrine.[65]

In fact, Sakyamuni Buddha's sin lay in leading his followers from idolatry to atheism because his first principle was Nothingness, by which the devil succeeded in 'eras[ing] out of the minds of some those excellent ideas of God which are so deeply ingraved there, and to imprint in the minds of others the worship of false gods under the shapes of a multitude of different creatures'.[66]

If the Jesuits were sometimes presenting one face to the Chinese and another to Europeans, they were consistent in their disdain for Buddhism in both their Western and Chinese writings. In *Simo zhenlun*, 'On the Four Last Things', the Belgian Philippe Couplet ridiculed the Buddhist idea of reincarnation: 'What the Buddhists state, on transcending the three worlds, or that even those in heaven cannot escape rebirth in the six categories of being, or that those in hell can be reborn in heaven; what ridiculous and false arguments! They are all fabrications of the devil.'[67] Or take the Chinese works by Andrea-Giovanni Lubelli, in which he claimed that Buddha was only a human being,[68] and that he should not be worshipped because he was like a rebellious official to an emperor-God.[69] Comparing Sakyamuni Buddha to a rebellious official was relegating Buddhism to a position subordinate to Christianity in the language of Confucian statecraft. As the reader may recall, this expression was ascribed to Matteo Ricci in his dialogue with Yang Tingyun, as recorded in the account of Yang's conversion, *Yang Qiyuan xiansheng chaoxing shiji*. Whether the actual expression stemmed from Ricci or Yang, it signified the centrality of the Jesuit Confucian–Christian strategy of conversion.

---

64 Le Comte, p. 321.   65 *Ibid.*, p. 323.   66 *Ibid.*, p. 325.   67 *Simo zhenlun*, preface.
68 *Tianzhu shengjiao xu yan* (1676), 4b–5b.   69 *Tianzhu shengjiao lueshuo* (1674), 18a–b.

We can, at this stage, come to some conclusions on the Jesuit knowledge of Buddhism:

1. The knowledge of Buddhist texts was minimal and superficial. In the Jesuit writings we have surveyed, only one text, the *Lotus Sutra*, was cited by title. But even in Ruggieri's dialogue, where this occurred, the text of the Sutra was never cited. In fact, no excerpt from a Buddhist work appeared in any of the Jesuit writings. There may be many reasons for this. The sheer volume of sutras (teachings by the Buddha) and sastras (treatises on Buddhist doctrines), the absence of a commonly acknowledged hierarchy of sutras in the Buddhist *Tripitaka*, the often contradictory and competing doctrines, and the difficult technical terms and metaphysical concepts no doubt all contributed to this textual ignorance. But compared to the assiduous and creative appropriation of Confucian texts by several generations of Jesuits in China, there is only one conclusion to be drawn. Their ignorance of Buddhist texts reflected the disinterest in Jesuit missionaries. In Ricci's words, Buddhism represented 'a babylon of doctrines so intricate that no one can understand or explain it well". Still, given a sympathetic reading, one could find someone like Semedo, who grasped the central idea of no-being and the sameness of all things in his brief discussion of Buddhism. Semedo, however, gave no reference to his source: whether it came from reading Buddhist texts or from conversing with practitioners.

2. While there are references to different Buddhist practices and beliefs, such as *nien-fo* (Buddha recitations) and meditations, Jesuit commentators seemed to have only a superficial knowledge of Buddhist schools. Neither Chan nor Pure Land Buddhism, the two surviving schools in Ming Buddhism, was named in Jesuit writings. References to the history of Buddhism were limited to stating the first introduction of Buddhism.

3. Refutation of Buddhist doctrines focused exclusively on Rebirth (samsara). The doctrines of nirvana, Emptiness (Sunyata), Buddha-nature (buddhata) or Dharma-body (dharmakaya) did not appear in Jesuit texts. There is little attempt to comprehend or refute the metaphysics of Buddhism beyond stating the truth of Greco-Christian metaphysics. As a religion based on an omnipotent First-Cause and the ultimate reality of the Self, Christianity stood at the other side of a chasm that separated it from the Buddhist idea of no-self and the reluctance to state primary causes.

4. The critique of Buddhist practices correctly identified the major soterio-logical liturgies such as funeral chants and Buddha-recitations that made Buddhism in the Ming dynasty a popular and laicized religion. Significantly, with the exception of one remark by Ricci that mentioned the anger of the Buddhists because Christian converts were required to destroy statutes of Guanyin,[70] the Jesuits in general failed to mention Guanyin even though her cult represented the most widespread form of popular Buddhist devotion in China. The obvious question arises: did the obvious similarity between the Marian and Guanyin cults discourage Jesuit commentary on this matter? Ricci's memoirs testified to the confusion during the first years of the mission:[71] some Chinese wondered whether the Jesuits worshipped a female deity when they saw a representation of the Virgin Mary; others confused the name of the Virgin in Chinese, *Tianzhu shengmu leng leng*, with sim-ilar appellations for female deities in popular Chinese and folk Buddhist beliefs.[72]

5. In terms of chronology, the most intense period of contact between Chris-tianity and Buddhism occurred during the first two generations of Jesuit missionaries. Ricci was the only Jesuit to have engaged in personal conver-sations, debates, and written polemics with leading Buddhist lay and clerical intellectuals.

The Jesuit encounter with Buddhism thus proceeded through stages: from similitude, differentiation, polemics, demonization, contempt, to indifference. Their evaluation of Buddhism also influenced missionaries of the mendi-cant orders, who borrowed generously from the commonplaces of earlier Jesuit/Chinese Christian anti-Buddhist polemics. The focus in the mendicant texts is on the refutation of Buddhist doctrines, specifically the doctrine of rebirth and vegetarianism, as exemplified by the Dominican Juan García's *Tianzhu shengjiao rumen wenda* (1642),[73] itself compiled from earlier Jesuit cate-chisms,[74] or by the Franciscan Pedro Piñuela's *Chu hui wenda* (1680),[75] whereas the Franciscan Agustín de San Pascual focused his arguments solely on the doctrine of reincarnation in *Renhun yicheng* (1680). Wary of the Jesuit way of proceeding, the mendicant orders kept a distinct clerical identity; they were

---

70 Storia, n. 673.　　71 *Ibid.*, n. 246, 247.

72 On Guanyin and Venerable Mother cults in China, which appeared to the Chinese to be akin to Marian devotion, see Yü, *Kuan-yin*, pp. 449–86.

73 The refutations are on pp. 8b–12a.　　74 HCC, p. 611.

75 The refutations are on pp. 18a-19a. Piñuela's catechism has been translated into Portuguese and analysed by Girard in *Os Religiosos Ocidentais na China*, pp. 317–441.

Western clerics, not Western literati; they served the church as missionaries, not the emperors as mandarins. While many mendicant friars criticized the Jesuit-mandarins at court, they themselves could not escape the dilemma that faced the first Jesuit missionaries. Or, as it was put to the Augustinian Miguel Rubio by a Chinese interlocutor: 'Your religion teaches fasting and uses prayer beads; how is this different from Buddhist monks?'[76]

---

76 *Shi ke wen* (1694), 2 vols. Here vol. 2, question 48. On the authorship of the work, see HCC, p. 145.

Bibliography

SERIES

Texts

Acta S. Congregationis de Propaganda Fide Ecclesiam Catholicam Ucrainae et Bielorusijae spectantia. Ed. A. Welykyi. 4 vols. (Rome, P. P. Basiliani, 1953–).

Bibliotheca reformatoria Neerlandica. Ed. Samuel Cramer and Fredrik Pijper. 10 vols. ('s-Gravenhage: M. Nijhoff, 1903–14).

Bibliotheca sanctorum, 12 vols. (Rome: Città nuova editrice, 1961–9), Index (1970), 2 appendix vols. (1987, 2000).

Calvin, John, *Ioannis Calvini Opera quae supersunt omnia.* Ed. G. Baum, E. Cunitz *et al.* 59 vols. (Braunschweig: C. A. Scwetschke, 1863–80).

Documenta Anabaptistica Neerlandica. Ed. Albert Fredrik Mellink. 5 vols. (Leiden, E. J. Brill, 1975–).

Documenta Indica. Ed. Joseph Wicki. 18 vols. (Rome: Monumenta Historica Soc. Iesu, 1948–).

Documenta Pontificum Romanorum historiam Ucrainae illustrantia (1075–1953). Ed. A. Welykyi. 2 vols. (Rome: P. P. Basiliani, 1953).

Hierarchia ecclesiastica Orientalis: series episcoporum Ecclesiarum christianarum Orientalium. Ed. Giorgio Fedalto. 2 vols. (Padua: Ed. Messagero, 1988).

Litterae nuntiorum apostolicorum historiam Ucrainae illustrantes (1550–1580). Ed. A. Welykyi. 13 vols. (Rome: P. P. Basiliani, 1959–).

Litterae S. Congregationis de Propaganda Fide Ecclesiam Catholicam Ucrainae et Bielorusjae spectantes (Rome: P. P. Basiliani, 1954–).

Luther, Martin, *D. Martin Luthers Werke. Kritische Gesamtausgabe.* 101 vols. (Weimar: Böhlau, 1883–1970).

> *Martin Luther. Studienausgabe.* Ed. Hans-Ulrich Delius. 6 vols. (Berlin: Evangelische Verlagsanstalt, 1979–99).

Monumenta Ucrainae historica. Ed. Andrii Sheptyts'kyi and O. Baran. 14 vols. (1075–1632). (Rome: 1964–).

Quellen und Forschungen zur Reformationsgeschichte (Gütersloh: Gerd Mohn, 1911–).

Quellen und Abhandlungen zur Schweizerischen Reformationsgeschichte. Series I, ed. Emil Elgi. 3 vols. (Basel: Basler Buch- und Antiquariatshandlung, 1901–5). Series II, 1 vol. (Leipzig: M. Heinsius, 1912).

Quellen zur Geschichte des kirchlichen Unterrichts in der evangelischen Kirche Deutschlands zwischen 1530 und 1600. Ed. Johann Michael Reu. 4 vols., in 9 (Gütersloh: C. Bertelsmann, 1904–35).

Schmauss, Johann Jakob (ed.), *Neue und vollständigere Sammlung der Reichs-Abschiede.* 4 vols. (Frankfurt a. M.: Koch, 1747; rpt. Osnabrück: Zeller, 1967).

Schriften des Vereins für Reformationsgeschichte (Gütersloh: Bertelsman, 1883–).

Schultz, Selina G. *et al.* (eds.), *Corpus Schwenckfeldianorum.* 19 vols. (Leipzig: Breitkopf und Hartel, 1907–61).

Sehling, Emil (ed.), *Die Evangelischen Kirchenordnungen des XVI. Jahrhunderts.* 13 vols. (Leipzig: O. R. Reisland, 1902–13; Tübingen: Mohr, 1955–80).

Travaux d'humanisme et Renaissance. 338 vols. (Geneva: E. Droz, 1950–)

Urkundliche Quellen zur Hessischen Reformationsgeschichte (Marburg: Elwert, 1915–).

Zwingli, Huldreich, *Huldreich Zwinglis sämtliche Werke.* Ed. Emil Egli, Georg Finsler *et al.* 12 vols. (Berlin: Schwetschke und Sohn, 1905–).

Zwingli, Ulrich, *Ulrich Zwingli Opera. Completa editio prima.* Ed. Johann Melchior Schuler and Johannes Schultheiss. 10 vols. (Turicil: apud Fridericum Schulthessiana, 1829–42).

Translations

Aquinas, Thomas, *The basic writings of Saint Thomas Aquinas.* Ed. A. C. Pegis. 2 vols. (New York: Random House, 1945).

Cambridge studies in early modern history (Cambridge: Cambridge University Press, 1970–).

Classics of the radical Reformation. Ed. John H. Yoder *et al.* 10 vols. (Scottdale, PA: Herald Press, 1973–).

Erasmus, Desiderius, *Collected works of Erasmus.* Ed. Richard Schoeck and Beatrice Corrigan. 84 vols. (Toronto: University of Toronto Press, 1974–).

Library of Christian Classics (Philadelphia: Westminster Press, 1953–).

Luther, Martin, *Luther's works. American edition.* Ed. Jaroslav Pelikan and Helmut Lehman. 55 vols. (St Louis; Philadelphia: Concordia Fortress Press, 1955–76).

New approaches to European history. Ed. William Beik and T. C. W. Blanning (Cambridge: Cambridge University Press, 1993–).

Studies in church history (London: Ecclesiastical History Society [various imprints], 1964–).

Studies in medieval and Reformation traditions: history, culture, religion, ideas (Formerly *Studies in medieval and Reformation thought*). 98 vols. (Leiden: E. J. Brill, 1966–).

LEXICA, DICTIONARIES, ENCYCLOPAEDIAS AND REFERENCE WORKS

Bibliographie hellénique ou description raisonnée des ouvrages publiés par des Grecs au XVIIe siècle. Ed. E. Legrand. vols. 1–4 (Paris: 1894–1903; Bruxelles: Reed, 1963).

The Blackwell dictionary of Eastern Christianity. Ed. K. Parry, D. J. Melling *et al.* (Oxford: Blackwell Publishers, 1999).

The Cambridge history of China. Ed. Denis Twitchett and John K. Fairbank. 15 vols. (Cambridge: Cambridge University Press, 1978–).

Diccionario histórico de la Compañía de Jesús. Ed. Joaquín Domínguez and Charles O'Neill. 4 vols. (Rome: Institutum Historicum S. I.; Madrid: Universidad pontificia Comillas, 2001).

Encyclopedia of witchcraft. Ed. Richard Golden. 4 vols. (St Barbara, CA: ABC-Clio, 2005).

Handbook of Christianity in China. Ed. Nicolas Standaert (Leiden: Brill, 2001).

Handbook of early modern history, 1400–1600. Late Middle Ages, Renaissance, and Reformation. Ed. Thomas A. Brady, Jr, Heiko A. Oberman, and James D. Tracy (Leiden: Brill, 1994).

Hierarchia ecclesiastica Orientalis: series episcoporum Ecclesiarum christianarum Orientalium. A cura di Giorgio Fedalto. 2 vols. (Padua: Ed. Messagero, 1988).

The Oxford encyclopedia of the Reformation. Ed. Hans J. Hillerbrand. 4 vols. (New York: Oxford University Press, 1996).

Hobson-Jobson, A glossary of colloquial Anglo-Indian words [. . .]. Ed. H. Yule and A. C. Burnell (rpt. New Delhi: Munshiram Manoharlal, 1979).

Kleines Wörterbuch des Christlichen Orients. Ed. J. Assfalg and Paul Krüger (Wiesbaden: Otto Harrassowitz, 1975).

FREQUENTLY CITED WORKS

Benedict, Philip, *Christ's churches purely reformed: a social history of Calvinism* (New Haven: Yale University Press, 2001).

Châtellier, Louis, *The Europe of the devout: the Catholic Reformation and the formation of a new society* (Cambridge: Cambridge University Press, 1989; French orig., 1987).

Grell, Ole Peter, and Porter, Roy (eds.), *Toleration in Enlightenment Europe* (Cambridge: Cambridge University Press, 2000).

Grell, Ole Peter, and Scribner, Robert (eds.), *Tolerance and intolerance in the European Reformation* (Cambridge: Cambridge University Press, 1996).

Hsia, R. Po-chia, *Social discipline in the reformation: central Europe, 1550–1750* (London and New York: Routledge, 1989).

  The world of Catholic renewal, 1540–1770. New Approaches to European History, 12 (Cambridge and New York: Cambridge University Press, 1998).

Monter, E. William, *Judging the French Reformation. Heresy trials by sixteenth-century parlements* (Cambridge, MA: Harvard University Press, 1999).

Pettegree, Andrew, *Foreign Protestant communities in sixteenth-century London* (Oxford: Clarendon Press, 1986).

Schilling, Heinz (ed.), *Kirchenzucht und Sozialdisziplinierung im frühneuzeitlichen Europa* (Berlin: Duncker & Humblot, 1994).

Schutte, Anne Jacobson, *Aspiring saints: pretense of holiness, Inquisition, and gender in the Republic of Venice, 1618–1750* (Baltimore: Johns Hopkins University Press, 2001).

Scribner, Robert W., *For the sake of the simple folk. Popular propaganda for the German Reformation* (Cambridge: Cambridge University Press, 1981).

Seebaß, Gottfried, *Müntzers Erbe: Werk, Leben, und Theologie des Hans Hut* (Göttingen: Gütersloher Verlagshaus, 2002).

Strauss, Gerald, *Luther's house of learning: indoctrination of the young in the German Reformation* (Baltimore: Johns Hopkins University Press, 1978).

Bibliography

Tedeschi, John, *The prosecution of heresy: collected studies on the Inquisition in early modern Italy* (Binghamton: Medieval and Renaissance Texts and Studies, 1991).

I MARTIN LUTHER, REFORMER

Editions

E var = *Martin Luthers sämtliche Werke, 6. Abteilung: Opera Latina varii argumenti.* 7 vols. (Frankfurt and Erlangen, 1865–73).
LW = *Luther's works.* American Edition, 55 vols. Ed. J. Pelikan and H. Lehmann (St Louis and Philadelphia, 1955–86).
StA = *Martin Luther. Studienausgabe.* 6 vols. (Berlin, 1979–99).
WA = *D. Martin Luthers Werke. Kritische Gesamtausgabe, Schriften.* 69 vols. (Weimar, 1883–2001).
WABr = *D. Martin Luthers Werke. Kritische Gesamtausgabe, Briefwechsel.* 18 vols. (Weimar, 1930–85).

Primary sources

Rogge, Joachim (ed.), *1521–1971: Luther in Worms. Ein Quellenbuch* (Wittenberg: Luther-Verlag, 1971).
Trüdinger, Karl, *Luthers Briefe und Gutachten zur Durchführung der Reformation* (Münster: Aschendorff, 1975).

Secondary sources

Arnold, Matthieu, *La correspondance de Luther: Etude historique, littéraire et théologique.* (Mainz: Verlag Philipp von Zabern, 1996).
Bayer, Oswald, *Promissio: Geschichte der reformatorischen Wende in Luthers Theologie* (Göttingen: Vandenhoeck & Ruprecht, 1971).
Bornkamm, Heinrich, *Martin Luther in der Mitte seines Lebens: Das Jahrzehnt zwischen dem Wormser und dem Augsburger Reichstag* (Göttingen: Vandenhoeck & Ruprecht, 1979).
Borth, Wilhelm, *Die Luthersache (causa Lutheri) 1517–1524: Die Anfänge der Reformation als Frage von Politik und Recht* (Lübeck: Mathiesen Verlag, 1970).
Brecht, Martin, *Martin Luther.* 3 vols. (Stuttgart: Calwer, 1981–7).
Cranz, F. Edward, *An essay on the development of Luther's thought on justice, law, and society.* 2nd edn. Ed. Gerald Christianson and Thomas M. Izbicki (Mifflintown, PA: Sigler Press, 1998).
Dieter, Theodor, *Der junge Luther und Aristoteles: Eine historisch-systematische Untersuchung zum Verhältnis von Theologie und Philosophie* (Berlin and New York: de Gruyter, 2001).
Ebeling, Gerhard, *Lutherstudien* (Tübingen: Mohr Siebeck, 1989).
Edwards, Mark U., Jr, *Luther and the false brethren* (Stanford: Stanford University Press, 1975).
Luther's last battles: politics and polemics, 1531–1546 (Ithaca: Cornell University Press, 1983).
Erikson, Erik H., *Young man Luther: a study in psychoanalysis and history* (New York: W. W. Norton, 1958).

Frank, Günter, *Die theologische Philosophie Philipp Melanchthons (1497–1560)* (Hildesheim: Benno, 1995).

Grane, Leif, *Martinus Noster: Luther in the German Reform movement 1518–1521* (Mainz: Verlag Philipp von Zabern, 1994).

Gritsch, Eric W., *Martin – God's court jester: Luther in retrospect* (Philadelphia: Fortress, 1983).

Hagen, Kenneth, *Luther's approach to Scripture as seen in his 'Commentaries' on Galatians 1519–1538* (Tübingen: Mohr Siebeck, 1993).

Haile, H. G., *Luther: an experiment in biography* (Garden City, NY: Doubleday, 1980).

Härle, Wilfried, 'Luther's reformatorische Entdeckung – damals und heute'. *Zeitschrift für Theologie und Kirche* 99 (2002): 278–95.

Headley, John M., *Luther's view of church history* (New Haven: Yale University Press, 1963).

Hendrix, Scott, 'American Luther research in the twentieth century'. *Lutheran Quarterly* 15 (2001): 1–23.

Luther and the papacy: stages in a Reformation conflict (Philadelphia: Fortress Press, 1981).

'Luther's contribution to the disunity of the Reformation'. In Scott Hendrix, *Tradition and authority in the Reformation* (Aldershot and Brookfield: Ashgate,1996), vol. 8, pp. 48–63.

Holl, Karl, *Luther: Gesammelte Aufsätze zur Kirchengeschichte*, vol. 1. 7th edn (Tübingen: Mohr Siebeck, 1948).

Junghans, Helmar, *Leben und Werk Martin Luthers von 1526 bis 1546: Festgabe zu seinem 500. Geburtstag*, 2 vols. (Göttingen: Vandenhoeck & Ruprecht, 1983).

Martin Luther: exploring his life and times, 1483–1546. Multimedia CD-ROM (Minneapolis: Fortress, 1998).

Martin Luther und Wittenberg (Munich: Koehler & Amelang, 1996).

'Die Mitte der Theologie Luthers'. *Zeichen der Zeit* 37 (1983): 190–4.

Kittelson, James, *Luther the reformer: the story of the man and his career* (Minneapolis: Augsburg, 1986).

'Luther on being "Lutheran"'. *Lutheran Quarterly* 17 (2003): 99–110.

Kohler, Erika, *Martin Luther und der Festbrauch* (Cologne and Graz: Böhlau Verlag, 1959).

Kolb, Robert, *Martin Luther as prophet, teacher, hero: images of the reformer, 1520–1620* (Grand Rapids: Baker, 1999).

Lienhard, Marc, *Luther, témoin de Jésus-Christ: les étapes et les thèmes de la christologie du réformateur* (Paris: Editions du Cerf, 1973).

Lindberg, Carter, 'Tainted greatness: Luther's attitudes toward Judaism and their historical reception'. In Nancy A. Harrowitz (ed.), *Tainted greatness: antisemitism and cultural heroes* (Philadelphia: Temple University Press, 1994), pp. 15–35.

Lohse, Bernhard, *Der Durchbruch der reformatorischen Erkenntnis bei Luther* (Darmstadt: Wissenschaftliche Buchgesellschaft, 1968).

Martin Luther: Einführung in sein leben und sein Werk. 3rd edn (Munich: C. H. Beck, 1997).

Martin Luther's theology: its historical and systematic development (Minneapolis: Fortress Press, 1999).

Marius, Richard, *Martin Luther: the Christian between God and death* (Cambridge, MA, and London: Harvard University Press, 1999).

McKim, Donald K. (ed.), *The Cambridge companion to Martin Luther* (Cambridge and New York: Cambridge University Press, 2003).

Moeller, Bernd, 'Die frühe Reformation in Deutschland als neues Mönchtum'. In Bernd Moeller, *Luther-Rezeption: Kirchenhistorische Aufsätze zur Reformationsgeschichte*, ed. Johannes Schilling (Göttingen: Vandenhoeck & Ruprecht, 2001), pp. 145–55.

Oberman, Heiko A., *Luther: man between God and the devil* (New Haven and London: Yale University Press, 1989).

Saak, Eric, *High way to heaven: the Augustinian platform between reform and Reformation, 1292–1524* (Leiden: Brill, 2002).

Schwarz, Reinhard, *Luther* (Göttingen: Vandenhoeck & Ruprecht, 1986).

Siggins, Ian, *Luther and his mother* (Philadelphia: Fortress Press, 1981).

Spitz, Lewis, *Luther and German humanism* (Aldershot and Brookfield: Ashgate, 1996).

Steinmetz, David, *Luther and Staupitz: an essay in the intellectual origins of the Protestant Reformation* (Durham, NC: Duke University Press, 1980).

Luther in context. 2nd edn (Grand Rapids: Baker, 2002).

Tracy, James D. (ed.), *Luther and the modern state in Germany* (Kirksville, MO: Sixteenth Century Journal Publishers, 1986).

Treu, Martin, *Katharina von Bora* (Wittenberg: Drei Kastanien Verlag, 1995).

Wendelborn, Gert, *Martin Luther: Leben und reformatorisches Werk* (Vienna: Böhlaus Nachfolger, 1983).

Wengert, Timothy J., 'Melanchthon and Luther / Luther and Melanchthon'. *Lutherjahrbuch* 66 (1999): 55–88.

Wicks, Jared, *Luther's reform: studies on conversion and the Church* (Mainz: Verlag Philipp von Zabern, 1992).

zur Mühlen, Karl-Heinz, *Nos extra nos: Luthers Theologie zwischen Mystik und Scholastik* (Tübingen: Mohr Siebeck, 1972).

2 EMERGENCE AND CONSOLIDATION OF PROTESTANTISM IN THE HOLY ROMAN EMPIRE TO 1600

Primary sources

Bekenntnisschriften der evangelisch-lutherischen Kirche, herausgegeben im Gedenkjahr der Augsburgischen Konfession 1930. 10th edn (Göttingen: Vandenhoeck & Ruprecht, 1986).

Niesel, Wilhelm (ed.), *Bekenntnisschriften und Kirchenordnungen der nach Gottes Wort reformierten Kirche, im Auftrag des Reformierten Bundes und des Reformierten Konventes der Bekenntnissynode der Deutschen Evangelischen Kirche* (Zurich: Evangelischer Verlag A. G. Zollikon, 1938).

Chemnitz, Martin, *Examination of the Council of Trent*. Trans. Fred Kramer. 4 vols. (St Louis: Concordia, 1971–86).

Loci Theologici. Translated by J. A. O. Preus. 2 vols. (St Louis: Concordia, 1989).

Cochrane, Arthur C., ed. *Reformed confessions of the sixteenth century* (Philadelphia: Westminster, 1966).

Erastus, Thomas, *The theses of Erastus touching excommunication*. Trans. Robert Lee (Edinburgh: Myles Macphail, 1844).

Fabian, Ekkehart, *Die Entstehung des Schmalkaldischen Bundes, und seiner Verfassung 1524/29–1531/35: Brück, Philipp von Hessen und Jakob Sturm*. 2nd edn (Tübingen: Osiander, 1962).

The Heidelberg catechism with commentary. Trans. Allen O. Miller and M. Eugene Osterhaven, comm. André Péry (Philadelphia: United Church Press, 1963).

Kolb, Robert, and Nestingen, James A. (eds.), *Sources and contexts of the Book of Concord* (Minneapolis: Fortress, 2001).

Kolb, Robert, and Wengert, Timothy J. (eds.), *The Book of Concord: the confessions of the Evangelical Lutheran Church* (Minneapolis: Fortress Press, 2000).

Luther, Martin. *D. Martin Luthers Werke*. Weimarer Ausgabe. 101 vols. (Weimar: Böhlau, 1883–1970).

Luther's works. Ed. Jaroslav Pelikan. 55 vols. (St Louis: Concordia Pub. House, 1955–86).

Melanchthon, Philip, *Loci communes, 1543*. Trans. J. A. O. Preus (St Louis: Concordia Publishing House, 1992).

Reu, Johann Michael (ed.), *Quellen zur Geschichte des kirchlichen Unterrichts in der evangelischen Kirche Deutschlands zwischen 1530 und 1600*. 4 vols. in 9 (Gütersloh: C. Bertelsmann, 1904–35).

Roeck, Bernd (ed.), *Gegenreformation und Dreissigjähriger Krieg 1555–1648*. Deutsche Geschichte in Quellen und Darstellung, vol 4 (Stuttgart: Reclam, 1996).

Rupp, E. Gordon, and Drewery, Benjamin (eds.), *Martin Luther* (London: Edward Arnold, 1970).

Schmauss, Johann Jakob (ed.), *Neue und vollständigere Sammlung der Reichs-Abschiede*. 4 vols. (Frankfurt a. M.: Koch, 1747; rpt. Osnabrück: Zeller, 1967).

Schwendi, Lazarus von, *Denkschrift über die politische Lage des Deutschen Reiches von 1574*. Ed. Eugen Frauenholz. Münchener historische Abhandlungen, series 2, vol. 10 (Munich: C. H. Beck, 1939).

Sehling, Emil (ed.), *Die Evangelischen Kirchenordnungen des XVI. [i.e. Sechszehnten] Jahrhunderts*. 13 vols. (Leipzig: O. R. Reisland, 1902–13; Tübingen: Mohr, 1955–80).

Secondary sources

Abray, Lorna Jane, *The people's Reformation: magistrates, clergy, and commons in Strasbourg, 1500–1598* (Ithaca: Cornell University Press, 1985).

Andresen, Carl (ed.), *Handbuch der Dogmen- und Theologiegeschichte*. Vol. 2: *Die Lehrentwicklung im Rahmen der Konfessionalität* (Göttingen: Vandenhoeck & Ruprecht, 1988).

Bierma, Lyle D., *German Calvinism in the confessional age: the covenant theology of Caspar Olevianus* (Grand Rapids: Baker Books, 1996).

Brady, Thomas A., Jr, 'In search of the godly city: the domestication of religion in the German urban reformation'. In R. Po-Chia Hsia (ed.), *The German people and the Reformation* (Ithaca: Cornell University Press, 1988), pp. 14–31.

Protestant politics: Jacob Sturm (1489–1553) of Strasbourg and the German Reformation (Atlantic Highlands: Humanities Press, 1995).

Turning Swiss: cities and empire, 1450–1550 (Cambridge and New York: Cambridge University Press, 1985).

Brandi, Karl, *Kaiser Karl V. Werden und Schicksal einer Persönlichkeit und eines Weltreiches.* 6th edn (Munich: F. Bruckmann, 1961).

Cameron, Euan, *European Reformation* (Oxford: Clarendon Press, 1991).

Cohn, Henry J., 'The territorial princes in Germany's second Reformation'. In Menna Prestwich (ed.), *International Calvinism, 1541–1715* (Oxford: Clarendon Press, 1985), pp. 139–65.

Dingel, Irene, *Concordia controversa: Die öffentliche Diskussionen um das lutherische Konkordienwerk am Ende des 16. Jahrhunderts* (Gütersloh: Gütersloher Verlagshaus, 1996).

Estes, James Martin, *Christian magistrate and state church: the reforming career of Johannes Brenz* (Toronto: University of Toronto Press, 1982).

Evans, R. J. W., *The making of the Habsburg monarchy, 1550–1700: an interpretation* (Oxford: Clarendon Press, 1979).

Forell, George Wolfgang, *Faith active in love: an investigation of principles underlying Luther's social ethics* (Minneapolis: Augsburg, 1959).

Hollweg, Walter, *Der Augsburger Reichstag von 1566 und seine Bedeutung für die Entstehung der Reformierten Kirche und ihres Bekenntnisses.* Beiträge zur Geschichte und Lehre der Reformierten Kirche, vol. 17 (Neukirchen-Vluyn: Neukirchener Verlag, 1964).

Hsia, R. Po-chia, *Social discipline in the Reformation: central Europe, 1550–1750* (London and New York: Routledge, 1989).

Jedin, Hubert, Latourette, Kenneth Scott, and Martin, Jochen (eds.), *Atlas zur Kirchengeschichte: Die christlichen Kirchen in Geschichte und Gegenwart.* Rev. edn (Freiburg im Breisgau: Herder, 1987).

Karant-Nunn, Susan C., *Luther's pastors: the Reformation in the Ernestine countryside.* Transactions of the American Philosophical Society, vol. 69, part 8 (Philadelphia: The American Philosophical Society, 1979).

Kittelson, James M., *Toward an established church: Strasbourg from 1500 to the dawn of the seventeenth century.* Veröffentlichungen des Instituts für Europäische Geschichte Mainz, vol. 182 (Mainz: Philipp von Zabern, 2000).

Klein, Thomas, *Der Kampf um die zweite Reformation in Kursachsen, 1586–1591.* Mitteldeutsche Forschungen, vol. 25 (Cologne: Böhlau, 1962).

Koch, Ernst, *Das konfessionelle Zeitalter – Katholizismus, Luthertum, Calvinismus (1563–1675)* (Leipzig: Evangelische Verlagsanstalt, 2000).

Kolb, Robert, *Martin Luther as prophet, teacher, hero: images of the reformer, 1520–1620* (Grand Rapids: Baker Books, 1999).

Lau, Franz, and Bizer, Ernst, *A history of the Reformation in Germany to 1555.* Trans. Brian A. Hardy (London: Adam & Charles Black, 1969).

May, Georg, *Die deutschen Bischöfe angesichts der Glaubensspaltung des 16. Jahrhunderts* (Vienna: Mediatrix-Verlag, 1983).

Münch, Paul, 'Volkskultur und Calvinismus: Zu Theorie und Praxis der "reformatio vitae" während der "Zweiten Reformation"'. In Heinz Schilling (ed.), *Die reformierte Konfessionalisierung in Deutschland – Das Problem der 'Zweiten Reformation'. Wissenschaftliches Symposion des Vereins für Reformationsgeschichte 1985,* Schriften des

Vereins für Reformationsgeschichte, no. 195 (Gütersloh: Gütersloher Verlagshaus, 1986), pp. 296–7.

Neveux, Jean Baptiste, *Vie spirituelle et vie sociale entre Rhin et Baltique au XVIIe siècle: de J. Arndt à P. J. Spencer* (Paris: C. Klincksieck, 1967).

Nischan, Bodo, *Prince, people, and confession: the Second Reformation in Brandenburg* (Philadelphia: University of Pennsylvania Press, 1994).

Oberman, Heiko A., *Luther: man between God and the devil*. Trans. Eileen Walliser-Schwarzbart (New Haven: Yale University Press, 1989).

Rabe, Horst, *Deutsche Geschichte 1500–1600* (Munich: C. H. Beck, 1991).

Rublack, Hans-Christoph (ed.), *Die lutherische Konfessionalisierung in Deutschland*. Schriften des Vereins für Reformationsgeschichte, no. 197 (Gütersloh: Mohn, 1992).

Rupp, E. Gordon, and Drewery, Benjamin (eds.), *Martin Luther* (London: Edward Arnold, 1970).

Schilling, Heinz (ed.), *Die reformierte Konfessionalisierung in Deutschland – Das Problem der 'Zweiten Reformation'*. Schriften des Vereins für Reformationsgeschichte, no. 195 (Gütersloh: Gütersloher Verlagshaus, 1986).

Aufbruch und Krise: Deutschland 1517–1648 (Berlin: Siedler, 1988).

Civic Calvinism in northwestern Germany and the Netherlands: sixteenth to nineteenth centuries. Sixteenth Century Essays & Studies, vol. 17 (Kirksville, MO: Sixteenth Century Journal Publishers, 1991).

Religion, political culture, and the emergence of early modern society: essays in German and Dutch history. Studies in Medieval and Reformation Thought, vol. 50 (Leiden: E. J. Brill, 1992).

Schmidt, Heinrich Richard, *Konfessionalisierung im 16. Jahrhundert*. Enzyklopädie deutsche Geschichte, vol. 12 (Munich: R. Oldenbourg Verlag, 1992).

Schorn-Schütte, Luise, *Evangelische Geistlichkeit in der Frühneuzeit, deren Anteil an der Entfaltung frühmoderner Staatlichkeit und Gesellschaft. Dargestellt am Beispiel des Fürstentums Braunschweig-Wolfenbüttel, der Landgrafschaft Hessen-Kassel und der Stadt Braunschweig*. Quellen und Forschungen zur Reformationsgeschichte, vol. 62 (Gütersloh: Gütersloher Verlagshaus, 1996).

Strauss, Gerald, *Luther's house of learning: indoctrination of the young in the German Reformation* (Baltimore: Johns Hopkins University Press, 1978).

Traitler, Hildegard, *Konfession und Politik. Interkonfessionalle Flugschriftenpolemik aus Süddeutschland und Österreich (1564–1612)*. European University Studies, series 3, vol. 400 (Frankfurt am Main, Bern, and New York: Peter Lang, 1989).

Vogler, Bernard, *Le clergé protestant rhénan au siècle de la Réforme, 1555–1619* (Paris: Ophrys, 1976).

Wengert, Timothy J., *Law and gospel: Philip Melanchthon's debate with John Agricola of Eisleben over poenitentia* (Grand Rapids: Baker, 1997).

Human freedom, Christian righteousness: Philip Melanchthon's exegetical dispute with Erasmus of Rotterdam (Oxford: Oxford University Press, 1998).

Wenz, Gunther, *Theologie der Bekenntnisschriften der evangelisch-lutherischen Kirche*. 2 vols. (Berlin: de Gruyter, 1996–1998).

Zeeden, Ernst Walter. *Konfessionsbildung: Studien zur Reformation, Gegenreformation, und katholischen Reform* (Stuttgart: Klett-Cotta, 1985).

3 THE RADICAL REFORMATION
Primary sources

Baring, Georg and Fellmann, Walter (eds.), *Denck, Hans. Schriften*. 2 vols. (Gütersloh: Bertelsmann, 1955–6).

Bergmann, Cornelius (ed.), *Die Täuferbewegung im Canton Zurich bis 1600*. Quellen und Abhandlungen zur Schweizerischen Reformationsgeschichte, 2 (Leipzig: M. Heinsius Nachf., 1916).

Bergsten, Torsten and Westin, Gunnar (eds.), *Hubmaier, Balthasar. Schriften*. Quellen zur Geschichte der Täufer, 9 (Gütersloh: Mohn, 1962).

Bräuer, Siegfried and Ullmann, Ullmann (eds.), *Müntzer, Thomas. Theologische Schriften aus dem Jahr 1523*. 2nd edn (Berlin: Evangelische Verlagsanstalt, 1982).

Chronicle of the Hutterian Brethren 1525–1665 (Rifton, NY: Plough Publishing House, 1989).

Cornelius, Carl Adolf (ed.), *Berichte der Augenzeugen über das münsterische Wiedertäuferreich*. Die Geschichtsquellen des Bistums Münster, 2. Veröffentlichung der Historischen Kommission für Westfalen, 3 (Münster: Druck und Verlag der Theissing'schen Buchhandlung, 1853).

Estep, William R. (ed. and trans.), *Anabaptist beginnings 1523–1533: a source book* (Nieuwkoop: DeGraaf, 1976).

Franck, Sebastian, *280 paradoxes or wondrous sayings*. Trans. E. J. Furcha (Lewiston, NY: Edwin Mellen Press, 1986).

Franz, Günther et al., *Wiedertäuferakten 1527–1626*. Urkundliche Quellen zur Hessischen Reformationsgeschichte, 4 (Marburg: Elwert, 1951).

Franz, Günther, and Kirn, Paul (eds.), *Thomas Müntzer:Schriften und Briefe. Kritische Gesamtausgabe*. Quellen und Forschungen zur Reformationsgeschichte, vol. 33 (Gütersloh: Mohn, 1968).

Furcha, E. J. (ed. and trans.), *Selected writings of Hans Denck* (Lewiston, NY: Edwin Mellen Press, 1989).

Haas, Martin (ed.), *Quellen zur Geschichte der Täufer in der Schweiz*. Vol. 4: *Täufergeschichte* (Winterthur: Hirzel, 1974).

Harder, Leland (ed.), *The sources of Swiss Anabaptism: the Grebel letters and related documents*. Classics of the Radical Reformation, 4 (Scottdale, PA: Herald Press, 1985).

Hegler, Alfred (ed.), *Sebastian Francks lateinische Paraphrase der Deutschen Theologie und seine holländische erhalten Traktate* (Tübingen: G. Schnürlen, 1901).

Hertzsch, Erich (ed.), *Karlstadts Schriften aus den Jahren 1523–1525* (Halle: Niemeyer, 1956).

Hinrichs, Carl (ed.), *Thomas Müntzer, Politische Schriften mit Kommentar*. Hallesche Monographen, 17 (Halle: Niemeyer, 1950).

Klassen, Walter (ed. and trans.), *The writings of Pilgram Marpeck*. Classics of the Radical Reformation, 2 (Scottdale, PA: Herald Press, 1978).

Liechty, Daniel (ed. and trans.), *Early Anabaptist spirituality: selected writings*. Classics of Western Spirituality (New York: Paulist Press, 1994).

Locke, John, *A letter on toleration* (London: Printed for A. Churchill, 1689).

The reasonableness of Christianity, as delivered in the scriptures (London: Printed for Awnsham and John Churchil, at the Black Swan in Pater-Noster Row, 1695).

Löffler, Klemens (ed.), *Die Wiedertäufer zu Münster, 1534–35: Berichte, Aussagen, und Aktenstücke von Augenzeugen und Zeitgenossen* (Jena: E. Diederichs, 1923).

Matheson, Peter (ed. and trans.), *The collected works of Thomas Müntzer* (Edinburgh: T. & T. Clark, 1988).

Mellink, Albert F. (ed.), *Documenta Anabaptistica Neerlandica.* 5 vols. (Leiden: Brill 1975–).

Muralt, Leonhard von, Schmid, Walter, Fast, Heinold, and Haas, Martin (eds.), *Quellen zur Geschichte der Täufer in der Schweiz* (Zurich: S. Hertzel, 1952–).

Peukert, Will Erich and Zeller, Winfried (eds.), *Valentin Weigel. Sämtliche Schriften* (Stuttgart, F. Frommann, 1962–).

Philips, Dirk, *Enchiridion or handbook for the Christian soldier.* Trans. Abraham B. Kolb (Elkart, Ind.: Mennonite Publishing Co., 1910).

Pipkin, H. Wayne, and Yoder, John H. (ed. and trans.), *Balthasar Hubmaier: theologian of Anabaptism.* Classics of the Radical Reformation, 5 (Scottdale, PA: Herald Press, 1989).

Quellen zur Geschichte der Täufer. Quellen und Forschungen zur Reformationsgeschichte (Gütersloh: Bertelsmann 1955–).

Riedemann, Peter, *Account of our religion, doctrine, and faith given by Peter Riedemann of the brothers whom men call Hutterians.* Trans. Kathleen Hasenberg. 2nd English edn. (Rifton, NY: Plough Publishing House, 1970).

Schultz, Selina G. *et al.* (eds.), *Corpus Schwenckfeldianorum.* 19 vols. (Leipzig: Breitkopf & Härtel, 1907–61).

Stupperich, Robert (ed.), *Die Schriften Bernhard Rothmanns* (Münster: Aschendorffer Verlagsbuchhandlung, 1970).

Waite, Gary K. (ed. and trans.), *The Anabaptist writings of David Joris, 1535–1543* (Waterloo, Ontario/Scottdale, PA: Herald Press, 1994).

Wenger, John C. (ed.), *Simons, Menno: the complete writings.* Trans. Leonard Verduin (Scottdale, PA: Herald Press, 1956).

Wollgast, Siegfried (ed.), *Franck, Sebastian, Paradoxa* (Berlin: Akademie Verlag, 1966).

Yoder, John H. (ed. and trans.), *The legacy of Michael Sattler.* Classics of the Radical Reformation, 1 (Scottdale, PA: Herald Press, 1973).

Zeller, Winfried (ed.), *Valentin Weigel. Handschriftliche Predigtensammlung, 1573–1574* (Stuttgart: Frommann, 1977–8).

Secondary sources

Allen, Wayne, 'Hans Denck: a first generation radical reformer' (Ph.D. dissertation, Rutgers University, 1985).

Armour, Rollin S., *Anabaptist baptism: a representative study* (Scottdale, PA: Herald Press, 1966).

Augustijn, Cornelis, 'Anabaptism in the Netherlands: another look'. *Mennonite Quarterly Review* 72 (1988): 197–210.

Bailey, Richard G., 'Melchior Hoffman: proto-Anabaptist and printer in Kiel, 1527–1629'. *Church History* 59 (1990): 175–90.

Bainton, Roland H., *David Joris, Widertäufer und Kämpfer für Toleranz im 16. Jahrhundert.* Supplement to Archiv für Reformationsgeschichte, 6 (Leipzig: Heinsius Nachf., 1935).

Barge, Hermann, *Andreas Bodenstein von Carlstadt*. 2 vols. (Leipzig: Friedrich Brandstetter, 1905).

Bauman, Clarence, *Gewaltlosigkeit im Taufertum: Eine Untersuchung zur theologischen Ethik des oberdeutschen Taufertums der Reformationszeit*. Studies in the history of Christian thought, vol. 3 (Leiden: Brill, 1968).

Beachy, Alvin J., *The concept of grace in the radical reformation* (Nieuwkoop: De Graaf, 1977).

Bender, Harold S., *Conrad Grebel, c. 1498–1526, founder of the Swiss brethren, sometimes called Anabaptists* (Goshen, IN: Mennonite Historical Society, 1950).

Bensing, Manfred, *Thomas Müntzer und der Thüringer Aufstand 1525* (Berlin: VEB Deutscher Verlag der Wissenschaften, 1966).

Bergsten, Torsten, 'Pilgram Marpeck und seine Auseinandersetzung mit Caspar Schwenckfeld'. *Kyrkohistorisk Åsskrift* 42 (1957): 39–100; 43 (1958): 53–87.

Balthasar Hubmaier, seine Stellung zu Reformation und Täufertum, 1551–1528 (Kassel: Oncken, 1961).

Blough, Neal, *Christologie Anabaptiste: Pilgram Marpeck et l'humanité du Christ* (Geneva: Labor et Fides, 1984).

Bornkamm, Heinrich, *Mystik, Spiritualismus und die Anfänge des Pietismus im Luthertum* (Giessen: A. Töpelmann, 1926).

Boyd, Stephan, *Pilgram Marpeck: his life and social theology* (Durham, NC: Duke University Press, 1991).

Bräuer, Siegfried, and Helmar Junghans (eds.), *Der Theologe Thomas Müntzer: Untersuchungen zu seiner Entwicklung und Lehre* (Berlin: Evangelische Verlagsanstalt, 1989).

Brendler, Gerhard. *Thomas Müntzer: Geist und Faust* (Berlin: VEB Deutscher Verlag der Wissenschaften, 1989).

Bubenheimer, Ulrich, *Consonantia Theologiae et Iurisprudentiae: Andreas Bodenstein von Karlstadt, Theologe und Jurist zwischen Scholastik und Reformation* (Tübingen: Mohr, 1977).

Thomas Müntzer: Herkunft und Bildung. Studies in Medieval and Reformation Thought, 46 (Leiden: Brill, 1989).

Burrage, Champlin, *The early English dissenters in light of recent research*. 2 vols. (Cambridge: Cambridge University Press, 1912).

Clasen, Claus-Peter, *Anabaptism: a social history 1525–1618* (Ithaca: Cornell University Press, 1972).

Davis, Kenneth Ronald, *Anabaptism and asceticism: a study in intellectual origins* (Scottdale, PA: Herald Press, 1974).

Dejung, Christoph, *Wahrheit und Häresie: Untersuchungen zur Geschichtsphilosophie bei Sebastian Franck* (Zurich: Dejung, 1979).

Depperman, Klaus, Packull, Werner, and Stayer, James, 'From monogenesis to polygenesis: the historical discussion of Anabaptist origins'. *Mennonite Quarterly Review* 49 (1975): 83–102.

Melchior Hoffman: social unrest and apocalyptic visions in the age of reformation. Trans. Malcolm Wren (London: T. and T. Clark, 1986).

Dipple, Geoffrey, *"Just as in the Time of the Apostles," Uses of History in the Radical Reformation* (Kitchener, Ont.: Pandora Press, 2005).

Doornkaat Koolman, J. Ten, *Dirk Philips, vriend en medewerker van Menno Simons, 1504–1568* (Haarlem: Willink, 1964).

Dülmen, Richard van, *Das Täuferreich zu Münster, 1534–1535. Berichte und Dokumente* (Munich: Deutscher Taschenbuch Verlag, 1974).

Egli, Emil. *Die Züricher Wiedertäufer zur Reformationszeit* (Zurich: Friedrich Schulthess, 1878).

Eire, Carlos M. Nieto, *War against the idols: the Reformation of worship from Erasmus to Calvin* (New York: Cambridge University Press, 1986).

Elliger, Walter, *Thomas Müntzer: Leben und Werk*. 3rd edn (Göttingen: Vandenhoeck & Ruprecht, 1975).

Erb, Peter (ed.), *Schwenckfeld and early Schwenkfeldianism: papers presented at the colloquium on Schwenckfeld and the Schwenkfelders* (Pennsburg, PA: Schwenkfelder Library, 1986.)

Etienne, Jacques, *Spiritualisme érasmien* (Louvain: Publication Universitaires de Louvain, 1956).

Fast, Heinold, *Der linke Flügel der Reformation: Glaubenszeugnisse der Täufer, Spiritualisten, Schwärmer und Antitrinitarier* (Bremen: Schemann, 1962).

Fischer, Hans, *Jakob Huter: Leben, Frömmigkeit, Briefe*. Mennonite Historical Series, 4 (Newton, KS: Mennonite Publication Office, 1956).

Fix, Andrew, 'Radical Reformation and second Reformation in Holland: the intellectual consequences of the sixteenth-century religious upheaval and the coming of a rational world view'. *Sixteenth Century Journal* 18 (1987): 63–80.

Prophecy and reason: The Dutch Collegiants in the early Enlightenment (Princeton: Princeton University Press, 1991).

Friedman, Jerome, *Michael Servetus: a case study of total heresy* (Geneva: Droz, 1978).

Friedmann, Robert, *Hutterite studies: essays by Robert Friedmann*. Ed. Harold S. Bender (Goshen, IN: Mennonite Historical Society, 1961).

The theology of Anabaptism: an interpretation. Studies in Anabaptist and Mennonite History 15 (Scottdale, PA: Herald Press, 1973).

Friesen, Abraham, *Thomas Müntzer, a destroyer of the godless: the making of a sixteenth-century revolutionary* (Berkeley: University of California Press, 1990).

Erasmus, the Anabaptists and the Great Commission (Grand Rapids: W. B. Eerdmans Pub., 1998).

Furcha, E. J., *Schwenckfeld's concept of the new man: a study in the anthropology of Caspar von Schwenckfeld as set forth in his major theological writings* (Pennsburg, PA: Board of Publication of the Schwenkfelder Church, 1970).

Gerbert, Camill, *Geschichte der Strassburger Sectenbewegung zur Zeit der Reformation 1524–1534* (Strasbourg: J. H. Ed. Heitz, 1889).

Geyer, Iris, *Thomas Müntzer im Bauernkrieg* (Besigheim: Verlag K. H. V., 1982).

Ginzburg, Carlo, *Il Nicodemismo: Simulazione e dissimulazione religiosa nell'Europa de '500* (Turin: Einaudi, 1970).

Goerters, J. F. G., 'Die Vorgeschichte des Täufertums in Zürich'. In L. Abramowski and J. F. G. Goerters (eds.), *Studien zur Geschichte und Theologie der Reformation* (Neukirch: Neukirchener Verlag, 1969).

Goertz, Hans-Jürgen, *Innere und aüssere Ordnung in der Theologie Thomas Müntzers* (Leiden: Brill, 1967).

Goertz, Hans-Jürgen (ed.), *Umstrittenes Täufertum* (Göttingen: Vandenhoeck & Ruprecht, 1975).

Die Täufer: Geschichte und Deutung (Munich: C. H. Beck, 1980).

Thomas Müntzer: Mystiker, Apokalyptiker, Revolutionär (Munich: Beck, 1989). [*Thomas Müntzer: apocalyptic, mystic, and revolutionary*. Trans. Jocelyn Jaquiery, ed. Peter Matheson (Edinburgh: T. & T. Clark, 1993).]

Gritsch, Eric, *The authority of the inner word: a theological study of the major German spiritual reformers in the sixteenth century* (New Haven: Yale University Press. 1959).

Thomas Müntzer, a tragedy of errors (Minneapolis: Fortress Press, 1989).

Gross, Leonard, *The golden years of the Hutterites: the witness and thought of the communal Moravian Anabaptists during the Walpot era, 1565–1578* (Scottdale, PA: Herald Press, 1980).

Grützmacher, Richard, *Wort und Geist: eine historische und dogmatische Untersuchung zum Gnadenmittel des Wortes* (Leipzig: A. Deichert, 1902).

Hall, Thor, 'Possibilities of Erasmian influence on Denck and Hubmaier'. *Mennonite Quarterly Review* 35 (1961): 149–70.

Hamilton, Alistair, *The family of love* (Cambridge: James Clark & Co., 1981).

Hasel, Gerhard F., 'Sabbatarian Anabaptists of the sixteenth century'. *Andrews University Seminar Studies* 5 (1967): 101–21; 6 (1968): 19–29.

Hegler, Alfred, *Geist und Schrift bei Sebastian Franck. Eine Studie zur Geschichte des Spiritualismus in der Reformationszeit* (Freiburg i. B.: J. C. B. Mohr, 1892).

Hillerbrand, Hans, *Bibliographie des Täufertums, 1520–1630*. Quellen zur Geschichte der Täufer 10 (Gütersloh: G. Mohn, 1962). [*Bibliography of Anabaptism, 1520–1630*. (Elkart, IN: Institute of Mennonite Studies, 1962).]

Anabaptist bibliography 1520–1630 (St Louis: Center for Reformation Research, 1991).

Hinrichs, Carl, *Luther und Müntzer: Ihre Auseinandersetzung über Obrigkeit und Widerstandsrecht*. Arbeiten zur Kirchengeschichte, 29 (Berlin: W. De Gruyter, 1952).

Horst, Irvin Buckwalter, *Erasmus, the Anabaptists, and the problem of religious unity* (Haarlem: Ijeenk Willink, 1967).

The radical brethren: Anabaptism and the English Reformation to 1558 (Nieuwkoop: DeGraaf, 1972).

Horst, Irvin Buckwalter (ed.) *Dutch dissenters: a critical companion to their history and ideas, with a bibliographical survey of recent research pertaining to the early Reformation in the Netherlands*. Kerkhistorische bijdragen, 13 (Leiden: Brill, 1986).

Hsia, Ronnie Po-chia, *Society and religion in Münster, 1535–1618* (New Haven: Yale University Press, 1984).

Jones, Rufus M., *Spiritual reformers in the sixteenth and seventeenth centuries* (London: Macmillan, 1914).

Kaczerowsky, Klaus, *Sebastian Franck: Bibliographie* (Wiesbaden: Pressler, 1976).

Kähler, Ernest, *Karlstadt und Augustin: Der Kommentar von Karlstadt zu Augustins Schrift, De Spiritu et Litera* (Halle: Niemeyer, 1952).

Karant-Nunn, Susan C., *Zwickau in transition, 1500–1547: the Reformation as an agent of change* (Columbus, OH: Ohio State University Press, 1987).

Kawerau, Peter, *Melchior Hofmann als religiöser Denker* (Haarlem: Bohm, 1954).

Keeney, William E., 'The writings of Dirk Philips'. *Mennonite Quarterly Review* 32 (1958): 298–306.

The development of Dutch Anabaptist thought and practice, 1539–1564 (Nieuwkoop: DeGraaf, 1968).

Kiwiet, Jan J., *Pilgram Marpeck, ein Führer in der Täuferbewegung der Reformationszeit* (Kassel: Oncken, 1957).

Klassen, Peter J., *The economics of Anabaptism, 1525–1560* (The Hague: Nijhoff, 1964).

Klassen, Walter, *Covenant and community: the life, writings and hermeneutics of Pilgram Marpeck* (Grand Rapids: Eerdmans, 1968).

Knörrlich, Wolfgang, *Kaspar Schwenckfeld und die Reformation in Schlesien* (Bonn: 1957).

Köhler, Walther, *Zwingli und Luther, ihr Streit über das Abendmahl nach seinen politischen und religiösen Beziehungen*. Quellen und Forschungen zur Reformationsgeschichte. Bd. 6–7, 2 vols. (Leipzig: Verein für Reformationsgeschichte, Vermittlungsverlag von M. Heinsius Nachfolger, 1924–53).

Koyré, Alexandre, *Mystiques, spirituals, alchimistes du xvie siècle allemande* (Paris: Gallimard, 1971).

Krahn, Cornelius, *Der Gemeindebegriff des Menno Simons im Rahmen seines Lebens und seiner Theologie* (Heidelberg: C. Krahn, 1936).

Menno Simons, 1496–1561: Ein Beitrag zur Geschichte und Theologie der Taufgesinnten (Karlsruhe: H. Schnieder, 1936).

Dutch Anabaptism: origin, spread, life, and thought 1450–1600 (The Hague: Nijhoff, 1968).

Krajewski, Ekkehard, *Leben und Sterben des Zürcher Täuferführer Felix Mantz* (Kassel: Oncken, 1957).

Kraus, C. Norman, 'Anabaptist influence on English Separatism as seen in Robert Browne'. *Mennonite Quarterly Review* 34 (1960): 5–19.

Krodel, Gottfried. 'Die Abendmahlslehre des Erasmus von Rotterdam und seine Stellung am Anfang des Abendmahlsstreits der Reformatoren' (Ph.D. dissertation: University of Erlangen, 1955).

de Lagarde, Georges, *La Naissance de l'esprit laïque au déclin du moyen âge*. 3rd edn. 5 vols. (Louvain: Nauwelaerts, 1956–63).

Lambert, Malcolm, *Medieval heresy: popular movements from Bogomil to Hus* (New York: Holmes and Meier Publishers, 1977).

Laube, Adolf, 'Thomas Müntzer und die frühburgerliche Revolution'. *Zeitschrift für Geschichtswissenschaft* 38 (1990): 128–41.

Lecler, Joseph, *Histoire de la tolérance au siècle de la Réforme*. 2 vols. (Paris: 1955).

Leff, Gordon, *Heresy in the later Middle Ages: the relation of heterodoxy to dissent ca. 1250–1450*. 2 vols. (New York: Barnes and Noble, 1967).

Liechty, Daniel, *Andreas Fischer and the Sabbatarian Anabaptists: an early Reformation episode in east central Europe*. Studies in Anabaptist and Mennonite History, 29 (Scottdale, PA: Herald Press, 1988).

Lienhard, Marc (ed.), *The origins and characteristics of Anabaptism*. International Archives of the History of Ideas, 87 (The Hague: Martinus Nijhoff, 1977).

Les Dissidents du XVIe siècle entre l'humanisme et le catholicisme: actes du colloque de Strasbourg (5–6 février 1982). Bibliotheca Dissidentium. Scripta et studia, 1 (Baden-Baden: V. Koerner, 1983).

Lindeboom, Johannes, *Stiefkindern van het christendom* (The Hague: Nijhof, 1929).

De confessioneele ontwikkeling der Reformatie in de Nederlanden (Gravenhage: M. Nijhoff, 1946).

Littell, Franklin H., *The Anabaptist vision of the church*, 2nd edn (Boston: Starr King Press, 1958).

Lohmann, Annemarie, *Zur geistigen Entwicklung Thomas Müntzers* (Leipzig and Berlin: B. G. Teubner, 1931).

Loserth, Johann, *Doctor Balthasar Hubmaier und die Anfänge der Wiedertäufer in Mähren* (Brünn: Verlag der Hist.-Statist Section, 1893).

Pilgram Marpecks Antwort auf Caspar Schwenckfelds Beurteilung des Buches des Beundesbezeugung von 1542 (Vienna: Carl Fromme, 1929).

Maier, Hans, *Der Mystische Spiritualismus Valentin Weigels* (Gütersloh: C. Bertelsmann, 1926).

Maier, Paul, *Caspar Schwenckfeld on the person and work of Christ: a study of Schwenckfeldian theology at its core* (Assen: Van Gorcum, 1959).

Maron, Gottfried, *Individualismus und Gemeinschaft bei Caspar Schwenckfeld* (Stuttgart: Evangelisches Verlagswerk, 1961).

Martin, Joseph, *Religious radicals in Tudor England* (London: Hambledon, 1989).

McLaughlin, Robert Emmet, *Caspar Schwenckfeld, reluctant radical: his life to 1540* (New Haven: Yale University Press, 1986).

The freedom of the spirit, social privilege, and religious dissent: Caspar Schwenckfeld and the Schwenckfelders. Bibliotheca Dissidentium, Scripta et Studia, 6 (Baden-Baden: Editions Valentin Koerner, 1996).

'Luther, Spiritualism and the Spirit'. In *Piety and Family in Early modern Europe. Essays in Honour of Steven Ozment*. Ed. Marc Forster et al. (Aldershot: Ashgate, 2005), pp. 28–49.

'Müntzer and Apocalypticism', *Archiv für Reformationsgeschichte* 95 (2004), pp. 98–131.

'Spiritualismus', *Theologische Realenzyklopedie* (Berlin and New York: Walter de Gruyter 2000), vol. 31, pp. 701–8.

'Reformation spiritualism: typology, sources and significance'. In *Radikalität und Dissent im 16. Jahrhundert*. Ed. Hans-Jürgen Goertz and James M. Stayer, *Zeitschrift für historische Forschung*, Beiheft 27 (Berlin: Duncker & Humblot, 2002), pp. 127–40.

Mehl, Oskar, *Thomas Müntzers Deutsche Messen und Kirchenämter, mit Singnoten, und liturgischen Abhandlungen* (Grimmen in Pommern: A. Waberg, 1937).

Mennonite encyclopedia, ed. Harold S. J. Bender and C. Henry Smith. 4 vols. (Hillsboro, KS: Mennonite Brethren Publishing House, 1955–9).

Mennonitischen lexikon, ed. Christian Hege and Christian Neff. 4 vols. (Frankfurt and Weierhof (Pfalz), 1913–67).

Moss, Jean Dietz, *Godded with God: Henrik Niclaes and his family of love* (Philadelphia: American Philosophical Society, 1981).

Müller, Jan-Dirk (ed.), *Sebastian Franck (1499–1542)*. Wolfenbüttler Forschungen, 56 (Wiesbaden: Harrassowitz, 1993).

Nicoladoni, Alexander, *Johannes Bünderlin von Linz und die oberösterreichischen Täufergemeinden in den Jahren 1525–1531* (Berlin: R. Gaertner, 1893).

Oakley, Francis, *The western Church in the later Middle Ages* (Ithaca: Cornell University Press, 1979).

Opel, Julius Ott, *Valentin Weigel. ein Beitrag zur Literatur- und Culturgeschichte Deutschlands im 17. Jahrhundert* (Leipzig: T. O. Weigel, 1864).

Ozment, Steven E., *Homo Spiritualis: a comparative study of the anthropology of Johannes Tauler, Jean Gerson, and Martin Luther (1509–16) in the context of their theological thought* (Leiden: Brill, 1969).

Mysticism and dissent: religious ideology and social protest in the sixteenth century (New Haven: Yale University Press, 1973).

Packull, Werner O., *Mysticism and the early south German-Austrian Anabaptist movement, 1525–1531*. Studies in Anabaptist and Mennonite History 19 (Scottdale, PA and Kitchener, Ontario: Herald Press, 1977).

Packull, Werner O., and Stayer, James (eds.), *The Anabaptists and Thomas Müntzer* (Dubuque and Toronto: Kendall Hunt Publishing Co., 1980).

Hutterite beginnings: communitarian experiments during the Reformation (Baltimore and London: Johns Hopkins University Press, 1995).

Pater, Calvin A., *Andreas Bodenstein von Karlstadt as the father of the Baptist movements: the emergence of lay Protestantism* (Toronto: University of Toronto Press, 1983).

Payne, John B., *Erasmus: his theology of the sacraments* (Richmond, VA: John Knox Press, 1970).

Peachy, Paul P., *Die Soziale Herkunft der Schweizer Täufer in der Reformationszeit* (Karlsruhe: Schneider, 1954).

Plümper, Hans-Dieter, *Die Gütergemeinschaft bei den Täufern des 16. Jahrhunderts* (Göttingen: Alfred Kümmerle, 1972).

Porter, Jack Wallace, 'Bernhard Rothmann, 1495–1535, royal orator of the Münster Anabaptist Kingdom'. (Ph.D. dissertation, University of Wisconsin-Madison, 1964).

Preus, James S., *Carlstadt's 'Ordinaciones' and Luther's 'Liberty'*, Harvard Theological Studies, 21 (Cambridge, MA: Harvard University Press, 1974).

Probleme des Müntzerbildes (Berlin: Akademie Verlag, 1988).

Roehrich, Gustave Guillaume, *Essay on the life, the writings, and the doctrine of the Anabaptist, Hans Denk*. Trans. Claude R. Foster, William F. Bogart, and Mildred M. Van Sice (Lanham, MD: University Press of America, 1983).

Sachsse, Carl D. *Balthasar Hubmaier als Theologe*. Neue Studien zur Geschichte der Theologie und der Kirche, 20 (Berlin: Trowitzsch 1914).

Schultz, Selina Gerhard, *Caspar Schwenckfeld von Ossig (1489–1561)*. 2nd edn, intro, biblio. Peter C. Erb (Norristown, PA: Board of Publication of the Schwenkfelder Church, 1977).

Schwarz, Reinhard, *Die apokalyptische Theologie Thomas Müntzers und der Taboriten*. Beiträge zur historischen Theologie, 55 (Tübingen: Mohr 1977).

Scott, Tom, *Thomas Müntzer: Theologie and revolution in the German Reformation* (New York: St Martin's Press, 1989).

Seebass, Gottfried, *Müntzer Erbe: Werk, Leben und Theologie des Hans Hut* (Göttingen: Gütersloher Verlagshaus, 2002).

Séguenny, André, *Homme charnel, homme spirituelle: sur la christologie de Caspar Schwenckfeld* (Wiesbaden: Steiner, 1975).

Séguenny, André, Rott, Jean, and Backus, Irena Dorota (eds.), *Bibliotheca dissidentium: répertoire des non-conformistes religieux des seizième et dix-septième siècles* (Baden-Baden: V. Koerner 1980–).

Shantz, Douglas H., *Crautwald and Erasmus: a study in humanism and radical reform in sixteenth century Silesia* (Baden-Baden: Editions Valentin Koerner, 1992).

Sider, Ronald J., *Andreas Bodenstein von Karlstadt: the development of his thought, 1517–1525* (Leiden: Brill, 1974).

Sider, Ronald J. (ed.), *Karlstadt's battle with Luther: documents in a liberal-radical debate* (Philadelphia: Fortress Press, 1978).

Snyder, C. Arnold, *The life and thought of Michael Sattler*. Studies in Anabaptist and Mennonite History, 26 (Scottdale PA: Herald Press, 1984).

Stayer, James M., *Anabaptists and the sword* (Lawrence, KS: Coronado, 1972).

The German Peasants' War and Anabaptist community of goods (Montreal and Kingston: McGill-Queen's University Press, 1991).

Steinmetz, Max, *Das Müntzerbild von Martin Luther bis Friedrich Engels* (Berlin: Deutscher Verlag der Wissenschaften, 1971).

Strübing, Andrea, *Eifriger als Zwingli. Die frühe Taüferbewegung in der Schweiz* (Berlin: Duncker & Humblot, 2003).

Vogler, Günter, *Thomas Müntzer* (Berlin: Dietz Verlag, 1989).

Voogt, Gerrit, *Constraint on trial. Dirck Volckhertsz and religious freedom.* Sixteenth Century Essays & Studies, 52 (Kirksville, MO: Truman State University Press, 2000).

Vos, K., 'Obbe Philipsz'. *Doopsgezinde Beijtragen*, 54 (1917): 124–38.

Waite, Gary K., *David Joris and Dutch Anabaptism, 1524–1543* (Waterloo, Ontario: Wilfrid Laurier University Press, 1990).

Wappler, Paul, 'Thomas Müntzer in Zwickau and die Zwickauer Propheten', Schriften des Vereins für Reformationsgeschichte, 182 (Gütersloh: Mohn, 1966).

Weeks, Andrew, *Valentin Weigel (1533–1588): German religious dissenter, speculative theorist, and advocate of tolerance* (Albany, NY: State University Press of New York, 2000).

Weigelt, Horst, 'Sebastian Franck und Caspar Schwenckfeld in ihren Beziehungen zueinander'. *Zeitschrift für bayerischen Kirchengeschichte* 39 (1970): 3–19.

Sebastian Franck und die lutherische Reformation (Gütersloh: Mohn, 1972).

Schwenckfelders in Silesia. Trans. Peter C. Erb (Pennsburg, PA: Schwenckfeld Library, 1985).

Weiss, Frederick Lewis, *The life, teachings, and works of Johannes Denck* (Strasbourg: 1924).

Williams, George, *The radical Reformation* (Philadelphia: Westminster Press, 1957).

Spiritual and Anabaptist writers: documents illustrative of the radical Reformation (Philadelphia: Westminster Press, 1962).

Windhorst, Christof, *Täuferisches Taufverständnis: Balthasar Hubmaiers Lehre zwischen traditioneller und reformatorischer Theologie.* Studies in Medieval and Reformation Thought, 16 (Leiden: Brill, 1976).

Wollgast, Siegfried, *Der deutsche Pantheismus im 16. Jahrhundert: Sebastian Franck und seine Wirkungen auf die Entwicklung der pantheistischen Philosophie in Deutschland* (Berlin: Deutscher Verlag der Wissenschaften, 1972).

4 LUTHERANISM IN THE SEVENTEENTH CENTURY

Arndt, Johannes, *Das Heilige Römische Reich und die Niederlande 1566 bis 1648. Politische und konfessionelle Verflechtung und Publizistik im Achtzigjährigen Krieg* (Cologne: Böhlau, 1998).

Asche, Matthias, and Schindling, Anton (eds.), *Dänemark, Norwegen und Schweden im Zeitalter der Reformation und Konfessionalisierung. Nordische Königreiche und Konfession 1500 bis 1650* (Münster: Aschendorff, 2003).

Axmacher, Elke, Arndt, Johann, and Gerhardt, Paul. *Studien zur Theologie, Frömmigkeit und geistlichen Dichtung des 17. Jahrhunderts* (Tübingen: Francke, 2001).

Bahlke, Joachim, and Strohmeyer, Arno (eds.), *Konfessionalisierung in Ostmitteleuropa. Wirkungen des religiösen Wandels im 16. und 17. Jahrhundert in Staat, Gesellschaft und Kultur* (Stuttgart: Steiner, 1999).

Balázs, Mihály, and Keserü, Gizella (eds.), *György Enyedi and central European Unitarianism in the 16–17th centuries* (Budapest: Balassi, 2000).

Behringer, Wolfgang, Lehmann, Hartmut, and Pfister, Christian (eds.), *Kulturelle Konsequenzen der Kleinen Eiszeit* (Göttingen: Vandenhoeck & Ruprecht, 2005).

Braekman, Emile Michel, *Le Protestantisme belge au 16e siècle. Belgique, Nord de la France, Refuge* (Carrières-sous-Poissy: La Cause, 1999).

Bußmann, Klaus (ed.), *1648. Krieg und Frieden in Europa* (Münster: Veranstaltungsgesellschaft 350 Jahre Westfälischer Friede, 1998).

Canning, Joseph, Lehmann, Hartmut, and Winter, Jay (eds.), *Power, violence and mass-death in pre-modern and modern times* (Aldershot: Ashgate, 2004).

Conrad, Anne (ed.), *'In Christo ist weder man noch weyb'. Frauen in der Zeit der Reformation und der katholischen Reform* (Münster: Aschendorff, 1999).

Dantine, Johannes (ed.), *Protestantische Mentalitäten* (Vienna: Passagen-Verlag, 1999).

Dietz, Burkhard, and Ehrenpreis, Stefan (eds.), *Drei Konfessionen in einer Region. Beiträge zur Konfessionalisierung im Herzogtum Berg* (Cologne: Rheinland-Verlag, 1999).

Driedger, Michael D., *Obedient heretics. Mennonite identities in Lutheran Hamburg and Altona during the confessional age* (Aldershot: Ashgate, 2002).

Frieß, Peer, and Ay, Karl-Ludwig (eds.), *Konfessionalisierung und Region* (Constance: UVK, Universität Verlag Konstanz, 1999).

Garber, Klaus (ed.), *Kulturgeschichte Ostpreußens in der frühen Neuzeit* (Tübingen: Niemeyer, 2001).

Greyerz, Kaspar von, Jakubowski-Tiessen, Manfred, Kaufmann, Thomas, and Lehmann, Hartmut (eds.), *Interkonfessionalität – Transkonfessionalität – binnenkonfessionelle Pluralität. Neue Forschungen zur Konfessionalisierungsthese* (Gütersloh: Gütersloher Verlags-Haus, 2003).

Religion und Kultur in Europa 1500–1800 (Göttingen: Vandenhoeck & Ruprecht, 2000).

Hey, Bernd (ed.), *Der Westfälische Frieden und der deutsche Protestantismus* (Bielefeld: Verlag für Regionalgeschichte, 1998).

Hsia, Ronnie Po-chia, *Calvinism and religious toleration in the Dutch golden age* (Cambridge: Cambridge University Press, 2004).

The world of Catholic renewal, 1540–1770 (Cambridge: Cambridge University Press, 1998).

Social discipline in the Reformation. Central Europe, 1550–1750 (London: Routledge, 1989).

Jakubowski-Tiessen, Manfred, and Lehmann, Hartmut (eds.), *Um Himmels Willen. Religion in Katastrophenzeiten* (Göttingen: Vandenhoeck & Ruprecht, 2003).

Die Krisen des 17. Jahrhunderts. Interdisziplinäre Perspektiven (Göttingen: Vandenhoeck & Ruprecht, 1999).

Jelsma, Auke, *Frontiers of the Reformation. Dissidence and orthodoxy in sixteenth-century Europe* (Aldershot: Ashgate, 1998).

Kaufmann, Thomas, *Dreißigjähriger Krieg und Westfälischer Frieden. Kirchengeschichtliche Studien zur lutherischen Konfessionskultur* (Tübingen: Mohr Siebeck, 1998).

Koch, Ernst, *Das konfessionelle Zeitalter. Katholizismus, Luthertum, Calvinismus (1563–1675)* (Leipzig: Evangelische Verlags-Anstalt, 2000).

Krusenstjern, Benigna von, and Medick, Hans (eds.), *Zwischen Alltag und Katastrophe. Der Dreißigjährige Krieg aus der Nähe* (Göttingen: Vandenhoeck & Ruprecht, 1999).

Lehmann, Hartmut, and Trepp, Anne-Charlott (eds.), *Im Zeichen der Krise. Religiosität im Europa des 17. Jahrhunderts* (Göttingen: Vandenhoeck & Ruprecht, 1999).

Das Zeitalter des Absolutismus. Gottesgnadentum und Kriegsnot (Stuttgart: Kohlhammer, 1980).

Nischan, Bodo, *Lutherans and Calvinists in the age of confessionalism* (Aldershot: Ashgate, 1999).

Rau, Susanne, *Geschichte und Konfession. Städtische Geschichtsschreibung und Erinnerungskultur im Zeitalter von Reformation und Konfessionalisierung in Bremen, Breslau, Hamburg and Köln* (Munich: Dölling and Galitz, 2002).

Reinhard, Wolfgang (ed.), *Bruno Gebhardt. Handbuch der deutschen Geschichte*, 10 (Stuttgart: Klett-Cotta, 2001).

Schilling, Heinz, *Die neue Zeit. Vom Christenheitseuropa zum Europa der Staaten, 1250–1750* (Berlin: Siedler, 1999).

Szabó, András (ed.), *Iter Germanicum. Deutschland und die Reformierte Kirche in Ungarn im 16.–17. Jahrhundert* (Budapest: Kálvin K., 1999).

Weigl, Andreas (ed.), *Wien im Dreißigjährigen Krieg. Bevölkerung, Gesellschaft, Kultur, Konfession* (Vienna: Böhlau, 2001).

5 COMMUNAL REFORMATION: ZWINGLI, LUTHER, AND THE SOUTH OF THE HOLY ROMAN EMPIRE

Primary sources

Egli, Emil, *Aktensammlung zur Geschichte der Zürcher Reformation in den Jahren 1519–1533* (Zurich, 1879; rpt. Aalen: Scientia, 1973).

Franz, Günther, *Quellen zur Geschichte des Bauernkrieges* (Munich: Oldenbourg, 1963).

Luther, Martin, *Werke*. Weimarer Ausgabe, 66 vols (Weimar: Böhlau, 1900–80).

Müntzer, Thomas, *Schriften und Briefe. Kritische Gesamtausgabe*. Ed. Günther Franz, Quellen und Forschungen zur Reformationsgeschichte, 33 (Gütersloh: Gerd Mohn, 1968).

[Schappeler, Christoph], *An die versamlung gemeyner Pawerschaft, so in Hochteütscher Nation/ vnd vil anderer ort/mit empo(e)rung vnd auffru(o)r entstanden* (Nuremberg 1525). Reprinted in Horst Buszello, *Der deutsche Bauernkrieg von 1525 als politische Bewegung* (Berlin: Colloquium, 1969), pp. 152–92.

Scott, Tom, and Scribner, Bob, *The German Peasants' War: a history in documents* (New Jersey: Humanities Press, 1991).

Seebass, Gottfried, *Artikelbrief, Bundesordnung und Verfassungsentwurf. Studien zu drei zentralen Dokumenten des südwestdeutschen Bauernkrieges* (Heidelberg: Carl Winter, 1988).

Wopfner, Hermann, *Quellen zur Geschichte des Bauernkrieges in Deutschtirol 1525, 1. Teil: Quellen zur Vorgeschichte des Bauernkrieges; Beschwerdeartikel aus den Jahren 1519–1525*. Acta Tirolensia, 3 (Innsbruck, 1908: rpt. Aalen: Scientia, 1973).

Zwingli, Huldrich, *Sämtliche Werke*. 14 vols. (Zurich: Berichthaus, 1905–68).

Secondary sources

Albert, Thomas D., *Der gemeine Mann vor dem geistlichen Richter. Kirchliche Rechtsprechung in den Diözesen Basel, Chur und Konstanz vor der Reformation*. Quellen und Forschungen zur Agrargeschichte, 45 (Stuttgart: Lucius & Lucius, 1998).

Bierbrauer, Peter, 'Das Göttliche Recht und die naturrechtliche Tradition'. In Peter Blickle (ed.), *Bauer, Reich und Reformation* (Stuttgart: Eugen Ulmer, 1982), pp. 210–34.

'Die Reformation in den Schaffhauser Gemeinden Hallau und Thayngen'. In Peter Blickle (ed.), *Zugänge zur bäuerlichen Reformation*. Bauern und Reformation, 1 (Zurich: Chronos, 1987), pp. 21–53.

Die unterdrückte Reformation. Der Kampf der Tiroler um eine neue Kirche (1521–1527) Bauern und Reformation, 2 (Zurich: Chronos, 1993).

Blickle, Peter, *The Revolution of 1525. The German Peasants' War from a new perspective*. Trans. Thomas A. Brady, Jr and H. C. Erik Midelfort (Baltimore and London: Johns Hopkins University Press, 1981).

Blickle, Peter (ed.), *Zugänge zur bäuerlichen Reformation*. Bauern und Reformation, 1 (Zurich: Chronos, 1987).

Communal Reformation. The quest for salvation in sixteenth-century Germany. Trans. Thomas Dunlap (New Jersey: Humanities Press, 1992).

Kommunalismus. Skizzen einer gesellschaftlichen Organisationsform. 2 vols. (Munich: Oldenbourg, 2000).

Die Reformation im Reich. 3rd edn (Stuttgart: Eugen Ulmer Verlag, 2000).

Der Bauernkrieg. Die Revolution des Gemeinen Mannes. 3rd edn (Munich: C. H. Beck, 2006).

Bookchin, Murray, *The Third Revolution*, vol. 1: *Popular movements in the revolutionary era* (London: Cassell, 1996).

Brady, Thomas A., Jr, *Ruling class, regime and Reformation at Strasbourg 1520–1550* (Leiden: E. J. Brill, 1978).

'From the sacral community to the common man: reflections on German Reformation studies'. *Central European History* 20 (1987): 229–45.

Protestant politics: Jacob Sturm (1489–1553) and the German Reformation (New Jersey: Humanities Press, 1995).

Brady, Thomas A., Jr, Oberman, Heiko A., and Tracy, James D. (eds.), *Handbook of European history 1400–1600. Late Middle Ages, Renaissance and Reformation*, vol. 2: *Visions, programs and outcomes* (Leiden: E. J. Brill, 1995).

Burgard, Paul, *Tagebuch einer Revolte. Ein städtischer Aufstand während des Bauernkrieges 1525*. Historische Studien, 29 (Frankfurt: Campus, 1998).

Burkhardt, Johannes, *Das Reformationsjahrhundert. Deutsche Geschichte zwischen Medienrevolution und Institutionenbildung 1517–1617* (Stuttgart: Kohlhammer, 2002).

Buszello, Horst, *Der deutsche Bauernkrieg als politische Bewegung mit besonderer Berücksichtigung der anonymen Flugschrift An die Versamlung gemayner Pawerschafft*. Studien zur europäischen Geschichte, 8 (Berlin: Colloquium, 1969).

Bibliography

Cameron, Euan, *The European Reformation* (Oxford: Clarendon Press, 1991).

Conrad, Franziska, *Reformation in der bäuerlichen Gesellschaft. Zur Rezeption reformatorischer Theologie im Elsaß*. Veröffentlichungen des Instituts für Europäische Geschichte Mainz, 116 (Stuttgart: Franz Steiner, 1989).

Dilcher, Gerhard, 'Die Kommune als europäische Verfassungsform'. *Historische Zeitschrift* 272 (2001): 667–74.

Dixon, C. Scott (ed.), *The German Reformation* (Oxford: Blackwell Publishers, 1999).

Dykema, Peter A., and Oberman, Heiko A. (eds.), *Anticlericalism in late medieval and early modern Europe*. Studies in Medieval and Reformation Thought, 51 (Leiden: E. J. Brill, 1993).

Edwards, Mark U., Jr, 'Die Gemeindereformation als Bindeglied zwischen der mittelalterlichen und der neuzeitlichen Welt'. *Historische Zeitschrift* 249 (1989): 95–103.

Printing, propaganda and Martin Luther (Berkeley: University of California Press, 1994).

Ehrenpreis, Stefan, and Lotz-Heumann, Ute, *Reformation und konfessionelles Zeitalter* (Darmstadt: Wissenschaftliche Buchgesellschaft, 2002).

Endres, Rudolf, 'Die Reformation im fränkischen Wendelstein'. In Peter Blickle (ed.), *Zugänge zur bäuerlichen Reformation*. Bauern und Reformation, 1 (Zurich: Chronos, 1987), 127–46.

Franz, Günther, *Der deutsche Bauernkrieg* (Munich: Oldenbourg, 1933).

Fuchs, Thomas, *Konfession und Gespräch. Typologie und Funktion der Religionsgespräche in der Reformationszeit*. Norm und Struktur, 4 (Cologne: Böhlau, 1995).

Fuchs, Walther Peter, 'Das Zeitalter der Reformation'. In *Gebhardt. Handbuch der deutschen Geschichte*. 9th edn, vol. 2 (Stuttgart: Union, 1970), pp. 2–117.

Fuhrmann, Rosi, *Kirche und Dorf. Religiöse Bedürfnisse und kirchliche Stiftung auf dem Lande vor der Reformation*. Quellen und Forschungen zur Agrargeschichte, 40 (Stuttgart: Gustav Fischer, 1995).

Gäbler, Ulrich, *Huldrych Zwingli. Eine Einführung in sein Leben und sein Werk* (Munich: C. H. Beck, 1983).

Gatz, Erwin, 'Gemeinde'. In *Lexikon für Theologie und Kirche*. 3rd edn, vol. 4 (Freiburg: Herder, 1995), p. 420.

Goertz, Hans-Jürgen, *Pfaffenhaß und groß Geschrei. Die reformatorischen Bewegungen in Deutschland 1517–1529* (Munich: C. H. Beck, 1987).

Antiklerikalismus und Reformation. Sozialgeschichtliche Untersuchungen (Göttingen: Vandenhoeck & Ruprecht, 1995).

Hamm, Berndt, *Zwinglis Reformation der Freiheit* (Neukirchen and Vluyn: Neukirchener Verlag, 1988).

Hamm, Berndt, Moeller, Bernd, and Wendebourg, Dorothea, *Reformationstheorien. Ein kirchengeschichtlicher Disput über Einheit und Vielfalt der Reformation* (Göttingen: Vandenhoeck & Ruprecht, 1995).

Bürgertum und Glaube. Konturen der städtischen Reformation (Göttingen: Vandenhoeck & Ruprecht, 1996).

Hardtwig, Wolfgang, *Genossenschaft, Sekte, Verein in Deutschland. Vom Spätmittelalter bis zur Französischen Revolution* (Munich: C. H. Beck, 1997).

Hillerbrand, Hans J. (ed.), *The Oxford encyclopedia of the Reformation* 4 vols. (New York: Oxford University Press, 1996).

Hollaender, Albert, '"Articles of *Almayne*": An English version of German Peasants' Gravamina, 1525'. In J. Conway Davies (ed.), *Studies presented to Sir Hilary Jenkinson* (London: Oxford University Press, 1957), pp. 164–77.

Hsia, Ronnie Po-chia (ed.), *The German people and the Reformation* (Ithaca: Cornell University Press, 1988).

Jussen, Bernhard, and Koslofsky, Craig (eds.), *Kulturelle Reformation. Sinnformationen im Umbruch 1400–1600*. Veröffentlichungen des Max-Planck-Instituts für Geschichte, 145 (Göttingen: Vandenhoeck & Ruprecht, 1999).

Köhler, Hans-Joachim, 'Erste Schritte zu einem Meinungsprofil der frühen Reformationszeit'. In Volker Press and Dieter Stievermann (eds.), *Martin Luther. Probleme seiner Zeit*. Spätmittelalter und Frühe Neuzeit, 16 (Stuttgart: Klett-Cotta, 1986), pp. 244–81.

Locher, Gottfried W., *Die Zwinglische Reformation im Rahmen der europäischen Kirchengeschichte* (Göttingen: Vandenhoeck & Ruprecht, 1979).

Lutz, Robert H., *Wer war der gemeine Mann? Der dritte Stand in der Krise des Spätmittelalters* (Munich and Vienna: Oldenbourg, 1979).

Moeller, Bernd, 'Zwinglis Disputationen. Studien zu den Anfängen der Kirchenbildung und des Synodalwesens im Protestantismus'. *Zeitschrift der Savigny-Stiftung für Rechtsgeschichte. Kanonistische Abteilung* 56 (1970): 275–324, and 60 (1974): 213–364.

Reichsstadt und Reformation. Bearbeitete Neuausgabe (Berlin: Evangelische Verlagsanstalt, 1987).

Neveux, Hugues, *Les révoltes paysannes en Europe XIVᵉ–XVIIᵉ siècle* (Paris: Albin Michel, 1997).

Oberman, Heiko A., 'The gospel of social unrest'. In Robert Scribner and Gerhard Benecke (eds.), *The German Peasant War of 1525. New viewpoints* (London: George Allen & Unwin, 1979), pp. 39–51.

Ozment, Steven E., *The Reformation in the cities. The appeal of Protestantism to sixteenth-century Germany and Switzerland* (New Haven: Yale University Press, 1975).

Politi, Giorgio, *Gli statuti impossibili. La rivoluzione tirolese del 1525 e il 'programma' di Michael Gaismair* (Turin: Enaudi, 1995).

Rabe, Horst, *Deutsche Geschichte 1500–1600. Das Jahrhundert der Glaubensspaltung* (Munich: C. H. Beck, 1991).

Rammstedt, Otthein, 'Stadtunruhen 1525'. In Hans-Ulrich Wehler (ed.), *Der Deutsche Bauernkrieg 1524–1526*. Geschichte und Gesellschaft, Sonderheft, 1 (Göttingen: Vandenhoeck & Ruprecht, 1975), pp. 239–76.

Ranke, Leopold von, *Deutsche Geschichte im Zeitalter der Reformation*. 4th edn (Leipzig: Duncker and Humblot, 1867), vol. 1.

Reinhard, Wolfgang, *Probleme deutscher Geschichte 1495–1806. Reichsreform und Reformation 1495–1555*. Gebhardt, Handbuch der deutschen Geschichte, 10th edn, vol. 9 (Stuttgart: Klett-Cotta, 2001).

Rublack, Hans Christoph, 'Is there a "new history" of the urban Reformation?' In E. I. Kouri and Tom Scott (eds.), *Politics and society in Reformation Europe. Essays for Sir Geoffrey Elton on his sixty-fifth birthday* (Houndmills: Macmillan, 1987), pp. 121–41.

Sabean, David W., *Landbesitz und Gesellschaft am Vorabend des Bauernkriegs. Eine Studie der sozialen Verhältnisse im südlichen Oberschwaben in den Jahren vor 1525*. Quellen und Forschungen zur Agrargeschichte, 26 (Stuttgart: Gustav Fischer, 1972).

Bibliography

Saulle Hippenmeyer, Immacolata, *Nachbarschaft, Pfarrei und Gemeinde in Graubünden 1400–1600*. Quellen und Forschungen zur Bündner Geschichte, 7 (Chur: Staatsarchiv Graubünden, 1997).

Schilling, Heinz, *Die Stadt in der Frühen Neuzeit*. Enzyklopädie deutscher Geschichte, 24 (Munich: Oldenbourg, 1993).

Schindling, Anton, and Ziegler, Walter (eds.), *Die Territorien des Reichs im Zeitalter der Reformation und Konfessionalisierung. Land und Konfession 1500–1650*. Katholisches Leben und Kirchenreform im Zeitalter der Glaubensspaltung, 49–53, 4 vols. (Münster: Aschendorff, 1989–93).

Schmidt, Heinrich Richard, *Reichsstädte, Reich und Reformation. Korporative Reichspolitik 1521–1529/30*. Veröffentlichungen des Instituts für Europäische Geschichte Mainz, 122 (Stuttgart: Franz Steiner, 1986).

'Die Häretisierung des Zwinglianismus im Reich seit 1525'. In Peter Blickle (ed.), *Zugänge zur bäuerlichen Reformation*. Bauern und Reformation, 1 (Zurich: Chronos, 1987), pp. 219–36.

Schulze, Winfried, 'Die veränderte Bedeutung sozialer Konflikte im 16. und 17. Jahrhundert'. In Hans-Ulrich Wehler (ed.), *Der Deutsche Bauernkrieg 1524–1526*. Geschichte und Gesellschaft, Sonderheft, 1 (Göttingen: Vandenhoeck & Ruprecht, 1975), pp. 277–302.

Schwarz, Reinhard, *Luther*. Die Kirche in ihrer Geschichte, III/1 (Göttingen: Vandenhoeck & Ruprecht, 1986).

Scott, Tom, 'The Peasants' War: a historiographical review'. *Historical Journal* 22 (1979): 693–720, 953–74.

Scribner, Robert W., *For the sake of the simple folk. Popular propaganda for the German Reformation* (Cambridge: Cambridge University Press, 1981).

The German Reformation (Houndmills: Macmillan, 1986).

Seebass, Gottfried, 'Reformation'. In *Theologische Realenzyklopädie*. 4th edn, vol. 28 (Berlin: de Gruyter, 1997).

Seibt, Ferdinand, *Utopica* (Düsseldorf: L. Schwann 1972).

Simon, Thomas, 'Gemeinwohltopik in der mittelalterlichen und frühneuzeitlichen Politiktheorie'. In Herfried Münkler and Harald Bluhm (eds.), *Gemeinwohl und Gemeinsinn* (Berlin: Akademie Verlag, 2001), pp. 129–46.

Smirin, Moisej M., *Die Volksreformation des Thomas Münzer und der große Bauernkrieg*. 2nd edn (Berlin: Dietz, 1956).

Stayer, James M., *The German Peasants' War and Anabaptist community of goods* (Montreal: McGill-Queen's University Press, 1991).

Steinmetz, Max. 'Über den Charakter der Reformation und des Bauernkrieges in Deutschland', *Wissenschaftliche Zeitschrift der Karl-Marx-Universität Leipzig* 14 (1965): 389–98.

Vasella, Oskar, 'Bauernkrieg und Reformation in Graubünden 1525–1526', *Zeitschrift für Schweizerische Geschichte* 20 (1940): 1–65.

Vogler, Günter, 'Marx, Engels und die Konzeption einer frühbürgerlichen Revolution in Deutschland', *Zeitschrift für Geschichtswissenschaft* 17 (1969): 704–17.

Die Gewalt soll gegeben werden dem gemeinen Volk. Der deutsche Bauernkrieg 1525. 2nd edn (Berlin: Dietz 1983).

Wandel, Lee Palmer, *Voracious idols and violent hands. Iconoclasm in Reformation Zurich, Strasbourg, and Basel* (Cambridge: Cambridge University Press, 1995).

Wehler, Hans-Ulrich (ed.), *Der Deutsche Bauernkrieg 1524–1526*. Geschichte und Gesellschaft, Sonderheft, 1 (Göttingen: Vandenhoeck & Ruprecht, 1975).

Wende, Peter (ed.), *Grosse Revolutionen der Weltgeschichte* (Munich: C. H. Beck, 2000).

Wohlfeil, Rainer, 'Der Speyrer Reichstag von 1526'. *Blätter für pfälzische Kirchengeschichte und religiöse Volkskunde* 43 (1976): 5–20.

6 THE CALVINIST REFORMATION IN GENEVA

Primary sources

Bèze, Théodore de, *Correspondance*. Ed. Henri Meylan, Alain Dufour *et al.* Travaux d'Humanisme et Renaissance (Geneva: Droz, 1960–).

Calvin, John, *Ioannis Calvini Opera quae supersunt omnia*. Ed. G. Baum, E. Cunitz, and E. Reuss. 59 vols. (Brunswick: Schwetschke, 1863–1900).

Registres de la Compagnie des Pasteurs de Genève au temps de Calvin. Ed. Jean-François Bergier, Robert M. Kingdon *et al.* Travaux d'Humanisme et Renaissance (Geneva: Droz, 1962–).

Registres du Consistoire de Genève au temps de Calvin. Ed. Thomas A. Lambert, Isabella M. Watt *et al.* Travaux d'Humanisme et Renaissance (Geneva: Droz, 1967–).

Les sources du droit du canton de Genève. Ed. Emile Rivoire and Victor van Berchem. Sammlung Schweizerischer Rechtsquellen, 12. Abteilung. 4 vols. (Aarau: Sauerländer, 1927–35).

Secondary sources

Armstrong, Elizabeth [Tyler], *Robert Estienne, royal printer: an historical study of the elder Stephanus*. Courtenay Studies in Reformation Theology, 6, rev. edn (Abingdon, Berks: The Sutton Courtenay Press, 1986). [First edition: Cambridge: Cambridge University Press, 1954.]

Cahier-Bucelli, Gabriella, 'Dans l'ombre de la Réforme: les membres de l'ancien clergé demeurés à Genève (1536–1538)', *Bulletin de la Société d'histoire et d'archéologie de Genève* 18 / 4 (1987): 367–90.

Chaix, Paul, *Recherches sur l'imprimerie à Genève de 1550 à 1564*. Travaux d'Humanisme et Renaissance, 16 (Geneva: Droz, 1964).

Doumergue, Emile, *Jean Calvin: les hommes et les choses de son temps*. 7 vols. (Lausanne: Bridel, and Neuilly-sur-Seine: 'La Cause', 1899–1927).

Dufour, Alain, 'Théodore de Bèze', *Histoire littéraire de la France*, vol. 42 (Paris: Boccard, 2002), pp. 315–470 + xiii.

Ganoczy, Alexandre, *Le jeune Calvin: genèse et évolution de sa vocation réformatrice*. Veröffentlichungen des Instituts für Europäische Geschichte, Mainz, 40. Abteilung Abendländische Religionsgeschichte, ed. Joseph Lortz (Wiesbaden: Steiner, 1966).

Gilmont, Jean-François, *Jean Crespin: un éditeur réformée du XVIe siècle*. Travaux d'Humanisme et Renaissance, 186 (Geneva: Droz, 1981).

Haag, Eugène and Emile, *La France protestante, ou vies des protestants français*. 1st edn, 10 vols. (Paris: Cherbuliez, 1846–59); 2nd edn, rev. Henri Bordier, 6 vols. (incomplete) (Paris: Sandoz et Fischbacher, 1877–88).

Kaden, Erich-Hans, *Le jurisconsulte Germain Colladon: ami de Jean Calvin et Théodore de Bèze.* Mémoires publiés par la Faculté de Droit, Genève, 41 (Geneva: Georg, 1974).

Kingdon, Robert M., *Adultery and divorce in Calvin's Geneva* (Cambridge, MA: Harvard University Press, 1995).

Geneva and the coming of the wars of religion in France, 1555–1563. Travaux d'Humanisme et Renaissance, 22 (Geneva: Droz, 1956).

Le livre du recteur de l'Académie de Genève, 1559–1578. Ed. Sven and Suzanne Stelling-Michaud. 6 vols. Travaux d'Humanisme et Renaissance (Geneva: Droz, 1959–81).

Martin, Charles, *Les Protestants Anglais réfugiés à Genève au temps de Calvin, 1550–1560* (Geneva: Jullien, 1915).

Monter, E. William, *Calvin's Geneva* (New York: John Wiley, 1967).

Muller, Richard A., *The unaccommodated Calvin: studies in the foundation of a theological tradition.* Oxford Studies in Historical Theology (New York: Oxford University Press, 2000).

Naphy, William G., *Calvin and the consolidation of the Genevan Reformation* (Manchester: Manchester University Press, 1994).

Olson, Jeannine E., *Calvin and social welfare: deacons and the bourse française* (Sellingsgrove, PA: Susquehanna University Press, 1989).

Roget, Amédée, *Histoire du peuple de Genève depuis la réforme jusqu'à l'Escalade.* 7 vols. (Geneva: Jullien, 1870–83).

Wendel, François, *Calvin: sources et évolution de sa pensée religieuse.* Etudes d'histoire et de philosophie religieuse publiés par la Faculté de Théologie Protestante de l'Université de Strasbourg, 41 (Paris: Presses Universitaires de France, 1950).

7 THE THEOLOGY AND LITURGY OF REFORMED CHRISTIANITY

Primary sources

[Bullinger, Heinrich], McCoy, Charles S. and Baker, J. Wayne, *Fountainhead of federalism: Heinrich Bullinger and the covenantal tradition* (Louisville, 1991). [Includes a translation of Bullinger's *De Testamentum seu fædere.*]

Calvin, Jean, *The Institutes of the Christian religion.* Ed. John T. McNeill. 2 vols. (Philadelphia, Library of Christian Classics, 1961). See also Wevers, Richard (ed.), *Calvin's Institutes. Latin–English search and browser programs.* CD-ROM (Calvin College, 1999) for a searchable text of the 1559 Latin edition and a corresponding English translation. For the 1536 edition of the *Institutes* in an English translation see the edition by Ford Lewis Battles (Grand Rapids, 1986).

New Testament commentaries. Ed. David W. and Thomas F. Torrance. 12 vols. (Grand Rapids: Eerdmans, 1959–72).

Three French treatises. Ed. Francis M. Higman (London: The Athlone Press, 1970).

Opera Calvini. Ed. G. Baum, E. Cunitz, and E. Reuss. Corpus Reformatorum, vols. 1–59 (Braunschweig, 1863–80).

Dordrecht, Synod of, *The Iudgement of the Synode Holden at Dort, Concerning the Five Articles, As Also Their Sentence Touching Conradus Vorstius* (London: John Bill, 1619).

Egli, Emil, *Actensammlung zur Geschichte der Züricher Reformation* (Zurich: Mayer & Zeller, 1879).

Egli, Emil, Finsler, Georg, Köler, Walter, Farner, Oskar, Blane, Fritz, von Muralt, Leonhart *et al.*, with the participation of the Zwingli Society, Zurich, (eds.), *Huldreich Zwinglis sämtliche Werke*. Corpus Reformatorum, vols. 88–101 (Berlin, Leipzig, and Zurich, Schwetschke und Sohn, 1905–).

Erasmus, Desiderius, *Les préfaces au Novum Testamentum*. Ed. Y. Delègue and J-P. Gillet (Geneva: Labor et Fides, 1990).

  Christian humanism and the Reformation. Selected writings. Ed. and trans. John C. Olin (New York: Harper and Row, 1965).

Foxe, John, *Actes and Monuments of John Foxe* (London: Richard Day, 1563).

Millet, Olivier (ed.), *Jean Calvin: Advertissement contre l'astrologie judiciaire* (Geneva: Droz, 1985).

Milton, A. (ed.), *The British Delegation and the Synod of Dort (1618–1619)* (Church of England Record Society 13) (Woodbridge: Boydell Press, 2005).

Pidoux, Pierre (ed.), *La forme des prières et chantz ecclésiastiques, 1542* facsimile edn (Kassel: n.p., 1959).

  Le psaultier huguenot du XVIe siècle, mélodies et documents. 2 vols. (Basel: Bärenreiter, 1962).

Piscator, Johannes, *Aphorismi doctrinae christianae* (Herborn: Corvinus, 1589). Translated into English and published as *Aphorismes of Christian religion* (London: Richard Field and Robert Dexter, 1596).

Schuler, Johann Melchior, and Schulthess, Johannes (eds.), *Ulrich Zwingli, Opera completa, editio prima*. 10 vols. (Turicil, 1829–42).

Secondary sources

Aeschbacher, Gerhard, 'Zwingli und die Musik im Gottesdienst', *Zwingliana* 19: 1–11.

Armstrong, Brian G., *Calvinism and the Amyraut heresy* (Madison, Milwaukee, and London: University of Wisconsin Press, 1969).

Baker, J. Wayne, *Heinrich Bullinger and the covenant: the other Reformed tradition* (Athens, OH: Ohio, 1980).

Bangs, C., *Arminius* (Nashville: Tennessee University Press, 1971).

Bedouelle, Guy, and Roussel, Bernard (eds.), *Le temps des Réformes et la Bible* (Paris: Beauchesne, 1989).

Benedict, Philip, *Christ's churches purely reformed. A social history of Calvinism* (New Haven and London: Yale University Press, 2002).

Bentley, Jerry, *Humanism and holy writ* (Princeton: Princeton University Press, 1983).

Bovet, Félix, *Histoire du Psautier des églises réformées* (Neuchâtel: J. Sandoz, 1872).

Boyle, Margery, *Erasmus on language and method in theology* (Toronto: Toronto University Press, 1977).

Bray, John S., *Theodore Beza's doctrine of predestination* (Nieuwkoop: De Graaf, 1975).

Büsser, Fritz, 'H. Bullingers 100 predigten über die Apokalypse', *Zwingliana* 27 (2000): 117–31.

Christ, Christine, 'Das Schriftverständnis von Zwingli und Erasmus im Jahre 1522', *Zwingliana* 16 (1983): 111–25.

Collinson, Patrick, *Godly people: essays in English Protestantism and Puritanism* (London: Hambledon Press, 1983).

Cummings, Brian, *The literary culture of the Reformation: grammar and grace* (Oxford: Oxford University Press, 2002).

Denis, Philippe, 'La prophétie dans les églises de la réforme au XVIe siècle', *Revue d'histoire ecclésiastique* 72 (1977): 289–316.

Douen, Emmanuel-Orentin, *Clément Marot et le Psautier Huguenot.* 2 vols. (Paris: Imprimerie Nationale, 1878–9).

Dowey, Edward A., *The knowledge of God in Calvin's theology* (New York: Columbia University Press, 1952).

Droz, Emile, 'Antoine Vincent. La propagande protestante par le Psautier'. In G. Berthoud (ed.), *Aspects de la propagande religieuse* (Geneva: Droz, 1957), pp. 276–93.

Eire, Carlos M. N., *War against the idols: the Reformation of worship from Erasmus to Calvin* (Cambridge: Cambridge University Press, 1986).

Elwood, Christopher, *The body broken. The Calvinist doctrine of the eucharist and the symbolization of power in sixteenth-century France* (Oxford: Oxford University Press, 1999).

Fitzer, Joseph, 'The Augustinian roots of Calvin's eucharistic thought', *Augustinian Studies* 7 (1986): 69–86.

Gäbler, Ulrich, *Huldrych Zwingli. His life and work* (Edinburgh: T. & T. Clark Ltd, 1986).

Garside Jr, Charles, *Zwingli and the arts* (New Haven and London: Yale University Press, 1966).

Gerrish, Brian A., *Grace and gratitude: the eucharistic theology of John Calvin* (Edinburgh: T. & T. Clark, 1993).

Gilmont, Jean-François, 'Les sermons de Calvin: de l'oral à l'imprimé', *Bulletin de la société de l'histoire du protestantisme français* 141 (1995): 139–62.

Girardin, Benoît, *Rhétorique et théologique* (Paris: Editions Beauchesne, 1979).

Hammann, Gottfried, *Entre la secte et la cité. Le projet d'Eglise du Réformateur Martin Bucer* (Geneva: Labor et Fides, 1984).

Hobbs, R. Gerald, 'Zwingli and the study of the Old Testament'. In E. J. Furcha (ed.), *Huldrych Zwingli, 1484–1531: a legacy of radical reform.* ARC Supplement No. 2 (Montreal: McGill University, 1985), pp. 144–78.

Hollweg, Walter, *Heinrich Bullingers Hausbuch: Eine Untersuchung über die Anfänge der reformierten Predigtliteratur* (Neukirchen-Vluyn: Neukirchener Verlag, 1956).

Höpfl, Harro, *The Christian polity of John Calvin* (Cambridge: Cambridge University Press, 1982).

Janson, Carol, 'Public places, private lives: the impact of the Dutch revolt on the Reformed churches in Holland'. In Arthur K. Wheelock Jr and Adele Seeff (eds.), *The public and private in Dutch culture of the Golden Age* (Newark: University of Delaware Press, 2000), pp. 191–205.

Jenny, Markus, *Luther, Zwingli, Calvin in ihren Liedern* (Zurich: Theologischer Verlag, 1983).

Kadane, Matthew, 'Les bibliothèques de deux théologiens réformés du XVIIe siècle', *Bulletin de la société de l'histoire du protestantisme français* 147 (2001): 67–100.

Koch, Ernst, *Der Theologie der Confessio Helvetica Posterior* (Neukirchen-Vluyn: Neukirchener Verlag, 1968).

Kroon, Marijn de, *Martin Bucer und Johannes Calvin*, trans. Hartmut Rudolph (Göttingen: Vandenhoeck & Ruprecht, 1991).

Laplanche, François, *Orthodoxie et prédication: l'œuvre d'Amyraut et la querelle de la grâce universelle* (Paris: P. U. F., 1965).

L'Ecriture, le sacré et l'histoire. Erudits et politiques protestants devant la Bible en France au XVIIe siècle (Amsterdam and Villeneuve d'Ascq: APA and Presses Universitaires de Lille, 1986).

Letham, Robert, 'The Fœdus operum: some factors accounting for its development', *Sixteenth Century Journal* 14 (1983): 457–67.

Locher, Gottfried, 'In spirit and in truth. How worship in Zurich changed at the Reformation'. In Gottfried Locher (ed.), *Zwingli's thought. New Perspectives* (Leiden: Brill, 1981), pp. 1–30.

MacCulloch, Diarmaid, *Reformation. Europe's house divided, 1490–1700* (London: Allen Lane, 2003).

McGiffert, Michael, 'Grace and works: the rise and division of covenant divinity in Elizabethan puritanism', *Harvard Theological Review* 75, 4 (1982): 463–502.

'From Moses to Adam: the making of the covenant of works', *Sixteenth Century Journal* 19 (1988): 131–55.

Marcus, Kenneth H., 'Hymnody and hymnals in Basel, 1526–1606', *Sixteenth Century Journal*, 32 (2001): 723–41.

Millet, Olivier, *Calvin et le dynamisme de la Parole* (Paris: Champion, 1992).

Milton, Anthony, *Catholic and Reformed. The Roman and Protestant churches in English Protestant thought, 1600–1640* (Cambridge: Cambridge University Press, 1995).

Moeller, Bernd, 'Zwingli's Disputationen: Studien zu den Anfängen der Kirchenbildung und des Synodalwesens im Protestantismus', *Zeitschrift der Savigny-Stiftung für Rechtsgeschichte* 56 (1970): 275–323.

Muller, Richard A., *Christ and the decree: Christology and predestination in Reformed theology from Calvin to Perkins* (Durham, NC: North Carolina University Press, 1986).

Post-Reformation Reformed dogmatics, vol. A: Prolegomena to theology (Grand Rapids: Eerdmans, 1987).

God, creation and providence in the thought of Jacob Arminius: Sources and directions of scholastic Protestantism in the era of early orthodoxy (Grand Rapids: Eerdmans, 1991).

'Calvin and the Calvinists', *Calvin Theological Journal* 30 (1995). 345–75, and 31 (1996): 125–60.

The unaccommodated Calvin: Studies in the foundation of a theological tradition (Oxford: Oxford University Press, 2000).

Neuser, Wilhelm Heinrich (ed.), *Calvinus Theologus*. 1st European Congress on Calvin research (Neukirchen-Vluyn: Neukirchener Verlag, 1976).

Calvinus ecclesiae doctor, 2nd International Congress on Calvin Research (Kampen: J. H. Kok, 1978).

Calvinus ecclesiae Genevensis custos, 3rd International Congress on Calvin Research. (Frankfurt-am-Main: Peter Lang, 1984).

Nischan, Bodo, 'The "Fractio Panis": a Reformed communion practice in late Reformation Germany', *Church History* 53 (1984): 17–29.

'The exorcism controversy and baptism in the late Reformation', *Sixteenth Century Journal* 18 (1987): 31–52.

Prince, people and confession. The second Reformation in Brandenburg (Philadelphia: Philadelphia University Press, 1994).

Parker, Thomas H. L., *The doctrine of the knowledge of God: a study in the theology of Calvin* (Edinburgh: Oliver & Boyd, 1952).

Patterson, W. B., *King James VI and I and the reunion of Christendom* (Cambridge: Cambridge University Press, 1997).

Pipkin, H. Wayne, 'The positive religious values of Zwingli's eucharistic writings'. In E. J. Furcha (ed.), *Huldrych Zwingli, 1484–1531: a legacy of radical reform*, ARC Supplement No. 2 (Montreal: McGill University, 1985), pp. 107–43.

Pollmann, Judith, 'Public enemies, private friends: Arnoldus Buchelius's experience of religious diversity in the early Dutch Republic'. In Arthur K. Wheelock Jr and Adele Seeff (eds.), *The public and private in Dutch culture of the golden age* (Newark: University of Delaware Press, 2000), pp. 181–90.

Potter, G. R., *Zwingli* (Cambridge: Cambridge University Press, 1976).

Huldrych Zwingli (London: Edward Arnold, 1978).

Prestwich, Menna (ed.), *International Calvinism, 1541–1715* (Oxford: Clarendon Press, 1985).

Rabil, Albert, *Erasmus and the New Testament: the mind of a Christian humanist* (San Antonio, TX: Trinity University Press, 1972).

Raitt, Jill, *The eucharistic theology of Theodore Beza* (Atlanta, GA: Scholars Press, 1972).

Rorem, Paul, *Calvin and Bullinger on the Lord's Supper* (Bramcote, Notts.: Grove Books, 1989).

Shapin, Steven, *A social history of truth: Civility and science in seventeenth-century England* (Chicago: Chicago University Press, 1994).

Sinnema, Donald, 'Reformed scholasticism and the Synod of Dort (1618–19)'. In B. J. Van der Walt (ed.), *John Calvin's Institutes: His opus magnum* (Potschefstroom: Potschefstroom University for Christian Higher Education, 1986), pp. 467–506.

Stephens, W. P., *The theology of Huldrych Zwingli* (Oxford: Clarendon Press, 1986).

Sunderland, Rosmarie, 'Huldrych Zwingli's Reformation. Changes in religious and social customs in sixteenth- and seventeenth-century Zürich and its environs' (Ph.D. dissertation: Fordham University, 2000).

Terry, Richard Runciman, *Calvin's first psalter* (London: E. Benn, 1932).

Tyacke, Nicholas, *Anti-Calvinists: The rise of English Arminianism, c.1590–1640* (Oxford: Clarendon Press, 1987).

Wallace, Dewey A., *Puritans and predestination: Grace in English protestant theology, 1525–1695* (Chapel Hill: North Carolina University Press, 1982).

Wandel, Lee Palmer, 'The reform of the images: New visualizations of the Christian community at Zürich', *Archiv für Reformationsgeschichte* 80 (1989): 105–24.

Weir, David A., *The origins of the federal theology in sixteenth-century Reformed thought* (Oxford: Oxford University Press, 1990).

White, Peter, *Predestination, policy and polemic: conflict and consensus in the English Reformation from the Reformation to the English Civil War* (Cambridge: Cambridge University Press, 1992).

Wright, D. F. (ed.), *Martin Bucer: Reforming church and community* (Cambridge: Cambridge University Press, 1994).

8 THE SECOND WAVE OF PROTESTANT EXPANSION

Primary sources

Kirk, James (ed.), *The second book of discipline* (Edinburgh: St Andrew Press, 1980).

Knox, John, *History of the Reformation in Scotland*. Ed. William Croft Dickinson, 2 vols. (London: Thomas Nelson and Sons, 1949).

Secondary sources

Benedict, Philip, *Rouen during the wars of religion* (Cambridge: Cambridge University Press, 1981).

The Huguenot population of France, 1600–1685: The demographic fate and customs of a religious minority. Transactions of the American Philosophical Society, vol. 18, part 5 (Philadelphia, American Philosophical Society, 1991).

Christ's churches purely reformed: A social history of Calvinism (New Haven: Yale University Press, 2001).

Benedict, Philip, Marnef, Guido, van Nierop, Henk, and Venard, Marc (eds.), *Reformation, revolt and civil war in France and the Netherlands 1555–1585*. Koninklijke Nederlandse Akademie van Wetenschappen, Afd. Letterkunde, new series, 176 (Amsterdam, 1999).

Bucsay, Mihaly, *Die Protestantismus in Ungarn 1521–1978: Ungarns Reformationskirchen in Geschichte und Gegenwart*, 2 vols. (Vienna: Böhlau, 1977).

Cameron, James (ed.), *The first book of discipline* (Edinburgh: St Andrew Press, 1972).

Chadwick, Owen, 'The making of a reforming prince: Frederick III, Elector Palatine'. In R. B. Knox (ed.), *Reformation, conformity and dissent: Essays in honour of Geoffrey Nuttall* (London: Epworth Press, 1977), pp. 44–69.

Cowan, Ian, *The Scottish Reformation: Church and society in sixteenth century Scotland* (New York: St Martin's, 1982).

Crouzet, Denis, *Les Guerriers de Dieu. La violence au temps des troubles de religion (vers 1525–vers 1610)*. 2 vols. (Seyssel: Champ Vallon, 1990).

La Genèse de la Réforme française 1520–1562 (Paris: SEDES, 1996).

Dickens, A. G., 'The early expansion of Protestantism in England 1520–1558', *Archiv für Reformationsgeschichte* 78 (1987): 187–222.

Diefendorf, Barbara, *Beneath the cross: Catholics and Huguenots in sixteenth-century Paris* (Oxford: Oxford University Press, 1991).

Donaldson, Gordon, *The Scottish Reformation* (Cambridge: Cambridge University Press, 1960).

Dufour, Alain, 'L'affaire de Maligny (Lyon, 4–5 septembre 1560) vue à travers la correspondance de Calvin et de Bèze', *Cahiers d'Histoire*, 8 (1963): 269–80.

Duke, Alastair, *Reformation and revolt in the Low Countries* (London: Hambledon Press, 1990).

Duke, Alastair, Lewis, Gillian, and Pettegree, Andrew (eds.), *Calvinism in Europe 1540–1620* (Cambridge: Cambridge University Press, 1994).

Fata, Márta, *Ungarn, das Reich der Stephanskrone, im Zeitalter der Reformation und Konfessionalisierung. Multiethnizität, Land und Konfession 1500 bis 1700* (Munster: Aschendorff Verlag, 2000).

Garrisson-Estèbe, Janine, *Protestants du Midi 1559–1598* (Toulouse: Privat, 1980).

Gelder, H. A. Enno van, *Revolutionnaire Reformatie. De vestiging van de Gereformeerde Kerk in de Nederlandse gewesten, gedurende de eerste jaren van de Opstand tegen Filips II, 1575–1585* (Amsterdam: P. N. van Kampen, 1943).

Gilmont, Jean-François (ed.), *La Réforme et le livre. L'Europe de l'imprimé (1517–v.1570)* (Paris: Editions du Cerf, 1990).

Glawischnig, Rolf, *Niederlande, Kalvinismus und Reichsgrafenstand 1559–1584: Nassau-Dillenberg unter Graf Johann VI* (Marburg: Elwert, 1973).

Haigh, Christopher, *English reformations: religion, politics and society under the Tudors* (Oxford: Oxford University Press, 1993).

Hollweg, Walter, *Der Augsburger Reichstag von 1566 und seine Bedeutung für die Entstehung der Reformierten Kirche und ihres Bekenntnisses* (Neukirchen: Neukirchener Verlag des Erziehungsvereins, 1964).

Jobert, Ambroise, *De Luther à Mohila. La Pologne dans la crise de la Chrétienté 1517–1648* (Paris: Institut d'Etudes Slaves, 1974).

Kaplan, Benjamin J., *Calvinists and libertines: Confession and community in Utrecht, 1578–1620* (Oxford: Clarendon Press, 1995).

Kingdon, Robert M., *Geneva and the coming of the wars of religion in France, 1555–1563* (Geneva: Librairie Droz, 1956).

Kirk, James, *Patterns of reform: continuity and change in the Reformation kirk* (Edinburgh: T. & T. Clark, 1989).

Lubieniecki, Stanislas, *History of the Polish Reformation and nine related documents*, trans. George Huntston Williams (Minneapolis: Fortress Press, 1995).

Maag, Karin (ed.), *The Reformation in eastern and central Europe* (Aldershot: Ashgate, 1997).

MacCulloch, Diarmaid, *Thomas Cranmer: A life* (New Haven: Yale University Press, 1996).

Tudor church militant: Edward VI and the Protestant Reformation (London: Allen Lane, 1999).

Marnef, Guido, *Antwerp in the age of Reformation: underground protestantism in a commercial metropolis, 1550–1577* (Baltimore: Johns Hopkins University Press, 1996).

Merczyng, Henryk, *Zbory I sentorowie protestanccy w Dawnej Rzeczpospolitej* (Warsaw: A. Gins, 1904).

Nischan, Bodo, *Prince, people and confession: The second Reformation in Brandenburg* (Philadelphia: University of Pennsylvania Press, 1994).

Pettegree, Andrew, *Emden and the Dutch revolt: exile and the development of Reformed Protestantism* (Oxford: Clarendon Press, 1992).

Pettegree, Andrew (ed.), *The early Reformation in Europe* (Cambridge: Cambridge University Press, 1992).

Press, Volker, *Calvinismus und Territorialstaat: Regierung und Zentralbehörden der Kurpfalz 1559–1619* (Stuttgart: E. Klett, 1971).

Prestwich, Menna (ed.), *International Calvinism 1541–1715* (Oxford: Clarendon Press, 1985).

Ridley, Jasper, *John Knox* (Oxford: Oxford University Press, 1968).

Schaab, Meinrad (ed.), *Territorialstaat und Calvinismus* (Stuttgart: Kohlhammer, 1993).

Schilling, Heinz, *Konfessionskonflikt und Staatsbildung: Eine Fallstudie über das Verhältnis von religiösem und sozialem Wandel in der Frühneuzeit am Beispiel der Grafschaft Lippe* (Guterslöh: Mohn, 1981).

Schilling, Heinz (ed.), *Die reformierte Konfessionalisierung in Deutschland – Das Problem der 'Zweiten Reformation'* (Guterslöh: Mohn, 1986).

Schramm, Gottfried, *Die polnische Adel und die Reformation 1548–1607* (Wiesbaden: F. Steiner, 1965).

'Reformation und Gegenreformation in Krakau: Die Zuspitzung des konfessionellen Kampfes in der polnischen Hauptstadt', *Zeitschrift für Ostforschung* 19 (1970): 1–41.

Tazbir, Janusz, 'La géographie du protestantisme polonais aux XVIe–XVIIe siècles', in *Miscellanea historiae ecclesiasticae V*. Bibliothèque de la Revue d'Histoire Ecclesiastique, 61 (Louvain, 1974), pp. 143–58.

9 REDEFINING CATHOLICISM: TRENT AND BEYOND

Primary sources

Botero, Giovanni, *Della ragion di stato con tre libri delle cause della grandezza della città, due Aggiunte e un Discorso sulla popolazione di Roma*. Ed. Luigi Firpo (Turin: Unione tipografico-editrice torinese, 1948).

Canisius, Peter, *Catechismi Latini et Germanici*. Ed. Friedrich Streicher. 2 vols. (Rome: Pontificia Universitas Gregoriana, 1933–6).

Caussin, Nicholas, *La cour sainte*. 2nd edn (Paris: Sébastian Chappelet, 1625).

Decrees of the Ecumenical Councils. Vol. 2. Ed. Norman Tanner and Giuseppe Alberigo (Washington: Georgetown University Press, 1990).

de Sales, Francis, *Introduction to the devout life*. Ed. and trans. John K. Ryan (New York: Doubleday, 1989).

Jansenius, Cornelius, *Augustinus*. 3 vols. in 1 (Louvain: Jacobi Zegeri, 1640; rpt. Frankfurt: Minerva, 1964).

Lipsius, Justus, *Politicorum sive civilis doctrinae libri sex* (Frankfurt: Joannes Wechel, 1590).

Loyola, Ignatius, *Saint Ignatius of Loyola. Personal writings*. Ed. Joseph A. Munitiz and Philip Endean (Harmondsworth: Penguin Books, 1996).

Pascal, Blaise, *Pensées and other writings* (New York: Oxford University Press, 1999).

The provincial letters (New York: Viking Penguin, 1982).

Polanco, Juan Alfonso, *Breve directorium ad confessarii ac confitentis munus recte obeundum* (Antwerp: Joannes Bellerum, 1564).

Puente, Luis de la, *Perfección del cristiano en todos los estados*. 4 vols. (Valladolid and Pamplona: Juan Godinez de Millis, 1612–16).

Secondary sources

Bergin, Joseph, *The making of the French episcopate, 1589–1661* (New Haven: Yale University Press, 1996).

Bireley, Robert, *The refashioning of Catholicism, 1450–1700: A reassessment of the Counter Reformation* (Basingstoke and Washington: Palgrave and Catholic University of America Press, 1999).

Religion and politics in the age of the Counterreformation: Emperor Ferdinand II, William Lamormaini, S. J., and the formation of imperial policy (Chapel Hill: University of North Carolina Press, 1981).

Black, Christopher, *Italian Confraternities in the sixteenth century* (Cambridge: Cambridge University Press, 1989).

Bossy, John, *Christianity in the west, 1400–1700* (New York: Oxford University Press, 1985).

Châtellier, Louis, *The Europe of the devout: The Catholic Reformation and the formation of a new society* (Cambridge: Cambridge University Press, 1989). (French orig., 1987.)

Comerford, Kathleen M., and Pabel, Hilmar M. (eds.), *Early modern Catholicism: Essays in honor of John W. O'Malley, S. J.* (Toronto: University of Toronto Press, 2001).

Delumeau, Jean, *Catholicism between Luther and Voltaire: a new view of the Counter-Reformation* (London: Burns and Oates and Philadelphia: Westminster Press, 1977). (French orig., 1971.)

Evans, R. J. W., *The making of the Habsburg monarchy, 1550–1700: an interpretation* (Oxford: Clarendon Press, 1979).

Evennett, H. Outram, *The spirit of the Counter-Reformation.* Ed. John Bossy (Cambridge: Cambridge University Press, 1968).

Forster, Marc, *Catholic revival in the age of the Baroque: religious identity in southwest Germany, 1550–1750* (Cambridge: Cambridge University Press, 2001).

Fragnito, Gigliola, *La Bibbia al rogo: La censura ecclesiastica e i volgarizzamenti della Scrittura (1471–1605)* (Bologna: Il Mulino, 1997).

Headley, John M., and Tomaro, John B. (eds.), *San Carlo Borromeo: Catholic reform and ecclesiastical politics in the second half of the sixteenth century* (Washington: The Folger Shakespeare Library, and London, Associated University Presses, 1988).

Hsia, R. Po-Chia. *Social discipline in the Reformation: Central Europe, 1550–1750* (London: Routledge, 1989).

Jedin, Hubert, *Geschichte des Konzils von Trient.* 4 vols. (Freiburg im Breisgau: Herder, 1958–75). (Eng. trans., *A history of the Council of Trent.* 2 vols. London, 1957–61.)

Jedin, Hubert, and Dolan, John (eds.), *History of the Church,* Vol. 5: *Reformation and Counter Reformation* (New York: Seabury Press, 1980). (German orig., 1967.)
Katholische Reform oder Gegenreformation? (Lucerne: Josef Stocker, 1946).

Kamen, Henry, *The phoenix and the flame: Catalonia and the Counter-Reformation* (New Haven: Yale University Press, 1993).

O'Malley, John W., *Trent and all that: renaming Catholicism in the early modern era* (Cambridge, MA: Harvard University Press, 2000).

Prodi, Paolo, and Reinhard, Wolfgang (eds.), *Das Konzil von Trent und die Moderne* (Berlin: Duncker and Humblot, 2001). (Italian edn, *Il concilio di Trento e il moderno.* Bologna, 1996.)

Rapley, Elizabeth, The dévotes: *women and church in seventeenth-century France* (Montreal: McGill-Queen's University Press, 1990).

Reinhard, Wolfgang. 'Papal power and family strategy in the sixteenth and seventeenth centuries'. In Ronald G. Asch and Adolf M. Burke (eds.), *Princes, patronage, and the nobility: the court at the beginning of the modern age, c1450–1650* (Oxford: Oxford University Press, 1991), pp. 329–56.

Reinhard, Wolfgang, 'Gegenreformation als Modernisierung? Prologemena zu einer Theorie des Konfessionellen Zeitalters,' *Archiv für Reformationsgeschichte* 68 (Gütersloh, 1977) pp. 226–52.

Reinhard, Wolfgang, and Schilling, Heinz (eds.), *Die katholische Konfessionalisierung.* Reformationsgeschichtliche Studien und Texte, 135 (Münster: Aschendorff, 1995).

Ridder-Symoens, Hilde de (ed.), *A history of the university in Europe*, Vol. 2: *Universities in early modern Europe* (Cambridge: Cambridge University Press, 1996).

Tallon, Alain, *Le concile de Trente* (Paris: Cerf, 2000).

La France et le Concile de Trente, 1518–1563 (Paris/Rome: École française de Rome, 1997).

Taveneaux, René, *Catholicisme dans la France classique, 1610–1715* (Paris: Société d'édition d'enseignement supérieur, 1980).

Tedeschi, John, *The prosecution of heresy: collected studies on the Inquisition in early modern Italy* (Binghamton: Medieval and Renaissance Texts and Studies, 1991).

10 NEW RELIGIOUS ORDERS FOR MEN
Primary sources

Caragnoni, Constanzo (ed.), *I frati cappuccini. Documenti e testimonianze del primo secolo.* 3 vols. in 4. (Perugia: Edizione Frate Indovino, 1988–91).

Ganss, George *et al.* (eds. and trans.), *Ignatius of Loyola: the Spiritual Exercises and selected works* (Mahwah, NJ: Paulist Press, 1991).

Hudon, William (ed. and trans.), *Theatine spirituality: selected writings* (Mahwah, NJ: Paulist Press, 1996).

Sántha, Georgius, and Vilá Palá, Claudius (eds.), *Epistolarium coaetanorum S. Josephi Calasanctii 1600–1648*. 6 vols. (Rome: Editiones Calasanctianae, 1977–81).

Secondary sources

Alden, Dauril, *The making of an enterprise: the Society of Jesus in Portugal, her empire, and beyond, 1540–1750* (Stanford: Stanford University Press, 1993).

Andrés Martín, Meliquiades, *La teología española en el siglo XVI*. 2 vols. (Madrid: La Editorial católica, 1976–7).

Bangert, William, SJ, *A history of the Society of Jesus*, rev. edn (St Louis: Institute of Jesuit Sources, 1986).

Berthelot de Chesnay, Charles, *Les missions de saint Jean Eudes* (Paris: Procure des Eudistes, 1967).

Bertier de Sauvigny, Guillaume de, *Au service de l'église de France: les Eudistes, 1680–1791* (Paris: S. P. M., 1999).

Bireley, Robert, *The Jesuits and the Thirty Years War: kings, courts, and confessors* (Cambridge: Cambridge University Press, 2003).

Boureau, René, *L'Oratoire en France* (Paris: Le Cerf, 1991).

Brémond, Henri, *Histoire littéraire de sentiment religieux en France depuis la fin des guerres de religion jusqu' à nos jours*. 12 vols. (Paris: Bloud et Gay, 1916–33).

Châtellier, Louis, *The Europe of the devout: the Catholic reformation and the formation of a new society*. Trans. Jean Birrell (Cambridge: Cambridge University Press, 1989).

The religion of the poor. Rural missions in Europe and the foundation of modern Catholicism, c. 1500–c. 1800. Trans. Brian Pearce (Cambridge: Cambridge University Press, 1997).

Cistellini, Antonio, *San Filippo Neri: L'oratorio e la congregazione oratoriana: storia e spiritualità*. 3 vols. (Brescia: Morcelliana, 1989).

Contrisciani, Romano, *Perfil historico de los Barnabitas* (Palencia: Editorial Barnabita, 1968).

Conwell, Joseph F., *Impelling spirit: revisiting a founding experience, 1539. Ignatius of Loyola and his companions* (Chicago: Loyola University Press, 1997).

Coste, Pierre, *The life and work of St. Vincent de Paul.* Trans. J. Leonard. 3 vols. (London: Oates & Washbourne, 1934–5).

Criscuolo, Vincenzo, *I cappuccini e la congregazione dei Vescovi e regolari.* Vol. 1: *1573–1595.* Vol. 2: *1596–1605.* Vol. 3: *1606–1612* (Rome: Istituto storico dei Cappuccini, 1989–91).

Crisógono de Jésus Sacramentado, *The life of St. John of the Cross.* Trans. Kathleen Pond (New York: Harper, 1958).

Cushner, Nicholas, *Soldiers of God: the Jesuits in colonial America, 1565–1761* (Buffalo: Language Communications, 2002).

Cuthbert of Brighton. *The Capuchins: a contribution to the history of the Counter-Reformation.* 2 vols. (London: Longmans and Green, 1929).

DeMolen, Richard L. (ed.), *Essays on the religious orders of the Catholic Reformation* (New York: Fordham University Press, 1993).

Dizionario degli istituti di perfezione. Ed. Guerrino Pelliccia and Giancarlo Rocca. 9 vols. (Rome: Edizione Paoline, 1974–97).

Domínguez, Joaquín, and O'Neill, Charles (eds.), *Diccionario histórico de la Compañía de Jesús.* 4 vols. (Rome: Institutum Historicum S. I., and Madrid: Universidad pontificia Comillas, 2001).

Duchet-Suchaux, Gaston and Monique, *Les ordres religieux: guide historique* (Paris: Flammarion, 1993).

Feingold, Mordechai (ed.), *Jesuit science and the Republic of Letters* (Cambridge, MA: MIT Press, 2003).

Gagliano, Joseph, and Ronan, Charles, *Jesuit encounters in the new world: Jesuit chroniclers, geographers, educators, and missionaries in the Americas, 1549–1767* (Rome: Institutum Historicum S. I., 1997).

Garrido, Pablo. *Santa Teresa, San Juan de la Cruz y los Carmelitas españoles* (Madrid: Universidad pontificia de Salamanca, 1982).

Gentili, Antonio M., *The Barnabites: a historical profile.* Trans. S. Zanchetta and A. Bianco (Youngstown, NY: The North American Voice of Fatima, 1980).

Giordano, Francesco, *Il Calasanzio e l'origine della scuola popolare* (Genoa: A. G. I. S., 1960).

Guibert, Joseph de, *The Jesuits: their spiritual doctrine and practice.* Trans. William J. Young (Chicago: Loyola University Press, 1964).

Hostie, Raymond, *Vie et mort des ordres religieux: approches psychosociologiques* (Paris: Desclée de Brouwer, 1972).

Knowles, Dom David, *From Pachomius to Ignatius. A study in the constitutional history of the religious orders* (Oxford: Oxford University Press, 1966).

Lach, Donald, *Asia in the making of Europe.* 9 vols. in 3 (Chicago: University of Chicago Press, 1965–93).

Lemoine, Robert, *Le monde de religieux: l'époque moderne 1563–1789.* Histoire du droit et des institutions de l'église en occident, 15 (in 2 parts) (Paris: Editions Cujas, 1976).

Llompart, G., *Gaetano da Thiene. Estudios sobre un reformador religioso* (Wiesbaden: Steiner, 1969).

Lucas, Thomas, *Landmarking: city, church and Jesuit urban strategy* (Chicago: Loyola University Press, 1997).

McCoog, Thomas, *The Society of Jesus in Ireland, Scotland and England, 1541–1588. 'Our way of proceeding?'* (Leiden: E. J. Brill, 1996).

McCoog, Thomas (ed.), *The Mercurian project: forming Jesuit culture, 1573–1580* (St Louis: Institute of Jesuit Sources, 2004).

McCormick, Ignatius (ed. and trans.), *The Capuchin reform: essays in commemoration of its 450th anniversary 1528–1978.* In Analecta ordinis minorum Capuccinorum 94 (1978) (Pittsburgh: North American Capuchin Project, 1983).

McMahon, Norbert, *St. John of God* (New York: McMullen Books, 1953).

Melchior de Pobladura, *Historia generalis ordinis fratrum minorum Capuccinorum.* 4 vols. (Rome: Institutum historicum ordinis fratrum minorum capuccinorum, 1947–51).

Michelini, Vittorio, *Barnabiti: Chierici regolari di S. Paolo alle radice della congregatione, 1533–1983* (Milan: Nuove edizione Duomo, 1983).

Nimmo, Duncan, *Reform and division in the medieval Franciscan order from Saint Francis to the foundation of the Capuchins* (Rome: Capuchin Historical Institute, 1987).

O'Malley, John (ed.), *Catholicism in early modern history: a guide to research.* Reformation guides to research, 2 (St Louis: Center for Reformation Research, 1988).

The first Jesuits (Cambridge, MA: Harvard University Press, 1993).

O'Malley, John et al. (eds.), *The Jesuits: cultures, sciences and the arts, 1540–1773* (Toronto: Toronto University Press, 1999).

The Jesuits II: Cultures, sciences and the arts, 1540–1773 (Toronto: Toronto University Press, forthcoming).

Paschini, Pio, *S. Gaetano Thiene, Gian Pietro Carafa, e le origini dei chierici regolari teatini* (Rome: Scuola tipografica Pio X, 1926).

Polgar, László, *Bibliographie sur l'histoire de la Compagnie de Jésus, 1901–1980.* 6 vols. (Rome: Institutum Historicum S. I., 1981–90).

Ponnelle, Louis, and Bordet, Louis, *St. Philip Neri and the Roman society of his times, 1515–1595.* Trans. Ralph Francis Kerr (London: Sheed and Ward, 1932; rpt. 1979).

Rigault, G., *Histoire générale de l'institut des frères des écoles chrétiennes.* 9 vols. (Paris: Plon, 1937–53).

Sántha, György, Ahuilera, César, and Centelles, Julián, *San José de Calasanz. Su obra, escritos* (Madrid: Biblioteca de Autores christianos, 1956).

Scaduto, Mario, *Storia della Compagnia di Gesù in Italia. L'epoca di Giacomo Lainez, 1556–1565.* Vol. 3: *Il governo.* Vol. 4: *L'azione.* Vol. 5: *L'opera di Francesco Borgia, 1562–1572* (Rome: Institutum Historicum S. I., 1964–92).

Smet, Joachim, *The Carmelites: a history of the brothers of our Lady of Mount Carmel.* 4 vols. (Barrington, IL: Carmelite Provincial House, 1975–82).

Trevor, Meriol, *Apostle of Rome: a life of Philip Neri, 1515–1591* (London: Macmillan, 1966).

Urbanelli, Callisto, *Storia dei Cappuccini delle Marche.* 3 vols. in 4 (Ancona: Curia provinciale Frati cappuccini, 1978–84).

Velasco Bayón, Balbino, *Historia del Carmelo Español.* 3 vols. (Rome: Institutum carmelitanum, 1990–4).

Williams, Charles E., *The French Oratorians and absolutism, 1611–1641* (New York: Peter Lang, 1989).

Wittkower, Rudolf, and Jaffe, Irma (eds.), *Baroque art: the Jesuit contribution* (New York: Fordham University Press, 1972).

Journals devoted to the history of early modern religious orders

Archivum Historicum Societatis Iesu
Archivum Scholarum Piarum
Carmelus
Collectanea Franciscana [Capuchins]
Oratorium: Archivum Historicum Oratorii Sancti Philippi Neri
Regnum Dei: Collectanea Theatina

II FEMALE SANCTITY, 1500–1660

Primary sources

Beilin, Elaine V. (ed.), *The examinations of Anne Askew: women writers in English 1350–1850* (New York and Oxford: Oxford University Press, 1996).
Pozzi, Giovanni (ed.), *Maria Maddalena de' Pazzi. Le parole dell'estasi* (Milan: Adelphi, 1984).
Sastre, Làzaro, 'Proceso de la beata de Piedrahita'. *Archivio dominicano. Anuario* 11 (1990): 350–401.
'Proceso de la beata de Piedrahita (II)'. *Archivio dominicano. Anuario* 12 (1991): 337–86.

Secondary sources

Addante, Pietro, *San Francesco di Paola* (Cinisello Balsamo: Edizioni Paoline, 1988).
Ahlgren, Gillian T. W., *Francisca de los Apostoles. A visionary voice for reform in sixteenth-century Toledo.* In Mary E. Giles (ed.), *Women in the Inquisition. Spain and the New World* (Baltimore and London: Johns Hopkins University Press, 1999), pp. 119–33.
Baernstein, Renée, *A convent tale. A century of sisterhood in Spanish Milan* (New York and London: Routledge, 2002).
Bainton, Roland, *Women of the Reformation in Germany and Italy* (Minneapolis: Augsburg Publication House, 1971).
Barone, Giulia, *La canonizzazione di Francesca Romana (1608): la riproposta di un modello agiografico medievale*, in *Finzione e società*, pp. 264–79.
Bell, Rudolph, *Holy anorexia.* Epilogue William N. Davis (Chicago: Chicago University Press, 1985).
Biblioteca Sanctorum Orientalium, Enciclopedia dei santi: le chiese orientali, vol. 2 (Rome: Città Nuova, 1998–9).
Bilinkoff, Iody, 'Charisma and controversy. The case of Maria', *Archivio dominicano. Anuario* 10 (1989): 55–66.
Bloch, Marc, *Les rois thaumaturges. Etude sur le caractère surnaturel attribué à la puissance royale particulièrement en France et en Angleterre.* Preface J. Le Goff (Paris: Gallimard, 1983; orig. edn 1923).

The royal touch: sacred monarchy and scrofula in England and France. Trans. J. E. Anderson (London: Routledge and Kegan Paul, 1973).

Bonora, Elena, *I conflitti della Controriforma. Santità e obbedienza nell'esperienza religiosa dei primi barnabiti* (Florence: Le Lettere, 1998).

Børresen, Kari E., and Vogt, Kari (ed.), *Women's studies of the Christian and Islamic traditions: ancient, medieval and Renaissance foremothers* (Dordrecht and Boston: Kluwer Academic, 1993).

Brown, Judith, *Immodest acts. The life of a lesbian nun in Renaissance Italy* (New York and Oxford: Oxford University Press, 1986).

Bucuré, Miriam, 'Camilla Battista Varano da Camerino: Istruzioni al discepolo. Dos dominicos testigos de un texto de espiritualidad francescana a principio de la etad moderna', *Memorie domenicane* 32 (2001): 263–338.

Bynum Walker, Caroline, *Holy feast and holy fast. The religious significance of food to medieval women* (Berkeley and London: University of California Press, 1987).

Jesus as mother. Studies in the spirituality of the high Middle Ages (Berkeley and London: University of California Press, 1982).

Cantù, Francesca, *Rosa da Lima e il 'Mistico giardino' del Nuovo Mondo: identità e trasfigurazione di una santa nell'immaginario sociale peruviano,* in *Ordini religiosi, santità e culti: prospettive di ricerca tra Europa e America Latina.* Atti del Seminario di Roma 21–22 giugno 2001, a cura di Gabriella Zarri (Galatina: Congedo Editori, 2003). (Pubblicazioni del Dipartimento di studi storici dal Medioevo all'Età contemporanea dell'Università di Lecce. Saggi e Ricerche 52.)

Certeau, Michel de, *La fable mystique: XVIe–XVIIe siècle* (Paris, Gallimard, 1982).

The mystic fable. Trans. Michael B. Smith (Chicago: Chicago University Press, 1992).

Le possession de Loudun (Paris: Gallimard/Julliard, 1990).

The possession at Loudun. Trans. Michael B. Smith; foreword Stephen Greenblatt (Chicago: University of Chicago Press, 2000).

Craveri, Marcello, *Sante e streghe: biografie e documenti dal 14 al 17 secolo* (Milan: Feltrinelli, 1980).

Devos, Roger, *Vie religieuse féminine et société: L'origine sociale des Visitandines d'Annecy aux XVIIe et XVIIIe siècles* (Annecy: Académie Salésienne, 1973).

Dinzelbacher, Peter, *Heilige oder Hexen? Schicksale auffälliger Frauen in Mittelalter und Frühneuzeit* (Zurich: Artemis & Winkler Verlag, 1995).

Dunn-Lardeau, Brenda (ed.), *Legenda aurea: sept siècles de diffusion.* Actes du Colloque international sur la *Legenda aurea,* Université du Québec, Montreal, 11–12 May 1983 (Montreal: Bellarmin, 1986).

Erasmo da Rotterdam, *Vita di san Girolamo.* Ed. and trans. Anna Morisi Guerra (L'Aquila and Rome: Japadre Editore, 1988).

Fedotov, Georgij, *I santi dell'antica Russia.* Preface by Gabriele De Rosa, Postface Sisto Dalla Palma. Ed. Maria Pia Pagani (Milan: Aquilegia Editori, 2000; orig. edn Paris: YMCA Press, 1931).

Fiorani, Luigi, and Prosperi, Adriano (eds.), *Roma la città del papa: vita civile e religiosa dal giubileo di Bonifacio 8 al giubileo di papa Wojtyla. Storia d'Italia.* Annali, (Turin: Einaudi, 2000).

Geary, Patrick J., *Furta sacra: thefts of relics in the central Middle Ages* (Princeton: Princeton University Press, 1990).

Giles, Mary E. (ed.), *Women in the Inquisition. Spain and the New World* (Baltimore and London: Johns Hopkins University Press, 1999).

Gregory, Brad S., *Salvation at stake. Christian martyrdom in early modern Europe.* Harvard Historical Studies, 132 (Cambridge, MA, and London: Harvard University Press, 1999).

Grisar, Joseph, *Maria Wards Institut vor Römischen Kongregationen (1616–1630)* (Rome: Pontificia Università Gregoriana, 1966).

Hamilton, Alastair, *Heresy and mysticism in sixteenth-century Spain: The Alumbrados* (Toronto and Buffalo: University of Toronto Press, 1992).

Herlihy, David, 'Did women have a Renaissance?' *Medievalia et Humanistica* 13 (1985): 15–16.

Hsia, R. Po-chia, *The world of Catholic renewal (1450–1770)* (Cambridge: Cambridge University Press, 1998).

Kagan, Richard, *Lucrecia's dreams. Politics and prophecy in sixteenth-century Spain* (Berkeley: University of California Press, 1990).

Kelly, Joan, 'Did women have a Renaissance?' In Joan Kelly, *Women, history and theory* (Chicago: University of Chicago Press, 1984), pp. 19–50.

Konrad, Anne, *Zwischen Kloster und Welt. Ursulinen und Jesuitinnen in der Katolischen Reformbewegung des 16./17. Jahrhunderts* (Mainz: Zabern, 1991).

Lavenia, Vincenzo, 'I diavoli di Carpi e il Sant'Uffizio (1636–1639)'. In Mario Rosa (ed.), *Eretici esuli e indemoniati nell'età moderna.* Biblioteca della Rivista di Storia e Letteratura religiosa. Studi, 9 (Florence: Olschki, 1999), pp. 77–139.

Maggi, Armando, *Maria Maddalena de' Pazzi.* Intro. and trans. Armando Maggi. Preface E. Ann Matter (New York: Mahwah, 2000).

Satan's rhetoric, a study of Renaissance demonology (Chicago: University of Chicago Press, 2002).

Malena, Adelisa, *L'eresia dei perfetti. Inquisizione romana ed esperienze mistiche nel Seicento italiano* (Rome: Edizioni di Storia e Letteratura, 2003).

Matter, E. Ann, 'Prophetic patronage as repression: Lucia Brocadelli da Narni and Ercole d'Este'. In Scott L. Waugh and Peter D. Diehl (eds.), *Christendom and its discontents. Exclusion, persecution, and rebellion, 1000–1500* (Cambridge: Cambridge University Press, 1996), pp. 105–19.

Matter, E. Ann, and Galluzzi, Maria Domitilla, 'Creative women'. In E. A. Matter and J. Coakley (eds.), *Medieval and early modern Italy. A religious and artistic Renaissance* (Philadelphia: University of Pennsylvania Press, 1994).

Mellinghoff-Bourgerie, Viviane, *François de Sales, 1567–1622: un homme de lettres spirituelles: culture, tradition, épistolarité.* Travaux d'humanisme et Renaissance, 330 (Geneva: Droz, 1999).

Morisi, Guerra Anna, 'La leggenda di San Girolamo. Temi e problemi tra umanesimo e controriforma', *Clio* 23 (1987): 5–33.

Muñoz, Fernandez Angela, *Beatas santas neocastellanas: ambivalencia de la religion correctoras del poder (ss XIV–XVII)* (Madrid: Comunedad de Madrid, 1994).

Niccoli, Ottavia, 'Introduzione'. In Ottavia Niccoli (ed.), *Rinascimento al femminile* (Rome and Bari: Laterza, 1991). Spanish edn, *La mujer del Renacimiento.* Edicion de Ottavia Niccoli (Madrid: Alianza Editorial, 1993).

Ori, Anna Maria, 'La principessa in Convento'. In Anna Maria Ori (ed.), *Le Clarisse in Carpi. Cinque secoli di storia XVI–XX*, vol. I. *Saggi*. Ed. Gabriella Zarri. Fondazione Cassa di Risparmio di Carpi (Reggio Emilia: Diabasis, 2003), pp. 178–283.

Polizzotto, Lorenzo, *The elect nation. The Savonarolan movement in Florence, 1494–1545* (Oxford and New York: Oxford University Press, 1994).

Pomata, Gianna, 'A Christian utopia of the Renaissance. Elena Duglioli's spiritual and physical motherhood (ca. 1510–1520)'. In Kaspar von Greyerz, Hans Medick, and Patrice Veit, *Von der dargestellten Person zum erinnerten Ich. Europaische Selbstzeugnisse als historische Quellen (1500–1850)* (Cologne, Weimar, and Vienna: Böhlau, 2001), pp. 323–53.

Prodi, Paolo, Zarri, Gabriella, Mezzadri, Luigi, and Castenetto, D., *Angela Merici. Vita della chiesa e spiritualità nella prima metà del Cinquecento. Convegno di studi storici (Mascalucia 21–22 iuglio 1997)*. Ed. Cataldo Naro (Caltanissetta and Rome: Salvatore Sciascia Editore, 1998).

Prosperi, Adriano, *Tribunali della coscienza. Inquisitori, confessori missionari* (Turin: Einaudi, 1997).

Ranft, Patricia, *A woman's way. The forgotten history of women spiritual directors* (New York: Palgrave, 2000).

Rapley, Elisabeth, *The dévotes: women and church in seventeenth-century France* (Montreal and Ithaca, 1990).

Renoux, Christian, 'Canonizzazione e santità femminile in età moderna'. In Luigi Foriani and Adriano Properi (eds.), *Roma, la città del papa: vita civile e religiosa dal giubileo di Bonifacio VIII al iubileo di papa Wojtyla* (Turin: Einaudi, 2000), pp. 731–51.

Rhodes, Elisabeth, 'Y yo dije, "Sì senor". Ana Domenge and the Barcelona Inquisition'. In Mary E. Giles (ed.), *Women in the Inquisition* (Baltimore: Johns Hopkins University Press, 1999), pp. 134–54.

Romeo, Giovanni, *Esorcisti, confessori e sessualità femminile nell'Italia della Controriforma. A proposito di due casi modenesi del primo Seicento* (Florence: Le Lettere, 1998).

Roper, Lyndal, *Oedipus and the devil: witchcraft, sexuality and religion in early modern Europe* (London and New York: Routledge, 1994).

Rudi, R. Tat'iana, 'La santità femminile nell'antica Rus'. In Adalberto Mainardi (ed.), *Forme della santità russa. Atti del Convegno ecumenico internazionale di spiritualità ortodossa sezione russa* (Bose: Edizioni QiQajon, 2002), pp. 211–28.

Ryan, Frances, and Rybolt, E. John (eds.), *Vincent de Paul and Louise de Marillac: rules, conferences, and writings*. Intro. Hugh F. O'Donnell. Preface Amin A. de Tarrazi (New York: Paulist Press, 1995).

Sastre, Làzaro, 'Proceso de la beata de Piedrahita', *Archivio dominicano. Anuario* 11 (1990): 350–401.

'Proceso de la beata de Piedrahita (II)', *Archivio dominicano. Anuario* 12 (1991): 337–86.

Scaraffia, Lucetta, and Zarri, Gabriella (eds.), *Donne e fede, santità e vita religiosa in Italia* (Rome and Bari: Laterza, 1994). English trans. *Women and faith: Catholic religious life in Italy from late antiquity to the present* (Cambridge, MA: Harvard University Press, 1999).

Scattigno, Anna, 'Carissimo figliolo in Cristo'. In Lucia Ferrante, Maura Palazzi, and Gianna Pomata (eds.), *Ragnatele di rapporti: patronato e reti di relazione nella storia delle donne* (Turin: Rosenberg & Sellier, 1988).

Schutte, Anne Jacobson, *Aspiring saints: pretense of holiness, inquisition and gender in the Republic of Venice, 1618–1750* (Baltimore: Johns Hopkins University Press, 2001).

Schutte, Anne Jacobson (ed.), *Autobiography of an aspiring saint: Cecilia Ferrazzi. The other voice in early modern Europe* (Chicago: Chicago University Press, 1996).

Slade, Carole, *St. Teresa of Avila: author of a heroic life* (Berkeley: University of California Press, 1995).

Solfaroli Camillocci, Daniela, *I devoti della carità: le confraternite del Divino Amore nell'Italia del primo Cinquecento* (Naples: La città del sole, 2002).

Surtz, Ronald, 'Writing and sodomy in the Inquisitorial trial (1495–1496) of Tecla Servent'. In Eukene Lacarra Lanz (ed.), *Marriage and sexuality in medieval and early modern Iberia* (New York and London: Routledge, 2002), pp. 197–213.

Tedeschi, John, *The prosecution of heresy. Collected studies on the Inquisition in early modern history*. Medieval and Renaissance texts and studies (Binghamton, NY: 1991).

Vauchez, André, *La sainteté en Occident aux derniers siècles du Moyen Age d'apres les proces de canonisation et les documents hagiographiques* (Ecole Française de Rome, Palais Farnese, 1981).

Sainthood in the later Middle Ages. Trans. Jean Birrell (New York: Cambridge University Press, 1997).

Les laïcs au Moyen Age: pratiques et experiences religieuses (Paris: Cerf, 1987).

The laity in the Middle Ages: religious beliefs and devotional practices. Ed., intro. Daniel. E. Bornstein. Trans. Margery J. Schneider (Notre Dame: University of Notre Dame Press, 1993).

Saints, prophètes et visionnaires: le pouvoir surnaturel au Moyen Age (Paris: Albin Michel, 1999).

Waugh, Scott, L., and Diehl, Peter D. (eds.), *Christendom and its discontents. Exclusion, persecution, and rebellion, 1000–1500* (Cambridge: Cambridge University Press, 1996).

Weber, Alison, *Teresa of Avila and the rhetoric of femininity* (Princeton: Princeton University Press, 1990).

Weinstein, Donald, *Savonarola and Florence: prophecy and patriotism in the Renaissance* (Princeton: Princeton University Press, 1970).

Girolamo Savonarola: piety, prophecy and politics in Renaissance Florence. Bridwell Library religious studies (Dallas: Bridwell Library, 1994).

Zarri, Gabriella, 'L'altra Cecilia: Elena Duglioli dall'Olio (1472–1520)'. In Carla Bernardini (ed.), *Indagini per un dipinto. La Santa Cecilia di Raffaello*. A cura di A. Emiliani (Bologna: ALFA, 1983), pp. 83–118. Now in Zarri, *Le sante vive*, pp. 165–96.

Le sante vive. Cultura e religiosità femminile nella prima età moderna (Turin: Rosenberg & Sellier, 1990).

'Le sante vive. Per una tipologia della santità femminile nel primo Cinquecento', *Annali dell'Istituto Storico Italo-Germanico in Trento*, 6 (1980), pp. 372–445.

'Living saints. A typology of female sanctity in the early sixteenth century'. In Daniel Bornstein and Roberto Rusconi (eds.), *Women and religion in medieval and Renaissance Italy* (Chicago and London: University of Chicago Press, 1996), pp. 219–303.

'Lucia da Narni e il movimento femminile savonaroliano'. In Gigliola Fragnito and Mario Miegge (eds.), *Girolamo Savonarola da Ferrara all'Europa* (Florence: SISMEL, 2001), pp. 99–116.

'Pietà e profezia alle corti padane: le pie consigliere dei principi'. In *Il Rinascimento alle corti padane. Società e cultura* (Bari: De Donato, 1977), pp. 201–37. Also in Zarri, *Le sante vive*, pp. 51–85.

'The thirth status'. In Anne Jacobson Schutte, Thomas Kuehn, and Silvana Seidel Menchi (eds.), *Time, space, women's lives in early modern Europe*. Sixteenth Century Essays and Studies, 57 (Kirksville, Truman State University Press, 2001), pp. 181–99.

'Ursula and Catherina: the marriage of virgins in the sixteenth century'. In E. A. Matter and E. J. Coakley (eds.), *Creative women in medieval and early modern Italy. A religious and artistic renaissance* (Philadelphia: University of Pennsylvania press, 1994).

Zarri, Gabriella (ed.), *Finzione e santità tra medioevo ed età moderna* (Turin: Rosenberg & Sellier, 1991).

Zemon Davis, Natalie, *Society and culture in early modern France: eight essays* (Stanford: Stanford University Press, 1975).

12 TRIDENTINE WORSHIP AND THE CULT OF SAINTS

Manuscript

Rome (Vatican)

ACCS, Archivio della congregazione per le cause dei santi (ex Riti)
Decreta servorum dei, vol. 1
Index processum beatificationis et canonizationis qui in Archivio Secreto Vaticano et in Archivio Sacrae Congregationis pro Causis Sanctorum asservantur, (1588–1982), ed. I. Beaudoin
Positiones decretorum et rescriptorum 1798

BAV, Biblioteca Apostolica Vaticana
Urbin. lat. 1095

Rome

BVR, Biblioteca Vallicelliana, Rome
Ms H. 14.
Ms. G. 91

Renoux, C. *Sainteté et mystique féminines à l'âge baroque.* (Unpublished thèse de doctorat, Université de Paris I, 1995.)

Printed

Acta SS, *Acta sanctorum, Octobris VII* (Brussels: Bollandists, 1845).

Bascapè, C., *Vita et rebus gestis Caroli S. R. E. Cardinalis tituli S. Praxedis Archiepiscopi Mediolani libri septem* (Ingolstadt: D. Sartori, 1592; rpt. Milan: Veneranda Fabbrica del Duomo, 1965. With Italian translation on facing pages), 559, 561.

Benedict XIV, *De Servorum Dei beatificatione et beatorum canonizatione.* 4 vols. (Bologna: Longhi, 1734–8), vol. 3 (1737).

Bondoni, G., *Del Tribunale della Sagra Rota Romana. Memorie storiche colle rispettive bolle de'Pontefici* (Rome: Pallotta, 1854).

Campi, P. M., *Dell'historia ecclesiastica di Piacenza.* 3 vols. (Piacenza: Giovanni Bazachi, 1651–62).

Castellino, L., *Elucidarium theologicum de certitudine gloriae sanctorum canonizatorum. Sacrorum Scripturarum, Pontificum, Conciliorum, Sanctorum Patrum, celeberrimorumque*

Doctorum, monumentis locupletatum. In quo ad gloriam, beatificationem, canonizationem, venerationem, atque miracula sanctorum spectantia, clara methodo explicantur (Rome: G. Facciotti, 1628).

Contelori, F., *Tractatus et praxis de canonizatione sanctorum* (Lyon: L. Durand, 1634).

Jacobilli, L., *Vite de'santi e beati dell'Umbria e di quelli corpi de'quali riposano in essa provincial*. 3 vols. (Foligno: A. Alteri, 1647–61).

Secondary sources

Amiet, R, *Missels et Bréviaires imprimés (supplément aux catalogues de Weale et Bohatta); Propres des Saints (editio princeps)*. (Paris: CNRS, 1990).

Bailey, G. A. *Art on the Jesuit missions in Asia and Latin America 1542–1773* (Toronto, Buffalo, London: University of Toronto Press, 1999).

Batiffol, P. *History of the Roman Breviary* (London: Longmans, Green and Co, 1912) trans. with added chapter of the 3rd French edition of 1911.

Bäumer, S, *Histoire du Bréviaire*, 2 vols., an update of the German edn. of 1895 by R. Biron (Paris: Letouzey et Ané, 1905).

Bibliotheca sanctorum, 12 vols (Rome: Città Nuova Editrice, 1961–69), Index (1970), 2 appendix vols (1987, 2000).

Bohatta, H. *Bibliographie der Breviere 1501–1850*, repr. of 2nd edn. 1937 (Stuttgart and Nieuwkoop: Hiersemann/De Graaf, 1963).

Brown, P. *The cult of saints: its rise and function in Latin Christianity* (London and Chicago: SCM Press/University of Chicago press, 1981).

Burke, P. 'How to be a Counter-Reformation saint'. In P. Burke, *The historical anthropology of early modern Italy: essays on perception and communication* (Cambridge: Cambridge University Press, 1987), pp. 48–62.

Bury, M. *The print in Italy 1550–1620* (London: The British Museum, 2001).

Dall'Aglio, S. *Savonarola e il savonarolismo* (Bari: Cacucci, 2005).

Dandelet, T. *Spanish Rome 1500–1700* (New Haven and London, 2001), pp. 170–87.

De Maio, R. 'L'ideale eroico nei processi di canonizzazione della Controriforma'. In R. De Maio, *Riforme e miti nella chiesa del Cinquecento* (Naples: Guida, 1973), pp. 253–72.

Ditchfield, S. 'Martyrs on the move: relics as vindicators of local diversity in the Tridentine Church. In D. Wood (ed.), *Martyrs and martyrologies*. Studies in Church History, 30 (Oxford: Blackwell, 1993), pp. 283–94.

Liturgy, sanctity and history in Tridentine Italy: Pietro Maria Campi and the preservation of the particular (Cambridge: Cambridge University Press, 1995).

'Giving Tridentine worship back its history'. In R. N. Swanson (ed.), *Continuity and change in Christian worship*. Studies in Church History, 35 (Woodbridge: Boydell Press, 1999), 199–226.

'Of dancing cardinals and mestizo madonnas: reconfiguring the history of Roman Catholicism in the early modern period', *Journal of Early Modern History*, 8, 3–4 (2004), 386–408.

Finucane, R. 'Saint-making at the end of the sixteenth century: how and why Jacek of Poland (d. 1257) became St Hyacinth in 1594', *Hagiographica* 9 (2002), 207–58.

Focke, F. and Heinrichs, H. 'Das Kalendarium des Missale Pianum vom Jahre 1570 und seine Tendenzen', *Theologisches Quartalschrift*, 120 (1939), 383–400, 461–9.

Gentilcore, D. *From bishop to witch: the system of the sacred in early modern Terra d'Otranto*, (Manchester: Manchester University Press).

Gotor, M. 'La fabbrica dei santi: la riforma urbaniana e il modello tridentino'. In L. Fiorani and A. Prosperi (eds.) *Roma, la città del papa. Vita civile e religiosa dal giubileo di Bonifacio VIII al giubileo di papa Wojtyla*. Storia d'Italia, Annali 16 (Turin: Einaudi, 2000), pp. 679–727

I beati del papa: santità, inquisizione e obbedienza in età moderna (Florence; Olschki, 2002).

Chiesa e santità nell'Italia moderna (Rome and Bari: Laterza, 2004).

Index ac status causarum (Vatican City: Congregatio de causis sanctorum, 1999).

Klauser, T. *A short history of the Western liturgy: an account and some reflections*, 2nd edn. of 5th German edn. 1965 (Oxford: Oxford University Press, 1979).

Leuschner, E. *Antonio Tempesta. Ein Bahnbrecher des römischen Barock und seine europäische Wirkung* (Petersberg: Michael Imhof, 2005).

Lockhart, J. *The Nahuas after the conquest. A social and cultural history of the Indians of Central Mexico, sixteenth through eighteenth centuries* (Stanford; Stanford University Press, 1992).

MacCulloch, D. *Reformation: Europe's house divided 1490–1700* (London: Allen Lane, 2003).

Mureddu, D., Salvi, D. and Stefani, G. (eds.) '*Sancti innumerabiles*'. *Scavi nella Cagliari del Seicento: testimonianze e verifiche* (Oristano: Editrice S'Alvure, 1988).

Papa, G. 'La sacra congregazione dei Riti nel primo periodo di attività (1588–1634)'. In *Miscellanea in occasione del IV centenario della Congregazione per le Cause dei Santi (1588–1988)* (Vatican City: Congregazione per le cause dei Santi, 1988), pp. 13–52.

Le cause di canonizzazione nel primo periodo della Congregazione dei Riti (1588–1634) (Vatican City: Urbaniana University Press, 2001).

Parker, G. *The Thirty Years' War*, (London / New York: Routledge, 1984).z

Prosperi, A. *Tribunali della coscienza. Inquisitori, confessori e missionari* (Turin: Einaudi, 1996).

Renoux, C., 'Sainteté et mystique féminines à l'âge baroque' (Unpublished thèse de doctorat: Université de Paris I, 1995).

Sallmann, J.-M. *Naples et ses saints à l'âge baroque (1540–1750)*, (Paris: Presses Universitaires de France, 1994).

Schmid, J. 'Weitere Beiträge zur Geschichte des römischen Breviers und Missale', *Theologisches Quartalschrift* 67 (1885): 468–87, 624–37.

Schutte, A. J. *Aspiring saints: pretense of holiness, inquisition and gender in the republic of Venice, 1618–1750* (Baltimore: Johns Hopkins University Press, 2001).

Sluhovsky, M. *Patroness of Paris. Rituals of devotion in early modern France* (Leiden: Brill, 1998).

Strasser, U. 'Bones of contention: cloistered nuns, decorated relics and the contest over women's place in the public sphere of Counter-Reformation Munich', *Archiv für Reformationsgeschichte* 90 (1999): 255–88.

Taylor, W. *Magistrates of the sacred: priests and parishioners in eighteenth-century Mexico* (Stanford: Stanford University Press, 1996).

Turnbull, S. 'The veneration of the martyrs of Ikitsuki (1609–1645) by the Japanese "Hidden Christians"'. In D. Wood (ed.) *Martyrs and martyrologies*. Studies in Church History, 30 (Oxford: Blackwell, 1993), pp. 295–310.

Veraja, F. *La beatificazione. Storia, problemi, prospettive* (Rome: S. Congregazione per le cause dei Santi, 1983).

Villalon, L. J. A., 'San Diego of Alcalá and the politics of saint-making in Counter-Reformation Europe', *Catholic Historical Review* 83 (1997): 691–715.

Suggested further reading

Benvenuti, A., Boesch Gajano, S., Ditchfield, S., Rusconi, R., Scorza Barcellona, F. and Zarri, G. *Storia della santità nel cristianesimo occidentale* (Rome: Viella, 2005).

Beyer, J., Burkardt, A., Van Lieburg F. and Wingens, M. (eds.) *Confessional sanctity (c.1500–1800)* (Mainz am Rhein: Verlag Philipp von Zabern, 2003).

Boesch Gajano, S. and Michetti, R. (eds.) *Raccolte agiografiche e identità politiche in Europa fra medioevo ed età moderna* (Rome: Carocci, 2002).

Boesch Gajano, S. and Sebastiani, L. (eds.) *Culto dei santi, istituzioni e classi sociali in età preindustriale* (L'Aquila / Rome: Japadré editore, 1984).

Delooz, P. 'Towards a sociological study of canonized sainthood in the Catholic church'. In S. Wilson (ed. & intr.) *Saints and the cults: studies in religious sociology, folklore and history* (Cambridge: Cambridge University Press, 1983), pp. 189–216.

Frazier, A. K. *Possible lives: authors and saints in Renaissance Italy* (New York: Columbia University Press, 2005).

Greer, A., *Mohawk saint: Catherine Tekakwitha and the Jesuits* (New York / Oxford: Oxford University Press, 2004).

Greer, A. and Bilinkoff, J. (eds.), *Colonial saints: discovering the holy in the Americas* (New York / London: Routledge, 2003).

Heming, C. P. *Protestants and the cult of saints in German-speaking Europe, 1517–1531* (Kirksville, MI: Truman State University Press, 2003).

Johnson, T. 'Holy fabrications: the catacomb saints and the Counter-Reformation in Bavaria' *Journal of Ecclesiastical History* 47 (1996): 274–97.

Sodano, G. *Modelli e selezione del santo moderno: periferia napoletana e centro Romano* (Naples: Liguori editore, 2002).

Soergel, P. M. *Wondrous in His saints: Counter-Reformation propaganda in Bavaria* (Berkeley, Los Angeles and London: University of California Press, 1993).

Suire, E. *La sainteté française de la Réforme catholique (XVIe–XVIIIe siècles): d'après les textes hagiographiques et les procès de canonisation* (Pessac: Presses universitaires de Bordeaux, 2001).

13 PEACE WITHOUT CONCORD: RELIGIOUS TOLERATION IN THEORY AND PRACTICE

Primary sources

Castellio, Sebastianus, *Contra libellum Calvini in quo ostendere conatur haereticos jure gladii coercendos esse* (s.l. = Gouda?, 1612).

Castellion, Sébastien, *De haereticis an sint persequendi, et omnino quomodo sit cum eis agendum, Luteri et Brentii aliorumque multorum tum veterum tum recentiorum sententiae.* Ed. Sake van der Woude (Geneva: E. Droz, 1954).

Celsi, Mino, *In haereticis coërcendis quatenus progredi liceat. Poems – Correspondence.* Ed. Peter G. Bietenholz. Corpus Reformatorum Italicorum (Naples: Prismi editrice; Chicago: The Newberry Library, 1982), pp. 9–400.

Erasmus, Desiderius, *Collected works of Erasmus*, vol. 9: *The correspondence of Erasmus*. Trans. R. A. B. Mynors, annotated Peter G. Bietenholz (Toronto: Toronto University Press, 1989).

Collected works of Erasmus, vol. 7: *The correspondence of Erasmus*. Trans. R. A. B. Mynors, annotated Peter G. Bietenholz (Toronto: Toronto University Press, 1987).

More, Thomas, *Utopia*. Ed. George M. Logan and Robert M. Adams (Cambridge: Cambridge University Press, 1989).

Williams, Roger, *The bloudy tenent of persecution for cause of conscience discussed: and Mr. Cotton's letter examined and answered*. Ed. Edward Bean Underhill. Hanserd Knollys Society (London: printed for the Society by J. Haddon, 1848).

Secondary sources

Augustijn, C., *Erasmus en de Reformatie. Een onderzoek naar de houding die Erasmus ten opzichte van de Reformatie heeft aangenomen* (Amsterdam: H. J. Paris, 1962).

Ayers, Michael, 'Theories of knowledge and belief'. In Daniel Garber and Michael Ayers (eds.), *The Cambridge history of seventeenth century philosophy*, 2 (Cambridge: Cambridge University Press, 1998).

Bainton, Robert, 'The parable of the tares as the proof text for religious liberty to the end of the sixteenth century'. *Church History* 1 (1932): 67–88.

Bainton, Roland H., *The travail of liberty. Nine biographical studies* (Philadelphia: The Westminster Press, 1951).

Barbers, Meinulf, *Toleranz bei Sebastian Franck. Untersuchungen zur allgemeinen Religionsgeschichte*. Neue Folge, Heft 4 (Bonn: Röhrscheid, 1964).

Bateman, John J., 'From soul to soul: persuasion in Erasmus' Paraphrases on the New Testament', *Erasmus in English* 15 (1987–8), pp. 7–16.

Benedict, Philip, '*Un roi, une loi, deux fois*: parameters for the history of Catholic-Reformed co-existence in France, 1555–1685'. In Ole Peter Grell and Bob Scribner (eds.), *Tolerance and intolerance in the European Reformation* (Cambridge: Cambridge University Press, 1996), pp. 65–93.

Berner, Hans, Gäbler, Ulrich, and Guggisberg, Hans Rudolf, 'Schweiz'. In Anton Schindling and Walter Ziegler (eds.), *Die Territorien des Reichs im Zeitalter der Reformation und Konfessionalisierung. Land und Konfession 1500–1650*, vol. 5: *Der Südwesten* (Münster: Aschendorff Verlag, 1993), pp. 278–323.

Binder, Ludwig, *Grundlagen und Formen der Toleranz in Siebenbürgen bis zur Mitte des 17. Jahrhunderts*. Siebenbürgisches Archiv Dritte Folge, 11 (Cologne and Vienna: Böhlau, 1976).

Bossy, John, *Peace in the Post-Reformation. The Birkbeck Lectures 1995* (Cambridge: Cambridge University Press, 1998).

Bouwsma, William J., *John Calvin. A sixteenth-century portrait* (New York and Oxford: Oxford University Press, 1988).

Brady, Jr., Thomas A., 'Settlements: the Holy Roman Empire'. In Thomas A. Brady, Jr, Heiko A. Oberman, and James D. Tracy (eds.), *Handbook of European history 1400–1600. Late Middle Ages, Renaissance and Reformation*, vol. 2: *Visions, programs and outcomes* (Leiden: E. J. Brill, 1995), pp. 349–83.

Briggs, E. R., 'An apostle of the incomplete reformation: Jacopo Aconcio (1500–1567)', *Proceedings of the Huguenot Society of London* 22 (1976): 481–95.

Cargill Thompson, W. D. J., *The political thought of Martin Luther* (Brighton: Harvester Press, 1984).

Carlin, Norah, 'Toleration for Catholics in the Puritan revolution'. In Ole Peter Grell and Bob Scribner (eds.), *Tolerance and intolerance in the European Reformation* (Cambridge: Cambridge University Press, 1996), pp. 216–30.

Christin, Olivier, 'From repression to pacification: French royal policy in the face of Protestantism'. In Philip Benedict, Guido Marnef, Henk van Nierop, and Marc Venard (eds.), *Reformation, revolt and civil war in France and the Netherlands 1555–1585* (Amsterdam: Koninklijke Nederlandse Akademie van Wetenschappen, 1999), pp. 201–14.

Coles, Paul, *The Ottoman impact on Europe* (London: Thames and Hudson, 1968).

Collinson, Patrick, *The birthpangs of Protestant England. Religious and cultural change in the sixteenth and seventeenth centuries. The Third Anstey Memorial Lectures in the University of Kent at Canterbury 12–15 May 1986* (Houndmills and London: Macmillan, 1988).

'The cohabitation of the faithful with the unfaithful'. In Ole Peter Grell and Roy Porter (eds.), *Toleration in Enlightenment Europe* (Cambridge: Cambridge University Press, 2000), pp. 51–76.

Davies, Norman, *God's playground. A history of Poland*, vol. 1: *The origins to 1795* (Oxford: Clarendon Press, 1981).

Dickmann, Fritz, 'Das Problem der Gleichberechtigung der Konfessionen im Reich im 16. und 17. Jahrhundert'. In Heinrich Lutz (ed.), *Zur Geschichte der Toleranz und Religionsfreiheit* (Darmstadt: Wissenschaftliche Buchgesellschaft, 1977), pp. 203–51.

Elton, G. R., 'Persecution and toleration in the English Reformation'. In W. J. Sheils (ed.), *Persecution and toleration. Studies in Church History*, 21 (Oxford: Basil Blackwell, 1984), pp. 163–87.

Estes, James M., 'Luther's first appeal to secular authorities for help with church reform, 1520'. In Robert J. Bast and Andrew C. Gow (eds.), *Continuity and change. The harvest of late-medieval and Reformation history. Essays presented to Heiko A. Oberman on his 70th birthday* (Leiden: E. J. Brill, 2000), pp. 48–76.

Ferguson, Wallace K., 'The attitude of Erasmus toward toleration'. In *Persecution and liberty: Essays in honor of George Lincoln Burr* (New York: The Century Company, 1931), pp. 171–81.

Fimpel, Ludwig, *Mino Celsis Traktat gegen die Ketzertötung: ein Beitrag zum Toleranzproblem des 16. Jahrhunderts.* Basler Beiträge zur Geschichtswissenschaft, 56 (Basel: Helbing & Lichtenhahn, 1967).

Fletcher, Anthony, 'The enforcement of the Conventicle Act 1664–1679'. In W. J. Sheils (ed.), *Persecution and toleration. Studies in Church History*, 21 (Oxford: Basil Blackwell, 1984), pp. 235–46.

Furcha, E. J., '"Turks and heathen are our kin": the notion of tolerance in the works of Hans Denck and Sebastian Franck'. In Cary J. Nederman and John Christian Laursen (eds.), *Difference and dissent. Theories of toleration in medieval and early modern Europe* (Lanham: Rowman & Littlefield Publishers, Inc., 1996), pp. 83–97.

Garrisson, Janine, *L'Edit de Nantes: chronique d'une paix attendue* (Paris: Fayard, 1998).

L'Edit de Nantes et sa révocation: histoire d'une intolérance (Paris: Editions du Seuil, 1985).

Grell, Ole Peter, and Porter, Roy (eds.), *Toleration in Enlightenment Europe* (Cambridge: Cambridge University Press, 2000).

Guggisberg, Hans R., *Sebastian Castellio 1515–1563. Humanist und Verteidiger der religiösen Toleranz im konfessionellen Zeitalter* (Göttingen: Vandenhoeck & Ruprecht, 1997).

'Wandel der Argumente für religiöse Toleranz und Glaubensfreiheit im 16. und 17. Jahrhundert'. In Heinrich Lutz (ed.), *Zur Geschichte der Toleranz und Religionsfreiheit* (Darmstadt: Wissenschaftliche Buchgesellschaft, 1977), pp. 455–81.

Güldner, Gerhard, *Das Toleranz-Problem in den Niederlanden im Ausgang des 16. Jahrhunderts* (Lübeck and Hamburg: Matthiesen Verlag, 1968).

Hamilton, Bernard, *The medieval inquisition*. Foundations of medieval history (London: Edward Arnold, 1981).

Heckel, Martin, *Deutschland im konfessionellen Zeitalter*. Deutsche Geschichte, 5 (Göttingen: Vandenhoeck & Ruprecht, 1983).

Hofmann, Manfred, 'Erasmus and religious toleration', *Erasmus of Rotterdam Society Yearbook* 2 (1982), pp. 80–106.

Höpfl, Harro (ed. and trans.), *Luther and Calvin on secular authority*. Cambridge Texts in the History of Political Thought (Cambridge: Cambridge University Press, 1991).

Hsia, R. Po-chia, and Lehmann, Hartmut (eds.), *In and out of the ghetto: Gentile–Jewish relations in late medieval and early modern Germany* (Washington, DC: German Historical Institute; and Cambridge: Cambridge University Press, 1995).

Huseman, William H., 'The expression of the idea of toleration in French during the sixteenth century', *Sixteenth Century Journal* 15 (1984): 293–310.

Israel, Jonathan I., *Locke, Spinoza and the philosophical debate concerning toleration in the Early Enlightenment (c. 1670–c.1750)*. Koninklijke Nederlandse Akademie van Wetenschappen, Mededelingen van de Afdeling Letterkunde, Nieuwe Reeks, vol. 62, no. 6 (Amsterdam: Koninklijke Nederlandse Akademie van Wetenschappen, 1999).

'Spinoza, Locke and the Enlightenment battle for toleration'. In Ole Peter Grell and Roy Porter (eds.), *Toleration in Enlightenment Europe* (Cambridge: Cambridge University Press, 2000), pp. 102–13.

Jahns, Sigrid, 'Die Reichsjustiz als Spiegel der Reichs- und Religionsverfassung'. In Klaus Bussman and Heinz Schilling (eds.), *1648. Krieg und Frieden in Europa, Vol. I: Politik, Religion, Recht und Gesellschaft* (Münster and Osnabrück: Veranstaltungsgesellschaft 350 Jahre Westfälischer Friede, 1998), pp. 455–63.

Jordan, W. K., *The development of religious toleration in England from the beginning of the English Reformation to the death of Queen Elizabeth* (London: George Allen & Unwin, 1932).

Jordt-Jørgensen, Kai Eduard, *Ökumenische Bestrebungen unter den polnischen Protestanten bis zum Jahre 1645* (Copenhagen: Busck, 1942).

Katz, Jacob, *Exclusiveness and tolerance: studies in Jewish–Gentile relations in medieval and modern times*. Scripta Judaica, 3 (Oxford: Oxford University Press, 1961).

Kenny, Anthony, *Thomas More* (Oxford: Oxford University Press, 1983).

Kriegel, Maurice, *Les Juifs à la fin du Moyen Age dans l'Europe méditerranéenne* (Paris: Hachette, 1979).

Lambert, M. D., *Medieval heresy: popular movements from Bogomil to Hus* (London: Edward Arnold, 1977).

Laursen, John Christian, 'Spinoza on toleration: arming the state and reining in the magistrate'. In Cary J. Nederman and John Christian Laursen (eds.), *Difference and dissent. Theories of toleration in medieval and early modern Europe* (Lanham: Rowman & Littlefield Publishers, Inc., 1996), pp. 185–204.

Lecler, Joseph, *Histoire de la tolérance au siècle de la Réforme* (Paris: Albin Michel, 1994).

Lienhard, Marc, 'De la tolérance à l'intolérance: Comment et pourquoi Luther a-t-il changé à partir de 1525?' In Jean Delumeau (ed.), *Homo religiosus* (Paris: Fayard, 1997), pp. 637–40.

MacCulloch, Diarmaid, 'Archbishop Cranmer: concord and tolerance in a changing church'. In Ole Peter Grell and Bob Scribner (eds.), *Tolerance and intolerance in the European Reformation* (Cambridge: Cambridge University Press, 1996), pp. 199–215.

Montaigne, Michel de, *Les Essais, édition conforme au texte de l'exemplaire de Bordeaux*. Ed. Pierre Villey and V.-L. Saulnier, 3rd edn, 2 vols. (Paris: Presses Universitaires de France, 1978), vol. 1, Book II, Ch. XIX, 'De la liberté de conscience', p. 668.

Mout, M. E. H. N., 'Limits and debates: a comparative view of Dutch toleration in the sixteenth and early seventeenth centuries'. In C. Berkvens-Stevelinck, J. Israel, and G. H. M. Posthumus Meyjes (eds.), *The emergence of tolerance in the Dutch Republic* (Leiden: E. J. Brill, 1997), pp. 37–47.

Müller, Michael G., 'Protestant confessionalism in the towns of Royal Prussia and the practice of religious toleration in Poland-Lithuania'. In Ole Peter Grell and Bob Scribner (eds.), *Tolerance and intolerance in the European Reformation* (Cambridge: Cambridge University Press, 1996), pp. 262–81.

Nolte, Hans-Heinrich, *Religiöse Toleranz in Russland 1600–1750*. Göttinger Bausteine zur Geschichtswissenschaft, vol. 41 (Göttingen: Musterschmidt-Verlag, 1969).

Nugent, Donald, *Ecumenism in the age of the Reformation: the Colloquy of Poissy* (Cambridge, MA: Harvard University Press, 1974).

Orr, Robert R., *Reason and authority: the thought of William Chillingworth* (Oxford: Clarendon Press, 1967).

Pánek, Jaroslav, 'The question of tolerance in Bohemia and Moravia in the age of the Reformation'. In Ole Peter Grell and Bob Scribner (eds.), *Tolerance and intolerance in the European Reformation* (Cambridge: Cambridge University Press, 1996), pp. 231–48.

Péter, Katalin, 'Tolerance and intolerance in sixteenth-century Hungary'. In Ole Peter Grell and Bob Scribner (eds.), *Tolerance and intolerance in the European Reformation* (Cambridge: Cambridge University Press, 1996), pp. 249–61.

Pettegree, Andrew, 'The politics of toleration in the Free Netherlands, 1572–1620'. In Ole Peter Grell and Bob Scribner (eds.), *Tolerance and intolerance in the European Reformation* (Cambridge: Cambridge University Press, 1996), pp. 182–98.

Foreign Protestant communities in sixteenth-century London (Oxford: Clarendon Press, 1986).

Po-Chia Hsia, R., and van Nierop, H. F. K. (eds.), *Calvinism and religious toleration in the Dutch Golden Age* (Cambridge: Cambridge University Press, 2002).

Roellenbleck, Georg, 'Jean Bodin et la liberté de conscience'. In Hans R. Guggisberg, Frank Lestringant, and Jean-Claude Margolin (eds.), *La liberté de conscience (XVIe–XVIIe siècles)*. Actes du Colloque de Mulhouse et Bâle (1989). Etudes de philologie et d'histoire, 44 (Geneva: Droz, 1991), pp. 97–106.

Rupp, Gordon, 'Luther and government'. In Helmut Koenigsberger (ed.), *Luther* (London: Macmillan, 1973), pp. 125–49.

Schilling, Heinz, 'Confessionalization in the Empire: religious and societal change in Germany between 1555 and 1620'. In Heinz Schilling, *Religion, political culture and the emergence of early modern society*. Essays in German and Dutch History (Leiden: E. J. Brill, 1992), pp. 205–45.

Schindling, Anton, 'Andersgläubige Nachbarn. Mehrkonfessionalität und Parität in Territorien und Städten des Reichs'. In Klaus Bussman and Heinz Schilling (eds.), *1648. Krieg und Frieden in Europa vol. I Politik, Religion, Recht und Gesellschaft* (Münster and Osnabrück: Veranstaltungsgesellschaft 350 Jahre Westfälischer Friede, 1998), pp. 465–73.

Schmidt, Georg, 'Der Westfälische Friede als Grundgesetz des komplementären Reichs-Staats'. In Klaus Bussman and Heinz Schilling (eds.), *1648. Krieg und Frieden in Europa vol. I Politik, Religion, Recht und Gesellschaft* (Münster and Osnabrück: Veranstaltungsgesellschaft 350 Jahre Westfälischer Friede, 1998), pp. 447–54.

Der Dreissigjährige Krieg (Munich: Verlag C. H. Beck, 1995).

Schormann, Gerhard, *Der Dreissigjährige Krieg* (Göttingen: Vandenhoeck & Ruprecht, 1985).

Simon, Matthias, *Der Augsburger Religionsfriede: Ereignis und Aufgabe* (Augsburg: Evangelisch-lutherische Gesamtkirchenverwaltung, 1955).

Šmahel, František, *Husitské Čechy* (Prague: Nakladatelsví Lidové Noviny, 2001).

Stegmann, André, *Edits des guerres de religion.* Textes et documents de la Renaissance, 2 (Paris: Librairie philosophique J. Vrin, 1979).

Sutherland, N. M., 'Persecution and toleration in Reformation Europe'. In W. J. Sheils (ed.), *Persecution and toleration.* Studies in Church History, 21 (Oxford: Basil Blackwell, 1984), pp. 153–61.

Tazbir, Janusz, *A state without stakes: Polish religious toleration in the sixteenth and seventeenth centuries.* Trans. Alexander T. Jordan. The Library of Polish Studies, 3 (New York: Kośiuszko Foundation, 1973).

Tyacke, Nicholas, 'The "rise of Puritanism" and the legalizing of dissent, 1571–1719'. In Ole Peter Grell, Jonathan I. Israel, and Nicholas Tyacke (eds.), *From persecution to toleration. The Glorious Revolution and religion in England* (Oxford: Clarendon Press, 1991), pp. 17–49.

Válka, Josef, 'Tolerance, čikoexistence?' *Studia comeniana et historica* 18 (1988): 63–75.

Verbeek, Theo, 'Descartes et les exigences de la liberté'. In Henry Méchoulan (ed.), *Amsterdam XVIIe siècle. Marchands et philosophes: les bénéfices de la tolérance.* Série Mémoires, 23 (Paris: Editions Autrement, 1993), pp. 154–60.

De vrijheid van de filosofie: reflecties over een Cartesiaans thema. Questiones infinitae, 8 (Utrecht: Universiteit Utrecht, Faculteit der Wijsbegeerte, 1994).

'Le contexte néerlandais de la politique cartésienne', *Archives de Philosophie* 53 (1990): 357–70.

Wanegffelen, Thierry, *Ni Rome, ni Genève. Des fidèles entre deux chaires en France au XVIe siècle.* Bibliothèque littéraire de la Renaissance Série III, 36 (Paris: Honoré Champion éditeur, 1997).

L'Edit de Nantes.Une histoire européenne de la tolérance du XVIe au XXe siècle (Paris: Livre de poche, 1998).

Whaley, Joachim, 'A tolerant society? Religious toleration in the Holy Roman Empire, 1648–1806'. In Ole Peter Grell and Roy Porter (eds.), *Toleration in Enlightenment Europe* (Cambridge: Cambridge University Press, 2000), 175–95.

Worden, Blair, 'Toleration and the Cromwellian Protectorate'. In W. J. Sheils (ed.), *Persecution and toleration.* Studies in Church History, 21 (Oxford: Basil Blackwell, 1984), pp. 199–233.

Wyrwa, Tadeusz, 'La liberté de conscience en Pologne à la charnière des XVIe et XVIIe siècles'. In Hans R. Guggisberg, Frank Lestringant, and Jean-Claude Margolin (eds.), *La liberté de conscience (XVIe–XVIIe siècles)*. Actes du Colloque de Mulhouse et Bâle (1989). Etudes de philologie et d'histoire, 44 (Geneva: Droz, 1991), pp. 257–67.

14 IMPOSING CHURCH AND SOCIAL DISCIPLINE

Becker, T. P., *Konfessionalisierung in Kurköln: Untersuchungen zur Durchsetzung der katholischen Reform in den Dekanaten Ahrgau und Bonn anhand von Visitationsprotokollen 1583–1761* (Bonn: Edition Röhrscheid, 1989).

Benedict, Philip, *Christ's churches purely reformed: A social history of Calvinism* (New Haven and London: Yale University Press, 2002).

Black, C. F., *Italian confraternities in the sixteenth century* (Cambridge: Cambridge University Press, 1989).

Bossy, John, *Christianity in the West, 1400–1700* (Oxford and New York: Oxford University Press, 1985).

'The social history of confession in the age of the Reformation', *Transactions of the Royal Historical Society 5th series*, 25 (1975): 21–38.

Brecht, Martin, *Kirchenordnung und Kirchenzucht in Württemberg vom 16. bis zum 18. Jahrhundert* (Stuttgart: Calwer Verlag, 1967).

'Lutherische Kirchenzucht bis in die Anfänge des 17. Jahrhunderts im Spannungsfeld von Pfarramt und Gesellschaft'. In Hans-Christoph Rublack (ed.), *Die lutherische Konfessionalisierung in Deutschland: Wissenschaftliches Symposion des Vereins für Reformationsgeschichte 1988* (Gütersloh: Gütersloher Verlagshaus, 1992), pp. 400–23.

'Protestantische Kirchenzucht zwischen Kirche und Staat: Bemerkungen zur Forschungssituation'. In Heinz Schilling (ed.), *Kirchenzucht und Sozialdisziplinierung im frühneuzeitlichen Europa* (Berlin: Duncker & Humblot, 1994), pp. 41–8.

Burnett, A. N., 'Church discipline and moral reformation in the thought of Martin Bucer', *Sixteenth Century Journal* 22 (1991): 439–56.

Cameron, James, 'Godly nurture and admonition in the Lord: Ecclesiastical discipline in the Reformed tradition'. In Leif Grane and Kai Hørby (eds.), *Die dänische Reformation vor ihrem internationalen Hintergrund* (Göttingen: Vandenhoeck & Ruprecht, 1990), pp. 264–76.

Chareyre, Philippe, '"The great difficulties one must bear to follow Jesus Christ": Morality at sixteenth-century Nîmes'. In R. A. Mentzer (ed.), *Sin and the Calvinists: Moral control and the consistory in the Reformed tradition* (Kirksville: Sixteenth Century Journal Publishers, 1994), pp. 63–95.

Châtellier, Louis, *The Europe of the devout: the Catholic Reformation and the formation of a new society* (Cambridge: Cambridge University Press; Paris: Editions de la Maison des Sciences de l'Homme, 1989).

Davis, K. R., 'No discipline, no church. An Anabaptist contribution to the Reformed tradition', *Sixteenth Century Journal* 13 (1982): 43–58.

Davis, N. Z., 'Poor relief, humanism, and heresy'. In N. Z. Davis, *Society and culture in early modern France* (Stanford: Stanford University Press, 1987), pp. 17–64.

Delumeau, Jean, *L'aveu et le pardon: Les difficultés de la confession, 13e–18e siècles* (Paris: Fayard, 1990).

Sin and fear: The emergence of a western guilt culture, 13th–18th centuries (New York: St Martin's Press, 1990).

Dixon, C. S., *The Reformation and rural society: The parishes of Brandenburg–Ansbach–Kulmbach, 1528–1603* (Cambridge: Cambridge University Press, 1996).

Donnelly, J. P., and Maher, M. W. (eds.), *Confraternities and Catholic reform in Italy, France, and Spain* (Kirksville: Thomas Jefferson University Press, 1999).

Fehler, T. G., *Poor relief and Protestantism: The evolution of social welfare in sixteenth-century Emden* (Aldershot: Ashgate, 1999).

Franz, Günther, *Die Kirchenleitung in Hohenlohe in den Jahrzehnten nach der Reformation: Visitation, Konsistorium, Kirchenzucht und die Festigung des landesherrlichen Kirchenregiments 1556–1586* (Stuttgart: Calwer Verlag, 1971).

Freitag, Werner, *Pfarrer, Kirche und ländliche Gesellschaft: Das Dekanat Vechta 1400–1803* (Bielefeld: Verlag für Regionalgeschichte, 1998).

Friedeburg, Robert von, 'Anglikanische Sittenzucht und nachbarschaftliche Sittenreform: Reformierte Sittenzucht zwischen Staat, Kirche und Gemeinde in England 1559–1642'. In Heinz Schilling (ed.), *Kirchenzucht und Sozialdisziplinierung im frühneuzeitlichen Europa* (Berlin: Duncker & Humblot, 1994), pp. 153–82.

'Kirchenzucht'. In *Die Religion in Geschichte und Gegenwart: Handwörterbuch für Theologie und Religionswissenschaft*, 4th edn, vol. 4 (Tübingen: Mohr Siebeck, 2001), cols. 1367–74.

'Reformation of manners and the social composition of offenders in an East Anglian cloth village', *Journal of British Studies* 29 (1990): 347–85.

Sündenzucht und sozialer Wandel: Earls Colne (England), Ipswich und Springfield (Neuengland) c. 1524–1690 im Vergleich (Stuttgart: Steiner, 1993).

Goertz, Hans-Jürgen, '3. Reformationszeit'. In 'Kirchenzucht'. In *Theologische Realenzyklopädie*, 19 (Berlin and New York: Walter de Gruyter, 1990), pp. 176–83.

'Kleruskritik, Kirchenzucht und Sozialdisziplinierung in den täuferischen Bewegungen der Frühen Neuzeit'. In Heinz Schilling (ed.), *Kirchenzucht und Sozialdisziplinierung im frühneuzeitlichen Europa* (Berlin: Duncker & Humblot, 1994), pp. 183–98.

Gordon, Bruce, *Clerical discipline and the rural Reformation: The synod in Zürich, 1532–1580* (Bern and New York: Lang, 1992).

'Die Entwicklung der Kirchenzucht in Zürich am Beginn der Reformation'. In Heinz Schilling (ed.), *Kirchenzucht und Sozialdisziplinierung im frühneuzeitlichen Europa* (Berlin: Dunker & Humblot, 1994), pp. 65–90.

Gorski, P. S., *The disciplinary revolution: Calvinism and the rise of the state in early modern Europe* (Chicago and London: University of Chicago Press, 2003).

Götze, Ruth, *Wie Luther Kirchenzucht übte* (Göttingen: Vandenhoeck & Ruprecht, 1958).

Graham, M. F., 'Social discipline in Scotland, 1560–1610'. In R. A. Mentzer (ed.), *Sin and the Calvinists: Moral control and the consistory in the Reformed tradition* (Kirksville: Sixteenth Century Journal Publishers, 1994), pp. 129–57.

The uses of reform: 'Godly discipline' and popular behavior in Scotland and beyond, 1560–1610 (Leiden: Brill, 1996).

Greaves, R. L., 'Church courts'. In *The Oxford encyclopedia of the Reformation*, 1 (New York and Oxford: Oxford University Press, 1996), pp. 435–40.

Grell, O. P., and Cunningham, Andrew (eds.), *Health care and poor relief in Protestant Europe, 1500–1700* (London and New York: Routledge, 1997).

'The religious duty of care and the social need for control in early modern Europe', *Historical Journal* 39 (1996): 257–63.

Headley, J. M., and Tomato, J. B. (eds.), *San Carlo Borromeo: Catholic reform and ecclesiastical politics in the second half of the sixteenth century* (Washington: Folger Shakespeare Library, 1988).

Heiß, Gernot, 'Konfessionsbildung, Kirchenzucht und frühmoderner Staat: Die Durchsetzung des "rechten" Glaubens im "Zeitalter der Glaubensspaltung" am Beispiel des Wirkens der Jesuiten in den Ländern Ferdinands I'. In H. C. Ehalt (ed.), *Volksfrömmigkeit* (Cologne and Vienna: Böhlau, 1989), pp. 191–220.

Holzem, Andreas, 'Katholische Konfession und Kirchenzucht: Handlungsformen und Deliktfelder archidiakonaler Gerichtsbarkeit im 17. und 18. Jahrhundert', *Westfälische Forschungen* 45 (1995): 295–332.

Religion und Lebensformen. Katholische Konfessionalisierung im Sendgericht des Fürstbistums Münster 1570–1800 (Paderborn: Ferdinand Schöningh, 2000).

Houlbrooke, Ralph, *Church courts and the people during the English Reformation, 1520–1570* (Oxford: Oxford University Press, 1979).

Houston, Rab, 'The consistory of the Scots Church, Rotterdam: An aspect of "civic Calvinism", c. 1600–1800', *Archiv für Reformationsgeschichte / Archive for Reformation History* 87 (1996): 362–92.

Hsia, R. P., *Social discipline in the Reformation: Central Europe, 1550–1750* (London and New York: Routledge, 1989).

Ingram, Martin, *Church courts, sex and marriage in England, 1570–1640* (Cambridge: Cambridge University Press, 1987).

'History of sin or history of crime? The regulation of personal morality in England, 1450–1750'. In Heinz Schilling (ed.), *Institutionen, Instrumente und Akteure sozialer Kontrolle und Disziplinierung im frühneuzeitlichen Europa / Institutions, instruments and agents of social control and discipline in early modern Europe* (Frankfurt a.M.: Vittorio Klostermann, 1999), pp. 87–103.

Jütte, Robert, 'Disziplinierungsmechanismen in der städtischen Armenfürsorge der Frühneuzeit'. In Christoph Sachße and Florian Tennstedt (eds.), *Soziale Sicherheit und soziale Disziplinierung: Beiträge zu einer historischen Theorie der Sozialpolitik* (Frankfurt a.M.: Suhrkamp, 1986), pp. 101–18.

Kingdon, R. M., *Adultery and divorce in Calvin's Geneva* (Cambridge, MA, and London: Harvard University Press, 1995).

'Calvinist discipline in the Old World and the New'. In H. R. Guggisberg and G. G. Krodel (eds.), *Die Reformation in Deutschland und Europa: Interpretationen und Debatten* (Gütersloh: Gütersloher Verlagshaus, 1993), pp. 665–79.

'The control of morals in Calvin's Geneva'. In L. P. Buch and J. W. Zophy (eds.), *The social history of the Reformation* (Columbus, OH: Ohio State University Press, 1972), pp. 3–16.

'The Genevan consistory in the time of Calvin'. In Andrew Pettegree, Alistair Duke, and Gillian Lewis (eds.), *Calvinism in Europe, 1540–1620* (Cambridge: Cambridge University Press, 1994), pp. 21–34.

Kirk, James, '"The polities of the best Reformed kirks": Scottish achievements and English aspirations in church government after the Reformation', *Scottish Historical Review* 59 (1980): 22–53.

Kittelson, J. M., 'Successes and failures in the German Reformation: The report from Strasbourg', *Archiv für Reformationsgeschichte / Archive for Reformation History* 73 (1982): 153–75.

'Visitations and popular religious culture: further reports from Strasbourg'. In K. C. Sessions and P. N. Bebb (eds.), *Pietas et societas: New trends in Reformation social history* (Kirksville: Sixteenth Century Journal Publishers, 1988), pp. 89–103.

Köhler, Walter, *Zürcher Ehegericht und Genfer Konsistorium*, Vol. 1: *Das Zürcher Ehegericht und seine Auswirkungen in der deutschen Schweiz zur Zeit Zwinglis* (Leipzig: Heinsius, 1932).

Konersmann, Frank, *Kirchenregiment und Kirchenzucht im frühneuzeitlichen Kleinstaat: Studien zu den herrschaftlichen und gesellschaftlichen Grundlagen des Kirchenregiments der Herzöge von Pfalz-Zweibrücken 1410–1793* (Cologne: Rheinland-Verlag, 1996).

'Kirchenvisitation als landesherrliches Kontrollmittel und als Regulativ dörflicher Kommunikation: Das Herzogtum Pfalz-Zweibrücken im 16. und 17. Jahrhundert'. In Andreas Blauert and Gerd Schwerhoff (eds.), *Kriminalitätsgeschichte: Beiträge zur Sozial- und Kulturgeschichte der Vormoderne* (Constance: Universitätsverlag Konstanz, 2000), pp. 603–25.

'Presbyteriale Bußzucht aus zivilisationsgeschichtlicher Perspektive: Kirchenzucht pfälzischer und provenzalischer Presbyterien zwischen 1580 und 1780'. In Heinz Schilling (ed.), *Institutionen, Instrumente und Akteure sozialer Kontrolle und Disziplinierung im frühneuzeitlichen Europa / Institutions, instruments and agents of social control and discipline in early modern Europe* (Frankfurt a.M.: Vittorio Klostermann, 1999), pp. 105–46.

Kooi, Christine, 'Pharisees and hypocrites: A public debate over church discipline in Leiden, 1586', *Archiv für Reformationsgeschichte / Archive for Reformation History* 88 (1997): 258–78.

Lang, P. T., 'Reform im Wandel: Die katholischen Visitationsinterrogatorien des 16. und 17. Jahrhunderts'. In E. W. Zeeden and P. T. Lang (eds.), *Kirche und Visitation: Beiträge zur Erforschung des frühneuzeitlichen Visitationswesens in Europa* (Stuttgart: Klett-Cotta, 1984), pp. 131–89.

Leith, J. H., '1. Begriff, 2. Theologischer Überblick'. In 'Kirchenzucht'. In *Theologische Realenzyklopädie*, 19 (Berlin and New York: Walter de Gruyter, 1990), pp. 173–6.

Lenman, Bruce, 'The limits of godly discipline in the early modern period with particular reference to England and Scotland'. In Kaspar von Greyerz (ed.), *Religion and society in early modern Europe, 1500–1800* (London: Allen & Unwin, 1984), pp. 124–45.

Lindberg, Carter, *Beyond charity: Reformation initiatives for the poor* (Minneapolis: Fortress, 1993).

Link, Christoph, 'V. Reformation und Neuzeit'. In 'Bann'. In *Theologische Realenzyklopädie*, 5 (Berlin and New York: Walter de Gruyter, 1980), pp. 182–90.

Littleton, Charles, 'Ecclesiastical discipline in the French church of London and the creation of community', *Archiv für Reformationsgeschichte / Archive for Reformation History* 92 (2001): 232–63.

Lotz-Heumann, Ute, 'Social control and church discipline in Ireland in the sixteenth and early seventeenth centuries'. In Heinz Schilling (ed.), *Institutionen, Instrumente und Akteure sozialer Kontrolle und Disziplinierung im frühneuzeitlichen Europa / Institutions, instruments and agents of social control and discipline in early modern Europe* (Frankfurt a.M.: Vittorio Klostermann, 1999), pp. 275–304.

'The concept of "confessionalization": a historiographical paradigm in dispute', *Memoria y Civilización* 4 (2001): 93–114.

Marchant, R. A., *The church under the law: justice, administration and discipline in the diocese of York, 1560–1640* (Cambridge: Cambridge University Press, 1969).

The Puritans and the church courts in the diocese of York, 1560–1642 (London: Longmans, 1960).

Mentzer, R. A., 'Disciplina nervus ecclesiae: the Calvinist reform of morals at Nîmes', *Sixteenth Century Journal* 18 (1987): 89–115.

'Ecclesiastical discipline and communal reorganisation among the Protestants of southern France', *European History Quarterly* 21 (1991), pp. 163–83.

'Marking the taboo: excommunication in French Reformed churches'. In R. A. Mentzer, (ed.), *Sin and the Calvinists: Morals control and the consistory in the Reformed tradition* (Kirksville: Sixteenth Century Journal Publishers, 1994), pp. 97–128.

Monter, E. W., 'The consistory of Geneva, 1559–1569', *Bibliothèque d'Humanisme et Renaissance* 38 (1976): 467–84.

Müller, Siegfried, 'Die Konfessionalisierung in der Grafschaft Oldenburg: Untersuchungen zur "Sozialdisziplinierung" einer bäuerlichen Gesellschaft in der Frühen Neuzeit', *Archiv für Reformationsgeschichte / Archive for Reformation History* 86 (1995): pp. 257–319.

Münch, Paul, 'Kirchenzucht und Nachbarschaft: Zur sozialen Problematik des calvinistischen Seniorats um 1600'. In E. W. Zeeden and P. T. Lang (eds.), *Kirche und Visitation: Beiträge zur Erforschung des frühneuzeitlichen Visitationswesens in Europa* (Stuttgart: Klett-Cotta, 1984): 216–48.

Zucht und Ordnung: Reformierte Kirchenverfassungen im 16. und 17. Jahrhundert (Nassau-Dillenburg, Kurpfalz, Hessen-Kassel, and Stuttgart: Klett-Cotta, 1978).

Naphy, W. G., *Calvin and the consolidation of the Genevan Reformation* (Manchester: Manchester University Press, 1994).

Neuser, Wilhelm, 'Dogma und Bekenntnis in der Reformation: Von Zwingli und Calvin bis zur Synode von Westminster'. In Bernhard Lohse *et al.*, *Die Lehrentwicklung im Rahmen der Konfessionalität, Handbuch der Dogmen- und Theologiegeschichte*, vol. 2, 2nd edn (Göttingen: Vandenhoeck & Ruprecht, 1998), pp. 167–351.

O'Day, Rosemary, 'Geschichte der bischöflichen Kirchenvisitation in England, 1500–1689'. In E. W. Zeeden, and P. T. Lang (eds.), *Kirche und Visitation: Beiträge zur Erforschung des frühneuzeitlichen Visitationswesens in Europa* (Stuttgart: Klett-Cotta, 1984), pp. 191–215.

Parker, C. H., *The reformation of community. Social welfare and Calvinist charity in Holland, 1572–1620* (Cambridge: Cambridge University Press, 1998).

'Two generations of discipline: moral reform in Delft before and after the synod of Dort', *Archiv für Reformationsgeschichte / Archive for Reformation History* 92 (2001): 215–31.

Parker, Geoffrey, 'The "kirk by law established" and origins of "the taming of Scotland": Saint Andrews, 1559–1600'. In R. A. Mentzer (ed.), *Sin and the Calvinists: Morals control and the consistory in the Reformed tradition* (Kirksville: Sixteenth Century Journal Publishers, 1994), pp. 159–97.

Pettegree, Andrew, *Foreign Protestant communities in sixteenth-century London* (Oxford: Clarendon Press, 1986).

Bibliography

Pfister, Ulrich, 'Reformierte Sittenzucht zwischen kommunaler und territorialer Organisation. Graubünden, 16.–18. Jahrhundert', *Archiv für Reformationsgeschichte / Archive for Reformation History* 87 (1996): 287–333.

Pollmann, Judith, 'Off the record: problems in the quantification of Calvinist church discipline', *Sixteenth Century Journal* 33 (2002): 423–38.

Prak, Maarten, 'The carrot and the stick: social control and poor relief in the Dutch republic, sixteenth to eighteenth centuries'. In Heinz Schilling (ed.), *Institutionen, Instrumente und Akteure sozialer Kontrolle und Disziplinierung im frühneuzeitlichen Europa / Institutions, instruments and agents of social control and discipline in early modern Europe* (Frankfurt a.M.: Vittorio Klostermann, 1999), pp. 149–66.

Pullan, Brian, 'Catholics and the poor in early modern Europe', *Transactions of the Royal Historical Society* 26 (1976): 15–34.

Reinhard, Wolfgang, 'Reformation, Counter-Reformation, and the early modern state: a reassessment', *Catholic Historical Review* 75 (1989): 383–404.

'Was ist katholische Konfessionalisierung?' In Wolfgang Reinhard and Heinz Schilling (eds.), *Die katholische Konfessionalisierung: Wissenschaftliches Symposion der Gesellschaft zur Herausgabe des Corpus Catholicorum und des Vereins für Reformationsgeschichte* (Gütersloh: Gütersloher Verlagshaus, 1995), pp. 419–52.

'Zwang zur Konfessionalisierung? Prolegomena zu einer Theorie des konfessionellen Zeitalters', *Zeitschrift für historische Forschung* 10 (1983): 257–77.

Roodenburg, Herman, *Oonder censuur: De kerkelijke tucht in de gereformeerde gemeente van Amsterdam, 1578–1700* (Hilversum: Verloren, 1990).

'Reformierte Kirchenzucht und Ehrenhandel: Das Amsterdamer Nachbarschaftsleben im 17. Jahrhundert'. In Heinz Schilling (ed.), *Kirchenzucht und Sozialdisziplinierung im frühneuzeitlichen Europa* (Berlin: Duncker & Humblot, 1994), pp. 129–52.

Roper, Lyndal, *The holy household: women and morals in Reformation Augsburg* (Oxford: Clarendon Press, 1989).

Schaab, Meinrad, 'Obrigkeitlicher Calvinismus und Genfer Gemeindemodell: Die Kurpfalz als frühestes reformiertes Territorium im Reich und ihre Einwirkungen auf Pfalz-Zweibrücken'. In Meinrad Schaab (ed.), *Territorialstaat und Calvinismus* (Stuttgart: W. Kohlhammer Verlag, 1993), 34–86.

Schilling, Heinz, 'Confessional Europe'. In T. A. Brady, Jr, H. A. Oberman, and J. D. Tracy (eds.), *Handbook of European History, 1400–1600: Late middle ages, Renaissance and Reformation*, vol. 2: *Visions, programs and outcomes* (Leiden: Brill, 1995), pp. 641–75.

'Confessionalization in the empire: religious and societal change in Germany between 1555 and 1620'. In Heinz Schilling, *Religion, political culture and the emergence of early modern society: essays in German and Dutch history* (Leiden: Brill, 1992), pp. 205– 45.

'Die Konfessionalisierung von Kirche, Staat und Gesellschaft: Profil, Leistung, Defizite und Perspektiven eines geschichtswissenschaftlichen Paradigmas'. In Wolfgang Reinhard and Heinz Schilling (eds.), *Die katholische Konfessionalisierung: Wissenschaftliches Symposion der Gesellschaft zur Herausgabe des Corpus Catholicorum und des Vereins für Reformationsgeschichte* (Gütersloh: Gütersloher Verlagshaus, 1995), pp. 1–49.

'"History of crime" or "history of sin"? Some reflections on the social history of early modern church discipline'. In E. I. Kouri and Tom Scott (eds.), *Politics and society in Reformation Europe: essays for Sir Geoffrey Elton on his 65th birthday* (London: Macmillan, 1987), pp. 289–310.

'Calvinism and the making of the modern mind: ecclesiastical discipline of public and private sin from the sixteenth to the nineteenth century'. In Heinz Schilling, *Civic Calvinism in northwestern Germany and the Netherlands: Sixteenth to nineteenth centuries* (Kirksville: Sixteenth Century Journal Publishers, 1991), pp. 41–68.

'Die Frühneuzeitliche Formierung und Disziplinierung von Ehe, Familie und Erziehung im Spiegel calvinistischer Kirchenratsprotokolle'. In Paolo Prodi (ed.), *Treueformeln, Glaubensbekenntnisse und Sozialdisziplinierung zwischen Mittelalter und Neuzeit* (Munich: Oldenbourg, 1993), pp. 199–235.

'Die Kirchenzucht im frühneuzeitlichen Europa in interkonfessionell vergleichender und interdisziplinärer Perspektive: Eine Zwischenbilanz'. In Heinz Schilling (ed.), *Kirchenzucht und Sozialdisziplinierung im frühneuzeitlichen Europa* (Berlin: Duncker & Humblot, 1994), pp. 11–40.

'Profil und Perspektiven einer interdisziplinären und komparatistischen Disziplinierungsforschung jenseits einer Dichotomie von Gesellschafts- und Kulturgeschichte'. In Heinz Schilling (ed.), *Institutionen, Instrumente und Akteure sozialer Kontrolle und Disziplinierung im frühneuzeitlichen Europa / Institutions, instruments and agents of social control and discipline in early modern Europe* (Frankfurt a.M.: Vittorio Klostermann, 1999), pp. 3–36.

'Reform and supervision of family life in Germany and the Netherlands'. In R. A. Mentzer (ed.), *Sin and the Calvinists: Morals control and the consistory in the Reformed tradition* (Kirksville: Sixteenth Century Journal Publishers, 1994), pp. 15–61.

'Reformierte Kirchenzucht als Sozialdisziplinierung? Die Tätigkeit des Emder Presbyteriums in den Jahren 1557–1562'. In Heinz Schilling and W. Ehbrecht (eds.), *Niederlande und Nordwestdeutschland: Studien zur Regional- und Stadtgeschichte Nordwestkontinentaleuropas im Mittelalter und in der Neuzeit* (Cologne, Vienna, and Böhlau, 1983), pp. 261–327.

'Sündenzucht und frühneuzeitliche Sozialdisziplinierung: Die calvinistische, presbyteriale Kirchenzucht in Emden vom 16. bis 19. Jahrhundert'. In Georg Schmidt (ed.), *Stände und Gesellschaft im Alten Reich* (Stuttgart: Steiner, 1989), pp. 265–302.

Schilling, Heinz (ed.), *Institutionen, Instrumente und Akteure sozialer Kontrolle und Disziplinierung im frühneuzeitlichen Europa / Institutions, instruments and agents of social control and discipline in early modern Europe* (Frankfurt a.M.: Vittorio Klostermann, 1999). *Kirchenzucht und Sozialdisziplinierung im frühneuzeitlichen Europa* (Berlin: Duncker & Humblot, 1994).

Schilling, Heinz, and Scherneck, Heike, 'Auswahlbibliographie'. In Heinz Schilling (ed.), *Kirchenzucht und Sozialdisziplinierung im frühneuzeitlichen Europa* (Berlin: Duncker & Humblot, 1994), pp. 219–32.

Schmidt, H. R., *Dorf und Religion: Reformierte Sittenzucht in Berner Landgemeinden der Frühen Neuzeit* (Stuttgart, Jena, and New York: Gustav Fischer Verlag, 1995).

'Gemeinde und Sittenzucht im protestantischen Europa der frühen Neuzeit'. In Peter Blickle (ed.), *Theorien kommunaler Ordnung in Europa* (Munich: Oldenbourg, 1996), pp. 181–214.

'Pazifizierung des Dorfes: Struktur und Wandel von Nachbarschaftskonflikten vor Berner Sittengerichten 1570–1800'. In Heinz Schilling (ed.), *Kirchenzucht und Sozialdisziplinierung im frühneuzeitlichen Europa* (Berlin: Duncker & Humblot, 1994), pp. 91–128.

'Sozialdisziplinierung? Ein Plädoyer für das Ende des Etatismus in der Konfessionalisierungsforschung', *Historische Zeitschrift* 265 (1997): 639–82.

Schmidt, M., 'Visitation'. In *Die Religion in Geschichte und Gegenwart: Handwörterbuch für Theologie und Religionswissenschaft*, 3rd edn, vol. 6 (Tübingen: J. C. B. Mohr (Paul Siebeck), 1962), cols. 1412–13.

Schnabel-Schüle, Helga, 'Calvinistische Kirchenzucht in Württemberg? Zur Theorie und Praxis der württembergischen Kirchenkonvente', *Zeitschrift für württembergischen Landesgeschichte* 49 (1990): 169–223.

'Der große Unterschied und seine kleinen Folgen: Zum Problem der Kirchenzucht als Unterscheidungskriterium zwischen lutherischer und reformierter Konfession'. In Monika Hagenmaier and Sabine Holtz (eds.), *Krisenbewußtsein und Krisenbewältigung in der Frühen Neuzeit / Crisis in early modern Europe: Festschrift für Hans-Christoph Rublack* (Frankfurt a.M.: Lang, 1992), pp. 197–214.

'Kirchenzucht als Verbrechensprävention'. In Heinz Schilling (ed.), *Kirchenzucht und Sozialdisziplinierung im frühneuzeitlichen Europa* (Berlin: Duncker & Humblot, 1994), pp. 49–64.

Schulze, Winfried, 'Gerhard Oestreichs Begriff "Sozialdisziplinierung in der Frühen Neuzeit"', *Zeitschrift für historische Forschung* 14 (1987): 265–302.

Sharpe, J. A., *Defamation and sexual slander in early modern England: the church courts at York* (York: University of York, Borthwick Institute of Historical Research, 1980).

Strauss, Gerald, *Luther's house of learning: indoctrination of the young in the German Reformation* (Baltimore and London: Johns Hopkins University Press, 1978).

'Success and failure in the German Reformation', *Past and Present* 67 (1975): 30–63.

'Visitations'. In *The Oxford encyclopedia of the Reformation*, vol. 4 (New York and Oxford: Oxford University Press, 1996), pp. 238–43.

Tentler, T. N., 'The summa for confessors as an instrument of social control'. In Charles Trinkaus and Heiko Oberman (eds.), *The pursuit of holiness in late medieval and Renaissance religion* (Leiden: Brill, 1974), pp. 103–26.

Todd, Margo, *The culture of Protestantism in early modern Scotland* (New Haven and London: Yale University Press, 2002).

Tolley, Bruce, *Pastors and parishioners in Württemberg during the late Reformation, 1581–1621* (Stanford: Stanford University Press, 1995).

Venard, Marc (ed.), *Geschichte des Christentums*, vol. 8: *Die Zeit der Konfessionen (1530–1620/30)*. German edition by Heribert Smolinsky (Freiburg, Basel, and Vienna: Herder, 1992).

Vogler, Bernard, and Estèbe, Jean, 'La genèse d'une société protestante: Etude comparée de quelques registres consistoriaux languedociens et palatins vers 1600', *Annales. Economies, Sociétés, Civilisations* 31 (1976): 362–88.

Wandel, L. P., 'Church discipline', in: *The Oxford encyclopedia of the Reformation*, vol. 1 (New York and Oxford: Oxford University Press, 1996), pp. 327–9.

Zeeden, E. W., and Lang, P. T. (eds.), *Kirche und Visitation: Beiträge zur Erforschung des frühneuzeitlichen Visitationswesens in Europa* (Stuttgart: Klett-Cotta, 1984).

Zeeden, E. W., and Molitor, Hans Georg (eds.), *Die Visitation im Dienste der kirchlichen Reform*. 2nd edn (Münster: Aschendorff, 1977).

15 PERSECUTIONS AND MARTYRDOM

Primary sources

[Allen, William], *Briefe Historie of the Glorious Martyrdom of XII Reverend Priests* ([Rheims: Jean Foigny], 1582).

Aussbund: Etlicher schöner Christlicher Geseng . . . (n.p., 1583).

Chauncy, Maurice, *Historia aliquot nostri saeculi martyrum cum piis tum lectu jucunda nunquam antehac typis excusa* (Mainz: Franciscus Behem, 1550).

Circignani, Niccolo, *Ecclesiae militantis triumphi sive Deo amabilium martyrum gloriosa pro Christi fide Certamina* . . . ([Rome: Franciscus Zannettus?], 1583).

Ecclesiae Anglicanae trophaea sive Sanctorum martyrum . . . (Rome: Franciscus Zannettus, 1584).

Cramer, Samuel (ed.), *Het offer des heeren* [1570]. In *Bibliotheca reformatoria Neerlandica* (The Hague: Martinus Nijhoff, 1904), vol. 2.

Crespin, Jean, *Actes des Martyres deduits en sept livres, depuis le temps de Wiclef et de Hus, jusques à present.* . . . ([Geneva]: Jean Crespin, 1564).

Dit is een devote meditacie op die passie ons liefs heeren . . . [1518]. *Bijdragen voor de geschiedenis van het Bisdom van Haarlem* 11 (1884): 324–43.

Etliche schöne Christliche Geseng, wie sie in der Gefengkniß zu Passaw im Schloß von den Schweitzer Brüdern durch Gottes gnad geticht und gesungen worden (n.p., 1564).

Eyn new warhafftig und wunderbarlich geschicht oder hystori, von Jörgen Wagner zu München in Bayern als eyn Ketzer verbrandt im Jar M. D.xxvii [Nuremberg: Hans Hergot, 1527].

Field, Richard S., *Fifteenth century woodcuts and metalcuts from the National Gallery of Art, Washington, D.C.* (Washington, D.C., n.d.).

Foxe, John, *Actes and Monuments of these latter and perilous dayes, touching matters of the Church* . . . (London: John Daye, 1563).

Geisberg, Max, *The German single-leaf woodcut: 1500–1550.* Ed. Walter Strauss. 4 vols. (New York: Hacker, 1974).

[Gibbons, John, and Fenn, John] (eds.), *Concertatio Ecclesiae catholicae in Anglia, adversos Calvinos papistas et Puritanos* . . . (Trier: Edmund Hatotus, 1583).

[Graveneck, Klaus von], *Ayn newes wunderbarlichs geschicht von Michel Sattler zü Rottenburg am Necker* . . . [Nuremberg: Hans Eichenauer, 1528].

Gregory, Brad S. (ed.), *The forgotten writings of the Mennonite martyrs, Documenta Anabaptistica Neerlandica* (Leiden: E. J. Brill, 2002), vol. 8.

Harpsfield, Nicholas, *The life and death of Sir Thomas More* . . . Ed. Elsie Vaughan Hitchcock. Early English Text Society, no. 186 (London: Oxford University Press, 1932).

Hide, Thomas, *A Consolatorie Epistle to the afflicted Catholikes* ([London], 1579).

[à Kempis, Thomas], *A full devoute and gostely treatyse of the Imytacyon and folowynge the blessed lyfe of our moste mercyfull Savyour cryste* . . . (London: Richard Pynson, 1517).

Luther, Martin, *Ein Brief an die Christen in Niederland*. In *WA*, vol. 12, pp. 77–80.

Von Bruder Henrico in Ditmar verbrannt samt den zehnten Psalmen ausgelegt. In *WA*, vol. 18, pp. 224–40.

Tröstung an die Christen zu Halle. In *WA*, vol. 23, pp. 391–5.

Von Er Lenhard Keiser ynn Beyern umb des Evangelii willen verbrandt Eine selige geschicht. In *WA*, vol. 23, pp. 452–76.

Muralt, Leonhard von, and Schmid, Walter (eds.), *Quellen zur Geschichte der Täufer in der Schweiz: Zürich* (Zurich: S. Hirzel, 1952), vol. 1.

[Persons, Robert], *A Treatise of Three Conversions of England from Paganisme to Christian Religion* . . . 2 vols. ([St Omer: F. Bellet], 1603–4).

Pijper, Fredrik (ed.), *Der actus und handlung der degradation und verprenung der Christlichen Ritter und merterer Augustiner ordens geschehen zu Brussel* . . . [Speyer: Johann Eckhart, 1523]. In *Bibliotheca Reformatoria Neerlandica* (The Hague: Martinus Nijhoff, 1911), vol. 8.

Pole, Reginald, 'Cardinal Pole's speech to the citizens of London, in behalf of religious houses'. In John Strype (ed.), *Ecclesiastical memorials* (Oxford: Clarendon Press, 1822), vol. 3, pt. II, pp. 482–510.

Pollen, John H. (ed.), *Unpublished documents relating to the English martyrs: volume 1, 1584–1603, Publications of the Catholic Record Society* (London: J. Whitehead and Son, 1908), vol. 5.

Rab, Christoph, in [Crespin, Jean, and Goulart, Simon], *Märtyrbuch: Darinnenmerckliche, denckwürdige Reden und Thaten viler heiligen Märtyrer beschriben werden* . . . (Herborn: [Christoph Rab], 1590).

Rabus, Ludwig, *Historien der Heyligen Außerwölten Gottes Zeügen, Bekennern und Martyrern* . . . 8 vols. (Strasbourg: Samuel Emmel, 1552–8).

[Sattler, Michael], *Brüderlich vereynigung etzlicher kinder Gottes, sieben Artickel betreffend* . . . [Worms: Peter Schöffer the Younger, *c.* 1527–9].

Schornbaum, Karl, ed., *Quellen zur Geschichte der Täufer: Bayern* (Gütersloh: Bertelsmann, 1951), vol. 5, pt. II.

Sévert, Jacques, *L'Anti-Martyrologe, ou Verite Manifestee contre les Histoires des Supposes Martyrs de la Religion pretendue reformée* . . . (Lyon: Simon Rigaud, 1622).

[Southwell, Robert], *An Epistle of Comfort, to the reverend Priestes, and to the Honorable, Worshipful, and other of the Laye sort restrained in Durance for the Catholicke Fayth* [London, 1587/8].

[Tyndale, William], *An exposicion upon the v. vi. vii. chapters of Mathew* . . . [Antwerp: J. Grapheus? 1533].

van Braght, Thieleman Jans, *Het Bloedig Tooneel, of Martelaers Spiegel der Doops-Gesinde of Weereloose Christenen* . . . 2 vols. (Amsterdam: J. vander Deyster *et al.*, 1685).

Van Engen, John (ed. and trans.), *Devotio moderna: basic writings* (New York: Paulist Press, 1988).

van Haemstede, Adriaen Cornelis, *De Gheschiedenisse ende den doodt der vromer Martelaren* . . . ([Emden: Gilles van der Erve], 1559).

[Verstegan, Richard], *Theatrum crudelitatum haereticorum nostri temporis* (Antwerp: Adrien Hubert, 1587).

Warhaffte hystorien. Von dem frummen zeügen und marterer Christi Johansen Heüglin von Lindaw . . . [Nuremberg: Jobst Gutknecht, 1527].

Secondary sources

Allison, A. F., and Rogers, D. M. (eds.), *The contemporary printed literature of the English Counter-Reformation between 1558 and 1640.* 2 vols. (Aldershot: Scolar Press, 1989–94).

De Backer, Augustin, *Essai bibliographique sur le livre 'De imitatione Christi".* (1864; rpt. Amsterdam: Desclée de Brouwer, 1966).

Bibliography

Burke, Peter, 'How to be a Counter-Reformation saint'. In Kaspar Von Greyerz (ed.), *Religion and society in early modern Europe, 1500–1800* (London: German Historical Institute, 1984), pp. 45–55.

Clasen, Claus Peter, 'Executions of Anabaptists, 1525–1618: a research report'. *Mennonite Quarterly Review* 47 (1973): 115–52.

Decavele, Johan, *De dageraad van de reformatie in Vlaanderen (1520–1565)*. 2 vols. (Brussels: Paleis der Academiën, 1975).

Dillon, Anne, *The construction of martyrdom in the English Catholic community, 1535–1603* (Aldershot: Ashgate Press, 2002).

Dyck, Cornelius J., 'The suffering church in Anabaptism', *Mennonite Quarterly Review* 59 (1985): 5–23.

El Kenz, David. *Les bûchers du roi: La culture protestante des martyres 1523–1572* (Seyssel: Champs Vallon, 1997).

Freedburg, David, 'The representation of martyrdoms during the early Counter-Reformation in Antwerp', *Burlington Magazine* 118 (1976): 128–38.

Gilmont, Jean-François, *Jean Crespin: Un éditeur réformé du XVIe siècle* (Geneva: Droz, 1981).

Goosens, Aline, *Les inquisitions modernes dans Les Pays-Bas meridionaux (1520–1633)*. 2 vols. (Brussels: Editions de l'Université de Bruxelles, 1997–8).

Gougaud, Louis, *Dévotions et pratiques ascétiques du moyen âge* (Paris: Desclée de Brouwer, 1925).

Gregory, Brad S., *Salvation at stake: Christian martyrdom in early modern Europe* (Cambridge, MA: Harvard University Press, 1999).

Grell, Ole Peter, and Scribner, Bob (eds.), *Tolerance and intolerance in the European Reformation* (Cambridge: Cambridge University Press, 1996).

Hebenstreit-Wilfert, Hildegard, 'Märtyrerflugschriften der Reformationszeit'. In Hans-Joachim Köhler (ed.), *Flugschriften als Massenmedium der Reformationszeit* (Stuttgart: Klett-Cotta, 1981), pp. 397–446.

Herz, Alexandra, 'Imitators of Christ: the martyr-cycles of late sixteenth century Rome seen in context', *Storia dell'arte* 62 (1988): 53–70.

Highley, Christopher, and King, John N. (eds.), *John Foxe and his world* (Aldershot: Ashgate, 2002).

Hofman, Bert, 'Gereformeerden en doopsgezinden in de spiegel van de schriftuurlijke liederen in de zesitende eeuw', *Doopsgezinde Bijdragen*, new series, 20 (1994): 61–9.

Hsia, R. Po-chia, *The world of Catholic renewal, 1540–1770* (Cambridge: Cambridge University Press, 1998).

Jelsma, A. J., *Adriaan van Haemstede en zijn martelaarsboek* (The Hague: Boekencentrum, 1970).

Kieckhefer, Richard, *Repression of heresy in medieval Germany* (Philadelphia: University of Pennsylvania Press, 1979).

Kolb, Robert, *For all the saints: changing perceptions of martyrdom and sainthood in the Lutheran reformation* (Macon, GA: Mercer State University Press, 1987).

Kreider, Alan F., '"The servant is not greater than his master": the Anabaptists and the suffering church', *Mennonite Quarterly Review* 58 (1984): 5–29.

Lieseberg, Ursula, *Studien zum Märtyrerlied der Täufer im 16. Jahrhundert* (Frankfurt am Main: Peter Lang, 1991).

Loades, David (ed.), *John Foxe and the English Reformation* (Aldershot: Scolar Press, 1997).
John Foxe: an historical perspective (Aldershot: Ashgate, 1999).

Lovatt, Roger, 'The *Imitation of Christ* in late medieval England', *Transactions of the Royal Historical Society*, 5th series, 18 (1968), pp. 97–121.

Mâle, Emile, *L'art religieux de la fin du XVIe siècle, du XVIIe siècle et du XVIIIe siècle: Etude sur l'iconographie après le concile de Trent.* 2nd edn (Paris: Armand Colin, 1951), pp. 109– 49.

McCabe, William H., *An introduction to Jesuit theater.* Ed. Louis J. Oldani (St Louis: Institute of Jesuit Resources, 1983).

Mentzer, Raymond F., *Heresy proceedings in Languedoc, 1500–1560* (Philadelphia: American Philosophical Society, 1984).

Monter, William, 'Heresy executions in reformation Europe'. In Ole Peter Grell and Robert Scribner (eds.), *Tolerance and intolerance in the European Reformation* (Cambridge: Cambridge University Press, 1996), pp. 48–65.

Judging the French Reformation: heresy trials by sixteenth-century parlements (Cambridge, MA: Harvard University Press, 1999).

Moore, R. I., *The formation of a persecuting society: power and deviance in western Europe, 950–1250* (New York: Blackwell, 1987).

Moreau, E. de, *Histoire de l'église de Belgique* (Brussels: L'Edition universelle, 1952), vol. 5.

Nalle, Sara Tilghman, *Mad for God: Bartolomé Sánchez, the secret messiah of Cardenete* (Charlottesville: University Press of Virginia, 2001).

Nicholls, David, 'The theatre of martyrdom in the French Reformation', *Past and Present* 121 (1988): 49–73.

Nuttall, Geoffrey F., 'The English martyrs 1535–1680: a statistical review', *Journal of Ecclesiastical History* 22 (1971): 191–7.

Packull, Werner O., *Hutterite beginnings: Communitarian experiments during the Reformation* (Baltimore: Johns Hopkins University Press, 1995).

Pettegree, Andrew, *Emden and the Dutch revolt: exile and the development of Reformed Protestantism* (Oxford: Clarendon Press, 1992).

Pollard, A. W. *et al.* (eds.), *A short-title catalogue of books printed in England, Ireland, Scotland and Wales, and of English books printed abroad, 1475–1640.* 2nd edn, 3 vols. (London: Bibliographical Society, 1976–91).

Reames, Sherry L., *The Legenda aurea: a reexamination of its paradoxical history* (Madison: University of Wisconsin Press, 1985).

Rush, Alfred C., 'Spiritual martyrdom in St. Gregory the Great', *Theological Studies* 23 (1962): 569–89.

Seidel Menchi, Silvana (ed.), *Ketzerverfolgung im 16. und frühen 17. Jahrhundert* (Wolffenbüttel: Harrassowitz, 1992).

Tedeschi, John, *The prosecution of heresy: collected studies on the Inquisition in early modern Italy* (Binghamton, NY: Medieval and Renaissance Texts and Studies, 1991).

Valentin, Jean-Marie, *Le théatre des jésuites dans les pays de langue allemande (1554–1680).* 3 vols. (Berne: Peter Lang, 1978).

van de Wiele, Johan, 'De inquisitierechtbank van Pieter Titelmans in de zestiende eeuw in Vlaanderen', *Bijdragen en mededelingen betreffende de geschiedenis der Nederlanden* 97 (1982): 19–63.

Vander Haeghen, Ferdinand *et al.* (eds.), *Bibliographie des martyrologes protestants néerlandais*. 2 vols. (The Hague: Martinus Nijhoff, 1890).

Vander Haeghen, Ferdinand, and Lenger, Marie-Thérèse (eds.), *Bibliotheca belgica*. 7 vols. (Brussels: Culture et civilisation, 1964–75).

White, Helen, *Tudor books of saints and martyrs* (Madison: University of Wisconsin Press, 1963).

Winston-Allen, Anne, *Stories of the rose: the making of the rosary in the Middle Ages* (University Park, PA: Pennsylvania State University Press, 1997).

Wood, Diana (ed.), *Martyrs and martyrologies*. Studies in Church History, 30 (Oxford: Blackwell, 1993).

16 THE MEDITERRANEAN INQUISITIONS OF EARLY MODERN EUROPE

Secondary sources

Amiel, Charles (ed.), *Relation de l'Inquisition de Goa par Charles Dellon (1687)* (Paris: Chandeigne, 1997).

Bailey, Michael, *Battling demons: witchcraft, heresy and reform in the late Middle Ages* (University Park, PA: Pennsylvania State University Press, 2003).

Bennassar, Bartolomé and Lucile, *Les Chrétiens d'Allah* (Paris: Perrin, 1989).

Bethencourt, Francisco, *L'Inquisition à l'époque moderne. Espagne, Portugal, Italie XVe–XIXe siècle* (Paris: Fayard, 1995).

'Les hérétiques et l'Inquisition portugaise: représentations et pratiques de persecution'. In S. Seidel Menchi (ed.), *Ketzerverfolgung im 16. und frühen 17. Jahrhundert* (Wiesbaden: Harrassowitz, 1992), pp. 103–17.

Carrasco, Rafael, *Inquisición y represión sexual en Valencia* (Barcelona: Laertes, 1985).

Contreras, Jaime, *El Santo Oficio de la Inquisición de Galicia (poder, sociedad y cultura)* (Madrid: Akal, 1982).

Sotos contra Riquelmes (Madrid: Anaya & M. Muchnik, 1992).

Dedieu, Jean-Pierre, *L'administration de la foi. L'Inquisition de Tolède, XVI–XVIIe siècle* (Madrid: Casa de Velázquez, 1989).

Del Col, Andrea, *Domenico Scandella known as Menocchio: his trials before the Inquisition (1583–1599)*. Trans. J. and A. Tedeschi (Binghamton: MRTS, 1996).

Di Simplicio, Oscar, *Inquisizione Stregoneria Medicina. Siena e il suo stato 1580–1721* (Siena: Il leccio, 2000).

Firpo, Massimo, and Marcatto, Domenico (eds.), *Il processo inquisitoriale del Cardinal Giovanni Morone*. 6 vols. (Rome: Istituto storico italiano per l'età moderna e contemporanea, 1981–95).

Fragnito, Gigliola, *La Bibbia al rogo: La censura ecclesiastica e i volgarizzamenti della Scrittura (1471–1605)* (Bologna: Il Mulino, 1997).

Fragnito, Gigliola (ed.), *Church, censorship and culture in early modern Italy* (Cambridge: Cambridge Univesity Press, 2001).

García Cárcel, Ricardo, *Orígines de la Inquisición española: El tribunal de Valencia (1478–1530)* (Barcelona: Ediciones Península, 1976).

Herejía y sociedad. La Inquisición en Valencia 1530–1609 (Barcelona: Ediciones Península, 1980).

Ginzburg, Carlo, *The cheese and the worms* (Baltimore: Johns Hopkins University Press, 1980). *The night battles* (Baltimore: Johns Hopkins University Press, 1983).

Godman, Peter, *The saint as censor: Robert Bellarmine between Inquisition and Index* (Leiden: Brill, 2001).

Grendler, Paul, *The Roman Inquisition and the Venetian press, 1540–1605* (Princeton: Princeton University Press, 1977).

Haliczer, Stephen, *Inquisition and society in the kingdom of Valencia, 1478–1834* (Berkeley: University of California Press, 1990).

Henningsen, Gustav, 'El "banco de datos" del Santo Oficio: las relaciones de causas de la Inquisición española (1550–1700)', *Boletín de la Real Academia de la Historia* 174 (1977): 547–70.

The witches' advocate: Basque witchcraft and the Spanish Inquisition (Reno, NV: University of Nevada Press, 1980).

Henningsen, Gustav, and Tedeschi, John (eds.), *The Inquisition in early modern Europe: studies in sources and methods* (DeKalb, IL: Northern Illinois University Press, 1986).

'The database of the Spanish Inquisition: the *relaciones de causas* project revisited'. In H. Mohnhaupt and D. Simon (eds.), *Vorträge zur Justizforschung. Geschichte und Theorie.* 2 vols. (Frankfurt-am-Main: V. Klostermann, 1993), vol. 2, pp. 43–85.

Ioly Zorattini, P. C., *Processi del S. Uffizio di Venezia contra Ebrei e Giudaizzanti.* 8 vols. (Florence: L. S. Olschki, 1980–).

Kamen, Henry, *The Spanish Inquisition* (New Haven: Yale University Press, 1997).

Lea, Henry Charles, *A history of the Spanish Inquisition.* 4 vols. (New York: Macmillan, 1908–12).

Martin, John, *Venice's hidden enemies* (Berkeley: University of California Press, 1993).

Monter, William, *Frontiers of heresy: the Spanish Inquisition from the Basque lands to Sicily* (Cambridge: Cambridge University Press, 1990).

Judging the French Reformation: heresy trials by sixteenth-century French parlements (Cambridge, MA: Harvard University Press, 1999).

'The Roman Inquisition and Protestant heresy executions in 16th century Europe'. In *Atti del Simposio internazionale sull'Inquisizione (29–31 ottobre 1998).* Ed. Agostino Borromeo (Vatican City: Biblioteca Apostolica Vaticana, Studi e testi, 2003), pp. 535–44.

Nalle, Sara, *God in La Mancha, 1500–1650* (Baltimore: Johns Hopkins University Press, 1992).

Mad for God: Bartolomé Sánchez, secret messiah of Cadenete (Charlottesville, VA: University Press of Viginia, 2001).

Nardon, Franco, *Benandanti e inquisitori nel Friuli del Seicento* (Trieste: Edizioni Università di Trieste, 1999).

Netanyahu, Benjamin, *Origins of the Spanish Inquisition.* 2nd edn (New York: 2000).

Paiva, José, *Bruxaria e superstição num pais sem 'caça às bruxa'* (Lisbon: Notícias, 1997).

Pardo Tomás, José, *Ciencia y censura. La Inquisición española y los libros científicos en los siglos XVI y XVII* (Madrid: Consejo Superior de Investigaciones Científicas, 1991).

Prosperi, Adriano, *Tribunali della coscienza. Inquisitori, confessori, missionary* (Turin: G. Einaudi, 1996).

Pullan, Brian, *The Jews of Europe and the Inquisition of Venice 1550–1670* (Totowa, NJ: Barnes and Noble, 1983).

Redondi, Pietro, *Galileo heretic* (Princeton: Princeton University Press, 1987; Italian edn, 1983).

Romeo, Giovanni, *Inquisitori, esorcisti e streghe nell'Italia dalla Contrariforma* (Florence: Sansoni, 1990).

Saraiva, Antonio, *Inquisição e critãos novos* (Porto: Editorial Inova, 1969).

Schutte, Anne J. (ed. and trans.), *Autobiography of an aspiring saint* (Chicago: University of Chicago Press, 1996).

Seidel Menchi, Silvana, *Erasmo in Italia, 1520–1580* (Turin: Bollati Boringhieri, 1987).

Tedeschi, John A., *The prosecution of heresy: collected studies on the Inquistion in early modern Italy* (Binghamton, NY: Medieval Texts and Studies, 1991).

Tellechea Idígoras, José Ignacio, *Fray Bartolomé Carranza y Cardenal Pole: un Navarro en la restauración católica de Inglaterra (1554–1558)* (Pamplona: Diputación Foral de Navarra, Institución Príncipe de Viana, Consejo Superior de Investigaciones Científicas, 1977).

Vincent, Bernard, *Minorias y marginados en la España del siglo XVI* (Granada, 1987).

17 RELIGIOUS COLLOQUIES AND TOLERATION

Augustijn, C., 'Die Religionsgespräche der vierziger Jahre'. In G. Müller (dir.), *Die Religionsgespräche der Reformationszeit* (Gütersloh: Güterslöher Verlaghaus G. Mohn, 1980), pp. 43–53.

Barta, G. *et al.* (eds.), *Kurze Geschichte Siebenbürgens* (Budapest: Akadémiai Kiadó, 1990).

Benedict, P., '*Un roi, une loi, deux fois*: parameters for the history of Catholic–Protestant coexistence in France, 1555–1685'. In Ole Peter Grell and Robert Scribner (eds.), *Tolerance and intolerance in the European Reformation* (Cambridge: Cambridge University Press, 1996), pp. 65–93.

Binder, L., *Grundlagen und Formen der Toleranz in Siebenbürgen bis zur Mitte des 17. Jahrhundert* (Cologne: Böhlau, 1976).

Brunner, O., Conze, W., and Koselleck, R. (eds.), *Geschichtliche Grundbegriffe* (Stuttgart: E. Klett, 1972).

Carbonnier-Burkardt, Marianne, 'Les préambules des édits de pacification (1562–1598)'. In M. Grandjean and B. Roussel (eds.), *Coexister dans l'intolérance. L'édit de Nantes (1598)*. (Geneva: Labor et Fides, 1998), pp. 75–92.

Christin, O., 'La formation étatique de l'espace savant : les colloques religieux des XVIe–XVIIe siècles', *Actes de la Recherche en Sciences sociales* (133): 53–61.

La paix de religion. L'autonomisation de la raison politique au XVIe siècle (Paris: Le Seuil, 1997).

'Peace must come from us: friendship pacts between the confessions during the Wars of Religion'. In R. Whelan and C. Baxter (eds.), *Toleration and religious identity. The Edict of Nantes and its implications in France, Britain and Ireland* (Dublin: Four Court Press, 2003), pp. 92–103.

Crouzet, D., *La sagesse et le malheur. Michel de L'Hospital, chancelier de France* (Seyssel: Champ Vallon, 1998).

Descimon, R. (ed.), *Michel de l'Hospital. Discours pour la majorité de Charles IX et trois autres discours* (Paris: Imprimerie nationale, 1993).

Diestelkamp, B. (ed.), *Die Politische Funktion des Reichskammergericht* (Cologne: Böhlau, 1993).

Dompnier, B., *Le venin de l'hérésie. Image du protestantisme et combat catholique au XVIIe siècle* (Paris: Le Centurion, 1985).

Duffy, E., *The stripping of the altars. Traditional religion in England 1400–1580* (New Haven: Yale University Press, 1992).

Dufour, A., 'Das Religionsgespräch von Poissy. Hoffnungen der Reformierten und der "Moyenneurs"'. In G. Müller (dir.), *Die Religionsgespräche der Reformationszeit* (Gütersloh: Güterslöher Verlaghaus G. Mohn, 1980), pp. 117–26.

Fischer, R. (ed.), *Appenzeller Land. Landschaft, Geschichte, Kultur* (Bühl / Baden, 1978).

Fischer, R. *et al.* (eds.), *Appenzeller Geschichte. Zur 450-Jahrfeier des Appenzellerbundes* (Appenzell: Kantonskanzleien, 1964–93).

Foa, J., 'Le métier de la dispute'. MA University of Lyon-II.

Fuchs, T., *Konfession und Gespräch. Typologie und Funktion der Religionsgespräche in der Reformationszeit* (Cologne: Böhlau, 1995).

Fumaroli, M. (ed.), *Histoire de la rhétorique dans l'Europe moderne* (Paris: Presses Universitaires de France, 1999).

Grandjean, M., and Roussel, B. (eds.), *Coexister dans l'intolérance. L'édit de Nantes (1598)* (Geneva: Labor et Fides, 1998).

Grell, Ole Peter, and Scribner, Robert (eds.), *Tolerance and intolerance in the European Reformation* (Cambridge: Cambridge University Press, 1996).

Guggisberg, H. R., 'Wandel der Argumente für religiöse Toleranz und Glaubensfreiheit im 16. Jahrhundert'. In H. Lutz (ed.), *Zur Geschichte der Toleranz und Religionsfreiheit* (Darmstadt: Wissenschaftliche Buchgesellschaft, 1977), pp. 455–81.

Harding, R. H., 'The mobilization of confraternities against the Reformation in France', *Sixteenth Century Journal* 11 (1980): 85–107.

Hartweg, F., 'Luther et l'autorité temporelle'. In J.-M. Valentin, *Luther et la Réforme. Du commentaire de l'Epître aux Romains à la Messe allemande* (Paris: Editions Desjonquères, 2001).

Head, R. C., 'Fragmented dominion, fragmented churches: the institutionalization of the Landfrieden in the Thurgau, 1531–1660' (forthcoming).

'Religious coexistence and confessional conflict in the Vier Dörfer: practices of toleration in Eastern Switzerland, 1525–1615'. In John C. Laursen and Cary J. Nederman (eds.), *Beyond the persecuting society: religious toleration before the Enlightenment* (Philadelphia: University of Pennsylvania Press, 1997), pp. 145–65.

Heckel, M., 'Die Reformationsprozesse im Spannungfeld des Reichskirchensystems'. In B. Diestelkamp (ed.), *Die Politische Funktion des Reichskammergericht.* (Cologne: Böhlau, 1993), pp. 9–40.

Huseman, W. H., 'The expression of the idea of toleration in French during the sixteenth century', *Sixteenth Century Journal* 15 (1984): 294–310.

Jouanna, A. (ed.), *Histoire et dictionnaire des guerres de religion* (Paris: Robert Laffont, 1998).

Kaplan, B., 'Fictions of privacy: house chapels and the spatial accommodation of religious dissent in early modern Europe'. *American Historical Journal* 107 (2002): 1031–64.

Koslofsky, C., *The reformation of the dead: death and ritual in early modern Germany, 1450–1700* (Basingstoke: Macmillan, 2000).

Kunisch, Johannes, *Neue Studien zur frühneuzeitlichen Reichsgeschichte* (Berlin: Duncker und Humblot, 1987).

Laursen, John C., and Nederman, Cary J., (eds.), *Beyond the persecuting society: religious toleration before the Enlightenment* (Philadelphia: University of Pennsylvania Press, 1997).

Luria, K., 'Separated by death? Burials, cemeteries, and confessional boundaries in seventeenth-century France', *French Historical Studies*, 24 (2001): 185–222.

Lutz, H. (ed.), *Zur Geschichte der Toleranz und Religionsfreiheit* (Darmstadt: Wissenschaftliche Buchgesellschaft, 1977).

Margolin, J.-C., 'L'apogée de la rhétorique humaniste'. In M. Fumaroli (ed.), *Histoire de la rhétorique dans l'Europe moderne* (Paris: Presses Universitaires de France, 1999).

Müller, G. (ed.), *Die Religionsgespräche der Reformationszeit* (Gütersloh: Güterslöher Verlaghaus G. Mohn, 1980).

Müller, M., 'Protestant confessionalisation in the towns of Royal Prussia and the practice of religious toleration in Poland-Lithuania'. In Ole Peter Grell and Robert Scribner (eds.), *Tolerance and intolerance in the European Reformation* (Cambridge: Cambridge University Press, 1996), pp. 262–81.

Peter, K., 'Tolerance and intolerance in sixteenth-century Hungary'. In Ole Peter Grell and Robert Scribner (eds.), *Tolerance and intolerance in the European Reformation* (Cambridge: Cambridge University Press, 1996).

Scheurmann, I. (ed.), *Frieden durch Recht. Das Reichskammergericht von 1495 bis 1806* (Mainz: P. von Zabern, 1994).

Schreiner, K., 'Tolerantz'. In O. Brunner, W. Conze, and R. Koselleck (eds.), *Geschichtliche Grundbegriffe* (Stuttgart: E. Klett, 1972–97), pp. 445–605.

Schulze, Winfried, 'Concordia, Discordia, Tolerantia. Deutsche Politik im konfessionellen Zeitalter'. In Johannes Kunisch (ed.), *Neue Studien zur frühneuzeitlichen Reichsgeschichte. Zeitschrift für historische Forschung*, Beiheft 3 (Berlin, Duncker and Humblot, 1987). pp. 43–79.

Tazbir, J., *Geschichte der polnische Toleranz* (Warsaw: Verlag Interpress, 1977), pp. 52–67.

Turchetti, M., *Concordia o tolleranza. François Bauduin (1520–1573) e i Moyenneurs* (Geneva: Droz, 1984).

Valentin, J.-M., *Luther et la Réforme. Du commentaire de l'Epître aux Romains à la Messe allemande* (Paris: Editions Desjonquères, 2001).

Walder, E. (ed.), *Religionsvergleiche des 16. Jahrhunderts* (Bern: H. Lang 1945).

Wanegffelen, T., *L'édit de Nantes. Une histoire européenne de la tolérance (XVI–XX siècle)* (Paris: Le Livre de Poche, 1998).

Ni Rome ni Genève, Des fidèles entre deux chaires en France au XVIe siècle (Paris: Honoré Champion, 1997), p. 131.

Warmbrunn, P., *Zwei Konfessionen in einer Stadt. Das Zusammenleben von Katholiken und Protestanten in den paritätischen Reichsstädten Augsburg, Biberach, Ravensburg und Dinkelsbühl von 1548 bis 1648* (Wiesbaden: F. Steiner, 1983).

Whelan, R., and Baxter, C. (eds.), *Toleration and religious identity. The Edict of Nantes and its implications in France, Britain and Ireland* (Dublin: Four Court Press, 2003).

18 WESTERN CHRISTIANITY AND EASTERN ORTHODOXY
Dictionaries and reference works

Albert, M., Beylot, R. et al., *Christianismes orientaux. Introduction à l'étude des langues et des littératures* (Paris: Cerf, 1993).

The Blackwell dictionary of Eastern Christianity. Ed. K. Parry, D. J. Melling et al. (Oxford: Blackwell, 1999).

Handbuch der Ostkirchenkunde (Düsseldorf: Patmos, 1984–9), vols. 1–2.

Hierarchia ecclesiastica orientalis: series episcoporum ecclesiarum christianarum orientalium. Ed. Giorgio Fedalto. 2 vols. (Padua: Messagero, 1988).

Janin, R., *Les Eglises orientales et les rites orientaux*. 5th edn (Paris: Letouzey et Ané, 1997).

Kleines Wörterbuch des christlichen Orients. Ed. J. Assfalg and Paul Krüger (Wiesbaden: Otto Harrassowitz, 1975).

Legrand, E., *Bibliographie hellénique ou description raisonnée des ouvrages publiés par des Grecs au XVe et XVIe siècles*. Vols. 1–4 (Paris: 1888–1906; Paris: Reed, 1962).

Bibliographie hellénique ou description raisonnée des ouvrages publiés par des Grecs au XVIIe siècle. Vols. 1–4 (Paris: 1894–1903; Brussels: Reed, 1963).

Primary sources

Acta S. Congregationis de Propaganda Fide Ecclesiam Catholicam Ucrainae et Bielorusjae spectantia. Ed. A. Welykyj. Vol. 1 (Rome: P. P. Basiliani, 1953).

Acta et Scripta Theologorum Wirtembergensium et Patriarchae Constantinopolitani D. Hieremiae (Wittenberg, 1584).

Allatius, L., *De ecclesiae occidentalis atque orientalis perpetua consensione* (Cologne, 1648).

Artykuly na które caucij potrzebuiemy od panów Rzymian pierwei anizli do iednosci s Kościołem Rzymskim przestapiemy. In *Documenta Unionis Berestensis eiusque auctorum (1590–1600)*. Ed. A. G. Welykyi (Rome, 1970), pp. 61–7; Latin trans. pp. 68–75.

Baronius, C., *Discours véritable de la réunion des églises d'Alexandrie et de Russie à la saincte église catholique, apostolique et romaine . . . Discours de l'origine des Russiens et de leur miraculeuse conversion, et de quelques actes mémorables de leurs rois. Traduict en françois du latin de . . . Cesar Baronius, par M. Marc Lescarbot* (Paris: C. Morel, 1599).

Congregationes particulares Ecclesiam Catholicam Ucrainae et Bielorusjae spectantes. Vol. 1 (1622–1728). Ed. A. Welykyi (Rome: P. P. Basiliani, 1956).

[Crusius, Martinus], *Turcograeciae libri octo, a Martino Crusio, . . . edita, quibus Graecorum status sub imperio Turcico in politia et ecclesia . . . describitur* (Basle: L. Ostenius, 1584).

Documenta Pontificum Romanorum historiam Ucrainae illustrantia (1075–1953). Vol. 1 (1622–1728). Ed. A. Welykyi (Rome: P. P. Basiliani, 1953).

Documenta Unionis Berestensis eiusque auctorum (1590–1600). Ed. A. Welykyi (Rome: P. P. Basiliani, 1970).

Epistolae Josephi Velamin Rutskyj, metropolitae Kioviensis catholici (1613–1637). Ed. T. T. Haluscynskyj and A. G. Welykyi (Rome: P. P. Basiliani, 1956).

Epistolae metropolitarum Kioviensium Catholicorum Raphaelis Korsak, Antonii Sielava, Gabrielis Kolenda (1637–1674). Ed. A. Welykyi (Rome: P. P. Basiliani, 1956).

Gerlach, M. Samuel, *Stephan Gerlachs des Aelteren Tagebuch* (Frankfurt am Main, 1674).

Gerlach, Stephan, *Türckisches Tagebuch* (Frankfurt am Main, 1673).

Lasicki, Jan, *De Russorum, Moscovitarum et Tartarorum religione, sacrificiis, nuptiarum, funerum Ritue diversis scriptoribus* (Spira: B. d'Albinus, 1582).

Litterae Basilianorum in terris Ucrainae et Bielarusjae. Vol. 1: 1601–1730. Ed. A. Welykyi (Rome: P. P. Basiliani, 1979).

Litterae episcoporum historiam Ucrainae illustrantes (1600–1900). Vol. 1: 1600–1640. Ed. A. Welykyi (Rome: P. P. Basiliani, 1972). Vol. 2: 1641–1664. Ed. A. Welykyi (Rome: P. P. Basiliani, 1973).

Litterae nuntiorum apostolicorum historiam Ucrainae illustrantes. Ed. A. Welykyi (Rome: P. P. Basiliani, 1959–61), vols. 1–8.

Litterae S. Congregationis de Propaganda Fide Ecclesiam Catholicam Ucrainae et Bielorusjae spectantes. Ed. A. Welykyi (Rome: P. P. Basiliani, 1954), vol. 1.

Moghila, P., *La confession orthodoxe de Pierre Moghila*. Latin text. Ed. A. Malvy and M. Viller. Orientalia Christiana, 10, no. 39 (Rome and Paris: Pont. Institutum Orientalium Studiorum, 1927).

Monumenta Ucrainae historica, vol. 2 (1624–1648): *Zibrav mitr. A. Shupticki?*(Rome, 1965); vols. 9–10 (1075–1632): *Supplementum* (Rome, 1971).

Papadopoulos, T. H., *Studies and documents relating to the history of the Greek Church and people under Turkish domination* (Brussels, 1952).

[Socolovius, S.], *Censura orientalis ecclesiae de praecipuis nostri saeculi haereticorum dogmatibus, Hieremiae constantinopolitano patriarchae, judicii et mutuae communionis causa, ab orthodoxae doctrinae adversariis non ita pridem oblatis, ab eodem patriarcha . . . ad Germanos graece conscripta, a Stanislao autem Socolovio . . . ex graeco in latinum conversa* (Paris: A. Sittart, 1854).

Vetera monumenta Poloniae et Lithuaniae gentiumque finitarum historiam illustrantia. Ed. A. Theiner. Vols 1–4 (Rome: Vatican Press, 1860–4).

Secondary sources

Amman, A. M., 'Der Aufenhalt der ruthenischen Bischofe H. Pociej und C. Terlecki in Rom im Dezember und Januar 1595–1596'. *Orientalia Christiana Periodica* 11 (1945): 105–40.

Baan, I., 'La pénétration de l'Uniatisme en Ukraine sub-carpathique au XVIIe siècle'. *XVIIème Siècle* 2003/3 (juillet–septembre). Numéro spécial: 'La frontière entre les chrétientés grecque et latine au XVIIème siècle. De la Lithuanie à l'Ukraine subcarpathique', pp. 515–26.

Bendza, M., 'Orthodox–protestantische Unionstendenzen im 16. Jh. in Polen', *Ostkirchliche Studien* 35/1 (1986): 3–16.

'Diecezja Przemyska w latach 1596–1681'. *Studium historyczno-kanoniczne* (Warsaw, 1982).

Benz, E., *Wittenberg und Byzanz. zur Begegnung und Auseinandersetzung der Reformation und der östlich-orthodoxen Kirche*. 2nd edn (Munich: Wilhelm Fink Verlag, 1971).

Bogovic, M., *Katolicka crkva i pravoslavije u Dalmaciji za vrieme mletacke vladavine*. Analecta Croatica Christiana, 14 (Zagreb: Kršćanska sadašnost, 1982).

Buri, V., *L'unione della chiesa copta con Roma sotto Clemente VIII* (Rome: Institutum Orientalium Studiorum, 1931).

Chodynicki, K., *Kościół prawoslawny a Rzeczpospolita Polska. Zarys historyczny. 1370–1632* (Warsaw: Sklad gl. Kasa im. Mianowskiego, 1934).

Croce, G., 'Les Eglises orientales'. In Jean Mayeur (ed.), *Histoire du christianisme des origines à nos jours* (Paris: Desclée, 1997), vol. 9, *L'Age de raison (1620–1750)*, pp. 540–612.

'Orient et Occident'. In Jean Mayeur (ed.), *Histoire du christianisme des origines à nos jours* (Paris: Desclée, 1997), vol. 9, *L'Age de raison (1620–1750)*, pp. 603–9.

Daugsch, W., 'Toleranz in Fürstentum Siebenbürgen. Politische und Gesellschaftliche Voraussetzungen der Religionsgesetzgebung im 16. und 17. Jh.', *Kirche im Osten* 26 (1983): 35–72.

Dmitriev, M. V., 'Les confréries de Ruthénie dans la deuxième moitié du Xve siècle – une "Réforme orthodoxe"?' In M. Derwich and M. Dmitriev (eds.), *Etre catholique, être orthodoxe, être protestant dans l'Europe médiévale et moderne* (Warsaw: Wydawnictwo Uniwersitetu Wrocławskiego, 2003).

Mezhdu Rimom i Tsargradom. Genesis Brestskoï tserkovnoï unii 1595–1596 gg. (Moscow: Izdvo MGU, 2003).

Dmitriev, M. V., Florja, B. N., and Yakovenko, S. G., *Brestskaia unia 1596 g. i obshchestvenno-politicheskaia bor'ba na Ukraine i v Belorussii v kontse XVI–nachape XVII v.* Part 1: *Brestskaia unia 1596 g. Istoricheskie prichiny* (Moscow, 1996).

Dmitriev, M. V., Zabrovskiï, L. V., Turilov, A. A., and Florja, B. N., *Brestskaia unia 1596 g. i obshchestvenno-politicheskaia bor'ba na Ukraine i v Belorussii v kontse XVI–XVII v.* Part 2: *Brestskaia unia 1596 g. Istoricheskie posledstviia sobytnia* (Moscow, 1999).

Draganovic, K., 'Massenübertritte von Katholiken zur "Orthodoxie" im kroatischen Sprachgebiet zur Zeit der Türkenherrschaft'. *Orientalia Christiana Periodica* 3 (1937): 181–232.

Ducellier, A., 'L'Orthodoxie'. In Jean Mayeur (ed.), *Histoire du christianisme des origines à nos jours* (Paris: Desclée, 1992), vol. 8: M. Venard (ed.), *Le Temps des confessions (1530–1620/30)*, pp. 323–50.

Dujcev, I., *Il cattolicesimo in Bulgaria nel secolo XVII* (Rome, 1937).

Dziegielewski, J., *O tolerancje dla zdominowanych. Polityka wyznaniowa Rzeczypospolitej w latach panowania Wladysława IV* (Warsaw: Panstwowe Wydawnictwo Nauka, 1986).

Fedalto, G., *Ricerche storiche sulla posizione giuridica ed ecclesiastica dei Greci a Venezia nei secoli XV e XVI* (Florence: Olschki, 1967).

Le Chiese d'Oriente, vol. 2: *Dalla caduta di Costantinopoli alla fine del Cinquecento* (Milan: Jaca, 1993); vol. 3: *Dal Seicento ai nostri giorni* (Milan: Jaca, 1994).

Massimo Margunio e il suo commento al 'De Trinitate' di S. Agostino (1588) (Brescia: Paideia, 1967).

Florja, B. N., 'Les conflits religieux entre adversaires et partisans de l'Union dans la "conscience de masse" du peuple en Ukraine et en Biélorussie (première moitié du XVIIe siècle)', *XVIIème Siècle* 2003/3 (juillet–septembre). Numéro spécial: 'La frontière entre les chrétientés grecque et latine au XVIIème siècle. De la Lithuanie à l'Ukraine subcarpathique', pp. 431–48.

Geanakoplos, D. J., *Byzantine East and Latin West* (Oxford: Blackwell, 1966).

Greek scholars in Venice (Cambridge, MA: Harvard University Press, 1962).

Interaction of the 'sibling' Byzantine and Western cultures in the Middle Ages and Italian Renaissance (330–1600) (New Haven: Yale University Press, 1976).

Golubev, S. T., *Kievskii mitropolit Petr Mogila i ego spodvizhniki. Opyt istoricheskogo issledovaniya*. (Kiev, 1893–8), vols. 1–2.

Gudziak, B. A., *Crisis and reform. The Kyivan Metropolitanate, the Patriarchate of Constantinople, and the genesis of the Union of Brest*. Harvard Series on Ukrainian Studies (Cambridge, MA: Harvard University Press, 1998).

Halecki, O., *From Florence to Brest (1439–1596)*. 2nd edn (Hamden, CT: Archon, 1968).

Hering, G., 'Orthodoxie und Protestantismus'. *Jahrbuch der Österreichischen Byzantinistik* 31 (1981): 823–74.

Ökumenisches Patriarchat und europäische Politik. 1620–1638. Veröffentlichungen des Instituts für Europäische Geschichte, 45 (Wiesbaden: Steiner, 1968).

Heyberger, B., *Les Chrétiens du Proche-Orient au temps de la Réforme catholique* (Rome: Ecole française de Rome, Palais Farnèse, 1994).

'Réforme catholique et union des Eglises orientales (XVIe–XVIIIe siècles)'. In Jean Delumeau (ed.), *Homo religiosus. Autour de Jean Delumeau* (Paris: Fayard, 1997), pp. 292–8.

Iorga, N., *Byzance après Byzance* (Paris: Balland, 1992).

Isaievych, I., 'Between Eastern tradition and influences from the West: confraternities in early modern Ukraine and Byelorussia'. In G. Brogi Bercoff (ed.), *La percepzione del Medioevo nell'epoca del Barrocco: Polonia, Ucraina, Russia*, Atti del Congresso tenutosi a Urbino, 3–8 iuglio 1989 (= *Ricerche Slavistiche* 37 (1990)) (Rome, 1990), pp. 269–93.

Jobert, A., *De Luther à Mohila: la Pologne dans la crise de la chrétienté, 1517–1648* (Paris: Institut d'études slaves, 1974).

Karalevskij, C., 'L'istruzione di Clemente VIII, "Super aliquibus ritibus Graecorum (1595)"' and 'Le Congregazioni per la riforma dei Greci (1593)', *Bessarione* 17 (1913): 344–65, 466–81.

Krajcar, J., 'Konstantin Basil Ostrozski and Rome in 1582–1584', *OCP* 35 (1969): 193–214.

'The last princes of Sluck and the West', *Journal of Byelorussian Studies* 3 (1975): 269–87.

'A report on the Ruthenians and their errors, prepared for the Fifth Lateran Council', *OCP* 29 (1963): 79–94.

'The Ruthenian Patriarchate: some remarks on the project for its establishment in the 17th century', *OCP* 30 (1960): 65–84.

Lapinski, A., *Zygmunt Stary a kościół prawoslawny*. Rozprawy historyczne Towarzystwa naukowego Warszawskiego, vol. 19, part 1 (Warsaw: Nakl. Tow. Naukowego Warszawskiego, 1937).

Lewicki, K., *Ksiaze Konstanty Ostrogski a Unja*. Archiwum Towarzystwa naukowego we Lwowie, Part II, vol. 11, part 1 (Brzeska, 1596; rpt. Lwow: Nakl. Tow. Naukowego Warszawskiego, 1933).

Litwin, H., 'Catholicization among the Ruthenian nobility and assimilation processes in the Ukraine during the years 1569–1648', *Acta Poloniae Historica* 55 (1987): 57–83.

Martel, A., *La langue polonaise dans les pays ruthènes*. Travaux et mémoires de l'Université de Lille. Nouvelle série: droit et lettres, 20 (Lille, 1938).

Medlin, W. K., and Patrinelis, C. G., *Renaissance influences and religious reforms in Russia: Western and post-Byzantine impacts on culture and education (16th–17th centuries)* (Geneva: Droz, 1971).

Milash, N., *Pravoslavna Dalmatsiia. Istoriïski pregled* (Belgrade, 1989).

Milev, N. I., *Katolishkata propaganda v Blgariya prez 3 XVII vek.* (Sofia, 1914).

Mironowicz, A., *Prawosławie i unia za panowania Jana Kazimierza* (Białystok: Orthdruk, 1997).

Murko, M., *Die Bedeutung der Reformation und Gegenreformation für das geistige Leben der Südslaven. Slavia*, IV, nos. 3–4; V (1926–7), nos. 1–4 (Prague: Druck der Ceská grafická, 1927).

Peri, V., 'Chiesa latina e chiesa greca nell'Italia posttridentina (1564–1596)'. In *Convegno storico interecclesiale, La chiesa greca in Italia dall'VIII al XVI secolo.* Italia sacra, 20–2 (Padua: Antenore, 1973).

'Inizi e finalità ecumeniche del Collegio Greco in Roma'. *Aevum* 44 (1970): 1–71.

'La Congregazione dei Greci (1573) e i suoi primi documenti'. In G. Forschielli and Alphonso Stickler (eds.), *Studia Gratiana* (Bologna: Institutum Iuridicum Universitatis Studiorum Bononiensis, 1967), Collectanea Stephan Kuttner, vol. 3, pp. 129–256.

'La lettura del Concilio di Firenze nella prospettiva unionistica romana'. In G. Alberigo (ed.), *Christian unity. The Council of Ferrara-Florence, 1438/39–1989* (Leuven: Leuven University Press, 1991), pp. 593–611.

Ricerche sull'editio princeps degli atti greci del Concilio di Firenze. Studi e testi, 275 (Vatican City: Biblioteca Apostolica Vaticana, 1975).

Pierling, P., *Antonio Possevino. Missio Moscovitica* (Paris: Leroux, 1882).

Rome et Moscou (1547–1579) (Paris: Leroux, 1883).

La Russie et le Saint-Siège, études diplomatiques, vols. 1–2 (Paris: Plon-Nouritt, 1896).

Platania, G., 'Politica e religione nella Polonia dell'ultimo Wasa'. In G. Platania, '*Rzeczpospolita', Europa e Santa Sede tra intese ed ostilità (Saggi sulla Polonia del Seicento)* (Viterbo: Sette Città, 2000), pp. 23–78.

Plokhy, S. N., *Papstvo i Ukraina. Politika Rimskoï kurin na ukrainskikh zemlyakh v XVI–XVII vv.* (Kiev, 1989).

The Cossacks and religion in early modern Ukraine (Oxford: Oxford University Press, 2001).

Podskalsky, G., *Griechische Theologie in der Zeit der Turkenherrschaft (1453–1821). Die Orthodoxie im Spannungsfeld der nachreformatorischen Konfessionen des Westens* (Munich: C. H. Beck, 1988).

'Die Union von Brest aus der Sicht des Ekumenischen Patriarchats (Konstantinopel) im 17. Jahrhundert'. *Orientalia Christiana Periodica* 61 (1995): 555–70.

Polcin, S., *Une tentative d'Union au XVIe siècle: la mission religieuse du Père Antoine Possevin S. J. en Moscovie (1581–1582)* (Rome: Pont. Institutum Orientalium Studiorum, 1957).

Praszko, I., *De Ecclesia Ruthena Catholica sede metropolitana vacante, 1655–1665* (Rome: Typographia augustiniana, 1944).

Przekop, E., 'Die "Rebaptizatio Ruthenorum" auf dem Gebiet Polens vor der Union von Brest (1596)', *Ostkirchliche Studien* 29 (1980): 272–82.

Radonih, J., *Shtamparije i shkole Rimske kuriye i Italiyi i juzhnoslovenskim zemlyama u XVII veku* (Belgrade, 1949).

Rimska kuriya i juzhnoslovenskie zemlye od XVI do XIX veka (Belgrade, 1950).

Runciman, S., *The great church in captivity. A study of the patriarchate of Constantinople from the eve of the Turkish conquest to the Greek war of independence* (Cambridge: Cambridge University Press, 1968).

Sawicki, J., 'Die "Rebaptizatio Ruthenorum" im lichte der polnischen Synodalgesetzgebung im XV. und XVI. Jh.'. In Congressus Historiae Slavicae Salisburgensis, *Geschichte der Ost- und Westkirche in ihren wechseleitigen Beziehungen*. Annales Instituti Slavici, vols. 1–3 (Wiesbaden: Otto Harrassowitz, 1967).

Sherrard, P., *The Greek East and the Latin West. A study in the Christian tradition* (London: Oxford University Press, 1959).

Shmurlo, E. F., *Rimskaia kuriia na russkom pravoslavnom vostoke v 1609–1654 godakh*. Parts I and II (Prague, 1928).

Simrak, J., *Crkevna uniija u sjevernoj Dalmaciji u XVII vieku* (Sibenik, 1929).

De relationibus Slavorum meridionalium cum Sancta Romana Sede Apostolica, saeculis XVII–XVIII, vol. 1 (Agram: Zagreb Hrvatska Bogoslovska Akademija, 1926).

Slijepchevih, B., *Istorija srpske pravoslavne tsrkve*. Vol. 1: *Od pokrshtavaniya srba do kraia XVIII veka* (Belgrade, 1991).

Snegarov, I., *Istoriia na Okhridskata arkhiepiskopiia patriarshiia ot padaneto i pod turtsite do neïnoto unishozhenie (1394–1767)* (Sofia: Pechatnica P. Glushkov, 1932).

Spremih, M., *Srbi i Florentinska unija tsrkava 1439 godine*. Zbornik radova Vizantoloshkog instituta, 24/25 (Belgrade, 1986), pp. 413–22.

Stanimirov, S., *Politicheskata deïnost na Blgarite katolitsi prez 30-te–7-te godini na XVII vek*. Nauka i izkustvo (Sofia, 1988).

Stökl, G., *Die deutsch-slavische Südostgrenze des Reiches im 16. Jahrhundert* (Breslau: Priebatsch, 1940).

Suttner, E., 'Anfänge einer zum Calvinismus tendierenden Theologie in der Orthodoxie Siebenbürgens in der zweiten Hälfte des 17. Jahrhunderts', *Jahrbuch der Österreichischen Byzantinistik* 32 (1982): 153–61.

'Die Konfrontation der Ostkirchen mit westlicher Theologie unter osmanischer Herrschaft'. In *Die Türken in Europa* (Göttingen, 1979), pp. 97–106.

Beiträge zur Kirchengeschichte der Rumänen (Vienna and Munich: Herold, 1978).

'Brachte die Union von Brest Einigung oder Trennung für die Kirche', *Ostkirchliche Studien* 39 (1990): 3–21.

'Gründe für den Miserfolg der Brester Union', *Der Christliche Osten* 45 (1990): 230–41.

Sysyn, F. E., 'The formation of modern Ukrainian religious culture: the sixteenth and seventeenth centuries'. In G. A. Hosking (ed.), *Church, nation and state in Russia and Ukraine* (New York: St Martin's Press, 1991), pp. 1–22.

'Peter Mohyla and the Kiev Academy in recent western works: divergent views on 17th century Ukrainian culture', *Harvard Ukrainian Studies* 8 (1984): 155–87.

Vodoff, W., 'La tolérance religieuse dans la Grande-Principauté de Lituanie (XVe–XVIe siècles)', *Etudes Danubiennes* 2 (1986): 98–105.

Vries, W. de, *Rom und die Patriarchate des Ostens* (Munich: Freiburg, 1963).

Wagner, O., 'Reformation und Orthodoxie in Ostmitteleuropa im 16. Jahrhundert', *Zeitschrift für Ostforschung* 35 (1986): 18–61.

Ware, T., *Eustratios Argenti* (Oxford: Clarendon Press, 1964).

Welykyi, A. G., 'Un progetto anonimo di Pietro Mohyla sull'unione delle chiese nell'anno 1645', *Analecta Ordinis S. Basilii Magni* 6 (1963): 451–67; also in *Mélanges Eugène Tisseraut*. Studi e testi, 233, vol. 3, pp. 451–73.

Wendebourg, D., *Reformation und Orthodoxie: der Ökumenische Briefwechsel zwischen der Leitung der Württembergischen Kirche und Patriarch Jeremias II. von Konstantinopel in den Jahren 1573–1581* (Göttingen: Vandenhoeck & Ruprecht, 1986).

Yakovenko, S. G., *Pravoslavnaia ierarkhiia Rechi Pospolitoï i plany tserkovnoï unii v 1590–1594 gg.* Katolitsizm i pravoslavie v Sredine veka (Slavane i ikh sosedi, 3) (Moscow, 1991), pp. 41–58. 'Proekty pereneseniia patriarshego prestola v predely Rechi Pospolitoï (80-e gody XVI v.).'

In *Rimsko-Konstantinopol'skoe nasledie na Rusi: ideia vlasti i politicheskaia praktika* (Moscow, 1995), pp. 318–21.

'Rimskaia kuriia i plany tserkovnoï unii na vostochnoslavyanskikh zemlyakh (60-e gody XVI v.)'. In A. I. Klibanov (ed.), *Tserkov', obshchestvo i gosudarstvo v feodalnoï Rossii Sb. stateï* (Moscow, 1990), pp. 253–60.

Zachariades, G. E., *Tübingen und Konstantinopel. Martin Crusius und seine Verhandlungen mit der griechisch-orthodoxen Kirche.* Schriftenreihe der Deutsch-Griechischen Gesellschaft, 7 (Göttingen: Gerstung und Lehmann, 1941).

Zhukovich, P. N., *Seïmovaya bor'ba pravoslavnogo zapadnorusskogo dvorianstva s tserkovnoï unieï (do 1609 g.)* (St Petersburg, 1901).

Seïmovaya bor'ba pravoslavnogo zapadnorusskogo dvorianstva s tserkovnoï unieï (s 1609 g.) Parts 1–6 (St Petersburg, 1903–12).

Zhukovskiï, A., *Petro Mogila i pytannia ednosti cerkov.* Ukrains'kiï Vilniï Universitet Monograph series, 17 (Paris, 1969).

19 THE REFORMATION AND THE VISUAL ARTS

Primary sources

Bodenstein von Karlstadt, Andreas, *Von Abthuhung der Bilder* (Wittenberg, 1522).

Calvin, John, *Institutes of the Christian religion*, vol. 1. Ed. John T. McNeill. Trans. Ford Lewis Battles (Philadelphia: Westminster Press, 1960), Book I, Chapter XI, paragraph 12, p. 112.

Luther, Martin, *Vom Abendmahl Christi, Bekenntnis*, (1528). In Otto Clemen (ed.), *Luthers Werke in Auswahl*, vol. 3. 5th edn (Berlin: Walter de Gruyter, 1959), p. 514.

Tanner, Norman P., SJ, *Decrees of the ecumenical councils.* 2 vols. (London: Sheed and Ward, 1990).

The life of Teresa of Jesus: the autobiography of Teresa of Avila. Trans. E. Allison Peers (New York: Image Books, 1991).

Secondary sources

Alpers, Svetlana, *Rembrandt's enterprise: the studio and the market* (Chicago: University of Chicago Press, 1988).

Andersson, Christiane, 'Popular imagery in German Reformation broadsheets'. In Gerald P. Tyson and Sylvia Wagonheim (eds.), *Print and culture in the Renaissance: essays on the advent of printing in Europe* (Newark: University of Delaware Press, 1986), pp. 120–50.

Ångström, Inge Lena, *Altartavlor i Sverige under renässans och barock: Studier i deras ikonografi och stil 1527–1686* (Stockholm: Almqvist & Wiksell International, 1992).

Aston, Margaret, *England's iconoclasts: laws against images* (Oxford: Clarendon Press, 1988).

Bailey, Gauvin Alexander, *Art on the Jesuit missions in Asia and Latin America, 1542–1773* (Toronto: University of Toronto Press, 1999).

Bangs, Jeremy Dupertuis, *Church art and architecture in the Low Countries before 1566*. Sixteenth Century Essays & Studies, 37 (Kirksville: Sixteenth Century Journal, 1997).

Baumstark, Reinhold (ed.), *Rom in Bayern: Kunst und Spiritualität der ersten Jesuiten* (Munich: Hirmer, 1997).

Belkin, Kristin Lohse, *Rubens* (London: Phaidon, 1998).

Belting, Hans, *Bild und Kult: eine Geschichte des Bildes vor dem Zeitalter der Kunst* (Munich: Beck, 1990).

Likeness and presence: a history of the image before the era of art. Trans. E. Jephcott (Chicago: University of Chicago Press, 1994).

Blickle, Peter, Holenstein, A., Schmidt, H. R., and Sladeczek, F-J. (eds.), *Macht und Ohnmacht der Bilder: Reformatorischer Bildersturm im Kontext der europäischen Geschichte*. Beiheft der Historischen Zeitschrift, 33 (Munich: Oldenbourg, 2002).

Campenhausen, Hans Freiherr von, 'Die Bilderfrage in der Reformation', *Zeitschrift für Kirchengeschichte* 68 (1957): 96–128.

Carruthers, Mary, *The book of memory: a study of memory in medieval culture* (Cambridge and New York: Cambridge University Press, 1990).

Christensen, Carl C., *Art and the Reformation in Germany* (Athens: Ohio University Press, 1979).

Dempsey, Charles, *Annibale Carracci and the beginnings of Baroque style*. 2nd edn (Fiesole: Cadmo, 2000).

'Mythic inventions in Counter-Reformation painting'. In P. A. Ramsey (ed.), *Rome in the Renaissance: the city and the myth* (Binghamton: Center for Medieval and Early Renaissance Studies, 1982), pp. 55–75.

Duffy, Eamon, *The stripping of the altars: traditional religion in England, c. 1400–c.1580* (New Haven: Yale University Press, 1992).

Finney, Paul Corby (ed.), *Seeing beyond the word: visual arts and the Calvinist tradition* (Grand Rapids: Eerdmans, 1999).

Gagnon, François Marc, *La conversion par l'image: un aspect de la mission des jésuites auprès des Indiens du Canada au XVIIe siècle* (Montreal: Bellarmin, 1975).

Göttler, Christine, *Die Kunst des Fegefeuers nach der Reformation: Kirchliche Schenkungen, Ablaß und Almosen in Antwerpen und Bologna um 1600* (Mainz: Verlag Philipp von Zabern, 1996).

Griffiths, Antony, *Prints and printmaking: an introduction to the history and techniques* (New York: Alfred A. Knopf, 1980).

The Grove Dictionary of Art Online. Ed. L. Macy <http://www.groveart.com>.

Halewood, William, *Six subjects of Reformation art: a preface to Rembrandt* (Toronto: University of Toronto Press, 1982).

Hall, Marcia, *Renovation and Counter-Reformation: Vasari and Duke Cosimo in Santa Maria Novella and Santa Croce 1565–1577* (Oxford and New York: Oxford University Press, 1979).

Hoffmann, Werner (ed.), *Luther und die Folgen für die Kunst* (Munich: Prestel Verlag, 1983).

Humfrey, Peter, and Kemp, Martin (eds.), *The altarpiece in the Renaissance* (Cambridge and New York: Cambridge University Press, 1990).

Jones, Pamela, *Federico Borromeo and the Ambrosiana: art patronage and reform in seventeenth-century Milan* (Cambridge and New York: Cambridge University Press, 1993).

Kaufmann, Thomas DaCosta, *Court, cloister, and city: the art and culture of central Europe 1450–1800* (Chicago: University of Chicago Press, 1995), ch. 9.

Kessler, Herbert, and Wolf, Gerhard (eds.), *The holy face and the paradox of representation.* Villa Spelman Colloquia, 6 (Baltimore: Johns Hopkins University Press, 1998).

Knipping, J. B., *The iconography of the Counter-Reformation in the Netherlands.* 2 vols. (Leiden: B. De Graf-Nieuwkoop & A. W. Sijthoff, 1974).

Lavin, Irving, *Bernini and the unity of the visual arts.* 2 vols. (New York and London: Oxford University Press & The Pierpont Morgan Library, 1980).

Lawrence, Cynthia, 'Before *The Raising of the Cross*: the origins of Rubens's earliest Antwerp altarpieces', *Art Bulletin* 81 (1999): 267–96.

Mâle, Emile, *L'art religieux de la fin du XVIe siècle, du XVIIe siècle et du XVIIIe siècle: Etude sur l'iconographie après le concile de Trente.* 2nd edn (Paris: A. Colin, 1951).

Melion, Walter, 'Artifice, memory, and Reformatio in Hieronymus Natalis's *Adnotationes et meditationes in Evangelia*', *Renaissance and Reformation* 22 (1998): 5–34.

'The art of vision in Jerome Nadal's *Adnotationes et meditationes in Evangelia*'. In Jerome Nadal, *Annotations and meditations on the liturgical gospels*, vol. 1: *The infancy narratives.* Ed. and trans. F. Homann, SJ (Philadelphia: St Joseph's Press, 2003).

The meditative art: prints and prayer in the Netherlands, 1550–1625 (Philadelphia: St Joseph's Press, forthcoming).

Mikalski, Sergiusz, *The Reformation and the visual arts: the Protestant image question in western and eastern Europe* (London and New York: Routledge, 1993).

Norman, Larry F. (ed.), *The theatrical Baroque* (Chicago: The David and Alfred Smart Museum of Art, University of Chicago, 2001).

Pelikan, Jaroslav, *Imago Dei: the Byzantine apologia for icons* (Princeton: Princeton University Press, 1990).

Phillips, John, *The reformation of images: destruction of art in England, 1535–1660* (Berkeley: University of California Press, 1973).

Prodi, Paolo, 'Ricerche sulla teorica delle arti figurative nella riforma cattolica'. *Archivio Italiano per la Storia della Pietà* 4 (1965): 121–212.

Rice, Louise, *The altars and altarpieces of New St. Peter's: outfitting the Basilica, 1621–1666* (Cambridge and New York: Cambridge University Press, with the American Academy in Rome, 1997).

Scharfe, Martin, *Evangelische Andachtsbilder: Studien zu Intention und Funktion des Bildes in der Frömmigkeitsgeschichte vornehmlich des schwäbischen Raumes* (Stuttgart: Verlag Müller & Graf, 1968).

Schmidt, Ph., *Die Illustration der Lutherbibel 1522–1700* (Basel: Friedrich Reinhardt, 1962).

Scribner, R. W., *For the sake of simple folk: popular propaganda for the German Reformation* (Cambridge and New York: Cambridge University Press, 1981; 2nd edn. Oxford and New York: Clarendon Press, 1994).

Smith, Jeffrey Chipps, *German sculpture of the later Renaissance c. 1520–1580: art in an age of uncertainty* (Princeton: Princeton University Press, 1994).

Sensuous worship: Jesuits and the art of the early Catholic Reformation in Germany (Princeton and Oxford: Princeton University Press, 2002).

Spence, Jonathan, *The memory palace of Matteo Ricci* (New York: Viking Penguin, 1984).

Stirm, Margarethe, *Die Bilderfrage in der Reformation* (Gütersloh: Gütersloher Verlaghaus Mohn, 1977).

Thulin, Oskar, *Cranach Altäre der Reformation* (Berlin: Evangelische Verlagsanstalt, 1955).

Vargas Ugarte, Ruben, SJ, *Los Jesuitas del Peru y el Arte* (Lima: 1963).

Visser 'T Hooft, W. A., *Rembrandt and the gospel* (Philadelphia: Westminster Press, 1957).

Wandel, Lee Palmer, *Voracious idols and violent hands: iconoclasm in Reformation Zurich, Strasbourg, and Basel* (New York and Cambridge: Cambridge University Press, 1995).

Wencelius, Léon, *L'esthétique de Calvin* (Geneva: Droz, 1979).

Wittkower, Rudolf, *Bernini: the sculptor of the Roman Baroque* (London: Phaidon, 1997 (1955)).

Wittkower, Rudolf, and Jaffe, Irma B. (eds.), *Baroque art: the Jesuit contribution* (New York: Fordham University Press, 1972).

Zell, Michael, *Reframing Rembrandt: Jews and the Christian image in seventeenth-century Amsterdam* (Berkeley: University of California Press, 2002).

20 RITUAL IN EARLY MODERN CHRISTIANITY

Primary sources

Baumgartner, Mira (comp.), *Die Täufer und Zwingli: Eine Dokumentation* (Zurich: Theologischer Verlag, 1993).

Bray, Gerald (ed.), *Documents of the English Reformation* (Minneapolis: Fortress Press, 1994).

The first and second Prayer Books of Edward VI (London: J. M. Dent & Sons, 1977; reprint of 1910 edition).

Hooker, Richard, *Of the laws of ecclesiastical polity*. Ed. R. W. Church (Oxford: Clarendon Press, 1905).

Registers of the Consistory of Geneva in the time of Calvin, vol. 1: *1542–1544*. Ed. Thomas A. Lambert and Isabella M. Watt. Trans. M. Wallace McDonald (Grand Rapids: William B. Eerdmans, 2000).

Zwingli, Ulrich. *Huldreich Zwingli's sämtliche Werke*. Ed. Emil Egli. Corpus Reformatorum, 88–101 (Zurich: Theologischer Verlag, 1905–).

Secondary sources

Altenburg, Jörg Jarnut, and Steinhoff, Hans-Hugo (eds.), *Feste und Feiern im Mittelalter* (Sigmaringen: Jan Thorbecke, 1991).

Bell, Catherine, *Ritual theory, ritual practice* (Oxford and New York: Oxford University Press, 1992).

Catterall, Douglas, 'The rituals of Reformed discipline: managing honor and conflict in the Scottish Church of Rotterdam, 1643–1665', *Archive for Reformation History* 94 (2003): 194–222.

Châtellier, Louis, *The Europe of the devout: the Catholic Reformation and the formation of a new society* (Cambridge and New York: Cambridge University Press, 1989).

Christian, William A., Jr, *Local religion in sixteenth-century Spain* (Princeton: Princeton University Press, 1981; rpt. 1989).

Cramer, Peter, *Baptism and change in the Early Middle Ages, c. 200–c. 1150* (Cambridge and New York: Cambridge University Press, 1993).

Deroo, André, *Saint Charles Borromée: Cardinal réformateur, docteur de la pastorale, 1538–1584* (Paris: Editions Saint-Paul, 1963).

Ehrstein, Glenn, *Theater, culture, and community in Reformation Berne, 1523–1555* (Leiden: Brill, 2002).

Garside, Charles, *Zwingli and the arts* (New Haven: Yale University Press, 1966).

Gonzalez, Justo L., *The story of Christianity*, vol. 1: *The early church to the dawn of the Reformation* (New York: Harper and Row, 1984).

Houston, Robert A., 'The Consistory of the Scots Church, Rotterdam: An Aspect of "Civic Calvinism", c. 1600–1800,' *Archive for Reformation History* 87 (1996), 362–92.

Hughes, Philip, *The church in crisis: a history of the general councils, 325–1870* (New York: Image Books, 1961).

Junghans, Helmar, 'Luthers Gottesdienstreform – Konzept oder Verlegenheit?' In Michael Beyer and Günther Wartenberg (eds.), *Spätmittelalter, Luthers Reformation, Kirche in Sachsen*: Arbeiten zur Kirchen- und Theologiegeschichte, 8 (Leipzig: Evangelische Verlagsanstalt, 2001), pp. 193–205.

Wittenberg als Lutherstadt (Berlin: Union Verlag, 1979).

Jungman, Joseph A., *The mass of the Roman rite: its origin and development*, 2 vols. Trans. Francis A. Brunner (New York: Benziger, 1951, 1955).

Karant-Nunn, Susan C., *The reformation of ritual: an interpretation of early modern Germany* (London and New York: Routledge, 1997).

'"Suffer the little children to come unto me, and forbid them not": The social location of baptism in early modern Germany'. In Robert J. Bast and Andrew C. Gow (eds.), *Continuity and change: the harvest of late medieval and Reformation history* (Leiden: Brill, 2000), pp. 359–78.

Lockyer, Roger, *Tudor and Stuart Britain, 1471–1714* (London: Longmans, 1964).

Lotz-Heumann, Ute, 'The concept of "confessionalisation": a historiographical paradigm in dispute', *Memoria y Civilización* 4 (2001): 93–114.

Manschreck, Clyde, *Melanchthon, the quiet Reformer* (New York and Nashville: Abingdon Press, 1958).

Mentzer, Raymond A., Jr, 'The Reformed churches of France and the visual arts'. In Paul Corby Finney (ed.), *Seeing beyond the word: visual arts and the Calvinist tradition* (Grand Rapids: William B. Eerdmans, 1999), pp. 199–230.

Muir, Edward, *Ritual in early modern Europe*. New Approaches to European History, 11 (Cambridge and New York: Cambridge University Press, 1997).

Naphy, W. G., 'Baptism, church riots and social unrest in Calvin's Geneva'. *Sixteenth Century Journal* 26 (1995): 87–97.

Oettinger, Rebecca Wagner. *Music as propaganda in the German Reformation*. St Andrews Studies in Reformation History (Aldershot: Ashgate, 2001).

Old, Hughs Oliphant, *The shaping of the Reformed baptismal rite in the sixteenth century* (Grand Rapids, Michigan: William B. Eerdmans, 1992).

O'Malley, John W., *Trent and all that: renaming Catholicism in the early modern era* (Cambridge, MA: Harvard University Press, 2000).

Pelikan, Jaroslav, *The Christian tradition: a history of the development of doctrine*, vol. 1: *The emergence of the Catholic tradition (100–600)* (Chicago: University of Chicago Press, 1971).

The Christian tradition: a history of the development of doctrine, vol. 3: *The growth of medieval theology (600–1300)* (Chicago: University of Chicago Press, 1978).

Reinhard, Wolfgang (ed.), *Bekenntnis und Geschichte: Die Confessio Augustana im historischen Zusammenhang*. Schriften der Philosophischen Fakultäten der Universität Augsburg, 20 (Augsburg: Vögel, 1981).

'Gegenreformation als Modernisierung? Prolegomena zu einer Theorie des konfessionellen Zeitalters', *Archiv für Reformationsgeschichte* 68 (1977): 226–52.

'Konfession and Konfessionalisierung in Deutschland'. In Wolfgand Reinhard, *Bekenntnis und Geschichte: Die Confessio Augustana im historischen Zusammenhang*. Schriften der Philosophischen Fakultäten der Universität Augsburg, 20 (Augsburg: Vögel, 1981), pp. 165–89.

Scheible, Heinz, *Melanchthon: Eine Biographie* (Munich: C. H. Beck, 1997).

Schilling, Heinz, 'Confessional Europe'. In Thomas A. Brady, Jr, Heiko A. Oberman, and James D. Tracy (eds.), *Handbook of European history 1400–1600: Late Middle Ages, Renaissance and Reformation*, vol. 1 (Leiden: Brill, 1995), pp. 641–75.

Konfessionskonflikt und Staatsbildung: Eine Fallstudie über das Verhältnis von religiösem und sozialem Wandel in der Frühneuzeit am Beispiel der Grafschaft Lippe (Gütersloh: Gütersloher Verlagshaus Mohn, 1981).

'The Reformation and the rise of the early modern state'. In James D. Tracy (ed.), *Luther and the modern state in Germany* (Kirksville: Sixteenth Century Journal Publishers, 1986), pp. 21–30.

Seebaß, Gottfried, *Müntzers Erbe: Werk, Leben und Theologie des Hans Hut* (Gütersloh: Gütersloher Verlagshaus, 2002).

Smith, Jeffrey Chipps, *Sensuous worship: Jesuits and the art of the early Catholic Reformation in Germany* (Princeton: Princeton University Press, 2002).

Soergel, Philip M., *Wondrous in his saints: propaganda for the Catholic Reformation in Reformation Germany* (Berkeley: University of California Press, 1993).

Spierling, Karen E., 'Daring insolence toward God? The perpetuation of Catholic baptismal traditions in sixteenth-century Geneva', *Archive for Reformation History* 93 (2002): 97–125.

Stell, Christopher, 'Puritan and nonconformist meetinghouses in England'. In Paul Corby Finney (ed.), *Seeing beyond the word: visual arts and the Calvinist tradition* (Grand Rapids: William B. Eerdmans, 1999), pp. 49–81.

Taylor, Larissa J. (ed.), *Preachers and people in the Reformation and early modern period* (Leiden: Brill, 2001).

Veit, Patrice, *Das Kirchenlied in der Reformation Martin Luthers* (Stuttgart: Franz Steiner, 1986).

von Greyerz, Kaspar, *Religion und Kultur: Europa 1500–1800* (Göttingen: Vandenhoeck and Ruprecht, 2000).

Wandel, Lee Palmer, 'Envisioning God: image and liturgy in Reformation Zurich'. *Sixteenth Century Journal* 24 (1993): 21–40.

Wendebourg, Dorothea, 'Luthers Reform der Messe – Bruch oder Kontinuität?' In Bernd
Moeller (ed.), *Die frühe Reformation in Deutschland als Umbruch*. Schriften des Vereins für
Reformationsgeschichte, 199 (Gütersloh: Gütersloher Verlagshaus, 1998), pp. 289–306.

Williams, George Huntston, *The radical Reformation* 3rd edn (Kirksville: Sixteenth Century
Journal Publishers, 1992).

21 MUSIC AND RELIGIOUS CHANGE

Primary sources

Baini, Giuseppe, *Memorie storico-critiche della vita e delle opere di Giovanni Pierluigi da Palestrina*
(Rome: Dalla Società tipografica, 1828).

Luther, Martin, *Table talk*. Trans.William Hazlitt (London: Fount/Harper Collins, 1995).

Robinson, Hastings (ed.), *The Zurich letters: comprising the correspondence of several English
bishops and others with some of the Helvetian reformers, during the early part of the reign of
Queen Elizabeth* (Cambridge: Cambridge University Press, 1842).

Stetten, Paul von, *Geschichte der Heil. Röm. Reichs Freyen Stadt Augspurg, Aus Bewährten Jahr-
Büchern und Tüchtigen Urkunden gezogen*. 2 vols. (Frankfurt am Main and Leipzig: In
der Merz- und Mayerischen Buch-Handlung, 1743).

Secondary sources

Arnold, Denis, *Giovanni Gabrieli and the music of the Venetian high Renaissance* (London and
New York: Oxford University Press, 1979).

Atlas, Allan W., *Renaissance music: music in western Europe, 1400–1600* (New York: Norton,
1998).

Blankenburg, Walter, *Johann Walter: Leben und Werk* (Tutzing: Hans Schneider, 1991).

Blume, Friedrich et al., *Protestant church music: a history* (New York: Norton, 1974).

Bukofzer, Manfred F., *Music in the Baroque era from Monteverdi to Bach* (New York: Norton,
1947).

Castagna, Paulo, 'The use of music by the Jesuits in the conversion of the indigenous
peoples of Brazil'. In John O'Malley et al. (eds.), *The Jesuits: cultures, sciences, and the
arts 1540–1773* (Toronto: University of Toronto Press, 1999), pp. 641–58.

Crook, David, *Orlando di Lasso's imitation Magnificats for Counter-Reformation Munich*
(Princeton: Princeton University Press, 1994).

Culley, Thomas D., SJ, *Jesuits and music: I. A study of the musicians connected with the German
College in Rome during the 17th century and of their activities in northern Europe*. Sources
and Studies for the History of the Jesuits, vol. 2 (Rome: Jesuit Historical Institute; St
Louis: St Louis University, 1970).

Danckwardt, Marianne, 'Konfessionelle Musik?' In Wolfgang Reinhard and Heinz Schillings
(eds.), *Die katholische Konfessionalisierung. Wissenschaftliches Symposon der Gesellschaft
zur Herausgabe des Corpus Catholicorum und des Vereins für Reformationsgeschichte 1993*.
Schriften des Vereins für Reformationsgeschichte, 198 (Gütersloh: Gütersloher Verlagshaus, 1995), pp. 371–83.

Davis, Natalie Zemon, 'Strikes and salvation at Lyon'. In Natalie Zemon Davis, *Society and
culture in early modern France* (Stanford: Stanford University Press, 1975), pp. 1–16.

Dürr, Alfred, and Walther Killy (eds.), *Das protestantische Kirchenlied im 16. und 17. Jahrhundert: Text-, musik- und theologiegeschichtliche Probleme* (Wiesbaden: In Kommission bei O. Harrassowitz, 1986).

Dyer, Joseph, 'Roman Catholic church music'. In Stanley Sadie et al., *The new Grove dictionary of music and musicians*, 2nd edn (London, Macmillan, 2001), vol. 21, pp. 544–70.

Fellerer, Karl Gustav (ed.), *Geschichte der katholischen Kirchenmusik*. 2 vols. (Kassel: Bärenreiter, 1972–6).

Fisher, Alexander J. *Music and religious identity in Counter-Reformation Augsburg, 1580–1630* (Aldershot: Ashgate, 2004).

Hayburn, Robert F., *Papal legislation on sacred music, 95 A.D. to 1977 A.D.* (Collegeville, MN: Liturgical Press, 1979).

Hsia, R. Po-Chia, *The world of Catholic renewal, 1540–1770*. New Approaches to European History, 12 (Cambridge and New York: Cambridge University Press, 1998).

Jedin, Hubert, 'Catholic Reformation or Counter-Reformation?' Trans. David M. Luebke. In Luebke (ed.), *The Counter-Reformation: the essential readings* (Malden, MA: Blackwell, 1999), pp. 21–45.

Kendrick, Robert L., *Celestial sirens: nuns and their music in early modern Milan* (Oxford and New York: Oxford University Press, 1996).

Kerman, Joseph, *The masses and motets of William Byrd* (Berkeley: University of California Press, 1981).

'On William Byrd's *Emendemus in melius*'. In Dolores Pesce (ed.), *Hearing the motet: essays on the motet of the middle ages and Renaissance* (New York and Oxford: Oxford University Press, 1997), pp. 329–47.

Kurtzman, Jeffrey G., *The Monteverdi Vespers of 1610: music, context, performance* (Oxford and New York: Oxford University Press, 1999).

Le Huray, Peter, *Music and the Reformation in England, 1549–1660* (London: Oxford University Press, 1967).

Lockwood, Lewis, *The Counter Reformation and the masses of Vincenzo Ruffo* (Vienna: Universal Edition, 1970).

McNaspy, C. J., *Lost cities of Paraguay: art and architecture of the Jesuit reductions, 1607–1767* (Chicago: Loyola University Press, 1982).

Monson, Craig A., *Disembodied voices: music and culture in an early modern Italian convent* (Berkeley: University of California Press, 1995).

'Byrd, the Catholics, and the motet: the hearing reopened'. In Dolores Pesce (ed.), *Hearing the motet: essays on the motet of the Middle Ages and Renaissance* (New York and Oxford: Oxford University Press, 1997), pp. 348–74.

'The Council of Trent revisited', *Journal of the American Musicological Society* 55 (2002): 1–37.

Moser, Dietz-Rudiger, *Verkündigung durch Volksgesang: Studien zur Liedpropaganda und -katechese der Gegenreformation* (Berlin: Erich Schmidt Verlag, 1981).

Moser, Hans Joachim, *Die evangelische Kirchenmusik in Deutschland* (Berlin and Darmstadt: Carl Merseburger, 1954).

Nawrot, Piotr, *Música de vísperas en las reducciones de Chiquitos-Bolivia (1691–1767); obras de Domenico Zipoli y maestros jesuitas e indígenas anónimos* (Concepción, Bolivia: Archivo Musical Chiquitos, 1994).

Oettinger, Rebecca Wagner, *Music as propaganda in the German Reformation* (Aldershot: Ashgate, 2001).

O'Malley, John, SJ, 'Was Ignatius Loyola a church reformer? How to look at early modern Catholicism', *The Catholic Historical Review* 77 (1991): 177–93.

O'Regan, Noel, *Institutional patronage in post-Tridentine Rome: music at Santissima Trinità dei Pellegrini, 1550–1650*. Royal Musical Association Monographs, 7 (London: Royal Musical Association, 1995).

Perkins, Leeman L., *Music in the age of the Renaissance* (New York: Norton, 1999).

Reese, Gustave, *Music in the Renaissance*. Rev. edn (New York: Norton, 1959).

Roche, Jerome, *Palestrina* (London: Oxford University Press, 1971).

Lassus (London: Oxford University Press, 1982).

North Italian church music in the time of Monteverdi (Oxford: Oxford University Press, 1984).

Saunders, Steven, *Cross, sword, and lyre: sacred music at the imperial court of Ferdinand II of Habsburg (1619–1637)* (Oxford and New York: Oxford University Press, 1995).

Schalk, Carl F., *Luther on music: paradigms of praise* (St Louis: Concordia, 1988).

Schulenberg, David, *Music in the Baroque era from Monteverdi to Bach* (New York: Oxford University Press, 2001).

Scribner, Robert W., *For the sake of simple folk: popular propaganda for the German Reformation* (Oxford and New York: Oxford University Press, 1994).

Stevenson, Robert, *Music in Mexico: a historical survey* (New York: Crowell, [1952]).

Spanish cathedral music in the golden age (Berkeley: University of California Press, 1961).

'Victoria, Tomás Luis de'. In *The new Grove dictionary of music and musicians*, 2nd edn (London, Macmillan, 2001), vol. 26, pp. 531–7.

Strauss, Gerald, *Luther's house of learning. Indoctrination of the young in the German Reformation* (Baltimore: Johns Hopkins University Press, 1978).

Summers, William J., 'The Jesuits in Manila, 1581–1621: the role of music in rite, ritual, and spectacle'. In John O'Malley et al. (eds.), *The Jesuits: Cultures, sciences, and the arts 1540–1773* (Toronto: University of Toronto Press, 1999), pp. 659–79.

Temperley, Nicholas, *The music of the English parish church* (Cambridge: Cambridge University Press, 1979).

Ursprung, Otto, *Münchens musikalische Vergangenheit. Von der Frühzeit bis zu Richard Wagner* (Munich: Bayerland-Verlag, 1927).

Veit, Patrice, *Das Kirchenlied in der Reformation Martin Luthers: eine thematische und semantische Untersuchung*. Veröffentlichungen des Instituts für Europäische Geschichte Mainz, 120 (Wiesbaden: Steiner, 1986).

Walker, Paul (ed.), *Church, stage, and studio: music and its contexts in seventeenth-century Germany* (Ann Arbor: UMI Research Press, 1990).

Weber, Edith, *Le Concile de Trente et la musique: de la réforme à la contre-réforme* (Paris: H. Champion, 1982).

Weinmann, Karl, *Das Konzil von Trient und die Kirchenmusik* (Leipzig: Breitkopf & Härtel, 1919).

Wolkan, Rudolf, *Die Lieder der Wiedertäufer. Ein Beitrag zur deutschen und niederländischen Litteratur- und Kirchengeschichte* (Berlin: B. Behr, 1903).

22 DEMONOLOGY, 1500–1660

Primary sources (Demonologies)

Ady, Thomas, *A candle in the dark, or, a treatise concerning the nature of witches* (London: 1656).

Agrippa von Nettesheim, Henricus Cornelius, *De incertitudine et vanitate scientarum* [1526] (Cologne: 1544).

Über die Fragwürdigkeit, ja Nichtigkeit der Wissenschaften, Künste und Gewerbe (Berlin: Akademie Verlag, 1993).

Alciati, Andrea, *De lamiis seu strigibus* [1515]. In *Parergon Juris* [1530], lib. 8, cap. 22. In *Opera*, vol. 4 (Basel: 1582), lib. 8, cap. 22, Sp. 498. In Joseph Hansen and Johannes Franck, *Quellen und Untersuchungen zur Geschichte des Hexenwahns und der Hexenverfolgung im Mittelalter. Mit einer Untersuchung der Geschichte des Wortes Hexe* (Bonn: C. Georgi, 1901), pp. 310–12.

Aquinas, Thomas, [St], *Summa contra Gentiles*. In A. C. Pegis (ed.), *The basic writings of Saint Thomas Aquinas*. 2 vols. (New York: Random House, 1945), vol. 2, pp. 3–224.

Summa Theologiae [c. 1270] (London: Blackfriars, 1964–6).

Augustine [St], *De Doctrina Christiana*. In PL 34.

The city of God (London: 1968).

Binsfeld, Peter, *Tractatus de confessionibus maleficorum et sagarum* (Trier, 1589).

Bodin, Jean, *De la Démonomanie des Sorciers* (Paris, 1580).

On the demon-mania of witches. Trans. Randy A. Scott (Toronto: Centre for Reformation and Renaissance Studies, 1995).

Boguet, Henry, *Discours execrable des Sorciers* (Lyon, 1602).

An examen of witches. Trans. E. Allen Ashwin. Ed. Montague Summers (London: J. Rodker, 1929).

Bullinger, Heinrich, *Von Hexen und Unholden. Wider die schwartzen Künst, aberglaubig segnens, unwarhafftigs Warsagen und andere dergleichen von Gott verbottne Künst* [1571]. In *Theatrum de Veneficis* (Frankfurt a. Main: durch Nicolaum Basseum, 1586), pp. 298–306.

Burchard von Worms, *Decretorum libri viginti*. In PL 140 (Paris: 1880), Sp. 491–1090.

Cyrano de Bergerac, *Lettre contre les sorciers* [1654]. In Frederic Lachevre (ed.), *Les Œuvres Libertines de Cyrano de Bergerac*. Vol. 2 (Paris: 1912), pp. 211–18.

Como, Bernardo [Rategno] da, *Tractatus de strigiis* [c. 1508]. In *Lucerna inquisitorum haereticae pravitatis* (Mailand, 1566; rpt. Rome: 1584).

Daneau, Lambert, *Les Sorciers. Dialogue tres-utile et necessaire pour ce temps: auquel ce qui se dispute auiourdhui des Sorciers & Eriges, est traité bien amplement & resolu* (Genf: 1574).

A Dialogue of Witches (London, 1575).

Del Rio, Martin, *Disquisitionum magicarum libri sex* (Louvain, 1599–1600).

Disquisitionum magicarum libri sex. 3rd edn (Mainz, 1603).

Investigations into magic (part. trans.). Ed. and trans. Peter George Maxwell-Stuart (Manchester and New York: Manchester University Press, 2000).

Dodo, Vincentius, *Apologia Dodi contra li defensori de le strie, et principaliter contra questiones lamiarum fratris Samuelis de Cassinis* (Pavia, 1506). In Joseph Hansen and Johannes Franck, *Quellen und Untersuchungen zur Geschichte des Hexenwahns und der*

Hexenverfolgung im Mittelalter. Mit einer Untersuchung der Geschichte des Wortes Hexe (Bonn: C. Georgi, 1901), pp. 273–8.

Erastus, Thomas, *Disputatio de lamiis seu strigibus* De strigibus liber (Basel, 1572).

Ewich, Johann, *De sagarum [. . .] natura* (Bremen, 1584; rpt. in *Theatrum de Veneficis* (Frankfurt a. Main, 1586), pp. 325–55.

Gifford, George, *A discourse of the subtill practises of devilles by witches and sorcerers* (London, 1587).

Glanvill, Joseph, *Some philosophical considerations touching the being of witches and witchcraft* (London, 1665).

A blow at modern Sadducism (London, 1668).

Philosophical considerations against modern Sadducism in the matter of witches and apparitions. In *Essays on several important subjects in philosophy and religion* (London, 1676), essay VI.

Goedelmann, Johann Georg, *Tractatus de magis, veneficis et lamiis, recte cognoscendis et puniendis* (Nürnberg, 1584).

Greve, Johann, *Tribunal reformatum* (Hamburg, 1624).

Grillandus, Paulus, *Tractatus de hereticis et sortilegiis* [1525] (Lyon: 1536).

Guazzo, Francesco Maria, *Compendium maleficarum* (Mailand, 1608). Trans. E. A. Ashwin. Ed. Montague Summers (London: J. Rodker, 1929).

Gui, Bernardo, *Interrogatoria ad sortilegos et divinos et invocatores demonum* (1315). In Joseph Hansen and Johannes Franck, *Quellen und Untersuchungen zur Geschichte des Hexenwahns und der Hexenverfolgung im Mittelalter. Mit einer Untersuchung der Geschichte des Wortes Hexe* (Bonn: C. Georgi, 1901), pp. 47–8.

Hemmingsen, Nils, *Admonitio de superstitionibus magicis vitandis* (Copenhagen, 1575).

Hobbes, Thomas, *Leviathan or the Matter, Forme and Power of Commonwealth Ecclesiasticall and Civil* (London, 1651).

Hopkins, Mathew, *The Discoverie of Witches* (London, 1647).

James IV, King of Scotland, *Daemonologie, in forme of a dialoge* (Edinburgh, 1597).

[Kramer, Heinrich / Institoris], *Malleus Maleficarum* (Speyer, 1486).

Malleus Maleficarum. Facsimile edition. Ed. Günter Jerouschek (Hildesheim, 1992).

Malleus Maleficarum. English trans. Montague Summers (London, 1928).

Malleus Maleficarum. Kommentierte Neuübersetzung. New German trans. from Latin. Trans. Wolfgang Behringer, Günter Jerouschek, and Werner Tschacher. Intro. Wolfgang Behringer and Günter Jerouschek. Ed. Günter Jerouschek and Wolfgang Behringer. (Munich, 2000).

Lancre, Pierre de, *Tableau de l' Inconstance des mauvais Anges et Démons. Ou il est amplement traicté de la Sorcelerie & Sorciers [. . .]* (Paris, 1612).

On the Fickleness of Demons. English trans. Gerhild Scholz Williams (forthcoming).

Loos, Cornelius, *De vera et ficta [falsa] magia* (Cologne, 1592).

Magnus, Olaus, *Historia de gentibus septentrionalibus* (Rome, 1555).

Malleus Maleficarum (s.v. Kramer).

Milichius, Ludwig, *Der Zauber Teuffel* (1563).

Molitor, Ulrich, *De laniis et phitonicis mulieribus, Teutonice unholden vel hexen.* (s.l. [Constance] s.d. [1489]).

Montaigne, Michel de, *Essais* (Paris, 1588).

More, Henry, *An antidote against atheisme, or an appeal to the natural faculties of the minde of men, whether there be not a God* (London, 1653).

Naudé, Gabriel, *Apologie pour tous les grands personnages, qui ont esté sopconnez de magie* (Paris, 1625).

Nicolas of Cusa, *Opera*, II (Paris, 1514).

Nider, Johannes, *Formicarius* [1435] (Cologne, 1475).

Paracelsus, Theophrastus Bombastus von Hohenheim, *De sagis et earum operibus* [1538]. In *Sämtliche Werke*. Ed. Karl Sudhoff. 14 (Munich and Berlin: R. Oldenbourg, 1933), pp. 5–27.

Pico della Mirandola, Giovanni Francesco, *Dialogus in tres libros divisus, cuius titulus est Strix, sive de Ludificatione Daemonum*. (s.l. [Bologna] s.d. [1523]).

Praetorius, Anton, *Gründlicher Bericht von Zauberey und Zauberern* (Lich, 1598, 1602; Heidelberg, 1613; Frankfurt a. Main, 1629).

Prierias, Silvester, *De strigimagarum libri tres* (Rome, 1521).

Rémy, Nicolas, *Daemonolatriae libri tres* (Lyon, 1595).

Demonolatry. Trans. Montague Summers (London, 1930).

Rituale Romanum Pauli V Pontificis Maximi iussu editum (Rome, 1614).

Sawr, Abraham (ed.), *Theatrum de Veneficis* (Frankfurt a. Main, 1586).

Schultheis, Heinrich von, *Ausführliche Instruction, wie in Inquisition Sachen des grewlichen Lasters der Zauberey zu procedieren* (Cologne, 1634).

Scot, Reginald, *The discoverie of witchcraft* (London, 1584).

The discoverie of witchcraft, 3rd edn (London, 1665).

The discoverie of witchcraft. Intro. Montague Summers (New York: Dover, 1972).

[Spee, Friedrich], *Cautio Criminalis seu de processibus contra sagas liber [. . .], auctore incerto theologo romano* (Rinteln, 1631).

Spina, Bartolomeo, *De strigibus et lamiis* (Venice, 1523).

Stearne, John, *A confirmation and discovery of witchcraft [. . .]. Together with the confessions of those executed since May 1645* (London, 1648; Facsimile reprint Exeter: 'The Rota' at the University of Exeter, 1973).

Suarez, Francisco, *De malis angelis eorumque lapsu et culpa*. In *Opera Omnia* 2 (Paris, 1866).

Tanner, Adam, *Theologia Scholastica*. 4 vols. (Ingolstadt, 1626/7).

Theatrum Diabolorum (Frankfurt a. Main, 1569).

Theatrum de Veneficis (Frankfurt a. Main, 1586). s.v. Sawr.

Trithemius, Johannes, *Antipalus maleficorum (MS von 1508*. In *Joannis Trithemii, Paralipomena opusculorum [. . .]* (Mainz, 1605), pp. 273–426.

Wagstaffe, John, *The question of witchcraft debated. Or a discourse against their opinion that affirm witches* (London, 1669).

Webster, John, *The displaying of supposed witchcraft* (London, 1677).

Wecker, Johann, *Hexen-Büchlein, das ist: Ware entdeckung und erklärung [. . .] der Zauberey, und was von Zauberern, Unholden und Hengsten [!], Nachtschaden, Schützen, auch der Hexen händel, art, thun, lassen, wesen, artzeney [. . .] zu halten sey* (Colma, 1575).

Theatrum de Veneficis (Frankfurt a. Main, 1586), pp. 306–24.

Weyer, Johann, *De praestigiis daemonum* (Basel, 1563).

On witchcraft. An abridged translation of Johann Weyer's De praestigiis daemonum. Ed. Benjamin G. Kohl and H. C. Erik Midelfort (Asheville, NC: Pegasus Press, 1998).

De lamiis liber (Basel, 1577).

Witekind, Herman, *Christlich Bedencken und Erinnerung von Zauberey* (Heidelberg, 1585).

Secondary sources

Ankarloo, Bengt, Clark, Stuart, and Monter, William, *Magic and witchcraft in Europe*, vol. 4: *The period of the witch trials* (Philadelphia: University of Pennsylvania Press, 2002).

Bailey, Michael D., *Battling demons. Witchcraft, heresy, and reform in the late Middle Ages* (Philadelphia: University of Pennsylvania Press, 2003).

Behringer, Wolfgang, *Witchcraft persecutions in Bavaria* (Cambridge: Cambridge University Press, 1997).

Witches and witch-hunts. A global history (Cambridge: Polity Press, 2004).

'Detecting the ultimate conspiracy, or how Waldensians became witches'. In Barry Coward and Julian Swann (eds.), *Conspiracies and conspiracy theory in early modern Europe. From the Waldensians to the French Revolution* (Aldershot: Ashgate, 2004), pp. 13–34.

'Malleus Maleficarum'. In Richard Golden (ed.), *Encyclopedia of witchcraft* (St Barbara, CA: ABC-Clio, 2005).

Brown, Peter, 'Sorcery, demons and the rise of Christianity. From late antiquity into the Middle Ages'. In Peter Brown, *Religion and society in the age of Augustine* (London: Faber and Faber, 1972), pp. 119–46.

Caro Baroja, Julio, *Las Brujas y su Mundo* (Madrid: Revista de Occidente, 1961).

Certeau, Michel de, *La Possession de Loudon* (Paris, 1971).

Cervantes, Fernando, *The devil in the new world. The impact of diabolism in New Spain* (New Haven and London: Yale University Press, 1994).

Clark, Stuart, 'The scientific status of demonology'. In Brian Vickers (ed.), *Occult and scientific mentalities in the Renaissance* (Cambridge: Cambridge University Press, 1984), pp. 351–74.

Thinking with demons. The idea of witchcraft in early modern Europe (Oxford: Oxford University Press, 1996).

Cohn, Norman, *Europe's inner demons: an enquiry inspired by the great witch-hunt* (London: Heinemann for Sussex University Press, 1975).

Duhr, Bernhard, *Geschichte der Jesuiten in den Ländern deutscher Zunge*. 4 vols. (Freiburg: Herder Verlag, 1906–27).

Ernst, Cécile, *Teufelsaustreibung. Die Praxis der katholischen Kirche im 16. und 17. Jahrhundert* (Bern: H. Huber, 1972).

Ewen, Cecile L'Estrange, *Witchcraft and demonianism. A concise account derived from sworn depositions and confessions obtained in the courts of England and Wales* (London: Muller, 1933).

Golden, Richard (ed.), *Encyclopedia of witchcraft*. 4 vols. (St Barbara, CA: ABC-Clio, 2005).

Hansen, Joseph, and Franck, Johannes, *Quellen und Untersuchungen zur Geschichte des Hexenwahns und der Hexenverfolgung im Mittelalter. Mit einer Untersuchung der Geschichte des Wortes Hexe* (Bonn: C. Georgi, 1901; rpt. Hildesheim, 1963).

Harmening, Dieter, *Superstitio. Überlieferungs- und theoriegeschichtliche Untersuchungen zur kirchlich-theologischen Aberglaubensliteratur des Mittelalters* (Berlin: E. Schmidt, 1979).

Kamen, Henry, *The iron century: social change in Europe 1550–1660* (London: Weidenfeld and Nicolson, 1971).

Langton, Edward, *Essentials of demonology* (London: Epworth Press, 1949).

Lea, Henry Charles, *Materials toward a history of witchcraft*. Ed. Arthur C. Howland. 3 vols. (Philadelphia: University of Pennsylvania Press, 1939; rpt. New York and London, 1957).

Midelfort, H. C. Erik, 'The devil and German people: Reflections on the popularity of demon possession in sixteenth-century Germany'. In Steven Ozment (ed.), *Religion and culture in the Renaissance and Reformation* (Kirksville: Sixteenth Century Journal Publishers, 1989), pp. 99–119.

   A history of madness in sixteenth-century Germany (Stanford: Stanford University Press, 1999).

Monter, William, *Witchcraft in France and Switzerland. The borderlands during the Reformation* (Ithaca and London: Cornell University Press, 1976).

Mormando, Franco, *The preacher's demons. Bernardino of Siena and the social underworld of early Renaissance Italy* (Chicago: University of Chicago Press, 1999).

Normand, Lawrence, and Roberts, Gareth, *Witchcraft in early modern Scotland. James VI's 'Demonology' and the North Berwick witches* (Exeter: University of Exeter Press, 2000).

Pearl, Jonathan, *The crime of crimes. Demonology and politics in France, 1560–1620* (Waterloo, Ontario: Wilfrid Laurier University Press, 1999).

Rochelandet, Brigitte, *Sorcières, diables et bouchers en Franche-Comté* (Besançon: Cêtre, 1997).

Roper, Lyndal, *Oedipus and the devil. Witchcraft, sexuality and religion in early modern Europe* (London and New York: Routledge, 1994).

Sharpe, Jim, 'The devil in East Anglia: the Matthew Hopkins trials reconsidered'. In Jonathan Barry, Marianne Hester, and Gareth Roberts (eds.), *Witchcraft in early modern Europe* (Cambridge and New York: Cambridge University Press, 1996), pp. 237–56.

   Instruments of darkness. Witchcraft in England 1550–1750 (London: Penguin, 1996).

   Witchcraft in early modern England (London: Longmann, 2001).

Stephens, Walter, *Demon lovers. Witchcraft, sex, and the crisis of belief* (Chicago: University of Chicago Press, 2002).

Summers, Montague, *The history of witchcraft and demonology* (New York: A. A. Knopf, 1926).

Thorndike, Lynn, *History of magic and experimental science*. 8 vols. (New York: Macmillan, 1923–58).

Walker, Daniel P., *Spiritual and demonic magic from Ficino to Campanella* (London: Warburg Institute, University of London, 1958).

   The decline of hell. Seventeenth-century discussions of eternal torment (Chicago: University of Chicago Press, 1964).

   Unclean spirits. Possession and exorcism in France and England in the late sixteenth and early seventeenth centuries (London and Philadelphia: University of Pennsylvania Press, 1981).

Worobec, Christine D., *Possessed: Women, witches and demons in Imperial Russia* (Dekalb, IL: Northern Illinois University Press, 2001).

Zagorin, Perez, *Ways of lying. Dissimulation, persecution, and conformity in early modern Europe* (Cambridge, MA: Harvard University Press, 1990).

Zika, Charles, *Exorcising our demons. Magic, witchcraft and visual culture in early modern Europe* (Leiden and Boston: Brill, 2003).

23 SCIENCE AND RELIGION

Primary sources

Bacon, Francis, *The Instauratio magna. Last writings*. Ed. Graham Rees (Oxford: Clarendon Press, 2000).

New Atlantis and the Great Instauration. Ed. Jerry Weinberger (Arlington Heights, IL: H. Davidson, 1989).

Baillet, Adrien, *Vie de Monsieur Descartes* (1691; rpt. Hildesheim: Olms, 1972).

Copernicus, Nicolaus, *De revolutionibus orbium caelestium* (1543).

  On the revolutions. Trans. Edward Rosen (Baltimore: Johns Hopkins University Press, 1992).

Descartes, René, *Le monde*. Trans. Michael Sean Mahoney (New York: Abaris Books, 1979).

Ficino, Marsilio, *Theologia Platonica*. Ed. James Hankins with William Bowen. Trans. Michael J. B. Allen and John Warden (Cambridge, MA: Harvard University Press, 2001–).

Galilei, Galileo, *Dialogue concerning the two chief world systems*. Trans. Stillman Drake (Berkeley: University of California Press, 1962).

  'Letter to the Grand Duchess Christina'. In *Discoveries and opinions of Galileo*. Trans. Stillman Drake (New York: Doubleday, 1957).

Hooke, Robert, *Micrographia* (1665) (Facsimile, Lincolnwood, IL: Science Heritage, 1987).

Kepler, Johannes, *Secret of the universe. Mysterium cosmographicum*. Trans. A. M. Duncan (New York: Abaris Books, 1981).

  Harmonices mundi. The harmony of the world. Trans. E. J. Aiton *et al.* (Philadelphia: American Philosophical Society, 1997).

Lucretius, *De rerum natura. On the nature of things*. Trans. Martin Ferguson Smith (Indianapolis: Hackett Publishing, 2001).

Melanchthon, Philip, *Doctrinae physicae elementa* (Lyon: Jean de Tournes and Gul. Gazeius, 1552).

Newton, Isaac, *The Principia: mathematical principles of natural philosophy*. Trans. I. Bernard Cohen (Berkeley: University of California Press, 1999).

Plato, *Timaeus*. Trans. Donald Zeyl (Indianapolis: Hackett Publishing, 2000).

Pomponazzi, Pietro, 'De immortalitate animi'. 'On the immortality of the soul'. Trans. William Henry Hay II with John Herman Randall Jr. In Ernst Cassirer *et al.* (eds.), *The Renaissance philosophy of man* (Chicago: University of Chicago Press, 1948), pp. 257–381.

Titelmans, Frans, *Compendium naturalis philosophiae* (Paris: Michael de Roigny, 1582).

Secondary sources

Ariew, Roger, 'Descartes and scholasticism: the intellectual background to Descartes' thought'. In John Cottingham (ed.), *The Cambridge companion to Descartes* (Cambridge: Cambridge University Press, 1992), pp. 58–90.

Barker, Peter, 'The role of religion in the Lutheran response to Copernicus'. In Margaret Osler (ed.), *Rethinking the scientific revolution* (Cambridge: Cambridge University Press, 2000), pp. 59–88.

  'Stoic contributions to early modern science'. In Margaret Osler (ed.), *Atoms, pneuma and tranquillity: Epicurean and Stoic themes in European thought* (Cambridge: Cambridge University Press, 1991), pp. 135–54.

Bellucci, Dino, *Science de la nature et Réformation. La physique au service de la réforme dans l'enseignement de Philippe Melanchthon* (Rome: Edizioni Vivere In, 1998).

Bertoloni Meli, Domenico, 'Francesco Redi e Marcello Malpighi: ricerca anatomica e practica medica'. In Walter Bernardi and Luigi Guerrini (eds.), *Francesco Redi: un protagonista della scienza moderna* (Florence: Olschki, 1999), pp. 73–86.

Blackwell, Richard J., *Galileo, Bellarmine and the Bible* (Notre Dame: University of Notre Dame Press, 1991).

Blair, Ann, 'Mosaic physics and the search for a pious natural philosophy in the late Renaissance', *Isis* 91 (2000): 32–58.

The theater of nature: Jean Bodin and Renaissance science (Princeton: Princeton University Press, 1997).

'Tycho Brahe's critique of Copernicus and the Copernican system', *Journal of the History of Ideas* 51 (1990): 355–77.

Brooke, John Hedley, *Science and religion: a historical perspective* (Cambridge: Cambridge University Press, 1991).

Cohen, I. Bernard (ed.), *Puritanism and the rise of modern science* (New Brunswick, NJ: Rutgers University Press, 1990).

Cohen, I. Bernard, and Westfall, Richard (eds.), *Newton* (New York: Norton Critical Editions, 1995).

Courtenay, William, *Capacity and volition: a history of the distinction of absolute and ordained power* (Bergamo: Lubrina, 1990).

Cunningham, Andrew, 'How the Principia got its name; or, taking Natural Philosophy seriously', *History of Science* 29 (1991): 377–92.

Daston, Lorraine, and Park, Katharine (eds.), *Cambridge history of science* vol. 3: *Early modern science* (Cambridge: Cambridge University Press, 2006).

Dobbs, Betty Jo Teeter, 'Newton as final cause and first mover', *Isis* 85 (1994): 633–43.

Donnelly, John Patrick, 'Calvinist Thomism', *Viator* 7 (1976): 441–55.

Draper, John William, *The history of the conflict between science and religion* (1875; rpt. Westmead: Gregg International Publishers, 1970).

Fatio, Olivier (ed.), *Les églises face aux sciences du Moyen Age au XXe siècle.* Actes du Colloque de la Commission internationale d'histoire ecclésiastique comparée, 1989 (Geneva: Droz, 1991).

Feingold, Mordechai (ed.), *The new science and Jesuit science: seventeenth-century perspectives.* (Dordrecht: Kluwer, 2003).

Feldhay, Rivka, and Heyd, Michael, 'The discourse of pious science', *Science in Context* 3 (1989): 109–42.

Ferngren, Gary B., *Science and religion. A historical introduction* (Baltimore: Johns Hopkins University Press, 2002).

Ferrone, Vincenzo, and Firpo, Massimo, 'From Inquisitors to microhistorians: a critique of Pietro Redondi's *Galileo Eretico*', *Journal of Modern History* 58 (1986): 485–524.

Field, Judith V., *Kepler's geometrical cosmology* (Chicago: University of Chicago Press, 1988).

Findlen, Paula (ed.), *Athanasius Kircher. The last man who knew everything* (New York and London: Routledge, 2004).

Finocchiaro, Maurice (ed.), *The Galileo affair: a documentary history* (Berkeley: University of California Press, 1989).

Firpo, Luigi, 'The flowering and withering of speculative philosophy. Italian philosophy and the Counter-Reformation: the condemnation of Francesco Patrizi'. In Eric Cochrane (ed.), *The Late Italian Renaissance 1525–1630* (New York: Harper Torchbooks, 1970), pp. 266–86.

Fragnito, Gigliola (ed.), *Church, censorship and culture in early modern Italy.* Trans. Andrew Belton (Cambridge: Cambridge University Press, 2001).

Gamble, Richard C., *Calvin and science* (New York: Garland, 1992).

Gieryn, Thomas F., 'Distancing science from religion in seventeenth-century England', *Isis* 79 (1988): 582–93.

Gilly, Carlos, '"Theophrastia Sancta" – Paracelsianism as a religion in conflict with the established churches'. In Ole Peter Grell (ed.), *Paracelsus. The man and his reputation, his ideas and their transformation* (Leiden: Brill, 1998), pp. 151–85.

Gingerich, Owen, *An annotated census of Copernicus' De revolutionibus (Nuremberg, 1543) and (Basel, 1566)* (Leiden: Brill, 2002).

Gingerich, Owen and Westman, Robert, *The Wittich connection: conflict and priority in late 16th-century cosmology* (Philadelphia: American Philosophical Society, 1988).

Grant, Edward (ed.), *A source book in medieval science* (Cambridge, MA: Harvard University Press, 1974).

Gunnoe, Charles D. Jr, 'Paracelsus's biography among his detractors'. In Gerhild Scholz Williams and Charles D. Gunnoe Jr (eds.), *Paracelsian moments. Science, medicine and astrology in early modern Europe* (Kirksville, MO: Truman State University Press, 2002), 3–18.

Hankins, James, 'Marsilio Ficino as a critic of scholasticism', *Vivens Homo* 5 (1994): 325–34.

Harrison, Peter, *The Bible, Protestantism and the rise of natural science* (Cambridge: Cambridge University Press, 1998).

Heilbron, John L., *The sun in the Church. Cathedrals as solar observatories* (Cambridge, MA: Harvard University Press, 1999).

Helm, Jürgen, and Winkelmann, Annette (eds.), *Religious confessions and the sciences in the sixteenth century* (Leiden: Brill, 2001).

Hooykaas, Reijer, 'Science and reformation', *Cahiers d'histoire moderne* 3 (1956–57): 109–39. *Religion and the rise of modern science* (Edinburgh: Scottish Academic Press, 1972).

Hotson, Howard, *Paradise postponed. Johann Heinrich Alsted and the birth of Calvinist millenarianism* (Dordrecht: Kluwer, 2000).

Hunter, Michael, *The Royal Society and its fellows 1660–1700: the morphology of an early scientific institution* (Oxford: British Society for the History of Science, 1994).

Hunter, Michael, and Wootton, David (eds.), *Atheism from the Reformation to the Enlightenment* (Oxford: Clarendon Press, 1992).

Jolley, Nicholas, 'The reception of Descartes' philosophy'. In John Cottingham (ed.), *The Cambridge Companion to Descartes* (Cambridge: Cambridge University Press, 1992), pp. 393–423.

Knoeff, Rina, *Herman Boerhaave (1668–1738). Calvinist chemist and physician* (Amsterdam: Koninklijke Nederlandse Akademie van Wetenschappen, 2002).

Kraye, Jill, 'The philosophy of the Italian Renaissance'. In *The Renaissance and seventeenth-century rationalism, Routledge history of philosophy*, vol. 4. Ed. G. H. R. Parkinson (London and New York: Routledge, 1993), pp. 16–69.

Kristeller, Paul O., *Eight philosophers of the Italian Renaissance* (Stanford: Stanford University Press, 1964).

Kroll, Richard *et al.* (eds.), *Philosophy, science and religion in England 1640–1700* (Cambridge: Cambridge University Press, 1992).

Kusukawa, Sachiko, *The transformation of natural philosophy* (Cambridge: Cambridge University Press, 1995).

Lagrée, Jacqueline. *La religion naturelle* (Paris: Presses Universitaires de France, 1991).

Lattis, James, *Between Copernicus and Galileo: Christoph Clavius and the collapse of Ptolemaic cosmology* (Chicago: University of Chicago Press, 1994).

Lindberg, David, and Numbers, Ronald (eds.), *God and nature* (Berkeley: University of California Press, 1986).

Mayaud, Pierre Noël, *La condamnation des livres coperniciens et sa révocation à la lumière de documents inédits des Congrégations de l'Index et de l'Inquisition* (Rome: Editrice Pontificia Universita Gregoriana, 1997).

Mercer, Christia, 'The vitality and importance of early modern Aristotelianism'. In Tom Sorell (ed.), *The rise of modern philosophy: the tension between the new and traditional philosophies from Machiavelli to Leibniz* (Oxford: Clarendon Press, 1993), pp. 33–67.

Menn, Stephen, 'The intellectual setting'. In Daniel Garber and Michael Ayers (eds.), *The Cambridge history of seventeenth-century philosophy.* 2 vols. (Cambridge: Cambridge University Press, 1998), vol. 1, pp. 33–86.

Merton, Robert, *Science, technology and society in seventeenth-century England* (Atlantic Highlands, NJ: Humanities Press, 1978).

Methuen, Charlotte, *Kepler's Tübingen: stimulus to a theological mathematics* (Aldershot: Ashgate, 1998).

Mornet, Daniel, 'Les enseignements des bibliothèques privées (1750–1780)', *Revue d'Histoire littéraire de la France* 17 (1910): 449–96.

Osler, Margaret, 'Baptizing Epicurean atomism: Pierre Gassendi on the immortality of the soul'. In Margaret Osler and Paul Lawrence Farber (eds.), *Religion, science and worldview: essays in honor of Richard S. Westfall* (Cambridge: Cambridge University Press, 1985), pp. 163–84.

Peltonen, Markku (ed.), *Cambridge companion to Bacon* (Cambridge: Cambridge University Press, 1996).

Pine, Martin L., *Pietro Pomponazzi: radical philosopher of the Renaissance* (Padua: Editrice Antenore, 1986).

Redondi, Pietro, *Galileo heretic.* Trans. Raymond Rosenthal (London: Allen Lane, 1987).

Russo, François, 'Le rôle respectif du catholicisme et du protestantisme dans le développement des sciences aux XVIe et XVIIe siècles', *Journal of World History* 3 (1956): 854–80.

Sargent, Rose-Mary, *The diffident naturalist: Robert Boyle and the philosophy of experiment* (Chicago: University of Chicago Press, 1995).

Schmitt, Charles B., *Aristotle and the Renaissance* (Cambridge, MA: Harvard University Press, 1993).

'The rise of the philosophical textbook'. *Cambridge history of Renaissance philosophy* (Cambridge: Cambridge University Press, 1988), pp. 795–6.

Science in Context, 3 (1989), entitled 'After Merton': Protestant and Catholic science in seventeenth-century Europe.

Sciences et religions de Copernic à Galilée, 1540–1610: actes du colloque international organisé par l'Ecole française de Rome, en collaboration avec l'Ecole nationale des chartes et l'Istituto italiano per gli studi filosofici, avec la participation de l'Università di Napoli "Federico II", Rome, 12–14 décembre 1996 (Rome: Ecole Française de Rome, 1999).

Segre, Michael, *In the wake of Galileo* (New Brunswick: Rutgers University Press, 1991).

Shapin, Steven, *A social history of truth: civility and science in seventeenth-century England* (Chicago: University of Chicago Press, 1994).

Shea, William, 'Galileo and the Church'. In Daniel Lindberg and Ronald Numbers (eds.), *God and nature* (Berkeley: University of California Press, 1986), pp. 114–35.

Stephenson, Bruce, *The music of the heavens: Kepler's harmonic astronomy* (Princeton: Princeton University Press, 1994).

Thijssen, J. M. M. H., 'What really happened on 7 March 1277? Bishop Tempier's condemnation and its institutional context'. In Edith Sylla and Michael McVaugh (eds.), *Texts and contexts in ancient and medieval science: studies on the occasion of John E. Murdoch's seventieth birthday* (Leiden: Brill, 1997), pp. 84–105.

Vermij, Rienk, *The Calvinist Copernicans: the reception of the new astronomy in the Dutch Republic 1575–1750* (Amsterdam: Koninklijke Nederlandse Akademie van Wetenschappen, 2002).

Wallace, William A. 'The philosophical setting of medieval science'. In David Lindberg (ed.), *Science in the Middle Ages* (Chicago: University of Chicago Press, 1978).

Webster, Charles, *The great instauration: science, medicine and reform 1626–60* (London: Duckworth, 1975).

Westfall, Richard, *Science and religion in seventeenth-century England* (New Haven: Yale University Press, 1958).

Westman, Robert, 'The Melanchthon circle, Rheticus and the Wittenberg interpretation of the Copernican theory', *Isis* 66 (1975): 165–93.

White, Andrew Dickson, *A history of the warfare of science with theology in Christendom* (1896) (Buffalo: Prometheus Books, 1993).

Wojcik, Jan, *Robert Boyle and the limits of reason* (Cambridge: Cambridge University Press, 1997).

24 THE NEW CLERGIES

Secondary sources

Aretin, Karl Otmar Freiherr von, *Heiliges Römisches Reich 1776–1806*, vol. 1 (Wiesbaden: Kohlhammer Verlag, 1967).

Asch, Ronald G., ' "Lumine solis". Der Favorit und die politische Kultur des Hofes in Westeuropa'. In Michael Kaiser and Andreas Pečar (eds.), *Der zweite Mann im Staat. Oberste Amtsträger und Favoriten im Umkreis der Reichsfürsten in der Frühen Neuzeit*. Zeitschrift für Historische Forschung, Beiheft 32 (Berlin: Duncker and Humblot, 2003), pp. 21–38.

Bahlcke, Joachim, 'Geistlichkeit und Politik. Der ständisch organisierte Klerus in Böhmen und Ungarn in der Frühen Neuzeit'. In Joachim Bahlcke, Hans-Jürgen Bömelburg, and Norbert Kersken (eds.), *Ständefreiheit und Staatsgestaltung in Ostmitteleuropa* (Leipzig: Universitätsverlag, 1996), pp. 161–86.

Barrie-Curien, Victor, 'The English clergy 1560–1620: recruitment and social status', *History of European Ideas* 9 (1988): 451–63.

Baur, Jörg, 'Das kirchliche Amt im Protestantismus'. In Jörg Baur (ed.), *Das Amt im ökumenischen Kontext* (Stuttgart: Kohlhammer Verlag, 1980), pp. 103–38.

Beck, Rainer, *Unterfinning. Ländliche Welt vor Anbruch der Moderne* (Munich: Beck Verlag, 1993).

Becker, Thomas P., *Konfessionalisierung in Kurköln. Untersuchungen zur Durchsetzung der katholischen Reform in den Dekanaten Ahrgau und Bonn* (Bonn: Ed. Röhrscheid, 1989).

Bergin, Joseph, 'Between estate and profession: the Catholic parish clergy of early modern western Europe'. In Martin L. Bush (ed.), *Social orders and social classes in Europe since 1500: Studies in social stratification* (London and New York: Oxford University Press, 1992), pp. 66–85.

The making of the French episcopate 1589–1661 (New Haven: Yale University Press, 1996).

Burns, John (ed.), *The Cambridge history of political thought 1450–1700* (Cambridge: Cambridge University Press, 1991).

Collinson, Patrick, *The religion of Protestants* (Oxford: Oxford University Press, 1982).

Dickerhof, Harald, 'Die katholischen Gelehrtenschulen des konfessionellen Zeitalters im Heiligen Römischen Reich'. In Wolfgang Reinhard and Heinz Schilling (eds.), *Die katholische Konfessionalisierung* (Gütersloh: Gütersloher Verlagshaus, 1995), pp. 348–70.

Dreitzel, Horst, *Monarchiebegriffe in der Fürstengesellschaft. Semantik und Theorie der Einherrschaft in Deutschland von der Reformation bis zum Vormärz* (Cologne, Weimar, and Vienna: Böhlau Verlag, 1991).

Dürr, Renate, 'Images of the priesthood: an analysis of Catholic sermons from the late seventeenth century'. *Central European History* 33 (2000): 87–107.

Kirchenräume. Handlungsmuster von Pfarrern, Obrigkeiten und Gemeinden in Stadt und Kleinem Stift Hildesheim, 1550–1750 (Gütersloh: Gütersloher Verlagshaus, 2005).

Fagerberg, Holsten, *Reformationszeit*. TRE Vol. 2, 1978, 574.

Fantappie, Carlo, 'Istituzioni ecclesiastiche e istruzione secondaria nell' Italia moderna: I seminari-collegi vescovili', *Jahrbuch des deutsch-italienischen historischen Instituts in Trient* 15 (1989): 186–240.

Feldbauer, Otto, 'Der Priester als Vorbild und Spiegel. Die Konfessionalisierung des Pfarrklerus im Herzogtum/Kurfürstentum Bayern 1560–1685'. In P. Friess and A. Kießling (eds.), *Konfessionalisierung und Region* (Constance: Universitätsverlag Konstanz, 1999), pp. 247–73.

Fischer, Albert, *Reformatio und Restitutio. Das Bistum Chur im Zeitalter der tridentinischen Glaubenserneuerung. Zugleich ein Beitrag zur Geschichte der Priesterbildung und Pastoralreform 1601–1661* (Zurich: Chronos Verlag, 2000).

Freitag, Werner, *Pfarrer, Kirche, and ländliche Gesellschaft, Das Dekanat Vechta 1400–1803* (Bielefeld: Verlag für Regionalgeschichte, 1998).

Gatz, Erwin (ed.), *Der Diözesanklerus* (Freiburg, Basel, and Vienna: Verlag Herder, 1995).

Gugerli, David, *Zwischen 'Pfrund' und Predigt. Die protestantische Pfarrfamilie auf der Zürcher Landschaft im ausgehenden 18. Jahrhundert* (Zurich: Chronos Verlag, 1988).

Hahn, Alois, *Die Rezeption des tridentinischen Pfarrerideals im westtrierischen Pfarrklerus des 16. und 17. Jahrhunderts, Untersuchungen zur Geschichte des katholische Reform im Erzbistum Trier.* Publications de la Section Historique de l'Institut G.-D. de Luxembourg, 90 (Luxemburg: Linden, 1974).

Hengst, Karl, *Jesuiten an Universitäten und Jesuitenuniversitäten* (Munich: Schöningh Verlag, 1981).

Holzem, Andreas, *Religion und Lebensformen. Katholische Konfessionalisierung im Sendgericht des Fürstbistums Münster* (Paderborn: Schöningh Verlag, 2000).

Hsia, Ronnie Po-Chia, *Gegenreformation: Die Welt der katholischen Erneuerung 1540–1770* (Frankfurt a. Main: Fischer Verlag, 1998).

Social discipline in the Reformation. Central Europe 1550–1750 (London and New York: Oxford University Press, 1989).

Jedin, Hubert, 'Das Leitbild des Priesters nach dem Tridentinum und dem Vaticanum II'. *Theologie und Glaube* 60 (1970): 102–24.

Julia, Dominique, 'Il prete'. In Marc Vovelle (ed.), *L'uomo dell' Illuminismo* (Rome and Bari: University Press, 1992), pp. 399–443.

Kaufmann, Thomas, *Universität und lutherische Konfessionalisierung. Die Rostocker Theologieprofessoren und ihr Beitrag zur theologischen Bildung und kirchlichen Gestaltung im Herzogtum Mecklenburg zwischen 1550 und 1675* (Gütersloh: Gütersloher Verlagshaus, 1997).

Knetsch, Georg, 'Die Geistlichen in Frickenhausen/M. Grundlagen und Personen'. In Karl W. Wittstadt (ed.), *Kirche und ländliche Gesellschaft in Mainfranken von der Reformation bis zur neuesten Zeit* (Würzburg: Verlag der Universität Würzburg, 1988), pp. 110–230.

Millet, Hélène, and Moraw, Peter, 'Clerics in the state'. In Wolfgang Reinhard (ed.), *Power elites and state building* (New York: Oxford University Press, 1996).

Moser-Rath, Elisabeth, *Dem Kirchenvolk die Leviten gelesen: Alltag im Spiegel süddeutscher Barockpredigten* (Stuttgart: Kohlhammer Verlag, 1991).

O'Day, Rosemarie, *The English clergy. The emergence and consolidation of a profession 1558–1642* (Leicester: University Press, 1996).

Paiva, José Pedro, 'The Portuguese secular clergy in the sixteenth and seventeenth centuries'. In Eszter Andor and István Toth (eds.), *Frontiers of faith. Religious exchange and the constitution of religious identities 1400–1750* (Budapest: European Science Foundation, 2001), pp. 157–66.

Papenheim, Martin, *Karrieren in der Kirche: Bischöfe in Nord- und Süditalien 1676–1903* (Tübingen: Max Niemeyer Verlag, 2001).

Pfister, Ulrich, 'Pastors and priests in the early modern grisons: organized profession or side activity'. *Central European History* 33 (2000): 41–65.

Reinhard, Wolfgang, *Geschichte der Staatsgewalt. Eine vergleichende Verfassungsgeschichte Europas von den Anfängen bis in die Gegenwart* (Munich: Beck Verlag, 1999).

Riegg, Ernst, *Konfliktbereitschaft und Mobilität. Die protestantischen Geistlichen zwölf süddeutscher Reichsstädte* (Leinfelden-Echterdingen: DRW-Verlag, 2002).

Schindling, Anton, 'Schulen und Universitäten im 16. und 17. Jahrhundert: 10 Thesen zur Bildungsexpansion, Laienbildung und Konfessionalisierung nach der Reformation'. In Wolfgang Brandmüller (ed.), *Ecclesia militans. Studien zur Konzilien- und Reformationsgeschichte; Remigius Bäumer zum 70. Geburtstag gewidmet* (Paderborn: Schöningh Verlag, 1988), pp. 561–70.

Schmidt, Peter, *Das Collegium Germanicum in Rom und die Germaniker. Zur Funktion eines römischen Ausländerseminars 1552–1914* (Tübingen: Max Niemeyer Verlag, 1984).

Schorn-Schütte, Luise, and Scott Dixon, 'Introduction'. In Luise Schorn-Schütte and Scott Dixon (eds.), *The Protestant clergy of early modern Europe* (Houndmills: Palgrave Macmillan, 2003), pp. 1–38.

'Die Geistlichen vor der Revolution. Zur Sozialgeschichte der evangelischen Pfarrer und des katholischen Klerus am Ende des Alten Reiches'. In Helmut Berding, Etienne François, and Hans Peter Ullmann (eds.), *Deutschland und Frankreich im Zeitalter der französischen Revolution* (Frankfurt a. Main: Suhrkamp, 1989), pp. 216–44.

Evangelische Geistlichkeit in der Frühneuzeit. Deren Anteil an der Entfaltung frühmoderner Staatlichkeit und Gesellschaft. (16.–18. Jahrhundert) (Gütersloh: Gütersloher Verlagshaus, 1996).

'Matrimony as profession: the clergyman's wife'. In Silvana Seidel Menchi, Thomas Kuehn, and Anne Jacobson Schutte (eds.), *Time, space, and women's lives in early modern Europe* (Kirksville, MO: Truman State University Press, 2001), pp. 255–77.

'Priest, preacher, pastor: research on clerical office in early modern Europe', *Central European History* 33 (2000): 1–39.

'Zwischen "Amt" und "Beruf": Der Prediger als Wächter, "seelenhirt" oder Volkslehrer. Evangelische Geistlichkeit im Alten Reich und in der schweizerischen Eidgenossenschaft im 18. Jahrhundert'. In Luise Schorn-Schütte and Walter Sparn (eds.), *Protestantische Pfarrer. Zur sozialen und politischen Rolle einer bürgerlichen Gruppe in der deutschen Gesellschaft des 18. bis 20. Jahrhunderts* (Stuttgart: Kohlhammer Verlag, 1997), pp. 1–35.

Shoenberger, Cintia G., 'The confession of Magdeburg and the Lutheran doctrine of resistance' (Ph.D. dissertation: University of Columbia, 1972).

Skinner, Quentin, *The foundations of modern political thought* (Cambridge: Cambridge University Press, 1991).

Strom, Jonathan, *Orthodoxy and reform: the clergy in seventeenth century Rostock* (Tübingen: Mohr Siebeck, 1999).

Swanson, Richard N., 'Before the Protestant clergy: the construction and deconstruction of medieval priesthood'. In Scott Dixon and Luise Schorn-Schütte (eds.), *The Protestant clergy of early modern Europe* (Houndmills: Palgrave Macmillan, 2003), pp. 39–59.

Titze, Hartmut, 'Überfüllung und Mangel im evangelischen Pfarramt seit dem ausgehenden 18. Jahrhundert'. In Luise Schorn-Schütte and Walter Sparn (eds.), *Protestantische Pfarrer. Zur sozialen und politischen Rolle einer bürgerlichen Gruppe in der deutschen Gesellschaft des 18. bis 20. Jahrhunderts* (Stuttgart: Kohlhammer Verlag, 1997), pp. 56–76.

Turchini, Andrea, 'La nascità del sacerdozio come professione'. In Paolo Prodi (ed.), *Disciplina dell' anima, disciplina del corpo e disciplina della società tra medioevo ed età moderna* (Bologna: Il Mulino, 1994), pp. 225–56.

Vogler, Bernhard, *Le clergé protestant rhénan au siècle de la réforme (1555–1619)* (Paris: Ed. Ophrys).

Wahl, Johannes, *Lebensplanung und Alltagserfahrung. Württembergische Pfarrerfamilien im 17. Jahrhundert* (Mainz: Philipp v. Zabern, 2000).

Wendland, Andreas, 'Träger der Konfessionalisierung und spiritueller Habitus. Beobachtungen zur Kapuzinermission in den Drei Bünden im 17. Jahrhundert', *Wissenschaft und Weisheit. Franziskanische Studien zu Theologie, Philosophie und Geschichte* 76 (2004): 71–95.

25 WOMEN AND RELIGIOUS CHANGE

Primary sources

Apóstoles, Francisca de los, *The inquisition of Francisca: a sixteenth-century visionary on trial.* Ed. and trans. Gillian T. W. Ahlgren (Chicago: University of Chicago Press, 2005).

Arenal, Electa, and Schlau, Stacey (eds.), *Untold sisters: Hispanic nuns in their own works* (Albuquerque: University of New Mexico Press, 1989).

Bibliography

Beilin, Elaine V. (ed.), *The examinations of Anne Askew* (New York: Oxford University Press, 1996).

Collett, Barry, *A long and troubled pilgrimage: the correspondence of Marguerite D'Angoulême and Vittoria Colonna 1540–1545* (Princeton: Princeton Theological Seminary, 2000).

Dentière, Marie, *Epistle to Marguerite de Navarre and preface to a sermon by John Calvin*. Ed. and trans. Mary B. McKinley (Chicago: University of Chicago Press, 2004).

Ferrazzi, Cecelia, *Autobiography of an aspiring saint*. Ed. and trans. Anne Jacobson Schutte (Chicago: University of Chicago Press, 1996).

Irwin, Joyce (ed.), *Womanhood in radical Protestantism* (New York: E. Mellen, 1979).

Joldersma, Hermoine, and Grijp, Louis (eds. and trans.), *'Elisabeth's manly courage': testimonials and songs by and about martyred Anabaptist women* (Milwaukee: Marquette University Press, 2001).

Karant-Nunn, Susan C., and Wiesner-Hanks, Merry E. (eds. and trans.), *Luther on women: a sourcebook* (Cambridge: Cambridge University Press, 2003).

Matheson, Peter (ed. and trans.), *Argula von Grumbach: a woman's voice in the Reformation* (Edinburgh: T. & T. Clark, 1995).

Rhodes, Elizabeth (ed. and trans.), *'This tight embrace': Luise de Carvajal y Mendoza* (Milwaukee: Marquette University Press, 2000).

Riccoboni, Bartolomea, *Spiritual letters*. Ed. and trans. Daniel Bornstein (Chicago: University of Chicago Press, 2000).

Wiesner-Hanks, Merry E., and Skocir, Joan (eds. and trans.), *Convents confront the Reformation: Catholic and Protestant nuns in Germany* (Milwaukee: Marquette University Press, 1996).

Zell, Katharina Schütz, *Church mother: the writings of a Protestant reformer in sixteenth-century Germany*. Ed. and trans. Elsie Anne McKee (Chicago: University of Chicago Press, 2006).

Secondary sources

Baernstein, P. Renée, *A convent tale: a century of sisterhood in Spanish Milan* (New York: Routledge, 2002).

Bilinkoff, Jodi, *Related lives: confessors and their female penitents, 1450–1750* (Ithaca: Cornell University Press, 2005).

Brewer, Carolyn, *Shamanism, Catholicism, and gender relations in colonial Philippines, 1521–1695* (Aldershot: Ashgate, 2004).

Conrad, Anne, *Zwischen Closter und Welt: Ursulinen und Jesuitinnen in der Katholischen Reformbewegung des 16./17. Jahrhunderts* (Mainz: Zabern, 1991).

Conrad, Anne (ed.), *'In Christo ist weden man noch weyb': Frauen in der Zeit der Reformation und der katholischen Reform* (Münster i. W.: Aschendorff, 1999).

Crawford, Patricia, *Women and religion in England, 1500–1750* (London: Routledge, 1993).

Diefendorf, Barbara, *From penitence to charity: pious women and the Catholic Reformation in Paris* (Oxford: Oxford University Press, 2004).

Dinan, Susan E., and Meters, Debra (eds.), *Women and religion in old and new worlds* (London: Routledge, 2001).

Forster, Marc R., and Kaplan, Benjamin J. (eds.), *Piety and family in early modern Europe* (Aldershot: Ashgate, 2005).

Giles, Mary G. (ed.), *Women in the Inquisition: Spain and the New World* (Baltimore: Johns Hopkins University Press, 1998).

Greer, Allan, and Bilinkoff, Jodi (eds.), *Colonial saints: discovering the holy in the Americas, 1500–1800* (New York: Routledge, 2003).

Haliczer, Stephen, *Between exaltation and infamy: female mystics in the golden age of Spain* (New York: Oxford University Press, 2002).

Harrington, Joel F., *Reordering marriage and society in Reformation Germany* (Cambridge: Cambridge University Press, 1995).

Karant-Nunn, Susan C., *The reformation of ritual: an interpretation of early modern Germany* (London: Routledge, 1997).

Kendrick, Robert, *Celestial sirens: nuns and their music in early modern Italy* (Oxford: Oxford University Press, 1996).

Kingdon, Robert, *Adultery and divorce in Calvin's Geneva* (Cambridge, MA: Harvard University Press, 1995).

Kobelt-Groch, Marian, *Aufsässige Töchter Gottes: Frauen im Bauernkrieg und in den Taüferbewegungen* (Frankfurt: Campus, 1993).

Kreitzer, Beth, *Reforming Mary: Lutheran preaching on the Virgin Mary in the sixteenth century* (Oxford: Oxford University Press, 2004).

Lehfeldt, Elizabeth, *Religious women in golden age Spain: the permeable cloister* (Aldershot: Ashgate, 2005).

Leonard, Amy, *Nails in the wall: Catholic nuns in Reformation Germany* (Chicago: University of Chicago Press, 2005).

Lowe, K. J. P., *Nuns' chronicles and convent culture in Renaissance and Counter-Reformation Italy* (Cambridge: Cambridge University Press, 2003).

Marshall, Sherrin (ed.), *Women in Reformation and Counter-Reformation Europe: public and private worlds* (Bloomington: Indiana University Press, 1989).

McKee, Elsie Anne, *Katharina Schütz Zell*. 2 vols. (Leiden: Brill, 1999).

Monson, Craig (ed.), *The crannied wall: women, religion and the arts in early modern Europe* (Ann Arbor: University of Michigan Press, 1992).

Perry, Mary Elizabeth, *The handless maiden: Moriscos and the politics of religion in early modern Spain* (Princeton: Princeton University Press, 2005).

Peters, Christine, *Patterns of piety: women, gender, and religion in late medieval and Reformation England* (Cambridge: Cambridge University Press, 2003).

Ranft, Patricia, *Women and the religious life in premodern Europe* (New York: St Martin's, 1996).

Rapley, Elizabeth, *A social history of the cloister: daily life in the teaching monasteries of the Old Regime* (Montreal and Kingston: McGill-Queens University Press, 2001).

Roper, Lyndal, *The holy household: women and morals in Reformation Augsburg* (Oxford: Clarendon Press, 1989).

Snyder, C. Arnold, and Huebert Hecht, Linda A. (eds.), *Profiles of Anabaptist women: sixteenth-century reforming pioneers* (Waterloo, Ontario: Wilfried Laurier University Press, 1996).

Sperling, Jutta Gisela, *Convents and the body politic in Renaissance Venice* (Chicago: University of Chicago Press, 2000).

Strasser, Ulrike, *State of virginity: gender, religion, and politics in an early modern Catholic state* (Ann Arbor: University of Michigan Press, 2004).

Thompson, John Lee, *John Calvin and the daughters of Sarah: women in regular and exceptional roles in the exegesis of Calvin, his predecessors and his contemporaries* (Geneva: Droz, 1992).

Walker, Claire, *Gender and politics in early modern Europe: English convents in France and the Low Countries* (London, Palgrave-Macmillan, 2003).

Watt, Diane, *Sectaries of God: women prophets in late medieval and early modern England* (Rochester, NY: Boydell and Brewer, 1997).

Weaver, Elissa B., *Convent theatre in early modern Italy: spiritual fun and learning for women* (Cambridge: Cambridge University Press, 2002).

Weissler, Chava, *Voices of the matriarchs: listening to the prayers of early modern Jewish women* (Boston: Beacon Press, 1998).

Westphal, Siegrid. *Frau und lutherische Konfessionalisierung: Eine Untersuchung zum Fürstentum Pfalz-Neuburg, 1542–1614* (Frankfurt: Peter Lang, 1994).

Wiesner-Hanks, Merry E., *Christianity and the regulation of sexuality in the early modern world: regulating desire, reforming practice* (London: Routledge, 2000).

Wood, Jeryldene M., *Women, art, and spirituality: the Poor Clares of early modern Italy* (Cambridge: Cambridge University Press, 1996).

Woodford, Charlotte, *Nuns as historians in early modern Germany* (Oxford: Oxford University Press, 2003).

Wunder, Heide, *'Er ist die Sonn', sie ist der Mond': Frauen in der frühen Neuzeit* (Munich: C. H. Beck'sche, 1992).

Zarri, Gabriella, *Le sante vive. Profezie di corte e devozione feminille tra '400 e '500* (Turin: Rosenberg and Sellier, 1990).

Recinti: Donne, clausura, e matrimonio nella prima età moderna (Bologna: Il Mulino, 2000).

26 CHRISTIANITY AND JUDAISM

Primary sources

Buxtorf, Johann, *Synagoga Judaica. Noviter restaurata: Das ist: Erneuerte jüdische Synagog, oder Juden-Schul, darinnen der gantze jüdische Glaube, und Glaubens-Ubung . . . sowohl offentlich als Heimlich im Gebrauch sind* (Frankfurt; Leipzig: J. P. Kraussen, 1738).

Gans, David, *Zemah David: A chronicle of Jewish and world history* (Prague, 1592). [Hebrew]. Ed. Mordechai Breuer (Jerusalem: Magnes Press, 1983).

Luther, Martin, *D. Martin Luthers Werke: kritische Gesammtausgabe* (Weimar: H. Böhlau, 1883–).

Modena, Leon, *The autobiography of a seventeenth-century Venetian rabbi: Leon Modena's* Life of Judah. Ed. and trans. Mark R. Cohen (Princeton: Princeton University Press, 1988).

Rosheim, Joseph, *Joseph of Rosheim: historical writings* [Hebrew]. Ed., trans., and intro. Chava Fraenkel-Goldschmidt (Jerusalem: Magnes Press, 1996).

Troki, Isaac bar Avraham, *Hizzuk Emunah* [Hebrew] (New York: General Lainataip, 1932).

Secondary sources

Ben-Sasson, Haim Hillel, 'Jews and Christian sectarians: existential similarity and dialectical tensions in sixteenth-century Moravia and Poland-Lithuania', *Viator* 4 (1973): 369–85.

Bodian, Miriam, 'Biblical Hebrews and the rhetoric of republicanism: seventeenth-century Portuguese Jews on the Jewish community', *AJS Review* 22 (Fall/Winter 1997): 199–221.

'In the cross-currents of the Reformation: Crypto-Jewish martyrs of the Inquisition 1570–1670', *Past and Present* 178 (2002): 66–104.

Hebrews of the Portuguese nation: conversos and community in early modern Amsterdam (Bloomington: Indiana University Press, 1997).

Bonfil, Robert, 'Change in the cultural patterns of a Jewish society in crisis: Italian Jewry at the close of the sixteenth century', *Jewish History* 3 (1988): 11–30.

Breuer, Mordechai, 'Modernism and traditionalism in sixteenth-century Jewish historiography: a study of David Gans' *Tzemah David*'. In B. D. Cooperman (ed.), *Jewish thought in the sixteenth century* (Cambridge, MA: Harvard University Press, 1983): 49–88.

Carlebach, Elisheva, *Divided souls: converts from Judaism in Germany, 1500–1750* (New Haven: Yale University Press, 2001).

Cohen, Mark R., 'Leone da Modena's Riti: a seventeenth-century plea for social toleration of Jews', *Jewish Social Studies* 34 (1972): 287–319.

Dán, Robert, 'Isaac Troky and his "antitrinitarian" sources'. In *Occident and orient: a tribute to the Memory of A. Scheiber* (Leiden: Brill, 1988), pp. 69–82.

Fishman, Talya, 'Changing early modern Jewish discourse about Christianity: the efforts of Rabbi Leon Modena'. In David Malkiel (ed.), *The lion shall roar: Leon Modena and his world* (Jerusalem: Magnes Press, 2003), pp. 159–94.

Friedman, Jerome, *The most ancient testimony: sixteenth-century Christian Hebraica in the age of Renaissance nostalgia* (Athens, OH: Ohio University Press, 1983).

Gelderen, Martin van, *The political thought of the Dutch revolt, 1555–1590* (Cambridge: Cambridge University Press, 1992).

Goldberg, Jacob, '*De non tolerandis iudaeis*: on the introduction of the anti-Jewish laws into Polish towns and the struggle against them'. In Shmuel Yeivin (ed.), *Studies in Jewish history presented to Raphael Mahler on his seventy-fifth birthday* (Merhavyah: Sifriat po'alim, 1974), pp. 39–52.

'Die getauften Juden in Polen-Litauen im 16.–18. Jahrhundert', *Jahrbücher für Geschichte Osteuropas* 30 (1982): 54–99.

'Poles and Jews in the 17th and 18th centuries: rejection or acceptance?' *Jahrbücher für Geschichte Osteuropas* 21 (1974): 248–82.

Guldon, Zenon, and Wijaczka, Jacek, 'The accusation of ritual murder in Poland, 1500–1800', *Polin: A Journal of Polish-Jewish Studies* 10 (1997): 99–140.

Harrán, Don, 'Jewish musical culture: Leon Modena'. In Robert C. Davis and Benjamin Ravid (eds.), *The Jews of early modern Venice* (Baltimore: Johns Hopkins University Press, 2001), pp. 211–30.

Hsia, R. Po-chia, *The myth of ritual murder: Jews and magic in Reformation Germany* (New Haven and London: Yale University Press, 1988).

Hsia, R. Po-chia, and Lehmann, Hartmut (eds.), *In and out of the ghetto: Jewish–Gentile relations in late medieval and early modern Germany* (Cambridge: Cambridge University Press, 1995), pp. 13–28.

Israel, Jonathan, *European Jewry in the age of mercantilism, 1550–1750* (Oxford: Clarendon Press, 1985).

Kalik, Judith, 'Attitudes towards the Jews and Catholic identity in eighteenth-century Poland'. In Maria Craciun, Ovidiu Ghitta, and Graeme Murdock (eds.), *Confessional identity in east-central Europe* (Burlington, VT: Ashgate, 2002), pp. 181–93.

'The Catholic Church and the Jews in Poland' [Hebrew]. In Yisra'el Bartal and Israel Gutman, (eds.), *The broken chain: Polish Jewry through the ages*. 2 vols. (Jerusalem: Zalman Shazar, 1997), vol. 1, pp. 193–208.

Kaplan, Yosef, *From Christianity to Judaism: the story of Isaac Orobio de Castro*. Trans. Raphael Loewe (Oxford: Littman Library of Jewish Civilization, 1989).

Kaplan, Yosef, Méchoulan, Henri, and Popkin, Richard (eds.), *Menasseh ben Israel and his world* (Leiden: Brill, 1989).

Katchen, Aaron, *Christian Hebraists and Dutch rabbis: seventeenth-century apologetics and the study of Maimonides' Mishneh Torah* (Cambridge, MA: Harvard University Press, 1994).

Katz, David, *Philo-semitism and the readmission of the Jews to England, 1603–1655* (Oxford: Clarendon Press, 1982).

Katz, Jacob, *Exclusiveness and tolerance: studies in Jewish-Gentile relations in medieval and modern times* (West Orange, NJ: Behrman House, 1961).

Kohut, Zenon, 'The Khmelnytsky uprising, the image of the Jews, and the shaping of Ukrainian historical memory', *Jewish History* 17 (2003): 141–63.

Manuel, Frank, *The broken staff: Judaism through Christian eyes* (Cambridge, MA: Harvard University Press, 1992).

Oberman, Heiko, *The roots of anti-semitism in the age of Renaissance and Reformation*. Trans. J. Porter (Philadelphia: Fortress Press, 1984).

Popkin, Richard H., 'Some aspects of Jewish–Christian theological interchanges in Holland and England 1640–1700'. In Johannes van den Berg and Ernestine G. E. van der Wall (eds.), *Jewish–Christian relations in the seventeenth century: studies and documents* (Dordrecht: Kluwer, 1988), pp. 3–32.

Ravid, Benjamin, 'A tale of three cities and their *raison d'état*: Ancona, Venice, Livorno and the competition for Jewish merchants in the sixteenth century', *Mediterranean Historical Review* 6 (1991): 138–62.

'"How profitable the nation of the Jewes are": the *Humble Addresses* of Menasseh ben Israel and the *Discorso* of Simone Luzzatto'. In Judah Reinharz and Daniel Swetschinski (eds.), *Mystics, philosophers, and politicians: essays in Jewish intellectual history in honor of Alexander Altmann* (Durham, NC: Duke University Press, 1982), pp. 159–80.

'The Venetian government and the Jews'. In Robert C. Davis and Benjamin Ravid (eds.), *The Jews of early modern Venice* (Baltimore: Johns Hopkins University Press, 2001), pp. 3–30.

Rosenthal, Judah, 'Marcin Czechowic and Jacob of Belzyce: Arian–Jewish encounters in 16th century Poland', *Proceedings of the American Academy of Jewish Research* 34 (1966): 77–97.

Rosman, M. J., 'Jewish perceptions of insecurity and powerlessness in 16th–18th century Poland', *Polin: A Journal of Polish-Jewish Studies* 1 (1986): 19–27.

Ruderman, David, *Jewish thought and scientific discovery in early modern Europe* (Detroit: Wayne State University, 2001).

Stow, Kenneth, *Catholic thought and papal Jewry policy, 1555–1593* (New York: Jewish Theological Seminary of America, 1977).

'Conversion, Christian Hebraism, and Hebrew prayer in the sixteenth century', *Hebrew Union College Annual* 47 (1976): 217–36.

Tazbir, Janusz, 'Anti-Jewish trials in old Poland', *Scripta Hierosolymitana* 38 (1998): 233–45.

'Images of the Jew in the Polish commonwealth', *Polin: A Journal of Polish-Jewish Studies* 4 (1989): 20–1.

Teter, Magda. *Jews and heretics in Catholic Poland: A beleaguered Church in the post-Reformation era* (Cambridge: Cambridge University Press, 2006).

Yerushalmi, Yosef Hayim, *From Spanish court to Italian ghetto: Isaac Cardoso, a study in seventeenth-century Marranism and Jewish apologetics* (Seattle: University of Washington Press, 1981).

27 THE NATURALIZATION OF ANDEAN CHRISTIANITIES

Primary sources

Acosta, José de, *De Procuranda Indorum Salute* [1588]. Ed. Luciano Pereña *et al.* vol. 1: *Pacificación y colonización*. Madrid, 1984.

Historia natural y moral de las Indias [1590]. Ed. Edmundo O'Gorman. Rev. edn. Mexico, 1962.

Archivum Romanum Societatis Iesu, Rome. Peru 12, tomo 1. *Carta anua de la provincia del Perú del año de 1602*.

Archivum Romanum Societatis Iesu, Rome. Peru 15, tomo 4. *Carta anua de la provincia del Perú de los años de 1641, 1642 y 1643*.

Avila, Francisco de, *Tratado de los evangelios que nuestra Madre la Yglesia nos propone en todo el año . . .* (Lima, 1646–8).

'Aviso de el modo que havia en el govierno de los Indios en tiempo del Inga (Aviso de Chincha)'. Transcribed and edited in María Rostworowski de Diez Canseco, 'Mercaderes del valle de Chincha en la época prehispánica. Un documento y unos comentarios', *Revista Española de Antropología Americana* 5 (1970): 135–77.

Calancha, Antonio de la, *Corónica moralizada del Orden de San Agustín en el Perú* [1638]. Ed. Ignacio Prado Pastor. 6 vols. (Lima, 1974–82).

'Carta anua de la provincia del Perú del año de 1599. P. Rodrigo de Cabredo to P. Claudio Aquaviva, Lima, April 20, 1600'. In Antonio de Egaña and Enrique Fernández (eds.), *Monumenta Peruana (1600–1602)* (Rome, 1981).

'Carta anua de la provincia del Perú del año de 1602. P. Rodrigo de Cabredo to P. Claudio Aquaviva, Lima, April 28, 1603'. In Enrique Fernández (ed.), *Monumenta Peruana VIII (1603–1604)* (Rome, 1986).

Castro, Cristóbal, and Diego de Ortega Morejón, 'Relación y declaración del modo que este valle de Chincha y sus comarcanos se governavan . . .' [1558]. In H. Trimborn (ed.), *Quellen zur Kulturgeschichte des präkolumbinischen Amerika* (Stuttgart, 1938), pp. 236–46.

Castromonte, Juan de, See Durston, Alan.

Cieza de León, Pedro de, *Crónica del Perú: Primera parte* [1553] (Lima, 1995).

Durston, Alan, 'El Aptaycachana de Juan de Castromonte: Un manual sacramental quechua para la sierra central del Perú (ca. 1650)', *Bull. Inst. Fr. Etudes andines* 31/2 (2002): 219–92.

Estete, Miguel de, 'Noticia del Perú'. [c. 1535], *Colección de libros y documentos referentes a la historia del Perú*, 2nd series. (Lima, 1924), vol. 8, pp. 38–9.

Garcilaso de la Vega, El Inca, *Comentarios reales de los Incas* [1609], ed. César Pacheco Vélez (Lima, 1985).

Jesuita Anónimo, 'Relación de las costumbres antiguas de los naturales del Piru [ca. 1594–1606]'. Biblioteca Nacional de España, Madrid, Spain. Ms. 3177. Published in *Crónicas peruanas de interés indígena*. Ed. Francisco Esteve Barba (Madrid, 1968).

Lobo Guerrero, Bartholomé, *Constituciones synodales* [1613] (Lima, 1754).

Murúa, Martín de, *Historia general del Perú* [c. 1611]. Ed. Manuel Ballesteros Gaibrois (Madrid, 2001).

Ocaña, Diego de, Untitled but called the 'Relación del viaje de Fray Diego de Ocaña por el Nuevo Mundo (1599–1605)'. Biblioteca Universitaria, Universidad de Oviedo, Oviedo, Spain. M-215.

Oré, Luis Jerónimo de, *Symbolo Catholico Indiano* [1598]. Ed. Antonine Tibesar (Lima, 1992).

Pizarro, Hernando, 'Relación de Hernando Pizarro acerca de la conquista' [1533]. In *Colección de libros y documentos referents a la historia del Perú* 2nd series (Lima, 1920), vol. 3, pp. 167–80.

Polo de Ondegardo, Juan, 'Los errores y supersticiones de los indios sacadas del tratado y averiguación que hizo el Lizenciado Polo'. In Juan Guillermo Durán (ed.), *El catecismo del III Concilio Provincial de Lima y sus complementos pastorales (1584–1585)* (Buenos Aires, 1982), pp. 459–78.

'Instrucción contra las ceremonias y ritos que usan los Indios conforme al tiempo de su infidelidad'. In Juan Guillermo Durán (ed.), *El catecismo del III Concilio Provincial de Lima y sus complementos pastorales (1584–1585)* (Buenos Aires, 1982), pp. 447–55.

Ramos Gavilán, Alonso, *Historia del santuario de Nuestra Señora de Copacabana* [1621]. Ed. Ignacio Prado Pastor (Lima, 1988).

Salomon, Frank, and George L. Urioste (eds.), *The Huarochirí manuscript: a testament of ancient and colonial Andean religion* (Austin, 1991).

San Pedro, Juan de, *La persecución del demonio. Crónica de los primeros agustinos del norte del Perú* [c. 1560]. Ed. Eric E. Deeds (Málaga, 1992).

Santillán, Hernando de. 'Relación del origin, descendencia, política y gobierno de los Incas' [1563]. In Francisco Esteve Barba (ed.), *Crónicas peruanas de interes indígena* (Madrid, 1968), pp. 97–149.

Taylor, Gerald (ed.), *Ritos y tradiciones de Huarochirí del siglo XVII* (Lima, 1987).

Secondary sources

Abercrombie, Thomas A., *Pathways of memory and power: ethnography and history among an Andean people* (Madison: University of Wisconsin Press, 1998).

Amino, Tetsuya, 'Las lágrimas de Nuestra Señora de Copacabana: un milagro de la imagen de María y los indios en diáspora de Lima en 1591'. *The Journal of the Department of Liberal Arts* (University of Tokyo) 22 (1989): 35–65.

Barnadas, Josep M., 'La vida cotidiana en Bolivia'. In Enrique Dussel *et al.* (eds.), *Historia general de la Iglesia en América Latina* (Salamanca, 1987), pp. 137–45.

Barnes, Monica, 'Catechisms and confesionarios: distorting mirrors of Andean societies'. In Robert V. H. Dover, Katherine E. Seibold, and John H. McDowell (eds.), *Andean cosmologies through time: persistence and emergence* (Bloomington: Indiana University Press, 1992), pp. 67–94.

Borges, Pedro, *Métodos misionales en la cristianización de América, siglo XVI* (Madrid, 1960).

Brown, Peter. 'Conversion and Christianization in late antiquity: the case of Augustine'. Unpublished paper at the Shelby Cullom Davis Center for Historical Studies, Princeton University. 24 September 1999.

The rise of Western Christendom: triumph and diversity, A.D. 200–1000. 2nd edn (Oxford, 2003).

Burga, Manuel, *Nacimiento de una utopia. Muerte y resurrección de los Incas* (Lima, 1988).

'The triumph of colonial Christianity in the Central Andes: guilt, good conscience, and Indian piety'. In Mark D. Szuchman (ed.), *The middle period in Latin America: value and attitudes in the 17th to 19th centuries* (Boulder, CO, 1989), pp. 33–55.

Burkhart, Louise M., *The slippery earth: Nahua–Christian moral dialogue in sixteenth-century Mexico* (Tucson, 1989).

Holy Wednesday: a Nahua drama from early colonial Mexico (Philadelphia: University of Pennsylvania Press, 1996).

Before Guadalupe: the Virgin Mary in early colonial Nahuatl literature (Albany, NY, 2001).

Bushnell, Amy Turner, '"People of Reason": fixed settlement as a concomitant of conversion in Spanish America'. In James Muldoon (ed.), *Conversion in the Americas*, Forthcoming.

Cahill, David, 'Popular religion and appropriation: the example of Corpus Christi in Colonial Cuzco', *Latin American Research Review* 31/2 (1996): 67–110.

Celestino, Olinda, and Albert Meyers, *Las cofradías en el Perú, región central* (Frankfurt, 1981).

Cervantes, Fernando, *The devil in the New World: the impact of diabolism in New Spain* (New Haven and London, 1994).

Chipps Smith, Jeffrey, *Sensuous worship: Jesuits and the art of the early Catholic Reformation in Germany* (Princeton, 2002).

Christian Jr., William A., 'De los santos a María: Panorama de las devociones a santuarios españoles desde el principio de la Edad Media hasta nuestros días'. In C. Lison Tolosana (ed.), *Temas de antropología española* (Madrid, 1976), pp. 49–105.

Local religion in sixteenth-century Spain (Princeton, 1981).

Person and God in a Spanish valley. Rev. edn (Princeton, 1989 [1972]).

Clendinnen, Inga. 'Ways to the sacred: reconstructing "Religion" in sixteenth-century Mexico', *History and Anthropology* 5 (1990): 105–41.

Corsi, Elisabetta. 'Masons of faith. Images and sacred architecture of the Jesuits in late imperial Beijing'. Unpublished paper presented at the Workshop on Court, Ritual Community, and the City: Chinese and Christian Rituality in Late Imperial Beijing. Katholieke Universiteit Leuven, 18 June 2004. Leuven, Belgium.

Cummins, Thomas B. F., *Toasts with the Inca: Andean abstraction and colonial images on Quero vessels* (Ann Arbor, 2002).

'El lenguaje del arte colonial: Imagen, ekfrasis y idolatría'. *I Encuentro Internacional de Peruanistas: Estado de estudios históricos-sociales sobre el Perú a fines del siglo XX* (Lima, 1998), pp. 23–45.

'From lies to truth: colonial ekphrasis and the act of crosscultural translation', In Claire Farago (ed.), *Reframing the Renaissance: visual culture in Europe and Latin America 1450–1650*. (New Haven and London, 1995), pp. 152–74.

Cussen, Celia L. 'El Barroco por dentro y por fuera: Redes de devoción en Lima colonial', *Anuario Colombiano de Historia Social y de la Cultura* (Bogotá) 26 (1999): 215–25.

'The Search for Idols and Saints in Colonial Peru: Linking Extirpation and Beatification', *Hispanic American Historical Review* 85:3 (2005): 417–448.

Dean, Carolyn. 'Familiarizando el catolicismo en el Cuzco colonial'. In Jacques Decoster (ed.), *Incas e indios cristianos. Elites indígenas e identidades cristianas en los Andes colonials* (Cuzco, 2002), pp. 169–94.

'The renewal of Old World images and the creation of colonial Peruvian visual culture'. In Diana Fane (ed.), *Converging cultures: art and identity in Spanish America* (New York, 1996), pp. 171–82.

Dedenbach-Salazar Sáenz, Sabine, 'La comunicación con los dioses: Sacrificios y danzas en la época prehispánica según las "tradiciones de Huarochirí". In Max Peter Baumann (ed.), *Cosmología y música en los Andes* (Frankfurt and Madrid, 1996), pp. 175–96.

'La terminología cristiana en textos quechuas de instrucción religiosa en el siglo XVI'. In Mary H. Preuss (ed.), *Latin American Indian literatures: messages and meanings* (Lancaster, CA, 1997), pp. 195–209.

Delumeau, Jean, *La Peur en Occident, XIVe–XVIIe siècles: une cité assiégée* (Paris, 1978).

Deslandres, Dominique, *Croire et faire croire. Les missions françaises au XVIIe siècle* (Paris, 2003).

Ditchfield, Simon, 'La santità e il culto dei santi fra universalità e particolarismi'. In Anna Benvenuti *et al.* (eds.), *Storia della santità nel cristianesimo occidentale* (Rome, forthcoming).

Liturgy, sanctity and history in Tridentine Italy: Pietro Maria Campi and the preservation of the particular (Cambridge, 1995).

Duverger, Christian, *La conversión de los indios de Nueva España: Con el texto de los Colquios de los Doce de Bernardino de Sahagún* (Mexico, 1993 [1987]).

Duviols, Pierre, *La Lutte contre les réligions autochtones dans le Pérou colonial* (Lima, 1971).

'Estudio preliminar'. In Pierre Duviols (ed.), *Procesos y visitas de idolatrías: Cajatambo, siglo XVII* (Lima, 2003), pp. 19–162.

'Los nombres Quechua de Viracocha, supuesto "Dios Creador" de los evangelizadores'. *Allpanchis* 10 (1977): 53–64.

Estenssoro Fuchs, Juan Carlos, *Del paganismo a la santidad: La incorporación de los indios del Perú al catolicismo, 1532–1750* (Lima, 2003).

'Les Pouvoirs de la Parole. La prédication au Pérou de l'évangélisation à l'utopie'. *Annales* (1996): 1225–57.

Garland Ponce, Beatriz. 'Las cofradías de Lima durante la Colonia'. In *La venida del Reino: religión, evangelización y cultura en América, siglos XVI–XX* (Cusco, 1994).

Ginzburg, Carlo, 'Ticiano, Ovidio y los códigos de la representación erótica en el siglo XVI'. In *Mitos, emblemas, indicios. Morfología e historia* (Barcelona, 1999), pp. 117–34.

Gose, Peter, 'Oracles, divine kingship, and political representation in the Inka state'. *Ethnohistory* 43/1 (1994): 1–32.

'Converting the ancestors: indirect rule, settlement consolidation, and the struggle over burial in colonial Peru, 1532–1614'. In Kenneth Mills and Anthony Grafton (eds.), *Conversion: old worlds and new* (Rochester, NY, 2003), pp. 140–74.

Graubart, Karen B., 'Indecent living: indigenous women and the politics of representation in early colonial Peru', *Colonial Latin American Review* 92 (2000): 213–35.

Griffiths, Nicholas, *The cross and the serpent: religious repression and resurgence in colonial Peru* (Norman, OK, 1996).

Gruzinski, Serge, *La Guerre des images de Christophe Colomb à Blade Runner, 1492–2019* (Paris, 1990).

Man-Gods in the Mexican highlands: Indian power and colonial society, 1520–1800 (Stanford, 1989).

Helms, Mary W., *Craft and the kingly ideal: art, trade, and power* (Austin, TX).

Hyland, Sabine, *The Jesuit and the Incas: the extraordinary life of Padre Blas Valera, S. J.* (Ann Arbor, MI, 2003).

Julien, Catherine J., *Reading Inca history* (Iowa City, 2000).

Die Inka (Munich, 1998).

Keatinge, Richard W. 'The nature and role of religious diffusion in the early stages of state formation: an example from Peruvian prehistory'. In Grant D. Jones and Robert R. Kautz (eds.), *The transition to statehood in the new world* (Cambridge, 1981), pp. 172–87.

Klor de Alva, J. Jorge, 'Spiritual conflict and accommodation in New Spain: toward a typology of Aztec responses to Christianity'. In G. A. Collier, R. I. Rosaldo, and J. D. Wirth (eds.), *The Inca and Aztec states 1400–1800: anthropology and history* (New York, 1982), pp. 345–65.

Kubler, George, *The shape of time: remarks on the history of things* (New Haven and London, 1962).

'The Quechua in the colonial world'. In Julian H. Steward (ed.), *The handbook of South American Indians* (Washington, DC, 1946), vol. 2, pp. 331–410.

Lamb, Ursula, 'Religious conflicts in the conquest of Mexico', *Journal of the History of Ideas* 17 (1956): 526–39.

MacCormack, Sabine, *Religion in the Andes: vision and imagination in early colonial Peru* (Princeton, 1991).

'"The heart has its reasons": predicaments of missionary Christianity in early colonial Peru', *Hispanic American Historical Review* 65 (1985): 443–66.

'From the sun of the Incas to the virgin of Copacabana', *Representations* 8 (1984): 30–60.

Mannheim, Bruce, 'A semiotic of Andean dreams'. In Barbara Tedlock (ed.), *Dreaming: Anthropological and psychological interpretations* (Cambridge, 1987), pp. 132–53.

Mariátegui, José Carlos, *Siete ensayos de interpretación de la realidad peruana* (Lima, 1973 [1928]).

Marzal, Manuel M., *La transformación religiosa peruana [1983]* (Lima, 1988).

'Una hipótesis sobre la aculturación religiosa andina', *Revista de la Universidad Católica* 2 (1977): 95–131.

Menegon, Eugenio, 'Deliver us from evil: confession and salvation in seventeenth- and eighteenth-century Chinese Catholicism'. Unpublished essay presented at the Workshop on Court, Ritual Community, and the City: Chinese and Christian Rituality in Late Imperial Beijing. Katholieke Universiteit Leuven, Leuven, Belgium, 17 June 2004.

Millones, Luis. *De la evangelización a la religiosidad popular peruana: el culto a las imágenes sagradas* (Málaga, 1998).

'Los ganados del señor: mecanismos de poder en las comunidades andinas, siglos XVIII y XIX'. *América Indígena* 39/1 (1979): 107–45.

'Introducción al studio de las idolatrías'. *Letras* (Papel no. 27 del Instituto de Literatura, Universidad Nacional Mayor de San Marcos, Lima, Peru) 78–9 (1969): 5–40.

Millones, Luis (ed.), *El retorno de la huacas: Estudios y documentos sobre el Taqui Oncoy, siglo XVI* (Lima, 1990).

Mills, Kenneth. 'Diego de Ocaña's hagiography of new and renewed devotion in colonial Peru'. In Allan Greer and Jodi Bilinkoff (eds.), *Colonial saints: discovering the holy in the Americas, 1500–1800* (New York, 2003), pp. 51–76.

Idolatry and its enemies: colonial Andean religion and extirpation, 1640–1750 (Princeton, 1997).

An evil lost to view? An investigation of post-evangelisation Andean religion in mid-colonial Peru (Liverpool, 1994).

'The limits of religious coercion in mid-colonial Peru', *Past and Present* 145 (1994): 84–121.

'"A very subtle idolatry": an authentic testimony of colonial Andean religion'. In Mario J. Valdes and Djelal Kadir (eds.), *History of Latin American literary cultures* (Oxford University Press, in press).

Mills, Kenneth, Taylor, William B., and Lauderdale Graham, Sandra (eds.), *Colonial Latin America: a documentary history* (Wilmington, DE, 2003).

Mills, Kenneth, and Grafton, Anthony, 'Introduction'. In *Conversion: old worlds and new*.

Morote Best, Efraín, 'Dios, la virgen y los santos (en los relatos populares)', *Tradición* (Cusco) 5, 11, nos. 12–14 (1953): 76–104.

Patterson, Thomas C., 'Pachacamac: an Andean oracle under Inca rule'. In D. Peter Kvietok and Daniel H. Sandweiss (eds.), *Recent studies in Andean prehistory and protohistory* (Ithaca, NY, 1985), pp. 169–75.

Platt, Tristan, 'The Andean soldiers of Christ: confraternity organization, the mass of the sun and regenerative warfare in rural Potosí (18th to 20th centuries)', *Journal de la Société des Américanistes* 73 (1987): 139–92.

Redden, Andrew, 'Satan's fortress: the devil in the Andes'. Unpublished MS.

'The Sun God and the Queen of Hell: the devil in the colonial Peruvian middle ground'. Unpublished MS.

Ricard, Robert, *The spiritual conquest of Mexico: an essay on the apostolate and the evangelizing methods of the mendicant orders in New Spain, 1523–1572* [1933]. Trans. Lesley Byrd Simpson (Berkeley, 1966).

Rostworowski de Diez Canseco, María. *Pachacamac y el Señor de los Milagros: Una trajectoria milenaria* (Lima, 1992).

Sahlins, Marshall, *Islands of history* (Chicago, 1985).

Saignes, Thierry, 'The colonial condition in the Quechua-Aymara heartland (1570–1780)'. In Frank Salomon and Stuart B. Schwartz (eds.), *The Cambridge history of the native peoples of the Americas*, vol 3: *South America*, part 2 (Cambridge, 1999), pp. 59–137.

Salles Reese, Verónica, *From Viracocha to the Virgin of Copacabana: representations of the sacred at Lake Titicaca* (Austin, TX, 1997).

Sallnow, Michael J., *Pilgrims of the Andes. Regional cults in Cuzco* (Washington, DC, 1987).

Salomon, Frank, 'Introductory essay'. In Frank Salomon and George L. Urioste (eds.), *The Huarochirí manuscript: a testament of ancient and colonial Andean religion* (Austin, TX, 1991), pp. 1–38.

'Nightmare victory: the meanings of conversion among Peruvian Indians (Huarochirí, 1608?)', 1992 Lecture Series, Working paper no. 7. Department of Spanish and Portuguese, University of Maryland, College Park, 1990.

Spalding, Karen, *Huarochirí: an Andean society under Inca and Spanish rule* (Stanford, 1984).

'The crises and transformations of invaded societies: Andean area (1500–1580)'. In Frank Salomon and Stuart B. Schwartz (eds.), *The Cambridge history of the native peoples of the Americas.* Vol. 3: *South America*, part 1 (Cambridge, 1999), pp. 904–72.

Szeminski, Jan, 'From Inca gods to Spanish saints and demons'. In Stephen Kaplan (ed.), *Indigenous responses to western Christianity* (New York, 1995), pp. 56–74.

Taylor, William B., 'Process in place: toward a history of devotional landscapes in Mexico'. Unpublished paper. Commentary for 'Devotional landscapes: mapping the shrines and saints of New Spain' symposium. Geographic Information Center, University of California at Berkeley. 27 February 2004.

Magistrates of the sacred: priests and parishioners in eighteenth-century Mexico (Stanford, 1996).

'Santiago's horse: Christianity and colonial Indian resistance in the heartland of New Spain'. In William B. Taylor and Franklin G. Y. Pease (eds.), *Violence, resistance, and survival in the Americas: native Americans and the legacy of conquest* (Washington, DC, 1994), pp. 153–89.

Thompson, E. P., *Customs in common: studies in traditional popular culture* (New York, 1993).

Topic, John R., Topic, Theresa Lange, and Melly Cava, Alfredo, 'Catequil: the archaeology, ethnohistory, and ethnography of a major provincial Huaca'. In William H. Isbell and Helaine Silverman (eds.), *Andean archaeology I: Variations in sociopolitical organization* (New York, 2002), pp. 303–35.

Urbano, Henrique, 'Introducción'. In Henrique Urbano and Ana Sánchez (eds.), *Antigüedades del Perú* (Madrid, 1992), pp. 7–38.

Urton, Gary, *The history of a myth: Pacariqtambo and the origin of the Inkas* (Austin, 1990).

Vargas Ugarte, Rubén (ed.), *Concilios Limenses (1551–1772)*. 3 vols. (Lima, 1951–4).

Varón, Rafael, 'Cofradías de indios y poder local en el Perú colonial: Huaraz, siglo XVII'. *Allpanchis* 17/20 (1982): 127–46.

Županov, Ines G., *Disputed mission: Jesuit experiments and Brahmanical knowledge in seventeenth-century India* (New Delhi, Oxford, and New York, 1999).

28 BETWEEN ISLAM AND ORTHODOXY: PROTESTANTS AND CATHOLICS IN SOUTH-EASTERN EUROPE

Basic works

Andor, Eszter, and Tóth István György (eds.), *Frontiers of faith. Cultural transfer and construction of religious identities. 1400–1750* (Budapest: Central European University / European Science Foundation, 2001).

Bérenger, Jean, *Tolérance ou paix de religion en Europe centrale (1415–1792)* (Paris: Champion-Slatkine, 2000).

Bibliography

Evans, Robert, J. W., Thomas, T. V. (eds.), *Crown, church and estates. Central European politics in the sixteenth and seventeenth centuries* (London and New York: St Martin's Press, 1991).

Fodor, Pál, *In quest of the golden apple: imperial ideology, politics and military administration in the Ottoman Empire* (Istanbul: Isis, 2000).

Frazee, Charles A., *Catholics and sultans: the church and the Ottoman Empire, 1453–1923* (Cambridge: Cambridge University Press, 1983).

Jačov, Marko, *Le missioni cattoliche nei Balcani durante la guerra di Candia (1645–1669)*. 2 vols. Studi e Testi, 352–3 (Rome, Cittá del Vaticano: Biblioteca Apostolica Vaticana, 1992).

Metzler, Josef (ed.), *Sacrae Congregationis de Propaganda Fide Memoria rerum, 350 years in the service of the missions, 1622–1972*. 3 vols. (Rome, Freiburg, and Vienna: Herder, 1972).

Tóth, István György (ed.), *Litterae missionariorum de Hungaria et Transylvania. 1572–1717* (with English introduction). 2 vols. (Rome: Accademia d'Ungheria, 2003).

Further reading

Alzati, Cesare, *Terra romena tra Oriente e Occidente. Chiese ed etnie nel tardo '500* (Milan: Jaca Book, 1981).

Andrić, Ivo, *The development of spiritual life in Bosnia under the influence of Turkish rule* (Durham, NC: Duke University Press, 1990).

Baán, István, 'La pénétration de l'uniatisme en Ukraine subcarpathique au XVIIe siècle', *XVII siècle* 55 (2003): 515–26.

Benda, Kálmán (ed.), *Documenta Hungarorum in Moldavia*. 2 vols (Budapest: Magyarságkutató, 1989).

Bitskey, István, *Il Collegio Germanico-Ungarico di Roma. Contribuito alla storia della cultura ungherese in etá barocca* (Rome: Viella, 1996).

Carter, Francis W., *Dubrovnik (Ragusa): a classic city-state* (London: Seminar Press, 1972).

Châline, Olivier, *La reconquête catholique de l'Europe centrale. XVIe–XVIIIe siècle* (Paris: Cerf, 1998).

Craciun, Maria-Ghitta, Ovidiu (ed.), *Ethnicity and religion in central and eastern Europe* (Cluj-Napoca: Cluj University Press, 1995).

Church and society in central and eastern Europe (Cluj-Napoca: European Studies Foundation Publishing, 1998).

Dávid, Géza-Fodor Pál (ed.), *Ottomans, Hungarians and Habsburgs in central Europe: the military confines in the era of Ottoman conquest* (Leiden, E. J. Brill, 2000).

Dimitrov, Bozhidar, *Bulgaria and the Vatican* (Sofia: Academia, 2002).

Fermendžin, Eusebius, *Acta Bosniae* (Zagrabiae: Societas typographica, 1892).

Acta Bulgariae (Zagrabiae: Academia scientiarum, 1887).

Hegyi, Klára-Zimányi Vera, *The Ottoman Empire in Europe* (Budapest: Corvina, 1986).

Heyberger, Bernard, *Les chrétiens du Proche-Orient au temps de la réforme catholique* (Rome: Ecole Française de Rome, 1994).

Hupchick, D. P., *The Bulgarians in the seventeenth century. Slavic Orthodox society and culture under Ottoman rule* (Jefferson: McFarland, 1993).

Jačov, Marko, *I Balcani tra Impero Ottomano e potenze europee (secoli XVI e XVII), il ruolo della diplomazia pontificia* (Cosenza: Periferia, 1997).

Bibliography

Le missioni cattoliche nei Balcani tra le due guerre: Candia (1645–1669), Vienna e Morea (1683–1699): Studi e Testi, 386 (Rome, Città del Vaticano: Biblioteca Apostolica Vaticana, 1998).

Korade, Mijo, Aleksic, M., and Matos, J., *Jesuits and Croatian culture* (Zagreb: Most; the Bridge, 1992).

Krekić, Bariša, *Dubrovnik: a Mediterranean urban society, 1300–1600* (Brookfield: Variorum, 1997).

Lukács, László (ed.), *Monumenta Antiquae Hungariae* 4 vols. (Rome: Institutum Historicum Societatis Iesu, 1969–86).

Malcolm, Noel, *Bosnia. A short history* (London: Macmillan, 1994).

Paiva, José Pedro (ed.), *Religious ceremonials and images: power and social meaning (1400–1750)* (Coimbra: European Science Foundation, 2002).

Peris, Lucian, *Le missioni gesuite in Transilvania e Moldavia nel Seicento* (Cluj-Napoca: Studii Europene, 1998).

Pinson, Mark (ed.), *The Muslims of Bosnia-Hercegovina, their historic development from the Middle Ages to the dissolution of Yugoslavia* (Cambridge, MA: Harvard University Press, 1994).

Setton, Kenneth Meyer, *The papacy and the Levant, 1204–1571*. 4 vols. (Philadelphia: American Philosophical Society, 1976–84).

Venice, Austria and the Turks in the seventeenth century (Philadelphia: American Philosophical Society, 1991).

Tollet, Daniel, 'La reconquête catholique en Europe Centrale (fin XVIIe siècle–début XVIIIe siècle)', *Mélanges de l'Ecole Française de Rome* 109 (1997): 825–52.

Tóth, István György, 'Between Islam and Catholicism: Bosnian Franciscan missionaries in Ottoman Hungary', *Catholic Historical Review* 89 (2003): 409–33.

Literacy and written culture in early modern central Europe (Budapest: Central European University Press, 2000).

Politique et religion en Hongrie du XVIIe siècle (Paris: Champion-Slatkine, 2004).

Tóth, István György (ed.), *Relationes missionariorum de Hungaria et Transylvania. 1627–1707* (Rome: Accademia d'Ungheria, 1994).

Zlatar, Zdenko, *Our kingdom come, the Counter-Reformation, the Republic of Dubrovnik and the liberation of the Balkan Slavs* (Boulder, CO: Columbia University Press, 1992).

29 CHRISTIANITY SHAPED BY THE CHINESE

Primary sources

Elia, Pasquale M. d' (ed.), *Fonti Ricciane* 3 vols. (Rome: La Libreria dello stato, 1942–9).

Ricci, Matteo, *The true meaning of the Lord of Heaven (T'ien-chu shih-i).* Ed. E. Malatesta. Trans. Douglas Lancashire and Peter Hu Kuo-chen (St Louis and Taibei: The Institute of Jesuit Sources; Ricci Institute, 1985).

Trigault, Nicolas, and Ricci, Matteo, *De Christiana expeditione apud Sinas, suscepta ab Societate Iesu, ex P. Matthaei Ricii eiusdem Societatis Commentariis, libri V, in quibus Sinensis regni mores, leges atque instituta et novae illius Ecclesiae difficillima primordia accurate et summa fide describuntur* (Augsburg: Christoph Mangium, 1615).

China in the sixteenth century: the journals of Matthew Ricci: 1583–1610 Trans. Louis J. Gallagher (New York: Random House, 1953).

Secondary sources

100 Roman documents concerning the Chinese Rites Controversy (1645–1941) Ed. Ray R. Noll. Trans. Donald F. St. Sure (San Francisco: Ricci Institute, 1992).

Bettray, Johannes, *Die Akkomodationsmethode des P. Matteo Ricci S. J. in China* (Rome: Gregoriana, 1955).

Brockley, Liam M., *'The harvest of the vine: the Jesuit missionary enterprise in China, 1579–1710'* (Ph.D. dissertation: Brown University, 2002).

Chow Kai-wing, 'Writing for success: printing, examinations and intellectual change in late Ming China', *Late Imperial China* 17 (1996): 120–57.

Engelfriet, Peter M., *Euclid in China: the genesis of the first translation of Euclid's Elements in 1607 and its reception up to 1723* (Leiden: Brill, 1998).

Gernet, Jacques, *Chine et christianisme: action et réaction* (Paris: Gallimard, 1982).
  China and the Christian impact: a conflict of cultures Trans. Janet Lloyd (Cambridge: Cambridge University Press, 1985).

Golvers, Noël, *François de Rougemont, S. J., missionary in Ch'ang-shu (Suchou): a study of the account book (1674–1676) and the Elogium* (Leuven: Leuven University Press, 2000).

Jami, Catherine, Engelfriet, Peter, and Blue, Gregory (eds.), *Statecraft & intellectual renewal in late Ming China: the cross-cultural synthesis of Xu Guangqi (1562–1633)* (Leiden: Brill, 2001).

Lamalle, Edmond, 'La propagande du P. N. Trigault en faveur des missions de Chine (1616)', *Archivum Historicum Societatis Iesu* 9 (1940): 49–120.

Leung, Yuen-sang P., 'Towards a hyphenated identity: Li Zhizao's search for a Confucian-Christian synthesis', *Monumenta Serica* 39 (1990–91): 115–30.

Margiotti, Fortunato, *Il Cattolicismo nello Shansi dalle origini al 1738* (Rome: Edizioni 'Sinica Franciscana', 1958).

Menegon, Eugenio, 'Ancestors, virgins, and friars: the localization of Christianity in late Imperial Mindong (Fujian, China) 1632–1863' (Ph.D. dissertation: University of California, Berkeley 2002).

Peterson, Willard J., 'Why did they become Christians? Yang T'ing-yün, Li Chih-tsao, and Hsü Kuang-ch'i'. In Charles Ronan and Bonnie Oh (eds.), *East meets west: the Jesuits in China, 1582–1773* (Chicago: Loyola University Press, 1988), pp. 129–52.

Rambo, Lewis, *Understanding religious conversion* (New Haven and London: Yale University Press, 1993).

Rule, Paul, *K'ung-tzu or Confucius? The Jesuit interpretation of Confucianism* (Sydney: Allen & Unwin, 1986).

Sebes, Joseph, 'The precursors of Ricci'. In Charles Ronan and Bonnie Oh (eds.), *East meets west: the Jesuits in China, 1582–1773* (Chicago: Loyola University Press, 1988), pp. 19–61.

Spence, Jonathan D., *The search for modern China* (New York: Norton, 1990).
  The memory palace of Matteo Ricci (London: Faber and Faber, 1985).

Standaert, Nicolas, 'Christianity as a religion in China', *Cahiers d'Extrême-Asie* 12 (2001): 1–21.
  'Jesuit corporate culture as shaped by the Chinese'. In John W. O'Malley et al. (eds.), *The Jesuits: cultures, sciences, and the arts, 1540–1773* (Toronto: University of Toronto Press, 1999), pp. 352–63.
  Yang Tingyun, Confucian and Christian in late Ming China: his life and thought (Leiden: Brill, 1988).

Standaert, Nicolas (ed.), *Handbook of Christianity in China*, vol. 1: *635–1800* (Leiden: Brill, 2001).

The Cambridge history of China, vol. 7: *The Ming dynasty, 1368–1644, Part 1*. Ed. Denis Twitchett and Frederick W. Mote (Cambridge: Cambridge University Press, 1988).

The Cambridge history of China, vol. 8: *The Ming dynasty, 1368–1644, Part 2*. Ed. Denis Twitchett and Frederick W. Mote (Cambridge: Cambridge University Press, 1998).

Übelhör, Monika, 'Geistesströmungen der späten Ming-Zeit die das Werken der Jesuiten in China begünstigten', *Saeculum* 23 (1972): 172–85.

'Hsü Kuang-ch'i und seine Einstellung zum Christentum', *Oriens Extremus* 15 (1968): 191–257 (I); 16 (1969): 41–74 (II).

Van Engen, John, 'The Christian Middle Ages as an historiographical problem', *American Historical Review* 91 (1986): 519–552.

Yang, C. K., *Religion in Chinese society: the first comprehensive sociological analysis of Chinese religious behavior* (Berkeley: University of California Press, 1961).

Zürcher, Erik, 'Bouddhisme et christianisme'. In Erik Zürcher, *Bouddhisme, christianisme et société chinoise* (Paris: Conférences, essais et leçons du Collège de France, 1990), pp. 11–42.

'Christian social action in late Ming Times: Wang Zheng and his "humanitarian society"'. In Jan A. M. De Meyer and Peter M. Engelfriet (eds.), *Linked faiths: essays on Chinese religions and traditional culture in honour of Kristofer Schipper* (Leiden: Brill, 1999), pp. 269–86.

'Confucian and Christian religiosity in late Ming China', *Catholic Historical Review* 83 (1997): 614–53.

'Jesuit accommodation and the Chinese cultural imperative'. In David E. Mungello (ed.), *The Chinese Rites Controversy: its history and meaning*. Monumenta Serica Monograph Series, 33 (Nettetal: Steyler Verlag, 1994), pp. 31–64.

'The Jesuit mission in Fujian in late Ming Times: levels of response'. In E. B. Vermeer (ed.), *Development and decline of Fukien province in the 17th and 18th centuries* (Leiden: Brill, 1990), pp. 417–57.

'The Lord of heaven and the demons: strange stories from a late Ming Christian manuscript'. In G. Naundorf et al. (eds.), *Religion und Philosophie in Ostasien (Festschrift für H. Steiniger)* (Würzburg: Königshausen & Neumann, 1985), pp. 357–76.

30 RECEPTION OF HINDUISM AND BUDDHISM

HINDUISM

Primary sources

Amiel, C., and Lima, A. (eds.), *L'Inquisition de Goa, La relation de Charles Dellon (1687)* (Paris: Editions Chandeigne, 1997).

Archivum Romanum Societatis Iesu. Rome: Goa 51, fols. 29r–31v.

Baldaeus, Philip, *A True and exact description of the most celebrated east-India coasts of Malabar [. . .]* (Amsterdam: 1672) (New Delhi: Asian Educational Services, 1996).

Barbosa, Duarte, *O Livro do Duarte Barbosa* (Lisbon, 2000).

Bernier, François, *Travels in the Mogul empire, 1656–1668* (New Delhi: Asian Educational Services, 1996).

Burnell, A. C., *The voyage of J. H. van Linschoten to the East Indies*. 2 vols. (Amsterdam, 1596; New Delhi: Asian Educational Services, 1988).

Carré, Abbé, *The travels of the Abbé Carré, 1672 to 1674*. 3 vols. (New Delhi: Asian Educational Services, 1990).

Castro, Xavier de, and Dejanirah Couto (eds.), *Voyage à Mozambique & Goa: la relation de Jean Mocquet (1607–1610)* (Paris: Chandeigne, 1996).

Castro, Xavier de, and Bouchon, Geneviève (eds.), *Voyage de Pyrard de Laval aux Indes orientales (1601–1611)*. 2 vols. (Paris: Chandeigne, 1998).

Charpentier, Jarl, *The Livro da Seita dos Indios Orientais of Father Jacobo Fenicio, S. J.* (Brit. Mus. MS Sloane 1820) (Uppsala: Almquist & Wiksells, 1933).

'Moraes to the members in Portugal, Cap Comorim, Dec. 15, 1547'. Archivum Romanum Societatis Iesu. Rome: N. N. 66 I, fol. 226v.

Paulinus a Sancto Bartholomaeo, Systema Brahmanicum (Rome: Apud A. Fulgonium, 1791).

Rivara, J. H. da Cunha, *Archivo Portuguez Oriental* (New Delhi: Asian Educational Services, 1992). fasc. 6.

Sousa, Manuel Faria y, *Asia Portuguesa*. 3 vols. (Lisbon: En la Officina de Henrique Valente de Oliveira, 1666–75).

Tavernier, Jean-Baptiste, *Les Six voyages de Jean-Baptiste Tavernier*. 2 vols. (Paris: G. Clouzier, 1676).

Valle, Pietro della, *The travels of Pietro della Valle in India*. 2 vols. (London: Printed for the Hakluyt Society, 1892; New Delhi: Asian Educational Services, 1991).

Wicki, Joseph (ed.), *Documenta Indica*. 18 vols. (Rome: Monumenta Historica Soc. Iesu, 1968), vol. 10.

    P. Diogo Gonçalves S. I. Historia do Malavar (Quakernbrück: Robert Kleinert, 1955)

    Tratado do Pe. Gonçalo Fernandes Trancoso sobre o Hinduísmo (Maduré, 1616; Lisboa, 1973).

Secondary sources

Carletti, Francesco, *Ragionamenti del mio viaggio intorno al mondo* (Turin: G. Einaudi, 1989).

Couto, Diogo do, *Da Asia, Decada Quinta Parte Segunda* (Lisbon: Livraria Sam Carlos, 1974).

Dalmia, Vasudha, and Stietencron, Heinrich von (eds.), *Representing Hinduism: the construction of religious traditions and national identity* (London: Sage, 1995).

Delgado, S. R., *Glossário Luso-Asiático*. 2 vols. (Coimbra: Imprensa da Universidade, 1919–21), vol. 1.

Halbfass, Wilhelm, *India and Europe: an essay in understanding* (New York: State University of New York Press, 1988).

King, Richard, *Orientalism and religion, postcolonial theory, India and 'the mystic east'* (New Delhi: Oxford University Press, 1999).

Loureiro, Rui Manuel, 'O Descobrimento da Civilização Indiana nas Cartas dos Jesuítas (século XVI)'. In *Fundação Oriente, Encontro sobre Portugal e India* (Lisbon: Fundação Oriente, 2000), pp. 107–25.

Matos, Luis de (ed.), *Imagens do Oriente no século XVI* (Lisbon: Imprensa Nacional, 1985).

Mitter, Partha, *Much maligned monsters* (Oxford: Clarendon Press, 1977).

Mota, Maria Manuela, 'Códice Casanatense: an Indo-Portuguese portrait of life in 16th-century India'. In José Pereira and Pratapaditya Pal (eds.), *India and Portugal: cultural interactions* (Mumbai: Marg, 2001) pp. 34–46.

Nabokov, Isabelle, *Religion against the self: an ethnography of Tamil rituals* (New York: Oxford University Press, 2000).

Pagden, Anthony, *The fall of natural man: the American Indian and the origins of comparative ethnology.*

Rajamanickam, S., SJ (ed.), *Roberto de Nobili on adaptation (Informatio)* (Palayamkottai: De Nobili Research Institute, 1971).

Rubies, Joan-Pau, 'The Jesuit discovery of Hinduism: Antonio Rubino's account of the history of religion of Vijayanagara (1608)', *Archiv für Religionsgeschichte* 3 (2001).

Travel and ethnology in the Renaissance, south India through European eyes, 1250–1625 (Cambridge: Cambridge University Press, 2000).

Smith, Wilfred Cantewell, *The meaning and end of religion: a revolutionary approach to the great religious traditions* (Minneapolis: Fortress, 1962).

Sontheimer, Günter D., and Kulke, Hermann (eds.), *Hinduism reconsidered* (New Delhi: Manohar Publications, 1991).

Subrahmanyam, Sanjay, *The career and legend of Vasco da Gama* (Cambridge: Cambridge University Press, 1997), pp. 131–3.

Sweetman, Will, 'Unity and plurality: Hinduism and the religious of India in early European scholarship', *Religion* 31 (2001): 209–24.

Yule, H., and Burnell, A. C. (eds.), *Hobson-Jobson, a glossary of colloquial Anglo-Indian words [. . .]* (rpt. New Delhi: Munshiram Manoharlal, 1979).

Županov, Ines G., *Disputed mission: Jesuit experiments and brahmanical knowledge in seventeenth-century India* (New Delhi: Oxford University Press, 1999).

BUDDHISM

Primary sources

Chen Yuan, ed., *Kangxi yu Luoma shijie guanxi wenshu yingyin ben* (1932), rpt. in *Zhongguo shixue congshu xubian* 23 (Taipei: Xuesheng shuju, 1973).

Cruz, Gaspar da Cruz, *Tratado das coisas da China* (Evora, 1569–70), ed. Rui Manuel Loureiro (Macau: Instituto cultural de Macau, 1997).

Magalhães, Gabriel de SJ, *Nova Relação da China*. Trans. Lussís Gonzaga Gomes (Macau: Fundação Macau, 1997).

Ricci, Matteo, *Storia dell'introduzione del Cristianesimo in Cina*, 3 vols. Ed. Pasquale M. D'Elia (Rome: Libreria dello Stato, 1942–9).

Semedo, Álvaro, SJ, *Relação de Grande Monarquia da China* (Macau: Fundação Macau, 1994).

Yin Guangren and Zhang Rulin, *Aomen zhilue, 'A record of Macau'*. Ed. Zhao Chunchen (Macao: Instituto Cultural de Macao, 1992).

Secondary sources

Cha Shijie, 'Ming mo fo jiao dui Tianzhu jiao de pi xie yun dong chu tan', in *Ming Qing zhiji Zhongguo wenhua di zhuan bian yu yan xu* (Taipei, 1990).

Girard, Pascale, *Os Religiosos Ocidentais na China na época moderna* (Macau: Fundação Macau, 1999).

Hsu, Sung-peng, *A Buddhist leader in Ming China: the life and thought of Han-shan Te-ch'ing* (University Park, PA: Pennsylvania State University Press, 1979).

Kern, Iso, *Buddhistische Kritik am Christentum im China des 17. Jahrhunderts* (Bern, Frankfurt, and Vienna: P. Lang, 1992).

Mungello, D. E., *The forgotten Christians of Hangzhou* (Honolulu: University of Hawaii Press, 1994).

Shi Guoxiang, *Zi bo da chi yanjiu* (Taipei: Dongchu, 1987).

Shi Shengyan, *Mingmo Zhongguo Fojiao zi yanjiu* (Taipei: Xueshen, 1988).

Mingmo Zhungguo Fojiao yanjiu (Biography of Zhiyu) (Taipei: Dongchu, 1988)

Standaert, Nicolas, *Yang Tingyun, Confucian and Christian in Late Ming China: his life and thought* (Leiden: E. J. Brill, 1988).

Yü, Chün-Fang, *The renewal of Buddhism in China: Chu-hung and the Late Ming synthesis* (New York: Columbia University Press, 1981).

Index

Surnames are alphabetized under their first capitalized major element (Salazar y Frias, Alonso; Cloche, Abraham de La). Page numbers in italics refer to illustrations.